MENTAL HEALTH ACT
MANUAL

by

Richard M. Jones, M.A. (Kent and Brunel), Solicitor

President, Institute of Mental Health Act Practitioners
Consultant, Morgan Cole, Solicitors

Seventh Edition

Sweet & Maxwell

Published in 2001 by
Sweet & Maxwell Ltd of
100 Avenue Road, Swiss Cottage,
London NW3 3PF
http://www.sweetandmaxwell.co.uk
Selwood Systems, Midsomer Norton
Printed and bound in Great Britain by
MPG Books Ltd, Bodmin, Cornwall

No natural forests were destroyed to
make this product: only farmed
timber was used and re-planted.

ISBN 0 421 759100

**A catalogue record for this book is
available from the British Library**

1002624615

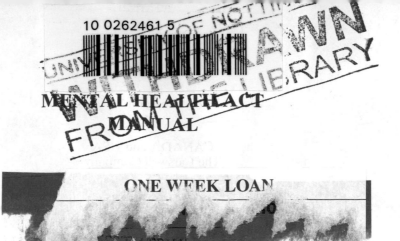

MENTAL HEALTH ACT MANUAL

AUSTRALIA
LBC Information Services
Sydney

CANADA and USA
The Carswell Company
Toronto

NEW ZEALAND
Brooker's
Auckland

SINGAPORE and MALAYSIA
Sweet & Maxwell Asia
Singapore and Kuala Lumpur

PREFACE

This edition aims to follow its predecessors by providing material and analysis that will assist those who either have responsibility for implementing or for providing advice on the Mental Health Act. The major development since the publication of the previous edition has been the bringing into force on October 2, 2000, of the Human Rights Act 1998. Schedule 1 to the 1998 Act, which sets out the relevant Articles of the European Convention of Human Rights, is reproduced in an annotated form in Part 6. Commentary on the implications of the Act for mental health law is made throughout the text.

During the course of the training that I provide on mental health law, I am frequently asked to indicate where practitioners can find material that explains relevant common law principles. Much of what is required can be found in this Manual. Common law rules relating to consent to medical treatment are considered in the General Note to Part IV of the Act. This coverage includes a new section on "The medical treatment of children". An account of common law powers of detention can be found in the General Note to section 5 under the heading "Further powers to detain and control patients" and in the General Note to section 131. Uncertainty about the scope of common law powers has lead to patients being detained under the Mental Health Act on every occasion where restraint has had to be used. The use of restraint should only be followed by detention under the Act in the circumstances set out in the General Note to paragraph 19.8 of the *Code of Practice*.

Sources of information for those who take an interest in mental health law have improved significantly in recent years. Those who have access to the internet can benefit from two websites that provide comprehensive sources of material on mental health law and related matters. The websites are those of Dave Sheppard Associates (*www.davesheppard.co.uk*) and of Mark Walton (*www.markwalton.net*). The Journal of Mental Health Law was launched in 1999 with the objective of providing "a forum for the publication of high quality research material, analysis and commentary in the area of mental health law". It has already achieved a considerable reputation (details from Northumbria Law Press, University of Northumbria at Newcastle, Newcastle upon Tyne, NE1 8ST). Another important development is the publication of a set of law reports, the Mental Health Law Reports, which reproduces the full text of cases relating to all aspects of mental health law. The reports are edited by Kris Gledhill, a barrister who specialises in this area of law (details from Southside Legal Publishing Limited, 66 Grove Park, London SE5 8LF).

The amendments made to this Act by the Care Standards Act 2000, which are due to come into effect on April 1, 2002, have been incorporated into this edition. Subject to this exception, I have attempted to state the law as it is today.

Richard Jones
18 Meadowside
Penarth
Vale of Glamorgan

July 31, 2001

CONTENTS

CONTENTS

TABLE OF CASES

Table of Cases

Table of Cases

Table of Cases

Table of Cases

Table of Cases

EUROPEAN COURT OF HUMAN RIGHTS CASES

Cases including United Kingdom citations are also included in the United Kingdom
section

Table of Cases

PART 1

MENTAL HEALTH ACT 1983

(1983 c. 20)

ARRANGEMENT OF SECTIONS

1

PART IV

CONSENT TO TREATMENT

PART V

MENTAL HEALTH REVIEW TRIBUNALS

Constitution, etc.

PART VI

REMOVAL AND RETURN OF PATIENTS WITHIN UNITED KINGDOM, ETC.

Removal to Scotland

Removal to and from Northern Ireland

Removal to and from Channel Islands and Isle of Man

Removal of aliens

Return of patients absent without leave

General

PART VII

MANAGEMENT OF PROPERTY AND AFFAIRS OF PATIENTS

PART VIII

MISCELLANEOUS FUNCTIONS OF LOCAL AUTHORITIES AND THE SECRETARY OF STATE

Approved social workers

Visiting patients

After-care

Functions of the Secretary of State

PART IX

OFFENCES

PART X

MISCELLANEOUS AND SUPPLEMENTARY

Miscellaneous provisions

Supplemental

SCHEDULES

An Act to consolidate the law relating to mentally disordered persons.

[May 9, 1983]

GENERAL NOTE

1–002   The origins of modern mental health legislation lie with the Mental Health Act 1959 which repealed all existing legislation dealing with mental illness and mental deficiency. It was based on the *Report of the Royal Commission on the Law Relating* *to Mental Illness* (Cmnd. 169) and incorporated the principles that no one should be admitted to hospital if care in the community would be more appropriate, and that where admission to hospital was required compulsion, which was to be a medical instead of a judicial matter, should if possible be avoided. In January 1975 the Labour Government announced its intention to review the 1959 Act in the light of the many changes which had taken place in treatment and care, in the patterns of services for the mentally disordered, and in public attitudes. An interdepartmental Committee of civil servants was set up to undertake the review and it considered a number of suggestions for amending the Act including comprehensive reviews which had been carried out by the Royal College of Psychiatrists and by MIND in Volume 1 of its publication, *A Human Condition*. It also considered that part of the *Report of the Committee on Mentally Abnormal Offenders*, Cmnd. 6244 (The Butler Report) which reviewed Pt V of the 1959 Act which is concerned with offenders.

The Committee's suggestions were set out in a consultative document, *A Review of the Mental Health Act 1959* (HMSO, 1976) and comments were invited from interested bodies and individuals. Following the publication of the consultative document two further major contributions to the debate came in the form of the second volume of MIND's, *A Human Condition*, on offender patients and the British Association of Social Workers' document, "Mental Health Crisis Services—A New Philosophy."

In 1978 the Government published its response to this consultative exercise in a **1–003** White Paper, *The Review of the Mental Health Act 1959* (Cmnd. 7320). Some of the proposals in this White Paper were set out in a tentative form because they were either not put forward in the consultative document or were not fully developed at that time. Comments on these proposals were invited but before the Government could translate its proposals into an amending Bill a change of government took place. Further consultations then took place and the Conservative Government's conclusions were embodied in a Bill which was published in November 1981, together with an accompanying White Paper, *Reform of Mental Health Legislation* (Cmnd. 8405). This Bill, which was scrutinised by a Special Standing Committee of the House of Commons, was enacted in October 1982 as the Mental Health (Amendment) Act 1982. It made substantial amendments to the 1959 Act as well as introducing new powers relating to the treatment and discharge of mentally disordered patients. In Cmnd. 8405 the Government announced its intention to introduce a consolidation measure soon after the Royal Assent had been given to the 1982 Act and a Consolidation Bill was introduced in the House of Lords on January 20, 1983. It was referred to the Joint Committee on Consolidation Bills which reported on February 9, 1983 (HL 81, HC 193). The Bill received the Royal Assent on May 9, 1983. The background to this Act is analysed by Clive Unsworth in *The Politics of Mental Health Legislation*, 1987.

Although this Act conveniently brings together the law relating to mentally disordered persons, the fact that certain provisions of the 1959 Act are not repealed might cause confusion. In particular, section 8 which deals with the welfare functions of local authorities, and section 128 which is concerned with sexual offences relating to mentally disordered patients will remain in the 1959 Act until consolidated elsewhere.

Scope of the Act
According to the Court of Appeal the "policy and objects" of this Act are "to **1–004** regulate the circumstances in which the liberty of persons who are mentally disordered may be restricted and, where there is conflict, to balance their interests against those of public policy" (*R. v. Secretary of State for the Home Department, ex p. K* [1990] 3 All E.R. 562, 570 *per* McCowan L.J.).

Judicial interpretation
"There is ... no canon of construction which presumes that Parliament intended **1–005** that people should, against their will, be subjected to treatment which others,

however professionally competent, perceive, however sincerely and however correctly, to be in their best interests. What there is is a canon of construction that Parliament is presumed not to enact legislation which interferes with the liberty of the subject without making it clear that this was its intention. It goes without saying that, unless clear statutory authority to the contrary exists, no one is to be detained in hospital or to undergo medical treatment or even to submit himself to a medical examination without his consent. That is as true of a mentally disordered person as of anyone else" (*R. v. Hallstrom, ex p. W (No. 2); R. v. Gardner, ex p. L* [1986] 2 All E.R. 306, 314, *per* McCullough J.).

Injunctions to support an authority's performance of its duties under this Act

1–006   In *Broadmoor Hospital Authority v. R* [2000] All E.R. 727, the issue before the Court of Appeal was whether a statutory body is entitled to be granted an injunction in civil proceedings to support its performance of its statutory duties. The court held that:

(i) if a public body is given a statutory responsibility which it is required to perform in the public interest, then, in the absence of an implication to the contrary in the statute, it has standing to apply to the court for an injunction to prevent interference with its performance of its public responsibilities and the court should grant such an application when it appears to the court to be just and convenient to do so; and

(ii) conduct outside a hospital can affect what happens within the hospital and if this is so jurisdiction exists in the court to provide protection by injunction. However there would need to be a substantial risk to the hospital's powers being prejudiced for the court to exercise its discretion to issue an injunction. *Per* Lord Woolf at 736:
"If for example an individual was causing interference with the discipline of a special hospital by writing letters to the patients then notwithstanding the ability of the authority to censor correspondence, in the appropriate situation an injunction against the individual could be granted to reduce the risk of discipline being undermined and treatment interfered with."

Injunctions granted against mentally incapable persons

1–007   In *Wookey v. Wookey* [1991] 3 All E.R. 365, the Court of Appeal held that an injunction ought not to be granted against a person who is incapable of understanding what he is doing or that it is wrong, because such a person is incapable of complying with it. The appropriate way of dealing with the problem behaviour of a mentally incapable person is the use of the powers under this Act. However, an interlocutory injunction might be appropriate if the court considers that the mental condition of the person against whom an injunction is sought should be investigated.

In *P v. P (Contempt of Court: Mental Capacity)* [1999] 2 F.L.R. 897, the Court of Appeal considered the degree of capacity which an individual must have in order to be subject to the contempt jurisdiction. The court held that it was not necessary for the person to comprehend the meaning or significance of courts or of the legal process. What was required was that a potential contemnor should understand that an order has been made forbidding him to do certain things and that if he did them he may very well be punished.

Applications for injunctions and ouster orders relating to mentally disordered persons are considered by District Judge Gordon Ashton in "Injunctions and Mental Disorder" [2000] Fam. Law 29–42.

The protection of mentally incapable adults

1–008   See the note under this heading in the General Note to section 8.

Voting

The law relating to the right of patients in psychiatric hospitals to vote has been **1–009** changed by the Representation of the People Act 2000. New section 3A of the Representation of the People Act 1983 (as inserted by section 2 of the 2000 Act) essentially excludes those patients who have been detained in psychiatric hospitals as a consequence of criminal activity from voting in parliamentary and local government elections. Other patients, both detained and informal, will be entitled to be registered to vote pursuant to either new section 7 of the 1983 Act (as inserted by section 4 of the 2000 Act) or to new section 7A of the 1983 Act (as inserted by section 5 of the 2000 Act).

Marriage

The marriage of patients detained under this Act is provided for under section 1 of **1–010** the Marriage Act 1983. Guidance on the relevant procedure is contained in paragraphs 5 to 7 DHSS Circular No. LAC (84)9:

"The Marriage Act also permits the marriages of patients detained in hospital under the Mental Health Act 1983 to take place in hospital. It does, however, exclude from these provisions those detained under the shorter-term provisions, *i.e.* sections 2, 4, 5, 35, 36, or 136 of the Mental Health Act 1983.

When a detained person wishes to be married in hospital the notice of marriage required by section 27 of the Marriage Act 1949 must be accompanied by a statement made in the prescribed form by the hospital managers not more than 21 days before the date on which notice of the marriage is given:

i. identifying the establishment where the person is detained; and
ii. stating that the hospital managers have no objection to that establishment being specified in the notice of marriage as the place where that marriage is to be solemnised.

A copy of this form is at Annex B. Further copies are obtainable from the local Superintendent Registrar.

Hospitals will wish to arrange careful counselling for any detained patient who wishes to marry, and possibly for their prospective spouses, so that both parties may consider the matter fully."

Anyone, including the doctor in charge of the patient's treatment, who does not believe that the patient is capable of giving a valid consent to the marriage, may enter a caveat with the Superintendent Registrar before the ceremony. The Superintendent Registrar will give the person who gave notice of marriage an opportunity to answer the objection and to produce evidence in rebuttal of the grounds alleged. If the Superintendent Registrar is in doubt whether or not the caveat ought to obstruct the issue of a certificate for marriage, he may refer the matter to the Registrar General. There is a right of appeal to the Registrar General against a Superintendent Registrar's refusal to issue his certificate for marriage by reason of a caveat.

The impact that the Human Rights Act 1998 will have on the marital rights of detained patients is considered in the note on Article 12 of the European Convention on Human Rights.

Diplomatic immunity

By virtue of the Diplomatic Privileges Act 1964, "the person of a diplomatic agent **1–011** shall be inviolate. He shall not be liable to any form of arrest or detention. The receiving State shall treat him with due respect and shall take all appropriate steps to prevent any attack on his person, freedom or dignity" (s.2, Sched. 1, art. 29). Article 1(e) defines a "diplomatic agent" as "the head of the mission or a member of the diplomatic staff of the mission" and article 37 extends the provisions of article 29 to "the members of the family of a diplomatic agent forming part of his household" who are not nationals of the receiving State. Diplomats and their families should not therefore be made subject to the provisions of this Act unless the inviolability afforded by the 1964 Act has been lifted. According to Dr David Pariente, the legal department of the Foreign and Commonwealth Office has advised that such inviolability "can only be lifted by the State which the diplomat represents; in normal circumstances the State's consent must be obtained from the appropriate Head of Mission, usually an Ambassador, with whose agreement the provisions of the Mental Health Act can then be exercised. Irreversible and hazardous treatments would require his consent. In cases of extreme emergency, where immediate detention of the diplomat is the only way to protect human safety, such action would be justifiable on the basis of the inherent right of self-defence, or the duty to protect human life. In such a case the Foreign and Commonwealth Office should be informed immediately." Dr Pariente further reports that the Medical Defence Union has "advised that the consent of the Head of Mission should be sought in writing; and that the issue of breach of confidentiality should not present a problem to a doctor who was clearly acting in the best interests of the patient" ("Diplomatic immunity and the Mental Health Act 1983" (1991) *Psychiatric Bulletin* 15, 207–209). An approved social worker faced with the possibility of making an application in respect of a person who is covered by the 1964 Act would be best advised to contact the Foreign and Commonwealth Office which could request the relevant Head of Mission to provide the necessary consent.

International

1–012 The only international instrument against which U.K. mental health law can be judicially tested is the European Convention for the Protection of Human Rights and Fundamental Freedoms (more commonly known as the European Convention on Human Rights). Although the Convention has not been incorporated into U.K. domestic law, the Human Rights Act 1998 provides for improved access to the rights and freedoms guaranteed under it. A note on the Human Rights Act, together with Schedule 1 to the Act, which sets out the relevant Articles of the European Convention on Human Rights, is reproduced below. Case law on the Convention had a significant influence on the drafting of this Act and the Convention places an important constraint on the scope of any changes that can be made to the Act. For an analysis of the rights of mentally disordered people under the Convention, see C. Baker (ed.), *Human Rights Act 1998: A Practitioner's Guide* (1998), Chap. 10.

On December 17, 1991, the General Assembly of the United Nations adopted 25 Principles for the Protection of Persons with Mental Illness and for the Improvement of Mental Health. Principle 22 requires Member States to "ensure that appropriate mechanisms are in force to promote compliance with [the] Principles, for the inspection of mental health facilities, for the submission, investigation and resolution of complaints and for the institution of appropriate disciplinary or judicial proceedings for professional misconduct or violation of the rights of a patient." Copies of this document can be obtained from the United Nations Information Centre, 20 Buckingham Gate, London SW1E 6LB. The United Nations also adopted, on December 20, 1971, a Declaration on the Rights of Mentally Retarded Persons. This Declaration is reproduced in the "International" section of the *Encyclopedia of Social Services and Child Care Law*, Sweet & Maxwell, 1993.

COMMENCEMENT

1–013 Most of this Act came into force on September 30, 1983 (s.149(2)). Sections 35, 36, 38 and 40(3) came into force on October 1, 1984 (s.149(3) and S.I. 1984 No. 1537). The provisions for approved social workers (ss.114 and 145(1)) came into force on October 28, 1984 (Sched. 5, para. 4). The amendments made to this Act by the Mental Health (Patients in the Community) Act 1995 came into force on April 1, 1996 (*ibid.*, s.7(2)).

TRANSITIONAL PROVISIONS

Detailed transitional provisions are set out in Schedule 5. General continuity **1–014** between the repealed legislation and this Act is provided for in paragraphs 1 and 3 which specify that periods of time which began under the repealed legislation are to be re-calculated under the corresponding provisions of this Act and that anything done under the repealed legislation, *e.g.* detention for treatment under the 1959 Act, does not cease to have effect because of the repeal of that legislation.

EXTENT

This Act applies to Scotland and Northern Ireland only to the extent provided for **1–015** in sections 146 and 147, respectively. The whole of this Act was extended to the Isles of Scilly on March 12, 1985, by the Isles of Scilly (Mental Health) Order 1985 (S.I. 1985 No. 149) with the modification that the expression "local social services authority" in the Act shall, in relation to the Isles, mean the Council of the Isles constituted under the Isles of Scilly Order 1978 (S.I. 1978 No. 1844).

ABBREVIATIONS

In the annotations the following abbreviations are used: **1–016**

Aarvold Committee: Report on the Review of Procedures for the Discharge and Supervision of Psychiatric Patients subject to Special Restrictions (Cmnd. 5191).

Butler Committee: Report of the Committee on Mentally Abnormal Offenders (Cmnd. 6244).

Code of Practice: The *Code of Practice* published under section 118(4) of this Act.

Cmnd. 7320: Reform of the Mental Health Act 1959.

Cmnd. 8405: Reform of the Mental Health Legislation.

Memorandum: Mental Health Act 1983: Memorandum on Parts I to VI, VIII and X. Department of Health and Welsh Office, 1998. The Memorandum, which describe the main provisions of this Act, "is for the guidance of all those who work with the Act" (*ibid.*, para. 1).

Consultative Document: A review of the Mental Health Act 1959 (HMSO, 1976).

The Reed Committee: Review of Health and Social Services for Mentally Disordered Offenders and others requiring similar services, Chairman: Dr John Reed, HMSO, 1992.

Royal Commission: Report of the Royal Commission on the Law Relating to Mental Illness and Mental Deficiency 1954–1957, Chairman—Lord Percy (Cmnd. 169).

Special Standing Committee: The special Standing Committee which considered the Mental Health (Amendment) Bill.

PARLIAMENTARY DEBATES

Hansard, HL Vol. 437, col. 1533; Vol. 438, col. 519; Vol. 440, cols 616, 833; Vol. 441, **1–017** col. 1049; Vol. 442, col. 342; HC Vol. 40, col. 642; Vol. 41, col. 260.

PART I

APPLICATION OF ACT

Application of Act: "mental disorder"

1–018   **1.**—(1) The provisions of this Act shall have effect with respect to the reception, care and treatment of mentally disordered patients, the management of their property and other related matters.

(2) In this Act—

"mental disorder" means mental illness, arrested or incomplete development of mind, psychopathic disorder and any other disorder or disability of mind and "mentally disordered" shall be construed accordingly;

"severe mental impairment" means a state of arrested or incomplete development of mind which includes severe impairment of intelligence and social functioning and is associated with abnormally aggressive or seriously irresponsible conduct on the part of the person concerned and "severely mentally impaired" shall be construed accordingly;

"mental impairment" means a state of arrested or incomplete development of mind (not amounting to severe mental impairment) which includes significant impairment of intelligence and social functioning and is associated with abnormally aggressive or seriously irresponsible conduct on the part of the person concerned and "mentally impaired" shall be construed accordingly;

"psychopathic disorder" means a persistent disorder or disability of mind (whether or not including significant impairment of intelligence) which results in abnormally aggressive or seriously irresponsible conduct on the part of the person concerned;

and other expressions shall have the meanings assigned to them in section 145 below.

(3) Nothing in subsection (2) above shall be construed as implying that a person may be dealt with under this Act as suffering from mental disorder, or from any form of mental disorder described in this section, by reason only of promiscuity or other immoral conduct, sexual deviancy or dependence on alcohol or drugs.

DEFINITION

1–019   patient: s.145(1).

GENERAL NOTE

1–020   Apart from indicating the extent of this Act, this section defines the generic term "mental disorder" and three of the four specific categories of mental disorder. The definitions of "severe mental impairment", "mental impairment", and "psychopathic disorder" are remarkably similar in their scope in that all three definitions refer to "abnormally aggressive or seriously irresponsible conduct" and can also include "impairment of intelligence".

Sections 16, 25F and 72(5) provide for the reclassification of the form of mental disorder from which a detained patient, a patient who is subject to supervised discharge or a patient who is subject to guardianship is said to be suffering.

The Human Rights Act 1998
The terms of this section are consistent with the interpretation given by the **1–021**
European Court of Human Rights to the phrase "persons of unsound mind"
contained in Article 5(1)(e) of the European Convention on Human Rights: see the
note on *Winterwerp v. Netherlands* (1979) 2 E.H.R.R. 387 under the heading
"persons of unsound mind" in Article 5(1)(e).

Subsection (1)
In *R. v. Kirklees MBC* [1992] 2 F.L.R. 117, 120, Kennedy J., speaking *obiter*, said **1–022**
that this provision "seems to suggest that the provisions of [this] Act never do apply if
the person admitted to hospital for assessment turns out not to be a mentally
disordered person". The *Kirklees* case is considered in the General Note to section
131.

Subsection (2)
Mental disorder: More than one of the conditions set out in this definition may **1–023**
affect the patient at any one time. For many of the purposes of this Act a diagnosis of
"mental disorder" is not sufficient and a diagnosis of one of the four specific
categories of mental disorder—mental illness, mental impairment, severe mental
impairment or psychopathic disorder—is required. In *St George's Healthcare NHS
Trust v. S* [1998] 3 All E.R. 673, 696, CA, Judge L.J. said that the court did not doubt
"that reactive depression (not merely a transient sense of being 'a little down' or 'fed
up with everything') is capable of amounting to a mental disorder."
Mental illness: This category of mental disorder, which is the diagnosis identified in
the overwhelming majority of formal admissions under this Act, is not defined, nor is
any attempt made in the *Code of Practice* to provide guidance on this term. Its
"operational definition and usage is a matter for clinical judgment in each case"
(*Memorandum*, para. 8). Anorexia nervosa is a mental illness for the purposes of this
Act (*Re KB (Adult) (Mental Patient: Medical Treatment)* (1994) 19 B.M.L.R. 144,
Ewbank J.)
The Royal Commission felt that "the term 'mental illness' would be used in the
same sense as at present, including the mental infirmity of old age" (para. 17(a)). This
"lay view" of mental illness has received judicial blessing from Lawton L.J. who, in *W
v. L* [1974] Q.B. 711, 719, CA, said that the words "mental illness" are "ordinary
words of the English language. They have no particular medical significance. They
have no particular legal significance. How should the court construe them? The
answer ... is ... that ordinary words of the English language should be construed in
the way that ordinary sensible people would construe them. That being in my
judgment the right test, then I ask myself, what would the ordinary sensible person
have said about the patient's condition in this case if he had been informed of his
behaviour to the dogs [he hanged one dog and strangled another], the cat [this he
tortured before cutting its throat] and his wife [he placed a knife at her throat]? In my
judgment such a person would have said: 'Well, the fellow is obviously mentally ill.'
... It is that application of the sensible person's assessment of the condition, plus the
medical indication [of an E.E.G. test], which in my judgment brought the case within
the classification of mental illness." This unsatisfactory formulation, which has been
described as "the-man-must-be-mad" test (Brenda Hoggett, *Mental Health Law*,
1990, p. 48), is analysed by Michael Cavadino in "Mental Illness and Neo-
Polonianism" (1991) 2 *Journal of Forensic Psychiatry* 294–304. Also note the
following dictum of Bowen L.J. in *Edgington v. Fitzmaurice* (1885) 29 Ch.D. 459 at
483: "the state of a man's mind is as much a fact as the state of his digestion". The
Butler Committee considered that the expression mental illness "denotes a disorder
which has not always existed in the patient but has developed as a condition overlying
the sufferer's usual personality" (para. 1.13).

The following attempt by the DHSS to define mental illness, which is contained in Appendix II of its *Consultative Document*, provides a guide to the symptoms that are associated with the legal category of "mental illness":

"*Mental illness* means an illness having one or more of the following characteristics:

(i) More than temporary impairment of intellectual functions shown by a failure of memory, orientation, comprehension and learning capacity;

(ii) More than temporary alteration of mood of such degree as to give rise to the patient having a delusional appraisal of his situation, his past or his future, or that of others or to the lack of any appraisal;

(iii) Delusional beliefs, persecutory, jealous or grandiose;

(iv) Abnormal perceptions associated with delusional misinterpretation of events;

(v) Thinking so disordered as to prevent the patient making a reasonable appraisal of his situation or having reasonable communication with others."

This definition "has been criticised by some psychiatrists because it is restrictive in some places and over-inclusive in others, and because it seems to exclude the commonest psychiatric disorder encountered in practice which is depression", (*Assessment of Mental Capacity: Guidance for doctors and lawyers*, A Report of the British Medical Association and The Law Society, 1995, para. 3:2:1).

The Government abandoned its search for a definition of mental illness partly because of "the difficulties of producing a definition which would be likely to stand the test of time" and partly because of the fact that there apparently had "not been much evidence that the lack of definition of mental illness leads to any particular problems", (Cmnd. 7320, para. 1.17.)

In art. 3(1) of the Mental Health (Northern Ireland) Order 1986 (S.I. 1986 No. 595 (N.I. 4)) mental illness is defined as "a state of mind which affects a person's thinking, perceiving, emotion or judgment to the extent that he requires care or medical treatment in his own interests or the interests of other persons."

1–024 *Arrested or incomplete development of mind: I.e.* mental handicap. This phrase "would seem to cover any appreciable failure to meet the normal milestones of mental development, whether this is caused by genetic or constitutional factors, or by environmental shortcomings in childhood, or by damage to or disease of the brain" (Brenda Hoggett, *Mental Health Law*, 1996, p. 39). It does not cover an injury to, or the degeneration of, a mind which has reached full development, *e.g.* brain injury to an adult or senile dementia. An account of the legal and medical definitions of mental handicap can be found in G. Ashton and A. Ward, *Mental Handicap and the Law* (1992), pp. 9–18. Also see the *Code of Practice* at paragraph 30.5 and the note on "severe mental impairment", below.

Any other disorder or disability of mind: The conditions that will come within this wide residual category will, to a certain extent, depend upon how broad a view is taken of "mental illness." They could include "neuroses, personality disorders, behaviour disorders, disability resulting from head injuries and transient mental disturbances" (L. Gostin and P. Fennell, *Mental Health: Tribunal Procedure* (2nd ed., 1992), p. 183). In *R. v. Ireland; R. v. Burstow* [1997] 4 All E.R. 225 at 231, HL, Lord Steyn said that neuroses "must be distinguished from simple states of fear, or problems in coping with everyday life. Where the line is to be drawn must be a matter of psychiatric judgment." The Minister of Health, speaking on the Committee stage of the 1959 Act, said that this category would cover "disabilities arising from head injuries or encephalitis or mental enfeeblement as the aftermath of mental illness." (Standing Committee, February 12, 1959.)

In the context of the *McNaghten* rules Devlin J. said that "mind" should be "used in the ordinary sense of the mental faculties of reason, memory and understanding"

(*R. v. Kemp* [1957] 1 Q.B. 399 at 407). This statement was approved by Lord Diplock in *R. v. Sullivan* [1983] 2 All E.R. 673, HL at 677. In *Vernon v. Bosley (No. 1)* [1997] 1 All E.R. 577, 597, CA, Evans L.J. described the phrase "disorder of the mind" as being "no more than a metaphor, although a dramatic and useful one".

A person who suffers from a disorder which comes within this category is eligible for detention under sections 2, 4, 5, 135 and 136 of this Act.

Severe mental impairment: The intention behind the definitions of "mental impairment" and "severe mental impairment" is to "distinguish the small minority of people with learning disabilities who need to be detained in hospital or received into guardianship, from the great majority who do not" (*Memorandum*, para. 8). However, as the definition of "mental disorder" includes those who are suffering from "arrested or incomplete development of mind" which need not necessarily be "associated with abnormally aggressive or seriously irresponsible conduct," people with a learning disability will continue to be liable to be detained under those provisions of this Act which do not require a specific diagnosis. Also see the note on "arrested or incomplete development of mind," above.

In *Megarry v. Chief Adjudication Officer, The Times*, November 11, 1999, the Court of Appeal held that a high intelligence quotient was not sufficient to deprive an autistic child of entitlement to disability living allowance as a person suffering from "severe impairment of intelligence and social functioning" within the meaning of regulation 12(5) of the Social Security (Disability Living Allowance) Regulations (S.I. 1991 No. 2890). *Per* Simon Brown L.J.:

> "In most cases, no doubt, the measurement of IQ will be the best available method of measuring intelligence. But among the dictionary definitions of intelligence one finds reference not merely to the functions of understanding and intellect but also to the qualities of insight and sagacity. It seems to me that in the case of an autistic child those qualities may well be lacking and to the extent that they are there will be a functional impairment which overlaps both limbs of the regulation, *i.e.* both intelligence and social functioning."

In *R. v. Hall (John Hamilton)* (1988) 86 Cr.App.R. 159, the Court of Appeal considered a similar definition of severe mental impairment in the context of a criminal prosecution brought under the Sexual Offences Act 1956. It was submitted on behalf of the appellant that a person whose incomplete development produced severe impairment of intelligence and social functioning as compared with normally developed members of the public, but only moderate impairment when compared with *other* mental defectives, was not to be regarded as suffering from severe mental impairment. The Court regarded the submission as untenable. On a natural reading of the definition it was clear that severe impairment was to be measured against the standard of normal persons.

Includes: What follows is not an exclusive list of attributes associated with this disorder.

Impairment: This term is used by the World Health Organisation in its *Inter-* **1–025** *national Classification of Impairments, Disabilities and Handicaps* (1979) to describe any loss or abnormality of psychological, physiological or anatomical structure or function. It was criticised by some of the professional bodies which gave evidence to the Special Standing Committee on the ground that it implied a reduction from a higher level of function which does not apply to the majority of cases of mental handicap.

Social functioning: This phrase appears to cover all aspects of a person's social behaviour.

Is associated with: The abnormally aggressive or seriously irresponsible conduct need not be as a result of the impairment: an association is sufficient. An amendment by Mr Christopher Price M.P. to insert "recent" after this phrase was defeated by the Special Standing Committee. He was concerned that "is associated with" could be construed as "has been associated with", and that an event of seriously irresponsible or abnormally aggressive conduct that has occurred in the patient's past could be used to satisfy the test of association. The Minister for Health responded to this concern by stating that the definition had the effect of "asking people to determine the current state of the patient when deciding whether to detain him. They should not be asking whether he is being violent at that moment but whether his state of mind makes him liable to be violent or seriously irresponsible unless a detention order is made ... A patient's past conduct may be highly relevant as evidence ... for those who must appraise his conduct and state of mind" (sitting of May 11, 1982).

Abnormally aggressive or seriously irresponsible conduct: The use of this phrase, which was taken from the definition of psychopathy in the 1959 Act, was criticised by a number of witnesses to the Special Standing Committee on the ground that it may result in mentally impaired patients being confused with patients who are suffering from psychopathic disorder.

What is "abnormally aggressive" or "seriously irresponsible" must, to a certain extent, depend upon the cultural and social context within which the behaviour occurs. In *R. v. Trent Mental Health Review Tribunal, ex p. Ryan* [1992] C.O.D. 157, Nolan L.J. said: "No doubt whether the conduct is the result of the disorder ... is a medical question. Whether it amounts to seriously irresponsible or abnormally aggressive behaviour seem to me ... to raise questions other than of a purely clinical nature".

In *Re F (Mental Health Act: Guardianship)* [2000] 1 F.L.R. 192, the Court of Appeal adopted a restrictive construction of the phrase "seriously irresponsible conduct" by holding that a seventeen year old patient's natural desire to return home, albeit to an inadequate home where the patient had been exposed to chronic neglect and sexual exploitation, could not be labelled as irresponsible conduct. *Per* Thorpe L.J. at 198:

> "The urge to return [home] is almost universal ... The deficiencies of the home are more apparent to other adults than to the young who have known no other. Furthermore, any measure of irresponsibility must depend upon an evaluation of the consequences of return ... Clearly each case must depend on its particular facts and we would not wish to be taken as offering any general guideline."

Although Thorpe L.J. emphasised that the court had reached its conclusions "on the special facts of a difficult and unusual case", the court's finding is significant because the urge to return home is not the only " almost universal" urge that might effect a patient: the urge to love and be loved falls into this category. As it clearly possible for a patient to express such an urge in a seriously irresponsible manner, the fact that the nature of the urge is "almost universal" does not exclude the patient from being assessed as involving him or herself in "seriously irresponsible conduct". When determining whether a patient's conduct falls into this category, a clinician should pay special attention to the consequences of the expression of the urge for the patient and/or others. The clinician should refrain from categorising the patient's conduct as being "seriously irresponsible" in the absence of a clear opinion based on reliable evidence that the patient's conduct would result or is resulting in a significant risk to his or her health or safety or to the health or safety of others. *Re F* is considered by R. Sandland in "Mental Health Act Guardianship and the Protection of Children" (2000) 4 Journal of Mental Health Law 186–195.

Phil Fennell has said that "it is a moot point whether it can be seriously irresponsible conduct for a person who is unable to care for themselves to fail to remedy neglect by the person who looks after them". Fennell argues that the point involves three questions, none of which has a clear answer: "First, can passive endurance of neglect be conduct? Second, can irresponsibility include irresponsibility to oneself? Third, how bad does the conduct have to be to be serious?": see

P. Fennell, "The Beverley Lewis case: Was the Law to Blame" *New Law Journal*, November 17, 1989, pp. 1557–1558 and "Falling Through the Legal Loopholes" *Social Work Today*, Nov. 30, 1989, pp. 18–20. Dr Yvonne Wiley argues that to use the concept of "passive irresponsibility" would be contrary to the spirit of this Act because "the implication would be that every person suffering from severe mental handicap would immediately be included in the Act because they are unable by reason of their intellectual deficit to be responsible ("The Beverley Lewis Case: An Outline of Some of the Medico–Legal Aspects", in *A Double Challenge: Working with People who have both Learning Difficulties and a Mental Illness*, C.C.E.T.S.W. Paper 19.27, 1992, pp. 13–15). Given the judgment of the Court of Appeal in *Re F (Mental Health Act: Guardianship)*, above, this opinion must be correct. The Law Commission's view is that unless "the meaning of these words are distorted, the vast majority of those with a learning disability (mental handicap) will be excluded from guardianship" (*Mental Incapacity*, 1995, para. 2.21). However, it has been reported that a failure by the patient to protect himself from the abusive behaviour of others has been used as evidence of "seriously irresponsible conduct" on the part of the patient (Helen Whitworth and Shashi Singhal, "The use of guardianship in mental handicap services" (1995) 19 *Psychiatric Bulletin* 725–727).

The Mental Health Act Commission has defined the terms "abnormally aggressive" and "seriously irresponsible" as follows: "'abnormally aggressive conduct' is behaviour which is mostly unpredictable and severe, causing damage or distress and occurring either recently or persistently or with excessive severity. Examples are: damaging others by physical acts, throwing objects to cause damage to others. 'Seriously irresponsible conduct' is behaviour which frequently constitutes a serious or potentially serious danger, where the person concerned does not show appropriate regard to its consequences. Examples are: absconding, arson, life-endangering self-neglect, (*Mental Health Act 1983: Section 118—Draft Code of Practice*, 1985, paras 1.10.4, 5). The *Code of Practice* gives guidance on these terms at paragraph 29.5.

Mental impairment: The distinction between "severe mental impairment" and **1–026** "mental impairment" is one of degree in that while the former includes a *"severe* impairment of intelligence and social functioning," the latter includes a *"significant* impairment of intelligence and social functioning." A slight impairment would not be sufficient for either definition. Whether an impairment is considered to be slight, significant or severe is a matter for clinical judgment.

Psychopathic disorder: "Since its introduction more than 90 years ago the term 'psychopathic disorder' has been subject to a variety of different practical usages: it has been taken to cover a narrow or broad group of mental disorders, and to indicate differences either of causation or of clinical manifestation from other mental disorders. In consequence there is now a multiplicity of opinions as to the aetiology, symptoms and treatment of 'psychopathy,' which is only to be understood by reference to the particular sense in which the term is being employed by the psychiatrist in question" (*Butler Committee*, para. 5.2). Its analysis of the term "psychopathic disorder" led the Butler Committee to conclude that, "it is no longer a useful or meaningful concept" (para. 5.23). The "Report of the Department of Health and Home Office Working Group on Psychopathic Disorder" (1994) states in paragraphs 2.2 and 2.3:

> "What constitutes psychopathic disorder and how it should be managed and treated has, over the years, been the subject of intensive debate without any general agreement being reached. It is now generally accepted that the term 'psychopathic disorder' does not represent a single clinical disorder but is a legal category describing a number of severe personality disorders, which contribute to the person committing anti-social acts, usually of a recurrent or episodic type.

One important feature may be an inability to relate to others, and to take account of their feelings and safety. It has often proved difficult to influence this behaviour by means of social, penal and medical interventions.

Thus people in the category of psychopathic disorder are not a homogenous group for which established treatment techniques have proved successful. Both for this reason, and because people in the group often behave in an aggressive and unpredictable manner, their management presents particular difficulty."

The Working Group concluded that "there was a persuasive argument for substituting the term 'personality disorder' for 'psychopathic disorder' in the statutory definition provided that 'personality disorder' was not defined further" (para. 10.17). Also see, John Reed, "Psychopathy—A Clinical and Legal Dilemma" (1996) 168 *British Journal of Psychiatry* 4–9 and Part 6 of the Report of the Committee of Inquiry into the Personality Disorder Unit, Ashworth Special Hospital (1999).

Bearing in mind the exclusions contained in subsection (3), the definition used here enables a patient to be diagnosed as a psychopath largely on the basis of his behaviour. Although the definition does not refer to the treatability of the condition, the effect of sections 3, 37 and 47 is that psychopathic (and mentally impaired) patients cannot be compulsorily admitted to hospital for treatment unless it can be shown that the medical treatment is likely to alleviate or prevent a deterioration of their condition. It is possible for a patient to be diagnosed as suffering from both psychopathic disorder and mental illness (*W v. L*, above).

The category of "psychopathic disorder" is not used in the mental health legislation in Scotland or Northern Ireland: see section 1 of the Mental Health (Scotland) Act 1984 and article 3 of the Mental Health (Northern Ireland) Order 1986. Dr Rosemarie Cope reports that forensic psychiatrists are divided on the question of whether the category should remain within this Act ("A survey of forensic psychiatrists' views on psychopathic disorder", *The Journal of Forensic Psychiatry*, Vol. 4, No. 2, 215–235).

Persistent . The disorder must have existed for "a considerable period before a patient can be classified as having psychopathic disorder" (*Memorandum*, para. 11).

Results in: Implies a stronger causal relationship than is the case with the term "associated with" which is used in the definitions of impairment.

Abnormally aggressive or seriously irresponsible conduct: See above.

Subsection (3)

1–027   *By reason only:* Thus a person cannot be treated as being mentally disordered for any of the purposes of this Act solely on the ground that he is promiscuous, immoral, a sexual deviant or an alcohol or drub abuser. There must be other independent evidence to justify a finding of mental disorder. In *R. v. Mental Health Act Commission, ex p. X* (1988) 9 B.M.L.R. 77, 84, DC, Stuart Smith L.J. said that "where the mental disorder is quite distinct from the sexual deviancy or other matter referred to in section 1(3) ... , and the proposed treatment is solely for the purpose of dealing with the sexual deviancy or other section 1(3) condition, it is difficult to see how this can be treatment for mental disorder. In practice however it seems likely that the sexual problem will be inextricably linked with mental disorder, so that treatment for one is treatment for the other.... "

Sexual deviancy: In *R. v. Mental Health Review Tribunal, ex p. Clatworthy* [1985] 3 All E.R. 699, Mann J. made the following *obiter* observations, at 701, 702: "It may at once be observed that the effect of subsection (3) is apparently to prevent there being a condition of psychopathic disorder when the abnormally aggressive or seriously irresponsible conduct consequent upon the persistent disorder or disability of mind is conduct which is the manifestation of sexual deviancy. It may also be observed that it can be contended that sexual deviancy does not mean tendency to deviation but means indulgence in deviation." It is submitted that: (1) these observations are defective in that they fail to have regard to the phrase "by reason only"; and (2) the correct interpretation of this provision is to be found in the Scottish case of *W (a Patient) v. Secretary of State for Scotland, The Times,* April 21, 1999, Inner House, where section 1(3) of the Mental Health (Scotland) Act 1984 (which in all material respects is identical to subsection (3) of this section) was interpreted as meaning that a person could not be deemed to mentally disordered by virtue of a sexual deviancy which was unrelated to a mental disorder, but that a patient's detention was not prevented by the Act where a mental disorder manifested itself in deviant sexual behaviour.

Dependence on alcohol or drugs: This exclusion does not rule out the possibility of a person being treated as being mentally disordered under this Act if he is suffering from a mental disorder arising from or suspected to arise from alcohol or drug dependence or from the withdrawal of alcohol or a drug.

PART II

COMPULSORY ADMISSION TO HOSPITAL AND GUARDIANSHIP

GENERAL NOTE

The principles that underpin this Part were identified by Sir Thomas Bingham **1–028** M.R. in the following extract from his judgment in *Re S.-C. (Mental Patient: Habeas Corpus)* [1996] 1 All E.R. 532, CA, at 534, 535:

"[N]o adult citizen of the United Kingdom is liable to be confined in any institution against his will, save by the authority of law. That is a fundamental constitutional principle, traceable back to Ch. 29 of Magna Carta 1297 (25 Edw. 1 c. 1), and before that to Ch. 39 of Magna Carta (1215). There are, of course, situations in which the law sanctions detention. The most obvious is in the case of those suspected or convicted of crime. Powers then exist to arrest and detail. But the conditions in which those powers may be exercised are very closely prescribed by statute and the common law. ... [Mental patients] present a special problem since they may be liable, as a result of mental illness, to cause injury either to themselves or to others. But the very illness which is the source of the danger may deprive the sufferer of the insight necessary to ensure access to proper medical care, whether the proper medical care consists of assessment or treatment, and, if treatment, whether in-patient or out-patient treatment.

Powers therefore exist to ensure that those who suffer from mental illness may, in appropriate circumstances, be involuntarily admitted to mental hospitals and detained. But, and it is a very important but, the circumstances in which the mentally ill may be detained are very carefully prescribed by statute. Action may only be taken if there is clear evidence that the medical condition of a patient justifies such action, and there are detailed rules prescribing the classes of person who may apply to a hospital to admit and detain a mentally disordered person. The legislation recognises that action may be necessary at short notice and also recognises that it will be impracticable for a hospital to investigate the background facts to ensure that all the requirements of the Act are satisfied if they appear to be so. Thus we find in the statute a panoply of powers combined with detailed safeguards for the protection of the patient."

In *St George's Healthcare NHS Trust v. S* [1998] 3 All E.R. 673, the Court of Appeal held that this Act cannot be deployed to achieve the detention of an individual against her will merely because her thinking process is unusual, even apparently bizarre and irrational, and contrary to the views of the overwhelming majority of the community at large. It could only be used to justify the detention of a mentally disordered person who fell within the prescribed conditions.

A patient who is detained under this Act, in spite of his detention, retains all civil rights which are not taken away expressly or by necessary implication (*Raymond v. Honey* [1982] 1 All E.R. 756, HL). The extent to which this Act provides implied authority for staff to override the civil rights of patients is outlined in the note on "act purporting to be done in pursuance of this Act" in section 139(1). If a patient considers that his detention is unlawful he can attempt to secure his release by means of habeas corpus or judicial review proceedings: see the General Note to section 65 under the heading "Habeas Corpus and Judicial Review".

The legal authorisation for conveying a compliant mentally incapable patient to hospital for treatment for his mental disorder and for his detention there is to be found in the common law doctrine of necessity: see *R. v. Bournewood Community and Community NHS Trust, ex p. L* [1998] 3 All E.R. 289, HL, which is considered in the General Note to section 131. If the patient subsequently become non-compliant to being in hospital, consideration should be given to detaining him under this Part (*Code of Practice*, para. 19.2).

Powers, other than those contained in this Act, that are available to individuals to control and detain patients are set out in the General Note to section 5. Although the European Convention on Human Rights, in Article 5(1), states that a person of unsound mind can only be detained "in accordance with a procedure prescribed by law", the European Court of Human Rights has held that this provision does not apply to cases of emergency confinement (*X v. United Kingdom* (1981) 4 E.H.R.R. 181).

A person who meets the statutory criteria for detention can be compulsorily detained and treated in accordance with the terms of this Act, even though the person had previously made an advance directive refusing treatment for mental disorder: see the note on "Advance Directives" in the General Note to Part IV.

A person of any age (including a child) can be detained under this Part. Section 25 of the Children Act 1989 which sets restrictions on the use of secure accommodation for children, does not apply to a child who is detained under any provision of this Act (Children (Secure Accommodation) Regulations 1991 (S.I. 1991 No. 1505), reg. 5). A child is not a privately fostered child for the purposes of Part IX of the Children Act 1989 while he is liable to be detained under this Act (*ibid.* Sched. 8, para. 4).

In the "Report by the Committee for Privileges on Parliamentary Privilege and the Mental Health Act" June 18, 1984, HL (254) the Committee for Privileges was of the view that the provisions of this Act override any previously existing privilege of Parliament or peerage so far as it conflicts with the liability of mentally disordered peers to compulsory detention in hospital under sections 2 to 6. The procedure for vacating the seat of a Member of the House of Commons who has been detained under this Act is set out in section 141.

For the purpose of admissions to hospital or guardianship under this Part, documentation must be in the form set out in the Mental Health (Hospital, Guardianship and Consent to Treatment) Regulations 1983 (S.I. 1983 No. 893) (*ibid.* regs 4, 5).

Procedure for hospital admission

Admission for assessment

1–029   **2.**—(1) A patient may be admitted to a hospital and detained there for the period allowed by subsection (4) below in pursuance of an application (in this Act referred to as "an application for admission for assessment") made in accordance with subsections (2) and (3) below.

(2) An application for admission for assessment may be made in respect of a patient on the grounds that—

(a) he is suffering from mental disorder of a nature or degree which warrants the detention of the patient in a hospital for assessment (or for assessment followed by medical treatment) for at least a limited period; and

(b) he ought to be so detained in the interests of his own health or safety or with a view to the protection of other persons.

(3) An application for admission for assessment shall be founded on the written recommendations in the prescribed form of two registered medical practitioners, including in each case a statement that in the opinion of the practitioner the conditions set out in subsection (2) above are complied with.

(4) Subject to the provisions of section 29(4) below, a patient admitted to hospital in pursuance of an application for admission for assessment may be detained for a period not exceeding 28 days beginning with the day on which he is admitted, but shall not be detained after the expiration of that period unless before it has expired he has become liable to be detained by virtue of a subsequent application, order or direction under the following provisions of this Act.

DEFINITIONS

patient: s.145(1).   1–030
hospital: ss.34(2), 145(1).
mental disorder: ss.1, 145(1).
medical treatment: s.145(1).

GENERAL NOTE

This section, which is considered in chapter 2 of the *Code of Practice*, authorises **1–031** the compulsory admission of a patient to hospital for assessment (or for assessment followed by treatment), and for detention for this purpose for up to 28 days. If, after the 28 days have elapsed, the patient is to remain in hospital, he must do so either as an informal patient or be detained for treatment under section 3, if the conditions of that section are satisfied. Patients detained under this section are subject to the consent to treatment provisions contained in Part IV of this Act (s.56(1)).

In *R. v. Wilson, ex p. Williamson* [1996] C.O.D. 42, Tucker J. held that an application made under this section "is only intended to be of short duration for a limited purpose—assessment of the patient's condition with a view to ascertaining whether it is a case which would respond to treatment, and whether an [application] under section 3 would be appropriate. It was intended that the assessment should take place within 28 days, without any extension of time unless it was necessary for the purpose of replacing the nearest relative. Although there is nothing to suggest that section 2 is a once and for all procedure, there is nothing in the Act which justifies successive or back to back, applications under this section. .... The powers under section 2 can only be used for the limited purpose for which they were intended, and cannot be utilised for the purpose of further detaining a patient for the purposes of assessment beyond the 28 day period, or used as a stop-gap procedure."

The *Williamson* case provides authority for the proposition that an application under section 2 cannot be used for an improper purpose. Tucker J. identified two examples of such a purpose: (1) using a second application under section 2 in order to extend the 28-day assessment period; and (2) using an application under section 2 as a "stop-gap" procedure in circumstances where it is not possible to proceed with a section 3 application because of a nearest relative objection (also see para. 19 of the *Memorandum*). The fact that a second use of section 2 was involved in the *Williamson* case is not relevant to (2) as the rationale for finding the use of the section to be improper is that those who had made the decision to use section 3 must have reached the conclusion that the patient does not require detention for assessment: also see the note on "Section 2 or section 3", below.

Subsection (4) prevents a second application under section 2 from being made during the currency of an existing application, and it is not possible to use the holding powers provided for in section 5 while the patient is liable to be detained (s.5(1)(6)). Neither is it possible to use the holding powers to extend the 28-day period once the section 2 has expired (see the *Williamson* case, above).

It is submitted that an application for a second section 2 can be made if a significant change in the patient's situation can be said to justify the need for a reassessment. For example, a patient is detained under section 2 in city A, is discharged, and then moves to city B where his mental health deteriorates to the extent that he is subject to a second application under section 2. In these circumstances the second section 2 could be in close proximity to the first section 2.

An application under this section should be the usual method of detaining a patient who requires to be assessed. An emergency application under section 4 should only be used where the need for the patient's admission is so urgent that it is not practicable to obtain the second medical recommendation that is required for an admission under this section.

An order for the patient's discharge from this section can be made at any time prior to the expiration of the 28-day period by his reasonable medical officer, the hospital managers or, subject to section 25, his nearest relative (s.23(2)(a)). The patient can seek to obtain his own discharge by making an application to a Mental Health Review Tribunal within 14 days of his admission (s.66(1)(a), 2(a)). The approved social worker applicant is not required to identify a relevant change in the patient's circumstances before making an application under this section in respect of a patient who has been discharged from detention by a tribunal and is now living in the community: see *R. v. East London and City Mental Health NHS Trust, ex p. Brandenburg* [2001] EWCA Civ 239, which is considered in the General Note to section 3.

There is nothing to prevent a patient who has been detained under this section from being arrested in respect of a criminal offence.

The Human Rights Act 1998

1–032   See the note under this heading in the General Note to section 3.

Section 2 or section 3

1–033   The advice contained in chapter 5 of the previous edition of the *Code of Practice*, which is largely replicated in chapter 5 of the current edition, has been interpreted as requiring section 3 to be used as the admission section for patients who are "well known" to the mental health service. This interpretation has been reinforced by concern expressed by the Mental Health Commission over the "misuse" of section 2 where section 3 would have been more appropriate to admit such patients (see, for example, paragraph 3.1 of the Commission's Sixth Biennial Report, 1993–1995; also see the note on paragraph 5.3a of the *Code of Practice*) and the widely held, but totally erroneous view expressed by some practitioners that treatment under Part IV cannot be given to patients detained under section 2.

This Act provides two routes which can be used to detain and treat patients: section 2 which provides for the assessment and treatment of patients for a non-renewable period of up to 28 days, and section 3 which provides for the patient's detention and treatment for a potentially unlimited period. A patient whose current mental health and circumstances require him to be subject to the very significant procedure of compulsory detention surely needs to be assessed, however well known he might be to the mental health service. Something has happened in that patient's life to justify intervention under this Act and that "something" and its impact upon the patient needs to be assessed. The extent of any prior knowledge that might exist about the patient does not deflect from the need to assess the patient's *current* situation. This strongly suggests that the intention of Parliament was for section 2 to be used as the initial section to detain patients, because that section specifically provides for the patient's assessment, and that an application under section 3 be made if the assessment leads the clinical team to conclude that the patient needs a further period of treatment whilst being detained. Other factors which support this approach are:

(i) the finding of Tucker J. in *R. v. Wilson, ex p. Williamson*, above, that the purpose of section 2 is to ascertain whether an application under section 3 would be appropriate;

(ii) the fact that a well known patient can be detained under section 4 (an assessment section) in emergency situations;

(iii) dicta in a number of cases where the judges have assumed that section 2 can be used to admit a well known patient: see, for example, *R. v. Bournewood Community and Mental Health NHS Trust, ex p. L* [1998] 3 All E.R. 289, HL, where, at the Court of Appeal, Lord Woolf M.R. said that it would have been possible to use section 2 to admit the patient who had been in very close contact with the mental health services for most of his life ([1998] 1 All E.R. 634 at 641) and *R. v. East London and City Mental Health NHS Trust, ex p. Brandenburg*, above, where the Court of Appeal assumed that it could be appropriate to detain a patient under section 2 subsequent to his discharge by a tribunal.

(iv) the fact that section 25I of this Act provides for the "suspension" of a patient's supervised discharge in the event of his subsequent admission under section 2. The Act therefore contemplates section 3 (which the patient must be subject to if an application for supervised discharge is to be made) being followed by section 2 in circumstances where the patient is being closely supervised in the community;

(v) the fact that section 3(2)(c) states that an application under section 3 should only be made if the necessary treatment can only be provided under that section suggests that such an application should only be made if a judgment has been reached that the patient needs to be treated under detained powers for a period longer than that provided for in section 2. This is because both sections provide clinicians with identical powers to treat the patient. A judgment about the use of section 3 would normally be made in the context of the patient's detention under section 2 (see (i), above);

(vi) the meaning of the term "assessment" in section 2 is probably not confined to the process involved in identifying the specific form of mental disorder that the patient is suffering from: see the note on "assessment" in section 2(2)(a); and

(vii) section 29(4) allows for the extension of the patient's detention under section 2 if a displacement application is made to the county court on the ground that the patient's nearest relative has unreasonably objected to a section 3 application being made. The court must receive the application before the expiration of the section 2. This provision, and the absence of any remedy to an applicant who proceeds straight to section 3 and is then faced with an objection from the nearest relative, is a clear indication that this Act was drafted on the assumption that an application under section 2 would precede an application under section 3. Also note Stuart-Smith L.J.'s comment in *R. v. Central London County Court* [1999] 3 All E.R. 991, CA, that the extension of time provided for by section 29(4) should be utilised if an application for the displacement of a nearest relative is made: see the General Note to section 29.

Using section 2 as the initial detaining power will enable the approved social worker to avoid the difficult situation that can occur when an application under section 3 is met by an unexpected objection by the patient's nearest relative. In these circumstances the approved social worker cannot respond by making an application under section 2 (see the *Williamson* case, above).

The use of section 3 without it being preceded by an application under section 2 could be appropriate if the patient had been the subject of a full multi-disciplinary assessment during a period of in-patient care as an informal patient, or if such an assessment was made while the patient was detained under a relevant provision under Part III (*e.g.* s.35)

The deteriorating patient

1–034   See the note under this heading in the General Note to section 3.

Subsection (1)

1–035   *Detained There:* The patient can be granted leave of absence from the detaining hospital under section 17.

Application: An application under this section can be made by either the patient's nearest relative or by an approved social worker (s.11(1)). It will be addressed to the managers of the hospital to which admission is sought (s.11(2)). If the applicant is an approved social worker he must inform the nearest relative that the application is to be or has been made (s.11(3)). The patient's nearest relative cannot prevent an approved social worker making an application. In deciding whether he should make an application an approved social worker is required to have regard to any wishes expressed by relatives of the patient (s.13(1)). This does not mean that the approved social worker is placed under a legal obligation to consult with the patient's relatives before he makes an application. The applicant must have seen the patient within the previous 14 days (s.11(5)) and an approved social worker applicant must interview the patient before he makes the application (s.13(2)). The patient has to be admitted to hospital within 14 days of the time when he was last medically examined prior to the recommendations required by subsection (3) being made (s.6(1)(a)). It is possible to make an application in respect of a person who is already receiving hospital treatment as an in-patient on an informal basis (s.5(1)). An application for the admission of a ward of court cannot be made without the leave of the High Court (s.33(1)).

The effect of an application for admission for assessment is set out in section 6.

Subsection (2)

Paragraph (a)

1–036   *Is suffering:* See the note on "The deteriorating patient" in the General Note to section 3.

In *R. v. Kirklees M.B.C., ex p. C* [1993] 2 F.L.R. 187, 190, CA, Lloyd L.J., speaking *obiter*, said that "having regard to the definition of patient in section 145 there is, in my view, power to admit a patient for assessment under section 2, if he appears to be suffering from mental disorder, on the ground that he or she is so suffering, even though it turns out on assessment that [he or] she is not. Any other construction would unnecessarily emasculate the beneficial power under section 2 and confine assessment to choice of treatment." In *St George's Healthcare NHS Trust v. S*, [1998] 3 All E.R. 673, the Court of Appeal confirmed this approach by holding that the identification of the presence of mental disorder for the purposes of this section cannot be a final concluded diagnosis: the final diagnosis may or may not confirm that provisional view.

Mental disorder: A specific diagnosis of the category of mental disorder from which the patient is suffering is not required. It is therefore possible for a person with a learning disability whose condition is not associated with "abnormally aggressive or seriously irresponsible conduct" to be the subject of an application under this section.

Nature or Degree: The meaning of this phrase is considered in the note on section 3(2)(a).

Which warrants the detention of the patient in a hospital: These words "are intended to restrict the use of [this] section to patients who are thought to be suffering from a form of mental disorder which would justify admission under the Act" (*Memorandum*, para. 19). The use of restraint on a patient should not automatically lead to his admission under this Act: see the General Note to paragraph 19.8 of the Code of Practice.

The detention must be related to or linked with mental disorder. The patient's need for treatment for an unrelated physical disorder does not provide the necessary warrant (*St George's Healthcare NHS Trust v. S*, above). In the *St George's* case the Court of Appeal declared an admission under this section to be unlawful because the grounds prescribed in this paragraph were not established. *Per* Judge L.J., at 697:

"The contemporaneous documents themselves demonstrate that those involved in the decision to make an application for admission failed to maintain the distinction between the urgent need of [the patient] for treatment arising from her pregnancy, and the separate question whether her mental disorder (in the form of depression) warranted her detention in hospital. From the reasoning to be found in them, the conclusion that the detention was believed to be warranted in order that adequate provision could be made to deal with [the patient's] pregnancy and the safety of her unborn child is unavoidable."

Assessment: An application under this section would be unlawful if the patient was not going to be subjected to an assessment for his mental disorder after admission (*St George's Healthcare NHS Trust v. S*, above).

It is unclear whether "assessment" is confined to the process involved in enabling the medical staff to identify the specific statutory form of mental disorder that the patient is suffering from, or whether it has a broader meaning which incorporates an evaluation of the patient's response to diagnostic investigations and to being treated. (It should be noted that as the definition of "medical treatment" includes nursing, the treatment of the patient will commence as soon as he has been admitted under this section.) As the latter interpretation is consistent with the situation that generally obtains in medical practice, there is no reason to prevent a patient whose specific diagnosis is well known from being the subject of an application under this section. Support for this interpretation can be found in the following comment made by Woolf M.R. in *B v. Barking Havering and Brentwood Community Healthcare NHS Trust* [1999] 1 F.L.R. 106 at 114: "Often assessment or monitoring of progress will be an important part of treatment. This will certainly be the case where ... there is an evolving programme of treatment."

If the detaining hospital cannot provide the appropriate staffing and equipment to enable a full assessment to be undertaken, the patient can be granted leave of absence under section 17 to a hospital that is able to provide such facilities.

Or for assessment followed by medical treatment: Treatment under this section need not be confined to treatment which is an inherent part of the assessment process.

Paragraph (b)

There is no requirement for the two recommending doctors to agree on the nature **1–037** of the risk justifying detention under this section. A study into the statutory justifications for detention under this section given by recommending doctors found that "the majority of patients (67 per cent) were detained for both the protection of others and in the interests of their own health or safety, 32 per cent were detained only for their own protection and a minority (1 per cent) were detained solely for the protection of others" (M. Dixon *et al.*, "Formal Justifications for Compulsory Psychiatric Detention", (2000) Med. Sci. Law, 40(4), 319–326).

Health: The patient's mental, as well as physical health is covered by this term. This interpretation is adopted by the Mental Health Act Commission in its *Second Biennial Report*, 1985–1987, at paragraph 11.3 and in the judgment of Judge L.J. in the *St George's* case, noted above. The opinion that is sometimes heard from practitioners that an application under this section can only be made if the patient is either a danger to himself or others, or is engaging in seriously disruptive behaviour, is incorrect as an application under this section can be made to prevent a deterioration of the patient's health. This is the approach taken by the *Code of*

Practice at paragraph 2.10 and by the Law Society Mental Health and Disability Committee which has stated that the "avoidance of deterioration should certainly be considered to be in the interests of the patient's health ..." (House of Commons Health Committee Fifth Report, Community Supervision Orders, Vol. II, p. 109). Also see the note on "the deteriorating patient" in the General Note to section 3.

Safety: With the patient being exposed to the risk of being harmed, either through his own acts or omissions or through the act or omissions of others if he is not detained.

Protection of other persons: "The protection of 'other persons' does not necessarily mean the public at large because it could simply relate to an individual person or persons rather than to the public at large, nor is there the requirement that such persons should be protected 'from serious harm'," *per* Harrison J. in *R. v. North West London Mental Health NHS Trust, ex p. Stewart* (1996) 39 B.M.L.R. 105. Although the matter is not free from doubt, it is likely that this phrase covers both protection from physical harm and protection from serious emotional harm. This approach is taken by the *Code of Practice* at paragraph 2.9 where it refers to the risk of "serious persistent psychological harm to others". Although this provision does not make explicit reference to the protection of a person's property, actual or threatened damage to a person's property is likely to cause that person emotional harm.

Although an unborn child is not a "person" in need of protection, the "health or safety" of the potential mother can be assessed on the basis that she is heavily pregnant (*St George's Healthcare NHS Trust v. S*, above). *Per* Judge L.J. at 696: "Those responsible have to deal in realities, and [the patient] was dangerously ill [with pre-eclampsia]. Although the risks were caused by her pregnancy, the potential damage could have fallen within section 2(2)(b)." Also see the note on "The Human Rights Act 1998" under section 3.

Paragraphs 34 and 35 of the First Report of the House of Commons Health Committee for the session 1993–1994 summarise the evidence that the Committee received on the linkage between mental illness and violence:

"The Department of Health states that there are no sound studies giving an account of the relationship between mental illness and crime. The best predictor of violence is whether a person has a past history of actual or attempted violence, whether they are mentally ill or not. A few submissions suggest that violence is more likely in schizophrenics if the illness is linked with alcohol or drug misuse, or where care and support is lacking. Studies are also cited showing that psychosis or multiple disorders are more likely to increase the risk of violent crime and that a person is twice as likely to be convicted of a violent crime if he or she is diagnosed as schizophrenic as opposed to another mental disorder. However, the DoH points out that there are no studies showing the factors associated with future anti-social behaviour in a random sample of schizophrenic patients. Similarly, the Chief Medical Officer states that violence seems to be more closely associated with some mental disorders than in the general population, but that the picture is complex and unclear.

The evidence is clear that there is a far higher risk of a mentally ill person committing self-harm than harming others; the risk of suicide is about 100 times greater than the risk of violence to others. The National Schizophrenia Fellowship quotes figures showing that less than 0.01 per cent of schizophrenics kill another person, about 10 per cent kill themselves and about 20 per cent severely harm themselves" (*Better Off in the Community?: The Care of People Who are Seriously Mentally Ill*, Vol. I).

The factors to be taken into account when making decisions about patients who present risks are identified at paragraph 3.3.2 of the Report of the *Panel of Inquiry appointed by the West Midlands Regional Health Authority, South Birmingham Health Authority and the Special Hospitals Service Authority to investigate the case of Kim Kirkman* (1991). Also see paragraphs 23 to 32 of NHS Executive Guidelines HSG(94)27.

Subsection (3)
Written recommendations: Made either separately or jointly (section 11(7)).　　**1–038**
Two registered medical practitioners: Complying with the provisions of section 12.

Subsection (4)
Not exceeding 28 days: The patient can cease to be liable to be detained before the **1–039** 28 days expire if an order for his discharge is made under section 23. The 28-day period can be extended if an application is made to the county court under certain circumstances for an acting nearest relative to be appointed (s.29(4)) or if the patient is absent without leave and the provisions of section 21 apply (see the note on "a patient" in s.21(1)).
Beginning with: Including the day on which the patient was admitted (*Hare v. Gocher* [1962] 2 Q.B. 641). The authority to detain the patient will expire at midnight on the twenty-eighth day.
Under the following provisions of this Act: The use of the term "following" prohibits a further application under this section being made during the currency of an existing section 2 application (*R. v. Wilson, ex p. Williamson*, above).

Admission for treatment
3.—(1) A patient may be admitted to a hospital and detained there for the **1–040** period allowed by the following provisions of this Act in pursuance of an application (in this Act referred to as "an application for admission for treatment") made in accordance with this section.
(2) An application for admission for treatment may be made in respect of a patient on the grounds that—
   (a) he is suffering from mental illness, severe mental impairment, psychopathic disorder or mental impairment and his mental disorder is of a nature or degree which makes it appropriate for him to receive medical treatment in a hospital; and
   (b) in the case of psychopathic disorder or mental impairment, such treatment is likely to alleviate or prevent a deterioration of his condition; and
   (c) it is necessary for the health or safety of the patient or for the protection of other persons that he should receive such treatment and it cannot be provided unless he is detained under this section.
(3) An application for admission for treatment shall be founded on the written recommendations in the prescribed form of two registered medical practitioners, including in each case a statement that in the opinion of the practitioner the conditions set out in subsection (2) above are complied with; and each such recommendation shall include—
   (a) such particulars as may be prescribed of the grounds for that opinion so far as it relates to the conditions set out in paragraphs (a) and (b) of that subsection; and
   (b) a statement of the reasons for that opinion so far as it relates to the conditions set out in paragraph (c) of that subsection, specifying whether other methods of dealing with the patient are available and, if so, why they are not appropriate.

DEFINITIONS

1–041   patient: s.145(1).
hospital: ss.34(2), 145(1).
severe mental impairment: ss.1, 145(1).
psychopathic disorder: ss.1, 145(1).
mental impairment: ss.1, 145(1).
mental disorder: ss.1, 145(1).
medical treatment: s.145(1).

GENERAL NOTE

1–042   This section, which is considered in chapter 2 of the *Code of Practice*, provides for
the compulsory admission of a patient to hospital for treatment and for his
subsequent detention, which can last for an initial period of up to six months
(s.20(1)). The authority to detain a patient under this section can be renewed
(s.20(2)). Patients admitted under this section are subject to the consent to treatment
provisions contained in Part IV of this Act (s.56(1)). There is no legal rule which: (1)
prevents an application under this section from being made at any time after a section
4 admission has been made (*Re Makin*, May 4, 2000); or (2) prevents a patient who
has been detained under this section from being subsequently detained under section
2, a situation which is allowed for in section 25 I(1)(b).
    In *R. v. Hallstrom, ex p. W; R. v. Gardner, ex p. L* [1986] 2 All E.R. 306, McCullough
J. held that admission under this section only covered those whose mental condition
was believed to require a period of in-patient treatment. (This finding was approved
by the Court of Appeal in *B v. Barking Havering and Brentwood Community
Healthcare NHS Trust* [1999] 1 F.L.R. 106.) His Lordship said, at 315:

> "In my judgment, the key to the construction of section 3 lies in the phrase
> 'admission for treatment'. It stretches the concept of 'admission for treatment' too
> far to say that it covers admission for only so long as it is necessary to enable leave
> of absence to be granted [under section 17], after which the necessary treatment
> will begin. 'Admission for treatment' under section 3 is intended for those whose
> condition is believed to require a period of treatment as an in-patient. It may be
> that such patients will also be thought to require a period of out-patient treatment
> thereafter, but the concept of 'admission for treatment' has no applicability to
> those whom it is intended to admit and detain for a purely nominal period during
> which no necessary treatment will be given."

    The "nominal period" in *Hallstrom* was an overnight admission. In *Re Shearon*
[1996] C.O.D. 223, the Divisional Court held that whilst an admission for one week is
a relatively small part of the initial six-month period of detention authorised by this
section, there was no possible reason for stigmatising a genuine initial one week's
intended in-patient treatment as "a purely nominal period during which no necessary
treatment will be given". The court further held that the fact that the application was
made simultaneously with the institution of a parallel Care Plan did not invalidate the
admission and render it unlawful.
    The *Hallstrom* decision also prevents an application under this section being made
if the prime motivation for such action is to enable an application for supervised
discharge to be made in respect of the patient. Those who are involved in either
making an application or providing medical recommendations under this section
should only do so if, at the time when the application is made or the medical
recommendation is signed, they genuinely believe that the person concerned
requires treatment while being detained as an in-patient in a hospital.
1–043   In *R. v. East London and City Mental Health NHS Trust, ex p. Brandenburg* [2001]
EWCA Civ 239, the patient had been detained in hospital under section 2. He was
subsequently re-detained under this section on the sixth day of a seven day deferred
discharge that had been ordered by the Mental Health Review Tribunal. The patient

appealed on the ground that it is unlawful once a tribunal has ordered the discharge of a patient to apply to re-admit him, or to accede to such an application, unless it is demonstrated that there has been a relevant change of circumstances. The Court of Appeal held that as long as the professionals concerned are acting objectively and bona fide there is no requirement under this Act of a change in the patient's circumstances before an application under sections 2 or 3 can be made in respect of a patient who has been discharged by a tribunal. However, the statutory scheme does not leave it open to professionals effectively to overrule a decision to discharge taken by the tribunal: due regard must be paid to such a decision. A recent decision to discharge a patient, if the circumstances have not apparently changed, must be accorded very great weight if the decision to make an application in respect of the patient is not to be perceived as an illicit overruling of the tribunal's decision. A decision to make an application within days of the tribunal's decision, particularly if the patient has remained in hospital because the discharge has been deferred, would be capable of being challenged unless the applicant was aware of relevant facts relating to the patient which were not known to the tribunal. *Per* Lord Phillips M.R.: "In such a situation there is likely to have been … a difference of view between the patient's responsible medical officer and the tribunal as to whether or not the criteria justifying detention were established. Under the statutory scheme, where such a conflict exists, it is the opinion of the tribunal that is to prevail. In such circumstances I do not see how an approved social worker can properly be satisfied, as required by section 13, that an 'application ought to be made' unless aware of circumstances not known to the tribunal which invalidate the decision of the tribunal. In the absence of such circumstances an application by an approved social worker should, on an application for judicial review, be held unlawful on the ground of irrationality" (paras. 31,32). In this context "circumstances" could include a significant deterioration in the patient's mental condition, statements made by the patient which contradict relevant evidence that was relied on by the tribunal, the withdrawl of an after-care facility such as specialist accommodation that featured strongly in the patient's after-care plan, the discovery that the patient had not been taking prescribed medication for his mental disorder whilst he was in hospital, and the identification of a important aspect of the patient's psychiatric history that was not known to the tribunal.

In *R. (on the application of Wirral Health Authority and Wirral Borough Council) v. Dr Finnegan and D.E.* [2001] EWHC Admin 312, Scott Baker J. said that an application made immediately after a tribunal's decision to discharge would not usurp the tribunal's decision where it can be shown: "(a) that efforts were made to see if the decision of the tribunal could be implemented; and (b) there were genuine grounds for thinking, and in the event it has proved to be the case, that the tribunal's decision was unlawful" (para. 83).

Where a patient is admitted to hospital under this section, any previous application that had been made in respect of him under this Part of the Act (*i.e.* an application under section 2 or 4 or a guardianship application under section 7) is automatically cancelled (s.6(4)).

An order for the patient's discharge from this section can be made by his responsible medical officer, the hospital managers or, subject to section 25, his nearest relative (s.23(2)(a)). A patient can seek to obtain his own discharge by making an application to a Mental Health Review Tribunal within the first six months of admission (s.66(1)(b), 2(b)) and during each period of renewal (s.66(1)(f), 2(f), 20(2)). In certain circumstances the patient will have his case automatically referred to a tribunal (s.68).

There is nothing to prevent a patient who has been detained under this section from being arrested in respect of a criminal offence. If the patient is subsequently remanded into custody or sentenced under the criminal law, the provisions of section 22 will apply.

Where a patient who has been detained under this section ceases to be so detained and leaves hospital, he has to be offered appropriate after-care services (s.117).

The deteriorating patient

1–044   The "Committee of Inquiry into the events leading up to and surrounding the fatal incident at the Edith Morgan Centre, Torbay, on September 1, 1993" examined the issue of the "sectionability" of a patient whose mental health is likely to deteriorate: see *The Falling Shadow: One Patient's Mental Health Care 1978–1993*, 1995, pp. 153–169. The Committee disagreed with the view expressed by the *Internal Review of Legal Powers on the Care of Mentally Ill People in Community* that a patient could not be admitted under compulsory powers "simply on the grounds that his or her past medical history suggests that he or she will relapse in the future" (Department of Health, 1993, para. 3.2). The conclusion that the Committee reached was that "there is probably no legal impediment to the readmission of a ['revolving door'] patient ... at the point of loss of insight when he refuse[s] further medication" (p. 160). In fact, this conclusion does not conflict with the statement made by the *Internal Review* as a patient who has lost insight would not be detained "simply" on the ground of his medical history.

The Committee found the case of *Devon C.C. v. Hawkins* [1967] 2 Q.B. 26, to be "highly pertinent" to the issue. In this case the question before the court was whether a person who was taking drugs which successfully controlled his epilepsy could be said to be "suffering from" that disease. The answer given by the then Lord Chief Justice, Lord Parker, was in the affirmative. His Lordship said that "so long as drugs are necessary to prevent the manifestation of disease, the disease in my judgment remains". In other words, so the Committee stated, what the patient "was 'suffering from' rested on a prognosis of what would occur in the future if medication was withdrawn" (p. 155).

Although it might be the case that a person with a history of mental illness who is being successfully medicated for that illness can be said to be "suffering from" that illness, it does not follow that merely because that person stops taking his medication the illness becomes one of a "nature or degree which makes it appropriate for him to receive medical treatment in a hospital" (s.3(2)(a)) or one of a "nature or degree which warrants the detention of the patient in a hospital for assessment" (s.2(2)(a)). While a patient whose symptoms are being well controlled by medication cannot be said to be suffering from a "degree" of mental disorder sufficient to justify detention, can that patient be detained because of the "nature" of his disorder? This question was considered by Popplewell J. in *R. v. The Mental Health Review, Tribunal for the South Thames Region, ex p. Smith* which is noted under subsection (2)(a).

The course of a patient's mental illness is never entirely predictable and this Act requires the professionals involved in assessing a patient for possible compulsory admission to exercise their judgment to determine whether the patient's condition and situation at the time of the assessment meet the statutory criteria for admission. If it is the case that a mere failure to continue with medication would be sufficient to satisfy the statutory criteria with respect to a patient who has a history of admissions subsequent to previous failures to continue with medication, this would lead to a personal examination of the patient by the recommending doctors under section 12(2) and the interviewing of the patient by the approved social worker under section 13(2) becoming sterile exercises. One of the objectives of the examinations and interview of such a patient would be to identify whether there is any evidence (apart from the cessation of medication) to suggest that it is likely that history will repeat itself in that the symptoms of the patient's mental disorder will reappear. If there is such evidence, the "nature" of the patient's mental disorder could lead professionals to conclude that detention in hospital is either "appropriate" or "warranted" even though there is no current manifestation of the disorder (the "degree").

It is suggested that the following approach should be taken by those involved in the assessment of a "revolving door" patient who has ceased to take medication for his mental disorder:

(1) a withdrawal from medication is a significant, but not a determining factor in the assessment;

(2) the role of the professionals involved in the assessment is to assess the patient's response to the withdrawal and to identify the reasons for his decision to cease taking medication; and

(3) although it would not be possible to determine that the provisions of either section 2(2)(a) or 3(2)(a) are satisfied solely on the ground that the patient has ceased to take medication, an evaluation of the patient's history, and, in particular, of his reaction to withdrawal from medication in the past, could lead to a decision that the "nature" of the his mental disorder justifies an application being made in respect of him.

Clearly, the greater the knowledge that the doctors and the approved social worker have of the patient's psychiatric history, the easier it will be to determine when to intervene by sectioning him. An approved social worker could only proceed to make an application if such action was considered to be "the most appropriate way of providing the care and medical treatment of which the patient stands in need" (s.13(2)).

Section 2 or section 3

The question whether it is appropriate to detain patient under this section or under **1–045** section 2 is considered in the General Note to section 2 under this heading.

The Human Rights Act 1998

In *Winterwerp v. Netherlands* (1979) 2 E.H.R.R. 387, the European Court of **1–046** Human Rights held, *inter alia,* that in order for the detention of a person of unsound mind to be lawful the mental disorder from which the patient is suffering must be of a kind or degree warranting compulsory confinement: see the note on Article 5 (1)(e) of the European Convention on Human Rights under the heading "persons of unsound mind". This finding is reflected in the phrase "nature or degree" in subsection (2)(a). The Court has confirmed that the detention of a patient under Article 5 may be justified on the ground of protecting the public (*Litwa v. Poland,* April 4, 2000).

The question whether the continued detention of an asymptomatic patient contravenes Article 5 was considered by the Court of Appeal in *R. (on the application of H.) v. Mental Health Review Tribunal, North and North East London Region* [2001] EWCA Civ 415, where Lord Phillips M.R. said:

"The circumstances of the present case ... are not uncommon. A patient is detained who is unquestionably suffering from schizophrenia. While in the controlled environment of the hospital he is taking medication, and as a result of the medication is in remission. So long as he continues to take the medication he will pose no danger to himself or to others. The nature of the illness is such, however, that if he ceases to take the medication he will relapse and pose a danger to himself or to others. The professionals may be uncertain whether, if he is discharged into the community, he will continue to take the medication. We do not believe that Article 5 requires that the patient must always be discharged in such circumstances. The appropriate response should depend upon the result of weighing the interests of the patient against those of the public having regard to the particular facts. Continued detention can be justified if, but only if, it is a proportionate response having regard to the risks that would be involved in discharge" (para. 33).

His Lordship also said, *obiter,* that Article 5 does not require a "patient to be discharged whenever any one of the three criteria in section 3 cannot be demonstrated on balance of probability. Detention cannot be justified under Article 5(1)(e) unless the patient is "of unsound mind", but once that is established we do not consider that the Convention restricts the right to detain a patient in hospital, as does section 3, to circumstances where medical treatment is likely to alleviate or prevent a deterioration of the condition. Nor is it necessary under the Convention to demonstrate that such treatment cannot be provided unless the patient is detained in hospital" (para. 32).

The finding of the Court of Appeal in *St George's Healthcare NHS Trust v. S,* above, that a unborn child is not a "person" in need of protection for the purposes of sections 2(2)(b) and 3(2)(c) could be challenged on the ground that a failure to protect the unborn child constitutes a violation of the child's right to life under Article 2 of the Convention. In *H v. Norway* (1990) app. no. 17004/90, the Commission said that each State had a wide discretion as to at what age an unborn child could be lawfully aborted, and that termination at 14 weeks was within that discretion. The position may be different where the child is capable of a viable existence outside the womb because the Commission stated that it would not exclude that in certain circumstances an unborn child may enjoy protection under Article 2 notwithstanding that there is "in the Contracting States a considerable divergence of views on whether or to what extent Article 2 protects the unborn child".

If a patient has been assessed as either needing a particular treatment or requiring a specialist opinion, an excessive delay in providing that treatment or opinion could give rise to a claim under Article 8(1) of the Convention if the delay has a serious impact on the patient's health: see *Passannante v. Italy* (1998) 26 E.H.R.R. CD 153, noted under Article 8(1).

Although Article 5 is not concerned with the suitability of the treatment that the detained patient receives or the conditions of his detention, subject to the requirement that he be detained in a hospital, clinic or other appropriate institution (*Ashingdane v. United Kingdom* (1985) 7 E.H.R.R. 528, at para. 44), the medical treatment of a patient can constitute "inhuman or degrading treatment" under the Convention if it reaches a minimum level of severity (see the General Note to Art. 3).

A failure or refusal to provide treatment that is discriminatory will be unlawful, either under Article 14 of the Convention or the Disability Discrimination Act 1995.

Subsection (1)

1–047   *Detained There:* The patient can be granted leave of absence from the detaining hospital under section 17.

The period allowed: An initial period of six months renewable for a further six months and thereafter renewable at yearly intervals (s.20(1), (2)).

Application: An application can be made by either the patient's nearest relative or by an approved social worker (s.11(1)). It will be addressed to the managers of the hospital to which admission is sought (s.11(2)). If an approved social worker makes the application he must consult with the patient's nearest relative if this is practicable and he cannot proceed with the application if the nearest relative objects (s.11(4)). The positive consent of the nearest relative to the application is not required. The applicant must have seen the patient within the previous 14 days (s.11(5)) and an approved social worker applicant must interview the patient before he makes an application (s.13(2)). The patient must be admitted to hospital within 14 days of the time when he was last medically examined prior to the recommendations required by subsection (3) being made (s.6(1)(a)). It is possible to make an application in respect of a person who is already receiving hospital treatment as an in-patient on an informal basis (section 5(1)). An application for the admission of a ward of court cannot be made without the leave of the High Court (s.33(1)).

The effect of an application for admission for treatment is set out in section 6.

Subsection (2)

Paragraph (a)
Suffering from: See the note on "The deteriorating patient" in the General Note to **1–048**
this section. A patient whose condition does not fall within one of the four specific
categories of mental disorder but only comes within the phrase "any other disorder
or disability of mind" (see the definition of mental disorder in s.1(2)) cannot be
detained under this section. Both recommending doctors must state that at the time
when the medical recommendation are made that the patient is suffering from the
same form of mental disorder (s.11(6)).

Of a Nature or Degree: The meaning of this phrase was considered by Popplewell J.
in *R. v. Mental Health Review Tribunal for the South Thames Region, ex p. Smith*
[1999] C.O.D. 148. His Lordship held that:

(1) although the wording of this phrase is disjunctive, in very many cases the
nature and degree of the patient's mental disorder will be inevitably bound up
so that it matters not whether the issue is dealt with under nature or degree;
(2) the word "nature" refers to the particular mental disorder from which the
patient suffers, its chronicity, its prognosis, and the patient's previous response
to receiving treatment for the disorder; and
(3) the word "degree" refers to the current manifestation of the patient's disorder.

This criterion can therefore be satisfied in respected of an well known asymptomatic patient who has ceased to take medication for his mental disorder and who has
a history of a significant deterioration in his mental health after ceasing to take such
medication. This interpretation is supported by the following comment made by
Hale L.J. in *Smirek v. Williams*, April 7, 2000, CA: "There are, of course, mental
illnesses which come and go, but where there is a chronic condition, where there is
evidence that it will soon deteriorate if medication is not taken, I find it impossible to
accept that that is not a mental illness of a nature or degree which makes it
appropriate for the patient to be liable to be detained in hospital for medical
treatment if the evidence is that, without being detained in hospital, the patient will
not take that treatment" (para.19).

Appropriate for him to receive medical treatment in a hospital: And not in the
community or under guardianship. It is unlawful to detain a patient under this section
if the intention is to immediately send him on leave of absence under section 17 (*R. v.
Hallstrom,* above).

An assessment of the patient's response to being treated can be a part of the
medical treatment that the patient receives: see the comment made by Woolf M.R. in
B v. Barking Havering and Brentwood Community Healthcare NHS Trust [1999] 1
F.L.R. 106, CA, noted under "assessment" in section 2(2)(a).

Paragraph (b)
The suggestion in the *Consultative Document* that the "treatability test" set out in **1–049**
this paragraph might apply to all four categories of mental disorder was rejected
because "there is a possibility that such a requirement would preclude the
compulsory admission of some severely [mentally impaired] people or of mentally ill
persons suffering from illnesses who are unlikely to benefit from treatment in the
sense that their condition may not improve; these people might nevertheless need to
be admitted on occasions, for example, to tide them over a crisis" (para. 2.40). *The
Memorandum,* at paragraph 16, states that the test will be satisfied if treatment "is
likely to enable the patient to cope more satisfactorily with his disorder or its
symptoms, or if it stops his condition from becoming worse."

In *R. v. Canons Park Mental Health Review Tribunal, ex p. A* [1994] All E.R. 659,
CA, Roch L.J., at pages 679, 680, suggested the following "principles" that should be
applied to the treatability test:

"First, if a tribunal were to be satisfied that the patient's detention in hospital was simply an attempt to coerce the patient into participating in group therapy, then the tribunal would be under a duty to direct discharge. Second, treatment in hospital will satisfy the treatability test although it is unlikely to alleviate the patient's condition, provided that it is likely to prevent a deterioration. Third, treatment in hospital will satisfy the treatability test although it will not immediately alleviate or prevent deterioration in the patient's condition, provided that alleviation or stabilisation is likely in due course. Fourth, the treatability test can still be met although initially there may be some deterioration in the patient's condition, due for example to the patient's initial anger at being detained. Fifth, it must be remembered that medical treatment in hospital covers nursing and also includes care, habilitation and rehabilitation under medical supervision. Sixth, the treatability test is satisfied if nursing care etc. are likely to lead to an alleviation of the patient's condition in that the patient is likely to gain an insight into his problem or cease to be unco-operative in his attitude towards treatment which would potentially have a lasting benefit."

In the Scottish case of *R. v. Secretary of State for Scotland*, 1998 S.C. 49, 2 Div., the court identified a seventh principle namely "that the patient's condition includes the symptoms or manifestations of it and behaviour caused by it, so that, if there was treatment likely to alleviate or prevent the deterioration of such symptoms, manifestations or behaviour, that would suffice to demonstrate treatability". This case was appealed to the House of Lords where it was held that the term "medical treatment" was "wide enough to include treatment which alleviates or prevents a deterioration of the symptoms of the disorder, not the disorder itself which gives rise to them" (*per* Lord Hope at 497) and that the treatability test could be satisfied in circumstances where "the anger management of the [patient] in the structured setting of the State Hospital in a supervised environment resulted in his being less physically aggressive" (*per* Lord Hutton at 515) (*Reid v. Secretary of State for Scotland* [1999] 1 All E.R. 481). *Reid* is considered in the notes to section 72(1)(b). *Canons Park* and *Reid* were considered by Elias J. in *R. (on the application of Wheldon) v. Rampton Hospital Authority* [2001] EWHC Admin 134; [2001] M.H.L.R. 19. His Lordship said that it "is plain from both these authorities that the concept [or treatability] is a very wide one, and that the responsible medical officer making the assessment can look to the future and consider whether the treatment is likely, in the future, to achieve beneficial results" (para. 14). If the doctor has reason to believe that further and different treatment might alleviate the patient's condition or prevent a deterioration of it, the test will be satisfied.

Although a patient who is suffering from mental illness or severe mental impairment does not have to satisfy the "treatability test" on admission, the authority to detain such a patient can only be renewed if his responsible medical officer certifies either: (a) that treatment is likely to alleviate or prevent a deterioration of his condition; or (b) that if discharged he would be unlikely to be able to cope for himself, to obtain the care which he needs or to guard himself against serious exploitation (s.20(3)(4)). If a patient who is suffering from mental illness or severe mental impairment is reclassified to the effect that he is suffering from psychopathic disorder or mental impairment, the authority to detain the patient ceases unless his responsible medical officer certifies that the "treatability test" is satisfied (s.16(2)).

Likely to: Which suggests a high degree of probability; a mere hope or possibility is not sufficient.

Alleviate: But not necessarily cure the patient's condition.

Prevent a Deterioration: The test set out in this paragraph would be satisfied if it was considered likely that medical treatment, which is given a very wide definition in section 145(1), would stabilise the patient's condition.

It should be noted that the courts have occasionally been presented with medical evidence in support of the contention that psychiatric in-patient units have the capacity to bring about a significant deterioration in the behaviour of certain categories of patient (see, for example, *R. v. Brand*, March 16, 1999, CA).

Condition: Means "the mental disorder on grounds of which the application for [the patient's] admission and detention has been made", *per* Hoffmann L.J. in *B v. Croydon Health Authority* [1995] 1 All E.R. 683 at 687.

Paragraph (c)
There is no requirement for the two recommending doctors to agree on the nature **1–050** of the risk which justifies detention under this section.

Necessary: A stronger term than "ought" in section 2(2)(b). The necessity must relate to both compulsion and treatment.

Health: See the note on section 2(2).

Safety: With the patient being exposed to the risk of being harmed if he is not detained.

Protection of other persons: See the note on section 2(2).

And that it cannot be provided: By, for example, an informal admission. The use of restraint on a patient should not automatically lead to his admission under this Act: see the General Note to paragraph 19.8 of the *Code of Practice*.

Unless he is detained under this section: See the General Note to section 2 under the heading "Section 2 or section 3".

Subsection (3)
Written recommendations: Made either separately or jointly (s.11(7)). **1–051**
Two registered medical practitioners: Complying with the provisions of section 12.

Admission for assessment in cases of emergency

4.—(1) In any case of urgent necessity, an application for admission for **1–052** assessment may be made in respect of a patient in accordance with the following provisions of this section, and any application so made is in this Act referred to as "an emergency application".

(2) An emergency application may be made either by an approved social worker or by the nearest relative of the patient; and every such application shall include a statement that it is of urgent necessity for the patient to be admitted and detained under section 2 above, and that compliance with the provisions of this Part of this Act relating to applications under that section would involve undesirable delay.

(3) An emergency application shall be sufficient in the first instance if founded on one of the medical recommendations required by section 2 above, given, if practicable, by a practitioner who has previous acquaintance with the patient and otherwise complying with the requirements of section 12 below so far as applicable to a single recommendation, and verifying the statement referred to in subsection (2) above.

(4) An emergency application shall cease to have effect on the expiration of a period of 72 hours from the time when the patient is admitted to the hospital unless—

(a) the second medical recommendation required by section 2 above is given and received by the managers within that period; and

(b) that recommendation and the recommendation referred to in subsection (3) above together comply with all the requirements of section 12 below (other than the requirement as to the time of signature of the second recommendation).

35

(5) In relation to an emergency application, section 11 below shall have effect as if in subsection (5) of that section for the words "the period of 14 days ending with the date of the application" there were substituted the words "the previous 24 hours".

DEFINITIONS

1–053 application for admission for assessment: ss.2, 145(1).
patient: s.145(1).
approved social worker: s.145(1).
nearest relative: ss.26(3), 145(1).
hospital: ss.34(2), 145(1).

GENERAL NOTE

1–054 This section, which is considered in Chapter 6 of the *Code of Practice*, provides, in a case of urgent necessity, for the compulsory admission of a person to hospital for assessment for a period of up to 72 hours. The Royal Commission expected the equivalent procedure in the 1959 Act to be used only in exceptional circumstances: "It is important that the emergency procedure should not be used except in real emergencies when action to remove the patient must be taken before there is time to obtain the two medical recommendations required under the normal procedure [*i.e.* admission under s.2]" (para. 409). The emergency procedure was used far more frequently than the Royal Commission envisaged, and it became the most widely used form of compulsory admission. This situation caused concern and in 1966, the Ministry of Health instituted an inquiry to try and establish why the procedure was being used so frequently. That enquiry found, *inter alia*, that: (1) many medical and social work professionals were largely ignorant of the relevant legislative provisions; (2) those involved in compulsory admissions considered that the emergency procedure, being quicker, easier and of shorter duration than the normal procedure, was a more humane method of admitting formally; and (3) the emergency procedure was administratively more convenient than the normal procedure. In 1974 the Hospital Advisory Service added its voice to the disquiet that was being expressed about the emergency procedure, and in 1976 the Royal College of Psychiatrists said that the advantages of the emergency procedure had "led to misuse and abuse in some areas".

Most of the criticism of the emergency procedure has been based upon the frequency of its use but, as Philip Bean has pointed out, one cannot say that the emergency procedure is being misused because there is a high percentage of admissions under this procedure because "it may be that the high percentage of admissions reflects a psychiatric reality, *i.e.* that there are a large number of emergencies which required short-term admissions" (*Compulsory Admissions to Mental Hospitals*, 1980, p. 69). However, the existence of large regional variations in the use of the emergency procedure does suggest that it had been used inappropriately on many occasions. Although pressure from the Mental Health Act Commission has been largely responsible for a decrease in both the number and proportion of applications under this section, such applications should be made in psychiatric emergencies where the patient's urgent need for treatment outweighs the desirability of waiting for a medical examination by a second doctor.

An application under this section cannot be renewed at the end of the 72 hour period. If compulsory detention is to be continued the application must either be "converted" into a section 2 application under the provisions of subsection (4), in which case the patient can be detained for 28 days beginning with the date of his admission under this section, or an application for treatment should be made under section 3. This Act does not contain a procedure under which a section 4 application can be converted into a section 3 application by the addition of a second medical recommendation: the criteria for admission under each section are quite distinct.

As the nearest relative of a detained patient has to give not less than 72 hours' notice of his intention to discharge the patient (s.25), only the responsible medical officer and the hospital managers have the power to order the discharge of a patient detained under this section (s.23). A patient detained under this section can seek his own discharge by making an application to a Mental Health Review Tribunal. If the second medical recommendation provided for in subsection (4) is not forthcoming, the application to the tribunal will lapse.

Patients admitted under this section are *not* subject to the consent to treatment provisions contained in Pt IV of this Act and are therefore in the same position as an informal patient in so far as consent to treatment is concerned (s.56(1)(a)).

Subsection (1)

Application: The applicant must have seen the patient within the previous 24 hours **1–055** (s.11(5)) and the patient must be admitted to hospital within 24 hours beginning from the time when he was medically examined or when the application was made, whichever is the earlier (s.6(1)(b)). These time limits were introduced by the 1982 Act to help "to prevent [this section] being used for cases other than those of real emergency" (Cmnd. 7320, para. 2.6). Although an approved social worker applicant is not required to consult with the patient's nearest relative prior to the application being made, the duty of the approved social worker under section 11(3) to inform the nearest relative of an application under section 2 is triggered if the application is "converted" to a section 2 application under the provisions of subsection (4). An application for the admission of a ward of court cannot be made without the leave of the High Court (s.33(1)).

The effect of an application made under this section is set out in section 6.

Subsection (2)

Approved social worker: An approved social worker applicant must comply with **1–056** the requirements of section 13. The assessment of people with mental health problems prior to possible admission under this Act is covered by the *Code of Practice* at paragraphs 2.1 *et seq.*

Urgent necessity ... undesirable delay: The use of this section should be confined to cases of real emergency where the delay that would be caused by waiting for a second medical opinion would be undesirable because of the patient's urgent need for medical treatment in a hospital. If a patient who has been detained in a general hospital under section 5(2) needs to be transferred to a psychiatric hospital urgently, an application under this section can be made if the criteria in this subsection are satisfied. The statement made by the Mental Health Act Commission in paragraph 3 of its Guidance Note "Use of the Mental Health Act 1983 in general hospitals without a psychiatric unit" (March, 2001), that this section "cannot be used in the case of in-patients" is not correct (see s.5(1)).

The delay involved in obtaining a second medical recommendation could depend, *inter alia*, on local geography, the administrative procedures adopted locally to respond to crises, or on the hour at which the crisis occurs. "It is wrong for patients to be admitted under section 4 ... because it is more convenient for the second doctor to examine the patient in ... hospital" (*Code of Practice*, para. 6.4). If an approved social worker is unable to persuade a doctor approved under section 12 to visit the patient with a view to making an application under section 2, an application under this section should not automatically follow as the social worker would need to be satisfied that it is "necessary or proper" for the application to be made (s.13(1)). If approved social workers consider that they are being forced to make inappropriate use of this section because of difficulties in obtaining the second medical recommendation required by section 2, they should try to resolve the difficulty at local level or, if this turns out to be unproductive, inform the Mental Health Act Commission which is required to keep this Act under review.

It is difficult to envisage a nearest relative applicant being aware of the distinction between an application made under this section and an application made under section 2.

Subsection (3)

1–057   *One of the medical recommendations:* A medical recommendation provided under this section cannot be used to support a subsequent application made under section 3: see the General Note to this section.

If practicable: The applicant should ascertain whether it is practicable to involve a doctor who has prior knowledge of the patient.

Subsection (4)

1–058   *Period of 72 hours:* If the application is "converted" into a section 2 application under this subsection, the 28 days period provided for in section 2 will run from the time of the patient's admission to hospital under this section. Note that the provisions of section 11(3) could not be fulfilled unless an approved social worker applicant had been informed of the "conversion" by the hospital authorities.

An approved social worker or a nearest relative applicant should not complete an application form for an admission under section 2 if a "conversion" is effected under this subsection.

Second medical recommendation . . . is given: An appropriate second doctor should examine the patient as soon as possible after admission, to decide whether the patient should be detained under section 2 (*Code of Practice*, para. 6.8).

Hospital: Local social services authorities must be informed of those hospitals where arrangements are in force for the reception, in cases of special urgency, of patients requiring treatment for mental disorder (s.140).

Application in respect of patient already in hospital

1–059   **5.**—(1) An application for the admission of a patient to a hospital may be made under this Part of this Act notwithstanding that the patient is already an in-patient in that hospital or, in the case of an application for admission for treatment that the patient is for the time being liable to be detained in the hospital in pursuance of an application for admission for assessment; and where an application is so made the patient shall be treated for the purposes of this Part of this Act as if he had been admitted to the hospital at the time when that application was received by the managers.

(2) If, in the case of a patient who is an in-patient in a hospital, it appears to the registered medical practitioner in charge of the treatment of the patient that an application ought to be made under this Part of this Act for the admission of the patient to hospital, he may furnish to the managers a report in writing to that effect; and in any such case the patient may be detained in the hospital for a period of 72 hours from the time when the report is so furnished.

(3) The registered medical practitioner in charge of the treatment of a patient in a hospital may nominate one (but not more than one) other registered medical practitioner on the staff of that hospital to act for him under subsection (2) above in his absence.

(4) If, in the case of a patient who is receiving treatment for mental disorder as an in-patient in a hospital, it appears to a nurse of the prescribed class—

(a) that the patient is suffering from mental disorder to such a degree that it is necessary for his health or safety or for the protection of others for him to be immediately restrained from leaving the hospital; and

(b) that it is not practicable to secure the immediate attendance of a practitioner for the purpose of furnishing a report under subsection (2) above, the nurse may record that fact in writing; and in that event the patient may be detained in the hospital for a period of six hours from the time when that fact is so recorded or until the earlier arrival at the place where the patient is detained of a practitioner having power to furnish a report under that subsection.

(5) A record made under subsection (4) above shall be delivered by the nurse (or by a person authorised by the nurse in that behalf) to the managers of the hospital as soon as possible after it is made; and where a record is made under that subsection the period mentioned in subsection (2) above shall begin at the time when it is made.

(6) The reference in subsection (1) above to an in-patient does not include an in-patient who is liable to be detained in pursuance of an application under this Part of this Act and the references in subsections (2) and (4) above do not include an in-patient who is liable to be detained in a hospital under this Part of this Act.

(7) In subsection (4) above "prescribed" means prescribed by an order made by the Secretary of State.

DEFINITIONS

    patient: s.145(1).   **1–060**
    hospital: ss.34(2), 145(1).
    application for admission for treatment: ss.3, 145(1).
    application for admission for assessment: ss.2, 145(1).
    the managers: s.145(1).
    mental disorder: s.145(1).

GENERAL NOTE

This section provides for applications for compulsory detention under section 2 or **1–061** 3 of this Act to be made in respect of mentally disordered patients who are already receiving treatment in hospital as informal patients. It also sets out the procedures that can be used if it is considered that a patient might leave the hospital before there is time to complete an application under either section 2 or section 3.

Patients who are detained under the provisions of subsection (2) or (4) of this section are not subject to the consent to treatment provisions contained in Part IV of this Act (s.56(1)(b)). Treatment of such patients without their consent can therefore only be given under common law powers: see the General Note to Part IV and Chapter 15 of the *Code of Practice*.

A person who has been detained under either subsection (2) or subsection (4) may be retaken if he absents himself from the hospital without leave as long as the relevant period of detention has not expired (s.18(5)).

Further powers to detain and control patients

The courts have held that where a patient has been detained under this Act, there **1–062** is an implied power to exercise control over that patient: see the note on "act purporting to be done in pursuance of this Act" in section 139(1). Both statute and the common law provide further powers that can be used to detain and/or control mentally disordered patients. They are:

(1) Under section 3(1) of the Criminal Law Act 1967 "a person may use such force as is reasonable in the circumstances in the prevention of crime, or in effecting or assisting the lawful arrest of offenders or suspected offenders or persons unlawfully at large". This provision enables a member of staff to use reasonable force in an attempt to prevent a patient from committing an assault or any other criminal offence such as theft or the possession of an unauthorised offensive weapon. It does not apply where the patient is insane within the meaning of the M'Naghten rules because such a patient is not capable of committing a crime. Not many hospital patients would meet

the criteria for being insane within the meaning of the M'Naghten rules. The test established by the House of Lords in the M'Naghten case [1843–60] All E.R. 229, is that "it must be clearly proved that, (A) at the time of the committing of the act, the party accused was labouring under such a defect of reason, from disease of the mind, (B) as not to know (1) the nature and quality of the act he was doing wrong, or, if he did know it, (2) that he did not know he was doing what was wrong". The judges added (3) that if the defendant "labours under [a] partial delusion only, and is not in other respects insane, we think he must be considered in the same situation as to responsibility as if the facts with respect to which the delusion exists were real". Extract taken from G. Williams, *Textbook of Criminal Law*, 2nd ed., 1983, p. 643. Prof. Williams inserted the lettering and numbering. If the patient is insane, the common law authorise reasonable force to be used in self-defence or in the defence of others.

(2) In the case of *Albert v. Lavin* [1981] 3 All E.R. 878, the House of Lords confirmed that "every citizen in whose presence a breach of the peace is being, or reasonably appears to be about to be, committed has the right to take reasonable steps to make the person who is breaking or threatening to break the peace refrain from doing so; and these reasonable steps in an appropriate case include detaining him against his will" (*per* Lord Diplock at 880). A breach of the peace, which can take place in public or on private property, is not necessarily a crime. It occurs when "harm is actually done or its likely to be done to a person or in his presence to his property or a person is in fear of being so harmed through an assault, an affray, an unlawful assembly or other disturbance" (*R. v. Howell* [1982] Q.B. 416, 427, *per* Watkins L.J.). Breach of the peace is limited to violence or threats of violence: harm to property will constitute a breach only if done or threatened in the owner's presence because the natural consequence of such harm is likely to be a violent retaliation (*Percy v. Director of Public Prosecutions* [1995] 3 All E.R. 124, DC). A breach of the peace can occur on private premises even if the only persons likely to be affected by the breach are inside the premises and no member of the public outside the premises is involved (*McConnell v. Chief Constable of the Greater Manchester Police* [1990] 1 All E.R. 423, CA).

(3) In the leading speech in *Black v. Forsey*, 1987 S.L.T. 681, HL, a case under the Mental Health (Scotland) Act 1984, Lord Keith said that the common law confers upon a private individual power to detain, in a situation of necessity, a person of unsound mind who is a danger to himself or others. A person exercising the power must be able to justify his action, if challenged, by proving the mental disorder of the detainee and the necessity of detention. In the opinion of Lord Griffiths the power is "confined to imposing temporary restraint on a lunatic who has run amok and is a manifest danger either to himself or to others—a state of affairs as obvious to a layman as to a doctor. Such a common law power is confined to the short period of confinement necessary before the lunatic can be handed over to a proper authority."

The powers noted above allow for an informal patient to be detained or secluded for a limited period only: they cannot be used as an alternative to procedures set out in this Act. Brenda Hoggett suggests that the powers "can probably be summed up by the proposition that there is a right to restrain a patient who is doing, or is about to do, physical harm to himself, to another person, or to property" as long as "the force used is no more than is in fact necessary to accomplish the object for which it is allowed" and the reaction is "in proportion to the harm threatened" (*Mental Health Law*, 1996, p. 140: also see, Phil Fennell, "Detention and Control of Informal Mentally Incapable Patients" [1984] J.S.W.L. 345).

Apart from the powers noted under (2) and (3) above, the extent to which common law powers enable informal patients to be controlled is not entirely clear. In *Pountney v. Griffiths* [1976] A.C. 314, the House of Lords noted that it had been conceded by counsel for a Broadmoor patient that hospital staff have "powers of control over all mentally disordered patients, whether admitted voluntary or compulsorily, though the nature and duration of the control varies with the category to which a patient belongs". The Report of the Committee of Inquiry into Complaints about Ashworth Hospital, Cm. 2028, considered that this "statement would be likely to receive the endorsement of the courts today" (p. 196). If an informal patient is unable to accept the control and discipline which is considered to be in the interests of either himself or the hospital, he should be asked to leave or, alternatively, consideration should be given to making an application for his compulsory detention if the necessary grounds exist.

The emergency medical treatment of a patient whose mental disorder precludes any rational communication with him is justified under the common law doctrine of necessity if such action is in the patient's best interests: see the note on "the treatment of incapable patient's" in the General Note to Part IV. Advice on caring for patients who present staff with particular management problems is contained in chapter 19 of the *Code of Practice*. The searching of patients and their belongings is considered in chapter 25 of the *Code*.

The Human Rights Act 1998

The powers contained in subsections (2) and (4) of this section do not violate the **1–063** European Convention on Human Rights because the procedural safeguards established under Convention case law do not apply to emergency situations (*Winterwerp v. Netherlands* (1979) 2 E.H.R.R. 387, noted under Art. 5(1)(e)). The use by staff of common law powers to detain and control patients in emergency situations whilst awaiting the presence of either a doctor or a specialist nurse who has the power to act under either subsection (2) or (4) of this section is also allowable under Convention law. However, such powers should only be used as a "safety net" to cover situations were it is not possible to immediately invoke the statutory powers. In other words, to be consistent with the Convention, common law powers should not be used as an alternative to the powers contained in this Act. The use of these powers must also be a proportionate response to the threat posed by the patient.

Doctors and nurses who use the holding powers contained in this section are exercising "functions of a public nature" and are therefore "public authorities" for the purposes of section 6 of the 1998 Act (s.6(3)(b)).

Subsection (1)

In-patient: The combined effect of this subsection and subsection (6) is that: **1–064**

(1) an application for compulsory admission to hospital under this Part can be made in respect of a person notwithstanding that he is already an in-patient in hospital;

(2) an application for compulsory admission cannot be made in respect of patients who are already in hospital under compulsory powers except that an application for admission for treatment under section 3 can be made in respect of a patient detained under an application for assessment under section 2; and

(3) where an application is made in respect of a patient already in hospital, it is treated for the purposes of this Part as if the patient were admitted to the hospital at the time when that application was received by the managers. Note that a patient who is admitted under an emergency application for assessment under section 4 can have the application "converted" into one for admission for assessment under section 2 (s.4(4)).

Subsection (2)

This subsection, which is considered in chapter 8 of the *Code of Practice*, enables **1–065** an informal patient to be detained for up to 72 hours if the doctor in charge of his treatment reports that an application under section 2 or 3 ought to be made. It cannot be used to prolong the detention of a patient where the authority to detain is about to expire (subs. (6)) or to provide time for an application to be made to the county court pursuant to section 29(4) to displace a nearest relative after the expiration of the 28 day period of detention provided for under section 2 (*McDougall v. Sefton Area Health Authority*, April 9, 1987, McNeill J., cited in L. Gostin, *Mental Health Services-Law and Practice*, 1986, at para. 10.04). The detention of the patient under this provision cannot be renewed on the expiration of the 72-hour period. The use of this provision has been audited by P. Mason and R. Turner, "Audit of the use of doctors' holding power under section 5(2) of the Mental Health Act 1983" (1994) *Health Trends* 44–46 and by E. Salib and B. Iparragirre, "Detention of in-patients under section 5(2) of the Mental Health Act 1983", (1998) Med. Sci. Law, 10–16. A study by I. Ebrahim and C. Botha found that 53 per cent of detentions under this provision are followed by applications under either section 2 or 3 ("Section 5(2) of the Mental Health Act 1983 in Practice: An Audit and a Review", (2000) Med. Sci. Law, 40(4), 313–318).

The Mental Health Act Commission reports that it advised a NHS trust "that consecutive applications of section 5(2) are uncommon and hardly every necessary if assessments are carried out promptly" (*M.H.A.C. Seventh Biennial Report*, 1995–1997, para. 3.2). It is submitted that, following the decision in *R. v. Wilson, ex p. Williamson* (noted in the General Note to s.2), this practice is unlawful.

In its Second Biennial Report 1985–87, the Commission said, at paragraph 17.4, that it viewed an application under section 4 as being "inappropriate following use of section 5(2)." In its Third Biennial Report 1987–89, the Commission, at paragraph 14.5, revised its view to the extent that it regarded the use of section 4 in such circumstances as being "inappropriate in most cases". The view expressed by the Commission in its Second Biennial Report is to be preferred because the 72 hour period allowed for under this provision should provide sufficient time for the two medical recommendations required for an application under section 2 or 3 to be obtained.

The purpose of this holding power is to prevent a patient from discharging himself from hospital before there is time to arrange for an application under section 2 or 3 to be made. As soon as the power is invoked, arrangements should be made for the patient to be assessed by a potential applicant and potential recommending doctors.

The "Inquiry into the Care and Treatment of Gilbert Kopernik-Steckel" recommended that the Mental Health Act Commission should produce advice on the use of statements in a patient's file such as "For section 5(2) if he tries to leave", instructions from one clinician to another which were considered by many medical and nursing staff to override professional judgment. Although statements which appear to fetter the judgment of the "section 5(2) doctor" should be avoided, there is nothing objectionable in the responsible medical officer making a record to the effect that "Section 5(2) should be considered if the patient makes an attempt to leave".

There is no procedure for discharging the patient from the holding power. The power will automatically lapse if:

(a) the result of the assessment is a decision not to make an application under section 2 or 3; or

(b) the power is invoked by a doctor who has been nominated under subsection (3) and the patient's responsible medical officer subsequently decides that no assessment for possible detention needs to be carried out (also see the *Code of Practice* at para. 8.3); or

(c) an application under section 2 or 3 is made; or

(d) the patient is discharged from the hospital for clinical reasons before an assessment can be undertaken, *e.g.* the patient's violent conduct results in an arrest and removal to police custody.

If an approved social worker concludes at the assessment that an application in respect of the patient is not required and the assessing doctor holds a contrary view, there is nothing in this provision that prevents the assessment from being prolonged to enable the patient's nearest relative to consider whether he or she wishes to make an application.

The Mental Health Act Commission has "found instances where section 5(2) appears either to be used simply as a three day holding power, or lasts three days by default because the responsible medical officer has not informed the records officer as soon as a decision is taken not to proceed with assessment for compulsory detention or because the assessment process is not begun as soon as the section 5(2) is implemented." This finding led the Commission to recommend that "a record be kept of the date and time of both beginning and end of the holding power under section 5(2)" (Fifth Biennial Report 1991–1993, para. 3.5(e)). In their research into the use of this provision P. Bean and P. Mounser found evidence of it "being used as a quick and easy way of detaining patients compulsorily" and as "a trial period of compulsory detention" (*Discharged From Mental Hospitals* (Macmillan, 1993), pp. 82–86).

The relationship between this provision, the nurses "holding power" under subsection (4) and the common law is discussed in the following extract from paragraph 14.4. of the Third Biennial Report of the Mental Health Act Commission:

"It is the Commission's view that section 5(2) of the Act was not intended to provide legal authority for seclusion of informal patients but to provide for the temporary detention of patients pending the conclusion of the necessary interviews, examinations and other procedures of compulsory detention. If nursing staff of the appropriate level consider that detention is necessary to prevent the patient from leaving the hospital, section 5(4) may be used to authorise up to six hours' detention pending the arrival of the Responsible Medical Officer or his or her nominated deputy. If the Responsible Medical Officer or the nominated deputy considers an application for compulsory admission ought to be made then the patient may be held for up to 72 hours while such an application is made. [At one hospital visited] there appeared to be a misconception that the implementation of a section 5(2) or (4) was necessary to 'cover' staff against the risk of legal action on the part of a secluded patient. It is the Commission's experience that situations occur where patients become violent but evince no intention of leaving the hospital. In such a case it would be difficult for a nurse to justify the use of a section 5(4), although detention under section 5(2) might be justified if the violent conduct provided grounds for a view that the patient should be detained under section 2 or 3. Seclusion may be justified under common law if it is immediately necessary to prevent the patient from behaving dangerously to himself or others, or to prevent the commission of a crime or a breach of the peace, but then detention is only justified until the risk of such conduct has passed. The common law should not be used to justify protracted periods of seclusion. In cases where common law powers are invoked, the reasons for seclusion should be fully documented, and consideration ought to be given to the question whether the patient needs to be detained under statutory powers."

In-patient in a hospital: The patient could be receiving treatment in a general **1–066** hospital for a physical condition: see the note on "medical practitioner in charge," below.

A patient who is being treated in an out-patient department or in a day hospital cannot be detained under this provision. A mentally capable informal in-patient is "one who has understood and accepted the offer of a bed, and who has freely appeared on the ward and who has co-operated in the admission procedure" (the definition contained in the second edition of the *Code of Practice*, at para. 8.4). A suggested definition of a mentally incapable informal in-patient is: a compliant patient who has arrived at the ward and who has offered no resistance (either verbal or physical) to the admission procedure.

As the power contained in this subsection only applies if the patient is an informal in-patient, it is necessary to identify how a patient can divest himself of his in-patient status. Can, for example, an in-patient avoid being held under this provision by the simple expedient of saying to the doctor who is about to invoke the power, "I discharge myself"? It is highly unlikely that the courts would find that a patient could end his in-patient status in this manner as such a finding would have the effect of totally subverting Parliament's intention in enacting this provision. It is submitted that a patient does not lose his in-patient status until he has physically removed himself from the hospital.

In *R. v. Wilson, ex p. Williamson* [1996] C.O.D. 42, the court declared that the patient's detention under section 2 of this Act was unlawful. Counsel for the hospital managers stated that this provision would not be available following the court's decision because it was "designed for the patient who had been a voluntary patient" and that to use the provision in respect of a patient who had been detained in the hospital unlawfully would be to "take advantage of unlawful status" and would make the hospital managers vulnerable to judicial review on the ground that they were "using it for improper purposes". Although counsel's points have some substance, the correctness of his opinion must be doubted because a patient who has been unlawfully detained is clearly an "in-patient" if he has been admitted to the hospital, and it surely cannot be "improper" for the patient's consultant to utilise the only provision that is available to him to prevent a patient, who might have been diagnosed as being either dangerous or suicidal, from being discharged. The *Memorandum* states, at paragraph 47, that this provision can be used if an application is found to be fundamentally defective. In *R. v. Birmingham Mental Health Trust, ex p. Phillips*, May 25, 1995 the fact that the patient had been made the subject of this provision immediately after it was discovered that the application under section 2 that had been made in respect of her was invalid, was accepted by Tucker J. without comment.

It appears: Although this provision does not state that the patient must have been "personally examined" by the doctor, the *Code of Practice*, at paragraph 8.10, states that such an examination must take place. It would clearly not be possible to follow this guidance, other than in a superficial sense, in a situation where the patient suddenly decides that he wishes to leave the hospital immediately. In any event, it is the "attendance" of the doctor on the ward that is the pre-condition to invoking the holding power (subs. (4)(b)).

1–067   *Medical practitioner in charge:* In most cases this will be the consultant psychiatrist on the staff of the hospital under whose care the patient has been admitted. Paragraph 26 of the *Memorandum* states: "It may occasionally be necessary to make a report under section 5(2) in respect of a patient who is not in a psychiatric hospital or the psychiatric wing of a general hospital. Where a patient is receiving psychiatric treatment (even though he may also be receiving non-psychiatric treatment) the doctor in charge of the treatment for the purposes of section 5(2) will be the consultant or senior psychiatrist concerned. But where an in-patient is not receiving psychiatric treatment, the doctor who is in charge of the treatment the patient is receiving would have power to furnish the report. Where such a report is made by a non-psychiatrist, a senior psychiatrist should see the patient as soon as possible to determine whether the patient should be detained further."

If a patient is receiving out-patient treatment for his mental disorder at the time of his admission to a general hospital for treatment for a physical disorder, it is arguable that the patient's consultant psychiatrist has the power to invoke this provision. For a survey of general hospital in-patients detained under this provision, see C. Buller *et al.* (1996) 20 *Psychiatric Bulletin* 733–737. This research found evidence of frequent breaches of the *Code of Practice*.

The use of the holding powers in small mental nursing homes was considered by the Mental Health Act Commission in its Second Biennial Report at paragraph 19.2:

"In most of the small [mental nursing homes] visited general medical care is provided by general practitioners and medication for mental illness is reviewed by consultants at hospital outpatient clinics. Since these homes employ no medical staff, there would appear to be no-one to act as responsible medical officer under section 5(2) and follow up the report under section 5(4)."

The inference in this statement that a patient's general practitioner cannot invoke this provision is not correct because there is nothing in this Act that prevents such a doctor from being the "medical practitioner in charge of the treatment of the patient". It is also the case that an informal patient cannot have a "responsible medical officer" (s.34(1)).

An application ought to be made: The appropriate form, (see below) requires the doctor to state his or her reasons for believing that an application ought to be made. It is a misuse of this provision for it to be used as a means of restraining the patient from leaving hospital in circumstances where the medical practitioner does not consider that the patient ought to be *detained* for either assessment or treatment. If an application is made under section 2 or 3 during the 72-hour period the application will commence from the time when it was completed and not from the time when the holding power was invoked.

Report: Using Form 12 of Schedule 1 to the Mental Health (Hospital, Guardian- **1–068** ship and Consent to Treatment) Regulations 1983. Subject to subsection (3), the power to furnish a report under this provision cannot be delegated.

Detained in the hospital: The patient can be detained in any part of the hospital which is managed by the relevant hospital managers. If it is necessary to lock a ward door in order to detain the patient, the guidance set out in paragraphs 19.24 *et seq.* of the *Code of Practice* should be followed.

A patient who is detained under this provision cannot be transferred to another hospital under regulation 7 of the 1983 Regulations because such a person is not "liable to be detained in a hospital by *virtue of an application*" under this Part (s.19(1)(a), (2)(a)). The Mental Health Act Commission's Guidance Note entitled "Issues Surrounding Sections 17, 18 and 19 of the Mental Health Act 1983" states:

"The question sometimes arises whether there are circumstances in which [a patient who has been detained under section 5(2)] can be moved to another hospital—for example to a more appropriate environment or to obtain treatment not available in the detaining hospital. In the opinion of the Commission, a patient held under section 5(2) might lawfully be taken to another hospital with their full consent—for example to a more appropriate environment or to another site under the control of the same managers. In the absence of consent there may be circumstances of pressing need in which a transfer might be lawful under common law—for example in order to allow a patient to receive the physical treatment necessary to save life or to prevent serious and possible permanent suffering."

A number of points arise from this passage. They are:

(1) the section 5(2) will automatically lapse if the patient is moved from the hospital named on the Form 12 because this provision only provides authority for the patient to be detained in "the hospital" *i.e.* the hospital which was

providing in-patient treatment to the patient at the time when the power was invoked;

(2) a mentally capable consenting patient or a mentally incapable compliant patient who has been detained under this provision can be moved to another hospital under common law powers if there is a clinical justification for such action. Consideration would have to be given to invoking this provision if the patient made an attempt to leave that other hospital; and

(3) there is no authority to support the Commission's implied contention that the common law can be used to move a mentally capable patient to another hospital in the absence of his consent and without an application under section 2 or section 3 having been made in respect of him. The common law doctrine of necessity can only be invoked in respect of a mentally incapable patient: see the discussion on "The treatment of incapable patients" in the General Note to Part IV.

If a patient who has been detained under this provision needs to be transferred to another hospital urgently and there is not sufficient time to conform with the provisions of section 2, an application under section 4 can be made in respect of him if the criteria set out in section 4(2) can be satisfied.

72 hours: This is the maximum period during which a patient can be detained. The authority to detain under this provision is not renewable.

If a patient who has been detained under this section absents himself from the hospital without leave, he cannot be retaken once the 72 hour period has expired (s.18(5)).

Time when the report is ... furnished: In the Scottish case of *Milborrow, Applicant*, 1996 S.C.L.R. 315, Sh.Ct, it was held that a report is "furnished" to the hospital managers when it is committed to the internal mailing system operated by those managers. This finding is consistent with one of the dictionary definitions of "furnish" which is "to provide or supply" (*Shorter O.E.D.*). Regulation 3(1) of the Mental Health (Hospital, Guardianship and Consent to Treatment) Regulations 1983, which is concerned with the method of delivery of documents that are required to be "served", appears to apply to external rather than internal communications. The requirement on Form 12 for the patient's consultant to identify the time when his signature was appended supports this interpretation. If regulation 3(1) applied, the form would have needed to identify the time when an authorised person received it.

If the patient is intent of leaving the hospital immediately, the common law powers outlined in the General Note to this section will usually provide authority for the patient to be detained for the short period that is required to complete Form 12. It is submitted that once Form 12 has been completed, the patient can be detained even though he might have left the ward area. However, if the patient has left the hospital before the completion of Form 12, the hospital managers cannot subsequently detain him and return him to hospital on the authority of the Form 12. This is because by leaving hospital the patient relinquishes his in-patient status which is an essential pre-condition to the use of this subsection. As a patient who is not "liable to be detained" he could not be returned to hospital under the auspices of section 18.

Subsection (3)

1–069 This subsection was introduced by the 1982 Act to lessen the pressures on medical practitioners to contravene the provisions of subsection (2) by, for example, allowing persons other than the "medical practitioner in charge", such as a night duty doctor, to sign the relevant form or by the consultant signing a number of blank forms for use when emergencies occurred. Only the "medical practitioner in charge" or his nominated deputy have authority to detain a patient under subsection (2).

May nominate: The nomination should be put in writing and conveyed to all relevant staff: a nomination by telephone is of doubtful legality. It is the doctor in charge of the patient's treatment and not the hospital managers who must make the nomination. The nominated doctor cannot himself delegate to another because of the legal principle *delegatus non potest delegare.*

Only one doctor may be nominated to act for the consultant during any particular period of time. A nomination "to Dr A or, in Dr A's absence, to Dr B" would be unlawful.

On the staff of that hospital: The doctor must be contracted to undertake clinical responsibilities at that hospital. He or she must be a fully registered person within the meaning of the Medical Act 1956 (Interpretation Act 1978, Sched. 1).

To act for him: The nominated doctor should exercise his own judgment when exercising his powers under subsection (2). He can be advised, but not required to consult with a senior colleague before exercising his powers. The Mental Health Act Commission has said that, in so far as it is possible, the doctor who is nominated by the consultant should be another consultant or senior registrar (MHAC—CPC/1). Also see "Section 5(2): Who Acts as the Consultant's Nominated Deputy", Sally-Ann Cooper and Ruth Harper, *Psychiatric Bulletin* (1992), 16, 759–761 and G. E. P. Vincenti, "Who acts as the consultant's nominated deputy?" (1993) 17 *Psychiatric Bulletin* 771.

Subsection (4)

This subsection, which is considered in Chapter 9 of the *Code of Practice*, provides **1–070** for nurses of a prescribed class to invoke a "holding power" in respect of a patient for a period of not more than six hours. During this period the "medical practitioner in charge" or his nominated deputy should examine the patient with a view to making a report under subsection (2). A nurse invoking this provision is entitled to "use the minimum force necessary to prevent the patient from leaving hospital" (*Code of Practice*, para. 9.6). For a study of the application of this provision, see N. Pym *et al.* (1999) "A review of 100 applications of section 5(4) Mental Health Act", 13 Nursing Standard 20, 37–40.

Receiving treatment for mental disorder: This power can only be used in respect of patients who are receiving hospital treatment for mental disorder on an informal basis (subs. (6)).

In-patient in a hospital: Although this power can be invoked in any hospital where the patient is receiving treatment for mental disorder, it is unlikely that a non-psychiatric ward will be staffed with nurses of the "prescribed class".

Nurse: Exercising the holding power "is the personal decision of the nurse who cannot be instructed to exercise [it] by anyone else" (*Code of Practice*, para. 9.1).

Prescribed class: See subsection (7).

Degree: The patient cannot be made subject to this holding power if he is not exhibiting any manifestations of his mental disorder: see the note on "of a nature or degree" in section 3(2)(a).

Record: Using Form 13 of Schedule 1 to the Mental Health (Hospital, Guardianship and Consent to Treatment) Regulations 1983. Although this form does not require the nurse to state his reasons for invoking this power, the *Code of Practice*, at paragraph 9.4, recommends that they be recorded in the patient's notes.

Immediately restrained from leaving the hospital: The power to detain the patient takes effect at the time when the nurse makes her report. It can only be used if the patient is indicating either verbally or otherwise that he wishes to leave the hospital.

Immediate attendance of a practitioner: It is submitted that the nurses' holding power need not be invoked if either the patient's consultant or his nominated doctor is in the hospital building and can attend at the ward within a few minutes of the crises occurring. A combination of the common law powers outlined in the General Note to this section and the legal maxim *de minimis non curat lex* (the law does not take account of trifles) would enable the patient to be held during this brief period.

Detained in the hospital: See the note on subsection (2).

Six hours: This is the maximum, and non-renewable period during which a patient can be detained. The nurse, or another nurse of the prescribed class, should let the managers know when the power has lapsed by delivering the prescribed form to them (reg. 4(5) and Form 16 of Schedule 1 to S.I. 1983 No. 893). The equivalent power under Scot's law allows for the patient to be detained for two hours (Mental Health (Scotland) Act 1984, s.25(2)).

In the sample studied by N. Pym *et al.*, see above, all uses of this provision were followed by use of the doctor's holding power provided for in subsection (2). In 95 per cent of the cases studied, the doctor provided his report under subsection (2) within three hours of the invoking of this provision.

From the time when that fact is so recorded: The record should be made immediately after the nurse has decided to exercise the "holding power". The power will end six hours later or on the earlier arrival of one of the two doctors entitled to make a report under subsection (2). If that doctor decides not to exercise his powers under subsection (2), the patient can either leave the hospital or remain as an informal patient.

Earlier arrival . . . of a practitioner: Who should quickly decide whether he should invoke his powers under subsection (2) as his arrival on the ward ends the power to detain.

Subsection (5)

1–071 This subsection provides that where the "holding power" provided for in subsection (4) is followed by a report made under subsection (2), the period of 72 hours provided for in subsection (2) runs from the time when the record required by subsection (4) is made.

Subsection (7)

1–072 *Prescribed:* The Mental Health (Nurses) Order 1998 (S.I. 1998 No. 2625) prescribes the class of nurse for the purposes of subsection (4) of this section as:

"a nurse registered in any part of the register maintained under section 7 of the Nurses, Midwives and Health Visitors Act 1997 which is mentioned in paragraph (2).
    (2) The parts of the register are:—
      (a) part 3 (first level nurses trained in the nursing of persons suffering from mental illness);
      (b) part 4 (second level nurses trained in the nursing of persons suffering from mental illness (England and Wales));
      (c) part 5 (first level nurses trained in the nursing of persons suffering from learning disabilities);
      (d) part 6 (second level nurses trained in the nursing of persons suffering from learning disabilities);
      (e) part 13 (nurses qualified following a course of preparation in mental health nursing);
      (f) part 14 (nurses qualified following a course of preparation in learning disabilities nursing)".

Secretary of State: The functions of the Minister, so far as exercisable in relation to Wales, are exercised by the National Assembly for Wales (S.I. 1999 No. 672, art. 2, Sched. 1).

Effect of application for admission

1–073 **6.**—(1) An application for the admission of a patient to a hospital under this Part of this Act, duly completed in accordance with the provisions of this Part of this Act, shall be sufficient authority for the applicant, or any person authorised by the applicant, to take the patient and convey him to the hospital at any time within the following period, that is to say—

(a) in the case of an application other than an emergency application, the period of 14 days beginning with the date on which the patient was last examined by a registered medical practitioner before giving a medical recommendation for the purposes of the application;

(b) in the case of an emergency application, the period of 24 hours beginning at the time when the patient was examined by the practitioner giving the medical recommendation which is referred to in section 4(3) above, or at the time when the application is made, whichever is the earlier.

(2) Where a patient is admitted within the said period to the hospital specified in such an application as is mentioned in subsection (1) above, or, being within that hospital, is treated by virtue of section 5 above as if he had been so admitted, the application shall be sufficient authority for the managers to detain the patient in the hospital in accordance with the provisions of this Act.

(3) Any application for the admission of a patient under this Part of this Act which appears to be duly made and to be founded on the necessary medical recommendations may be acted upon without further proof of the signature or qualification of the person by whom the application or any such medical recommendation is made or given or of any matter of fact or opinion stated in it.

(4) Where a patient is admitted to a hospital in pursuance of an application for admission for treatment, any previous application under this Part of this Act by virtue of which he was liable to be detained in a hospital or subject to guardianship shall cease to have effect.

DEFINITIONS

patient: s.145(1).   **1–074**
hospital: ss.34(2), 145(1).
the managers: s.145(1).
application for admission for treatment: ss.3, 145(1).

GENERAL NOTE

This section authorises the applicant or anyone authorised by him or her to take **1–075** the patient and convey him to hospital within specified periods, and authorises the hospital managers to detain the patient once he has been admitted. It also enables the hospital managers to act on statutory documents that appear to be valid and provides for the termination of existing applications subsequent to a patient's admission for treatment under section 3.

A duly completed application (subs. (1)) provides authority for the patient to be detained in the hospital named in the application (subs. (2)). Either section 17 or 19 of this Act will have to be used if the patient needs to be cared for in another hospital, even if that hospital is managed by the same hospital managers (s.19(3)). Health authorities and NHS Trusts, who have a duty to provide an ambulance service, must transport the patient to hospital if this proves to be necessary: see paragraph 31 of the *Memorandum*, quoted below.

The legality of a patient's detention in circumstances where the requirements of this Act relating to applications have not been fulfilled is considered in the following passage from the judgment of Laws J. in *R. v. Managers of South Western Hospital, ex p. M* [1994] 1 All E.R. 161, 176:

"Section 6(1) and (2) confer authority to convey or detain the patient in hospital where the application is 'duly completed in accordance with the provisions of this Part of this Act.' In my judgment this is an objective requirement and means that the application must not only *state* that the relevant provisions (which include the requirements of section 11(4)) have been fulfilled, but also that it be the case that they have actually been fulfilled. Here they were not; section 11(4) was not complied with. It follows, in my judgment, that the managers were not authorised to detain the applicant unless they were entitled to act upon [the approved social worker's] application by virtue of section 6(3). The contrast between section 6(1) and section 6(3) is of course between the words 'duly completed' and 'appears to be made.' In my judgment, where an application on its face sets out all the facts which, if true, constitute compliance with the relevant provisions of Part II of the Act (again, including section 11(4)) it is an application which 'appears to be duly made' within section 6(3). If any of the facts thus stated are not true, then although the application *appears* to be duly made, it is not duly completed for the purposes of section 6(1) and 6(2). Here, [the approved social worker's] application did state all the facts which, if true, constituted compliance with the relevant statutory provisions. Accordingly it was an application which appeared to be duly made. It follows that, although the managers were not authorised to detain the patient by section 6(2) standing alone, they were entitled to act upon the application, and thus to detain the patient, by virtue of section 6(3). Accordingly, the applicant's detention is not unlawful."

In *Re S-C (Mental Patient: Habeas Corpus)* [1996] 1 All E.R. 532, CA, Sir Thomas Bingham M.R. said, at 542, 543, that he "would accept almost everything in [the passage quoted above] as correct with the exception of the last sentence. The judge goes straight from a finding that the hospital managers were entitled to act upon an apparently valid application to the conclusion that the applicant's detention was therefore not unlawful. That is, in my judgment, a non sequitur. It is perfectly possible that the hospital managers were entitled to act on an apparently valid application, but that the detention was in fact unlawful. If that were not so the implications would, in my judgment, be horrifying. It would mean that an application which appeared to be in order would render the detention of a citizen lawful even though it was shown or admitted that the approved social worker purporting to make the application was not an approved social worker, that the registered medical practitioners whose recommendations founded the application were not registered medical practitioners or had not signed the recommendations, and that the approved social worker had not consulted the patient's nearest relative or had consulted the patient's nearest relative and that relative had objected. In other words, it would mean that the detention was lawful even though every statutory safeguard built into the procedure was shown to have been ignored or violated. Bearing in mind what is at stake, I find that conclusion wholly unacceptable." The other members of the Court of Appeal agreed with this finding.

In *R. v. Central London County Court, ex p. London* [1999] 3 All E.R. 991, CA, Stuart-Smith L.J., in giving the leading judgment, said that he understood the Court of Appeal in *Re S-C* to have interpreted the phrase used by Laws J. which they had criticised as meaning that the patient's *continued* detention is not unlawful, rather than the original detention was not unlawful (at para. 32). The court held, *obiter*, that hospital managers would have acted lawfully in accepting an application that was made subsequent to an order of county court made under section 29 displacing the patient's nearest relative on an interim basis, even if it was subsequently found that the court had no jurisdiction to make the order.

1–076 The following propositions can be said to represent the law on this issue:

(1) an application for admission made by an approved social worker or a nearest relative setting out all the relevant facts which, if true, constituted compliance with the relevant provisions of this Part of this Act, is an application which "appears to be duly made" for the purposes of subsection (3);

(2) after having carefully checked (*per* Neill L.J. in *Re S-C* at 544) the documentation for obvious errors, the hospital managers are entitled to act on the application without further proof of the facts stated therein. *Per* Sir Thomas Bingham M.R. at 537:

> "[Section 6] provides protection for a hospital to which a patient is admitted or in which a patient is detained. Such a hospital is not at risk of liability for false imprisonment if it turns out that the approved social worker does not meet the definition in section 145(1), or if the recommendations which purport to be signed by registered medical practitioners are in truth not signed by such, although appearing to be so. That is obviously good sense. A mental hospital is not obliged to act like a private detective; it can take documents at face value. Provided they appear to conform with the requirements of the statute, the hospital is entitled to act on them."; and

(3) if, subsequent to having accepted an application, the hospital managers discover that the application is fundamentally defective (*e.g.*, a relative who is not the patient's "nearest relative" has been consulted under section 11(4)), this has the effect of rendering the continued detention of the patient unlawful. In these circumstances the hospital managers should:

(a) inform the patient of the situation and of the need for him to obtain legal advice;
(b) make an appropriate note on the patient's file; and
(c) exercise their power under section 23 to discharge the patient from his liability to be detained. If the patient is not discharged an application for either *habeas corpus* or judicial review could be made: see the General Note to section 65.

A report could be issued under section 5(2) or (4) in respect of the patient if the appropriate requirements were satisfied: see the note on "in-patient in a hospital" in section 5(2) and the *Memorandum* at paragraph 47.

If there is a genuine dispute about whether a provision of this Act has been complied with (*e.g.* the patient's nearest relative disputes the ASW's assertion on the application form that the consultation required by section 11(4) took place), the hospital managers should not attempt to resolve the dispute but should leave the patient to consider challenging the detention. "There is, in my judgment, no means by which managers can investigate the truth or otherwise of assertions that the form has not been duly made, let alone is there any guidance as to the manner in which they should adjudicate on such issue and come to a conclusion contrary to that which appears on the face of the application form" (*In the Matter of Darren Simpson-Cleghorn* [1997] C.O.D. 221, *per* Turner J.). Although this case was decided before the judgment of the Court of Appeal in *Re S.-C.*, it is submitted that the comment of Turner J. remains valid.

Subsection (1)

An application: Comprises the application form and the medical recommendation **1–077** form(s).

Duly completed: This is an objective requirement. It is possible to amend incorrect or defective applications and medical recommendations under section 15.

Applicant: Who will be the patient's nearest relative or an approved social worker (ss.4(2), 11(1)). Where the approved social worker is the applicant "he has a professional responsibility for ensuring that all the necessary arrangements are made for the patient to be conveyed to hospital" (*Code of Practice*, para. 11.1). A nearest relative applicant should receive professional assistance (*ibid.* para. 11.2).

Any person authorised by the applicant: Such as the police or a member of the ambulance service. Paragraph 31 of the *Memorandum* states: "Where it is necessary to provide transport to take the patient to hospital, this comes within the duty of Health Authorities and NHS Trusts to provide ambulance services. If the patient is likely to be unwilling to be moved, the applicant should provide the ambulance attendant or escort with written authority." The provision of written authority is a matter of good practice and is not a legal requirement.

Where delegation takes place the approved social worker "retains ultimate responsibility to ensure that the patient is conveyed in a lawful and humane manner, and should give guidance to those asked to assist" (*Code of Practice*, para. 11.4).

If it is not practicable for the approved social worker to attend at the hospital named in the application because it is located far away from the approved social worker's home area, the statutory documentation should be handed to the person who has been authorised by the approved social worker to convey the patient to the hospital.

To take the patient: If an application is not "duly completed" there is no authority for an approved social worker, medical practitioner or authorised person to take the patient to hospital against his will. If such persons were asked to leave the patient's home before the application is "duly completed" they would be trespassers if they remained and the householder would be entitled to use reasonable force in ejecting them: see *Townley v. Rushworth*, 62 L.G.R. 95, DC, where an attempt was made to detain a patient on an emergency application before the medical recommendation had been completed. *Per* Lord Parker C.J. at 98: "Unless it is to be said that a householder is to sit down and submit, not only to his liberty being infringed in his own house, but also to assault by injection, and to his liberty being removed in hospital, I cannot say that to hit out with the fist is an unreasonable use of force." Professionals would not become trespassers if one co-owner gave them permission to stay, despite the fact that the other co-owner requested that they leave: see the note on "enter and inspect" in section 115. A duly completed application does not provide authority for the applicant to force his way into the patient's home. If force is required an approved social worker should apply for a warrant under section 135(1).

1–078   *Convey him:* Using such force as is reasonably necessary to achieve the objective. If the patient is likely to be violent or dangerous police assistance should be requested (*Code of Practice*, para. 11.7). An applicant who conveys a patient to hospital has all the powers that a policeman has when taking a person into custody (s.137(2)). A patient who is being conveyed to hospital is deemed to be in legal custody (s.137(1)) and if he escapes he may be retaken within 14 days after the last medical examination for the purposes of a medical recommendation for section 2 or 3 patients, or within 24 hours from the medical examination, or the time when the application was made, whichever is the earlier, for a section 4 patient (s.138). If forcible entry is required to retake a patient who is liable to be detained, a warrant should be applied for under section 135(2). Guidance on the arrangements for conveying the patient to hospital is contained in chapter 11 of the *Code of Practice*.

To hospital: Which will be the hospital named on the application. It is unlawful to convey a patient to hospital on the authority of an application which does not state the name of the potential admitting hospital. The named hospital is not under a legal obligation to admit the patient and the duly completed application does not provide authority to convey the patient to another hospital. It is therefore essential for the recommending doctor to have ensured that a bed is available for the patient in the named hospital. In its eighth Biennial Report 1997–1999, the Mental Health Act Commission suggests that if a patient cannot be admitted to hospital in an emergency for want of a bed "the approved social worker should complete the application, making it out to a hospital specified to the relevant health authority in the notice required to be given under section 140 of the Act, and convey the patient to that hospital" (para. 4.45). This advice is subject to the criticism that the managers of the hospital specified in the section 140 notice are not legally obliged to admit the patient and, in any event, it might be clinically inappropriate for the patient to be admitted to that hospital.

If the patient requires emergency treatment for a physical injury or disorder, he could be taken to and treated in an A. and E. Department under common law powers before being transported to the hospital named in the application. If the patient requires a period of in-patient treatment for a physical injury or disorder, it would be unlawful for him to be admitted to the psychiatric hospital named in the application and then immediately transferred to a general hospital on section 17 leave (*R. v. Hallstrom, ex p. W* [1986] Q.B. 1090). It is also clearly unlawful for the patient to be admitted directly to the general hospital after having been given a "notional" leave of absence from the psychiatric hospital. If the patient named in the application is mentally competent, he could be admitted directly to the general hospital with his agreement and then taken to the psychiatric hospital before the expiry of the fourteen day period provided for in paragraph (a). If the patient is unwilling to be admitted formally to the general hospital, he could be "sectioned" to that hospital and treated there for both his psychiatric and physical conditions. The exercise of this option would be facilitated if the psychiatric hospital had made a service level agreement with the general hospital for the provision of psychiatric treatment and Mental Health Act administration services at that hospital. In these circumstances the general hospital would be the hospital named in the application and the patient's responsible medical officer would be the psychiatrist who is in charge of the treatment of the patient's mental disorder. The treatment of a mentally capable patient's physical condition could only proceed with his consent: see the General Note to Part IV. To enable the managers of the general hospital to deal appropriately with any application for discharge that such a patient might make, it is suggested that the managers should attempt to appoint the committee that has been established by the managers of the psychiatric hospital to hear such applications, to hear applications on their behalf.

Paragraph (a)
Beginning with the date: Including the date on which the patient was last examined **1–079**
(*Hare v. Gocher* [1962] 2 Q.B. 641).
Last examined by a registered medical practitioner: The relevant date is that of the last medical examination and not the day on which the medical recommendation form was signed by the doctor. If the medical practitioners examined the patient separately, not more than five days must have elapsed between the respective examinations (s.12(1)).
The applicant must have seen the patient within the period of 14 days ending with the day of the application (s.11(5)).

Paragraph (b)
Whichever is the earlier: As an emergency application must be "founded on" the **1–080**
medical recommendation (s.4(3)), it should not be signed until the medical recommendation has been given.

Subsection (2)
"A person who is detained in hospital under section 6(2) is lawfully detained. If he **1–081**
goes absent without leave, he is then at large . . . , and, since he ought not to be at large and is, by virtue of section 18(1), liable to be taken into custody and returned to the hospital, he would inevitably appear to be *unlawfully* at large [within section 17(1)(d) of the Police and Criminal Evidence Act 1984] until he is taken into custody"; *per* Lord Lowry in *D'Souza v. Director of Public Prosecutions* [1992] 4 All E.R. 545 at 553, 544. The *D'Souza* case is considered in the General Note to section 135.
Sufficient authority for the managers: The application will be served by delivering it to an officer of the managers (S.I. 1983 No. 893, reg. 3(2)). That officer will scrutinise the documents to ensure that the application has been "duly made" (subs. (3)). Even if the application has been properly completed, there is no obligation placed on the managers by this Act to accept the application and detain the patient.
Where a patient has been admitted to hospital under sections 2, 3, or 4, or detained

pursuant to a report under section 5(2), a record of admission shall be made by the managers in the form set out in Form 14 of Schedule 1 to the Mental Health (Hospital, Guardianship and Consent to Treatment) Regulations 1983 (*ibid.* reg. 4(3)).

To detain the patient: The courts have held that the express power to detain a patient for treatment necessarily implies a power to control that patient: see the note on "act purporting to be done in pursuance of this Act" in section 139(1).

Subsection (3)

1–082 *Appears to be duly made:* If on careful checking the application appears to be duly made, the hospital managers can act on it; see the General Note to this section.

Subsection (4)

1–082.1 A similar provision relating to the making of a hospital order or a guardianship order by a court under section 37 can be found in section 40(5). For the effect that reception into guardianship has on existing applications, see section 8(5).

Guardianship

Application for guardianship

1–083 **7.**—(1) A patient who has attained the age of 16 years may be received into guardianship, for the period allowed by the following provisions of this Act, in pursuance of an application (in this Act referred to as "a guardianship application") made in accordance with this section.

(2) A guardianship application may be made in respect of a patient on the grounds that—

(a) he is suffering from mental disorder, being mental illness, severe mental impairment, psychopathic disorder or mental impairment and his mental disorder is of a nature or degree which warrants his reception into guardianship under this section; and

(b) it is necessary in the interests of the welfare of the patient or for the protection of other persons that the patient should be so received.

(3) A guardianship application shall be founded on the written recommendations in the prescribed form of two registered medical practitioners, including in each case a statement that in the opinion of the practitioner the conditions set out in subsection (2) above are complied with; and each such recommendation shall include—

(a) such particulars as may be prescribed of the grounds for that opinion so far as it relates to the conditions set out in paragraph (a) of that subsection; and

(b) a statement of the reasons for that opinion so far as it relates to the conditions set out in paragraph (b) of that subsection.

(4) A guardianship application shall state the age of the patient or, if his exact age is not known to the applicant, shall state (if it be the fact) that the patient is believed to have attained the age of 16 years.

(5) The person named as guardian in a guardianship application may be either a local social services authority or any other person (including the applicant himself); but a guardianship application in which a person other than a local social services authority is named as guardian shall be of no effect unless it is accepted on behalf of that person by the local social services authority for the area in which he resides, and shall be accompanied by a statement in writing by that person that he is willing to act as guardian.

DEFINITIONS   **1–084**
    patient: s.145(1).
    mental disorder: ss.1, 145(1).
    severe mental impairment: ss.1, 145(1).
    psychopathic disorder: ss.1, 145(1).
    local social services authority: s.145(1).

GENERAL NOTE

The guardianship powers in this Act are largely based on recommendations made   **1–085**
by the Royal Commission (paras 387, 399, 400, 411). The "Commission argued that
care outside hospital should usually be on the basis of persuasion to accept help and
advice and take advantage of arrangements for employment and training. However,
the Commission recommended that where a person's unwillingness to receive
training or social help could not be overcome by persuasion it would be appropriate
to place him under guardianship if this offered the prospect of success. The
Commission suggested that care under guardianship might be more appropriate for
some people, particularly those with mild or chronic forms of mental illness, than
compulsory admission to or continued detention in hospital. ... The use of
guardianship powers has declined steadily since their introduction and practice
varies considerably between local authorities. The Royal Commission expected that
as community psychiatric services developed guardianship would become more
frequent, but this hope has not been borne out" (Cmnd. 7320, paras 4.5, 4.7).

The White Paper that preceded this Act stated that guardianship powers are
needed for "a very small number of mentally disordered people who do not require
treatment in hospital, either formally or informally, [but who] nevertheless need
close supervision and some control in the community as a consequence of their
mental disorder. These include people who are able to cope provided that they take
their medication regularly, but who fail to do so, and those who neglect themselves to
the point of seriously endangering their health" (Cmnd. 8405, para. 43).

The House of Commons' Health Committee in its report on *Community
Supervision Orders* found that "guardianship is only infrequently used in practice.
There has been limited growth in its use in recent years, from about 80 cases in 1984
to 233 new cases in the year ending March 31, 1992. On average it is applied annually
to only one or two cases in each local authority, although this average figure conceals
considerable variation between authorities. The Department of Health could not
explain these variations but other witnesses suggested a number of reasons including
a lack of awareness and understanding of the provisions, insufficient resources to
discharge the responsibility under guardianship and a lack of powers to compel
compliance with a guardianship order" (Fifth Report, Session 1992–93, Vol. 1, para.
27). Guardianship is used predominantly for mentally ill people who are over 65
years of age (National Health Act Guardianship: A Discussion Paper, Department
of Health, 1994, p. 5). The reception of a patient into guardianship does not carry with
it resource implications for the local authority (apart from associated administrative
costs) because the fact that a patient is subject to guardianship does not provide that
patient with an entitlement to receive community care services under the National
Health Service and Community Care Act 1990.

The *Code of Practice*, at paragraph 13.1, states that the "purpose of guardianship is   **1–086**
to enable patients to receive community care where it cannot be provided without the
use of compulsory powers. It enables the establishment of an authoritative
framework for working with a patient with a minimum of constraint to achieve as
independent a life as possible within the community. Where it is used it must be part
of the patient's overall care and treatment plan." Guardianship is compared with
supervised discharge in paragraph 8 of the supplement to the *Code of Practice* and in
the General Note to "After-Care Under Supervision" which precedes section 25A.

A comprehensive bibliography on guardianship is contained in *Research on
Guardianship for Mentally Ill People*, Dr Brian Cox, DH/SSI, 1994. Dr Cox's study

examines how social workers view the use of guardianship to meet the needs of clients with a mental illness and reviews previous research. The literature on guardianship is reviewed in chapter 2 of H. Richards and C. McGregor, *Guardianship in Scotland*, HMSO 1992. Paragraphs 2.19 to 2.22 of the Law Commission's *Mental Incapacity*, 1995, provide a brief historical perspective. Reasons for the sparing use that is made of guardianship are considered by M. J. Gunn in "Mental Health Act Guardianship: Where now" [1986] J.S.W.L. 144 and by Mike Fisher in "Guardianship under the Mental Health Legislation: A Review" [1988] J.S.W.L. 316. There is a marked variation in the use of guardianship by local authorities: see Jenny Shaw *et al.*, "Guardianship under the Mental Health Act 1983" (2000) 24, *Psychiatric Bulletin* 51–52.

This section specifies the circumstances whereby a patient aged 16 or over may be received into the guardianship of a local social services authority or a person who is acceptable to the authority. A patient shall cease to be subject to guardianship if an order for his discharge is made by his responsible medical officer, by the responsible local social services authority or by his nearest relative (s.23(2)(b)). A discharge by the nearest relative cannot be barred by anyone. A patient can attempt to seek his own discharge from guardianship by making an application to a Mental Health Review Tribunal within the first six months of reception into guardianship (s.66(1)(c), (2)(c)), and during each period of renewal (ss.66(f), 2(f), 20(2)). There is no automatic reference of guardianship cases to the Mental Health Review Tribunal. As the nearest relative has an unfettered right to order the patient's discharge from guardianship he is not given the power to apply to a tribunal.

There is no statutory obligation similar to that contained in section 132 for detained patients, to provide information to patients under guardianship and their nearest relatives. "However, it is clearly within the spirit of the Act that this should be done, and leaflets and draft covering letters for this purpose have ... been provided for the use of local social services authorities" (DHSS Circular No. HC (83)17, para. 8).

A patient who is subject to guardianship cannot receive direct payments under the terms of the Community Care (Direct Payments) Act 1996 (Community Care (Direct Payments) Regulations 1997 (S.I. 1997 No. 734), reg. 2).

If a patient who has been made the subject of an application under this section is remanded into custody or sentenced under the criminal law, the provisions of section 22 will apply.

Under section 19 and regulations 7 to 9 of the Mental Health (Hospital, Guardianship and Consent to Treatment) Regulations 1983 detained patients and patients who are subject to guardianship may be transferred between hospitals and guardians or between detention in hospital and guardianship: see the notes to section 19.

The Human Rights Act 1998 and the protection of mentally incapable adults

1–087 See the notes on section 8 under these headings.

The National Assistance Act 1948

1–088 It is possible for persons who are not necessarily mentally disordered to be compulsorily admitted to a hospital or a residential care facility under the provisions of section 47 of the National Assistance Act 1948. The use of this provision is, in practice, usually confined to cases where elderly people, usually living alone, are unable to care for themselves adequately. Under section 47 a district council or London borough council (in Wales, the councils of counties and county boroughs) may make an application to a magistrates' court to remove a person from his home on the grounds (i) that the person is suffering from grave chronic disease *or*, being aged, infirm or physically incapacitated, is living in insanitary conditions; *and* (ii) that the person is unable to devote to himself, and is not receiving from other persons, proper care and attention; *and* (iii) that his removal from home is necessary, either in his own interests or for preventing injury to the health of, or serious nuisance to, other persons. The local authority can only make an application under section 47 if the community physician has certified to the authority that he is satisfied after "thorough enquiry and consideration" that it is necessary to remove the person from the premises in which he is residing "in the interests" of the person or "for preventing injury to the health of, or serious nuisance to, other persons." The community physician is an employee of the health service and not the local authority. If, after hearing oral evidence, the court finds that the grounds are satisfied, and that it is "expedient" to do so, it may order that an officer of the applicant local authority remove the person to "a suitable hospital or other place". The "other place" is usually residential accommodation or a nursing home. The order, which provides authority for the person's "detention and maintenance" in the specified place, lasts for an initial period of up to three months, with the court having power to extend it for further periods of up to three months. Six weeks after the making of the order the person who was removed, or someone acting on his behalf, may apply to the court for the order to be revoked. If it is thought necessary to remove the person from his home without delay, section 1 of the National Assistance (Amendment) Act 1951 enables the court, or a single justice, to make an *ex parte* order under section 47. If granted, the order provides authority for the person to be detained for an initial period of three weeks. An application under section 1 may be made by either the community physician or the local authority. The 1948 Act does not provide authority for medical treatment to be given to the person concerned without his consent.

Subsection (1)

Patient: As a patient under guardianship is not "liable to be detained" for the **1–089** purposes of section 56(1), he is not subject to the consent to treatment provisions contained in Part IV of this Act.

It is an offence under this Act to neglect or ill-treat a patient who is under guardianship (s.127(2)).

Attained the age: At the commencement of his sixteenth birthday (Family Law Reform Act 1969, s.9(1)). Where on September 30, 1983, a person who was not then 16 years old was subject to guardianship, the authority for his guardianship terminated on that day (s.148(1), Sched. 5, para. 8(1)).

In *Re F (Mental Health Act. Guardianship)* [2000] 1 F.L.R. 192, the Court of Appeal held that wardship should not have been rejected by the judge as a more appropriate remedy than guardianship for a seventeen year old patient. An immediate consequence of wardship would have been the appointment of the Official Solicitor as her guardian *ad litem*, thereby securing the benefit of separate representation for the child. *Per* Thorpe L.J. at 199: "[Guardianship] is not a child-centred Jurisdiction and the child lacks the benefit of independent representation." An application for guardianship cannot be made in respect of a ward of court (s.33(3)).

Care proceedings under section 31 and Schedule 3, paragraph 5 of the Children Act 1989 could be brought in respect of a child under 16 who requires supervision and control in the community as a consequence of mental disorder.

A child is not a privately fostered child for the purposes of Part IX of the Children Act 1989 while he is subject to guardianship (*ibid*. Sched. 8, para. 4).

Period allowed: A patient may be kept under guardianship for an initial period of up to six months from the day on which the application was accepted (s.20(1)). The authority for guardianship may be renewed for a further period of six months, and then for yearly periods (s.20(2)).

An application: The application is addressed to the local social services authority and it must be received within 14 days of the second medical examination (s.8(2)). The application must be in the form set out in Form 17 (for a nearest relative applicant) or Form 18 (for an approved social worker applicant) of Schedule 1 to S.I.

1983 No. 893 (*ibid.* reg. 5(1)(a)). There is no time limit within which an application must be accepted.

Subsection (2)

1–090   *A guardianship application may be made:* There is no requirement for the patient to consent to the guardianship. The application may be made by either the patient's nearest relative or by an approved social worker (s.11(1)). The applicant must have personally seen the patient within 14 days of making the application (s.11(5)). An approved social worker cannot make an application if the nearest relative objects (s.11(4)) and he or she must comply with the provisions of section 13(1). The application must either be sent to the local social services authority named as guardian or to the social services authority for the area in which the individual named as guardian resides (s.11(2)).

The power of the nearest relative to veto a guardianship application made by an approved social worker can cause difficulty as "often social workers are concerned not that the patient may act irresponsibly, but that the relatives may act irresponsibly towards the patient. Where there is a caring relative, guardianship may not be needed. It is where there is a nearest relative who is neglectful, exploitive, or unable to care, that guardianship may well be required, but the relative has a power of veto which can only be overridden by the county court in the limited circumstances [set out in section 29]" (Phil Fennell, "The Beverley Lewis Case: was the law to blame" *New Law Journal*, November 17, 1989, pp. 1557–1558).

If an approved social worker considers that a nearest relative's likely objection to a guardianship application would place his client at risk, the following legal options could be considered. In cases of urgency, an application to a magistrate for a warrant under section 135 could be followed by an application under section 2 for the patient to be detained in hospital for up to 28 days. Alternatively, an application made under section 2 could be made direct from the community. In both cases it is assumed that the grounds for an section 2 application could be satisfied and that the patient was assessed as requiring a period of hospital treatment as an in-patient. A nearest relative does not have the right to veto applications under either section 135 or section 2. Immediately after the completion of the section 2 application, the approved social worker could make an application to the county court under section 29(3)(c) for the nearest relative to be displaced. An application under that provision has the effect of extending the life of the section 2 order until the application to the county court is disposed of (s.29(4)), although it should be noted that the nearest relative could use his power under section 23 to discharge the patient from the section 2 during this period. While this application is pending the responsible medical officer could consider granting the patient leave of absence under section 17 to a non-hospital setting. The patient could then be transferred into the guardianship of the local social services authority under section 19 and regulation 7(3) of the Mental Health (Hospital, Guardianship and Consent to Treatment) Regulations 1983. If the application to the county court was successful the nearest relative would lose his power to discharge the patient from the guardianship.

Is suffering: The patient must be suffering from one of the specific forms of mental disorder at the time when the medical recommendation is signed. A person who has lost mental capacity as a result of a physical disorder (*e.g.*, a stroke) but is not mentally disordered could not be the subject of an application under this section.

Mental disorder: There is no requirement that the specific form of mental disorder be amenable to treatment.

Severe mental impairment . . . mental impairment: It is therefore not possible for a person with a learning disability whose impairment is not associated with abnormally aggressive or seriously irresponsible conduct to be placed under guardianship; see the note on "abnormally aggressive and seriously irresponsible conduct" in section 1.

The restrictive construction given to the term "seriously irresponsible conduct" by the Court of Appeal in *Re F (Mental Health Act: Guardianship)* [2000] 1 F.L.R. 192, which is noted under section 1, will lead to a diminution of the use of guardianship for persons with a learning disability, because prior to this decision this term had been broadly interpreted to protect patients who are vulnerable and subject to abuse and neglect: see H. Whitworth and S. Singhai (1995) "The use of guardianship in mental handicap services", 19 *Psychiatric Bulletin* 725–727.

Nature or degree: The meaning of this phrase is considered in the note on section 3(2)(a).

Interests of the welfare of the patient: All factors which might affect the well-being of the patient are covered by this phrase, including his need to be protected from exploitation. The wording is wide enough to encompass the need to prevent the person's welfare being prejudiced at some time in the future. In these circumstances the recommending doctors would need to be satisfied that there is a real risk of such an eventuality occurring, *e.g.* an attempt by a relative to remove a mentally incompetent resident from a care setting to accommodation where the patient's welfare might be seriously prejudiced. Consideration should be given to making an application to the Court of Protection in respect of patients who are incapable, by reason of mental disorder, of managing their financial affair.

Protection of other persons: It is submitted that "protection" is not limited to protection from physical harm, but could include protection from serious emotional harm. Support for this interpretation can be found in paragraph 2.9 of the *Code of Practice*.

Subsection (3)

Written recommendations: Made either separately or jointly (s.11(7)) using either **1–091** Form 17 or Form 18 of Schedule 1 to the Mental Health (Hospital, Guardianship and Consent to Treatment) Regulations 1983 (*ibid.* reg. 5(1)(c)).

Two registered medical practitioners: Complying with the provisions of section 12.

Subsection (5)

This subsection provides for the guardian to be either a local social services **1–092** authority or a person who is accepted by the authority to act in that capacity. Neither the authority nor the individual is placed under any legal obligation to accept the duties of guardian.

Guardian: The powers of guardians are set out in section 8(1). For the duty of the local social services authority to arrange for the patient to be visited, see regulation 13 of the 1983 Regulations. If the patient is hospitalised, the local authority has duties placed upon it by section 116.

Local social services authority: This does not have to be the authority for the area where the patient lives. If the application is accepted, the authority will become "the responsible local social services authority" (s.34(3)). Although Directors of Social Services may decline any guardianship proposal, they are required to take over the role of guardian where a private guardianship arrangement has broken down in the circumstances set out in section 10.

Or any other person: "The local social services authority should consider the suitability of any proposed guardian before accepting the application. Any guardian should be a person who can appreciate the special disabilities and needs of a mentally disordered person and who will look after the patient in an appropriate and sympathetic way. The guardian should display an interest in promoting the patient's physical and mental health and in providing for his occupation, training, employment, recreation and general welfare in a suitable way. The local social services authority must satisfy itself that the proposed guardian is capable of carrying out his functions and should assist the guardian with advice and other facilities. Regulation 12 [of the Mental Health (Hospital, Guardianship and Consent to Treatment) Regulations 1983] provides that they can call for reports and information from the guardian, as they may require; the guardian also has a duty to inform them of his address, the address of the patient and of the nominated medical attendant, and if the patient should die" (*Memorandum*, para. 42). The local social services authority is the guardian in the overwhelming majority of cases (*Mentally Incapacitated and*

Other Vulnerable Adults: Public Law Protection, The Law Commission Consultation
Paper No. 130 (1993), para. 4.7).

If an approved social worker considers that a private guardian has performed his
functions negligently or in a manner contrary to the interests of the welfare of the
patient, he can apply to the county court under section 10(3) for the guardianship to
be transferred to another person or to the local social services authority.

Accepted: The acceptance should be recorded on Form 21 and the receipt of the
medical recommendations recorded on Form 15: see regulation 5(3)(4) of the Mental
Health (Hospital, Guardianship and Consent to Treatment) Regulations 1983.

The area: i.e. the area where the person named as guardian resides.

Resides: Temporary absences from the place where a person lives does not affect
residence, as long as there is an intention to return (*R. v. St Leonard's Shoreditch
(Inhabitants)* (1865) L.R. 1 Q.B. 21). Also note Widgery L.J.'s statement in *Fox v.
Stirk* [1970] 2 Q.B. 463 at 477: "A man cannot be said to reside in a particular place
unless in the ordinary sense of the word one can say that for the time being he is
making his home in that place."

Willing to act as guardian: The statement that the person is willing to act as
guardian must be in the form set out in either Form 17 or 18 of Schedule 1 to the
Mental Health (Hospital, Guardianship and Consent to Treatment) Regulations
1983 (*ibid.* reg. 5(1)(b)). The duties of private guardians are set out in *ibid.* regulation
12.

Effect of guardianship application, etc.

1–093   **8.**—(1) Where a guardianship application, duly made under the provisions
of this Part of this Act and forwarded to the local social services authority
within the period allowed by subsection (2) below is accepted by that
authority, the application shall, subject to regulations made by the Secretary
of State, confer on the authority or person named in the application as
guardian, to the exclusion of any other person—

    (a) the power to require the patient to reside at a place specified by the
authority or person named as guardian;

    (b) the power to require the patient to attend at places and times so
specified for the purpose of medical treatment, occupation, education
or training;

    (c) the power to require access to the patient to be given, at any place
where the patient is residing, to any registered medical practitioner,
approved social worker or other person so specified.

(2) The period within which a guardianship application is required for the
purposes of this section to be forwarded to the local social services authority
is the period of 14 days beginning with the date on which the patient was last
examined by a registered medical practitioner before giving a medical
recommendation for the purposes of the application.

(3) A guardianship application which appears to be duly made and to be
founded on the necessary medical recommendations may be acted upon
without further proof of the signature or qualification of the person by whom
the application or any such medical recommendation is made or given, or of
any matter of fact or opinion stated in the application.

(4) If within the period of 14 days beginning with the day on which a
guardianship application has been accepted by the local social services
authority the application, or any medical recommendation given for the
purposes of the application, is found to be in any respect incorrect or

defective, the application or recommendation may, within that period and with the consent of that authority, be amended by the person by whom it was signed; and upon such amendment being made the application or recommendation shall have effect and shall be deemed to have had effect as if it had been originally made as so amended.

(5) Where a patient is received into guardianship in pursuance of a guardianship application, any previous application under this Part of this Act by virtue of which he was subject to guardianship or liable to be detained in a hospital shall cease to have effect.

DEFINITIONS

local social services authority: s.145(1).   **1–094**
medical treatment: s.145(1).
patient: s.145(1).
approved social worker: s.145(1).
hospital: ss.34(2), 145(1).

GENERAL NOTE

This section confers specific powers on the patient's guardian. The 1959 Act gave   **1–095** the guardian the power that a father has over a child of 14. These powers were therefore very wide, as well as being somewhat ill-defined, and it was felt that they were out of keeping, in their paternalistic approach, with modern attitudes to the care of the mentally disordered. Subsection (1) replaces these general powers with specific powers limited to restricting the liberty of the person under guardianship only to the extent necessary to ensure that various forms of treatment, social support, training, education or occupation are undertaken. These powers are considered in paragraph 13.8 of the *Code of Practice.* Apart from the power to return an absconding patient to the place where he is required to reside, there "are no other specific sanctions if a patient does not act as required by his guardian, but in appropriate cases the extra authority of guardianship has been found sufficient for a social worker or relative to persuade a patient to modify his behaviour" (Mental Health (Amendment) Bill: Notes on Clauses, House of Commons, DHSS, March 1992, p. 46). The patient's guardian, who is subject to the duties laid down in Part III of the Mental Health (Hospital Guardianship and Consent to Treatment) Regulations 1983, does not have any power to use or dispose of the patient's property or to carry out any financial transactions on the patient's behalf.

It is an offence for anyone to ill-treat or wilfully to neglect a patient subject to his guardianship or otherwise in his custody or care (s.127(2)).

The protection of mentally disordered adults

In *Re F (Adult: Court's Jurisdiction)* [2000] 2 F.L.R. 512, CA, the local authority   **1–096** were unable to use guardianship to protect the welfare of T, aged 18, because the Court of Appeal had found that her behaviour did not constitute "seriously irresponsible conduct" as required in the definition of "mental impairment": see *Re F (Mental Health Act: Guardianship)* [2000] 1 F.L.R. 192, noted under "abnormally aggressive or seriously irresponsible conduct" in section 1(2). The authority was concerned that T, who was being accommodated in one of the authority's establishments contrary to her mother's wishes, would be at risk of neglect and exposure to sexual exploitation if she were to return to her home. In order to protect T from this risk the authority sought declarations, the effect of which were to keep her in specialist accommodation and to restrict and supervise her contact with her natural family. In determining the question of the jurisdiction of the High Court to make such declarations, the Court held that:

(i) the application of the common law doctrine of necessity (see *F. v. West Berkshire Health Authority (Mental Health Act Commission intervening)*

[1989] 2 All E.R. 545, HL, noted in General Note to Part IV under "The treatment of incapable patients") is not limited to medical and similar emergencies; it embraces the problems that arose in this case;

(ii) the doctrine, which can be invoked by both an authority and an individual, may properly be invoked side by side with this Act (see *R. v. Bournewood Community and Mental Health NHS Trust, ex p. L* [1998] 3 All E.R. 289, HL, noted in the General Note to s.131) ;

(iii) the jurisdiction of the High Court under its inherent jurisdiction to grant relief by way of declarations is not therefore excluded by this Act; and

(iv) in making a declaration the judge will be guided by the patient's best interests on an application of a welfare test analogous to that applied in wardship. *Per* Sedley L.J. at 529: "[N]either the mother nor the (imaginary) sister nor the local authority possesses by virtue of their status any power to detain T. Nor, however, does T have the capacity to chose one of them as an appropriate carer. If the role of carer is contested, it is the court alone which has the power—and in my judgment the duty—to make that choice in T's best interests. From the choice will follow the exercise of care; and from the exercise of care, if absolutely necessary, some restraint may follow."

A declaration that had the effect of detaining the patient would risk violating Article 5 of the European Convention on Human Rights; see the notes on Article 5 and on "The Human Rights Act 1998", below.

Whether the power to make a declaration is in accord with Article 8 of the Convention was considered in the following passage of the judgment of Sedley L.J. at 531,532: "The family life for which Article 8 requires respect is not a propriety right vested in either parent or child: it is as much an interest of society as of individual family members, and its principle purpose, at least where there are children, must be the safety and welfare of the child. It needs to be remembered that the tabulated right is not to family life as much as respect for it. The purpose, in my view, is to ensure within proper limits the entitlement of individuals to the benefit of what is benign and positive in family life. It is not to allow other individuals, however closely related and well-intentioned, to create or perpetuate situations which jeopardise their welfare. As the European Court of Human Rights said in *Marckx v. Belgium* (1979) 2 E.H.R.R. 330, Article 8(1) 'does not merely compel the state to abstain from ... interference; in addition to this primarily negative undertaking, there may be positive obligations inherent in an effective "respect" for family life'. In the present state of the law as it affects T, it is upon the court and the local authority that any such positive obligation comes to rest. One of the advantages of a declaratory remedy, and in particular of an interim declaration, is that the court itself can do much to close the so-called *Bournewood* gap in the protection of those without capacity." See further D. Hewitt, "Widening the 'Bournewood Gap'?", (2000) 4 Journal of Mental Health Law, 196–204.

The wardship jurisdiction of the High Court should be invoked if the individual that needs protecting is a child and intervention under the Children Act 1989 is either not possible or inappropriate (*Re F (Mental Health Act: Guardianship)*, above).

The Human Rights Act 1998

1–097   Guardianship proceedings must comply with the standards of Article 6(1) of the European Convention on Human Rights because such proceedings involve the determination of a civil right (see the note on Art. 6). The fact that the initial determination of the guardianship application is made by an administrative body (the local authority) does not contravene Article 6(1) provided that there is a right of appeal to a court (the Mental Health Review Tribunal) which provides the guarantees of that Article (see for example, *Le Compte, Van Leuven and De Meyer v.*

Belgium (1981) 4 E.H.R.R. 1, para. 51). The state must ensure that the appeal is heard within a reasonable time (*Buchholz v. Germany* (1981) 3 E.H.R.R. 597, para. 50). A patient who has been placed under guardianship will be afforded the protections of Article 5 of the Convention if he is being detained in the place where he is being cared for. The European Court of Human Rights has held that for a patient to be detained for the purposes of Article 5, there is no need to show that the patient was subject to a direct physical restraint to prevent him from leaving that place. When determining this issue the court will have regard to the patient's actual situation, taking into account such factors as the type, duration, effects and manner of the restrictions placed upon him: see *Ashingdane v. United Kingdom* (1985) 7 E.H.R.R. 528, noted under Article 5(1)(e) under the heading "detention". The court is likely to find that a patient under guardianship is being detained if: (i) he is required to reside in a particular establishment under subsection (1)(a); (ii) he would not be allowed to leave that establishment on the ground that such a move would prejudice his health or welfare; and (iii) he is either exhibiting signs of non-compliance at being there, has absconded and been brought back to the establishment under the terms of section 18(4), or if his freedom of association with his family is being restricted as a means of denying him the opportunity to leave the premises.

This Act violates Article 5 in so far as it applies to a "detained" guardianship patient in that:

1. Article 5(2) is not complied with as there is no provision that requires the patient to be informed of the reasons for his detention (see the note on section 132); and
2. The lack of an automatic reference to a tribunal, equivalent to that contained in section 68 for patients detained under section 3, contravenes Article 5(4).

In *Aerts v. Belgium* (2000) 29 E.H.R.R. 50, the Court held that, in principle, the detention of a mentally disordered person will only be lawful for the purposes of Article 5 if effected in "a hospital, clinic or other appropriate institution" (para.46).

The patient's private or local authority guardian is exercising functions of a public nature in respect of the patient and is therefore a "public authority" for the purposes of section 6 of the 1998 Act.

A local authority acting as the patient's guardian could use its implied power to act for the welfare of the patient to restrict or deny access to the patient (*R. v. Kent County Council, ex p. Marston*, noted under s.1(1)(a)). Such action would constitute an interference with the patient's private life under Article 8(1) and would need to be justified under Article 8(2).

Admission to hospital of patients under guardianship
If a patient under guardianship is admitted for psychiatric treatment as an informal **1–098** patient, he will remain subject to guardianship unless he is discharged from it (s.23) or transferred to hospital under the procedure set out in regulation 8(3) of the Mental Health (Hospital, Guardianship and Consent to Treatment) Regulations 1983. The guardianship will also remain in force if the patient is admitted for assessment under section 2 or 4, but it will cease to have effect if the patient is admitted for treatment under section 3 (s.6(4)) or is transferred to hospital under regulation 8(3). If the patient is admitted informally he could be made subject to the holding powers provided for in section 5(2) and (4).

Subsection (1)
Secretary of State: The functions of the Minister, so far as exercisable in relation to **1–099** Wales, are exercised by the National Assembly for Wales (S.I. 1999 No. 672, art. 2, Sched. 1).

Accepted by that authority: The power to accept guardianship could be delegated by the social services committee to a sub-committee or to an officer under section 101 of the Local Government Act 1972.

Paragraph (a)

1–100   The guardian may exercise powers over the patient in addition to the specific powers contained in this provision. In *R. v. Kent C.C., ex p. Marston*, July 9, 1997, Owen J. said that he could "find no difficulty in accepting that section 7 of necessity implies a statutory duty to act for the welfare of the patient". His Lordship further stated that "the extent and consequences of that duty are not so clear. An example, of no relevance here, would be seen if a patient were to be given a sexually provocative magazine. I would have no difficulty in accepting that the guardian would a duty to monitor the effects and if necessary to remove the magazine." This finding was endorsed by Simon Brown L.J. who said, in refusing leave to appeal on September 5, 1997, that it is implicit in section 7 "that the guardian is entitled in certain respects to act so as to promote the welfare of the patient. Owen J. recognised, as I would too, that the precise extent and consequence of such an implicit duty to act for the welfare of the patient is not clear. I envisage that that may well need clarification at some future date. For example, if there were good reason to suppose that an authority was acting in some totalitarian fashion or was not properly having regard to the interests of its patients, then it seems to me clear that someone would have the standing, would have a sufficient interest to bring the case before the court so that the matter could be properly investigated and the true extent of the authority's discretion be clarified". In *Marston*, Owen J. upheld the decision of the local authority, acting as the patient's guardian, to refuse to disclose to the patient's former foster brother where the patient was living. The foster brother was ultimately intent on taking over the care of the patient and the local authority had received medical advice that this would be contrary to the patient's interests. The patient, who was mentally incapable, had expressed no interest in seeing his former foster brother. His Lordship also said that as the patient needed protection, the guardian had a right to see letters addressed to him and that whether "the guardian would be entitled to censor them would depend what was in them". However, as the patient was unable to read, the right to see the letters would not have to be exercised. The decision in *Marston* suggests that a guardian has an implied power to make decisions concerning the daily living arrangements of clients who are mentally incapable. Such decisions should be "necessary in the interests of the welfare" of the client (cf. s.7(2)(b)).

The power: With the exception of the power to retake a patient, noted below, the powers given to the guardian under this provision are not capable of direct enforcement, but rely on the co-operation of the patient.

Require: This power cannot be used to override the refusal of the owner of premises to provide accommodation for the patient.

1–101   *Reside:* The *Memorandum* envisages that this power would "be used to discourage the patient from sleeping rough or living with people who may exploit or mistreat him, or to ensure that he resides in a particular hostel or other facility" (para. 40). There is no power to require that the patient resides with a particular person.

There no prohibition on charging a person who is subject to guardianship for the accommodation in which he is required to reside, as long as the accommodation is not being provided as an after-care service under section 117 of this Act. Section 21(8) of the National Assistance Act 1948 states:

"Nothing in this section shall authorise or require a local authority to make any provision authorised or required to be made (whether by that or by any other authority) by or under any enactment not contained in this Part of this Act or authorised or required to be made under the National Health Service Act 1977."

It has been argued that section 21(8) has the effect of prohibiting a local authority from charging for accommodation in guardianship cases. This argument is erroneous as, unlike section 117, neither this section nor section 7 "authorise or require" the provision of accommodation. Requiring a patient to reside in accommodation is not the same as requiring the accommodation to be provided.

If the patient leaves the place where he is required to reside without his guardian's consent, he can be taken into custody and returned to that place within the period specified in section 18(4). An application could be made to a magistrate under section 135(2) if it is not possible to obtain access to where the patient is staying. Anyone obstructing a person authorised by section 18(3) to return the patient would be guilty of an offence under section 129. It is an offence under section 128 to induce or knowingly to assist a person under guardianship to absent himself without leave of the guardian.

The person in control of the premises where the patient is required to reside has the power "under general law ... to control who is allowed to be there and in what circumstances"; *per* Hale J. in *Cambridgeshire C.C. v. R (an Adult)* [1995] 1 F.L.R. 50 at 55. In *Re D-R (Adult: Contact)* [1999] 1 F.L.R. 1161, where the Court of Appeal, in refusing an application of the father of a mentally incompetent child for a declaration that the child's mother was acting unlawfully in refusing him direct contact with his daughter, held that there is no presumption of the right to contact between a parent and an adult child, even one under a disability. Any restriction on access between a relative and the patient would need to be justified under Article 8(2) of the European Convention on Human Rights.

This Act does not contain a specific power that enables a patient to be taken and conveyed under guardianship to a specified place from which he has not absconded. Guardianship should therefore not be used to take a non-compliant mentally capable person from his home into residential care. It is submitted that a similar power to that expressly provided in section 6(1) for the taking and conveying of detained patients cannot be implied in relation to mentally capable patients under guardianship. In the words of McCullough J.: "there is a canon of construction that Parliament is presumed not to enact legislation which interferes with the liberty of the subject without making it clear that this was its intention" (see the note on Judicial Interpretation in the General Note to this Act and para. 19.5 of the *Second Biennial Report* of the Mental Health Act Commission).

If a mentally *incapable* person is living at home in circumstances where: (1) that person's behaviour poses a significant risk either to himself or to others; (2) all reasonable steps have been taken to reduce the risk to an acceptable level; (3) there has been a failure to reduce the risk to such a level; (4) the person concerned is unwilling to be moved from his home; and (5) the person's identified needs do not require an admission to hospital for medical treatment, it is submitted that a combination of the common law doctrine of necessity (*F v. West Berkshire Health Authority (Mental Health Act Commission Intervening)* [1989] 2 All E.R. 545) and the guardian's implied duty to act for the welfare of the patient (*R. v. Kent C.C., ex p. Marston*, above), enables guardianship to be used to convey that person to a suitable place of safety (*e.g.* a residential care home) if such a move was deemed to be in the patient's best interests. However, given the uncertain nature of the law, it would be advisable for a local authority to seek a declaration from the High Court in these circumstances: see the General Note to this section under the heading "The protection of mentally disordered adults".

The guardian owes a duty of care to the patient and must take reasonable steps to ensure that the patient avoids injury or does not cause injury to others by, for example, wandering from the premises onto the road. Although guardianship does not provide for the detention of the patient, Lord Woolf has stated that "it must be at least arguable" that the common law doctrine of necessity entitles whoever has the care of a mentally incapable patient in a community placement to take steps which amount in law, to his detention (*R. v. Bournewood Community and Mental Health Trust, ex p. L* [1998] 1 All E.R. 634 at 646, CA). This point was not considered when the case reached the House of Lords where it was held, *inter alia*, that a patient is "detained" if there is *in fact* a complete deprivation of, or restraint upon his liberty ([1998] 3 All E.R. 289). It is submitted that if a mentally incapable patient is being detained in a community setting and that patient is exhibiting signs of non-compliance:

(i) a guardianship application should be made in respect of the patient as this would: (a) provide a degree of protection for the patient through the formal reviewing of his situation; (b) provide explicit authority for the patient to be returned to the designated place of residence if he absented himself from that place without authority; and (c) would be evidence of the good faith of those who have responsibility for the patient's welfare;

(ii) staff caring for the patient would have authority under the common law doctrine of necessity to restrain the patient from leaving the designated place of residence if such action is required for his own protection; and

(iii) in cases where (a) there is a conflict between the local authority and the patient's carer as to where the patient should reside; (b) where the patient has to be restrained from leaving the home on a frequent basis; or (c) the patient cannot be the subject of a guardianship application because of the ruling in *Re F (Mental Health Act: Guardianship)* (noted under "abnormally aggressive or seriously irresponsible conduct" in s.1(2)), the authority should apply to the High Court for a declaration as to the lawfulness of the detention: see *Re F (Adult: Court's Jurisdiction)* which is considered in the General Note to this section.

At a place: Although McCullough J. made the *obiter* comment in *R. v. Hallstrom, ex p. W.L.; R. v. Gardner, ex p. L* [1986] 2 All E.R. 306, 312 that "there is nothing in [the Mental Health Act 1983] which appears to prevent a guardian from requiring his patient to reside in a hospital", this practice is contrary to the intention of the Act if the patient is likely to require long term hospital care. This is the approach adopted by the *Code of Practice* at paragraph 13.10(a). The White Paper that preceded the 1982 Act suggests that guardianship was envisaged as an alternative to treating a person in hospital rather than as a procedure that could be used to ensure that a person received in-patient care (Cmnd. 8405 para. 43). A patient under guardianship could be required to reside in an appropriately registered residential care home or mental nursing home.

There is nothing to prevent a patient who is subject to guardianship from being admitted to hospital for treatment for either a physical or a psychiatric disorder. In the event of such an admission taking place a local authority acting as the guardian of a patient is required to comply with section 116 of this Act. See the note on "Admission to hospital of patients under guardianship", above, for the legal consequences of a patient being admitted to hospital for psychiatric treatment under compulsory powers.

The responsible social services authority must arrange for the patient to be visited at not more than three monthly intervals (Mental Health (Hospital, Guardianship and Consent to Treatment) Regulations 1983, reg. 13).

Paragraph (b)

1–102   *Attend at places:* "These might include a local authority day centre, or a hospital, surgery or clinic" (*Memorandum*, para. 40).

For the purposes of medical treatment: Neither the guardian, nor the patient's nearest relative, can consent to treatment on the patient's behalf. In *T v. T* [1988] 1 All E.R. 613, 617 Wood J. said: "The wording of section 8 will be seen to be much more restricted than the wider powers of the guardian under section 34 of the [Mental Health Act 1959]. One important effect is to remove the guardian's implicit power to consent to treatment on behalf of the patient. In my judgment there is no power to consent to [abortion] to be found in section 8 ..., and indeed, on a construction of the statute as a whole I am satisfied that medical treatment means psychiatric treatment."

A patient under guardianship is subject to common law rules relating to the provision of medical treatment and is not subject to the Consent to Treatment provisions contained in Part IV of this Act: see section 56(1) and the General Note to Part IV. If a patient's psychiatric condition is deteriorating because he refuses to accept treatment, consideration should be given to admitting him to hospital under section 2 (with the guardianship order remaining in force) or to transferring him to hospital under regulation 8(3) of the Mental Health (Hospital, Guardianship and Consent to Treatment) Regulations 1983 (with the guardianship order ceasing to have effect).

Although guardianship does not provide authority for a mentally capable patient to be treated in the absence of his consent, the existence of guardianship can have the effect of persuading the patient to co-operate with his treatment. For an example of this, see L. Blom-Cooper *et al.*, *The Falling Shadow*, 1995, p. 90.

The responsible social services authority must arrange for a medical practitioner approved under section 12 of this Act to visit the patient at least once a year: see regulation 13 of the 1983 Regulations.

Require the patient to attend: If the patient refuses to attend, guardianship does not provide authority for force to be used to secure attendance.

Paragraph (c)
Require access to the patient: This provision, which could be used to ensure that the **1–103** patient did not neglect himself, does not include a power to force entry if this is denied. If entry is denied consideration should be given to utilising the procedure set out in section 135 of this Act. A refusal to permit an authorised person to have access to the patient is an offence under section 129.

Subsection (2)
Beginning with: Including the date on which the patient was last examined by a **1–104** medical practitioner (*Hare v. Gocher* [1962] 2 Q.B. 641).

Subsection (3)
Appears to be duly made: An incorrect or defective application can be amended **1–105** under subsection (4).

Subsection (4)
Accepted by the local social services authority: The authority may authorise an **1–106** officer or class of officers to consent under this provision to any amendment of a guardianship application which it has accepted or any medical recommendation given for the purposes of that application (Mental Health (Hospital, Guardianship and Consent to Treatment) Regulations 1983, reg. 5(2)).

Incorrect or defective: See the notes to section 15(1).

Amended: This provision provides a means of righting accidental mistakes that were made when the statutory documentation was completed: it is not a device for overcoming a fundamental defect in the application (see the General Note to s.15).

The amended application must comply with all the requirements for making an application. Minor mistakes which are not rectified within the 14-day period would not invalidate the application. An application which contains an unrectifiable error (*e.g.* a relative who was not the patient's nearest relative was consulted under section 11(4)) should be discharged under section 23 as soon as the error is discovered.

By whom it was signed: i.e. the applicant or the recommending doctor. An unsigned application or medical recommendation cannot be remedied under this provision.

Regulations as to guardianship

1–107   **9.**—(1) Subject to the provisions of this Part of this Act, the Secretary of State may make regulations—

(a) for regulating the exercise by the guardians of patients received into guardianship under this Part of the Act of their powers as such; and

(b) for imposing on such guardians, and upon local social services authorities in the case of patients under the guardianship of persons other than local social services authorities, such duties as he considers necessary or expedient in the interest of the patients.

(2) Regulations under this section may in particular make provision for requiring the patients to be visited, on such occasions or at such intervals as may be prescribed by the regulations, on behalf of such local social services authorities as may be so prescribed, and shall provide for the appointment, in the case of every patient subject to the guardianship of a person other than a local social services authority, of a registered medical practitioner to act as the nominated medical attendant of the patient.

DEFINITIONS

1–108   patients: s.145(1).
local social services authority: s.145(1).

GENERAL NOTE

1–109   This section, which gives power to the Secretary of State (or, in relation to Wales, the National Assembly for Wales (S.I. 1999 No. 672, art. 2, Sched. 1) to make regulations for regulating guardianship, applies to patients who have been under guardianship by a guardianship order made by a court under section 37 (Sched. 1, Pt I, para. 1).

The Mental Health (Hospital, Guardianship and Consent to Treatment) Regulations 1983 (S.I. 1983 No. 893) came into operation on September 30, 1983.

Subsection (1)

1–110   *Powers:* These are set out in section 8.

Subsection (2)

1–111   *Visited:* A person who refuses to allow an authorised person to visit a patient commits an offence under section 129.
Nominated medical attendant: Is defined in section 34(1).

Transfer of guardianship in case of death, incapacity, etc., of guardian

1–112   **10.**—(1) If any person (other than a local social services authority) who is the guardian of a patient received into guardianship under this Part of this Act—

(a) dies; or

(b) gives notice in writing to the local social services authority that he desires to relinquish the functions of guardian,

the guardianship of the patient shall thereupon vest in the local social services authority, but without prejudice to any power to transfer the patient into the guardianship of another person in pursuance of regulations under section 19 below.

(2) If any such person, not having given notice under subsection (1)(b) above, is incapacitated by illness or any other cause from performing the functions of guardian of the patient, those functions may, during his incapacity, be performed on his behalf by the local social services authority or by any other person approved for the purposes by that authority.

(3) If it appears to the county court, upon application made by an approved social worker, that any person other than a local social services authority having the guardianship of a patient received into guardianship under this Part of this Act has performed his functions negligently or in a manner contrary to the interests of the welfare of the patient, the court may order that the guardianship of the patient be transferred to the local social services authority or to any other person approved for the purpose by that authority.

(4) Where the guardianship of a patient is transferred to a local social services authority or other person by or under this section, subsection (2)(c) of section 19 below shall apply as if the patient had been transferred into the guardianship of that authority or person in pursuance of regulations under that section.

DEFINITIONS
    local social services authority: s.145(1).   **1–113**
    patient: s.145(1).
    approved social worker: s.145(1).

GENERAL NOTE
    This section provides for the transfer of guardianship in circumstances where the **1–114** guardian of a patient dies, becomes incapacitated, wishes to relinquish his functions, or is found to be performing his functions negligently. It applies to patients who have been placed on guardianship orders made by a court under section 37 (Sched. 1, Pt I, para. 1).

    It is also possible for a patient to be transferred from one guardian to another under the provisions of section 19.

Documents
    When a patient is transferred under this section "the documents authorising **1–115** guardianship or detention, including the authority for transfer, should be sent to the hospital or guardian to which the patient is transferred. The former hospital or guardian should retain copies of these documents" (*Memorandum*, para. 93).

Subsection (1)
    This subsection provides for the automatic transfer of guardianship from a private **1–116** guardian to a local social services authority. Guardianship could subsequently be transferred to another local social services authority or to a person under regulation 8 of the Mental Health (Hospital, Guardianship and Consent to Treatment) Regulations 1983.
    Notice in writing to the local social services authority: The notice should be sent to the authority for the area in which the guardian resides and not to the authority for the area in which the patient resides, if different.

Shall thereupon: The authority cannot resist a notice of relinquishment.

Subsection (2)

1–117   This subsection allows the local social services authority, or a person authorised by the authority, to act temporarily on behalf of a guardian who is ill or is otherwise incapacitated.

May, during his incapacity, be performed: The local social services authority is not placed under a duty to take over the functions of an incapacitated guardian.

On his behalf: "The authority or person acting as guardian ... acts as an agent for the real guardian and may not go against any wishes or instructions he may express" (*Memorandum*, para. 87).

The local social services authority: See the note on subsection (1) and paragraph 87 of the *Memorandum* which refers to the guardian's functions being performed on his behalf by the "responsible social services authority," *i.e.* the local authority for the area where the guardian lives (s.34(3)(b)).

Subsection (3)

1–118   This subsection empowers an approved social worker to apply to the county court for an order transferring the guardianship of the patient to a local social services authority or to a person approved by that authority.

County court: The procedure on an application to the county court is set out in the Civil Procedure Rules 1998 (S.I. 1998 No. 3132), Sched. 2, CCR Ord. 49, r. 12.

General provisions as to applications and recommendations

General provisions as to applications

1–119   **11.**—(1) Subject to the provisions of this section, an application for admission for assessment, an application for admission for treatment and a guardianship application may be made either by the nearest relative of the patient or by an approved social worker; and every such application shall specify the qualification of the applicant to make the application.

(2) Every application for admission shall be addressed to the managers of the hospital to which admission is sought and every guardianship application shall be forwarded to the local social services authority named in the application as guardian, or, as the case may be, to the local social services authority for the area in which the person so named resides.

(3) Before or within a reasonable time after an application for the admission of a patient for assessment is made by an approved social worker, that social worker shall take such steps as are practicable to inform the person (if any) appearing to be the nearest relative of the patient that the application is to be or has been made and of the power of the nearest relative under section 23(2)(a) below.

(4) Neither an application for admission for treatment nor a guardianship application shall be made by an approved social worker if the nearest relative of the patient has notified that social worker, or the local services authority by whom that social worker is appointed, that he objects to the application being made and, without prejudice to the foregoing provision, no such application shall be made by such a social worker except after consultation with the person (if any) appearing to be the nearest relative of the patient unless it appears to that social worker that in the circumstances such consultation is not reasonably practicable or would involve unreasonable delay.

(5) None of the applications mentioned in subsection (1) above shall be

made by any person in respect of a patient unless that person has personally seen the patient within the period of 14 days ending with the date of the application.

(6) An application for admission for treatment or a guardianship application, and any recommendation given for the purposes of such an application, may describe the patient as suffering from more than one of the following forms of mental disorder, namely mental illness, severe mental impairment, psychopathic disorder or mental impairment; but the application shall be of no effect unless the patient is described in each of the recommendations as suffering from the same form of mental disorder, whether or not he is also described in either of those recommendations as suffering from another form.

(7) Each of the applications mentioned in subsection (1) above shall be sufficient if the recommendations on which it is founded are given either as separate recommendations, each signed by a registered medical practitioner, or as a joint recommendation signed by two such practitioners.

DEFINITIONS

application for admission for assessment: s.145(1).   **1–120**
application for admission for treatment: s.145(1).
nearest relative: ss.26(3), 145(1).
approved social workers: s.145(1).
the managers: s.145(1).
hospital: ss.34(2), 145(1).
local social services authority: s.145(1).
patient: s.145(1).
mental disorder: ss.1, 145(1).
severe mental impairment: ss.1, 145(1).
psychopathic disorder: ss.1, 145(1).
mental impairment: ss.1, 145(1).

GENERAL NOTE

This section contains general provisions relating to applications for admission for **1–121** assessment, applications for admission for treatment, and guardianship applications.

Although primary responsibility for checking that the statutory forms have been completed correctly rests with the applicant, hospital managers and local social services authorities should each designate an officer to scrutinise the documents as soon as they have been completed and to take any necessary action if they have been improperly completed: see regulation 4(2) and 5(2) of the Mental Health (Hospital, Guardianship and Consent to Treatment) Regulations 1983.

The Human Rights Act 1998

The approach taken to the interpretation of the phrase "not reasonably **1–122** practicable" in subsection (4) is consistent with Article 8(2) of the European Convention on Human Rights and the judgment of the European of Human Rights in *JT v. United Kingdom,* March 30, 2000.

Subsection (1)

Application: An application in respect of a ward of court cannot be made without **1–123** the leave of the High Court (s.33(1)). The procedure for making an application and recording an admission is set out in regulation 4 of the Mental Health (Hospital, Guardianship and Consent to Treatment) Regulations 1983.

May be made either by: The approved social worker is "usually the right applicant" (*Code of Practice,* para. 2.35). Neither the approved social worker nor the nearest relative can prevent the other from making an application. An application which is signed by a person who is neither an approved social worker nor the patient's nearest relative is invalid and incapable of being rectified under section 15.

Nearest relative: Or an acting nearest relative appointed by the court under section 29. It is possible for a nearest relative to authorise some other person to act for him under regulation 14 of the 1983 Regulations.

Approved social worker: Section 13 places a duty on an approved social worker to make an application if certain criteria are satisfied. The great majority of applications for compulsory admission are made by approved social workers.

Subsection (2)

1–124   *Application:* If it has not been possible to identify the name of the patient by the time the application is made, it is suggested that the phrase "the patient known by the name of John [or Mary] Smith" be entered in the patient name space on the appropriate application form. A note of the real name of the patient should be attached to the application as soon as it is discovered.

The managers: Who are the detaining authority (*R. v. South Western Hospital Managers, ex p. M* [1994] 1 All E.R. 161). The application shall be served by delivering it to an officer of the managers of the hospital to which it is proposed that the patient shall be admitted (Mental Health (Hospital, Guardianship and Consent to Treatment) Regulations 1983, reg. 3(2)). Hospital managers are not obliged to admit patients in respect of whom applications under Pt II of this Act have been made. In Volume 2 of his *A Human Condition* (1977), Larry Gostin refers to the opinion that Sir Geoffrey Howe Q.C., M.P. gave to the North West Thames Regional Health Authority in 1974 on the role of hospital managers in respect of hospital admissions. Sir Geoffrey concluded that a hospital consultant had no right to admit a patient, except with the authority of the hospital managers (*ibid.* pp. 53, 59).

Hospital: As the application does not authorise the applicant to take the patient to any hospital other than the hospital specified in the application, it is suggested that the name of the hospital should not be written on the application form until the recommending doctor has confirmed that a hospital bed has been arranged for the patient (see para. 2.22d of the *Code of Practice*). For the patient who also needs treatment for a physical injury or disorder, see the note on "to hospital" in section 6(1).

Local social services authority for the area in which the person so named resides: A guardianship application does not take effect until it is accepted by the authority. If it is accepted, the authority will become the "responsible local social services authority" for the purposes of this Part of the Act (s.34(3)).

Resides: Temporary absence from the place where a person lives does not affect residence, as long as there is an intention to return (*R. v. St Leonard's Shoreditch (Inhabitants)* (1865) L.R. 1 Q.B. 21). In *Fox v. Stirk* [1970] Q.B. 463 at 477, Widgery L.J. said: "A man cannot be said to reside in a particular place unless in the ordinary sense of the word one can say that for the time being he is making his home in that place."

Subsection (3)

1–125   This subsection requires an approved social worker who makes an application for admission for assessment to take such steps as are practicable to inform the patient's nearest relative that the application is either about to be or has been made and of his power to discharge the patient.

Within a reasonable time: Given that an application deprives a patient of his liberty, it is unlikely that a court would consider a delay of more than 24 hours to be reasonable.

Admission . . . for assessment: Under either section 4 or section 2 (*Re Makin*, May 4, 2000, Burton J.).

That social worker: The duty is placed upon the approved social worker who made the application.

Such steps as are practicable: This could include telephoning to inform a nearest relative who resides at some distance from the admitting hospital or asking a social worker from the area where the nearest relative resides to inform him of the application. The actual giving of the information need not necessarily be undertaken by the approved social worker who made the application (*R. v. Managers of South Western Hospital, ex p. M* [1994] 1 All E.R. 161, Laws J.).

Inform: The information could be given either orally or in writing.

Appearing to be the nearest relative: The approved social worker should take reasonable steps to discover the identity of the nearest relative, using the formula set out in section 26. If the approved social worker makes a genuine mistake and informs a person who is not, in fact, the patient's nearest relative, that mistake does not have the effect of invalidating the section 2 application: see *R. v. Birmingham Mental Health Trust, ex p. Phillips*, May 25, 1995, where Tucker J. refused applications for *habeas corpus* and Judicial Review that had been made on behalf of a patient who had been detained under section 2 in circumstances where the patient's mother had been incorrectly identified as the patient's nearest relative (the nearest relative was the patient's father). Tucker J. also said that a subsequent application that had been made to the County Court under section 29 of this Act had also not been invalidated by the mistake.

The power ... under section 23(2)(a): Of the nearest relative to order the patients discharge from hospital. It is suggested that the approved social worker should also inform the nearest relative of the power of the patient's responsible medical officer under section 25(1) to prevent the discharge from taking place.

Subsection (4)

This subsection provides that: (1) an application by an approved social worker for **1–126** admission for treatment or for guardianship must be preceded by a consultation with the patient's nearest relative unless this is impracticable or would involve unreasonable delay; and (2) the application cannot proceed if the patient's nearest relative objects.

If the nearest relative of a patient who is detained under section 2 objects to an application being made under section 3, the patient can continue to be detained beyond the 28-day period provided for in section 2 if an approved social worker applies during the currency of the section 2 to the county court for the nearest relative to be displaced under ground (c) or (d) of section 29(3). Once steps have been taken to make an application under section 3 it is not possible for an approved social worker to overcome a nearest relative's objection by making an application under section 2 in respect of the patient (*R. v. Wilson, ex p. Williamson*, noted in the General Note to s.2).

Objects: Unreasonable objection by a nearest relative to an application is one of the grounds in section 29(3) which enables a county court to transfer the powers of the nearest relative to an "acting nearest relative".

The approved social worker should provide the nearest relative with sufficient information to enable him or her to form an opinion (*Re Whitbread*, below). It is not necessary for the approved social worker to ask the nearest relative the specific question of whether there is an objection to the application being made. (*Re GM (Patient: Consultation)* [2000] M.H.L.R. 41). The approved social worker can proceed if the relative either does not express an objection to the application or is unwilling to form an opinion.

If a nearest relative objects to an application being made but subsequently withdraws that objection, it is advisable for the approved social worker to obtain a signed written statement to that effect; *per* Simon Brown L.J. in *Re Shearon* [1996] C.O.D. 223, DC.

Consultation: In *Re Whitbread (Mental Patient: Habeas Corpus)*, (1998) 39 B.M.L.R. 94, the Court of Appeal held that the consultation with the nearest relative can take place before the applicant has seen the patient in accordance with subsection (5). *Per* Phillips L.J.: "No express provision is made as to when [the] consultation should take place. Counsel for the respondents conceded that a nexus must exist between the consultation and the application that is subsequently made. The consultation must relate to that application. It must place the nearest relative in a position, if so minded, to object to that application . . . Provided that the social worker explains to the nearest relative that he or she is considering making an application and why, the nearest relative will be afforded the opportunity for objecting to the application that the Act requires." His Lordship also said: "The consultation will have two objectives. The first will be to provide information to the social worker to assist with the decision of whether to apply for admission. The second will be to put the nearest relative in a position to object to an application".

In *Re Briscoe* [1998] C.O.D. 402, Tucker J. said: "Lest I needed to be instructed as to the meaning of the word 'consultation', counsel thoughtfully provided the ruling of Webster J. in the case of *R. v. Secretary of State for Social Services, ex p. Association of Metropolitan Authorities* [1986] 1 All E.R. 164 where at page 167 Webster J. said this: 'But in any context the essence of consultation is the communication of a genuine invitation to give advice and a genuine consideration of that advice.' Therefore merely informing the nearest relative will not suffice." The process of consultation might well involve the approved social worker in divulging confidential information about the patient to the nearest relative. The transmission of such information should only be to the extent necessary to provide the nearest relative with a genuine opportunity to object to the application.

In *R. v. Managers of South Western Hospital*, above, Laws J. said at 175, 176, that the approved social worker is not prevented in suitable circumstances from carrying out his duty to consult through the medium of another. He developed this point by stating that "ordinarily, it will clearly be desirable for the consultation to be carried out directly by the approved social worker. But there may be circumstances in which that will be difficult, or even well-nigh impossible. What is important is that the consultation be full and effective, to ensure that the nearest relative has the opportunity to play his full part in the process. . . . I do not suggest that an approved social worker has a wholly free hand to appoint, as it were, a delegate for the purposes of consultation. It remains throughout the approved social worker's responsibility". As an approved social worker will have the knowledge and experience to engage in a "full and effective" consultation with the nearest relative, an attempt should be made to consult through the medium of another approved social worker.

Although there appears to be no legal reason to prevent an approved social worker undertaking the consultation through correspondence, this practice is unlikely to result in the "full and effective" consultation advocated by Laws J.

1–127 *(If any):* The application can proceed without consultation having taken place if it appears to the approved social worker that the patient has no nearest relative. Reasonable steps must be taken by the approved social worker to ascertain the identity of the patient's nearest relative.

Appearing to be the nearest relative: These words "cannot in my judgment, embrace a situation where, on the facts known to the social worker, the person in question is legally *incapable* of being the statutory nearest relative having regard to the terms of section 26"; *per* Laws J. in *R. v. Managers of South Western Hospital*, above at 175. In this case the patient's mother, who was ordinarily resident in the Republic of Ireland, was incorrectly deemed to be the patient's nearest relative (see s.26(5)(a)).

This section does not impose a duty of reasonable inquiry on the approved social worker applicant in deciding who is the patient's nearest relative. A court cannot inquire into the reasonableness of the approved social worker's decision, it can only inquire into the honesty of his assertion that it appeared that that relative was the nearest relative (*Re D (Mental Patient: Habeas Corpus)* [2000] 2 F.L.R. 848, CA).

In the absence of action being taken under section 29 to displace the nearest relative or of the nearest relative agreeing to transfer his functions to another under regulation 14 of the Mental Health (Hospital, Guardianship and Consent to

Treatment) Regulations 1983, the approved social worker should consult with the person who he has identified as being the patient's nearest relative using the formula set out in section 26, even though, from a professional perspective, it might be inappropriate for that person to be consulted. However, the consultation need not take place if the approved social worker considers that it is not "reasonably practicable" to undertake the consultation; see below.

Not reasonably practicable: It would clearly not be practicable for an approved social worker to consult with a nearest relative who is mentally incapable of being consulted or who is implacably opposed to being consulted. Neither would it be practicable to consult in a situation where a patient who is not known to the clinical team is either unable or unwilling to give the approved social worker information to enable him to identify the nearest relative.

The Mental Health Act Commission states that it has been informed of many instances "where it has been inappropriate for a person to remain as the nearest relative ... , for instance if the patient has been abused, physically, emotionally or sexually by the nearest relative or, for instance, where the patient and the nearest relative have severed all emotional links" (*Fourth Biennial Report*, 1989–1991, para. 11.3(d)). "As a result, in a small minority of cases, an abusing or potentially abusing person can establish or re-establish contact with the patient in the most vulnerable of circumstances" (*Eighth Biennial Report*, 1997–1999, para. 4.46).

It is submitted that: (1) there is clear judicial authority to support the contention that it will not always be "practicable" to consult with a nearest relative in the circumstances identified by the Commission; and (2) the advice contained in paragraph 2.16 of the *Code of Practice* that "practicability refers to the availability of the nearest relative" is incorrect.

The word "practicable" was considered in *Owen v. Crown House Engineering* [1973] 3 All E.R. 618, NIRC, where, at 622, Sir Hugh Griffiths, giving the judgment of the court said:

"It is important not to equate 'practicable' with 'possible'. When considering whether a course of action is possible, it is not permissible to consider the results of that course of action; if it can be done, it must be done. But when considering whether a course of action is practicable it may be permissible to look at the end result. Like so many other words of the English language, 'practicable' will take considerable colour from the context in which it is used."

In *Re P (Adoption)(Natural Father's Rights)* [1994] 1 F.L.R. 771, Ewbank J. said that he found this statement to be a "valuable exposition" of the meaning of "practicable". His Lordship held in adoption proceedings that if the consequences of ascertaining the wishes and feelings of an unmarried father, who was unaware of the child's birth, would be detrimental to the child, the court would be prepared to say that it was not "practicable" (the term used in Schedule 2 to the Adoption Rules 1984) to obtain them.

The meaning of "practicable" was also considered in *Dedman v. British Building and Engineering Appliances Ltd* [1974] 1 W.L.R. 171, CA, where Scarman L.J. said at 179:

"The word 'practicable' is an ordinary English word of great flexibility: it takes its meaning from its context. But, whenever used, it is a call for the exercise of common sense, a warning that sound judgment will be impossible without compromise. Sometimes the context contemplates a situation rarely to be achieved though much to be desired: the word then indicates one must be satisfied with less than perfection ... sometimes ... what the context requires may have been possible, but may not for some reason have been 'practicable'. Whatever its context, the quality of the word is that there are circumstances in which we must be content with less than 100 per cent: and it calls for judgment to determine how much less."

These cases strongly suggest that it would not be "practicable" for an approved social worker applicant to consult with a nearest relative if such consultation would have an adverse effect on the patient's situation by, for example, causing significant emotional distress to the patient or by placing the patient at risk of harm.

The approach taken to the interpretation of this provision by the *Code of Practice* and the Mental Health Act Commission conflicts with the requirement of Article 8(2) of the European Convention on Human Rights that any interference with a person's private life must be "necessary in a democratic society ... for the protection of [the person's] health ..." in that a consultation which would be likely to have an adverse effect on the patient's emotional health or safety would not serve to protect the patient's health. It is also inconsistent with the decision of the European Court of Human Rights in *JT v. United Kingdom*, March 30, 2000, which is noted in the General Note to section 29.

A decision that it would not be practicable to consult with the nearest relative should never be made on the sole ground that an objection to the application is anticipated.

Undesirable delay: Given the circumstances of most guardianship applications and applications for treatment, it is unlikely that this situation would often obtain. It could occur if tracing the whereabouts of the nearest relative would involve an excessive amount of investigative work on the part of the approved social worker.

Subsection (5)

1–128 *Personally seen:* An intermediary cannot be used (*R. v. Managers of South Western Hospital*, above).

The relationship between this provision and section 13(2), which requires an approved social worker to interview the patient before making an application, was examined in the following passage from Phillips L.J.'s judgment in *Re Whitbread*, above: "In my judgment section 11(5) and section 13(2) do not necessarily refer to the same event. The precondition to an application imposed by section 11(5) applies whether the application is made by the nearest relative or by the social worker and thus must be appropriate to either. It seems to me that the object of section 11(5) is to ensure that the view of an applicant that an application is desirable is informed by recent face to face contact with the patient. So far as the social worker is concerned, this may or may not be the occasion upon which the interview required by section 13(2) takes place. I consider that the Act permits an application to follow from an interview that takes place more than 14 days before the application, provided that the social worker has confirmed his conclusion that an application is desirable by face to face contact with the patient within 14 days of the application."

14 days ending with the date of the application: With the exception of an emergency application, once an application has been completed the patient must be taken to the hospital named in the application within 14 days of the second medical recommendation being made (s.6(1)(a)).

Subsection (6)

1–129 *More than one:* The use of this phrase clearly indicates that a recommending doctor can certify that a patient is suffering from more than one form of mental disorder. The wording of Form 11 of S.I. 1983 No. 893, which requires the recommending doctor to indicate whether the patient is suffering from either mental illness/severe mental impairment or psychopathic disorder/mental impairment, cannot have the effect of constraining the discretion that this provision gives to a recommending doctor regarding the identification of the mental disorder(s) from which the patient is suffering. It is therefore lawful for the doctor to state on Form 11 that the patient is suffering from both a mental illness and a psychopathic disorder.

Suffering from the same form of mental disorder: Although the recommending doctors can each state that the patient is suffering from more than one of the forms of mental disorder specified in this subsection, they must both agree on at least one of them. An application would not be invalidated if one of the recommending doctors made a general diagnosis as to the form of mental disorder and the other made a specific diagnosis coming within the same form, *e.g.* if Dr A. diagnosed mental illness and Dr B. diagnosed paranoid schizophrenia, a form of mental illness; see the note on section 37(2).

General provisions as to medical recommendations

12.—(1) The recommendations required for the purposes of an appli- **1–130** cation for the admission of a patient under this Part of this Act (in this Act referred to as "medical recommendations") shall be signed on or before the date of the application, and shall be given by practitioners who have personally examined the patient either together or separately, but where they have examined the patient separately not more than five days must have elapsed between the days on which the separate examinations took place.

(2) Of the medical recommendations given for the purposes of any such application, one shall be given by a practitioner approved for the purposes of this section by the Secretary of State as having special experience in the diagnosis or treatment of mental disorder; and unless that practitioner has previous acquaintance with the patient, the other such recommendation shall, if practicable, be given by a registered medical practitioner who has such previous acquaintance.

(3) Subject to subsection (4) below, where the application is for the admission of the patient to a hospital which is not a [registered establishment], one (but not more than one) of the medical recommendations may be given by a practitioner on the staff of that hospital, except where the patient is proposed to be accommodated under section [18A(4), 65 or 66] of the National Health Service Act 1977 [or paragraph 14 of Schedule 2 to the National Health Service and Community Care Act 1990] (which relate to accommodation for private patients).

(4) Subsection (3) above shall not preclude both the medical recommendations being given by practitioners on the staff of the hospital in question if—

(a) compliance with that subsection would result in delay involving serious risk to the health or safety of the patient; and

(b) one of the practitioners giving the recommendations works at the hospital for less than half of the time which he is bound by contract to devote to work in the health service; and

(c) where one of those practitioners is a consultant, the other does not work (whether at the hospital or elsewhere) in a grade in which he is under that consultant's directions.

(5) A medical recommendation for the purposes of an application for the admission of a patient under this Part of this Act shall not be given by—

(a) the applicant;

(b) a partner of the applicant or of a practitioner by whom another medical recommendation is given for the purposes of the same application;

(c) a person employed as an assistant by the applicant or by any such practitioner;

(d) a person who receives or has an interest in the receipt of any payments made on account of the maintenance of the patient; or

(e) except as provided by subsection (3) or (4) above, a practitioner on the staff of the hospital to which the patient is to be admitted,

or by the husband, wife, father, father-in-law, mother, mother-in-law, son, son-in-law, daughter, daughter-in-law, brother, brother-in-law, sister or sister-in-law of the patient, or of any person mentioned in paragraphs (a) to (e) above, or of a practitioner by whom another medical recommendation is given for the purposes of the same application.

(6) A general practitioner who is employed part-time in a hospital shall not for the purposes of this section be regarded as a practitioner on its staff.

(7) Subsections (1), (2) and (5) above shall apply to applications for guardianship as they apply to applications for admission but with the substitution for paragraph (e) of subsection (5) above of the following paragraph—

"(e) the person named as guardian in the application."

AMENDMENT
In subs. (3) the words in square brackets were inserted by the National Health Service and Community Care Act 1990, s.66(1), Sched. 9, para. 24(1) and the Care Standards Act 2000, s.116, Sched. 4, para. 9(2). The numbers in square brackets were substituted by the Health Act 1999 (Supplementary, Consequential, etc., Provisions) Order 2000 (S.I. 2000 No. 90), Sched. 1, para. 16(2).

DEFINITIONS
1–131   patient: s.145(1).
mental disorder: ss.1, 145(1).
hospital: ss.34(2), 145(1).
mental nursing home: s.145(1).
registered establishment: s.34(1).

GENERAL NOTE
1–132   This section specifies the requirements that apply to medical recommendations. The assessment by doctors of the needs of a person with mental health problems, where it may lead to an application for admission to hospital under this Act is considered in chapter 2 of the *Code of Practice*. Chapter 4 of the *Code* is concerned with the provision of medical recommendations by doctors in private practice. Guidance for general practitioners on the process involved in undertaking mental health assessments under this Act was published by the Department of Health on July 12, 2001. A doctor who makes a recommendation under this section must be a fully registered person within the meaning of the Medical Act 1983 (Interpretation Act 1978, s.5, Sched. 1).

There is no provision in this Act which allows for the withdrawal of a valid medical recommendation after it has been provided to a potential applicant. In a case known to the author, a request for the return of a recommendation was made subsequent to the recommending doctor being subjected to pressure from members of the patient's family. An attempt to withdraw a recommendation would be a factor that the potential applicant would take into account before making a decision about the appropriateness of making an application in respect of the patient.

Duty of care owed by recommending doctors
1–133   In *M (A Minor) v. Newham L.B.C.* [1995] 3 All E.R. 353, HL, the local authority, in exercising functions under the child care legislation, arranged for a child whom they suspected was being sexually abused to be interviewed by a social worker and a child psychiatrist. The House of Lords held that the social worker and the psychiatrist "did

not, by accepting the instructions of the local authority, assume any general professional duty of care to the [child]. The professionals were employed or retained to advise the local authority in relation to the well-being of the [child] but not to advise or treat [the child]"; *per* Lord Browne-Wilkinson at 384. As reference was made in both the Court of Appeal and in the House of Lords to *Everett (pauper) v. Griffiths* [1920] 3 K.B. 163, CA; [1921] 1 A.C. 631, a case decided under the Lunacy Act 1890 where the House of Lords assumed that a recommending doctor owed a duty of care to the patient, without deciding the point (in *De Freville v. Dill* (1927) 96 L.J.K.B. 1056, McCardie J. considered *Everett* and held that such a duty did exist), it could be argued that the decision in the *Newham* case determines the liability of doctors and approved social workers undertaking assessments under this Act. However, the legal position of professionals performing functions under the child care legislation and under this Act is quite different. Approved social workers and doctors who undertake assessments under this Act are not involved in either reporting to or advising their employer or any other body. The approved social worker is undertaking an independent legal function when determining whether to make an application and the role of the recommending doctors is to support the application if it is considered that the statutory criteria are satisfied. When carrying out these functions the approved social worker and the doctors have, it is submitted, assumed personal responsibility towards the patient to take reasonable care. It follows that an action for negligence could be brought where the professional fails to exercise such care. As Atkin L.J. pointed out in the Court of Appeal in *Everett* at 212, section 330 of the Lunacy Act 1890 (now to be found in an amended form in section 139 of this Act) assumes that professionals performing functions under this Act consider themselves bound to exercise reasonable care.

Atkin L.J.'s judgment in *Everett* included the following noteworthy passages:

"Grievous as is the wrong of unjust imprisonment of an alleged criminal, I apprehend that its colours pale beside the catastrophe of unjust imprisonment on an unfounded finding of insanity. Modern organisation has no doubt done much to remove the horrors that were associated with Bedlam in the days when the victims were subject to public exhibition. Probably even now the insane ward or reception ward is not without its revolting incidents. But it is the effect on the mind sane, even if feeble, that knows itself wrongly adjudged unsound that produces the most poignant suffering" (at 211). His Lordship concluded his judgment by aserting that "it is just as it is convenient that the law should impose a duty to take reasonable care that such persons, if sane, should not suffer the unspeakable torment of having their sanity condemned and their liberty restricted; and I am glad to record my opinion, ineffectual though it may be, that for such an injury the English law provides a remedy" (at 233).

At the House of Lords, Lord Haldane described this as " powerful piece of reasoning displaying anxiety to guard against a possible miscarriage of justice" ([1921] 1 A.C. 631 at 652).

Subsection (1)
This subsection provides that where the two recommending doctors examine the **1–134** patient separately not more than five days must have elapsed between the days on which the separate examinations took place.

Recommendations. Incorrect or defective recommendations can be rectified under section 15. Recommendations must be in the forms prescribed by Schedule 1 to the Mental Health (Hospital, Guardianship and Consent to Treatment) Regulations 1983.

Application for the admission: Or a guardianship application (subs. (7)).

On or before the date of the application: An applicant should not sign an application and then try to obtain the medical recommendation to support it.

Personally examined: The personal examination should be accompanied by such further enquiries as are necessary: see *Hall v. Semple* (1862) 3 F. & F. 337, 354 *per* Crompton J., cited in M. Jones, *Medical Negligence* (1996), at para. 4–111.

A personal examination of the patient must always precede the making of a medical recommendation, even though the patient might be well known to the doctor (*Code of Practice*, para. 2.23). In *Routley v. Worthing Health Authority*, July 14, 1983, CA, a patient was applying for leave to sue doctors who, it was alleged, had failed to examine him before they had signed medical recommendations. Counsel for the doctors suggested that "examined" meant "observation sufficient to form a clinical judgment, having regard to the doctor's knowledge of the history." It is submitted that this definition is defective in that it fails to incorporate an attempt by the doctor to conduct an interview with the patient.

An examination of an unconscious or highly intoxicated patient would not enable the doctor to ascertain whether the criteria for admission under this Act were established. Such a patient could be admitted to hospital and treated under common law powers.

If the doctor is unable to gain access to the patient, consideration should be given to invoking section 135(1) of this Act.

Five days: i.e. five clear days between the days on which the medical examinations took place. The relevant dates are the dates when the examinations took place and not the dates when the medical recommendations were signed.

Subsection (2)

1–135   *Any such application:* Including a guardianship application (subs. (7)).

Approved: Approval is delegated to Health Authorities in England by the National Health Service (Functions of Health Authorities and Administration Arrangements) (England) Regulations 2001 (S.I. 2001 No. 747), reg. 3, Sched. 1 and it can be given only—

"(a) after carrying out such consultations, and the obtaining of such advice, as the Secretary of State may direct; and
(b) for such periods as the Secretary of State may direct" (reg. 4(7)).

The Authority can arrange for approval to be exercised—

"(a) by another Health Authority,
(b) by a Special Health Authority,
(c) jointly with any one or more of the following—
    (i) Primary Care Trusts, and
    (ii) other Health Authorities,
or
(d) on behalf of the Authority by a committee, sub-committee or officer of the Authority" (reg. 5(1)).

The approval is not limited in its effect to the area of the Authority (reg. 3(3)).

Department of Health Circular No. HSG(96)3 states that the "Royal College of Psychiatrists together with the Royal College of General Practitioners have reviewed the criteria for approval and the Department of Health endorses the changes." Annex A of the Circular lays down the qualifications and experience required for approval and the necessary training which must be undertaken before approval is given.

In most of the 10 local authority areas inspected by the Social Services Inspectorate in *Detained: Inspection of compulsory mental health admissions* (2001) "problems in the availability of section 12 doctors had been raised frequently by the Mental Health Act Commission in the course of its regular visits, and by local social services managers, with little positive result" (para. 4.21).

Secretary of State: The functions of the Minister, so far as exercisable in relation to Wales, are exercised by the National Assembly for Wales (S.I. 1999 No. 672, art. 2, Sched. 1).

Special experience in the diagnosis or treatment of mental disorder: In *R. v. Trent Regional Health Authority, ex p. Somaratne* (1993) 18 B.M.L.R. 143, Potts J. held that the "special experience" referred to in this subsection does no more than provide a minimum threshold required before approval can be granted and is, therefore, not the only matter which the Health Authority can take into account. This finding was reversed by a majority in the Court of Appeal (1994) 31 B.M.L.R. 140 where it was held that "special experience" is the sole criterion for approving a doctor and that having "special experience" requires examination of the doctor's current knowledge and skills in the diagnosis and treatment of mental disorder. The Health Authority has to consider the doctor's qualifications and experience and not his overall suitability for appointment. Following this decision the doctor made a fresh application for approval to the Health Authority and this application was refused. An application for a judicial review of this decision was made and judgment was given by Latham J. [1996] C.O.D. 138. In dismissing the application his Lordship held that:

(1) the Health Authority was entitled to take into account the doctor's age because this issue was only considered in the context of the length of the approval that might be granted; and

(2) the authority was entitled to issue guidance to members of its Mental Health Approval Panel taking into account the number of psychiatrists in any given area and adjusting the standard to be applied in considering "special experience", provided that this was applied generally and that the adjustment was directed to consideration of experience only. In this case there was no shortage of approved doctors in the relevant areas which would justify departing from what would otherwise be considered an appropriate standard of experience.

The other such recommendation: The recipients of a survey undertaken by E. K. Ung questioned the "independence" of the second medical opinion ("Who should act as the second medical recommendation for sections 2 and 3 of the Mental Health Act", *Psychiatric Bulletin* (1993), 17, 466–468).

Shall, if practicable: This wording suggests that an application would be unlawful if neither medical recommendation came from a doctor with previous acquaintance of the patient in circumstances where it would have been practicable to obtain such a recommendation. Such an assumption was made by the Divisional Court in *R. v. D'Souza* [1992] Crim.L.R. 119.

Note that the test is one of practicability, and not "exceptional circumstances" as stated in the *Code of Practice* at paragraph 2.29. It is important not to equate "practicable" with "possible"; see the cases noted under "not reasonably practicable" in section 11(4). It is submitted that, in the context of this provision, judgments about practicability have to be made in the following situations:

(a) is it practicable to involve a doctor with previous acquaintance with the patient given the time that it will take for that doctor to attend upon the patient; and

(b) is it practicable to involve such a doctor given the patient's need for a specialist assessment (*e.g.* the approved social worker might conclude that the patient's disturbed behaviour and violent fantasies require an assessment from both a general and a forensic psychiatrist, neither of whom were previously acquainted with the patient.)

If it is not possible to obtain a recommendation from a doctor who knows the patient, the applicant must explain why this was the case: see Forms 1, 2, 8 and 9 of S.I.

1983 No. 983. If neither of the recommending doctors know the patient, it is suggested that the "approved" doctor should attempt to consult with the patient's general practitioner over the telephone before he signs a recommendation. Advice on the provision of the second medical recommendation is contained in paragraph 2.29 of the *Code of Practice.*

In circumstances where general practitioners have organised themselves into large rotas or co-operatives to provide emergency out-of-hours services, the Department of Health has advised the Mental Health Act Commission that the deputising doctor cannot be considered "to have prior knowledge of the patient simply because he has access to the patient's records" and that the G.P.s deputising/answering service should contact the actual G.P. if it appears from the telephone call that a mental health assessment is likely (M.H.A.C., Sixth Biennial Report, 1993–1995, para. 8.1).

Previous acquaintance: This doctor could be the patient's G.P. or a medical member of a Community Mental Health Team. A doctor who had provided a medical recommendation in respect of the patient on a previous occasion could be said to have had "previous acquaintance with the patient".

Subsection (3)

1–136   This subsection provides that the general rule for a patient who is to be admitted to hospital as a National Health Service patient is that only one of the two medical recommendations may come from a doctor on the staff of the hospital to which the patient is to be admitted. There is no requirement in this section that a recommending doctor must be on the staff of the admitting hospital and there is no prohibition against both medical recommendations being given by doctors who are on the staff of the same non-admitting hospital. If the patient is admitted to a N.H.S. hospital as a private patient or is admitted to a registered establishment, neither recommendation may come from a doctor on the staff of the hospital or establishment. This subsection and subsection (4) do not apply to guardianship applications (subs. (7)).

Practitioner on the staff of that hospital: Note subsection (6). Whether a doctor is "on the staff of" a hospital is a question of fact which can be determined by asking the following question: "Is the doctor employed or contracted to undertake clinical responsibilities at the hospital?" If the answer is in the affirmative, that doctor is on the staff of the hospital even though the majority of his clinical responsibilities might be undertaken elsewhere.

Hospital means, *inter alia,* "any institution for the reception and treatment of persons suffering from illness" (National Health Service Act 1977, s.128(1) and s.145(1) of this Act). It is submitted that: (1) the phrase "that hospital" refers to the institution, *i.e.* a building or collection of buildings that are referred to by a common name; (2) the fact that the building or buildings might be managed by more than one NHS trust is not relevant for the purposes of this provision; and (3), the Mental Health Act Commission is correct in its view that this provision does not "preclude the second medical recommendation from being provided by a doctor on the staff of another hospital but employed by the same Trust as the first," (M.H.A.C., Sixth Biennial Report, 1993–1995, para. 3.3; also see para. 2.30 of the *Code of Practice*).

Subsection (4)

1–137   This subsection specifies when both medical recommendations in respect of national health service patients may come from doctors on the staff of the admitting hospital. All three conditions must be satisfied before the recommendations can be given.

Delay: If the patient has been admitted for assessment under section 2 there should be ample time to comply with the provisions of subsection (3) if an application for treatment under section 3 is being considered.

Under the consultant's directions: A query was raised at the Special Standing Committee as to the relationship between a doctor's independent clinical judgment and his position of being under the "direction" of a consultant. The Under-Secretary of State responded by saying that "it was commonsense to say in this context that 'direction' means that a junior doctor, a registrar working as part of a consultant's team, finally has to accept the directions, advice or instructions of the consultant. If the doctor believes that those instructions are wholly wrong, he must decide whether to obey them" (sitting of May 18, 1982).

Subsection (5)

This subsection disqualifies certain doctors from providing medical recommenda- **1–138** tions to support applications for admission to hospital and guardianship applications.

Application for the admission: And a guardianship application (subs. (7)).

Paragraph (b)

Partner: This means professional partner. Two doctors working in the same G.P. **1–139** partnership are therefore precluded from making recommendations in respect of the same application.

Paragraph (d)

Thus a doctor who has a financial interest in a registered establishment cannot **1–140** provide a medical recommendation in respect of a patient who is to be admitted to that establishment. A doctor who is on the staff of the registered establishment is precluded from providing a medical recommendation by virtue of subsection (3). Although the *Code of Practice*, at paragraph 4.3, states that it is "undesirable" for a doctor to recommend the admission of a patient whom he intends to treat as a private patient, this practice is not unlawful. The General Medical Council "Blue Book" *Professional Conduct and Discipline: Fitness to Practice* (April 1992) provides that a

> "doctor who recommends that a patient should attend at, or be admitted to, any private hospital, nursing home or similar institution, whether for treatment by that doctor or by another person, must do so only in such a way as will best serve, and will be seen to best serve, the medical interests of the patient ... When doctors have a financial interest in an organisation to which they propose to refer a patient for admission or treatment, whether by reason of capital investment or a remunerative position, they should always disclose that they have such an interest before making the referral" (para. 115).

There is nothing to prevent a doctor who comes within the scope of this provision from providing a report under section 20 for the continued detention of the patient.

Receives or has an interest in: This would cover a doctor who has made a capital investment in the organisation that controls the registered establishment or who receives any income from that organisation.

Paragraph (e)

A practitioner by whom another medical recommendation is given: The effect of **1–141** this provision is that two doctors who come within the prohibited relationships cannot provide the medical recommendations for the same application. This paragraph is substituted for guardianship applications (subs. (7)).

Subsection (6)

It is therefore possible for the medical recommendations to be given by a hospital **1–142** consultant and the patient's G.P. even if the G.P. happens to work part-time in the hospital in question.

Subsection (7)

The doctors who provide medical recommendations for guardianship can be **1–143** employed at the same hospital, even if one works under the direction of the other.

Duty of approved social workers to make applications for admission or guardianship

1–144　**13.**—(1) It shall be the duty of an approved social worker to make an application for admission to hospital or a guardianship application in respect of a patient within the area of the local social services authority by which that officer is appointed in any case where he is satisfied that such an application ought to be made and is of the opinion, having regard to any wishes expressed by relatives of the patient or any other relevant circumstances, that it is necessary or proper for the application to be made by him.

(2) Before making an application for the admission of a patient to hospital an approved social worker shall interview the patient in a suitable manner and satisfy himself that detention in a hospital is in all the circumstances of the case the most appropriate way of providing the care and medical treatment of which the patient stands in need.

(3) An application under this section by an approved social worker may be made outside the area of the local social services authority by which he is appointed.

(4) It shall be the duty of a local social services authority, if so required by the nearest relative of a patient residing in their area, to direct an approved social worker as soon as practicable to take the patient's case into consideration under subsection (1) above with a view to making an application for his admission to hospital; and if in any such case that approved social worker decides not to make an application he shall inform the nearest relative of his reasons in writing.

(5) Nothing in this section shall be construed as authorising or requiring an application to be made by an approved social worker in contravention of the provisions of section 11(4) above, or as restricting the power of an approved social worker to make any application under this Act.

DEFINITIONS
1–145　approved social worker: s.145(1).
hospital: ss.34(2), 145(1).
patient: s.145(1).
local social services authority: s.145(1).
medical treatment: s.145(1).
nearest relative: ss.26(3), 145(1).

GENERAL NOTE
1–146　This section places a duty on an approved social worker to make an application for admission to a hospital or a guardianship application in respect of a patient if he considers that such an application ought to be made and if, after taking into account the views of relatives and any other relevant circumstances, he considers that it is necessary or proper for him to do so. It also provides an approved social worker with a discretion to make applications outside his employing local authority's area and requires a local authority to direct an approved social worker to consider making an application for admission to a hospital at the request of a patient's nearest relative. None of the provisions of this section apply to a nearest relative applicant. The assessment by approved social workers of the needs of a person with mental health problems, where it may lead to an application for admission under this Act is considered in Chapter 2 of the *Code of Practice*. Paragraph 3.19 of the *Code* is concerned with assessments made in prison or in a court.

The British Association of Social Workers has suggested that the role of the approved social worker in compulsory admissions should be:

"(a) to investigate the client's social situation and how that has developed; and to estimate, in consultation with others involved, the extent to which the social and environmental pressures have contributed to the client's observed behaviour;

(b) to apply professional skill to help modify any contributory personal relationship or environmental factors;

(c) to mobilise the resources of the health service, the community service and acknowledge and use the community as a therapeutic resource;

(d) to ensure that any intervention is the least restrictive necessary in the circumstances;

(e) to ensure strict compliance with the law." ("Review of the Mental Health Act 1959—Further Evidence" 1980, p. 25.)

Paragraph 14 of D.H.S.S. Circular No. LAC (86) 15 states that approved social workers

> "should have a wider role than reacting to requests for admission to hospital, making the necessary arrangements and ensuring compliance with the law. They should have the specialist knowledge and skills to make appropriate decisions in respect of both clients and their relatives and to gain the confidence of colleagues in the health services with whom they are required to collaborate. They must be familiar with the day to day working of an integrated mental health service and be able to assess what other services may be required and know how to mobilise them. They should have access to, consultation with and supervision from qualified and experienced senior officers. Their role is to prevent the necessity for compulsory admission to hospital as well as to make application where they decide this is appropriate".

There is no requirement for an approved social worker to identify a change in the patient's circumstances before proceeding to make an application under sections 2 or 3 in respect of a patient who has been discharged by a tribunal (*R. v. East London and City Mental Health NHS Trust, ex p. Brandenburg*, [2001] EWCA Civ 239, noted in the General Note to s.3). Also see the note on "necessary or proper", below.

Some suggestions for a "Code of Practice" which provides guidance to approved social workers in assessing the need for compulsory admission have been made by Fisher, Newton and Sainsbury in *Mental Health Social Work Observed*, 1984, pp. 185–190. The role of the approved social worker in the assessment of individuals for possible compulsory admission to hospital under this Act is examined by M. Sheppard in *Mental Health: The Role of the Approved Social Worker*, Joint Unit for Social Services Research/Community Care, 1990 and by B. Hatfield *et al.*, "The 1983 Mental Health Act in five local authorities: a study of the practice of approved social workers" (1992) 38 Int. J. Soc. Psychiatry 189–207. In *Detained: Inspection of compulsory mental health admissions* (2001), the Social Services Inspectorate examines the role played by approved social workers in ten local authority areas. Suggestions for a risk management strategy for approved social workers are made by Curran *et al.* in "Approved Social Workers: safety and professional support" (1995) 35 Med. Sci. Law 261–268.

The Human Rights Act 1998
An approved social worker who is performing functions under this Act is **1–147** exercising "functions of a public nature" and is therefore a "public authority" for the purposes of the 1998 Act (s.6(3)(b)).
If an approved social worker acts in an arbitrary fashion by, for example, resorting

to making an application for detention in bad faith or making an application in circumstances where such action is a disproportionate response to the patient's situation, he will have violated Article 5(1) of the European Convention on Human Rights: see *Tsirlis and Kouloumpas v. Geece* (1997) 25 E.H.R.R. 198 (para. 56). In *Litwa v. Poland,* April 4, 2000, the Court, in reiterating that a necessary element of the "lawfulness" of a detention within the meaning of Article 5(1)(e) is the absence of arbitrariness, said that "the detention of an individual is such a serious measure that it is only justified where other, less severe measures have been considered and found to be insufficient to safeguard the individual or public interest which might require that the person concerned be detained. That means that it does not suffice that the deprivation of liberty is executed in conformity with national law but it must also be necessary in the circumstances" (para.78).

The giving of "reasons" to a nearest relative for a decision not to make an application in respect of the patient could constitute an interference with the patient's right to respect for his private life under Article 8(1). Either the reasons should be drafted in a manner which would not constitute such a violation or a justification for the violation must be found in Article 8(2).

Subsection (1)

1–148   *Duty of an approved social worker:* Also see the note on section 114(2). The duty is placed on the approved social worker and not on his employing authority. An approved social worker is therefore personally liable for his actions whilst carrying out functions under this Act. He should exercise his own judgment, based upon social and medical evidence, and not act at the behest of his employers, medical practitioners or other persons who might be involved with the patient's welfare. In *St George's Healthcare NHS Trust v. S* [1998] 3 All E.R. 673 at 694, CA, Judge L.J. said: "[The provisions of section 13] make clear that the social worker must exercise her own independent judgment on the basis of all the available material, including her interview and assessment of the 'patient', and personally make the appropriate decision. When doing so she is required to take account of the recommendations made by the medical practitioners". It is submitted that the approved social worker owes a duty of care to those people who he assesses for possible admissions under this Act: see the note on "Duty of care owed by recommending doctors" in the General Note to section 12.

Speaking of the role of the approved social worker's precursor, Devlin L.J., said: "It is the business of the duly authorised officer, rather than that of the doctor, to see that statutory powers are not used for the purpose [of hospital treatment] unless the circumstances warrant it" (*Buxton v. Jayne* [1960] 1 W.L.R. 783, 784).

The duty placed on the approved social worker by this section does not affect the provisions as to consultation with nearest relatives set out in section 11(4) (subs. (5)).

Make an application: If the approved social worker makes an application he should fully record his reasons for taking such action. This was the approach taken by the Local Ombudsman in his investigation into complaint 87/B/1308 where a failure by approved social workers to make adequate records of the circumstances of the compulsory admission of a patient was sufficient for the Ombudsman to find that the employing local authority was guilty of maladministration.

The approved social worker is obliged, as far as he is able, to ensure that the medical recommendations upon which the application is founded comply with the provisions of section 12. He should not make an application and then look for the medical recommendations to support it because his application is "founded on" the medical recommendations: see Forms 2, 6 and 9 of S.I. 1983 No. 893.

Patient within the area of the local social services authority: This would include a patient who is temporarily in that area (for example, on holiday).

Ought to be made: In the case of an application for admission to hospital, the approved social worker can only be satisfied that an application ought to be made if the requirements of subsection (2) have been met.

Having regard to: The approved social worker must take the wishes of relatives and other relevant circumstances into account when he considers whether he should proceed to make an application.

For a dramatic illustration of the need for approved social workers and other professionals to listen to, and to take account of, the views of family members and others with close knowledge of the patient, see chapter 17 of L. Blom-Cooper *et al.*, *The Falling Shadow*, 1995.

The approved social worker should not challenge the diagnosis set out in the medical recommendations but, because mental disorder alone does not render a person liable to detention, he is entitled to take the view that it is not appropriate to make an application. The view of the *Royal Commission* was that "medical and non-medical opinions should supplement each other; each person should be expected to contribute to the final decision only what is appropriate to his own knowledge or experience or to his relationship with the patient" (para. 390).

Relatives: As defined in section 26(1).

Other relevant circumstances: Which could include the provisions that have to be satisfied before an emergency application under section 4 of this Act can be made.

Necessary or proper: In *St George's Healthcare NHS Trust v. S*, above, Judge L.J. said, at 695: "In deciding whether it is 'necessary or proper' to make an application under section 2, the approved social worker has to approach the individual 'patient' as she is, or at any rate as on the best analysis she can make at the time, the patient appears to be." In this case the Court of Appeal held that facts that the patient was heavily pregnant and adamantly refusing treatment for her pre-eclampsia were, at least potentially, of compelling importance to the approved social worker who had to make an informed judgment under this provision. To require the approved social worker to make such a judgment by ignoring the reality of the patient's situation "would be absurd". However, the patient's pregnancy was not sufficient on its own to bring the provisions of this section into play. Also see the notes on section 2(2).

By him: If the approved social worker decides not to make an application it would be improper for that decision to be reviewed by another approved social worker in the absence of any change in circumstances or fresh evidence or concern that the approved social worker had acted negligently. A procedure which allowed for the automatic review of the decisions of approved social workers would undermine the independent nature of the approved social worker's role. For a contrary view, see "Disagreements between psychiatrists and social workers over compulsory admissions under the Mental Health Act", R. G. Sammut and H. Sergeant, *Psychiatric Bulletin* (1993), 17, 462–465.

The use of the phrase "necessary or proper for the application to be made *by him*" enables the approved social worker to conclude that although an application ought to be made, it would be more appropriate for the application to be made by another approved social worker exercising his powers under subsection (3).

If an approved social worker considers that he would find it difficult to make an independent or impartial assessment of the patient or that he would be perceived to be so acting, he should ask another approved social worker to undertake the assessment; see the note on section 114(2).

Subsection (2)

It is possible to have a single interview under this provision doubling as a section **1–149** 4/2 interview in the first instance, followed without further interview, by a section 3 application (*Re GM (Patient: Consultation* [2000] M.H.L.R. 41, May 4, 2000). *Per* Burton J.:

> "It seems to me entirely possible, provided that a necessary and suitable interview is carried out, for the social worker to have acquired the necessary knowledge, either retaining it in her memory or if necessary reflecting back on

any notes, so that there is sufficient to justify an initial section 2 or 4 application, but subsequently, when it comes to a section 3 application, for her to be able to draw on that same knowledge when she comes to consider section 3 ... In those circumstances there is nothing which prevents the use, for the purpose of a subsequent section 3 admission, of any proper information available on an earlier section 2/4 admission, just as there is no prohibition upon the social worker using acquired knowledge prior to the interview for the purposes of the interview itself ..." (paras 69, 70).

In this case the patient was the subject of an application under section 3 whilst he was being detained under section 4. A fresh interview would be required if the patient attained informal status subsequent to the expiry or discharge of the initial detaining section and before the need for a further period of detention arose. This is because the attaining of informal status should trigger a fresh enquiry, via an interview, as to the appropriateness of a further period of detention.

Where a person requests an approved social worker to undertake a mental health assessment in respect of a member of that person's family, and the approved social worker concludes that an assessment for possible admission under this Act is required, the person who made the request should be informed as to the possible outcomes of the assessment: see the report of the Local Government Ombudsman into complaint No. 97/A/2239. In his report into complaint No. 97/A/1082, the Ombudsman found maladministration in a case where: (1) a family had been given inadequate notice of a planned assessment of a patient for possible admission under this Act; and (2) no less than three home care staff were present when the assessment took place.

Before making an application: The interview required by this provision can take place more than 14 days before the application, provided that the approved social worker has confirmed his conclusion that an application is necessary by having face to face contact with the patient within 14 days of the application as required by section 11(5): *Re Whitbread* (*Mental Patient: Habeas Corpus*), 39 B.M.L.R. 94, 1997 CA, which is considered in the notes to section 11(4)(5).

Hospital: This subsection does not apply to guardianship applications. A recommending doctor has responsibility for ensuring that a hospital bed is available for the patient (*Code of Practice*, 2.22d).

Interview: The approved social worker should explain the purpose of interview to the patient who should ordinarily be given the opportunity of speaking to the approved social worker alone (*Code of Practice* para. 2.13). It is submitted that, in the context of this Act, an attempt by an approved social worker to communicate with a patient would be sufficient to constitute an interview and that this would be the case even if the patient was either unable or unwilling to respond. There is no obligation placed on the approved social worker to warn the patient that he or she may be the subject of a particular section (see the note on para. 2.11 of the *Code*).

An interview cannot take place with an unconscious or highly intoxicated patient. In these circumstances the doctor could use his common law powers to treat the patient, with the approved social worker intervening only when the patient recovers. If an unconscious patient requires immediate hospital treatment he could be taken to hospital under common law powers.

If the approved social worker is unable to gain access to premises in order that he might interview the person, he cannot force entry but should consider making an application to a magistrate under section 135(1).

Suitable manner: These words, which are considered in paragraph 2.12 of the *Code of Practice*, were added to this section as a result of an amendment moved at the Special Standing Committee by Mr Tom Benyon M.P. who stressed the need for those who are involved in the management of deaf psychiatric patients having either the use of an interpreter or a fluency in British Sign Language. He also drew the Committee's attention to a number of cases where patients had been compulsorily detained under the 1959 Act in circumstances where a lack of speech had been mistakenly attributed to mental disorder. Other M.P.s were concerned that approved social workers should be sensitive to the difficulties faced by members of ethnic minorities who might not speak English or who might not speak it well. The words "suitable manner" should direct the approved social worker's attention to the particular needs of all groups, including children, who might have difficulties in communicating effectively. The difficulties that face approved social workers in accessing impartial interpreters for people with mental health problems whose first language is not English are described by Joan Rapaport in "Am I making myself clear?", *Professional Social Work*, February, 2001.

Satisfy himself: The approved social worker would need to consult with others who **1–150** have been involved with the patient's welfare. Speaking of the role that approved social workers should take in compulsory admissions the Under-Secretary of State said that he would "expect the [approved social worker], the doctor and others to discuss what should be done" (Special Standing Committee, Sitting of May 27, 1982). A doctor who has made a recommendation might be reluctant to meet with the approved social worker to discuss the case and, if the case is one of sufficient urgency, the social worker might have to make an application without the benefit of a discussion with him. If an approved social worker considers that he has been forced by these circumstances to make an "improper" application he should, in the first instance, attempt to resolve the difficulty by involving relevant bodies at the local level. If the difficulties persist, the social worker should consider contacting the Mental Health Act Commission which has a duty under section 121(2)(b) to keep matters relating to the detention of patients under review.

An approved social worker should not make an application solely because a doctor has made a recommendation; he must exercise his own judgment as to whether the provisions of this section have been satisfied (*Buxton v. Jayne*, above).

All the circumstances of the case: These will include "the past history of the patient's mental disorder, his present condition and the social, familial, and personal factors bearing on it, the wishes of the patient and his relatives, and medical opinion. To do this he will need to consult all those professionally involved in the case (for example the doctor or a community psychiatric nurse) and the patient's main carer(s). In order to assess the available options the approved social worker will have to inform himself as to the availability and suitability of other means of giving the patient care and medical treatment, such as treatment as an informal patient, day care, out-patient treatment, community psychiatric nursing support, crisis intervention centres, primary health care support, local authority social services provision, and support from friends, relatives and voluntary organisations" (*Memorandum*, para. 34). The factors to be taken into account at assessment are considered in chapter 2 of the *Code of Practice*.

The most appropriate way: The approved social worker is placed under an obligation to satisfy himself of the appropriateness of detention in the light of his knowledge of the alternative forms of intervention that would be available for the patient: see the note on "all the circumstances of the case", above. He is not placed under an obligation to actively seek out alternatives before making an application.

At the Special Standing Committee (May 27, 1982), Mr David Ennals M.P. said: "My criticism of [this] formulation is that it starts from the supposition that the hospital is the most appropriate place, and then looks outward to see whether it is not. I should like to reverse that to see whether the community could provide the appropriate environment, given the circumstances of the case."

A comprehensive knowledge of local resources available for the mentally disordered is essential if an informed judgment is to be made: see the extract from paragraph 34 of the *Memorandum*, noted above. The approved social worker's view as to why there was no alternative to compulsory hospitalisation should be recorded in the client's case notes: see the Local Ombudsman's investigation into Complaint 87/B/1308, noted under subsection (1), above.

If a patient vacillates between consenting and refusing to consent to admission to hospital as an informal patient, it is suggested that the patient should be admitted informally if this is possible, with the powers contained in section 5 being used if this proves to be necessary.

Care and medical treatment: This means care and medical treatment for the patient's mental disorder, and not for a medical disorder which is unconnected with her mental condition (*St George's Healthcare NHS Trust v. S* [1998] 3 All E.R. 673, CA). It is therefore unlawful for an application to be made in circumstances where there is no intention to either assess or treat the patient's mental disorder. Despite the confirmation of the legal position given in the *St George's* case, it is the author's experience that this Act is still invoked to "authorise" the removal of mentally incompetent patients from their homes where the sole cause of concern is the patient's need for hospitalisation to treat a physical disorder. The common law provides a justification for the patient's removal to hospital in these circumstances; see the note on "The treatment of mentally incapable patients" in the General Note to Part IV.

Subsection (3)

1–151   *May:* The approved social worker is not placed under a *duty* to make an application outside the area of his appointing authority. An approved social worker may wish to make an application outside the area of his authority "if, for example, a patient is admitted informally to a hospital outside his local authority and then needs to be detained. In such a case it would be desirable for an approved social worker from the local authority in which the patient is normally resident to make the application for an assessment even though the patient is technically the responsibility of the local authority in which the hospital is situated" (*Memorandum*, para. 35). This power should only be exercised following consultation between approved social workers of the relevant authorities.

Subsection (4)

1–152   *Local social services authority:* Guidance to local authorities on their obligations under this section is set out in paragraph 2.38 of the *Code of Practice*.

Required: The communication can be either written or verbal. It might not always be clear whether a communication from a nearest relative amounts to a request to a local authority to act under the provisions of this subsection. It is submitted that if a nearest relative indicates his concern about the patient by saying, for example, that the patient "ought to be in hospital" or that "something ought to be done" about the patient, the nearest relative should be informed of his power under this subsection and asked whether he wishes to exercise it. If a local social services authority is repeatedly asked by a particular nearest relative to direct an approved social worker to consider the patient's case, the authority is not required, on each occasion when the request is made, to ensure that an approved social worker interviews the patient "in a suitable manner" to comply with subsection (1). Although such an interview is a pre-condition to the making of an application, it is not a pre-condition to "taking the case into consideration under subsection (1)". Frequent interviews could clearly be prejudicial to a patient's mental health, especially if the patient was receiving treatment for mental disorder as an informal hospital in-patient; also see the note on "take the patient's case into consideration", below.

Nearest relative: Or acting nearest relative appointed by the court under section 29. It is submitted that this provision should apply if the approach to the local authority is made by someone acting on behalf of the nearest relative, *e.g.* a general practitioner.

Patient: If the local social services authority considers that the person concerned is not "a person suffering or appearing to be suffering from mental disorder," which is the definition of "patient" in section 145(1), the provisions of this subsection will not apply.

Direct: Once the direction has been made, the approved social worker must exercise his own judgment in considering whether to make an application.

Take the patient's case into consideration: Which does not necessarily mean that the approved social worker undertakes an assessment of the patient or even interviews the patient: see the notes on "required", above, and on paragraph 2.38 of the *Code of Practice*. The effect of a nearest relative's request under this provision is to require an approved social worker to consider whether an application under this Act should be made in respect of the patient. The extent and nature of the inquiries made by the approved social worker would depend upon the knowledge that the social services department has about the patient. If the patient has been the subject of a recent mental health assessment, the approved social worker's obligation would be confined to identifying whether there has been a change in the patient's situation that would justify a reassessment. If the patient is not known to the department, the patient's general practitioner should be contacted to ascertain whether the patient is mentally disordered as the obligation under this section only arises if this is the case. It could be that the nearest relative is the mentally disordered member of the "patient's" family.

Hospital: The provision does not apply to a nearest relative who wants a guardianship application to be made.

Inform: The approved social worker should write to the nearest relative immediately after the decision not to make an application has been made. It is the approved social worker, and not the local authority, who has to inform the nearest relative. If the approved social worker decides not to make an application, the nearest relative could proceed to make an application himself if the required medical recommendation(s) had been made. If the nearest relative's application was made under either section 2 or 3 of this Act, a local authority social worker would be required to provide the hospital managers with a social circumstances report under section 14.

Reasons: Giving "reasons" need not necessarily involve the approved social worker in revealing confidential information because statements of a general nature such as "I took medical advice and was informed that Mr X is not mentally disordered within the meaning of the Mental Health Act 1983," or "Mr X agreed to enter hospital as an informal patient," or "In my opinion it is appropriate for Mr X to continue to receive treatment at home," would constitute a "reason" for the purposes of this subsection. Also see the note on "The Human Rights Act 1998", above.

Subsection (5)

Section 11(4): Which provides: (1) that the approved social worker must consult **1–153** with the patient's nearest relative before making an application for treatment or guardianship, if this is practicable; and (2) that the social worker cannot proceed if the nearest relative objects.

Social reports

14. Where a patient is admitted to a hospital in pursuance of an application **1–154** (other than an emergency application) made under this Part of this Act by his nearest relative, the managers of the hospital shall as soon as practicable give notice of that fact to the local social services authority for the area in which the patient resided immediately before his admission; and that authority shall as soon as practicable arrange for a social worker of their social services department to interview the patient and provide the managers with a report on his social circumstances.

DEFINITIONS
  patient: s.145(1). **1–155**
  hospital: ss.34(2), 145(1).

nearest relative: ss.26(3), 145(1).
the managers: s.145(1).
local social services authority: s.145(1).

GENERAL NOTE

1–156   This section places a duty on social services authorities to provide hospital managers with a report on a patient's social circumstances if the patient has been admitted to a hospital or registered establishment pursuant to an application made by his nearest relative under either section 2 or 3 of this Act.

If a patient who is the subject of a report under this section makes an application to a Mental Health Review Tribunal, the hospital managers could send the report to the tribunal if it contains material which is relevant to the tribunal's deliberations.

Other than an emergency application: It is unclear whether this section requires a social circumstances report to be made where an emergency application has been converted into a 28 day order by the addition of the second medical recommendation required by section 2 (s.4(4)). Good practice suggests that it should be.

Nearest relative: Or an acting nearest relative appointed by the County Court under section 29. It is presumably assumed that an approved social worker applicant would automatically provide the hospital with the information that would be contained in a social circumstances report.

Area in which the patient resided: This need not necessarily be the place where the patient was staying immediately prior to his admission, as temporary absences from the place where a person lives does not affect residence, as long as there is an intention to return (*R. v. St Leonard's Shoreditch (Inhabitants)* (1865) L.R. 1 Q.B. 21). Also note Widgery L.J.'s statement that "a man cannot be said to reside in a particular place unless in the ordinary sense of the word one can say that for the time being he is making his home in that place" (*Fox v. Stirk* [1970] 2 Q.B. 463, 477).

Social worker: Who need not be an approved social worker.

Interview the patient: A person who refuses to grant the social worker access to the patient commits an offence under section 129(1)(b).

Report on his social circumstances: This could include an account of the patient's family and social relationships (including the attitude of carers), his history of mental disorder, his previous contact with the local authority, his access to community resources, his employment record, his financial situation and his accommodation. The report should also contain an account of the circumstances of the admission. If the nearest relatives' application was made after an approved social worker had refused to make one, it is suggested that that social worker should prepare the report which would include an account of the reasons for his decision.

Rectification of applications and recommendations

1–157   **15.**—(1) If within the period of 14 days beginning with the day on which a patient has been admitted to a hospital in pursuance of an application for admission for assessment or for treatment the application, or any medical recommendation given for the purposes of the application, is found to be in any respect incorrect or defective, the application or recommendation may, within that period and with the consent of the managers of the hospital, be amended by the person by whom it was signed; and upon such amendment being made the application or recommendation shall have effect and shall be deemed to have had effect as if it had been originally made as so amended.

(2) Without prejudice to subsection (1) above, if within the period mentioned in that subsection it appears to the managers of the hospital that one of the two medical recommendations on which an application for the admission of a patient is founded is insufficient to warrant the detention of the patient in pursuance of the application, they may, within that period, give notice in writing to that effect to the applicant; and where any such notice is

given in respect of a medical recommendation, that recommendation shall be disregarded, but the application shall be, and shall be deemed always to have been, sufficient if—

(a) a fresh medical recommendation complying with the relevant provisions of this Part of this Act (other than the provisions relating to the time of signature and the interval between examinations) is furnished to the managers within that period; and

(b) that recommendation, and the other recommendation on which the application is founded, together comply with those provisions.

(3) Where the medical recommendations upon which an application for admission is founded are, taken together, insufficient to warrant the detention of the patient in pursuance of the application, a notice under subsection (2) above may be given in respect of either of those recommendations; but this subsection shall not apply in a case where the application is of no effect by virtue of section 11(6) above.

(4) Nothing in this section shall be construed as authorising the giving of notice in respect of an application made as an emergency application, or the detention of a patient admitted in pursuance of such an application, after the period of 72 hours referred to in section 4(4) above, unless the conditions set out in paragraphs (a) and (b) of that section are complied with or would be complied with apart from any error or defect to which this section applies.

DEFINITIONS

patient: s.145(1).   **1–158**
hospital: ss.34(2), 145(1).
application for admission for assessment: ss.2, 145(1).
application for admission for treatment: ss.3, 145(1).
the managers: s.145(1).

GENERAL NOTE

This section, which does not apply to documents issued by a court, to documents **1–159** given in support of either a patient's transfer under section 19 or the renewal of the patient's detention under section 20, or to documents relating to guardianship or supervised discharge applications, provides for admission documents which are found to be incorrect or defective to be rectified after they have been acted upon. A rectified document is treated as if it had been correctly completed at the time when it was signed. If a document which contains a minor irregularity is not rectified under subsection (1) within the 14-day period, the application is not invalidated by virtue of the *de minimis* principle.

Rectification cannot be used to enable "a fundamentally defective application to be retrospectively validated" (*per* Sir Thomas Bingham M.R. in *Re S.-C.* (*Mental Patient: Habeas Corpus*) [1996] 1 All E.R. 532, 537, CA) or to "cure a defect which arises because a necessary event in the procedural chain leading to the detention has simply not taken place at all. It is essentially concerned with correction of errors on the face of the document" (*R. v. South Western Hospital Managers, ex p. M* [1994] 1 All E.R. 161, *per* Laws J. 177). If an admission document reveals a fundamental breach of law or procedure which is incapable of rectification under this section, either the hospital managers or the patient's responsible medical officer should exercise their powers under section 23 to discharge the patient from the section; see below. If the patient is discharged he could be made the subject of a report under either section 5(2) or (4) and prevented from leaving hospital if it was considered that the appropriate requirements were satisfied; see the note on "in-patient in a hospital" in section 5(2). This advice is reproduced in an extended form in the General Note to section 6. The *Memorandum*, at paragraph 47, contains similar advice.

The Mental Health Act Commission has published a Guidance Note on "Scrutinising and Rectifying Statutory Forms for Admission under the Mental Health Act". Paragraph 5 of this document suggests that hospital managers need not discharge a patient from detention even if there has been a "clear and fundamental breach" of this Act. One of the reasons given in support of this opinion is that it "may be argued that, notwithstanding a fundamental defect, the application continues to constitute a valid authority for the patient's detention until such time as it is set aside by the court". The validity of this opinion must be doubted. The Court of Appeal, in *Re S.-C.*, above, held that the continued detention of a patient who has been the subject of fundamentally defective application is unlawful. In order to avoid a possible claim for unlawful imprisonment, hospital managers should act to regularise the patient's situation by exercising their power of discharge under section 23 as soon as the error is discovered. A fresh application could be made in respect of the patient if the relevant statutory criteria were satisfied. The *Memorandum*, at paragraph 47, states that if an application is found to be fundamentally defective "authority for the patient's detention can only be obtained through a new application".

The hospital managers should nominate an officer to undertake the task of scrutinising admission documents as soon as the patient is admitted, or, if he is already in hospital, as soon as the documents are received: see reg. 4(2) of the Mental Health (Hospital, Guardianship and Consent to Treatment) Regulations 1983. A local social services authority can nominate a person to carry out a similar function in respect of guardianship applications: *ibid.*, reg. 5(2).

As to the use of obsolete or defective forms, see the General Note to Schedule 1 to the Mental Health (Hospital, Guardianship and Consent to Treatment) Regulations 1983.

A person who wilfully makes a false entry or statement in an application commits an offence under section 126(4).

This section is considered in chapter 12 of the *Code of Practice* and by K. Keyword in "Rectification of incorrect documentation under the Mental Health Act 1983", *Journal of Forensic Psychiatry* (1996), 7:79–91.

Documents

1–160   When a patient is transferred under section 10 or 19, "the documents authorising guardianship or detention, including the authority for transfer, should be sent to the hospital or guardian to which the patient is transferred. The former hospital or guardian should retain copies of these documents" (*Memorandum*, para. 93).

Subsection (1)

1–161   *Beginning with:* Including the day on which the patient was admitted to hospital (*Hare v. Gocher* [1962] 2 Q.B. 641).

Admitted to a hospital: Or a registered establishment (s.34(2)).

Incorrect: In that had the facts been correctly stated, the admission would have been justified, *e.g.* mis-stating dates, names or places. Rectification can only be used to ensure that the relevant form reflects the factual situation that obtained when the form was completed.

Defective: Probably means that incomplete information has been provided, *e.g.* leaving a space blank, omitting to insert a date or failing to delete one or more alternatives in places where only one can be correct. It does not mean that a completed form which accurately reflects the factual situation can be altered to provide legal justification for detention.

The application or recommendation: This section does not allow for the rectification of forms used in the exercise of the holding powers provided for in section 5.

Consent of the managers: Or an officer acting on their behalf (Mental Health (Hospital, Guardianship and Consent to Treatment) Regulations 1983, reg. 4(2)).

Amended: The amended application or medical recommendation must comply with the relevant provisions of this Act.

By whom it was signed: It is submitted that an unsigned application or medical recommendation cannot be remedied under this section and that an application or medical recommendation which is signed by a person who is not empowered to do so under this Act is also incapable of rectification. This is the view adopted by the *Memorandum* at paragraph 46. A check therefore needs to be made to confirm that the application is signed by someone who appears to be an approved social worker, a nearest relative or an acting nearest relative and that the medical recommendations are signed by practitioners who are not excluded by section 12. When performing this task the scrutinising officer can take certain statements at face value: see the note on regulation 3(4) of the 1983 Regulations.

Subsection (2)
This subsection provides a remedy if *one* of the medical recommendations **1–162** required under section 2 or 3 of this Act is found to be insufficient to warrant the detention of the patient. It could be used if, for example, a doctor who gives a medical recommendation for admission for treatment on Form 11 of the 1983 Regulations fails to convince the scrutineer that he has considered other methods of care or treatment. The hospital managers must notify the applicant (not the doctor concerned) and if a fresh medical recommendation is received within 14 days of the patient's admission, the application is treated as if it had been validly made from the date when it was completed.
One of the two medical recommendations: As Eldergill has pointed out, it seems that neither this subsection nor subsection (3) allows for the remedying of a defective joint medical recommendation (A. Eldergill, *Mental Health Review Tribunals* (1997), p. 269).
Insufficient: This procedure cannot be used if the signatory is disqualified from making a recommendation by reason of section 12.
The applicant: And not to the doctor who signed the recommendation. The *Memorandum*, at paragraph 23, recommends that the doctor should be informed of the action taken.
A fresh medical recommendation: Not necessarily by the same doctor.

Subsection (3)
This subsection allows for the procedure set out in subsection (2) to be used when **1–163** both recommendations are good in themselves but taken together are insufficient.
Insufficient: If, for example, neither recommending doctor is "approved," under section 12. The fresh recommendation and the existing one taken together must comply with all the requirements of the Act (subs. (2)(b)), except the requirements about the interval between recommendations and the time of the signature (subs. (2)(a)).
No effect by virtue of section 11(6): A new recommendation under this subsection cannot be sought where an application under section 3 is defective because the recommending doctors do not agree about the form of the mental disorder from which the patient suffers.

Subsection (4)
This subsection provides that this section cannot be used to rectify an emergency **1–164** application after it has expired unless it has been "converted" under the provisions of section 4(4).

Position of patients subject to detention or guardianship

Reclassification of patients
16.—(1) If in the case of a patient who is for the time being detained in a **1–165** hospital in pursuance of an application for admission for treatment, or subject to guardianship in pursuance of a guardianship application, it

appears to the appropriate medical officer that the patient is suffering from a form of mental disorder other than the form or forms specified in the application, he may furnish to the managers of the hospital, or to the guardian, as the case may be, a report to that effect; and where a report is so furnished, the application shall have effect as if that other form of mental disorder were specified in it.

(2) Where a report under subsection (1) above in respect of a patient detained in a hospital is to the effect that he is suffering from psychopathic disorder or mental impairment but not from mental illness or severe mental impairment the appropriate medical officer shall include in the report a statement of his opinion whether further medical treatment in hospital is likely to alleviate or prevent a deterioration of the patient's condition; and if he states that in his opinion such treatment is not likely to have that effect the authority of the managers to detain the patient shall cease.

(3) Before furnishing a report under subsection (1) above the appropriate medical officer shall consult one or more other persons who have been professionally concerned with the patient's medical treatment.

(4) Where a report is furnished under this section in respect of a patient, the managers or guardian shall cause the patient and the nearest relative to be informed.

(5) In this section "appropriate medical officer" means—

(a) in the case of a patient who is subject to the guardianship of a person other than a local social services authority, the nominated medical attendant of the patient; and

(b) in any other case, the responsible medical officer.

DEFINITIONS

1–166   patient: s.145(1).
hospital: ss.34(2), 145(1).
application for admission for treatment: ss.3, 145(1).
mental disorder: ss.1, 145(1).
the managers: s.145(1).
psychopathic disorder: ss.1, 145(1).
mental impairment: ss.1, 145(1).
severe mental impairment: ss.1, 145(1).
nearest relative: ss.26(3), 145(1).
the nominated medical attendant: s.34(1).

GENERAL NOTE

1–167   This section provides for the reclassification of the stated form of mental disorder of a patient who is detained for treatment or is subject to guardianship. A far simpler method of effecting a reclassification is provided for on the renewal of the patient's detention (s.20(9)). Either the patient or his nearest relative has a right to appeal to a Mental Health Review Tribunal within 28 days of a report under this section being furnished by the appropriate medical officer (s.66(1)(d) (2)(d)). A tribunal has the power to reclassify a patient under section 72(5). The tribunal can use this power even if the application is made subsequent to the patient being reclassified under this section.

A doctor who disagrees with the decision of a tribunal to reclassify a patient cannot immediately exercise his power under this section to reverse the tribunal's decision in the absence of some change in circumstance. For a change in circumstance to justify the use of this section in this situation the change must be "of a significant kind which would enable a tribunal to take a different view if the matter was referred to them again. That may be because of further evidence that has emerged about the patient, and it may be because of further information that is available to the doctor who has the responsibility of the patient which was not available to him before he gave evidence to the tribunal, and of which therefore the tribunal was deprived." If a doctor found himself in the position where he did not think that the decision of the tribunal could properly be sustained, the remedy was for the doctor or the NHS Trust to apply for judicial review of the decision of the tribunal (*R. v. Pathfinder NHS Trust, ex p. W* [2000] 3 C.C.L.R. 271, Kay J.).

This section applies to patients who have been made subject to hospital or guardianship orders by a court under section 37, subject to the modification that in subsection (1) for references to an application for admission or a guardianship application there shall be substituted references to the order or direction under Part III of this Act by virtue of which the patient is liable to be detained or subject to guardianship (Sched. 1, Pt 1, paras 2, 3). It does not apply to restricted patients (Sched. 1, Pt II).

The procedure for the reclassification of patients under this section is set out in regulation 6 of the Mental Health (Hospital, Guardianship and Consent to Treatment) Regulations 1983.

Subsection (1)

Subject to guardianship: The reclassification of a guardianship patient has no legal **1–168** effect because section 7 makes no distinction between the various categories of mental disorder.

Appropriate medical officer: Is defined in subsection (5). He is placed under an obligation to consult before furnishing a report (subs. (3)).

A form of mental disorder other than the form or forms specified: If a patient is classified as suffering from two categories of mental disorder, there is no obligation to reclassify the patient by deleting reference to the category of disorder from which the patient continues to suffer but which would not on its own justify detention because, for example, the disorder is not of a nature or degree which makes it appropriate for him to receive treatment (*R. v. Anglia and Oxfordshire Mental Health Review Tribunal, ex p. Hagen* [2000] C.O.D. 352, CA).

He may furnish: Using either Form 22 or 23 set out in Schedule 1 of the 1983 Regulations. If the doctor who makes a report under section 20, renewing the authority to detain a patient or keep him subject to guardianship, states in his report that the patient is suffering from a form of mental disorder other than that specified on the original application, this has the effect of automatically reclassifying the patient (s.20(9)).

In the Scottish case of *Milborrow, Applicant*, 1996 S.C.L.R. 315, Sh.Ct, it was held that a report is "furnished" to the hospital managers when it is committed to the internal mailing system operated by those managers: see the note on section 5(2).

Shall have effect as if that other form of mental disorder were specified in it: Thus a patient's mental disorder could be reclassified more than once.

Subsection (2)

This subsection provides that where a patient's diagnosis has been changed from **1–169** either mental illness or severe mental impairment to either psychopathic disorder or mental impairment and a report to that effect has been made under subsection (1), the authority to detain the patient terminates unless the patient's responsible medical officer certifies that further medical treatment in hospital is likely to alleviate or prevent a deterioration of the patient's condition.

Detained in a hospital: This subsection does not apply to patients who are subject to guardianship.

Likely to alleviate or prevent a deterioration: For comment on this "treatability test" for psychopathic and mentally impaired patients, see the notes on section 3(2)(b).

Subsection (3)

1–170   *Consult:* "[T]he essence of consultation is the communication of a genuine invitation to give advice and a genuine consideration of that advice"; *per* Webster J. in *R. v. Secretary of State for Social Services, ex p. Association of Metropolitan Authorities* [1986] 1 All E.R. 164 at 167.

One or more other persons: Although Parliamentarians who spoke on this provision, which derives from the 1982 Act, referred to it in terms of placing a duty on the appropriate medical officer to consult with professionals from *other* disciplines, the wording of this subsection is such that the duty could be discharged by the medical officer consulting with other medical practitioners who have been involved with the patient's treatment.

Professionally concerned: In respect of a patient who is being treated in hospital, it is submitted that it is not sufficient for the person consulted merely to have been working on the ward where the patient is being treated: he or she must have had a particular involvement with the patient's treatment.

Subsection (4)

1–171   *Nearest relative:* Or acting nearest relative appointed by the county court under section 29.

Leave of absence from hospital

1–172   **17.**—(1) The responsible medical officer may grant to any patient who is for the time being liable to be detained in a hospital under this Part of this Act leave to be absent from the hospital subject to such conditions (if any) as that officer considers necessary in the interests of the patient or for the protection of other persons.

(2) Leave of absence may be granted to a patient under this section either indefinitely or on specified occasions or for any specified period; and where leave is so granted for a specified period, that period may be extended by further leave granted in the absence of the patient.

(3) Where it appears to the responsible medical officer that it is necessary so to do in the interests of the patient or for the protection of other persons, he may, upon granting leave of absence under this section, direct that the patient remain in custody during his absence; and where leave of absence is so granted the patient may be kept in the custody of any officer on the staff of the hospital, or of any other person authorised in writing by the managers of the hospital or, if the patient is required in accordance with conditions imposed on the grant of leave of absence to reside in another hospital, of any officer on the staff of that other hospital.

(4) In any case where a patient is absent from a hospital in pursuance of leave of absence granted under this section, and it appears to the responsible medical officer that it is necessary so to do in the interests of the patient's health or safety or for the protection of other persons, that officer may, subject to subsection (5) below, by notice in writing given to the patient or to the person for the time being in charge of the patient, revoke the leave of absence and recall the patient to the hospital.

(5) A patient to whom leave of absence is granted under this section shall not be recalled under subsection (4) above after he has ceased to be liable to be detained under this Part of this Act; [...].

AMENDMENT

In subs. (5) the words omitted were repealed by the Mental Health (Patients in the Community) Act 1995, s.3(1).

DEFINITIONS

DEFINITIONS
    patient: s.145(1).   **1–173**
    hospital: ss.34(2), 145(1).
    absent without leave: ss.18(6), 145(1).
    responsible medical officer: s.34(1).

GENERAL NOTE
    This section provides for a patient to be granted leave of absence from the hospital **1–174**
in which he is liable to be detained for a specified or for an indefinite period and
subject to such conditions as are considered to be necessary. It provides the only
lawful authority for a detained patient to be absent from the hospital where he is
detained. A patient who has been granted leave of absence under this section
continues to be "liable to be detained" and is therefore subject to the consent to
treatment provisions in Part IV of the Act (s.56(1)). The *Code of Practice* states that
the patient should be recalled to hospital if it becomes necessary to treat him without
his consent (para. 20.8). A section 3 patient who has been granted leave under this
section can have his detention renewed under section 20 if his responsible medical
officer considers that there is a legitimate in-patient element to his treatment (*R. v.
BHB Community Healthcare NHS Trust, ex p. Barker*, noted under s.20(4)(c)).
    Further provisions relating to ground access, leave of absence and the escorting of
patients from Ashworth, Broadmoor and Rampton Hospitals can be found in the
Safety and Security in Ashworth, Broadmoor and Rampton Hospitals Directions
2000. These Directions, which were made by the Secretary of State for Health under
sections 16D, 17 and 126(4) of the National Health Service Act 1997 and section 4(5)
of the Regulation of Investigatory Powers Act 2000, can be found at
http:/www.doh.gov.uk/hospitaldirections/.
    A patient who has been granted leave of absence to reside in the community has
been discharged *from the hospital* for the purposes of the social security legislation,
although he has not been discharged *from the section* that provides the authority for
his continued liability to be detained.
    The duty to provide aftercare services applies to a patient on leave of absence (see
the note on "cease to be detained" in s.117(1)) and such a patient can be the subject of
an application for supervised discharge (s.25A(9)).
    Advice on this section is contained in chapter 20 of the *Code of Practice* and in the
Mental Health Act Commission's Guidance Note "Issues Surrounding Sections 17,
18 and 19 of the Mental Health Act 1983". Attached to the Guidance Note is a sample
"Record of Granting Section 17 Leave of Absence".
    A patient who has been granted leave of absence under this section cannot receive
direct payments under the terms of the Community Care (Direct Payments) Act 1996
(Community Care (Direct Payments) Regulations 1997 (S.I. 1997 No. 734), reg. 2).
    Paragraph 9.1(g) of Department of Health Circular HSC 1999/222 states that staff
should "be aware of the child protection and child welfare issues in granting leave of
absence under [this section]."
    It is an offence to induce or help a patient absent himself without leave or to
harbour or prevent a patient being returned to hospital (s.128).
    For a retrospective case study of the use of this section over a 10-year period, see J.
Milton "Section 17 of the Mental Health Act" (1998) 22 *Psychiatric Bulletin*,
415–418.
    This section applies without modification to patients who have been made subject
to hospital or guardianship orders by a court under section 37 (Sched. 1, Pt 1, para. 1).
It also applies, with subsections (1), (4) and (5) modified as set out below, to patients
who are subject to special restrictions (Sched. 1, Pt II, paras 2, 3):

    "(1) The responsible medical officer may [with the consent of the Secretary of
    State] grant to any patient who is for the time being liable to be detained in a
    hospital under this Part of this Act leave to be absent from the hospital subject to

such conditions (if any) as that officer considers necessary in the interests of the patient or for the protection of other persons."

"(4) In any case where a patient is absent from a hospital in pursuance of leave of absence granted under this section, and it appears to the responsible medical officer [or the Secretary of State] that it is necessary so to do in the interests of the patient's health or safety or for the protection of other persons, that officer [or the Secretary of State] may, subject to subs. (5) below, by notice in writing given to the patient or to the person for the time being in charge of the patient, revoke the leave of absence and recall the patient to the hospital."

"(5) A patient to whom leave of absence is granted under this section shall not be recalled [by the responsible medical officer] under subs. (4) above after [the expiration of the period of [twelve] months beginning with the first day of his absence on leave]."

The transfer of patients between hospitals

1–175   It is lawful to use this section to grant a patient "trial leave" to a hospital other than the one in which he is formally detained (subs. (3)). Such leave can be useful step in a patient's rehabilitation programme. In these circumstances the consultant at the base hospital continues to be the patient's responsible medical officer. Although day-to-day functions relating to the care of the patient can be delegated to a consultant at the second hospital, the responsibilities of the responsible medical officer to renew the patient's detention and to issue certificates under Part IV of this Act cannot be delegated. If the trial leave is successful the patient could then be transferred to the second hospital under section 19.

The Department of Health recommends, in circular HSG(96) 28, that where an unrestricted patient is to move from one hospital to another he should be transferred at the outset under section 19 rather than using the provisions of this section. The rationale for this recommendation is that by using section 19 "the managers and medical staff at the second hospital will clearly assume responsibility for the patient and there will be no need to agree treatment and other matters with the responsible medical officer at the first hospital". It is suggested that this advice should not be followed if the patient's stay in the second hospital is likely to be of limited duration. The Mental Health Commission's Guidance Note, noted above, suggests that leave of absence should also be used "where a patient is progressing to a unit with lesser security and leave is used for a time to assess their suitability for this environment" (para. 7).

The Human Rights Act 1998

1–176   A patient who has been granted leave of absence under this section continues to be "detained" for the purposes of Article 5 of the European Convention on Human Rights: see *L. v. Sweden*, app. no. 10801/84, noted under the heading "detention" in the note on Article 5(1)(e). In this case the European Commission held that the granting of leave of absence with a condition that the patient accepts medication will not contravene the Convention if one of the grounds in Article 8(2) is satisfied. The principles that apply when determining whether an interference under Article 8(2) is justified have been articulated by Hale L.J. in *Re W. & B. (Children): Re W. (Children)* [2001] EWCA Civ 747 and by Newman J. in *R. (on the application of N.) v. Ashworth Special Hospital Authority and the Secretary of State for Health* [2001] EWHC Admin 339: see the notes on Article 8(2).

Subsection (1)

1–177   *The responsible medical officer may grant:* The permission of the Home Secretary is required for restricted patients: see the General Note to this section and the notes on section 41(3)(c)(i). The granting of leave of absence for patients detained at

Ashworth, Broadmoor and Rampton Hospitals must be preceded by a risk assessment by the responsible medical officer and a recommendation by the hospital's security director (Safety and Security in Ashworth, Broadmoor and Rampton Hospitals Directions 2000, para. 33).

The responsible medical officer does not have the power to delegate his functions under this section and the exercise of his discretion cannot be fettered by either the hospital managers or the hospital management. There is no appeal from the responsible medical officer's decision. The advice of the Mental Health Act Commission on the procedure to be adopted on the granting of leave of absence is contained in the following extract from paragraph 9.7 of its *Fourth Biennial Report*, 1989–1991: "Leave of absence from hospital under section 17 is often a major component of rehabilitation programmes. Such leave may cover periods of absence from a single night up to [a year]. Short term absences of only a few hours also feature extensively in treatment plans and are sometimes regarded as a form of parole arranged at ward level in the hospital. The Act, however, describes leave of absence without mention of its duration whilst its granting is the prerogative solely of the responsible medical officer. The occurrence of any untoward incidents during absence from hospital could raise the question of its planning and authorisation. On the other hand the requirement to obtain responsible medical officer agreement for every activity outside the hospital would seriously curtail any patient's involvement in the social programme and other rehabilitative activities which are often arranged at short notice by ward staff. The recommendation of the Commission is that all absences from hospital should be regarded as constituting leave with a need for responsible medical officer authorisation but that such leave should be agreed periodically, the weekly multi-disciplinary conference being an ideal occasion, with a written statement of the maximum licence that is granted for a defined period and with any related conditions. Staff implementing the treatment programme would then be free to arrange absences from hospital within the known limits and without need to obtain further more detailed authorisations." A similar proposal involving the drawing up of a "protocol" for the granting of leave to each patient is made by L. Blom-Cooper *et al.* in *The Falling Shadow*, 1995, at p. 138. The Mental Health Act Commission states that the patient's responsible medical officer "may instruct nursing staff not to implement any authorised leave on medical grounds at their discretion" (MHAC, *Sixth Biennial Report*, para. 9.4).

Any patient who is ... liable to be detained: The frequently expressed opinion that it is not lawful to grant leave under this section to a patient who is liable to be detained under section 2 is erroneous. A patient who has been detained under section 5(2) cannot be granted leave of absence because such a patient does not have a responsible medical officer: see the definition of responsible medical officer in section 34(1).

Leave to be absent: There is no legal obligation to obtain the patient's consent to the leave. "Leave of absence can be given either for a temporary absence, or on a specific occasion, after which the patient is expected to return to hospital, or as a period of trial of the patient's suitability for discharge" (*Memorandum*, para. 67). Leave of absence can be used to enable a patient to receive treatment for a physical disorder in a general hospital or to move a patient presenting severe management problems from a district hospital to a regional secure unit. This latter practice has been criticised by the Mental Health Act Commission: see the Commission's *Fourth Biennial Report* 1989–1991, para. 9.7 and *Sixth Biennial Report*, 1993–1995, at para. 9.4. Also see, A.J.B. James *et al.*, "Minimum and medium security—the interface: use of section 17 trial leave" (1996) 20 *Psychiatric Bulletin*, 201–204.

From the hospital: Which is the hospital named in the application or order which provides authority for the patient's detention. With the exception of a restricted patient who is detained in a named hospital unit (see the note on "such hospital as may be prescribed" in s.45A(3)) and a patient who moves between high security psychiatric services and other services provided at the same hospital (s.145(1AA)), leave is not required for the patient to move from one hospital building to another or to have access to the grounds of the hospital; also see paragraph 20.1 of the *Code of Practice*. A decision to allow the patient to leave the ward area, but not the hospital, is a clinical decision that should be made following a risk assessment. Every absence from the hospital, however brief, requires leave to be given under this section.

A particular difficulty has arisen where a single hospital site contains a psychiatric and a general facility and the two facilities are administered by different NHS Trusts. In this situation, should a detained patient who needs treatment for a physical disorder at the general facility be sent to that facility under the authority of section 17 leave? As this Act was not drafted in contemplation of NHS trusts the answer to this question is not easy to determine.

An argument against granting the patient formal leave of absence is that leave under this section is leave from the *hospital* and not from the NHS trust. The definition of hospital in section 145 refers back to the National Health Service Act 1977 which, in section 128 of that Act, defines a hospital as, *inter alia*, "any institution for the reception and treatment of persons suffering from illness". This definition is very broad. It is submitted that a collection of buildings located on a common site which are used for the treatment of patients constitute a single "hospital", even though the buildings might be managed by different NHS trusts. On this argument, how can a patient be granted leave of absence *from* the hospital if he does not leave the hospital site?

An argument in favour of granting leave is that if the patient moves from a part of the hospital that is managed by the NHS trust that is detaining him to a part of the hospital that is managed by another NHS trust, the staff of that other trust would not be authorised to detain him. This is because the application for the patient's detention would not have been addressed to the Hospital Managers of that other trust: see the General Note to section 6. It would seem that the appropriate way to respond to this unsatisfactory situation is to avoid any element of doubt in the minds of the staff of the non-detaining trust by moving the patient to the premises of that trust under the authority of a leave of absence.

The view of the Mental Health Act Commission "is that where there is more than one Trust on a hospital site, section 17 leave will not be required to move from one Trust to another but such authority will be required to leave the hospital site" (MHAC Guidance Note, noted above). Eldergill's opinion is that section 17 leave is required in these circumstances. He argues that "where two or more NHS Trusts manage different parts of an institution which is a hospital for the purposes of the National Health Services Act 1997, each separately managed part is a hospital for the purposes of the admission, detention and discharge provisions of the Mental Health Act 1983" (A. Eldergill, *Mental Health Review Tribunals* (1998), p. 141).

Leave of absence cannot be given to a patient to reside at a separately located residential unit which is staffed by nurses and is managed by the same NHS Trust that manages the hospital where the patient is detained. In these circumstances the legal position of the patient is that he remains an in-patient of the hospital; also see the note on "discharge" in section 73(1).

Conditions: For example, to live with a particular person or at a specified place, to be a patient at another hospital (see subs. (3)), to receive visits from a social worker and to attend for medical treatment.

Section 2(3)(b) of the Care Standards Act 2000 requires all establishments that can accept people who are "liable to be detained" under this Act to be registered as an independent hospital under that Act. However, in order to allow patients who have been granted leave under this section to be provided with care and accommodation in a registered care home, section 2(6) of the Act exempts anyone on such leave from the definition of "liable to be detained". A condition of leave requiring a patient to reside in a registered care home is therefore lawful.

Subsection (2)

Specified occasions: Such as visits to the patient's home or shopping expeditions. **1–178** The responsible medical officer should consider whether a condition that the patient be escorted should be attached to such leave.

Extended: Leave can be extended in the absence of the patient from the hospital.

Subsection (3)

This subsection "states that the responsible medical officer may direct that the **1–179** patient must remain in custody during his leave if it is necessary in the interest of the patient or for the protection of other persons. The patient may be kept in the custody of an officer on the staff of the hospital or of any other person authorised in writing by the managers of the hospital. These kinds of arrangement would allow detained patients to have escorted leave for outings, to attend other hospitals for treatment, or to have home visits on compassionate grounds. If a patient is granted leave of absence on condition that he stays in another hospital, he may be kept in the custody of any officer on the staff of the other hospital" (*Memorandum*, para. 68).

Remain in custody: If the patient escapes from such custody he can be re captured immediately: there is no need to wait for him to fail to return to his "base" hospital. For provisions relating to the powers of the person having custody of the patient, see sections 137 and 138.

Officer on the staff of the hospital: "Officer" is not defined in this Act and could include an employee who is neither a nurse nor a doctor.

Subsection (4)

This subsection provides for the revocation of leave of absence. Leave of absence **1–180** may only be revoked and the patient recalled to hospital when it is necessary in the interests of his health or safety or for the protection of other persons *that he again becomes an in-patient*. It is therefore unlawful to recall a patient to hospital to facilitate the renewal of the patient's detention under section 20 (*R. v. Hallstrom, ex p. W; R. v. Gardner, ex p. L* [1986] 2 All E.R. 306). A patient who is on leave of absence can have his detention renewed under s.20 if his treatment programme contains an element of in-patient care (*B v. Barking Havering and Brentwood Community Healthcare NHS Trust*, noted under section 20(4)(c)).

The Mental Health Act Commission interprets this provision "as meaning that it had been medically established and confirmed that the patient's mental state was such as to justify his compulsory hospitalisation (*Winterwerp v. The Netherlands* (1979, 2 E.H.R.R. 387)" (House of Commons Health Committee, Fifth Report, Community Supervision Orders, Vol. II, p. 19).

Revoke: Leave of absence can only be revoked if the provisions of this subsection can be satisfied. The Mental Health Act Commission has stated that it "may therefore be unlawful to resolve leave and recall a patient solely for the administration of treatment without consent or for the procedures under section 58 to be carried out" (Fourth Biennial Report 1989–1991, para. 6.10). The recall of a patient for the purpose of administering treatment would be lawful in the following circumstances. If receiving treatment is a condition of the patient's leave of absence, a breach of that condition should trigger a review of the patient's situation. A recall could result from that review if the responsible medical officer considered that the patient needed a further period of in-patient treatment on the ground that such action was in the interests of the patient's health or safety, or was for the protection of other persons.

Subsection (5)

This subsection provides that a patient cannot be recalled to hospital after a period **1–181** of 12 months has elapsed since the first day of leave or the authority to detain lapses, whichever is the earlier. In other words, the maximum period of leave that can be granted to a patient is the unexpired term of his current period of detention. Prior to its amendment by the Mental Health (Patients in the Community) Act 1995, this provision limited leave of absence to a maximum period of six months. Although the Department of Health's Internal Review was clear that the removal of the six-month limit "would be a simple change giving useful flexibility to ensure the continuation of care after patients were discharged", they recognised that "it will not achieve this by itself". It recommended "that extended leave is operated (even if the conditions remain formally subject to the RMO's discretion) in accordance with the principles of the care programme approach. In particular ... there should always be a named key worker and a clear treatment plan negotiated with the patient and agreed with the other professionals and agencies concerned. It can *never* be acceptable for leave to be allowed to lapse without proper provision having been made for follow-up care" (Legal Powers on the Care of Mentally Ill People in the Community, 1993, para. 8.9).

A restricted patient can be recalled by his responsible medical officer at any time up to 12 months from the first day of his absence on leave. The Home Secretary can recall such a patient at any time (see the General Note to this section).

Return and readmission of patients absent without leave

1–182   **18.**—(1) Where a patient who is for the time being liable to be detained under this Part of this Act in a hospital—

(a) absents himself from the hospital without leave granted under section 17 above; or

(b) fails to return to the hospital on any occasion on which, or at the expiration of any period for which, leave of absence was granted to him under that section, or upon being recalled under that section; or

(c) absents himself without permission from any place where he is required to reside in accordance with conditions imposed on the grant of leave of absence under that section,

he may, subject to the provisions of this section, be taken into custody and returned to the hospital or place by any approved social worker, by any officer on the staff of the hospital, by any constable, or by any person authorised in writing by the managers of the hospital.

(2) Where the place referred to in paragraph (c) of subsection (1) above is a hospital other than the one in which the patient is for the time being liable to be detained, the references in that subsection to an officer on the staff of the hospital and the managers of the hospital shall respectively include references to an officer on the staff of the first-mentioned hospital and the managers of that hospital.

(3) Where a patient who is for the time being subject to guardianship under this Part of this Act absents himself without the leave of the guardian from the place at which he is required by the guardian to reside, he may, subject to the provisions of this section, be taken into custody and returned to that place by any officer on the staff of a local social services authority, by any constable, or by any person authorised in writing by the guardian or a local social services authority.

[(4) A patient shall not be taken into custody under this section after the later of—

(a) the end of the period of six months beginning with the first day of his absence without leave; and

(b) the end of the period for which (apart from section 21 below) he is liable to be detained or subject to guardianship;

and, in determining for the purposes of paragraph (b) above or any other provision of this Act whether a person who is or has been absent without leave is at any time liable to be detained or subject to guardianship, a report furnished under section 20 or 21B below before the first day of his absence without leave shall not be taken to have renewed the authority for his detention or guardianship unless the period of renewal began before that day.]

(5) A patient shall not be taken into custody under this section if the period for which he is liable to be detained is that specified in section 2(4), 4(4) or 5(2) or (4) above and that period has expired.

(6) In this Act "absent without leave" means absent from any hospital or other place and liable to be taken into custody and returned under this section, and related expressions shall be construed accordingly.

AMENDMENT

Subs. (4) was substituted by the Mental Health (Patients in the Community) Act 1995, s.2(1).

DEFINITIONS

patient: s.145(1).   **1–183**
hospital: ss.34(2), 145(1).
approved social worker: s.145(1).
the managers: s.145(1).
local social services authority: s.145(1).

GENERAL NOTE

This section, which should be read with sections 21, 21A and 21B, identifies the **1–184** action that can be taken when a detained patient or a patient subject to guardianship absents himself without leave. A patient who has been admitted for treatment (s.3) or received into guardianship (s.7) can be taken into custody at any time up to six months from the date on which he absconded or, if later, the end of the existing authority for his detention in hospital or guardianship (subs. 4). A patient who has been detained under one of the short term provisions of this Act cannot be taken into custody after the authority to detain him has expired (subs. (5)). Guidance on this section is contained in chapter 21 of the *Code of Practice*.

Sube Banerjee *et al.* in *Deaths of Detained Patients: A Review of Reports to the Mental Health Act Commission*, Mental Health Foundation, 1995, express concern at their finding that "a high proportion of sudden deaths occurred after the patient had absconded from hospital (41 per cent of probable suicides; 30 per cent of accidental deaths). Patients often died within a very short time of leaving. Probably in many cases the patient absconded with a specific intention of self harm" (p. 25). The authors state that units "with a high level of absconding are advised to review both the physical environment and care policies" and that there "is no value in waiting several hours to see if the patient returns voluntarily; a detained patient's absence should trigger a search at once" (p. 26). Also see the Mental Health Act Commission's report *Deaths of Detained Patients in England and Wales* (2001). In the opinion of the Butler Committee "absconding often results either from mistaken diagnosis leading to inappropriate disposal to the hospital system or from the patient's inability to accept and co-operate in treatment" (*Butler Committee*, para. 14.14).

Those persons who have the power under subsection (1) to return the absconder to hospital are not provided with a power under this section to force entry onto premises where the absconder is staying. If a power of entry is needed an application should be made under section 135(2) of this Act for a warrant authorising a policeman to enter the premises to remove the patient or, alternatively, the police might be able to use their powers under section 17(1)(d) of the Police and Criminal Evidence Act 1984; see the General Note to section 135.

It is an offence for a person to induce or knowingly to assist a detained patient to absent himself without leave, knowingly to harbour the patient whilst he is at large, or to help the patient to avoid being retaken (s.128). The patient who absents himself without leave does not thereby commit an offence (*R. v. Criminal Injuries Compensation Board, ex p. Lawton* [1972] 3 All E.R. 582, *per* Lord Widgery C.J., at 584).

This section applies to patients who have been placed under hospital or guardianship orders by a court under section 37 with the modification that subsection (5) shall be omitted (Sched. 1, Pt 1, paras 2, 4). For patients who are subject to special restrictions subsections (3), (4) and (5) shall be omitted and in subsection (1) the words "subject to the provisions of this section" shall be omitted (Sched. 1, Pt II, paras 2, 4). This section also applies to patients who have been sentenced and who remain liable to be detained by virtue of section 22 (s.22(2)(b)).

Subsection (1)

1–185   This subsection and subsection (2) do not apply to patients under guardianship.

Absents himself from ... hospital: For a description of the response of hospitals and the police following a patient absconding from a psychiatric hospital, see B. Andoh, "Hospital and Police Procedure when a Patient Absconds from a Mental Hospital" (1994) 34 Med.Sci.Law 130–136.

Taken: The patient may be taken into custody in, and returned to England or Wales from, any other part of the United Kingdom or the Channel Islands or the Isle of Man (s.88).

Returned: The patient must have absented himself from the hospital or place where he is required to reside.

Custody ... officer on the staff of the hospital: See the notes on section 17(3).

Authorised in writing: The authorisation can be transmitted by fax.

Subsection (2)

1–186   This subsection provides that if a patient has been granted leave of absence on condition that he resides in a hospital other than the one in which he is formally liable to be detained, he can be taken into custody by an officer on the staff of the hospital where he is on leave, or by a person authorised by the managers of that hospital.

Subsection (3)

1–187   *Taken into custody:* If access to the patient is denied consideration will have to be given to obtaining a warrant under section 135(2): see the General Note to this section.

Returned to that place: There is no power to take the patient to a new place of residence.

Officer on the staff of the local social services authority: Who should, but need not be a social worker.

Subsection (4)

1–188   The Parliamentary Under-Secretary of State for Health, Mr John Bowis M.P., explained the rationale for this provision (*Hansard*, H.C., Vol. 262, col. 164):

> "[It] ends a loophole in the 1983 Act relating to the return to hospital, or guardianship, of ... patients who are absent without leave. Restricted patients who abscond can be returned to hospital at any time, but under section 18(4), as it stands, an unrestricted patient who is not returned within 28 days simply ceases to be liable to be detained—regardless of the state of his or her mental health or the original period of detention. That is clearly unsatisfactory, so the Bill provides for an unrestricted patient to be returned to hospital or

guardianship at any time up to six months from going absent without leave, or within the existing period of detention or guardianship if that is longer. Where a patient is returned after more than 28 days, his or her condition must be reassessed by the RMO. The new limits improve the protection given by the Act to detained patients and the public while taking proper account of patients' civil liberties."

The reference to the existing state of the law as representing a "loophole" or being an "anachronism" (*per* Baroness Cumberlege, *Hansard*, H.L., Vol. 562, col. 936) is hardly appropriate because the use of such language gives the impression that the provisions that this amendment replaced, which had their origins in the Lunacy Act 1890, remained on the statute book as a result of governmental and legislative oversight. In fact, arguments for amending the pre-existing law were examined in *A Review of the Mental Health Act 1959*, DHSS, 1976 at paragraphs 10.4 to 10.6, and both the 28 day period and the fact that it applied both to patients who had been detained for treatment and to hospital order patients were considered in detail in the White Paper, *Review of the Mental Health Act 1959*, Cmnd. 7320, at paragraphs 8.18 to 8.24. At that time the Government concluded that arguments in favour of the existing law outweighed arguments for change.

Shall not be taken into custody: But see subsection (5). A patient who is subject to restrictions can be retaken at any time: see the General Note to this section.

Beginning with the first day of his absence without leave: Including the first day of the patient's absence without leave (*Hare v. Gocher* [1962] 2 Q.B. 641). The effect of this provision is that the patient could be retaken long after the expiration of his period of detention or guardianship.

Shall not be taken to have renewed the authority: If at the time when the person goes absent the authority for detention of guardianship has been renewed, but the new period has yet to begin, the renewal is ignored and the sixth month limit for returning the patient applies.

Subsection (5)

This subsection provides that a patient cannot be taken into custody under this **1–189** section if the period of his detention under one of the following powers has expired: admission for assessment (s.2(4)), emergency admission (s.4(4)), or the detention of an in-patient by a doctor (s.5(2)) or nurse (s.5(4)).

Regulations as to transfer of patients

19.—(1) In such circumstances and subject to such conditions as may be **1–190** prescribed by regulations made by the Secretary of State—

(a) a patient who is for the time being liable to be detained in a hospital by virtue of an application under this Part of this Act may be transferred to another hospital or into the guardianship of a local social services authority or of any person approved by such an authority;

(b) a patient who is for the time being subject to the guardianship of a local social services authority or other person by virtue of an application under this Part of this Act may be transferred into the guardianship of another local social services authority or person, or be transferred to a hospital.

(2) Where a patient is transferred in pursuance of regulations under this section, the provisions of this Part of this Act (including this subsection) shall apply to him as follows, that is to say—

(a) in the case of a patient who is liable to be detained in a hospital by virtue of an application for admission for assessment or for treatment and is transferred to another hospital, as if the application were an application for admission to that other hospital and as if the patient had been admitted to that other hospital at the time when he was originally admitted in pursuance of the application;

(b) in the case of a patient who is liable to be detained in a hospital by virtue of such an application and is transferred into guardianship, as if the application were a guardianship application duly accepted at the said time;

(c) in the case of a patient who is subject to guardianship by virtue of a guardianship application and is transferred into the guardianship of another authority or person, as if the application were for his reception into the guardianship of that authority or person and had been accepted at the time when it was originally accepted;

(d) in the case of a patient who is subject to guardianship by virtue of a guardianship application and is transferred to a hospital, as if the guardianship application were an application for admission to that hospital for treatment and as if the patient had been admitted to the hospital at the time when the application was originally accepted.

(3) Without prejudice to subsections (1) and (2) above, any patient, who is for the time being liable to be detained under this Part of this Act in a hospital vested in the Secretary of State for the purposes of his functions under the National Health Service Act 1977 or any accommodation used under Part I of that Act by the managers of such a hospital [or in a hospital vested in a National Health Service trust] [or Primary Care Trust], may at any time be removed to any other such hospital or accommodation [which is managed by the managers of, or is vested in the National Health Service trust [or Primary Care Trust] for, the first-mentioned hospital]; and paragraph (a) of subsection (2) above shall apply in relation to a patient so removed as it applies in relation to a patient transferred in pursuance of regulations made under this section.

(4) Regulations made under this section may make provision for regulating the conveyance to their destination of patients authorised to be transferred or removed in pursuance of the regulations or under subsection (3) above.

AMENDMENTS

In subs. (3) the words in square brackets were inserted and substituted by the National Health Service and Community Care Act 1990, s.66(1), Sched. 9, para. 24(2). The references to Primary Care Trusts were inserted by the Health Act 1999 (Supplementary, Consequential, etc., Provisions) Order 2000 (S.I. 2000 No. 90) Sched. 1, para. 16(3).

DEFINITIONS

1–191   patient: s.145(1).
hospital: ss.34(2), 145(1).
local social services authority: s.145(1).
application for admission for assessment: ss.2, 145(1).
application for admission for treatment: ss.3, 145(1).
the managers: s.145(1).

GENERAL NOTE

1–192   This section empowers the Secretary of State (or, in relation to Wales, the National Assembly for Wales (S.I. 1999 No. 672, art. 2, Sched. 1)) to regulate the circumstances in which detained patients and patients who are subject to guardianship may be transferred between hospitals or guardians or between detention in hospital and guardianship. The patient's nearest relative, who has the power to discharge the patient from either detention or guardianship, should "normally be consulted before a patient is transferred to another hospital or to guardianship, and he should be notified when the transfer has taken place" (*Memorandum*, para. 84). The Government has recommended that this section, rather than section 17, should be used where it is intended to move an unrestricted detained patient from one hospital to another, unless he can be discharged and can continue as an informal patient: see the General Note to section 17 under the heading "The transfer of patients between hospitals".

This section applies to patients who are subject to hospital or guardianship orders made by a court under section 37, with the modification that subsection (2) shall read as follows:

"(2) Where a patient is transferred in pursuance of regulations under this section, the provisions of this Part of this Act (including this subsection) shall apply to him [as if the order or direction under Part III of this Act by virtue of which he was liable to be detained or subject to guardianship before being transferred were an order or direction for his admission or removal to the hospital to which he is transferred, or placing him under the guardianship of the authority or person into whose guardianship he is transferred, as the case may be]." (Sched. 1, Pt 1, paras 2, 5.)

For restricted patients subsections (1), (2) and (3) shall read as follows:

"(1) In such circumstances and subject to such conditions as may be prescribed by regulations made by the Secretary of State—
  (a) a patient who is for the time being liable to be detained in a hospital by virtue of an application under this Part of this Act may [with the consent of the Secretary of State] be transferred to another hospital [...]
(2) Where a patient is transferred in pursuance of regulations under this section, the provisions of this Part of this Act (including this sub-section) shall apply to him [as if the order or direction under Part III of this Act by virtue of which he was liable to be detained before being transferred were an order or direction for his admission or removal to the hospital to which he is transferred].
(3) Without prejudice to subsections (1) and (2) above, any patient, who is for the time being liable to be detained under this Part of this Act in a hospital vested in the Secretary of State for the purposes of his functions under the National Health Service Act 1977 or any accommodation used under Part I of that Act by the managers of such a hospital or in a hospital vested in a National Health Service trust [or Primary Care Trust], may at any time [, with the consent of the Secretary of State,] be removed to any other such hospital or accommodation which is managed by the managers of, or is vested in the National Health Service Trust [or Primary Care Trust] for, the first-mentioned hospital; and paragraph (a) of subsection (2) above shall apply in relation to a patient so removed as it applies in relation to a patient transferred in pursuance of regulations made under this section." (Sched. 1, Pt II, paras 2, 5.)

The effect of these provisions is that any transfer of a restricted patient between hospitals, even where the hospitals are administered by the same NHS Trust, is subject to the agreement of the Home Secretary.

Provisions relating to the transfer of patients to and from high security hospitals are contained in section 123.

Subsection (1)

1–193   *Regulations:* See regulations 7 to 9 of the Mental Health (Hospital, Guardianship and Consent to Treatment) Regulations 1983.

Paragraph (a)

1–194   *By virtue of an application:* Therefore patients who are detained in hospital but who have not been made subject to an application are excluded, *e.g.* patients detained under sections 5(2), (4), 135 and 136.

The Mental Health Act Commission in its Guidance Note entitled "Issues Surrounding Sections 17, 18 and 19 of the Mental Health Act 1983" impliedly contends that in circumstances of "pressing need" the transfer of a mentally capable section 5(2) patient from one hospital to another might be lawful under the common law in the absence of that patient's consent. For an expression of doubt as to the correctness of this opinion, see the note on "detained in the hospital" in section 5(2).

Transferred to another hospital: Including a high security hospital. An alternative course of action would be to grant the patient leave of absence under section 17, with the condition that he resides at another hospital: see the General Note to section 17 under the heading "The transfer of patients between hospitals".

Transferred to hospital: The procedure for effecting such a transfer is very similar to the procedure for making an application under section 3: see regulation 8(3) of the 1983 Regulations. If a patient is transferred from guardianship to hospital under regulation 8(3) he has a right to make an application to a Mental Health Review Tribunal (s.66(1)(e)). If he does not exercise this right within six months of the transfer, the hospital managers will automatically refer the case to the tribunal (s.68(1)).

Transferred into the guardianship of another: Transfer from one guardian to another can, in certain circumstances, also take place under section 10.

Subsection (2)

Paragraph (a)

1–195   *Transferred:* Using the procedure set out in regulation 7(2) and Form 24 of the 1983 Regulations. Transfer to another hospital managed by the same managers is allowed for without formality under subsection (3).

Hospital: Or registered establishment (s.34(2)).

Paragraph (b)

1–196   *Hospital:* Or registered establishment.

Transferred into guardianship: Using the procedure set out in regulation 7(3) and Form 25 of the 1983 Regulations. Fresh medical recommendations are not required on such a transfer.

As if the application were a guardianship application: The original application will have either been for assessment under section 2 or for treatment under section 3 (subs. (2)(a)). If a patient who has been admitted to hospital under section 3 is transferred into guardianship under this provision, the patient's nearest relative would have had the opportunity to exercise his right to object to the application being made (s.11(4)). The nearest relative of a patient who has been admitted under section 2 has no such right. A section 2 patient who is transferred into guardianship will not have been identified as suffering from a specific form of mental disorder. Such an identification will be made if the guardianship is renewed under section 20(6)(7).

At the said time: This is the time when the application for admission to hospital was made.

Paragraph (c)
Transferred: Using the procedure set out in regulation 8(2) and Form 26 of the **1–197** 1983 Regulations.

Paragraph (d)
If a patient is transferred under this paragraph, it would appear that the **1–198** three-month period relating to the administration of medicine specified in section 58(1)(b) of this Act would commence from the first occasion when medicine was administered to the patient during the period when he was subject to guardianship.
Transferred: Using the procedure set out in regulation 8(3) and Form 27 of the 1983 Regulations. Medical recommendations are required on such a transfer: see regulation 8(3)(b) and Forms 28 and 29 and the note on subsection (1)(b).
Hospital: Or registered establishment (s.34(2)).
At the time when the application was originally accepted: The guardian should ensure that this date is communicated to the hospital managers.

Subsection (3)
This subsection enables a patient to be transferred to another hospital, or other **1–199** accommodation managed by the same managers without any special procedure being followed. It does not apply to patients who have been detained under section 5(2) or (4) because "paragraph (a) of subsection (2)", which "shall" apply to patients transferred under this provision, does not apply to patients who have been made subject to the holding powers.
Hospital: A patient who is transferred under this provision is treated as if he had been admitted to the hospital to which he has been transferred at the time of the original application.
Vested in the Secretary of State: Or in the National Assembly for Wales for the purposes of its functions under the National Health Service Act 1977 (S.I. 2000 No. 253, Sched. 3).

Duration of detention or guardianship and discharge

Duration of authority
20.—(1) Subject to the following provisions of this Part of this Act, a **1–200** patient admitted to hospital in pursuance of an application for admission for treatment, and a patient placed under guardianship in pursuance of a guardianship application, may be detained in a hospital or kept under guardianship for a period not exceeding six months beginning with the day on which he was so admitted, or the day on which the guardianship application was accepted, as the case may be, but shall not be so detained or kept for any longer period unless the authority for his detention or guardianship is renewed under this section.
(2) Authority for the detention or guardianship of a patient may, unless the patient has previously been discharged, be renewed—
(a) from the expiration of the period referred to in subsection (1) above, for a further period of six months;
(b) from the expiration of any period of renewal under paragraph (a) above, for a further period of one year,
and so on for periods of one year at a time.

(3) Within the period of two months ending on the day on which a patient who is liable to be detained in pursuance of an application for admission for treatment would cease under this section to be so liable in default of the renewal of the authority for his detention, it shall be the duty of the responsible medical officer—

(a) to examine the patient; and

(b) if it appears to him that the conditions set out in subsection (4) below are satisfied, to furnish to the managers of the hospital where the patient is detained a report to that effect in the prescribed form;

and where such a report is furnished in respect of a patient the managers shall, unless they discharge the patient, cause him to be informed.

(4) The conditions referred to in subsection (3) above are that—

(a) the patient is suffering from mental illness, severe mental impairment, psychopathic disorder or mental impairment, and his mental disorder is of a nature or degree which makes it appropriate for him to receive medical treatment in a hospital; and

(b) such treatment is likely to alleviate or prevent a deterioration of his condition; and

(c) it is necessary for the health or safety of the patient or for the protection of other persons that he should receive such treatment and that it cannot be provided unless he continues to be detained;

but, in the case of mental illness or severe mental impairment, it shall be an alternative to the condition specified in paragraph (b) above that the patient, if discharged, is unlikely to be able to care for himself, to obtain the care which he needs or to guard himself against serious exploitation.

(5) Before furnishing a report under subsection (3) above the responsible medical officer shall consult one or more other persons who have been professionally concerned with the patient's medical treatment.

(6) Within the period of two months ending with the day on which a patient who is subject to guardianship under this Part of this Act would cease under this section to be so liable in default of the renewal of the authority for his guardianship, it shall be the duty of the appropriate medical officer—

(a) to examine the patient; and

(b) if it appears to him that the conditions set out in subsection (7) below are satisfied, to furnish to the guardian and, where the guardian is a person other than a local social services authority, to the responsible local social services authority a report to that effect in the prescribed form;

and where such a report is furnished in respect of a patient, the local social services authority shall, unless they discharge the patient, cause him to be informed.

(7) The conditions referred to in subsection (6) above are that—

(a) the patient is suffering from mental illness, severe mental impairment, psychopathic disorder or mental impairment and his mental disorder is of a nature or degree which warrants his reception into guardian-ship; and

(b) it is necessary in the interests of the welfare of the patient or for the protection of other persons that the patient should remain under guardianship.

(8) Where a report is duly furnished under subsection (3) or (6) above, the authority for the detention or guardianship of the patient shall be thereby renewed for the period prescribed in that case by subsection (2) above.

(9) Where the form of mental disorder specified in a report furnished under subsection (3) or (6) above is a form of disorder other than that specified in the application for admission for treatment or, as the case may be, in the guardianship application, that application shall have effect as if that other form of mental disorder were specified in it; and where on any occasion a report specifying such a form of mental disorder is furnished under either of those subsections the appropriate medical officer need not on that occasion furnish a report under section 16 above.

(10) In this section "appropriate medical officer" has the same meaning as in section 16(5) above.

DEFINITIONS

patient: s.145(1). **1–201**
hospital: ss.34(2), 145(1).
application for admission for treatment: ss.3, 145(1).
the managers: s.145(1).
severe mental impairment: ss.1, 145(1).
psychopathic disorder: ss.1, 145(1).
mental impairment: ss.1, 145(1).
mental disorder: ss.1, 145(1).
medical treatment: s.145(1).
local social services authority: s.145(1).
responsible medical officer: s.34(1).
responsible local social services authority: s.34(1).

GENERAL NOTE

This section provides for patients who have been detained for treatment or placed **1–202** under guardianship to be detained or kept under guardianship for an initial period of up to six months. It also sets out the criteria that have to be satisfied if the authority to detain a patient or keep him in guardianship is to be renewed. Renewal can be for one further period of six months and subsequently for periods of one year at a time. If the authority to detain the patient is not renewed, "this fact should be made clear to him, whether he wishes to leave or stay on as an informal patient" (*Memorandum*, para. 301).

The finding of McCullough J. in *R. v. Hallstrom, ex p. W*; *R. v. Gardner, ex p. L* [1986] 2 All E.R. 306, that a decision to renew the authority to detain a patient cannot be made at a time when the patient is on leave of absence was overruled by the Court of Appeal in *B v. Barking Havering and Brentwood Community Healthcare NHS Trust* [1999] 1 F.L.R. 106. A renewal can be made while the patient is on leave of absence if the patient's treatment taken as a whole also requires an in-patient element: see the note on subsection (4)(c).

This section applies to patients who are subject to hospital or guardianship orders made by a court under section 37, with the modification that subsections (1) and (9) shall read as follows:

"(1) Subject to the following provisions of this Part of this Act, a patient admitted to hospital in pursuance of an application for admission for treatment, and a patient placed under guardianship in pursuance of a guardianship application, may be detained in a hospital or kept under guardianship for a period not exceeding six months beginning with the [date of the relevant order or direction under Part III of this Act] but shall not be so detained or kept for any longer period unless the authority for his detention or guardianship is renewed under this section."

"(9) Where the form of mental disorder specified in a report furnished under subs. (3) or (6) above is a form of disorder other than that specified in [the relevant order or direction under Part III of this Act, that order or direction] shall have effect as if that other form of mental disorder were specified in it; and where on any occasion a report specifying such a form of mental disorder is furnished under either of those subsections the appropriate medical officer need not on that occasion furnish a report under s.16 above" (Sched. 1, Pt I, para. 6).

All patients, except those placed under hospital orders, have a right to apply to a Mental Health Review Tribunal within six months of the application or guardianship order being made. A hospital order patient has a right to apply to a tribunal during the second months of his detention. Further applications can be made by all patients on every occasion when authority to detain or keep a patient under guardianship is renewed under this section (s.66, as applied by Sched. 1).

The Human Rights Act 1998
1–203   It is has been argued that the lack of any involvement of the hospital managers as detaining authority in the decision to renew the patient's detention (see the *Warlingham Park Hospital* case, noted under subs. (3)) might constitute a violation of Article 5(1) of the European Convention of Human Rights as interpreted by the European Court of Human Rights in *Winterwerp v. Netherlands* (1979) 2 E.H.R.R. 397 (Philip Fennell, "The Third Way in Mental Health Policy: Negative Rights, Positive Rights and the Convention", (1999) 26 *Journal of Law and Society*, 103–127).

A finding by a responsible medical officer that the patient is no longer suffering from a mental disorder (see subs.(4)(a)) does not require the patient's immediate release from detention if that patient poses a risk to the public: see the note on section 23 under this heading.

Subsection (1)
1–204   *Subject to the following provisions of this part of this act:* Note especially the powers of discharge granted by section 23.

Beginning with: Including the day on which the patient was admitted to hospital or the day on which the guardianship application was accepted by the local social services authority (*Hare v. Gocher* [1962] 2 Q.B. 641).

Subsection (3)
1–205   This subsection requires the responsible medical officer to examine a patient detained for treatment during the two months preceding the day on which the authority for his detention is due to expire. If the responsible medical officer considers that the conditions set out in subsection (4) are satisfied, the authority to detain the patient is renewed when Form 30 has been completed and delivered to the hospital managers.

Although the responsible medical officer's report provides authority for the patient's continued detention (see the note on "furnish", below), this section does not require that the report should have been considered by the managers before renewal can take place: *R. v. Managers of Warlingham Park Hospital, ex p. B* (1994) 22 B.M.L.R. 1, CA. *Per* Sir Thomas Bingham M.R. at 11: "In my judgment it is essential to distinguish between the authority to detain, which section 20 makes dependent on the due furnishing of a report, and the decision whether or not to discharge, assuming that there was a continued authority to detain, which is plainly entrusted, as section 23 makes plain, to the managers." As Phil Fennell has pointed out, this decision identifies the responsible medical officer as "effectively the detaining authority, as the mere furnishing of his or her report is enough to renew the detention. The original detaining authority, the managers, do not have to have considered the report and satisfied themselves that the conditions of detention continue to be met before the current period of detention expires. Nor do they have to have exercised their discretion over whether to discharge before the expiry of the detention" (All E.R. Rev. 1995, p. 384).

Two months: This time limit applies to the examination of the patient by the responsible medical officer, the forming of the responsible medical officer's opinion and the furnishing of the report to the managers of the hospital where the patient is detained.

The day on which: The period of detention can be extended by virtue of section 21.

Liable to be detained: This covers patients who are actually detained and those who would be detained if they were not currently on leave of absence under section 17 (*B v. Barking and Brentwood Community Healthcare Trust*, noted under subs. (4)(c)).

Responsible medical officer: There is nothing to prevent a doctor on the staff of a registered establishment who would have been prevented from making a medical recommendation on the patient by virtue of section 12(5)(d) from furnishing a report in respect of the patient under this provision. The duty of the responsible medical officer under this section cannot be delegated.

Furnish: In the Scottish case of *Milborrow, Applicant*, 1996 S.C.L.R. 315, Sh.Ct, it was held that a report is "furnished" to the hospital managers when it is committed to the internal mailing system operated by those managers: see the note on section 5(2).

The furnishing of the responsible medical officer's report gives authority for the continued detention of the patient: see subs. (8) and *R. v. Managers of Warlingham Park Hospital*, above. Per Sir Thomas Bingham M.R. at 11: "If the authorised period of detention expires without there being a report duly furnished ..., any detention after the expiry date will plainly be unlawful and render the managers at risk of successful action." The date of the renewal is the date on which the authority to detain was due to expire and not the date of the report. The patient's right to apply to a Mental Health Review Tribunal arises from the date of the renewal (s.66(1)(f), (2)(f)).

Managers of the hospital where the patient is detained: It is submitted that a report under this provision can be made if the patient is "liable to be detained" under section 17 leave in a second hospital: see the note on subsection (4)(c).

A report: See the Mental Health (Hospital, Guardianship and Consent to Treatment) Regulations 1983, regulation 10, and Form 30. The report, which should be kept with the patient's admission documents, requires the hospital managers to consider whether they should exercise their power of discharge in respect of the patient. The exercise of the managers' power to review the detention of a patient who has been the subject of a renewal report is considered in the *Code of Practice* at paragraph 23.7. The *Memorandum*, at paragraph 100, states that the managers should "give the patient a hearing unless he or she does not wish to contest the renewal".

A Form 30 which is defective because of a minor error or slip of the pen would not render the renewal unlawful. If the form is fundamentally defective in some way, for example it was signed by a person who is not the patient's responsible medical officer or it was completed after the authority for the patient's detention had expired, the renewal would be unlawful. Although minor errors cannot be formally rectified under section 15, it would be sensible for an error on the form to be corrected and initialled.

Unless they discharge the patient: Under section 23(2)(a).

Subsection (4)

This subsection specifies the conditions which have to be satisfied if the authority **1–206** to detain a patient who has been admitted for treatment is to be renewed. The alternative to condition (b) for patients who are mentally ill or severely mentally impaired was introduced because "the health and social services authorities have a clear responsibility to care for the mentally ill and severely mentally handicapped and, where necessary, to protect the public from their actions. There will be a few cases where continued detention may be necessary but where there can be little expectation of treatment having a beneficial effect" (Cmnd. 7320, para. 2.44).

In *R. v. Canons Park Mental Health Review Tribunal, ex p. A* [1994] 2 All E.R. 659, 671, CA, Roch L.J. said that "the alteration of the wording of section 3(2) of the 1983 Act made in section 20(4) of the Act would seem to indicate Parliament's intention that mentally disordered persons should not be detained in hospital beyond the initial six months' period unless medical treatment in the hospital is likely to alleviate or prevent a deterioration of the patient's condition unless the patient suffers from mental illness or severe mental impairment and would not be able to look after himself or be looked after in the community if discharged from hospital; that patients suffering from psychopathic disorders and mental impairment should cease to be detained once medical treatment in hospital is unlikely to alleviate or prevent deterioration in their conditions. That intention may owe as much to a policy that such patients should not occupy valuable hospital places and use scarce resources when no alleviation or stabilisation of their conditions was likely as to any concept of personal liberty."

Paragraph (a)

1–207   *Appropriate for him to receive medical treatment in a hospital:* It can be appropriate: (1) for a patient who has been granted substantial leave to be absent from the hospital to receive the required medical treatment in that hospital; and (2) for the medical treatment to be focused on assessing the patient's mental condition and monitoring her progress towards achieving the eventual aim of total rehabilitation into the community (*B v. Barking Havering and Brentwood Community Healthcare NHS Trust*, noted under para. (c)). As this provision refers to *a* hospital rather than *the* hospital, this provision can be satisfied where the patient is receiving treatment for his mental disorder at a hospital where he is required to be as a condition of leave of absence. Also see *R. (on the application of Epsom and St Helier NHS Trust) v. The Mental Health Review Tribunal*, which is noted under paragraph (c).

Paragraph (b)

1–208   *Likely to alleviate or prevent a deterioration:* This "treatability test", which only applies to psychopathic and mentally impaired patients on admission, applies to all patients on renewal, unless the alternative test for mentally ill and severely mentally ill patients is satisfied. For comment on the "treatability test", see the notes to sections 3(2)(b) and 72(1)(b).

Paragraph (c)

1–209   The effect of this paragraph is that it is not possible to renew the detention of a patient if there is no longer a need for the patient's treatment to contain an element of in-patient care. In *B v. Barking Havering and Brentwood Community Healthcare NHS Trust* [1999] 1 F.L.R. 106, the patient had been granted leave of absence under section 17. At the time of the renewal of her detention under this section she had been granted leave for five days a week and for four hours a day on the remaining two days. The patient challenged the legality of the renewal on the ground that it contravened the ruling of McCullough J. in *R. v. Hallstrom, ex p. W, R. v. Gardner, ex p. L* [1986] 2 All E.R. 206, that a patient's detention could not be renewed whilst she was "liable to be detained" during a period of leave of absence. In overruling McCullough J. on this point, the Court of Appeal held that as long as the patient's medical treatment viewed as a whole involved treatment as an in-patient, the requirements of this section could be met. The fact that the patient happened to be away from hospital at the time of renewal did not mean that she was no longer "detained" for treatment. This was the case even where the activities which took place as part of the in-patient treatment might all individually be capable of being performed without the treatment taking place in the hospital if, for the treatment as a whole to be successful, there was a need for an in-patient element to the treatment. Such a renewal would be lawful even if the periods of in-patient care could be classified as being for the purposes of assessment, rather than actual treatment.

In *R. (on the application of Epsom and St Helier NHS Trust) v. The Mental Health Review Tribunal*, above, Sullivan J. said that *Barking* is authority for the proposition that the whole course of the patient's treatment must be examined: the past, present and future. With regard to the prospect of treatment at some future stage, if the timing of that treatment is very uncertain it might not be appropriate for the patient to continue to be liable to detention. This case is considered further in the note on section 72(1)(b) under the heading "appropriate for him to be liable to be detained in a hospital for medical treatment".

Health or safety of the patient or for the protection of other persons: See the notes on section 3(2)(c).

Continues to be detained: Or liable to be recalled to receive the in-patient element of her treatment plan: see the *Barking* case, above.

This ground could be satisifed in relation to a potentially dangerous patient who is compliant with medication and who is willing to remain in hospital as an informal patient. This is because an essential element of the patient's treatment is his preparation for eventual discharge from the hospital. A key element of such preparation is the granting of leave of absence to the patient. Given that the patient would pose a potential risk to the public, it would not be appropriate to grant leave in the absence of a mechanism that would enable staff to require the patient to return to the hospital should he exhibit a reluctance to do so. Section 17 provides such a mechanism. This ground is therefore satisfied because an essential element of the patient's total treatment programme, the testing out of his readiness for discharge, can only be put in place if he were a detained patient who could be granted leave under section 17.

Unlikely to be able to care for himself, to obtain the care that he needs or to guard against serious exploitation: These words are capable of very wide interpretation.

Subsection (5)

One or more other persons: See the note on section 16(3). **1–210**

Subsection (6)

This subsection provides for the the patient's appropriate medical officer to renew **1–211** the authority for guardianship.

The day on which: The period of guardianship can be extended under section 21.

Appropriate medical officer: Is defined in section 16(5) (subs. (10)).

A report: See regulation 10, and Form 31 of the 1983 Regulations. The report is not rectifiable: see the note on "report" in subsection (3).

Furnished: The appropriate medical officer's report gives authority for the continued guardianship of the patient (subs. (8)).

Local social services authority: Which "should give the patient a hearing unless he or she does not wish to contest the renewal" (*Memorandum*, para. 100).

Unless they discharge the patient: Under section 23(2)(b). The *Code of Practice* does not provide any guidance on the procedure that should be followed by the guardian when reviewing the patient's continued need for guardianship. A local authority guardian should require the social worker who has lead responsibility for the patient's welfare to provide a report on the patient's response to being subject to guardianship.

Subsection (7)

This subsection specifies that the conditions for making a guardianship application **1–212** have to be satisfied if the authority for guardianship is to be renewed.

Subsection (8)

1–213   *Renewed:* For the recording of the renewal, see regulation 10 and Form 30 or 31 of the 1983 Regulations.

Subsection (9)

1–214   This subsection provides that if the doctor who makes a report under this section states in his report that the patient is suffering from a form of mental disorder other than that specified in the original application, this has the effect of reclassifying the patient. There is therefore no need for the doctor to make a separate report under section 16. A reclassification under this procedure does not give rise to an additional right of application to a tribunal, and there is no legal obligation to inform either the patient or his nearest relative that the reclassification has taken place. Good practice suggests that the patient should be informed of the reclassification.

   A form of disorder other than that specified in the application: If a patient is classified as suffering from two categories of mental disorder, there is no obligation to reclassify the patient by deleting reference to the category of disorder from which the patient continues to suffer but which would not on its own justify detention because, for example, the disorder is not of a nature or degree which makes it appropriate for him to receive medical treatment (*R. v. Anglia and Oxfordshire Mental Health Review Tribunal, ex p. Hagen* [2000] C.O.D. 352, CA).

[Special provisions as to patients absent without leave

1–215   **21.**—(1) Where a patient is absent without leave—

   (a) on the day on which (apart from this section) he would cease to be liable to be detained or subject to guardianship under this Part of this Act; or

   (b) within the period of one week ending with that day,

he shall not cease to be so liable or subject until the relevant time.

   (2) For the purposes of subsection (1) above the relevant time—

   (a) where the patient is taken into custody under section 18 above, is the end of the period of one week beginning with the day on which he is returned to the hospital or place where he ought to be;

   (b) where the patient returns himself to the hospital or place where he ought to be within the period during which he can be taken into custody under section 18 above, is the end of the period of one week beginning with the day on which he so returns himself; and

   (c) otherwise, is the end of the period during which he can be taken into custody under section 18 above.]

AMENDMENT

This section was substituted by the Mental Health (Patients in the Community) Act 1995, s.2(2).

DEFINITIONS

1–216   patient: s.145(1).
absent without leave: ss.18(6), 145(1).
hospital: ss.34(2), 145(1).

GENERAL NOTE

1–217   This section extends the authority for detention or guardianship of a patient who is absent without leave for up to one week after his return to hospital or place where he ought to be. It applies to patients who have been placed under hospital or guardianship orders by a court (Sched. 1, para. 1).

   Government guidance on the return of patients absent without leave is reproduced in the General Note to section 21B.

Subsection (1)

A patient: Although it is a commonly held view that this section does not apply to **1–218** patients who are detained under section 2 (see, for example, Mental Health Act Commission Practice Note No. 4, para. 9ii), the wording of this subsection does not have such an effect.

Relevant time: This allows for the patient's medical officer to examine the patient and decide whether he wishes to make a report renewing the detention or guardianship under section 20(3) or 20(6). The making of such a report is authorised by section 21A(2) and the date of the renewal is provided for in section 21A(3). This provision also allows time for professionals to consider the appropriateness of making an application under section 3 in respect of a patient who has been detained under section 2.

Taken into custody under section 18: Although a section 2 patient cannot be taken into custody after the section expires (s.18(5)), a section 3 or guardianship patient can be taken into custody long after the detention or guardianship has expired (s.18(4)).

[Patients who are taken into custody or return within 28 days

21A.—(1) This section applies where a patient who is absent without leave **1–219** is taken into custody under section 18 above, or returns himself to the hospital or place where he ought to be, not later than the end of the period of 28 days beginning with the first day of his absence without leave.

(2) Where the period for which the patient is liable to be detained or subject to guardianship is extended by section 21 above, any examination and report to be made and furnished in respect of the patient under section 20(3) or (6) above may be made and furnished within the period as so extended.

(3) Where the authority for the detention or guardianship of the patient is renewed by virtue of subsection (2) above after the day on which (apart from section 21 above) that authority would have expired, the renewal shall take effect as from that day.]

AMENDMENT

This section was substituted by the Mental Health (Patients in the Community) Act 1995, s.2(2).

DEFINITIONS

    patient: s.145(1).   **1–220**
    absent without leave: s.18(6), 145(1).
    hospital: ss.34(2), 145(1).

GENERAL NOTE

If a section 3 or guardianship patient who has absconded returns to the hospital or **1–221** place where he is required to be not more than 28 days after absconding, or is taken into custody during that period, this section enables the patient's medical officer to renew the detention or guardianship under section 20 without further formality. If the authority to detain the patient (or the authority for guardianship) expired during his absence, or has less than seven days to run on his return, section 21 extends it for up to a week from the date of his return.

Government guidance on the return of patients absent without leave is reproduced in the General Note to section 21B.

Subsection (1)

Beginning with: Including the first day of his absence without leave (*Hare v.* **1–222** *Gocher* [1962] 2 Q.B. 641).

Subsection (2)

1–223   *Report:* On Form 30 of S.I. 1983 No. 893.

Subsection (3)

1–224   *Renewal:* The renewal has effect from the date when the authority for detention or guardianship would have expired if it had not been extended by section 21.

[Patients who are taken into custody or return after more than 28 days

1–225   **21B.**—(1) This section applies where a patient who is absent without leave is taken into custody under section 18 above, or returns himself to the hospital or place where he ought to be, later than the end of the period of 28 days beginning with the first day of his absence without leave.

(2) It shall be the duty of the appropriate medical officer, within the period of one week beginning with the day on which the patient is returned or returns himself to the hospital or place where he ought to be—

(a) to examine the patient; and

(b) if it appears to him that the relevant conditions are satisfied, to furnish to the appropriate body a report to that effect in the prescribed form;

and where such a report is furnished in respect of the patient the appropriate body shall cause him to be informed.

(3) Where the patient is liable to be detained (as opposed to subject to guardianship), the appropriate medical officer shall, before furnishing a report under subsection (2) above, consult—

(a) one or more other persons who have been professionally concerned with the patient's medical treatment; and

(b) an approved social worker.

(4) Where the patient would (apart from any renewal of the authority for his detention or guardianship on or after the day on which he is returned or returns himself to the hospital or place where he ought to be) be liable to be detained or subject to guardianship after the end of the period of one week beginning with that day, he shall cease to be so liable or subject at the end of that period unless a report is duly furnished in respect of him under subsection (2) above.

(5) Where the patient would (apart from section 21 above) have ceased to be liable to be detained or subject to guardianship on or before the day on which a report is duly furnished in respect of him under subsection (2) above, the report shall renew the authority for his detention or guardianship for the period prescribed in that case by section 20(2) above.

(6) Where the authority for the detention or guardianship of the patient is renewed by virtue of subsection (5) above—

(a) the renewal shall take effect as from the day on which (apart from section 21 above and that subsection) the authority would have expired; and

(b) if (apart from this paragraph) the renewed authority would expire on or before the day on which the report is furnished, the report shall further renew the authority, as from the day on which it would expire, for the period prescribed in that case by section 20(2) above.

(7) Where the authority for the detention or guardianship of the patient would expire within the period of two months beginning with the day on which a report is duly furnished in respect of him under subsection (2) above, the report shall, if it so provides, have effect also as a report duly furnished under section 20(3) or (6) above; and the reference in this subsection to

authority includes any authority renewed under subsection (5) above by the report.

(8) Where the form of mental disorder specified in a report furnished under subsection (2) above is a form of disorder other than that specified in the application for admission for treatment or guardianship application concerned (and the report does not have effect as a report furnished under section 20(3) or (6) above), that application shall have effect as if that other form of mental disorder were specified in it.

(9) Where on any occasion a report specifying such a form of mental disorder is furnished under subsection (2) above the appropriate medical officer need not on that occasion furnish a report under section 16 above.

(10) In this section—

"appropriate medical officer" has the same meaning as in section 16(5) above;

"the appropriate body" means—
(a) in relation to a patient who is liable to be detained in a hospital, the managers of the hospital; and
(b) in relation to a patient who is subject to guardianship, the responsible local social services authority; and

"the relevant conditions" means—
(a) in relation to a patient who is liable to be detained in a hospital, the conditions set out in subsection (4) of section 20 above; and
(b) in relation to a patient who is subject to guardianship, the conditions set out in subsection (7) of that section.]

AMENDMENT
This section was substituted by the Mental Health (Patients in the Community) Act 1995, s.2(2).

DEFINITIONS
    patient: s.145(1).   **1–226**
    absent without leave: ss.18(6), 145(1).
    hospital: ss.34(2), 145(1).

GENERAL NOTE
If a section 3 or guardianship patient who has absconded is taken into custody, or **1–227** returns to the hospital or place where he is required to be, later than 28 days after absconding, the patient's medical officer must comply with the provisions of this section if the patient's detention or guardianship is to be renewed under section 20. If the authority to detain the patient (or the authority for guardianship) expired during his absence, or has less than seven days to run on his return section 21 extends it for up to a week from the day of his return.

The following guidance on the return of patients absent without leave is to be found in Annex B to EL (97) 26:

"*General*
1. Section 2 of the Mental Health (Patients in the Community) Act 1995 amends the time limit (previously 28 days) stipulated in section 18 of the 1983 Act for the return of patients who are absent without leave. . . . In common with the rest of the Act the new time limits come into force on April 1, 1996.
2. Under the new provisions a patient may be returned for up to six months after going absent, or until the expiry date of the current authority for his or her detention or guardianship if that is later. If at the time the patient goes absent the authority for detention or guardianship has been renewed in accordance with

section 20, but the new period has yet to begin, the renewal is ignored and the six month limit for returning the patient applies.

3. The new limits do not apply to patients subject to restrictions under section 41 or 49 of the Act who continue to be liable to be returned at any time. They also do not apply to patients who are released from prison while still liable to detention under the Act; as previously they may be returned to hospital under section 22 within 28 days of their release.

Patients returned/returning within 28 days

4. Where a patient is returned (or returns) within 28 days of going absent, and the current authority for detention or guardianship has not expired, that authority remains in force until its original expiry date. If the authority has expired, or has less than seven days to run, the Act extends it by up to a week from the date of the patient's return. Within that time the appropriate medical officer may examine the patient and make a renewal report under section 20. The new period of detention or guardianship will then run from the date the original period ended. Otherwise the patient will cease to be detained or subject to guardianship.

Patients returned/returning after 28 days

5. Where a patient is returned (or returns) more than 28 days after going absent (but within the periods defined in paragraph 2 above) section 21B stipulates that the appropriate medical officer must examine the patient within a week of his or her return. Again if the authority for detention or guardianship has expired, or has less than seven days to run, the Act extends it by up to a week. The medical officer must decide, in the light of his or her examination of the patient, whether the conditions for continuing liability to detention or guardianship are met and, if they are, must make a report to the hospital managers or local social services authority. The effect of such a report is explained in paragraphs 6 and 7 below. In the case of patients who are liable to be detained (but not those subject to guardianship) the RMO must consult an approved social worker, and another professional concerned with the patient's medical treatment, before making a report. The patient must be informed that the report has been made (in the case of both guardianship and detention). If a report is not made the liability to detention or guardianship will end (even if the original expiry date has not been reached).

6. If the report under section 21B is made before the date when the original authority would have expired its effect is to restore that authority, which then runs until the original expiry date. However if the original authority has less than two months to run the medical officer may specify that the report should also have the effect of a renewal report under section 20. The authority for detention or guardianship is then renewed for the appropriate period (six or 12 months) prescribed by section 20(2).

7. If the report under section 21B is made after the date when the original authority would have expired it automatically has the effect of a section 20 renewal report. The new authority (whether for six or 12 months) then runs from the expiry date of the old one.

8. The report under section 21B may specify a different form of mental disorder to that which appeared in the original application. The appropriate medical officer does not then need to submit a separate reclassification report under section 16 of the Act unless the section 21B report also serves as a section 20 renewal report as described above.

Related provisions

9. A patient who has the authority for his or her detention or guardianship renewed after being absent without leave may then apply to a Mental Health

Review Tribunal. There is no right to a Tribunal if the authority is simply restored under section 21 B.

10. The 1995 Act also makes provision for patients who are taken into custody abroad. In addition it amends the provisions on consent to treatment in the 1983 Act to take account of the new time limits for returning absent patients."

FORMS
Annex A to EL (97) 26 provides guidance on the use of forms when this section is invoked:

"1. Section 21 B provides that the appropriate medical officer's report after examining the patient on return to hospital must be in the "prescribed form". Two forms are being introduced, one for use when a patient is liable to be detained (form 31A) and one for when a patient is subject to the guardianship provisions (form 31B).

2. There are three instances when the new forms should be used:

(a) patient returns/is returned to hospital/guardianship within the final two months of detention complete form 31A or form 31B (the form may provide that it will act as renewal of detention/guardianship under section 20);

(b) patient returns/is returned to hospital/guardianship before the final two months of detention complete form 31A or 31B (a further form will be required under section 20 when the patient's detention/guardianship is due for renewal);

(c) patient returns/is returned to hospital after authority for detention/ guardianship has expired but within the time limit laid down in section 18(4), as amended, complete form 31A or 31B (this will act as authority to renew detention/guardianship for the period prescribed by section 20(2) from the date of expiry of the original detention. A further form under section 20 will be required at the end of this period).

3. The authority for the continued detention of the patient will not take effect until the forms are received by the Managers. The Managers' role in respect of a report under section 21(B) is somewhat different to their role in respect of a report under section 20 because the report renews the detention under section 21B without giving the mangers the express option of discharging the patient. The same is true of the local authority in renewing guardianship.

4. The new forms 31A or 31B should not be used for patients who on return from absence without leave have a maximum of seven days before their liability to detention or guardianship expires.* Such patients have their liability to detention or guardianship extended by a week on return to hospital or to the place, where they ought to be by virtue of section 21(1)(b) and (2)(a) or (b). Once they have returned their detention or guardianship may be renewed during that week under section 20 using form 30 or 31."

[*The advice contained in paragraph 4 is wrong. Forms 31A or 31B should be used in *all* cases where a patient has been absent without lease for more than 28 days: see the footnote to paragraph 77 of the *Memorandum*.]

Subsection (1)
Beginning with: See the note on section 21(1).   **1–228**

Subsection (2)
Appropriate medical officer, relevant conditions, appropriate body: See subsection **1–229** (10).

Furnish to the appropriate body: Even if the unexpired period of detention or guardianship is longer than the one week provided for in this subsection. The appropriate medical officer must comply with subsection (3) prior to furnishing a report in respect of a patient who is liable to be detained.

In the Scottish case of *Milborrow, Applicant*, 1996 S.C.L.R. 315, Sh.Ct, it was held that a report is "furnished" to the hospital managers when it is committed to the internal mailing system operated by those managers; see the note on sections 5(2).

Cause him: The appropriate body must arrange for the patient to be informed.

Prescribed form: See the General Note to this section.

Subsection (3)

1–230   *Professional concerned with patient's medical treatment:* Not necessarily in the hospital.

An approved social worker: Who need not have been involved in the patient's admission.

Subsection (4)

1–231   This subsection states that if the patient's liability to be detained or to be subject to guardianship would have extended beyond the one week period provided for in subsection (2), the detention or guardianship will end in the absence of a report being made by the appropriate medical officer under that subsection.

Subsection (5)

1–232   If a patient's liability to be detained or to be subject to guardianship would have expired before the end of the one week period provided for in subsection (2), and a report is furnished under that provision, the period of renewal shall be the period provided for in section 20(2). The date of the renewal is established by subsection (6).

Subsection (6)

1–233   This subsection provides that where the authority for detention or guardianship of a patient has been renewed in the circumstances set out in subsection (5), the renewal has effect from the day on which the detention or guardianship would have expired. If this renewed authority is due to expire before the day on which the report under subsection (2) is made, a further period of renewal for the prescribed period is authorised by the subsection (2) report.

Subsection (7)

1–234   This provision avoids the need for two reports renewing a patient's detention or guardianship, one under subsection (2) and the other under section 20(3) or (6), if the authority for the patient's detention or guardianship would expire within two months of the report being made under subsection (2).

Subsection (8)

1–235   If the doctor who makes a report under subsection (2) states in his report that the patient is suffering from a form of mental disorder other than that specified in the original application, this provision has the effect of reclassifying the patient. Such a reclassification gives rise to a right to make an application to a tribunal (s.66(1)(fb)).

Special provisions as to patients sentenced to imprisonment, etc.

1–236   **22.**—(1) Where a patient who is liable to be detained by virtue of an application for admission for treatment or is subject to guardianship by virtue of a guardianship application is detained in custody in pursuance of any sentence or order passed or made by a court in the United Kingdom (including an order committing or remanding him in custody), and is so detained for a period exceeding, or for successive periods exceeding in the aggregate, six months, the application shall cease to have effect at the expiration of that period.

(2) Where any such patient is so detained in custody but the application does not cease to have effect under subsection (1) above, then—

(a) if apart from this subsection the patient would have ceased to be liable to be so detained or subject to guardianship on or before the day on which he is discharged from custody, he shall not cease and shall be deemed not to have ceased to be so liable or subject until the end of that day; and

(b) in any case, sections 18[, 21 and 21A] above shall apply in relation to the patient as if he had absented himself without leave on that day.

[(3) In its application by virtue of subsection (2) above section 18(4) above shall have effect with the substitution of the words "end of the period of 28 days beginning with the first day of his absence without leave." for the words from "later of" onwards.]

AMENDMENTS

The words in square brackets in subs. (2), and subs. (3), were inserted by the Mental Health (Patients in the Community) Act 1995, s.2(3).

DEFINITIONS

patient: s.145(1).   **1–237**
application for admission for treatment: ss.3, 145(1).
absent without leave: ss.18(6), 145(1).

GENERAL NOTE

This section provides that if a patient who is the subject of an application for **1–238** treatment or a guardianship application is sentenced, or committed or remanded to custody, by a court for a period of more than six months, the application will cease to have effect at the expiration of the period spent in custody. If the patient is detained in custody for less than six months and would, in the ordinary course of events, have ceased to be liable to be detained for treatment or subject to guardianship prior to his discharge from custody, subsections (2) and (3) provide that he does not cease to be so liable or subject until end of the day on which he is discharged, and for the purposes of sections 18, 21 and 21A of this Act he will be treated as if he had absconded himself without leave on that day, *i.e.* the patient can be taken into custody within 28 days of his release (s.18(4), as substituted by subs. (3) of this section) and the authority has 7 days during which the application can be renewed (s.21) if it is due for renewal at that time. If the renewal report is furnished after the expiration of the previous period of detention or guardianship, the report is deemed to have been furnished on the final day of that period (s.21A).

This section applies to patients who have been placed under hospital or guardianship orders by a court under section 37, with the modification that for references to an application for admission or a guardianship application there shall be substituted references to the order or direction under Part III of this Act by virtue of which the patient is liable to be detained or subject to guardianship (Sched. 1, Pt I, paras 2, 7). For restricted patients the section applies with the modification that subsection (1) and paragraph (a) of subsection (2) shall be omitted (Sched. 1, Pt II, paras 2, 7), *i.e.* the restriction order will not cease if the patient is detained in custody for more than six months.

Subsection (1)

United Kingdom: This means Great Britain and Northern Ireland (Interpretation **1–239** Act 1978, s.5, Sched. 1).

Subsection (2)
1–240   This subsection covers the situation where a patient is released before he has been in custody for a continuous period exceeding six months: see the General Note to this section.

Subsection (3)
1–241   The effect of this subsection was explained by the Parliamentary Under-Secretary of State for Health, Baroness Cumberlege (*Hansard*, HL, Vol. 564, col. 174):

> "At present, section 22 of the Mental Health Act 1983 states that when a patient who has been subject to imprisonment is released, he should be treated as though he were absent without leave under section 18 of the 1983 Act. This is a legal device to provide a period of 28 days in which such patients could be returned to detention in hospital. However, as your Lordships know, clause 2 of this Bill [now s.18(4)] extends the period of time in which an absconding patient can be returned to hospital from 28 days to at least six months. An unintentional consequence of this is to extend the period of time within which a released prisoner could be returned to detention under the 1983 Act. I am sure your Lordships will agree that this is undesirable, both in its own right, and because it would be inconsistent with the provisions laid out in the earlier amendments relating to prisoners subject to supervision applications. The effect of the amendment, therefore, is to retain for the purposes of section 22 the period of 28 days within which a person who has been released from prison may be returned to hospital. This is followed by a period of seven days during which the responsible medical officer must examine the patient and determine whether his liability to detention should be renewed."

Discharge of patients
1–242   **23.**—(1) Subject to the provisions of this section and section 25 below, a patient who is for the time being liable to be detained or subject to guardianship under this Part of this Act shall cease to be so liable or subject if an order in writing discharging him from detention or guardianship (in this Act referred to as "an order for discharge") is made in accordance with this section.
(2) An order for discharge may be made in respect of a patient—
(a) where the patient is liable to be detained in a hospital in pursuance of an application for admission for assessment or for treatment by the responsible medical officer, by the managers or by the nearest relative of the patient;
(b) where the patient is subject to guardianship, by the responsible medical officer, by the responsible local social services authority or by the nearest relative of the patient.
(3) Where the patient is liable to be detained in a [registered establishment] in pursuance of an application for admission for assessment or for treatment, an order for his discharge may, without prejudice to subsection (2) above, be made by the Secretary of State and, if the patient is maintained under a contract with a [National Health Service trust][, [Health Authority, Special Health Authority or Primary Care Trust], by that National Health Service trust, [Health Authority, Special Health Authority or Primary Care Trust].]
(4) The powers conferred by this section on any authority, [trust] or body

of persons may be exercised [subject to subsection (5) below] by any three or more members of that authority [trust] or body authorised by them in that behalf or by three or more members of a committee or sub-committee of that authority [trust] or body which has been authorised by them in that behalf.

[(5) The reference in subsection (4) above to the members of an authority, trust or body or the members of a committee or sub-committee of an authority, trust or body,—

(a) in the case of [a [Health Authority, Special Health Authority or Primary Care Trust]] or a committee or sub-committee of [a [Health Authority, Special Health Authority or Primary Care Trust]], is a reference only to the chairman of the authority [or trust] and such members (of the authority [trust], committee or sub-committee, as the case may be) as are not also officers of the authority [or trust], within the meaning of the National Heath Service Act 1977; and

(b) in the case of a National Health Service trust or a committee or sub-committee of such a trust, is a reference only to the chairman of the trust and such directors or (in the case of a committee or sub-committee) members as are not also employees of the trust.]

AMENDMENTS

The amendments to this section were made by the National Health Service and Community Care Act 1990, s.66(1), Sched. 9, para. 24(3), the Health Authorities Act 1995, s.2(1), Sched. 1, para. 107(2), the Health Act 1999 (Supplementary, Consequential, etc., Provisions) Order 2000 (S.I. 2000 No. 90), Sched. 1, para. 13(4), and the Care Standards Act 2000, s.116, Sched. 4, para. 9(2).

DEFINITIONS

patient: s.145(1). **1–243**
hospital: ss.34(2), 145(1).
application for admission for assessment: ss.2, 145(1).
the managers: s.145(1).
nearest relative: ss.26(3), 145(1).
local social services authority: s.145(1).
application for admission for treatment: ss.3, 145(1).
responsible medical officer: s.34(1).
Health Authority: s.145(1).
Special Health Authority: s.145(1).
registered establishment: s.34(1).

GENERAL NOTE

This section provides for the discharge of detained patients and patients who are **1–244** subject to guardianship to be ordered by the patient's responsible medical officer, the hospital managers (or the responsible local social services authority for guardianship patients) or the patient's nearest relative. The term "discharge" means discharge from detention or guardianship, and not discharge from hospital. This section applies to patients who have been placed under hospital or guardianship orders made under section 37 with the modification that subsection (2) shall read as follows:

"(2) An order for discharge may be made in respect of a patient—
(a) where the patient is liable to be detained in a hospital in pursuance of an application for admission [...] for treatment by the responsible medical officer, by the managers [...],
(b) where the patient is subject to guardianship, by the responsible medical officer, by the responsible local social services authority [...]."
(Sched. 1, Pt I, paras 2, 8.)

It also applies to restricted patients with the modification that subsections (1) and (2) shall read as follows:

"(1) Subject to the provisions of this section and section 25 below, a patient who is for the time being liable to be detained [...] under this Part of this Act shall cease to be so liable or [...] if an order in writing discharging him from detention [...] (in this Act referred to as "an order for discharge") is made [with the consent of the Secretary of State] in accordance with this section.

(2) An order for discharge may be made in respect of a patient—

(a) where the patient is liable to be detained in a hospital in pursuance of an application for admission [...] for treatment by the responsible medical officer, by the managers [...];

(b) [...]." (Sched. 1, Pt II, paras 2, 7.)

The Home Secretary has his own powers to discharge restricted patients under section 42(2).

Guidance on the discharge of all types of patients from hospital is contained in Department of Health circulars LAC(89)7 and HC(89)5 and in the accompanying booklet, *Discharge of Patients from Hospital*. The aftercare of patients who have been discharged from hospital is considered in chapter 27 of the *Code of Practice*.

The Human Rights Act 1998

1–245 In *Winterwerp v. Netherlands* (1979) 2 E.H.R.R 387, the European Court of Human Rights held that the validity of the continued confinement of a mentally disordered person depends upon the persistence of such a disorder: see the notes on Article 5(1)(e) of the European Convention on Human Rights. In a subsequent decision of the Court it was held that it does not automatically follow that a finding by an expert authority that the mental disorder which justified a patient's compulsory confinement no longer persists, compels his immediate and unconditional release into the community (*Johnson v. United Kingdom* (1997) 27 E.H.R.R. 296). The effect of this decision is that if a patient who is deemed to pose a risk to the public is found no longer to be mentally disordered, his discharge from detention can be delayed for a limited period until such time as appropriate after-care facilities are put in place. In *Johnson* the Court said that the authority "should be able to retain some measure of supervision over the progress of the person once he is released into the community ..." (para. 63). It follows that the patient's discharge from detention could be preceded by a period of leave of absence under section 17 as a means of judging the adequacy of the after-care arrangements.

The question whether a decision not to discharge a patient because of a failure to put in place appropriate after-care facilities in the community violates Article 5 was considered by the Court of Appeal in *R v. Camden and Islington Health Authority, ex p. K.* [2001] EWCA Civ 240. This case is considered in General Note to section 117 under this heading.

The persons and bodies who have the power to discharge the patient under this provision are "public authorities" for the purposes of section 6 of the 1998 Act.

Subsection (1)

1–246 *Order in writing:* Managers should ensure that a suitable form is available (*Code of Practice*, para. 22.10). There are forms which *may* be used by the nearest relative: see the Mental Health (Hospital, Guardianship and Consent to Treatment) Regulations 1983, 15(1)(2), Forms, 34, 35. The order must be served in the manner prescribed by *ibid.* regulation 3(3).

Discharging him from detention or guardianship: Paragraph 301 of the *Memorandum* states that when "a patient is discharged from detention, or the authority for his detention expires, this fact should be made clear to him, whether he wishes to leave hospital or to stay on as an informal patient." The power to discharge can be exercised at any time during the person's detention or guardianship.

Subsection (2)

Order for discharge: There are no statutory criteria governing the exercise of this **1–247** power. In its *First Biennial Report*, 1983–1985, the Mental Health Act Commission stated that the hospital managers "have the right and duty to end a deprivation of liberty as soon as it appears not, or no longer, to be justified by the Act" (para. 8.13).

In *R. v. Riverside Mental Health Trust, ex p. Huzzey* (1998) 43 B.M.L.R. 167, Latham J. identified the criteria that hospital managers must use when considering the continued detention of a section 3 patient where the nearest relative's application for discharge had been subject to a "barring report" made under section 25. His Lordship said:

"[S]ection 23 provides, *inter alia*, a general discretion in the managers to discharge a patient. No criteria are set out as to what should or should not be taken into account by managers when considering decision as to whether or not to discharge. The question of what are the relevant considerations has to be answered by looking at the general scheme of the Act. Clearly the criteria set out in section 3 are of fundamental importance. If the criteria for admission no longer exist, I cannot see how any decision by managers not to discharge could be other than perverse. Section 23 implicitly recognises that managers have a discretion to discharge even if those criteria have been met. Where ... a nearest relative has sought to obtain a discharge order but has been confronted by a barring report, those facts must equally be relevant and material considerations. In my view, the managers are not only entitled to, but must, consider whether or not they are persuaded by the barring report that the patient, if discharged, would be likely to act in a manner dangerous to other persons or to himself. For if they are not so persuaded, they will have reached the position that the nearest relative would have been entitled to an order for discharge if the responsible medical officer had not come to what they have decided was an erroneous conclusion as to the danger presented by the patient. That cannot be anything other than a relevant and material consideration, and would be likely, in almost all circumstances, to mean that discharge should be ordered."

In this case Latham J. held that the failure of the managers to apply their minds to the question of the patient's dangerousness meant that their decision not to order discharge was irrational and had to be quashed. His Lordship also held that as the medical reports which had been placed before the managers justified the continued detention of the patient on the basis of his need for further *assessment*, the patient's continued detention under section 3 could not be justified. This aspect of His Lordship's judgment must be considered in the light of Lord Woolf's subsequent finding in *B. v. Barking Havering and Brentwood Community Healthcare NHS Trust* [1999] 1 F.L.R. 106 at 114, that often "assessment or monitoring of progress will be an important part of treatment. This will certainly be the case where ... there is an evolving programme of treatment".

Although the *Huzzey* case was concerned with the power of hospital managers under this section, the approach taken by Latham J. is equally applicable to the power of the patient's responsible medical officer to order discharge. Hospital managers and the responsible medical officer should therefore assess the need for the patient's continued detention by considering whether: (1) the patient is still suffering from mental disorder; (2) his disorder continues to be of a nature or degree which makes assessment or assessment followed by medical treatment (for section 2 patients) or treatment (for section 3 patients) in a hospital appropriate; (3) the treatability test for psychopathic or mentally impaired patients who have been detained under section 3 continues to apply (see s.3(2)(b)), or, on a section 20 renewal, the provisions of section 20(4)(b), or the alternative to the treatability test for mentally ill or severely mentally impaired patients contained in section 20(4), apply; and (4) detention in a hospital is still necessary in the interests of the patient's own health or safety or for the protection of others. For patients who have been granted leave of absence under section 17, the additional question that will need to be considered is whether the patient's responsible medical officer continues to need to have a power of recall either in the interests of the patient's own health or safety or for the protection of others. If the nearest relative's order for the patient's discharge has been confronted by a barring report, the hospital managers must, in addition to considering the admission criteria, also ask themselves whether the patient would be likely to act in a manner dangerous to other persons or to himself if he were to be discharged (*Huzzey*, above). The patient should be discharged if any of these questions can be answered in the negative.

The solicitors for the Trust in the *Huzzey* case have reported that the patient "was awarded £24,000 compensatory damages and £2,000 aggravated damages by way of compensation for his 87-day detention, around £300 per day. This compensation was set by a jury and seems to reflect the fact that the unit was a medium secure unit and that he was detained with fellow patients in circumstances where his treatment and period of detention were being questioned by him. His detention had also been subject to publicity in the press" (Radcliffe's Mental Health Briefing Note No. 37).

Liable to be detained in a hospital: Or a registered establishment (s.34(2)).

Application for admission for assessment: This includes an emergency application made under section 4 because such an application is "an application for admission for assessment" (see s.4(1)) which is founded on a single medical recommendation.

Responsible medical officer: The responsible medical officer "may discharge patient without reference to the hospital managers" (*Memorandum*, para. 102) or anybody else. As the patient is legally detained by the hospital managers (s.6(2)), the responsible medical officer should inform an appropriate officer of the managers of the fact that the patient has been discharged from detention. "There are no statutory criteria governing the exercise of this power. Its exercise is wholly within the responsible medical officer's discretion subject, in my judgment, to the usual restrictions of lawfulness and so forth. [I]f it is exercised for reasons based on error of law it is susceptible to challenge by judicial review" (*R. (on the application of Wirral Health Authority and Wirral Borough Council) v. Dr Finnegan and D.E.* [2001] EWHC Admin 312, *per* Scott Baker J. at para. 68). The responsible medical officer, who has a continuing duty to consider whether the admission conditions remain satisfied (*R. (on the application of C) v. Mental Health Review Tribunal London South and South West Region*, December 21, 2000, *per* Scott Baker J., at para. 20), can discharge the patient at any time.

A restricted patient may only be discharged with the consent of the Home Secretary: see the General Note to this section.

1–248 *The managers:* Who can delegate their functions under subsection (4). The patient's responsible medical officer has no power to prevent the managers from exercising their powers of discharge, even if he considers that the patient is dangerous. Advice to hospital managers on their responsibilities under this section is contained in chapter 23 of the *Code of Practice.*

As hospital managers are not constrained by statutory requirements in the exercise of their discretion to discharge, it is submitted that a reasonable exercise of that discretion would enable the managers to exercise options which are broadly similar to the powers enjoyed by the Mental Health Review Tribunal in that they can

(i) adjourn the consideration of the patient's case if, for example, an important piece of information concerning the patient has not been provided to them; (ii) order that the discharge of the patient be subject to the achievement of a condition, such as obtaining a place for the patient in a hostel; (iii) order that the patient be discharged on a specified future date (which must not be a date after that on which the authority for the patient's detention expires) to allow time for preparations for the discharge to be put in place; and (iv) make an unenforceable recommendation in respect of the patient, such as a recommendation that supervised discharge be considered for the patient. The managers could reconvene in the event of a recommendation not being complied with.

A patient can make an application to the managers for his discharge as often as he likes during a period of detention. No formal procedure is laid down for the hearing of a patient's application. In fact, there is no explicit requirement that a hearing should take place at all. Although David Hewitt has said that "it is difficult to see how the ... requirements of the Code [of Practice] can be fulfilled without some form of oral hearing" (see below, p. 327), having a hearing is not always the most appropriate mechanism for managers to use when exercising their review function. For example, if a patient makes frequent applications to managers in the absence of any change of circumstances between applications, or if the patient does not wish to challenge the renewal of his detention under section 20, or if the patient makes an application to managers immediately after an unsuccessful application to a Mental Health Review Tribunal without any change in his circumstances, managers might think it appropriate to exercise their review function by considering written reports from the relevant professionals. As managers, when exercising their power under this section are acting in a quasi-judicial capacity, they must abide by the rules of natural justice: see the General Note to paragraph 23.16 of the *Code of Practice*. The *Code* states, at paragraph 22.6, that the managers should provide written reasoned decisions, a copy of which should be placed with the patient's records.

NHS Management Executive, TEL (94)2, paragraph 10 states:

"From April 14, 1994 existing arrangements for funding clinical negligence will be extended to cover the costs of any successful litigation Trusts may face as a consequence of the exercise of their statutory duties under section 23 of the Mental Health Act 1983. This takes into account the fact that from that date responsibility for decisions taken under section 23 rest with the Trust, rather than with individual non-executive directors."

In its *Second Biennial Report* 1985–1987 at paragraph 19.3, the Mental Health Act Commission suggest that, in order to avoid any potential conflict of interest, the powers of discharge of the managers of a mental nursing home [now a registered establishment] could be carried out by people who are neither on the staff of the mental nursing home nor have a financial interest in it. Also see the Commission's *Third Biennial Report*, 1987–1989, at page 55.

The National Association of Health Authorities and Trusts has published a pamphlet on the responsibilities of managers under this section: see *Duties of Managers for the review of detention under the provisions of the Mental Health Act*, C. Williamson and C. Vellenoweth, 1996. The review function of managers is also considered by Hazel Rumsey in "Hot Seat", *Health Services Journal*, February 22, 1996, pp. 32–33 and by David Hewitt in "Managers' Review Hearings Under the Mental Health Act", [1995] Litigation 323. For a defence of the role of the managers in reviewing the detention of patient's, see Patricia Gregory, "Who can best protect patient's rights?", *Psychiatric Bulletin* (2000) 24, 366–367. A forthright response is provided by Harry Kennedy at *ibid.*, 361–361.

Nearest relative: Who does not have the power to order the discharge of a patient who is subject to a hospital order (with or without restrictions) or to a guardianship order made by a court under Part III of this Act: see the General Note to this section. For service of the order of discharge, see regulation 3(3) of the Mental Health (Hospital, Guardianship and Consent to Treatment) Regulations 1983. The order *may* be in the form set out in Form 34 (for detained patients) or Form 35 (for patients subject to guardianship) of Schedule 1 to the Regulations (*ibid*. reg. 15(1)(2)). Under the provisions of section 25, seventy two hours' notice of the nearest relative's intention to order the patient's discharge must be given to the hospital managers. The patient's responsible medical officer can nullify the discharge if he reports to the managers during the 72 hour period that, in his opinion, the patient would be dangerous if discharged. A nearest relative can be replaced if he has exercised or is likely to exercise his power under this provision "without due regard to the welfare of the patient or the interests of the public" (s.29(3)(d)). The nearest relative has no power to order the discharge of a mentally incapacitated informal patient from hospital: see the note on section 29(3)(d).

A doctor may visit and examine the patient for the purpose of advising a nearest relative on the exercise of his right of discharge (s.24(1)(2)).

Guardianship: The responsible medical officer has no power to prevent a nearest relative obtaining the discharge of a patient who is subject to guardianship. The nearest relative could be displaced if the discharge was either contrary to the welfare of the patient or to the interests of the public (s.29(3)(d)).

Responsible local social services authority: Is defined in section 34(3). "The power of discharge can be exercised by three or more members of the local social services authority or by three or more members of a committee or sub-committee of the authority" (*Memorandum*, para. 106). This function may also be delegated to an officer of the authority (Local Government Act 1972, s.101(10)).

Subsection (3)

1–249　*Registered establishment:* For powers relating to patients detained in such establishments, see section 24(3)–(4).

Subsection (4)

1–250　Neither this subsection nor subsection (5) shall apply to the exercise by the National Assembly for Wales of the powers conferred by this section (S.I. 2000 No. 253, Sched. 3).

May be exercised: If delegation takes place under this provision, responsibility for ensuring that the requirements of this section are complied with remains with the delegating body. Hospital managers have been advised to appoint a small committee or sub-committee to carry out their functions under this section (Cmnd. 7320, para. 3.19). The Mental Health Act Commission recommends that "one manager at least should be a non-executive member of the responsible Trust Board" (MHAC, *Fourth Biennial Report*, 1989–1991, para. 14.2).

Three or more members of that authority trust or body: Not officers (subs. (5)). This Act does not require a committee that exercises functions under this provision to reach a unanimous decision.

Trust: The impact that the Mental Health (Amendment) Act 1994 has had on the performance by NHS Trusts of their powers under this section is explained in the following extract from NHS Management Executive letter TEL (94)2: "The Mental Health (Amendment) Act 1994, changes the definition of 'the managers' of a Trust in section 145(1) of the Mental Health Act 1983 from 'the directors of the Trust' to 'the Trust'. The result is that NHS Trusts will, from April 14, 1994 [the commencement date of the 1994 Act], be able to delegate the managers' duties under section 23 of the 1983 Act to a committee or sub-committee made up wholly or partly of non-executive directors of the Trust, or wholly of persons who are not directors of the Trust. No executive director of the Trust or other person who is an employee of the Trust may sit on such a committee or sub-committee [see subs. (5)]. Non-executive directors of Trusts will no longer be personally liable for decisions taken about the discharge of detained patients. Liability will rest with the Trust as a body. Trusts should now appoint a committee or sub-committee to undertake the duties of the managers under section 23 of the Mental Health Act 1983. The committee or sub-committee should be made up of informed non-executive directors of the Trust and/or other appointed and informed outside persons. Any person who acts as a manager should be fully informed about the functions of managers."

The authority for NHS trusts to appoint committees of the trust "consisting wholly or partly of directors of the trust or wholly of persons who are not directors of the trust" is contained in regulation 15 of the National Health Service Trusts (Membership and Procedure) Regulations 1990 (S.I. 1990 No. 2024).

Visiting and examination of patients

24.—(1) For the purpose of advising as to the exercise by the nearest **1 251** relative of a patient who is liable to be detained or subject to guardianship under this Part of this Act of any power to order his discharge, any registered medical practitioner authorised by or on behalf of the nearest relative of the patient may, at any reasonable time, visit the patient and examine him in private.

(2) Any registered medical practitioner authorised for the purposes of subsection (1) above to visit and examine a patient may require the production of and inspect any records relating to the detention or treatment of the patient in any hospital [or to any after-care services provided for the patient under section 117 below].

(3) Where application is made by the Secretary of State or a [Health Authority, Special Health Authority [, Primary Care Trust] or National Health Service trust] to exercise, in respect of a patient liable to be detained in a [registered establishment], any power to make an order for his discharge, the following persons, that is to say—

(a) any registered medical practitioner authorised by the Secretary of State or, as the case may be, that [Health Authority, Special Health Authority [, Primary Care Trust] or National Health Service trust]; and

(b) any other person (whether a registered medical practitioner or not) authorised under [Part II of the Care Standards Act 2000] to inspect the home,

may at any reasonable time visit the patient and interview him in private.

(4) Any person authorised for the purposes of subsection (3) above to visit a patient may require the production of and inspect any documents constituting or alleged to constitute the authority for the detention of the patient under this Part of this Act; and any person so authorised, who is a registered medical practitioner, may examine the patient in private, and may require the production of and inspect any other records relating to the treatment of the patient in the home [or to any after-care services provided for the patient under section 117 below].

AMENDMENT

In subs. (3) the words in square brackets were substituted by the Health Authorities Act 1995, s.2(1), Sched. 1, para. 107(3), the Health Act 1999 (Supplementary, Consequential, etc., Provisions) Order 2000 (S.I. 2000 No. 90) Sched. 1, para. 13(5) and the Care Standards Act 2000, s.79, Sched. 3, para. 9. The words in square brackets in subss. (2) and (4) were inserted by the Mental Health (Patients in the Community) Act 1995, s.1(2), Sched. 1, para. 1.

DEFINITIONS
1–252 nearest relative: ss.26(3), 145(1).
patient: s.145(1).
hospital: ss.34(2), 145(1).
registered establishment: s.34(1).

GENERAL NOTE
1–253 This section provides for the visiting and examination of patients and for the production of documents in connection with the power to order the discharge of a patient from detention or guardianship. Subsections (3) and (4) apply to patients who have been placed under hospital, restriction or guardianship orders by a court under sections 37 or 41 (Sched. 1, Pt I, para. 1, Pt II, para. 1).

A person who fails to allow the visiting, interviewing or examination of a patient or who refuses to produce any document for inspection commits an offence under section 129.

Subsection (1)
1–254 *Nearest relative:* Or acting nearest relative appointed by a county court under section 29.
Power to order his discharge: Under section 23(2).

Subsection (3)
1–255 *Secretary of State:* This subsection shall have effect as if it applied to an application by the National Assembly for Wales as well as to an application by the Secretary of State (S.I. 2000 No. 253, Sched. 3).

Restrictions on discharge by nearest relative
1–256 **25.**—(1) An order for the discharge of a patient who is liable to be detained in a hospital shall not be made by his nearest relative except after giving not less than 72 hours' notice in writing to the managers of the hospital; and if, within 72 hours after such notice has been given, the responsible medical officer furnishes to the managers a report certifying that in the opinion of that officer the patient, if discharged, would be likely to act in a manner dangerous to other persons or to himself—

    (a) any order for the discharge of the patient made by that relative in pursuance of the notice shall be of no effect; and

    (b) no further order for the discharge of the patient shall be made by that relative during the period of six months beginning with the date of the report.

(2) In any case where a report under subsection (1) above is furnished in respect of a patient who is liable to be detained in pursuance of an application for admission for treatment the managers shall cause the nearest relative of the patient to be informed.

DEFINITIONS
1–257 patient: s.145(1).
hospital: ss.34(2), 145(1).
nearest relative: ss.26(3), 145(1).
the managers: s.145(1).
application for admission for treatment: ss.3, 145(1).
responsible medical officer: s.34(1).

GENERAL NOTE
1–258 This section states that a nearest relative must give 72 hours' notice to the hospital managers of his or her intention to order the discharge of the patient from detention

and that the order for discharge, when made, will have no effect if in the meantime the responsible medical officer has reported to the managers that, in his opinion, the patient, if discharged, would be likely to act in a manner dangerous to other persons or to himself. If the responsible medical officer makes such a report it will have the effect of preventing the nearest relative from exercising his powers of discharge for the next six months. In the case of a patient detained for treatment, the nearest relative has a right to apply to a Mental Health Review Tribunal if such a report is made (s.66(1)(g), (2)(d)).

In *Gary Kinsey v. North Mersey Community NHS Trust*, June 21, 1999, CA, Sedley L.J. said that the responsible medical officer's power to issue a "barring order" is "there to ensure that the mere desire of, in particular, a closest relative to have a patient out does not defeat the purpose of the Act which, both in the interests of the patient and the interests of the public, has ultimate regard to the patient's mental state".

The *Code of Practice*, at paragraph 23.8*b*, states that the hospital managers must consider holding a review of the patient's detention if the responsible medical officer makes a report under this provision. The criteria that hospital managers must use when reviewing the detention of a patient subsequent to such a report being made were identified in *R. v. Riverside Mental Health Trust, ex p. Huzzey* (1998) 43 B.M.L.R. 167, which is considered in the note on "the managers" in section 23(2). Also see paragraph 23.12 of the *Code of Practice*.

Subsection (1)
Order for the discharge: Under section 23(2)(a). **1–259**
Liable to be detained in a hospital: This section does not affect the right of a nearest relative to order the discharge of a patient who is subject to guardianship (s.23(2)(b)).

Nearest relative: Or acting nearest relative appointed by the county court under section 29.

72 hours' notice: Paragraph 105 of the *Memorandum* states: "The 72 hour period starts to run from the time when the notice is received by an authorised person, or is delivered by post at the hospital to which it is addressed. Therefore all hospitals in which patients are detained should have suitable arrangements for opening post, whether delivered by hand or by the Post Office, at weekends and during holidays. As soon as the notice is received, the time of receipt should be recorded and the responsible medical officer should be informed." This guidance must be read subject to the decision of the Court of Appeal in *Gary Kinsey v. North Mersey Community NHS Trust,* which is noted under regulation 3(3) of the Mental Health (Hospital, Guardianship and Consent to Treatment) Regulations 1983. The notice may be in the form set out in Form 34 of Schedule 1 to the Regulations (*ibid.* reg. 15(1)).

Responsible medical officer: There is nothing to prevent a doctor on the staff of a registered establishment who would have been prevented from making a medical recommendation in respect of the patient by virtue of section 12(5)(d) from making a report under this section.

Furnishes to the managers a report: The responsible medical officer must use Form 36 of Schedule 1 to the Regulations (*ibid.* reg. 15(3)).

Likely to act: The prospect of dangerous behaviour must be a probability, and not a mere possibility.

Dangerous: The Butler Committee equated "dangerousness with a propensity to cause serious physical injury or lasting psychological harm" (para. 4.10). In *Re Whitbread* [1999] C.O.D. 370, Mr David Pannick Q.C., sitting as a deputy judge of the High Court, upheld the decision of hospital managers who had concluded that the dangerousness test was satisfied in a case where there was a "very high level of probability that lasting psychological harm could be caused to others if the barring order were to be lifted".

Some of the problems in defining dangerousness are identified by J. Atkinson and L. Patterson in *Review of Literature Relating to Mental Health Legislation* (2001): "Inherent in the problem of defining dangerousness is the difficulty of using the same word to describe harm to others and harm to self. This includes whether it is reasonable to describe 'self-neglect' as 'dangerous' as well as concerns about whether different levels of dangerousness should apply to the risk of the individual harming him/herself or others. Dangerousness is also usually situation-specific and may require complicated formulae to determine risk, for example when the likelihood of danger is high but in a rare situation" (para. 2.11).

For an analysis of dangerousness and risk assessment/management, see J. H. M. Crichton (ed.), *Psychiatric Patient Violence: Risk and Response* (1995) and D. Chiswick "Dangerousness", Ch. 8 in D. Chiswick and R. Cope, *Seminars in Practical Forensic Psychiatry* (1995).

During the period of six months: The disqualification from ordering the patient's discharge is not affected by any change in the patient's legal status. Therefore a nearest relative who has been made the subject of a responsible medical officer's report under this section, subsequent to ordering the discharge of a patient who has been detained under section 2 of this Act is barred from ordering the discharge of the patient for the full six month period even though the section 2 is immediately followed by an application under section 3 or if the patient is discharged from the hospital and the section only to be re-admitted under a fresh application shortly thereafter.

Beginning with: Including the date of the report (*Hare v. Gocher* [1962] 2 Q.B. 641).

Subsection (2)

1–260   *Cause the nearest relative to be informed:* So that the nearest relative could consider applying to a Mental Health Review Tribunal (s.66(1)(g), (2)(d)). The nearest relative of a patient who has been detained for assessment does not have an equivalent right to apply. The patient must be discharged by the tribunal if the provisions of section 72(1)(b)(iii) are satisfied.

[After-care under supervision

GENERAL NOTE

1–261   Sections 25A to 25J were inserted by the Mental Health (Patients in the Community) Act 1995 which came into force on April 1, 1996.

The people for whom after-care under supervision (referred to hereafter as "supervised discharge") is targeted have been described as "the small group of so-called 'revolving door patients'. Typically, such a patient will be someone who:

● is compulsorily admitted to hospital for treatment for mental illness;

● responds to the treatment and improves;

● is discharged into the community with a care plan;

● fails to continue to comply with the care plan, and consequently deteriorates;

● is formally re-admitted to hospital, where the whole cycle begins again",

(*Legal Powers on the Care of Mentally Ill People in the Community*, Report of the Internal Review, Department of Health, August 1993, para. 2.1).

The Government took the view that this group of patients, 20 or so in each Health District (*per* Mr John Bowis M.P., Parliamentary Under-Secretary of State for Health, *Hansard*, HC, Vol. 262, col. 183), needed "an especially high degree of supervision" (*ibid.* Standing Committee F, col. 93) if they are to live successfully in community settings.

The potential benefits to patients of an increased level of supervision was not the sole factor which prompted the Government to legislate. The Government, it was said, "must never forget our obligation to reassure the public as a whole that such supervised care will be effective, because without public confidence and support, mental health policy cannot function in the interests of patients. It is a chicken-and-egg scenario—the egg of mental health policy and the chicken of supportive public opinion" (*ibid. Hansard*, HC, Vol. 262, col. 157).

The approach that has been adopted as a means of ensuring that such patients receive the supervision they are deemed to require is to provide a mechanism which requires patients who are subject to section 117 of this Act to receive their after-care services under supervision. "The central principle of [supervised discharge] is that supervision cannot be separated from the after-care services which it exists to support"; *per* Baroness Cumberlege, Parliamentary Under-Secretary of State for Health, *Hansard*, HL, Vol. 564, col. 189. Such supervision will "reflect the objectives of the care programme approach and be part of a comprehensive multi-disciplinary approach to care" (*ibid.* col. 1243).

The procedure for supervised discharge set out in sections 25A to 25J reflects the fact that it "must be health led ... and will involve health decisions on discharge and management—largely taken by health workers, especially community psychiatric nurses"; *per* Mr John Bowis M.P., Standing Committee F, col. 93. An application for supervision can only be made in respect of mentally disordered patients aged 16 or over who, after leaving hospital, will receive after-care services under section 117. The application is made by the patient's responsible medical officer and addressed to the Health Authority which is to be responsible (with the appropriate local authority) for providing after-care services for the patient. Before accepting the application, the Health Authority is required to consult with the local authority. The responsible medical officer must be satisfied that the application is justified by the risk of harm or serious exploitation to the patient, or by the risk to other people. Prior to submitting the application the responsible medical officer must consult widely (consultation is a significant feature at other stages in the procedure) and find two professionals, one being an approved social worker, to provide supporting recommendations.

The application must identify who is to be the patient's community responsible medical officer and the patient's supervisor. The community responsible medical officer, who must be approved under section 12 of this Act, is responsible for the medical care of the patient in the community. The supervisor, who must be a person who is professionally concerned with any of the after-care services provided to the patient, has a responsibility to ensure that the patient receives after-care services.

The application will be accompanied by a copy of the patient's after-care plan and will identify any requirement that the patient has to abide by. The requirements that can be imposed on the patient relate to place of residence and attendance for medical treatment, occupation, education or training. If a patient refuses to comply with a requirement he can be "taken and conveyed" to the place where he is required to be. The patient cannot be forced to receive medical treatment.

If a patient refuses to receive after-care services, or fails to comply with a requirement, the Health Authority and local authority are required to review both services and requirements. If they consider that it might be appropriate for the patient to return to hospital for treatment under compulsory powers, an approved social worker will be informed.

Supervision will last for an initial period of six months, after which it may be renewed (if the conditions for renewal are satisfied) for a further period of six months and subsequently for periods of a year at a time. The supervision will end if the community responsible medical officer so directs, or if the patient is detained under section 3 or is received into guardianship.

Patients must be informed of their rights to apply to a Mental Health Review Tribunal for supervision to be terminated. A tribunal considering an application from a patient detained in hospital for treatment may, if it does not discharge the patient itself, recommend that the patient's responsible medical officer considers making an application for supervised discharge.

It will be some time before the effectiveness of supervised discharge can be judged. In the meantime it is appropriate to reflect on the concerns expressed by the Internal Review that "legal powers can never be a substitute for properly planned and delivered services, that the solutions of choice are those which are agreed with the patient and take the maximum account of his or her wishes and aspirations, and that any legal power should be used only to the minimum extent necessary to support the achievement of its aim" (para. 8.19).

Guidance on supervised discharge is contained in a supplement to the *Code of Practice* which was published in February 1996 and which came into effect on April 1, 1996 on the implementation of the 1995 Act. This guidance remains extant (*ibid.* para. 28.9).

A patient who is subject to supervised discharge cannot receive direct payments under the terms of the Community Care (Direct Payments) Act 1996 (Community Care (Direct Payments) Regulations 1997 (S.I. 1997 No. 734), reg. 2).

Comparison with Guardianship

1–262 The Mental Health Act Commission in its evidence to the House of Commons Health Committee's Inquiry into Supervision Orders said that in its view, "there are sufficient powers in the Mental Health Act which, if used properly, would be able to address the needs of the majority of the identified group of patients. The problem is that they are not being utilised properly in many cases and in particular, guardianship is currently (as it has been for the last thirty years) severely under-utilised" (MHAC, May 1993, para. 4*a*).

Guardianship was also considered by the Internal Review which concluded that it "cannot see guardianship offering a ready answer to the problems of the patients with whom we have been concerned. They are, in particular, a group whose *health* care needs are of central importance, and this suggests that local authorities may not be best placed (and may find it difficult) to take the lead in their care" (para. 7.4).

Apart from the contentious power to "take and convey", the requirements that can be attached to supervised discharge are almost identical to the powers given to a patient's guardian by section 8. The principal difference between the two powers can be found in the procedure for making applications. As the Mental Health Act Commission has pointed out in "many ways after-care under supervision can with reasonable fairness be characterised as a form of medical guardianship—the applicant is the patient's doctor and not an approved social worker and the application for its imposition is made to the relevant District Health Authority and not a Local Authority" (MHAC, Memorandum to the Secretary of State on the Mental Health (Patients in the Community) Bill, 1995, p. 3).

Other distinguishing factors are: (1) while guardianship is a "free standing" power that can be used whether or not the patient has been detained, an application for supervised discharge can only be made in respect of detained patients or patients who are liable to be detained; and (2) if a patient under guardianship refuses medical treatment for mental disorder there is a power to transfer him to hospital under rule 8(3) of the Mental Health (Hospital, Guardianship and Consent to Treatment) Regulations 1983: a similar procedure does not exist for patients under supervised discharge.

The Government view is that guardianship is suited to patients with "a lower risk factor and fewer medical needs" than patients who will be subject to supervised discharge which will have "a different focus from guardianship and can work alongside it"; *per* Baroness Miller, *Hansard*, HL, Vol. 563, col. 1263. The Mental Health Act Commission has expressed the hope that "in appropriate cases doctors will not feel compelled by the new provisions to ignore the possible use of guardianship as an alternative" (MHAC, Public Position Paper on the Mental Health (Patients in the Community) Bill, 1995, para. 2.5). Also see paragraph 8 of the supplement to the *Code of Practice*.

Jurisdiction of the Mental Health Act Commission
In its Public Position Paper on the Mental Health (Patients in the Community) **1–263**
Bill, *ibid.*, the Mental Health Act Commission advocated that consideration should
be given by Parliament to an

"extension of its remit to patients under supervised after-care so as to enable it to
ensure (so far as possible)—
    that the new powers are correctly exercised and applied in strict accordance with
    the statutory requirements, and
    that, by a process of observation and monitoring over the years, the use of the
    powers is of benefit to the patients involved and to the community into which the
    patients have been discharged" (para. 3.1).

Although the Government resisted various attempts that were made to amend the
Bill to extend the Commission's remit, the Commission's existing remit enables it to
monitor supervised discharge as follows:
    (1) under section 120(1) the Secretary of State has delegated to the Commission his
duty to "keep under review the exercise of the powers and the discharge of the duties
conferred or imposed by this Act so far as relating to the detention of patients or to
patients liable to be detained under this Act". As an application for supervised
discharge can only be made in respect of a detained patient or a patient who is liable
to be detained, that part of this Act which is concerned with the making of
applications comes within the Commission's remit;
    (2) the Commission has the power to visit and interview detained patients who are
subject to supervision applications (s.120(1)(a)); and,
    (3) the Commission can investigate a complaint made by a patient or other person
about the exercise of the powers supervised discharge in so far as the complaint arises
from a period when the patient was detained or liable to be detained (s.120(1)(b)(ii)).

Partnership arrangements
Sections 25A to 25H are prescribed as NHS functions which may be the subject of **1–264**
partnership arrangements with local authorities under the Health Act 1999 (NHS
Bodies and Local Authority Partnership Arrangements Regulations 2000 (S.I. 2000
No. 617), reg. 5 and the National Health Service Bodies and Local Authorities
Partnership Arrangements (Wales) Regulations 2000 (S.I. 2000 No. 2993), reg. 5.
Local authorities are allowed to make payments to NHS bodies toward expenditure
incurred by them in connection with the performance of their functions under these
sections (National Health Service (Payments by Local Authorities to NHS Bodies)
(Prescribed Functions) Regulations 2000 (S.I. 2000 No. 618), reg. 2 and the National
Health Service (Payments by Local Authorities to Health Authorities) (Prescribed
Functions) (Wales) Regulations 2001 (S.I. 2001 No. 1543), reg. 2).

Primary Care Trusts
Health Authority functions under the following sections are to be exercised by **1–265**
Primary Care Trusts in England : sections 25A(6) to (8), 25C(6), 25D(1), 25E, 25F(1)
and (4), 25G(3) and (8) and 25H(6) (Primary Care Trusts (Functions) (England)
Regulations 2000 (S.I. 2000 No. 695), reg. 3(2)(b), Sched. 2).

The Human Rights Act 1998
See the note on section 25D. **1–266**

Application for supervision
    25A.—(1) Where a patient— **1–267**
    (a) is liable to be detained in a hospital in pursuance of an application for
        admission for treatment; and
    (b) has attained the age of 16 years,
an application may be made for him to be supervised after he leaves hospital,
for the period allowed by the following provisions of this Act, with a view to

securing that he receives the after-care services provided for him under section 117 below.

(2) In this Act an application for a patient to be so supervised is referred to as a "supervision application"; and where a supervision application has been duly made and accepted under this Part of this Act in respect of a patient and he has left hospital, he is for the purposes of this Act "subject to after-care under supervision" (until he ceases to be so subject in accordance with the provisions of this Act).

(3) A supervision application shall be made in accordance with this section and sections 25B and 25C below.

(4) A supervision application may be made in respect of a patient only on the grounds that—

(a) he is suffering from mental disorder, being mental illness, severe mental impairment, psychopathic disorder or mental impairment;

(b) there would be a substantial risk of serious harm to the health or safety of the patient or the safety of other persons or of the patient being seriously exploited, if he were not to receive the after-care services to be provided for him under section 117 below after he leaves hospital; and

(c) his being subject to after-care under supervision is likely to help to secure that he receives the after-care services to be provided.

(5) A supervision application may be made only by the responsible medical officer.

(6) A supervision application in respect of a patient shall be addressed to the Health Authority which will have the duty under section 117 below to provide after-care services for the patient after he leaves hospital.

(7) Before accepting a supervision application in respect of a patient a Health Authority shall consult the local social services authority which will also have that duty.

(8) Where a Health Authority accept a supervision application in respect of a patient the Health Authority shall—

(a) inform the patient both orally and in writing—
    (i) that the supervision application has been accepted; and
    (ii) of the effect in his case of the provisions of this Act relating to a patient subject to after-care under supervision (including, in particular, what rights of applying to a Mental Health Review Tribunal are available);

(b) inform any person whose name is stated in the supervision application in accordance with sub-paragraph (i) of paragraph (e) of section 25B(5) below that the supervision application has been accepted; and

(c) inform in writing any person whose name is so stated in accordance with sub-paragraph (ii) of that paragraph that the supervision application has been accepted.

(9) Where a patient in respect of whom a supervision application is made is granted leave of absence from a hospital under section 17 above (whether before or after the supervision application is made), references in—

(a) this section and the following provisions of this Part of this Act; and
(b) Part V of this Act,

to his leaving hospital shall be construed as references to his period of leave expiring (otherwise than on his return to the hospital or transfer to another hospital).]

AMENDMENT
This section was inserted by the Mental Health (Patients in the Community) Act 1995, s.1.

DEFINITIONS
    patient: s.145(1).   **1–268**
    application for admission for treatment: ss.3, 145(1).
    hospital: ss.34(2), 145(1).
    mental disorder: ss.1, 145(1).
    severe mental impairment: ss.1, 145(1).
    psychopathic disorder: ss.1, 145(1).
    mental impairment: ss.1, 145(1).
    responsible medical officer: s.34(1).
    local social services authority: s.145(1).

GENERAL NOTE
    This section, which should be read with sections 25B and 25C, identifies who can be **1–269** made subject to an application for supervised discharge, who can make an application and what grounds must be satisfied if an application is to be made. Its provisions are modified in respect of patients subject to community care orders in Scotland who intend to reside in England or Wales: see the Mental Health (Patients in the Community) (Transfers from Scotland) Regulations 1996 (S.I. 1996 No. 295).
    It applies to patients who are subject to hospital orders and their equivalent made under Part III (Sched. 1, Part 1, paras 2, 8A) but not to patients who are subject to restriction orders (s.41(3)(aa)).
    Guidance on this section is contained in paragraph 13 *et seq.* of the supplement to the *Code of Practice.*

Delegation of functions
    The functions placed on the Health Authority by subsections (6), (7) and (8) of this **1–270** section may be delegated to a body with whom the Authority has contracted to provide section 117 services. This will in most cases be a NHS trust, but could be an independent or voluntary sector provider. Most delegations will be in this form although the Health Authority does have the alternative of delegating to:

    (i) another Health Authority;
    (ii) a committee or sub-committee, or an officer, of the Health Authority or another Health Authority;
    (iii) a joint committee, or joint sub-committee, of the Health Authority and one or more other Health Authorities;
    (iv) a Special Health Authority; or
    (v) an officer of a Special Health Authority (Mental Health (After-care under Supervision) Regulations 1994 (S.I. 1994 No. 294), reg. 2).

Subsection (1)
    Liable to be detained . . . for treatment: There is no need for the patient to have had a **1–271** history of previous compulsory admissions. Although the patient must be liable to be detained at the time when the application is made, the application is not invalidated if the patient subsequently attains informal status. Section 117 would apply to such a patient on his eventual discharge from hospital (s.117(1)).
    Age of 16 years: It might be possible to bring proceedings under section 31 and Schedule 3, paragraph 5 of the Children Act 1989 in respect of a child under 16 who

requires supervision and control in the community as a consequence of mental disorder. If an application is made in respect of a ward of court, supervised discharge is subject to any order which the court may make in the exercise of its wardship jurisdiction (s.33(4)).

After he leaves hospital: Note, however, that it is possible to make an application in respect of a patient who has left hospital having been granted leave of absence under section 17 (subs. (9)). If an application is accepted in respect of such a patient, the application is "suspended" until the leave has expired (subs. (9)).

Period allowed: See section 25G.

Subsection (2)

1–272   *And he has left hospital:* Although section 117 is a continuing duty in respect of any patient who may be discharged and falls within that section (*R. v. Ealing District Health Authority, ex p. Fox* [1993] 3 All E.R. 170), a supervision application does not come into effect until either the patient has left hospital (subs. (1)) or his leave of absence has expired (subs. (9)).

Until he ceases to be so subject: See section 25H.

Subsection (4)

Paragraph (a)

1–273   *Mental disorder:* Supervised discharge "is available for patients suffering from any form of mental disorder but is primarily intended for those with severe mental illness" (*Memorandum*, para. 113).

Paragraph (b)

1–274   *Substantial risk of serious harm:* The court's have interpreted "substantial risk" in the context of section 2(2) of the Contempt of Court Act 1981, as a risk that is more than remote and not merely minimal (*Att.-Gen. v. English* [1982] 2 All E.R. 903 at 919 and *Att.-Gen. v. News Group Newspapers Ltd* [1986] 2 All E.R. 833 at 841).

The aim of supervised discharge is to respond to the particular needs of "revolving door" patients. It is likely that most of these patients will meet this criterion because they will have had a history of defaulting on medication which will have led to them becoming ill enough to trigger compulsory admissions. This history would make the risk "substantial" and the process of becoming ill again would cause "serious harm" to the health of the patient.

Health: As this term covers both physical and mental health, a substantial risk of harm resulting from neglect of the patient's physical well-being comes within the scope of this provision.

Of other persons: A substantial risk of serious psychological harm to a potential carer of the patient would suffice.

Seriously exploited: Baroness Cumberlege, in responding to a criticism that this phrase is "capable of many interpretations" said that the Government

"are trying to identify a small group of mentally disordered patients whose care in the community is less effective than it should be because of a repeating pattern in which they fail to comply with their treatment plan and then have to be readmitted to hospital. There will be mentally disordered patients who are at risk of exploitation who will fall into this group. Such risks might be that they could be lured into prostitution or that they are exposed to the risks of drug abuse" (*Hansard*, HL, Vol. 563, col. 108). The risk of economic exploitation could be added to this list.

Paragraph (c)

1–275   *Likely to help to secure:* This convoluted formulation probably means that the responsible medical officer, having considered the general effectiveness of supervised discharge, has concluded that the making of an application will assist the care team in their task of ensuring that the patient receives the after-services he is deemed to need. Research studies suggest that patients on supervised discharge have increased community survival rates (S. Davies *et al.*, "Section 25 Aftercare under supervision; the first eighteen months", *Medicine, Science and the Law* 39 (1999) 214–218 and D. Franklin *et al.*, "Consultant psychiatrists' experiences of using supervised discharge", *Psychiatric Bulletin* (2000) 24, 412–415).

An application for supervised discharge should not be used as a device for ensuring that the patient is provided with after-care services: see paragraph 7 of the supplement to the *Code of Practice*.

Subsection (5)
  A supervision application may be made: Using Form 1S (S.I. 1996 No. 294, reg. 3,   **1–276**
Sched. 2).
  The responsible medical officer: The discretion to make an application cannot be delegated.

Subsection (6)
  Health Authority: See the General Note to this section under the heading   **1–277**
"Delegation of functions". A report renewing supervision is addressed to the Health Authority and the local authority (s.25G(3)).

Subsection (7)
  Consult: A requirement that the Health Authority obtain the agreement of the   **1–278**
local authority to the making of a supervision application was not felt to be necessary because "in practice the statement of services to be provided, which has to be submitted with the supervision application, will need to have been agreed with the local authority's representatives so far as the social services element is concerned"; *per* Baroness Cumberlege, *Hansard*, HL, Vol. 563, col. 117.

Subsection (8)
  Accepts: There is no maximum period within which an application must be   **1–279**
accepted. There appears to be nothing to prevent an application being accepted in respect of an in-patient who had ceased to be liable to be detained after the application had been made. The acceptance of the application does not have the effect of automatically discharging the section 3. If the Health Authority accepts the application it has a duty to secure that the patient under supervision has a community responsible medical officer and a supervisor (s.117(2A)).

Paragraph (a)
  Inform the patient: The applicant should also be informed.   **1–280**
  Rights of applying to a mental health review tribunal: Under section 66(1)(ga), (2)(c).

Paragraph (b)
  Inform: The method to be used when informing the "lay carer" is not prescribed.   **1–281**

Paragraph (c)
  ANY PERSON. *i.e.* the patient's nearest relative.   **1–282**

Subsection (9)
  The rationale for this provision was explained by Baroness Cumberlege: "[Subsec-   **1–283**
tion (9)] puts beyond doubt that a supervision application can be made for patients who have been granted leave of absence from hospital and who may be made subject to aftercare under supervision without having first to return to hospital, once their period of liability to detention comes to an end. That has always been our policy intention. Under the existing Act patients who are on leave of absence are entitled to section 117 aftercare, but remain liable to recall to hospital and are subject to the

consent to treatment provisions in the Act. This means medication can be administered without their consent, although that would usually be given in hospital. When their period of detention ends, we foresee that some patients who are on their way to successful rehabilitation at the end of their period of liability to detention, but who still require supervision, could be made subject to the new power at that stage. Such aftercare services would then have to be provided under supervision. The patient would have the right to appeal against the decision to a mental health review tribunal in the same way as any patient for whom a supervision application has been accepted."

[Making of supervision application

1–284   **25B.**—(1) The responsible medical officer shall not make a supervision application unless—

(a) subsection (2) below is complied with; and

(b) the responsible medical officer has considered the matters specified in subsection (4) below.

(2) This subsection is complied with if—

(a) the following persons have been consulted about the making of the supervision application—

   (i) the patient;

   (ii) one or more persons who have been professionally concerned with the patient's medical treatment in hospital;

   (iii) one or more reasons who will be professionally concerned with the after-care services to be provided for the patient under section 117 below; and

   (iv) any person who the responsible medical officer believes will play a substantial part in the care of the patient after he leaves hospital but will not be professionally concerned with any of the after-care services to be so provided;

(b) such steps as are practicable have been taken to consult the person (if any) appearing to be the nearest relative of the patient about the making of the supervision application; and

(c) the responsible medical officer has taken into account any views expressed by the persons consulted.

(3) Where the patient has requested that paragraph (b) of subsection (2) above should not apply, that paragraph shall not apply unless—

(a) the patient has a propensity to violent or dangerous behaviour towards others; and

(b) the responsible medical officer considers that it is appropriate for steps such as are mentioned in that paragraph to be taken.

(4) The matters referred to in subsection (1)(b) above are—

(a) the after-care services to be provided for the patient under section 117 below; and

(b) any requirements to be imposed on him under section 25D below.

(5) A supervision application shall state—

(a) that the patient is liable to be detained in a hospital in pursuance of an application for admission for treatment;

(b) the age of the patient or, if his exact age is not known to the applicant, that the patient is believed to have attained the age of 16 years;

(c) that in the opinion of the applicant (having regard in particular to the patient's history) all of the conditions set out in section 25A(4) above are complied with;

(d) the name of the person who is to be the community responsible medical officer, and of the person who is to be the supervisor, in relation to the patient after he leaves hospital; and

(e) the name of—

    (i) any person who has been consulted under paragraph (a)(iv) of subsection (2) above; and

    (ii) any person who has been consulted under paragraph (b) of that subsection.

(6) A supervision application shall be accompanied by—

(a) the written recommendation in the prescribed form of a registered medical practitioner who will be professionally concerned with the patient's medical treatment after he leaves hospital or, if no such practitioner other than the responsible medical officer will be so concerned, of any registered medical practitioner; and

(b) the written recommendation in the prescribed form of an approved social worker.

(7) A recommendation under subsection (6)(a) above shall include a statement that in the opinion of the medical practitioner (having regard in particular to the patient's history) all of the conditions set out in section 25A(4) above are complied with.

(8) A recommendation under subsection (6)(b) above shall include a statement that in the opinion of the social worker (having regard in particular to the patient's history) both of the conditions set out in section 25A(4)(b) and (c) above are complied with.

(9) A supervision application shall also be accompanied by—

(a) a statement in writing by the person who is to be the community responsible medical officer in relation to the patient after he leaves hospital that he is to be in charge of the medical treatment provided for the patient as part of the after-care services provided for him under section 117 below;

(b) a statement in writing by the person who is to be the supervision in relation to the patient after he leaves hospital that he is to supervise the patient with a view to securing that he receives the after-care services so provided;

(c) details of the after-care services to be provided for the patient under section 117 below; and

(d) details of any requirements to be imposed on him under section 25D below.

(10) On making a supervision application in respect of a patient the responsible medical officer shall—

(a) inform the patient both orally and in writing;

(b) inform any person who has been consulted under paragraph (a)(iv) of subsection (2) above; and

(c) inform in writing any person who has been consulted under paragraph (b) of that subsection,

of the matters specified in subsection (11) below.

(11) The matters referred to in subsection (10) above are—

(a) that the application is being made;

(b) the after-care services to be provided for the patient under section 117 below;

(c) any requirements to be imposed on him under section 25D below; and
(d) the name of the person who is to be the community responsible medical officer, and of the person who is to be the supervisor, in relation to the patient after he leaves hospital.]

AMENDMENT
This section was inserted by the Mental Health (Patients in the Community) Act 1995, s.1.

DEFINITIONS
1–285   responsible medical officer: s.34(1)
supervision application: ss.25A(2), 145(1).
patient: s.145(1).
medical treatment: s.145(1).
hospital: ss.34(2), 145(1).
nearest relative: ss.26(3), 145(1)
application for admission for treatment: ss.3, 145(1).
community responsible medical officer: s.34(1)
supervisor: s.34(1)
approved social worker: s.145(1).

GENERAL NOTE
1–286   This section requires the patient's responsible medical officer to ensure that consultation takes place and to consider the patients after-care plan and any requirements to be imposed on him, before making an application for supervised discharge. It also specifies the contents of an application and the documents that must accompany it, and requires the application to be supported by recommendations from a doctor and an approved social worker. Finally, it requires the responsible medical officer to inform the patient and others that the application has been made. Its provisions are modified in respect of patients subject to community care orders in Scotland who intend to reside in England or Wales: see the Mental Health (Patients in the Community) (Transfers from Scotland) Regulations 1996 (S.I. 1996 No. 295).
Guidance on this section is contained in paragraph 20 *et seq.* of the supplement to the *Code of Practice.*

Subsection (1)
1–287   *Shall not:* This section is mandatory.

Subsection (2)
1–288   *Have been consulted:* The wording of this provision does not require the responsible medical officer to have personally undertaken the consultations. The consultations must be carried out before the application is made. Guidance on consultation is given in paragraphs 20 to 26 of the supplement to the *Code of Practice.*

Paragraph (a)
1–289   (i) *The patient:* Whose agreement to the application is not required.
(ii) *Professionally concerned with the patient's medical treatment:* This person need not be another doctor.
(iii) *Professionally concerned with the after-care services:* The patient's potential supervisor could come within this category. As the supervisor will play a central role in the patient's care in the community, it would seem sensible to consult with him or her.
(iv) *Substantial part in the care of the patient:* This is a judgment for the responsible medical officer to make. A carer who would do no more than call in occasionally to "keep an eye" on the patient would not qualify. More than one person could fall into this category.

Paragraph (b)
 To consult: Subject to subsection (3). **1–290**
 Nearest relative: Who has a right to make an application to a Mental Health Review Tribunal if the application is accepted (s.66(1)(ga)(i)).

Paragraph (c)
 Taken into account: This phrase is superfluous given that "in any context the **1–291** essence of consultation is the communication of a genuine invitation to give advice and a genuine consideration of that advice" (*R. v. Secretary of State for Social Services, ex p. Association of Metropolitan Authorities* [1986] 1 All E.R. 164 *per* Webster J. at 167).

Subsection (3)
 That paragraph shall not apply: In many cases the patient's nearest relative will be **1–292** a person who will play "a substantial part" in the care of the patient and will therefore have been consulted under paragraph (a)(iv).
 Propensity to violent or dangerous behaviour: An unfortunate label to attach to a patient who is about to be discharged into the community. The matters which the responsible medical officer is likely to want to consider when addressing this issue are identified in paragraph 27 of the supplement to the *Code of Practice.*
 Baroness Cumberlege when responding to Baroness Jay's statement that if "people are identified as having a propensity to violent or dangerous behaviour they would appear, prima facie, to be unsuitable for ... release", said that she was "advised that the word 'propensity' would bear its ordinary dictionary meaning of an inclination, bent, tendency or disposition. It is not possible to say in general terms how strong that propensity would need to be because the Bill deliberately leaves that to the judgment of the responsible medical officer. Clearly the responsible medical officer would wish to consider, for example, what was known about the patient's history; the seriousness of any past violence; against whom it had been directed; how the patient had responded to treatment; and how must light consultation with the nearest relative was likely to shed on the assessment of the patient's present condition and needs" (*Hansard*, HL, Vol. 563, col. 1644). Her Ladyship had previously stated that if "there is a serious risk of violence which could not be contained by supervision it is highly unlikely that a supervision application would be made" (*ibid.* Vol. 563, col. 1235).

Subsection (4)
 After-care services to be provided: These should be described in a written after-care **1–293** plan for the patient.
 Any requirements to be imposed on him: As the responsible medical officer has to consider this matter before an application has been made, the after-care bodies could only realistically be expected to have given consideration to their joint power under section 25D to impose requirements if both authorities had agreed to delegate their respective duties to members of the care team who constructed the patient's after-care plan. This was the assumption made by Mr John Bowis M.P.: "The care plan that is put in place before the supervision application is made will include any requirements that those responsible for care believe will help the patient to comply with it. Details will be attached to the application, which will have been the subject of consultation with all those concerned, including the patient (*Hansard*, HC, Standing Committee F, col. 83).

Subsection (5)

Paragraph (d)
 The Health Authority with section 117 responsibilities has a duty to ensure that a **1–294** patient subject to supervised discharge has a community responsible medical officer and a supervisor (s.117(2A)).

Community responsible medical officer: There is nothing to prevent the same person being the patient's community responsible medical officer, responsible medical officer and supervisor (s.34(1A)). The professional responsibilities of the community responsible medical officer are outlined in paragraph 44 of the supplement to the *Code of Practice*.

Supervisor: Baroness Cumberlege outlined the role and liability of the supervisor:

> "The supervisor will, of course, play a crucial role in the successful working of the new power. It is he or she who will keep closely in touch with a patient, co-ordinating the care which the patient is to receive, convening meetings of the care team, alerting colleagues to any modifications that may be necessary and checking that any requirements laid upon the patient are followed. If found to be necessary, it will be the supervisor in the first instance who will invoke the power to convey the patient.
>
> It is essential that the person who is to play this important role is identified early on and before the patient is discharged from hospital. The whole application process is founded on the understanding that there has been full consultation between the hospital responsible medical officer and the future care team and that one of the multi-disciplinary team has agreed to act as a supervisor for the patient. Indeed, the Health Authority could not accept an application without that degree of clarity. The nomination of the supervisor must follow from the consultation and discussion which have preceded the application and upon which the care plan has been based.
>
> Having explained how we see the supervisor's role and how important it is to have it identified and formalised at the outset, I believe that my noble friend may have concerns about what legal liabilities this key role will attract, as he mentioned this afternoon. I think I can reassure him on that point. While the supervisor will have professional liabilities and responsibilities along with other professionals in the care team, there will be no additional liability of the kind I think my noble friend has in mind. The supervisor would, of course, be personally liable in cases involving, for example, serious professional negligence, indiscipline or the abuse of patients. But, in general, liability would fall on the bodies responsible for providing the section 117 aftercare services, not the supervisor personally, just because he or she fulfils that role. This is the normal relationship between public bodies and the professional staff they employ, and in this respect the supervisor is in the same position as other professionals" (*Hansard*, Vol. 563, col. 1238).

Baroness Miller said that the Government "envisage the supervisor being the same person as the key worker under the care programme approach in most cases and, again, in most cases this will be a community psychiatric nurse. But we do not want to restrict who may be the supervisor ... In some cases that person might be a social worker rather than a nurse, but in others the patient's doctor might be better placed to perform the role. Nor would we want to exclude other possible but perhaps unusual arrangements such as, for example, a clinical psychologist being nominated" (*ibid*. Vol. 565, col. 1241).

The professional responsibilities of the supervisor are outlined in paragraph 43 of the supplement to the *Code of Practice*.

Subsection (6)

1–295 *Shall be accompanied by:* Unlike applications for the admission of a patient to hospital, there are no restrictions on the timing of recommendations made under this provision. As there is no requirement equivalent to that contained in section 12(1) for the recommendations to be signed "on or before the date of the application", it is possible for the recommendations to be completed after the application has been signed. Good professional practice suggests that the recommendations be based on a recent assessment of the patient.

Any registered medical practitioner: Not coming within the categories set out in section 25C(9). The doctor, who is given powers in respect of the patient by section 25C(3)(5), must use form 2S (S.I. 1996 No. 294, reg. 3, Sched. 2). Section 12, which is concerned with medical recommendations made in support of applications for admission to hospital and guardianship applications, does not apply to applications for supervised discharge.

Professionally concerned: The recommending doctor "should normally be the community responsible medical officer unless the patient's responsible medical officer will also be acting in that role" (*Memorandum*, para. 121).

Any registered medical practitioner: This could include a doctor who is professionally accountable to the applicant.

An approved social worker: Who need not have had a professional involvement with the patient's care. The approved social worker, who is given powers in respect of the patient by section 25(4)(5), must use Form 3S (S.I. 1996 No. 294, *ibid.*).

Subsection (9)
Community responsible medical officer ... supervisor: These terms are defined in **1–296** section 34(1). A procedure for changing the patient's CRMO and supervisor is set out in section 25E(9)–(11).

Subsection (10)

Paragraph (b)
Inform: "We think there should be flexibility in the way [informal carers] are **1–297** informed"; *per* Baroness Cumberlege, *Hansard*, HL, Vol. 563, col. 1227. Guidance on this provision is contained in paragraphs 37 to 39 of the supplement to the *Code of Practice.*

[Supervision applications: supplementary
25C.—(1) Subject to subsection (2) below, a supervision application, and **1–298** the recommendation under section 25B(6)(a) above accompanying it, may describe the patient as suffering from more than one of the following forms of mental disorder, namely, mental illness, severe impairment, psychopathic disorder and mental impairment.

(2) A supervision application shall be of no effect unless the patient is described in the application and the recommendation under section 25B(6)(a) above accompanying it as suffering from the same form of mental disorder, whether or not he is also described in the application or the recommendation as suffering from another form.

(3) A registered medical practitioner may at any reasonable time visit a patient and examine him in private for the purpose of deciding whether to make a recommendation under section 25B(6)(a) above.

(4) An approved social worker may at any reasonable time visit and interview a patient for the purpose of deciding whether to make a recommendation under section 25B(6)(b) above.

(5) For the purpose of deciding whether to make a recommendation under section 25B(6) above in respect of a patient, a registered medical practitioner or an approved social worker may require the production of and inspect any records relating to the detention or treatment of the patient in any hospital or to any after-care services provided for the patient under section 117 below.

(6) If, within the period of 14 days beginning with the day on which a supervision application has been accepted, the application, or any recommendation accompanying it, is found to be in any respect incorrect or defective, the application or recommendation may, within that period and with the consent of the Health Authority which accepted the application, be amended by the person by whom it was made or given.

(7) Where an application or recommendation is amended in accordance with subsection (6) above it shall have effect, and shall be deemed to have had effect, as if it had been originally made or given as so amended.

(8) A supervision application which appears to be duly made and to be accompanied by recommendations under section 25B(6) above may be acted upon without further proof of—

(a) the signature or qualification of the person by whom the application or any such recommendation was made or given; or

(b) any matter of fact or opinion stated in the application or recommendation.

(9) A recommendation under section 25B(6) above accompanying a supervision application in respect of a patient shall not be given by—

(a) the responsible medical officer;

(b) a person who receives or has an interest in the receipt of any payments made on account of the maintenance of the patient; or

(c) a close relative of the patient, of any person mentioned in paragraph (a) or (b) above or of a person by whom the other recommendation is given under section 25B(6) above for the purposes of the application.

(10) In subsection (9)(c) above "close relative" means husband, wife, father, father-in-law, mother, mother-in-law, son, son-in-law, daughter, daughter-in-law, brother, brother-in-law, sister or sister-in-law.]

AMENDMENT

This section was inserted by the Mental Health (Patients in the Community) Act 1995, s.1.

DEFINITIONS

1–299   supervision application: ss.25A(2) 145(1).
patient: s.145(1)
mental disorder: ss.1, 145(1)
severe mental impairment: ss.1, 145(1).
psychopathic disorder: ss.1, 145(1).
mental impairment: ss.1, 145(1).
approved social worker: s.145(1).
hospital: ss.34(2), 145(1).
responsible medical officer: s.34(1).

GENERAL NOTE

1–300   This section requires the applicant and the doctor making the medical recommendation to state that the patient is suffering from the same form of mental disorder, provides those who make recommendations with a right to have access to the patient and to examine relevant documentation, allows for the rectification of defective application documents, and prohibits certain persons from making recommendations. Its provisions are modified in respect of patients subject to community care orders in Scotland who intend to reside in England or Wales: see the Mental Health (Patients in the Community) (Transfers from Scotland) Regulations 1996 (S.I. 1996 No. 295).

Subsections (3), (4)
    Access: Any person refusing access to the patient without reasonable cause **1–301**
commits an offence under section 129(1)(b).

Subsection (5)
    Records: A person who refuses to produce records without reasonable cause **1–302**
commits an offence under section 129(1)(c).

Subsection (6)
    Beginning with: Including the day on which the supervision application was **1–303**
accepted (*Hare v. Gocher* [1962] 2 Q.B. 641).
    Incorrect or defective: Rectification cannot be used to cure a genuine deficiency
which would, otherwise, invalidate the application, such as a failure by the applicant
and the recommending doctor to agree on the form of the patient's mental disorder
(subs. (2)).
    Health Authority: The Health Authority can delegate this function to a body with
whom the Authority has contracted to provide section 117 services or to a person or
body listed in the General Note to section 25A under the heading "Delegation of
functions" (Mental Health (After-care under Supervision) Regulations 1996 (S.I.
1996 No. 294), reg. 2).

Subsection (9)

Paragraph (a)
    Responsible medical officer: Despite what is said in paragraph 30 of the supplement **1–304**
to the *Code of Practice*, this provision does not prevent a doctor who works under the
direction of the responsible medical officer from providing a recommendation.

Paragraph (b)
    See the notes on section 12(5)(d).   **1–305**

Paragraph (c)
    Close relative: See subsection (10).   **1–306**

|Requirements to secure receipt of after-care under supervision
    25D.—(1) Where a patient is subject to after-care under supervision (or, if **1–307**
he has not yet left hospital, is to be so subject after he leaves hospital), the
responsible after-care bodies have power to impose any of the requirements
specified in subsection (3) below for the purpose of securing that the patient
receives the after-care services provided for him under section 117 below.
    (2) In this Act "the responsible after-care bodies", in relation to a patient,
means the bodies which have (or will have) the duty under section 117 below
to provide after-care services for the patient.
    (3) The requirements referred to in subsection (1) above are—
    (a) that the patient reside at a specified place;
    (b) that the patient attend at specified places and times for the purpose of
        medical treatment, occupation, education or training; and
    (c) that access to the patient be given, at any place where the patient is
        residing, to the supervisor, any registered medical practitioner or any
        approved social worker or to any other person authorised by the
        supervisor.
    (4) A patient subject to after-care under supervision may be taken and
conveyed by, or by any person authorised by, the supervisor to any place

where the patient is required to reside or to attend for the purpose of medical treatment, occupation, education or training.

(5) A person who demands—

(a) to be given access to a patient in whose case a requirement has been imposed under subsection (3)(c) above; or

(b) to take and convey a patient in pursuance of subsection (4) above,

shall, if asked to do so, produce some duly authenticated document to show that he is a person entitled to be given access to, or to take and convey, the patient.]

AMENDMENT

This section was inserted by the Mental Health (Patients in the Community) Act 1995.

DEFINITIONS

1–308   patient: s.145(1).

subject to after-care under supervision: ss.25A(2), 145(1A).

hospital: ss.34(2), 145(1).

medical treatment: s.145(1).

supervisor: s.34(1).

GENERAL NOTE

1–309   This section enables the Health Authority and the local authority to jointly impose certain "requirements" on a patient who is subject to supervised discharge. Its provisions are modified in respect of patients subject to community care orders in Scotland who intend to reside in England or Wales: see the Mental Health (Patients in the Community) (Transfers from Scotland) Regulations 1996 (S.I. 1996 No. 295). Details of the requirements to be imposed must accompany the application (s.25B(9)(d)) and they can be subsequently modified under the review procedure set out in section 25E. The requirements are very similar to the powers given to a patient's guardian under section 8. The major difference between guardianship powers and supervision requirements is that the latter can be enforced by means of a power to "take and convey" a reluctant patient to the place where he is required to be. This power was keenly debated in Parliament and Ministers were repeatedly called upon to explain the Government view:

"We are providing for a reserve power, as it were, which would be available to the supervisor of that small group of vulnerable, and sometimes unpredictable patients, in order to overcome a temporary unwillingness to co-operate. The power would be temporary to enable supervisors to overcome a temporary problem and assist people in complying with the terms of the care plan to which they have agreed in such a way that by the time that they have been conveyed they will, it is hoped, have resumed their agreement to co-operate with the care plan. If they continue refusing to co-operate, it will be clear that supervised discharge is not working and a patient's plan may be eligible for reassessment. In that case, under the existing terms of the Act, the patient's case can be reconsidered"; *per* Mr John Bowis, M.P., *Hansard*, HC Standing Committee F, col. 94.

"Although we envisage the comparatively rare use of the power to convey a patient, we do see it as an important feature of the new provisions. It will enable a supervisor, or any person authorised by the supervisor, to take the patient to the place where he or she is required, under the terms of the supervision arrangements, to live or attend for treatment or rehabilitation. While it is true that ultimately supervision will succeed only with the patient's participation, the power to convey will give useful backing to the care team, for example where there is a temporary reluctance to co-operate. We have followed the form of the existing Mental Health Act power for conveying a patient to hospital following an application for detention. I do not believe that this power will be misused because to do so would be so obviously self-defeating"; *per* Baroness Cumberlege, *Hansard*, HL Vol. 563, col. 154.

"It is not for politicians to decide on behalf of a professional when to use the power. The professional in charge of the patient must make that decision. Perhaps the patient might have a cold, for example, on the first occasion that he showed reluctance, and the professional would not worry too much about failure to comply. If the patient subsequently refused to go for treatment or training, the supervisor might tell the patient, this is getting serious, you must come with me. I have the power to convey you, will you please come? I hope that such a reminder will be sufficient. However, if the patient showed a stronger reluctance, the professional might consider using the power of conveyance. I hope that it will not be necessary to do that. The provision aims to strengthen the supervisor and protect the patient"; *per* Mr John Bowis M.P., *Hansard*, HC Standing Committee F, col. 96.

"[In the absence of such a power] one of two things will happen. First, the patient will be taken in for assessment each time that a risk is perceived to exist. When the conditions of the care plan are not complied with, a risk will be deemed to exist. Therefore, the patient's ability to remain in the community will be weakened. That is the first option available if there is no provision to comply with the care agreement. It means that patients could be subject to the powers to convey in the Mental Health Act 1983, which, under sections 2 or 3, mean that someone can be taken in for treatment or assessment. That will reduce a patient's potential to stay in the community. Alternatively, a second option could be chosen. A patient could be told that, however much he fails to comply with the conditions that he agreed to before he was discharged, nothing will be done about it. If he does not comply with the conditions, he will be told that there is now power halfway between leaving him in the community or taking him back in. Our proposal is designed to create a halfway stage. It will strengthen the supervisor and put a little more pressure on a patient to comply with the terms and conditions to which he agreed before a supervised discharge. I hope that that will work"; *per* Mr John Bowis M.P., *Hansard*, Vol. 262, col. 164.

Although subsection (4) provides the supervisor, or someone authorised by the supervisor, with a power to override a patient's objection to going to the place where he is required to be, it does not authorise the patient's detention once he has arrived at that place. There can be no implied power to detain associated with this provision because "there is a canon of construction that Parliament is presumed not to enact legislation which interferes with the liberty of the subject without making it clear that this was its intention" (*R. v. Hallstrom, ex p. W; R. v. Gardner, ex p. L* [1986] 2 All E.R. 306, *per* McCullough J. at 314). This provision can be compared with section 6 which provides hospital managers with an explicit power to detain a patient who has been subject to an application for admission to hospital.

Presumably the expectation is that once the patient arrives at the place where he is required to be he will be willing to remain there and co-operate with whatever activity is planned for him. If the patient cannot be persuaded to stay, he cannot be prevented from leaving the premises immediately after his arrival there. The take and convey power cannot be immediately reused to return the patient to the premises as this would have the effect of detaining him there. As the power to take and convey is most likely to be used in respect of patients who have stopped taking their medication, and as there is no power to treat such patients without their consent once they have arrived at the place where they are to receive the treatment, using this power could "be a classic case of taking a horse to water but not being able to make it drink"; *per* Baroness Jay, *Hansard*, HL, Vol. 563, col. 152. However, research suggests that the use of supervised discharge has been successful in improving medication compliance (Donna Franklin *et al.*, "Consultant psychiatrists' experiences of using supervised discharge", *Psychiatric Bulletin* (2000) 24, 412–415).

The Human Rights Act 1998

1–310 A requirement that the patient continues to accept medication will not contravene the European Convention on Human Rights if one of the grounds in Article 8(2) of the Convention is satisfied (see the note on Art. 8(2)).

On a number of occasions during the passage of the Mental Health (Patients in the Community) Bill the Government was pressed to confirm that the power to take and convey did not breach Articles 5 and 8 of the Convention. Such confirmation was repeatedly provided; see, for example, Mr John Bowis MP at *Hansard*, HL, Standing Committee F, col. 94. Article 5 exists to protect the freedom and security of the individual from arbitrary detention and Article 8 provides that everyone has a right to his private and family life.

It is clear that supervision by itself is not caught by Article 5 because the restrictions attached to supervised discharge could not be characterised as a deprivation of liberty: see the decisions of the European Commission of Human Rights in *L v. Sweden* (app. no. 10801/84) and *W v. Sweden* (app. no. 12778/87). The power to take and convey is a form of psychiatric arrest and for such an arrest to be lawful under the Convention the person concerned must be reliably shown to be of unsound mind of a nature or degree warranting detention, entailing "the establishment of a true mental disorder before a competent authority on the basis of objective expertise" (*Winterwerp v. The Netherlands* (1979) 2 E.H.R.R. 387, para. 39). In *X v. the United Kingdom* (1981) 1 B.M.L.R. 98, the court held at 112, 113, that "where a provision of domestic law is designed, among other things, to authorise emergency confinement of persons capable of presenting a danger to others, it would be impracticable to require a thorough medical examination prior to any arrest or detention". If the power to take and convey is to escape contravening the Convention by virtue of the decision in *X.*, it would need to be shown that a failure by a patient to comply with a requirement constituted an emergency. Although it might be possible to argue that a failure by a patient to take his medication creates an emergency if such action had in the past led to the patient or others being placed at risk, it would be difficult to make a similar argument in the case of a patient who refuses to comply with a requirement to take up his place in a day centre.

Guidance on the take and convey power is contained in paragraphs 48 to 50 of the supplement to the *Code of Practice*. The power is used rarely (Vanessa Pinfold *et al.*, "Supervised Discharge Orders in England", *Psychiatric Bulletin* (1999) 23, 199–203).

Subsection (1)

1–311 *Responsible after-care bodies have power to impose:* This is a power which must be exercised jointly. The function of the Health Authority under this provision can be delegated to a body with whom the Authority has contracted to provide section 117 services or to a person or body listed in the General Note to section 25A under the heading "Delegation of functions". If the Health Authority makes such a delegation, the local authority can also delegate its function under the provision to the same person or body (Mental Health (After-care under Supervision) Regulations 1996 (S.I. 1996 No. 294), reg. 2). Also see the note on "Any requirements to be imposed on him" in section 25B(4).

Securing that the patient receives . . . after care services: As the patient's supervisor is appointed "with a view to securing that [the patient] receives the after-care services . . . provided" (s.25B(9)(b)), the supervisor's view on the imposition of requirements should always be sought.

Subsection (3)
Requirements: The requirements should be specific enough to enable the patient to **1–312**
be clear about what is required of him. A requirement merely to "attend at a day
centre" would not satisfy this test and would be incapable of being enforced. A rigid
requirement, such as an obligation to attend a day centre "every Wednesday", should
be avoided because if that day proved to be inconvenient an alternative day could not
be substituted until the provisions of section 25E(5)(b),(6) had been complied with.
A more appropriate formulation would be a requirement to attend a day centre
"once a week on a day to be notified by [the supervisor] to [the patient]".

Paragraph (a)
Reside at a specified place: Which could be a private house, Housing Association **1–313**
accommodation, a hostel or a registered establishment. A hospital, which is an
institution provided for the treatment of patients (National Health Service Act 1977,
s.128), cannot be designated as a place of residence under this provision. There is no
power to require that the patient resides with a particular person.
The patient's agreement to live at the specified place is not required: "It is simply
inconceivable that health authorities or local authorities would want to make a
patient live in an unacceptable place, but if the patient's agreement is stipulated in
the Bill he would be able to overturn the requirement and undermine the supervised
discharge arrangement simply by withdrawing his agreement"; *per* Mr John Bowis
M.P., *Hansard*, HC, Standing Committee F, col. 88.

Paragraph (b)
Attend: But not reside. **1–314**
Medical treatment: A patient under supervised discharge is subject to common law
rules relating to the provision of medical treatment. see the General Note to Part IV.
The power in this section "cannot be used to require the patient to accept medication
in the community, and compulsory medication is no part of the Bill's provisions. I
know that that is something that some, including the British Medical Association,
would like, but we are advised that it would risk being in breach of our human rights
convention obligations, as well as being opposed by substantial bodies of medical
opinion"; *per* Mr John Bowis M.P., *Hansard*, HC Vol. 262, col. 163.

Paragraph (c)
Access to the patient is given: This power does not authorise the supervisor to use **1–315**
force to gain entry. If access to the patient is denied and it is considered that action to
obtain access should be taken, an approved social worker should be asked to consider
whether grounds exist for making an application to a magistrate under section 135(1)
for a warrant to remove the patient to a place of safety. A refusal to allow access to
the patient by an authorised person without reasonable cause constitutes an offence
under section 129(1)(b). Also see paragraph 51 of the supplement to the *Code of
Practice*.
Any place where the patient is residing: Which will not necessarily be the place
where the patient is required to reside under paragraph (a).
Authorised: The authorisation should be in writing (see subs. (5)).

Subsection (4)
The "take and convey" power is considered in the General Note to this section. **1–316**
May be: The supervisor is not obliged to use this power if a patient breaches a
requirement.
Taken and conveyed: As the use of this power will follow a refusal on the part of the
patient to comply with a requirement, it will trigger a review under section 24E.

If the medical condition of a patient who is reluctant to be taken and conveyed suggests that a period of hospitalisation might be appropriate, the supervisor should consider asking for an assessment to be made for a possible compulsory admission to hospital.

Any person authorised: The authorisation, which should be in writing (see subs. (5)), can be given to any person who the supervisor considers suitable to perform the task. "[T]he power to convey includes the right to ask a constable to assist. However, that will not happen in many cases. I believe that telling the patient that the supervisor has the power to convey will help to overcome any temporary lack of co-operation"; *per* Mr John Bowis, M.P., *Hansard*, HC, Standing Committee F, col. 96.

A patient being taken and conveyed is deemed to be in legal custody and the person who is conveying the patient is granted the powers of a policeman (s.137). If the patient "escapes" during the course of his conveyance he can be retaken by the person who was conveying him, by a policeman or by an approved social worker (s.138(1)). Section 138 does not provide authority for a forced entry to the place where the patient is believed to be.

Subsection (5)

1–317   *Demands:* A verbal demand would be sufficient.

Duly authenticated document: Authenticated by the supervisor, who is the person who possesses the relevant powers. It would be prudent for the supervisor to prepare such documentation for possible use during periods when he is absent from work.

[Review of after-care under supervision, etc.

1–318   **25E.**—(1) The after-care services provided (or to be provided) under section 117 below for a patient who is (or is to be) subject to after-care under supervision, and any requirements imposed on him under section 25D above, shall be kept under review, and (where appropriate) modified, by the responsible after-care bodies.

(2) This subsection applies in relation to a patient who is subject to after-care under supervision where he refuses or neglects—

(a) to receive any or all of the after-care services provided for him under section 117 below; or

(b) to comply with any or all of any requirements imposed on him under section 25D above.

(3) Where subsection (2) above applies in relation to a patient, the responsible after-care bodies shall review, and (where appropriate) modify—

(a) the after-care services provided for him under section 117 below; and

(b) any requirements imposed on him under section 25D above.

(4) Where subsection (2) above applies in relation to a patient, the responsible after-care bodies shall also—

(a) consider whether it might be appropriate for him to cease to be subject to after-care under supervision and, if they conclude that it might be, inform the community responsible medical officer; and

(b) consider whether it might be appropriate for him to be admitted to a hospital for treatment and, if they conclude that it might be, inform an approved social worker.

(5) The responsible after-care bodies shall not modify—

(a) the after-care services provided (or to be provided) under section 117 below for a patient who is (or is to be) subject to after-care under supervision; or

(b) any requirements imposed on him under section 25D above, unless subsection (6) below is complied with.

(6) This subsection is complied with if—

   (a) the patient has been consulted about the modifications;

   (b) any person who the responsible after-care bodies believe plays (or will play) a substantial part in the care of the patient but is not (or will not be) professionally concerned with the after-care services provided for the patient under section 117 below has been consulted about the modifications;

   (c) such steps as are practicable have been taken to consult the person (if any) appearing to be the nearest relative of the patient about the modifications; and

   (d) the responsible after-care bodies have taken into account any views expressed by the persons consulted.

(7) Where the patient has requested that paragraph (c) of subsection (6) above should not apply, that paragraph shall not apply unless—

   (a) the patient has a propensity to violent or dangerous behaviour towards others; and

   (b) the community responsible medical officer (or the person who is to be the community responsible medical officer) considers that it is appropriate for steps such as are mentioned in that paragraph to be taken.

(8) Where the responsible after-care bodies modify the after-care services provided (or to be provided) for the patient under section 117 below or any requirements imposed on him under section 25D above, they shall—

   (a) inform the patient both orally and in writing;

   (b) inform any person who has been consulted under paragraph (b) of subsection (6) above; and

   (c) inform in writing any person who has been consulted under paragraph (c) of that subsection,

that the modifications have been made.

(9) Where—

   (a) a person other than the person named in the supervision application becomes the community responsible medical officer when the patient leaves hospital; or

   (b) when the patient is subject to after-care under supervision, one person ceases to be, and another becomes, the community responsible medical officer,

the responsible after-care bodies shall comply with subsection (11) below.

(10) Where—

   (a) a person other than the person named in the supervision application becomes the supervisor when the patient leaves hospital; or

   (b) when the patient is subject to after-care under supervision, one person ceases to be, and another becomes, the supervisor,

the responsible after-care bodies shall comply with subsection (11) below.

(11) The responsible after-care bodies comply with this subsection if they—

   (a) inform the patient both orally and in writing;

   (b) inform any person who they believe plays a substantial part in the care of the patient but is not professionally concerned with the after-care services provided for the patient under section 117 below; and

(c) unless the patient otherwise requests, take such steps as are practicable to inform in writing the person (if any) appearing to be the nearest relative of the patient,

of the name of the person who becomes the community responsible medical officer or the supervisor.]

AMENDMENT
This section was inserted by the Mental Health (Patients in the Community) Act 1995, s.1.

DEFINITIONS
1–319   patient: s.145(1).
subject to after-care under supervision: ss.25A(2), 145(1A).
responsible after-care bodies: ss.25D, 145(1).
community responsible medical officer: s.34(1).
hospital: ss.34(2), 145(1).
approved social worker: s.145(1).
nearest relative: ss.26(3), 145(1).

GENERAL NOTE
1–320   This section requires the relevant Health Authority and local authority to keep under review and, where appropriate, modify both the after-care services provided to, and any requirements imposed on a patient who is subject to supervised discharge. If the patient refuses to receive an after-care service or to comply with a requirement, the authorities must consider whether they should recommend to the patient's community responsible medical officer that the supervision should end or whether they should inform an approved social worker that, in their view, the patient should be admitted to hospital under section 3 for treatment. Guidance on this section is contained in paragraph 44 *et seq.* of the supplement to the *Code of Practice*.
The section also requires the two authorities to inform the patient and others on a change of the patient's community responsible medical officer or supervisor.

Delegation of functions
1–321   The functions placed on the Health Authority by subsections (1), (3), (4), (6), (8) and (11) of this section can be delegated to a body with whom the Authority has contracted to provide section 117 services or to a person or body listed in the General Note to section 25A under this heading. If the Health Authority makes such a delegation, the local authority can delegate its functions under those subsections to the same person or body (Mental Health (After-care under supervision) Regulations 1994 (S.I. 1996 No. 294), reg. 2). Neither the Health Authority nor the local authority can delegate the functions under subsections (1) and (3) so far as they relate to the review and modification of section 117 services (*ibid.*, reg. 2(5)).

Patients moving within England and Wales
1–322   The following procedure could be adopted if a patient who is subject to supervised discharge intends to move outside the area of the after-care bodies:

(i) the supervisor contacts the relevant Health Authority and local authority before the patient moves to inform them of the patient's history and the existence of the supervised discharge. There will also "need to be direct contact between the present community responsible medical officer and his counterpart in the new area" (*Memorandum*, para. 131);

(ii) the two authorities consider whether they wish to continue with the supervised discharge;

(iii) if the decision is not to continue with the supervised discharge the existing CRMO could be requested to end the supervised discharge using the procedure under section 25H. If the supervised discharge is ended, it cannot be revived;

(iv) if the decision is to continue with the supervised discharge the Health Authority should:
  (a) identify a new CRMO and a new supervisor for the patient (subss. (10) and (11) of this section);
  (b) use the procedure set out in this section to identify new requirements and a new after-care plan for the patient; and
  (c) request the after-care bodies to forward copies of the statutory documentation so that the renewal date for the supervised discharge can be identified.

It is important to note that the identity of the bodies with responsibility to provide after-care services under section 117 does not change on a change of the patient's place of residence (*R. v. Mental Health Review Tribunal, ex p. Hall* [1993] 3 All E.R. 132, noted under s.117(2)). Also see paragraph 54 of the supplement to the *Code of Practice*.

Subsection (1)

Or to be provided: "In the great majority of cases the sequence of events will be, **1–323** broadly, that the care plan will have been drawn up and agreed, the supervision application made and then accepted by the Health Authority, and the patient leaves hospital and returns to the community where he will be subject to aftercare under supervision. However, it is possible that the care plan may need to be revised before discharge from hospital—perhaps a hostel place has fallen through, or the care team has to change. It therefore seems sensible to build in the possibility that the aftercare services could be modified before the patient leaves hospital. Changes as needed could also be made to the requirements in . . . section 25D. Any other approach would mean that the original care plan and requirements would take effect when the patient leaves hospital and would then need immediate review and change"; *per* Baroness Cumberlege, *Hansard*, HL, Vol. 563, cols 1256, 1257.

Responsible after-care bodies: See section 25D(2).

Subsection (2)

Refuses or neglects: Professional discretion should be used to ensure that the **1–324** provisions of this section are not triggered if the patient offers a reasonable excuse for his failure.

Subsection (3)

The responsible after-care bodies shall review: See the General Note to this section **1–325** under the heading "Delegation of functions" and the note on section 25B(4).

Modify . . . the after care services: This option is subject to the local authority's duty under section 47 of the National Health Service and Community Care Act 1990 to assess the social care needs of any person who appears to them to need community care services and decide in the light of the assessment whether such services should be provided. Services provided under section 117 are "community care services" under the 1990 Act (*ibid.* s.46(3)).

Modify . . . any requirements: This can only be done if the two authorities agree to the modification (s.24D(1)).

Subsection (4)

Paragraph (a)

They conclude: A joint decision is required. **1–326**

Community responsible medical officer: Who has the power to end the supervision under section 25H(1).

Paragraph (b)
1–327   *They conclude:* See above.
An approved social worker: And not the patient's nearest relative who is also a potential applicant under this Act.
   If the approved social worker is involved in the patient's care, he has an ongoing duty under section 13(1) of this Act to make an application for an admission to hospital or a guardianship application if he considers that such an application ought to be made.

Subsection (5)
1–328   *Shall not:* The provisions of subsection (6) are mandatory.

Subsection (6)
1–329   *Consulted:* "In practice, we envisage that when the patient is subject to after-care under supervision [consultation] will fall to the supervisor"; *per* Baroness Cumberlege, *op. cit.,* col. 1257.

Subsection (7)
1–330   See the notes on section 25B(3).

Subsection (8)

Paragraph (b)
1–331   *Inform:* Either orally or in writing.

Paragraph (c)
1–332   *Inform in writing:* There is no requirement for the information to be given orally.

Subsection (11)

Paragraph (c)
1–333   *Unless the patient otherwise requests:* There is no power in this provision similar to that provided for in section 25(3) to override the patient's objection.

[Reclassification of patient subject to after-care under supervision
1–334   **25F.**—(1) If it appears to the community responsible medical officer that a patient subject to after-care under supervision is suffering from a form of mental disorder other than the form or forms specified in the supervision application made in respect of the patient, he may furnish a report to that effect to the Health Authority which have the duty under section 117 below to provide after-care services for the patient.
   (2) Where a report is so furnished the supervision application shall have effect as if that other form of mental disorder were specified in it.
   (3) Unless no-one other than the community responsible medical officer is professionally concerned with the patient's medical treatment, he shall consult one or more persons who are so concerned before furnishing a report under subsection (1) above.
   (4) Where a report is furnished under subsection (1) above in respect of a patient, the responsible after-care bodies shall—
      (a) inform the patient both orally and in writing; and
      (b) unless the patient otherwise requests, take such steps as are practicable to inform in writing the person (if any) appearing to be the nearest relative of the patient,
that the report has been furnished.]

AMENDMENT
This section was inserted by the Mental Health (Patients in the Community) Act 1995, s.1.

DEFINITIONS
community responsible medical officer: s.34(1).   **1–335**
patient: s.145(1).
subject to after-care under supervision: ss.25A(2), 145(1A).
supervision application ss.25A(2), 145(1).
medical treatment: s.145(1).
responsible after-care bodies: ss.25D, 145(1).
nearest relative: ss.26(3), 145(1).

GENERAL NOTE
This section provides for the reclassification of the stated form of mental disorder **1–336** of a patient who is subject to supervised discharge. Reclassification has no legal consequences as section 25A makes no distinction between the various categories of mental disorder. Either the patient or, if he has been informed of the report, the patient's nearest relative has a right to apply to a Mental Health Review Tribunal within 28 days of the report being furnished (s.66(1)(gb), (2)(d)). Guidance on this section is given in paragraph 57 of the supplement to the *Code of Practice*.
If a patient is reclassified on the renewal of the supervision there is no need for a further report to be made under this section (s.25G(10)).

Delegation of functions
The functions placed on the Health Authority by subsections (1) and (4) of this **1–337** section can be delegated to a body with whom the Authority has contracted to provide section 117 services or to a person or body listed in the General Note to section 25A under this heading. If the Health Authority makes such a delegation, the local authority can delegate its function under subsection (4) to the same person or body (Mental Health (After-care under Supervision) Regulations 1996 (S.I. 1996 No. 294, reg. 2).

Subsection (1)
He may: In *R. v. Anglia and Oxfordshire Mental Health Review Tribunal, ex p.* **1–338** *Hagen* [2000] C.O.D. 352, Collins J. said that he could see no reason, in principle, why this section should not be construed in a similar manner to the construction that he had given to section 72(5) of this Act: see the note on that provision under "the Tribunal may".
Furnish a report: Using Form 45 (S.I. 1996 No. 294, reg. 3, Sched. 2).

[Duration and renewal of after-care under supervision
    25G.—(1) Subject to sections 25H and 25I below, a patient subject to **1–339** after-care under supervision shall be so subject for the period—
    (a) beginning when he leaves hospital; and
    (b) ending with the period of six months beginning with the day on which
        the supervision application was accepted,
but shall not be so subject for any longer period except in accordance with the following provisions of this section.
    (2) A patient already subject to after-care under supervision may be made so subject—
    (a) from the end of the period referred to in subsection (1) above, for a
        further period of six months; and

(b) from the end of any period of renewal under paragraph (a) above, for a further period of one year,

and so on for periods of one year at a time.

(3) Within the period of two months ending on the day on which a patient who is subject to after-care under supervision would (in default of the operation of subsection (7) below) cease to be so subject, it shall be the duty of the community responsible medical officer—

(a) to examine the patient; and

(b) if it appears to him that the conditions set out in subsection (4) below are complied with, to furnish to the responsible after-care bodies a report to that effect in the prescribed form.

(4) The conditions referred to in subsection (3) above are that—

(a) the patient is suffering from mental disorder, being mental illness, severe mental impairment, psychopathic disorder or mental impairment;

(b) there would be a substantial risk of serious harm to the health or safety of the patient or the safety of other persons, or of the patient being seriously exploited, if he were not to receive the after-care services provided for him under section 117 below;

(c) his being subject to after-care under supervision is likely to help to secure that he receives the after-care services so provided.

(5) The community responsible medical officer shall not consider whether the conditions set out in subsection (4) above are complied with unless—

(a) the following persons have been consulted—

(i) the patient;

(ii) the supervisor;

(iii) unless no-one other than the community responsible medical officer is professionally concerned with the patient's medical treatment, one or more persons who are so concerned;

(iv) one or more persons who are professionally concerned with the after-care services (other than medical treatment) provided for the patient under section 117 below; and

(v) any person who the community responsible medical officer believes plays a substantial part in the care of the patient but is not professionally concerned with the after-care services so provided;

(b) such steps as are practicable have been taken to consult the person (if any) appearing to be the nearest relative of the patient; and

(c) the community responsible medical officer has taken into account any relevant views expressed by the persons consulted.

(6) Where the patient has requested that paragraph (b) of subsection (5) above should not apply, that paragraph shall not apply unless—

(a) the patient has a propensity to violent or dangerous behaviour towards others; and

(b) the community responsible medical officer considers that it is appropriate for steps such as are mentioned in that paragraph to be taken.

(7) Where a report is duly furnished under subsection (3) above, the patient shall be thereby made subject to after-care under supervision for the further period prescribed in that case by subsection (2) above.

(8) Where a report is furnished under subsection (3) above, the responsible after-care bodies shall—

(a) inform the patient both orally and in writing—
  (i) that the report has been furnished; and
  (ii) of the effect in his case of the provisions of this Act relating to making a patient subject to after-care under supervision for a further period (including, in particular, what rights of applying to a Mental Health Review Tribunal are available);
(b) inform any person who has been consulted under paragraph (a)(v) of subsection (5) above that the report has been furnished; and
(c) inform in writing any person who has been consulted under paragraph (b) of that subsection that the report has been furnished.

(9) Where the form of mental disorder specified in a report furnished under subsection (3) above is a form of disorder other than that specified in the supervision application, that application shall have effect as if that other form of mental disorder were specified in it.

(10) Where on any occasion a report specifying such a form of mental disorder is furnished under subsection (3) above the community responsible medical officer need not on that occasion furnish a report under section 25F above.]

AMENDMENT
This section was inserted by the Mental Health (Patients in the Community) Act 1995, s.1.

DEFINITIONS
  patient: s.145(1).   **1–340**
  subject to after-care under supervision: ss.25A(2), 145(1A).
  hospital: ss.34(2), 145(1).
  supervision application: ss.25A(2), 145(1).
  community responsible medical officer: s.34(1).
  responsible after-care bodies: ss.25D, 145(1).
  mental disorder: ss.1, 145(1).
  mental impairment: ss.1, 145(1).
  psychopathic disorder: ss.1, 145(1).
  severe mental impairment: ss.1, 145(1).
  supervisor: s.145(1).
  medical treatment: s.145(1).
  nearest relative: ss.26(3), 145(1).

GENERAL NOTE
This section states that the initial period of supervised discharge can last for a **1–341** maximum of six months. The patient's community responsible medical officer can, following consultation, renew the supervision for a further period of six months and thereafter for periods of one year at a time. These periods are the same as the renewal periods for a patient who is detained for treatment under section 3. If the supervision is renewed the persons identified in subsection (8) must be informed. Guidance on this section is given in paragraphs 58 *et seq.* of the supplement to the *Code of Practice*. The provisions of this section are modified in respect of patients subject to community care orders in Scotland who intend to reside in England or Wales: see the Mental Health (Patients in the Community) (Transfers from Scotland) Regulations 1996 (S.I. 1996 No. 295).

Either the patient or, if he has been informed of the report, the patient's nearest relative can apply to a Mental Health Review Tribunal on a report being made under this section (s.66(1)(gc), (2)(fa)).

Delegation of functions

1–342 The functions placed on the Health Authority by subsections (3) and (8) of this section can be delegated to a body with whom the Authority has contracted to provide section 117 services or to a person or body listed in the General Note to section 25A under this heading. If the Health Authority makes such a delegation, the local authority can delegate its functions under those subsections to the same person or body (Mental Health (After-care under Supervision) Regulations 1996 (S.I. 1996 No. 294), reg. 2).

Subsection (1)

1–343 *Beginning when he leaves hospital:* Or when his period of leave of absence expires (s.25A(9)).

Beginning with: Including the day on which the supervision application was accepted (*Hare v. Gocher* [1962] 2 Q.B. 641). Although the patient will not be subject to supervised discharge until he leaves hospital, the six-month period commences from the day on which the supervision application was accepted.

Subsection (3)

1–344 *To furnish to the responsible after-care bodies:* Although neither the Health Authority nor the local authority have the power to discharge the patient from supervision, they will need to establish a mechanism for scrutinising the report to ensure that it complies with this section.

Prescribed form: Which is Form 5S (S.I. 1996 No. 294, reg. 3, Sched. 2).

Subsection (4)

1–345 The criteria for renewal replicate the grounds for making a supervision application: see section 25A(4). If the form of mental disorder specified in the report differs from the form of mental disorder specified in the application, see subsections (8) and (9).

Subsection (5)

1–346 Although the requirement to consult does not apply if the supervised discharge is allowed to lapse, good practice suggests that the persons identified in this provision are informed of the decision not to renew the supervision.

Shall not: This provision is mandatory. For paragraphs (a), (b) and (c), see the notes on section 25B(2).

Consult . . . the nearest relative: Subject to subsection (6).

Subsection (6)

1–347 See the notes on section 25B(3).

Subsection (7)

1–348 The renewal of supervised discharge must be recorded in the form set out in Part II of Form 5S (S.I. 1996 No. 294, *ibid.*).

Subsection (8)

1–349 *Responsible after-care bodies:* Who will need to identify a mechanism for fulfilling their responsibilities under this provision: see the General Note to this section under the heading "Delegation of functions" and the note on section 25B(4).

Paragraph (a)

1–350 *Rights of applying to a mental health review tribunal:* Under section 66(1)(gc).

Paragraph (b)

1–351 *Inform:* Either orally or in writing.

Paragraph (c)
Inform in writing: There is no requirement for the information to be given orally. **1–352**

Subsection (9)
A reclassification effected through this provision does not give rise to an additional **1–353** right to make an application to a tribunal.

[Ending of after-care under supervision
25H.—(1) The community responsible medical officer may at any time **1–354** direct that a patient subject to after-care under supervision shall cease to be so subject.

(2) The community responsible medical officer shall not give a direction under subsection (1) above unless subsection (3) below is complied with.

(3) This subsection is complied with if—
(a) the following persons have been consulted about the giving of the direction—
  (i) the patient;
  (ii) the supervisor;
  (iii) unless no-one other than the community responsible medical officer is professionally concerned with the patient's medical treatment, one or more persons who are so concerned;
  (iv) one or more persons who are professionally concerned with the after-care services (other than medical treatment) provided for the patient under section 117 below; and
  (v) any person who the community responsible medical officer believes plays a substantial part in the care of the patient but if not professionally concerned with the after-care services so provided;
(b) such steps as are practicable have been taken to consult the person (if any) appearing to be the nearest relative of the patient about the giving of the direction; and
(c) the community responsible medical officer has taken into account any views expressed by the persons consulted.

(4) Where the patient has requested that paragraph (b) of subsection (3) above should not apply, that paragraph shall not apply unless—
(a) the patient has a propensity to violent or dangerous behaviour towards others; and
(b) the community responsible medical officer considers that it is appropriate for steps such as are mentioned in that paragraph to be taken.

(5) A patient subject to after-care under supervision shall cease to be so subject if he—
(a) is admitted to a hospital in pursuance of an application for admission for treatment; or
(b) is received into guardianship.

(6) Where a patient (for any reason) ceases to be subject to after-care under supervision the responsible after-care bodies shall—
(a) inform the patient both orally and in writing;
(b) inform any person who they believe plays a substantial part in the care of the patient but is not professionally concerned with the after-care services provided for the patient under section 117 below; and
(c) take such steps as are practicable to inform in writing the person (if any) appearing to be the nearest relative of the patient,

that the patient has ceased to be so subject.

(7) Where the patient has requested that paragraph (c) of subsection (6) above should not apply, that paragraph shall not apply unless subsection (3)(b) above applied in his case by virtue of subsection (4) above.]

AMENDMENT
This section was inserted by the Mental Health (Patients in the Community) Act 1995, s.1.

DEFINITIONS
1–355   community responsible medical officer: s.34(1).
patient: s.145(1).
subject to after-care under supervision: ss.25A(2), 145(1A).
supervisor: s.34(1).
medical treatment: s.145(1).
nearest relative: ss.26(3), 145(1).
hospital: ss.34(2), 145(1).
responsible after-care bodies: s.145(1).

GENERAL NOTE
1–356   This section states that supervised discharge ends:

(1) if, following consultation, a direction to that effect is made by the patient's community responsible medical officer;
(2) if the patient is detained for treatment; or
(3) if the patient is received into guardianship.

Supervised discharge also ends if the patient's community responsible medical officer decides not to exercise his power under section 25G to renew the supervision. Supervision can be ended by the Mental Health Review Tribunal (s.72(4A)), but not by the body which accepts the application for supervised discharge (*i.e.* the Health Authority) and not by the patient's nearest relative. For the ending of supervised discharge subsequent to the patient moving within England and Wales, see the General Note to section 25E.

The ending of supervision does not affect the continuing duty of the Health Authority and the local authority under section 117 to provide after-care services until the person concerned is no longer in need of them.

Guidance on this section is given in paragraph 65 *et seq.* of the supplement to the *Code of Practice.*

Subsection (1)
1–357   *At any time:* There are no circumstances that oblige the community responsible medical officer to discharge the supervision.
Direct: Using Form 6S (S.I. 1996 No. 294, reg. 3, Sched. 2).

Subsection (2)
1–358   *Shall not:* The provisions of subsection (3) are mandatory.

Subsection (3)
1–359   See the notes on section 25B(2).

Subsection (4)
1–360   See the notes on section 25B(3).

Subsection (5)

Admission for treatment: A further application for supervised discharge can be **1–361** made before the patient is discharged from hospital. Supervised patients who are detained under section 2 have their supervision requirements placed in suspension by virtue of section 25I.

Received into guardianship: This course of action would be appropriate if the patient requires a degree of structure in the provision of after-care services but does not meet the risk criterion for renewal set out in section 25G(4)(b).

Subsection (6)

The responsible after care bodies: The function of the Health Authority under this **1–362** subsection can be delegated to a body with whom the Authority has contracted to provide section 117 services or to a person or body listed in the General Note to section 25A under the heading "Delegation of functions". If the Health Authority makes such a delegation, the local authority can delegate its functions under this subsection to the same person or body (Mental Health (After-care under Supervision) Regulations 1996 (S.I. 1996 No. 294), reg. 2).

Paragraph (b)

Inform: Either orally or in writing. **1–363**

Paragraph (c)

Inform in writing: There is no requirement for the nearest relative to be given the **1–364** information orally.

[Special provisions as to patients sentenced to imprisonment, etc.

25I.—(1) This section applies where a patient who is subject to after-care **1–365** under supervision—

(a) is detained in custody in pursuance of any sentence or order passed or made by a court in the United Kingdom (including an order committing or remanding him in custody); or

(b) is detained in hospital in pursuance of an application for admission for assessment.

(2) At any time when the patient is detained as mentioned in subsection (1)(a) or (b) above he is not required—

(a) to receive any after-care services provided for him under section 117 below; or

(b) to comply with any requirements imposed on him under section 25D above.

(3) If the patient is detained as mentioned in paragraph (a) of subsection (1) above for a period of, or successive periods amounting in the aggregate to, six months or less, or is detained as mentioned in paragraph (b) of that subsection, and, apart from this subsection, he—

(a) would have ceased to be subject to after-care under supervision during the period for which he is so detained; or

(b) would cease to be so subject during the period of 28 days beginning with the day on which he ceases to be so detained,

he shall be deemed not to have ceased, and shall not cease, to be so subject until the end of that period of 28 days.

(4) Where the period for which the patient is subject to after-care under supervision is extended by subsection (3) above, any examination and report

to be made and furnished in respect of the patient under section 25G(3) above may be made and furnished within the period as so extended.

(5) Where, by virtue of subsection (4) above, the patient is made subject to after-care under supervision for a further period after the day on which (apart from subsection (3) above) he would have ceased to be so subject, the further period shall be deemed to have commenced with that day.]

AMENDMENT

This section was inserted by the Mental Health (Patients in the Community) Act 1995.

DEFINITIONS

1–366   patient: s.145(1).
subject to after-care under supervision: ss.25A(2), 145(1A).
hospital: ss.34(2), 145(1).
application for admission for assessment: ss.2, 145(1).

GENERAL NOTE

1–367   This section has the effect of placing supervised discharge in suspension if the patient is given a custodial sentence or is detained in hospital for assessment under section 2. The practical effect of admitting a patient to hospital either informally or under sections 4, 135 or 136 is also to put the arrangements for supervised discharge into suspension: see paragraph 70 of the supplement to the *Code of Practice*.

Subsection (1)

1–368   *United Kingdom:* Means Great Britain and Northern Ireland (Interpretation Act 1978, s.5, Sched. 1).

Application for admission for assessment: This provision was explained by Mr John Bowis M.P. (*Hansard*, HC, Standing Committee F, cols 107, 108):

"As a general rule, we would expect that a patient who was subject to the new power would be readmitted only when a need for further treatment had been established. Section 3 would normally be used in preference to section 2, but we cannot be certain that section 2 will not be used in some cases. Those would include emergency admissions under section 4 which are subsequently converted to section 2. That could have the consequence of vulnerable people being returned to the community without the special support that the Bill supplies.

The amendment deals with that by extending to patients who are admitted for assessment the provision which new section 25I(1) already makes for those who are detained in custody. The effect is to put the supervision arrangements into suspense while the patient is in hospital and then to reactivate them when he or she is discharged. If the supervision would otherwise have lapsed while the patient was in hospital, it is extended for 28 days after his or her discharge."

Subsection (3)

1–369   If a patient who is subject to supervised discharge is detained in custody for a period of six months or less or is detained in hospital under section 2, and the patient's supervision would have ended during the period in custody or within 28 days of his ceasing to be detained under section 2, this subsection provides that in both cases the supervision stays in place until 28 days after the patient has ceased to be detained. Formalities for the renewal of the supervised discharge can be completed during this period (subs. (4)). A renewal could not be effected during the period when the patient was detained or in custody because section 117 services are not being "provided for him" during this period: see section 25G(4)(b).

Six months or less: "The amendment does not apply to those sentenced to longer periods in custody essentially because if someone has been out of touch with the specialist services for a long period, the presumption that he or she is still suffering from the conditions which led to aftercare under supervision being arranged become hard to sustain. However, if the sentence was more than six months but less than a year and supervision had not expired while the person was in custody, it would still be reactivated when he or she left prison"; *per* Baroness Cumberlege, *Hansard*, HL, Vol. 544, col. 171.

Subsection (5)
If a patient has had his period of supervision extended by virtue of subsection (3), a renewal of his supervision is deemed to have started on the day on which it would have expired had it not been for subsection (3).   **1–370**

[Patients moving from Scotland to England and Wales

25J.—(1) A supervision application may be made in respect of a patient who is subject to a community care order under the Mental Health (Scotland) Act 1984 and who intends to leave Scotland in order to reside in England and Wales.   **1–371**

(2) Sections 25A to 25I above, section 117 below and any other provision of this Act relating to supervision applications or patients subject to after-care under supervision shall apply in relation to a patient in respect of whom a supervision application is or is to be made by virtue of this section subject to such modifications as the Secretary of State may by regulations prescribe.]

AMENDMENT
This section was inserted by the Mental Health (Patients in the Community) Act 1995, s.1.

DEFINITIONS
supervision application: ss.25A(2), 145(1).   **1–372**
patient: s.145(1).
subject to after-care under supervision: ss.25A(2), 145(1A).

GENERAL NOTE
The effect of this section was explained by Baroness Cumberlege (*Hansard*, HL,   **1–373**
Vol. 564, col. 173):

"[This section enables] an application for aftercare under supervision [to] be made in respect of a patient subject to a community care order. The modifications which need to be made to the procedure to cover the fact that the patient is moving, not from being detained in hospital, but from being subject to a Scottish community care order, will be prescribed in the regulations. In practice we see this working as follows. If the care team in Scotland believes it is in the patient's best interest to move to England or Wales, it will make contact with a section 12 approved doctor south of the Border. This is likely to be the same person who will eventually be the patient's community responsible medical officer after the transfer has taken place. This doctor will then make the application to the health authority which will have to be supported by two recommendations, one from an approved social worker and the other from a registered medical practitioner who has knowledge of the patient's history.
The significant difference from the general arrangement in [section 25A] is that the application is made not by a doctor who has been looking after the patient in hospital, but by one who is likely to be his or her responsible medical officer in the community. So far as the supporting medical recommendation is

concerned, it would obviously make sense for this to be given by the special medical officer who is the Scottish equivalent of the community responsible medical officer and that is what we expect to happen in the ordinary way. There would have to be full consultation on both sides of the Border and the transfer would take place when all concerned were ready for it to go ahead. The patient would become subject to aftercare under supervision upon taking up residence in England or Wales. He or she would have an immediate right to a Mental Health Review Tribunal.

It would only be practicable to apply these provisions to patients who agree to the transfer. The new powers rely on the sanction of the patient's possible return to hospital rather than any more direct form of compulsion, so it is not feasible to legislate for patients who abscond.

Although the number of patients who are likely to be affected by such transfers is probably very small, we feel that we need this new provision to ensure that a patient does not lose the support and supervision he or she may need simply as a result of moving to the other side of the Border."

Guidance on this section is given in paragraphs 55 and 56 of the Supplement to the *Code of Practice* and in the *Memorandum* at paragraph 132.

An application for a community care order can be made in respect of a patient who is subject to supervised discharge and who intends to leave England and Wales in order to reside in Scotland: see section 35K of the Mental Health (Scotland) Act 1984 and the Mental Health (Patients in the Community) (Transfer from England and Wales to Scotland) Regulations 1996 (S.I. 1996 No. 742).

For the procedure to be used where a patient moves within England and Wales, see the General Note to section 25E.

Subsection (1)

1–374   *A supervision application may be made:* Using Form 1S (S.I. 1996 No. 294, reg. 3, Sched. 2).

Intends to leave: The application must be made before the patient leaves Scotland.

Subsection (2)

1–375   *Secretary of State:* The functions of the Minister, so far as exercisable in relation to Wales, are exercised by the National Assembly for Wales (S.I. 1999 No. 672, art. 2, Sched. 1).

By regulations prescribe: See the Mental Health (Patients in the Community) (Transfers from Scotland) Regulations 1996 (S.I. 1996 No. 295).

Functions of relatives of patients

Definition of "relative" and "nearest" relative

1–376   **26.**—(1) In this Part of this Act "relative" means any of the following persons:—

(a) husband or wife;
(b) son or daughter;
(c) father or mother;
(d) brother or sister;
(e) grandparent;
(f) grandchild;
(g) uncle or aunt;
(h) nephew or niece.

(2) In deducing relationships for the purposes of this section, any relationship of the half-blood shall be treated as a relationship of the whole blood, and an illegitimate person shall be treated as the legitimate child of

[(a) his mother, and

(b) if his father has parental responsibility for him within the meaning of section 3 of the Children Act 1989, his father.]

(3) In this Part of this Act, subject to the provisions of this section and to the following provisions of this Part of this Act, the "nearest relative" means the person first described in subsection (1) above who is for the time being surviving, relatives of the whole blood being preferred to relatives of the same description of the half-blood and the elder or eldest of two or more relatives described in any paragraph of that subsection being preferred to the other or others of those relatives, regardless of sex.

(4) Subject to the provisions of this section and to the following provisions of this Part of this Act, where the patient ordinarily resides with or is cared for by one or more of his relatives (or, if he is for the time being an in-patient in a hospital, he last ordinarily resided with or was cared for by one or more of his relatives) his nearest relative shall be determined—

(a) by giving preference to that relative or those relatives over the other or others; and

(b) as between two or more such relatives, in accordance with subsection (3) above.

(5) Where the person who, under subsection (3) or (4) above, would be the nearest relative of a patient—

(a) in the case of a patient ordinarily resident in the United Kingdom, the Channel Islands or the Isle of Man, is not so resident; or

(b) is the husband or wife of the patient, but is permanently separated from the patient, either by agreement or under an order of a court, or has deserted or has been deserted by the patient for a period which has not come to an end; or

(c) is a person other than the husband, wife, father or mother of the patient, and is for the time being under 18 years of age;

(d) [...]

the nearest relative of the patient shall be ascertained as if that person were dead.

(6) In this section "husband" and "wife" include a person who is living with the patient as the patient's husband or wife, as the case may be (or, if the patient is for the time being an in-patient in a hospital, was so living until the patient was admitted), and has been or had been so living for a period of not less than six months; but a person shall not be treated by virtue of this subsection as the nearest relative of a married patient unless the husband or wife of the patient is disregarded by virtue of paragraph (b) of subsection (5) above.

(7) A person, other than a relative, with whom the patient ordinarily resides (or, if the patient is for the time being an in-patient in a hospital, last ordinarily resided before he was admitted), and with whom he has or had been ordinarily residing for a period of not less than five years, shall be treated for the purposes of this Part of this Act as if he were a relative but—

(a) shall be treated for the purposes of subsection (3) above as if mentioned last in subsection (1) above; and

(b) shall not be treated by virtue of this subsection as the nearest relative of a married patient unless the husband or wife of the patient is disregarded by virtue of paragraph (b) of subsection (5) above.

AMENDMENTS
In subsection (2) the words in square brackets were substituted by the Children Act 1989 (Consequential Amendment of Enactments) Order 1991 (S.I. 1991 No. 1881), art. 3.
In subsection (5), para. (d) was repealed by the Children Act 1989, s.108(7), Sched. 15.

DEFINITIONS

1–377   hospital: ss.34(2), 145(1).
patient: s.145(1).

GENERAL NOTE

1–378   This section, which defines "relative" and "nearest relative" for the purposes of Part II of this Act, also applies to patients who have been placed under hospital or guardianship orders by a court under section 37, (Sched. 1, Pt 1, para. 1).
A person who has been identified as the patient's nearest relative is not legally obliged to act as such. He or she can authorise any person (other than the patient or a person disqualified under subsection (5)) to perform the functions of the nearest relative. The authority can be revoked at any time. Both the authority and the revocation must be in writing: see regulation 14 of the Mental Health (Hospital, Guardianship and Consent to Treatment) Regulations 1983.
A nearest relative who provides a substantial amount of care on a regular and unpaid basis for the patient has a right to request the local authority that is assessing the patient's need for community care services to assess his or her ability to provide and to continue to provide such care (Carers (Recognition and Services) Act 1995, s.1).
The leave of the court is required before the nearest relative of a ward of court exercises his functions under this Act (s.33(2)).

The Human Rights Act 1998

1–379   The patient's nearest relative, as a person who has the power to exercise "functions of a public nature", is a "public authority" for the purposes of section 6 of the 1998 Act (*ibid.*, s.6(3)(b)). Also see the note on section 29.

Subsection (1)

1–380   If a relative of a patient is not one of the relatives specified in this subsection, that person cannot be a relative for the purposes of this section. However, such a person could be appointed by the county court to be the patient's acting nearest relative under section 29 or authorised by the nearest relative to act as such under regulation 14 of the 1983 Regulations. For the occasions when relatives will be disregarded for the purposes of ascertaining the patient's "nearest relative", see subsection (5). The remaining notes on this subsection are concerned with the definitions of relative as they affect the identification of the patient's nearest relative.
Husband or wife: Even if the marital partner is under the age of 18 (subs. (5)(c)). If the patient is unmarried or if the marital partner can be disregarded under subsection (5)(b), a person who had been living with the patient as the patient's husband or wife for at least six months will be treated as if he or she were the patient's husband or wife (subs. (6)).
Son or daughter: An adopted child is treated as if he were the child of his adoptive parents (Adoption Act 1976, s.39(1)) and an unmarried mother's child is treated as if he were the child of his mother (subs. (2)) and, if he has parental responsibility for him, his father. The child must be over the age of 18 (subs. (5)(c)). A step-child is not a relative for the purposes of this provision but could become a nearest relative under the provisions of subsection (7), by being appointed as an acting nearest relative under section 29 or by being authorised to act as such under regulation 14 of the 1983 Regulations.

Father or mother: Even if the parent is under the age of 18 (subs. (5)(c)). An unmarried father is to be disregarded unless he has parental responsibility (subs. (2)). In cases where a child is in the care of a local authority by virtue of a care order or where a guardian for the child has been appointed or where a residence order has been made in respect of the child, the local authority (s.27), guardian (s.28) or person named in the residence order (s.28) is deemed to be the child's nearest relative.

Subsection (2)

Relationship of the half-blood: In order to determine whether a relationship exists **1–381** for the purposes of this section, if a patient has both a full-blood relative and a half-blood relative, they are both treated as full-blood relatives. Whole blood relatives are preferred to half-blood relatives for the purposes of determining the patient's nearest relative under subsection (3).

Parental responsibility: An unmarried father can acquire parental responsibility for his child under the following provisions of the Children Act 1989: by obtaining a residence order (s.12(1)); by virtue of an order of the court (s.4(1)(a)); by making an agreement with the mother in the "prescribed form" (s.4(1)(b)); by being appointed the child's guardian by the court (s.5(1)); or by being appointed as the child's guardian by the mother or another guardian (s.5(3)(4)). The appointment as guardian will not take effect while the mother is alive (s.5(8)). An unmarried father's parental responsibility for his child can be ended on the application of the child or any person with parental responsibility (s.4(3)). It will also end when the child reaches 18 (s.91(7), (8)) or is adopted (Adoption Act 1976, s.12(1)).

Subsection (3)

Nearest relative: This subsection states that the general rule for determining the **1–382** patient's nearest relative is to take whoever comes first on the list of relatives set out in subsection (1), with preference being given to relatives of the whole blood, and that if there is more than one relative coming within the same category the elder or eldest is to take priority regardless of the sex of the relative. The remainder of this section contains the exceptions to this rule.

If the patient has no nearest relative or if it is not reasonably practicable to ascertain whether he has such a relative, or who that relative is, an application may be made to the county court for the appointment of an acting nearest relative under section 29(3)(a).

The patient cannot choose his nearest relative who must be identified by applying subsections (3) to (6) to the patient's family and social situation. The fact that a relative is either mentally disordered, mentally incapable or detained under this Act does not disqualify him from being a nearest relative, although there could be grounds for removing him under section 29(3)(b).

It is possible for a nearest relative to authorise another person to perform the functions of nearest relative on his behalf: see the General Note to this section.

Elder or eldest: Thus the elder or eldest wife of a polygamous marriage would normally become her husband's nearest relative.

Subsection (4)

This subsection provides that if the patient is either living with or being cared for by **1–383** a relative, that relative becomes the patient's nearest relative.

Ordinarily resides: General guidance about what is meant by this phrase has been given by Lord Scarman in *Shah v. Barnet L.B.C.* [1983] 1 All E.R. 226 at 235, HL: "Unless ... it can be shown that the statutory framework or the legal context in which the words are used requires a different meaning, I unhesitatingly subscribe to the view that 'ordinarily resident' refers to a man's abode in a particular place or country which he has adopted voluntarily and for settled purposes as part of the regular order of his life for the time being, whether short or long duration."

A person may change his place of ordinary residence during the course of a day, *e.g.* a son who leaves the parental home and moves into a flat of his own with no intention of returning. But each case has to be judged on its own facts and the fact that a person has left his home does not necessarily mean that he has established an ordinary residence elsewhere. McCullough J. examined this issue in *R. v. Liverpool C.C., ex p. F*, April 16, 1997, a case where the patient had left the parental home in acrimonious circumstances and had gone to live with his grandmother, as well as staying at a number of other places. His Lordship said that those who were charged with the task of identifying the identity of the patient's nearest relative should have considered "not just the choice between whether he was ordinarily resident with his mother or with his grandmother. They should have considered also the possibility that he may not have been ordinarily resident anywhere and should have specifically asked themselves—bearing in mind his itinerant lifestyle, his lack of stability and the condition of his mental health—whether he really had settled down sufficiently at his grandmother's for her home to be regarded as his place of ordinary residence."

If a patient leaves home, but takes up no other place of ordinary residence and no relative is caring for him, his nearest relative can be identified by applying the general rule set out in subsection (3) to his situation.

Cared for: In *Re D (Mental patient: habeas corpus)* [2000] 2 F.L.R. 848, the Court of Appeal held that: (a) the words "ordinarily" qualifies "resided with" but not "cared for"; and (b) although the words "cared for" are not defined in this Act, they are clear and everyday words set in a context where the approved social worker applicant has to act in a pragmatic and common sense manner in a situation which is fraught with emotion and difficulty. In order to justify a finding that the relative is caring for the patient, the services provided by the relative must be more than minimal and they need not have been provided over the long term. In this case the court was asked to consider the situation of a relative who assisted the patient in managing his financial affairs, checked whether he was eating appropriately and took away and cleaned his soiled clothing and bed clothes. In finding that this relative was caring for the patient the court said that there "was more than sufficient evidence to pass the 'cared for' test, wherever one sets the threshold of services amounting to 'cared for'. In other words, the services were not merely minimal. They were services which were substantial and sustained."

The patient may be "cared for" by a relative even if they do not share a residence. In *R. v. Liverpool C.C.*, above, McCullough J. held that the quality of regularity identified by Lord Scarman in the *Shah* case, above, is equally important when considering whether there has been a change in the identity of the person who is to be regarded as caring for the patient. His Lordship said: "In such a case it will be necessary to take into account the duration, continuity and quality of the care afforded by the relative under consideration as having assumed the role ... and also the intention of the patient himself."

Subsection (5)

1–384   This subsection, which disqualifies certain persons from acting as a patient's nearest relative, is applied to persons who have been deemed to be the patient's nearest relative by virtue of section 28 (s.28(2)).

Paragraph (a)—United Kingdom: This means Great Britain and Northern Ireland (Interpretation Act 1978, s.5, Sched. 1). It is easier for a person to lose their ordinary/habitual residence in a country than to acquire it. In *C v. S (A Minor) (Abduction)* [1990] 2 F.L.R. 442 at 454, HL, Lord Brandon said:

"[T]he question whether a person is or is not habitually resident in a specified country is a question of fact to be decided by reference to all the circumstances of any particular case .... A person may cease to be habitually resident in country A in a single day if he or she leaves it with a settled intention not to return to it but to take up long term residence in country B instead. Such a person cannot, however, become habitually resident in country B in a single day. An appreciable period of time and a settled intention will be necessary to enable him or her to become so. During that appreciable period of time the person will have ceased to be habitually resident in country A but not yet have become habitually resident in country B."

Not so resident: A patient's nearest relative who is abroad on holiday is not disqualified under this provision.

Paragraph (b)—deserted: A desertion involves one partner leaving the other without that person's consent or a reasonable excuse. A person who has been disqualified from being a patient's nearest relative under this provision can resume that role as soon as the desertion comes to an end.

Paragraph (c)—under 18 years of age: Means before the commencement of his eighteenth birthday (Family Law Reform Act 1969, s.9(1)).

Subsection (6)

Living with the patient as the patient's husband or wife: This phrase applies to **1–385** heterosexual relationships only: see *Harrogate B.C. v. Simpson* (1984) 17 H.L.R. 205, CA, a case involving the interpretation of a similar phrase in section 50(3) of the Housing Act 1980. *Per* Ewbank J.: "I agree that the expression 'living together as husband and wife' ... is not apt to include a homosexual relationship. The essential characteristics of living together as husband and wife, in my judgment, is that there should be a man and a woman ... ." This decision was approved by the House of Lords in *Fitzpatrick v. Sterling Housing Association Ltd* [1999] 4 All E.R. 705.

Married patient: The cohabitee of a married patient cannot be the nearest relative of that patient unless the patient's spouse can be disregarded because of permanent separation or desertion.

In *Mummery v. Mummery* [1942] P. 107, a case on desertion, Lord Merriman P. doubted that it was possible to "give a completely exhaustive definition of cohabitation". This statement was cited in *Kimber v. Kimber* [2000] 1 F.L.R. 383, where H.H. Judge Tyrer identified the following factors as being relevant to the question of determining whether a man and a woman are living together as husband and wife:

(a) are the parties living together in the same household;
(b) do they share daily tasks and duties;
(c) is there stability and a degree of permanence in the relationship;
(d) is the way in which financial matters are being handled an indication of the cohabitation;
(e) do the parties have a sexual relationship with each other;
(f) are there children of the relationship;
(g) what is the intention and motivation of the parties; and
(h) would a reasonable person of normal perceptions consider that the parties were cohabiting.

H.H. Judge Tyrer said that these factors "cannot be complete nor comprehensive ...". It is submitted that although not all factors need to be present before a couple can be said to be living together as husband and wife, factor (a) must be present in all cases.

Subsection (7)

This subsection provides that a person who has been living with the patient for five **1–386** years or more shall be treated as if he were a relative who came last on the hierarchy of relatives set out in subsection (1). By virtue of subsection (4) that person as a relative who "ordinarily resides" with the patient becomes the patient's nearest relative, unless a relative who came higher in the hierarchy is either living with or caring for the patient.

There may be difficulties in identifying the patient's nearest relative in cases where the patient has been residing with a number of people for five years or more in a communal living situation. This could occur where, for example, the patient is a member of a religious community or if he lives in a group home. In this situation the provisions of subsection (3) would apply and the eldest person who had become a "relative" under this subsection would become the patient's nearest relative.

A particular difficulty has arisen with the identification of the nearest relative of an elderly patient who is the resident of a residential care home. Although the question of whether a person ordinarily resides with others is a question of fact which must be determined in each case (see the note on "ordinarily resides" in subs. (4)), it would be difficult to argue that the residents of many such homes do not "ordinarily reside" with each other in that they will usually eat together, use common facilities and generally live a communal life. Such a finding would not be appropriate in a case where the residents lived in self-contained units within the home and only had contact with each other for social purposes. If the patient is found to have ordinarily resided with a number of fellow residents for more than five years the combined effect of subsections (3) and (4) is to identify the eldest of these residents as the patient's nearest relative. It might well be the case that this person is not best qualified to act as the patient's nearest relative and in these circumstances he or she could be asked to use the simple procedure set out in regulation 14 of Mental Health (Hospital, Guardianship and Consent to Treatment) Regulations 1983 to nominate some other person to take over the responsibilities of nearest relative.

If a relative or a spouse of a patient who has been living in a communal situation has had a substantial and sustained contact with the patient by, for example, taking the patient out on trips or entertaining the patient at his or her home, it might be possible to argue that that person was caring for the patient for the purposes of subsection (4). In these circumstances that person would take precedence over the "five year" person by virtue of subsection (3).

It is submitted that: (1) a landlord and tenant can only be considered as "ordinarily residing" together if they live in the same accommodation and there is a substantial sharing of household facilities and functions; and (2) patients in registered nursing homes or registered mental nursing homes cannot be said to be ordinarily residing together as the primary purpose of such homes is to treat patients and not to provide them with a place of residence.

Ordinarily resides: This provision does not require the patient and the person with whom he has resided for five years or more to regard each other as husband or wife, or to be lovers, or even to be friends.

Five years: Temporary separations resulting, for example, from separate holidays being taken should be disregarded in calculating this period.

This provision caters for the situation where an adult mentally disordered ex-patient has been "fostered" to carers under an adult placement scheme. It seems inappropriate that carers have to wait for five years before one of them is entitled to exercise the functions of nearest relative. It also appears to cover the situation of a child who has been placed with foster parents under either Part III or Part IX of the Children Act 1989. If the child remains at that home on reaching adulthood, the period when the child was fostered should be included in the calculation of the five-year period.

Married patient: The "five year" person cannot be the nearest relative of a married patient unless the patient's spouse can be disregarded because of permanent separation or desertion.

[Children and young persons in care

1–387   **27.** Where—

    (a) a patient who is a child or young person is in the care of a local authority by virtue of a care order within the meaning of the Children Act 1989; or—

(b) the rights and powers of a parent of a patient who is a child or young person are vested in a local authority by virtue of section 16 of the Social Work (Scotland) Act 1968,

the authority shall be deemed to be the nearest relative of the patient in preference to any person except the patient's husband or wife (if any).]

AMENDMENT
This section was substituted by the Children Act 1989, s.108(5), Sched. 13, para. 48(1).

DEFINITIONS
patient: s.145(1).   **1–388**
nearest relative: ss.26(3), 145(1).

GENERAL NOTE
If an unmarried child is in the care of a local authority by virtue of a care order (in **1–389** England or Wales) or if parental rights and powers in respect of a child have been vested in a local authority (in Scotland), this section identifies that authority as the child's nearest relative. It would clearly be appropriate for the local authority to delegate its functions under this provision to an officer.
This section applies to children who have been placed under hospital or guardianship orders by a court under section 37 (Sched. 1, Pt 1, para. 1).
Child: Is defined in the Children Act 1989 as a person under the age of eighteen (s.105(1)).
Care order: A care order is defined in section 31(11) of the Children Act 1989 to include an interim care order made under section 38 of that Act.

Nearest relative of minor under guardianship, etc.
28.—[(1) Where   **1–390**
(a) a guardian has been appointed for a person who has not attained the age of eighteen years; or
(b) a residence order (as defined by section 8 of the Children Act 1989) is in force with respect to such a person,

the guardian (or guardians, where there is more than one) or the person named in the residence order shall, to the exclusion of any other person, be deemed to be his nearest relative.]
(2) Subsection (5) of section 26 above shall apply in relation to a person who is, or who is one of the persons, deemed to be the nearest relative of a patient by virtue of this section as it applies in relation to a person who would be the nearest relative under subsection (3) of that section.
[(3) In this section "guardian" does not include a guardian under this Part of this Act.]
(4) In this section "court" includes a court in Scotland or Northern Ireland, and "enactment" includes an enactment of the Parliament of Northern Ireland, a Measure of the Northern Ireland Assembly and an Order in Council under Schedule 1 of the Northern Ireland Act 1974.

AMENDMENTS
Subsections (1) and (3) were substituted by the Children Act 1989, s.108(5), Sched. 13, para. 48.

DEFINITIONS
patient: s.145(1).   **1–391**
nearest relative: ss.26(3), 145(1).

1–392   This section provides for a person who has been appointed as a child's guardian (other than under this Act) or a person who is named in a residence order which has been made in respect of a child, to be that child's nearest relative. It applies to children who have been placed under hospital or guardianship orders by a court under section 37 (Sched. 1, Pt 1, para. 1).

Subsection (1)
1–393   *Attained the age:* At the commencement of his eighteenth birthday (Family Law Reform Act 1969, s.9(1)).
      Guardian: A guardian can only be appointed under section 5 of the Children Act 1989 (*ibid.*, s.5(13)).
      Guardians, where there is more than one: Thus two persons, as co-guardians, could have equal powers as the patient's nearest relative. Compare this with section 26(3) where only a sole nearest relative is contemplated.
      Residence order: If more than one person is named in the residence order, those named will have equal powers as the patient's nearest relative.

Subsection (2)
1–394   This provides that section 26(5), which disqualifies certain persons from acting as a patient's nearest relative, applies to the person or persons deemed to be the patient's nearest relative by virtue of subsection (1).

Subsection (3)
1–395   *Guardian under this part of this Act:* Such a person could become a patient's nearest relative if, apart from his guardianship responsibilities under this Act, he would be nearest relative by virtue of either being the person named or appointed under subsection (1) or by being identified as nearest relative under section 26.

Appointment by court of acting nearest relative
1–396   **29.**—(1) The county court may, upon application made in accordance with the provisions of this section in respect of a patient, by order direct that the functions of the nearest relative of the patient under this Part of this Act and sections 66 and 69 below shall, during the continuance in force of the order, be exercisable by the applicant, or by any other person specified in the application, being a person who, in the opinion of the court, is a proper person to act as the patient's nearest relative and is willing to do so.
      (2) An order under this section may be made on the application of—
      (a) any relative of the patient;
      (b) any other person with whom the patient is residing (or, if the patient is then an in-patient in a hospital, was last residing before he was admitted); or
      (c) an approved social worker;
but in relation to an application made by such a social worker, subsection (1) above shall have effect as if for the words "the applicant" there were substituted the words "the local social services authority."
      (3) An application for an order under this section may be made upon any of the following grounds, that is to say—
      (a) that the patient has no nearest relative within the meaning of this Act, or that it is not reasonably practicable to ascertain whether he has such a relative, or who that relative is;
      (b) that the nearest relative of the patient is incapable of acting as such by reason of mental disorder or other illness;

(c) that the nearest relative of the patient unreasonably objects to the making of an application for admission for treatment or a guardianship application in respect of the patient; or

(d) that the nearest relative of the patient has exercised without due regard to the welfare of the patient or the interests of the public his power to discharge the patient from hospital or guardianship under this Part of this Act, or is likely to do so.

(4) If, immediately before the expiration of the period for which a patient is liable to be detained by virtue of an application for admission for assessment, an application under this section, which is an application made on the ground specified in subsection (3)(c) or (d) above, is pending in respect of the patient, that period shall be extended—

(a) in any case, until the application under this section has been finally disposed of; and

(b) if an order is made in pursuance of the application under this section, for a further period of seven days;

and for the purposes of this subsection an application under this section shall be deemed to have been finally disposed of at the expiration of the time allowed for appealing from the decision of the court or, if notice of appeal has been given within that time, when the appeal has been heard or withdrawn, and "pending" shall be construed accordingly.

(5) An order made on the ground specified in subsection (3)(a) or (b) above may specify a period for which it is to continue in force unless previously discharged under section 30 below.

(6) While an order made under this section is in force, the provisions of this Part of this Act (other than this section and section 30 below) and sections 66, 69, 132(4) and 133 below shall apply in relation to the patient as if for any reference to the nearest relative of the patient there were substituted a reference to the person having the functions of that relative and (without prejudice to section 30 below) shall so apply notwithstanding that the person who was the patient's nearest relative when the order was made is no longer his nearest relative; but this subsection shall not apply to section 66 below in the case mentioned in paragraph (h) of subsection (1) of that section.

DEFINITIONS

    patient: s.145(1).   **1–397**

    nearest relative: ss.26(3), 145(1).

    hospital: ss.34(2), 145(1).

    approved social worker: s.145(1).

    local social services authority: s.145(1).

    mental disorder: ss.1, 145(1).

    application for admission for treatment: ss.3, 145(1).

    application for admission for assessment: ss.2, 145(1).

GENERAL NOTE

    The section gives the county court power to make an order directing that the **1–398** functions of the nearest relative shall be exercised by another person, or by a local social services authority. An application to the court can be made concurrently with, or subsequent to, an application under section 3 (s.30(4) and *R. v. Central London County Court, ex p. London* [1999] 3 All E.R. 991, CA). An applicant can only rely on the grounds set out in subsection (3): an application cannot be made on the general ground that the person's past or present behaviour makes him unsuited to act as the patient's nearest relative. If the court makes an order under this section it has no further role to play in respect of any subsequent application for treatment or guardianship that is made in respect of the patient.

In *Barnet LBC v. Robin* (1999) 2 C.C.L.R. 454, the Court of Appeal, without having heard full argument on the point, was prepared to proceed on the basis that an appeal of an order made under this section can be made to the Court of Appeal on both matters of law and of fact.

A nearest relative who has been supplanted by an order under this section can apply to a Mental Health Review Tribunal for the patient's case to be reviewed: see subsection (6) and section 66(1)(h), (2)(g). The acting nearest relative has a separate power to apply to a tribunal (subs. (1)).

The provisions of section 38 of the County Court Act 1984 provide the county court with the power to make an interim order when considering an application under this section. A decision of the hospital managers to rely on such an order for the purposes of the admission and detention of a patient is lawful (*R. v. Central London County Court*, above). In *R. v. Uxbridge County Court, ex p. Binns*, August 11, 2000, the court made an *ex parte* order appointing the local authority as the acting nearest relative of the patient. Two hours notice of the application was given to the nearest relative, who was not served with any papers. The displaced nearest relative was given permission to apply to the court after giving notice to the local authority, to vary or discharge the order. On an application for judicial review of the order Hidden J. held that:

(i) section 38 of the 1984 Act is broad enough to encompass a temporary order which was both interlocutory and conditional and was not for a specified period;

(ii) there is nothing in Ord. 49 r. 12 of the County Court Rules which is inconsistent with the general provisions of Part 23 of the Civil Procedure Rules which, *inter alia,* entitle a person against whom an order is made without notice to apply to set aside or vary it (para. 23.10(1)); require the order to contain a statement of the right to make an application to set aside or vary it (para. 23.9(3)); and provide a power in the court to re-list an application where an order had been made in the absence of a respondent either at the application of that person or of the court's own motion (para. 23.11(2)); and

(iii) since the Mental Health Act 1983 does not set out a complete code governing the making of orders displacing the nearest relative of a patient, then the submission that the granting of permission to apply would necessarily be *ultra vires* section 30 is an incorrect one.

In the *Central London County Court* case, above, Stuart-Smith L.J. said: "unless there are cogent reasons to the contrary, it is preferable that questions under section 29(3)(c) should be finally determined before an application is made under section 3, and the machinery of extension of detention under section afforded by section 29(4) should be used" (para. 24). His Lordship also said, *obiter*, that it was arguable that the hospital managers would be bound to release the patient from detention if the court eventually made no order for displacement (para. 22).

In *Surrey County Council Social Services v. McMurray*, November 11, 1994, CA, Hale J., in dismissing an appeal by a nearest relative against an order that had been made under this section, said that "the displacement of a person as nearest relative in no way takes away his legitimate interest in the welfare of his daughter, which should always be paid proper respect by the authorities in making decisions about and arrangements for her care."

Section 30 gives the county court power to discharge or vary an order made under this section, and also specifies the duration of such an order if the duration has not been established under subsection (5) of this section. An order made under this section does not expire on the transfer of the patient under section 19.

It is *prima facie* a contempt of court to publish information relating to proceedings brought under this section where the county court is sitting in private: see section 12 of the Administration of Justice Act 1960 and *Pickering v. Liverpool Daily Post and Echo Newspapers plc and others* [1991] 1 All E.R. 622, HL.

The Human Rights Act 1998

In *J.T. v. United Kingdom* (1997) E.H.R.L.R. 437, the Commission declared **1–399** admissible the applicant's complaint that the automatic appointment of her nearest relative under section 26, the lack of a means available to her under this section to change the identity of that relative combined with the powers and access to personal information of the nearest relative, amounted, in the light of her reasonable fears surrounding her relationship with her nearest relative, to an interference in her private life which is not justified under Article 8(2) of the European Convention on Human Rights. A friendly settlement to this application was reached (Judgment, March 30, 2000) with the Government undertaking to amend this Act by: (i) providing the detained patient with the power to make an application to the court to have the nearest relative replaced where the patient reasonably objected to a certain person acting in that capacity; and (ii) providing for the exclusion of certain persons from acting as nearest relative. The displacement of the nearest relative which was justified under Article 8(2) would not contravene the Convention.

The question whether a patient who has had his detention under section 2 extended by virtue of subsection (4) of this section retains his right to apply to a Mental Health Review Tribunal after the 14 day period specified in section 66(2) has expired is undecided. Article 5(4) of the Convention provides a detained patient with the right to have the lawfulness of his detention decided speedily. As section 3(1) of the 1998 Act requires a court to interpret this Act, so far as is possible to do so, in a way which is compatible with Convention rights, it is likely that a court would find that a patient has a right of application in these circumstances.

Subsection (1)

County court: For the procedure on an application to the county court, see section **1–400** 31 and the Civil Procedure Rules 1998 (S.I. 1998 No. 3132), Sched. 2, CCR Ord. 49, r. 12. The court has the power to make an interim order when considering an application: see the General Note to this section. Applications should be listed on an emergency basis if time is of the essence. Applications without notice are governed by the provisions of Part 23 of the Civil Procedure Rules.

In *B(A) v. B(L) (Mental Health Patient)* [1980] 1 W.L.R. 116, the Court of Appeal held that under the provisions of the relevant county court rule (which is preserved by the Civil Procedure Rules, above) it was sufficient that the medical reports were handed to the legal adviser of the nearest relative in circumstances where the adviser could give advice and take instructions.

Jurisdiction under this section can only be exercised by a circuit judge (Practice Direction: Allocation of Cases to Levels of Judiciary, para. 11.1).

May: The judge has a discretion as to whether or not to make an order displacing the nearest relative notwithstanding that one of the grounds set out in subsection (3) has been satisfied (*Barnet L.B.C. v. Robin*, above).

Functions of the nearest relative: The nearest relative retains his power of discharge under section 23 during the currency of an application under this section.

In *R. v. Birmingham Mental Health Trust, ex p. Phillips*, May 25, 1995, Tucker J. refused applications for *habeas corpus* and judicial review that had been made in respect of a patient who had been detained under section 2 and whose nearest relative had been wrongly identified for the purposes of section 11(3). His Lordship said that an application that was subsequently made under this section to displace that relative was not invalildated by the mistake.

Sections 66 and 69: Which are concerned with applications to Mental Health

Review Tribunals. Subsection (6) provides the supplanted nearest relative with a right to make an application to a tribunal.

Exercisable by the applicant: Except where the applicant is an approved social worker (subs. (2)).

Willing to do so: The consent of the relevant person or local services authority should be obtained prior to the application being made to the county court.

Subsection (2)

1–401 *Relative of the patient:* Is defined in section 26(1). The patient cannot apply under this provision and cannot compel another person to make an application on her behalf.

Residing: It is not necessary for the applicant to be ordinarily residing with the patient.

Approved social worker: An approved social worker applicant acts in a personal capacity and is not therefore bound to follow the advice of his managers. As an employee of the social services authority the approved social worker should receive the legal advice and support that the authority would normally provide to any employee who is involved in legal proceedings by virtue of the nature of their employment.

Local social services authority: If a local authority is appointed as nearest relative it must comply with its responsibilities under section 116.

Subsection (3)

1–402 *May be made:* There is no requirement to make an application in any of the situations specified in this provision.

Paragraph (a)

1–403 There is no obligation placed on an approved social worker to seek an order under this section if the patient has no nearest relative. Approved social worker should consider acting on this ground if the patient is likely to be detained for a lengthy period, or if a suitable person comes forward who is willing to perform the functions of the nearest relative.

Paragraph (b)

1–404 *Incapable:* This ground is only available if the person concerned is unable to perform the functions of nearest relative. It does not cover the situation of a nearest relative who exercises his functions in an irresponsible manner.

If an approved social worker concludes that it is not practicable to consult with the patient's nearest relative under section 11(4) because of that person's mental incapacity, an application under section 3 can proceed without an application being made to the court under this provision.

Paragraph (c)

1–405 *Unreasonably objects:* At the date of the hearing. In *W v. L* [1974] Q.B. 711 the Court of Appeal held that the proper test for the county court to apply is an objective one: the court should ask what an objectively reasonable person would do in all the circumstances, and not ask whether the actual nearest relative involved in the case was behaving reasonably from his own subjective point of view. The court stated that this test is similar to the test in adoption cases in which the House of Lords have approved the following statement: "... in considering whether she is reasonable or unreasonable we must take into account the welfare of the child. A reasonable mother surely gives great weight to what is better for the child. Her anguish of mind is quite understandable: but still it may be unreasonable for her to withhold consent": see *Re W (An Infant)* [1971] 2 All E.R. 49, 55, *per* Lord Hailsham L.C. citing Lord Denning M.R. in *Re L (An Infant)* (1962) 106 Sol.Jo. 611. The Court in *Re W* held that two reasonable parents can perfectly reasonably come to opposite conclusions on the same set of facts without forfeiting their title to be regarded as reasonable. The question before a court hearing an application under this provision is therefore whether a nearest relative's objection comes within the band of possible reasonable decisions and not whether it is right or mistaken. *Per* Lord Hailsham in *Re W* at 56: "Not every reasonable exercise of judgment is right, and not every mistaken exercise of judgment is unreasonable. There is a band of decisions within which no court should seek to replace the individuals judgment with his own." In *Smirek v. Williams*, April 7, 2000, CA, Hale L.J. said that, in her view, "it cannot possibly be outside that band of reasonable decisions for the [nearest relative] to agree with, and rely upon, a recent decision of a Mental Health Review Tribunal unless there has since been a change in the circumstances leading to that decision." As the nearest relative is objecting to an application being made and as an approved social worker applicant is required by section 13(1) to consider all "relevant circumstances", it would seem that a reasonable nearest relative is entitled to consider all the circumstances of the case and not just the medical evidence.

The *obiter* comment of Lawton L.J. in *B(A) v. B(L) (Mental Health Patient)*, above, that "the judge must have some evidence that compulsory admission to hospital and detention is necessary" suggests that a court hearing an application under this paragraph should consider the merits for detaining the patient by reference to the statutory criteria before moving on to considering the reasonableness of the nearest relative's decision. The judge should not be concerned to establish whether the technical requirements of this Act relating to applications for detention or guardianship have been satisfied. In the words of Lawton L.J. at 121: "The object of an application under [this paragraph] is to enable the provisions of [section 3] to be brought into operation, and until an application has been dealt with under [this section the approved social worker] is not in a position to make an application under [section 3]. It follows, so it seems to me, that if there were any defects for the purposes of [section 3] in the form of the reports tendered to the county court judge they were irrelevant for the purposes of ... the application. The county court judge had to look at the reports for their medical content; he was not concerned with their statutory form."

The operation of this provision is examined by D. Hewitt in "A tendency to laugh and sing: the unreasonable relative and the Mental Health Act" [1992] 5 Litigation 183 and by S. Simblet in "Displacing the 'unreasonable' nearest relative" (1999) 143(7) S.J. 156–158.

Paragraph (d)
Without due regard: The test is an objective one (*Surrey County Council Social Services v. McMurray*, November 11, 1994, CA). **1–406**

Power to discharge the patient: From detention or guardianship using the power contained in section 23. When considering an application under this paragraph the judge should consider not only the history of the matter but also the situation with which he is faced at the date of the hearing (*Barnet L.B.C. v. Robin*, above).

Although applications under this provision can only be made in respect of detained patients and patients subject to guardianship, the author is aware of a case where the judge ordered that the patient's nearest relative be displaced in circumstances where the patient was neither detained nor subject to guardianship. The motive for making the application was a desire to prevent the nearest relative from discharging the patient *from hospital*, and not from detention or guardianship. No relative has the power to insist on the discharge of an informal patient from hospital in the absence of either the patient's valid consent to such a discharge or the acquiescence of a mentally incapacitated patient. If there is a dispute between the relatives and the hospital, or between relatives, as to the appropriate future care of a mentally incapacitated patient, the High Court has jurisdiction to adjudicate on the issue by exercising its jurisdiction to grant declaratory relief (*Re S (Hospital Patient: Court's Jurisdiction)* [1995] 3 All E.R. 290, CA).

Subsection (4)

1–407　This subsection provides that if the patient is detained for assessment and an application is made to the county court on ground (c) or (d) before the 28 days provided for in section 2 expire, the period for which the patient may be detained is extended until the application is finally disposed of and, if an order is made, for a further period of seven days to enable the formalities of a section 3 application to be complied with. An authenticated copy of the application to the court should be placed with the patient's statutory documentation as this provides the hospital managers with continued authority for the patient's detention. The relationship between this section and section 66, which, *inter alia*, requires a section 2 patient to make his application to a Mental Health Review Tribunal within 14 days of his admission, is unclear: see the note on section 66(2) and on "The Human Rights Act 1998", above.

A nearest relative is not deprived of his power of discharge under section 23 during the period of the extended section 2. The patient's responsible medical officer could prevent such a discharge taking effect if the provisions of section 25 apply.

Immediately before the expiration of the period for which a patient is liable to be detained: Where a Mental Health Review Tribunal has ordered the discharge of the patient from section 2 and has exercised its power under section 72(3) to delay the discharge to a specified future date, the provisions of this subsection will apply if an application under this section is made to the county court before that date (*Re Whitbread* [1999] C.O.D. 370).

Paragraph (a)—finally disposed of: The detention continues during the period for lodging an appeal, and if an appeal is lodged, the time taken to determine it.

Subsection (5)

1–408　"[This subsection] provides that an order made on [grounds (3)(a) or (b)] may specify a period for which the order will remain in force, unless it is discharged. One example of a way in which a court might use this power would be to specify that the order should cease on the date when the eldest child of the patient reached 18, so that he could then take on the role of nearest relative" (*Memorandum*, para. 108).

Subsection (6)

1–409　This subsection specifies the functions of an acting nearest relative and provides that an order made under this section remains in force notwithstanding that the person who was the patient's nearest relative when the order was made is no longer his nearest relative, for example as a result of the death of that person.

Shall not apply ... in the case mentioned in paragraph (h): This means that a supplanted nearest relative has a right to apply to a Mental Health Review Tribunal for the patient's case to be reviewed. The application may be made within twelve months of the date of the county court order and in any subsequent period of twelve months (s.66(1)(h), (2)(g)).

Discharge and variation of orders under s.29

1–410　**30.**—(1) An order made under section 29 above in respect of a patient may be discharged by the county court upon application made—

(a) in any case, by the person having the functions of the nearest relative of the patient by virtue of the order;

(b) where the order was made on the ground specified in paragraph (a) or paragraph (b) of section 29(3) above, or where the person who was the nearest relative of the patient when the order was made has ceased to be his nearest relative, on the application of the nearest relative of the patient.

(2) An order made under section 29 above in respect of a patient may be varied by the county court, on the application of the person having the

functions of the nearest relative by virtue of the order or on the application of an approved social worker, by substituting for the first-mentioned person a local social services authority or any other person who in the opinion of the court is a proper person to exercise those functions, being an authority or person who is willing to do so.

(3) If the person having the functions of the nearest relative of a patient by virtue of an order under section 29 above dies—

(a) subsections (1) and (2) above shall apply as if for any reference to that person there were substituted a reference to any relative of the patient, and

(b) until the order is discharged or varied under those provisions the functions of the nearest relative under this Part of this Act and sections 66 and 69 below shall not be exercisable by any person.

(4) An order under section 29 above shall, unless previously discharged under subsection (1) above, cease to have effect at the expiration of the period, if any, specified under subsection (5) of that section or, where no such period is specified—

(a) If the patient was on the date of the order liable to be detained in pursuance of an application for admission for treatment or by virtue of an order or direction under Part III of this Act (otherwise than under section 35, 36 or 38) or was subject to guardianship under this Part of this Act or by virtue of such an order or direction, or becomes so liable or subject within the period of three months beginning with that date, when he ceases to be so liable or subject (otherwise than on being transferred in pursuance of regulations under section 19 above);

(b) if the patient was not on the date of the order, and has not within the said period become, so liable or subject, at the expiration of that period.

(5) The discharge or variation under this section of an order made under section 29 above shall not affect the validity of anything previously done in pursuance of the order.

DEFINITIONS
    patient: s.145(1). **1–411**
    nearest relative: ss.26(3), 145(1).
    approved social worker: s.145(1).
    application for admission for treatment: ss.3, 145(1).

GENERAL NOTE
    This section provides for the discharge or variation of an order made by a county **1–412** court under section 29 for the appointment of an acting nearest relative. It also, in subsection (4), specifies the duration of an order.

Subsection (1)
    Paragraph (a) or (b): A nearest relative who is displaced on ground (c) or (d) **1–413** cannot apply for the order to be discharged.

Subsection (4)
    This subsection "means that the order lasts either for the period specified under **1–414** section 29(5) or until the patient is discharged from hospital or guardianship if he was detained in hospital for treatment or subject to guardianship at the time the order was made or became so within the following three months. However, the order does not

lapse in the event of a transfer between hospital and guardianship, or between hospitals or guardians," (*Memorandum*, para. 109).

Supplemental

Procedure on applications to county court

1–415   **31.** County court rules which relate to applications authorised by this Part of this Act to be made to a county court may make provision—

    (a) for the hearing and determination of such applications otherwise than in open court;

    (b) for the admission on the hearing of such applications of evidence of such descriptions as may be specified in the rules notwithstanding anything to the contrary in any enactment or rule of law relating to the admissibility of evidence:

    (c) for the visiting and interviewing of patients in private by or under the directions of the court.

DEFINITION

1–416   patient: s.145(1).

GENERAL NOTE

1–417   This section is applied to patients who have been placed under hospital or guardianship orders by a court under section 37 (Sched. 1, Pt I, para. 1).

County court rules: See the Civil Procedure Rules 1998 (S.I. 1998 No. 3132), Sched. 2, CCR Ord. 49, r. 12.

Otherwise than in open court: The publication of information relating to proceedings brought under this Act before a county court sitting in private is prima facie a contempt of court: see section 12 of the Administration of Justice Act 1960 and *Pickering v. Liverpool Daily Post and Echo Newspapers plc* [1991] 1 All E.R. 622, HL.

Regulations for purposes of Part II

1–418   **32.**—(1) The Secretary of State may make regulations for prescribing anything which, under this Part of this Act, is required or authorised to be prescribed, and otherwise for carrying this Part of this Act into full effect.

(2) Regulations under this section may in particular make provision—

    (a) for prescribing the form of any application, recommendation, report, order, notice or other document to be made or given under this Part of this Act;

    (b) for prescribing the manner in which any such application, recommendation, report, order, notice or other document may be proved, and for regulating the service of any such application, report, order or notice;

    (c) for requiring [such bodies as may be prescribed by the regulations] to keep such registers or other records as may be [so prescribed] in respect of patients liable to be detained or subject to guardianship [or to after-care under supervision] under this Part of this Act, and to furnish or make available to those patients, and their relatives, such written statements of their rights and powers under this Act as may be so prescribed;

    (d) for the determination in accordance with the regulations of the age of any person whose exact age cannot be ascertained by reference to the registers kept under the Births and Deaths Registration Act 1953; and

(e) for enabling the functions under this Part of this Act of the nearest relative of a patient to be performed, in such circumstances and subject to such conditions (if any) as may be prescribed by the regulations, by any person authorised in that behalf by that relative;

and for the purposes of this Part of this Act any application, report or notice the service of which is regulated under paragraph (b) above shall be deemed to have been received by or furnished to the authority or person to whom it is authorised or required to be furnished, addressed or given if it is duly served in accordance with the regulations.

(3) Without prejudice to subsections (1) and (2) above, but subject to section 23(4) above, regulations under this section may determine the manner in which functions under this Part of this Act of the managers of hospitals, local social services authorities, [Health Authorities, Special Health Authorities[, Primary Care Trusts] or National Health Service trusts] are to be exercised, and such regulations may in particular specify the circumstances in which, and the conditions subject to which, any such functions may be performed by officers of or other persons acting on behalf of those managers and authorities.

AMENDMENTS
The amendments to this section were made by the Health Authorities Act 1995, s.2(1), Sched. 1, para. 107(4), the Mental Health (Patients in the Community) Act 1995, s.2(1), Sched. 1, para. 2 and the Health Act 1999 (Supplementary, Consequential, etc., Provisions) Order 2000 (S.I. 2000 No. 90), Sched. 1, para. 16(6).

DEFINITIONS
the managers: s.145(1).   **1–419**
hospital: ss.34(2), 145(1).
local social services authority: s.145(1).
patient: s.145(1).
nearest relative: ss.26(3), 145(1).
Health Authority: s.145(1).
Special Health Authority: s.145(1).

GENERAL NOTE
The Mental Health (Hospital Guardianship and Consent to Treatment) Regu- **1–420** lations 1983 (S.I. 1983 No. 893) and the Mental Health (After-care under Supervision) Regulations 1996 (S.I. 1996 No. 294) have been made under this section.

Subsection (1)
Secretary of State: The functions of the Minister, so far as exercisable in relation to **1–421** Wales, are exercised by the National Assembly for Wales (S.I. 1999 No. 672, art. 2, Sched. 1).

Special provisions as to wards of court
33.—(1) An application for the admission to hospital of a minor who is a **1–422** ward of court may be made under this Part of this Act with the leave of the court; and section 11(4) above shall not apply in relation to an application so made.

(2) Where a minor who is a ward of court is liable to be detained in a hospital by virtue of an application for admission under this Part of this Act, any power exercisable under this Part of this Act or under section 66 below in relation to the patient by his nearest relative shall be exercisable by or with the leave of the court.

(3) Nothing in this Part of this Act shall be construed as authorising the making of a guardianship application in respect of a minor who is a ward of court, or the transfer into guardianship of any such minor.

[(4) Where a supervision application has been made in respect of a minor who is a ward of court, the provisions of this Part of this Act relating to after-care under supervision have effect in relation to the minor subject to any order which the court may make in the exercise of its wardship jurisdiction.]

AMENDMENT
Subsection (4) was inserted by the Mental Health (Patients in the Community) Act 1995, s.2(1), Sched. 1, para. 3.

DEFINITIONS
1–423 hospital: ss.34(2), 145(1).
nearest relative: ss.26(3), 145(1).
supervision application: ss.25A, 145(1).

GENERAL NOTE
1–424 This section provides that the leave of the court must be obtained before a ward of court can be compulsorily detained in hospital (subs. (1)), and before the ward's nearest relative exercises his powers (subs. (2)). It also prohibits the reception or transfer of a ward of court into guardianship (subs. (3)) and makes any power or duty exercisable in respect of a ward who is subject to supervised discharge subject to the wardship court's jurisdiction (subs. (4)).

Interpretation of Part II
1–425 **34.**—(1) In this Part of this Act—

"the community responsible medical officer", in relation to a patient subject to after-care under supervision, means the person who, in accordance with section 117(2A)(a) below, is in charge of medical treatment provided for him;]
"the nominated medical attendant", in relation to a patient who is subject to the guardianship of a person other than a local social services authority, means the person appointed in pursuance of regulations made under section 9(2) above to act as the medical attendant of the patient;
["registered establishment" means an establishment—
(a) which would not, apart from subsection (2) below, be a hospital for the purposes of this Part; and
(b) in respect of which a person is registered under Part II of the Care Standards Act 2000 as an independent hospital in which treatment or nursing (or both) are provided for persons liable to be detained under this Act;]
"the responsible medical officer" means [(except in the phrase "community responsible medical officer")]—
(a) in relation to a patient [who is] liable to be detained by virtue of an application for admission for assessment or an application for admission for treatment [or who is to be subject to after-care under supervision after leaving hospital], the registered medical practitioner in charge of the treatment of the patient;

(b) in relation to a patient subject to guardianship, the medical officer authorised by the local social services authority to act (either generally or in any particular case or for any particular purpose) as the responsible medical officer.

["the supervisor", in relation to a patient subject to after-care under supervision, means the person who, in accordance with section 117(2A)(b) below, is supervising him.]

[(1A) Nothing in this Act prevents the same person from acting as more than one of the following in relation to a patient, that is—

(a) the responsible medical officer;

(b) the community responsible medical officer; and

(c) the supervisor.]

(2) Except where otherwise expressly provided, this Part of this Act applies in relation to a [registered establishment] as it applies in relation to a hospital, and references in this Part of this Act to a hospital, and any reference in this Act to a hospital to which this Part of this Act applies, shall be construed accordingly.

(3) In relation to a patient who is subject to guardianship in pursuance of a guardianship application, any reference in this Part of this Act to the responsible local social services authority is a reference—

(a) where the patient is subject to the guardianship of a local social services authority, to that authority;

(b) where the patient is subject to the guardianship of a person other than a local social services authority, to the local social services authority for the area in which that person resides.

AMENDMENTS
The amendments to this section were made by the Mental Health (Patients in the Community) Act 1995, s.2(1), Sched. 1, para. 4 and the Care Standards Act 2000, s.116, Sched. 4, para. 9(4).

DEFINITIONS
patient: s.145(1). **1–426**
local social services authority: s.145(1).
application for admission for assessment: ss.2, 145(1).
application for admission for treatment: ss.3, 145(1).
mental nursing home: s.145(1).
hospital: s.145(1).

GENERAL NOTE
This section also applies to patients who have been placed under hospital or **1–427** guardianship orders made by a court under section 37. (Sched. 1, Pt I, para. 1) and to restricted patients with the modification that in subsection (1) the definition of "the nominated medical attendant" and subsection (3) shall be omitted (Sched. 1, Pt II, paras 2, 8).

The Human Rights Act 1998
The community responsible medical officer, the nominated medical attendant and **1–428** the responsible medical officer are exercising "functions of a public nature" and are therefore "public authorities" for the purposes of section 6 of the 1998 Act (s.6(3)(b)).

Subsection (1)

1–429   *The nominated medical attendant:* Is appointed by a private guardian under the Mental Health (Hospital, Guardianship and Consent to Treatment) Regulations 1983, reg. 12(a).

Medical practitioner in charge of the treatment of the patient: Who will not be professionally accountable for the patients' treatment to any other doctor. This will usually be the consultant psychiatrist on the staff of the hospital under whose care the patient has been admitted. However, determining such a person is a question of fact and the medical practitioner need not necessarily have consultant status. For example, where the patient's consultant is not available because of sickness or annual leave, the doctor who is for the time being in charge of the patient's treatment ("who should normally be another consultant or specialist registrar approved under section 12(2)"—*Memorandum*, para. 60) would exercise the functions of the responsible medical officer. The responsible medical officer is not required to be approved under section 12(2), although this will normally be the case. The community responsible medical officer of a patient who is subject to supervised discharge must be approved under section 12(2).

Although this definition identifies the responsible medical officer as having a lead role in relation to the clinical team treating the patient, it should not be taken to imply that the doctor in question is granted powers additional to the specific powers that this Act confers on the responsible medical officer. In particular, the status of responsible medical officer does not:

(i)   confer on the doctor overall management responsibility for all of the treatments that the patient receives; or

(ii) provide the doctor with further powers over the provision of resources that might be of benefit to the patient (*R. (on the application of F.) v. Oxfordshire Mental Healthcare NHS Trust and Oxfordshire NHS Health Authority* [2001] EWHC Admin 535).

The responsibilities of a responsible medical officer are not delegable.

Paragraph (b)—authorised ... to act: There is no requirement for the responsible medical officer to be "in charge of the treatment" of a guardianship patient. "It is for the local social services authority to decide who is to act as the responsible medical officer, either generally for a particular patient, or on a specific occasion. The responsible local social services authority should wherever practicable nominate a consultant psychiatrist who has been involved in the patient's treatment" (*Memorandum*, para. 43).

Subsection (2)

1–430   *Registered establishment:* Registered by the National Care Standards Commission (for England) or the National Assembly for Wales (for Wales).

Subsection (3)

1–431   *Responsible local social services authority:* Renewal reports must be addressed to this authority which has the power to discharge the patient from guardianship by virtue of section 23(2)(b).

Resides: Temporary absences from the place where a person lives does not affect residence, as long as there is an intention to return (*R. v. St Leonard's Shoreditch (Inhabitants)* (1865) L.R. 1 Q.B. 21). Also note Widgery L.J.'s statement that "A man cannot be said to reside in a particular place unless in the ordinary sense of the word one can say that for the time being he is making his home in that place" (*Fox v. Stirk* [1970] 1 Q.B. 463, 477).

PART III

PATIENTS CONCERNED IN CRIMINAL PROCEEDINGS OR UNDER SENTENCE

GENERAL NOTE

1–432   This Part deals with the circumstances in which patients may be admitted to and detained in hospital or received into guardianship on the order of a court, or may be transferred to hospital or guardianship from penal institutions on the direction of the

Home Secretary. Guidance on professional responsibilities to patients who are concerned in criminal proceedings is contained in chapter 3 of the *Code of Practice*. The admission of patients from prison or a remand centre is considered in chapter 7 of the *Code*.

Home Office Circular No. 66/90 (as supplemented by Home Office Circular No. 12/95) draws the attention of the courts and those services responsible for dealing with mentally disordered people who come into contact with the criminal justice system to the legal powers that exist and to the desirability of ensuring effective co-operation between agencies. Phil Fennell examines the recommendations contained in this circular and considers some of the issues involved in diverting mentally disordered offenders from the penal system in "Diversion of Mentally Disordered Offenders from Custody" [1991] Crim.L.R. 333–348.

The Lord Chancellor's Department's Best Practice Advisory Group has produced a bulletin on "Mentally Disordered Offenders" (undated). The aim of the bulletin is to "heighten awareness of the problem of mentally disordered offenders and to encourage courts, with the aid of suggestions of best practice, to initiate action where possible and where resources allow" (p. 1).

Under section 4 of the Criminal Justice Act 1991 where an offender is or appears to be mentally disordered, the court shall obtain and consider a medical report on the offender's mental condition before passing a custodial sentence (subs. (1)). The report, which can be made or submitted orally or in writing, must be that of a doctor who is approved under section 12 of this Act. This requirement does not apply to murder cases or to cases where a sentence of life imprisonment is imposed by virtue of section 2(2) of the Crime (Sentences) Act 1997 (subs. (1)) and the court need not obtain a report if it is "of the opinion that it is unnecessary" to obtain one (subs. (2)). The court is also required to consider any information before it which relates to the offender's mental condition and the likely effect of a custodial sentence on that condition and on any treatment which may be available for it (subs. (3)).

The functions of the Home Secretary

Through inadvertence, the functions of the Home Secretary under this Part, in so **1–433** far as they are exercisable in relation to Wales, were transferred to the National Assembly for Wales under the National Assembly for Wales (Transfer of Functions) Order 1999 (S.I. 1999 No. 672) art. 2, Sched. 1. These functions (subject to a number of exceptions that are noted in the appropriate sections) were transferred back to the Home Secretary by a means of a variation to the Order by the National Assembly of Wales (Transfer of Functions) Order 2000 (S.I. 2000 No. 253), art. 4, Sched. 3. The period between the two transfer orders was covered by arrangements being put in place under section 41 of the Government of Wales Act 1998 enabing Home Office officials to exercise the functions on behalf of the Assembly.

Notification of hospital orders and hospital directions to the Home Office

Paragraph 190 of the *Memorandum* states: **1–434**

> "When a patient is admitted to hospital under a hospital order, the hospital is asked to send to the Home Office a copy of each order. This applies both to hospital orders made together with a restriction order and to those made without, but not to interim hospital orders, place of safety orders, remands to hospital or patients admitted by direction of the Home Secretary. However, if a patient originally admitted to hospital in one of the latter ways subsequently becomes subject to a hospital order, the hospital should notify the Home Office as if the patient were a new admission. The hospital should also notify the Home Office of hospital and limitation directions. The address to which copies of hospital orders should be sent is:

> Home Office
> Research and Statistics Directorate

Offenders and Corrections Unit
Room 262
Queen Anne's Gate
London
SW1H 9AT"

The Criminal Procedure (Insanity) Act 1964

1–435 The Criminal Procedure (Insanity) Act 1964, as amended by the Criminal Procedure (Insanity and Unfitness to Plead) Act 1991, makes provision for persons who are found unfit to be tried, or not guilty by reason of insanity, in respect of criminal charges. The disposals available to the court where the accused has been found unfit to be tried or unfit by reason of insanity and the changes introduced by the 1991 Act are set out in Home Office Circular No. 93/1991 and Department of Health Circular LASSL (91)12. The 1991 Act has been analysed by Stephen White at [1992] Crim.L.R. 4–14, by Phil Fennell at (1992) M.L.R., Vol. 55, 547–555, and by Adrian James at (1993) *Journal of Forensic Psychiatry*, 4, 285–294.

The Criminal Evidence (Amendment) Act 1997

1–436 The Criminal Evidence (Amendment) Act, which came into force on March 19, 1997, enables the police to take non-intimate samples without consent, for DNA profiling purposes, from persons who were convicted before April 10, 1995 of one of the offences listed in Schedule 1 to the Act (broadly sex, violent and burglary offences) and who are serving a sentence of imprisonment, or are detained under Part III of this Act, in respect of such an offence at the time when it is sought to take a sample. The Act also enables non-intimate samples to be taken without consent from persons detained under this Part who have been acquitted on grounds of insanity or found unfit to plead. Guidance on the Act is contained in Home Office Circulars 27/1997.

The Sex Offenders Act 1997

1–437 The Sex Offenders Act 1997, which came into force on September 1, 1997, imposes requirements on sex offenders, including those under 18, to notify the police of their name and address and of any subsequent changes of these. The purpose is to ensure that information on sex offenders contained within the Police National Computer is fully up to date. The Act applies to people who are subject to detention in hospital or guardianship under this Part following conviction or cautioning for a relevant offence. Guidance to hospital managers and local authority social services departments on the Act is contained in Local Authority Social Services Letter (97) 17/HSG (97) 37.

The Criminal and Court Services Act 2000

1–438 Sections 67 and 68 of this Act (which have not come into force) impose on the "responsible authority" for any area certain obligations in relation to sexual or violent offenders. The "responsible authority" is the chief officer of police and the local probation board established by section 4 of the Act acting jointly. The responsible authority is required to establish arrangements for the purpose of assessing and managing the risks posed in the area concerned by relevant sexual and violent offenders. A violent or sexual offender who has been made subject to a hospital or guardianship order under this Part falls into this category. The effectiveness of the arrangements must be monitored and reports on the discharge of this function must be published at intervals of 12 months. Section 69 (which has not come into force) places a duty on the local probation board to ascertain whether victims of sexual or violent offences wish to make representations about any conditions or requirements that should be imposed on the offender on his or her release.

Remands to hospital

Remand to hospital for report on accused's mental condition
35.—(1) Subject to the provisions of this section, the Crown Court or a **1–439**
magistrates' court may remand an accused person to a hospital specified by
the court for a report on his mental condition.
(2) For the purposes of this section an accused person is—
(a) in relation to the Crown Court, any person who is awaiting trial before
the court for an offence punishable with imprisonment or who has
been arraigned before the court for such an offence and has not yet
been sentenced or otherwise dealt with for the offence on which he
has been arraigned;
(b) in relation to a magistrates' court, any person who has been convicted
by the court of an offence punishable on summary conviction with
imprisonment and any person charged with such an offence if the
court is satisfied that he did the act or made the omission charged or
he has consented to the exercise by the court of the powers conferred
by this section.
(3) Subject to subsection (4) below, the powers conferred by this section
may be exercised if—
(a) the court is satisfied, on the written or oral evidence of a registered
medical practitioner, that there is reason to suspect that the accused
person is suffering from mental illness, psychopathic disorder, severe
mental impairment or mental impairment; and
(b) the court is of the opinion that it would be impracticable for a report
on his mental condition to be made if he were remanded on bail;
but those powers shall not be exercised by the Crown Court in respect of a
person who has been convicted before the court if the sentence for the
offence of which he has been convicted is fixed by law.
(4) The court shall not remand an accused person to a hospital under this
section unless satisfied, on the written or oral evidence of the registered
medical practitioner who would be responsible for making the report or of
some other person representing the managers of the hospital, that arrangements have been made for his admission to that hospital and for his
admission to it within the period of seven days beginning with the date of the
remand; and if the court is so satisfied it may, pending his admission, give
directions for his conveyance to and detention in a place of safety.
(5) Where a court has remanded an accused person under this section it
may further remand him if it appears to the court, on the written or oral
evidence of the registered medical practitioner responsible for making the
report, that a further remand is necessary for completing the assessment of
the accused person's mental condition.
(6) The power of further remanding an accused person under this section
may be exercised by the court without his being brought before the court if
he is represented by counsel or a solicitor and his counsel or solicitor is given
an opportunity of being heard.

(7) An accused person shall not be remanded or further remanded under this section for more than 28 days at a time or for more than 12 weeks in all; and the court may at any time terminate the remand if it appears to the court that it is appropriate to do so.

(8) An accused person remanded to hospital under this section shall be entitled to obtain at his own expense an independent report on his mental condition from a registered medical practitioner chosen by him and to apply to the court on the basis of it for his remand to be terminated under subsection (7) above.

(9) Where an accused person is remanded under this section—

(a) a constable or any other person directed to do so by the court shall convey the accused person to the hospital specified by the court within the period mentioned in subsection (4) above; and

(b) the managers of the hospital shall admit him within that period and thereafter detain him in accordance with the provisions of this section.

(10) If an accused person absconds from a hospital to which he has been remanded under this section, or while being conveyed to or from that hospital, he may be arrested without warrant by any constable and shall, after being arrested, be brought as soon as practicable before the court that remanded him; and the court may thereupon terminate the remand and deal with him in any way in which it could have dealt with him if he has not been remanded under this section.

DEFINITIONS

1–440   hospital: ss.55(5), 145(1).
psychopathic disorder: ss.1, 145(1).
severe mental impairment: ss.1, 145(1).
mental impairment: ss.1, 145(1).
the managers: s.145(1).

GENERAL NOTE

1–441   This section gives effect to the recommendation of the Butler Committee that courts should have the option of remanding an accused person to hospital for the preparation of a report on his mental condition (*Butler Committee*, paras 12.8 to 12.11). Magistrates' courts and the Crown Court have this power if they are satisfied, on the evidence of an approved doctor, that there is reason to suspect that the accused is suffering from one of the four categories of mental disorder and that it would be impracticable for a report on his mental condition to be made if he were remanded on bail. The remand, which can last for a maximum of 12 weeks, cannot be made unless the court is also satisfied that arrangements have been made for the accused's admission to hospital. The court may terminate the remand at any time. Advice on this section is contained in paragraphs 17.1 to 17.5 of the *Code of Practice*.

The power to remand to hospital should be used as an alternative to a remand to prison, and not as an alternative to a remand on bail. The Butler Committee emphasised that where it is possible to do so, the first choice of the courts should "always to be to give bail" (para. 12.10). A remand under this section would be appropriate where it was felt that the accused person might be likely to break a condition of bail that he should reside in a hospital. Under such a bail condition, the hospital authorities do not have the power to prevent the accused person from leaving the hospital. A remand under this section provides such a power.

The effect of subsections (3) and (4) of this section "is expected to be that the initiative for a remand to hospital will generally come either from the defendant's legal representative (who may already have taken steps to obtain the necessary evidence from an approved medical practitioner before suggesting to the court that remand to hospital might be appropriate) or from the medical officer of the prison to which the defendant has been remanded in custody at an earlier court appearance. Prison medical officers are being asked to explore the possibility of a remand to hospital in appropriate cases. Prison medical officers will of course continue to comply to the best of their ability with requests from the courts for medical reports on prisoners remanded in custody for that purpose. If the court itself is considering the suitability of a remand to hospital and no prior arrangements with a hospital have been made, it will generally be necessary to adjourn the case so that the necessary medical recommendation can be sought and arrangements made for the defendant to be admitted to a hospital" (Home Office Circular No. 71/1984, Annex, paras 24, 25).

This section does not provide the remanding court with a power to either grant the patient leave of absence under section 17 or to transfer him to another hospital under section 19. If the patient is subsequently made subject to an application under Part II, his responsible medical officer cannot exercise these powers: see point (6), below.

The *Memorandum* states that if "the accused person absconds, he may be arrested without warrant by any constable and is then to be brought before the court that remanded him, which may decide on some alternative approach to his case" (para. 147).

A person remanded under this section is not subject to the consent to treatment provisions contained in Part IV of this Act (s.56(1)(b)). This has led to the practice of using either section 2 or section 3 of this Act to bring the patient within the scope of Part IV. Although this practice has been regarded by legal commentators as being legally questionable, the decision in *R. v. North West London Mental Health NHS Trust, ex p. Stewart* [1997] 4 All E.R. 871, CA, noted under section 42(3), where the court held that the powers under Part II and Part III of this Act can co-exist and operate independently of each other, has confirmed that the either section 2 or section 3 can be used during the currency of a section 35. This was a pragmatic decision of the Court of Appeal that does not sit easily with the scheme of this Act. The following arguments can be made in support of the contention that the practice of "double detention" in these circumstances was unlawful:

(1) the specific exclusion of patients remanded under this section from Part IV of this Act is a clear indication of Parliament's intention that this section should not carry with it a power to impose treatment. In the House of Lords debate on this provision Lord Belstead, speaking for the Government, said that "this power is intended to be used only for diagnostic purposes ... [T]here need be no concern that a remand for a medical report would otherwise expose a person to the risk of receiving unnecessary treatment without his consent because ... there is no intention that a person remanded under this clause should be regarded as 'detained for treatment' for the purposes of clause 38: this is expressly excluded by subsection (9)(b) of that clause" (HL Vol. 426, No. 28, cols 769, 770). Clause 38(9)(b) was subsequently enacted as section 56(1)(b);

(2) if Parliament had intended that a power to treat a patient without consent could be added to this section by the use of Part II of this Act, why did it create two separate remand powers, one under section 36 authorising treatment without consent and exercisable only by the Crown Court and the other under this section not authorising treatment without consent and exercisable by the Crown Court or the magistrates' court;

(3) it would be difficult to justify making an application under section 2 because the criteria set out in subsection (2)(a) and (b) of that section cannot be

satisfied in that the patient is already being assessed and is subject to detention;

(4) a patient who has been remanded under this section and subsequently made subject to an application under section 2 or section 3 could be discharged from the section by a Mental Health Review Tribunal, but would continue to be liable to be detained by virtue of his remand under this section;

(5) a patient who has been remanded under this section and subsequently made subject to an application under section 2 or section 3 could have his remand terminated (see subss (7)–(8)), yet remain liable to be detained by virtue of section 2 or section 3;

(6) if a patient who has been remanded under this section is also made subject to an application under section 2 or section 3 it will not be possible for the patient's responsible medical officer to exercise some of the key powers under Part II of this Act (*e.g.* granting the patient leave of absence under section 17 or transferring the patient to another hospital or into guardianship under section 19) because the patient continues to be subject to the terms of the remand and the hospital managers have admitted him on the basis that they shall "therefore detain him in accordance with the provisions of *this* section" (subs. (9));

(7) the scenarios identified in (4), (5) and (6) would cause difficulties for the person who is charged under section 132 with giving the patient an explanation of his legal position, as subsection (1)(a) of that section clearly envisages a patient being detained under one provision of this Act at a time; and

(8) there is a canon of construction that Parliament is presumed not to enact legislation which interferes with the liberty of the subject without making it clear that this was its intention; see the note on Judicial Interpretation in the General Note to this Act.

Support for the practice of making an application under section 3 in respect of a patient who has been remanded under this section is given by the *Code of Practice* at paragraph 17.3 and in paragraph 9.4 the Fourth Biennial Report of the Mental Health Act Commission 1989–1991, which states that "the Commission takes the view that in certain rare instances, the use of … [section 3 concurrent with section 35] may be appropriate". J. Gunn and P. Joseph conclude from their research that "the vast majority of psychiatrists, whether they use section 35 or not, do not object to the principle of dual detention" ("Remands to hospital for psychiatric reports: a study of psychiatrists' attitudes to section 35 of the Mental Health Act 1983", *Psychiatric Bulletin* (1993) 17, 197–198). The joint Home Office and Department of Health review of health and social services for mentally disordered offenders suggests that this section be amended to enable a hospital to give treatment (Final Summary Report, Cm. 2088, para. 9.6ii).

If the remanded patient is mentally incapable of giving a valid consent to the proposed treatment, the common law authorises the administration of treatment provided it is in the patient's best interests: see the General Note to Part IV and Ch. 15 of the *Code of Practice*.

Section 22(1) of the Crime (Sentences) Act 1997 ensures that any time spent in hospital under this section before a sentence of imprisonment is passed may be subject to a direction under section 9 of that Act that the time count as part of the sentence, and that credit be given for any early release days which the offender might earn under section 13 of that Act.

A patient who has been remanded under this section has no right to apply to a Mental Health Review Tribunal.

Family Law Act 1996

1–442   If a person is arrested under a power of arrest or an arrest warrant which has been either attached to, or issued in respect of, an occupation order or a non-molestation order which has been made under Part IV of the Family Law Act 1996, then the court can make an order under this section if there is reason to suspect that the arrested person is suffering from mental illness or severe mental impairment (*ibid.* s.48(4)).

The 12-week time limit on remands made under this section does not apply to remands for medical reports made under section 48(1) of the 1996 Act (*C.W. v. A.W.* [2001] EWCA Civ 197).

Contempt of Court Act 1981
Under section 14(4A) of the Contempt of Court Act 1981 the High Court has the **1–443** power to make an order under this section where there is reason to suspect that a person who could be committed to prison for contempt of court is suffering from mental illness or severe mental impairment.

Subsection (1)
This subsection "provides an alternative to remanding the accused person in **1–444** custody for a medical report, in circumstances where it would not be practicable to obtain the report if he were remanded on bail (for instance, if he decided to break a condition of bail that he should reside at a hospital, the hospital would be unable to prevent him from discharging himself)" (Home Office Circular No. 71/1984, Annex, para. 1).

Hospital: Or a registered establishment (ss.34(2), 55(5)). For responsibility for returning the patient to court, see the General Note to section 38.

Report: Advice on the content of the report is given in paragraph 17.4 of the *Code of Practice.*

Subsection (2)

Paragraph (a)
Offence punishable with imprisonment: This section applies to a person who has **1–445** been accused, but not convicted, of murder (subs. (3)).

Paragraph (b)
Magistrates' court: If a person is remanded under this section by the magistrates **1–446** court and the case is subsequently committed to the Crown Court, the jurisdiction of the magistrates to make a further remand ends. Section 48 has been used to secure the persons immediate return to the hospital on a subsequent remand into custody (A. Akinkunmi and K. Murray, "Inadequacies in the Mental Health Act 1983 in relation to Mentally Disordered Remand Prisoners", 37 Med. Sci. Law (1997) 53–57).

Offence punishable on summary conviction with imprisonment: The offence could have been committed by a person under the age of 21 (s.55(2)).

Satisfied that he did the act: Without convicting him.

Consented: The consent relates to the making of the order and not to the extension of the order under subsection (5). A withdrawal of consent is therefore not relevant to the question of renewal.

Subsection (3)
Paragraph (a)—evidence: For general provisions as to medical evidence, see **1–447** section 54.

Registered medical practitioner: Who must have been approved by the Secretary of State under s.12 (s.54(1)).

Reason to suspect: A firm diagnosis is not required.

Paragraph (b)—impracticable: This presumably refers to the impracticability of preparing a sufficiently thorough report if the accused were granted bail.

Fixed by law: Although the power to remand to hospital is not available in respect of a person who has been *convicted* of murder who must be sentenced to life imprisonment (Murder (Abolition of Death Penalty) Act 1965, s.1(1)), a remand under this section can be made in a murder trial before conviction.

Subsection (4)

1–448   *Or of some other person:* Who need not be a doctor.

Admission to that hospital: "Normally the local psychiatric hospital or unit in a general hospital will be able to provide adequate arrangements for the assessment of mentally disordered persons, but in addition most regional health authorities are able to provide secure hospital accommodation in cases where this is necessary, and places may be sought in a special hospital in respect of persons who are thought to require treatment in conditions of special security because of their violent, dangerous, or criminal propensities," (Home Office Circular No. 66/90, para. 8(ii)).

Beginning with: Including the date of the remand (*Hare v. Gocher* [1962] 2 Q.B. 641).

Place of safety: Is defined in section 55(1).

Subsection (5)

1–449   *It may:* See the note on "consented" in subsection (2).

Further remand him: Up to a maximum of 12 weeks in all (subs. (7)).

Subsection (7)

1–450   *At any time:* "It will be open to the responsible medical officer in every case to inform the court if the object of the remand is achieved before the expiry of the stipulated time, so that the adjourned hearing may be brought forward accordingly or if necessary an alternative form of remand, either in custody or on bail, may be substituted" (*Butler Committee*, para. 12.9).

Subsection (8)

1–451   This provision was successfully moved during the passage of the 1982 Act against Government advice. The Government view was that it would be unlikely to be of great benefit to the accused person, firstly because he already has the right to commission his own private medical report and, secondly, because the court is unlikely to end his remand on the basis of such a report.

Apply to the court on the basis of it: Once the accused has received his private medical report he has the right to apply to the court to seek an end to the remand even if the reports that the court has asked for are not available.

Subsection (9)

1–452   *Convey:* Paras 31 to 33 of the Annex to Home Office Circular No. 71/1984 are concerned with the question of who is responsible for returning the patient to court:

> "31. The effect of a remand to hospital or an interim hospital order (like that of the transfer of a remand prisoner to hospital by direction of the Home Secretary under section 48 of the Act) is that the patient will remain throughout under the jurisdiction of the court before which he was remanded to appear or committed for trial. It follows that responsibility for complying with any subsequent direction by that court for the production of the patient will rest with the managers of the hospital to which he has been admitted. Normally, therefore, it will fall to hospital staff to escort the patient to court. An exception may arise where the patient is very violent or dangerous, in which case the police may be asked by the hospital managers to assist. It is open to the court to renew a remand or an interim hospital order in the patient's absence provided that the patient is legally represented and that his legal representative is present in court and is given the opportunity of being heard.
> 32. Once the patient has arrived at court the normal arrangements for the

detention there of defendants remanded in custody should apply, and the Home Secretary would be grateful for the co-operation of the courts and of the police with members of hospital staff in this respect.

33. In cases where it appears likely that the accused person's trial may last for some time, the responsible medical officer or the managers of the hospital may advise the court of difficulty over producing him in court from the hospital each day and enquire whether in these circumstances the court would consider remanding the accused person in custody or on bail for the duration of the trial, after his initial production in court by the hospital. At this point the court would have power to order further remands in whatever manner it thinks appropriate."

Also see paragraph 29.6 of the *Code of Practice*. For general provisions relating to conveyance, see section 137.

Hospital specified by the court: "Remands to hospital may sometimes entail a requirement of secure custody. It will be for the court to decide whether the defendant should be sent on remand to a local psychiatric hospital or whether there is need for the greater security afforded by the regional secure units. Exceptionally the security of a special hospital might be required" (*Butler Committee*, para. 12.12). Presumably the doctor referred to in subsection (3) would give evidence on this point.

Remand of accused person to hospital for treatment

36.—(1) Subject to the provisions of this section, the Crown Court may, 1–453 instead of remanding an accused person in custody, remand him to a hospital specified by the court if satisfied, on the written or oral evidence of two registered medical practitioners, that he is suffering from mental illness or severe mental impairment of a nature or degree which makes it appropriate for him to be detained in a hospital for medical treatment.

(2) For the purposes of this section an accused person is any person who is in custody awaiting trial before the Crown Court for an offence punishable with imprisonment (other than an offence the sentence for which is fixed by law) or who at any time before sentence is in custody in the course of a trial before that court for such an offence.

(3) The court shall not remand an accused person under this section to a hospital unless it is satisfied, on the written or oral evidence of the registered medical practitioner who would be in charge of his treatment or of some other person representing the managers of the hospital, that arrangements have been made for his admission to that hospital and for his admission to it within the period of seven days beginning with the date of the remand; and if the court is so satisfied it may, pending his admission, give directions for his conveyance to and detention in a place of safety.

(4) Where a court has remanded an accused person under this section it may further remand him if it appears to the court, on the written or oral evidence of the responsible medical officer, that a further remand is warranted.

(5) The power of further remanding an accused person under this section may be exercised by the court without his being brought before the court if he is represented by counsel or a solicitor and his counsel or solicitor is given an opportunity of being heard.

(6) An accused person shall not be remanded or further remanded under this section for more than 28 days at a time or for more than 12 weeks in all; and the court may at any time terminate the remand if it appears to the court that it is appropriate to do so.

(7) An accused person remanded to hospital under this section shall be entitled to obtain at his own expense an independent report on his mental condition from a registered medical practitioner chosen by him and to apply to the court on the basis of it for his remand to be terminated under subsection (6) above.

(8) Subsections (9) and (10) of section 35 above shall have effect in relation to a remand under this section as they have effect in relation to a remand under that section.

DEFINITIONS

1–454   hospital: ss.55(5), 145(1).
severe mental impairment: ss.1, 145(1).
the managers: s.145(1).
responsible medical officer: s.55(1).

GENERAL NOTE

1–455   This section empowers the Crown Court to remand an accused person, who is in custody either awaiting trial or during the course of a trial and who is suffering from mental illness or severe mental impairment, to hospital for treatment for a maximum of 12 weeks. It provides an alternative to the Home Secretary's power under section 48 to transfer unsentenced prisoners to hospital. Where the accused person is in urgent need of treatment and is not due to appear before the Crown Court in the immediate future, the procedure under section 48 is to be preferred. Also note paragraph 36 of Home Office Circular No. 71/1984 which states: "Section 36 provides the Crown Court with an alternative to the procedure laid down by the Criminal Procedure (Insanity) Act 1964 of finding a defendant under disability ('unfit to plead'). The power in section 36 can be used in cases in which if the defendant could receive treatment in hospital for a period it might be possible to proceed with the full trial. The Crown Court may prefer in appropriate cases to proceed in this way rather than under the Criminal Procedure (Insanity) Act, under which the defendant would thereafter have to be detained as a restricted patient (which may not be appropriate in relation to the nature of the alleged offence)." Advice on this section is contained in paragraphs 17.1 to 17.5 of the *Code of Practice.*

As this Act does not provide for the application of Part II to a patient who has been remanded under this section, there is no power to grant the patient leave of absence under section 17 or transfer the patient to another hospital under section 19.

A person remanded under this section as a "patient liable to be detained under this Act" is subject to the consent to treatment provisions contained in Part IV of this Act (s.56(1)). He has no right to apply to a Mental Health Review Tribunal.

Section 22(1) of the Crime (Sentences) Act 1997 ensures that any time spent in hospital under this section before a sentence of imprisonment is passed may be subject to a direction under section 9 of that Act that the time count as part of the sentence, and that credit be given for any early release days which the offender might earn under section 13 of that Act.

Subsection (1)

1–456   *Crown Court:* But not the magistrates' court. However, such courts have the alternative, under section 37(3), of making a hospital order in respect of a defendant charged but unconvicted.

Accused person: See subsection (2).

Hospital: Or a registered establishment (ss.34(2), 55(5)). For responsibility for returning the patient to court, see the General Note to section 38.

Evidence: For general provisions relating to medical evidence, see section 54.

Two registered medical practitioners: At least one of whom must have been approved by the Secretary of State under section 12 (s.54(1)). There is no prohibition on both of the doctors being on the staff of the same hospital.

Mental illness or severe mental impairment: A consultative paper on the recommendations of the Butler Committee, prepared jointly by the Home Office, DHSS, the Welsh Office and the Lord Chancellor's Office said, at paragraph 18, that it "is thought unlikely ... that persons suffering from psychopathic disorder or [mental impairment] would have a sufficiently clear-cut need for treatment in hospital to make it necessary for these categories to be included in this [section]". However, the *Review of Health and Social Services for Mentally Disordered Offenders and others requiring similar services, Final Summary Report,* Cm. 2088 recommended that the ambit of this section be extended to include people with mental impairment or psychopathic disorders (para. 9.6 iv).

Subsection (2)
Fixed by law: Unlike section 35, this section does not apply to a person who has **1–457** been charged with murder. If such a person is in need of urgent treatment and is either mentally ill or severely mentally impaired he could be removed to hospital under section 48 if he is awaiting trial having been remanded in custody by a magistrates' court.

Subsection (3)
Or of some other person: Who need not be a doctor. **1–458**
Beginning with: Including the date of the remand (*Hare v. Gocher* [1962] 2 Q.B. 641).
Place of safety: Is defined in section 55(1).

Subsection (4)
A further remand is warranted: Because the criteria set out in subsection (1) still **1–459** apply.

Subsection (7)
See the notes on section 35(8). **1–460**

Subsection (8)
See the extract from the Home Office Circular No. 71/1984 noted under section **1–461** 35(9).

Hospital and guardianship orders

Powers of courts to order hospital admission or guardianship
37.—(1) Where a person is convicted before the Crown Court of an **1–462** offence punishable with imprisonment other than an offence the sentence for which is fixed by law, [or falls to be imposed under [section 109(2) of the Powers of Criminal Courts (Sentencing) Act 2000]], or is convicted by a magistrates' court of an offence punishable on summary conviction with imprisonment, and the conditions mentioned in subsection (2) below are satisfied, the court may by order authorise his admission to and detention in such hospital as may be specified in the order or, as the case may be, place him under the guardianship of a local social services authority or of such other person approved by a local social services authority as may be so specified.
[(1A) In the case of an offence the sentence for which would otherwise fall to be imposed under subsection (2) of [section 110 or 111 of the Powers of Criminal Courts (Sentencing) Act 2000], nothing in that subsection shall prevent a court from making an order under subsection (1) above for the admission of the offender to a hospital.]
[(1B) For the purposes of subsections (1) and (1A) above, a sentence falls

to be imposed under section 109(2), 110(2) of the Powers of Criminal Courts (Sentencing) Act 2000 if it is required by that provision and the court is not of the opinion there mentioned.]

(2) The conditions referred to in subsection (1) above are that—

(a) the court is satisfied, on the written or oral evidence of two registered medical practitioners, that the offender is suffering from mental illness, psychopathic disorder, severe mental impairment or mental impairment and that either—

(i) the mental disorder from which the offender is suffering is of a nature or degree which makes it appropriate for him to be detained in a hospital for medical treatment and, in the case of psychopathic disorder or mental impairment, that such treatment is likely to alleviate or prevent a deterioration of his condition; or

(ii) in the case of an offender who has attained the age of 16 years, the mental disorder is of a nature or degree which warrants his reception into guardianship under this Act; and

(b) the court is of the opinion, having regard to all the circumstances including the nature of the offence and the character and antecedents of the offender, and to the other available methods of dealing with him, that the most suitable method of disposing of the case is by means of an order under this section.

(3) Where a person is charged before a magistrates' court with any act or omission as an offence and the court would have power, on convicting him of that offence, to make an order under subsection (1) above in his case as being a person suffering from mental illness or severe mental impairment, then, if the court is satisfied that the accused did the act or made the omission charged, the court may, if it thinks fit, make such an order without convicting him.

(4) An order for the admission of an offender to a hospital (in this Act referred to as "a hospital order") shall not be made under this section unless the court is satisfied on the written or oral evidence of the registered medical practitioner who would be in charge of his treatment or of some other person representing the managers of the hospital that arrangements have been made for his admission to that hospital [...], and for his admission to it within the period of 28 days beginning with the date of the making of such an order; and the court may, pending his admission within that period, give such directions as it thinks fit for his conveyance to and detention in a place of safety.

(5) If within the said period of 28 days it appears to the Secretary of State that by reason of an emergency or other special circumstances it is not practicable for the patient to be received into the hospital specified in the order, he may give directions for the admission of the patient to such other hospital as appears to be appropriate instead of the hospital so specified; and where such directions are given—

(a) the Secretary of State shall cause the person having the custody of the patient to be informed, and

(b) the hospital order shall have effect as if the hospital specified in the directions were substituted for the hospital specified in the order.

(6) An order placing an offender under the guardianship of a local social services authority or of any other person (in this Act referred to as "a

guardianship order") shall not be made under this section unless the court is satisfied that that authority or person is willing to receive the offender into guardianship.

(7) A hospital order or guardianship order shall specify the form or forms of mental disorder referred to in subsection (2)(a) above from which, upon the evidence taken into account under that subsection, the offender is found by the court to be suffering; and no such order shall be made unless the offender is described by each of the practitioners whose evidence is taken into account under that subsection as suffering from the same one of those forms of mental disorder, whether or not he is also described by either of them as suffering from another of them.

(8) Where an order is made under this section, the court [shall not:

(a) pass sentence of imprisonment or impose a fine or make a probation order in respect of the offence,

(b) if the order under this section is a hospital order, make a referral order (within the meaning of [the Powers of Criminal Courts (Sentencing) Act 2000]) in respect of the offence, or

(c) make in respect of the offender [a supervision order (within the meaning of that Act) or an order under section 105 of that Act (binding over of parent or guardian)],

but the court may make any other order which it] has power to make apart from this section; and for the purposes of this subsection "sentence of imprisonment" includes any sentence or order for detention.

AMENDMENTS
The words in square brackets in subs. (1), and subs. (1A) were inserted by the Crime (Sentences) Act 1997, s.55, Sched. 4, para. 12(1)(2). The words omitted in subs. (4) were repealed by *ibid.*, s.56(2), Sched. 6. In subsection (8) the words in square brackets were substituted by the Youth Justice and Criminal Evidence Act 1999, s.67, Sched. 4, para. 11. Subs. (1B) was inserted, and the references in subss. (1), (1A) and (8) to Powers of Criminal Courts (Sentencing) Act 2000 were made by s.165, Sched. 9, para. 90 of that Act.

DEFINITIONS
    hospital: ss.55(5), 145(1).   **1–463**
    local social services authority: s.145(1).
    psychopathic disorder: ss.1, 145(1).
    severe mental impairment: ss.1, 145(1).
    mental impairment: ss.1, 145(1).
    medical treatment: s.145(1).
    patient: s.145(1).
    the managers: s.145(1).
    place of safety: s.55(1).

GENERAL NOTE
This section empowers a Crown Court or magistrates' court to make a hospital or **1–464** guardianship order as an alternative to a penal disposal for offenders who are found to be suffering from mental disorder at the time of sentencing such as to warrant their detention in hospital or reception into guardianship. No causal relationship has to be established between the offender's mental disorder and his criminal activities. The effect of hospital and guardianship orders are set out in section 40 and in the

judgment of the Court of Appeal in *R. v. Birch*, noted below. An offender's nearest relative has no role to play in the making by the court of a hospital or guardianship order (s.40(4)).

When a person is made subject to a hospital order or guardianship order under this section any previous application or order made in respect of that person ceases to have effect (s.40(5)).

"Court reports under section 37 of the Mental Health Act should spell out the nature of the disorder and the criteria used in relation to treatability" (recommendation viii of a joint DHSS/Home Office consultation document on "Offenders Suffering from Psychopathic Disorder", 1986).

Hospital orders

1–465   The purpose and effect of a hospital order are explained in the following passage from the judgment of the Court of Appeal in *R. v. Birch* (1989) 11 Cr.App.R.(S.) 202, 210:

> "Once the offender is admitted to hospital pursuant to a hospital order or transfer order without restriction on discharge, his position is almost exactly the same as if he were a civil patient. In effect he passes out of the penal system and into the hospital regime. Neither the court nor the Secretary of State has any say in his disposal. Thus, like any other mental patient, he may be detained only for a period of six months, unless the authority to detain is renewed, an event which cannot happen unless certain conditions, which resemble those which were satisfied when he was admitted, are fulfilled. If the authority expires without being renewed, the patient may leave. Furthermore, he may be discharged at any time by the hospital managers or the 'responsible medical officer'. . . .
>
> Another feature of the regime which affects the disordered offender and the civil patient alike is the power of the responsible medical officer to grant leave of absence from the hospital for a particular purpose, or for a specified or indefinite period of time: subject always to a power of recall . . . .
>
> There are certain differences between the positions of the offender and of the civil patient, relating to early access to the [Mental Health] Review Tribunal and to discharge by the patient's nearest relative, but these are of comparatively modest importance. In general the offender is dealt with in a manner which appears, and is intended to be, humane by comparison with a custodial sentence. A hospital order is not a punishment. Questions of retribution and deterrence, whether personal or general, are immaterial. The offender who has become a patient is not kept on any kind of leash by the court, as he is when he consents to a probation order with a condition of in-patient treatment. The sole purpose of the order is to ensure that the offender receives the medical care and attention which he needs in the hope and expectation of course that the result will be to avoid the commission by the offender of further criminal acts."

The Court of Appeal has said that where a court is considering making a hospital order the defendant should, except in the rarest circumstances, be represented by counsel (*R. v. Blackwood* (1974) 59 Cr.App.R. 170).

The court can make a hospital order in the case of an offender who is subject to an interim hospital order made under section 38, without his being brought before the court (s.38(2)).

A patient who has been placed under a hospital order is subject to the consent to treatment provisions in Part IV of this Act (s.56(1)).

Where the Crown Court makes a hospital order, it may also make an order under section 41, restricting the discharge of the offender from hospital, if it considers that it is necessary for the protection of the public from serious harm so to do.

Either the patient or his nearest relative can apply to a Mental Health Review Tribunal in the period between six and twelve months after the making of the hospital order and in any subsequent period of one year (ss.66(1)(f), (2)(f), 40(4), 69(1)(a), Sched. 1, Pt 1, paras 2, 6, 9).

Health Authorities and local social services authorities have a duty to provide after-care services for hospital order patients who cease to be liable to be detained and leave hospital (s.117).

Appeals

A hospital order is a form of sentence and is therefore appealable to the Court of **1–466** Appeal (Criminal Appeal Act 1968, s.50(1)). Section 11(3) of the 1968 Act provides for the court to substitute a hospital order for a prison sentence on an appeal (*R. v. Smith* [2001] EWCA Crim. 743). Rights of appeal are described in paragraph 178 of the *Memorandum* and in leaflet 12 prepared by the Department of Health.

The issue of adducing fresh medical evidence to the Court of Appeal was considered by Hutchinson L.J. in the following passage of the judgment of the Court of Appeal in *R. v. Hassall*, April 23, 1998:

"In relation to fresh medical evidence the authorities establish that it is permissible in appropriate cases to seek to adduce before the Court of Appeal fresh evidence going to the question of sentence and there are authorities which indicate that, in relation to medical evidence, that has been done. In particular we have in mind the decision of this court in the case of *De Silva* (1994) 15 Cr.App.R.(S.) 296. However, it is also clear from another decision of this court in the case of *Mundle*, CA Monday 8th July 1996, that the correct principle to be observed when deciding whether such evidence can be adduced is this, and we quote from the judgment of the court given by Lord Justice Phillips. He said this: 'It seems to me that in principle that submission is well-founded and were the court to be persuaded that on the facts prevailing at the time of the sentence a hospital order should have been imposed but that by some evidential mischance it was not, then a hospital order ought to be imposed at the appellate stage. We do not, however, consider as a matter of principle, that if, after sentence, an appellant's mental condition deteriorates to the state where a hospital order would be appropriate at the time of the appeal, although it was not appropriate at the time that the original sentence was imposed, it is appropriate to substitute a hospital order for the sentence imposed. So, the issue that arises is whether on the evidence we are persuaded that at the time of sentencing, in January, the appellant's mental condition was such as to justify the imposition of a hospital order.'"

The Court of Appeal has allowed appeals against the imposition of restriction orders because of the progress that the patient had made since the trial: see, for example, *R. v. Crookes*, April 20, 1999.

Guardianship orders

Little use has been made of guardianship orders by the courts even though, in the **1–467** view of the Butler Committee, they "offer a useful form of control of some mentally disordered offenders who do not require hospital treatment [and are] particularly suited to the needs of subnormal offenders including those inadequate offenders who require help in managing their affairs" (para. 15.8). The nature and purpose of guardianship orders are described in paragraph 13.11 of the *Code of Practice*.

Paragraph 8(iv)(c) of Home Office Circular No. 66/90 states that "the purpose of guardianship is primarily to ensure that the offender receives care and protection rather than medical treatment, although the guardian does have powers to require the offender to attend for medical treatment. The effect of a guardianship order is to give the guardian power to require the offender to live at a specific place (this may be used to discourage the offender from sleeping rough or living with people who may exploit or mistreat him, or ensure that he resides at a particular hostel), to attend specific places at specified times for medical treatment, occupation, education, or training, and to require access to the offender to be given at the place where the offender is living to any doctor, approved social worker, or other person specified by the guardian. This power could be used, for example, to ensure the offender did not neglect himself".

The effect of a guardianship order made by a court is similar to that of civil guardianship, except that the patient's nearest relative has no power to discharge him (s.40(2)(4), Sched. 1, Pt I, paras 2, 8).

The provisions of section 39A of this Act apply where a court is minded to make a guardianship order.

A patient who has been made subject to a guardianship order can apply to a Mental Health Review Tribunal within the first six months of the order (s.69(1)(b)), and during each renewal period (ss.66(1)(f), 2(f), 40(4), Sched. 1, Pt 1, paras 2, 6, 9). The patient's nearest relative can apply within the first twelve months of the order and in any subsequent 12-month period (s.69(1)(b)).

A guardianship order patient cannot receive direct payments under the terms of the Community Care (Direct Payments) Act 1996 (Community Care (Direct Payments) Regulations 1997 (S.I. 1997 No. 734), reg.2).

Sentencing options

1–468   In *R. v. Birch*, above, the Court of Appeal said that in a case involving a degree of mental disorder the judge has available to him a variety of options, which he may conveniently approach in the following order:

"First, he should decide whether a period of compulsory detention is apposite. If the answer is that it is not, or may not be, the possibility of a probation order with a condition of in or out-patient treatment should be considered ....

Secondly, the judge will ask himself whether the conditions contained in section 37(2)(a) for the making of a hospital order are satisfied. Here the judge acts on the evidence of the doctors. If left in doubt, he may wish to avail himself of the valuable provisions of sections 38 and 39 (which are not used as often as they might be) to make an interim hospital order, giving the court and the doctors further time to decide between hospital with or without restrictions and some other disposal, and to require the Health Authority to furnish information on arrangements for the admission of the offender. If the judge concludes that the conditions empowering him to make an order are satisfied, he will consider whether to make such an order, or whether 'the most suitable method of disposing of the case' (s.37(2)(b)) is to impose a sentence of imprisonment.

Finally, he should consider whether the further condition imposed by section 41(1) is satisfied. If it is, then he may make a restriction order; but he is not obliged to do so, and may again consider sending the offender to prison, either for life or for a fixed term (*Speake* (1957) 41 Cr.App.R. 222, a pre-1959 case which we believe to be still good law). If he does decide on a restriction order, he must then choose between an unlimited order, or one for a fixed term" (at 212, 213).

The Court of Appeal went on to say, at 215, that the choice of prison as an alternative to hospital may arise "in two quite different ways:

(1) If the offender is dangerous and no suitable secure hospital accommodation is available. Here the judge will be driven to impose a prison sentence, see section 37(4) and *Jones* (1976) *Current Sentencing Practice*, F.2.3(b). (2) Where the sentencer considers that notwithstanding the offender's mental disorder there was an element of culpability in the offence which merits punishment. This may happen where there is no connection between the mental disorder and the offence, or where the defendant's responsibility for the offence is 'diminished' but not wholly extinguished. That the imposition of a prison sentence is capable of being a proper exercise of discretion is shown by *Morris* [1961] 2 Q.B. 237 and *Gunnell* (1966) 50 Cr.App.R. 242. Nevertheless the more recent decision in *Mbatha* (1985) 7 Cr.App.R.(S.) 373 strongly indicates that even where there is culpability, the right way to deal with a dangerous and disordered person is to make an order under sections 37 and 41.

In the absence of any question of culpability and punishment, the judge should not impose a sentence of imprisonment simply to ensure that if the [Mental Health] Review Tribunal finds that the conditions under section 73 are satisfied and is therefore constrained to order a discharge, the offender will return to prison rather than be set free: *Howell* (1985) 7 Cr.App.R.(S.) 360 and *Cockburn* (1967) Cr.App.R. 134."

In *R. v. Moses (Anthony)* [1996] 2 Cr.App.R.(S.) 407, the Court of Appeal said that the authorities of *Howell* and *Mbatha*, above, are to the effect that the court should make a hospital order in preference to passing a life sentence where the unanimous medical opinion was that a hospital order was appropriate, and the conditions under section 37 were satisfied.

The court cannot defer sentence on the basis of the offender undertaking to undergo treatment at a psychiatric hospital (*R. v. Skelton* [1983] Crim.L.R. 686).

Family Law Act 1996

Under section 51 of the Family Law Act 1996 a magistrates' court has the power to **1–469** make a hospital order or a guardianship order under this section, instead of a committal to custody, where there has been a breach of one of the following orders or requirements:

(a) an occupation order or non-molestation order made under Part IV of the 1996 Act;

(b) an exclusion requirement included by virtue of section 38A of the Children Act 1989 in an interim care order made under section 38 of that Act; or

(c) an exclusion requirement included by virtue of section 44A of the Children Act 1989 in an emergency protection order made under section 44 of that Act.

Contempt of Court Act 1981

Under section 14(4) of the Contempt of Court Act 1981 the High Court can make a **1–470** hospital order (but not a restriction order) or a guardianship order in the case of a person suffering from mental illness or severe mental impairment as an alternative to committing that person to prison for contempt of court.

The Human Rights Act 1998

If an offender satisfies the criteria for a hospital order set out in subsection (2) but **1–471** is not made the subject of such an order because of an inability to identify a hospital that would be willing to accept him (see subs.(4)), he could claim that Article 5(1) of the European Convention on Human Rights had been violated if he was subsequently incarcerated in a non-therapeutic environment (*Aerts v. Belgium* (2000) 29 E.H.R.R. 50, noted under Article 5(1)(e)).

Also see the note on section 3.

Subsection (1)

Convicted: Note that under section 51, it is possible for a court to make a hospital **1–472** order in respect of a transfer direction patient in his absence and without convicting him.

Fixed by law: This section does not apply to persons who have been convicted of murder who must be sentenced to life imprisonment (Murder (Abolition of Death Penalty) Act 1965, s.1(1)).

Imposed under section 109(2) of the Powers of Criminal Courts (Sentencing) Act 2000: Where the court must impose a life sentence unless the court considers that there are exceptional circumstances relating either to the offence or to the offender. If a life sentence is not imposed because of the presence of exceptional circumstances, the court has a discretion to make an order under this section. The provisions of section 45A(1), below, prevent the court from treating the offender's mental disorder as an exceptional circumstance justifying the making of a hospital order (*R. v. Newman* [2000] Crim.L.R. 309, CA). The Home Secretary could use his power under section 47 to transfer an offender who had been sentenced to life imprisonment to hospital.

Magistrates' court: Or youth court for those under the age of 18. If a magistrates' court believes that an order under this section should be made on a juvenile, it must remit the case to the youth court (Powers of Criminal Courts (Sentencing) Act 2000, s.8).

Although a magistrates' court does not have the power to attach a restriction order under section 41 to a hospital order made under this section, it may, instead of making a hospital order or other disposition, commit him to the Crown Court for sentencing under section 43 with a view to a hospital order with restrictions being made.

Offence punishable on summary conviction with imprisonment: For young offenders, see section 55(2).

The court may by order: A hospital order can be made despite the fact that there is no causal connection between the offender's mental disorder and the offence in respect of which the order is made (*R. v. McBride* [1972] Crim.L.R. 322). In *R v. Smith* [2001] EWCA Crim. 743, the Court of Appeal said that such is the wording of this section "that it seems that a hospital order may be made even though the mental disorder suffered by the defendant has developed since the date of the offence" (*per* Keene L.J. at para.9). The offender's consent to the order is not required (*R. v. Gunnee* [1972] Crim.L.R. 261).

Hospital: Or a registered establishment (ss.34(2), 55(5)). A court may request information about the availability of hospital places under section 39. The offender can be admitted to a hospital which is not situated in the locality where he is normally resident (*R. v. Marsden (Practice Note)* [1968] 1 W.L.R. 785).

Place him under ... guardianship: See the General Note to this section. The guardian must be willing to receive the offender into guardianship. The powers of the guardian and the effect of the guardianship order are set out in section 40. Note that there is no power to convey the person made subject to the guardianship order to the place where he is required to reside. The agreement of the offender to the placement should therefore be obtained. There is no provision for returning the offender to court on any subsequent failure by the offender to comply with the provisions of the guardianship order.

Local social services authority: Who "should appoint a named person to respond to requests from the court" (*Code of Practice*, para. 3.6).

Subsection (1A)

1–473   *Subsection 2 of section 110 or 111 of the Powers of Criminal Courts (Sentencing) Act 2000:* Which require the court to impose mandatory custodial sentences for the offences of drug trafficking and repeated domestic burglary except where the court is of the opinion that there are particular circumstances which relate to any of the offences or to the offender; and would make it unjust to do so in all the circumstances.

Subsection (2)

Paragraph (a)

1–474   *Evidence:* For general requirements as to medical evidence, see section 54. In *R. v. Crozier* (1990) 12 Cr.App.R.(S.) 206, the Court of Appeal applied *W v. Egdell* [1990] 1 All E.R. 835, CA (noted under s.76) by holding that, given the particular circumstances of the case, a psychiatrist who had prepared a medical report for the defence had acted responsibly and reasonably when he handed a copy of his report to counsel for the prosecution. This was a case where the strong public interest in the disclosure of the psychiatrist's opinion overrode his duty of confidence to his client. The psychiatrist was "firmly of the view that the appellant suffers from psychopathic disorder, continues to be a danger to the public and should be kept in a secure hospital without limit of time. He held this opinion so strongly that he felt impelled to ensure that the court became aware of it"; *per* Watkins L.J. at 213.

Two registered medical practitioners: One of whom must be approved under section 12 (s.54(1)). This section does not place any constraints upon the timing of the medical examinations of the offender. The Court of Appeal has advised that the trial judge should hear evidence from the doctor who will be treating the offender (*R. v. Blackwood*, above). Unlike the position under Part II of this Act (see s.12(3)(5)(d)), the two doctors could be on the staff of the same hospital and could have a financial interest in the matter. Guidance on medical assessments under this Part of this Act is contained in paragraphs 3.7 to 3.10 of the *Code of Practice*.

Suffering from: The offender's mental condition at the time when the offence was committed is not at issue. The Court of Appeal has said that the condition could have developed since the date of the offence (*R. v. Smith*, above). The two medical practitioners must agree on of the form of mental disorder from which the offender is suffering (subs. (7)). In *R. v. Nigel Gordon Smith*, July 30, 1974, (unreported), the court noted that it did not matter if one of the doctors made a general diagnosis as to the form of mental disorder (*e.g.* mental illness), and the other doctor made a specific diagnosis coming within the same form (*e.g.* paranoid schizophrenia). This case is referred to by L. Gostin in *A Human Condition*, (1977) Vol. 2, at p. 31.

Nature or degree: The meaning of this phrase is considered in the note on section 3(2)(a).

Likely to alleviate or prevent a deterioration: For comment on this "treatability test" for psychopathic and mentally impaired patients, see the note on section 3(2)(b).

Attained the age: At the commencement of his sixteenth birthday (Family Law Reform Act 1969, s.9(1)). Also see section 55(7).

Warrants his reception into guardianship: Compare with the criteria set out in section 7(2) for guardianship applications made under Part II of this Act.

Paragraph (b)

Nature of the offence: "Although hospital orders are frequently made in cases **1–475** involving grave offences of violence, the gravity of the offences is not an important consideration in making a hospital order (except in so far as it indicates a need for detention in secure conditions). Hospital orders have been upheld or imposed on appeal on offenders whose offences would not have justified a substantial term of imprisonment" (D. A. Thomas, *Principles of Sentencing* (2nd ed., 1979) p. 299).

Most suitable method of disposing of the case: Note subsection (8).

Subsection (3)

This provision, which empowers magistrates to make a hospital or guardianship **1–476** order without proceeding to conviction where the defendant is suffering from mental illness or severe impairment, applies only where the court is satisfied that the defendant did the act or made the omission charged. It is considered by A. Samuels in "Hospital Orders Without Conviction" [1995] Crim. L.R. 220. A person subject to hospital order made under this provision is to be treated as though he were an offender for the purposes of section 142 of the Magistrates' Courts Act 1980 (*R. v. Thames Magistrates' Court, ex p. Ramadan*, below). "In trivial cases the magistrates may properly have recourse to the expedient of adjourning the proceedings *sine die* or of simply not proceeding" (*Butler Committee*, para. 10.34).

In *R. v. Lincolnshire (Kesteven) Justices, ex p. O'Connor* [1983] 1 W.L.R. 335, DC, the accused's mental disorder was such that he was unable to understand what it meant to consent to summary trial. The magistrates decided that as they were unable to try the case, it followed that they had no power to make a hospital order under this provision. The Divisional Court held that the magistrates could have made a hospital order without holding a trial. "In our judgment the words of [section 37(3)] are clear. It gives the justices power in an appropriate case to make a hospital order without convicting the accused. No trial is therefore called for. The circumstances in which it will be appropriate to exercise this unusual power are bound to be very rare and will usually require ... the consent of those acting for the accused if he is under a disability so that he cannot be tried;" per Lord Lane L.C.J. at 338.

O'Connor was considered by the Divisional Court in *R. v. Ramsgate Justices, ex p. Kazmarek* (1985) 80 Cr.App.R. 366, and in *R. v. Chippenham Magistrates' Court, ex p. Thompson* (1996) 32 B.M.L.R. 69. In *Kazmarek* it was held that in the case of an offence triable either summarily or on indictment where the accused elects trial by jury, this subsection can apply because the magistrates "would have power, on convicting him of that offence" to make a hospital order. *Kazmarek* was distinguished in *Thompson* where the court held that this subsection cannot apply in the case of an offence triable *only* on indictment in the Crown Court because in such a case the magistrates could not convict the offender of that offence.

Did the act or made the omission charged: In *R. v. Egan* (1996) 35 B.M.L.R. 103, the Court of Appeal held that the use of an identical phrase in section 4A(2) of the Criminal Procedure (Insanity) Act 1964, meant that the prosecution is required to prove all the ingredients of the offence, not just the *actus reus*. In *Attorney-General's Reference (No. 3 of 1998)* [1999] 3 All E.R. 40, the Court of Appeal held that in determining whether a defendant "did the act or made the omission charged" for the purposes of section 2(1) of the Trial of Lunatics Act 1883, the prosecution was only required to prove the ingredients which comprise the *actus reus* of the offence. Judge L.J. in giving the judgment of the court, said that the decision in *Egan* "appears to have been decided *per incuriam*" (at 48). In *R. v. Antoine* [2000] 2 All E.R. 208, the House of Lords held that the decision in *Attorney-General's Reference (No. 3 of 1998)* was correct and that *R. v. Egan* should not be followed.

The court may: Having heard the evidence required by subsection (4).

Make such an order: An order under this subsection can be made even though the court has not proceeded to trial. It can therefore be made in cases where the defendant is unable, by virtue of his mental disorder, to give his consent as to the mode of trial (*R. v. Lincolnshire (Kesteven) Justices,* above.)

Without convicting him: The person has the same right of appeal against the order as if it had been made on his conviction (s.45). Although a person dealt with under this provision is not convicted, the order is a "conviction" for the purposes of the Rehabilitation of Offenders Act 1974, section 1(4), because it includes a finding that the person did the act or made the omission charged. A criminal records entry will therefore be made.

A person who is made subject to a hospital order under this provision is an "offender" for the purposes of section 142 of the Magistrates' Courts Act 1980. Under section 142: "A magistrates' court may vary or recind ... [an] order ... made by it when dealing with an offender ..." There are sound practical reasons for treating a defendant, made subject to a hospital order, as an offender for the purposes of section 142. If having made a hospital order the magistrates discovered information which suggested that the defendant might not suffer from mental illness, or might not have done the acts complained of, or, as in the present case, that arrangements could not in fact be made for his admission to hospital, it was highly desirable that there should be a procedural means by which the magistrates could rectify the error (*R. v. Thames Magistrates' Court, ex p. Ramadan* [1999] Crim. L.R. 498, DC).

Subsection (4)

1–477   This subsection applies both to orders made following conviction under subsection (1) and to orders made under subsection (3) (*R. v. Thames Magistrates' Court, ex p. Ramadan,* above).

Evidence: Whether a restriction order under section 41 is appropriate is not a matter for the doctor; it is a matter for the judge: see the cases cited under "evidence in section 41(2).

An order ... shall not be made: A hospital order can only be made if a suitable hospital has agreed to make a bed available for the offender. Courts have occasionally been placed in the position of not being able to give effect to orders made under this section because of pressure from nursing staff who consider that certain offenders should not be sent to secure units without an accompanying increase in staffing levels. This situation was considered by Lawton L.J. in *R. v. Harding* (*Bernard*), *The Times*, June 15, 1983, CA. His Lordship said that the time had come for those who in the past had been obstructive to the use of secure units to appreciate that once a court had made an order under this section, anyone who obstructed the execution of that order or counselled or procured others to obstruction, might be guilty of contempt of court.

"If there is difficulty in obtaining a bed, the doctor may need to seek the help of the Health Authority" (*Memorandum*, para. 172).

Registered medical practitioner: Who could be one of the doctors giving evidence under subsection (2)(a).

Some other person: Who need not be a doctor.

28 days: The Secretary of State has been given the power to reduce this period under section 54A.

Beginning with: Including the date of the making of the order (*Hare v. Gocher* [1962] 2 Q.B. 641).

Conveyance ... and detention: General provisions relating to conveyance and detention are set out in section 137.

Place of safety: Is defined in section 55(1). Home Office Circular No. 66/1980 draws attention to the problem which can arise when a hospital order has been made and the defendant is committed to a place of safety under this subsection pending admission to hospital, but the hospital subsequently withdraws its undertaking to admit him. If no alternative placement is arranged before the 28 days currency of the "place of safety" direction expires, the defendant must be released, and the hospital order is frustrated. A change of procedure was introduced in 1979 in the Crown Court, which attempts to deal with this problem. The Crown Court has power, under section 11(2) of the Courts Act 1971, to vary sentence on a defendant within 28 days, and the purpose of the new procedure is to ensure that the court is forewarned of the possible frustration of a hospital order and so has the opportunity to pass an alternative sentence before the authority to detain the person is extinguished. The Lord Chief Justice has directed that an additional direction be given by the court under this section, addressed to the governor of the prison which is to hold the person pending admission to hospital, which reads as follows: "but if at any time it appears to the person in whose custody the defendant is detained in a place of safety that the defendant might not be admitted to hospital in pursuance of this order within 28 days of this date, that person shall within 21 days of this date (or at once if it becomes apparent only after 21 days that the defendant might not be admitted to hospital) report the circumstances to the Chief Clerk of the Court and unless otherwise directed by the Chief Clerk shall bring the defendant before the Court forthwith so as to enable it within 28 days of this date to make such order as may be necessary." Magistrates' courts have re-sentencing powers, analogous to those of the Crown Court, under section 142 of the Magistrates' Courts Act 1980: see the note on subsection (3), above.

A patient who is detained in a place of safety is not subject to the Consent to Treatment provisions contained in Part IV of this Act (s.56(1)(b)). However, following the decision by the Court of Appeal in *R. v. North West London Mental Health NHS Trust, ex p. Stewart* [1997] 4 All E.R. 871, it seems that a patient who has been detained in a place of safety which is a hospital could be brought within the scope of Part IV if he was made the subject of an application under section 3: see the General Note to section 35. There are no provisions for discharge or leave of absence from a place of safety.

If a patient escapes from a place of safety section 138 allows for him to be retaken, subject to the time limits set out in section 18(4). A restriction order patient may be retaken at any time.

Subsection (5)

1–478 "This provision is intended to meet the case of a hospital which has agreed to accept the patient being unavoidably unable to do so, *e.g.* because of a fire or an epidemic; but in practice it is generally easier for the patient to be returned to court for a further order to be made so as to give a further 28 day period in which a bed may become available. The Crown Court hospital order form 5034 is designed to facilitate this procedure" (Home Office Circular No. 69/1983, para. 5).

Secretary of State: See the General Note to this Part.
28 days: See the note on subsection (4) above.

Subsection (6)

1–479 This subsection provides that the court cannot make a guardianship order without the consent of the potential guardian. The consent of the offender is not required.

Subsection (7)

1–480 It follows from this subsection "that a hospital order cannot contain within it, as a classified form of mental disorder, one which is not agreed to by the two medical practitioners" (*R. v. Anglia and Oxfordshire Mental Health Review Tribunal, ex p. Hagan*, [2000] C.O.D. 352, *per* Collins J.).

Subsection (8)

1–481 *Any other order:* For example, a compensation order or an order disqualifying the offender from driving.

Interim hospital orders

1–482 **38.**—(1) Where a person is convicted before the Crown Court of an offence punishable with imprisonment (other than an offence the sentence for which is fixed by law) or is convicted by a magistrates' court of an offence punishable on summary conviction with imprisonment and the court before or by which he is convicted is satisfied, on the written or oral evidence of two registered medical practitioners—

   (a) that the offender is suffering from mental illness, psychopathic disorder, severe mental impairment or mental impairment; and

   (b) that there is reason to suppose that the mental disorder from which the offender is suffering is such that it may be appropriate for a hospital order to be made in his case,

the court may, before making a hospital order or dealing with him in some other way, make an order (in this Act referred to as "an interim hospital order") authorising his admission to such hospital as may be specified in the order and his detention there in accordance with this section.

   (2) In the case of an offender who is subject to an interim hospital order the court may make a hospital order without his being brought before the court if he is represented by counsel or a solicitor and his counsel or solicitor is given an opportunity of being heard.

   (3) At least one of the registered medical practitioners whose evidence is taken into account under subsection (1) above shall be employed at the hospital which is to be specified in the order.

   (4) An interim hospital order shall not be made for admission of an offender to a hospital unless the court is satisfied, on the written or oral

evidence of the registered medical practitioner who would be in charge of his treatment or of some other person representing the managers of the hospital, that arrangements have been made for his admission to that hospital and for his admission to it within the period of 28 days beginning with the date of the order; and if the court is so satisfied the court may, pending his admission, give directions for his conveyance to and detention in a place of safety.

(5) An interim hospital order—

(a) shall be in force for such period, not exceeding 12 weeks; as the court may specify when making the order; but

(b) may be renewed for further periods of not more than 28 days at a time if it appears to the court, on the written or oral evidence of the responsible medical officer, that the continuation of the order is warranted;

but no such order shall continue in force for more than [twelve months] in all and the court shall terminate the order if it makes a hospital order in respect of the offender or decides after considering the written or oral evidence of the responsible medical officer to deal with the offender in some other way.

(6) The power of renewing an interim hospital order may be exercised without the offender being brought before the court if he is represented by counsel or a solicitor and his counsel or solicitor is given an opportunity of being heard.

(7) If an offender absconds from a hospital in which he is detained in pursuance of an interim hospital order, or while being conveyed to or from such a hospital, he may be arrested without warrant by a constable and shall, after being arrested, be brought as soon as practicable before the court that made the order; and the court may thereupon terminate the order and deal with him in any way in which it could have dealt with him if no such order had been made.

AMENDMENT

In subsection (5) the words in square brackets were substituted by the Crime (Sentences) Act 1997, s.49(1).

DEFINITIONS

psychopathic disorder: ss.1, 145(1).   **1–483**
mental impairment: ss.1, 145(1).
severe mental impairment: ss.1, 145(1).
hospital: ss.55(5), 145(1).
hospital order: ss.37, 145(1).
the managers: s.145(1).

GENERAL NOTE

The Butler Committee "gained the impression that many doctors found it difficult **1–484** to decide whether to recommend that a hospital order should be made where they have been able to examine the patient only briefly in a prison hospital under the pressure of impending court proceedings, since it was often impossible to know how he would react subsequently to the psychiatric hospital regime" (para. 12.5). This section responds to this concern by empowering a Crown Court or magistrates' court to send a convicted offender to hospital for up to twelve months to enable an assessment to be made on the appropriateness of making a hospital order or direction in respect of him. If the court makes an order under this section "the offender's response in hospital can be evaluated without any irrevocable commitment on either side to this method of dealing with the offender if it should prove unsuitable" (Home Office Circular No. 71/1984, Annex, para. 15). An examination of the use of this section in the Trent Regional Secure Unit found that it had been utilised principally to assess the treatability of patients under the category of psychopathic disorder ("Interim Hospital Order—a Regional Secure Unit experience", A. Kaul (1994) 34 Med.Sci. Law, 233–236).

An offender who is placed under an interim hospital order made under this section is subject to the consent to treatment provisions contained in Part IV of this Act (ss.40(4), 56(1)). Otherwise, the legal position of a patient subject to an interim hospital order differs markedly from that of a patient subject to a hospital order; see the note on section 40(3). As an interim hospital order is a form of sentence it is appealable (Criminal Appeal Act 1968, s.50(1)).

Section 22(1) of the Crime (Sentences) Act 1997 ensures that any time spent in hospital under this section before a sentence of imprisonment is passed may be subject to a direction under section 9 of that Act that the time count as part of the sentence, and that credit be given for any early release days which the offender might earn under section 13 of that Act.

If the offender absconds, "he may be arrested without warrant by any constable and is then to be brought before the court that made the order, which may decide on an alternative way of dealing with him" (*Memorandum*, para. 156).

Appeals

1–484.1　Under section 11(3) of the Criminal Appeals Act 1968 an interim hospital order may only be made by the Court of Appeal if it first quashes the trial judge's sentence. The Court of Appeal has described this state of affairs as being "obviously unsatisfactory" (*R. v. Cooper* [2001] EWCA Crim 47, *per* Hooper J. at para. 18).

Family Law Act 1996

1–485　Under section 51 of the Family Law Act 1996 a magistrates' court has the power to make an interim hospital order under this section, instead of a committal to custody, where there has been a breach of one of the following orders or requirements:

(a) an occupation order or non-molestation order made under Part IV of the 1996 Act;
(b) an exclusion requirement included by virtue of section 38A of the Children Act 1989 in an interim care order made under section 38 of that Act; or
(c) an exclusion requirement included by virtue of section 44A of the Children Act 1989 in an emergency protection order made under section 44 of that Act.

Contempt of Court Act 1981

1–486　Under section 14(4) of the Contempt of Court Act 1981 the High Court can make an order under this section where there is reason to suspect that a person who could be committed to prison for contempt of court is suffering from mental illness or severe mental impairment.

Responsibility for returning the patient to court

1–487　See paragraphs 31 to 33 of Home Office Circular No. 71/1984 which are reproduced in the note on section 35(9).

Subsection (1)

1–488　*Convicted by a magistrates' court:* A magistrates' court cannot make an interim hospital order in respect of an unconvicted person.

Offence punishable with imprisonment: This is construed in accordance with section 47(5) (s.55(6)).

Fixed by law: This section does not apply to persons who have been convicted of murder.

Offence punishable on summary conviction with imprisonment: See section 55(2).

Evidence: For general requirements as to medical evidence, see section 54.

Two registered medical practitioners: One of whom must be approved by the Secretary of State under section 12, (s.54(1)). Also note subsection (3).

Is suffering from: It is not sufficient that the doctors have a mere reason to suspect that the offender is suffering from one of the four forms of mental disorder.

Hospital order: Or a hospital direction and a limitation direction (s.45A(8)).

Dealing with him in some other way: The court has a complete discretion as to how it will deal with the offender once the interim hospital order has come to an end.

Interim hospital order: The effect of such an order is set out in s.40(3). Neither the patient nor the patient's nearest relative has a right to apply to a Mental Health Review Tribunal, no-one has the right to discharge the patient, and the patient may not be granted leave of absence.

Hospital: an establishment registered under the Care Standards Act 2000 (ss.34(2), 55(5)). A court may request information about the availability of hospital places under section 39.

Subsection (4)

Registered medical practitioners who would be in charge of his treatment: Who **1–489** could be the doctor referred to in subsection (3).

Some other person: Who need not be a doctor.

28 days: The Secretary of State has been given the power to reduce this period (s.54A).

Beginning with the date of the order: Including the date of the order (*Hare v. Gocher* [1962] 2 Q.B. 641).

Conveyance . . . and detention: For general provisions relating to conveyance and detention, see section 137. Also see the extract from Home Office Circular No. 71/1984 noted under section 35(9), and paragraph 28.6 of the *Code of Practice*.

Place of safety: See the note on section 37(4). A significant difference between a patient who is in a place of safety under section 37(4) and a patient who is in a place of safety under this provision, is that the latter is subject to the consent to treatment provisions contained in Part IV of this Act: see section 56(1)(b).

Subsection (5)

This provides that if doubts remain as to the appropriateness of a hospital order (or **1–490** a hospital direction and a limitation direction (s.45A(8))) after three months, the interim hospital order can be renewed at monthly intervals up to an overall total of 12 months.

12 weeks: This requirement does not apply to the remand of an accused person under section 48(1) of the Family Law Act 1996 (*Williams v. Williams* [2001] EWCA Civ 197).

The responsible medical officer: Is the medical practitioner in charge of the treatment of the patient (s.55(1)).

Information as to hospitals

39.—(1) Where a court is minded to make a hospital order or interim **1–491** hospital order in respect of any person it may request—

(a) the [Health Authority] for [the area] in which that person resides or last resided; or—

(b) any other [Health Authority] that appears to the court to be appropriate,

to furnish the court with such information as [that Health Authority have] has or can reasonably obtain with respect to the hospital or hospitals (if any) in [their area] or elsewhere at which arrangements could be made for the admission of that person in pursuance of the order, and [that Health Authority shall] comply with any such request.

(2) […]

AMENDMENTS

The amendments to this section were made by the Health Authorities Act 1995, ss.2(1), 5(1), Sched. 1, para. 107(5), Sched. 3.

DEFINITIONS

1–492   hospital order: ss.37, 145(1).

interim hospital order: ss.38, 145(1).

hospital: ss.55(5), 145(1).

Health Authority: s.145(1).

GENERAL NOTE

1–493   This section provides that whenever a court is considering making a hospital order, a hospital and a limitation direction (s.45A(8)) or an interim hospital order, it may ask the appropriate Health Authority to provide information as to the availability of suitable hospital places for the person in question. It "obliges . . . Health Authorities to inform the court as to the facilities they provide for detained patients, including those who may require treatment in appropriate conditions of security; and it will also enable the . . . Health Authority to advise in cases where there is some room for doubt as to the patient's normal place of residence or other factor determining the appropriate hospital within whose catchment area he falls. The intention is to provide a court with all possible assistance short of removing the obligation in section 37(4) of the 1983 Act to be satisfied that the necessary arrangements have been made before making a hospital order, in cases where the necessary criteria for a hospital order are satisfied and it is minded to make one, but no hospital place has been made available. . . . Health Authorities have been encouraged to make standing arrangements for meeting such requests for information from courts, and it is intended that these arrangements will reduce the number of cases in which a hospital order appears suitable but the court is frustrated in the search for a place. In cases where it is desired to make use of this provision, the clerk of the court should contact the . . . Health Authority covering the area from which the offender appears to come. (There is no longer any scope for disputes between . . . Health Authorities as to responsibility for dealing with the enquiry, as any Authority approached by the court is under a statutory duty to provide information about hospitals 'in [their area] or elsewhere' at which arrangements could be made for the person to be admitted. If the Authority first contacted believes it to be more appropriate for another Authority to respond, it will only be able to pass on responsibility if the second Authority agrees)" (Home Office Circular No. 66/90, para. 15).

Health Authorities are required by section 140 to notify relevant social services authorities of those hospitals where patients can be treated in cases of special urgency.

Subsection (1)

1–494   *Hospital order or interim hospital order:* But not a remand under sections 35 or 36.

It may request: The Mental Health Act Commission reports that only limited use has been made of this power (Mental Health Act Commission, Third Biennial Report 1987–89, para. 11.2). According to one experienced magistrate, invoking this section "can be quite effective in producing a bed" (Joy Major "What can a magistrate do", in *The Mentally Disordered Offender*, Ed. K. Herbst and J. Gunn, Butterworth—Heinemann, 1991, at p. 52).

For the area: "There may sometimes be doubt as to the patient's normal place of residence or as to other factors which affect the appropriate hospital for admission and in this case it will fall to the Health Authority to advise the court. A court requesting information should get in touch with the Regional Mental Health Lead at the respective Regional Office of the NHS Executive [or, for Wales, the National Assembly] for details of the relevant Health Authority contact" (*Memorandum,* para. 173).

Resides: Temporary absences from the place where a person lives does not affect residence, as long as there is an intention to return (*R. v. St Leonard's Shoreditch (Inhabitants)* (1865) L.R. 1 Q.B. 21). Also note Widgery L.J.'s statement in *Fox v. Stirk* [1970] 2 Q.B. 463 at 477 that: "A man cannot be said to reside in a particular place unless in the ordinary sense of the word one can say that for the time being he is making his home in that place."

Hospital: Or registered establishment (ss.34(2), 55(5)).

[Information to facilitate guardianship orders

39A. Where a court is minded to make a guardianship order in respect of **1–495** any offender, it may request the local social services authority for the area in which the offender resides or last resided, or any other local social services authority that appears to the court to be appropriate—

   (a) to inform the court whether it or any other person approved by it is willing to receive the offender into guardianship; and

   (b) if so, to give such information as it reasonably can about how it or the other person could be expected to exercise in relation to the offender the powers conferred by section 40(2) below;

and that authority shall comply with any such request.]

AMENDMENT
This section was inserted by the Criminal Justice Act 1991, s.27(1).

DEFINITIONS
   local social services authority: s.145(1). **1–496**
   guardianship order: ss.37, 145(1).

GENERAL NOTE
This section enables the court to find out whether the relevant local social services **1–497** authority or a private guardian approved by the authority is willing to receive the offender into guardianship and, if this were to happen, how the authority or guardian might exercise their guardianship powers in relation to the offender.

"If the reporting doctors wish to recommend community care from the local social services authority with or without guardianship, they should consult the local social services authority for the offender's home area" (*Memorandum,* para. 174).

Effect of hospital orders, guardianship orders and interim hospital orders

40.—(1) A hospital order shall be sufficient authority— **1–498**

   (a) for a constable, an approved social worker or any other person directed to do so by the court to convey the patient to the hospital specified in the order within a period of 28 days; and

   (b) for the managers of the hospital to admit him at any time within that period and thereafter detain him in accordance with the provisions of this Act.

(2) A guardianship order shall confer on the authority or person named in the order as guardian the same powers as a guardianship application made and accepted under Part II of this Act.

(3) Where an interim hospital order is made in respect of an offender—

(a) a constable or any other person directed to do so by the court shall convey the offender to the hospital specified in the order within the period mentioned in section 38(4) above; and

(b) the managers of the hospital shall admit him within that period and thereafter detain him in accordance with the provisions of section 38 above.

(4) A patient who is admitted to a hospital in pursuance of a hospital order, or placed under guardianship by a guardianship order, shall, subject to the provisions of this subsection, be treated for the purposes of the provisions of this Act mentioned in Part I of Schedule 1 to this Act as if he had been so admitted or placed on the date of the order in pursuance of an application for admission for treatment or a guardianship application, as the case may be, duly made under Part II of this Act, but subject to any modifications of those provisions specified in that Part of that Schedule.

(5) Where a patient is admitted to a hospital in pursuance of a hospital order, or placed under guardianship by a guardianship order, any previous application, hospital order or guardianship order by virtue of which he was liable to be detained in a hospital or subject to guardianship shall cease to have effect; but if the first-mentioned order, or the conviction on which it was made, is quashed on appeal, this subsection shall not apply and section 22 above shall have effect as if during any period for which the patient was liable to be detained or subject to guardianship under the order, he had been detained in custody as mentioned in that section.

[(6) Where—

(a) a patient admitted to a hospital in pursuance of a hospital order is absent without leave;

(b) a warrant to arrest him has been issued under section 72 of the Criminal Justice Act 1967; and

(c) he is held pursuant to the warrant in any country or territory other than the United Kingdom, any of the Channel Islands and the Isle of Man,

he shall be treated as having been taken into custody under section 18 above on first being so held.]

AMENDMENT

Subs. (6) was inserted by the Mental Health (Patients in the Community) Act 1995, s.2(4).

DEFINITIONS

1–499   hospital order: ss.37, 145(1).
approved social worker: s.145(1).
the managers: s.145(1).
hospital: ss.55(5), 145(1).
hospital order: s.55(4).
guardianship order: ss.37, 55(4), 145(1).
interim hospital order: ss.38, 145(1).
patient: s.145(1).
application for admission for treatment: ss.3, 145(1).

GENERAL NOTE

1–500   This section provides that, with very few exceptions, a patient who is admitted to hospital under a hospital order without restrictions or placed under guardianship by a guardianship order is treated the same as a patient who has been admitted to hospital or placed under guardianship under Part II of this Act. The necessary modifications to the provisions of Part II are made by Part I of Schedule I and are noted in subsection (4). The effect of a hospital and guardianship order was considered by the Court of Appeal in *R. v. Birch* (1989) 11 Cr.App.R.(S.) 202, noted in the General Note to section 37.

Any reference to hospital orders and guardianship orders in subsection (2), (4) or (5) of this section shall be construed as including a reference to any order or directions under this Part having the same effect as a hospital or guardianship order (s.55(4)).

Subsection (1)

Constable: Means the office of constable, and not the rank of constable (Police Act **1–501** 1996, s.29, Sched. 4).

Convey the patient to hospital: For general provisions relating to conveyance, see section 137. Before proceeding to convey the patient to hospital the authorised person should confirm with the hospital that it is still willing to accept the patient because this section does not give authority to convey the patient *from* hospital if admission is refused.

Within a period of 28 days: If the hospital specified in the order withdraws its agreement to accept the patient, the person having custody of him should bring him back to the Crown Court within the 28 day period so that the court can vary the sentence under section 11(2) of the Courts Act 1971: see the note on section 37(4).

Detain him: A patient placed under a hospital order is subject to the consent to treatment provisions contained in Pt IV of this Act (s.56(1)).

Subsection (2)

Same powers: As contained in section 8(1). A patient placed under a guardianship **1–502** order is not subject to the consent to treatment provisions contained in Pt IV of this Act because he is not a patient who is "liable to be detained" (s.56(1)).

Subsection (3)

This subsection sets out the effect of an interim hospital order made under section **1–503** 38. Apart from coming within the scope of Part IV of this Act, an interim hospital order patient is treated very differently from a hospital order patient. This is because an interim hospital order patient is not to be treated as if he had been admitted in pursuance of an application for admission for treatment. The consequences of this are that neither the patient nor his nearest relative can apply to a Mental Health Review Tribunal, no-one has the right to discharge the patient and the patient may not be granted leave of absence or be transferred to another hospital. Although applications have been made to the court for authority to either grant the patient leave of absence or to transfer the patient, this Act does not provide the court with the power to make such orders.

Convey the offender to the hospital: As to who is responsible for conveying the patient back to court, see the note on section 35(9).

Within the period mentioned in section 38(4). 28 days.

Shall admit him: The hospital specified in an interim hospital order cannot subsequently withdraw its agreement to accept the offender.

Detain him: A patient placed under an interim hospital order as a "patient liable to be detained under this Act" is subject to the consent to treatment provisions contained in Pt IV of this Act (s.56(1)).

Subsection (4)

Hospital order: With two exceptions, the effect of this subsection is to place a **1–504** patient who has been placed under a hospital order in the same legal position as a patient who has been admitted to hospital for treatment under section 3 of this Act. The two exceptions are: (1) the nearest relative of a hospital order patient cannot order his discharge under section 23 (Sched. 1, paras 2, 8); and (2) unlike a section 3 patient, the hospital order patient cannot apply to a Mental Health Review Tribunal within the first six months of his detention (Sched. 1, paras 2, 9). The first occasion on which either the hospital order patient or his nearest relative can apply to a tribunal occurs in the period between six and 12 months of the order being made (ss.66(1)(f), 66(2)(f), 69(1)). A hospital order patient could have his case automatically referred to a tribunal under section 68(2). A hospital order patient can apply to the hospital managers for his discharge at any time (s.23).

Guardianship order: The effect of a guardianship order made under section 37 is essentially the same as if the patient had been made the subject of a guardianship application under section 7. The major difference between the two is that with a guardianship order the power of the nearest relative to discharge the patient from guardianship does not apply (Sched. 1, paras 2, 8).

Subsection (5)

1–505   *Cease to have effect:* Unless a restriction order made in respect of the patient under section 41 is in force at the material time (s.41(4)).

Subsection (6)

1–506   This subsection is concerned with the taking into custody of absconding patients who have gone abroad.

Restriction orders

Power of higher courts to restrict discharge from hospital

1–507   **41.**—(1) Where a hospital order is made in respect of an offender by the Crown Court, and it appears to the court, having regard to the nature of the offence, the antecedents of the offender and the risk of his committing further offences if set at large, that it is necessary for the protection of the public from serious harm so to do, the court may, subject to the provisions of this section, further order that the offender shall be subject to the special restrictions set out in this section, either without limit of time or during such period as may be specified in the order; and an order under this section shall be known as "a restriction order".

(2) A restriction order shall not be made in the case of any person unless at least one of the registered medical practitioners whose evidence is taken into account by the court under section 37(2)(a) above has given evidence orally before the court.

(3) The special restrictions applicable to a patient in respect of whom a restriction order is in force are as follows—

(a)   none of the provisions of Part II of this Act relating to the duration, renewal and expiration of authority for the detention of patients shall apply, and the patient shall continue to be liable to be detained by virtue of the relevant hospital order until he is duly discharged under the said Part II or absolutely discharged under section 42, 73, 74 or 75 below;

[(aa): none of the provisions of Part II of this Act relating to after-care under supervision shall apply;]

(b)   no application shall be made to a Mental Health Review Tribunal in respect of a patient under section 66 or 69(1) below;

(c)   the following powers shall be exercisable only with the consent of the Secretary of State, namely—

    (i) power to grant leave of absence to the patient under section 17 above;

    (ii) power to transfer the patient in pursuance of regulations under section 19 above [or in pursuance of subsection (3) of that section]; and

    (iii) power to order the discharge of the patient under section 23 above;

and if leave of absence is granted under the said section 17 power to recall the patient under that section shall vest in the Secretary of State as well as the responsible medical officer; and

    (d) the power of the Secretary of State to recall the patient under the said section 17 and power to take the patient into custody and return him under section 18 above may be exercised at any time;

and in relation to any such patient section 40(4) above shall have effect as if it referred to Part II of Schedule 1 to this Act instead of Part I of that Schedule.

(4) A hospital order shall not cease to have effect under section 40(5) above if a restriction order in respect of the patient is in force at the material time.

(5) Where a restriction order in respect of a patient ceases to have effect while the relevant hospital order continues in force, the provisions of section 40 above and Part I of Schedule 1 to this Act shall apply to the patient as if he had been admitted to the hospital in pursuance of a hospital order (without a restriction order) made on the date on which the restriction order ceased to have effect.

(6) While a person is subject to a restriction order the responsible medical officer shall at such intervals (not exceeding one year) as the Secretary of State may direct examine and report to the Secretary of State on that person; and every report shall contain such particulars as the Secretary of State may require.

AMENDMENTS
In subs. (3), para. (aa) was inserted by the Mental Health (Patients in the Community) Act 1995, s.2(1), Sched. 1, para. 5. The words in square brackets in para. (c)(ii) were inserted by the Crime (Sentences) Act 1997, s.49(2).

DEFINITIONS
hospital order: ss.37, 55(4), 145(1).   **1–508**
patient: s.145(1).
hospital: ss.55(5), 145(1).
hospital order: s.55(4).
guardianship order: s.55(4).
responsible medical officer: s.55(1).

GENERAL NOTE
This section empowers the Crown Court, having made a hospital order under **1–509** section 37, to make a further order (a "restriction order") restricting the patient's discharge, transfer or leave of absence from hospital for a specified or unlimited period without the consent of the Home Secretary. A restriction order can only be made where it is necessary to protect the public from serious harm. Magistrates' courts may only commit a convicted offender to the Crown Court with a view to a restriction order being made (s.43(1)). A restriction order may be terminated at any time by the Home Secretary under section 42(1).

For a study which examines the characteristics of offenders who had been made the subject of restriction orders and follows their progress on discharge from hospital, see Robert Street, *The Restricted Hospital Order: From Court to Community*, Home Office Research Study 186, 1998. The use of restriction orders is considered by G. Robertson in "The Restricted Hospital Order", *Psychiatric Bulletin* (1989), 13, 4–11. Sentencing options available to a judge in cases where the offender is mentally disordered are set out in the General Note to section 37 and in Appendix 7 to the *Memorandum*.

The nature of a restriction order was considered by the Court of Appeal in *R. v. Birch* (1989) 11 Cr.App.R.(S.) 202, at 211–212:

"A restriction order has no existence independently of the hospital order to which it relates; it is not a separate means of disposal. Nevertheless, it fundamentally affects the circumstances in which the patient is detained. No longer is the offender regarded simply as a patient whose interests are paramount. No longer is the control of him handed over unconditionally to the hospital authorities. Instead the interests of public safety are regarded by transferring the responsibility for discharge from the responsible medical officer and the hospital to [...] the Secretary of State and the Mental Health Review Tribunal. A patient who has been subject to a restriction order is likely to be detained for much longer in hospital than one who is not, and will have fewer opportunities for leave of absence".

In this case the court made the following observations, at 213–215, on the principles to be observed in deciding whether a restriction order is appropriate:

"[The judge] is required to choose between an order without restrictions, which may enable the author of a serious act of violence to be at liberty only a matter of months after he appears in court, and a restriction order which may lead the offender to be detained for a long time: longer in some cases than the period which he would serve if sent to prison: see *Haynes* (1981) 3 Cr.App.R.(S.) 330. It is moreover a choice which depends on a prognosis, the ultimate responsibility for which is left with the judge.

This responsibility may be hard to discharge, since the judge will often have nothing on which to base his decision, if he feels reservations about the medical evidence, apart from the considerations stated by the statute, namely the nature of the offence and the antecedents of the offender: which will often consist only of a single episode of fatal violence and a blank criminal record. Where there is a trial the judge can form an impression of [the] defendant as the case unfolds which may enable him to make his own assessment of his dangerousness. But in the more usual case where a plea of guilty to manslaughter on the grounds of diminished responsibility is accepted by the prosecution and the court, this opportunity is largely absent, and did not exist at all in the present case, where the appellant was too distressed to remain for the hearing in the Crown Court ....

Nevertheless, section 41(1) is there and the judge must apply it. Quite plainly the addition of the words 'from serious harm' has greatly curtailed the former jurisdiction to make a restriction order: most particularly because the word 'serious' qualifies 'harm' rather than 'risk.' Thus the court is required to assess not the seriousness of the risk that the defendant will re-offend, but the risk that if he does so the public will suffer serious harm. The harm in question need not, in our view, be limited to personal injury. Nor need it relate to the public in general, for it would in our judgment suffice if a category of persons, or even a single person, were adjudged to be at risk: although the category of persons so protected would no doubt exclude the offender himself. Nevertheless the potential harm must be serious, and a high possibility of a recurrence of minor offences will no longer be sufficient.

Thus we do not consider that cases such as *Smith* (1974) *Current Sentencing Practice* F.2.4(b), *Toland* (1973) *ibid.* F.2.4(c) (appellant was a recidivist young

burglar, described as 'an anti-social person ... a pest') and *Eaton* (1975) *ibid.*
F.2.4(d) (restriction order on appellant with behavioural difficulties, who had
broken two panes in a telephone kiosk), would be decided the same way under the
new legislation in the absence of special factors. This was, as it seems to us,
precisely the result which the 1983 Act was intended to achieve.

Khan (1987) 9 Cr.App.R.(S.) 455 was, if we correctly understand the facts, a case
where the offences themselves, whilst not of great gravity, included reckless
driving of a very bad nature by a very disturbed young man with a megalomaniac
approach to his driving prowess which, if repeated, would create a risk of serious
harm to the public. We pause to note that there is nothing in the Act which requires
a causal connection between the offender's mental state and what the professionals call the 'index offence'. It is sufficient for section 41 that the defendant is
a convicted offender, and that the conditions of section 41 are satisfied: see *Hatt*
[1962] Crim.L.R. 647.

It would however be a mistake to equate the seriousness of the offence with the
probability that a restriction order will be made. This is only one of the factors
which section 41(1) requires to be taken into account. A minor offence by a man
who proves to be mentally disordered and dangerous may properly leave him
subject to a restriction. In theory the converse is also true. *Courtney* (1987) 9
Cr.App.R.(S.) 404 shows that a serious offence committed by someone who is
adjudged to have a very low risk of re-offending may lead to an unrestricted
hospital order.

Nevertheless, the court will need to be very sure of its ground in such a case, and **1–510**
we consider that there is nothing in the 1983 Act to derogate from the following
statement of principle by Lord Parker C.J., in *Gardiner* (1967) 51 Cr.App.R. 187:

'Thus, for example, in the case of crimes of violence, and of the more serious
sexual offences, particularly if the prisoner has a record of such offences, or if
there is a history of mental disorder involving violent behaviour, it is suggested
that there must be compelling reasons to explain why a restriction order should
not be made.'

In this connection we should mention the possible effect on the judge's
discretion of the fact that the restricted patient may now be released, through the
medium of the Review Tribunal, earlier than he might have been under the former
regime. On the argument of the present appeal, counsel were disposed to agree
that the judge should leave this out of account; just as, when sending an offender to
prison or to detention under section 53(2) of the Children and Young Persons Act
1933, he should concentrate on fixing the right terms, without allowance for the
possibility that through parole or executive action by the Home Secretary the
offender might be released before the expiry of such term.

At the time we were inclined to agree, but now we are not so sure. We are not
here concerned with a free discretionary release acting upon a term fixed judicially,
but rather with a judicial decision by the Mental Health Review Tribunal based on
statutory norms, co-existing with the Secretary of State's discretion. When
weighing up the respective merits of prison and hospital, and of restricted and
unrestricted hospital orders, we see no reason why the practical effect of all the
orders which the Court might be contemplating should not be taken into account:
and the Review Tribunal's powers have an important effect in minimising the
starkness of the practical difference between restricted and unrestricted orders,
and in qualifying the relative merits, so far as public safety is concerned, of hospital
and prison, with or without a subsequent transfer under section 47. ...

Finally we would make two further points on section 41. First, the sentencer
should not impose a restriction order simply to mark the gravity of the offence
(although this is an element in the assessment of risk), nor as a means of
punishment: for a restriction order merely qualifies a hospital order and a hospital

order is not a mode of punishment. Secondly, the observations of Lord Parker C.J., in *Gardiner* (*supra*) as to the imprudence in any but the most exceptional case of imposing a restriction for a fixed period rather than for an unlimited period still hold good under the 1983 Act: *Haynes* (1981) 3 Cr.App.R.(S.) 330."

In *R. v. Paul Martin*, November 6, 1998, CA, Judge L.J. said: "There should normally be some proportionate relationship, in our judgment, between the instant offence and the history of offending, together with an assessment of risk on the basis of medical examinations before a section 41 restriction order is made." The severity of an assault cannot be predicted solely on the basis of what has occurred in the past (*R. v. James Kamara*, [2000] M.H.L.R. 9, CA). *Per* Scott Baker J.: "Sometimes the extent of the injury that results from an assault is a matter of chance. There are cases in this court's experience where one punch has led to death and others where a grave and sustained assault has led to minimal injury. The court has to look not just at what has happened in the past but at the risk of what may happen in the future."

The risk that the offender may be released prematurely by a Mental Health Review Tribunal is not a ground for passing a life sentence rather than making a hospital order with restrictions: *R. v. Mitchell* [1997] 1 Cr.App.R.(S.) 90, where the Court of Appeal said that the case of *Fleming* (1993) 14 Cr.App.R.(S.) 151 (where a sentence of life imprisonment was imposed despite the existence of unanimous medical opinions recommending a hospital order with restrictions), should be disregarded. In *Mitchell* the court pointed out that the release procedures in respect of those detained under a hospital order with restrictions, and those detained under sentence of life imprisonment, are substantially similar in practice. The approach adopted in *Mitchell* was followed in *R. v. Hutchinson* [1997] 1 Cr.App.R.(S.) 60, CA. Also see the note on "sentencing options" in the General Note to section 37 and the note on "the court may by order" in section 37(1).

A restriction order remains in force even if the patient is subsequently imprisoned for an offence committed after his conditional discharge (*R. v. Mersey Mental Health Review Tribunal, ex p. K* [1990] 1 All E.R. 694, CA), and the patient may be recalled to hospital on the expiry of his prison sentence (*R. v. Secretary of State for the Home Department, ex p. K* [1990] 1 All E.R. 703).

If a court is considering making an order under this section the defendant should be represented by counsel (*R. v. Blackwood* (1974) 59 Cr.App.R. 170).

A patient who is subject to a restriction order may apply to a Mental Health Review Tribunal in the period between six and 12 months of the order and in any subsequent period of one year (s.70) and the Home Secretary may, and in some circumstances must, refer such patients to a tribunal (s.71). The patient's nearest relative has no power to apply to a tribunal. The powers of a tribunal when considering the case of a restricted patient are set out in section 73.

In subsections (3) to (5) of this section any reference to a hospital order, a guardianship order or a restriction order are to be construed as including a reference to any order or direction under this Part having the same effect as such orders (s.55(4)).

Subsection (1)

1–511   *Hospital order is made:* The offender must therefore have satisfied the conditions of section 37(2). Although this section implies that the offender will be kept in secure accommodation, this might not be necessary in all cases. The Butler Committee gave the following example of a restricted patient who might not need to be accommodated in secure accommodation: "the persistent molester of small children may need the continuing supervision after discharge which a restriction order allows, and should not be permitted simply to walk out of hospital whenever he wishes, but is unlikely to need the secure containment of bolts and bars" (para. 14.21).

Before it makes an order under this section the court should ensure that the receiving hospital has the facilities for keeping the offender in the degree of custody that the court considers necessary (*R. v. Morris* [1961] 2 Q.B. 237).

Section 47 of the Crime (Sentences) Act 1997 provides that where a court makes an order under this section it has the power to order that the patient be admitted to and detained in a named hospital unit. A named hospital unit can be any part of a hospital which is treated as a separate unit. The effect of this power is considered in paragraph 11 of Home Office Circular 52/1997 which is reproduced in the note on section 45A(3).

Crown Court: A Crown Court has jurisdiction to make a restriction order in respect of an offence which only became triable by that court under the provisions of section 40 of the Criminal Justice Act 1998. Section 40 enables a summary only offence to be included in an indictment in certain specified circumstances (*R. v. Avbunudje* [1999] 2 Cr.App.R.(S.) 189, CA). Although a magistrates' court cannot make a restriction order, it does have the power to commit the offender to the Crown Court with a view to such an order being made by that court (s.43(1)).

Nature of the offence ... the antecedents of the offender: See the statement of Lord Parker C.J. in *R. v. Gardiner* which is reproduced in the General Note to this section.

Antecedents: Street reports that this term is "construed by the judges to include not just previous convictions, but also accounts of previous unprosecuted dangerous behaviour made in psychiatric reports (subject to any objection by defence counsel), and some [judges] said that evidence of failure of previous treatment might also be significant. A history of violence would cause particular concern, especially if it appeared that the violence was escalating in seriousness" (*The Restricted Hospital Order: From Court to Community*, p. 40, noted in the General Note to this section).

The public: The public does not include an unborn child, who, when born, could be protected by the provisions of the Children Act 1989 (*R. v. Michelle Louise Jones* [2000] M.H.L.R. 12, CA).

Serious harm: The insertion of this phrase into the 1982 Act gave effect to recommendation of the Butler Committee which proposed that the equivalent section in the 1959 Act should be revised to make it clear that the intention of a restriction order is to protect the public from serious harm. The Committee wished to ensure that a court would not impose restrictions on "the petty recidivist because of the virtual certainty that he will persist in similar offences in the future" (*ibid.* para. 14.24) or on the offender who has become a "social nuisance" by virtue of his criminal activities.

"Serious harm" refers to possible serious harm to the public in the future rather than to proven serious harm to the public in the past and an offender who has no history of serious violence but who, on the medical evidence, has a potentiality for causing serious harm could be made the subject of an order under this section (*R. v. James Kamara* [2000] M.H.L.R. 9, CA. The word "serious" qualifies "harm" rather than "risk": see *R. v. Birch* which is noted in the General Note to this section.

The fact that a "very experienced psychiatrist" was of the opinion that the existence of a restriction order was "a hindrance rather than a help" to the successful rehabilitation of a very vulnerable mentally impaired patient resulted in the Court of Appeal quashing the order in *R. v. Mahmood*, April 11, 2000. Also see *R. v. Cox*, March 25, 1999 where the Court of Appeal said that risk of serious harm to the public must be real, rather than fanciful or remote. In *R. v. Natasha Beaumont*, July 8, 1998, CA, Moses J. said that "setting fire to premises, even if it is difficult for them to ignite successfully, is likely to cause, in our judgment serious harm to others who may be affected by [the] fire".

It is not necessary that the harm should be purely physical: a risk of serious psychological harm will suffice (*R. v. Melbourne*, January 25, 2000, CA).

Without limit of time: The view of the medical witness as to the appropriateness of an order without limit of time should be obtained by the judge before such an order is made (*Application for Permission (Kenneally)*) [2001] EWHC Admin 219, *per* Latham L.J. at para. 14).

It is not necessary to wait until someone is actually seriously injured before making a hospital order with an indefinite restriction order (*R. v. Nwohia* [1996] 1 Cr.App.R.(S.) 170, CA).

During such period: A study by Crystal Romilly *et al.* found that in the 10 years following the introduction of this Act 73 restriction orders of limited duration were imposed. This represents 5 per cent of all restriction orders. The average duration of these orders was 3.1 years ("Limited duration restriction orders: what are they for?" (1997) *Journal of Forensic Psychiatry* 562–572). In *R. v. Nwohia*, above, the Court of Appeal said that "unless there is some foundation in the medical evidence for saying that the patient can be cured within a particular period, it would be indeed unwise to put a limit on the restriction orders." In *R. v. Gardiner*, above, Lord Parker C.J. said, at 469: "Since in most cases the prognosis cannot be certain, the safer course is to make a restriction order unlimited in point of time. The only exception is where the doctors are able to assert confidently that recovery will take place within a fixed period when the restriction order can properly be limited to that period." This formulation has been criticised as seeming to be "faulty in attempting to equate complete recovery from mental disorder with duration of dangerousness. An offender may cease to be dangerous and yet continue to suffer from some degree of mental disorder; indeed many mentally disordered offenders will never be entirely free from mental disorder" (Cmnd. 7320, para. 5.27). The Butler Committee recommended that the power to make orders of limited duration should be removed from the statute book (para. 14.25) but this was rejected because in "certain cases where there is a good ground for expectation that an offender will soon recover from the disorder that has prompted his offence (for example, in cases of endogenous depression) it may be possible for the court, in the light of medical evidence, to make a reasonable prediction of when an offender will cease to be dangerous" (Cmnd. 7320, para. 5.28).

In *R. v. Haynes* (1981) 3 Cr.App.R.(S.) 330, the Court of Appeal held that it was wrong for the court to seek to equate the length of a restriction order with the length of the term of imprisonment which would have been appropriate to the offence.

Subsection (2)

1–512   *One of the registered medical practitioners:* Who need not necessarily be approved by the Secretary of State under section 12. In *R. v. Blackwood* (1974) 59 Cr.App.R. 170, the Court of Appeal stressed the desirability of the doctor who gives oral evidence being on the staff of the admitting hospital.

Evidence: In *R. v. Birch*, above, the Court of Appeal, at 212, gave the following answer to the question whether a Crown Court judge had jurisdiction to make a restriction order in circumstances where those doctors who expressed an opinion on the matter were unanimous that the patient was not dangerous: "It is in our judgment quite clear that the answer is 'yes'. There is a contrast between the language of sections 37(2) and 41(1) and (2). Before a hospital order can be made, the Court must be satisfied of the stated conditions 'on the written or oral evidence of two practitioners'. But where a restriction order is in question, section 41(2) requires no more than that the Court shall hear the oral evidence of one of the medical practitioners. It need not follow the course which he recommends. Section 41(1) makes the assessment of the risk, in the light of the factors there identified, one for the court. In our judgment *R. v. Blackwood* (1974) 59 Cr.App.R. 170 and *R. v. Royse* (1981) 3 Cr.App.R.(S.) 58 are just as good law under the 1983 Act as they were under the earlier statute."

The finding in *Birch* was applied in *R. v. Crookes*, April 20, 1999, where the Court of Appeal said that the judge was right to impose a restriction order in a case where the medical evidence was unanimous in recommending that such an order was not necessary. In this case the judge felt that none of the doctors was able to explain to his satisfaction why a young man with no record of violent, and not seen as in any way dangerous, could suddenly react with an outburst of potentially lethal ferocity. Note, however, that in *R. v. Reynolds, The Times*, November 1, 2000, Judge Fawcus, in giving the judgment of the Court of Appeal, said that "one really must import into [this subsection] that on hearing the evidence there must be at least some basis upon which the doctor is able to say, and persuade the court, that a restriction order is appropriate." His Honour went on to say that this did not mean that in appropriate circumstances a judge might not be prepared to accept the oral evidence that he had before him. It would appear that *Birch* was not cited to the court in *Reynolds*. It is submitted that the decision in *Birch* should be followed: the question whether a restriction order is appropriate is a matter for the judge, not the doctors.

Subsection (3)

This subsection specifies the restrictions that are placed upon patients who are **1–513** subject to restriction orders. They are: (1) there is no periodic review of the authority to detain under section 20; (2) the patient cannot be discharged, transferred to another hospital (even if managed by the same hospital managers) or granted leave of absence without the consent of the Home Secretary; (3) the patient cannot be made subject to supervised discharge; and (4) the authority to detain lasts as long as the restriction order is in force: the patient cannot obtain his discharge under the provisions of sections 17(5) or 18(4). As section 16 does not apply to restricted patients, it is not possible for the responsible medical officer to reclassify the form of mental disorder from which the patient is suffering. The patient's nearest relative does not have the power to discharge the patient (s.40(4), Sched. 1, Pt II, paras 2,7). The Home Secretary may, at any time, discharge a restricted patient from hospital either absolutely or subject to conditions (s.42).

Requests to the Home Secretary "for consent to leave of absence, transfer or discharge should be sent to the Home Office by the responsible medical officer or the managers. When consent to transfer is given, the document in which consent is given should be attached to the authority for transfer (form 24) and sent with it to the receiving hospital, a copy being kept by the hospital which the patient is leaving" (*Memorandum*, para. 183).

Paragraph (a)

Provisions ... relating to the duration, renewal and expiration of authority for the **1–514** *detention of patients:* The effect of this provision is that no one is under any statutory obligation to consider whether the criteria for detaining the patient still apply.

Liable to be detained: The patient is subject to the consent to the treatment provisions contained in Pt IV of this Act (s.56(1)).

Paragraph (b)

No application shall be made: This paragraph only refers to a patient in his capacity **1–515** as a restricted patient detained, or liable to be detained, pursuant to the hospital order. It does not apply to the patient's detention under section 3, if such an application has been made in respect of him. A patient so detained has a right to apply to a Mental Health Review Tribunal under section 66(1)(b) (*R. v. North West London Mental Health NHS Trust, ex p. Stewart, The Times*, August 15, 1996, *per* Harrison J., whose decision on the ability of Parts II and III of this Act to coexist and operate independently of each other was affirmed by the Court of Appeal at [1997] 4 All E.R. 871).

Paragraph (c)

The Secretary of State: See the General Note to this Part. "The Home Secretary is **1–516** not concerned with the medical treatment a patient receives nor with his day to day management ... The only point at which the Home Secretary will become involved is if the management of the patient involves his leaving the hospital. As this could pose a risk to the public, the Home Secretary's consent is required" (Robert Baxter, "The mentally disordered offender in hospital: the role of the Home Office" in *The Mentally Disordered Offender*, (Ed. K. Herbst and J. Gunn) (1991), p. 136).

Leave of absence: In June 1996 the Home Office issued guidance which sets out to responsible medical officers in special hospitals, secure units and other psychiatric hospitals, the framework for making a request for leave for restricted patients.

In *R. (on the application of Hurlock) v. Dr Page and the Secretary of State for the Home Department* [2001] EWHC Admin 380, para. 22, Ouseley J. said that section 17 and this provision cannot arguably be read as imposing an obligation to grant a patient unescorted leave of absence as an alternative to a conditional discharge granted by a Mental Health Review Tribunal where those conditions are not yet fulfilled.

Transfer the patient: "In preparing a transfer report the responsible medical officer should have regard to the type of questions that annual statutory reports [under sections 41(6) and 49(3)] cover. In particular the transfer report should provide an account of the patient's mental disorder and his response to treatment in hospital—in effect, to address the question what has changed? It should aim, where possible, to provide an adequate explanation of how the patient came to commit his offence and of any previous serious offences; it should describe the patient's progress in hospital and, in particular, the changes which lead the responsible medical officer and his clinical team to the view that the patient no longer requires treatment in a special hospital and can be safely managed in conditions of lesser security" (*Restricted Patients Detained in Special Hospitals: Information for the Special Hospitals Service Authority*, Home Office, undated, para. 6.3).

Order the discharge: The commonly held view that hospital managers lack jurisdiction to review the detention of restricted patients is incorrect. An approach that managers could adopt when faced with a request for a review by a restricted patient is set out in General Note to paragraph 23.1 of the *Code of Practice*.

Subsection (5)

1–517   This subsection provides that when a restriction order ceases to have effect either through lapse of time or by virtue of the direction of the Home Secretary (s.42(1)), the patient is to be treated as if he had been admitted to hospital under a hospital order without restrictions made on the date on which the restriction order ceased to have effect. If the patient has been conditionally discharged from hospital before the restrictions end, he will cease to be liable to be detained (s.42(5)).

Cease to have effect: The patient can apply to a Mental Health Review Tribunal within six months of the restriction order ceasing to have effect (s.69(2)(a)).

Subsection (6)

1–518   This subsection, which was enacted in response to recommendation 114 of the Butler Committee, is aimed at preventing restricted patients being detained for unjustifiably long periods. As a patient who has been conditionally discharged from a restriction order remains subject to that order (see s.42(2)), this provision applies to such patients. If the Home Secretary, having considered the responsible medical officer's report and having weighed all the other evidence about the patients medical condition that is available to him, is satisfied that the patient is no longer suffering from mental disorder, he should discharge him: see the note to section 42(2).

Secretary of State: The Secretary of State referred to is the Home Secretary.

Report: "Guidance has been issued by the Home Office on the points it considers in the light of reports on patients. It is helpful if the reports cover such issues as whether any information has come to light since the last report which increases understanding of the patient's offence, whether the motivation for behaviour which has put others at risk is understood, whether there is evidence that the patient has a persistent pre-occupation with a particular type of victim or violent/sexual/arsonist activity, what the chances of circumstances similar to those surrounding the offence are of arising again and similar offences occurring. It is important for the Home Office to know what effects any prescribed medication may have had, whether any symptoms remain, how important the medication is for continued stability, whether mental stability has been maintained in differing circumstances, and whether the patient has insight. In cases of mental impairment it is important to know the extent to which a patient has benefited from training, whether his behaviour is more socially acceptable, and whether he is explosive or impulsive. In cases of psychopathic disorder it is important for the responsible medical officer to describe the extent to which the patient may be more mature, predictable, and concerned about others, whether he is more tolerant of frustration and stress, takes into account the consequences of his actions, and learns from experience.

In all cases it is helpful to know whether a patient has greater insight into his condition and whether he is more realistic and reliable, whether drugs or alcohol have affected him in the past or contributed towards his offence. The annual report should also consider how the patient has responded to stressful situations in the hospital in the past and whether his responses have changed—for example, how likely he is to resort to physical or to verbal aggression. If the patient is a sex offender it is important to consider whether he has shown in the hospital (or on visits outside) an undesirable interest in the type of person he has previously been known to favour as his victim, what form any sexual activity might have taken, and what the results have been of any psychological tests or therapeutic treatment.

The annual report should be based on an assessment of the patient by the clinical team responsible for his treatment, and it should advise the Home Secretary on whether it is considered that the patient should or should not continue to be detained and for what reasons, and whether continued detention in a special hospital is necessary" (Home Office, above, paras 5.3 to 5.5).

Powers of Secretary of State in respect of patients subject to restriction orders

42.—(1) If the Secretary of State is satisfied that in the case of any patient a **1–519** restriction order is no longer required for the protection of the public from serious harm, he may direct that the patient shall cease to be subject to the special restrictions set out in section 41(3) above; and where the Secretary of State so directs, the restriction order shall cease to have effect, and section 41(5) above shall apply accordingly.

(2) At any time while a restriction order is in force in respect of a patient, the Secretary of State may, if he thinks fit, by warrant discharge the patient from hospital, either absolutely or subject to conditions; and where a person is absolutely discharged under this subsection, he shall thereupon cease to be liable to be detained by virtue of the relevant hospital order, and the restriction order shall cease to have effect accordingly.

(3) The Secretary of State may at any time during the continuance in force of a restriction order in respect of a patient who has been conditionally discharged under subsection (2) above by warrant recall the patient to such hospital as may be specified in the warrant.

(4) Where a patient is recalled as mentioned in subsection (3) above—

(a) if the hospital specified in the warrant is not the hospital from which the patient was conditionally discharged, the hospital order and the restriction order shall have effect as if the hospital specified in the warrant were substituted for the hospital specified in the hospital order;

(b) in any case, the patient shall be treated for the purposes of section 18 above as if he had absented himself without leave from the hospital specified in the warrant, and, if the restriction order was made for a specified period, that period shall not in any event expire until the patient returns to the hospital or is returned to the hospital under that section.

(5) If a restriction order in respect of a patient ceases to have effect after the patient has been conditionally discharged under this section, the patient shall, unless previously recalled under subsection (3) above, be deemed to be absolutely discharged on the date when the order ceases to have effect, and shall cease to be liable to be detained by virtue of the relevant hospital order accordingly.

(6) The Secretary of State may, if satisfied that the attendance at any place in Great Britain of a patient who is subject to a restriction order is desirable in the interests of justice or for the purposes of any public inquiry, direct him to be taken to that place; and where a patient is directed under this subsection to be taken to any place he shall, unless the Secretary of State otherwise directs, be kept in custody while being so taken, while at that place and while being taken back to the hospital in which he is liable to be detained.

DEFINITIONS

1–520   patient: s.145.
restriction order: ss.41, 55(4), 145(1).
hospital: ss.55(5), 145(1).
hospital order: ss.37, 55(4), 145(1).
absent without leave: ss.18(6), 145(1).

GENERAL NOTE

1–521   This section empowers the Home Secretary to take the following action in respect of patients who have been placed on restriction orders: (1) to direct that the order shall cease to have effect; (2) to discharge the patient from hospital absolutely; and (3) to discharge the patient from hospital subject to conditions.

A restriction order cannot cease to have effect by inference or implication (*R. v. Secretary of State for the Home Department, ex p. Didlick* (1993) 16 B.M.L.R. 71, DC). *Per* Rougier J. at 75: "In my opinion subsection (1) and (2) [of section 42] indicate clearly that before a restriction order can be brought to an end, the Secretary of State must either make a declaration to that effect or must discharge the patient absolutely. Each of these is a positive act. There is no room, in my opinion, for the situation whereby a restriction order ceases to have effect by inference or implication. It follows, therefore, that, by merely allowing the conditions under which the applicant was discharged to lapse, the Secretary of State did not thereby bring to an end the operation of the restriction order."

Any reference in this section to a hospital order, a guardianship order or a restriction order shall be construed as including a reference to any other order or direction under this Part having the same effect as such orders (s.55(4)).

The Human Rights Act 1998

1–522   The granting of a conditional discharge to the patient under subsection (2), with a condition that the patient accepts medication, will not contravene the European Convention on Human Rights if one of the grounds in Article 8(2) of the Convention is satisfied (see the note on Art. 8(2)).

The exercise by the Home Secretary of his power of recall under subsection (3) will, except in emergency cases, constitute a violation of Article 5(1) of the Convention in the absence of an up to date report on the patient's medical condition (see the notes on subs. (3) and Art. 5).

One of the consequences of the decision of the Court of Appeal in *R. v. North West London Mental Health NHS Trust*, noted under subsection (3), is that a conditionally discharged patient who is brought back to hospital under either section 2 or section 3, can be discharged from that section by a Mental Health Review Tribunal but be liable to be re-detained by the Home Secretary using his recall power under subsection (3). It is questionable whether it could be successfully claimed that the tribunal in such a case has the power to order the discharge of the patient as required by Article 5(4) of the Convention, if the order can be immediately overridden by the Home Secretary.

Although the Home Secretary should discharge a patient as soon as he is satisfied that the patient is no longer mentally disordered, the discharge need not be absolute (see the note on subs.(2)).

Subsection (1)

This subsection enables the Home Secretary to lift the restrictions from a patient **1–523** who is subject to a restriction order, if he considers that they are no longer necessary to protect the public from serious harm.

Secretary of State: See the General Note to this Part.

Is satisfied: The Home Secretary will receive advice from the responsible medical officer (s.41(6)).

In June 1972 a committee was set up under the chairmanship of Sir Carl Aarvold to advise whether any changes, within the existing law, were required in the procedures for the discharge and supervision of patients who had been placed on restriction orders. The committee, which reported in January 1973 (*Report on the Review of Procedures for the Discharge and Supervision of Psychiatric Patients subject to Special Restrictions* (Cmnd. 5191)), recommended that special precautions needed to be taken in the discharge of a patient who had been identified by his responsible medical officer as requiring "special care in assessment" because of an unfavourable or unpredictable psychiatric prognosis and an indication of risk of the patient harming other persons. This recommendation was accepted by the Government and an Advisory Board on Restricted Patients has been established to advise the Home Secretary on proposals for the granting of leave, transfer or discharge of restricted patients where the risk of serious re-offending is considered particularly difficult to assess. The Board consists of eight members; two lawyers (one of them (a judge) is chairman), two experienced forensic psychiatrists, two senior social work representatives (one from the social services and the other from the probation service) and two members with special experience of the criminal justice system: see Annex C to *Mentally Disordered Offenders: Restricted patients detained in special hospitals— Information for the Special Hospitals Service Authority* (Home Office, undated). Reference to the Board is made only in a comparatively small number of cases. As a purely advisory body the board is not bound by the rules of natural justice, and its decisions are not amenable to judicial review (*R. v. Secretary of State for Home Department, ex p. Powell,* December 21, 1978 (unreported): a transcript of this case is reproduced as Appendix C to L. Gostin and E. Rassaby, *Representing the Mentally Ill and Handicapped,* 1980). Also see, Robert Baxter, "The mentally disordered offender in hospital: the role of the Home Office" in *The Mentally Disordered Offender,* (ed. K. Herbst and J. Gunn) (1991), p. 139, F. Egglestone, "The Advisory Board on Restricted Patients", in *Principles and Practice of Forensic Psychiatry,* (ed. R. Bluglass and P. Bowden) (1990) and *R. v. Secretary of State for the Home Department, ex p. Harry* [1998] 3 All E.R. 360, noted in the General Note to section 73.

The Butler Committee identified two main elements that need to be satisfied before a "restricted patient" is discharged: "from a medical point of view he must have sufficiently recovered his health; and from the point of view of society there must be, so far as can be assessed, little risk of further serious offending" (para. 7.24).

Protection of the public: In *R. v. Parole Board, ex p. Bradley* [1990] 3 All E.R. 828, 836, DC, Stuart-Smith L.J., on examining this provision, said that "the precise level of risk is not (surely cannot be) spelt out."

The restriction order shall cease to have effect: And the patient will continue to be detained as if he had been admitted to hospital under a hospital order made without restrictions (s.41(5)).

Subsection (2)

1–524   This subsection enables the Home Secretary to order the absolute or conditional discharge of a restricted patient. The Mental Health Review Tribunal has a similar power under section 73. Detailed notes of guidance for professionals on pre-discharge, supervision and after care arrangements for restricted patients who are conditionally discharged were issued with DHSS Circular No. LAC (87)3/HN (87)5. The guidance for social supervisors was updated in 1997.

A patient who has been conditionally discharged under this provision is not subject to the consent to treatment provisions contained in Part IV of this Act (s.56(1)(c)). However, as it is usually a condition of discharge that the patient takes such medication as may be prescribed by his responsible medical officer, a patient who fails to take his medication risks being recalled to hospital.

The Home Secretary will only be prepared to consider authorising the conditional discharge of a life sentence prisoner who has been transferred to hospital under sections 47 and 49 of this Act if the case is "exceptional" and the Lord Chief Justice and the trial judge so recommend: see the note on section 50(1)(b).

If the Home Secretary, after having weighed all the evidence about a patient's mental condition, is satisfied that the patient is no longer suffering from mental disorder, he should discharge the patient: see the *obiter* observations of Lawton L.J. in *Kynaston v. Secretary of State for Home Affairs* (1981) 73 Cr.App.R. 281, CA. This course of action would appear to be required by the European Convention on Human Rights: see article 5(1) and the decision of the European Court of Human Rights in *Winterwerp v. The Netherlands* (1979) 2 E.H.R.R. 387. The patient's discharge need not be absolute (*R. v. Merseyside Mental Health Review Tribunal, ex p. K* [1990] 1 All E.R. 694, CA and *Johnson v. United Kingdom* (1997) 27 E.H.R.R. 296).

A conditionally discharged patient cannot receive direct payments under the terms of the Community Care (Direct Payments) Act 1996 (Community Care (Direct payments) Regulations 1997 (S.I. 1997 No. 734), reg.2).

If he thinks fit: The Home Secretary is not bound by any statutory criteria when exercising his judgment under this provision. This contrasts with the power of the Mental Health Review Tribunal under section 73 where the tribunal is required to apply specific criteria in its decision making over restricted patients. Regular reports on the patient, prepared by his responsible medical officer, will be submitted to the Home Secretary under section 41(6).

Discharge the patient from hospital: Discharge means release from hospital and not that the patient should remain in the same or another hospital (*Secretary of State for the Home Department v. Mental Health Review Tribunal for the Mersey Regional Health Authority* [1986] 3 All E.R. 233). A patient cannot be conditionally discharged to premises which are managed by the detaining hospital and staffed by nurses of that hospital even if such premises are located some distance from the main hospital complex.

Absolutely: An absolute discharge has the effect of extinguishing both the hospital order and the restriction order. Such action would not preclude continuing contact between the patient and his supervisors on a non-statutory basis.

Subject to conditions: "The conditions which the Home Secretary would normally think it appropriate to attach to a conditional discharge are that the patient should live in a particular household and be under the supervision of a psychiatrist and a responsible person (usually a probation officer or social worker) who would undertake to submit reports to the Home Secretary on the patient's progress from time to time and to inform the Home Secretary and the responsible medical officer if the patient's mental condition appeared to be deteriorating" (*Memorandum*, para. 186). A condition that the patient refrains from entering a particular locality (e.g. the area where the patient's victim lives) could be attached to the discharge if this was felt to be a proportionate response to the circumstances of the case.

The main purpose of a conditional discharge is to provide compulsory supervision of the patient in the community. The supervisor will "assist the patient to settle down in the community and to this end to help him cope with his problems by providing him with professional guidance, support and control while he does so." He is "sometimes in a position to recognise that the discharged patient may be moving into a similar situation to that which originally precipitated an offence of violence; or to perceive other signs indicating the likelihood of a repetition of dangerous behaviour. Where this is so he can take steps to warn the patient and if necessary arrange for him to be recalled to hospital" (*Butler Committee*, para. 4.31). The *Butler Committee* agreed, at paragraph 8.7, with the recommendation of the Advisory Board on Restricted Patients that "supervision should be undertaken by the person who can bring most to the case in the way of knowledge, expertise and resources in the particular circumstances of the case. The arrangements may need to take particular account of the needs of public safety" (para. 4.8).

Paragraphs 16 and 17 of Supervisions and *After-Care of Conditionally Discharged Restricted Patients—Notes for the Guidance of Social Supervisors*, Home Office, Department of Health, Welsh Office, 1997, state: "The Home Secretary will usually decide to make a restricted patient's discharge from hospital subject to certain conditions. The conditions usually imposed by the Home Secretary are those of residence at a stated address, supervision by a local social worker or probation officer and psychiatric supervision. Tribunals also are likely to make discharge directions conditional either for the protection of the public or of the patient himself, and to impose similar conditions. If they do not, the Home Office, using powers under section 73(4) of the 1983 Act, usually requires social and psychiatric supervision.

The purpose of the formal supervision resulting from conditional discharge is to protect the public from further serious harm in two ways: first by assisting the patient's successful reintegration into the community after what may have been a long period of detention in hospital under conditions of security: second, by close monitoring of the patient's mental health or of a perceived increase in the risk of danger to the public so that, in the event of subsequent deterioration in the patient's mental health or of a perceived increase in the risk of danger to the public, steps can be taken to assist the patient and protect the public. Conditional discharge also allows a period of assessment of the patient in the community before a final decision is taken whether to remove the control imposed by the restriction order by means of an absolute discharge."

The role of the Home Office has been described as follows: "Under normal circumstances, while a patient is conditionally discharged, the Home Office will receive reports on him quarterly from his doctor and social supervisor, sometimes half-yearly if, after a number of years, he has made good progress and gives rise to no cause for concern. Usually after a period of about five years, successful rehabilitation, an absolute discharge will be considered on the recommendation of his supervisors, though this may sometimes be done after about two years when the patient's offending history is less serious. More difficult or troubling cases may take longer" (Robert Baxter, "The mentally disordered offender in hospital: the role of the Home Office," in *The Mentally Disordered Offender*, Ed. K. Herbst and J. Gunn, Butterworth—Heinemann, 1991, p. 143).

A summary of the study *The Discharge and Supervision of Restricted Patients* by Susanne Dell and Adrian Grounds has been published as Research Findings No. 19 by the Home Office Research and Statistics Department. Also see, Edward Petch, "The supervision of restricted patients in the community" (1996) 7 *Journal of Forensic Psychiatry* 369–375.

A conditionally discharged patient has a right to apply to a Mental Health Review Tribunal under section 75(2).

Subsection (2)

Subject to conditions: See *R. v. Secretary of State for the Home Department, ex p.* **1–525** *Didlick*, noted in the General Note to this section. Although this section does not provide the Home Secretary with an express power either to vary conditions after discharge or to impose further conditions, such a power can be inferred from the general purpose of a conditional discharge because the absence of such a power would lead to the patient being recalled to hospital for the sole purpose of varying the conditions of the discharge.

Subsection (3)

1–526   *The Secretary of State may:* In *R. v. Secretary of State for the Home Department, ex p. K* [1990] 3 All E.R. 562, the Court of Appeal affirmed the decision of McCullough J. ([1990] 1 All E.R. 703), by holding that there is no requirement in this provision that the Home Secretary could only issue a warrant to recall a patient who had been conditionally discharged if there was medical evidence before him that the patient was then suffering from mental disorder. "The clear intention [of this provision] is that the Secretary of State be empowered in his discretion at any time during the continuance of a restriction order in respect of a patient to recall the patient to hospital. In exercising that discretion, the Secretary of State will no doubt find it necessary to balance the interests of the patient against those of public safety"; *per* McCowan L.J., at 570. The exercise of the Home Secretary's discretion can only be challenged if it can be shown that he ignored the public law constraints recognised in *Associated Provincial Picture Houses Ltd v. Wednesbury Corporation* [1948] 1 K.B. 223 and *Padfield v. Ministry of Agriculture, Fisheries and Food* [1968] A.C. 997, *i.e.* that he took into account material he ought not to have taken into account or did not take into account material he ought to have taken into account or reached a decision which, on the material before him, no Secretary of State could have reached or that he used his discretion in a manner which did not promote the policy and objects of the Act. McCullough J., at first instance, held that it would be unlawful for the Secretary of State to recall a restricted patient to hospital when only the previous week or month he had been conditionally discharged from hospital by direction of a tribunal unless meanwhile something had happened which justified the belief that a different view might now be taken about one of the factors on which his release had depended. These observations were not repeated or approved (nor disapproved) in the Court of Appeal. They were referred to and implicitly approved by the Court of Appeal in *R. v. East London and City Mental Health NHS Trust, ex p. Brandenburg* [2001] EWCA Civ 239, where the court held that an application to re-detain a patient only a matter of days after a decision by a tribunal to discharge him from detention could be challenged in the absence of circumstances not known to the tribunal which invalidated its decision. The *Brandenburg* case is considered in the General Note to section 3.

Following the decision of the Court of Appeal in *K.*, the patient complained to the European Commission on Human Rights, arguing that because there had been no medical evidence at the time it was issued, the warrant of recall was an illegal deprivation of his liberty in violation of the European Convention on Human Rights, Article 5(1). The Commission declared K.'s application admissible and the European Court on Human Rights subsequently held that, in the absence of an emergency, there had been a breach of Article 5(1) in recalling K. without up to date medical evidence to demonstrate that that he was suffering from a true mental disorder (*Kay v. United Kingdom* (1998) 40 B.M.L.R. 20). The recall of conditionally discharged patients should conform with this judgment.

The *Notes for the Guidance of Social Supervisors*, above, state, at paragraph 71: "It is not possible to specify all the circumstances in which the Home Secretary may decide to exercise his power under [this provision] to recall to hospital a conditionally discharged patient, but in considering the recall of a patient he will always have regard to the safety of the public. A report to the Home Office must always be made in a case in which:

(a) there appears to be an actual or potential risk to the public;

(b) contact with the patient is lost or the patient is unwilling to co-operate with supervision;

(c) the patient's behaviour or condition suggests a need for further inpatient treatment in hospital;

(d) the patient is charged with or convicted of an offence".

If the patient will not return to hospital willingly on being told of his recall, then the police, to whom a copy of the warrant will have been sent, should be informed. There is no power of entry attached to a recall warrant. If it is not possible to gain access to a patient who has been recalled, an application may be made to a magistrate under section 135(2).

At any time: The Home Secretary's discretion to recall the patient can be exercised at any time and need not be triggered by a breach of the patient's conditions of discharge. There is no legal requirement for the Home Secretary to consult with the patient's responsible medical officer prior to the issue of recall warrant.

Recall the patient: A recall is a form of legal authority which authorises the compulsory readmission and detention of the patient and the reinstatement of the regime of control under section 41: see the *Dlodlo* case, noted below. Procedures for informing restricted patients of the reasons for their recall are contained in Department of Health Circular No. HSG(93)20. The Annex to this circular identifies a three-stage procedure that should be applied when a patient is recalled:

"*Stage 1*: The person returning the patient to hospital should inform him/her in simple terms that he/she is being recalled to hospital by the Home Secretary under section 42(3) of the Mental Health Act 1983 and that, to the extent that this is possible, a further explanation will be given later. The reason(s) for recalling the patient should be explained to the nearest relative, if one is available, within 72 hours.

Stage 2: An explanation should be given to the patient of the reason(s) for his/her recall as soon as possible after re-admission to hospital and in any event within 72 hours. This should be done by the responsible medical officer or deputy, an approved social worker, or an appropriate administrator representing the hospital managers. The person giving the explanation should ensure, so far as the patient's mental condition allows, that the patient understands the reason(s).

Stage 3: A written explanation of the reason(s) for recall should be provided for the patient within 72 hours of being re-admitted to hospital. Written information on the reason(s) should also be given to the patient's nearest relative (subject to the patient's consent)."

A conditionally discharged patient who has been recalled to hospital must have his case referred to a Mental Health Review Tribunal by the Home Secretary within a month of his return to hospital (s.75(1)). The patient may apply to the tribunal between six and 12 months after his recall and during each subsequent 12 month period (ss.70, 75(1)(b)). Also see paragraphs 29.2 to 29.5 of the *Code of Practice*.

As "recall" must be understood as authorising not only the physical recall of the patient, but also the reinstatement of a regime of control in respect of the patient, the Home Secretary may issue a warrant for the recall of a patient to a hospital in which the patient is already detained under section 3 of this Act (*Dlodlo v. Mental Health Review Tribunal for the South Thames Region* (1996) 36 B.M.L.R. 145, CA). In this case a restriction order patient was transferred to a local hospital. The patient was given a conditional discharge by a Mental Health Review Tribunal, but, on becoming ill, he was re-admitted to the local hospital under section 3. The re-admission was followed by the issue of a warrant for the patients recall. The legality of using section

3 to detain a restriction order patient who had been conditionally discharged was confirmed by the Court of Appeal in *R. v. North West London Mental Health NHS Trust, ex p. Stewart* [1997] 4 All E.R. 871, where it was held that Parts II and III of this Act are not mutually exclusive but contain powers which can coexist and operate independently of each other.

The D.H.S.S. and the Home Office in their *Notes for the Guidance of Supervising Psychiatrists*, 1987 state: "If the supervising psychiatrist has reason to fear for the safety of the patient or of others, he may decide to take immediate local action to admit the patient to hospital for a short period either with the patient's consent or using civil powers such as those under sections 2, 3 or 4 of the Mental Health Act 1983. Whether or not such action is taken, and even if the social supervisor does not share the supervising psychiatrist's concern, the supervising psychiatrist should report to the Home Office at once so that consideration should be given to the patient's formal recall to hospital" (para. 49). If the patient is admitted to hospital "it is generally inappropriate for a conditionally discharged patient to remain in hospital for more than a short time informally or under civil powers of detention, and the Home Secretary would usually wish to consider the issue of a warrant of recall if the period of in-patient treatment seemed likely to be protracted" (para. 52).

For an audit of the recall of all restricted patients to Ashworth Special Hospital during the period 1981–1991, see Dolan *et al.* (1993) "An audit of recalls to a Special Hospital, *The Journal of Forensic Psychiatry*, Vol. 4, No. 2, 249–260.

Hospital: Or a registered establishment (s.34(2)). "It is open to the Home Secretary to recall the patient to any hospital. If a patient has returned to the community from a special hospital via an R.S.U. or local psychiatric hospital, or if the patient has not previously been detained in a special hospital, the Home Secretary may decide to recall him to a special hospital if in his view this is necessary for the protection of the public. While the Home Office will always seek to act wherever possible with the agreement of the hospital managers or of the hospital consultant responsible for the patient's treatment, the final decision on the recall of a restricted patient rests with the Home Secretary and is not dependent on the consent of the hospital to which the patient is recalled" (*Restricted Patients Detained in Special Hospitals: Information for the Special Hospitals Service Authority*, Home Office, undated, para. 7.4). There is no statutory requirement for the Home Secretary to obtain the agreement of the hospital doctors to re-admit a recalled patient.

The legality of recalling a patient to a hospital other than the hospital named in the restriction order was confirmed in the *Dlodlo* case, noted above.

Subsection (4)

1–527   *Paragraph (b):* This paragraph provides: (1) that a recalled patient can be taken into custody and conveyed to the specified hospital by any approved social worker, officer on the staff of the hospital or any other person authorised by the hospital managers; and (2) that a patient whose restriction order was made for a specified period shall not cease to be liable to be detained if that period expires after the recall has been issued and before the patient can be returned to hospital.

Subsection (5)

1–528   This subsection provides that if a restriction order ceases to have effect while the patient is on conditional discharge from hospital he will cease to be liable to be detained.

Subsection (6)

1–529   *Great Britain:* England, Wales and Scotland (Union with Scotland Act 1706, preamble, art. 1).

Taken to that place: See section 137 for general provisions relating to custody, conveyance and detention.

Power of magistrates' courts to commit for restriction order
   43.—(1) If in the case of a person of or over the age of 14 years who is   **1–530**
convicted by a magistrates' court of an offence punishable on summary
conviction with imprisonment—
   (a) the conditions which under section 37(1) above are required to be
       satisfied for the making of a hospital order are satisfied in respect of
       the offender; but
   (b) it appears to the court, having regard to the nature of the offence, the
       antecedents of the offender and the risk of his committing further
       offences if set at large, that if a hospital order is made a restriction
       order should also be made,
the court may, instead of making a hospital order or dealing with him in any
other manner, commit him in custody to the Crown Court to be dealt with in
respect of the offence.
   (2) Where an offender is committed to the Crown Court under this
section, the Crown Court shall inquire into the circumstances of the case and
may—
   (a) if that court would have power so to do under the foregoing provisions
       of this Part of this Act upon the conviction of the offender before that
       court of such an offence as is described in section 37(1) above, make a
       hospital order in his case, with or without a restriction order;
   (b) if the court does not make such an order, deal with the offender in any
       other manner in which the magistrates' court might have dealt with
       him.
   (3) The Crown Court shall have the same power to make orders under
sections 35, 36 and 38 above in the case of a person committed to the court
under this section as the Crown Court has under those sections in the case of
an accused person within the meaning of section 35 or 36 above or of a
person convicted before that court as mentioned in section 38 above.
   (4) The power of a magistrates' court under [section 3 of the Powers of
Criminal Courts (Sentencing) Act 2000] (which enables such a court to
commit an offender to the Crown Court where the court is of the opinion
that greater punishment should be inflicted for the offence than the court has
power to inflict) shall also be exercisable by a magistrates' court where it is of
the opinion that greater punishment should be inflicted as aforesaid on the
offender unless a hospital order is made in his case with a restriction order.
   (5) The power of the Crown Court to make a hospital order, with or
without a restriction order, in the case of a person convicted before that
court of an offence may, in the same circumstances and subject to the same
conditions, be exercised by such a court in the case of a person committed to
the court under section 5 of the Vagrancy Act 1824 (which provides for the
committal to the Crown Court of persons who are incorrigible rogues within
the meaning of that section).

AMENDMENT
   The words in square brackets in subs. (4) were substituted by the Powers of
Criminal Courts (Sentencing) Act 2000, s.165, Sched. 9, para. 91.

DEFINITIONS
   hospital order: ss.37, 145(1).   **1–531**
   restriction order: ss.41, 145(1).

GENERAL NOTE
1–532   A magistrates' court has no power to make a restriction order. If such a court is satisfied that the conditions exist in which it could make a hospital order, but also feels that a restriction order should be made in addition, it may commit an offender (if over 14 years of age) to the Crown Court under this section. The magistrates may direct that the offender be detained in a hospital, pending the hearing of the case by the Crown Court (s.44). If the Crown Court decides not to make a hospital order, it can deal with the offender in any way in which the magistrates' court could have dealt with him (subs. (2)) or it can remand him under section 35 or 36 or it can make an interim hospital order in respect of him (subs. (3)).

Subsection (1)
1–533   *Age:* See section 55(7). A person attains the age of 14 at the commencement of his fourteenth birthday (Family Law Reform Act 1969, s.9(1)).

Convicted: The magistrates' must have convicted the offender. In *R. v. Horseferry Road Magistrates' Court, ex p. K* [1996] 3 All E.R. 719, 735, DC, Forbes J. said that this Act "makes *no* provision for committal to the Crown Court by the magistrates for imposition of a restriction order under section 41 upon a person who has been acquitted of an offence by reason of insanity. The magistrates only have such a power to commit to the Crown Court for that purpose in the case of a person *convicted* of an imprisonable offence, whether indictable or summary only". His Lordship said that this state of affairs represented an "obvious legislative lacuna."

Magistrates' court: Or youth court for those under the age of 18.

Offence punishable on summary conviction with imprisonment: For young offenders, see section 55(2).

Risk of his committing further offences: The magistrates' court does not need to be satisfied as to the "serious harm" test set out in section 41(1).

Commit him in custody: Or order him to be admitted to a hospital if the conditions of section 44 are satisfied. Note that the Home Secretary has power to transfer a mentally ill or severely mentally impaired offender from custody to hospital under section 48(2)(b).

Subsection (2)
1–534   *Committed to the Crown Court under this section:* Or under section 3 of the Powers of Criminal Courts (Sentencing) Act 2000 (subs. (4)).

Committal to hospital under s.43
1–535   **44.**—(1) Where an offender is committed under section 43(1) above and the magistrates' court by which he is committed is satisfied on written or oral evidence that arrangements have been made for the admission of the offender to a hospital in the event of an order being made under this section, the court may, instead of committing him in custody, by order direct him to be admitted to that hospital, specifying it, and to be detained there until the case is disposed of by the Crown Court, and may give such directions as it thinks fit for his production from the hospital to attend the Crown Court by which his case is to be dealt with.

(2) The evidence required by subsection (1) above shall be given by the registered medical practitioner who would be in charge of the offender's treatment or by some other person representing the managers of the hospital in question.

(3) The power to give directions under section 37(4) above, section 37(5) above and section 40(1) above shall apply in relation to an order under this section as they apply in relation to a hospital order, but as if references to the

period of 28 days mentioned in section 40(1) above were omitted; and subject as aforesaid an order under this section shall, until the offender's case is disposed of by the Crown Court, have the same effect as a hospital order together with a restriction order, made without limitation of time.

DEFINITIONS

hospital: ss.55(5), 145(1).   **1–536**
hospital order: ss.37, 145(1).
restriction order: ss.41, 145(1).
guardianship order: ss.37, 145(1).
the managers: s.145(1).

GENERAL NOTE

If a magistrates' court on committing an offender to the Crown Court under **1–537** section 43, is satisfied that arrangements have been made for the admission of the offender to a hospital, it may direct him to be admitted to that hospital until the case is disposed of by the Crown Court. Paragraphs 166 and 167 of the *Memorandum* state: "[I]f a considerable time elapses between the hearing by the magistrates and the hearing by the Crown Court, the hospital authorities should arrange for two fresh medical reports to be submitted to the court (one by a doctor approved under section 12). They should also arrange for at least one doctor to be available to give oral evidence. After appearing before the Crown Court the patient will not be liable to be taken back to the hospital compulsorily unless that court makes a hospital order.

It while the patient is detained under section 44 his mental condition deteriorates to such an extent that he is unlikely to be fit to appear before the Crown Court on the day of the hearing, the court should be notified immediately. In those circumstances the court may either adjourn the case or, if the patient is suffering from mental illness or severe mental impairment, it may make a hospital order, with or without a restriction order, in his absence under powers conferred by section 51. The court can make a hospital order in the patient's absence only if it is satisfied, on the written or oral evidence of at least two doctors, that the patient is suffering from mental illness or severe mental impairment of a nature or degree which makes it appropriate for the patient to be detained in hospital for medical treatment. In informing the court of a patient's unfitness to appear, the hospital authorities should enquire whether it is likely to wish to proceed in the patient's absence, and if so they should arrange for two doctors, one of whom must be a doctor approved under section 12 of the Act, to attend at the court to give evidence of the patient's mental state."

Subsection (1)

Magistrates' court: Or youth court for those under the age of 18.   **1–538**
Admitted to that hospital: Which will "normally be the hospital which had already agreed to admit the patient in the event of the magistrates' court itself making a hospital order" (*Memorandum*, para. 165). Once the offender has been admitted to the hospital, subsections (5) and (6) of section 51 shall apply to him as if he were a person subject to a transfer direction made under section 47 (s.51(3)).
Directions as it thinks fit for his production from the hospital: It will be the hospital's duty to arrange for the offenders attendance at the court with an appropriate escort. It "will not be necessary to obtain the Home Secretary's consent to leave of absence from the hospital for this purpose" (*Memorandum*, para. 166).

Subsection (2)

Some other person: Who need not be a doctor.   **1–539**

Subsection (3)

This subsection provides that the magistrates' court can direct that the offender be **1–540** detained in a place of safety pending his admission to hospital. It also authorises a constable, approved social worker or any other person directed to do so by the court to convey the offender to hospital at any time and not within the 28-day period provided for by section 40(1). Subject to this exception, an order under this section has the same effect as a restriction order made without limit of time.

Appeals from magistrates' courts

1–541   **45.**—(1) Where on the trial of an information charging a person with an offence a magistrates' court makes a hospital order or guardianship order in respect of him without convicting him, he shall have the same right of appeal against the order as if it had been made on his conviction; and on any such appeal the Crown Court shall have the same powers as if the appeal had been against both conviction and sentence.

   (2) An appeal by a child or young person with respect to whom any such order has been made, whether the appeal is against the order or against the finding upon which the order was made, may be brought by him or by his parent or guardian on his behalf.

DEFINITIONS

1–542   hospital order: ss.37, 145(1).
   guardianship order: ss.37, 145(1).
   child: s.55(1).
   young person: s.55(1).
   guardian: s.55(1).

GENERAL NOTE

1–543   This section provides a right of appeal for a person who has been made the subject of a hospital order or a guardianship order made by a magistrates' court under section 37(3).

   "If a patient appeals from the decision of a magistrates' court to the Crown Court he must be present in court when his appeal is heard. On the day of the hearing, of which the hospital authorities will be notified by the Crown Court, he will be taken to the court with an escort. If the patient appeals to the Court of Appeal, he will not necessarily have to appear before the court, but if the court orders him to be present he will similarly be taken with an escort. If he is subject to a restriction order the Home Office should be notified as soon as it is known that the Court of Appeal wishes him to be present in court; the Home Secretary will then issue a direction under section 42(6) authorising his production before the court. If any patient who is required to appear before the court is, in the opinion of the responsible medical officer, unfit to appear, the Crown Court or the Registrar of Criminal Appeal, as the case may be, will be notified immediately" (Home Office Circular No. 69/1983, para. 33).

Subsection (1)

1–544   *Conviction and sentence:* "This is necessary to enable the Crown Court to rehear the case completely so as to ascertain whether the facts proved justify a conviction, since it could not otherwise be justified in substituting a sentence for the hospital order or guardianship order" (*ibid.* para. 31).

[Hospital and limitation directions

Power of higher courts to direct hospital admission

1–545   **45A.**—(1) This section applies where, in the case of a person convicted before the Crown Court of an offence the sentence for which is not fixed by law—

(a) the conditions mentioned in subsection (2) below are fulfilled; and

(b) except where the offence is one the sentence for which falls to be imposed under section 2 of the Crime (Sentences) Act 1997, the court considers making a hospital order in respect of him before deciding to impose a sentence of imprisonment ("the relevant sentence") in respect of the offence.

(2) The conditions referred to in subsection (1) above are that the court is satisfied, on the written or oral evidence of two registered medical practitioners—

(a) that the offender is suffering from psychopathic disorder;

(b) that the mental disorder from which the offender is suffering is of a nature or degree which makes it appropriate for him to be detained in a hospital for medical treatment; and

(c) that such treatment is likely to alleviate or prevent a deterioration of his condition.

(3) The court may give both of the following directions, namely—

(a) a direction that, instead of being removed to and detained in a prison, the offender be removed to and detained in such hospital as may be specified in the direction (in this Act referred to as a "hospital direction"); and

(b) a direction that the offender be subject to the special restrictions set out in section 41 above (in this Act referred to as a "limitation direction").

(4) A hospital direction and a limitation direction shall not be given in relation to an offender unless at least one of the medical practitioners whose evidence is taken into account by the court under subsection (2) above has given evidence orally before the court.

(5) A hospital direction and a limitation direction shall not be given in relation to an offender unless the court is satisfied on the written or oral evidence of the registered medical practitioner who would be in charge of his treatment, or of some other person representing the managers of the hospital that arrangements have been made—

(a) for his admission to that hospital; and

(b) for his admission to it within the period of 28 days beginning with the day of the giving of such directions;

and the court may, pending his admission within that period, give such directions as it thinks fit for his conveyance to and detention in a place of safety.

(6) If within the said period of 28 days it appears to the Secretary of State that by reason of an emergency or other special circumstances it is not practicable for the patient to be received into the hospital specified in the hospital direction, he may give instructions for the admission of the patient to such other hospital as appears to be appropriate instead of the hospital so specified.

(7) Where such instructions are given—

(a) the Secretary of State shall cause the person having the custody of the patient to be informed, and

(b) the hospital direction shall have effect as if the hospital specified in the instructions were substituted for the hospital specified in the hospital direction.

241

(8) Section 38(1) and (5) and section 39 above shall have effect as if any reference to the making of a hospital order included a reference to the giving of a hospital direction and a limitation direction.

(9) A hospital direction and a limitation direction given in relation to an offender shall have effect not only as regards the relevant sentence but also (so far as applicable) as regards any other sentence of imprisonment imposed on the same or a previous occasion.

(10) The Secretary of State may by order provide that this section shall have effect as if the reference in subsection (2) above to psychopathic disorder included a reference to a mental disorder of such other description as may be specified in the order.

(11) An order made under this section may—

(a) apply generally, or in relation to such classes of offenders or offences as may be specified in the order;

(b) provide that any reference in this section to a sentence of imprisonment, or to a prison, shall include a reference to a custodial sentence, or to an institution, of such description as may be so specified; and

(c) include such supplementary, incidental or consequential provisions as appear to the Secretary of State to be necessary or expedient.]

AMENDMENT
This section was inserted by the Crime (Sentences) Act 1997, s.46.

DEFINITIONS
1–546   psychopathic disorder: ss.1, 145(1).
mental disorder: ss.1, 145(1).
hospital: ss.55(5), 145(1).
medical treatment: s.145(1).
managers: s.145(1).
place of safety: s.55.

GENERAL NOTE
1–547   This section empowers the Crown Court, when imposing a prison sentence on an offender convicted of an offence other than one of which the sentence is fixed by law, to give a direction for immediate admission to and detention in a specified hospital (a "hospital direction"), together with a direction that they be subject to the special restrictions set out in section 41 (a "limitation direction"). This option is only available if the offender is diagnosed as suffering from psychopathic disorder (with or without an additional category of mental disorder). The responsible medical offices will have the option of seeking the patient's transfer to prison at any time before his release date if no further treatment is necessary, or is likely to be beneficial.

The purpose and application of the power to make a hospital direction is considered in paragraphs 2 to 5 of Home Office Circular No.52/1997:

"It is the Government's policy that an offender needing specialist care and treatment for mental disorder should where possible receive it in hospital rather than in custodial care, wherever this is consistent with the needs of protecting the public. The hospital direction does not represent a departure from that policy. The advice given on inter-agency provision for dealing with mentally disordered offenders in Home Office Circulars 66/1990 and 12/1995 remains in force. Except where the law requires the imposition of a life sentence, courts retain the option of making a hospital order under section 37 of the 1983 Act, with or without a restriction order under section 41 of that Act.

The hospital direction is intended to give the courts greater flexibility in dealing with cases where they conclude that a prison sentence is the appropriate disposal in spite of evidence that the offender is mentally disordered. That will be either because the offender falls to be sentenced under the automatic life sentence provision in section 2 of the Crime (Sentences) Act 1997, or because the court is satisfied that a prison sentence with a hospital direction will be the most effective way to protect the public from further harm.

When sentencing mentally disordered offenders, the court is bound by the requirement in section 4 of the Criminal Justice Act 1991 to consider any information before it which relates to the defendant's mental condition. Except where the sentence is fixed by law, the court is required to consider the effect of a custodial sentence on the offender's mental disorder and on the treatment which may be available for it before passing such a sentence.

The hospital direction does not disturb this arrangement. Section 45A(1)(b) of the 1983 Act requires the court to consider making a hospital order in all cases (other than those where the sentence is fixed by law and offenders sentenced under section 2 of the Crime (Sentences) Act 1997) before attaching a hospital direction to a prison sentence. Existing procedures for giving medical evidence need not change, since the requirements for making a hospital direction are the same as those for making a restricted hospital order. The court will simply have the new option of directing to hospital when it concludes that a custodial sentence is appropriate."

In practice, the powers granted by this section are rarely used.

The effect of hospital and limitation directions are set out in section 45B. A person who is detained in hospital under this section will continue to qualify for early release days under the Crime (Sentences) Act 1997, without reference to his behaviour (*ibid.*, s.22(2)). If the offender is detained in hospital on the date his sentence would otherwise expire, a release supervision order will come into effect (see s.16 of the 1997 Act) and he will be supervised by either a probation officer or a social worker of a local authority social services department (*ibid.* s.22(4)).

A hospital direction and limitation direction constitute a sentence for the purpose of the Criminal Appeal Act 1968 (*ibid.* s.50(1)). The right of a patient who is subject to directions made under this section to apply to a Mental Health Review Tribunal is governed by section 73. The powers of a tribunal on hearing such an application are set out in section 74.

Subsection (1)

Fixed by law: This section does not apply to persons who have been convicted of **1–548** murder who must be sentenced to life imprisonment (Murder (Abolition of Death Penalty) Act 1965, s.1).

Section 2 of the Crime (Sentences) Act: Under which a mandatory life sentence must be imposed for a second serious offence. By virtue of section 2(4) of the Act, such a sentence is not regarded as a sentence fixed by law.

Hospital order: The court must have considered making a hospital order before imposing a sentence of imprisonment and attaching a hospital direction. The court is bound to consider the defendant's mental condition prior to sentence: see section 4 of the Criminal Justice Act 1991 noted in the General Note to this Part.

Subsection (2)

Two registered medical practitioners: One of whom must be approved under **1–549** section 12 of this Act (s.54(1)).

Psychopathic disorder: See subsection (10).

Alleviate or prevent a deterioration of his condition: See *R. v. Canons Park Mental Health Review Tribunal, ex p. A* [1994] 2 All E.R. 659, CA, noted under section 3(2)(b).

Subsection (3)

Both of the ... directions: The court cannot make a hospital direction without a **1–550** limitation direction.

Such hospital as may be prescribed: By virtue of section 47 of the Crime (Sentences) Act 1997, the court has the power to order that the patient be admitted to and detained in a named hospital unit. A named hospital unit can be any part of a hospital which is treated as a separate unit. The effect of specifying a hospital unit is considered in paragraph 11 of the Home Office Circular 52/1997:

"The amendment introduced by the 1997 Act provides that where a patient is detained in a named hospital unit, the Home Secretary's consent is required for any leave or transfer from the named unit. His consent to transfer is required irrespective of whether the transfer is to another unit in the same hospital or to another hospital. The purpose of the power is to ensure that where the Home Secretary or a court concludes that a restricted patient needs to be detained under a particular level of security for the protection of the public, the Home Secretary's consent is required before the patient can be moved from that level of security. It is a matter for the discretion of the court or the Home Secretary when making an order or direction, to decide whether a hospital unit should be specified, or whether to leave future accommodation within the hospital at the discretion of the hospital managers. It may be appropriate to specify a unit if the risk of serious harm to others if the offender were to abscond is assessed as high."

Subsection (5)

1–551 *Hospital:* "If there is difficulty in obtaining a bed, the doctor may need to seek the help of the Health Authority" (*Memorandum*, para. 172).
Beginning with: Including the day on which the directions were given (*Hare v. Gocher* [1962] 2 Q.B. 641).

Subsections (6), (7)

1–552 *Secretary of State:* The functions of the Minister under these provisions, so far as exercisable in relation to Wales, are exercised by the National Assembly for Wales (S.I. 1999 No. 672, art. 2, Sched. 1, as varied by S.I. 2000 No. 253, art. 4, Sched. 3).

Subsection (8)

1–553 This provides that sections 38(1) and (5) and 39 apply in respect of the giving of a hospital and a limitation direction as they do to the making of a hospital order. Those sections relate to the making of an interim hospital order and the acquisition of information from health authorities on the availability of facilities.

Subsection (9)

1–554 This provides that where a hospital and a limitation direction are made, they apply to all existing prison sentences passed on the offender.

Subsections (10), (11)

1–555 *Secretary of State:* See the General Note to this Part.

[Effect of hospital and limitation directions

1–556 **45B.**—(1) A hospital direction and a limitation direction shall be sufficient authority—
  (a) for a constable or any other person directed to do so by the court to convey the patient to the hospital specified in the hospital direction within a period of 28 days; and
  (b) for the managers of the hospital to admit him at any time within that period and thereafter detain him in accordance with the provisions of this Act.

(2) With respect to any person—
(a) a hospital direction shall have effect as a transfer direction; and
(b) a limitation direction shall have effect as a restriction direction.
(3) While a person is subject to a hospital direction and a limitation direction the responsible medical officer shall at such intervals (not exceeding one year) as the Secretary of State may direct examine and report to the Secretary of State on that person; and every report shall contain such particulars as the Secretary of State may require.]

AMENDMENT
This section was inserted by the Crime (Sentences) Act 1997, s.46.

DEFINITIONS   **1–557**
  hospital direction: ss.45A(3)(a), 145(1).
  limitation direction: ss.45A(3)(b), 145(1).
  hospital: ss.55(5), 145(1).
  managers: s.145(1).
  transfer direction: ss.47, 145(1).
  restriction direction: ss.49, 145(1).
  responsible medical offices: s.55(1).

GENERAL NOTE
The effect of hospital and limitation directions is set out in paragraphs 7 and 8 of **1–558**
the Home Office Circular 52/1997:

> "The hospital direction has the effect of ordering the offender's admission to a named hospital for treatment within 28 days, as if a hospital order had been made. Once there, the offender will be managed as if admitted under a transfer direction made under section 47 of the 1983 Act. When making a hospital direction the court must at the same time make a limitation direction. This has the same effect as a restriction direction under section 49 of the 1983 Act. The offender is made subject to the restrictions set out in section 41 of the 1983 Act.
>
> An offender who is subject to hospital and limitation directions may serve his entire sentence in hospital if the responsible medical officer is satisfied that he is benefiting from treatment. Alternatively he may, on the recommendation of the responsible medical officer or a Mental Health Review Tribunal, be transferred to prison at any time during sentence by warrant of the Home Secretary under section 50(1) of the 1983 Act. Transfer to prison will be considered by the Home Secretary on receipt of medical evidence that the patient no longer requires treatment in hospital for mental disorder, or that no other effective treatment can be given in hospital. Any subsequent transfer back to hospital would be considered under section 47 of the 1983 Act."

Subsection (3)
Secretary of State: See the General Note to this Part.   **1–559**

Detention during Her Majesty's pleasure

Persons ordered to be kept in custody during Her Majesty's pleasure
46.—(1) The Secretary of State may by warrant direct that any person **1–560**
who, by virtue of any enactment to which this subsection applies, is required to be kept in custody during Her Majesty's pleasure or until the directions of Her Majesty are known shall be detained in such hospital (not being a

[registered establishment]) as may be specified in the warrant and, where that person is not already detained in the hospital, give directions for his removal there.

(2) The enactments to which subsection (1) above applies are section 16 of the Courts-Martial (Appeals) Act 1968, section 116 of the Army Act 1955, section 116 of the Air Force Act 1955 and section 63 of the Naval Discipline Act 1957.

(3) A direction under this section in respect of any person shall have the same effect as a hospital order together with a restriction order, made without limitation of time; and where such a direction is given in respect of a person while he is in the hospital, he shall be deemed to be admitted in pursuance of, and on the date of, the direction.

AMENDMENTS
This section is prospectively repealed by the Armed Forces Act 1996, s.35(2), Sched. 7, Pt III.
The words in square brackets in subsection (1) were substituted by the Care Standards Act 2000, s.116, Sched. 4, para. 9(2).

DEFINITIONS
1–561   hospital: ss.55(5), 145(1).
hospital order: ss.37, 145(1).
restriction order: ss.41, 145(1).
registered establishment: ss.34(1), 145(1).

GENERAL NOTE
1–562   This section provides that a serviceman who has been ordered to be detained "during Her Majesty's pleasure" (*i.e.* indefinitely) may be directed by the Home Secretary to be detained in a hospital (but not a registered establishment). Such a direction has the same effect as a restriction order made with limit of time under section 41.

Subsection (1)
1–563   *Secretary of State:* See the General Note to this Part.

Subsection (3)
1–564   *Direction:* The patient may make an application to a Mental Health Review Tribunal within six months of the date of the direction (s.69(2)(b)).
Same effect as a hospital order: The patient will be subject to the consent to treatment provisions contained in Part IV of this Act.

Transfer to hospital of prisoners, etc.

Removal to hospital of persons serving sentences of imprisonment, etc.
1–565   **47.**—(1) If in the case of a person serving a sentence of imprisonment the Secretary of State is satisfied, by reports from at least two registered medical practitioners—

   (a) that the said person is suffering from mental illness, psychopathic disorder, severe mental impairment or mental impairment; and

   (b) that the mental disorder from which that person is suffering is of a nature or degree which makes it appropriate for him to be detained in a hospital for medical treatment and, in the case of psychopathic disorder or mental impairment, that such treatment is likely to alleviate or prevent a deterioration of his condition;

the Secretary of State may, if he is of the opinion having regard to the public interest and all the circumstances that it is expedient so to do, by warrant direct that that person be removed to and detained in such hospital [...] as may be specified in thé direction; and a direction under this section shall be known as "a transfer direction".

(2) A transfer direction shall cease to have effect at the expiration of the period of 14 days beginning with the date on which it is given unless within that period the person with respect to whom it was given has been received into the hospital specified in the direction.

(3) A transfer direction with respect to any person shall have the same effect as a hospital order made in his case.

(4) A transfer direction shall specify the form or forms of mental disorder referred to in paragraph (a) of subsection (1) above from which, upon the reports taken into account under that subsection, the patient is found by the Secretary of State to be suffering; and no such direction shall be given unless the patient is described in each of those reports as suffering from the same form of disorder, whether or not he is also described in either of them as suffering from another form.

(5) References in this Part of this Act to a person serving a sentence of imprisonment include references—

   (a) to a person detained in pursuance of any sentence or order for detention made by a court in criminal proceedings (other than an order under any enactment to which section 46 above applies);

   (b) to a person committed to custody under section 115(3) of the Magistrates' Courts Act 1980 (which relates to persons who fail to comply with an order to enter into recognisances to keep the peace or be of good behaviour); and

   (c) to a person committed by a court to a prison or other institution to which the Prison Act 1952 applies in default of payment of any sum adjudged to be paid on his conviction.

AMENDMENT

The words omitted from subsection (1) were repealed by the Crime (Sentences) Act 1997, s.56(2), Sched. 6.

DEFINITIONS

   psychopathic disorder: ss.1, 145(1).   **1–566**
   severe mental impairment: ss.1, 145(1).
   mental impairment: ss.1, 145(1).
   hospital: ss.55(5), 145(1).
   medical treatment: s.145(1).
   mental nursing home: s.145(1).
   hospital order: ss.37, 145(1).
   patient: s.145(1).

GENERAL NOTE

   This section enables the Home Secretary to direct that a person serving a sentence **1–567** of imprisonment or other detention be removed to and detained in a hospital. A direction made under this section (a "transfer direction") has the same effect as a hospital order made without restrictions under section 37 (a "notional section 37") (subs. (3)). A patient who has been made subject to a transfer direction can therefore be discharged at any time by his responsible medical officer or the hospital managers, can be transferred under the provisions of section 19, will be able to apply to a Mental

Health Review Tribunal and will be subject to the consent to treatment provisions contained in Part IV of this Act. The making of a transfer direction can result in the patient remaining in hospital under compulsory powers long after the day on which he would have been released from prison had such a direction not been made. When giving a transfer direction the Home Secretary may, and in most cases will, also impose the restrictions provided for under section 49 (so that the patient cannot be transferred to another hospital, sent on leave or discharged without his consent). In practice, the only occasion when a direction under section 49 (a "restriction direction") will not be made is if the prisoner is very close to his earliest date of release. The Home Secretary must make a restriction direction in respect of certain prisoners (s.49(1)). The following studies have examined the operation of this section: D. Hargreaves, "The transfer of severely mentally ill prisoners from HMP Wakefield: a descriptive study", (1997) 8 *Journal of Forensic Psychiatry* 62–73; P. Huckle, "A survey of sentenced prisoners transferred to hospital for urgent psychiatric treatment over a three year period in one region" (1997) 37 Med. Sci. Law, 37–40; and R. Huws *et al.*, "Prison transfers to special hospitals since the introduction of the Mental Health Act 1983" (1997) 8 Journal of Forensic Psychiatry 74–84. The legal powers that have been available in England and Wales to transfer sentenced prisoners to hospital under the Mental Health Acts of 1959 and 1983 are reviewed by A. Grounds in "Transfers of Sentenced Prisoners to Hospital" [1990] Crim.L.R. 544–551.

"In practice, where a prison medical officer considers that a person may require transfer to hospital they arrange for a doctor outside the prison service to provide a second opinion and complete the appropriate forms for submission to C3 Division in the Home Office. Negotiations for a hospital bed are usually initiated by the prison medical officer, if the second doctor reporting to the Home Office is not able to offer one. In cases of difficulty C3 Division assists in locating appropriate placements for prisoners requiring transfer to hospital. In any event it is C3 Division which exercises the Home Secretary's powers under the Act and determines the validity of the transfer request and the suitability of the hospital place offered in line with the need to ensure the protection of the public." (*Review of Health and Social Services for Mentally Disordered Offenders and others requiring similar services.* Vol. 2, para. 3.8.) The part of C3 Division which carries out the Home Secretary's responsibilities for mentally disordered offenders is now known as the "Mental Health Unit".

A person who is detained in hospital under this section will continue to qualify for early release days under the Crime (Sentencers) Act 1997, without reference to his behaviour (*ibid.*, s.22(2)). If the offender is detained in hospital on the date his sentence would otherwise expire, a release supervision order will come into effect (*ibid.* s.16) and he will be supervised by either a probation officer or a social worker of a local authority social services department (*ibid.* s.22(4)).

Under section 22(2)(b) of the Prison Act 1952, the Home Secretary may, if he is satisfied that a prisoner requires "medical investigation or observation or medical or surgical treatment of any description," direct the prisoner "to be taken to a hospital or other suitable place for the purpose of the investigation, observation or treatment".

Health Authorities and local social services authorities have a duty to provide after-care services for patients who cease to be liable to be detained and leave hospital after having been transferred by the Home Secretary under this section (s.117).

For the supervision in the community of a patient who has been transferred under this section and has been made the subject of a restriction direction under section 49, see the note on section 50(1)(b).

Subsection (1)

1–568   *Sentence of imprisonment:* See section 55(6) and subsection (5).
Secretary of State: See the General Note to this Part.

Is satisfied: In *R. v. Secretary of State for the Home Office, ex p. Gilkes*, January 21, 1999, Dyson J. said: "If the reports are manifestly unreliable, then the Secretary of State cannot reasonably be satisfied that [paragraphs (a) an (b) are satisfied] on the basis of the reports, and a decision to rely on them in such circumstances will be capable of successful challenge by judicial review. A medical report may be unreliable for a number of reasons. It may on its face not address the relevant statutory criteria. It may be based on an assessment which is so out of date that the mere fact of a lapse of time will be sufficient to render it unreliable. It may be unreliable to rely on a report based on an assessment conducted an appreciable, but not inordinate, time before the decision to transfer where the mental disorder is a fluctuating and unstable condition and/or where there has been a change of circumstances since the assessment was made. In each case, it will be for the Secretary of State to consider whether in his judgment the medical report is one on which he can safely and properly rely so as to be satisfied that the conditions set out in paragraphs (a) and (b) ... are met. One of the considerations that will be uppermost in his mind is whether the assessment on which the report is based is sufficiently recent to provide reliable evidence of the patient's current mental condition." In this case, Dyson J. further held that: (1) although it is incorrect to say that it can never be reasonable for the Secretary of State, when considering whether to make a transfer direction, to rely on a medical report made for the purposes of section 37, the Secretary of State should be slow to conclude that such a report can be safety relied on; and (2) it is not the case that it is only in exceptional cases that the Secretary of State can lawfully make a transfer direction close to the prisoner's release date.

Two registered medical practitioners: One of whom must be approved by the Secretary of State under section 12 (s.54(1)).

Appropriate for him to be detained ... for medical treatment: See the note on section 48(1).

The Secretary of State may: "The Secretary of State is never obliged to act under section 47, even if he thinks that the necessary preconditions are fulfilled" (*R. v. Secretary of State for the Home Department, ex p. K* [1990] 1 All E.R. 703, 716, *per* McCullough J. at 716).

Hospital: Including a registered establishment (ss.34(2), 55(5)).

Subsection (2)

14 days: After which "a fresh direction will be necessary if the patient has not been **1–569** admitted to the hospital or [registered establishment]" (*Memorandum*, para. 195).

Beginning with: Including the day on which the transfer direction is given (*Hare v. Gocher* [1962] 2 Q.B. 641).

Received into the hospital: The Butler Committee was informed that although there is no requirement under this section for the consent of the receiving hospital to be obtained, the Home Secretary observes the practice of seeking such consent before directing transfers from prison (para. 2.29). The procedure for effecting a transfer to hospital is set out in paragraph 194 of the *Memorandum*: "If transfer to a hospital is recommended, the Health Authority for the patient's home area will be sent copies of the medical reports and will be asked to say which hospital can admit the patient. In the case of a prisoner suffering from mental illness, this will be done by the prison medical officer at the same time as he sends the report to the Home Office; the Health Authority should notify both the Home Office and the prison which hospital will take the patient. In the case of prisoners suffering from other forms of mental disorder, the approach to the Health Authority will be made by the Home Office itself after preliminary consideration of the reports; the notification of the vacancy should be sent to the Home Office. On being informed that a vacancy is available, the Home Office will if satisfied that it is right to do so issue a transfer direction—*i.e.* a warrant directing the patient's transfer."

Subsection (3)

1–570   *Transfer direction:* The patient may make an application to a Mental Health Review Tribunal within six months of the date of the direction, once during the following six months, and at yearly intervals thereafter (s.69(2)(b)).

Same effect as a hospital order: The patient can therefore be discharged by his responsible medical officer or by the hospital managers (s.40(4)) and can continue to be detained in a hospital beyond the time set by the sentencing court for his release from prison.

Subsection (4)

1–571   *Suffering from:* See the note on section 37(2).

Subsection (5)

1–572   *Any sentence or order for detention made by a court in criminal proceedings:* These words are wide enough to cover detention during Her Majesty's pleasure (*R. v. Secretary of State for the Home Department, ex p. Hickey (No. 1)* [1995] 1 All E.R. 479, *per* Rose L.J. at 488).

Removal to hospital of other prisoners

1–573   **48.**—(1) If in the case of a person to whom this section applies the Secretary of State is satisfied by the same reports as are required for the purposes of section 47 above that that person is suffering from mental illness or severe mental impairment of a nature or degree which makes it appropriate for him to be detained in a hospital for medical treatment and that he is in urgent need of such treatment, the Secretary of State shall have the same power of giving a transfer direction in respect of him under that section as if he were serving a sentence of imprisonment.

(2) This section applies to the following persons, that is to say—

(a) persons detained in a prison or remand centre, not being persons serving a sentence of imprisonment or persons falling within the following paragraphs of this subsection;

(b) persons remanded in custody by a magistrates' court;

(c) civil prisoners, that is to say, persons committed by a court to prison for a limited term (including persons committed to prison in pursuance of a writ of attachment), who are not persons falling to be dealt with under section 47 above;

(d) persons detained under the Immigration Act 1971.

(3) Subsections (2) to (4) of section 47 above shall apply for the purposes of this section and of any transfer direction given by virtue of this section as they apply for the purposes of that section and of any transfer direction under that section.

DEFINITIONS

1–574   severe mental impairment: ss.1, 145(1).
hospital: ss.55(5), 145(1).
medical treatment: s.145(1).
transfer direction: ss.47, 145(1).
civil prisoner: s.55(1).

GENERAL NOTE

1–575   This section, which only applies to persons suffering from mental illness or severe mental impairment, empowers the Home Secretary to direct the removal from prison to hospital of certain categories of *unsentenced* prisoners. A person removed to hospital under this section is placed in the same position as a person who has been made the subject of a transfer direction under section 47: see the note on section 47(3). The use of this section is considered by R. Mackay and D. Machin in "Transfers from prison to hospital – the operation of section 48 of the Mental Health Act 1983", Home Office, 1998 and by the same authors in "The Operation of Section 48 of the Mental Health Act 1983", (2000) Brit.J.Criminol. 40: 727–745.

A transfer direction made in respect of persons coming within categories (a) or (b) of subsection (2) *must* be made subject to the restrictions provided for in section 49 (s.49(1)). The Home Secretary has a discretion to direct that persons coming within categories (c) or (d) be made subject to such restrictions.

"It is important for responsible medical officers to bear in mind that prisoners transferred to hospital under [this section] will, in most cases, not have been tried and convicted, and consequentially they should be returned to court as soon as possible. If the responsible medical officer believes the patient is not fit to return to court, there is provision under section 51(5) for the court to make a hospital order in the patient's absence and without convicting him" (*Restricted Patients Detained in Special Hospitals: Information for the Special Hospitals Service Authority*, Home Office, undated, para. 5.11).

L. Birmingham states that the "main disadvantage of section 48 as a diversion mechanism is that if for any reason the subject ceases to be a prisoner on remand (for example, is bailed or the case collapses) the powers conveyed under section 48 cease with immediate effect. If there is a real risk of his happening a concurrent civil order (section 3 of the MHA) can be imposed" ("Diversion from custody", (2001) Advances in Psychiatric Treatment, 7, 198–207).

Health Authorities and local social services authorities have a duty to provide after-care services for patients who have ceased to be liable to be detained and leave hospital after having been transferred under this section (s.117).

Section 22(1) of the Crime (Sentences) Act 1997 ensures that any time spent in hospital under this section before a sentence of imprisonment is passed may be subject to a direction under section 9 of that Act that the time count as part of the sentence, and that credit be given for any early release days which the offender might earn under section 13 of that Act.

Subsection (1)

Secretary of State: See the General Note to this Part.   **1–576**

Appropriate for him to be detained ... for medical treatment: But not for assessment. The Reed Committee said that "it is not always feasible for thorough assessments to be undertaken in prison: a hospital can usually offer greater flexibility and specialised expertise, especially in cases where diagnosis is problematic." (*Review of Health and Social Services for Mentally Disordered Offenders and others requiring similar services, Final Summary Report*, Cm. 2088, para. 9.6 v.) The Committee recommended that the ambit of this section be extended to people who required assessment and to people who suffer from any of the four specific forms of mental disorder defined in section 1(2) (para. 9.6 iv).

Urgent need of such treatment: The Home Office informed the *Butler Committee* that the procedure under this section is adopted only where a prisoner's condition is such that immediate removal to a hospital is necessary and that normally when he is well enough he is either produced at court from hospital or returned to prison to await trial (*ibid.*, para. 3.38). The Reed Committee was "concerned ... that the requirement under section 48 that the need for treatment should be 'urgent' is often interpreted narrowly". The Committee concluded that this section "should be applied where a doctor would recommend in-patient treatment if a person were seen as an out-patient in the community" (Final Summary Report, *supra*, para. 9.6 iv).

Transfer direction: Which will cease to have effect unless the prisoner is admitted to hospital within 14 days of it being given (s.47(2)).

Subsection (2)

1-577   *Paragraph (a):* Persons coming within this category, who will be awaiting trial or sentence in the Crown Court, are subject to the further provisions contained in section 51.

Paragraph (b): Persons coming within this category are subject to the further provisions contained in section 52.

Paragraphs (c) and (d): Persons coming within these categories are subject to the further provisions contained in section 53.

Subsection (3)

1-578   *Transfer direction given by virtue of this section:* The patient may make an application to a Mental Health Review Tribunal within six months of the date of the direction (s.69(2)(b)). Also note section 74(4).

Restriction on discharge of prisoners removed to hospital

1-579   **49.**—(1) Where a transfer direction is given in respect of any person, the Secretary of State, if he thinks fit, may by warrant further direct that that person shall be subject to the special restrictions set out in section 41 above; and where the Secretary of State gives a transfer direction in respect of any such person as is described in paragraph (a) or (b) of section 48(2) above, he shall also give a direction under this section applying those restrictions to him.

(2) A direction under this section shall have the same effect as a restriction order made under section 41 above and shall be known as "a restriction direction".

(3) While a person is subject to a restriction direction the responsible medical officer shall at such intervals (not exceeding one year) as the Secretary of State may direct examine and report to the Secretary of State on that person; and every report shall contain such particulars as the Secretary of State may require.

DEFINITIONS

1-580   transfer direction: ss.47, 145(1).
responsible medical officer: s.55(1).

GENERAL NOTE

1-581   This section provides that the Home Secretary may, and in respect of certain prisoners must, add an order restricting the patient's discharge from hospital (a "restriction direction") to a transfer direction made under section 47. The effect of a restriction direction is explained in the following passage from the judgment of the Court of Appeal in *R. v. Birch* (1989) 11 Cr.App.R.(S.) 202, 212: "If the transfer direction under section 47 is coupled with a restriction direction by the Home Secretary under section 49 (as in practice it usually is), the offender's position is in many ways the same as if he had been sent straight to hospital with order under sections 37 and 41, but the following special provisions apply: (1) Where the offender was sentenced to a fixed term of imprisonment, the restriction will automatically lift on the expiry of his sentence (allowing for remission): section 50(2). (2) Where the responsible medical officer or the [Mental Health] Review Tribunal concludes that the offender no longer requires treatment in hospital for mental disorder or that no effective treatment for his disorder can be given, the Secretary of State may: (a) release him on parole (if he is eligible), (b) return him to prison to serve out his sentence, or (c) take no action."

"In some cases . . . it is clear that on mental health grounds the patient should not be returned to prison as this would lead to a relapse, and that his return to the community should be from hospital. The Home Secretary's freedom of action is itself limited in these cases because of his duty to ensure the court's sentence is carried out. For this reason, prisoners who have been transferred to hospital are considered for rehabilitative leave in the community on a similar basis to those detained in prison" (Robert Baxter, "The mentally disordered offender in hospital: the role of the Home Office" in *The Mentally Disordered Offender* (ed. K. Herbst and J. Gunn) (1991), p. 135).

Section 47 of the Crime (Sentences) Act 1997 provides that where the Home Secretary makes an order under this section he has the power to order that the patient be admitted to and detained in a named hospital unit. A named hospital unit can be any part of a hospital which is treated as a separate unit. The effect of this power is considered in paragraph 11 of Home office Circular 52/1997 which is reproduced in the note on section 45A(3).

A patient who is subject to a restriction direction may apply to a Mental Health Review Tribunal within six months of the date of the direction, once during the following six months, and at yearly intervals thereafter (s.69(2)(b)).

For the supervision in the community of patients who have been transferred under section 47 together with a direction made under this section, see the note on section 50(1)(b).

Technical lifer
A "technical lifer" is a person who, although sentenced to life imprisonment **1–582** (whether discretionary or mandatory) will in certain circumstances be treated on his transfer to hospital as though he had originally been made the subject of a hospital order under section 37 of this Act in conjunction with a restriction order. In *R. v. Secretary of State for the Home Department, ex p. Pilditch* [1994] C.O.D. 352, Home Office policy relating to the granting of "technical lifer" status was identified in the Department's affidavit which stated:

> "Consideration is given to treating as a 'technical lifer' any transferred life sentence prisoner where it is clear that, even though he was suffering from a mental disorder, the court did not make a hospital order. In practice, 'technical lifer' status has been conferred by the Home Office where the court has not made a hospital order because:
> (a) of the unavailability of a suitable hospital bed;
> (b) of the unavailability of medical reports to the court;
> (c) reports which were prepared appear (in hindsight) not to have recorded accurately the patient's mental state at the time of the offence;
> (d) the offender, although mentally disordered, refused to allow a diminished responsibility defence and was as a result, convicted of murder (for which a life sentence is mandatory)."

In *R. v. Secretary of State for the Home Department, ex p. Williams*, June 21, 1994, the court referred to an affidavit sworn by a Home Office official which stated that in cases which are being considered for "technical lifer" status "the Home Office consults the trial Judge and the Lord Chief Justice to establish whether they consider that a hospital order would have been made had the Court been in a position to do so. If they consider "that a hospital order would have been made, the Home Secretary may then agree to confer 'technical lifer' status ... The effect of being classified as a 'technical lifer' is that the patient is treated, for the purposes of discharge, as though a hospital order under section 37 and a restriction order under section 41 of the 1983 Act had been made instead of the imposition of a sentence of imprisonment. He is treated with a view to rehabilitation and eventual release direct from hospital into the community. His case will not be referred to the Parole Board and he will not be released on life licence."

In *Williams* the court was informed that the Home Office has an equivalent system for determinate sentence prisoners: "... the Home Office does in fact recognise that there may be exceptional circumstances in which a determinate sentence prisoner should be rehabilitated through the hospital system and not returned to prison, even though his earliest date of release is someway ahead. This would be justifiable in cases where there was clear evidence that the sentencing Court did not dispose of the case by means of a hospital order for the kind of reason which influences the Home Office in conferring 'technical lifer' status on a transferred life sentence prisoner."

Subsection (1)

1–583　*Secretary of State:* See the General Note to this Part.

If he thinks fit: The Home Secretary is not bound by any statutory criteria when exercising his judgment under this provision.

May: In the majority of cases, when a sentenced prisoner is transferred to hospital a restriction direction is added by the Home Secretary (Cmnd. 7320, para. 5.40).

Subsection (2)

1–584　*Restriction direction:* For further provisions, see section 50. The Home Secretary does not have the power to make a time limited restriction direction.

Subsection (3)

Report: See the note on section 41(6).

Further provisions as to prisoners under sentence

1–585　**50.**—(1) Where a transfer direction and a restriction direction have been given in respect of a person serving a sentence of imprisonment and before the expiration of that person's sentence the Secretary of State is notified by the responsible medical officer, any other registered medical practitioner or a Mental Health Review Tribunal that that person no longer requires treatment in hospital for mental disorder or that no effective treatment for his disorder can be given in the hospital to which he has been removed, the Secretary of State may—

    (a)　by warrant direct that he be remitted to any prison or other institution in which he might have been detained if he had not been removed to hospital, there to be dealt with as if he had not been so removed; or

    (b)　exercise any power of releasing him on licence or discharging him under supervision which would have been exercisable if he had been remitted to such a prison or institution as aforesaid,

and on his arrival in the prison or other institution or, as the case may be, his release or discharge as aforesaid, the transfer direction and the restriction direction shall cease to have effect.

(2) A restriction direction in the case of a person serving a sentence of imprisonment shall cease to have effect on the expiration of the sentence.

(3) Subject to subsection (4) below, references in this section to the expiration of a person's sentence are references to the expiration of the period during which he would have been liable to be detained in a prison or other institution if the transfer direction had not been given [...].

[(3A) In applying subsection (3) above account shall be taken of any early release days awarded to the person under section 11 of the Crime (Sentences) Act 1997 (read with section 22 of that Act).]

(4) For the purposes of section 49(2) of the Prison Act 1952 (which provides for discounting from the sentences of certain prisoners periods while they are unlawfully at large) a patient who, having been transferred in

pursuance of a transfer direction from any such institution as is referred to in that section, is at large in circumstances in which he is liable to be taken into custody under any provision of this Act, shall be treated as unlawfully at large and absent from that institution.

[(5) The preceding provisions of this section shall have effect as if—

(a) the reference in subsection (1) to a transfer direction and a restriction direction having been given in respect of a person serving a sentence of imprisonment included a reference to a hospital direction and a limitation direction having been given in respect of a person sentenced to imprisonment;

(b) the reference in subsection (2) to a restriction direction included a reference to a limitation direction; and

(c) references in subsections (3) and (4) to a transfer direction included references to a hospital direction.]

AMENDMENTS

In subsection (3) the words omitted were repealed by the Criminal Justice Act 1991, s.101(2), Sched. 13.

Subsections (3A) and (5) were inserted by the Crime (Sentences) Act 1997, s.55, Sched. 4, para. 12(4)(5).

DEFINITIONS

transfer direction: ss.47, 145(1). **1–586**
restriction direction: ss.49, 145(1).
hospital: ss.55(5), 145(1).
mental disorder: ss.1, 145(1).
patient: s.145(1).
responsible medical officer: s.55(1).
hospital direction: s.145(1).
limitation direction: s.145(1).

GENERAL NOTE

This section provides that if the Home Secretary is informed that a patient who has **1–587** been placed on a restriction direction or a hospital and limitation direction no longer requires treatment he may either direct that the patient be returned to prison to serve the remainder of his sentence or release him from hospital on the same terms on which he could be released from prison. It also provides for a restriction direction or a hospital direction to cease to have effect on what would have been the patient's earliest date of release if he had remained in prison. Paragraph 197 of the *Memorandum* states:

> "Hospitals will be notified at the time of transfer of the date on which restrictions will expire. But if a patient has been absent without leave before that date the period of absence does not count towards the period of sentence. If any such patient is absent without leave for more than 24 hours, the hospital should inform the Home Office of the absence and when he returns to the hospital. The Home Office will then advise the hospital of the effect on the period of restriction."

If a patient subject to a restriction direction is in hospital when the restrictions cease to have effect, he will remain in hospital as a detained patient subject to a hospital order made under section 37 (s.41(5)).

The Home Secretary "also has the power, under section 42(2), on his own motion at any time, and under section 74(2), to authorise the Mental Health Review Tribunal to arrange for the discharge of a prisoner who has been transferred to a mental hospital" (*R. v. Secretary of State for the Home Department, ex p. Hickey* (*No. 1*) [1995] 1 All E.R. 479, 483, CA, *per* Rose L.J.).

Subsection (1)

1–588   *Transfer direction and a restriction direction:* See subsection (5)(a).

Serving a sentence of imprisonment: See section 55(6).

Expiration of that person's sentence: Taking into account remission (subs. (3)) and early release days (subs. (3A)) and adding periods of absence without leave from the hospital (subs. (4)). A prisoner's sentence continues to run during any period of transfer to a hospital (*Hickey*, above, at 484).

Secretary of State: See the General Note to this Part.

Notified by the responsible medical officer: The responsible medical officer should notify the Home Office at once in writing if he considers that a patient meets the criteria set out in this subsection: see the *Memorandum* at para. 198. The Home Secretary occasionally encounters difficulty in agreeing to responsible medical officers' requests for remission under this section or section 51 "where evidence about the patient's mental condition does not seem to support the psychiatrist's request" (*Review of Health and Social Services for Mentally Disordered Offenders and others requiring similar services*, Vol. 2, para. 3.18, HMSO, 1993).

May: Once the medical precondition is satisfied, the Home Secretary must either send the person back to prison, or he must release him under subsection (1)(b) (*Hickey*, above, at 485).

Paragraph (a)

1–589   Once a life sentenced patient no longer requires treatment in hospital, the normal course is for the Home Secretary to remit him to prison under this paragraph where he would be eligible for a Discretionary Life Panel or Parole Board hearing as appropriate in the normal manner.

Paragraph (b)

1–590   The Criminal Justice Act 1991 placed a statutory responsibility on the probation service to provide supervision in the community following the release of all prisoners sentenced to a term of imprisonment of 12 months or more and of all young offenders under the age of 22 sentenced to a term of imprisonment. The Home Office view is that such prisoners who are transferred to psychiatric hospital under section 47/49 of this Act during the course of their sentence fall to be supervised by the probation service if they are still in hospital on the date of their release, in the same way as if the person has been released from prison.

The licence under the Criminal Justice Act will be issued on the date restrictions cease, even if the person is to remain in hospital after that date. The probation service is also responsible for providing supervision to transferred life sentence prisoners: see Home Officer Probation Circular No. 90/1995.

In 1985, the Home Secretary made the following policy statement on life sentence prisoners in response to a Parliamentary Question by Mr John Wheeler M.P.:

"When life sentence prisoners transferred to hospital under the Mental Health Act 1983 are to be released, it has hitherto been the practice to discharge such persons on a warrant of conditional discharge under section 42(3) of the Act. I now intend to use the powers available to me under section 50(1)(b) of the Act, which enables me to release such persons under the same arrangements as those they would have been subject to had they remained in, or been returned to, prison. This means that, in future, such persons will normally be released on life licences under the provisions of section 61 of the Criminal Justice Act 1967 [now see section 34 of the Criminal Justice Act 1991] in accordance with the sentencing Courts' intention, *i.e.* on the recommendation of the Parole Board and after consultation with the Lord Chief

Justice and, if available, the trial judge. In exceptional cases, where the Lord Chief Justice and the trial judge so recommend, I will be prepared to consider whether it would be more appropriate to authorise discharge under section 42(2) of the 1983 Act.

Under the new procedure, a life sentence prisoner who has been transferred to hospital, can be released on life licence without having to return to prison before release. Persons released on life licence under these arrangements will be subject to recall to prison under the provisions of section 62 of the 1967 Act [now see section 39 of the Criminal Justice Act 1991]. Should their mental condition be such that they are recommended for transfer to hospital this could very quickly be effected under the provisions of section 47 of the 1983 Act."

This policy was challenged in *R. v. Secretary of State for the Home Department, ex p. Stroud* [1993] C.O.D. 75. The applicant stated that a life prisoner released from prison on licence under section 61 of the Criminal Justice Act 1967 remains subject to supervision for the rest of his life whereas release under section 42(2) or 74(2) of this Act allowed for the possibility of an eventual absolute discharge either by the Home Secretary or by a Mental Health Review Tribunal. He contended that the normal rule of practice set out in the policy statement deprived life sentence prisoners of the potential benefit of absolute discharge and thus the Home Secretary had fettered his discretion unlawfully. Henry J. held, in refusing the application for judicial review, that there was no illegality in the policy which had been adopted for legitimate reasons to ensure consistency of treatment between all those sentenced to life imprisonment. *Stroud* is analysed by Michael Gunn at (1993) *Journal of Forensic Psychiatry*, Vol. 4, No. 2, pp. 330–334.

In *R. v. Secretary of State for the Home Department, ex p. Hickey (No. 1)* [1995] 1 All E.R. 479, the principal question before the Court of Appeal was whether a prisoner sentenced either to a discretionary life term or to be detained during Her Majesty's pleasure, transferred subsequently to a hospital by the Home Secretary under sections 47 and 49 of this Act, and who has served the tariff part of his sentence, can require the Home Secretary so to act that his case is considered by the Parole Board in accordance with the Criminal Justice Act 1991, notwithstanding that he is still in hospital needing, and receiving, treatment. The court held that a person who had been made the subject of such a transfer was governed by the regime laid down in this Act and had no right to have his case referred to the Parole Board under the release provisions of the 1991 Act.

Discretionary and mandatory life prisoners who have been transferred to hospital under this Act, and whom it is not appropriate to remit to prison even though they no longer require, or can effectively be given, hospital treatment will be referred by the Home Secretary to the Parole Board under section 34 of the 1991 Act, while they remain in hospital, in the same way as if they had been remitted to prison (245 HC Official Report (6th series) written answers, col. 9, 20 June 1994 and *Hickey*, above, at 485, 486).

Although the Home Secretary will consider all requests put to him by the responsible medical officer to discharge life sentenced patients direct from hospital under this paragraph, he has a discretion to act on these requests. However, where a Mental Health Review Tribunal notifies the Home Secretary that the conditions of paragraphs (a) and (b) of section 74 of the Act are satisfied, then he would, if the person had passed tariff, refer the case to the Discretionary Life Panel or Parole Board whilst the person remained in hospital even if he did not agree with the tribunal's recommendation (letter from the Home Office to responsible medical officers in Special Hospitals and R.S.U.s, dated March 14, 1995. Also see Elizabeth Sadler, "Life-sentenced prisoners transferred to hospital" (1995) *Journal of Forensic Psychiatry*, Vol. 6, No. 3, 577–580) and the note on "technical lifer" in the General Note to section 49.

Subsection (2)
   Restriction direction: See subsection (5)(b).   **1–591**

Subsections (3)(4)

1–592   *Transfer direction:* See subsection (5)(c).

Further provisions as to detained persons

1–593   **51.**—(1) This section has effect where a transfer direction has been given in respect of any such person as is described in paragraph (a) of section 48(2) above and that person is in this section referred to as "the detainee".

(2) The transfer direction shall cease to have effect when the detainee's case is disposed of by the court having jurisdiction to try or otherwise deal with him, but without prejudice to any power of that court to make a hospital order or other order under this Part of this Act in his case.

(3) If the Secretary of State is notified by the responsible medical officer, any other registered medical practitioner or a Mental Health Review Tribunal at any time before the detainee's case is disposed of by that court—

    (a) that the detainee no longer requires treatment in hospital for mental disorder; or

    (b) that no effective treatment for his disorder can be given at the hospital to which he has been removed,

the Secretary of State may by warrant direct that he be remitted to any place where he might have been detained if he had not been removed to hospital, there to be dealt with as if he had not been so removed, and on his arrival at the place to which he is so remitted the transfer direction shall cease to have effect.

(4) If (no direction having been given under subsection (3) above) the court having jurisdiction to try or otherwise deal with the detainee is satisfied on the written or oral evidence of the responsible medical officer—

    (a) that the detainee no longer requires treatment in hospital for mental disorder; or

    (b) that no effective treatment for his disorder can be given at the hospital to which he has been removed,

the court may order him to be remitted to any such place as is mentioned in subsection (3) above or[, subject to section 25 of the Criminal Justice and Public Order Act 1994,] released on bail and on his arrival at that place or, as the case may be, his release on bail the transfer direction shall cease to have effect.

(5) If (no direction or order having been given or made under subsection (3) or (4) above) it appears to the court having jurisdiction to try or otherwise deal with the detainee—

    (a) that it is impracticable or inappropriate to bring the detainee before the court; and

    (b) that the conditions set out in subsection (6) below are satisfied,

the court may make a hospital order (with or without a restriction order) in his case in his absence and, in the case of a person awaiting trial, without convicting him.

(6) A hospital order may be made in respect of a person under subsection (5) above if the court—

    (a) is satisfied, on the written or oral evidence of at least two registered medical practitioners, that the detainee is suffering from mental illness or severe mental impairment of a nature or degree which makes it appropriate for the patient to be detained in a hospital for medical treatment; and

(b) is of the opinion, after considering any depositions or other documents required to be sent to the proper officer of the court, that it is proper to make such an order.

(7) Where a person committed to the Crown Court to be dealt with under section 43 above is admitted to a hospital in pursuance of an order under section 44 above, subsections (5) and (6) above shall apply as if he were a person subject to a transfer direction.

AMENDMENT

In subs. (4) the words in square brackets were inserted by the Criminal Justice and Public Order Act 1994, s.168(2), Sched. 10, para. 51.

DEFINITIONS

transfer direction: ss.47, 145(1).　　　　　　　　　　　　　　　　　**1–594**
hospital order: ss.37, 145(1).
responsible medical officer: s.55(1).
hospital: ss.55(5), 145(1).
mental disorder: ss.1, 145(1).
restriction order: ss.41, 145(1).
severe mental impairment: ss.1, 145(1).
medical treatment: s.145(1).

GENERAL NOTE

This section provides that a transfer direction made in respect of a person detained **1–595** in a prison or remand centre shall cease to have effect when the case has been finally dealt with by the appropriate court (subs. (2)). The linked restriction direction will also cease to have effect at that time. In the meanwhile the Home Secretary has power to direct the patient's return to prison (subs. (3)). If the Home Secretary does not exercise this power the court can, on receiving the requisite evidence, either order the patient to be returned to prison or released on bail (subs. (4)). The transfer direction will cease to have effect if the Home Secretary or court exercise their powers under subsections (3) and (4). If the patient has not been sent back to prison or released on bail the court can make a hospital order in respect of a mentally ill or severely mentally impaired patient in his absence and without convicting him (subss. (5), (6)).

The Human Rights Act 1998

The power of the court under subsections (5) and (6) to make a hospital order in **1–596** the absence of a conviction or a finding that the person concerned "did the act or made the omission charged" (as required by, for example, s.37(3)), would appear to be a breach of Article 6 of the European Convention on Human Rights in that the court has passed sentence in the absence of a trial.

Subsection (3)

Secretary of State: See the General Note to this Part.　　　　　　　　**1–597**
Notified by the responsible medical officer: See the note on section 50(1).

Subsection (4)

Written or oral evidence: For general requirements as to medical evidence, see **1–598** section 54.

Subsection (5)

1–599 *Hospital order (with or without a restriction order):* A judge, prior to the imposition of a restriction order under section 41, following the making of a hospital order under this provision, is not obliged to resolve any factual dispute between the Crown case and the defence case before he makes a finding that the "serious harm" criterion in section 41(1) is satisfied (*R. v. Kingston Crown Court, ex p. Mason*, July 27, 1998, CA). *Per* Rose L.J.: "In my judgment, it was not incumbent on the judge, in the absence of the applicant [who could not be tried because of his aversion to women], to embark on an elaborate fact finding exercise: the outcome was inevitable …."

Subsection (6)

1–600 *Two registered medical practitioners:* One of whom must be approved by the Secretary of State under section 12 (s.54(1)).

Further provisions as to persons remanded by magistrates' courts

1–601 **52.**—(1) This section has effect where a transfer direction has been given in respect of any such person as is described in paragraph (b) of section 48(2) above; and that person is in this section referred to as "the accused".

(2) Subject to subsection (5) below, the transfer direction shall cease to have effect on the expiration of the period of remand unless the accused is committed in custody to the Crown Court for trial or to be otherwise dealt with.

(3) Subject to subsection (4) below, the power of further remanding the accused under section 128 of the Magistrates' Courts Act 1980 may be exercised by the court without his being brought before the court; and if the court further remands the accused in custody (whether or not he is brought before the court) the period of remand shall, for the purposes of this section, be deemed not to have expired.

(4) The court shall not under subsection (3) above further remand the accused in his absence unless he has appeared before the court within the previous six months.

(5) If the magistrates' court is satisfied, on the written or oral evidence of the responsible medical officer—

(a) that the accused no longer requires treatment in hospital for mental disorder; or

(b) that no effective treatment for his disorder can be given in the hospital to which he has been removed,

the court may direct that the transfer direction shall cease to have effect notwithstanding that the period of remand has not expired or that the accused is committed to the Crown Court as mentioned in subsection (2) above.

(6) If the accused is committed to the Crown Court as mentioned in subsection (2) above and the transfer direction has not ceased to have effect under subsection (5) above, section 51 above shall apply as if the transfer direction given in his case were a direction given in respect of a person falling within that section.

(7) The magistrates' court may, in the absence of the accused, inquire as examining justices into an offence alleged to have been committed by him and commit him for trial in accordance with section 6 of the Magistrates' Courts Act 1980 if—

(a) the court is satisfied, on the written or oral evidence of the responsible medical officer, that the accused is unfit to take part in the proceedings; and

(b) where the court proceeds under subsection (1) of that section, the accused is represented by counsel or a solicitor.

DEFINITIONS

transfer direction: ss.47, 145(1).　　　　　　　　　　　　　　　　　　　1–602

responsible medical officer: s.55(1).

hospital: ss.55(5), 145(1).

mental disorder: ss.1, 145(1).

GENERAL NOTE

This section provides that a transfer direction made in respect of a person who has **1–603**
been remanded in custody by a magistrates' court ceases to have effect at the
expiration of the period of remand unless the accused is then committed in custody to
the Crown Court (subs. (2)). However, if the magistrates' court further remands the
accused under subsection (3) the direction will not expire. Alternatively, if the court
is satisfied, on receiving the requisite evidence, that the accused no longer requires
treatment in hospital it may direct that the transfer direction shall cease to have effect
(subs. (5)). The court also has power to conduct committal proceedings in the
absence of the accused if it is satisfied that he is unfit to take part in the proceedings
(subs. (7)).

Subsection (4)

Months: Means calendar months (Interpretation Act, s.5, Sched. 1).　　　**1–604**

Subsection (5)

Written or oral evidence: See section 54.　　　　　　　　　　　　　　**1–605**

Further provisions as to civil prisoners and persons detained under the Immigration Act 1971

53.—(1) Subject to subsection (2) below, a transfer direction given in **1–606**
respect of any such person as is described in paragraph (c) or (d) of section
48(2) above shall cease to have effect on the expiration of the period during
which he would, but for his removal to hospital, be liable to be detained in
the place from which he was removed.

(2) Where a transfer direction and a restriction direction have been given
in respect of any such person as is mentioned in subsection (1) above, then, if
the Secretary of State is notified by the responsible medical officer, any other
registered medical practitioner or a Mental Health Review Tribunal at any
time before the expiration of the period there mentioned—

(a) that that person no longer requires treatment in hospital for mental
disorder; or

(b) that no effective treatment for his disorder can be given in the hospital
to which he has been removed,

the Secretary of State may by warrant direct that he be remitted to any place
where he might have been detained if he had not been removed to hospital,
and on his arrival at the place to which he is so remitted the transfer direction
and the restriction direction shall cease to have effect.

DEFINITIONS

transfer direction: ss.47, 145(1).　　　　　　　　　　　　　　　　　　　**1–607**

hospital: ss.55(5), 145(1).

restriction direction: ss.49, 145(1).
responsible medical officer: s.55(1).
mental disorder: ss.1, 145(1).

GENERAL NOTE

1–608   This section provides that a transfer direction made in respect of a civil prisoner or a person detained under the Immigration Act 1971 ceases to have effect on the expiration of the period of detention that would have occurred had the removal to hospital not taken place (subs. (1)). Where a transfer direction *and* a restriction direction have been made the Home Secretary has power to direct that the patient be returned to prison, and on his arrival there both the transfer direction and the restriction direction shall cease to have effect (subs. (2)).

Subsection (2)

1–609   *Secretary of State:* See the General Note to this Part.

Supplemental

Requirements as to medical evidence

1–610   **54.**—(1) The registered medical practitioner whose evidence is taken into account under section 35(3)(a) above and at least one of the registered medical practitioners whose evidence is taken into account under sections 36(1), 37(2)(a), 38(1)[, 45A(2)] and 51(6)(a) above and whose reports are taken into account under sections 47(1) and 48(1) above shall be a practitioner approved for the purposes of section 12 above by the Secretary of State as having special experience in the diagnosis or treatment of mental disorder.

(2) For the purposes of any provision of this Part of this Act under which a court may act on the written evidence of—

(a) a registered medical practitioner or a registered medical practitioner of any description; or

(b) a person representing the managers of a hospital,

a report in writing purporting to be signed by a registered medical practitioner or a registered medical practitioner of such a description or by a person representing the managers of a hospital may, subject to the provisions of this section, be received in evidence without proof of the signature of the practitioner or that person and without proof that he has the requisite qualifications or authority or is of the requisite description; but the court may require the signatory of any such report to be called to give oral evidence.

(3) Where, in pursuance of a direction of the court, any such report is tendered in evidence otherwise than by or on behalf of the person who is the subject of the report, then—

(a) if that person is represented by counsel or a solicitor, a copy of the report shall be given to his counsel or solicitor;

(b) if that person is not so represented, the substance of the report shall be disclosed to him or, where he is a child or young person, to his parent or guardian if present in court; and

(c) except where the report relates only to arrangements for his admission to a hospital, that person may require the signatory of the report to be called to give oral evidence, and evidence to rebut the evidence contained in the report may be called by or on behalf of that person.

AMENDMENT
In subs. (1) the figure in square brackets was inserted by the Crime (Sentences) Act 1997, s.55, Sched. 4, para. 12(6).

DEFINITIONS
mental disorder: ss.1, 145(1).   **1–611**
the managers: s.145(1).
hospital: ss.55(5), 145(1).
child: s.55(1).
young person: s.55(1).
guardian: s.55(1).

GENERAL NOTE
This section specifies when medical evidence must be given by a doctor who has **1–612**
been approved by the Secretary of State under section 12, and provides for the circumstances when written evidence by a doctor or a person representing the managers of a hospital may be accepted by a court.
"Medical reports should normally be submitted in writing to the court in advance of the hearing, and the doctors should be prepared to give oral evidence if required. They maybe asked to do so at comparatively short notice, especially in the Crown Court" (*Memorandum*, para. 171).

Subsection (1)
The general requirement relating to civil admissions under Pt II of this Act that the **1–613**
two doctors making medical recommendations cannot be on the staff of the same hospital (s.12(3)) and the prohibition on a recommending doctor having a financial interest in the hospital that will be treating the patient (s.12(5)(d)) do not apply to medical recommendations made under this Part.
Approved ... by the Secretary of State: Or by the National Assembly for Wales (S.I. 2000 No. 253, Sched. 3).

Subsection (3)
This subsection has been enacted because medical reports "may contain facts or **1–614**
comments which might cause distress not only to the accused but also to his relatives. If the accused wishes, however, he may insist that the medical practitioner should give oral evidence, and he may then call evidence in rebuttal" (Home Office Circular No. 69/1983, para. 44).

[Reduction of period for making hospital orders
54A.—(1) The Secretary of State may by order reduce the length of the **1–615**
periods mentioned in sections 37(4) and (5) and 38(4) above.
(2) An order under subsection (1) above may make such consequential amendments of sections 40(1) and 44(3) above as appear to the Secretary of State to be necessary or expedient.]

AMENDMENT
This section was inserted by the Criminal Justice Act 1991, s.27(2).

GENERAL NOTE
This section enables the Secretary of State to reduce, by statutory instrument, the **1–616**
time periods for the admission of mentally disordered offenders to hospital.

Secretary of State: See the General Note to this Part.

Interpretation of Part III
1–617   **55.**—(1) In this Part of this Act—
"child" and "young person" have the same meaning as in the Children
and Young Persons Act 1933;
"civil prisoner" has the meaning given to it by section 48(2)(c) above;
"guardian", in relation to a child or young person, has the same meaning
as in the Children and Young Persons Act 1933;
"place of safety", in relation to a person who is not a child or young
person, means any police station, prison or remand centre, or any
hospital the managers of which are willing temporarily to receive
him, and in relation to a child or young person has the same
meaning as in the Children and Young Persons Act 1933;
"responsible medical officer", in relation to a person liable to be
detained in a hospital within the meaning of Part II of this Act,
means the registered medical practitioner in charge of the treatment of the patient.

(2) Any reference in this Part of this Act to an offence punishable on
summary conviction with imprisonment shall be construed without regard to
any prohibition or restriction imposed by or under any enactment relating to
the imprisonment of young offenders.

(3) Where a patient who is liable to be detained in a hospital in pursuance
of an order or direction under this Part of this Act is treated by virtue of any
provision of this part of this Act as if he had been admitted to the hospital in
pursuance of a subsequent order or direction under this Part of this Act or a
subsequent application for admission for treatment under Part II of this Act,
he shall be treated as if the subsequent order, direction or application had
described him as suffering from the form or forms of mental disorder
specified in the earlier order by direction or, where he is treated as if he had
been so admitted by virtue of a direction under section 42(1) above, such
form of mental disorder as may be specified in the direction under that
section.

(4) Any reference to a hospital order, a guardianship order or a restriction
order in section 40(2), (4) or (5), section 41(3) to (5), or section 42 above or
section 69(1) below shall be construed as including a reference to any order
or direction under this Part of this Act having the same effect as the
first-mentioned order; and the exceptions and modifications set out in
Schedule 1 to this Act in respect of the provisions of this Act described in
that Schedule accordingly include those which are consequential on the
provisions of this subsection.

(5) Section 34(2) above shall apply for the purposes of this Part of this Act
as it applies for the purposes of Part II of this Act.

(6) References in this Part of this Act to persons serving a sentence of
imprisonment shall be construed in accordance with section 47(5) above.

(7) Section 99 of the Children and Young Persons Act 1933 (which relates
to the presumption and determination of age) shall apply for the purposes of
this Part of this Act as it applies for the purposes of that Act.

DEFINITIONS

    hospital: s.145(1).   **1–618**

    the managers: s.145(1).

    patient: s.145(1).

    application for admission for treatment: ss.3, 145(1).

    mental disorder: ss.1, 145(1).

    hospital order: ss.37, 145(1).

    guardianship order: ss.37, 145(1).

    restriction order: ss.41, 145(1).

Subsection (1)

Under section 107(1) of the Children and Young Persons Act 1933, "child" means **1–619** a person under the age of 14 years, "young person" means a person who has attained the age of 14 years and is under the age of 17 years, "guardian," in relation to a child or young person, includes any person who, in the opinion of the relevant court, has for the time being the care of the child or young person, and "place of safety" means a community home provided by a local authority or a controlled community home, any police station, or any hospital, surgery, or any other suitable place, the occupier of which is willing temporarily to receive a child or young person.

Medical practitioner in charge of the treatment of the patient: See the note on section 34(1).

Subsection (4)

Having the same effect: An interim hospital order made under section 38 does not **1–620** have the same effect as a hospital order made under section 37. There are fundamental differences between the two orders: see the note on section 40(3).

PART IV

CONSENT TO TREATMENT

GENERAL NOTE

The extent to which the 1959 Act gave authority to the responsible medical officer **1–621** to treat a detained patient without his consent was unclear. The opinion of the Department of Health and Social Security was that where the purpose of detention was treatment, the Act gave implied authority for treatment to be imposed. During the 1970s the correctness of this opinion was questioned by a number of commentators: see paragraphs 3.57 to 3.59 of the *Butler Committee* and chapter 11 of Phil Fennell's *Treatment Without Consent: Law Psychiatry and the Treatment of Mentally Disordered People since 1895* (1996).

The purpose of this Part is to clarify the extent to which treatment for mental disorder can be imposed on detained patients. Where this Part applies its provisions override the common law. It provides for two categories of treatment which have different legal consequences. They are: (1) the most serious treatments which require the patient's consent *and* a second opinion (s.57); and (2) other serious treatments which require the patient's consent *or* a second opinion (s.58). Treatments that do not come within either of these categories can be imposed on a detained patient who understands the nature and purpose of the treatment, but expressly withholds consent (s.63). The safeguards provided for by sections 57 and 58 can be overridden if the treatment is required urgently (s.62). Guidance on the provisions contained in this Part is contained in chapter 16 of the *Code of Practice.* The Mental Health Act Commission has issued guidance which has been issued as DHSS Circular No. DDL (84)4. The Commission has also provided "Advice to Second Opinion Appointed Doctors" (1999).

The "sectioning" of compliant mentally incapable patients

1–622   There appears to be a widespread practice of making applications to detain patients who require medical treatment for their mental disorder despite the fact that such patients are both mentally incapable and compliant, in that they are not exhibiting dissent to being in hospital at the time when the application is made. In particular, it is felt that a compliant mentally ill patient who needs to be given ECT as a treatment for depression must be detained under this Act before the treatment can be given, even though the effect of the depression has been to render the patient mentally incapable. As the provision of medical treatment to a mentally incapable patient, using force if necessary (*Re MB (Medical Treatment)* 2 F.L.R. 426), is authorised under the common law if the treatment is considered to be in the patient's best interests (see the note on "The treatment of incapable patients", below), the sectioning of the patient for the purpose of providing "authority" for medical treatment for his mental disorder to be given is unnecessary. Such action is also almost certainly unlawful because the "sectioning" of a compliant incapable patient would not be "warranted" for the purposes of section 2 (see s.2(2)(a)) and it would not be possible to satisfy the requirement in section 3 that the treatment "cannot be provided" unless the patient is detained under that section (see s.3(2)(c)). It would also not be possible for an approved social worker to claim under section 13(1) that it was "necessary and proper" for an application to be made as it is neither necessary nor legally proper to make an application in respect of a patient who is not attempting to leave the hospital and whose medical treatment is authorised under common law. The detention of a compliant mentally incapable informal patient is authorised under the common law doctrine of necessity: see *R. v. Bournewood Community and Mental Health NHS Trust, ex p. L* [1998] 3 All E.R. 289, HL which is considered in the General Note to section 131. In *Bournewood,* Lord Steyn said, at 308: "The general effect of the decision of the House is to leave compliant patients without the safeguards enshrined in the 1983 Act. This is an unfortunate result."

The Common Law

1–623   If the patient comes within the scope of section 56, the scheme set out in this Part overrides the common law in respect of treatments given for the patient's mental disorder. As treatments given for physical disorders, and treatments given for mental disorders to patients who do not come within the scope of section 56 are governed by the common law, an account of common law rules is given below. Common law rules are also considered in chapter 15 of the *Code of Practice.*

Medical treatment under common law—an overview

1–624   General propositions relating to medical treatment under common law can be found in the judgments of Lord Donaldson M.R. in *Re T (Adult: Refusal of Medical Treatment)* [1992] 4 All E.R. 649, CA and Butler-Sloss L.J. in *Re M.B. (Medical Treatment)* [1997] 2 F.L.R. 426, CA. They are:

1. It is a criminal and tortious assault to perform physically invasive medical treatment, however minimal the invasion might be, without the patient's consent if the patient has the capacity to decide.
2. Prima facie every adult has the right and capacity to decide whether or not he will accept medical treatment, even if a refusal may risk permanent injury to his health or even lead to premature death (or to the death or injury to the child that a woman bears). Furthermore, it matters not whether the reasons for the refusal were rational or irrational, unknown or even non-existent. This is so notwithstanding the very strong public interest in preserving the life and health of all citizens. However the presumption of capacity to decide, which stems from the fact that the patient is an adult, is rebuttable.

3. Irrationality is here used to connote a decision which is so outrageous in its defiance of logic or of accepted moral standards that no sensible person who had applied his mind to the question to be decided could have arrived at it. It might be otherwise if a decision is based on a misperception of reality (*e.g.* the blood is poisoned because it is red). Such a misperception will be more readily accepted to be a disorder of the mind. Although it might be thought that irrationality sits uneasily with competence to decide, panic, indecisiveness and irrationality in themselves do not as such amount to incompetence, but they may be symptoms or evidence of incompetence. The graver the consequences of the decision, the commensurately greater the level of competence is required to take the decision.

4. A person lacks capacity if some impairment or disturbance of mental functioning renders the person unable to make a decision whether or not to consent to or refuse treatment. This can occur by reason of long-term mental incapacity or retarded development or by temporary factors such as unconsciousness or confusion or the effects of fatigue, shock, pain or drugs. Those concerned must be satisfied that such temporary factors are operating to such a degree that the ability to decide is absent. Another such influence may be panic induced by fear. Again, careful scrutiny of the evidence is necessary because fear of an operation may be a rational reason for refusal to undergo it. Fear may also, however, paralyse the will and thus destroy the capacity to make a decision. (For a further consideration of capacity, see below.)

5. If an adult patient did not have the capacity to decide at the time of the purported refusal and still does not have that capacity, it is the duty of the doctors to treat him in whatever way they consider, in the exercise of their clinical judgment, to be in his best interests.

6. Doctors faced with a refusal of consent have to give very careful and detailed consideration to what was the patient's capacity to decide at the time when the decision was made. It may not be a case of capacity or no capacity. It may be a case of reduced capacity. What matters is whether at that time the patient's capacity was reduced below the level needed in the case of a refusal of that importance, for refusals can vary in importance. Some may involve a risk to life or of irreparable damage to health. Others may not.

7. In some cases doctors will not only have to consider the capacity of the patient to refuse treatment, but also whether the refusal has been vitiated because it resulted not from the patient's will, but from the will of others. It matters not that those others sought, however strongly, to persuade the patient to refuse, so long as in the end the refusal represented the patient's independent decision. If, however, his will was overborne, the refusal will not have represented a true decision. In this context the relationship of the persuader to the patient—for example, spouse, parents or religious adviser—will be important, because some relationships more readily lend themselves to overbearing the patient's independent will than do others.

8. In all cases doctors will need to consider what is the true scope and basis of the refusal. Was it intended to apply in the circumstances which have arisen? Was it based upon assumptions which in the event have not been realised? A refusal is only effective within its true scope and is vitiated if it is based upon false assumptions.

9. A refusal can take the form of a declaration of intention never to consent in the future or never to consent in some future circumstances (This proposition was identified by Thorpe J. in *Re C* (*Adult: Refusal of Medical Treatment*) [1994] 1 All E.R. 819; see further, the note on Advance Directives, below).

10. In cases of doubt as to the effect of a purported refusal of treatment, where failure to treat threatens the patient's life or threatens irreparable damage to

his health, doctors and health authorities should not hesitate to apply to the courts for assistance. The practice to be followed when it is necessary to seek declarations from the courts is set out in *St George's Healthcare NHS Trust v. S* [1998] 3 All E.R. 673, CA, at 702. Courts have a discretion to grant interim declarations (CPR, r. 25.1(b)). In extreme emergencies where there is no time to seek the assistance of the court, any doubt that may exist about the patient's capacity must be resolved in favour of society's interest in upholding the concept that all human life is sacred and that it should be preserved if at all possible.

The Department of Health has produced a *Reference Guide to Consent for Examination or Treatment* (2001) which provides guidance on English law concerning consent to physical interventions on patients.

Capacity

1–625   Central to the propositions noted above is the issue of whether the patient has the capacity to decide whether or not he will accept medical treatment. The fact that a patient has been detained under this Act does not, of itself, rebut the presumption of capacity. The test of capacity was considered in *Re C*, above, where C, a Broadmoor patient with paranoid schizophrenia, sought court recognition of his capacity to refuse amputation of a gangrenous foot which was said to be life threatening. Thorpe J. held that "the question to be decided is whether it had been established that C's capacity is so reduced by his chronic mental illness that he does not sufficiently understand the nature, purpose and effects of the proffered amputation". The answer to this question depended upon whether C had been able to follow the decision making process of: "first, comprehending and retaining treatment information, second, believing it and, third, weighing it in the balance to arrive at choice". Applying this test Thorpe J. held that he was "completely satisfied that the presumption that C has the right of self-determination has not been displaced". Although C's general capacity had been impaired by schizophrenia, his Lordship was satisfied that C "has understood and retained the relevant treatment information, that in his own way he believes it, and that in the same fashion he has arrived at a clear choice". The decision-making process identified by Thorpe J. was affirmed by the Court of Appeal in *Re M.B. (Medical Treatment)*, above, where the court said, in relation to the first element of the process, that the information about treatment provided to the patient should focus on the likely consequences of having or not having the treatment in question, and that, in relation to the third element, if a compulsive disorder or phobia from which the patient suffers stifles belief in the information presented to her, then the decision may not be a true one. In this case the Court of Appeal held that the patient's extreme needle phobia rendered her temporarily incompetent.

In *B v. Croydon District Health Authority* (1994) 22 B.M.L.R. 13. Thorpe J. returned to the second element of the decision making process that he had identified in *Re C*. He said, at 20, that there is a difference between outright disbelief (due to mental disorder) which meant being "impervious to reason, divorced from reality, or incapable of adjustment after reflection", and "the tendency which most people have when undergoing medical treatment to self assess and then puzzle over the divergence between medical and self assessment". As Phil Fennell has said, the requirement to believe the treatment information "does not mean that, in order to be capable, the patient must accept the medical evaluation of having the treatment or not having it and of the trade-off between risks and benefits" (*Treatment Without Consent*, 1996, p. 257).

The *Croydon* case was concerned with whether a twenty-four year old detained patient suffering from a borderline personality disorder who had stopped eating should be force fed. Although Thorpe J. found B to be mentally capable, Hoffmann L.J., at the Court of Appeal, said that he found it hard to accept that "someone who acknowledges that in refusing food at the critical time she did not appreciate the extent to which she was hazarding her life, was crying out inside for help but unable to break out of the routine of punishing herself, could be said to be capable of making a true choice as to whether to eat" ([1995] 1 All E.R. 683, at 689).

When reaching a decision about a patient's capacity the doctor should consider whether the patient has a capacity which is commensurate with the gravity of the decision which he is purporting to make. The more serious the decision, the greater the capacity required: see proposition 6 noted above. If the doctor concludes that the patient has capacity and that patient is refusing a particular treatment, the doctor is not only entitled to withhold treatment, he is bound to respect the patient's wishes. In these circumstances, a declaration that it is lawful for the doctor to abide by the patient's refusal is unnecessary (*Re J.T. (Adult: Refusal of Medical Treatment)* [1998] 1 F.L.R. 48, Wall J.).

The standard to be used when deciding whether adequate information has been given to a patient was decided by the House of Lords in *Sidaway v. Bethlam Royal Hospital Governors* [1985] 1 All E.R. 643, which is considered in the note on section 57(2) under the heading "consented to it".

It has been noted that competency is rarely questioned when a patient consents to treatment (B. Hoffman and J. Srinivasan (1992) "A study of competence to consent to treatment in a psychiatric hospital", *Canadian Journal of Psychiatry* 37, 179–182).

For general guidance for doctors and lawyers, see *Assessment of Mental Capacity*, British Medical Association, 1995.

The treatment of incapable patients

The question of the lawfulness of treating patients who are incapable of giving **1–626** consent because they are unconscious in circumstances where the operation or other treatment cannot safely be delayed until consciousness is recovered or because they cannot satisfy the capacity test identified by Thorpe J. in *Re C*, above, was considered by the House of Lords in *F v. West Berkshire Health Authority and another (Mental Health Act Commission intervening)* [1989] 2 All E.R. 545. Their Lordships held:

(1) Under the common law doctrine of necessity a doctor can lawfully operate on, or give other treatment to, adult patients who are incapable, for one reason or another, of consenting to his doing so, provided that the operation or other treatment concerned is in the best interests of such patients. The operation or other treatment will be in the best interests of patients if, but only if, it is carried out in order either to save their lives or ensure improvement or prevent deterioration in their physical or mental health. *Per* Lord Brandon at 551: "In many cases . . . it will not only be lawful for doctors, on the ground of necessity, to operate on or give other medical treatment to adult patients disabled from giving their consent: it will be their common law duty to do so". In *Re Y (Mental Incapacity: Bone Marrow Transplant)* [1996] 2 F.L.R. 787, Connell J. held that it was in the best interests of a mentally incapacitated patient to donate bone marrow to her gravely ill sister. Having heard evidence that the death of the sister would have a particularly adverse effect upon the mother, with whom the patient enjoyed a very close relationship, and, in particular, would significantly handicap her ability to visit the patient, the judge said that the procedure would be to the patients "emotional, psychological and social benefit". The patient's best interests "are not limited to best medical interests" (*per* Butler-Sloss L.J. in *Re M.B. (Medical Treatment)*, above); they encompass "medical, emotional and all other welfare issues" (*per* Butler-Sloss L.J. in *Re A (Male Sterilisation)* [2000] 1 F.L.R. 549, CA, at 555). Welfare considerations should not be confused with social considerations, although whether the interests of third parties should ever be considered in a case concerned with the best interests of a patient ought to be left open (*Re A, per* Thorpe L.J. at 558).

In *Re A*, Thorpe L.J., at 560, said that:

"the first instance judge with the responsibility to make an evaluation of the best interests of a claimant lacking capacity should draw up a balance sheet. The first entry should be of any factor or factors of actual benefit .... Then on the other sheet the judge should write any counterbalancing dis-benefits to the applicant ... Then the judge should enter on each sheet the potential gains and losses in each instance making some estimate of the extent of the possibility that the gain or loss might accrue. At the end of that exercise the judge should be better placed to strike a balance between the sum of the certain and possible gains against the sum of the certain and possible losses. Obviously, only if the account is in relatively significant credit will the judge conclude that the applicant is likely to advance the best interests of the claimant".

The best interests principle is equally applicable to decisions to initiate, or to discontinue life support systems to the patient, as it is to other forms of treatment (*Airdale NHS Trust v. Bland* [1993] 1 All E.R. 821, HL). In *Re D* (*Medical Treatment: Mentally Disabled Patient*) [1998] 2 F.L.R. 22, Sir Stephen Brown P. granted a declaration that, "notwithstanding the [patient's] inability to consent to or refuse medical treatment, it is lawful as being in the best interests of the patient that the [NHS trust] do not impose haemodialysis upon him in circumstances in which, in the opinion of the medical practitioners responsible for such treatment, it is not reasonably practicable so to do". This was a case where it had proved to be impossible to treat a gravely ill physically protesting incompetent patient and the doctors sought a declaration to protect themselves from any liability arising from a failure to carry out the treatment.

If a patient suddenly becomes severely mentally disturbed, a doctor could provide emergency treatment in the absence of the patient's consent if: (1) the patient's behaviour precludes rational communication with him; and (2) a reasonable person would conclude that such action would be in the patient's best interests: see Lord Goff's analysis of the doctrine of necessity in the *F.* case, above, at 565 *et seq.*

1–627 In *Re H* (*Mental Patient*) (1992) 8 B.M.L.R. 71, the court refused to distinguish between proposed diagnostic procedures and proposed therapeutic procedures. *Per* Nicholas Wilson Q.C. sitting as a deputy judge in the High Court: "The same criterion governs their lawfulness; and, as to whether a procedure is in the best interests of a patient, surely there is always a balance to be struck, in relation to treatment just as much as to diagnosis, between possible risks and possible benefits."

(2) A doctor will be deemed to have acted in the best interests of an incapable patient and will be immune from liability in trespass to the person if he establishes that he acted in accordance with a practice accepted at the time as proper by a responsible body of medical opinion skilled in the particular form of treatment in question (*Bolam v. Friern Hospital Management Committee* [1957] 2 All E.R. 118). Note, however, that in *Bolitho (administratrix of the estate of Bolitho (deceased)) v. City and Hackney Health Authority* [1997] 4 All E.R. 771, the House of Lords held that in a rare case, if it could be demonstrated that the professional opinion given in an action for negligence was not capable of withstanding logical analysis, the judge would be entitled to hold that the body of opinion was not responsible.

In *F*, Lord Goff emphasised the need for consultation in cases where serious treatment is being considered: "No doubt, in practice, a decision [in the case of serious treatment] may involve others beside the doctor. It must surely be good practice to consult relatives and others who are concerned with the care of the patient. Sometimes, of course, consultation with a specialist or specialists will be required; and in others, especially where the decision involves more than a purely medical opinion, an inter-disciplinary team will in practice participate in the decision. It is very difficult, and would be unwise, for a court to do more than to stress that, for those who are involved in these important and sometimes difficult decisions, the overriding consideration is that they should act in the best interests of the person who suffers from the misfortune of being prevented by incapacity from deciding for himself what should be done to his own body in his own best interests," (at 567).

In *Re S (Sterilisation: Patient's Best Interests)* [2000] 2 F.L.R. 389, the Court of Appeal held that in determining the welfare of the patient, the test established in *Bolam* is applied only at the outset to ensure that the treatment proposed is recognised as proper by a responsible body of medical opinion. The test has no part to play in the subsequent decision of choosing between two or more possible treatments both or all of which would satisfy the best interests test. In deciding what is the best treatment for a mentally incompetent patient the doctor must have regard to the patient's welfare as the paramount consideration. "That embraces issues far wider than the medical. Indeed it would be undesirable and probably impossible to set bounds to what is relevant to a welfare determination" *per* Thorpe L.J. at 403.

(3) Special considerations apply in the case of an operation for the sterilisation of an adult woman or in the case of an operation on an organ transplant donor (*per* Lord Bridge in *F* at 549), where it is proposed to sterilise a mentally incapable male patient (*Re A. (Male Sterilisation*, above), where it is proposed to withdraw artificial feeding from a patient in a persistent vegetative state (*Airedale N.H.S. Trust v. Bland*, above) and where it is proposed to harvest bone marrow (*Re Y (Mental Incapacity: Bone Marrow Transplant)*, above). No court now has jurisdiction either by statute or derived from the Crown as *parens patriae* to give or withhold consent to such operations in the case of a mentally incapable adult as it would in wardship proceedings in the case of a child. However, the High Court does have jurisdiction to make a declaration that the proposed operation is lawful on the ground that in the circumstances it is in the best interests of the patient. Although a declaration is not necessary to establish the lawfulness of the operation, doctors are strongly advised to obtain declarations in these cases if they are to avoid the prospect of being sued for unlawful trespass to the patient's person on the ground that the operation was not in the patient's best interests.

The procedure for applying a declaration in sterilisation cases is set out in a Practice Note of the Official Solicitor dated June 1996: see [1996] 2 F.L.R. 111. The Practice Note is issued for the guidance of practitioners and is not intended to be a mandatory code (*J v. C* (note) [1990] 3 All E.R. 735, *per* Thorpe J.). For a case where the court refused the local authority's application for a declaration authorising sterilisation, see *Re L.C. (Medical Treatment: Sterilisation)* [1997] 2 F.L.R. 258, where Thorpe J. said that leave "could not be justified upon the basis of some vague and unsubstantiated fear that [the woman] would be exposed to risks [of pregnancy] from which she is presently protected". A similar approach was taken in *Re S (Medical Treatment: Adult Sterilisation)* [1998] 1 F.L.R. 944, where Johnson J. refused to grant a declaration on an application by the woman's mother in "the absence of any risk [of pregnancy] that can be called identifiable rather than speculative". A sterilisation can be in the best interests of an incompetent woman even if the risk of pregnancy is small (*Re W (An Adult: Mental Patient) (Sterilisation)* [1993] 1 F.L.R. 381).

A declaration is not required if a proposed abortion complies with the terms of the Abortion Act 1967 (*Re SG (Adult Mental Patient: Abortion)* [1991] 2 F.L.R. 329) or where the incidental result of a hysterectomy performed for therapeutic reasons would be sterilisation as long as two doctors are satisfied that: (i) the operation was necessary for therapeutic purposes; (ii) it was in the best interests of the patient; and (iii) that there was no practicable, less intrusive means of treating the condition (*Re GF (Medical Treatment)* [1992] 1 F.L.R. 293). Judicial guidance on the procedure to be followed generally in cases where there is a concern about a patient's competence to consent to or refuse treatment is given in *St George's Healthcare NHS Trust v. S* [1998] 3 All E.R. 673 at 702–704.

In *Re H (Mental Patient)*, above, the judge held that a C.T. scan for a schizophrenic patient with a suspected brain tumour was not one of those cases where it was necessary or desirable to grant a declaration. He did not wish to "send a signal" that this and similar procedures should be delayed pending a costly application to the court.

Reasonable force can be used to ensure that the patient accepts treatment. There must be a necessity to act and the action taken must be such as a reasonable person would in all the circumstances take, acting in the best interests of the patient (*Norfolk and Norwich Healthcare (NHS) Trust v. W* [1996] 2 F.L.R. 613). The extent of force or compulsion that may become necessary can only be judged in each individual case and by health professionals. It may become for them a balance between continuing treatment which is forcibly opposed and deciding not to continue with it (*Re MB (Medical Treatment)*, above, at 439).

If a mentally incompetent patient is resisting being taken to hospital for treatment for a physical condition in a situation where: (1) it would be in the best interests of the patient to receive the treatment; and (2) treatment outside of the hospital is considered to be inappropriate because of either therapeutic or safety reasons, the common law doctrine of necessity would provide authority for an appropriate degree of force to be used to transfer the patient to the hospital (see *Re M.B.*, above). The provisions of Part II of this Act would have to be invoked if the patient required treatment for a mental disorder.

Appendix B of the NHS Management Executive Booklet, "A Guide to Consent for Examination and Treatment", which was published with Department of Health Circular No. HC(90)2, sets out a form which can be used where medical or dental treatment is proposed to be given to a patient who is unable to consent because of mental disorder.

The treatment of capable patients

1–628   If a patient has the mental capacity to exercise a choice he "*must* consent if medical treatment of him is to be lawful, although the consent need not be in writing and may sometimes be inferred from the patient's conduct in the context of the surrounding circumstances. Treating him without his consent or despite a refusal of consent will constitute the civil wrong of trespass to the person and may constitute a crime" *per* Lord Donaldson M.R. in *Re T*, above, at 653. For the nature of the information about treatment that must be provided to a patient in order that a valid consent be obtained, see the note on "consented to it" in section 57(2).

The consent of the patient can be vitiated by outside influence. In *Re T*, above, Lord Donaldson said, at 662, that, while it is acceptable for the patient to receive advice or for the patient to have been subject to the strong persuasion of others in reaching a decision, such persuasion must not "overbear the independence of the patient's decision". His Lordship identified the "real question" in each such case as being: "does the patient really mean what he says or is he merely saying it for a quiet life, to satisfy someone else or because the advice and persuasion to which he has been subjected is such that he can no longer think and decide for himself? In other words, is it a decision expressed in form only, not in reality?" His Lordship identified two aspects of the effect of outside influences which could be of "crucial importance": the strength of will of the patient and the relationship of the "persuader" to the patient. With regard to the former, a patient who is "very tired, in pain or depressed will be much less able to resist having his will overborne than one who is rested free from pain and cheerful". As far as the relationship issue is concerned, his Lordship spoke of the potential strength of the parental and marital relationship, especially with regard to arguments based on religious belief. These factors should make the doctor alert to the possibility that "the patient may not mean what he says". Other outside influences that would vitiate a patient's consent include fraud, misrepresentation and duress.

The statement in the *Code of Practice*, at paragraph 15.25, that it is permissible to give treatment to a non-consenting capable patient who is suffering from a "mental disorder which is leading to behaviour that is an immediate serious danger to himself or to other people" is open to doubt. In any event, a patient whose mental disorder is leading to such behaviour is unlikely to possess the high level of capacity that would be required in such a situation: see the discussion on "capacity", above. Support for the contention that it is not permissible to provide emergency treatment to a non-consenting capable patient in circumstances where it would have been possible to ascertain the wishes of the patient can be found in the following passage from Lord Mustill's judgment in *Airedale NHS Trust v. Bland*, above, at pp. 889, 890 under the heading "Emergencies": "Although the consent of the patient is normally essential to the immunity of the doctor from criminal (and also from civil) process there are occasions when the law permits him to proceed without it. Notably, where urgent action is imperative in the interests of the patient, and because the patient is unconscious, or disorientated, or for some other reason the consent cannot be obtained until it is too late."

The unlikelihood of the courts departing from the principle of patient autonomy is emphasised by *S. v. S., W. v. Official Solicitor* [1972] A.C. 24, where the House of Lords considered whether it was right to order blood tests on two children to help establish whether or not they were legitimate. Lord Reid examined the legal position and said, at 43:

"There is no doubt that a person of full age and capacity cannot be ordered to undertake a blood test against his will . . . The real reason is that English law goes to great lengths to protect a person of full age and capacity from interference with his personal liberty. We have too often seen freedom disappear in other countries not only by coups d'etat but by gradual erosion; and often it is the first step that counts. So it would be unwise to make even minor concessions."

In *St George's Healthcare NHS Trust v. S.* [1998] 3 All E.R. 673, 686, Judge L.J. said that "the importance of this salutary warning remains undiminished."

Patient autonomy extends to the decision by a patient to discontinue life support (*Re A.K. (Medical Treatment: Consent)* [2001] 1 F.L.R. 120). *Per* Hughes J., at 135: [T]he continuation of invasive ventilation, if it is clearly established that an adult patient of full capacity has withdrawn his consent to it, is not simply not the duty of the doctor but is positively unlawful."

The consent can be evidenced by the patient's signature on a consent form but this evidence can be negatived by, for example, evidence of duress or incapacity. A patient's consent can be inferred from his behaviour, such as the patient holding out his hand to receive tablets. A patient's consent can be withdrawn at any time prior to or during treatment. In *Re A.K.*, above, the patient withdrew his consent to being connected to a ventilator by the only means of communication available to him, which was the movement of one eyelid.

Dr Gareth Jones has reported that "[s]ome significant proportion of patients with chronic schizophrenia suffer from defects of cognitive function so grave as to throw into doubt their ability to give informed consent to treatment, in particular the prescription of neuroleptis to reduce the risk of relapse ("Informed Consent in Chronic Schizophrenia" (1995) 167 *British Journal of Psychiatry* 565–568).

The medical treatment of children

The legal position relating to the medical treatment of children under common **1–629** law, which is considered in chapter 31 of the *Code of Practice*, can be summarised as follows:

(1) A child aged 16 or 17 who is capable of expressing his or her own wishes can give a valid consent to medical treatment (Family Law Reform Act 1969, s.8(1)). As the definition of treatment in section 8 does not include the

donations of blood or organs, capacity to consent to these procedures falls within the *Gillick* principles: see point (4) below. A parent cannot override such a child's consent if the child is deemed to be mentally capable of consenting to the proposed treatment. The test established in *Re C (Refusal of Medical Treatment)*, see point (5) below, should be used to determine whether the child has the required capacity. If a 16 or 17 year old child is found to be mentally incapable of consenting to the treatment, the consent of a person or body with parental responsibility should be obtained. The right and the duty to give consent to medical treatment is an incident of parental responsibility vested in the parent (*Re A. (Conjoined Twins: Surgical Separation)* [2000] 4 All E.R. 961, at 992, *per* Ward L.J.). The court can be asked to consent to the treatment in exceptional cases. "[W]here major surgical or other procedures (such as an abortion) were proposed, and whereby the parents or those in loco parentis were prepared to give consent but the child (having sufficient understanding to make an informed decision) was not, the jurisdiction of the court should always be invoked"; *per* Nolan L.J. in *Re W(A Minor)(Medical Treatment)* [1992] 4 All E.R. 627, CA, at 648,649.

(2) Medical treatment should only be proposed for a child of any age if the treatment is considered to be in the child's best interests. By analogy with the position pertaining to mentally incapable adults, a treatment will be in the best interests of the child if it is required to save life or to ensure improvement or prevent deterioration in the child's physical or mental health: see "The treatment of incapable patients", above. A treatment that is deemed to be either "inhuman or degrading" would violate Article 3 of the European Convention on Human Rights.

(3) A child under the age of 16 can give a valid consent to medical treatment if the child is deemed to be mentally competent to consent to the proposed treatment. A child is mentally capable if he or she is deemed to be "*Gillick* competent" to consent to the treatment: see *Gillick v. West Norfolk and Wisbech Area Health Authority* [1985] 3 All E.R. 402, HL.

(4) A child is "*Gillick* competent" if the treating doctor concludes that the child has reached an age where she has sufficient understanding and intelligence to enable her to understand fully what is proposed and to be capable of making up her mind on the matter. The child must be able to understand the nature of the proposed treatment, its side effects and the consequences of not receiving it (*Re R (A Minor)(Wardship: Medical Treatment)* [1992] 1 F.L.R. 190). It is therefore possible for a child to be found to be competent to make a decision in respect of a treatment that may have minor consequences, but not to be competent to make a decision in respect of a treatment that may have major consequences. In *Re R*, Lord Donaldson said: "'*Gillick* competence' is a developmental concept and will not be lost on a day-to-day or week-to-week basis. In the case of mental disability, that disability must also be taken into account, particularly where it is fluctuating in its effect" (at 200). The challenges that professionals face when assessing the competence of children are considered by Professor John Pearce in "Consent to treatment during childhood" (1994) *British Journal of Psychiatry*, 165, 713–716 and by Dr Mike Shaw in "Competence and consent to treatment in children and adolescents", Advances in Psychiatric Treatment (2001), 7, 150–159. Also see *Consent, Rights and Choices in Health Care for Children and Young People* (2001), British Medical Association.

(5) The clinician needs to consider whether the decision is really that of the child. "The real question in each case is, 'Does the patient really mean what he says or is he merely saying it for a quiet life, to satisfy someone else or because the

advice and persuasion to which he has been subjected is such that he can no longer think and decide for himself?' In other words, 'Is it a decision expressed in form only, not in reality?'" *per* Lord Donaldson M.R. in *Re T (Adult: Refusal of Medical Treatment)* [1992] 4 All E.R. 649,662. His Lordship further stated that when considering the effect of outside influences, two aspects can be of "crucial importance". They are "the strength of will of the patient" and the "relationship of the 'persuader' to the patient." With regard to the latter his Lordship said that the "influence of parents on their children ... can be, but is by no means necessarily, much stronger than would be the case in other relationships."

(6) The three stage test identified by Thorpe J. in *Re C (Refusal of Medical Treatment)* [1994] 1 All E.R. 819 (noted under "Capacity", above) should be used to determine whether a child is "*Gillick* competent" as the test provides a practical dimension to the determination of capacity. This approach was taken by Wall J. in *Re C (Detention: Medical Treatment)* [1997] 2 F.L.R. 180.

(7) The refusal of a "*Gillick* competent" child or of a mentally capable 16- or 17-year-old child to accept treatment can be overridden by a mentally competent person with parental responsibility for the child, a local authority if the child is subject to a care order, or the court (*Re W (A Minor)(Medical Treatment)*, above. *Per* Lord Donaldson M.R. at 639,670: "No minor of whatever age has power by refusing consent to treatment to override a consent to treatment by someone who has parental responsibility for the minor and *a fortiori* a consent by the court. Nevertheless such a refusal is a very important consideration in making clinical judgments and for parents and the court in deciding whether themselves to give consent. Its importance increases with the age and maturity of the minor." A decision to override the child's refusal of consent must be exercised on the basis that the welfare of the child is paramount. In *Re W.*, Nolan L.J. suggested that the power to override should only used if there is "a serious and imminent risk that the child will suffer grave and irreversible mental harm" if the treatment is not provided (at 648).

(8) In the case of married parents, if the parents disagree a doctor may proceed to treat the child on the authority of the consent of one parent alone (Children Act 1989, s.2(7)).

(9) The High Court, in the exercise of its inherent jurisdiction, has the discretion to make an order that would have the effect of overriding the expressed wishes of a parent or a competent child. In reaching a decision the court will regard the welfare of the child as the paramount consideration (*Re T (A Minor)(Wardship: Medical Treatment)* [1997] 1 AllE.R. 906, CA). *Per* Butler-Sloss J. at 913: "The consent or refusal of consent of the parents is an important consideration to weigh in the balancing exercise to be carried out by the judge. In that context, the extent to which the court will have regard to the view of the parent will depend upon the court's assessment of that view. But as Bingham MR said in *Re Z (A Minor)(Freedom of Publication)* [1995] All E.R. 961, CA, the court decides and in doing so may overrule the decision of a reasonable parent." There have been a number of occasions when the court has used this jurisdiction to override the wishes of parents who are Jehovah's Witnesses who have refused consent to life-saving blood transfusion for their children; see, for example, *Re E (A Minor)(Wardship: Medical Treatment)* [1993] 1 F.L.R. 386. *Per* Ward J. at 394: "[The] court, exercising its prerogative of protection, should be very slow to allow an infant to martyr himself."

(10) Section 2(9) of the Children Act 1989 states that a person "who has parental authority for a child may not surrender or transfer any part of that

275

responsibility to another but may arrange for some or all of it to be met by one or more persons acting on his behalf." This provision enables a parent to delegate authority to consent to treatment to a person who has temporary charge of the child, for example a nanny, relative or headmaster of a boarding school.

(11) A person who does not have parental responsibility for a child but has care of the child, may "do what is reasonable in all the circumstances of the case for the purposes of safeguarding or promoting the child's welfare" (Children Act 1989, s.3(5)). This would enable a temporary carer, who has neither parental responsibility nor delegated authority, to give a valid consent to medical treatment if it was not possible to contact the child's parents. The Law Commission suggested that it would be reasonable for someone caring for a child while parents were away to arrange emergency medical treatment but not major elective surgery (Law Commission Report 172, *Review of Child Law: Guardianship and Custody* (1988), para. 2.16).

(12) Under common law a doctor may lawfully treat a child in an emergency even though he is unable to obtain a valid consent, if he considers the treatment to be in the best interests of the child. In exceptional cases, emergency treatment can be provided in the face of parental opposition. Per Lord Templeman in the *Gillick* case, above, at 432: "I accept that where there is no time to obtain a decision from the court, a doctor may safely carry out treatment in an emergency if the doctor believes the treatment to be vital to the survival or health of an infant and notwithstanding the opposition of a parent or the impossibility of alerting the parent before the treatment is carried out".

(13) In non-emergency situations, if there is no one with parental responsibility who is prepared to give the necessary consent, an application should be made either within the court's inherent jurisdiction for leave to carry out the proposed treatment or for a "specific issue order" under Part II of the Children Act 1989.

(14) Reasonable force can be used to ensure that either a mentally incapable or a refusing capable child (where consent has been given under (6), above) accepts treatment. The Court of Appeal has said: "The extent of force or compulsion which may become necessary can only be judged in each individual case by the health professionals. It may become for them a balance between continuing treatment which is forcibly opposed and deciding not to continue with it" (*Re MB (Medical Treatment)* [1997] 2 F.L.R. 426 at 439).

Advance directives

1–630   *Re C (Adult: Refusal of Medical Treatment)*, above, was the first occasion when an English Court had been invited to rule directly on the legal validity of an advance directive. Thorpe J. held that a refusal of treatment "can take the form of a declaration of intention never to consent in the future or never to consent in some future circumstances". The effect of this finding is that a valid advance refusal of treatment made when the patient was capable, survives any supervening incapacity, even if the refusal leads to the patient's death. His Lordship accepted that a patient might have capacity to make a present refusal but lack the capacity to make an anticipatory refusal. In *Re C* Thorpe J. also held that the High Court has power, exercising its inherent jurisdiction, to determine the effect of a purported advance directive as to future medical treatment.

An advance directive:

(i) can only be effective if it was made when the patient had the capacity to make it;
(ii) need not be in writing;
(iii) cannot be used to require a doctor to carry out a positive act which is contrary to his clinical judgment;

(iv) can be overridden by the provisions of sections 58, 62 and 63 of this Act, so that a directive which refuses treatment for mental disorder will be rendered ineffective if a detained patient comes within the scope of Part IV;

(v) will be ineffective if at the time when it was made the patient did not appreciate the implications of refusing treatment;

(vi) can be made by a detained patient who possesses the required capacity; and

(vii) can be revoked if the patient has the necessary capacity to do so.

The Law Commission in its report on *Mental Incapacity* (1995), at paragraph 5.21, states that, as was "made clear in *Re T*, 'doctors will need to consider what is the true scope and basis of the decision'. They must ask whether the patient has refused consent to the treatment or procedure which it is now desired to carry out, in the circumstances in which it would now be carried out. Inevitably, problems of evidence will sometimes arise".

The House of Lords Select Committee on Medical Ethics which was appointed in February 1993 called for a *Code of Practice* on advance directives for health professionals. Such a code has been prepared by a multi professional group which was established by the British Medical Association. The *Code* is published as *Advance Statements About Medical Treatment*, 1995. For advance directives and psychiatric treatment, see A. Halpern and G. Szmukler, "Psychiatric advance directives: reconciling autonomy and non-consensual treatment" (1997) 21 *Psychiatric Bulletin* 323–327.

Patients to whom Part IV applies
56.—(1) This Part of this Act applies to any patient liable to be detained **1–631** under this Act except—

(a) a patient who is liable to be detained by virtue of an emergency application and in respect of whom the second medical recommendation referred to in section 4(4)(a) above has not been given and received;

(b) a patient who is liable to be detained by virtue of section 5(2) or (4) or 35 above or section 135 or 136 below or by virtue of a direction under section 37(4) above; and

(c) a patient who has been conditionally discharged under section 42(2) above or section 73 or 74 below and has not been recalled to hospital.

(2) Section 57 and, so far as relevant to that section, sections 59, 60 and 62 below, apply also to any patient who is not liable to be detained under this Act.

DEFINITIONS
patient: s.145(1). **1–632**
hospital: ss.64(1), 145(1).

GENERAL NOTE
The section establishes that the provisions of this Part shall apply to all detained **1–633** patients, except those mentioned in paragraphs (a) to (c) of subsection (1), and provides for the safeguards for the most serious treatments to apply to informal patients. The treatment of patients who fall outside the scope of this Part is governed by common law rules which are described in the General Note to this Part.

Subsection (1)
Patient: Of any age. **1–634**
Liable to be detained: It is submitted that the provisions of this Part do not apply until the patient has been detained in the hospital named in the application or order: see ss.6(2), 37(1), Form 14 of S.I. 1983 No. 893 and paragraph (b), below, in so far as it

relates to section 37(4). Patients who have been granted leave of absence under section 17 continue to be "liable to be detained" under this Act and are therefore subject to the provisions of this Part. It is therefore important that during such leave of absence the patient's General Practitioner is informed of the content of any certificates given on Form 38 or Form 39 of the Mental Health (Hospital, Guardianship and Consent to Treatment) Regulations 1983 as he will be bound by them.

Patients who are subject to guardianship and informal patients are not "liable to be detained" and do not, therefore, come within the scope of this Part.

Hospital: Or a registered establishment (s.64(1)).

Subsection (2)

1–635   This subsection extends the protection provided by section 57 to informal patients. It was enacted as a result of an opposition amendment to the 1982 Act which found favour with the Minister for Health who accepted the argument that "if a course of treatment is so drastic that a detained patient's consent alone should not justify it and that there should be further safeguards, it is difficult to see why the same provisions should not apply to an informal patient" (HC Vol. 29, col. 81).

Treatment requiring consent and a second opinion

1–636   **57.**—(1) This section applies to the following forms of medical treatment for mental disorder—

(a) any surgical operation for destroying brain tissue or for destroying the functioning of brain tissue; and

(b) such other forms of treatment as may be specified for the purposes of this section by regulations made by the Secretary of State.

(2) Subject to section 62 below, a patient shall not be given any form of treatment to which this section applies unless he has consented to it and—

(a) a registered medical practitioner appointed for the purposes of this Part of this Act by the Secretary of State (not being the responsible medical officer) and two other persons appointed for the purposes of this paragraph by the Secretary of State (not being registered medical practitioners) have certified in writing that the patient is capable of understanding the nature, purpose and likely effects of the treatment in question and has consented to it; and

(b) the registered medical practitioner referred to in paragraph (a) above has certified in writing that, having regard to the likelihood of the treatment alleviating or preventing a deterioration of the patient's condition, the treatment should be given.

(3) Before giving a certificate under subsection (2)(b) above the registered medical practitioner concerned shall consult two other persons who have been professionally concerned with the patient's medical treatment, and of those persons one shall be a nurse and the other shall be neither a nurse nor a registered medical practitioner.

(4) Before making any regulations for the purpose of this section the Secretary of State shall consult such bodies as appear to him to be concerned.

DEFINITIONS

1–637   medical treatment: ss.56, 145(1).
mental disorder: ss.1, 145(1).
patient: s.145(1).
responsible medical officer: s.64(1).

GENERAL NOTE

This section, which is considered by the *Code of Practice* at paragraphs 16.6 to 16.8, **1–638** provides that certain of the most serious forms of medical treatment for mental disorder can only be given if the patient consents to the treatment and three independent people appointed by the Mental Health Act Commission, one being a doctor, have certified that the patient understands the treatment and has consented to it. If the patient is not capable of consenting to the treatment, or if he does not consent to it, the treatment cannot proceed. The independent doctor must also certify that the treatment should be given on the ground that it will have a beneficial effect. Before he issues his certificate the doctor must consult with two persons, other than the patient's doctor, who have been professionally concerned with the patient's treatment. The certificate of consent and the certificate relating to the need for treatment together make up Form 37 of Schedule 1 to the Mental Health (Hospital Guardianship, and Consent to Treatment) Regulations 1983.

This section applies to informal patients (s.56(2)) as well as to patients who are liable to be detained under the long term provisions of this Act (s.56(1)). It does not apply to patients who are detained under the powers set out in paragraphs (a) to (c) of section 56(1) and only the consent of such patients is required before the treatments covered by this section can be given. In view of the argument accepted by the Minister for Health relating to informal patients (see the note on s.56(2)) this exclusion would appear to have been an oversight and, although it is highly unlikely that the very serious forms of treatment provided for in this section would ever be given to patients who are being detained under one of these powers, the protection given by this section should be afforded to all categories of mentally disordered patients.

In *X v. A, B and C and the Mental Health Act Commission* (1991) 9 B.M.L.R. 91, Morland J. held that the only legal relationship between the three persons appointed under subsection (2)(a) and the Mental Health Act Commission is that of appointees and appointor. It is the Commission on behalf of the Secretary of State who appoints the panel. It then becomes the exclusive function of the panel to carry out their responsibilities and the Commission have no further responsibility or duty in relation to a person who is aggrieved by the actions of the panel. When carrying out their functions under subsection (2)(a) the panel had to discharge duties which had quasi-judicial hallmarks and which were in the field of public administrative law. Consequently no common law duty of care is owed by the panel in private law to the patient. *Per* Morland J. at 96: "It may very well be although I reach no definitive conclusion about it, that a doctor giving an opinion, which was negligent, that electro-convulsive therapy should be given, that that opinion, being in the certificate given under section 58(3)(b) could be in breach of a common law duty in private law. In my judgment the reason for that is that the doctor, *qua* doctor, is giving a medical opinion about a patient, albeit not his. Similar considerations would apply to a doctor's certificate ... given under section 57(2)(b)."

If a patient is given treatment under this section, his responsible medical officer must provide the Mental Health Act Commission with reports on the treatment and the patient's condition (ss.61, 121(2)(b)).

The Human Rights Act 1998
See the note on "appointed ... by the Secretary of State" in subsection (2). **1–639**

Subsection (1)
Medical treatment for mental disorder: See the note on section 63. **1–640**
Paragraph (a): The total number of patients referred to the Mental Health Act Commission in relation to psychosurgery during the periods covered by the Commission's Biennial Reports is: 1983–1985 (57), 1985–1987 (54), 1987–1989 (52), 1989–1991 (65), 1991–1993 (46), 1993–1995 (3) and 1995–1997 (30). Of these 334 referrals, psychosurgery was authorised in 272 cases. Only two detained patients

have been referred under this provision (MHAC, *Eighth Biennial Report*, 1997–1999, para. 6.46). The most frequent reason given for non-authorisation was that the patient lacked the capacity to give valid consent.

The Commission has adopted the following procedure for psychosurgery patients referred under this section: "When the RMO, or the unit where the operation is to take place (as in the case of patients from abroad) contacts the Commission, a doctor is appointed who will carry out the first part of the procedure within two months of the proposed date of the operation. The appointed doctor will discuss with the patient's consultant psychiatrist the proposals for psychosurgery and may visit. There may be reasons why the appointed doctor will advise against proceeding to the second stage. It sometimes happens that further treatment recommended by the specialist psychiatrist has not yet begun and the visiting doctor may advise waiting until such further treatments have been completed. Otherwise the doctor accompanied by non medical appointees will visit the patient within six weeks prior to the proposed operation and consult the relevant professionals. If all three decide to certify under ... section 57(2) and the appointed doctor decides to certify under sub-section (b) of the same section, then the certification will be notified immediately to those concerned and subsequently the certificate sent to the Commission office" (MHAC, *Fourth Biennial Report, 1989–1991*, para. 6.2).

Paragraph (b)—Other forms of treatment: Regulation 16 of the Mental Health (Hospital, Guardianship and Consent to Treatment) Regulations 1983 specifies "the surgical implantation of hormones for the purposes of reducing male sex drive" as a form of treatment to which this section shall apply. The patient must be mentally disordered as well as having an abnormal sex drive for him to come within the scope of this Part of the Act (s.1(3)). In *R. v. Mental Health Act Commission, ex p. X* (1988) 9 B.M.L.R. 77, 85, DC, Stuart-Smith L.J. said that where a mentally disordered patient is sexually deviant "it seems likely that the sexual problem will be inextricably linked with the mental disorder, so that the treatment for the one is treatment for the other ... " The interpretation of the terms "surgical implantation" and "hormone" were considered by the Divisional Court in this case which is analysed by Phil Fennell at [1988] Crim.L.R. 660–676. The Court decided that the term "hormone" included synthetically produced hormones as well as the naturally occurring substance, but did not include hormone analogues, such as Goserelin, which are separate substances well known at the time the regulations were made. It was therefore held that Goserelin, even though approximately 100 times more powerful than the naturally occurring substance, is not a hormone within the meaning of regulation 16. *Per* Stuart-Smith L.J. at 83: "If Parliament passes legislation on the control of leopards, it is not to be presumed that leopards include tigers on the basis that they are larger and fiercer." On the question whether a particular procedure comes within the scope of "surgical implant", the Court held that "in the end it is ... a question of fact and degree". The Court took the view that a wide bore disposable syringe used for implanting the Goserelin was more like a conventional injection and could not be described as "surgical". It would appear that an incision must be made if an implant is to be categorised as being "surgical". The effect of this judgment is that if the administration of Goserelin is used as a treatment for mental disorder, it is governed by section 58(1)(b).

There have only been four referrals (only one of which was proceeded with) of patients for hormone implantation and there have been no referrals since 1988. "This is probably because the most widely used sexual suppressant, Cyproterone Acetate, is administered by mouth" (Phil Fennell, *Treatment Without Consent: Law Psychiatry and the Treatment of Mentally Disordered People since 1845* (1996), p. 188).

Regulations: See subsection (4). The *Code of Practice* can also specify treatments to which this section will apply (s.118(2)).

Secretary of State: The functions of the Minister under this section, so far as exercisable in relation to Wales, are exercised by the National Assembly for Wales (S.I. 1999 No. 672, art. 2, Sched. 1).

Subsection (2)

Registered medical practitioner: See the note on section 58(3)(a). **1–641**

Appointed ... by the Secretary of State: The Mental Health Act Commission will appoint the doctor and the two other persons referred to in this paragraph (s.121(2)(a) and S.I. 1983 No. 892, art. 3(2)(a)). The persons appointed need not be members of the Commission. They must be allowed to interview the patient and inspect his records, and the doctor must be allowed to examine the patient: see section 119 for registered establishments and the direction of the Secretary of State, reproduced in the note on section 120(4), for hospitals. The three appointed persons have a duty to act fairly (*R. v. Mental Health Act Commission, ex p. X*, above). Having been appointed these people do not act under the Commission's direction, but are exercising their own independent judgment. Therefore their decisions cannot be appealed against to the Commission. As the appointed persons are discharging a public law function their decisions can be challenged by way of a judicial review (see *X v. A, B and C and Mental Health Act Commission*, noted in the General Note to this section). The appointed persons are "public authorities" for the purposes of section 6 of the Human Rights Act 1998 because they "exercise functions of a public nature" (*ibid.*,s.6(3)(b)). Also see the note under this heading in section 58(3)(a).

Consented to it: Patients must consent themselves: consent delegated to another is not lawful. The word "consent" is not defined in this Act. The *Code of Practice* identifies the "basic principles" of consent at paragraph 15.13. The Government has stated that "valid consent implies the ability, given an explanation in simple terms to understand the nature, purpose and effect of the proposed treatment" (Cmnd. 7320, para. 6.23). The consent should be given in an atmosphere which is uncontaminated by fear or intimidation. "An apparent consent will not be a true consent if it has been obtained by fraud, misrepresentation, duress or fundamental mistake"; *per* Stuart-Smith L.J. in *R. v. Mental Health Act Commission, ex p. X*, above, at 85.

An explanation in "broad terms" of the nature of the procedure which is intended and its likely effects would be sufficient for the consent to be "real" (*Chatterton v. Gerson* [1981] 1 Q.B. 432, 442, *per* Bristow J.). This approach was endorsed by the House of Lords in *Sidaway v. Bethlam Royal Hospital Governors* [1985] 1 All E.R. 643, where it was held that the decision on what risks should be disclosed to a patient was primarily a matter of clinical judgment and in making that judgment a doctor was required to act in accordance with a practice accepted at the time as proper by a responsible body of medical opinion. It would not matter that there may be another body of responsible medical opinion which takes a different view. However, Lords Bridge and Keith, speaking with the majority, considered the court might in certain circumstances come to the conclusion that disclosure of a particular risk was so obviously necessary to an informed choice on the part of the patient that no reasonably prudent medical man would fail to make it. This approach was endorsed by the House of Lords in *Bolitho (administratrix of the estate of Bolitho (deceased) v. City and Hackney Health Authority* [1997] 4 All E.R. 771, where it was held that in a rare case, if it could be demonstrated that the medical opinion was not capable of withstanding logical analysis, the judge would be entitled to hold that the body of opinion was not reasonable or responsible. *Bolitho* and *Sidaway* were considered by the Court of Appeal in *Pearce v. United Bristol Healthcare NHS Trust* (1999) 48 B.M.L.R. 118, where Lord Woolf held that:

"If there is a significant risk which would affect the judgment of a reasonable patient then in the normal course it is the responsibility of a doctor to inform the patient of that significant risk, if the information is needed so that the patient can determine for him or herself as to what course that he or she should adopt."

In *Re R* (*A Minor*) (*Wardship: Medical Treatment*) [1991] 4 All E.R. 177, 187, CA, a case concerning the capacity of a child to consent to treatment, Lord Donaldson M.R., said, that "what is involved is not merely an ability to understand the nature of the proposed treatment—in this case compulsory medication—but a full understanding and appreciation of the consequences both of the treatment in terms of intended and possible side effects and, equally important, the anticipated consequences of a failure to treat". Also note Stuart-Smith L.J.'s statement in *R. v. Mental Health Act Commission, ex p. X*, above, at 87 that he could not "accept that a patient must understand the precise physiological process involved before he can be said to be capable of understanding the nature and likely effects of the treatment or can consent to it".

The Mental Health Act Commission has said that the "knowledge communicated by the therapist may vary in detail from 'broad terms' to great detail, depending on the patient's ability and the complexity of the treatment being offered, with the final criteria ... being that the patient 'is capable of understanding the nature, purpose, and likely effects' of the treatment" (M.H.A.C., *Third Biennial Report*, 1987–1989, para. 7.6(h)).

Both the patient's consent and the doctor's certificate may apply to a plan of treatment (s.59). The patient can withdraw his consent to treatment under section 60.

Paragraph (a)—Certified in writing: "This certificate is not a substitute for a standard consent form which should be obtained" (*Memorandum*, para. 218). The certificate must be in the form set out in Form 37 of the Mental Health (Hospital, Guardianship and Consent to Treatment) Regulations 1983 (s.64(2) and reg. 16(1)). The appointed persons have to be satisfied as to the patient's capacity and to the fact of consent before a certificate can be issued. In forming a view as to whether the patient has consented to the treatment the appointed persons would need to be satisfied that the patient had been provided with sufficient information to enable a valid consent to be given. In other words, the appointed persons must be satisfied that the patient knew what he was consenting to. It is the responsibility of the doctor proposing to treat the patient to ensure that sufficient information has been provided.

"The Commission-appointed doctors undertaking section 57 visits have been advised to set a time limit on the validity of Form 37, *i.e.* stating that the certificate 'remains valid for only 8 weeks from the date of this certificate'. It remains the view of the Commission as stated in its Fifth Report that a new Form 37 would be necessary if an operation was postponed for more than 8 weeks after certification. Consent of the patient to treatment is essential for a certificate to be issued", (Mental Health Act Commission, Sixth Biennial Report, 1993–1995, para. 5.1). Also see the note on "certified", below.

The Commission has the power to withdraw the authority to treat provided by the certificate by issuing a notice under section 61(3).

Capable of understanding: In *R. v. Mental Health Act Commission, ex p. X*, above, Stuart-Smith L.J. noted, *obiter*, at 85, that the words in this subsection "are 'capable of understanding' and not 'understands'. Thus the question is capacity and not actual understanding." In paragraph 6.12 of its Fourth Biennial Report 1989–1991, the Mental Health Act Commission states that the judgment in this case "appeared to suggest that consent rests not on actual understanding but simply on the patient's intellectual capacity to understand." The Commission reported that it had "taken legal advice on this approach and advised all [Second Opinion Appointed Doctors] to continue with their approach of requiring both a capacity and adequate understanding of the treatment and its consequences." It is submitted that the Commission's advice is correct as Stuart-Smith L.J.'s remarks do little more than distinguish the two elements of this provision, *i.e.* the patient's capacity and the patient's consent. In any event Stuart-Smith L.J.'s formulation, at 86, of the requirements of a valid consent—"No doubt consent has to be an informed consent in that [the patient] knows the nature and likely effect of the treatment"—is supportive of the Commission's approach.

The test under common law for determining whether a patient has the capacity to consent is that set out by Thorpe J. in *Re C (Adult: Refusal of Medical Treatment)* [1994] 1 All E.R. 819 which is considered in the General Note to this Part and at paragraph 15.10 of the *Code of Practice*.

Nature, purpose and likely effects of the treatment: This formulation is declaratory of the common law position relating to information that must be given to a patient before a valid consent can be obtained (*Re C (Refusal of Medical Treatment)* above, *per* Thorpe J. at 824).

Paragraph (b): In *R. v. Mental Health Act Commission, ex p. X*, above, Stuart-Smith L.J. took the view that a doctor appointed by the Commission must first have regard to the likelihood that the treatment will alleviate or prevent a deterioration in the patient's condition. If he decides that no benefit would accrue to the patient, then he must refuse to issue the certificate. If he decides that the patient would benefit from the treatment, the doctor may then have regard to what he conceives to be the treatment's disadvantages. In circumstances where the doctor concludes that the disadvantages outweigh the advantages of treatment he should discuss the perceived disadvantages with the patient's responsible medical officer.

For the appointed doctors duty of care in private law to the patient, see the remarks of Morland J. in *X v. A, B, and C and the Mental Health Act Commission*, reproduced in the General Note to this section.

Certified: Using Form 37 of the 1983 Regulations (s.64(2) and reg. 16(1)). During the passage of the 1982 Act the Minister for Health said that there "is nothing in the [Act] to stop an independent psychiatrist putting a time limit on a certificate. If he thinks that it is an unusual or difficult decision he can specify whatever time limit he deems appropriate" (HC, Vol. 29, col. 58).

The doctor is not required to give reasons for his decision (*R (on the application of W) v. Feggetter*, November 30, 2000).

Having regard to: The doctor "does not have to have regard only to the likelihood of the treatment alleviating the patient's condition or preventing its deterioration. It is plain that these are two matters that he must have regard to"; *per* Stuart-Smith L.J. in *R. v. Mental Health Act Commission, ex p. X*, above at 89.

Subsection (3)

Shall consult: This Act does not place an obligation on any person to act as a **1–642** consultee. The "essence of consultation is the communication of a genuine invitation to give advice and a genuine consideration of that advice"; *per* Webster J. in *R. v. Secretary of State for Social Services, ex p. Association of Metropolitan Authorities* [1986] 1 All E.R. 164 at 167. Consultation could take place over the telephone.

"The responsible medical officer will need to provide the appointed medical practitioner with the relevant documents and the names of professionals involved with the case" (*Memorandum*, para. 219). The appointed doctor is under no obligation to accept the nurse or "other person" put forward by the responsible medical officer. The roles and responsibilities of the "statutory consultees" are discussed in paragraphs 16.34 to 16.37 of the *Code of Practice*.

Two other persons: Consultation with more than two persons could take place if this was felt to be desirable.

Who have been professionally concerned: And will therefore have some direct knowledge of the patient's history and condition and be in a position to comment on the issues identified by the *Code of Practice* at paragraph 16.34.

The fact that consultation must take place with two persons who *have been* concerned with the patient's medical treatment, rather than with persons who *are* so concerned, means that a consultation can take place with a person who has no current involvement with the patient. Such a consultation can only take place if identifying the person concerned was a reasonable action for the authorities to take given the non-availability of a person with a current involvement in the patient's treatment (*R (on the application of W.) v. Feggetter*, above).

With the patient's medical treatment: The purpose of this provision is to ensure that the patient is treated by a multi-disciplinary team and that members of the team are consulted on issues relating to the treatment of the patient. It is therefore not sufficient for the two people consulted merely to have had general responsibilities on the ward where the patient is being treated: a particular involvement with the patient's treatment is required.

Nurse: Means a qualified nurse whose name appears on the register maintained by the Central Council for Nursing, Midwifery and Health Visiting (Nurses, Midwives and Health Visitors Act 1979, s.10). "Under Part IV the nurse consulted can be any Registered nurse, first or second level, providing that they are professionally concerned with the care of the patient. Student nurses can act neither as a nurse nor a third person. Good practice, rather than the law, may suggest that the nurse consulted should, wherever possible, be a first level nurse on an appropriate part of the register held by the UKCC: that is a registered mental nurse or registered nurse for the mentally handicapped" (Mental Health Act Commission, Third Biennial Report, 1987–89, para. 7.6(d)).

The other: The Mental Health Act Commission in its Fifth Biennial Report 1991–1993 at paragraph 7.16, reports that identifying the "other person" is a "major source of difficulty for Appointed Doctors when undertaking second opinion visits". While recognising that the issue has not yet been tested in the courts the Commission has "concluded that to require the statutory 'other' consultee to be invariably professionally qualified and included in a professional register would be unnecessarily restrictive". At the same time the Commission expressed its "grave doubts about the validity of some certificates which, for example, refer to the 'ward clerk', 'Gymnasium technician' and 'Occupational Therapy Aid' ". The Commission suggests that "the appointed doctor should endeavour to meet with somebody whose qualifications, experience and knowledge of the patient should enable them to make an effective contribution to the work of the multidisciplinary team." As Parliament has required the "other person" to be "professionally concerned", as opposed to being merely "concerned" with the patient's medical treatment, it would seem that the other person must hold a recognised qualification which is directly relevant to the "medical treatment" of the patient as defined in section 145(1). Persons falling into this category could include psychologists, occupational therapists, pharmacists, psychotherapists, physiotherapists, art/music therapists and social workers.

In the sample studied by Phil Fennell, by far the largest category of "other persons" consulted was that of social worker. He reports that "the duty to consult the other professional is becoming seen as a tiresome formality" (*Treatment Without Consent*, 1996, p. 208). This attitude is partly due to the difficulties in finding another person to consult, which does call into question the extent to which multidisciplinary care is being provided to patients.

Treatment requiring consent or a second opinion

1–643   **58.**—(1) This section applies to the following forms of medical treatment for mental disorder—

    (a) such forms of treatment as may be specified for the purposes of this section by regulations made by the Secretary of State;

    (b) the administration of medicine to a patient by any means (not being a form of treatment specified under paragraph (a) above or section 57 above) at any time during a period for which he is liable to be detained as a patient to whom this Part of this Act applies if three months or more have elapsed since the first occasion in that period when medicine was administered to him by any means for his mental disorder.

(2) The Secretary of State may by order vary the length of the period mentioned in subsection (1)(b) above.

(3) Subject to section 62 below, a patient shall not be given any form of treatment to which this section applies unless—

(a) he has consented to that treatment and either the responsible medical officer or a registered medical practitioner appointed for the purposes of this Part of this Act by the Secretary of State has certified in writing that the patient is capable of understanding its nature, purpose and likely effect and has consented to it; or

(b) a registered medical practitioner appointed as aforesaid (not being the responsible medical officer) has certified in writing that the patient is not capable of understanding the nature, purpose and likely effects of that treatment or has not consented to it but that, having regard to the likelihood of its alleviating or preventing a deterioration of his condition, the treatment should be given.

(4) Before giving a certificate under subsection (3)(b) above the registered medical practitioner concerned shall consult two other persons who have been professionally concerned with the patient's medical treatment, and of those persons one shall be a nurse and the other shall be neither a nurse nor a registered medical practitioner.

(5) Before making any regulations for the purposes of this section the Secretary of State shall consult such bodies as appear to him to be concerned.

DEFINITIONS
   medical treatment: s.145(1).   **1–644**
   mental disorder: ss.1, 145(1).
   patient: ss.56, 145(1).
   responsible medical officer: s.64(1).

GENERAL NOTE
   This section, which is considered by the *Code of Practice* at paragraphs 16.9 to **1–645**
16.14, provides that certain forms of treatment shall not be given to a patient unless
the patient consents *or* an independent medical practitioner appointed by the Mental
Health Act Commission has certified that either the patient is incapable of giving his
consent or that the patient should receive the treatment even though he has not
consented to it. If the patient consents to the treatment, either the patient's
responsible medical officer or an independent medical practitioner must certify that
the consent has been properly given. There were 10,216 referrals to the Commission
for a second opinion under this section between July 1995 and April 1997 (MHAC,
Seventh Biennial Report, 1995–1997, para. 5.2)).
   If a patient is given treatment under this section, his responsible medical officer
must provide the Mental Health Act Commission with reports on the treatment and
the patient's condition (ss.61, 121(2)(b)).
   The role of nurses in administering medicine under this section is considered in the
Mental Health Act Commission's Guidance Note, concerning "Nurses, the Adminis-
tration of Medicine for Mental Disorder and the Mental Health Act."

The Human Rights Act 1998
   See the note on "appointed ... by the Secretary of State" in subsection (3)(a).   **1–646**

Subsection (1)

1–647   *Medical treatment for mental disorder:* See the note on section 63.

Paragraph (a)

1–648   *Such forms of treatment:* Regulation 16 of the Mental Health (Hospital, Guardian-ship and Consent to Treatment) Regulations 1983 specifies "electro-convulsive therapy" as a form of treatment to which this section shall apply.

There appears to be a widespread practice of making applications to detain patients who require ECT treatment for their depression despite the fact that such patients are both mentally incapable and compliant at the time when the application is made. This practice is unnecessary and almost certainly unlawful: see the note on "The 'sectioning' of compliant mentally incapable patient" in the General Note to this Part.

Regulations: See subsection (5). There is no power equivalent to that contained in section 118(2) for treatments to be specified for the purposes of this section by the *Code of Practice.*

Secretary of State: The functions of the Minister under this section, so far as exercisable in relation to Wales, are exercised by the National Assembly for Wales (S.I. 1999 no. 672, art. 2, Sched. 1).

Paragraph (b)

1–649   This paragraph enables a course of medication to be imposed on a patient coming within the scope of this Part for up to three months without the patient's consent and without the need to obtain an independent medical opinion. The protection provided by this section does not come into play until three months have elapsed since the commencement of the treatment. Authorisation for imposing treatment on the patient during the initial three months is given by section 63.

Medicine: Or any combination of medicines. Drugs should be designated on certificates by the classes described in the British National Formulary rather than individually (Circular No. DDL (84) 4, para. 17). Phil Fennell reports that the "most striking aspect of the medication cases [he studied] was the surprisingly high number of occasions where BNF recommended dose limits were exceeded (12 per cent of the medicines cases), and in a small number of cases the very large margin by which they were exceeded" (*Treatment Without Consent*, 1996, p. 216).

A medicine is identified by its chemical composition and not by its method of administration. Ordinary food in liquid form, such as would be used in the tube feeding of a patient with anorexia nervosa, is therefore not a medicine within the meaning of this section (*B v. Croydon Health Authority* [1995] 1 All E.R. 683, CA). For the administration of placebos, see the note on "consented" in subsection (3)(a)).

The taking of any necessary blood or urine samples either to evaluate the patient's suitability to be given a medicine or to monitor the patient's response to having been given a medicine is "medical treatment" for the purposes of section 63 (*B v. Croydon Health Authority*, above).

Patient: See section 56(1).

Three months or more: "The three months gives time for the psychiatrist to consider a treatment programme which suits the patient. Three months seems to fit in best with both clinical experience and clinical practice. It is long enough to allow a proper valuation and assessment of what, if any, long term treatment may be needed. It is also short enough to ensure that patient's consent, or a second opinion, is obtained before a long term course of drug treatment gets too far ahead"; *per* the Under-Secretary of State, Special Standing Committee, June 29, 1982.

The three-month period must be continuous. The period is not broken on: (1) the patient being granted leave of absence; (2) the patient being transferred to another hospital whilst continuing to be liable to be detained; (3) the authority to detain the patient being renewed under section 20; (4) a change of medication; (5) the medi-cation not being administered continuously; and (6) the section under which the patient is detained being changed. The *Memorandum* states that "there can only be one three month period for drug treatment in any continuous period of detention, including such a period during which detention under one section is immediately followed by detention under another section" (para. 220). As the medication must be given "at any time during a period for which [the patient] is liable to be detained" the three month period will clearly be broken by the patient's discharge from detention.

The Mental Health Act Commission has expressed its "concern that the provisions of [this] Act ... allow prolonged treatment without consent or a second medical opinion in a few cases where relatively prolonged periods of detention ... , each of less than three months' duration, are interrupted by brief periods of discharge from detention" (M.H.A.C., Sixth Biennial Report, 1993–1995, para. 3.8).

The fact that medication administered to a patient within the three month period will continue to have an effect on the patient after the period has expired is not legally relevant.

First occasion in that period: The three month period starts from the first occasion when medicine is given to a patient who is detained under a section which is not excluded by section 56(1). For example, if a patient is initially detained under section 4, which is subsequently converted to a section 2, and is then detained under section 3, the three month period will start from the first time that medicine was administered to the patient after the second medical recommendation referred to in section 4(4) was given and received. The period starts irrespective of whether the patient has consented to the treatment.

Subsection (3)

Paragraph (a)
Consented: See the note on "consented to it" in section 57(2). Both the patient's **1–650** consent and the medical practitioner's certificate may relate to a plan of treatment (s.59). A patient can withdraw his consent to treatment under section 60. Also note Lord Donaldson's remark in *Re R (A Minor) (Wardship: Medical Treatment)* [1991] 4 All E.R. 177, 184, CA, "that consent by itself creates no obligation to treat".

In paragraph 5.8 of its Sixth Biennial Report, 1993–1995, the Mental Health Act Commission makes the following comments about the covert administration of medication:

"One of the problems associated with covert administration is that it is clearly impossible to attempt to negotiate consent to such treatment and covert administration is seemingly precluded by paragraph 16.11 in the *Code of Practice* and by section 58(3)(a) of the Act, unless it has been certified as acceptable by a Second Opinion Doctor under section 58(3)(b). In contrast, it has been argued that a doctor may be entitled to withhold information from the patient under paragraph [15.14] of the Code but must be prepared to justify that decision. However, for that to be valid, the treatment must be 'in accordance with practice accepted at the time by a responsible body of medical opinion skilled in the particular form of treatment in question' (*Code of Practice* para. [15.21]). It would seem appropriate therefore for this matter to be considered by the Royal College of Psychiatrists and the Royal College of Nursing. Meanwhile, professional judgment must be relied upon in making decisions on this important ethical issue."

That the Commission should offer such equivocal advice on this issue is to be regretted. The quotation reproduced by the Commission is from the case of *Bolam v. Friern Hospital Management Committee* [1957] 1 W.L.R. 582, which laid down the general approach to be adopted by the courts to questions of medical negligence. The argument that this common law test can override the clear statutory language of subsection (3)(a) where it is stated that "a patient shall not be given ... treatment to which this section applies unless ... he has consented to that treatment" is clearly erroneous and should not be followed. It should also be noted that paragraph 15.21 of the Code is concerned with the treatment of patients who lack the capacity to consent.

In a later Biennial Report the Commission said that "as an inert substance, a placebo does not fall within the definition of 'medicine' and, therefore, falls outside the provisions of section 58" (*Eighth Biennial Report*, 1997–1999, para. 6.17). This approach fails to address the reality of the situation which is that a placebo is offered to the patient as a "medicine" which, hopefully, will lead to an improvement in his or her condition. It is instructive to note that the *Shorter Oxford English Dictionary* reports that a placebo was first described, in 1811, as "a medicine given more to please than to benefit the patient".

Registered medical practitioner: For this doctor's role in respect of scrutiny of the patient's detention documents, see below. The doctor cannot perform his functions under this section without visiting the patient (Circular DDL (84)(4), para. 24(f)).

Appointed ... by the Secretary of State: The Mental Health Act Commission will make the appointment (s.112(2)(a)) and S.I. 1983 No. 892, para. 3(2)(a)). The doctor, who may or may not be a member of the Commission, has a right of access to the patient and his records: see section 119 for registered establishments and the direction of the Secretary of State, reproduced in the note to section 120(4), for hospitals. Once appointed the doctor will not act under the Commission's direction, but will exercise his own independent judgment. His decision cannot therefore be appealed against to the Commission. As the doctor is discharging a public law function his decision can be challenged by way of a judicial review (*X. v. A. B. C. and the Mental Health Act Commission*, noted in the General Note to s.57). As a person who is exercising "functions of a public nature", the doctor is a "public authority" for the purposes of section 6 of the Human Rights Act 1998 (*ibid.*, s.6(3)(b)).

"I should say [the appointed doctor does not provide] a second opinion in the recognised technical or medical sense, because we do not wish the doctor who comes to advise to substitute his own opinion for that of the consultant who is directly responsible, but merely to say whether or not he thinks that, in the condition the patient is in, the line of medication proposed and the plan of treatment as a whole are in accordance with good medical practice"; *per* Viscount Colville of Culross, the first Chairman of the Mental Health Act Commission, HL, Vol. 468, No. 15, col. 1352. This approach is endorsed by the Commission in paragraph 11 of its "Advice to Second Opinion Appointed Doctors".

Paragraph 14 of the Mental Health Act Commission's guidance to SOADs states that the doctor should "confirm that the statutory detention forms are in order." For a comment on the role of the SOAD in so far as it relates to the scrutiny of documents, see the General Note to paragraph 16.26 of the *Code of Practice*. The policy that the Commission follows when complaints against SOADs are received is set out in Appendix 8.6 of the Commission's Sixth Biennial Report, 1993–1995. The Mental Health Act Commission does not appear to undertake any evaluation of the performance of appointed doctors.

Certified: Using Form 38 of the 1983 Regulations (s.64(2) and reg. 16(2)), irrespective of whether a standard consent form has also been used. The view expressed in the *Code of Practice* that the validity of Form 38 lapses if the patient has a new responsible medical officer is not correct (see the note on para. 16.9(b) of the *Code*). The *Code* is also incorrect when it implies that Form 38 lapses when the patient's detention is renewed (see the note on para. 16.35). The Mental Health Act Commission "has suggested that the form certifying the validity of the patient's consent should always be renewed by the responsible medical officer if there is a permanent change of responsible medical officer, a significant change of treatment or a break in the continuity of detention. However, it is also considered to be good practice if these forms are renewed at the times specified for the reports under section 61, *i.e.* at the time of renewal of detention. The Commission expects that the patient's consent status will be kept under close and regular review between such times, with appropriate records made as required by the *Code of Practice*" (MHAC, *Sixth Biennial Report*, 1993–1995, para. 5.12). As neither this Act nor the Mental Health (Hospital, Guardianship and Consent to Treatment) Regulations 1983 provide for the "renewal" of Form 38, the advice of the Mental Health Act Commission should not be followed. The validity of Form 38 will lapse in the following circumstances:

  (i) on the patient becoming mentally incapable of consenting to the treatment specified on the Form;
 (ii) on the withdrawl of the patient's consent to that treatment;
(iii) on the treatment specified on the Form changing; and
 (iv) on the ending of the patient's detention.

Although the Commission has expressed its concern that "the Forms 38 are not always signed by the current responsible medical officer" (*Eighth Biennial Report*, 1997–1999, para. 5.123), this is not a legal requirement.

The function of signing this form cannot be delegated. Unlike the consent forms used in general medicine, Form 38 does not require the signature of the patient.

The patient: Although this section does not specifically say that the patient should be interviewed, the *Code of Practice* states that this should happen (at para.16.26(b)).

Nature, purpose and likely effects of the treatment: See the note on section 57(2).

Paragraph (b)

The Minister of Health said that it would probably be very unusual for the psychiatrist who gives a certificate under this paragraph to give an open-ended opinion which would allow the treatment to go on for years. Most psychiatrists would be likely to suggest that a course of treatment should be tried for a finite period. (Special Standing Committee, June 29, 1982.) **1–651**

Registered medical practitioner: See the note on paragraph (a).

Certified: Using Form 39 of the 1983 Regulations (s.64(2) and reg. 16(2)). The second opinion appointed doctor will also complete the Mental Health Act Commission's internal administrative form (MHAC 2). The Mental Health Act Commission states that if the patient subsequently agrees to the treatment, the completion of the Form 38 under paragraph (a) will cancel the Form 39 and that should the patient subsequently refuse or become unable to consent, the Commission should be contacted for a further second opinion: see Form MHAC 1.

The doctor is not required to give reasons for his decision (*R. (on the application of W) v. Feggetter*, November 30, 2000).

The Commission has the power to the withdraw the authority to treat provided by Form 39 by issuing a notice under section 61(3).

Not consented to it: The 1978 White Paper suggested that the following principle be adopted in cases where the patient's consent is not forthcoming: "where it is not possible to agree with the patient the form the treatment is to take and the consultant feels the imposition of treatment is essential he should, wherever there is a choice, select the method of treatment the patient finds least objectionable or which would represent the minimum interference with the patient" (Cmnd. 7320, para. 6.18).

Likelihood: If there is some uncertainty about the effect of a particular form of medication, the medical practitioner should consider recommending to the Mental Health Act Commission that the treatment be subject to an early review under section 61.

The treatment should be given: A certificate should not be issued for the possible use of the medication at some unspecified time in the future.

Subsection (4)

1–652   See the notes on section 57(3).

Plans of treatment

1–653   **59.** Any consent or certificate under section 57 or 58 above may relate to a plan of treatment under which the patient is to be given (whether within a specified period or otherwise) one or more of the forms of treatment to which that section applies.

DEFINITION

1–654   patient: s.145(1).

GENERAL NOTE

1–655   This section enables any consent or certificate obtained for the purposes of section 57 or 58 to relate to a plan of treatment which would involve one or more of the treatments specified under the same section. Such a plan would allow for variations in treatment within the context of the treatment objectives and enable the responsible medical officer to respond rapidly to the patient's reaction to a particular drug or dosage. The plan could include a time scale for the administration of treatments. A patient may withdraw his consent to a plan of treatment under section 60(2). "Treatment plans are usually described in terms of the drug categories recorded in the British National Formulary" (Mental Health Act Commission, Fifth Biennial Report 1991–1993, para. 7.7).

"If a plan of treatment is being considered, the appointed medical practitioner will consider the whole plan, and accept or reject it as a whole. However, it is hoped that there will be scope for discussion between the responsible medical officer and the appointed doctor about details of the plan, so that a generally sound plan need not be rejected because of a minor disagreement. An outline of the plan of treatment will appear on the certificate, and will, of course, be described in detail in the patient's medical records" (*Memorandum*, para. 222).

Withdrawal of consent

1–656   **60.**—(1) Where the consent of a patient to any treatment has been given for the purpose of section 57 or 58 above, the patient may, subject to section 62 below, at any time before the completion of the treatment withdraw his consent, and those sections shall then apply as if the remainder of the treatment were a separate form of treatment.

(2) Without prejudice to the application of subsection (1) above to any treatment given under the plan of treatment to which a patient has consented, a patient who has consented to such a plan may, subject to section 62 below, at any time withdraw his consent to further treatment, or to further treatment of any description, under the plan.

DEFINITION

1–657   patient: ss.56, 145(1).

GENERAL NOTE

1–658   This section provides for a patient to withdraw his consent to treatment under sections 57 or 58 or to a plan of treatment. On the withdrawal of consent, the remainder of the treatment must be considered as a separate treatment for the purposes of those sections. "This means that if a patient withdraws his consent to a section 57 treatment it must not be given, or if a plan of treatment is in progress, the treatment must cease immediately unless one of the criteria for urgent treatment [set out in section 62] is met. If a patient withdraws consent to a treatment or a plan of treatment specified for section 58 the responsible medical officer must contact the Mental Health Act Commission immediately so that the requirements of that section can be complied with. Again, the responsible medical officer must cease administering the treatment unless section 62 applies" (*Memorandum*, para. 223). Advice on this section is contained in paragraph 16.19 of the *Code of Practice*.

Subsection (1)
Withdraw his consent: The withdrawal of consent can be made in writing, orally, or **1–659** through the patient's behaviour, *e.g.* by physically resisting the administration of the treatment.

Separate form of treatment: It is submitted that the three month period referred to in section 58(1)(b) is not re-activated on a patient withdrawing his consent to be treated by medication. A patient cannot therefore be treated for a fresh period of three months without his consent before the independent medical opinion referred to in section 58(3)(b) is obtained. This interpretation is favoured by the *Memorandum*; see *ibid.*

Review of treatment

61.—(1) Where a patient is given treatment in accordance with section **1–660** 57(2) or 58(3)(b) above a report on the treatment and the patient's condition shall be given by the responsible medical officer to the Secretary of State—

(a) on the next occasion on which the responsible medical officer furnishes a report [under section 20(3) or 21B(2) above renewing the authority for the detention of the patient]; and

(b) at any other time if so required by the Secretary of State.

(2) In relation to a patient who is subject to a restriction order [, limitation direction] or restriction direction subsection (1) above shall have effect as if paragraph (a) required the report to be made—

(a) in the case of treatment in the period of six months beginning with the date of the order or direction, at the end of that period;

(b) in the case of treatment at any subsequent time, on the next occasion on which the responsible medical officer makes a report in respect of the patient under section 41(6) [, 45B(3)] or 49(3) above.

(3) The Secretary of State may at any time give notice to the responsible medical officer directing that, subject to section 62 below, a certificate given in respect of a patient under section 57(2) or 58(3)(b) above shall not apply to treatment given to him after a date specified in the notice and sections 57 and 58 above shall then apply to any such treatment as if that certificate had not been given.

AMENDMENTS
In subsection (1) the words in square brackets were inserted by the Mental Health (Patients in the Community) Act 1995, s.2(5).

In subsection (2) the words in square brackets were inserted by the Crime (Sentences) Act 1997, s.55, Sched. 4, para. 12(7).

DEFINITIONS
limitation direction: s.145(1). **1–661**
patient: ss.56, 145(1).
responsible medical officer: s.64(1).
restriction direction: s.145(1).
restriction order: s.145(1).

GENERAL NOTE

1–662 This section provides for the periodic review by the Mental Health Act Commission of treatment which is being given under either section 57(2) (commonly psychosurgery) or section 58(3)(b) (ECT or medication after three months). A review is not required where a patient has consented to treatment being given to him under section 58(3)(a). A letter from the Chairman of the Commission dated September 1984 notified Health Authorities of the arrangements for reports to be given by responsible medical officers under this section and set out the form to be used for this purpose. This letter states that when a report has been given to the Commission, as required by this section, consent to continue treatment may be assumed unless the Commission gives notice of the withdrawal of consent. In its Fourth Biennial Report, 1989–1991, the Commission, at paragraph 6.4, states that there "is still some misunderstanding about the Commission's requirements of hospitals under section 61. Whereas some hospitals have been submitting reports regularly every few months, other hospitals have forwarded very few reports on forms MHAC 1. Hospital Managers should ensure that MHAC 1 forms are completed and returned to the Commission at the beginning of every period of renewable detention and to furnish additional reports if requested by the Second Opinion Appointed Doctor. Patients under restriction order must have a review of treatment reported on MHAC 1 annually when a report is sent to the Home Office. In addition hospitals are asked to inform the Commission when a detained patient receiving treatment on the authority of a Form 39 is discharged or consents to treatment. Hospitals are advised to institute a system at ward level for monitoring the cancellation or changes of Form 38 and Form 39 since at present ward records are often found to be unclear as to the current consenting status of the patient."

This section is considered at paragraphs 16.36 to 16.37 of the *Code of Practice*.

Subsection (1)

1–663 *Report on the treatment and the patient's condition:* The responsible medical officer should report on the treatment and the patient's response to it. There is no requirement under paragraph (a) for the responsible medical officer to report on an *informal* patient who has been treated under section 57. However, the Mental Health Act Commission can require such a report to be made under paragraph (b).

Secretary of State: The functions of the Secretary of State under this section are performed by the Mental Health Act Commission (s.121(2)(b)) and S.I. 1983 No. 892, para. 3(2)(b)).

On the next occasion: And on each subsequent occasion when the authority to detain the patient is renewed.

Any other time: It is likely that the Mental Health Act Commission will require a more frequent review than is provided for in paragraph (a) if the treatment is particularly hazardous or if there are other factors which suggest that special monitoring arrangements would be appropriate.

Subsection (2)

1–664 Specifies the timing of the treatment review in respect of patients who are subject to a restriction order, limitation direction or restriction direction.

Subsection (3)

1–665 This subsection provides that the Mental Health Act Commission may at any time give notice to the responsible medical officer that a certificate given under sections 57(2) or 58(3)(b) shall cease to apply after the date it specifies. If the responsible medical officer wished to continue with the treatment specified in the notice he would need to start afresh with the procedures laid down in sections 57 or 58, unless the criteria for urgent treatment set out in section 62(2) were satisfied.

Urgent treatment
62.—(1) Sections 57 and 58 above shall not apply to any treatment—   **1–666**
(a) which is immediately necessary to save the patient's life; or
(b) which (not being irreversible) is immediately necessary to prevent a serious deterioration of his condition; or
(c) which (not being irreversible or hazardous) is immediately necessary to alleviate serious suffering by the patient; or
(d) which (not being irreversible or hazardous) is immediately necessary and represents the minimum interference necessary to prevent the patient from behaving violently or being a danger to himself or to others.

(2) Sections 60 and 61(3) above shall not preclude the continuation of any treatment or of treatment under any plan pending compliance with section 57 or 58 above if the responsible medical officer considers that the discontinuance of the treatment or of treatment under the plan would cause serious suffering to the patient.

(3) For the purposes of this section treatment is irreversible if it has unfavourable irreversible physical or psychological consequences and hazardous if it entails significant physical hazard.

DEFINITIONS
  patient: ss.56, 145(1).   **1–667**
  responsible medical officer: s.64(1).

GENERAL NOTE
  This section, which is considered in the *Code of Practice* at paragraphs 16.40 and **1–668**
16.41, states that the procedural safeguards provided for in sections 57 and 58 shall not apply to certain categories of urgent treatment. It is not applicable to any treatment that does not come within the remit of either section 57 or 58.
  "When second opinion consultations are requested for medication it is unusual for emergency drugs to be given in the interval between the request for a consultation and the [second opinion doctor's] visit. When ECT is requested it is more common for one or two administrations of ECT to be required urgently before the consultation is undertaken. This usually happens with a very sick patient, where one treatment may be given within the two days taken to arrange the consultation, or perhaps a few more over an extended bank holiday weekend" (Mental Health Act Commission, Third Biennial Report 1987–1989, para. 7.6(j)).
  The Mental Health Act Commission has expressed its concern "about treatment given in emergency situations which fall outside the Consent to Treatment provisions of the Act. Some treatment is described as being given under the provisions of section 62 when in fact the patient is either not detained or is held under the short-term holding powers of the Act to which section 62 does not apply" (Fifth Biennial Report 1991–1993, para. 7.12). If treatment is to be given in these circumstances it must be justified under common law: see the General Note to this Part.
  Although there is no statutory form to be completed when this section is invoked, the *Code of Practice*, at paragraph 16.41, recommends that hospital managers should devise a form and ensure that it is completed by the patient's responsible medical officer on every occasion when treatment is given under this section.

Subsection (1)
  Note that the test in this provision is not one of mere necessity: the treatment must **1–669**
be *immediately* necessary. It is for the patient's responsible medical officer to determine whether the criteria set out in this subsection are satisfied.

Sections 57 and 58: It is highly unlikely that doctors would use this section to provide treatments covered by section 57 in the absence of a detained patient's consent.

Shall not apply: Which means that the treatment can be given to a detained patient without his consent by virtue of the power given to the patient's responsible medical officer by section 63. As section 63 does not apply to informal patients, the responsible medical officer must find a common law justification for proceeding without the patient's consent if he plans to give a section 57 treatment to a mentally incapable informal patient in any of the circumstances set out in paragraphs (a) to (d).

Treatment: This section provides authorisation for treatment to be given as a response to an immediate crisis. If it is proposed to continue with the treatment thereafter, the procedures set out under section 57 or 58 should be observed. "Our view, expressed in the First Biennial Report, remains that where this section is invoked a request should generally simultaneously be made for a second opinion, so that repeated use does not arise" (M.H.A.C., *Second Biennial Report*, 1985–87, para. 7.6).

Subsection (2)

1–670   This subsection provides that a course of treatment or a plan of treatment can continue notwithstanding that the patient has withdrawn his consent if the responsible medical officer considers that discontinuing the treatment or plan of treatment would cause the patient *serious* suffering.

Section 58: The responsible medical officer should immediately contact the Mental Health Act Commission and request a second opinion if the section 58 treatment is to continue.

Serious suffering: Treatment must cease as soon as its cessation would no longer cause the patient serious suffering.

Subsection (3)

1–671   Paragraph 6.25 of the White Paper Cmnd. 7320 contains the following definitions of "irreversible" and "hazardous" treatments: "irreversible treatments" are "treatments which necessitate the removal or destruction of brain tissue or are designed to effect irreversible change in cerebral or bodily functions"; "hazardous treatments" are "treatments where the risk of adverse reaction or the severity of such reaction would be disproportionate to the degree of benefit the treatment is likely to confer or the prospect of success."

Unfavourable: At the Special Standing Committee the Under-Secretary of State cited the removal of a brain tumour and the removal of a diseased thyroid as examples of treatments which are irreversible and which can be reasonably expected to have favourable consequences. (Sitting of June 29, 1982.)

Treatment not requiring consent

1–672   **63.** The consent of a patient shall not be required for any medical treatment given to him for the mental disorder from which he is suffering, not being treatment falling within section 57 or 58 above, if the treatment is given by or under the direction of the responsible medical officer.

DEFINITIONS

1–673   patient: ss.56, 145(1).
medical treatment: s.145(1).
mental disorder: ss.1, 145(1).
responsible medical officer: s.64(1).

GENERAL NOTE

This section, which is considered in the *Code of Practice* at paragraphs 16.38 and **1–674**
16.39, provides that the consent of a patient to whom this Part applies (see s.56(1)) is
not required for treatment which does not fall within sections 57 or 58. Treatment
should only be given under this section if it is considered by the treating doctor to be
in the patient's best interests. The Minister for Health's response to the argument
that detained patients should not be forced to receive treatment is contained in the
following passage from his speech to the Special Standing Committee: "[That
argument would] lead us to conclude that those who were forcibly detained and had
lost their liberty against their will ... should be kept in custody in places in which they
received no treatment despite the fact that those who looked after them would have
to gaze on them knowing perfectly well that some treatment could be given to
alleviate their suffering and distress and enable them eventually to recover their
liberty. Hospitals are places of treatment and we cannot have hospitals in which
people are locked up and left to wander about without receiving treatment" (sitting
of June 29, 1982). The Government's response to the criticism that this provision
might authorise a disturbingly wide range of interventions was given by Lord Elton,
who emphasised that it was not intended to apply to "borderline" or "experimental"
treatments, but to "things which a person in hospital for treatment ought to undergo
for his own good and for the good of the running of the hospital and for the good of
other patients ... perfectly routine, sensible treatment"(H.L. vol. 426, col. 107).

Although treatments which do not come within sections 57 or 58 may be given to a
patient without his consent "in practice it is impossible to undertake many of the
therapies concerned without a patient's co-operation" (Cmnd 8405, para. 37).

A complaint made by a patient about treatment that was given under this section
without his consent may be investigated by the Mental Health Act Commission
(s.120(1)(b)).

The Human Rights Act 1998

In *B v. Croydon Health Authority*, below, counsel for the patient submitted that if **1–675**
the meaning of "medical treatment for ... mental disorder" was wide enough to
include ancillary forms of treatment, this section would involve a breach of Article 8
of the European Convention on Human Rights. He referred to *Herczegfalvy v.
Austria* 15 E.H.R.R. 537 at 485 in which the European Court of Human Rights said
that a measure constituting an interference with private life and therefore prima facie
contrary to Article 8(1) (like involuntary tube feeding) can only be justified under
Article 8(2) if, among the other requirements of that Article, its terms are sufficiently
precise to enable the individual "to foresee its consequences for him". This
requirement is necessary to prevent such measures from being a source of arbitrary
power, contrary to the rule of law. In rejecting counsel's submission, Hoffmann L.J.
said: "In my judgment section 63 amply satisfies this test. There is no conceptual
vagueness about the notion of treating the symptoms or consequences of a mental
disorder, although naturally there will be borderline cases. But there is no question of
exercise of arbitrary power" (at 688).

Consent ... shall not be required: The consent of the patient should always be
sought (*Code of Practice*, para. 16.4).

Medical treatment ... for the mental disorder: The leading case on the meaning of
this phrase is *B v. Croydon Health Authority* [1995] 1 All E.R. 683, where the Court of
Appeal held that:

(1) a range of acts ancillary to the core treatment that the patient is receiving fall
within the term "medical treatment" as defined in section 145(1);
(2) treatment is capable of being ancillary to the core treatment if it is nursing and
care "concurrent with the core treatment or as a necessary prerequisite to such

treatment or to prevent the patient from causing harm to himself or to alleviate the consequences of the disorder ... " *per* Hoffmann L.J. at 687; and
(3) relieving the symptoms of the mental disorder is just as much a part of treatment as relieving its underlying cause.

Applying these findings to the case before it, the Court of Appeal held that the feeding by nasogastric tube of a patient suffering from borderline personality disorder was treatment which fell within the scope of this section because such treatment was aimed at treating a symptom of the disorder which was a refusal to eat in order to inflict self harm. Feeding by naso-gastic tube was held to constitute treatment for the mental disorder of anorexia nervosa in *Re K.B.* [1997] 2 F.L.R. 180. In *R. v. Collins and Ashworth Hospital Authority, ex p. Brady*, March 10, 2000, Kay J., held that as the patient's hunger strike was a manifestation or symptom of his personality disorder, the force feeding of the patient came within this section because it constituted a form of treatment for his disorder. David Pannick Q.C., in his comment on this case, states that "it is a considerable expansion of the section 63 principle to bring within its scope a person who would prefer to die rather than submit to control by those detaining him" ("State should not go out of its way to keep Brady alive", *The Times*, March 14, 2000). Although Douglas Brown J. suggested in *Re V.S. (Adult: Mental Disorder)* (1995) 3 Med. L. Rev. 292 that cases involving force-feeding under this section should routinely be brought before the court for consideration, it is submitted that such action should only be taken if there is uncertainty about the application of this section to a particular case.

In *Brady*, Kay J. further held that when a responsible medical officer is challenged by way of judicial review in respect of treatment given by him or under his direction which he seeks to justify by reference to this section, the test to be applied by the court is the "super *Wednesbury* test" appropriate to human rights cases rather than the "precedent fact" test established in *Khawaja v. Secretary of State for the Home Department* [1984] 1 A.C. 74. The "super *Wednesbury* test" was set out in *R. v. Ministry of Defence, ex p. Smith* [1996] Q.B. 517, 554 by Sir Thomas Bingham:

"The court may not interfere with the exercise of an administrative discretion on substantive grounds save where the court is satisfied that the decision is unreasonable in the sense that it is beyond the range of responses open to a reasonable decision-maker. But in judging whether the decision-maker has exceeded the margin of appreciation the human rights context is important. The more substantial the interference with human rights, the more the court will be required by way of justification before it is satisfied that the decision is reasonable in the sense outlined above."

A person detained under this Act cannot be forced into medical procedures unconnected with her mental condition unless she is deprived of her capacity to decide for herself, in which case the treatment would be authorised under common law (*St George's Healthcare NHS Trust v. S* [1998] 3 All E.R. 673, CA). Equally, it would be unlawful to treat a person under this Act in a situation where the patient's physical disorder was giving rise to symptoms that effected the patient's mental state, *e.g.* delirium. Such symptoms could not be treated under the Act as they are not symptoms of a mental disorder. Common law rules relating to medical treatment are set out in the General Note to this Part.

The *Croydon* case, above, was applied by Wall J. in *Tameside and Glossop Acute Services Trust v. C.H.* [1996] 1 F.L.R. 762. In this case a pregnant patient who was suffering from schizophrenia had been detained under section 3 of this Act. She had the delusional belief that the doctors who were caring for her wished to harm her baby. The baby was not developing well and the obstetrician took the view that if the pregnancy was allowed to continue the baby might die in the womb. For that reason the obstetrician wished to induce labour and, if necessary, perform a caesarean section. The trust sought a declaration that it would be lawful to carry out such treatment without the patient's consent and to use any necessary force to restrain her in order to facilitate the treatment. Wall J. held that there were "several strands in the evidence" which brought the proposed treatment within the scope of this section:

"First, there is the proposition that an ancillary reason for the induction and, if necessary, the birth by caesarean section is to prevent a deterioration in the [patient's] mental state. Secondly, there is the clear evidence of [the patient's psychiatrist] that in order for the treatment of her schizophrenia to be effective, it is necessary for her to give birth to a live baby. Thirdly, the overall structure of her treatment requires her to receive strong anti-psychotic medication. The administration of that treatment has been necessarily interrupted by her pregnancy and cannot be resumed until her child is born. It is not, therefore, I think stretching language unduly to say that achievement of a successful outcome of her pregnancy is a necessary part of the overall treatment of her mental disorder" (at 773).

His Lordship granted the declaration sought, distinguishing *Re C (Adult: Refusal of Medical Treatment),* [1994] 1 All E.R. 819 where a schizophrenic patient was held to have the mental capacity to refuse treatment for gangrene which was considered to be life threatening, on the ground that "C's gangrene was not likely to affect his mental condition: the manner in which the delivery of the [patient's] child is treated is likely to have a direct effect on her mental state". As the patient's pregnancy was neither a symptom nor a consequence of her mental disorder, this finding appears to allow a doctor to claim that the treatment of a condition which has no apparent connection with the patient's mental disorder comes within the scope of this section on the ground that such treatment will either enhance, or prevent a deterioration of, the patient's mental condition. Although it has been said that the decision of the Court of Appeal in *St George's Healthcare NHS Trust v. S,* above, would result in the *Tameside* case not being followed in future (see L. Jewell, "Treatment Without Consent" [1998] Fam. Law 774), this case did not overrule *Tameside* or subject the notion of "ancillary treatment" to analysis. In the *St George's* case, *B v. Croydon Health Authority* was cited as authority for the proposition that this section "may apply to the treatment of any condition which is integral to the mental disorder" (*per* Judge L.J. at 693). As the treatment of a condition that is "a necessary part of the overall treatment of [the] mental disorder" (see Wall J., above) is treatment which is "integral to the mental disorder", the judgments in the *St George's* and *Tameside* cases would appear to be compatible.

The reason why a declaration was sought in the *Tameside* case, above, was the fact that the obstetrician might have had to use force. Wall J. held that it was permissible, should the doctor deem it to be clinically necessary, to use restraint to the extent to which it may be reasonably required in order to achieve the delivery by the patient of a healthy baby. It is therefore lawful for doctors and nurses to use restraint, so far as reasonably required and clinically necessary, to administer treatment under this part. His Lordship agreed with counsel's proposition that "in cases in which the question of restraint arose or was likely to arise, and the doctor was doubtful about the lawfulness of the application of restraint or the use of force, an application should be made to the court for a declaration that the treatment would be lawful", (at 774).

It is submitted that "the mental disorder from which [the patient] is suffering" would include a category of mental disorder which was not identified on the application or order which authorised the patient's initial detention. A patient who was categorised as being psychopathic at the time of his detention could therefore be treated under this section for a subsequently diagnosed mental illness

By or under the direction of the responsible medical officer: A regime of behaviour modification instituted by a psychologist would not come within the scope of this section if it occurred without the concurrence of the patient's responsible medical officer.

Supplementary provisions for Part IV

1–676   **64.**—(1) In this Part of this Act "the responsible medical officer" means the registered medical practitioner in charge of the treatment of the patient in question and "hospital" includes a [registered establishment].

(2) Any certificate for the purposes of this Part of this Act shall be in such form as may be prescribed by regulations made by the Secretary of State.

AMENDMENT
   The words in square brackets in subs. (1) were substituted by the Care Standards Act 2000, s.116, Sched. 4, para. 9(2).

DEFINITIONS
1–677   patient: s.145(1).
   hospital: s.145(1).
   registered establishment: ss.34(1), 145(1).

Subsection (1)
1–678   *Medical practitioner in charge:* See the note on section 55(1).

Subsection (2)
1–679   *Secretary of State:* Or, in relation to Wales, the National Assembly for Wales (S.I. 1999 No. 672, art. 2, Sched. 1).

PART V

MENTAL HEALTH REVIEW TRIBUNALS

Constitution, etc.

Mental Health Review Tribunals

1–680   **65.**—[(1) There shall be tribunals, known as Mental Health Review Tribunals, for the purpose of dealing with applications and references by and in respect of patients under the provisions of this Act.

(1A) There shall be—

(a) one tribunal for each region of England, and

(b) one tribunal for Wales.

(1B) The Secretary of State—

(a) shall by order determine regions for the purpose of subsection (1A)(a) above; and

(b) may by order vary a region determined for that purpose;

and the Secretary of State shall act under this subsection so as to secure that the regions together comprise the whole of England.

(1C) Any order made under subsection (1B) above may make such transitional, consequential, incidental or supplemental provision as the Secretary of State considers appropriate.]

(2) The provisions of Schedule 2 to this Act shall have effect with respect to the constitution of Mental Health Review Tribunals.

(3) Subject to the provisions of Schedule 2 to this Act, and to rules made by the Lord Chancellor under this Act, the jurisdiction of a Mental Health

Review Tribunal may be exercised by any three or more of its members, and references in this Act to a Mental Health Review Tribunal shall be construed accordingly.

(4) The Secretary of State may pay to the members of Mental Health Review Tribunals such remuneration and allowances as he may with the consent of the Treasury determine, and defray the expenses of such tribunals to such amount as he may with the consent of the Treasury determine, and may provide for each such tribunal such officers and servants, and such accommodation, as the tribunal may require.

AMENDMENT
Subs. (1) was substituted by the Health Authorities Act 1995, s.2(1), Sched. 1, para. 107(6).

DEFINITION
patient: s.145(1).   1–681

GENERAL NOTE
The Royal Commission recommended that psychiatric patients should be **1–682** provided with a safeguard against unjustified detention or control under guardianship by means of an independent review of their cases from both medical and non-medical points of view. It proposed that the review should be undertaken by a local tribunal which would consist of medical and non-medical members selected from a panel of suitable people. This proposal was carried into effect by the 1959 Act which provided for the setting up of Mental Health Review Tribunals. Tribunals are empowered under this Act to review the cases of detained patients apart from those who are detained under sections 4, 5, 35, 36, 38, 135 and 136. Tribunals can also hear applications in relation to patients who are subject to guardianship, to guardianship orders made by a court or to supervised discharge. There is no jurisdiction over informal patients. Provisions relating to the constitution of Mental Health Review Tribunals are contained in Schedule 2. As it is a creature of statute a Mental Health Review Tribunal has no inherent jurisdiction. J. Peay, *Tribunals on Trial: A Study of Decision-Making under the Mental Health Act 1983*, 1989 provides a survey of the operation of tribunals. For a critique of the tribunal system, see H. Crimlisk and M. Phelan, "Mental Health Review Tribunals. Time for a change?" (1996) 169 Br. J. of Psychiatry 678–681.

Tribunals are obliged to follow the procedure laid down in the Mental Health Review Tribunal Rules 1983 and where the Rules are silent on a point of procedure the tribunal must follow the rules of natural justice, *i.e.* it should act in a fair and unbiased way and should provide an opportunity for each party to adequately state his case. The procedure of Mental Health Review Tribunals is considered by A. Eldergill in *Mental Health Review Tribunals: Law and Practice* (1998), by L. Gostin and P. Fennell in *Mental Health: Tribunal Procedure*, 1992, and by Judge Palmer in *Litigation*, Vol. 4, No. 4, pp. 136–143. For a study which examines the reasons for the delays in holding tribunal hearings, see S. Blumenthal and S. Wessely, *The Pattern of Delays in Mental Health Review Tribunals (Summary)*, HMSO, 1994. The same authors estimate that the direct and indirect costs of the tribunal system are over £12 million per year ("The cost of Mental Health Review Tribunals" (1994) *Psychiatric Bulletin* 18, 328–322).

In *W v. Egdell and others* [1989] 1 All E.R. 1089, 1095, Scott J. described the nature **1–683** of a hearing before a Mental Health Review Tribunal as inquisitional, not adversarial. Aldous L.J. has said that a tribunal "should apply its mind to the matters before it in each case. It should not feel itself fettered by a previous decision but of course it should pay due regard to it" (*R. v. South West Thames Mental Health Review Tribunal, ex p. Demetri* [1997] C.O.D. 44, CA). Also note Burton J.'s statement that "there is clear authority that a tribunal hearing is completely unfettered by any earlier tribunal, is not bound by its decision and must approach the case ... afresh in the light of the medical evidence which, of course, will include historical evidence of how the [patient] is and whether he qualifies under the Act at the date of the fresh tribunal, whatever may have been the position in the past" (*R v. The Mental Health Review Tribunal, ex p. Pearson,* July 14, 2000, at para. 9).

The proceedings in a Mental Health Review Tribunal can be challenged either by applying to the High Court for judicial review or by requiring the tribunal to state a case for the determination by the High Court on a point of law under section 78(8). In *Bone v. Mental Health Review Tribunal* [1985] 3 All E.R. 330, 334, Nolan J. said that "the procedure of an application for judicial review should be considered as an alternative to a case stated under section 78(8). I say this not only because the judicial review procedure allows a broader consideration of the issues, but also because it offers a much more comprehensive range of reliefs".

Although a tribunal has no powers itself to deal with the contempt of its proceedings, the ruling of the House of Lords in *Pickering v. Liverpool Daily Post and Echo Newspapers plc* [1991] 1 All E.R. 622 that Mental Health Review Tribunals were courts for the purposes of the law of contempt means that it is open to a party of the proceedings to apply to the Divisional Court for the committal of any party who is in contempt of the tribunal: see Gostin and Fennell, above, pp. 143–145, the note on rule 21(5) of the Mental Health Review Tribunal Rules 1983 and the note on "Contempt of Court" in the General Note to section 37.

The function of a tribunal is to review the justification for the patient's continued detention or guardianship at the time of the hearing. "It has no power to consider the validity of the admission which gave rise to the liability to be detained"; *per* Ackner L.J. in *R. v. Hallstrom, ex p. Waldron* [1986] 1 Q.B. 824 at 846. However, the circumstances of the admission would need to be taken account of when the tribunal considers the patient's condition at the time of the hearing: "as its name suggests, the Mental Health Review Tribunal is a body charged with reviewing the operative decisions of the responsible authorities to detain the patient, and its functions are to reappraise the patient's condition at the time of the hearing and in the light of its findings do one of three things—to direct discharge as of right, to direct discharge in the exercise of its discretion, or to do neither"; *per* Sedley J. in *R. v. Cannons Park Mental Health Review Tribunal, ex p. A* [1994] 1 All E.R. 481, at 490.

Although the *Hallstrom* case, above, confirmed that tribunals do not have jurisdiction to consider the legal validity of the patient's admission, Ackner L.J.'s *obiter* comment in that case that "the jurisdiction given to the tribunal is limited to entertaining applications made by a person who *is liable* to be detained" has been taken as providing authority for a tribunal either to refuse to consider a case where it considers that the patient's detention is invalid or to exercise its discretion under section 72(1) to discharge a patient subject to an "invalid" application on the ground that he is not "liable to be detained". It is submitted that a tribunal that adopts either of these options is acting unlawfully because: (1) a proper interpretation of this Act does not allow for such options being available to the tribunal as neither the Act nor the Mental Health Review Tribunal Rules provide for a tribunal to refuse to determine a validly made application or to adjudicate on the validity of the application or order; and (2) the consequence of acting in such a manner is to usurp the jurisdiction of the High Court to determine the legality of the application; also see the *Cooper* case cited in the General Note to section 72. The tribunal can also be said to be acting unwisely because, if it refuses to consider the application the patient remains liable to be detained and either the hospital managers or the patient's responsible medical officer will be placed under pressure to exercise their power of discharge under section 23. If the tribunal has formed an incorrect opinion as to the validity of the application (in the experience of the author, this has happened on a number of occasions) the patient will be discharged inappropriately. Although it has been argued that the decision of the Court of Appeal in *Re V.E.* [1973] 1 Q.B. 452 (a case on provisions of the Mental Health Act 1959 which are not replicated in this Act) is authority for the proposition that a tribunal which is satisfied that a patient's detention is invalid is obliged to direct his discharge (see A. Eldergill, *Mental Health Review Tribunals* (1998), p. 588), it is submitted that a better interpretation of this case is that it determined that a tribunal has an obligation to discharge a patient if it makes a finding that it is empowered to make and *the effect of that finding* is that there is no longer lawful authority to detain the patient.

By virtue of section 132(1)(b) of this Act hospital managers have a duty to inform patients of their right to make an application to a Mental Health Review Tribunal. Patients who are subject to supervised discharge must also be informed of their rights of applying to a tribunal: see sections 25A(8) and 25G(8).

Habeas Corpus and Judicial Review

If a patient considers that his initial admission was unlawful he can attempt to **1–684** secure his release by making an application to the High Court for a writ of *habeas corpus*. The writ of *habeas corpus* runs to the party having the applicant in his custody (the hospital managers) and not the doctor who made medical recommendation in support of an application under Part II of this Act (*R. v. South Western Hospital, Managers, ex p. M* [1994] 1 All E.R. 161). An alternative course of action for a person who considers that he has been wrongfully detained would be to make an application to the High Court for judicial review. An application for judicial review was successfully made in *R. v. Hallstrom, ex p. W* [1986] 2 All E.R. 306. In *Perkins v. Bath District Health Authority*; *R. v. Wessex Mental Health Review Tribunal, ex p. Wiltshire C.C.*, *The Times*, August 29, 1989, CA, Lord Donaldson M.R. expressed the view that a combination of *habeas corpus* and judicial review would "cover the entire field".

The distinction between the *habeas corpus* and judicial review procedures was explained by Lord Donaldson M.R. in the following extract from his judgment in *R. v. Secretary of State for the Home Department, ex p. Cheblak* [1991] 2 All E.R. 319 at 322, 323, a case where the applicant was seeking to challenge his arrest and the decision to deport him:

> "Although, as I have said, the two forms of relief which Mr. Cheblak seeks are interrelated on the facts of his case, they are essentially different. A writ of *habeas corpus* will issue where someone is detained without any authority or the purported authority is beyond the powers of the person authorising the detention and so is unlawful. *The remedy of judicial review* is available where the decision or action sought to be impugned is within the powers of the person taking it but, due to procedural error, a misappreciation of the law, a failure to take account of relevant matters, a taking account of irrelevant matters or the fundamental unreasonableness of the decision or action, it should never have been taken. In such a case the decision or action is lawful, unless and until it is set aside by a court of competent jurisdiction. In the case of detention, if the warrant, or the underlying decision to deport, were set aside but the detention continued, a writ of *habeas corpus* would issue."

The distinction between *habeas corpus* and judicial review as explained by Lord Donaldson M.R. was applied to this Act in *Re S-C (Mental Patient: Habeas Corpus)* [1996] 1 All E.R. 532, CA. In this case the patient was challenging the lawfulness of his detention on the ground that the application signed by the approved social worker was not "duly completed" as required by section 6(1) because a condition precedent relating to the section 3 application was not present in that the patient's nearest relative had not been consulted as required by section 11(4). The court held that as the patient's challenge was not directed to an administrative decision but to the jurisdiction of the hospital managers to detain him, an application for *habeas corpus* was the appropriate remedy rather than proceedings for judicial review. In *D.T. v. Chase Farm Hospital*, May 17, 2000, the applicant submitted that the court considering the remedy of *habeas corpus* is not limited to considering whether the procedural requisites for detention are met, but can also take action where there is inadequate evidence to justify the detention. Owen J., in refusing the application, held that although there was authority to support the contention that *habeas corpus* is available when there is no evidence to justify the decision to detain (*R. v. Board of Control, ex p. Rutty* [1956] 2 Q.B. 109), this does not support an argument that when a case before a tribunal is strong, but no decision has been given because the tribunal adjourned the hearing, the court hearing the application can consider the evidence, side-line the tribunal, and find that the tribunal should discharge. His Lordship said that in these circumstances "it is evident that the tribunal should make the decision."

In *B. v. Barking Havering and Brentwood Community Healthcare NHS Trust* [1999] 1 F.L.R. 106, CA, Lord Woolf M.R. referred to a passage in the judgment of Sir Thomas Bingham M.R. in *Re S.-C.*, above, where his Lordship said that on the facts of that case "an application for *habeas corpus* is *an* appropriate, and possibly even *the* appropriate course to pursue". Lord Woolf expressed his respectful disagreement with the suggestion that "possibly" an application for *habeas corpus* was the only procedure that was appropriate. While accepting that in *Re S.-C. habeas corpus* was an appropriate procedure, his Lordship suggested that judicial review was equally appropriate and would even have advantages over *habeas corpus*. His Lordship would discourage applications for *habeas corpus* unless it was clear that no other form of relief would be required. Where applications were made for both judicial review and *habeas corpus*, the proceedings should be harmonised if at all possible.

The court considering an application for judicial review is exercising a public law jurisdiction and is not required to grant the application even if unlawfulness is established. An application will only proceed if it is in the public interest to do so. The courts have shown a reluctance to grant applications if a tribunal hearing is imminent (see, for example, *R. v. North East Thames Mental Health Review Tribunal, ex p. Brown*, June 13, 2000). In order to succeed in an application for judicial review, one of the established grounds must be made out, namely that the tribunal has misdirected itself in law, has behaved with *Wednesbury* unreasonableness (see *Associated Provincial Picture Houses v. Wednesbury Corporation* [1948] 1 K.B. 223), or has failed to act with procedural fairness toward one of the parties. The courts are slow to interfere with a tribunal decision on the grounds of *Wednesbury* unreasonableness (see, for example, *R. v. Mental Health Review Tribunal, ex p. Haringey L.B.C.*, April 4, 1995); see further, Phil Fennell, "Judicial Review and Mental Health" from T. Buck, *Judicial Review and Social Welfare*, 1998, pp. 55–89.

The decision of a tribunal that has been quashed on judicial review becomes a nullity (*R. (on the application of Wirral Health Authority and Wirral Borough Council) v. Dr Finnegan and D.E.* [2001] EWHC Admin 312).

Legal Aid

1–685   The provision of legal aid for representation before Mental Health Review Tribunals is limited to legal practices specifically approved for this purpose by the Legal Services Commission; also see the General Note to the Mental Health Review Tribunal Rules 1983.

Council on Tribunals

1–686   The operation of the Mental Health Review Tribunal System is subject to the oversight of the Council on Tribunals: see the General Note to the Mental Health Review Tribunal Rules 1983. The Council published a Special Report on Mental Health Review Tribunals in 2000 (Cm. 4740).

The Human Rights Act 1998
The Mental Health Review Tribunal is a "public authority" for the purposes of the **1–687**
1998 Act (*ibid.,* s.6(3)(a)).

Subsection (1B)
Shall by order: The Mental Health Review Tribunals (Regions) Order 1998 (S.I. **1–688**
1998 No. 1460) determines the following regions for Mental Health Review
Tribunals from August 1, 1998: North London and East, Trent and Northern and
Yorkshire, South London and South and West and West Midlands and North West.
A separate tribunal office continues to operate for Wales. The addresses of these
offices are set out in Appendix 2 to the *Memorandum.*

Subsection (3)
Three or more of its members: It is rare for a tribunal to consist of more than three **1–689**
members.

Subsection (4)
Secretary of State: The functions of the Minister, so far as exercisable in relation to **1–690**
Wales, are exercised by the National Assembly for Wales (S.I. 1999 No. 672, art. 2,
Sched. 1).

Applications and references concerning Part II patients

Applications to tribunals
66.—(1) Where— **1–691**
 (a) a patient is admitted to a hospital in pursuance of an application for
   admission for assessment; or
 (b) a patient is admitted to a hospital in pursuance of an application for
   admission for treatment; or
 (c) a patient is received into guardianship in pursuance of a guardianship
   application; or
 (d) a report is furnished under section 16 above in respect of a patient; or
 (e) a patient is transferred from guardianship to a hospital in pursuance
   of regulations made under section 19 above; or
 (f) a report is furnished under section 20 above in respect of a patient and
   the patient is not discharged; or
 [(fa) a report is furnished under subsection (2) of section 21B above in
   respect of a patient and subsection (5) of that section applies (or
   subsections (5) and (6)(b) of that section apply) in the case of the
   report; or
 (fb) a report is furnished under subsection (2) of section 21B above in
   respect of a patient and subsection (8) of that section applies in the
   case of the report; or]
 (g) a report is furnished under section 25 above in respect of a patient
   who is detained in pursuance of an application for admission for
   treatment; or
 [(ga) a supervision application is accepted in respect of a patient; or
 (gb) a report is furnished under section 25F above in respect of a patient;
   or
 (gc) a report is furnished under 25G above in respect of a patient; or]
 (h) an order is made under section 29 above in respect of a patient who is
   or subsequently becomes liable to be detained or subject to guardianship under Part II of this Act,

an application may be made to a Mental Health Review Tribunal within the
relevant period—
>   (i) by the patient (except in the cases mentioned in paragraphs (g)
>   and (h) above) or, in the [cases mentioned in paragraphs (d), (ga),
>   (gb) and (gc), by his nearest relative if he has been (or was entitled
>   to be) informed under this Act of the report or acceptance] by his
>   nearest relative, and
>   (ii) in the cases mentioned in paragraphs (g) and (h) above, by his
>   nearest relative.

(2) In subsection (1) above "the relevant period" means—

(a) in the case mentioned in paragraph (a) of that subsection, 14 days
     beginning with the day on which the patient is admitted as so
     mentioned;

(b) in the case mentioned in paragraph (b) of that subsection, six months
     beginning with the day on which the patient is admitted as so
     mentioned;

(c) in the [cases mentioned in paragraphs (c) and (ga)] of that subsection,
     six months beginning with the day on which the application is
     accepted;

(d) in the cases mentioned in paragraphs (d) [, (fb)] [,(g) and (gb)] of that
     subsection, 28 days beginning with the day on which the applicant is
     informed that the report has been furnished;

(e) in the case mentioned in paragraph (e) of that subsection, six months
     beginning with the day on which the patient is transferred;

(f) in the case mentioned in paragraph (f) [or (fa) of that subsection, the
     period or periods] for which authority for the patient's detention or
     guardianship is renewed by virtue of the report;

[(fa) in the case mentioned in paragraph (gc) of that subsection, the further
     period for which the patient is made subject to after-care under
     supervision by virtue of the report;]

(g) in the case mentioned in paragraph (h) of that subsection, 12 months
     beginning with the date of the order, and in any subsequent period of
     12 months during which the order continues in force.

(3) Section 32 above shall apply for the purposes of this section as it
applies for the purposes of Part II of this Act.

AMENDMENTS
The amendments to this section were made by the Mental Health (Patients in the
Community) Act 1995, s.2(1), Sched. 1, para. 7, s.2(6).

DEFINITIONS
1–692   patient: s.145(1).
hospital: ss.79(6), 145(1).
application for admission for assessment: ss.2, 145(1).
application for admission for treatment: ss.3, 145(1).
nearest relative: ss.26(3), 145(1).

GENERAL NOTE
1–693   This section identifies the occasions on which a patient or his or her nearest relative
may make an application to a tribunal. Only one application may be made within the
specified period (s.77(2)).
In *R. v. The South Thames Mental Health Review Tribunal, ex p. M* [1998] C.O.D.
38, Collins J. held that the right of a patient to make an application to a tribunal is

founded on the patient's admission, which is something that happens in a moment of time, and not on his detention. Applying this ruling to the situation of a patient who is admitted and detained under section 2 and who is subsequently detained under section 3 during the currency of the section 2, his Lordship held that the following passage from paragraph 5.3 of the Code of Practice (1993 edition) is correct:

"Changing a patient's status from section 2 to section 3 will not deprive him of a Mental Health Review Tribunal hearing if the change takes place after a valid application has been made to the Tribunal but before it has been heard. The patient's right to apply for a Tribunal under section 66(1)(b) in the first period of detention after his change of status are unaffected."

His Lordship said that in these circumstances the tribunal must consider the patient's case by using the section 3 criteria set out in section 72(1)(b). The determination of the tribunal on the section 2 application cannot prevent the patient from making a subsequent section 3 application during the first six months of detention if the section 2 application is unsuccessful.

For patients who have been placed under hospital or guardianship orders by a court under section 37, this section reads as follows:

"(1) Where—
    (d) a report is furnished under section 16 above in respect of a patient; or
    (e) a patient is transferred from guardianship to a hospital in pursuance of regulations made under section 19 above; or
    (f) a report is furnished under section 20 above in respect of a patient and the patient is not discharged;
    (fa) a report is furnished under subsection (2) of section 21B above in respect of a patient and subsection (5) of that section applies (or subsections (5) and (6)(b) of that section apply) in the case of the report; or
    (fb) a report is furnished under subsection (2) of section 21B above in respect of a patient and subsection (8) of that section applies in the case of the report; or
    (ga) a supervision application is accepted in respect of a patient; or
    (gb) a report is furnished under section 25F above in respect of a patient; or
    (gc) a report is furnished under section 25G above in respect of a patient;
an application may be made to a Mental Health Review Tribunal within the relevant period by the patient or, in the cases mentioned in paragraphs (d), (ga), (gb) and (gc), by his nearest relative if he has been (or was entitled to be) informed under this Act of the report or acceptance, by his nearest relative.
(2) In subsection (1) above 'the relevant period' means—
    (d) in the cases mentioned in paragraphs (d) and (gb) of that subsection, 28 days beginning with the day on which the applicant is informed that the report has been furnished;
    (e) in the case mentioned in paragraph (e) of that subsection, six months beginning with the day on which the patient is transferred;
    (f) in the case mentioned in paragraph (f) [or (fa) of that subsection, the period or periods] for which authority for the patient's detention or guardianship is renewed by virtue of the report;
    (fa) in the case mentioned in paragraph (gc) of that subsection, the further period for which the patient is made subject to after-care under supervision by virtue of the report;
(3) Section 32 above shall apply for the purposes of this section as it applies for the purposes of Part II of this Act" (Sched. 1, Pt 1, paras 2, 9).

The effect of subsections (1)(f), (2)(f) is to enable a hospital order patient to make his first application to a tribunal during the *second* six months of his detention. The rationale for this is explained in the note to section 69(1). Thereafter the patient's entitlement to make applications corresponds to the entitlements accruing on renewal of the authority to detain Part II patients. A list of Part III patients who can make an application during the *first* six months of detention is set out in paragraph 243 of the *Memorandum*.

Applications by or on behalf of hospital and guardianship order patients can also be made under section 69. Applications by restricted patients are governed by sections 70 and 79.

Subsection (1)

1–694   *Paragraph (a)—application for admission for assessment:* If the patient's status changes to a section 3 patient, see *R. v. South Thames Mental Health Review Tribunal, ex p. M*, which is considered in the General Note to this section. Patients admitted under section 4 are not excluded as an application under that section is "an application for admission for assessment" (s.4(1)) which is founded on one medical recommendation. An application which was made immediately after the patient's admission would automatically lapse if the second medical recommendation required by s.4(4) was not forthcoming.

Paragraph (b)—application for admission for treatment: Made under section 3. If the patient does not make an application within six months of his admission (subs. (2)(b)), the hospital managers will automatically refer the case to the tribunal (s.68(1)). A patient who is subject to a hospital order can make his first application to a tribunal during the *second* six months of his detention under paragraph (f).

A conditionally discharged restriction order patient who has been made subject to an application under section 3 has a right to make an application under this paragraph (*R. v. North West London Mental Health NHS Trust, ex p. Stewart* [1997] C.O.D. 42).

Paragraph (c)—received into guardianship: Under section 7.

Paragraph (d)—report under section 16: Reclassifying the mental disorder of a detained patient or a patient subject to guardianship.

Paragraph (e): A patient who does not exercise his right to apply to a tribunal within six months of his transfer (subs. (2)(e)) will have his case automatically referred to a tribunal by the hospital managers (s.68(1)).

Paragraph (f)—report ... under section 20: Renewing the authority to detain a patient who has been admitted to hospital for treatment or renewing the authority for a patient's guardianship. In certain situations a patient who has been admitted to hospital for treatment will have his case automatically referred to a tribunal by the hospital managers (s.68(2)). See the note on section 68(1) for hospital order patients.

Paragraph (g)—report ... under section 25: By the responsible medical officer nullifying the nearest relative's power to discharge the patient.

Paragraph (ga)—supervision application . Made under section 25A. An application to the tribunal can be made before the patient leaves hospital if the application for supervised discharge has been accepted by the Health Authority.

Paragraph (gb)—report ... under section 25F: Reclassifying the mental disorder of a patient subject to supervised discharge.

Paragraph (gc)—report ... under section 25G: Renewing supervised discharge.

Paragraph (h)—order ... under section 29: By the County Court directing that the functions of the patient's nearest relative be exercised by an acting nearest relative.

An application: Only one application can be made during the period specified in subsection (2). Withdrawn applications do not count for this purpose (s.77(2)). The application should contain the information specified in rule 3 of the Mental Health Tribunal Rules 1983.

Nearest relative: Or, except in relation to paragraph (h), an acting nearest relative. Where an acting nearest relative has been appointed under section 29, that person exercises the right of the nearest relative to make applications to a tribunal under this section and under section 69 (s.29(1)). However, the supplanted nearest relative can make an application to a tribunal for the patient's discharge within the periods specified in subsection (2)(g) (s.29(6)). It would seem that section 29(6) was not drawn to the attention of the Court of Appeal in *Merrill v. County of Herefordshire District Council*, July 27, 1999 where Mummery L.J. said that "[a]lthough we have not had the benefit of full argument from both sides on this point, it would appear, as at present advised, that only the [acting nearest relative] can make an application to a Mental Health Review Tribunal ...".

If the patient is a ward of court the nearest relative cannot make an application to a tribunal without the leave of the High Court (s.33(2)).

The nearest relative could consider using his powers of discharge under section 23(2)(a) as an alternative to making an application to a tribunal.

Or, in the case mentioned in paragraph (d): The patient and the patient's nearest relative cannot both make an application on being told that the patient's mental disorder has been reclassified.

Subsection (2)
14 days: The question whether a patient who has been detained under section 2 is **1–695** entitled to apply to a tribunal in circumstances where the period of detention is extended by virtue of section 29(4) of this Act and the 14-day period has expired is undecided. The point was raised in *R. v. Wessex Mental Health Review Tribunal, ex p. Wiltshire County Council*, (1989) 4 B.M.L.R. 145, CA. It is likely that a court would find that the patient has a right to make an application in these circumstances: see the note on "The Human Rights Act 1998" in section 29.

Beginning with Means "including" (*Hare v. Gocher* [1962] 2 Q.B. 641).

References to tribunals by Secretary of State concerning Part II patients

67.—(1) The Secretary of State may, if he thinks fit, at any time refer to a **1–696** Mental Health Review Tribunal the case of any patient who is liable to be detained or subject to guardianship [or to after-care under supervision] under Part II of this Act.

(2) For the purpose of furnishing information for the purposes of a reference under subsection (1) above any registered medical practitioner authorised by or on behalf of the patient may, at any reasonable time, visit the patient and examine him in private and require the production of and inspect any records relating to the detention or treatment of the patient in any hospital [or to any after-care services provided for the patient under s.117 below].

(3) Section 32 above shall apply for the purposes of this section as it applies for the purposes of Part II of this Act.

AMENDMENT
The words in square brackets in subss. (1) and (2) were inserted by the Mental Health (Patients in the Community) Act 1995, s.2(1), Sched. 1, para. 8.

DEFINITIONS
hospital: ss.79(6), 145(1). **1–697**
patient: s.145(1).

GENERAL NOTE
This section enables the Secretary of State (or, in relation to Wales, the National **1–698** Assembly for Wales) to refer a patient who is liable to be detained, or subject to guardianship or to supervised discharge to a tribunal at any time. It applies to patients who have been placed under hospital or guardianship orders by a court under section 37 (Sched. 1, Pt 1, para. 1). The Home Secretary has a similar power to refer the case of a restricted patient to a tribunal under section 71(1).

Subsection (1)

1–699   *Secretary of State:* The functions of the Minister, so far as exercisable in relation to Wales, are exercised by the National Assembly for Wales (S.I. 1999 No. 672, art. 2, Sched. 1).

If he thinks fit: A reference could be made if the Secretary of State considered that there were good reasons for a tribunal hearing to take place before the date when the patient would be next eligible to make an application under section 66. "A request to the Secretary of State to refer a patient's case to the tribunal should state the reasons for giving the patient's case early consideration by the tribunal and why it would be unreasonable for the patient to wait until he next became eligible to apply to the tribunal" (L. Gostin and P. Fennell, *Mental Health: Tribunal Procedure* (1992), p. 79).

Subsection (2)

1–700   This subsection provides for a patient whose case has been referred to a tribunal under this section to call for an independent medical opinion. A failure to allow the doctor to examine the patient could amount to an offence under section 129.

Duty of managers of hospitals to refer cases to tribunal

1–701   **68.**—(1) Where a patient who is admitted to a hospital in pursuance of an application for admission for treatment or a patient who is transferred from guardianship to hospital does not exercise his right to apply to a Mental Health Review Tribunal under section 66(1) above by virtue of his case falling within paragraph (b) or, as the case may be, paragraph (e) of that section, the managers of the hospital shall at the expiration of the period for making such an application refer the patient's case to such a tribunal unless an application or reference in respect of the patient has then been made under section 66(1) above by virtue of his case falling within paragraph (d), (g) or (h) of that section or under section 67(1) above.

(2) If the authority for the detention of a patient in a hospital is renewed under section 20 [or 21B] above and a period of three years (or, if the patient has not attained the age of sixteen years, one year) has elapsed since his case was last considered by a Mental Health Review Tribunal, whether on his own application or otherwise, the managers of the hospital shall refer his case to such a tribunal.

(3) For the purpose of furnishing information for the purpose of any reference under this section, any registered medical practitioner authorised by or on behalf of the patient may at any reasonable time visit and examine the patient in private and require the production of and inspect any records relating to the detention or treatment of the patient in any hospital [or to any after-care services provided for the patient under section 117 below].

(4) The Secretary of State may by order vary the length of the periods mentioned in subsection (2) above.

(5) For the purposes of subsection (1) above a person who applies to a tribunal but subsequently withdraws his application shall be treated as not having exercised his right to apply, and where a person withdraws his application on a date after the expiration of the period mentioned in that subsection, the managers shall refer the patient's case as soon as possible after that date.

AMENDMENT
   In subss. (2) and (3) the words in square brackets were inserted by the Mental Health (Patients in the Community) Act 1995, s.2(1), Sched. 1, para. 9, s.2(7).

Definitions   **1–702**
   patients: s.145(1).
   hospital: ss.79(6), 145(1).
   application for admission for treatment: ss.3, 145(1).
   the managers: s.145(1).

General Note
   This section requires the hospital managers to refer a patient who has been **1–703**
admitted for treatment, or a patient who has been transferred from guardianship to
hospital, to a tribunal where no application or reference has been made during the
first six months of his detention or within six months of his transfer (subs. (1)). It also
requires the managers to refer to a tribunal a patient (including a hospital order
patient) whose authority to detain is being renewed and who has not had a tribunal
hearing during the preceding three years (or one year in case of a child under 16)
(subs. (2)). The purpose of these provisions is to "ensure that patients who lack the
ability or initiative to make an application to a tribunal … have the safeguard of an
independent review of their case" (Cmnd. 8405, para. 24). Under section 71(2), the
Home Secretary must refer the case of any restricted patient whose case has not been
considered by a tribunal for three years.
   The Law Society has established a panel of solicitors with relevant experience to
assist patients who are automatically referred to a tribunal under this section to find
legal representatives: see the General Note to the Mental Health Review Tribunal
Rules 1983.

Subsection (1)
   Patient: This subsection does not apply to hospital order patients or to patients who **1–704**
have been transferred from prison to hospital.
   Does not exercise his right to apply: Note subsection (5).

Subsection (2)
   Patient in a hospital: Including a patient who is subject to a hospital order made **1–705**
under section 37 (s.40(4)). See section 71(2), for patients subject to restriction orders
and prisoners transferred with restrictions.
   Is renewed: The reference should be made at the time when the patient's detention
is next renewed after the one or three year period has expired.
   Attained the age: At the commencement of his sixteenth birthday (Family Law
Reform Act 1969, s.9(1)).

Subsection (3)
   Medical practitioner: A failure to allow the medical practitioner to perform his **1–706**
functions under this section could amount to an offence under section 129.

Subsection (4)
   Secretary of State: The functions of the Minister, so far as exercisable in relation to **1–707**
Wales, are exercised by the National Assembly of Wales (S.I. 1999 No. 672, art. 2,
Sched. 1).
   By order: See section 143(1).

Applications and references concerning Part III patients

Applications to tribunals concerning patients subject to hospital and guardianship orders
   69.—(1) Without prejudice to any provision of section 66(1) above as **1–708**
applied by section 40(4) above, an application to a Mental Health Review
Tribunal may also be made—

    (a) in respect of a patient admitted to a hospital in pursuance of a hospital order, by the nearest relative of the patient in the period between the expiration of six months and the expiration of 12 months beginning with the date of the order and in any subsequent period of 12 months; and

    (b) in respect of a patient placed under guardianship by a guardianship order—

        (i) by the patient, within the period of six months beginning with the date of the order;

        (ii) by the nearest relative of the patient, within the period of 12 months beginning with the date of the order and in any subsequent period of 12 months.

(2) Where a person detained in a hospital—

    (a) is treated as subject to a hospital order or transfer direction by virtue of section 41(5) above, 82(2) or 85(2) below, [section 77(2) of the Mental Health (Scotland) Act 1984] or section 5(1) of the Criminal Procedure (Insanity) Act 1964; or

    (b) is subject to a direction having the same effect as a hospital order by virtue of section [45B(2),] 40(3), 47(3) or 48(3) above,

then, without prejudice to any provision of Part II of this Act as applied by section 40 above, that person may make an application to a Mental Health Review Tribunal in the period of six months beginning with the date of the order or direction mentioned in paragraph (a) above or, as the case may be, the date of the direction mentioned in paragraph (b) above.

AMENDMENTS

    In subs. (2)(a) the words in square brackets were substituted by the Mental Health (Scotland) Act 1984, s.127(1), Sched. 3, para. 49.

    In subs. (2)(b) the figure in square brackets was inserted by the Crime (Sentences) Act 1997, s.55, Sched. 4, para. 12(8).

DEFINITIONS

1–709   patient: s.145(1).
    hospital: ss.79(6), 145(1).
    hospital order: ss.37, 55(4), 145(1).
    guardianship order: s.55(4).
    transfer direction: ss.47, 145(1).
    nearest relative: ss.26(3), 145(1).

GENERAL NOTE

1–710   This section specifies when a tribunal application can be made by the nearest relative of a patient who has been placed under a hospital order made by a court under section 37. It also enables tribunal applications to be made in respect of guardianship order patients and provides an opportunity for certain other patients who have been admitted to hospital after having committed offences to have their cases reviewed by a tribunal. Applications by restricted patients are governed by sections 70 and 79.

Subsection (1)

1–711   This subsection provides that the nearest relative of a patient detained in hospital under a hospital order can apply to a tribunal during the *second* six months of the patient's detention, and thereafter at yearly intervals. Under the 1959 Act an application could be made to a tribunal within the first six months of the admission. Section 70 provides for a restricted patient to make his initial tribunal application during the second six months of his detention. The Government were advised that a continuance of the right of unrestricted patients to apply to a tribunal within the first six months of their detention would contravene article 14 of the European Convention on Human Rights which states that the "enjoyment of rights and freedoms set forth in [the] Convention shall be secured without discrimination on any ground." It was also pointed out during the Parliamentary debate on this provision that the patient's case would have been examined at the outset by the sentencing court which must have considered the medical evidence. These considerations led to this provision being enacted, together with Schedule 1, Pt 1, paragraphs 2 and 9, which have the effect of postponing the first opportunity for an unrestricted patient to apply to a tribunal from the first six months to the second six months of his detention: see the General Note to section 66.

Hospital order: See section 55(4).

Nearest relative: Or acting nearest relative appointed by the county court under section 29. The patient has a right to apply to a tribunal during the second six months of his detention and at yearly intervals thereafter by virtue of section 66(1)(f),(2)(f).

Beginning with: Including the date of the order (*Hare v. Gocher* [1962] 2 Q.B. 641).

Guardianship order: See section 55(4).

Within the period of six months: A patient who has been placed under a guardianship order can make subsequent applications to the tribunal by virtue of section 66(1)(f),(2)(f).

Subsection (2)

This subsection affects "certain categories of patient whose cases have not recently **1–712** been looked at by a court but who are, simply by reason of the way the [this Act is] put together, deemed to be detained as though subject to a fresh hospital order. I am referring chiefly to restricted patients whose restrictions expire or are removed; patients transferred from prison to hospital subject to restrictions, and whose restrictions subsequently expire; and patients transferred to the English hospital system from Scotland, Northern Ireland, the Isle of Man or the Channel Islands. As a result of [Sched. 1, Pt 1, paras 2, 9], such patients, who may already have been in hospital for a substantial period, would have a six months' gap during which they were not entitled to apply to a Tribunal and had not just had their cases looked at by a court ... [This subsection removes] that gap. In addition, [it] seeks to meet the concern which has been expressed ... about the position of patients immediately after they have been transferred from prison. Again, the grounds for their detention in hospital will not previously have been considered by a court. The Government now accept that such people should have an immediate right to a Tribunal hearing"; *per* Lord Belstead, HL Vol. 427, col. 868.

Section 5(1) of the Criminal Procedure (Insanity) Act: If such a patient does not exercise his right to apply to a tribunal within six months of the order being made, the Secretary of State will refer the patient to a tribunal (s.71(5)).

Applications to tribunals concerning restricted patients

70. A patient who is a restricted patient within the meaning of section 79 **1–713** below and is detained in a hospital may apply to a Mental Health Review Tribunal—

    (a) in the period between the expiration of six months and the expiration of 12 months beginning with the date of the relevant hospital order [, hospital direction] or transfer direction; and

    (b) in any subsequent period of 12 months.

AMENDMENT

In para. (b) the words in square brackets were inserted by the Crime (Sentences) Act 1997, s.55, Sched. 4, para. 12(9).

DEFINITIONS
1–714   patient: s.145(1).
restricted patient: s.79(1).
hospital: ss.79(6), 145(1).
hospital direction: s.145(1).

GENERAL NOTE
1–715   This section provides for a tribunal application to be made by a restricted patient during the second six months of the duration of the hospital order or transfer direction, and at yearly intervals thereafter. Tribunals hearing applications by restricted patients will be chaired by a lawyer who has had substantial experience in the criminal courts: see the note on section 78(4).

A tribunal considering an application made by a restricted patient under this section has no power pursuant to rule 16(1) of the Mental Health Review Tribunal Rules 1983 to adjourn the proceedings so as to monitor the patient's progress in the hope that a projected course of treatment would eventually permit it to discharge the patient (*R. v. Mental Health Review Tribunal, ex p. Secretary of State for the Home Department, The Times*, March 25, 1987).

A patient: The nearest relative of a restricted patient does not have a right to make an application to a tribunal.

Beginning with: Including the date of the hospital order or transfer direction (*Hare v. Gocher* [1962] 2 Q.B. 641).

References by Secretary of State concerning restricted patients
1–716   **71.**—(1) The Secretary of State may at any time refer the case of a restricted patient to a Mental Health Review Tribunal.

(2) The Secretary of State shall refer to a Mental Health Review Tribunal the case of any restricted patient detained in a hospital whose case has not been considered by such a tribunal, whether on his own application or otherwise, within the last three years.

(3) The Secretary of State may by order vary the length of the period mentioned in subsection (2) above.

(4) Any reference under subsection (1) above in respect of a patient who has been conditionally discharged and not recalled to hospital shall be made to the tribunal for the area in which the patient resides.

(5) Where a person who is treated as subject to a hospital order and a restriction order by virtue of an order under section 5(1) of the Criminal Procedure (Insanity) Act 1964 does not exercise his right to apply to a Mental Health Review Tribunal in the period of six months beginning with the date of that order, the Secretary of State shall at the expiration of that period refer his case to a tribunal.

(6) For the purposes of subsection (5) above a person who applies to a tribunal but subsequently withdraws his application shall be treated as not having exercised his right to apply, and where a patient withdraws his application on a date after the expiration of the period there mentioned the Secretary of State shall refer his case as soon as possible after that date.

DEFINITIONS
1–717   restricted patient: s.79(1).
hospital: ss.79(6), 145(1).
hospital order: ss.37, 145(1).
restriction order: ss.41, 145(1).
patient: s.145(1).

GENERAL NOTE

This section provides that the Home Secretary may, and in certain circumstances **1–718** must, refer the case of a restricted patient to a tribunal. The meaning of "restricted patient" is set out in section 79(1).

Subsection (1)

The nature of the Home Secretary's discretion under this provision was examined **1–719** in *R. (on the application of C.) v. The Secretary of State for the Home Department* [2001] EWHC Admin 501, where Collins J. held that:

    (i) the Home Secretary has a discretion to refer a case even where the tribunal has reached a decision, and even though the effect of the reference is to stultify the decision of that tribunal;

    (ii) the discretion is not untrammelled in that the Home Secretary must pay proper respect to the decision of the tribunal. He should not use his power merely because he disagreed with the decision reached by the tribunal; and

    (iii) a reference can be made: (a) where the decision of the tribunal has been ruled unlawful or stayed by the court on judicial review; (b) where the tribunal has imposed a condition that has proved impossible to put into effect; and (c) where there has been a material change of circumstances. With regard to (c), to be consistent with the patient's rights under Article 5 of the European Convention on Human Rights, a reference should only be made if the Home Secretary has formed the view that it is probable that the material in question would have affected the decision of the tribunal in that it would have decided either that a more onerous condition be imposed or that a conditional discharge would not have been ordered.

Subsection (5)

"[A]s a matter of policy, the Home Office will review the case of a patient who has **1–720** been found unfit to plead at six monthly intervals during the first two years after admission to hospital to establish whether he has become fit to stand trial. It is consequently important that responsible medical officers recognise that the first consideration is the patient's fitness for trial rather than his full recovery from mental disorder. Wherever possible, a court should have the opportunity of considering the evidence against a defendant. If he is convicted and remains sufficiently mentally disordered to warrant detention in hospital for treatment, it will be open to the courts to make a hospital order" (*Restricted Patients Detained in Special Hospitals: Information for the Special Hospitals Advisory Service*, Home Office, undated, para. 5.9).

Discharge of patients

Powers of tribunals

72.—(1) Where application is made to a Mental Health Review Tribunal **1–721** by or in respect of a patient who is liable to be detained under this Act, the tribunal may in any case direct that the patient be discharged, and—

    (a) the tribunal shall direct the discharge of a patient liable to be detained under section 2 above if they are satisfied—

        (i) that he is not then suffering from mental disorder or from mental disorder of a nature or degree which warrants his detention in a hospital for assessment (or for assessment followed by a medical treatment) for at least a limited period; or

        (ii) that his detention as aforesaid is not justified in the interests of his own health or safety or with a view to the protection of other persons;

    (b) the tribunal shall direct the discharge of a patient liable to be detained otherwise than under section 2 above if they are satisfied—

        (i) that he is not then suffering from mental illness, psychopathic disorder, severe mental impairment or mental impairment or from any of those forms of disorder of a nature or degree which makes it appropriate for him to be liable to be detained in a hospital for medical treatment; or

(ii) that it is not necessary for the health or safety of the patient or for the protection of other persons that he should receive such treatment; or

(iii) in the case of an application by virtue of paragraph (g) of section 66(1) above, that the patient, if released, would not be likely to act in a manner dangerous to other persons or to himself.

(2) In determining whether to direct the discharge of a patient detained otherwise than under section 2 above in a case not falling within paragraph (b) of subsection (1) above, the tribunal shall have regard—

(a) to the likelihood of medical treatment alleviating or preventing a deterioration of the patient's condition; and

(b) in the case of a patient suffering from mental illness or severe mental impairment, to the likelihood of the patient, if discharged, being able to care for himself, to obtain the care he needs or to guard himself against serious exploitation.

(3) A tribunal may under subsection (1) above direct the discharge of a patient on a future date specified in the direction; and where a tribunal do not direct the discharge of a patient under that subsection the tribunal may—

(a) with a view to facilitating his discharge on a future date, recommend that he be granted leave of absence or transferred to another hospital or into guardianship; and

(b) further consider his case in the event of any such recommendation not being complied with.

[(3A) Where, in the case of an application to a tribunal by or in respect of a patient who is liable to be detained in pursuance of an application for admission for treatment or by virtue of an order or direction for his admission or removal to hospital under Part III of this Act, the tribunal do not direct the discharge of the patient under subsection (1) above, the tribunal may—

(a) recommend that the responsible medical officer consider whether to make a supervision application in respect of the patient; and

(b) further consider his case in the event of no such application being made.]

(4) Where application is made to a Mental Health Review Tribunal by or in respect of a patient who is subject to guardianship under this Act, the tribunal may in any case direct that the patient be discharged, and shall so direct if they are satisfied—

(a) that he is not then suffering from mental illness, psychopathic disorder, severe mental impairment or mental impairment; or

(b) that it is not necessary in the interests of the welfare of the patient, or for the protection of other persons, that the patient should remain under such guardianship.

[(4A) Where application is made to a Mental Health Review Tribunal by or in respect of a patient who is subject to after-care under supervision (or, if he has not yet left hospital, is to be so subject after he leaves hospital), the tribunal may in any case direct that the patient shall cease to be so subject (or not become so subject), and shall so direct if they are satisfied—

(a) in a case where a patient has not yet left hospital, that the condition set out in section 25A(4) above are not complied with; or

(b) in any other case, that the conditions set out in section 25G(4) above are not complied with.]

(5) Where application is made to a Mental Health Review Tribunal under any provision of this Act by or in respect of a patient and the tribunal do not direct that the patient be discharged [or, if he is (or is to be) subject to after-care under supervision, that he cease to be so subject (or not become so subject)], the tribunal may, if satisfied that the patient is suffering from a form of mental disorder other than the form specified in the application, order or direction relating to him, direct that that application, order or direction be amended by substituting for the form of mental disorder specified in it such other form of mental disorder as appears to the tribunal to be appropriate.

(6) Subsections (1) to (5) above apply in relation to references to a Mental Health Review Tribunal as they apply in relation to applications made to such a tribunal by or in respect of a patient.

(7) Subsection (1) above shall not apply in the case of a restricted patient except as provided in sections 73 and 74 below.

AMENDMENTS

Subsections (3A) and (4A) and the words in square brackets in subsection (5) were inserted by the Mental Health (Patients in the Community) Act 1995, s 2(1), Sched. 1, para. 10.

DEFINITIONS   **1–722**
    patient: s.145(1).
    mental disorder: ss.1, 145(1).
    hospital: ss.79(6), 145(1).
    medical treatment: s.145(1).
    psychopathic disorder: ss.1, 145(1).
    severe mental impairment: ss.1, 145(1).
    mental impairment: ss.1, 145(1).
    subject to after-care under supervision: ss.25A(2), 145(1A).
    supervision application: ss.25A(2), 145(1).

GENERAL NOTE

This section empowers Mental Health Review Tribunals to discharge patients **1–723** from hospital, guardianship or supervised discharge and directs tribunals to discharge such patients if specified criteria are satisfied. For detained patients the actual discharge can take place at a specified future date (subs. (3)). This section also enables tribunals to reclassify the mental disorder of a patient who is not discharged (subs. (5)).

The tribunal's powers under this section are confined to granting or refusing relief in respect of persons who are liable to be detained: it has no power to consider the validity of the admission which gave rise to the liability to be detained (*R. v. Hallstrom, ex p. W* [1985] 3 All E.R. 775, *per* Ackner L.J. at 784 and *R. v. Mental Health Review Tribunal, ex p. Cooper*, unreported, February 14, 1990, Rose J).

The tribunal must give written reasons for its decision: see rule 23(2) of the Mental Health Review Tribunal Rules 1983 and the *Pickering* case, noted under subsection 1(b).

The Human Rights Act 1998

In *R. (on the application of H.) v. Mental Health Review Tribunal, North and East* **1–724** *London Region,* [2001] EWCA Civ 415, the Court of Appeal held that the provisions of this section and section 73, in so far as they place the burden on a patient to prove that the conditions for detention are no longer met, are incompatible with Articles 5(1) and 5(4) of the European Convention on Human Rights. *Per* Lord Phillips M.R.: "So far as 5(4) is concerned, it seems to us axiomatic that if the function of the tribunal is to consider whether the detention of the patient is lawful, it must apply the same test that the law required to be applied as a precondition to admission, unless it be the case that a patient once admitted can be lawfully detained provided that some other test is satisfied. [I]t is contrary to the Convention compulsorily to detain a patient unless it can be shown that the patient is suffering from a mental disorder that warrants detention. Inasmuch as sections 72 and 73 do not require the tribunal to discharge a patient if this cannot be shown we have concluded that they are incompatible with both Article 5(1) and 5(4)" (para.31).

The agreed proposed declaration of incompatibility reads as follows:

"A declaration under section 4 Human Rights Act 1998 that sections 72(1) and 73(1) Mental Health Act 1983 are incompatible with Articles 5(1) and 5(4) of the European Convention on Human Rights in that, for the Mental Health Review Tribunal to be obliged to order a patient's discharge, the burden is placed upon the patient to prove that the criteria justifying his detention in hospital for treatment no longer exist; and that Articles 5(1) and 5(4) require the Tribunal to be positively satisfied that all the criteria justifying the patient's detention in hospital for treatment continue to exist before refusing to order a patient's discharge."

The Court considered the practical implications of its decision:

"It does not follow from our conclusion that Article 5 requires that a patient be discharged whenever any one of the criteria in section 3 cannot be demonstrated on a balance of probability. Detention cannot be justified under Article 5(1)(e) unless a patient is "of unsound mind", but once that is established we do not consider that the Convention restricts the right to detain a patient in hospital, as does section 3, to circumstances where medical treatment is likely to alleviate or prevent a deterioration of the condition. Nor is it necessary under the Convention to demonstrate that such treatment cannot be provided unless the patient is detained in hospital (see s.3(2)(c)).

The circumstances of the present case ... are not uncommon. A patient is detained who is unquestionably suffering from schizophrenia. While in the controlled environment of the hospital he is taking medication, and as a result of the medication is in remission. So long as he continues to take the medication he will pose no danger to himself or others. The nature of the illness is such, however, that if he ceases to take the medication he will relapse and pose a danger to himself or others. The professionals may be uncertain whether, if he is discharged into the community, he will continues to take the medication. We do not believe that Article 5 requires that the patient must always be discharged in such circumstances. The appropriate response should depend upon the result of weighing the interests of the patient against those of the public having regard to the particular facts. Continued detention can be justified if, but only if, it is a proportionate response having regard to the risks that would be involved in discharge" (paras 32, 33).

The court said that it believed that "it is only rarely" that the provisions of this section and section 73 would constrain a tribunal to refuse an order of discharge where the continued detention of the patient infringes Article 5. *Per* Lord Phillips:

"Indeed, in our experience where a tribunal refuses an application for discharge it usually gives reasons for doing so that involve a positive finding that the patient is suffering from a mental disorder that warrants his or her continued detention" (para. 34).

The effect of this decision is that:

(i) The declaration of incompatibility does not affect "the validity, continuing operation or enforcement" of sections 72 and 73 (Human Rights Act 1998, s.4(6)).

(ii) Tribunals must therefore continue to apply the tests set out in sections 72(1) and 73(1).

(iii) Where a tribunal refuses an application for discharge it should make and record positive findings that each of the criteria for continued detention are met.

(iv) In the unlikely event of the tribunal refusing an application for discharge in a situation where it is unable to make a positive finding in respect of one or more of the criteria, the tribunal can express its finding in the "double negative" form.

If the tribunal is unable to make a positive finding in respect of an unrestricted patient in a case where applying the burden of proof has prevented his discharge, it should consider exercising its discretion under section 72(1) to discharge the patient. The Human Rights Act does not require that this discretion be exercised (*ibid.* s.4(6)). The tribunal does not have a discretionary power of discharge in respect of a restricted patient. If the patient would have been discharged if the burden of proof had not been placed on him, the patient's representative could request the Home Secretary to exercise his power of discharge under section 42(2).

The discharge on a future date (see subs. (3)) of a patient who is found by the tribunal not to be suffering from a mental disorder would be in danger of violating Article 5(1)(e) of the European Convention on Human Rights if the delay between the decision to discharge and the date of discharge was excessive: see *Johnson v. United Kingdom* (1997) 27 E.H.R.R. 296, noted in Article 5(1)(e) under the heading "persons of unsound mind". Also see the note on section 73 under this heading.

The question whether a decision not to discharge a patient who had been granted a conditional discharge by a tribunal due to a failure to put in place appropriate after-care facilities in the community would constitute a violation of Article 5 was considered by the Court of Appeal in *R. v. Camden and Islington Health Authority* [2001] EWCA Civ 240. This case is considered in the General Note to section 117 under this heading.

A submission that Article 5(4) of the Convention requires that subsection (3) be construed to apply to restricted patients was rejected by Collins J. in *R. v. Mental Health Review Tribunal for North East Thames Region, ex p. Smith, The Times,* February 20, 2001.

Subsection (1)

This subsection requires a tribunal to discharge an unrestricted patient if *any one* **1–725** of the criteria set out in (a)(i)(ii) or (b)(i)(ii)(iii) is satisfied. Although these criteria are in the negative, in *R. v. East London and City Mental Health NHS Trust, ex p. Brandenburg* [2001] EWCA Civ 239, Lord Phillips M.R. said that a "finding by a tribunal pursuant to section 72 that a patient must be discharged amounts, in terms, to a finding that one or more of the criteria necessary to found an admission under section 2 or section 3 are not present" (para. 18). The tribunal should express its reasons for justifying the continued detention of the patient as a positive finding that the patient suffers from a mental disorder that warrants his detention under this Act (see the note on "The Human Rights Act 1998", above). Where the mandatory discharge criteria are not satisfied, the tribunal is given a discretionary power to discharge the patient.

In *Reid v. Secretary of State for Scotland* [1999] 1 All E.R. 481 at 504–505, a case which was concerned with the interpretation of provisions in the Mental Health (Scotland) Act 1984 which are the equivalent to this section and to section 73, Lord Clyde identified the issues which had to be considered by the Sheriff:

"Firstly, so far as (a) is concerned, (1) he must first decide whether the appellant has at the time of the hearing a mental disorder. If he is satisfied that he has not, then he must order a discharge. (2) If the appellant has a mental disorder the Sheriff must identify the nature and degree of it. Then (3) he should turn to the matter of medical treatment in hospital. He will have to consider the nature and effectiveness of any possible treatment. Where the appellant is a psychopath or has a mental impairment which is not severe he must consider whether such treatment is likely to alleviate or prevent a deterioration of the condition. If he is satisfied that such treatment is not likely to do so, then he is bound to grant a discharge. (4) If he is not so satisfied, or if he is dealing with any other kind of mental disorder, he must consider the propriety of the appellant receiving the medical treatment in detention in hospital. In doing so he must look to the nature and degree of the mental disorder. If he is satisfied in the light of all the evidence before him and in the whole circumstances that the appellant is not suffering from mental disorder of a nature or degree which makes it appropriate for him to be detained in hospital for medical treatment, then he must discharge him. The circumstances which he may consider can include the matter of health and safety of the patient and the safety of other persons, including members of the public; that is to say the propriety as distinct from the necessity, of his continued detention in hospital. If he is satisfied that the requirements of paragraph (a) have been met then it is not necessary for him to consider paragraph (b) and he should turn to paragraph (c).

Secondly, if he is not satisfied that the provisions of paragraph (a) have been met, then he should turn to paragraph (b). The single question here is whether he is satisfied that it is not necessary for the health or safety of the patient or for the protection of the other persons that the patient should receive medical treatment in hospital. The standard here is one of necessity, not desirability. If he is so satisfied then he must discharge the appellant, and he should then turn to paragraph (c). If he is not so satisfied he must refuse the appeal.

Finally, if he has been satisfied on either (a) or (b) he must consider (c). Here the question is whether it is or is not appropriate for the patient to remain liable to be recalled to hospital for further treatment. In the light of his decision on this matter he will grant a conditional or absolute discharge."

Translated into the terms of this Act, the Sheriff becomes the tribunal, paragraph (a) becomes section 72(1)(b)(i), paragraph (b) becomes section 72(1)(b)(ii) and paragraph (c) becomes section 73(1)(b). *Reid* is further considered in the note on paragraph (b), below.

In *R. v. London South and South West Region Mental Health Review Tribunal, ex p. M* [2000] Lloyd's Rep. 143, Latham J. held, *inter alia*, that the question of whether the criteria were fulfilled was to be decided by the tribunal which were not bound by the views of any psychiatrists whose evidence is put before them.

This subsection only applies to restricted patients to the extent provided for in sections 73 and 74 (subs. (7)).

Application: Or a reference made by the Home Secretary (subs. (6)).

Patient: See the note on "any such patient" in section 73(2).

May in any case direct that the patient be discharged: The tribunal has power to discharge the patient even though the legal grounds for compulsory detention still subsist. The discharge could take place some time after the tribunal's decision (subs. (3)).

Although it has been held that discharge means "release from hospital" (*Secretary of State for the Home Department v. Mental Health Review Tribunal for the Mersey Regional Health Authority* [1986] 3 All E.R. 233, *per* Mann J. at 237), the scheme of this Act and, in particular, the use of the phrase "liable to be detained" in subsection (1)(b)(i), strongly suggest that discharge in this context means discharge from the patient's liability to be detained. In guardianship cases discharge means discharge from guardianship.

Paragraph (a)
As the criteria contained in this paragraph are similar to the grounds that have to **1–726** be satisfied on an application being made under section 2, reference should be made to the notes on section 2(2).

Shall direct: The tribunal *must* discharge the patient if any of the criteria set out in paragraphs (i) and (ii) are satisfied.

Satisfied: In the *Reid* case, above, Lord Clyde said that the standard of proof under the equivalent provision in the Mental Health (Scotland) Act 1984 "is the balance of probabilities" (at 504). This should be regarded as an authoritative statement of the legal position under this Act. Peay's research led her to the conclusion that, in practice, the standard applied is more "akin to 'beyond reasonable doubt' than to the civil standard theoretically to be applied" (J. Peay, *Tribunals on Trial*, 1989, p. 211).

Is not then suffering. The use of the term "then" means that the tribunal must consider "the question whether there should be discharge at the time the matter is before it. It is looking to the present tense in the sense that it is dealing with the patient's condition as it appears to it then" (*R. v. Mental Health Review Tribunal for North East Thames Region, ex p. Secretary of State for the Home Department*, The Times, February 20, 2001, *per* Collins J., at para. 22).

Given the decision of the Court of Appeal in *R. (on the application of H.) v. Mental Health Review Tribunal*, noted under "The Human Rights Act 1998", above, the tribunal should express its reasons for continuing the detention of the patient as a positive finding that the patient is suffering from a mental disorder that warrants his or her detention under this Act.

Nature or degree: See the note on paragraph (b)(i), below.

Detention: Or the patient's liability to be detained during a period of leave of absence granted under section 17: see the note on "liable to be detained", below, and the judgment of Lord Woolf in *B v. Barking Havering and Brentford Community Healthcare NHS Trust* [1999] 1 F.L.R. 106.

Paragraph (b)
As the criteria contained in this paragraph are similar to two of the grounds that **1–727** have to be satisfied on an application being made under section 3, reference should be made to the notes on section 3(2)(a), (b).

Shall direct: If either paragraph (i), (ii) *or* (iii) is satisfied the patient must be discharged. Where a tribunal is considering whether they are satisfied as to the matters specified in paragraph (b)(i) or (ii) they must bear in mind the distinction between the two matters and "one must somehow be able to read from the reasons the issue to which the reasons are directed" (*R. v. Mental Health Review Tribunal, ex p. Pickering* [1986] 1 All E.R. 99 at 104, *per* Forbes J). Logic requires paragraph (i) to be considered before paragraph (ii) (*R. v. Mental Health Review Tribunal, North and East London Region, ex p.H*, September 15, 2000).

In *R. v. Canons Park Mental Health Review Tribunal, ex p. A* [1994] 2 All E.R. 659, the Court of Appeal held that when deciding whether it must exercise its mandatory power to discharge a psychopathic [or a mentally impaired] patient the tribunal does not have to have regard to the treatability test as set out in section 3(2)(b). It need only have regard to the "appropriateness test" and the "safety test" which are each expressly referred to in this provision. This case was effectively overruled by *Reid v. Secretary of State for Scotland*, above, where the House of Lords was required to interpret an equivalent provision contained in section 64(1) of the Mental Health

(Scotland) Act 1984 in the case of a patient diagnosed as suffering from psychopathic disorder; also see the note on subsection (1), above. The findings of their Lordships as applied to this Act are that:

(1) a tribunal reviewing the detention of a psychopathic or mentally impaired patient under section 3 or 20 (or a mentally ill or severely mentally impaired patient whose detention has been renewed under section 20 and who does not satisfy the alternative to the "treatability" test set out in section 20(4)) must consider all three of the criteria laid down in this Act to justify compulsory detention, *i.e.* the "appropriateness", "safety" and "treatability" tests;

(2) no good purpose would be served by considering the "appropriateness" test first in those cases which must pass the "treatability" test. *Per* Lord Hope at 495: "It is only if the 'treatability' test is satisfied that it will be necessary to consider whether it is appropriate that that treatment should be received by that person in a hospital and, if so, whether it is necessary for his health or safety or for the protection of other persons that he should receive such treatment"; and

(3) the definition of "medical treatment" in section 145(1) is wide enough to include treatment which alleviates or prevents a deterioration of the symptoms of the mental disorder rather than the disorder itself. It was therefore possible for a tribunal to conclude that the "treatability" test was satisfied in respect of a patient whose anger management was improved because of the supervision that he received within the structured setting of a State Hospital. *Per* Lord Clyde at 505: "Views have evidently differed in the past as to the extent to which [patients suffering from psychopathic disorder] can benefit from medical treatment, although the hope must continue to be that medical science will progress to a greater understanding of the condition and the developing of ways of alleviating or resolving it. Moreover it may well be that generalisations cannot readily be made in regard to this difficult condition. While further study and research is continuing it may be the more difficult to affirm with confidence that the condition in any particular case is truly unresponsive to treatment or that no alleviation or stabilisation can be achieved in the secure environment of a hospital."

In *R. (on the application of Weldon) v. Rampton Hospital Authority* [2001] EWCA Admin 134, Elias J. held that the test was satisfied in a case where the treatment gave rise to "very limited benefits" to the patient.

Is not then suffering See the note under paragraph (a).

1–728 *Nature or degree:* The meaning of this phrase is considered in the note on section 3(2)(a). In *R. v. The Mental Health Review Tribunal or the South Thames Region, ex p. Smith,* [1999] C.O.D. 148, the tribunal refused to discharge the patient who was suffering from paranoid schizophrenia, the symptoms of which were well controlled by medication. On refusing the patient's application to judicially review this decision, Popplewell J. said:

"[At the time of the tribunal hearing the patient] was in a stable condition and it is quite clear that the illness was not of a degree which of itself made it appropriate for him to be liable to be detained. The reason for that was because he had a chronic condition which was static. However, the nature of the condition was that it might cease to be static so that the interpretation that nature is in some way unchanging in one view may be right, but the effect of the condition is that because of its very nature it may not remain static. It seems to me that if the facts upon which the tribunal rely have shown that it may not be static, that goes to the nature of the condition. The degree in the instant case, in relation to his condition, was not relevant because it was static and stable".

His Lordship continued:

"If one had simply to look at the degree it would have been right for the discharge to take place, but the nature of the condition was such that it was clear that he should not be discharged. It may well be in a great number of cases that nature and degree involve much the same questions … and it maybe that tribunals will be wise, if they have any doubts about it, to include them both [in their conclusions]."

The finding of Popplewell J. in *Smith* is consistent with the obligations placed on the tribunal by Article 5 of the European Convention on Human Rights: see *R. (on the application of H.) v. Mental Health Review Tribunal, North and East London Region,* CA, noted under "The Human Rights Act 1998", above.

Smith was followed by Latham J. in *R. v. London and South West Region Mental Health Review Tribunal, ex p. M.*, noted under subsection (1), where his Lordship, when considering the position of a patient with a history of relapsing, said:

"The correct analysis, in my judgment, is that the nature of the illness of a patient such as the applicant is that it is an illness which will relapse in the absence of medication. The question that then has to be asked is whether the nature of that illness is such as to make it appropriate for him to be liable to be detained in hospital for medical treatment. Whether it is appropriate or not will depend upon an assessment of the probability that he will relapse in the near future if he were free in the community."

The question whether the continued detention of an asymptomatic patient contravenes Article 5 of the European Convention on Human Rights was considered by the Court of Appeal in *R. (on the application of H.) v. Mental Health Review Tribunal, North and North East London Region* [2001] EWCA Civ 415, where Lord Phillips M.R. said:

"The circumstances of the present case, which are similar to those considered by Latham J. in *M*, are not uncommon. A patient is detained who is unquestionably suffering from schizophrenia. While in the controlled environment of the hospital he is taking medication, and as a result of the medication is in remission. So long as he continues to take the medication he will pose no danger to himself or to others. The nature of the illness is such, however, that if he ceases to take the medication he will relapse and pose a danger to himself or to others. The professionals may be uncertain whether, if he is discharged into the community, he will continue to take the medication. We do not believe that Article 5 requires that the patient must always be discharged in such circumstances. The appropriate response should depend upon the result of weighing the interests of the patient against those of the public having regard to the particular facts. Continued detention can be justified if, but only if, it is a proportionate response having regard to the risks that would be involved in discharge" (para. 33).

Appropriate for him to be liable to be detained in a hospital for medical treatment: In *R. (on the application of Epsom and St Helier NHS Trust) v. The Mental Health Review Tribunal* [2001] EWHC Admin 101, the Trust challenged the decision of the Mental Health Review Tribunal to discharge the patient. The tribunal's decision was made on the ground that as the patient, who had been granted leave of absence under section 17 to reside in a nursing home, was not receiving in-patient treatment it was not "appropriate for her to be liable to be detained in hospital for medical treatment" for the purposes of this provision. Sullivan J. held that:

1. The decision of the Court of Appeal in *B. v. Barking Havering and Brentwood Community Healthcare NHS Trust* [1999] 1 F.L.R. 106 is authority for the proposition that one has to look at the whole course of the patient's treatment. To do so, one has to look at the past present and future. "It is not enough to say that the patient is not receiving treatment at a particular time. If, for example, it was proposed that the patient should be admitted to hospital for in-patient treatment in the week following the expiration of a six-month period of liability to detention, it would be absurd if the tribunal could not take that fact into account. The timing of in-patient treatment, whether it falls within or outside a particular period of liability to detention might be dictated by factors other than the patient's own state of health, for example, resource availability or the availability of specialised staff, and so forth" (para. 47); and

2. It would be inconsistent with the scheme of the Act if the mere prospect, that at some unspecified future time in-patient treatment would or might be required, compelled a tribunal to reject a patient's application for discharge. "The matter has to be looked at in the round, including the prospect of future in-patient treatment, but there will come a time when, even though it is certain that treatment will be required at some stage in the future, the timing of that treatment is so uncertain that it is no longer 'appropriate' for the patient to continue to be liable to detention. It is the tribunal's function to use its expertise to decide whether the certainty, or the possibility, of the need for in-patient treatment at some future date makes it 'appropriate' that the patient's liability to detention shall continue" (para. 52). His Lordship further stated that the tribunal should look at "the reality of the situation" when making this decision and should not apply "artificial cut-offs" (para. 61).

It can be appropriate for a patient to be liable to be detained in hospital if the evidence is that, without being detained in hospital, the patient will not take the medication that is required to prevent the deterioration of a chronic mental illness (*Smirek v. Williams* [2000] M.H.L.R. 38, CA).

The phrase "liable to be detained" includes patients who have been granted leave of absence from hospital (*R. v. Hallstrom, ex p. W; R. v. Gardner, ex p. L* [1986] 2 All E.R. 306 at 312, *per* McCullough J.). A patient is therefore not entitled to be discharged on satisfying the tribunal that he no longer needs actual *detention* in order to receive the treatment that he needs if the tribunal considers that he needs to be liable to be detained (and therefore liable to be recalled) in order to receive it. The correctness of this interpretation was confirmed by Sullivan J. in *R. (on the application of Epsom and St Helier NHS Trust) v. The Mental Health Review Tribunal* [2001] EWHC Admin 101, where his Lordship concluded that the tribunal was right to reject an argument that the patient was "... automatically entitled to be discharged under section 72 purely by virtue of the fact that she is not receiving any element of in-patient treatment whilst on [section 17] leave" (para.46). His Lordship said that the tribunal should look at "the reality of the situation" in deciding whether it was "appropriate" that a patient who is on leave of absence should be "liable to be detained in hospital for medical treatment"; see above.

Protection of other persons: In *R. v. Parole Board, ex p. Bradley* [1990] 3 All E.R. 828, 836, DC, Stuart-Smith L.J. on examining this provision said that "the precise level of risk is not (surely cannot be) spelt out".

That he should receive such treatment: Compare with the criterion set out in paragraph (a)(ii). The patient will not gain his discharge if he satisfies the tribunal that treatment under detention is not necessary: he must show that medical treatment is not necessary.

Paragraph (g) of section 66(1): Which provides for an application to a tribunal to be made by a nearest relative on the issue by the responsible medical officer of a report under section 25, barring the nearest relative's discharge powers. The test in paragraph (iii) is much narrower than that in paragraph (ii). It implies a likely serious psychological or physical injury to the patient or to some other person: a mere suspicion that the patient might be dangerous is not sufficient; also see the note on "dangerous" in section 25(1). If it is satisfied that this paragraph applies, the tribunal must discharge the patient, even if detention is still justified under paragraphs (i) and (ii).

Subsection (2)
This subsection provides that if an application is made by a patient who is detained **1–729** for treatment and the tribunal does not have to discharge the patient under subsection (1)(b), the tribunal must *have regard* to the provisions of this subsection when exercising its general discretion to discharge.

Likelihood of medical treatment alleviating or preventing a deterioration: Six principles that should be applied to this "treatability test" were identified by Roch L.J. in *R. v. Canons Park Mental Health Review Tribunal, ex p. A*, above. They are reproduced in the note on section 3(2)(b). Speaking in the Divisional Court, Sedley J. said that "section 72(2) furnishes a wide region of discretion in which treatability is no more than a factor to which regard is to be had" ([1994] 1 All E.R. 481, 489).

Subsection (3)
A tribunal may: The power to defer discharge under this provision applies to **1–730** situations where the tribunal has either exercised its mandatory duty to discharge or its discretionary power to discharge under subsection (1) (*R. v. Mental Health Review Tribunal for the North Thames Region, ex p. P* [1996] C.O. D. 467). In this case Harrison J. doubted whether the exercise of the power to direct discharge on a future date was for a lawful purpose, since the treatment proposed to be given in the period before discharge was not connected with the criterion in subsection (1)(b)(iii), namely whether the patient was likely to act in a manner dangerous to herself or to other persons.

Direct the discharge of a patient under that subsection: I.e. under subsection (1) which is concerned with the powers of tribunals to discharge unrestricted patients. This subsection does not therefore apply to patients who are subject to restriction orders (*R. v. Oxford Mental Health Authority Review Tribunal, ex p. Smith*, January 25, 1995, CA).

The power to defer does not apply to patients who are subject to guardianship because applications under this section can only be made in respect of patients who are "liable to be detained" (subs. (1)).

On a future date: Which would enable preparations to be made to receive a patient back into the community. As a patient who is subject to a deferred discharge continues to be "liable to be detained", his responsible medical officer retains the power to grant leave of absence and to make an application for supervised discharge during the period of deferment. The power of deferred discharge could also be used if the tribunal came to the conclusion that the patient would be fit for discharge at the expiration of a further short period of treatment. It is submitted that Gostin and Fennell, above, are correct in arguing that a tribunal "could not specify a date for discharge after that on which the authority for a patient's detention expires" (at p. 91).

In *R. v. Wessex Health Review Tribunal, ex p. Wiltshire County Council*, above, the tribunal directed the patient's discharge from a section 2 order but directed that the patient's discharge be deferred "to give an adequate opportunity to those responsible to consider whether an application for treatment might be appropriate". Although counsel for the tribunal was prepared to accept that a tribunal cannot defer discharge under this provision to enable the authorities to decide whether there is some other basis for lawful detention, the Court of Appeal was not required to resolve the point.

It is likely that counsel's concession would be upheld if the point was required to be resolved.

Specified in the direction: The date specified in the direction cannot be changed by the tribunal subsequent to the communication to the patient of the decision to defer discharge: see *Secretary of State for the Home Department v. Oxford Regional Mental Health Review Tribunal* [1987] 3 All E.R. 12, noted under section 73(7).

Recommend: "The distinction between ordering and recommending is an important one and takes account of the need for agreement of others, *e.g.* the receiving hospital or social services department" (Cmnd. 7320, para. 6.5).

Further consider his case: The tribunal will set a time limit at the expiration of which it will reconsider the case. It may then decide to reconvene the hearing: see the Mental Health Review Rules 1983, rr. 24(4), 25(2). At such a hearing the tribunal has all the powers available that it enjoyed at the original hearing (*Mental Health Review Tribunal v. Hempstock* (1998) 39 B.M.L.R. 94). *Per* Kay J.: "[The tribunal] can, if it considers appropriate, order immediate discharge or future discharge. Clearly, the tribunal will only take either of those courses if it deems such a course right, applying the usual principles. Bearing in mind its earlier decision, it will no doubt be a rarity that it will reach such a conclusion after a short period particularly so far as immediate discharge is concerned."

Subsection (3A)

1–731   This subsection provides that if a tribunal decides not to direct the discharge of a patient who has been detained under section 3 or a hospital order patient, the tribunal can recommend to the patient's responsible medical officer that he makes an application for supervised discharge in respect of the patient. The tribunal can reconsider the case (and could discharge the patient) in the event of the recommendation not being complied with.

Patient: This subsection does not apply to patients who are subject to restriction orders (*R. v. Oxford Mental Health Review Tribunal, ex p. Smith*, above).

Further consider his case: See rules 24(4), 25(2), of the Mental Health Review Tribunal Rules noted under this heading in subsection (3).

Subsection (4)

1–732   This subsection enables the tribunal to discharge a patient under guardianship and directs the tribunal to discharge the patient if either of the criteria set out in paragraphs (a) or (b) is satisfied. The tribunal does not have the power either to defer the patient's discharge or to make recommendations with a view to facilitating discharge at a later date.

Paragraph (b)

1–733   *Welfare:* See the note on section 7(2).

Subsection (4A)

1–734   Under this subsection a tribunal has a general discretion to discharge a patient who is subject to supervised discharge and must discharge the patient if they are satisfied that either the application criteria or the renewal criteria are not complied with. The tribunal does not have the power to make recommendations with a view to facilitating the patient's discharge from supervised discharge at a later date.

The provisions of this subsection are modified in respect of patients subject to community care orders in Scotland who intend to reside in England or Wales; see the Mental Health (Patients in the Community) (Transfers from Scotland) Regulations 1996 (S.I. No. 295).

Subsection (5)

1–735   This subsection enables the tribunal to reclassify the form of mental disorder which is recorded in the application, order or direction. The reclassification, which can name an additional form of disorder which exists together with the other or can replace the previously recorded form with another (*Memorandum*, para. 64), has the same effect as a reclassification made by the patient's responsible medical officer under section 16, or community responsible medical officer under section 25F, with the exception that the reclassification does not give rise to a right to make an application to a tribunal.

In *R. v. Anglia and Oxfordshire Mental Health Review Tribunal, ex p. Hagan* [2000] C.O.D. 252, the Court of Appeal, in holding that a tribunal was not bound to reclassify a patient detained under a court order specifying that he suffered from two forms of mental disorder by deleting reference to one disorder from which the patient continued to suffer but which would not on its own justify detention, made the following findings on this provision:

  (i) its primary purpose is to enable a tribunal who has concluded that the form of mental disorder which requires the patient to continue to be detained is different from the form of mental disorder specified in an order (or application or direction), to substitute that mental disorder so as to in effect correct the order to accord with the position as it is now known to be;
 (ii) it ought to be construed as providing the tribunal with a discretion so that they are not obliged to reclassify a patient in a way different from that which he would have been classified as a civil patient;
(iii) in the context of a section 37 and 41, it ought to be construed as giving the tribunal a discretion not to delete a mental disorder from which a patient still suffers where deletion might frustrate their powers in relation to conditional discharge in the future; and
 (iv) reclassification relates to whether the patient suffers from a particular mental disorder; not whether he is detainable for that mental disorder if it stood alone; *per* Waller L.J.:
     "it ... seems to me that the reason why under section 16 a report may generate some other form of mental disorder being specified in the application has to do with the lawfulness or otherwise of continued detention pursuant to an application, and the purpose of substitution under section 72(5) has to do with ensuring that the order correctly reflects the basis for detention. But it does not follow in either case that the purpose of reclassification is to ensure that there is not described in the application or order a form of mental disorder from which the patient suffers and may need treatment if he continues to be detained on the basis of another form of mental disorder. Indeed the ordinary application of section 16 leads to that conclusion, and there is no reason why the tribunal, under section 72(5), should be obliged to reach a different conclusion."

In *R. v. South-West Thames Mental Health Review Tribunal, ex p. Demetri* [1997] C.O.D. 44, the Court of Appeal, in rejecting a submission that there is no power in a tribunal under this provision to reclassify restricted patients as suffering from some other form of mental disorder than that specified by the sentencing court in the original hospital order, confirmed that this subsection was the appropriate vehicle for dealing with the reclassification of patients detained in a mental hospital, whether under compulsory detention by way of an order of the court or otherwise. The application of this provision to restricted patients was probably unintentional because: (1) the reclassification of such patients has no legal consequences; and (2) neither the patient's responsible medical officer nor the Home Secretary enjoys a similar power. In *Demetri* the court said that the reasons given for the decision to reclassify must show that the tribunal turned its mind to the relevant legal matters that had to be considered under this Act.

A doctor who disagrees with the decision of a tribunal to reclassify a patient cannot use his power under section 16 to reverse the decision in the absence of a change of circumstance: see *R. v. Pathfinder NHS Trust, ex p. W.*, noted in the General Note to section 16. In the event of a further reclassification, the patient or his nearest relative has a right to make an application to a tribunal under section 66(1)(d), or (gb).

Power to discharge restricted patients

1–736   **73.**—(1) Where an application to a Mental Health Review Tribunal is made by a restricted patient who is subject to a restriction order, or where the case of such a patient is referred to such a tribunal, the tribunal shall direct the absolute discharge of the patient if satisfied—

(a) as to the matters mentioned in paragraph (b)(i) or (ii) of section 72(1) above; and

(b) that it is not appropriate for the patient to remain liable to be recalled to hospital for further treatment.

(2) Where in the case of any such patient as is mentioned in subsection (1) above the Tribunal are satisfied as to the matters referred to in paragraph (a) of that subsection but not as to the matter referred to in paragraph (b) of that subsection the Tribunal shall direct the conditional discharge of the patient.

(3) Where a patient is absolutely discharged under this section he shall thereupon cease to be liable to be detained by virtue of the relevant hospital order, and the restriction order shall cease to have effect accordingly.

(4) Where a patient is conditionally discharged under this section—

(a) he may be recalled by the Secretary of State under subsection (3) of section 42 above as if he had been conditionally discharged under subsection (2) of that section; and

(b) the patient shall comply with such conditions (if any) as may be imposed at the time of discharge by the Tribunal or at any subsequent time by the Secretary of State.

(5) The Secretary of State may from time to time vary any condition imposed (whether by the Tribunal or by him) under subsection (4) above.

(6) Where a restriction order in respect of a patient ceases to have effect after he has been conditionally discharged under this section the patient shall, unless previously recalled, be deemed to be absolutely discharged on the date when the order ceases to have effect and shall cease to be liable to be detained by virtue of the relevant hospital order.

(7) A Tribunal may defer a direction for the conditional discharge of a patient until such arrangements as appear to the Tribunal to be necessary for that purpose have been made to their satisfaction; and where by virtue of any such deferment no direction has been given on an application or reference before the time when the patient's case comes before the Tribunal on a subsequent application or reference, the previous application or reference shall be treated as one on which no direction under this section can be given.

(8) This section is without prejudice to section 42 above.

DEFINITIONS

1–737   restricted patient: s.79(1).
restriction order: ss.41, 145(1).
hospital: ss.79(6), 145(1).
relevant hospital order: s.79(2).

GENERAL NOTE

1–738   Under the Mental Health Act 1959 a patient subject to a restriction order had no right to apply for his discharge to a tribunal. He could only require that his case be referred to the tribunal by the Home Secretary in order that the advice of the tribunal be obtained. The decision whether or not he should be discharged rested with the Home Secretary. In *X v. U.K.* (1981) 4 E.H.R.R. 181 this state of the law was held by the European Court of Human Rights not to be in conformity with article 5(4) of the European Convention on Human Rights which entitles those detained on grounds of unsoundness of mind to a review of the lawfulness of their detention at periodic intervals before a court which must be empowered to order their discharge. This section, which specifies when a Mental Health Review Tribunal must direct either the absolute or conditional discharge of restricted patients, was enacted as a direct consequence of the ruling in *X v. U.K.*

The tribunal has no general discretion to order the discharge of a restricted patient where the statutory criteria are not met and has no power to adjourn the patient's application to give an opportunity for the patient's condition to improve or to see if an improvement already made is sustained (*R. v. Nottingham Mental Health Review Tribunal, ex p. Secretary of State for the Home Department*; *R. v. Trent Mental Health Review Tribunal, ex p. Secretary of State for the Home Department, The Times*, October 12, 1998, CA).

Although the tribunal has no power under this section equivalent to that under section 72(3) to make recommendations in relation to unrestricted patients (*R. v. Oxford Mental Health Authority Review Tribunal, ex p. Smith*, January 25, 1995, CA), the following Written Answer was given by Mr Douglas Hogg M.P. to a question on what would happen if a tribunal which had considered the case of a restricted patient included in its decision a recommendation that the patient be granted leave of absence or be transferred to another hospital or be transferred to guardianship:

"Any such recommendation received in the Home Office is acknowledged, and any comments are offered which can usefully be made at that stage. Correspondence with the tribunal is copied to the patient's responsible medical officer since it is for this officer to consider the recommendation in the first instance. If the responsible medical officer submits a proposal based on a tribunal's recommendation, full account is taken of the tribunal's views. At any subsequent hearing of the case, the statement which the Home Office provides will explain the outcome of any recommendation which the tribunal had made" (HC Vol. 121, Cols 261, 262, Oct. 28, 1987).

In *R. v. Secretary of State for the Home Department, ex p. Harry* [1998] 3 All E.R. 360, Lightman J. held that if the Home Secretary is not fully satisfied with a recommendation made by a tribunal concerning a patient's leave or transfer, he is not only entitled, but bound, to seek further advice from the Advisory Board on Restricted Patients (the role of the Board is considered in the note on s.42(1)). In reaching his decision on whether to accept the tribunal's recommendation the Home Secretary must "balance the patient's claim to liberty against the interests of everyone else to be safeguarded against the risks to which such liberty may give rise" (at 369). The following procedure, which was endorsed by Lightman J. at 370, will be used by the Home Secretary when making a reference to the Board:

"Where, after an extra-statutory recommendation by the Mental Health Review Tribunal, the Secretary of State seeks advice from the Advisory Board on whether to give his consent to the transfer of a patient, or grant leave of absence, pursuant to his powers under section 41(3)(c) of the Mental Health Act 1983, the Secretary of State accepts that the patient is entitled by reason of procedural fairness (subject to public interest immunity or some other substantial reason for departing from these principles which will normally be communicated to the patient's advisers): 1. To be told the gist of any new information before the Advisory Board on a relevant point and, in particular, to be told the gist of the report to the Advisory Board by its member who has visited the hospital. 2.

To make written representations to the Advisory Board in response to such material before the Advisory Board reaches a conclusion on its advice to the Secretary of State. 3. To be given a copy of the advice from the Advisory Board to the Secretary of State, and to be given an opportunity to make written representations on the matter to the Secretary of State before the Secretary of State reaches his conclusions. 4. To be given reasons for the decision of the Secretary of State. 5. To make thereafter, any further written representations to the Secretary of State, which will be considered, it being a continuing process of review by the Secretary of State of the need for, and application of, restrictions."

A tribunal cannot use its power under rule 16 of the Mental Health Review Tribunal Rules 1983 to adjourn an applicaton to enable it to decide whether an extra-statutory recommendation should be made (*R. (on the application of the Secretary of State for the Home Department) v. Mental Health Tribunal* [2001] A.C.D. 62).

There is no statutory disqualification of a president of a Mental Health Review Tribunal who has sat on the case of an applicant seeking discharge under this section, from sitting on a later application by the same patient (*R. v. Oxford Regional Mental Health Review Tribunal, ex p. Mackman, The Times,* June 2, 1986).

Guidance on pre-discharge, supervision and after-care arrangements for restricted patients who are conditionally discharged was issued with D.H.S.S. Circular No. LAC (87)3.

The Human Rights Act 1998

1–739   In *Johnson v. United Kingdom* (1997) 27 E.H.R.R. 296, the Court held that the absence of a power to ensure that the deferred conditional discharge of a patient who is found not to be suffering from mental disorder is not unreasonably delayed, is a violation of Article 5 of the Convention: see the notes on subss. (2) and (7) and the notes on Article 5(1)(e) under the heading "persons of unsound mind".

In *R. v. Camden and Islington Health Authority, ex p. K* [2001] EWCA Civ 240, the Court of Appeal said that the decision of the House of Lords in *Secretary of State for the Home Department v. Oxford Regional Mental Health Review Tribunal* [1987] 3 All E.R. 8, noted under subsection (7), to the effect that should it prove to be impossible to implement the conditions specified by a tribunal on a deferred conditional discharge, that tribunal could not consider whether to impose alternative conditions, may not be consistent with Article 5 as interpreted by the Court in *Johnson. Per* Lord Phillips M.R.: "If the tribunal imposes a condition which proves impossible of performance, too lengthy a period may elapse before the position is reconsidered as a result of a subsequent referral" (para. 35). In *K.*, Buxton and Sedley L.JJ.s did not accept a distinction that had been drawn by Lord Phillips M.R. between cases where the tribunal concludes that the patient is mentally ill, but can be treated in the community; and cases, such as *Johnson*, where the tribunal finds that the patient is no longer suffering from mental illness but nonetheless needs to be released into a controlled environment (see para. 32). *Per* Buxton L.J.: "In the latter case, the justification for the placing of continued detention on the subject relates, and can only relate, to the history of mental illness and, as in *Johnson*, to the prospect of recurrence. In both cases, there is continued detention; the role of the tribunal in both cases is to exercise the court-like functions required by Article 5(4), and under the jurisprudence of Article 5(4) the national authorities are equally bound to respect and act on the determination of the tribunal in either case" (para. 42). *Per* Sedley L.J.: "[T]he difference ... is one of degree, not kind" (para. 53).

The provisions of this section, in so far as they place the burden of proof on the patient to prove that the conditions of detention are no longer met, are incompatible with Article 5(1) and 5(4) of the Convention: see *R. (on the application of H.) v. Mental Health Review Tribunal, North and East London Region,* noted in section 72 under this heading.

The question whether a decision not to discharge a patient because of a failure to put in place appropriate after-care facilities in the community was considered in *R. v. Camden and Islington Health Authority, ex p. K.,* above. This case is considered in the General Note to section 117 under this heading.

The granting of a discharge with a condition that the patient continues to accept medication will not contravene the Convention if one of the grounds in Article 8(2) is satisfied (*L. v. Sweden,* noted under Art. 8(2) under "protection of health").

Subsection (1)

The effect of this subsection is that a tribunal must order the *absolute* discharge of a **1–740** restricted patient if they are satisfied:

(i) that he was not suffering from mental illness, psychopathic disorder, severe mental impairment or mental impairment *or* from any of those forms of disorder of a nature or degree which makes it appropriate for him to be liable to be detained in hospital for medical treatment;
or

(ii) that it is not necessary for the health and safety of the patient or for the protection of other persons that he should receive such treatment;
and

(iii) that it is not appropriate for the patient to remain liable to be recalled to hospital for further treatment.

A tribunal has no discretionary power of discharge in respect of restricted patients.

A tribunal is not obliged to order an absolute discharge if it finds that the patient is not mentally disordered: "Section 73(1)(a) imports section 72(1)(b)(i) and requires the tribunal to be satisfied both as to one or other part of paragraph (b)(i) *and* that it is not appropriate for the patient to remain liable to be recalled to hospital for further treatment. Even if satisfied that he is not then suffering from mental illness etc. in paragraph (b)(i) the tribunal, unless satisfied that it is not appropriate to recall a patient, are required to direct a conditional discharge under section 73(2)" (*R. v. Merseyside Mental Health Review Tribunal, ex p. K* [1990] 1 All E.R. 694, 699, CA, *per* Butler-Sloss L.J.).

The effect of the decision of the House of Lords in *Reid v. Secretary of State for Scotland* [1999] 1 All E.R. 481, on the interpretation of section 64(1) of the Mental Health (Scotland) Act 1984, is that the statement in paragraph 251 of the *Memorandum* that the absence of a "treatability test" from the criteria in this subsection means that the "fact that a restricted patient's condition is not benefiting from the treatment he is receiving does not automatically entitle him to be discharged" can no longer be regarded as an accurate statement of the legal position: see the notes on section 72(1)(b).

Restricted patient: A restricted patient who is no longer suffering from a mental disorder remains a "patient" for the purposes of this section until he is discharged absolutely (*R. v. Merseyside Mental Health Review Tribunal, ex p. K,* above). The relevant extract from the judgment of Butler-Sloss L.J. is reproduced in the note on "patient" in s.145(1); also see *Johnson v. United Kingdom,* noted under subsection (2).

Subject to a restriction order: Made under section 41.

Referred to such a tribunal: See the note on section 75(1).

Discharge: Means release from hospital, and not that the patient should remain in the same or another hospital (*Secretary of State for the Home Department* v. *Mental Health Review Tribunal for the Mersey Regional Health Authority,* above). There is no power to direct that the discharge takes effect on a future date.

Satisfied: On a balance of probabilities (see the note on s.72(1)(a)).

Matter mentioned in paragraph (b)(i) or (ii) of section 72(1): Reference should be made to the notes on this provision.

Recalled to hospital for further treatment: This paragraph is relevant only to the question of whether any discharge should be conditional or absolute. The tribunal would have to be satisfied at the time of the hearing that it would not be appropriate for the patient to remain liable to be recalled to hospital to receive treatment that might be required at some time in the future.

Subsection (2)

1–741   The effect of this subsection is that a tribunal must order the *conditional* discharge of a restricted patient if they are satisfied:

> (i) that he is not suffering from mental illness, psychopathic disorder, severe mental impairment or mental impairment *or* from any of those forms of disorder of a nature or degree which makes it appropriate for him to be liable to be detained in a hospital for medical treatment;
> *or*
> (ii) that it is not necessary for the health and safety of the patient or the protection of other persons that he should receive such treatment.

This provision "gives to the tribunal power to impose a conditional discharge and retain residual control over patients not then suffering from mental disorder or not to a degree requiring continued detention in hospital. This would appear to be a provision designed both for the support of the patient in the community and the protection of the public, and is an important discretionary power vested in an independent tribunal, one not lightly to be set aside in the absence of clear words"; *per* Butler-Sloss L.J. in *R. v. Merseyside Mental Health Review Tribunal, ex p. K*, above, at 699, 700.

Where a tribunal is satisfied under this subsection as to one or other of the matters referred to in paragraph (a) of subsection (1), it is mandatory that the tribunal "shall direct the conditional discharge of the patient." If the tribunal then proceeds to direct that the conditional discharge be deferred under subsection (7) for the purpose of making the necessary practical arrangements to enable the patient to comply with the conditions, it is not entitled later to reconsider the question whether the patient should in fact be conditionally discharged (*Secretary of State for the Home Department v. Oxford Regional Mental Health Review Tribunal* [1987] 3 All E.R. 8, HL).

In *Johnson v. United Kingdom* (1997) 27 E.H.R.R. 296, the European Court of Human Rights, having considered the case law on Article 5(1)(e) of the European Convention on Human Rights, held that a finding that a detained patient was no longer suffering from the mental disorder which led to his confinement need not inevitably lead to his immediate discharge. A tribunal is entitled to retain some measure of supervision over the progress of such a patient once he is released into the community and to that end make his discharge subject to conditions, such as residence in a hostel. The court further held that it is of paramount importance that the patient's discharge is not unreasonably delayed if such a condition is imposed and that safeguards should exist to prevent this; see further, Department of Health Circular LAC (2000) 3, paras. 11–13.

The patient must comply with any conditions laid down by the tribunal or subsequently imposed by the Home Secretary (subs. (4)).

Not as to the matter referred to in paragraph (b): In *R. v. Mental Health Review Tribunal, ex p. Cooper,* February 14, 1990, Rose J. held that the tribunal could direct a conditional discharge, rather than an absolute discharge, solely for therapeutic reasons and that it was not the case that the maintenance of liability to recall under paragraph (b) of subsection (1) of this section can only be proper if the applicant poses some danger to others.

Conditional Discharge: See subsection (4).

Subsection (3)
Thereupon: The absolute discharge of a restricted patient cannot be deferred **1–742**
under subsection (7).

Subsection (4)
May be recalled: And have his case referred to a tribunal under section 75(1)(a). **1–743**
Only the Home Secretary can recall the patient to hospital: see the note on section
42(3).
Conditions: The tribunal has a discretion as to the nature of the conditions that it
wishes to impose. A condition should only be imposed if there is sufficient evidence
to justify it and if it can be met within a reasonable time (*Hall*, below). The tribunal
should give reasons for its decision to impose a condition. The usual conditions relate
to supervision, residence and medical treatment. Although a condition may require
that the patient attends for treatment, treatment cannot be forced upon him in the
absence of his consent because conditionally discharged patients are not subject to
the consent to treatment provisions contained in Part IV of this Act (s.56(1)(c)). A
Health Authority is not placed under an absolute obligation to satisfy the conditions
imposed by the tribunal: see *R. v. Camden and Islington Health Authority, ex p. K.*
[2001] EWCA Civ 240, noted in the General Note to section 117.
A condition requiring that a patient who is conditionally discharged should remain
in a hospital is inconsistent with the duty to discharge albeit conditionally (*Secretary
of State for the Home Department v. Mental Health Review Tribunal for the Mersey
Regional Health Authority* [1986] 3 All E.R. 233). The fact that a facility is not called a
hospital does not necessarily mean that it is not a hospital as a matter of law. Hospital
means, *inter alia*, "any institution for the reception and treatment of persons suffering
from illness (National Health Service Act 1997, s.128(1) and s.145(1) of this Act). A
pre-discharge facility which is referred to as a hostel, which is located some distance
from the base hospital and which is both managed and staffed by that hospital would
be a hospital for the purposes of this Act if the "residents" were subject to medical
supervision: see the definition of "medical treatment" in section 145(1).
Also note the following comment by Lord Bridge in *Secretary of State for the Home
Department v. Oxford Regional Mental Health Review Tribunal* [1987] 3 All E.R. 8,
HL, at 12:

> "the tribunal may perfectly properly be satisfied that hospital detention is no
> longer necessary provided that the patient can be placed in a suitable hostel and
> required to submit to treatment as an out-patient by a suitable psychiatrist.
> These are matters to be secured by imposing appropriate conditions."

A conditionally discharged patient can apply to a tribunal for his absolute
discharge under section 75.
After a conditional discharge the patient's progress in the community will be
monitored by the Home Office in the same way as that of a patient conditionally
discharged by the Home Secretary, and the Home Secretary may vary conditions
imposed by the tribunal (subs. (5)).
A conditionally discharged patient cannot receive direct payments under the
terms of the Community Care (Direct Payments) Act 1996 (Community Care
(Direct Payments) Regulations 1997 (S.I. 1997 No. 734), reg. 2.
If any: The tribunal is not obliged to impose conditions on a conditionally
discharged patient.
Secretary of State: The Secretary of State can impose conditions even though the
tribunal has not.

Subsection (7)
A tribunal may defer: The purpose of the deferment under this provision is to **1–744**
enable arrangements to be made to satisfy the conditions which the tribunal has

attached to the patient's conditional discharge. A tribunal cannot subsequently reconvene to reconsider its original decision that the patient be discharged (*Secretary of State for the Home Department v. Oxford Regional Mental Health Review Tribunal*, above). This ruling may not be consistent with Article 5 of the European Convention on Human Rights: see the note on "The Human Rights Act 1998", above. As an alternative to using its power of deferment the tribunal could: (a) indicate the nature of the conditions that it was minded to impose; (b) adjourn the application to enable the feasibility of securing the achievement of the conditions to be assessed; and (c) determine the application at the adjourned hearing.

Once the tribunal has stipulated its conditions the burden is passed to the local authority and/or the Health Authority to make the necessary arrangements within a reasonable time (*Johnson v. U.K.*, below) and to the patient to co-operate with arrangements which are made. The tribunal does not have the power to police the work of the authorities required to make those arrangements or even to set a time limit. Therefore delay and non-compliance by the authorities could not convert the tribunal's lawful imposition of conditions into an unlawful decision (*R. v. Mental Health Review Tribunal and others, ex p. Hall* [1999] 4 All E.R. 883). *Per* Kennedy L.J.: "Section 73(7) even contemplates the possibility of a further application being made to a tribunal during a period of deferral, but there are safeguards against tardiness or the imposition of impracticable conditions which can be invoked. Legal safeguards are to be found in section 71(1) ... and in the provisions of the Local Authority Social Services Act 1970 (which enable pressure to be exerted on the local authority and/or Health Authority). There are also ... ways in which a Mental Health Review Tribunal which foresees problems can exercise its powers to ensure that they are addressed at an early date. The tribunal can adjourn pursuant to rule 16 of the Mental Health Review Tribunal Rules 1983, to enable those involved to produce a care plan, and that period of adjournment can be finite ... The tribunal can, if necessary, call for reports (rule 15) and even summon witnesses such as Directors of Social Services or Chairmen of Health Authorities but in the end the tribunal can only gather information and impose conditions. It may shame others into action, but it cannot otherwise ensure that its reasonable conditions are met within a reasonable time, and, if the statutory conditions are met it must discharge its own duty by ordering conditional discharge." His Lordship further noted that "nothing in any statutory provision, or any rule of procedure, requires the tribunal to have available a care plan setting out workable conditions before those conditions are imposed".

The deferment cannot be to a fixed date. *Per* Lord Bridge in the *Oxford* case at 13: "There is no authority for this in the Act or the rules and in the nature of the case it is impossible for a tribunal in making a deferred direction for conditional discharge to predict how long it will take to make the necessary arrangements. The decision should simply indicate that the direction is deferred until the necessary arrangements have been made to the satisfaction of the tribunal and specify what arrangements are required, which can normally be done, no doubt, simply by reference to the conditions to be imposed. Whoever is responsible for making the arrangements should then proceed with all reasonable expedition to do so and should bring the matter to the attention of the tribunal again as soon as practicable after it is thought that satisfactory arrangements have been made. Pursuant to rule 25 [of the Mental Health Review Tribunal Rules 1983] the tribunal may then decide that the arrangements are to their satisfaction without a further hearing."

A deferment should not result in the patient's discharge being unreasonably delayed: see the decision of the European Court of Human Rights in *Johnson v. United Kingdom*, noted under subsection (2). Subsequent to this decision the Department of Health issued Circular HSC 2000/003 which states that where "social services authorities are unable to implement conditions set by a MHRT they should follow guidance in Dr Graham Winyard's and Sir Herbert Laming's June 1997 letter

'Implementation of Mental Health Review Tribunals' Decisions'" (para. 13). If the relevant health or local authority finds it impossible to satisfy the conditions attached to the patient's conditional discharge, it should refer the matter to the Secretary of State to enable him to consider exercising his power to refer the case back to the tribunal under section 71(1). This action should also be taken if the patient's condition deteriorates after the tribunal has reached its decision to defer the conditional discharge: see *R. v. Ealing District Health Authority, ex p. Fox* [1993] 3 All E.R. 170, noted in the General Note to section 117.

A decision to defer must be communicated to the patient within the terms of rule 24(1) of the Mental Health Review Tribunal Rules 1983.

For the conditional discharge: A patient's absolute discharge cannot be deferred.

Such arrangements as appear to the tribunal to be necessary: It is unlawful for a tribunal to defer the conditional discharge of a patient if the purpose of the deferment is to secure his admission to another hospital: see *Secretary of State for the Home Department v. Mental Health Review Tribunal for the Mersey Regional Health Authority*, above, where Mann J. held that the tribunal had no power to defer the patient's conditional discharge until arrangements had been made for his admission to a less secure hospital, with a view to his subsequent discharge to a local hostel or to his home. If the tribunal is not satisfied that appropriate arrangements have been made, the order for conditional discharge will not take effect.

Have been made to their satisfaction: The wording of this provision clearly implies that the tribunal is required to formally indicate whether the arrangements that have been put in place to enable the patient to be discharged are satisfactory. As the Mental Health Review Tribunal Rules 1983 do not provide for such a procedure, there would appear to no reason to prevent the tribunal from directing that the decision to discharge take effect without a further hearing (see *ibid.*, r.25(1)) and from signifying their subsequent satisfaction with the arrangements by correspondence.

The previous application or reference: The patient cannot be discharged on the basis of the earlier deferred direction: the matter must be considered afresh.

Subsection (8)
Section 42: Which, *inter alia*, empowers the Home Secretary to discharge the **1–745** patient from hospital either absolutely or subject to conditions.

Restricted patients subject to restriction directions

74.—(1) Where an application to a Mental Health Review Tribunal is **1–746** made by a restricted patient who is subject to [a limitation direction or] a restriction direction, or where the case of such a patient is referred to such a tribunal, the Tribunal—

    (a) shall notify the Secretary of State whether, in their opinion, the patient would, if subject to a restriction order, be entitled to be absolutely or conditionally discharged under section 73 above; and

    (b) if they notify him that the patient would be entitled to be conditionally discharged, may recommend that in the event of his not being discharged under this section he should continue to be detained in hospital.

    (2) If in the case of a patient not falling within subsection (4) below—

    (a) the Tribunal notify the Secretary of State that the patient would be entitled to be absolutely or conditionally discharged; and

    (b) within the period of 90 days beginning with the date of that notification the Secretary of State gives notice to the Tribunal that the patient may be so discharged,

the Tribunal shall direct the absolute or, as the case may be, the conditional discharge of the patient.

(3) Where a patient continues to be liable to be detained in a hospital at the end of the period referred to in subsection (2)(b) above because the Secretary of State has not given the notice there mentioned, the managers of the hospital shall, unless the Tribunal have made a recommendation under subsection (1)(b) above, transfer the patient to a prison or other institution in which he might have been detained if he had not been removed to hospital, there to be dealt with as if he had not been so removed.

(4) If, in the case of a patient who is subject to a transfer direction under section 48 above, the Tribunal notify the Secretary of State that the patient would be entitled to be absolutely or conditionally discharged, the Secretary of State shall, unless the Tribunal have made a recommendation under subsection (1)(b) above, by warrant direct that the patient be remitted to a prison or other institution in which he might have been detained if he had not been removed to hospital, there to be dealt with as if he had not been so removed.

(5) Where a patient is transferred or remitted under subsection (3) or (4) above [the relevant hospital direction and the limitation direction or, as the case may be,] the relevant transfer direction and the restriction direction shall cease to have effect on his arrival in the prison or other institution.

(6) Subsections (3) to (8) of section 73 above shall have effect in relation to this section as they have effect in relation to that section, taking references to the relevant hospital order and the restriction order as references to [the hospital direction and the limitation direction or, as the case may be, to] the transfer direction and the restriction direction.

(7) This section is without prejudice to sections 50 to 53 above in their application to patients who are not discharged under this section.

AMENDMENT
In subss. (1), (5) and (6) the words in square brackets were inserted by the Crime (Sentences) Act 1997, s.55, Sched. 4, para. 12.

DEFINITIONS
1–747   restricted patient: s.79(1).
restriction direction: ss.49, 145(1).
restriction order: ss.41, 145(1).
hospital: ss.79(6), 145(1).
hospital direction: s.145(1).
limitation direction: s.145(1).
the managers: s.145(1).
transfer direction: ss.47, 145(1).

GENERAL NOTE
1–748   This section provides for the procedure to be adopted on an application to a Mental Health Review Tribunal by a patient who has been transferred from prison to hospital under either section 47 or 48, subject to the special restrictions set out in section 49, or has been made the subject of hospital and limitation directions under section 45A. It also applies to references to tribunals made in respect of such patients by the Home Secretary. A patient who has been transferred subject to a restriction direction ceases to be subject to restrictions on reaching what would have been his earliest date of release had he remained in prison (s.50(2)(3)).

The *Memorandum*, at paragraph 253, describes the effect of this section: "Patients subject to a restriction or a limitation direction are liable to resume serving their sentence of imprisonment if they no longer require treatment in hospital. Under these circumstances, the tribunal cannot therefore authorise discharge in the normal way. Instead, it has to notify the Home Secretary if it finds that the patient could otherwise be conditionally or absolutely discharged, and may at the same time recommend that if the patient cannot be conditionally discharged he should continue to be detained in hospital rather than being returned to prison. In the case of a patient who was originally a remand prisoner transferred under section 48, the Home Secretary has no discretion: unless the tribunal has made a recommendation for the patient's detention in hospital, he must return the patient to prison. In the case of a sentenced prisoner, however, it may be that the Home Secretary is able to agree to his discharge. The Home Secretary has 90 days from the date of notification of the tribunal's finding in which to give notice that the patient may be discharged: if he does not, the patient must be returned to prison unless that tribunal has made a recommendation that in those circumstances he should remain in hospital."

In *R. v. Secretary of State for the Home Department, ex p. Williams*, June 21, 1994, which is noted under the heading "Technical lifer" in the General Note to section 49, Buxton J. made the following comments on the function of the tribunal and the role of the Home Secretary in cases heard under this section: "Section 74 specifically deals with, and is limited to, transferred prisoners. That is persons sentenced to a prison term who have, however, been transferred to hospital for treatment. In such cases a restriction direction will normally be made. That direction is, by sections 50(2) and (3) of the 1983 Act, limited to the effective term of the prisoner's sentence. The whole arrangement operates within the context of a prison sentence, and provides for a particular way in which that sentence shall be served. The function of the tribunal is to make recommendations to the Secretary of State that the prisoner need no longer remain in hospital. That under section 74(2)(b), gives the Secretary of State the opportunity to cause the tribunal to direct the prisoner's discharge, but for the reasons given by [the Home Office] there is no rational reason why the Secretary of State should normally cause the prisoner's discharge just because the need for hospital treatment has passed. The prisoner remain subject to the period to which the court has sentenced him. The assumption must surely be that he should serve that period and not be excused it just because part of the period has been served in hospital in respect of an illness from which he has now recovered. That assumption is, in my view, reflected by the structure of section 74(2) and (3), which envisage the Secretary of State simply doing nothing in receipt of the recommendation for discharge with the result that the prisoner returns to prison and takes up again his life as an ordinary prisoner."

The policy of the Home Secretary on receiving a notification under paragraphs (a) and (b) of subs. (1) is set out in the note on section 50(1)(b).

The Human Rights Act 1998

In *Benjamin and Wilson v. United Kingdom*, app. no. 28212/85, the European **1–749** Commission on Human Rights declared admissible a complaint that that the purely advisory powers that the tribunal has under this section contravene Article 5(4) of the European Convention on Human Rights. The Government's response to this application is contained in the following passage of the Commission's decision:

"The Government informed the Commission that it is the practice and policy of the Secretary of State to follow recommendations of the Mental Health Review Tribunal as to discharge under section 74 of the 1983 Act, and it would be unlawful for the Secretary of State not to comply with his own policy."

Subsection (1)

Patient: See the note on "any such patient" in section 73(2).   **1–750**

Discharge: Means release from hospital; see the note on "discharge" in section 73(1).

Subsection (2)

1–751   *Beginning with:* Including the date of the notification (*Hare v. Gocher* [1962] 2 Q.B. 641).

    Conditional discharge: A patient who has been conditionally discharged under this provision is not subject to the consent to treatment provisions contained in Part IV of this Act (s.56(1)(c)).

Subsection (5)

1–752   *Relevant hospital direction . . . relevant transfer direction:* See section 79(2).

Subsection (6)

1–753   *Relevant hospital order:* See section 79(2).

Applications and references concerning conditionally discharged restricted patients

1–754   **75.**—(1) Where a restricted patient has been conditionally discharged under section 42(2), 73 or 74 above and is subsequently recalled to hospital—

    (a) the Secretary of State shall, within one month of the day on which the patient returns or is returned to hospital, refer his case to a Mental Health Review Tribunal; and

    (b) section 70 above shall apply to the patient as if the relevant hospital order [, hospital direction] or transfer direction had been made on that day.

    (2) Where a restricted patient has been conditionally discharged as aforesaid but has not been recalled to hospital he may apply to a Mental Health Review Tribunal—

    (a) in the period between the expiration of 12 months and the expiration of two years beginning with the date on which he was conditionally discharged; and

    (b) in any subsequent period of two years.

    (3) Sections 73 and 74 above shall not apply to an application under subsection (2) above but on any such application the Tribunal may—

    (a) vary any condition to which the patient is subject in connection with his discharge or impose any condition which might have been imposed in connection therewith; or

    (b) direct that the restriction order or restriction direction to which he is subject shall cease to have effect;

and if the tribunal give a direction under paragraph (b) above the patient shall cease to be liable to be detained by virtue of the relevant hospital order or transfer direction.

AMENDMENT

    In subsection (1)(b) the words in square brackets were inserted by the Crime (Sentences) Act 1997, s.55, Sched. 4, para. 12(13).

DEFINITIONS

1–755   restricted patient: s.79(1).
    hospital: ss.79(6), 145(1).
    hospital direction: s.145(1).
    relevant hospital order: s.79(2).
    relevant transfer direction: s.79(2).
    restriction order: ss.41, 145(1).
    restriction direction: ss.49, 145(1).

GENERAL NOTE
This section directs the Home Secretary to refer the case of a conditionally discharged restricted patient who has been recalled to hospital to a Mental Health Review Tribunal. It also provides for a tribunal application to be made by a conditionally discharged restricted patient who has not been recalled to hospital. On hearing such an application the tribunal has the power to vary the conditions of the discharge, to impose new conditions, or to direct that the restriction order or direction shall cease to have effect.

A restricted patient who is no longer suffering from a mental disorder remains a "patient" for the purposes of this section until he is discharged absolutely (*R. v. Merseyside Mental Health Review Tribunal, ex p. K* [1990] 1 All E.R. 694, CA).

The Human Rights Act 1998
Article 5(4) of the European Convention on Human Rights requires the tribunal **1–756** hearing of the recalled patient to take place speedily. In *X. v. United Kingdom*, app. no. 6998/75, para. 138, the Commission said that a delay of six months between the patient's recall to hospital by the Home Secretary and the hearing violated Article 5(4).

Subsection (1)
Restricted patient: Is a patient who is subject to a restriction order or direction **1–757** (s.79(1)).

Within one month: Disregarding the day of the patient's return to hospital (*Stewart v. Chapman* [1951] 2 K.B. 792). "In requiring the Secretary of State to refer the case to a Mental Health Review Tribunal within one month of the patient's recall, rather than sooner or later, Parliament was striking a balance between the need to have the question considered by a court at the earliest opportunity and the need to provide the tribunal with evidence of appropriate quality; such evidence would obviously include assessments made in hospital after recall" (*R. v. Secretary of State for the Home Department, ex p. K* [1990] 1 All E.R. 703, 712, per McCullough J.).

Refer his case to a Mental Health Review Tribunal: Which must arrange for a hearing to take place within eight weeks of the receipt of the reference (Mental Health Tribunal Rules 1983, r. 29(cc)). The tribunal will exercise its powers under section 73. In *R. v. Mental Health Review Tribunal for Merseyside, ex p. Kelly* [1998] 39 B.M.L.R. 114, Keene J. said that he could "see that in general terms the events leading up to a recall of a patient may not be relevant to the issues arising under section 72(1)(b)(i) and (ii) [see s.73(1)(a)] ... However, it is also true that such events prior to a patient's recall may be relevant. Diagnosis of and opinions as to such matters as are referred to in the relevant statutory paragraphs are not arrived at by ignoring events which have happened. The behaviour of the patient may well be material to such diagnosis and opinions. It will depend at least partly on how the expert witness or witnesses have arrived at their conclusions." In this case his Lordship declared that the decision of the tribunal was *ultra vires* in that it was contrary to the rules of natural justice because of a refusal by the tribunal to allow the cross-examination of the patient's responsible medical officer on statements that he had made in his report to the tribunal concerning allegations that had been made about the patient's conduct prior to his recall to hospital.

Subsection (2)
Conditionally discharged: A patient is conditionally discharged for the purposes of **1–758** calculating time under this provision, not on the date when the tribunal decided that he be discharged subject to conditions being met, but on the date when he actually leaves hospital once those conditions had been met (*R. v. Canons Park Mental Health Review Tribunal, ex p. Martins* (1995) 26 B.M.L.R. 134). In this case Ognall J.

followed Mann J.'s finding in *Secretary of State for the Home Department v. Mental Health Review Tribunal for the Mersey Regional Health Authority* [1986] 3 All E.R. 233, 237 that:

> "The word 'discharge' as employed in sections 72 to 75 of the Act of 1983 means, and in my judgment can only mean, release from hospital. The release may be absolute or it may be conditional."

Law and practice appear to differ on this point. Lucy Scott-Moncrieff, a very experienced practitioner of mental health law, has informed the author that the Home Office, hospitals and tribunals all regard the relevant date as being the date that the tribunal office sends written confirmation to the patient's responsible medical officer that the terms of the deferred conditional discharge have been met and that the patient is entitled to be discharged. The patient's actual date of discharge from the hospital can be delayed for some time after this authorisation has been received.

Not been recalled to hospital: A conditionally discharged restricted patient who has been brought back to hospital under either section 2 or section 3 has not been "recalled to hospital" as such a recall can only be made by the Home Secretary under section 42(3).

May apply: To the tribunal for the area in which he resides (s.77(4)).

Beginning with: Including the date of his conditional discharge (*Hare v. Gocher* [1962] 2 Q.B. 641) which is day when he leaves hospital: see the note on "conditionally discharged" above.

Subsection (3)

1–759   *May:* The tribunal is not bound by any criteria in the exercise of its discretion.

General

Visiting and examination of patients

1–760   **76.**—(1) For the purpose of advising whether an application to a Mental Health Review Tribunal should be made by or in respect of a patient who is liable to be detained or subject to guardianship [or to after-care under supervision (or, if he has not yet left hospital, is to be subject to after-care under supervision after he leaves hospital)] under Part II of this Act or of furnishing information as to the condition of a patient for the purposes of such an application, any registered medical practitioner authorised by or on behalf of the patient or other person who is entitled to make or has made the application—

(a) may at any reasonable time visit the patient and examine him in private, and

(b) may require the production of and inspect any records relating to the detention or treatment of the patient in any hospital [or to any after-care services provided for the patient under s.117 below].

(2) Section 32 above shall apply for the purposes of this section as it applies for the purposes of Part II of this Act.

AMENDMENTS

The words in square brackets in subs. (1) were inserted by the Mental Health (Patients in the Community) Act 1995, s.2(1), Sched. 1, para. 11.

DEFINITIONS

1–761   patient: s.145(1).
hospital: ss.79(6), 145(1).
subject to after-care under supervision: ss.25A(2), 145(1A).

GENERAL NOTE

A registered medical practitioner is given similar powers to those contained in this **1–762** section on an automatic tribunal reference made by the hospital managers (s.68(3)) and where the Secretary of State for Health refers a case to the tribunal (s.67(2)). A similar power is not provided for on a reference being made by the Home Secretary under section 71, although it is highly unlikely that access would be denied in such cases.

This section is applied to patients who have been placed under hospital, restriction or guardianship orders by a court under section 37 or 41 of this Act (Sched. 1, Pt 1, para. 1; Pt 2, para. 1). Its provisions are modified in respect of patients subject to community care orders in Scotland who intend to reside in England and Wales: see the Mental Health (Patients in the Community) (Transfers from Scotland) Regulations 1996 (S.I. 1996 No. 295).

A failure to allow medical practitioners or authorised persons to carry out their functions under this section could amount to an obstruction under section 129.

Subsection (1)

Furnishing information: In *W v. Egdell* [1990] 1 All E.R. 835, the Court of Appeal **1–763** held that where a doctor is called on to examine a patient with a view to providing an independent psychiatric report to support the patient's application to a Mental Health Review Tribunal, he owes a duty not only to his patient but also a duty to the public. His duty to the public would enable him to place before the proper authorities the results of his examination if, in his opinion, the public interest so required. This would be so whether or not the patient instructed him not to do so. *Per* Bingham L.J. at 852, 853: "There is one consideration [in this case] which in my judgment ... weighs the balance of public interest decisively in favour of disclosure. It may be shortly put. Where a man has committed multiple killings under the disability of serious mental illness, decisions which may lead directly or indirectly to his release from hospital should not be made unless a responsible authority is properly able to make an informed judgment that the risk of repetition is so small as to be acceptable. A consultant psychiatrist who becomes aware, even in the course of a confidential relationship, of information which leads him, in the exercise of what the court considers a sound professional judgment, to fear that such decisions may be made on the basis of inadequate information and with a real risk of consequent danger to the public is entitled to take such steps as are reasonable in all the circumstances to communicate the grounds of his concern to the responsible authorities." The *Egdell* case is examined by Andrew Grubb in the All E.R. Rev. 1990 at pp. 188–190.

General provisions concerning tribunal applications

77.—(1) No application shall be made to a Mental Health Review **1–764** Tribunal by or in respect of a patient except in such cases and at such times as are expressly provided by this Act.

(2) Where under this Act any person is authorised to make an application to a Mental Health Review Tribunal within a specified period, not more than one such application shall be made by that person within that period but for that purpose there shall be disregarded any application which is withdrawn in accordance with rules made under section 78 below.

(3) Subject to subsection (4) below an application to a Mental Health Review Tribunal authorised to be made by or in respect of a patient under this Act shall be made by notice in writing addressed to the tribunal for the area in which the hospital in which the patient is detained is situated or in

which the patient is residing under guardianship [or when subject to after-care under supervision (or in which he is to reside on becoming so subject after leaving hospital)] as the case may be.

(4) Any application under section 75(2) above shall be made to the tribunal for the area in which the patient resides.

AMENDMENT
In subsection (3) the words in square brackets were inserted by the Mental Health (Patients in the Community) Act 1995, s.2(1), Sched. 1, para. 12.

DEFINITIONS
1–765   patient: s.145(1).
hospital: ss.79(6), 145(1).
subject to after-care under supervision: ss.25A(2), 145(1A).

GENERAL NOTE
1–766   This section provides, *inter alia*, that there is no right to apply to a tribunal apart from those situations expressly provided for in this Act, that where the Act gives rise to a right to make an application within a specified period only one such application may be made within that period, and that where the tribunal authorises the withdrawal of an application the applicant can re-apply during the relevant period.

Subsection (2)
1–767   *Withdrawn in accordance with the rules:* See rule 19 of the Mental Health Review Tribunal Rules 1983. References cannot be withdrawn.

Subsection (3)
1–768   *Notice in writing:* See rule 3 of the Mental Health Review Tribunal Rules 1983.
Hospital in which the patient is detained: And not the hospital where the patient is residing subsequent to being granted leave of absence under section 17.

Subsection (4)
1–769   *Application under section 75(2):* By a restricted patient who has been conditionally discharged from hospital.
Resides: Temporary absences from the place where a person resides does not affect residence, as long as there is an intention to return to it (*R. v. St Leonard's Shoreditch* (*Inhabitants*) (1865) L.R. 1 Q.B. 21). Also note Widgery L.J.'s statement in *Fox v. Stirk* [1970] 2 Q.B. 463 at 477 that: "A man cannot be said to reside in a particular place unless in the ordinary sense of the word one can say that for the time being he is making his home in that place."

Procedure of tribunals
1–770   **78.**—(1) The Lord Chancellor may make rules with respect to the making of applications to Mental Health Review Tribunals and with respect to the proceedings of such tribunals and matters incidental to or consequential on such proceedings.

(2) Rules made under this section may in particular make provision—
(a) for enabling a tribunal, or the chairman of a tribunal, to postpone the consideration of any application by or in respect of a patient, or of any such application of any specified class, until the expiration of such period (not exceeding 12 months) as may be specified in the rules

from the date on which an application by or in respect of the same patient was last considered and determined by that or any other tribunal under this Act;

(b) for the transfer of proceedings from one tribunal to another in any case where, after the making of the application, the patient is removed out of the area of the Tribunal to which it was made;

(c) for restricting the persons qualified to serve as members of a tribunal for the consideration of any application, or of an application of any specified class;

(d) for enabling a tribunal to dispose of an application without a formal hearing where such a hearing is not requested by the applicant or it appears to the Tribunal that such a hearing would be detrimental to the health of the patient;

(e) for enabling a tribunal to exclude members of the public, or any specified class of members of the public, from any proceedings of the Tribunal, or to prohibit the publication of reports of any such proceedings or the names of any persons concerned in such proceedings;

(f) for regulating the circumstances in which, and the persons by whom, applicants and patients in respect of whom applications are made to a tribunal may, if not desiring to conduct their own case, be represented for the purposes of those applications;

(g) for regulating the methods by which information relevant to an application may be obtained by or furnished to the Tribunal, and in particular for authorising the members of a tribunal, or any one or more of them, to visit and interview in private any patient by or in respect of whom an application has been made;

(h) for making available to any applicant, and to any patient in respect of whom an application is made to a tribunal, copies of any documents obtained by or furnished to the Tribunal in connection with the application, and a statement of the substance of any oral information so obtained or furnished except where the Tribunal considers it undesirable in the interests of the patient or for other special reasons;

(i) for requiring a tribunal, if so requested in accordance with the rules, to furnish such statements of the reasons for any decision given by the Tribunal as may be prescribed by the rules, subject to any provision made by the rules for withholding such a statement from a patient or any other person in cases where the Tribunal considers that furnishing it would be undesirable in the interests of the patient or for other special reasons;

(j) for conferring on the tribunals such ancillary powers as the Lord Chancellor thinks necessary for the purposes of the exercise of their functions under this Act;

(k) for enabling any functions of a tribunal which relate to matters preliminary or incidental to an application to be performed by the chairman of the tribunal.

(3) Subsections (1) and (2) above apply in relation to references to Mental Health Review Tribunals as they apply in relation to applications to such tribunals by or in respect of patients.

(4) Rules under this section may make provision as to the procedure to be adopted in cases concerning restricted patients and, in particular—

(a) for restricting the persons qualified to serve as president of a tribunal for the consideration of an application or reference relating to a restricted patient;

(b) for the transfer of proceedings from one tribunal to another in any case where, after the making of a reference or application in accordance with section 71(4) or 77(4) above, the patient ceases to reside in the area of the tribunal to which the reference or application was made.

(5) Rules under this section may be so framed as to apply to all applications or references or to applications or references of any specified class and may make different provision in relation to different cases.

(6) Any functions conferred on the chairman of a Mental Health Review Tribunal by rules under this section may, if for any reason he is unable to act, be exercised by another member of that tribunal appointed by him for the purpose.

(7) A Mental Health Review Tribunal may pay allowances in respect of travelling expenses, subsistence and loss of earnings to any person attending the Tribunal as an applicant or witness, to the patient who is the subject of the proceedings if he attends otherwise than as the applicant or a witness and to any person (other than counsel or a solicitor) who attends as the representative of an applicant.

(8) A Mental Health Review Tribunal may, and if so required by the High Court shall, state in the form of a special case for determination by the High Court any question of law which may arise before them.

(9) [Part I of the Arbitration Act 1996] shall not apply to any proceedings before a Mental Health Review Tribunal except so far as any provisions of that Act may be applied, with or without modifications, by rules made under this section.

AMENDMENT
In subsection (9) the words in square brackets were substituted by the Arbitration Act 1996, s.107(1), Sched. 3, para. 40.

DEFINITION
1–771   patient: s.145(1).

GENERAL NOTE
1–772   The Mental Health Review Tribunal Rules 1983 (S.I. 1983 No. 942), the Mental Health Review Tribunal (Amendment) Rules 1996 (S.I. 1996 No. 314) and the Mental Health Review Tribunal (Amendment) Rules 1998 (S.I. 1998 No.1189) have been made under this section.

Subsection (2)
1–773   *Paragraph (a)—chairman of a tribunal:* See Schedule 2, para. 2.
Paragraph (b)—area of the tribunal: See section 65(1).

Subsection (4)
1–774   *Qualified to serve as president of a tribunal:* "The Government recognise that the power to release restricted patients who may have been convicted of very serious offences carries with it a formidable responsibility. We regard it as essential that the exercise of this responsibility ... should command the confidence not only of the public but also of members of the judiciary who, in the Crown Court, must decide in an individual case whether a restriction order ought to be made. Those considerations led us to conclude that when the tribunal exercises this ... jurisdiction it should

have in the chair as its president a lawyer with substantial judicial experience in the criminal courts ...";*per* Lord Belstead, HL Vol. 426, col. 761. Now see rule 8(3) of the Mental Health Review Tribunal Rules 1983.

Subsection (7)
  Loss of earnings: This would not cover the payment of a fee for representing the **1–775** client or acting as an expert witness.
  Attending: Expenses cannot be paid for preparatory work.

Subsection (8)
  State in the form of a special case: For the procedure to be adopted, see the Rules of **1–776** the Supreme Court, Ord. 56, rr. 7–12 (as reproduced in Schedule 1 to the Civil Procedure Rules 1998). Also see the General Note to section 65.

Interpretation of Part V
  79.—(1) In this Part of this Act "restricted patient" means a patient who is **1–777** subject to a restriction order [, limitation direction] or restriction direction and this Part of this Act shall, subject to the provisions of this section, have effect in relation to any person who
  (a) is subject to a direction which by virtue of section 46(3) above has the same effect as a hospital order and a restriction order; or
  (b) is treated as subject to a hospital order and a restriction order by virtue of an order under section 5(1) of the Criminal Procedure (Insanity) Act 1964 or section 6 or 14(1) of the Criminal Appeal Act 1968; or
  (c) is treated as subject to a hospital order and a restriction order or to a transfer direction and a restriction direction by virtue of section 82(2) or 85(2) below or [section 73(2) of the Mental Health (Scotland) Act 1984],
as it has effect in relation to a restricted patient.
  (2) Subject to the following provisions of this section, in this Part of this Act "the relevant hospital order" [, "the relevant hospital direction"] and "the relevant transfer direction," in relation to a restricted patient, mean the hospital order [, the hospital direction] or transfer direction by virtue of which he is liable to be detained in a hospital.
  (3) In the case of a person within paragraph (a) of subsection (1) above, references in this Part of this Act to the relevant hospital order or restriction order shall be construed as references to the direction referred to in that paragraph.
  (4) In the case of a person within paragraph (b) of subsection (1) above, references in this Part of this Act to the relevant hospital order or restriction order shall be construed as references to the order under the provisions mentioned in that paragraph.
  (5) In the case of a person within paragraph (c) of subsection (1) above, references in this Part of this Act to the relevant hospital order, the relevant transfer direction, the restriction order or the restriction direction or to a transfer direction under section 48 above shall be construed as references to the hospital order, transfer direction, restriction order, restriction direction or transfer direction under that section to which that person is treated as subject by virtue of the provisions mentioned in that paragraph.
  (6) In this Part of this Act, unless the context otherwise requires, "hospital" means a hospital [and the "responsible medical officer" means the responsible medical officer,] within the meaning of Part II of this Act.

[(7) In this Part of this Act any reference to the area of a tribunal is—
(a) in relation to a tribunal for a region of England, a reference to that region; and
(b) in relation to the tribunal for Wales, a reference to Wales.]

AMENDMENTS
In subsection (1)(c) the words in square brackets were substituted by the Mental Health (Scotland) Act 1984, s.127(1), Sched. 3, para. 50. The words in square brackets in subsections (1) and (2) were inserted by the Crime (Sentences) Act 1997, s.55, Sched. 4, para. 12(14)(15). Subsection (7) was inserted by the Health Authorities Act 1995, s.2(1), Sched. 1, para. 107(7) and the words in square brackets in subsection (6) were inserted by the Mental Health (Patients in the Community) Act 1995, s.2(1), Sched. 1, para. 13.

DEFINITIONS
1–778   patient: s.145(1).
restriction order: ss.41, 145(1).
restriction direction: ss.49, 145(1).
hospital order: ss.37, 145(1).
transfer direction: ss.47, 145(1).

Subsection (6)
1–779   *Hospital:* See section 34(2).

PART VI

REMOVAL AND RETURN OF PATIENTS WITHIN UNITED KINGDOM, ETC.

GENERAL NOTE
1–780   Paragraph 260 of the *Memorandum* states:

> "Part VI of the Act provides powers under which certain categories of detained patients (not those detained under section 35, 36 or 38), conditionally discharged patients and patients under guardianship may be moved between England and Wales and other parts of the United Kingdom, the Channel Islands and the Isle of Man, while remaining under detention or guardianship or continuing to be conditionally discharged; or may be retaken in those places when absent without leave from hospitals or institutions. It also provides powers for moving mentally disordered patients who are neither British citizens nor Commonwealth citizens with the right of abode here from hospitals in England and Wales to countries abroad."

Appendix 5 to the *Memorandum* gives a brief résumé of the procedures to be followed and the corresponding provisions in the Scotland and Northern Ireland mental health legislation.

There is no need to invoke the provisions of this Part if arrangements are made at the request of a patient or his relatives for him to go to another part of the United Kingdom, the Channel Islands or to the Isle of Man, and it is not necessary to keep the authority for detention in operation while he is being moved. In these circumstances, he may be discharged before leaving, and enter hospital or guardianship in the country of destination under the admission procedures of that country.

The procedure to be followed on the removal of a patient to England or Wales under this Part is set out in regulation 11 of the Mental Health (Hospital, Guardianship and Consent to Treatment) Regulations 1983.

Removal to Scotland

Removal of patients to Scotland

80.—(1) If it appears to the Secretary of State, in the case of a patient who **1–781**
is for the time being liable to be detained or subject to guardianship under
this Act (otherwise than by virtue of section 35, 36 or 38 above), that it is in
the interests of the patient to remove him to Scotland, and that arrangements have been made for admitting him to a hospital or, as the case may be,
for receiving him into guardianship there, the Secretary of State may
authorise his removal to Scotland and may give any necessary directions for
his conveyance to his destination.

(2) Subject to the provisions of subsection (4) below, where a patient
liable to be detained under this Act by virtue of an application, order or
direction under any enactment in force in England and Wales is removed
under this section and admitted to a hospital in Scotland, he shall be treated
as if on the date of his admission he had been so admitted in pursuance of an
application forwarded to the Health Board responsible for the administration of the hospital, or an order or direction made or given, on that date
under the corresponding enactment in Scotland, and, where he is subject to a
restriction order or restriction direction under any enactment in this Act, as
if he were subject to [a restriction order or restriction] direction under the
corresponding enactment in force in Scotland.

(3) Where a patient subject to guardianship under this Act by virtue of an
application, order or direction under any enactment in force in England and
Wales is removed under this section and received into guardianship in
Scotland, he shall be treated as if on the date on which he arrives at the place
where he is to reside he had been so received in pursuance of an application,
order or direction under the corresponding enactment in force in Scotland,
and as if the application had been forwarded or, as the case may be, the order
or direction had been made or given on that date.

(4) Where a person removed under this section was immediately before
his removal liable to be detained by virtue of an application for admission for
assessment under this Act, he shall, on his admission to a hospital in
Scotland, be treated as if he had been admitted to the hospital in pursuance
of an emergency recommendation under the [Mental Health (Scotland) Act
1984] made on the date of his admission.

(5) Where a patient removed under this section was immediately before
his removal liable to be detained under this Act by virtue of a transfer
direction given while he was serving a sentence of imprisonment (within the
meaning of section 47(5) above) imposed by a court in England and Wales,
he shall be treated as if the sentence had been imposed by a court in
Scotland.

(6) Where a person removed under this section was immediately before
his removal subject to a restriction order or restriction direction of limited
duration, [the restriction order or restriction direction to which he is subject
by virtue of subsection (2) of this section shall expire on the date on which
the first-mentioned order or direction would have expired if he had not been
so removed.]

(7) In this section "hospital" has the same meaning as in the [Mental
Health (Scotland) Act 1984].

In this section the words in square brackets were substituted by the Mental Health (Amendment) (Scotland) Act 1983, s.39(2), Sched. 2, para. 1 and the Mental Health (Scotland) Act 1984, s.127(1), Sched. 3, para. 51.

DEFINITIONS
1–782 patient: s.145(1).
hospital: subs. (7).
restriction order: ss.41, 145(1).
restriction direction: ss.49, 145(1).
application for admission for assessment: ss.2, 145(1).
transfer direction: ss.47, 145(1).

GENERAL NOTE
1–783 This section enables the Secretary of State (or, for certain categories of patient in relation to Wales, the National Assembly for Wales) to transfer a patient who is detained (otherwise than under section 35, 36 or 38) or subject to guardianship in England or Wales to Scotland without a break in the powers of detention or guardianship. The Secretary of State (or the National Assembly) must be satisfied that such a move is in the interests of the patient and that suitable arrangements have been made for admitting him to hospital or receiving him into guardianship in Scotland. On his arrival in Scotland the patient will become subject to the equivalent Scottish legislation.

"The views of the person exercising the functions of nearest relative should be ascertained and reported to the Secretary of State whenever it is desired to remove a patient under section 80 or 81" (*Memorandum*, para. 262).

Once the transfer of a detained patient has been agreed in principle between the sending and receiving hospitals, the sending hospital should write to: Department of Health, Mental Health Legislation Branch, Wellington House, 133–155 Waterloo Road, London SE1 8UG, Tel: 020 7972 2000.

For patients who are either detained or subject to guardianship in Wales, the information should be sent to: The National Assembly for Wales, Cathays Park, Cardiff CF10 3NQ, Tel: 029 20825111.

The sending hospital should provide the details set out in paragraph 4 of Appendix 5 to the *Memorandum*.
Full details of the proposed transfer of a restricted patient should be sent to: Mental Health Unit, Home Office, Queen Anne's Gate, London SW1H 9AT.

The Secretary of State for Scotland can transfer detained patients or patients subject to guardianship to England and Wales under section 77 of the Mental Health (Scotland) Act 1984. The procedure to be followed on such a transfer is set out in paragraphs 7 to 9 of Appendix 5 to the *Memorandum*.

Subsection (1)
1–784 *Secretary of State:* The functions of the Minister, so far as exercisable in relation to Wales, are exercised by the National Assembly for Wales (S.I. 1999 No. 672, art. 2, Sched. 1, as varied by S.I. 2000 No. 253, art. 4, Sched. 3) except in relation to a patient who is subject to one or more of the following, namely:

(a) a restriction order;
(b) a hospital direction;

(c) a limitation direction; or

(d) a restriction direction,

made under sections 41, 45A or, as the case may be, 49.

Remove him to Scotland: The position of the nearest relative on the patient's transfer to Scotland is covered by section 79 of the Mental Health (Scotland) Act 1984.

Hospital: See subs. (7).

Conveyance to his destination: General provisions relating to the custody, conveyance and detention of patients are contained in section 137.

Subsection (2)

Direction: See section 92(4).   **1–785**

Subsection (4)

Emergency recommendation: Made under section 24 of the Mental Health **1–786** (Scotland) Act 1984 and which authorises removal to hospital within three days and detention for a maximum of 72 hours. There is no equivalent in the Scottish legislation to an admission for assessment made under section 2 of this Act.

Subsection (5)

Transfer direction: See section 92(5).   **1–787**

Subsection (7)

Hospital: Is defined in section 125(1) of the 1984 Act as: "(a) any hospital vested in **1–788** the Secretary of State under the National Health Service (Scotland) Act 1978; (b) any private hospital registered under Part IV of [the 1984] Act; and (c) any State hospital."

[Transfer of responsibility for patients to Scotland

80A.—(1) If it appears to the Secretary of State, in the case of a patient **1–789** who—

(a) is subject to a restriction order under section 41 above; and

(b) has been conditionally discharged under section 42 or 73 above,

that a transfer under this section would be in the interests of the patient, the Secretary of State may, with the consent of the Minister exercising corresponding functions in Scotland, transfer responsibility for the patient to that Minister.

(2) Where responsibility for such a patient is transferred under this section, the patient shall be treated—

(a) as if on the date of the transfer he had been conditionally discharged under the corresponding enactment in force in Scotland; and

(b) as if he were subject to a restriction order under the corresponding enactment in force in Scotland.

(3) Where a patient responsibility for whom is transferred under this section was immediately before the transfer subject to a restriction order of limited duration, the restriction order to which he is subject by virtue of subsection (2) above shall expire on the date on which the first-mentioned order would have expired if the transfer had not been made.]

AMENDMENT

This section was inserted by the Crime (Sentences) Act 1997, s.48, Sched. 3, para. 1.

DEFINITIONS

1–790   patient: s.145(1).
restriction order: ss.41, 145(1).

GENERAL NOTE

1–791   This section makes provision for the transfer of responsibility for conditionally discharged restricted patients from England and Wales to Scotland. It enables the Home Secretary to authorise such a transfer where it appears to be in the interests of the patient, and where the Secretary of State for Scotland has consented to the transfer. The Secretary of State for Scotland is given a reciprocal power by section 77A of the Mental Health (Scotland) Act 1984. Supervisors of such patients "should initially approach the caseworker dealing with the patient in the Home Office Mental Health Unit" (*Memorandum*, Appendix 5, para. 2).

Subsection 2 provides that where responsibility for a patient has been transferred, the patient will be treated as if he had been conditionally discharged under the corresponding enactment in Scotland on the date of the transfer, and as if he were subject to a restriction order under that enactment.

Subsection 3 provides that where such a patient was immediately before the transfer subject to a restriction order of limited duration, the restriction order to which he becomes subject in Scotland will expire on the date the original restriction order would have expired.

Removal to and from Northern Ireland

Removal of patients to Northern Ireland

1–792   **81.**—(1) If it appears to the Secretary of State, in the case of a patient who is for the time being liable to be detained or subject to guardianship under this Act (otherwise than by virtue of section 35, 36 or 38 above), that it is in the interests of the patient to remove him to Northern Ireland, and that arrangements have been made for admitting him to a hospital or, as the case may be, for receiving him into guardianship there, the Secretary of State may authorise his removal to Northern Ireland and may give any necessary directions for his conveyance to his destination.

(2) Subject to the provisions of subsections (4) and (5) below, where a patient liable to be detained under this Act by virtue of an application, order or direction under any enactment in force in England and Wales is removed under this section and admitted to a hospital in Northern Ireland, he shall be treated as if on the date of his admission he had been so admitted in pursuance of an application made, or [a restriction order or a restriction direction] made or given, on that date under the corresponding enactment in force in Northern Ireland, and, where he is subject to a restriction order or restriction direction under any enactment in this Act, as if he were subject to an order or direction under the corresponding enactment in force in Northern Ireland.

(3) Where a patient subject to guardianship under this Act by virtue of an application, order or direction under any enactment in force in England and Wales is removed under this section and received into guardianship in Northern Ireland, he shall be treated as if on the date on which he arrives at the place where he is to reside he had been so received in pursuance of an application, order or direction under the corresponding enactment in force in Northern Ireland, and as if the application had been accepted or, as the case may be, the order or direction had been made or given on that date.

(4) Where a person removed under this section was immediately before his removal liable to be detained by virtue of an application for admission for assessment under this Act, he shall, on his admission to a hospital in

Northern Ireland, be treated as if he had been admitted to the hospital in pursuance of an application [for assessment under Article 4 of the Mental Health (Northern Ireland) Order 1986] made on the date of his admission.

(5) Where a person removed under this section was immediately before his removal liable to be detained by virtue of an application for admission for treatment under this Act, he shall, on his admission to a hospital in Northern Ireland, be treated as if [he were detained for treatment under Part II of the Mental Health (Northern Ireland) Order 1986 by virtue of a report under Article 12(1) of that Order made on the date of his admission.]

(6) Where a person removed under this section was immediately before his removal liable to be detained under this Act by virtue of a transfer direction given while he was serving a sentence of imprisonment (within the meaning of section 47(5) above) imposed by a court in England and Wales, he shall be treated as if the sentence had been imposed by a court in Northern Ireland.

(7) Where a person removed under this section was immediately before his removal subject to a restriction order or restriction direction of limited duration, [the restriction order or restriction direction] to which he is subject by virtue of subsection (2) above shall expire on the date on which [the first mentioned restriction order] or restriction direction would have expired if he had not been so removed.

(8) In this section "hospital" has the same meaning as in the Mental Health [(Northern Ireland) Order 1986].

AMENDMENT
In this section the words in square brackets were substituted by the Mental Health (Northern Ireland Consequential Amendments) Order 1986 (S.I. 1986 No. 596), art. 2.

DEFINITIONS
    patient: s.145(1).
    hospital: subs. (8).
    restriction order: ss.41, 145(1).
    restriction direction: ss.49, 145(1).
    application for admission for assessment: ss.2, 145(1).
    application for admission for treatment: ss.3, 145(1).
    transfer direction: ss.47, 145(1).

1–793

GENERAL NOTE
This section enables the Secretary of State (or, for certain categories of patient in relation to Wales, the National Assembly for Wales) to transfer a patient who is detained (otherwise than under section 35, 36 or 38) or subject to guardianship in England or Wales to Northern Ireland without a break in the powers of detention or guardianship. The Secretary of State (or the National Assembly) must be satisfied that such a move is in the interests of the patient and that suitable arrangements have been made for admitting him to hospital or receiving him into guardianship in Northern Ireland. On his arrival in Northern Ireland the patient will become subject to the equivalent Northern Irish legislation, and the application, order or direction made in England or Wales will cease to have effect.

1–794

Once the transfer of a detained patient has been agreed in principle between the sending and receiving hospitals, the sending hospital should contact either the Department of Health or the National Assembly. Details of the proposed transfer of a restricted patient should be sent to the Home Office: see the General Note to section 80.

Subsection (1)
1–795   *Secretary of State:* See the note on section 80(1).
Arrangements: For the transmission of information about these arrangements, see the general note to section 80.
Hospital: See subsection (8).

Subsection (6)
1–796   *Transfer direction:* See section 94(5).

Subsection (8)
1–797   *Hospital:* Is defined in article 2 of the 1986 Order.

[Transfer of responsibility for patients to Northern Ireland
1–798   **81A.**—(1) If it appears to the Secretary of State, in the case of a patient who—

(a) is subject to a restriction order or restriction direction under section 41 or 49 above; and

(b) has been conditionally discharged under section 42 or 73 above,

that a transfer under this section would be in the interests of the patient, the Secretary of State may, with the consent of the Minister exercising corresponding functions in Northern Ireland, transfer responsibility for the patient to that Minister.

(2) Where responsibility for such a patient is transferred under this section, the patient shall be treated—

(a) as if on the date of the transfer he had been conditionally discharged under the corresponding enactment in force in Northern Ireland; and

(b) as if he were subject to a restriction order or restriction direction under the corresponding enactment in force in Northern Ireland.

(3) Where a patient responsibility for whom is transferred under this section was immediately before the transfer subject to a restriction order or restriction direction of limited duration, the restriction order or restriction direction to which he is subject by virtue of subsection (2) above shall expire on the date on which the first-mentioned order or direction would have expired if the transfer had not been made.]

AMENDMENT
This section was inserted by the Crime (Sentences) Act 1997, s.48, Sched. 3, para. 2.

DEFINITIONS
1–799   patient: s.145(1).
restriction order: ss.41, 145(1).
restriction direction: ss.49, 145(1).

GENERAL NOTE
1–800   This section makes provision for the transfer of responsibility for conditionally discharged restricted patients from England and Wales to Northern Ireland. It is an equivalent provision to section 80A and reference should be made to the notes on that section.

Subsection (1)
Restriction direction: See section 94(4)(b).

Removal to England and Wales of patients from Northern Ireland

82.—(1) If it appears to the responsible authority, in the case of a patient **1–801** who is for the time being liable to be detained or subject to guardianship under the Mental Health [(Northern Ireland) Order 1986 (otherwise than by virtue of Article 42, 43 or 45 of that Order)], that it is in the interests of the patient to remove him to England and Wales, and that arrangements have been made for admitting him to a hospital or, as the case may be, for receiving him into guardianship there, the responsible authority may authorise his removal to England and Wales and may give any necessary directions for his conveyance to his destination.

(2) Subject to the provisions of [subsections (4) and (4A)] below, where a patient who is liable to be detained under the [Mental Health (Northern Ireland) Order 1986] by virtue of an application, order or direction under any enactment in force in Northern Ireland is removed under this section and admitted to a hospital in England and Wales, he shall be treated as if on the date of his admission he had been so admitted in pursuance of an application made, or an order or direction made or given, on that date under the corresponding enactment in force in England and Wales and, where he is [subject to a restriction order or restriction direction under any enactment in that Order, as if he were subject to a restriction order or restriction direction under the corresponding enactment in force in England and Wales].

(3) Where a patient subject to guardianship under the [Mental Health (Northern Ireland) Order 1986] by virtue of an application, order or direction under any enactment in force in Northern Ireland is removed under this section and received into guardianship in England and Wales, he shall be treated as if on the date on which he arrives at the place where he is to reside he had been so received in pursuance of an application, order or direction under the corresponding enactment in force in England and Wales and as if the application had been accepted or, as the case may be, the order or direction had been made or given on that date.

[(4) Where a person removed under this section was immediately before his removal liable to be detained for treatment by virtue of a report under Article 12(1) or 13 of the Mental Health (Northern Ireland) Order 1986, he shall be treated, on his admission to a hospital in England and Wales, as if he had been admitted to the hospital in pursuance of an application for admission for treatment made on the date of his admission.

(4A) Where a person removed under this section was immediately before his removal liable to be detained by virtue of an application for assessment under Article 4 of the Mental Health (Northern Ireland) Order 1986, he shall be treated, on his admission to a hospital in England and Wales, as if he had been admitted to the hospital in pursuance of an application for admission for assessment made on the date of his admission.]

(5) Where a patient removed under this section was immediately before his removal liable to be detained under the [Mental Health (Northern Ireland) Order 1986] by virtue of a transfer direction given while he was serving a sentence of imprisonment (within the meaning of [Article 53(5) of that Order)] imposed by a court in Northern Ireland, he shall be treated as if the sentence had been imposed by a court in England and Wales.

(6) Where a person removed under this section was immediately before his removal subject to [a restriction order or restriction direction] of limited

351

duration, the restriction order or restriction direction to which he is subject by virtue of subsection (2) above shall expire on the date on which the [first-mentioned restriction order or restriction direction] would have expired if he had not been so removed.

(7) In this section "the responsibility authority" means the Department of Health and Social Services for Northern Ireland or, in relation to a patient who is subject to [a restriction order or restriction direction], the Secretary of State.

AMENDMENTS

In this section the words in square brackets were substituted or inserted by the Mental Health (Northern Ireland Consequential Amendments) Order 1986 (S.I. 1986 No. 596), art. 2.

DEFINITIONS

1–802   patient: s.145(1).
hospital: ss.92(1), 145(1).
application for admission for assessment: ss.2, 145(1).
application for admission for treatment: ss.3, 145(1).
transfer direction: ss.47, 145(1).
restriction order: ss.41, 145(1).
restriction direction: ss.49, 145(1).

GENERAL NOTE

1–803   This section provides that a patient who is detained or subject to guardianship in Northern Ireland may be transferred to England or Wales without a break in the powers of detention or guardianship. On his arrival in England or Wales the patient will become subject to detention or guardianship under this Act. A patient who has been transferred under this section has a right to apply to a Mental Health Review Tribunal within six months of his transfer (ss.66(1), 69(2)(a)).

An equivalent power to transfer such patients from Scotland to England and Wales is to be found in section 77 of the Mental Health (Scotland) Act 1984.

Guidance on this section and on section 77 of the 1984 Act is contained in the *Memorandum* at paragraphs 263 to 265 and in Appendix 5.

Subsection (1)

1–804   *Responsible authority:* See subsection (7).

Patient: Section 92(3) and regulation 11(2) of the Mental Health (Hospital, Guardianship and Consent to Treatment) Regulations 1983 require the responsible medical officer (or nominated medical attendant) to record the form of mental disorder from which the patient is suffering on Form 32 as soon as possible after his arrival.

Subsection (2)

1–805   *Direction:* See section 94(4).

Date of his admission: Which must be recorded on Form 33 (reg. 11(3)).

Subsection (5)

1–806   *Transfer direction:* See section 94(4)(a).

Date on which he arrives: Which must be recorded on Form 33 (reg. 11(4)).

Subsection (6)

1–807   *Restriction direction:* See section 94(4)(b).

[Transfer of responsibility for patients to England and Wales from Northern Ireland

82A.—(1) If it appears to the relevant Minister, in the case of a patient **1–808** who—

    (a) is subject to a restriction order or restriction direction under Article 47(1) or 55(1) of the Mental Health (Northern Ireland) Order 1986; and

    (b) has been conditionally discharged under Article 48(2) or 78(2) of that Order,

that a transfer under this section would be in the interests of the patient, that Minister may, with the consent of the Secretary of State, transfer responsibility for the patient to the Secretary of State.

(2) Where responsibility for such a patient is transferred under this section, the patient shall be treated—

    (a) as if on the date of the transfer he had been conditionally discharged under section 42 or 73 above; and

    (b) as if he were subject to a restriction order or restriction direction under section 41 or 49 above.

(3) Where a patient responsibility for whom is transferred under this section was immediately before the transfer subject to a restriction order or restriction direction of limited duration, the restriction order or restriction direction to which he is subject by virtue of subsection (2) above shall expire on the date on which the first-mentioned order or direction would have expired if the transfer had not been made.

(4) In this section "the relevant Minister" means the Minister exercising in Northern Ireland functions corresponding to those of the Secretary of State.]

AMENDMENT

This section was inserted by the Crime (Sentences) Act 1997, s.48, Sched. 3, para. 3.

DEFINITIONS

    patient: s.145(1).   **1–809**
    restriction order: ss.41, 145(1).
    restriction direction: ss.41, 145(1).

GENERAL NOTE

This section enables the Home Secretary to authorise the transfer of a con- **1–810** ditionally discharged restricted patient from Northern Ireland to England and Wales. The expiry date of the original order or direction is not effected by the transfer.

Subsection (2)

Restriction direction: See section 94(4)(b).   **1–811**

Removal to and from Channel Islands and Isle of Man

Removal of patients to Channel Islands or Isle of Man

83. If it appears to the Secretary of State, in the case of a patient who is for **1–812** the time being liable to be detained or subject to guardianship under this Act (otherwise than by virtue of section 35, 36 or 38 above), that it is in the interests of the patient to remove him to any of the Channel Islands or to the Isle of Man, and that arrangements have been made for admitting him to a hospital or, as the case may be, for receiving him into guardianship there, the Secretary of State may authorise his removal to the island in question and may give any necessary directions for his conveyance to his destination.

DEFINITIONS
1–813   patient: s.145(1).
hospital: ss.92(1), 145(1).

GENERAL NOTE
1–814   This section provides for patients who are detained or subject to guardianship in England or Wales to be transferred to the Channel Islands or the Isle of Man by the Secretary of State (or, for certain categories of patient in relation to Wales, the National Assembly for Wales) without a break in the powers of detention or guardianship.
Secretary of State: See the note on section 80(1).
Arrangements: For the transmission of information about these arrangements, see the General Note to section 80.
Conveyance: General provisions relating to the custody, conveyance and detention of patients are contained in section 137.

[Transfer of responsibility for patients to Channel Islands or Isle of Man
1–815   **83A.** If it appears to the Secretary of State, in the case of a patient who—
   (a) is subject to a restriction order or restriction direction under section 41 or 49 above; and
   (b) has been conditionally discharged under section 42 or 73 above,
that a transfer under this section would be in the interests of the patient, the Secretary of State may, with the consent of the authority exercising corresponding functions in any of the Channel Islands or in the Isle of Man, transfer responsibility for the patient to that authority.]

AMENDMENT
This section was inserted by the Crime (Sentences) Act 1997, s.48, Sched. 3, para. 4.

DEFINITIONS
1–816   patient: s.145(1).
restriction order: ss.41, 145(1).
restriction direction: ss.49, 145(1).

GENERAL NOTE
1–817   This section provides for the Home Secretary to authorise the transfer of a conditionally discharged restricted patient from England and Wales to the Channel Island or the Isle of Man.

Removal to England and Wales of offenders found insane in Channel Islands and Isle of Man
1–818   **84.**—(1) The Secretary of State may by warrant direct that any offender found by a court in any of the Channel Islands or in the Isle of Man to be insane or to have been insane at the time of the alleged offence, and ordered to be detained during Her Majesty's pleasure, be removed to a hospital in England and Wales.
   (2) A patient removed under subsection (1) above shall, on his reception into the hospital in England and Wales, be treated as if he had been removed to that hospital in pursuance of a direction under section 46 above.

(3) The Secretary of State may by warrant direct that any patient removed under this section from any of the Channel Islands or from the Isle of Man be returned to the island from which he was so removed, there to be dealt with according to law in all respects as if he had not been removed under this section.

DEFINITIONS
hospital: ss.92(1), 145(1).   **1–819**
patient: s.145(1).

GENERAL NOTE
This section enables the Home Secretary to transfer to a hospital in England or **1–820**
Wales an offender who has been found to be insane by a court in the Channel Islands
or Isle of Man.
For procedure and tribunal rights, see the General Note to section 82.

Patients removed from Channel Islands or Isle of Man
85. (1) This section applies to any patient who is removed to England **1–821**
and Wales from any of the Channel Islands or the Isle of Man under a
provision corresponding to section 83 above and who immediately before his
removal was liable to be detained or subject to guardianship in the island in
question under a provision corresponding to an enactment contained in this
Act (other than section 35, 36 or 38 above).
(2) Where the patient is admitted to a hospital in England and Wales he
shall be treated as if on the date of his admission he had been so admitted in
pursuance of an application made, or an order or direction made or given, on
that date under the corresponding enactment contained in this Act and,
where he is subject to an order or direction restricting his discharge, as if he
were subject to a restriction order or restriction direction.
(3) Where a patient is received into guardianship in England and Wales,
he shall be treated as if on the date on which he arrives at the place where he
is to reside he had been so received in pursuance of an application, order or
direction under the corresponding enactment contained in this Act and as if
the application had been accepted or, as the case may be, the order or
direction had been made or given on that date.
(4) Where the patient was immediately before his removal liable to be
detained by virtue of a transfer direction given while he was serving a
sentence of imprisonment imposed by a court in the island in question, he
shall be treated as if the sentence had been imposed by a court in England
and Wales.
(5) Where the patient was immediately before his removal subject to an
order or direction restricting his discharge, being an order or direction of
limited duration, the restriction order or restriction direction to which he is
subject by virtue of subsection (2) above shall expire on the date on which
the first-mentioned order or direction would have expired if he had not been
removed.
(6) While being conveyed to the hospital referred to in subsection (2) or,
as the case may be, the place referred to in subsection (3) above, the patient
shall be deemed to be in legal custody, and section 138 below shall apply to
him as if he were in legal custody by virtue of section 137 below.
(7) In the case of a patient removed from the Isle of Man the reference in
subsection (4) above to a person serving a sentence of imprisonment

includes a reference to a person detained as mentioned in section 60(6)(a) of the Mental Health Act 1974 (an Act of Tynwald).

DEFINITIONS
1–822   patient: s.145(1).
hospital: ss.92(1), 145(1).
restriction order: ss.41, 145(1).
restriction direction: ss.49, 145(1).
transfer direction: ss.47, 145(1).

GENERAL NOTE
1–823   This section provides for a patient who is detained or subject to guardianship in the Channel Islands or the Isle of Man to be transferred to England or Wales without a break in the powers of detention or guardianship. On his arrival in this country the patient will be subject to the corresponding legislative provision in this Act. A patient who has been transferred under this section has a right of appeal to a Mental Health Review Tribunal within six months of his transfer (ss.66(1), 69(2)(a)).

For the procedure to be followed when a patient is transferred to England or Wales, see regulation 11 of the Mental Health (Hospital, Guardianship and Consent to Treatment) Regulations 1983.

Subsection (2)
1–824   *Direction:* See section 94(4).

Subsection (4)
1–825   *Transfer direction:* See section 94(5).

Subsection (5)
1–826   *Restriction direction:* See section 94(4)(b).

[Responsibility for patients transferred from Channel Islands or Isle of Man

1–827   **85A.**—(1) This section applies to any patient responsibility for whom is transferred to the Secretary of State by the authority exercising corresponding functions in any of the Channel Islands or the Isle of Man under a provision corresponding to section 83A above.

(2) The patient shall be treated—

(a) as if on the date of the transfer he had been conditionally discharged under section 42 or 73 above; and

(b) as if he were subject to a restriction order or restriction direction under section 41 or 49 above.

(3) Where the patient was immediately before the transfer subject to an order or direction restricting his discharge, being an order or direction of limited duration, the restriction order or restriction direction to which he is subject by virtue of subsection (2) above shall expire on the date on which the first-mentioned order or direction would have expired if the transfer had not been made.]

AMENDMENT
This section was inserted by the Crime (Sentences) Act 1997, s.48, Sched. 3, para. 4.

DEFINITIONS
1–828   patient: s/145(1).
restriction order: ss.41, 145(1).
restriction direction: ss.49, 145(1).

This section states that a patient who has been transferred from the Channel **1–829**
Islands or the Isle of Man under a provision that corresponds to section 83A, above,
shall be treated as if on the date of the transfer he was a conditionally discharged
restricted patient.

Removal of aliens

Removal of alien patients
86.—(1) This section applies to any patient who is neither a British citizen **1–830**
nor a Commonwealth citizen having the right of abode in the United
Kingdom by virtue of section 2(1)(b) of the Immigration Act 1971, being a
patient who is receiving treatment for mental illness as an in-patient in a
hospital in England and Wales or a hospital within the meaning of the
Mental Health Act [(Northern Ireland) Order 1986] and is detained
pursuant to—
 (a) an application for admission for treatment or [a report under Article
  12(1) or 13 of that Order];
 (b) a hospital order under section 37 above or [Article 44 of that Order];
  or
 (c) an order or direction under this Act (other than under section 35, 36
  or 38 above) or [under that Order (other than under Article 42, 43 or
  45 of that Order] having the same effect as such a hospital order.
 (2) If it appears to the Secretary of State that proper arrangements have
been made for the removal of a patient to whom this section applies to a
country or territory outside the United Kingdom, the Isle of Man and the
Channel Islands and for his care or treatment there and that it is in the
interests of the patient to remove him, the Secretary of State may, subject to
subsection (3) below—
 (a) by warrant authorise the removal of the patient from the place where
  he is receiving treatment as mentioned in subsection (1) above, and
 (b) give such directions as the Secretary of State thinks fit for the
  conveyance of the patient to his destination in that country or
  territory and for his detention in any place or on board any ship or
  aircraft until his arrival at any specified port or place in any such
  country or territory.
 (3) The Secretary of State shall not exercise his powers under subsection
(2) above in the case of any patient except with the approval of a Mental
Health Review Tribunal or, as the case may be, of the Mental Health Review
Tribunal for Northern Ireland.

In subs. (1) the words in square brackets were substituted by the Mental Health
(Northern Ireland Consequential Amendments) Order 1986 (S.I. 1986 No. 596), art.
2.

 patient: s.145(1). **1–831**
 hospital: ss.92(2), 145(1).
 application for admission for treatment: ss.3, 145(1).
 hospital order: ss.37, 145(1).

GENERAL NOTE

This section empowers the Home Secretary to authorise the removal to any country abroad of certain detained patients who do not have a right of abode in this country and who are receiving in-patient treatment for mental illness. Before he exercises his power the Home Secretary must have obtained the approval of a Mental Health Review Tribunal. The main purpose of this section is to "enable patients who are either irrationally opposed to their removal, or are unable to express a view, to be compulsorily removed to another country when this is judged to be in their best interests. It is also used to enable patients to be kept under escort on their journey home if this is necessary" (Cmnd. 7320, para. 8.26). There is nothing to prevent a patient who has been removed under this section from applying for re-admission to the United Kingdom. If the patient was subject to a hospital order with restrictions when he was removed, both the hospital order and the restriction order will remain in force (s.91(2)). Otherwise the application, order or direction will cease to have effect (s.91(1)).

"Proposals for the removal of such a person from a hospital or mental nursing home should be made in the first place to the Home Office (Mental Health Unit, Queen Anne's Gate, London SW1H 9AT). Details should be given of any arrangements which have been or could be made for the patient's care and treatment in the receiving country. The Home Office will, in consultation with the Department of Health, decide whether authority under section 86 should be issued or whether the patient should be repatriated under other powers. Application to the Home Office will not be necessary if the patient, whether or not accompanied by an escort, is able and willing to travel without powers of detention, and suitable arrangements have been made" (*Memorandum*, para. 268).

In *R. (on the application of X.) v. Secretary of State for the Home Department* (2001) 4 C.C.L.R. 92, the Court of Appeal held that where a person detained under this Act had no basis for remaining in the United Kingdom under the Immigration Act 1971, the Home Secretary was entitled to remove him under the provisions of that Act, and was not obliged to do so only in accordance with his power of removal under this section. *Per* Schiemann L.J. at para.28: "There appears to us no reason who the two regimes should not run in parallel in the case of a person who is both an immigrant and mentally ill. Clearly if the Home Secretary proposes to use his Immigration Act powers in relation to a mentally ill person that illness will be a factor which he must take into account." The statement provided by the chief immigration officer in this case stated that it is the practice of the Home Secretary to use this section only in cases of persons who have been granted leave to enter the United Kingdom.

It is possible for a patient who has been made subject to a hospital order or restriction order by a court to be transferred out of the United Kingdom by a warrant issued by the Home Secretary under the Repatriation of Prisoners Act 1984.

The steps that are required to arrange repatriation are considered by L. Green and T. Nayani in "Repatriating psychiatric patients", *Psychiatric Bulletin* (2000) 24, 405–408.

The Human Rights Act 1998

1–832 The removal of a patient under this section could involve a breach of Article 3 of the European Convention on Human Rights if there is a real risk of the patient being the subject of inhuman or degrading treatment in the country to which he is sent. In *R. (on the application of X.) v. Secretary of State for the Home Department*, above, Turner J., at first instance (*The Times*, June 14, 2000), held that the question whether or not there would be a violation of Article 3 of the European Convention on Human Rights if the applicant was returned to Malta on the basis that he would be subjected to inhuman or degrading treatment if so returned, was a question that had to be subjected to rigorous scrutiny (*R. v. Secretary of State for the Home Department, ex p. Turgut* [2001] 1 All E.R. 719, CA and *D v. United Kingdom* 24 E.H.R.R. 423). In *D* the court said: "... [T]he court emphasises that aliens who have served their prison sentences and are subject to expulsion cannot in principle claim any entitlement to remain in the territory of a Contracting State in order to continue to benefit from the medical, social or other forms of assistance provided by the expelling State during their stay in prison" (para. 54). The same principle would apply to persons who are detained under this Act. Turner J. held that the fact that the applicant would be subjected to stress as a result of a decision to deport him was not sufficient to constitute inhuman treatment; see further, the General Note to Article 3.

Subsection (1)

United Kingdom: Means Great Britain and Northern Ireland (Interpretation Act **1–833** 1978, s.5, Sched. 1).

Mental illness: This section only applies to patients who are currently receiving in-patient treatment for mental illness. It does not apply to detained patients who have been granted leave of absence. It could apply to a patient who was originally detained after being diagnosed as suffering from one of the other categories of mental disorder but who was subsequently reclassified as being mentally ill.

In-patient: The power to repatriate is not "appropriate for patients whose discharge is imminent. It would not be easy during a short period to become sufficiently well informed about the patient's situation to know whether removal is in his best interests, or to know whether adequate arrangements could be or have been made for the removal and his subsequent care and treatment. A minimum of six months as an in-patient is a useful guide" (Home Office Guidance to Staff, undated, para. 5).

Detained: This section does not apply to informal patients.

Subsection (2)

Proper arrangements: Inquiries "are best carried out by hospital trusts and staff **1–834** locally whose knowledge and understanding of the patient, his treatment and his requirements is up to date and comprehensive. It will be for the Home Secretary to be certain that all the information coming forward indicates that it is in the best interests of the patient to be removed (*ibid.* para. 3).

Although the Home Office will seek to facilitate appropriate liaison between the appropriate agencies, "in general, the mechanics for putting the arrangements into place should be negotiated direct between the health trust and the immigration service, each of whom will be familiar with their respective roles in this operation. With the exception of the direct control costs of the immigration service, all other costs involved will be the responsibility of the health trust (*ibid.* paras 7, 8).

In the interests of the patient remove him: Paragraph 269 of the *Memorandum* states:

"The types of cases in which it might be appropriate to propose repatriation include:

a. those where repatriation would be in the person's interest;
b. those where the person has been in hospital in this country for a considerable period (6 months or more), where there is little prospect of a substantial improvement in his condition and where repatriation would not be detrimental to him."

Conveyance ... and for his detention: General provisions relating to the custody, conveyance and detention of patients are contained in section 137.

Subsection (3)

The Approval of a Mental Health Review Tribunal: The "Home Secretary will **1–835** exercise his discretionary power to refer the patient to a tribunal. The tribunal will be asked for advice whether removal would be in the best interests of the patient and whether proper arrangements have been made for his care or treatment" (*Memorandum*, para. 267). There is no reference in Part V of this Act or in the Mental Health Review Tribunal Rules 1983 to the procedure to be adopted by a tribunal when considering a case that has been referred to it under this provision. It submitted that tribunals should adopt the procedure set out in Part VI of the 1983 Rules, in so far as it applies to references.

Return of patients absent without leave

Patients absent from hospitals in Northern Ireland
1–836   **87.**—(1) Any person who—
   (a) under [Article 29 or 132 of the Mental Health (Northern Ireland) Order 1986] (which provide, respectively, for the retaking of patients absent without leave and for the retaking of patients escaping from custody); or
   (b) under the said [Article 29 as applied by Article 31 of the said Order] (which makes special provision as to persons sentenced to imprisonment),
may be taken into custody in Northern Ireland, may be taken into custody in, and returned to Northern Ireland from, England and Wales by an approved social worker, by any constable or by any person authorised by or by virtue of the [said Order] to take him into custody.

   (2) This section does not apply to any person who is subject to guardianship.

AMENDMENT
   In subsection (1) the words in square brackets were substituted by the Mental Health (Northern Ireland Consequential Amendments) Order 1986 (S.I. 1986 No. 596), art. 2.

DEFINITIONS
1–837   patient: s.145(1).
   absent without leave: ss.18(6), 145(1).
   approved social worker: s.145(1).

GENERAL NOTE
1–838   This section permits a patient from Northern Ireland who has either escaped from custody or who is absent without leave from a hospital, to be taken into custody in England or Wales and returned to Northern Ireland. It does not apply to patients subject to guardianship. An equivalent provision in respect of patients from Scotland is made by section 84 of the Mental Health (Scotland) Act 1984.

Subsection (1)
1–839   *Returned:* For the powers of a constable or approved social worker on taking the patient into custody and returning him to Northern Ireland, see section 137.

Patients absent from hospitals in England and Wales
1–840   **88.**—(1) Subject to the provisions of this section, any person who, under section 18 above or section 138 below or under the said section 18 as applied by section 22 above, may be taken into custody in England and Wales may be taken into custody in, and returned to England and Wales from, any other part of the United Kingdom or the Channel Islands or the Isle of Man.

   (2) For the purposes of the enactments referred to in subsection (1) above,

in their application by virtue of this section to Scotland, Northern Ireland, the Channel Islands or the Isle of Man, the expression "constable" includes a Scottish constable, an officer or constable of the Royal Ulster Constabulary, a member of the police in Jersey, an officer of police within the meaning of section 43 of the Larceny (Guernsey) Law 1958 or any corresponding law for the time being in force, or a constable in the Isle of Man, as the case may be.

(3) For the purposes of the said enactments in their application by virtue of this section to Scotland or Northern Ireland, any reference to an approved social worker shall be construed as including a reference—

(a) in Scotland, to any mental health officer within the meaning of the Mental Health (Scotland) Act 1984];

(b) in Northern Ireland, to any [approved social worker within the meaning of the Mental Health (Northern Ireland) Order 1986.]

(4) This section does not apply to any person who is subject to guardianship.

AMENDMENT

In subsection (3)(a) the words in square brackets were substituted by the Mental Health (Scotland) Act 1984, s.127(1), Sched. 3, para. 52. In subsection (3)(b) the words in square brackets were substituted by the Mental Health (Northern Ireland Consequential Amendments) Order 1986 (S.I. 1986 No. 596), art. 2.

DEFINITION

approved social worker: s.145(1).   **1–841**

GENERAL NOTE

This section permits patients from England or Wales who are absent without leave **1–842**
from hospital or who have escaped from custody, to be taken into custody in, and returned to England and Wales from Scotland, Northern Ireland, the Channel Islands or the Isle of Man. It does not apply to patients who are subject to guardianship.

Patients absent from hospitals in the Channel Islands or Isle of Man

89.—(1) Any person who under any provision corresponding to section 18 **1–843**
above or 138 below may be taken into custody in any of the Channel Islands or the Isle of Man may be taken into custody in, and returned to the island in question from, England and Wales by an approved social worker or a constable.

(2) This section does not apply to any person who is subject to guardianship.

DEFINITION

approved social worker: s.145(1).   **1–844**

GENERAL NOTE

The purpose of this section is to ensure that a detained patient who absconds to **1–845**
England or Wales from the Channel Islands or the Isle of Man can be apprehended and returned to the island in question. It does not apply to patients who are subject to guardianship. Patients who abscond in the opposite direction are liable to be detained and returned under section 88.

Returned: For the powers of a constable or approved social worker, see section 137.

General

Regulations for purposes of Part VI

1–846   **90.** Section 32 above shall have effect as if references in that section to Part II of this Act included references to this Part of this Act and to [Part VII of the Mental Health (Scotland) Act 1984], so far as those Parts apply to patients removed to England and Wales thereunder.

AMENDMENT

In this section the words in square brackets were substituted by the Mental Health (Scotland) Act 1984, s.127(1), Sched. 3, para. 53.

DEFINITION

1–847   patient: s.145(1).

GENERAL NOTE

1–848   See the Mental Health (Hospital, Guardianship and Consent to Treatment) Regulations 1983.

General provisions as to patients removed from England and Wales

1–849   **91.**—(1) Subject to subsection (2) below, where a patient liable to be detained or subject to guardianship by virtue of an application, order or direction under Part II or III of this Act (other than section 35, 36 or 38 above) is removed from England and Wales in pursuance of arrangements under this Part of this Act, the application, order or direction shall cease to have effect when he is duly received into a hospital or other institution, or placed under guardianship, in pursuance of those arrangements.

(2) Where the Secretary of State exercises his powers under section 86(2) above in respect of a patient who is detained pursuant to a hospital order under section 37 above and in respect of whom a restriction order is in force, those orders shall continue in force so as to apply to the patient if he returns to England and Wales at any time before the end of the period for which those orders would have continued in force.

DEFINITIONS

1–850   patient: s.145(1).
hospital: ss.92(2), 145(1).
hospital order: ss.37, 145(1).
restriction order: ss.41, 145(1).

GENERAL NOTE

1–851   This section provides that, with one exception, when a patient is removed from England or Wales under a provision in this Part, any application, order or direction made in respect of him will cease to have effect on his arrival at his destination. The exception is that if a patient who is subject to a hospital order with restrictions is removed, both the hospital order and the restriction order will remain in force (subs. (2)).

Subsection (1)

1–852   *Section 35, 36 or 38:* Are concerned with remands to hospital for a report on an accused person's mental condition (s.35), remands to hospital for treatment (s.36) and interim hospital orders (s.38).

Interpretation of Part VI

92.—(1) References in this Part of this Act to a hospital, being a hospital in **1–853** England and Wales, shall be construed as references to a hospital within the meaning of Part II of this Act.

(2) Where a patient is treated by virtue of this Part of this Act as if he had been removed to a hospital in England and Wales in pursuance of a direction under Part III of this Act, that direction shall be deemed to have been given on the date of his reception into the hospital.

(3) A patient removed to England and Wales under this Part of this Act or under [Part VI of the Mental Health (Scotland) Act 1984] shall be treated for the purposes of this Act as suffering from such form of mental disorder as may be recorded in his case in pursuance of regulations made by virtue of section 90 above, and references in this Act to the form or forms of mental disorder specified in the relevant application, order or direction shall be construed as including references to the form or forms of mental disorder so recorded.

[(4) Sections 80 to 85A above shall have effect as if—

(a) any hospital direction under section 45A above were a transfer direction under section 47 above; and

(b) any limitation direction under section 45A above were a restriction direction under section 49 above.

(5) Sections 80(5), 81(6) and 85(4) above shall have effect as if any reference to a transfer direction given while a patient was serving a sentence of imprisonment imposed by a court included a reference to a hospital direction given by a court after imposing a sentence of imprisonment on a patient.]

AMENDMENTS

In subsection (3) the words in square brackets were substituted by the Mental Health (Scotland) Act 1984, s.127(1), Sched. 3, para. 54.

Subsections (4) and (5) were inserted by the Crime (Sentences) Act 1997, s.55, Sched. 4, para. 16.

DEFINITIONS
    patient: s.145(1).   **1–854**
    mental disorder: ss.1, 145(1).
    hospital direction: s.145(1).
    transfer direction: s.145(1).
    limitation direction: s.145(1).
    restriction direction: s.145(1).

Subsection (1)
    Hospital: See section 35(2).   **1–855**

PART VII

MANAGEMENT OF PROPERTY AND AFFAIRS OF PATIENTS

GENERAL NOTE

This Part deals with the management of the property and affairs of mentally **1–856** disordered people. The powers of the judge, the Master of the Court of Protection or the Public Guardianship Office are exercisable when the court is satisfied, after considering medical evidence, that "a person is incapable, by reason of mental disorder, of managing and administering his property and affairs." Anyone meeting these criteria is known as a "patient" (s.94(2)). There is no requirement that the person in respect of whom an order under this Part is made should either be liable to be detained, be subject to guardianship or be a hospital patient and there are no patients who become automatically subject to the jurisdiction of the Court. Sections 122 and 142 of this Act are also relevant to persons who are incapable of managing their own property and affairs.

The Court of Protection has extensive powers and it "is not limited in its jurisdiction to dealing with the patient's property or financial affairs, nor limited to dealing with such other matters as may be within its jurisdiction in their property or financial aspects ... [I]t has exclusive jurisdiction over all the property and all the affairs of the patient in all their aspects; but not the management or care of the patient's person"; *per* Ungoed-Thomas J., in *Re W (E.E.M.)* [1971] Ch. 123, 143. This interpretation was followed by the House of Lords in *F v. West Berkshire Health Authority (Mental Health Act Commission intervening)* [1989] 2 All E.R. 545, where it was held that this Act does not confer on a judge nominated under section 93(1) any jurisdiction to decide questions relating to the medical treatment of a patient. Although the Court of Protection has no legal powers over, or direct legal responsibility for, the care of the patient's person or for the patient's welfare other than in financial legal or property matters, the Court's legal officer has advised that "the Court does have a duty to exercise its jurisdiction for the patient's benefit in the wider sense and thus to take personal welfare matters into account in coming to decisions with regard to property and affairs. It seems unlikely that the Court could fulfil this responsibility without taking reasonable steps to inform itself about matters which affect the patient's person and his personal welfare. The Court therefore needs to know about a patient's personal welfare in order properly to exercise its jurisdiction. The degree to which enquiries need to be made will vary with every case" (*Looking After the Financial Affairs of People with Mental Incapacity*, National Audit Office, 1994, para. 4.1).

"The Court of Protection is an office of the Supreme Court of Judicature ... [W]ith the coming into effect on January 2, 1987 of the Public Trustee and Administration of Funds Act 1986, the Receivership and Protection Divisions (formerly part of the Court) became part of a new department called the Public Trust Office, whose head is a single official with the twin titles of Accountant General of the Supreme Court and Public Trustee. This new department also has responsibility for other parts of the Lord Chancellor's Department concerned with the administration of private moneys, namely the Public Trust Office. In his capacity as Public Trustee, he is sometimes appointed receiver by the Court. The Court of Protection is a separately constituted entity outside the Public Trust Office but that office carried out all the administrative functions of the Court"(*Heywood and Massey, Court of Protection Practice* (12th ed., 1991), p. 3). On April 2, 2001, the Public Trust Office ceased to exist. Its mental health functions were taken on by a new organisation, the Public Guardianship Office (*Making Changes: The Future of the Public Trust Office*, Lord Chancellor's Department, Dec. 2000, para. 2.01). The Public Guardianship Office is an Executive Agency of the Lord Chancellor's Department within the Court of Protection (P.G.O. Framework Document, paras 2.1, 4.10.1). Under current arrangements the judicial powers of the judge under this Part are exercised by the Master, Assistant Masters and nominated officers of the Court of Protection, while the administrative functions are carried out by the Public Guardianship Office. The Protection Division is the larger of the two Divisions in the Public Guardianship Office. It oversees the activities of private receivers appointed by the court. Its role is to ensure adequate supervision of receivers by means of issuing orders, authorities and directions and auditing receiver's annual income and expenditure accounts. Where there is no one available to act as a private receiver to a patient, the Public Guardianship Office is appointed as their receiver. In these circumstances the

Receivership Division carries out all those tasks that are necessary to manage the patient's personal financial affairs.

The Court of Protection Rules 2001 (S.I. 2001 No. 824), which came into force on April 1, 2001, regulate the procedure in respect of applications under this Part. Proceedings are normally started by a formal application (r. 7). The patient's nearest relative usually makes the application but some other person such as another relative, a doctor, a solicitor, a social worker or a friend, can also apply. If there is no one available to make an application, the Court can direct one of its own officers or the Official Solicitor to apply (r. 11). Although the help of a solicitor is recommended in complex cases or where large sums of money are involved, it is possible for an application to be made directly through the Court's personal application branch at Stewart House, 24 Kingsway, London WC2B 6JX.

There is no automatic review as to whether the Court's continued intervention is required. If a patient recovers his mental capacity he can either ask a solicitor to apply to the Court to determine the proceedings, or he can write to the Court making the request and giving the name of a doctor who will support the application with medical evidence of recovery.

Legal aid is not available in the Court of Protection. The fees payable to the Court are set out in the Court of Protection Rules. Under rule 83 it is possible for the Court to remit or postpone the payment of fees in cases of hardship.

The Law Commission has stated that the "present jurisdiction of the Court of Protection is arguably too limited, in that it can only address financial and business issues, and yet too wide, in that it does not cater for partial and limited interventions The present procedures do not appeal to many who might benefit from the exercise of the jurisdiction, and the status of the Court as an office of the Supreme Court is confusing and anomalous" (*Mental Incapacity*, (1995), para. 2.13).

Legal practitioners who come into contact with the court are referred to the standard legal text in this field: Heywood and Massey, *Court of Protection Practice*, above, and to A. Donnelly, *Court of Protection Handbook* (10th ed., 1995). An account of the work of the Court of Protection by Mrs A. B. Macfarlane, a former Master of the Court, can be found in the *Medico-Legal Journal*, Vol. 60, Pt 1, 1992, pp. 25–43. A critical analysis of the Court's practice and procedure is L. Gostin, *The Court of Protection* (1983). The Public Guardianship Office has published three booklets to assist those who become applicants or receivers: "Making an Application", "Handbook for Receivers" and "Duties of a Receiver". Copies of these publications can be obtained from Stewart House. For a readable and informative explanation of what can be done to take over the management of other people's money and financial affairs, see *Managing Other People's Money*, Penny Letts, Age Concern, 1998.

The Human Rights Act 1998
The right of a person to manage "his property and affairs" is a civil right for the **1–857** purposes of Article 6 of the European Convention on Human Rights (*Winterwerp v. Netherlands* (1979) 2 E.H.R.R. 387). Under rule 9(1) of the Court of Protection Rules 2001, an application for the appointment of a receiver for that person can be considered without a hearing. Under Convention caselaw, the right of access to a court is not absolute (*Golder v. United Kingdom* (1975) 1 E.H.R.R. 524). In *Ashingdane v. United Kingdom* (1985) 7 E.H.R.R. 528, the Court said:

> "The right of access ... may be subject to limitations ... Nonetheless, the limitations applied must not restrict or reduce the access left to the individual in such a way or to such an extent that the very essence of the right is impaired. Furthermore, a limitation will not be compatible with Article 6(1) if it does not pursue a legitimate aim and if there is not a reasonable relationship of

proportionality between the means employed and the aim sought to be achieved" (para.57).

The denial of a hearing under rule 9 must be tested by these criteria.

No public funding is available before the Court of Protection. Although the European Court of Human Rights has held that the State is not required to provide free legal aid for every dispute relating to a "civil right", Article 6(1) "may compel the State to provide for the assistance of a lawyer when such assistance proves indispensable for an effective access to court ... by reason of the complexity of the procedure or of the case" (*Airey v. Ireland* (1979) 2 E.H.R.R. 305, para. 26).

Appointees under the Social Security Regulations

1–858   If a person lacking capacity has little capital and receives income only from state benefits, the necessary financial arrangements can be made under regulation 33 of the Social Security (Claims and Payments) Regulations 1987 (S.I. 1987 No. 1968) which provides that the Secretary of State may appoint someone aged 18 or over (the "appointee") to act on behalf of the claimant. An appointment can be made where:

> "a person is, or is alleged to be, entitled to benefit, whether or not a claim for benefit has been made by him or on his behalf; and
>   that person is unable for the time being to act; and
>   no receiver has been appointed by the Court of Protection with power to claim or, as the case may be, receive benefit on his behalf."

Although medical evidence to support the applicant's view that the claimant is "unable ... to act" may be asked for, the Department of Social Security does not require medical evidence in all cases, and does not provide any standard form of medical certificate.

The appointee has no power to deal with the claimant's capital but can:

(a) exercise any rights and duties that the claimant has under the Social Security Acts and Regulations;

(b) receive any benefits payable to the claimant; and

(c) deal with the money received on the claimant's behalf in the interests of the claimant and his or her dependents.

The Secretary of State can revoke an appointment at any time.

The Law Commission has reported that many of its consultees "were very concerned about the apparently not uncommon practice of a nursing or residential home manages acting as [an] ... appointee for one or more residents." The Department of Social Security confirmed to the Commission "that its policy is always to seek a friend or relative to act as appointee, and to appoint a home manager only as a last resort" (*Mental Incapacity*, (1995), paras 4.26, 4.27). Government guidance on this issue is that proprietors and staff "should not become in the handling and management of residents' monies," (Centre for Policy on Ageing, *Home Life: a code of practice for residential care* (1984), p. 65, para. 56).

Concern has been expressed about the nature of the enquiries conducted before appointments are made, and about the absence of regular supervision or monitoring of the performance of appointees (R. Lavery and L. Lundy, "The Social Security Appointee System," [1994] J.Soc.Wel. and Fam.L. 313).

The Enduring Powers of Attorney Act 1985

1–859   Under the Powers of Attorney Act 1971 it is possible for a person (the donor) who wishes to put his property and financial affairs in the hands of a friend or adviser to grant that person a power of attorney. A power of attorney enables the attorney to make legally binding decisions on behalf of the donor. A major weakness of this power is that any subsequent mental incapacity of the donor automatically serves to revoke the power of attorney. This difficulty has been tackled by the Enduring Powers of Attorney Act 1985 which enables a donor to appoint an attorney whose authority will not be revoked by the donor's subsequent mental incapacity. The Act gives effect to the recommendations of the Law Commission report, *The Incapacitated Principal* (Law Comm. No. 122, Cmnd. 8977). The main benefit of this new power is that the delay and expense involved in an application to the Court of Protection for the appointment of a receiver in the event of the donor's mental incapacity is avoided. The Court of Protection does not permit "a patient [who is subject to the Court's jurisdiction] to execute an enduring power of attorney over any of his or her property, since this would conflict with the global approach it takes to each case" (Law Commission, *Mental Incapacity*, 1995, para. 2.11).

The Act creates a special power of attorney known as an enduring power of attorney. The instrument creating the power must be in the prescribed form (see the Court of Protection (Enduring Powers of Attorney) Rules 1994 (S.I. 1994 No. 3047) and executed by both the donor and the attorney. The authority conferred by the enduring power may be general or it may be subject to restrictions or conditions.

If the donor remains mentally capable, the enduring power can operate as an ordinary power of attorney or it can be drafted so that it will not operate until the donor becomes mentally incapable. In the event of the donor becoming mentally incapable the attorney must apply to the Court of Protection for the instrument to be registered. Before this application is made the attorney must give notice of his intention to do so to specified relatives and to the donor himself.

Relatives who have been given notice of the attorney's intention to apply for registration and the donor have an opportunity to make objections on a number of specified grounds. The procedures relating to the registration of an enduring power of attorney and the objections that can be made to registration are contained in the Court of Protection (Enduring Powers of Attorney) Rules 2001 (S.I. 2001 No. 825). If the power is successfully registered the attorney has full power to act under the terms of the instrument. While the instrument remains registered the donor may not, even if mentally capable, revoke or amend the power without the court's confirmation.

The 1985 Act is considered by S. M. Cretney and D. Lush in *Enduring Powers of Attorney*, 1996. The Public Guardianship Office has produced a helpful leaflet with the same title. It can be obtained from Stewart House, 24 Kingsway, London WC2B 6JX.

Judicial authorities and Court of Protection

93.—(1) The Lord Chancellor shall from time to time nominate one or **1–860** more judges of the Supreme Court (in this Act referred to as "nominated judges") to act for the purposes of this Part of this Act.

(2) There shall continue to be an office of the Supreme Court, called the Court of Protection, for the protection and management, as provided by this Part of this Act, of the property and affairs of persons under disability; and there shall continue to be a Master of the Court of Protection appointed by the Lord Chancellor under section 89 of the Supreme Court Act 1981.

(3) The Master of the Court of Protection shall take the oath of allegiance and judicial oath in the presence of the Lord Chancellor; and the Promissory Oaths Act 1868 shall have effect as if the officers named in the Second Part of the Schedule to that Act included the Master of the Court of Protection.

(4) The Lord Chancellor may nominate other officers of the Court of Protection (in this Part of this Act referred to as "nominated officers") to act for the purposes of this Part of this Act.

DEFINITION
property: s.112.

1–861

GENERAL NOTE

1–862   It is prima facie a contempt of court to publish information relating to proceedings heard in private brought under this Part of the Act: see section 12 of the Administration of Justice Act 1960 and *Pickering v. Liverpool Daily Post and Echo Newspapers plc* [1991] 1 All E.R. 622, HL.

Subsection (1)

1–863   *Lord Chancellor:* "Administratively, the Court of Protection is part of the Lord Chancellor's Department, but it is also an office of the Supreme Court and a court of law, with its own judiciary" (*Mentally Incapacitated Adults and Decision-Making: An Overview*, The Law Commission, 1991, para. 3.6).

Nominated judge: Who will be a judge of the Chancery Division of the High Court.

Subsection (2)

1–864   *Court of Protection:* The use of the term "court" is rather misleading as most matters under this Part are dealt with by post by the Public Guardianship Office. Very little work is, in practice, referred to a judge.

Property and affairs of persons: See the note on section 94(2).

Exercise of the judge's functions: "the patient"

1–865   **94.**—(1) [Subject to subsection 1A below] the functions expressed to be conferred by this Part of this Act on the judge shall be exercisable by the Lord Chancellor or by any nominated judge, and shall also be exercisable by the Master of the Court of Protection [, by the Public Trustee] or by any nominated officer, but—

   (a)   in the case of the Master [, the Public Trustee] or any nominated officer, subject to any express provision to the contrary in this Part of this Act or any rules made under this Part of this Act,

   [(aa) in the case of the Public Trustee, subject to any directions of the Master and so far only as may be provided by any rules made under this Part of this Act or (subject to any such rules) by directions of the Master,]

   (b)   in the case of any nominated officer, subject to any directions of the Master and so far only as may be provided by the instrument by which he is nominated;

and references in this Part of this Act to the judge shall be construed accordingly.

   [(1A) In such cases or circumstances as may be prescribed by any rules under this Part of this Act or (subject to any such rules) by directions of the Master, the functions of the judge under this Part of this Act shall be exercised by the Public Trustee (but subject to any directions of the Master as to their exercise).]

   (2) The functions of the judge under this Part of this Act shall be exercisable where, after considering medical evidence, he is satisfied that a person is incapable, by reason of mental disorder, of managing and administering his property and affairs; and a person as to whom the judge is so satisfied is referred to in this Part of this Act as a patient.

AMENDMENT

   The amendments to this section were made by the Public Trustee and Administration of Funds Act 1986, s.2.

DEFINITIONS
    nominated judge: s.112.   **1–866**
    nominated officer: s.112.
    mental disorder: ss.1, 145(1).
    property: s.112.

GENERAL NOTE
    "The nature of patients' incapacity and circumstances can vary. Patients may be **1–867**
elderly people with mental infirmity; or people with mental illness or mental
handicap; or people with brain damage as a result of accident or illness. Over 60 per
cent of patients live in private nursing homes or in National Health Service
accommodation; around 20 per cent live in their own homes; and a further 15 per cent
live in sheltered accommodation and local authority homes", (*Looking After the
Financial Affairs of People with Mental Incapacity*, National Audit Office, 1994, para.
1.5). The Public Accounts Committee has reported that over 70 per cent of the
patients under the Court's protection either have Alzheimer's disease or a
degenerative mental disease (House of Commons, Session 1993–1994, *Thirty-Ninth
Report*, para. 58).

Subsection (2)
    After considering medical evidence: There is no requirement that the medical **1–868**
evidence has to be provided by a doctor who has specialist knowledge of mental
disorder. As most cases are dealt with by post there is little opportunity available to
the court to test the validity of the medical evidence. Medical evidence from one
doctor would be sufficient (Court of Protection Rules 2001, r.34). Where conflicting
medical evidence is presented it is for the court to decide which to prefer. The court is
required to review a patient's case from time to time where a medical certificate
provided to it has expressed an opinion that there is a possibility of the patient's
mental recovery (*ibid.*, r.35(2)).
    Satisfied: The fact that some other person or body has been satisfied as to the
patient's mental disorder does not affect the requirement that the Court must
consider the medical evidence, unless the person concerned is already subject to the
jurisdiction of the Court (*Re S (F.G.)* [1973] 1 W.L.R. 179). Note that under section
98 the Court can accept jurisdiction in an emergency without making a formal
determination of the patient's mental capacity.
    A person: Who could be a child or a person who has never been able to manage his
or her affairs. A former Master of the Court of Protection has stated that the court is
only able to accept jurisdiction over the affairs of a child if satisfied "that the mental
disability will continue after the child reaches 18" ("Court of Protection" (1991) 33
L.S.Gaz. 15–16).
    Incapable: This Part of the Act does not provide for a partial intervention in a
person's affairs because the person concerned has partial or fluctuating capacity.
"There is authority to the effect that once under the jurisdiction of the Court of
Protection a patient cannot be bound by any act of his or her own done in relation to
his or her property, even if the act was in fact done when the patient had capacity to
do it, *Re Walker* [1905] 1 Ch. 160 and *Re Marshall* [1920] 1 Ch. 284" (Law
Commission, *Mental Incapacity*, 1995, p. 10n).
    Paragraph 3.2.2 of *Assessment of Mental Capacity: Guidance for doctors and
lawyers*, A Report of the British Medical Association and the Law Society, 1995,
states that "[a]ssessing a patient's capacity to manage and administer his or her
property and affairs is extremely subjective to the patient. The patient's ability to
cope depends largely on the value and complexity of the property and affairs, and the
extent to which the patient may be vulnerable to exploitation".
    Mental disorder: The fact that a person is suffering from mental disorder is not of

itself evidence of incapacity. The person concerned must have a mental disorder *and* be incapable of managing his property and affairs. There is no requirement that the person should be suffering from one of the specific forms of mental disorder set out in section 1(2).

Property and affairs: This expression relates solely to business matters, legal transactions and other dealings of similar kind. This Part of this Act does not confer on a judge nominated under section 93(1) any jurisdiction to decide questions relating to the medical treatment of a patient (*F v. West Berkshire Health Authority* (*Mental Health Act Commission intervening*) [1989] 2 All E.R. 545; also see the General Note to this Part).

A patient: There is no time limit to a determination that a person is a "patient" within the meaning of this Part of the Act. The definition of "patient" contained in section 145(1) does not apply to this Part.

General functions of the judge with respect to property and affairs of patient

1–869 **95.**—(1) The judge may, with respect to the property and affairs of a patient, do or secure the doing of all such things as appear necessary or expedient—
    (a) for the maintenance or other benefit of the patient,
    (b) for the maintenance or other benefit of members of the patient's family,
    (c) for making provision for other persons or purposes for whom or which the patient might be expected to provide if he were not mentally disordered, or
    (d) otherwise for administering the patient's affairs.

(2) In the exercise of the powers conferred by this section regard shall be had first of all to the requirements of the patient, and the rules of law which restricted the enforcement by a creditor of rights against property under the control of the judge in lunacy shall apply to property under the control of the judge; but, subject to the foregoing provisions of this subsection, the judge shall, in administering a patient's affairs, have regard to the interests of creditors and also to the desirability of making provision for obligations of the patient notwithstanding that they may not be legally enforceable.

DEFINITIONS
1–870 the judge: s.112.
property: s.112.
patient: s.112.
mental disorder: ss.1, 145(1).

GENERAL NOTE
1–871 The scope of this section was considered in *Re W (E.E.M.)* [1971] Ch. 123 where Ungoed-Thomas J. held that "benefit" in paragraphs (a) and (b) "is of wide significance comprehending whatever would be beneficial in any respect, material or otherwise." His Lordship also held that the reference to "requirements" in subsection (2) "must similarly and correspondingly bear its wide *prima facie* meaning." In *Re E (Mental Health Patient)* [1985] 1 All E.R. 609, the Court of Appeal held that the benefit of the patient, and of his or her family, is not confined to material benefit but extends to whatever may be meant by their true interests.

Although both this section and section 96 are "extremely wide and flexible" in their terms, in "the vast majority of cases, however, the Court of Protection exercises its jurisdiction by appointing a receiver to whom it grants specified powers over the patient's income" (Law Commission, *Mental Incapacity*, 1995, para. 8.37).

Rule 42 of the Court of Protection Rules 2001 enables the court to make immediate provision in respect of the matters referred to in subsection (1).

Subsection (1)

Property: Which includes papers held by the Official Solicitor in an action in which **1–872** he acts as the patient's next friend (*Re E, ibid*). In *Re E* the Court held that the parents of a patient had no absolute right to see such papers, although they were the patient's property, but must obtain the authority of the Court of Protection to order disclosure of them as necessary or expedient for the benefit of the patient.

Necessary or expedient: "[This section] does not provide that the requirements of the patients shall be the only consideration"; *per* Dunn L.J. in *Jones v. Jones* [1984] 3 All E.R. 1003, 1008.

Paragraph (b): In *Re B. (Deceased)* [1999] 2 All E.R. 425, Jonathan Parker J. said, at 434, 435, that it was "questionable, to say the least, whether the power to maintain a member of a patient's family empowers the Court of Protection to 'assume responsibility' for the maintenance of that person [for the purposes of section 1(1)(e) of the Inheritance (Provision for Family and Dependants) Act 1975]". On appeal, Robert Walker L.J. said: "there is nothing absurd (at any rate to lawyers familiar with the jurisdiction of the Court of Protection) in the notion of that court acting as the conscience of a patient and making provision for those to whom the patient, if of full mental capacity, would have felt a moral obligation . . ." ([2000] 1 All E.R. 665 at 673).

Paragraph (c): This is the only paragraph in this subsection under which gifts to charity, legatees or next of kin may be authorised. The will or gift must reflect the court's view of what the actual patient "might be expected to provide" and not (if different) what some reasonable person in the patient's position would have done (*Re D (J)* [1982] Ch. 237). In *Re C (A Patient)* [1991] 3 All E.R. 866, Hoffmann J. held that in the case of a person who has never enjoyed a rational mind the court when called upon to interpret the phrase "the patient might be expected to provide" should assume that the patient would have been a normal decent person who would have acted in accordance with contemporary standards of morality. In appropriate cases this could result in the patient making charitable gifts and bequests. For a discussion of *Re D (J)* and *Re C*, see Rod Edmunds, 'Statutory Wills for Mental Patients' (1992) *Journal of Forensic Psychiatry*, Vol. 3, No. 2, pp. 350–357. *Re C* was considered by Ferris J. in *Re S (Gifts by Mental Patient)* [1997] 1 F.L.R. 96 at 98, where his Lordship said that the discretionary jurisdiction under this section "is not an area in which judicial precedent really has any weight". On the question of dispositions to charity his Lordship said, at 99: "It seems to me that I ought not to authorise the making of dispositions to charity except to the extent that I have a reasonable degree of confidence that not only is it objectively reasonable but that it is something which the patient herself would have wished to be done if she were of full capacity and aware of the circumstances."

Subsection (2)

Subject to being satisfied that adequate means are available for the patient's **1–873** maintenance, the Court will have regard to the just and proper claims of creditors (*Re Seager Hunt* [1906] 2 Ch. 295).

Powers of the judge as to patient's property and affairs

96.—(1) Without prejudice to the generality of section 95 above, the judge **1–874** shall have power to make such orders and give such directions and authorities as he thinks fit for the purposes of that section and in particular may for those purposes make orders or give directions or authorities for—

(a) the control (with or without the transfer or vesting of property or the payment into or lodgment in the Supreme Court of money or securities) and management of any property of the patient;

(b) the sale, exchange, charging or other disposition of or dealing with any property of the patient;

(c) the acquisition of any property in the name or on behalf of the patient;

(d) the settlement of any property of the patient, or the gift of any property of the patient to any such persons or for any such purposes as are mentioned in paragraphs (b) and (c) of section 95(1) above;

(e) the execution for the patient of a will making any provision (whether by way of disposing of property or exercising a power or otherwise) which could be made by a will executed by the patient if he were not mentally disordered;

(f) the carrying on by a suitable person of any profession, trade or business of the patient;

(g) the dissolution of a partnership of which the patient is a member;

(h) the carrying out of any contract entered into by the patient;

(i) the conduct of legal proceedings in the name of the patient or on his behalf;

(j) the reimbursement out of the property of the patient, with or without interest, of money applied by any person either in payment of the patient's debts (whether legally enforceable or not) or for the maintenance or other benefit of the patient or members of his family or in making provision for other persons or purposes for whom or which he might be expected to provide if he were not mentally disordered;

(k) the exercise of any power (including a power to consent) vested in the patient, whether beneficially, or as guardian or trustee, or otherwise.

(2) If under subsection (1) above provision is made for the settlement of any property of a patient, or the exercise of a power vested in a patient of appointing trustees or retiring from a trust, the judge may also make as respects the property settled or trust property such consequential vesting or other orders as the case may require, including (in the case of the exercise of such a power) any order which could have been made in such a case under Part IV of the Trustee Act 1925.

(3) Where under this section a settlement has been made of any property of a patient, and the Lord Chancellor or a nominated judge is satisfied, at any time before the death of the patient, that any material fact was not disclosed when the settlement was made, or that there has been any substantial change in circumstances, he may by order vary the settlement in such manner as he thinks fit, and give any consequential directions.

(4) The power of the judge to make or give an order, direction or authority for the execution of a will for a patient—

(a) shall not be exercisable at any time when the patient is a minor, and

(b) shall not be exercised unless the judge has reason to believe that the patient is incapable of making a valid will for himself.

(5) The powers of a patient as patron of a benefice shall be exercisable by the Lord Chancellor only.

DEFINITIONS

1–875   the judge: s.112.
property: s.112.
patient: s.112.
will: s.112.
mental disorder: ss.1, 145(1).
nominated judge: s.112.

GENERAL NOTE

"It is clear ... that section 96 does not extend the powers conferred by section 95 **1–876** but enumerates a number of the ways in which those powers may be exercised. Any act or transaction mentioned in section 96 must still be justified under one or other of the paragraphs of section 95(1) and satisfy the order of priorities laid down by section 95(2)" (*Re C (A Patient)* [1991] 3 All E.R. 866, 869 *per* Hoffmann J.).

For applications under subsection (1)(d) and (e) of this section, see rule 18 of the Court of Protection Rules 2001. For transaction fees, see *ibid.*, rule 79.

Subsection (1)

In particular: What follows is not an exhaustive list of powers. The Court has **1–877** exclusive jurisdiction over all of the patient's property and affairs.

Paragraph (d)

For general guidance to solicitors as to the practice of the Court on dealing with **1–878** applications for settlements and gifts under this paragraph, see Practice Direction [1983] 3 All E.R. 255. Also see Practice Note 9, "Applications for the execution of statutory wills and codicils and for gifts, settlements and other similar dealings", which was issued by the Court in November 1987. A further Practice Note on the "Procedure for the settlement of personal injury awards to patients" was issued on November 15, 1996.

Settlement of any property: In *Re L (W.J.G.)* [1966] Ch. 135, Cross J., considered, at 144, 145, the approach to be adopted by a judge in determining whether and how he should exercise his discretion in regard to the making of a settlement under this paragraph and section 95(1)(c).

The gift of any property of the patient: The court has to answer the following question when determining whether a patient should make a gift: is the proposed gift such a gift as the patient might be expected to provide if she had ceased to be mentally disordered and was removed from any influence (*Re C.M.G.* [1970] 1 Ch. 574).

Paragraph (e)

"Where a patient's affairs are the subject of an order of the Court of Protection, **1–879** and such patient has expressed the desire to execute a will or codicil, arrangements may be made for this to be done under the directions of the Court who will, before giving directions, require to be satisfied by medical evidence that the patient is of testamentary capacity, *i.e.* that he understands (a) the nature of the document to be executed, (b) the extent of the property to be disposed of, and (c) the claims of those he proposes to benefit or exclude [which is the test established by *Banks v. Goodfellows* (1870) 5 Q.B. 549]" (*Heywood and Massey*, p. 189). Also see Practice Note 5, "Procedure for the execution of testamentary documents", which was issued by the Court in November 1987. If the patient is not of testamentary capacity consideration should be given to the possibility of the court directing the execution of a "statutory will" under this provision. The judge will not direct the execution of such a will without first being satisfied as to the matters set out in subsection (4). For the approach that the judge will adopt in such cases, see the note on section 95(1)(c). Guidance on the making of an application for the execution of a statutory will is contained in Practice Note 9, which is noted under paragraph (d), above. Additional guidance for use in cases where the application is made by an attorney under a registered enduring power of attorney is contained in Practice Note 9A, which was also issued in November 1987.

Under rule 19(4) of the Court of Protection Rules 2001 the court has a discretion as to which persons are to be made respondents to or given notice of an application for the execution of a will under this paragraph. In *Re B (Court of Protection: Notice of Proceedings)* [1987] 1 W.L.R. 552, Millett J. considered who should be notified of an application made under this paragraph. In the absence of emergency, the normal rule is that all those who might be materially and adversely affected by the court's exercise of its jurisdiction should be notified. In will cases such persons would normally include all those for whom the patient might, if in sound mind, have been expected to provide, beneficiaries under a previous will, and in the case of an intestacy, the next of kin.

In *Re D (J)* [1982] 2 All E.R. 37 at 42–43, Megarry V.-C. identified the five considerations which the court should have in mind when deciding on what provisions should be inserted in a will.

The power under this provision extends to the making of a codicil which amends an already existing will (s.112).

Paragraph (i)

1–880   *The conduct of legal proceedings:* Which need not be confined to proceedings relating to the management, protection or administration of the patient's property (*Re W (E.E.M.)* [1971] Ch. 123). L. Gostin states that in practice the patient's receiver "must have authorisation from the court before bringing or defending an action on behalf of the patient" (*The Court of Protection,* 1983, p. 42).

Paragraph (k)

1–881   Note rules 15 and 17 of the Court of Protection Rules 2001.

Subsection (3)

1–882   The provisions of this subsection do not prevent trustees of a settlement from distributing the capital of a trust property during the lifetime of the patient (*Re C.W.H.T.* [1978] Ch. 67).

Subsection (4)

1–883   *A minor:* Is a person who has not attained the age of 18 (Family Law Reform Act 1969, s.1).

Supplementary provisions as to wills executed under s.96

1–884   **97.**—(1) Where under section 96(1) above the judge makes or gives an order, direction or authority requiring or authorising a person (in this section referred to as "the authorised person") to execute a will for a patient, any will executed in pursuance of that order, direction authority shall be expressed to be signed by the patient acting by the authorised person, and shall be—

   (a) signed by the authorised person with the name of the patient, and with his own name, in the presence of two or more witnesses present at the same time, and

   (b) attested and subscribed by those witnesses in the presence of the authorised person, and

   (c) sealed with the official seal of the Court of Protection.

(2) The Wills Act 1837 shall have effect in relation to any such will as if it were signed by the patient by his own hand, except that in relation to any such will—

   (a) section 9 of that Act (which makes provision as to the signing and attestation of wills) shall not apply, and

   (b) in the subsequent provisions of that Act any reference to execution in the manner required by the previous provisions of that Act shall be construed as a reference to execution in the manner required by subsection (1) above.

(3) Subject to the following provisions of this section, any such will executed in accordance with subsection (1) above shall have the same effect

for all purposes as if the patient were capable of making a valid will and the will had been executed by him in the manner required by the Wills Act 1837.

(4) So much of subsection (3) above as provides for such a will to have effect as if the patient were capable of making a valid will—

(a) shall not have effect in relation to such a will in so far as it disposes of any immovable property, other than immovable property in England or Wales, and

(b) where at the time when such a will is executed the patient is domiciled in Scotland or Northern Ireland or in a country or territory outside the United Kingdom, shall not have effect in relation to that will in so far as it relates to any other property or matter, except any property or matter in respect of which, under the law of his domicile, any question of his testamentary capacity would fall to be determined in accordance with the law of England and Wales.

DEFINITIONS **1–885**
the judge: s.112.
will: s.112.
patient: s.112.
property: s.112.

GENERAL NOTE
If the formalities set out in subsection (1) of this section are complied with by a **1–886** Master of the Court of Protection the will must, by virtue of subsection (3), be treated as if it were duly made and the High Court has no jurisdiction to interfere with it (*Re Davey (decd.)* [1981] 1 W.L.R. 164).

Subsection (1)
Property: See the note on section 95(1). **1–887**
Sealed with the official seal: This provision does not require the will to have been sealed during the lifetime of the testator (*Re Hughes (deceased), The Times,* January 8, 1999).

Judge's powers in cases of emergency
98. Where it is represented to the judge, and he has reason to believe, that **1–888** a person may be incapable, by reason of mental disorder, of managing and administering his property and affairs, and the judge is of the opinion that it is necessary to make immediate provision for any of the matters referred to in section 95 above, then pending the determination of the question whether that person is so incapable the judge may exercise in relation to the property and affairs of that person any of the powers conferred on him in relation to the property and affairs of a patient by this Part of this Act so far as is requisite for enabling that provision to be made.

DEFINITIONS
the judge: s.112. **1–889**
mental disorder: ss.1, 145(1).
property: s.112.

GENERAL NOTE
This section enables the Court to act in an emergency without making a formal **1–890** determination of the patient's incapacity if it considers that it is necessary to make immediate provision. Also note the power contained in rule 42 of the Court of

Protection Rules to make immediate provision in relation to the property and affairs of the patient.

The Human Rights Act 1998

1–891   A failure to notify the mentally disordered person that an application to a judge under this section was about to be made would risk violating that person's right to a fair hearing under Article 6(1) of the European Convention on Human Rights: see *Winterwerp v. Netherlands* (1979) 2 E.H.R.R. 387, para. 74 and the notes on Article 6(1). The notification should advise the person of the desirability of obtaining legal advice.

   A Person: Not a "patient" as defined in section 94(2).

   Reason to believe: The Court is not obliged to hear medical evidence of incapacity.

   Any of the powers: But not including those powers specified in the third column of Schedule 3 (s.113).

Power to appoint receiver

1–892   **99.**—(1) The judge may by order appoint as receiver for a patient a person specified in the order or the holder for the time being of an office so specified.

   (2) A person appointed as receiver for a patient shall do all such things in relation to the property and affairs of the patient as the judge, in the exercise of the powers conferred on him by sections 95 and 96 above, orders or directs him to do and may do any such thing in relation to the property and affairs of the patient as the judge, in the exercise of those powers, authorises him to do.

   (3) A receiver appointed for any person shall be discharged by order of the judge on the judge being satisfied that the person has become capable of managing and administering his property and affairs, and may be discharged by order of the judge at any time if the judge considers it expedient to do so; and a receiver shall be discharged (without any order) on the death of the patient.

DEFINITIONS
1–893   the judge: s.112.
   patient: s.112.
   property: s.112.

GENERAL NOTE
1–894   This section empowers the Court to exercise its jurisdiction by appointing a receiver for the patient. The receiver acts under the direction of the Court and he will be discharged once the Court is satisfied that the patient is capable of managing his own affairs. A receiver will automatically be discharged on the death of the patient. The Court may allow the receiver to be remunerated for his services (Court of Protection Rules 2001 r. 43(1)) and the receiver is usually called upon to give security for the due performance of his duties (*ibid.*, r. 56). The receiver's "powers are limited and specified in the order appointing him and a further direction or authority of the Court is required for matters outside the scope of the order. Receivers are expected to visit the patient at least once a year and to account, usually annually, to the Court for their dealings with the patient's property" (*Mentally Incapacitated Adults and Decision-Making, supra*, para. 3.7). The Public Accounts Committee has stated that for "a receivership to be successful it is crucial that the receiver appointed is trustworthy and reliable. It is also important that the receiver is competent to manage the patient's affairs and should take an active interest in the patient's welfare" (House of Commons, Session 1993–1994, Thirty-ninth Report, para. 5). A former

Master of the Court of Protection has stated that "the receiver stands in the shoes of the patient and makes the decisions which the patient would make if they were capable of making them" (*Medico-Legal Journal*, Vol. 60, Pt 1, 1992, p. 26).

The Law Commission has reported that the case of *Re EG* [1914] 1 Ch. 927, has established that the receiver is a statutory agent of the patient, that the property of the person without capacity does not rest in the receiver, and that the receiver is not personally liable for the costs of those he employs in the course of acting for the person concerned (*Mental Incapacity*, 1995, para. 8.45).

Re EG also established that a solicitor instructed by the receiver in connection with the patient's affairs is the solicitor of the patient and not that of the receiver. For the question of who is the patient's solicitor in cases where more than one solicitor has been instructed to make an application for receivership or where a patient himself wishes to instruct another solicitor for a particular area of his affairs; see Practice Direction [1995] 2 F.L.R. 1036.

The procedure for making an application to appoint a receiver is set out in rule 7 of the Court of Protection Rules 2001. This rule provides, *inter alia*, that any application to the Court, other than a first application to appoint a receiver, may be by letter unless the court directs that a formal application shall be made. Where it is considered that a receiver should be appointed at once, the court should be asked to exercise its power under rule 42(1)(b) to appoint an interim receiver.

Receivership is the normal method of protecting a patient's estate and using it for his benefit. However, if the patient's assets do not exceed £10,000, the Court may make an order in summary manner pursuant to rule 8 of the Court of Protection Rules 2001 without appointing a receiver. This type of order, called a short order, can also be made if the patient's assets exceed £10,000 but the Court considers the appointment of a receiver to be unnecessary.

If the patient's sole asset consists of a pension or salary payable by a government department, the department concerned can administer the asset under section 142.

Subsection (1)

Appoint: Appointments of receivers under this section are not made subject to any **1–895** time limit.

Person: Who will usually be the person who made the application to the court. He or she can be a relative, a friend, an official of a local authority, or a professional adviser to the patient. "Some 19,000 receivers (68 per cent) are relatives or friends of the patient, some 4,000 (14 per cent) are professional people, such as solicitors and bank managers; and some 2,400 (9 per cent) are agents of local authorities. Where nobody willing and suitable can be found, the Public Trustee is appointed receiver. He is currently responsible for some 2,600 cases (9 per cent)" (NAO Report, para. 1.4).

Professional receivers may charge for their receivership work, but relatives and friends receive no payment other than out-of-pocket expenses.

Holder ... of an office: Who could be the Director of Social Services of a local authority. The expenses of an officer of a social services authority who is appointed receiver can be paid by virtue of section 49 of the National Assistance Act 1948.

Subsection (3)

Shall be discharged: On an application for the discharge of the receiver and the **1–896** restoration of the patient to the management of his own affairs the rules of natural justice, but not the rules of evidence, apply (*Re W.L.W.* [1972] Ch. 456).

Capable of managing. A patient can be capable of managing his affairs even though he continues to suffer from a mental disorder.

Expedient: This means expedient for the patient (*Re N. (decd.)* [1977] 1 W.L.R. 676).

Death of the patient: The receiver remains liable to account for money received prior to the patient's death (*Re Walker* (1907) 2 Ch. 120).

Vesting of stock in curator appointed outside England and Wales

1–897   **100.**—(1) Where the judge is satisfied—

(a) that under the law prevailing in a place outside England and Wales a person has been appointed to exercise powers with respect to the property or affairs of any other person on the ground (however formulated) that the other person is incapable, by reason of mental disorder, of managing and administering his property and affairs, and

(b) that having regard to the nature of the appointment and to the circumstances of the case it is expedient that the judge should exercise his powers under this section,

the judge may direct any stock standing in the name of the said other person or the right to receive the dividends from the stock to be transferred into the name of the person so appointed or otherwise dealt with as requested by that person, and may give such directions as the judge thinks fit for dealing with accrued dividends from the stock.

(2) In this section "stock" includes shares and also any fund, annuity or security transferable in the books kept by any body corporate or unincorporated company or society, or by an instrument of transfer either alone or accompanied by other formalities, and "dividends" shall be construed accordingly.

DEFINITIONS

1–898   the judge: s.112.
property: s.112.
mental disorder: ss.1, 145(1).

GENERAL NOTE

1–899   The "purpose of this section is that the Court in this country should be able to recognise judicially the operation of foreign law, whereunder some form of curatorship has been constituted for a mental patient, without itself having to go into the question of mental status and capacity" (Heywood and Massey, *Court of Protection Practice*, 12th ed., 1991, p. 35).

Subsection (1)

1–900   *The judge may direct:* See rule 73(2) of the Court of Protection Rules 1994. A transaction fee is payable (*ibid.*, r. 79).

Preservation of interests in patient's property

1–901   **101.**—(1) Where any property of a person has been disposed of under this Part of this Act, and under his will or his intestacy, or by any gift perfected or nomination taking effect on his death, any other person would have taken an interest in the property but for the disposal—

(a) he shall take the same interest, if and so far as circumstances allow, in any property belonging to the estate of the deceased which represents the property disposed of; and

(b) if the property disposed of was real property any property representing it shall so long as it remains part of his estate be treated as if it were real property.

(2) The judge, in ordering, directing or authorising under this Part of this

Act any disposal of property which apart from this section would result in the conversion of personal property into real property, may direct that the property representing the property disposed of shall, so long as it remains the property of the patient or forms part of his estate, be treated as if it were personal property.

(3) References in subsections (1) and (2) above to the disposal of property are references to—

    (a) the sale, exchange, charging or other dealing (otherwise than by will) with property other than money,

    (b) the removal of property from one place to another,

    (c) the application of money in acquiring property, or

    (d) the transfer of money from one account to another;

and references to property representing property disposed of shall be construed accordingly and as including the result of successive disposals.

(4) The judge may give such directions as appear to him necessary or expedient for the purpose of facilitating the operation of subsection (1) above, including the carrying of money to a separate account and the transfer of property other than money.

(5) Where the judge has ordered, directed or authorised the expenditure of money for the carrying out of permanent improvements on, or otherwise for the permanent benefit of, any property of the patient, he may order that the whole or any part of the money expended or to be expended shall be a charge upon the property, whether without interest or with interest at a specified rate; and an order under this subsection may provide for excluding or restricting the operation of subsection (1) above.

(6) A charge under subsection (5) above may be made in favour of such person as may be just, and in particular, where the money charged is paid out of the patient's general estate, may be made in favour of a person as trustee for the patient; but no charge under that subsection shall confer any right of sale or foreclosure during the lifetime of the patient.

DEFINITIONS   **1–902**

    property: s.112.

    will: s.112.

    the judge: s.112.

    patient: s.112.

GENERAL NOTE

    This section, which is concerned with the effect of dispositions made under this **1–903** Part on the law of succession, is considered in Heywood and Massey, *Court of Protection Practice*, at pp. 120 *et seq.*

Lord Chancellor's Visitors

  102.—(1) There shall continue to be the following panels of Lord **1–904** Chancellor's Visitors of patients constituted in accordance with this section, namely—

    (a) a panel of Medical Visitors;

    (b) a panel of Legal Visitors; and

    (c) a panel of General Visitors (being Visitors who are not required by this section to possess either a medical or legal qualification for appointment).

  (2) Each panel shall consist of persons appointed to it by the Lord

Chancellor, the appointment of each person being for such term and subject to such conditions as the Lord Chancellor may determine.

(3) A person shall not be qualified to be appointed—

(a) to the panel of Medical Visitors unless he is a registered medical practitioner who appears to the Lord Chancellor to have special knowledge and experience of cases of mental disorder;

(b) to the panel of Legal Visitors unless [he has a 10 year general qualification, within the meaning of section 71 of the Courts and Legal Services Act 1990].

(4) If the Lord Chancellor so determines in the case of any Visitor appointed under this section, he shall be paid out of money provided by Parliament such remuneration and allowances as the Lord Chancellor may, with the concurrence of the Treasury, determine.

AMENDMENT

The words in square brackets in subs. 3(b) were substituted by the Courts and Legal Services Act 1990, s.71(2), Sched. 10, para. 51.

DEFINITION

1–905 patient: s.112.

GENERAL NOTE

1–906 This section provides for the appointment and payment of Medical, Legal and General Visitors. The functions of Visitors are set out in section 103.

Subsection (1)

1–907 *Legal Visitors:* "The legal visitor over the last eight and a half years has only done three visits"; *per* Mrs. A. B. Macfarlane, "The Court of Protection," *Medico-Legal Journal*, Vol. 60, Pt. 1, 1992, p. 42.

Medical Visitors: See, Royal College of Psychiatrists, "Medical visitors and the Court of Protection", *Bulletin of the Royal College of Psychiatrists* (1983), 7, 34–35, and E.F. Carr, "The work of the Lord Chancellor's medical visitors", *Medicine, Science and the Law*, (1988), 28, 6–8.

General Visitors: Most General Visitors are former employees of the Public Trust Office and the Lord Chancellor's Department. A patient should receive a visit from a General Visitor if they are "a minor, if they are living in their own home or with a relative, if they are in a nursing home, other than a National Health Service hospital and are not being regularly visited by relatives or friends, or if their receiver is a local authority" (Thirty-fifth report of the Public Accounts Committee for Session 1998–1999, p. 15, n. 13).

Functions of Visitors

1–908 **103.**—(1) Patients shall be visited by Lord Chancellor's Visitors in such circumstances, and in such manner, as may be prescribed by directions of a standing nature given by the Master of the Court of Protection with the concurrence of the Lord Chancellor.

(2) Where it appears to the judge in the case of any patient that a visit by a Lord Chancellor's Visitor is necessary for the purpose of investigating any particular matter or matters relating to the capacity of the patient to manage and administer his property and affairs, or otherwise relating to the exercise in relation to him of the functions of the judge under this Part of this Act, the judge may order that the patient shall be visited for that purpose.

(3) Every visit falling to be made under subsection (1) or (2) above shall be made by a General Visitor unless, in a case where it appears to the judge that

it is in the circumstances essential for the visit to be made by a Visitor with medical or legal qualifications, the judge directs that the visit shall be made by a Medical or a Legal Visitor.

(4) A Visitor making a visit under this section shall make such report on the visit as the judge may direct.

(5) A Visitor making a visit under this section may interview the patient in private.

(6) A Medical Visitor making a visit under this section may carry out in private a medical examination of the patient and may require the production of and inspect any medical records relating to the patient.

(7) The Master of the Court of Protection may visit any patient for the purpose mentioned in subsection (2) above and may interview the patient in private.

(8) A report made by a Visitor under this section, and information contained in such a report, shall not be disclosed except to the judge and any person authorised by the judge to receive the disclosure.

(9) If any person discloses any report or information in contravention of subsection (8) above, he shall be guilty of an offence and liable on summary conviction to imprisonment for a term not exceeding three months or to a fine not exceeding level 3 on the standard scale or both.

(10) In this section references to patients include references to persons alleged to be incapable, by reason of mental disorder, of managing and administering their property and affairs.

DEFINITIONS
    the judge: s.112.   **1–909**
    property. s.112.
    standard scale: s.145(1).
    mental disorder: ss.1, 145(1).

GENERAL NOTE
    "The most important part of [the Visitors'] duty is to assist the Court in **1–910** determining what is the mental capacity of the person in question, whether in regard to an application for the appointment of a receiver or the discharge of a receiver on recovery, but many other matters arise in regard to which they visit the patient, under the directions of the Court, and report, *e.g.* testamentary capacity, suitability of accommodation, care and attention and ascertaining the patient's views in regard to any matter" (Heywood and Massey, p. 16).

    This section also applies to donors of enduring powers whether or not they are patients within the meaning of this Act (Enduring Powers of Attorney Act 1985, s.10).

Subsection (1)
    Patient: See subsection (10).   **1–911**

Subsection (5)
    Making a visit: The obstruction of a Visitor constitutes an offence under section **1–912** 129. It is also a contempt of court to interfere with the discharge of a Visitor's duties (*Re Anon* (1881) 18 Ch.D. 26, 27, *per* James L.J.).

Subsection (8)
    Report: When a patient is applying for the discharge of his receiver, the judge, save **1–913** in exceptional circumstances, should exercise his discretion so as to allow the

disclosure of the Visitor's report, and where disclosure is so ordered the patient should be able to test the report by putting questions to the Visitor (*Re W.L.W.* [1972] Ch. 456).

Disclosed: Written questions may be put to the Visitor following disclosure (Court of Protection Rules 1994, r. 31).

General powers of the judge with respect to proceedings

1–914   **104.**—(1) For the purposes of any proceedings before him with respect to persons suffering or alleged to be suffering from mental disorder, the judge shall have the same powers as are vested in the High Court in respect of securing the attendance of witnesses and the production of documents.

(2) Subject to the provisions of this section, any act or omission in the course of such proceedings which, if occurring in the course of proceedings in the High Court would have been a contempt of the Court, shall be punishable by the judge in any manner in which it could have been punished by the High Court.

(3) Subsection (2) above shall not authorise the Master, or any other officer of the Court of Protection to exercise any power of attachment or committal, but the Master or officer may certify any such act or omission to the Lord Chancellor or a nominated judge, and the Lord Chancellor or judge may upon such certification inquire into the alleged act or omission and take any such action in relation to it as he could have taken if the proceedings had been before him.

(4) Subsections (1) to (4) of section 36 of the Supreme Court Act 1981 (which provides a special procedure for the issue of writs of subpoena ad testificandum and duces tecum so as to be enforceable throughout the United Kingdom) shall apply in relation to proceedings under this Part of this Act with the substitution for references to the High Court of references to the judge and for references to such writs of references to such document as may be prescribed by rules under this Part of this Act for issue by the judge for securing the attendance of witnesses or the production of documents.

DEFINITIONS

1–915   mental disorder: ss.1, 145(1).
the judge: s.112.
nominated judge: s.112.

GENERAL NOTE

1–916   This section provides the Court of Protection judge with the same powers as are vested in the High Court to secure the attendance of witnesses and the production of documents. It also applies to proceedings under the Enduring Powers of Attorney Act 1985 with respect to donors of enduring powers whether or not they are patients within the meaning of this Act (*ibid.* s.10).

Subsection (1)

1–917   *Attendance of witnesses:* Rule 48 of the Court of Protection Rules 2001 provides for the issue of a witness summons.

Appeals

1–918   **105.**—(1) Subject to and in accordance with rules under this Part of this Act, an appeal shall lie to a nominated judge from any decision of the Master of the Court of Protection or any nominated officer.

(2) The Court of Appeal shall continue to have the same jurisdiction as to appeals from any decision of the Lord Chancellor or from any decision of a

nominated judge, whether given in the exercise of his original jurisdiction or on the hearing of an appeal under subsection (1) above, as they had immediately before the coming into operation of Part VIII of the Mental Health Act 1959 as to appeals from orders in lunacy made by the Lord Chancellor or any other person having jurisdiction in lunacy.

DEFINITIONS
    nominated judge: s.112.   **1–919**
    nominated officer: s.112.

GENERAL NOTE
    Subsection (1) of this section applies to any decision of the Master of the Court of **1–920** Protection or any nominated officer made in proceedings under the Enduring Powers of Attorney Act 1985 (*ibid.* s.10).

Subsection (1)
    Rules: See rules 54 and 55 of the Court of Protection Rules 2001.   **1–921**
    Appeal: On an appeal under this subsection the nominated judge has a complete discretion to consider the matter and he is in no way fettered by any decision of the Master or nominated officer (*Re D.* (J.) [1982] 2 All E.R. 37).

Rules of procedure
    106.—(1) Proceedings before the judge with respect to persons suffering **1–922** or alleged to be suffering from mental disorder (in this section referred to as "proceedings") shall be conducted in accordance with the provisions of rules made under this Part of this Act.
    (2) Rules under this Part of this Act may make provision as to—
    (a) the carrying out of preliminary or incidental inquiries;
    (b) the persons by whom and manner in which proceedings may be instituted and carried on;
    (c) the persons who are to be entitled to be notified of, to attend, or to take part in proceedings;
    (d) the evidence which may be authorised or required to be given in proceedings and the manner (whether on oath or otherwise and whether orally or in writing) in which it is to be given;
    (e) the administration of oaths and taking of affidavits for the purposes of proceedings; and
    (f) the enforcement of orders made and directions given in proceedings.
    (3) Without prejudice to the provisions of section 104(1) above, rules under this Part of this Act may make provision for authorising or requiring the attendance and examination of persons suffering or alleged to be suffering from mental disorder, the furnishing of information and the production of documents.
    (4) Rules under this Part of this Act may make provision as to the termination of proceedings, whether on the death or recovery of the person to whom the proceedings relate or otherwise, and for the exercise, pending the termination of the proceedings, of powers exercisable under this Part of this Act in relation to the property or affairs of a patient.
    (5) Rules under this Part of this Act made with the consent of the Treasury may—
    (a) make provision as to the scale of costs, fees and percentages payable in relation to proceedings, and as to the manner in which and funds out of which such costs, fees and percentages are to be paid;

(b) contain provision for charging any percentage upon the estate of the person to whom the proceedings relate and for the payment of costs, fees and percentages within such time after the death of the person to whom the proceedings relate or the termination of the proceedings as may be provided by the rules; and

(c) provide for the remission of fees and percentages.

(6) A charge upon the estate of a person created by virtue of subsection (5) above shall not cause any interest of that person in any property to fail or determine or to be prevented from recommencing.

(7) Rules under this Part of this Act may authorise the making of orders for the payment of costs to or by persons attending, as well as persons taking part in, proceedings.

DEFINITIONS

1–923   the judge: s.112.
mental disorder: ss.1, 145(1).
property: s.112.
patient: s.112.

GENERAL NOTE

1–924   The Court of Protection Rules 2001 (S.I. 2001 No. 824), which were made under this section, came into force on April 1, 2001. The Civil Procedure Rules 1998 do not apply to proceedings before the judge within the meaning of this Part (*ibid.* r. 2.1(2)).

This section applies to proceedings under the Enduring Powers of Attorney Act 1985 and to donors of enduring powers whether or not they are patients within the meaning of this Act (*ibid.* s.10).

Security and accounts

1–925   **107.**—(1) Rules under this Part of this Act may make provision as to the giving of security by a receiver and as to the enforcement and discharge of the security.

(2) It shall be the duty of a receiver to render accounts in accordance with the requirements of rules under this Part of this Act, as well after his discharge as during his receivership; and rules under this Part of this Act may make provision for the rendering of accounts by persons other than receivers who are ordered, directed or authorised under this Part of this Act to carry out any transaction.

GENERAL NOTE

1–926   In the majority of receivership cases a security bond is required to be taken out with a Guarantee Society.

Subsection (1)

1–927   *Giving of a security:* See the Court of Protection Rules 2001, rr. 56 to 61.

Subsection (2)

1–928   *Rendering of accounts:* See *ibid.*, rr. 61 to 66.

General provisions as to rules under Part VII

1–929   **108.**—(1) Any power to make rules conferred by this Part of this Act shall be exercisable by the Lord Chancellor.

(2) Rules under this Part of this Act may contain such incidental and supplemental provisions as appear requisite for the purposes of the rules.

See the General Note to section 106.   **1–930**

Effect and proof of orders, etc.
   109.—(1) Section 204 of the Law of Property Act 1925 (by which orders of **1–931**
the High Court are made conclusive in favour of purchasers) shall apply in
relation to orders made and directions and authorities given by the judge as
it applies in relation to orders of the High Court.
   (2) Office copies of orders made, directions or authorities given or other
instruments issued by the judge and sealed with the official seal of the Court
of Protection shall be admissible in all legal proceedings as evidence of the
originals without any further proof.

DEFINITION
   the judge: s.112.   **1–932**

GENERAL NOTE
   This section was considered by the Court of Appeal in *Pritchard v. Briggs* [1980] **1–933**
Ch. 338.

Reciprocal arrangements in relation to Scotland and Northern Ireland as
      to exercise of powers
   110.—(1) This Part of this Act shall apply in relation to the property and **1–934**
affairs in Scotland or Northern Ireland of a patient in relation to whom
powers have been exercised under this Part of this Act, or a person as to
whom powers are exercisable and have been exercised under section 98
above as it applies in relation to his property and affairs in England and
Wales [unless—
   (a) in Scotland, a [...] judicial factor has been appointed for him; or
   (b) in Northern Ireland, he is a patient in relation to whom powers have
       been exercised under Part VIII of the Mental Health (Northern
       Ireland) Order 1986, or a person as to whom powers are exercisable
       and have been exercised under Article 97(2) of that Order].
   (2) Where under the law in force in Scotland [...] with respect to the
property and affairs of persons suffering from mental disorder a [...]
[judicial factor] has been appointed for any person, the provisions of that law
shall apply in relation to that person's property and affairs in England and
Wales unless he is a patient in relation to whom powers have been exercised
under this Part of this Act, or a person as to whom powers are exercisable
and have been exercised under section 98 above.
   [(2A) Part VIII of the Mental Health (Northern Ireland) Order 1986 shall
apply in relation to the property and affairs in England and Wales of a
patient in relation to whom powers have been exercised under that Part, or a
person as to whom powers are exercisable and have been exercised under
Article 97(2) of that Order as it applies in relation to his property and affairs
in Northern Ireland unless he is a patient in relation to whom powers have
been exercised under this Part of this Act, or a person as to whom powers are
exercisable and have been exercised under section 98 above.]
   (3) Nothing in this section shall affect any power to execute a will under
section 96(1)(e) above [or Article 99(1)(e) of the Mental Health (Northern
Ireland) Order 1986] or the effect of any will executed in the exercise of such
a power.

(4) In this section references to property do not include references to land or interests in land but this subsection shall not prevent the receipt of rent or other income arising from land or interests in land.

AMENDMENTS
The amendments to this section were made by the Mental Health (Northern Ireland Consequential Amendments) Order 1986 (S.I. 1986 No. 596) and the Adults with Incapacity (Scotland) Act 2000, s.88(3), Sched. 4.

DEFINITIONS
1–935   patient: s.112.
mental disorder: ss.1, 145(1).
will: s.112.

Subsection (1)
1–936   *Property:* See section 112 and subsection (4).

Construction of references in other Acts to judge or authority having jurisdiction under Part VII

1–937   **111.**—(1) The functions expressed to be conferred by any enactment not contained in this Part of this Act on the judge having jurisdiction under this Part of this Act shall be exercisable by the Lord Chancellor or by a nominated judge.

(2) Subject to subsection (3) [and (3A)] below, the functions expressed to be conferred by any such enactment on the authority having jurisdiction under this Part of this Act shall, subject to any express provision to the contrary, be exercisable by the Lord Chancellor, a nominated judge, the Master of the Court of Protection [, by the Public Trustee] or a nominated officer.

[(2A) The exercise of the functions referred to in subsection (2) above by the Public Trustee shall be subject to any directions of the Master and they shall be exercisable so far only as may be provided by any rules made under this Part of this Act or (subject to any such rules) by directions of the Master.]

(3) The exercise of the functions referred to in subsection (2) above by a nominated officer shall be subject to any directions of the Master and they shall be exercisable so far only as may be provided by the instrument by which the officer is nominated.

[(3A) In such cases or circumstances as may be prescribed by any rules under this Part of this Act or (subject to any such rules) by directions of the Master, the functions referred to in subsection (2) above shall be exercised by the Public Trustee (but subject to any directions of the Master as to their exercise).]

(4) Subject to the foregoing provisions of this section—

(a)   references in any enactment not contained in this Part of this Act to the judge having jurisdiction under this Part of this Act shall be construed as references to the Lord Chancellor or a nominated judge, and

(b) references in any such enactment to the authority having jurisdiction under this Part of this Act shall be construed as references to the Lord Chancellor, a nominated judge, the Master of the Court of Protection or a nominated officer.

AMENDMENTS

The amendments to this section were made by the Public Trustee and Administration of Funds Act 1986, s.2.

DEFINITIONS

    the judge: s.112.   **1–938**

    nominated judge: s.112.

    nominated officer: s.112.

Interpretation of Part VII

112. In this Part of this Act, unless the context otherwise requires—   **1–939**

"nominated judge" means a judge nominated in pursuance of subsection (1) of section 93 above;

"nominated officer" means an officer nominated in pursuance of subsection (4) of that section;

"patient" has the meaning assigned to it by section 94 above;

"property" includes any thing in action, and any interest in real or personal property;

"the judge" shall be construed in accordance with section 94 above;

"will" includes a codicil.

GENERAL NOTE

Property: See the note on section 95(1).   **1–940**

Disapplication of certain enactments in relation to persons within the jurisdiction of the judge

113. The provisions of the Acts described in Schedule 3 to this Act which **1–941** are specified in the third column of that Schedule, so far as they make special provision for persons suffering from mental disorder, shall not have effect in relation to patients and to persons as to whom powers are exercisable and have been exercised under section 98 above.

DEFINITIONS

    mental disorder: ss.1, 145(1).   **1–942**

    patient: s.112.

GENERAL NOTE

"The reason and purpose of this section will not be readily apparent. The **1–943** enactment[s] mentioned in Schedule 3 made special provision, in the language of the day, as to what is to happen when a 'lunatic' or an 'idiot' has to do something, or suffer something being done, and in some instances provided as to how any money arising shall be dealt with or applied. Usually the enabling power was to the effect that the committee (if any) should act on behalf of the patient. The provisions of this Part of this Act, and in particular section 96(b) and (k), render unnecessary any special enabling provision in specific statutes, since under this Part of the Act anything which the patient can do can be done by his receiver under an order of the court" (Heywood and Massey, p. 329).

Approved social workers

Appointment of approved social workers

1–944   **114.**—(1) A local social services authority shall appoint a sufficient number of approved social workers for the purpose of discharging the functions conferred on them by this Act.

(2) No person shall be appointed by a local social services authority as an approved social worker unless he is approved by the authority as having appropriate competence in dealing with persons who are suffering from mental disorder.

(3) In approving a person for appointment as an approved social worker a local social services authority shall have regard to such matters as the Secretary of State may direct.

DEFINITIONS

1–945   local social services authority: s.145(1).
approved social worker: s.145(1).
mental disorder: s.145(1).

GENERAL NOTE

1–946   This section requires local authorities to appoint a sufficient number of approved social workers to carry out the functions given to them by this Act. Only social workers who have been approved by authorities as being competent can be appointed. Approved social workers replaced the mental welfare officers who were appointed under the 1959 Act on October 28, 1984. Anything done prior to October 28, 1984, by a mental welfare officer is not affected by this changeover (Sched. 5, para. 4(2)). The role of approved social workers is considered in the General Note to section 13.

The findings of a research project into the experience of social services departments in implementing this Act are contained in *Sectioned: Social Services and the 1983 Mental Health Act*, M. Barnes, R. Bowl and M. Fisher, 1990. A report of an inspection by the Social Services Inspectorate on key aspects of the work of approved social workers is *Approved Social Workers—Developing a Service*, Department of Health, 1991 and an examination of the provision of approved social workers, their location, numbers and workload can be found in "A Survey of Approved Social Work in England and Wales", P. Huxley and M. Kerfoot (1994) 24 *British Journal of Social Work*, 311–324. For an examination of the role of the approved social worker, see "The Approved Social Worker—Reflections on Origins," Pauline M. Prior (1992) 22 *British Journal of Social Work*, 105–119 and "'A Mere Transporter'—the Legal Role of the Approved Social Worker"*, Roger Hargreaves, (2000) 4 Journal of Mental Health Law 135–146.

The Human Rights Act 1998

1–947   See the note on section 13 under this heading.

Partnership arrangements

1–948   The function of the local authority under this section is not a local authority health related function which can be the subject of a partnership arrangement with NHS bodies under the Health Act 1999 (NHS Bodies and Local Authority Partnership Arrangements Regulations 2000 (S.I. 2000 No. 617), reg.6 and NHS Bodies and

Local Authority Partnership Arrangements (Wales) Regulations 2000 (S.I. 2000 No. 2993 (W.193)), reg. 6).

Subsection (1)

Local social services authority: Only social services authorities have the power to **1–949** appoint approved social workers. Although National Health Service Trusts, established under Part I of the National Health Service and Community Care Act 1990, have the power to employ social workers, those social workers cannot discharge the functions of approved social workers because they are not employed by the local authority: see the definition of "approved social worker" in section 145(1). Also see the note on "partnership arrangements", above.

Appoint: An approved social worker should be provided with documentary evidence of his appointment as some sections of this Act require the production of such documentation (see, for example, s.115). The document, which should be authenticated by a member or officer of the appointing local authority, could read as follows: "[Name of approved social worker] has been appointed by the [name of local authority] to act as an approved social worker under the Mental Health Act 1983 (Mental Health Act 1983, s.114)." It would be advisable to reproduce the provisions of section 115 of this Act, which provides an approved social worker with a power of entry and inspection, on the document.

Sufficient number: Guidance on the criteria to be adopted in ascertaining the number of approved social workers that need to be appointed is given in paragraph 8 of "Draft Guidelines for Approval of Social Workers under the Proposed Mental Health (Amendment) Act" published by the DHSS in December 1981: "Decline in the use of compulsory powers is a factor to be taken into account in deciding how many social workers an authority will need to train and approve under the amendment legislation, but it should be balanced by a proper assessment of the work to be undertaken and an appreciation of the role envisaged for them. Local social services authorities should establish criteria for deciding how many will be required to meet the demands in their area and generally speaking a count of the number of crises referred to the department is likely to be a better indicator than the recorded number of compulsory admissions to hospital."

As functions given to approved social workers may have to be discharged at any time of the day or night, local authorities should appoint sufficient approved social workers to provide a 24-hour approved social worker service. The *Report of the Inquiry into the Care and Treatment of Christopher Clunis*, HMSO, 1994, recommended, at paragraph 50.0.5(vi), that an "approved social worker should be contactable throughout the working day, as well as at night and during weekends and public holidays". The Department of Health has stated that local authorities have a responsibility to employ enough approved social workers "to provide a seven days a week assessment and emergency service" under this Act (*Building Bridges: A Guide to Arrangements for Inter-Agency Working for the Care and Protection of Severely Mentally Ill People* (1995), para. 2.2.2.). The *Code of Practice*, at paragraph 2.37, states that the obligation to provide a 24-hour service is "subject to resources".

Functions: The relevant sections are 4, 10, 11, 13, 14, 18, 25B, 25C, 29, 30, 40, 87, 89, 115, 135, 136 and 138.

Conferred on them: And not on the local authority.

Subsection (2)

Appointed: Although an approved social worker acts in a personal capacity when **1–950** carrying out his functions under this Act (see the note on "duty of an approved social worker" in s.13(1)), as an employee he will be protected by the doctrine of vicarious liability and the local authority will be liable for wrongs done by him while acting in the course of his employment. A legal action brought against either an approved social worker or his employing authority will succeed only if evidence of bad faith or lack of reasonable care is present (s.139).

In *Detained: Inspection of compulsory mental health admissions* (2001), the Social Services Inspectorate reports that a belief exists "that because approved social workers act as independent professionals under the Mental Health Act, their work did not require scrutiny and evaluation" (para. 5.17). This belief is erroneous because a local authority has a continuing obligation to ensure that any approved social worker that it appoints continues to possess "appropriate competence".

At the House of Lords Committee stage of the Mental Health (Amendment) Bill an attempt was made to amend this section so as to preclude a hospital social worker from acting as an approved social worker in cases where the patient would be admitted to the hospital where the social worker was employed. Lord Elton said, in resisting the amendment: "There may be cases where social workers based in a hospital and undertaking [approved social worker] duties find it difficult to act independently in making applications to that hospital, and that may well arise most often where the doctor with whom the social worker is working has made one of the medical recommendations ... It is our view that this sort of case should be a matter of good practice rather than legislation." (H.L. Vol. 426, col. 1167). During the course of his speech Lord Elton referred to advice that the DHSS had given to Directors of Social Services, in a letter dated April 16, 1974, on the appointment of hospital social workers to act as mental welfare officers in which it was stated that it should be made clear to each hospital social worker who is so appointed that if in any case he feels that he cannot act or be seen to act independently he should get advice from his superior officer as to whether another person should be appointed to act in his stead. National Health Service social workers were transferred to the employment of local social services authorities on April 1, 1974, by virtue of the National Health Service (Transfer of Social Services Staff) Order 1974 (S.I. 1974 No. 318), art. 3.

Approved by the authority: The fact that a social worker has been "approved by the authority" does not necessarily mean that he will be *appointed* under subsection (1). Paragraphs 8 to 12 of DHSS Circular No. LAC(86)15 (Welsh Office Circular No. 51/86) deal with approval arrangements.

Subsection (3)

1–951 *Such matters as the Secretary of State may direct:* The functions of the Secretary of State under this section, so far as exercisable in relation to Wales, are exercised by the National Assembly for Wales (S.I. 1999 No. 672, art. 2, Sched. 1).

Have regard to: The local authority need not have exclusive regard to the Secretary of State's directions. In planning law the obligation to "have regard to" a development plan has been held to mean that the planning authority was bound to consider the plan, along with other material considerations, but was not bound to follow it (*Simpson v. Edinburgh Corp.* 1960 S.C. 313). Under section 71(1) of the Housing Act 1985 a housing authority "shall have regard" to guidance given by the Secretary of State. Such guidance was described by Bridge L.J in *De Falco v. Crawley Borough Council* [1980] 1 All E.R. 913, 925, CA as having "no direct statutory force or effect." His Lordship said that "the local authority are not bound to follow [the guidance] in any particular case." Although the term "direct" is mandatory in tone it is submitted that a local authority is not bound to follow the directions of the Secretary of State made under this section and that "have regard to" should be interpreted in the manner identified in the cases mentioned above. This means that although this subsection places a local authority under an obligation to take the Secretary of State's directions into account when appointing approved social workers, it is not bound to follow the directions if it considers that they are outweighed by another material consideration, such as the need to appoint a sufficient number of approved social workers. The Secretary of State's directions are contained in paragraph 7 of DHSS Circular No. LAC(86)15 (Welsh Office Circular No. 51/86). In accordance with paragraph 7(b)(i) of this circular the Central Council for Education and Training in Social Work has published "Assuring Quality for Mental Health Social Work: Requirements for the Training of Approved Social Workers in England, Wales and Northern Ireland and of Mental Health Officers in Scotland" (2000).

Powers of entry and inspection

115. An approved social worker of a local social services authority may at **1–952** all reasonable times after producing, if asked to do so, some duly authenticated document showing that he is such a social worker, enter and inspect any premises (not being a hospital) in the area of that authority in which a mentally disordered patient is living, if he has reasonable cause to believe that the patient is not under proper care.

DEFINITIONS

approved social worker: s.145(1).   **1–953**
hospital: s.145(1).
local social services authority: s.145(1).
mental disorder: ss.1, 145(1).
patient: s.145(1).

GENERAL NOTE

This section provides approved social workers with a power to enter and inspect **1–954** premises where a mentally disordered patient is believed to be living. It does not provide the approved social worker with authority to remove the patient from the premises. The power does not apply to hospitals and it can only be exercised within the area of the approved social worker's employing authority.

A visiting headquarters, as defined by article 3 of the Visiting Forces and International Headquarters (Application of Law) Order 1999 (S.I. 1999 No. 1763), is exempted from the operation of this section (*ibid*. art. 12, Sched. 5).

The National Care Standards Commission and the National Assembly for Wales have the power to inspect establishments registered under the Care Standards Act 2000 by virtue of section 31 of that Act. The Mental Health Act Commission will visit patients who are detained in such establishments (s.120(1)(4)).

Partnership arrangement

This function of the local authority under this section is not a local authority health **1 955** related function which can be the subject of a partnership arrangement with NHS bodies under the Health Act 1999 (NHS Bodies and Local Authority Partnership Arrangements Regulations 2000 (S.I. 2000 No. 617), reg. 6 and NHS Bodies and Local Authority Partnerships Arrangements (Wales) Regulations 2000 (S.I. 2000 No. 2993 (W.193)), reg. 6).

All reasonable times: The reasonableness of the time will presumably depend upon the urgency of the situation.

After producing, if asked to do so: The right of entry is not dependent upon someone being available to whom the document can be produced (*Grove v. Eastern Gas Board* [1952] 1 K.B. 77).

Duly authenticated document: There is no statutory form for this document.

Enter and inspect: This section does not empower the approved social worker to force entry on to the premises, or to override the owner's refusal to give permission to enter. The Court of Appeal has held that a wife who is the co-owner of a house may give permission for a person to enter the house, and that person shall not be a trespasser, notwithstanding that the husband purports to refuse permission: see *Slade v. Guscott*, July 28, 1981, 78/0656, noted in L. Gostin, *Mental Health Services—Law and Practice*, 1986, at para. 21.13.5. There is also authority for the proposition that a co-occupier of premises can allow entry to another person: see the cases cited by Gostin, *ibid*.

If entry is refused, the approved social worker could point out to the person concerned that a refusal to allow the inspection to take place would constitute an offence under section 129. If this information fails to impress the obstructor and entry is still denied, the approved social worker should consider whether the facts of the case would justify him making an application to a justice of the peace under section 135(1) for a warrant authorising a policeman to enter the premises by force. The police also have a power under section 17(1)(e) of the Police and Criminal Evidence Act 1984 to enter premises without a warrant if such action is required to save "life or limb" or to prevent "serious damage to property".

Although it has been suggested that the long-recognised common law power to apprehend dangerous insane persons carries with it a power to force entry where necessary, it is submitted that, in the absence of express statutory authority, this power should not be relied on and the procedure set out in section 135 be followed if force is required (*cf.* D. Lanham *Arresting and Insane* [1974] Crim.L.R. 515).

Mentally disordered patient: The use of this phrase rather than the term "patient" (see s.145(1)), suggests that this section can only be invoked in respect of persons who have been diagnosed as being mentally disordered. If the patient is living in a nursing home or residential care home and there is some doubt as to whether he is mentally disordered, the health authority or the local authority could be asked to exercise their powers of inspection under the Registered Homes Act 1984; see the General Note to this section.

Visiting patients

Welfare of certain hospital patients

1–956   **116.**—(1) Where a patient to whom this section applies is admitted to a hospital or [, independent hospital or care home] in England and Wales (whether for treatment for mental disorder or for any other reason) then, without prejudice to their duties in relation to the patient apart from the provisions of this section, the authority shall arrange for visits to be made to him on behalf of the authority, and shall take such other steps in relation to the patient while in the hospital [independent hospital or care home] as would be expected to be taken by his parents.

(2) This section applies to—

[(a) a child or young person—

    (i) who is in the care of a local authority by virtue of a care order within the meaning of the Children Act 1989, or

    (ii) in respect of whom the rights and powers of a parent are vested in a local authority by virtue of s.16 of the Social Work (Scotland) Act 1968;]

(b) a person who is subject to the guardianship of a local social services authority under the provisions of this Act or the [Mental Health (Scotland) Act 1984]; or

(c) a person the functions of whose nearest relative under this Act or under the [Mental Health (Scotland) Act 1984] are for the time being transferred to a local social services authority.

AMENDMENTS

In subs. (2) the words in square brackets were substituted by the Mental Health (Scotland) Act 1984, s.127(1), Sched. 3, para. 55, the Courts and Legal Services Act 1990, s.116, Sched. 16, para. 42 and the Care Homes Act 2000, s.116, Sched. 4, para. 9(5).

DEFINITIONS

1–957

    patient: s.145(1).
    hospital: s.145(1).
    mental disorder: ss.1, 145(1).
    local social services authority: s.145(1).
    nearest relative: ss.26(3), 145(1).
    care home: s.145(1).
    independent hospital: s.145(1).

GENERAL NOTE

This section obliges local authorities to arrange for visits to be made to certain **1–958** categories of patients who have been admitted to hospitals, independent hospitals and care homes. It also requires local authorities to take other steps in relation to the patients as would be expected to be taken by patients' parents. There is no requirement that the patients concerned need to be receiving treatment for mental disorder. If a child is admitted to a hospital or mental nursing home in Scotland, an equivalent duty arises under section 10 of the Mental Health (Scotland) Act 1984.

Where a child is provided with accommodation by any Health Authority, Special Health Authority, NHS Trust or local education authority for a period of three months, section 85 of the Children Act 1989 requires that body to notify the appropriate local authority which shall take steps to ensure that the child's welfare is safeguarded. Similar responsibilities are placed on the proprietors of care homes and independent hospitals by section 86 of the 1989 Act.

Under section 17(1) of the Chronically Sick and Disabled Persons Act 1970 Health Authorities have to use their "best endeavours" to ensure that patients who are under 65 years of age and who suffer from a condition of chronic illness or disability are not cared for in part of a hospital which is normally used for the care of people who are over 65 years of age or are suffering from the effects of premature ageing.

The Secretary of State and, in relation to Wales, the National Assembly for Wales (S.I. 1999 No. 672, art. 2, Sched. 1) have the power to conduct, or assist other persons in conducting, research into this section so far as it relates to children looked after by local authorities (Children Act 1989, s.83).

Subsection (1)

Such other steps: Which could include discussing the patient's condition with the **1–959** hospital doctors and providing a child patient with toys and reading matter.

Subsection (2)

Paragraph (a)—child: This section does not apply to children who are wards of **1–960** court.

Paragraph (c)—for the time being transferred to a local social services authority: By virtue of section 29.

After-care

After-care

117.—(1) This section applies to persons who are detained under section 3 **1–961** above, or admitted to a hospital in pursuance of a hospital order made under section 37 above, or transferred to a hospital in pursuance of [a hospital direction made under section 45A above or] a transfer direction made under section 47 or 48 above, and then cease to be detained and [(whether or not immediately after so ceasing)] leave hospital.

(2) It shall be the duty of the [Health Authority] and of the local social services authority to provide, in co-operation with relevant voluntary agencies, after-care services for any person to whom this section applies until

such time as the [Health Authority] and the local social services authority are satisfied that the person concerned is no longer in need of such services [; but they shall not be so satisfied in the case of a patient who is subject to after-care under supervision at any time while he remains so subject.]

[(2A) It shall be the duty of the Health Authority to secure that at all times while a patient is subject to after-care under supervision—

(a) a person who is a registered medical practitioner approved for the purposes of section 12 above by the Secretary of State as having special experience in the diagnosis or treatment of mental disorder is in charge of the medical treatment provided for the patient as part of the after-care services provided for him under this section; and

(b) a person professionally concerned with any of the after-care services so provided is supervising him with a view to securing that he receives the after-care services so provided.

(2B) Section 32 above shall apply for the purposes of this section as it applies for the purposes of Part II of this Act.]

(3) In this [section "the Health Authority" means the Health Authority, and "the local social services authority" means the local social services authority, for the area] in which the person concerned is resident or to which he is sent on discharge by the hospital in which he was detained.

AMENDMENTS

The amendments to this section were made by the Health Authorities Act 1995, s.2(1), Sched. 1, para. 107(8), the Mental Health (Patients in the Community) Act 1995, s.2(1), Sched. 1, para. 15 and the Crime (Sentences) Act 1997, s.55, Sched. 4, para. 12(17).

DEFINITIONS

1–962
hospital: s.145(1).
hospital order: ss.37, 145(1).
transfer direction: ss.47, 145(1).
local social services authority: s.145(1), subs. (3).
Health Authority: s.145(1).

GENERAL NOTE

1–963
This section, which is considered in chapter 27 of the *Code of Practice*, imposes a duty to provide after-care services for certain categories of mentally disordered patients who have ceased to be detained and leave hospital. The Government argued that the inclusion of this section in the 1982 Act was unnecessary because a statutory duty already existed for local authorities to provide after-care facilities for mentally disordered patients. This duty is contained in paragraph 2(1) of Schedule 8 to the National Health Service Act 1977 which states: "A local social services authority may, with the Secretary of State's approval, and to such extent as he may direct shall, make arrangements for the purpose of the prevention of illness and for the care of persons suffering from illness and for the after-care of persons who have been so suffering." Approval for the provision by local authorities of after-care facilities for people who are or have been suffering from mental disorder was given by the Secretary of State in Appendix 3 to Department of Health Circular No. LAC(93)10 and in paragraph 3(2)(a) of that Appendix the Secretary of State directs local authorities to provide "centres (including training centres and day centres) or other facilities (including domiciliary facilities), whether in premises managed by the [local authority] or otherwise, for training or occupation of persons suffering from or who have been suffering from mental disorder". By virtue of section 22(1) of the 1977 Act a local authority acting under powers contained in Schedule 8 of that Act is required to co-operate with the health authority "in order to advance the health and welfare of

the people of England and Wales". The 1977 Act also places an obligation on Health Authorities to provide "services for the prevention of illness, the care of persons suffering from illness and the after care of persons who have suffered from illness" if these are considered appropriate as part of the health service (s.3(1)(e) and S.I. 1982 No. 287, regs 3(e)(v), 5).

The Government's argument that this section duplicates the provisions of the 1977 Act is not correct because while the 1977 Act directs local authorities and health authorities to provide for the after-care of the *generality* of mentally disordered persons, this section places a duty on local authorities and Health Authorities to consider the after-care needs of each *individual* to whom the section applies.

The nature of the obligation placed on authorities by this section was considered by Otton J. in *R. v. Ealing District Health Authority, ex p. Fox* [1993] 3 All E.R. 170. In this case a Mental Health Review Tribunal directed that the applicant, a restricted patient, be conditionally discharged, the discharge to be deferred pursuant to section 73(7) until the tribunal was satisfied that certain conditions could be met. In order for the conditions to be met and the conditional discharge to take effect, a consultant psychiatrist had to be found who would be prepared to act as the applicant's responsible medical officer. Neither the consultant forensic psychiatrist nor the consultant general psychiatrist for the applicant's home area was prepared to act as responsible medical officer as both were pessimistic about the applicant's capacity to progress in the community. The General Manager of the Health Authority wrote to the patient's responsible medical officer setting out the consultants' stance and it was this letter which formed the subject of the application for judicial review. The applicant sought a declaration that the Health Authority had erred in law in refusing to provide psychiatric supervision in the community; an order of *certiorari* to quash the health authority's decision not to provide psychiatric supervision; and an order of *mandamus* to compel the authority to provide psychiatric supervision.

Otton J. held that the applicant was entitled to an order of *certiorari* to quash the decision of the health authority not to provide psychiatric supervision in the community, and to a declaration in the following terms: "(1) that the [Health] Authority has erred in law in not attempting with all reasonable expedition and diligence to make arrangements so as to enable the applicant to comply with the conditions imposed by the mental health review tribunal; (2) that a ... Health Authority is under a duty under section 117 of the Mental Health Act 1983 to provide after-care services when a patient leaves hospital, and acts unlawfully in failing to seek to make practical arrangements for after-care prior to that patient's discharge from hospital where such arrangements are required by a Mental Health Review Tribunal in order to enable the patient to be conditionally discharged from hospital."

However, his Lordship, at 183, held "that it would not be appropriate to make an order of *mandamus* to compel the Health Authority at this stage to provide psychiatric supervision in the community for the applicant. ... Such an order would in effect compel a doctor to supervise a patient against the doctor's will where the doctor's refusal arises from an honestly held clinical judgment that the treatment is not in the patient's best interests or is not in the best interests of the community in which the supervision would take place."

His Lordship considered a "proper interpretation of this section to be that it is a **1–964** continuing duty in respect of any patient who may be discharged and falls within section 117, although the duty to any particular patient is only triggered at the moment of discharge" (at 181). His Lordship concluded, at 182, by stating that "the mere acceptance by the Health Authority of the doctors' opinions is not of itself a sufficient discharge of their obligations to proceed with reasonable expedition and diligence and to give effect to the arrangements specified and required by the mental health review tribunal .... In my judgment, if the ... Health Authority's doctors do not agree with the conditions imposed by the Mental Health Review Tribunal and are disinclined to make the necessary arrangements to supervise the applicant on his release, the ... health authority cannot let the matter rest there. The ... Health Authority is under a continuing obligation to make further endeavours to provide arrangements within its own resources or to obtain them from other health authorities who provide such services so as to put in place practical arrangements for enabling the applicant to comply with the conditions imposed by the Mental Health Review Tribunal or, at the very least, to make inquiry of other providers of such services. If the arrangements still cannot be made then the ... Health Authority should not permit an impasse to continue but refer the matter to the Secretary of State to enable him to consider exercising his power to refer the case back to the Mental Health Review Tribunal under section 71(1). Furthermore, it is not open to the ... Health Authority to contend that because there has been an intervening deterioration in the patient's condition that their obligations are at an end. This situation is met by informing the Secretary of State of the deterioration and to invite the Secretary of State to refer the case back to the Mental Health Review Tribunal under section 71." This finding was followed by Burton J. in *R. v. Camden and Islington Health Authority, ex p. K* [2000] 3 C.C.L.R. 256, where his Lordship said at 268:

> "There is no obligation on the Health Authority to instruct its own doctors or, *a fortiori*, doctors employed ... by a third party, who decline to take part in arrangements which have been prescribed as a condition by the tribunal, to do so. The most that can be expected from an authority is to clarify that such is indeed the position and, where appropriate, to expect the consultants who have declined themselves personally to take part to assist, in so far as they owe a duty either to their patient or to the authority, in exploring other possibilities."

His Lordship confimed that in these circumstances doctors are not "in any way estopped by the tribunal's decision from exercising their own professional judgment".

In *R. v. Mental Health Review Tribunal, ex p. Hall* [1999] 3 All E.R. 132, Scott Baker J. said, at 143:

> "In my judgment *ex p. Fox* supports the following propositions which I accept to be the law: (i) an authority's duty to provide after-care services includes a duty to set up the arrangements that will be required on discharge. It is not a duty that arises for the first time at the moment of discharge; (ii) an authority with a duty to provide after-care arrangements acts unlawfully by failing to seek to make arrangements for the fulfilling of conditions imposed by a Mental Health Review Tribunal ...; (iii) if such an authority is unable to make the necessary arrangements it must try to obtain them from another authority; (iv) if arrangements still cannot be made an impasse should not be allowed to continue; the case must be referred back to a Mental Health Review Tribunal through the Secretary of State."

The decisions in *Fox, Hall* and *K.* were considered by the Court of Appeal in *R. v. Camden and Islington Health Authority, ex p. K* [2001] EWCA Civ 240, where the court confirmed that this section does not impose on Health Authorities an absolute obligation to satisfy any conditions that a tribunal may specify as prerequisites to the discharge of a patient. *Per* Lord Phillips M.R.: "[This section] imposes on Health Authorities a duty to provide after care facilities for the benefit of patients who are discharged from mental hospitals. The nature and extent of those facilities must, to a degree, fall within the discretion of the Health Authority which must have regard to other demands on its budget" (para. 29). His Lordship endorsed a concession that had been made by the Health Authority that a failure to use reasonable endeavours to fulfil conditions imposed by a tribunal, in the absence of strong reasons, would be likely to be an unlawful exercise of discretion. A decision by a local authority not to provide a service under this section would need to be consistent with the authority's responsibilities under the National Health Service and Community Care Act 1990.

When the *Hall* case reached the Court of Appeal, the court held that once the tribunal has stipulated its conditions the burden is passed to the relevant authorities to make the necessary arrangements. The tribunal does not have any power to police the work of the authorities ((1999) 2 C.C.L.R. 383).

The duty of the after-care bodies to make arrangements for the discharge of the patient arises even though the professional involved in the patient's care consider that the patient is not ready to be discharged from detention: see, for example, the remarks of Hale L.J. in *Smirek v. Williams*, April 7, 2000, CA, at para. 16. If, in the opinion of the after-care bodies, there is not a realistic prospect of the patient being discharged in the foreseeable future, an after-care plan which is couched in general terms would be sufficient to discharge their obligations under this section. In *R. v. Mental Health Review Tribunal, ex p. Hall* (1999) 2 C.C.L.R. 383, 390, Kennedy L.J. said that the terms of paragraph 27.7 of the *Code of Practice* suggest that a care plan "at least in embryo" should be available before a tribunal hearing takes place.

Services provided under this section are "community care" services for the purposes of the National Health Service and Community Care Act 1990. A person who falls within subsection (1) of this section, as a person who "may be in need" of community care services (s.47(1)), must be assessed by the local authority. Under section 47(1)(b) of the 1990 Act the local authority "having regard to the results of that assessment, shall then decide whether his needs call for the provision by them of any such services". As section 117 places a *duty* on a local authority to provide after-care services, it is submitted that the correct interpretation of section 47(1)(b) is that when the assessment identifies a need for after-care services, then the authority must determine that such need calls for the provision of those services. Although the authority is placed under an obligation to provide a service that it has determined will meet an assessed need, it has a discretion in identifying the level and precise nature of the service to be provided given resource constraints. (*R. v. Gloucestershire C.C., ex p. Barry* [1997] 2 All E.R. 1, HL). A failure by a local authority to provide a care plan which complies with statutory guidance and to make a service delivery decision under section 47(1)(b) in respect of a patient who had been assessed as being fit for discharge from NHS premises, resulted in successful judicial review proceedings in *R. v. Sutton London Borough Council, ex p. Tucker* [1997] C.O.D. 144.

If a patient who is subject to this section is considered to be substantially at risk if he were not to receive after-care services after he leaves hospital, he can be made subject to application for supervised discharge if the patient's responsible medical officer believes that such supervision is likely to help secure that the patient receives such services: see section 25A *et seq.* "Patients should not be placed under supervised discharge simply with a view to ensuring that [after-care] services are provided for them, but only if they meet the [statutory] criteria" (Supplement to the *Code of Practice*, para. 7).

General guidance on the "Discharge of Patients from Hospital" can be found in **1–965** Department of Health Circular No. HC (89)5; LAC (89)7. Specific "Guidance on the discharge of mentally disordered people and their continuing care in the community" was issued by the NHS Executive as HSG(94)27. This guidance was circulated to local authorities in England with Local Authority Social Services Letter (94)4. Mentally ill patients who are discharged from hospital are subject to the Care Programme Approach which English authorities were required to introduce in 1991 (Health Circular (90)23/Local Authority Social Services Letter (90)11). In *R. v. Mental Health Review Tribunal, Torfaen County B.C. and Gwent Health Authority, ex p. Hall* (1999) 2 C.C.L.R. 361, Scott Baker J. rejected a suggestion that the Care Programme Approach does not apply to Wales. His Lordship said, at 375: "The CPA and the Welsh [Office Mental Illness Strategy] make essentially the same provision, see paragraphs 1.2 and 27.2 of the new Code of Practice and paragraphs 10,11 and 14 of WHC 95(40)." The Clinical Standards Advisory Group on Schizophrenia, HMSO, 1995, reported at Vol. 1, para. 4.39 that there had been a patchy implementation of the Care Programme Approach for section 117 patients. Similar findings were was made by the Social Services Inspectorate in *Social Services Departments and the Care Programme Approach: An Inspection*, Department of Health, 1995 and by the Sainsbury Centre for Mental Health in *Acute Problems* (2000). The Care Programme Approach was extended by NHS Management Executive Guideline HSG(94)5 which required Health Authorities to have in place by April 1 1994 contracts which ensure that "all provider units providing mental health care set up registers which identify and provide information on patients who are, or are liable to be, at risk of committing serious violence or suicide, or of serious self neglect, whether existing patients or newly accepted by the secondary psychiatric services". Revised guidance on the Care Programme Approach, *Effective Care Co-ordination in Mental Health Services: Modernising the Care Programme Approach* was published in 1999. Guidance on "Discharge Arrangements and Ongoing Care for Prisoners with Mental Illness: Liaison between the NHS and the Prison Service" is contained in a letter dated July 27, 2000, from the NHS Executive.

The relationship between the Care Programme Approach and this section is considered in paragraph 8 of the guidance attached to Health Circular No. HSG (94)27:

> "The Care Programme Approach applies whether or not a patient has been detained under the Mental Health Act, but health and local authorities also have a statutory duty under section 117 of the [Mental Health Act] to provide after-care services for patients (in all categories of mental disorder) who have been detained in hospital under section 3, 37 (whether or not with restrictions under section 41), 47 or 48 of the Act. To fulfil this duty authorities will need to ensure that the Care Programme Approach is fully implemented for mentally ill patients who have been detained, and that its principles are applied so far as they are relevant to the after-care of other detained patients. Authorities will need to establish mechanisms to monitor the application of the Care Programme Approach as a whole and should report on progress at regular intervals to authority members".

The *Report of the Inquiry into the Care and Treatment of Christopher Clunis*, HMSO, 1994, identified fourteen recommendations as a "guide to aftercare" at paragraph 44.0.3. A further recommendation that a "new form should be designed for use in all section 117 after care cases" (*ibid.*, para. 45.1.2(i)) has been acted on by the Government which has published an after-care form which is designed to be used for *all* patients discharged from psychiatric in-patient treatment. The form was attached to a letter sent by the Department of Health to the relevant statutory bodies on February 6, 1995. This letter states that the form "is not mandatory but its use is strongly recommended as good practice".

The Human Rights Act 1998

1–966   The question whether a decision not to discharge a patient who had been granted a conditional discharge by a tribunal due to a failure to put in place appropriate after-care facilities in the community would constitute a violation of Article 5 of the European Convention on Human Rights was considered by Lord Phillips M.R. in the following extract from his judgment in *R v. Camden and Islington Health Authority, ex p. K.*, above:

> "Where (i) a patient is suffering from mental illness and (ii) treatment of that illness is necessary in the interests of the patient's own health or for the

protection of others and (iii) it proves impossible or impracticable to arrange for the patient to receive the necessary treatment in the community, it seems to me that the three criteria identified by the European Court in *Winterwerp v. Netherlands* [see the note on Article 5(1)(e) under "detention"] are made out. Whether or not it is necessary to detain a patient in hospital for treatment may well depend upon the level of facilities available for treatment within the community. Neither Article 5 nor Strasbourg jurisprudence lays down any criteria as to the extent to which Member States must provide facilities for the care of those of unsound mind in the community, thereby avoiding the necessity for them to be detained for treatment in hospital.

If a Health Authority is unable, despite the exercise of all reasonable endeavours, to procure for a patient the level of care and treatment in the community that a tribunal considers to be a prerequisite to the discharge of the patient from hospital, I do not consider that the continued detention of the patient in hospital will violate the right to liberty conferred by Article 5.

Very different considerations apply to the factual situation such as that considered by the Strasbourg Court in *Johnson v. United Kingdom*. Where a patient has been cured of mental illness, he is no longer of unsound mind and the exception to the right to liberty provided for by Article 5(1)(e) does not apply. In *Johnson* the Court has recognised that, in such circumstances, it may nonetheless be legitimate to make discharge of the patient conditional rather than absolute and to defer, to some extent, the discharge to which the patient is entitled. The deferral must, however, be proportionate to its object and cannot become indefinite" (paras 33–35).

Neither Buxton nor Sedley L.JJ. followed the distinction drawn by Lord Phillips. Both were of the view that the difference between the *Winterwerp* class of case and the *Johnson* class of case is one of degree, not of kind and that once a tribunal has determined that a patient did not need to be detained, Article 5(4) requires that decision to be respected. Buxton L.J. said that the remedy would be against the public body that is detaining the patient and not the authority that is responsible for providing after-care under this section. Sedley L.J. took a contrary view in stating that the patient's remedy is an application for judicial review against the public body that is failing to put the tribunal's conditions into effect. His Lordship said:

"No judge can realistically sit as a court of appeal from a psychiatrist on a question of professional judgment. What a judge must be able to do is ensure that such judgment, to the extent that its exercise is a public law function, is made honestly, rationally and with due regard only to what is relevant. Within this boundary more than one legitimate judgment—that of the community psychiatrist as well as of the MHRT—may have to be accommodated for the purposes of Article 5(4), at least to the extent that the decision of the MHRT is explicitly dependent on the collaboration of the psychiatrist" (para. 55).

Charging for local authority services provided under section 117

In *R. v. London Borough of Richmond, ex p. Watson and other appeals* [2001] 1 All **1–967** E.R. 436, the Court of Appeal dismissed an appeal from the decision of Sullivan J. ([1999] 2 C.C.L.R. 402) by holding that as this section imposes a freestanding duty to provide after-care services, as opposed to being a "gateway" section which imposes a duty to ensure that after-care services are provided under such other enactments as may be appropriate, and as there is no express power to charge for services provided under it, such services must be provided free of charge. At the first instance hearing, Sullivan J. held that:

(i) if a charged for service is being provided to the patient prior to the patient's admission under one of the provisions set out in subsection (1), that service would have to be provided free of charge on the patient's discharge from hospital if the provision of the service was a component of the patient's after-care plan; and

(ii) the fact that a patient has either been granted leave of absence under section 17 or transferred from detention under section 3 into guardianship under the provisions of section 19, does not affect his entitlement to receive services under this section.

These findings, which are considered in Department of Health Circular LAC (2000) 3, are unaffected by the Court of Appeal's decision.

The following points arise from this decision: (1) this section does not provide the Government with a power to regulate its use; and (2) the National Assistance Act 1948 (Choice of Accommodation) Directions 1992, which only apply where accommodation is provided under section 21 of the 1948 Act, do not apply to accommodation provided under this section. Judgment in the Court of Appeal was given before the implementation of the Human Rights Act 1998. It could be argued that an informal patient who has been discharged from a psychiatric hospital and is being charged for residential accommodation that is being provided for his mental health needs would have a claim under Article 14 of the European Convention on Human Rights in that: (1) his Article 8 rights are invoked and: (b) he is suffering discrimination as a result of his non-detained status. Leave to appeal was granted by the House of Lords on June 7, 2001.

The finding of the Court of Appeal leads to the following consequences:

Case 1. A 50-year-old man with pre-senile dementia is admitted informally to hospital as a compliant mentally incompetent patient. He is assessed as requiring residential care on his discharge from hospital. He will almost certainly require such accommodation for the rest of his life. He will be charged for the accommodation by virtue of section 22 of the National Assistance Act.

Case 2. A 50-year-old man with pre-senile dementia and with identical needs to the man in Case 1 is admitted to hospital under section 3 of this Act because he happened not to be compliant when the crisis in his mental health occurred. He is assessed as requiring residential care on his discharge from hospital. He will almost certainly require such accommodation for the rest of his life. He will be provided with the accommodation without charge because he comes within the scope of section 117.

A similar result would arise if the patients were discharged from hospital with the support of a substantial package of domicillary care in circumstances where it was likely that such care would have to remain in place for many years if a further admission to hospital was to be avoided: case 1 would be charged for such services; case 2 would receive them free of charge.

In his Report on an Investigation into Complaint No. 98/B/0341, the Local Government Ombudsman found that a delay of over two years between legal advice being received which advised that charging for section 117 services was unlawful and the matter being reported to members constituted maladministration. He also recommended that the council reimburse all of the charges that had been levied on the complainant for after-care services provided under this section.

Partnership arrangements

1–968 This section is prescribed as a NHS function which may be the subject of a partnership arrangement with local authorities under the Health Act 1999 (NHS Bodies and Local Authority Partnership Arrangements Regulations 2000 (S.I. 2000 No. 617), reg. 5 and NHS Bodies and Local Authorities Partnership Arrangements (Wales) Regulations 2000 (S.I. 2000 No. 2993 (W.193)), reg. 5). Local authorities are allowed to make payments to NHS bodies toward expenditure incurred by them in connection with their performance under this section (National Health Service (Payments by Local Authorities to NHS Bodies) (Prescribed Functions) Regulations 2000 (S.I. 2000 No. 618), reg. 2 and the National Health Service (Payments by Local Authorities to Health Authorities) (Prescribed Functions) (Wales) Regulations 2001 (S.I. 2001 No. 1543), reg. 2).

Primary Care Trusts

Health Authority functions under subsections (2) and (2A) are to be exercised by **1–969** Primary Care Trusts in England in respect of patients who leave hospital and are resident in, or sent on discharge by that hospital to, the trust's area (Primary Care Trusts (Functions) (England) Regulations 2000 (S.I. 2000 No. 695), reg. 3(2)(b), (4)(c), Sched. 2).

Subsection (1)

Hospital order made under section 37: This section also applies to hospital order **1–970** patients who have been made subject to restriction orders under section 41. A person who is admitted to a hospital in pursuance of an admission order made otherwise than under section 14A of the Criminal Appeal Act 1968 shall be treated for the purposes of this Act as if he had been admitted in pursuance of a hospital order or, if the court so directs, a restriction order (Criminal Procedure (Insanity and Unfitness to Plead) Act 1991, Sched. 1, para. 2(1)).

Transfer direction made under section 47: This section also applies to transfer direction patients who have been made subject of restriction directions under section 49.

Cease to be detained: The duty to provide after-care services under this section extends to patients who, having been detained under section 3, are granted leave of absence under section 17 (*R. v. Richmond L.B.C., ex p. W.,* above). *Per* Sullivan J.: "In my view, this section is dealing with a practical problem: what after-care is to be provided for a patient who has suffered from mental illness requiring inpatient treatment when he actually leaves hospital? A person on leave under section 17 is in just as much, if not more, need of care after he leaves hospital as a person who leaves hospital subject to guardianship or supervision. For the purposes of section 17, he has ceased to be detained, and left hospital. It would be remarkable if, in such circumstances there was no duty to provide him with after-care under section 117, even though it would almost certainly have been a condition of his being given leave that he should reside in particular accommodation." His Lordship's reasoning on this point would also apply to a restricted patient who had been conditionally discharged from hospital.

Whether or not immediately after so ceasing: This section applies to a patient who has been detained under one of the sections mentioned in this subsection and who subsequently acquires informal status prior to leaving hospital. It also applies to a patient who having been discharged from the section 3, is re-detained under another provision of this Act (*e.g.* under section 5(2)) prior to his discharge from hospital.

Subsection (2)

Duty: In order to fulfil their obligations under this provision the health and social **1–971** services authorities must take reasonable steps to identify appropriate after-care facilities for the patient before his actual discharge from hospital (*R. v. Ealing District Health Authority, ex p. Fox,* above). Proper preparation by the after-care bodies is required where a patient who is subject to this provision makes an application to a Mental Health Review Tribunal. Careful investigation and research is needed to enable the bodies to present to the tribunal an up-to-date care plan with a proposal or options as to how it can be implemented (*R. v. Mental Health Review Tribunal, ex p. Hall,* above, at 145). A care plan "at least in embryo" should be put before the tribunal: see the statement made by Kennedy L.J. in the *Hall* case which is noted in the General Note to this section. The duty to provide after-care services is not broken by the patient's subsequent readmission to hospital for assessment under section 2. The duty would end on the patient's readmission under section 3: see the note under "Health Authority ... local social services authority", below.

In *R. v. Richmond LBC, ex p. A.,* noted under "Charging for local authority services provided under section 117", above, Otton L.J. said that although there is a positive duty to provide the after-care services there is clearly a discretion as to the level of provision, bearing in mind that the obligation is to each individual patient and is circumscribed by the need of the patient.

A person who is aggrieved by a failure by either the Health Authority or the local authority to meet its obligations under this section could consider the following options:

(1) making a complaint to the local authority under the machinery established by section 7B of the Local Authority Social Services Act 1970, the Local Authority Social Services (Complaints Procedure) Order 1990 (S.I. 1990 No. 2244) and the Complaints Procedure Directions 1990 or to the Health Authority under the terms of the Directions issued by the Secretary of State under section 1 of the Hospital Complaints Procedure Act 1985. Although the scope of the 1985 Act is confined to complaints made by people who either are or who have been hospital patients, the decision in the *Fox* case, above, confirms that the duty of the Health Authority under this section arises prior to the patient's discharge from hospital. If the complainant remains dissatisfied with the result of the investigation, he has a right to refer his complaint to the Commissioner for Local Administration, the Health Services Commissioner or the Mental Health Act Commission.

(2) requesting the Secretary of State to exercise his discretion under section 7D of the Local Authority Social Services Act 1970 to declare the local authority to be in default. This option is only available where it is alleged that the authority has not complied with its duty: it cannot be used to regulate the exercise of the authority's discretion under this section. A Health Authority can be declared to be in default under section 85 of the National Health Service Act 1977; and

(3) institute judicial review proceedings if it is alleged that either the Health Authority or the local authority has acted illegally, irrationally or with procedural impropriety. If a failure to comply with the requirements of this section results in a significant threat to the patient's mental health on his or her discharge from hospital, an urgent application for judicial review to obtain appropriate services can be made. An example of this occurred in *R. v. Wrexham Social Services and Housing Department, ex p. Edwards*, August 18, 2000 (noted by M.Mullins at Legal Action, Dec. 2000, 15) where Newman J. granted permission and an interim injunction requiring the provision of emergency interim accommodation and emergency support for the applicant.

When considering these alternatives the court will prefer the avenue of redress which is the most convenient, expeditious and effective (*R. v. London Borough of Sutton, ex p. Tucker* [1997] C.O.D. 144).

In *Clunis v. Camden and Islington Health Authority* [1998] 3 All E.R. 180, the Court of Appeal held that: (1) the duty under this section to provide after-care services does not give rise to a private law claim for damages if it is not fulfilled; and; (2) the primary method of enforcement of the duty is by complaint to the Secretary of State.

Health Authority ... local social services authority: In *R. v. Mental Health Review Tribunal, ex p. Hall*, above, Scott Baker J. held that for the purposes of this provision, the relevant health and social services authorities were those for the area in which the patient was resident at the time he was detained. If a patient with ordinary residence in one area is discharged to another area, it is the responsibility of the health and social services authorities for the area where the patient was resident before admission to make the necessary arrangements under this section. This is the case notwithstanding the fact that the patient might never return to that place of residence. His Lordship further held that if the patient had no place of residence at the time of his detention, the relevant authorities would be those for the area where he was sent on discharge; also see subs. (3). Scott Baker J.'s judgment is considered in

Department of Health Circular LAC (2000) 3. Paragraph 9 of the circular states: "Where a patient is discharged to an area different from that where he/she was resident at the time of admission, the 'responsible authorities' may need to purchase services in that area. They should inform the health and social services authorities in the receiving area of the arrangements made for the patient's after-care."

The responsibility of the relevant health and local authorities to provide after-care services under this section lasts until both authorities are satisfied that the patient no longer needs any after-care service for his mental health needs. The only occasion when responsibility for providing such services would be placed on new authorities is where the patient has moved to a new area and is subsequently detained under one of the provisions set out in subsection (1). Such an admission would trigger the duty under this section and require the preparation of a new after-care plan. The ruling in *Hall* would mean that the relevant after-care bodies would be the health and social services authorities for the area where the patient resided at the time of the subsequent admission.

After-care services: This section imposes a free-standing duty to provide after-care services: it is not a "gateway" section, which imposes a duty to ensure that services are provided under other relevant Acts, such as the National Assistance Act 1948 or the Chronically Sick and Disabled Person's Act 1970 (*R. v. London Borough of Richmond, ex p. W.*, noted under "Charging for local authority services provided under section 117", above). As after-care services are not defined, this section gives a considerable discretion to health and local authorities as to the nature of the services that can be provided. In *Clunis v. Camden and Islington Health Authority* (1998) 1 C.C.L.R. 215, 225, Beldam L.J. noted that:

"After-care services are not defined in the Act. They would normally include social work, support in helping the ex-patient with problems of employment, accommodation or family relationships, the provision of domiciliary services and the use of day centre and residential facilities."

In the *Richmond* case, above, the court confirmed that after-care services could include residential accommodation that is designed to care for people with mental health problems. The fact that a patient was receiving a service, such as residential care, for his mental health needs prior to his admission to hospital does mean that that service cannot be an "after-care" service for the purposes of this section on his discharge. The residential care would have been provided under the National Assistance Act 1948 prior to the admission, and under this section on discharge. In these circumstances, the patient could not be charged for the accommodation on his return to it from hospital.

The search for necessary after-care services should not be confined to those services and facilities provided directly by the health and social services authorities. Also see the note on "satisfied", below.

In order to help authorities develop their after-care services the Mental Health Act Commission has prepared a checklist of desirable features for an after-care policy: see Appendix 3 to the Commission's Third Biennial Report 1987–89.

Any person: The local authority and Health Authority must assess the particular after-care needs of each person to whom this section applies. No person is legally obliged to accept the after-care services that are offered to him.

If the person is a child, the local authority should ensure that it complies with its responsibilities under Part III of the Children Act 1989.

Satisfied: The relevant health and social services authorities can only be satisfied that the person concerned is no longer in need of after-care services if they have monitored that person's progress in the community since discharge. The duty to provide after care services continues until *both* authorities have come to a decision that the patient no longer needs *any* after-care service. In this context it is suggested that an after-care service is a service which: (1) is provided in response to an assessed mental health need of the patient; and (2) reduces the prospect of the patient being re-admitted to hospital for treatment for his or her mental disorder. Many patients will require such services for substantial periods. An unwillingness to receive after-care services should not be equated with an absence of need for such services. A patient's continued refusal to receive after-care services should be confirmed by professional inquiry at appropriate intervals.

Subject to after-care under supervision: The relevant Health Authority and local authority are required to keep under review after-care services provided for a patient who is subject to supervised discharge (s.25E).

Subsection (2A)

1–972   *Approved ... by the Secretary of State:* Or by the National Assembly for Wales (S.I. 2000 No. 253, Sched. 3).

Professionally concerned: See the note on "the other" in section 57(3).

Subsection (3)

1–973   *Health Authority ... local social services authority:* See the note on subsection (2).

Area in which the person concerned is resident: Reference should be made to Department of Health Circular No. LAC(93)7 which contains guidance on the identification of the ordinary residence of people who require services under the National Assistance Act 1948. The Department of Health will arbitrate in cases where there is a dispute about residence.

Functions of the Secretary of State

Code of practice

1–974   **118.**—(1) The Secretary of State shall prepare, and from time to time revise, a code of practice—

(a)   for the guidance of registered medical practitioners, managers and staff of hospitals and [, independent hospitals and care homes] and approved social workers in relation to the admission of patients to hospitals and [registered establishments] under this Act [and to guardianship and after-care under supervision under this Act]; and

(b)   for the guidance of registered medical practitioners and members of other professions in relation to the medical treatment of patients suffering from mental disorder.

(2) The code shall, in particular, specify forms of medical treatment in addition to any specified by regulations made for the purposes of section 57 above which in the opinion of the Secretary of State give rise to special concern and which should accordingly not be given by a registered medical practitioner unless the patient has consented to the treatment (or to a plan of treatment including that treatment) and a certificate in writing as to the matters mentioned in subsection (2)(a) and (b) of that section has been given by another registered medical practitioner, being a practitioner appointed for the purposes of this section by the Secretary of State.

(3) Before preparing the code or making any alteration in it the Secretary of State shall consult such bodies as appear to him to be concerned.

(4) The Secretary of State shall lay copies of the code and of any alteration in the code before Parliament; and if either House of Parliament passes a resolution requiring the code or any alteration in it to be withdrawn the Secretary of State shall withdraw the code or alteration and, where he

withdraws the code, shall prepare a code in substitution for the one which is withdrawn.

(5) No resolution shall be passed by either House of Parliament under subsection (4) above in respect of a code or alteration after the expiration of the period of 40 days beginning with the day on which a copy of the code or alteration was laid before that House; but for the purposes of this subsection no account shall be taken of any time during which Parliament is dissolved or prorogued or during which both Houses are adjourned for more than four days.

(6) The Secretary of State shall publish the code as for the time being in force.

AMENDMENT

In subs. (1)(a) the words in square brackets were inserted by the Mental Health (Patients in the Community) Act 1995, s.2(1), Sched. 1, para. 16 and the Care Standards Act 2000, s.116, Sched. 4, para. 9(6).

DEFINITIONS

the managers: s.145(1).   **1–975**
hospital: s.145(1).
mental nursing home: s.145(1).
approved social worker: s.145(1).
care home: s.145(1).
independent hospital: s.145(1)
registered establishment: s.145(1).
patient: s.145(1).
medical treatment: s.145(1).
mental disorder: ss.1, 145(1).

GENERAL NOTE

This section imposes a duty on the Secretary of State (and, in relation to Wales, the **1–976** National Assembly for Wales) to prepare, publish and from time to time revise, a Code of Practice for the guidance of those concerned with the admission, treatment, guardianship and after-care of mentally disordered patients. The Code, which cannot override the powers contained in this Act, is not mandatory in that professionals carrying out functions under this Act are not legally obliged to follow the advice contained in it. A failure to have regard to the Code could be used in legal proceedings as *prima facie* evidence of bad practice, although the effect of non-compliance will largely depend upon the nature of the provision in the Code that has not been followed. Such a failure could also influence the judgment of an employer, the local government ombudsman, the Health Service Commissions and the Mental Health Act Commission.

The Employment Protection Act 1975, section 6 provided for "Codes of Practice". In *Lewis Shops Group v. Wiggins* [1973] I.C.R. 335 at 338, a decision under the Industrial Relations Act 1971, Sir Hugh Griffiths, giving the judgment of the National Industrial Relations Court, said:

"But even in a case in which the Code of Practice is directly in point, it does not follow that a dismissal must as a matter of law be deemed unfair because an employer does not follow the procedures recommnded in the code .... The code is, of course, always one important factor to be taken into account in the case, but its significance will vary according to the particular circumstances of each individual case."

Certain passages of the *Code* go beyond the boundaries of guidance. In *R. v.*

Secretary for State for Health, ex p. Pfizer Ltd (1999) 2 C.C.L.R. 270, Collins J. held that Government guidance which is expressed in unqualified and mandatory language and which appeared to override the clinical judgment which a doctor was entitled to exercise in an individual case, was unlawful.

The guidance contained in the *Code* should not be followed if it is considered to be legally incorrect or if its application cannot be professionally justified (see, for example, para. 2.20.59 of the Report of the Committee of Inquiry into the Personality Disorder Unit, Ashworth Special Hospital (1999) where para. 26.3 of the *Code* was described as being "untenable" in the context of a special hospital). The *Code* "should be read in conjunction with the *Memorandum*" (*ibid.*, para. 3).

The Code can specify forms of treatment which give rise to special concern and which should not be given without the patient's consent and an independent second medical opinion (subs. (2)).

The latest edition of the *Code* was laid before Parliament on December 3, 1998 and came into force on April 1, 1999. It was considered by the First Standing Committee on Delegated Legislation, January 26, 1999. A supplement to the Code of Practice giving guidance on the supervised discharge arrangements introduced by the Mental Health (Patients in the Community) Act 1995, was published in February 1996 and became effective on April 1, 1996. This guidance remains extant (*Code of Practice*, para. 28.9).

An interesting account of the lengthy gestation period of the first edition of the *Code of Practice* can be found in "The Mental Health Act *Code of Practice*," Phil Fennell, *Modern Law Review*, Vol. 53, No. 4, July 1990, pp. 499–507. Also see Michael Caradino, "Commissions and Codes: A Case Study in Law and Public Administration," [1993] *Public Law*, pp. 333–345 and Genevra Richardson, *Law, Process and Custody: Prisoners and Patients*, 1993, pp. 221–223.

Subsection (1)

1–977   *Secretary of State:* Both the 1981 White Paper (Cmnd. 8405, para. 38) and Ministers speaking on the Mental Health (Amendment) Bill in Parliament (see, for example Kenneth Clarke's statement to the Special Standing Committee at its June 17, 1982 sitting, col. 592) assumed that it would be the responsibility of the Mental Health Act Commission to produce the *Code of Practice*. However, this duty is given directly to the Secretary of State who has a responsibility to consult under subsection (3). The function of submitting proposals as to the contents of the Code is delegated to the Management Board of the Mental Health Act Commission (S.I. 1983, No. 892, para. 3(2)(d) and S.I. 1983 No. 894, reg. 7(2)(a)).

The functions of the Secretary of State, so far as exercisable in relation to Wales, are exercised by the National Assembly for Wales (S.I. 1999 No. 672, art. 2, Sched. 1).

Revise: "At the beginning of 1990 the Secretary of State asked the [Mental Health Act] Commission to monitor the implementation of the *Code of Practice* and to advise Ministers of any changes to the Code which the Commission feels might be appropriate" (M.H.A.C. Sixth Biennial Report, 1993–1995, Appendix 1, para. 1.2).

Paragraph (a)—Guidance: Which need not be restricted to the exercise of powers or the discharge of duties under this Act.

Paragraph (b)— This provision is not limited to the hospital care of patients but will also cover care in the community. Given that "medical treatment" is defined very widely in section 145(1), the Code should cover most aspects of the care of mentally disordered people. The published Code adopts a far narrower focus.

Subsection (2)

1–978   *Specify forms of medical treatment:* The Code has not added to the forms of treatment covered by section 57.

Opinion of the Secretary of State: The function of proposing additional section 57 treatments has been delegated to the Management Board of the Mental Health Act Commission (S.I. 1983 No. 892, para. 3(2)(d) and S.I. 1983 No. 894, reg. 7(2)(a)).

Practitioner appointed ... by the Secretary of State: The appointment will be made by the Mental Health Act Commission (s.121(2)(a) and S.I. 1983 No. 892, para. 3(2)(a)).

Practitioners approved for Part IV and s.118

119.—(1) The Secretary of State may make such provision as he may with **1–979** the approval of the Treasury determine for the payment of remuneration, allowances, pensions or gratuities to or in respect of registered medical practitioners appointed by him for the purposes of Part IV of this Act and section 118 above and to or in respect of other persons appointed for the purposes of section 57(2)(a) above.

(2) A registered medical practitioner or other person appointed by the Secretary of State for the purposes of the provisions mentioned in subsection (1) above may, for the purpose of exercising his functions under those provisions, at any reasonable time—

(a) visit and interview and, in the case of a registered medical practitioner, examine in private any patient detained in a [registered establishment]; and

(b) require the production of and inspect any records relating to the treatment of the patient in that home.

AMENDMENT

The words in square brackets in subs. (2) were substituted by the Care Standards Act 2000, s.116, Sched. 4, para. 9(2).

DEFINITIONS

patient: s.145(1). **1–980**
nursing home: s.145(1).
registered establishment: ss.34(1), 145(1).

GENERAL NOTE

This section provides for the payment of medical practitioners appointed by the **1–981** Secretary of State to carry out certain functions under this Act, and for them to have access to detained patients cared for in registered establishments, and their records. For the right of access to detained patients cared for in hospitals, and their records, see the direction of the Secretary of State reproduced in the note on section 120(4).

Subsection (1)

Secretary of State: The functions of the Minister, so far as exercisable in relation to **1–982** Wales, are exercised by the National Assembly for Wales. The Treasury approval requirement continues to have effect so far as it relates to pensions (S.I. 1999 No. 672, art. 2, Sched. 1).

Subsection (2)

Anyone who obstructs a person in the exercise of his functions under this section **1–983** commits an offence under section 129.

General protection of detained patients

120.—(1) The Secretary of State shall keep under review the exercise of **1–984** the powers and the discharge of the duties conferred or imposed by this Act so far as relating to the detention of patients or to patients liable to be detained under this Act and shall make arrangements for persons authorised by him in that behalf—

(a) to visit and interview in private patients detained under this Act in hospitals and [registered establishments]; and

(b) to investigate—

    (i) any complaint made by a person in respect of a matter that occurred while he was detained under this Act in a hospital or [registered establishment] and which he considers has not been satisfactorily dealt with by the managers of that hospital or [registered establishment]; and

    (ii) any other complaint as to the exercise of the powers or the discharge of the duties conferred or imposed by this Act in respect of a person who is or has been so detained.

(2) The arrangements made under this section in respect of the investigation of complaints may exclude matters from investigation in specified circumstances and shall not require any person exercising functions under the arrangements to undertake or continue with any investigation where he does not consider it appropriate to do so.

(3) Where any such complaint as is mentioned in subsection (1)(b)(ii) above is made by a Member of Parliament and investigated under the arrangements made under this section the results of the investigation shall be reported to him.

(4) For the purpose of any such review as is mentioned in subsection (1) above or of carrying out his functions under arrangements made under this section any person authorised in that behalf by the Secretary of State may at any reasonable time—

(a) visit and interview and, if he is a registered medical practitioner, examine in private any patient in a [registered establishment]; and

(b) require the production of and inspect any records relating to the detention or treatment of any person who is or has been detained in a [registered establishment].

(5) [*Repealed by the Registered Homes Act 1984, s.57(3), Sched. 3.*]

(6) The Secretary of State may make such provision as he may with the approval of the Treasury determine for the payment of remuneration allowances, pensions or gratuities to or in respect of persons exercising functions in relation to any such review as is mentioned in subsection (1) above or functions under arrangements made under this section.

(7) The powers and duties referred to in subsection (1) above do not include any power or duty conferred or imposed by Part VII of this Act.

AMENDMENTS

The words in square brackets in subss. (1) and (4) were substituted by the Care Standards Act 2000. s.116, Sched. 4, para. 9(2).

DEFINITIONS

1–985   patients: s.145(1).

hospital: s.145(1).

the managers: s.145(1).

registered establishment: ss.34(1), 145(1).

GENERAL NOTE

1–986   This section places duties relating to the general protection of detained patients on the Secretary of State and the National Assembly for Wales. By virtue of section 121(2)(b), and S.I. 1983 No. 892, paragraph 3(2)(c), the Secretary of State has directed the Mental Health Act Commission to carry out the following duties on his behalf. The duties are: (1) to keep under review the exercise of the powers and duties contained in this Act which relate to detained patients and to patients liable to be detained; (2) to visit and interview patients detained under this Act in hospitals and registered establishments; and (3) to investigate complaints that come within the Commission's jurisdiction. The Commission does not have the power to directly enforce any recommendations that it might make arising from the exercise of these duties. During the course of their duties Commissioners will write reports which deal with the specific circumstances of individual patients. This Act does not place any obligation on the Commission to disclose such reports following a request by the patient or his advisers (*R. v. Mental Health Act Commission, ex p. X* (1988) 9 B.M.L.R. 77, DC). *Per* Stuart-Smith L.J. at 87: "Save where it is so ordered by the court disclosure of ... reports should remain a matter of discretion on the part of the Commission."

Subsection (1)
Secretary of State: The functions of the Minister under this section, so far as **1–987** exercisable in relation to Wales, are exercised by the National Assembly for Wales (S.I. 1999 No. 672, art. 2, Sched. 1).

Keep under review: The Commission does not have the power to discharge an inappropriately detained patient or to inspect and report on the general services that are available to mentally disordered patients.

A key mechanism that the Commission uses to fulfil its review function is the regular visiting of hospitals. The Commission also meets with representatives of local social services departments. Commission policies for these visits and meetings are set out in chapter 2 of its *Seventh Biennial Report* 1995–1997. "In their visits the Commission members will make themselves available to detained patients who wish to see them, will ensure that staff are helping patients to understand their legal position and their rights. They will look at patients' records of admission and renewal of detention and at records relating to treatment. They will also ensure that detained patients are satisfied with the handling of any complaints they may make" (Cmnd. 8405, para. 32).

Powers and ... duties: Excluding the powers or duties conferred or imposed by Part VII of this Act (subs. (7)).

Liable to be detained: For example, a patient on leave of absence.

Paragraph (a)
To visit and interview ... patients: In a letter to Health Authorities dated December **1–988** 21, 1984, the Chairman of the Mental Health Act Commission announced that the Commission has "decided as a matter of policy that a few visits [to hospitals] will take place without prior announcement" and that "visits may also take place at night."

Rights of access to patients and their records are conferred by subsection (4), for registered establishments, and by a direction of the Secretary of State (reproduced in the note on subsection (4)) for hospitals.

Detained under this Act: Although the duty to interview patients does not extend to patients who have been made subject to the guardianship provisions of this Act the Commission's policy is to "meet with clients [of social services departments], including those subject to guardianship, who have requested an interview" (Sixth Biennial Report, 1993–1995, Appendix 8.1, para. 15 iii). As the Commission does not have jurisdiction to examine the individual circumstances of patients subject to guardianship or to review the exercise by local authorities of their powers under guardianship, this aspect of the Commission's policy would appear to be *ultra vires*.

Paragraph (b)
Complaint: This paragraph "defines two types of complaints which the Com- **1–989** mission may investigate:

- any complaint made by a person in respect of a matter which occurred while he was detained under the Act, and which has not been dealt with to his satisfaction by the managers of a hospital or Registered Mental Nursing Home;
- any other complaint as to the exercise of powers and discharge of duties conferred or imposed by the Act in respect of a detained patient" (Mental Health Act Commission, Sixth Biennial Report, 1993–1995, para. 4.1)

The Commission has policies for the investigation of complaints, for the reinvestigation of complaints about Commissioners, and for the investigation of complaints against Second Opinion Approved Doctors. These are reproduced at *ibid*, Appendix 8, paras 4, 5 and 6.

The Commission need not investigate a complaint where it considers this course of action to be "appropriate" (subs. (2)).

The Report of the Committee of Inquiry into Complaints about Ashworth Hospital described the Commission's complaints jurisdiction as an "impossible task" (Cm. 2028, Vol. 1, p. 139). For a response, see W. Bingley and L. Blom-Cooper, "Sharp Eyes: Keen Ears" *Community Care*, October 15, 1992, p. 23. Chapter 24 *Code of Practice* considers the general issue of complaints.

Any person who obstructs the Commission in the exercise of its complaints jurisdiction could be guilty of an offence under section 129.

Sub-paragraph (i)

1–990   *A person:* The patient or ex-patient. Although the wording of this provision precludes a complaint being made in respect of a deceased patient, it is permissible for the Commission to continue to investigate a complaint which has been made by a patient who subsequently dies before the investigation has been completed.

"It is of course open to patients to instruct an agent to complain on their behalf under either section 120(1)(b)(i) or (ii), but this depends upon the patients having the necessary mental capacity to authorise an agent so to act" (Mental Health Act Commission, Second Biennial Report, 1985–1987, para. 6.4). It is the view of the Commission that it is not legally permissible for a nearest relative to make a complaint under paragraph (i) on behalf of a patient who lacks the capacity to give the necessary authorisation. The Commission has also considered a problem that arises as a result of the confidential nature of the relationship between the responsible medical officer and the patient: "If the complainant is a person other than the patient, and the patient is incapable of authorising the disclosure of confidential information to that person, then the Commission has taken the view that it must respect the patient's right to have that information remain confidential and have not disclosed it to the complainant" (*ibid*).

A matter: Which does not necessarily have to relate to the exercise of powers or the discharge of duties under this Act. It could include matters of clinical judgment. In its *Seventh Biennial Report* 1995–1997, the Commission stated that "it will no longer exclude consideration of complaints about clinical judgement when deciding whether to investigate a complaint" (para. 6.1).

That occurred: The Commission can investigate a complaint made by an ex-patient as long as the complaint relates to a period when the patient was detained under this Act.

He considers: i.e. the subjective opinion of the patient. If the person authorised by the Commission concludes that the patient's complaint has been satisfactorily dealt with by the managers, he need not undertake an investigation (subs. (2)).

By the managers: The patient cannot complain directly to the Commission in the first instance.

Sub-paragraph (ii)

Any other complaint: Which does not have to be made by the patient himself. **1–991**
Where a complaint falls into this category, it is not necessary for the complainant to
have first used the hospital or social services complaints machinery. See subsection
(3) for complaints made by a Member of Parliament.

Exercise of the powers or the discharge of the duties: In *R. v. Mental Health Act
Commission, ex p. Smith* (1998) 43 B.M.L.R. 174, complaints were made to the
Commission is respect of a hospital patient who had committed suicide during a
period when he was subject to detention under section 3 of this Act. There were four
essential complaints:

(i) it was said that the patient's original detention was neither appropriate nor
legal;
(ii) it was said that he was inappropriately detained in a secure unit for a period;
(iii) it was alleged that the patient was given drugs in such quantities that it was
unlikely that he could have given consent, and the level of dosage was
inappropriate; and
(iv) it was said that the patient was inadequately cared for during his detention,
and his condition was not adequately assessed for the purposes of determining whether there was any risk of self harm.

The Commission had always been prepared to accept jurisdiction to entertain
complaint (i), was persuaded that it had jurisdiction to accept complaint (iii), but only
to a limited extent, but considered that it did not have jurisdiction to entertain
complaints (ii) and (iv).

On a judicial review of the Commission's decision, Latham J. held that it is too
restrictive to construe this provision as referring only to the express powers and
duties set down in the Act. Rights and duties which flow necessarily and by necessary
implication from the patient's detention also come within its scope. It followed that
any complaints arising out of the exercise of the power to detain, manage and control,
and the duty to treat detained patients could be investigated by the Commission.
Accordingly, the Commission had jurisdiction to consider complaints (ii) and (iv),
and had an unrestricted jurisdiction to consider complaint (iii).

Person: Who could be dead at the time when the complaint is made.

Who is or has been so detained: The patient could be an informal patient at the time
when the complaint is made.

Subsection (2)

Shall not require: The Commission has a discretion not to investigate a complaint **1–992**
or to discontinue investigating a complaint.

Appropriate to do so: If, for example, the investigation would more appropriately
be made by the Health Service Commissioner.

Subsection (4)

Anyone who obstructs an authorised person in the exercise of his functions under **1–993**
this section commits an offence under section 129.

Secretary of State: The Mental Health Act Commission will perform this function
(s.121(2)(b) and S.I. 1983 No. 892, para. 3(2)(c)).

Registered establishment: As far as hospitals are concerned the Secretary of State
issued the following Direction to District Health Authorities and Special Health
Authorities as Annex A to D.H.S.S. Circular No. HC(83)19:

"The Secretary of State for Social Services, in exercise of the powers conferred on
him by section 17 of the National Health Service Act 1977 and all other powers
enabling him in that behalf, hereby gives the following Direction:—
1. In this Direction 'Authority' means a District Health Authority or special health

authority responsible for the administration of a health service hospital or special hospital.

2. Each Authority is hereby directed, in the exercise of functions which the Authority has been directed to exercise, to make arrangements to ensure that—

(1) any records which are required to be made under the Mental Health (Hospitals, Guardianship and Consent to Treatment) Regulations 1983 (S.I. 1983/893), and which relate to the detention or treatment of a patient in a hospital for which the Authority is responsible, are kept for a period of not less than 5 years commencing on the date on which the person to whom they relate ceases to be a patient in that hospital:

(2) any person—

    (a) authorised by the Mental Health Act Commission for the purpose of carrying out any review mentioned in section 120(1) of the Mental Health Act 1983 or of carrying out the functions of that Commission under arrangements made under that section; or

    (b) being a registered medical practitioner appointed by that Commission for the purposes of Part IV or section 118(2) of that Act; or

    (c) being a person appointed by that Commission for the purposes of section 57(2)(a) of that Act,

is able for the said purposes, at any reasonable time,—

    (i) to visit and interview, and if that person is a registered medical practitioner examine, in private any patient in a hospital for which the Authority is responsible;

    (ii) in the case of a practitioner or any other person to whom sub-paragraph (b) or (c) above applies, to require the production of and inspect any records relating to the treatment of that patient in that hospital; and

    (iii) in any other case, to require the production of and inspect any records relating to the detention or treatment of any person who is or has been detained in a hospital for which the Authority is responsible."

The Secretary of State issued the following Direction with Department of Health Circular No. HC(91)29: "That each NHS trust shall comply with the Direction set out at Annex A to HC(83)19 as if a reference in that Direction to an Authority included a reference to a NHS trust is responsible for the administration of a hospital." The equivalent Welsh Office circulars are WHC (83)25 and WHC (92)10.

Subsection (6)

1–994   *Secretary of State:* See subsection (1). With regard to the National Assembly for Wales, the Treasury approval requirement continues in effect so far as it relates to pensions (S.I. 1999 No. 672, art. 2, Sched. 1).

Subsection (7)

1–995   The Mental Health Act Commission has jurisdiction to review the exercise of the powers and duties exercised by a tribunal under Part V of the Act in so far as they relate to patients who are liable to be detained.

Mental Health Act Commission

1–996   **121.**—(1) Without prejudice to section 126(3) of the National Health Service Act 1977 (powers to vary or revoke orders or directions) there shall continue to be a [Special Health Authority] known as the Mental Health Act Commission established under section 11 of that Act.

(2) Without prejudice to the generality of his powers under section 13 of that Act, the Secretary of State shall direct the Commission to perform on his behalf—

    (a) the function of appointing registered medical practitioners for the purposes of Part IV of this Act and section 118 above and of appointing other persons for the purposes of section 57(2)(a) above; and

(b) the functions of the Secretary of State under sections 61 and 120(1) and (4) above.

(3) The registered medical practitioners and other persons appointed for the purposes mentioned in subsection (2)(a) above may include members of the Commission.

(4) The Secretary of State may, at the request of or after consultation with the Commission and after consulting such other bodies as appear to him to be concerned, direct the Commission to keep under review the care and treatment, or any aspect of the care and treatment, in hospitals [, independent hospitals and care homes] of patients who are not liable to be detained under this Act.

(5) For the purpose of any such review as is mentioned in subsection (4) above any person authorised in that behalf by the Commission may at any reasonable time—

(a) visit and interview and, if he is a registered medical practitioner, examine in private any patient in [an independent hospital or a care home]; and

(b) require the production of and inspect any records relating to the treatment of any person who is or has been a patient in [an independent hospital or a care home].

(6) The Secretary of State may make such provision as he may with the approval of the Treasury determine for the payment of remuneration, allowances, pensions or gratuities to or in respect of persons exercising functions in relation to any such review as is mentioned in subsection (4) above.

(7) The Commission shall review any decision to withhold a postal packet (or anything contained in it) under subsection (1)(b) or (2) of section 134 below if an application in that behalf is made—

(a) in a case under subsection (1)(b), by the patient; or

(b) in a case under subsection (2), either by the patient or by the person by whom the postal packet was sent;

and any such application shall be made within six months of the receipt by the applicant of the notice referred to in subsection (6) of that section.

(8) On an application under subsection (7) above the Commission may direct that the postal packet which is the subject of the application (or anything contained in it) shall not be withheld and the managers in question shall comply with any such direction.

(9) The Secretary of State may by regulations make provision with respect to the making and determination of applications under subsection (7) above, including provision for the production to the Commission of any postal packet which is the subject of such an application.

(10) The Commission shall in the second year after its establishment and subsequently in every second year publish a report on its activities; and copies of every such report shall be sent by the Commission to the Secretary of State who shall lay a copy before each House of Parliament.

(11) Paragraph 9 of Schedule 5 to the said Act of 1977 (pay and allowances for chairmen and members of [Special Health Authorities]) shall have effect in relation to the Mental Health Act Commission as if references in

413

sub-paragraphs (1) and (2) to the Chairman included references to any member and as if sub-paragraphs (4) and (5) were omitted.

AMENDMENTS
In subss. (1) and (11) the words in square brackets were substituted by the Health Authorities Act 1995, s.2(1), Sched. 1, para. 107(9). In subss. (4) and (5) the words in square brackets were substituted by the Care Standards Act 2000, s.116, Sched. 4, para. 9(7).

DEFINITIONS
1–997   hospital: s.145(1).
        patient: s.145(1).
        Special Health Authority: s.145(1).
        independent hospital: s.145(1).
        care home: s.145(1).

GENERAL NOTE
1–998   The Mental Health (Amendment) Act 1982 (Commencement No. 1) Order 1983 (S.I. 1983 No. 890) brought into force section 56(1) and (11) of the 1982 Act which provide for the establishment of the Mental Health Act Commission as a special health authority. This section provides for the continuance of the Commission. The Commission carries out certain functions on the Secretary of State's and the National Assembly for Wales's behalf (subs. (2)) and reviews the decision to withhold a postal packet if an application is made to it to do so (subs. (7)). A duty is also placed on the Commission to present a biennial report to Parliament on its activities (subs. 10)). The present structure of the Commission is described in paragraphs 1.6 to 1.12 of its *Eighth Biennial Report* 1997–1999. An account of the reasons for the creation of the Commission is given by M. Cavadino in "Commissions and Codes: A Case Study in Law and Public Administration" [1993] *Public Law*, 333–345. Also see, M. Barnes, "Citizens in detention: the role of the Mental Health Act Commission in protecting the rights of detained patients" (1996) 22 *Local Government Studies* 28–46.
     The functions of the Commission are:

(1) to keep under review the exercise of the powers and duties contained in this Act which relate to detained patients and to patients liable to be detained (s.120(1) and subs. (2)(b));
(2) to visit and interview patients detained under this Act in hospitals and registered establishments (s.120(1)(a) and subs. (2)(b));
(3) to investigate complaints that come within the Commission's jurisdiction (s.120(1)(b) and subs. (2)(b));
(4) to appoint medical practitioners and other persons for the purposes of providing a second opinion and verifying consent under the consent to treatment provisions contained in Part IV of this Act (subs. (2));
(5) to receive and examine reports on treatment given under the consent to treatment provisions (subs. (2));
(6) submitting proposals as to the content and revision of the *Code of Practice* published under section 118 of this Act (these functions have been delegated to the Commission's Management Board; see the note on s.118(1));
(7) submitting proposals, for the purposes of section 118(2) of forms of medical treatment in addition to any specified in regulations made for the purposes of section 57 which in the opinion of the Commission give rise to special concern (see the note on s.118(2));
(8) to review decisions of hospital managers to withhold the correspondence of detained patients (subs. (7)); and,
(9) to publish a biennial report on its activities (subs. (10)) (this function has been delegated to the Commission's Management Board).

Only the last two of these functions are performed by the Commission in its own right: all of the others are delegated powers exercised on behalf of the Secretary of State and the National Assembly for Wales. The Commission can also be directed by the Secretary of State to keep under review the care and treatment of informal patients in hospitals and mental nursing homes (subs. (4)). According to the Minister of State at the Department of Health, the Commission does not have jurisdiction to examine the physical environment of a hospital (Standing Committee G (Care Standards Bill), col.312).

The address of Mental Health Act Commission is: Maid Marian House, 56 Houndsgate, Nottingham, NG1 6BG. Tel: 0115 943 7100, Fax: 0115 943 7101.

As a special health authority the Commission has established a policy and procedure in accordance with the Hospital Complaints Procedure Act 1985, for complaints made against Commissioners: see the note on "complaint" in section 120(1)(b).

The Commission is a body which is subject to investigation by the Health Service Commissioner: see the Health Service Commissioners Act 1993, section 2 and the Health Service Commissioner for England (Mental Health Act Commission) Order 1993 (S.I. 1993 No. 1114). Complaints which allege that injustice or hardship has been sustained in consequence of maladministration by the Commission or its officers may, subject to the provisions of the 1993 Act, be investigated by the Commissioner (*ibid.* s.3).

The Human Rights Act 1998
As the Mental Health Act Commission performs functions of a public nature it is a **1–999** "public authority" for the purposes of section 6 of the 1998 Act.

Subsection (1)
Mental Health Act Commission: The Commission's constitution is provided for in **1–1000** the Mental Health Act Commission (Establishment and Constitution) Order 1983 (S.I. 1983 No. 892). The Mental Health Act Commission Regulations 1983 (S.I. 1983 No. 894), as amended by S.I. 1990 No. 1331 and S.I. 1995 No. 2630, deal with the appointment and tenure of office of the chairman and members of the Commission, and for meetings, and procedure of the Commission. Meetings of the Commission are open to the public (the Special Health Authorities (Establishment and Constitution Orders) Amendment Order 1998 (S.I. 1998 No. 1577), art. 5).

Subsection (2)
Generality of his powers: Section 13 of the National Health Service Act 1977 **1–1001** authorises the Secretary of State to direct a special health authority to exercise on his behalf such of his functions relating to the health service as are specified in the directions.

Secretary of State: The functions of the Minister under this section, so far as exercisable in relation to Wales, are exercised by the National Assembly for Wales (S.I. 1999 No. 672, art. 2, Sched. 1).

Shall direct: The Secretary of State's directions are contained in article 3 of S.I. 1983 No. 892.

The function of appointing: The Mental Health Act Commission performs a public law function when acting under this paragraph and no duty of care arises (*X v. A, B and C and the Mental Health Act Commission* (1991) 9 B.M.L.R. 91.)

Subsection (4)
Direct: The Secretary of State has not issued a direction under this provision. The **1–1002** Government announced that it did not intend to invoke this power straight away "since the Commission's first priority must be the responsibilities for detained patients"; *per* Lord Trefgarne, H.L. Vol. 435, col. 541. In May 1996 the Mental Health Act Commission requested the Secretary of State to extend its remit to cover certain

aspects of the treatment of informal patients and children who are detained in hospital under child care law. The request was declined (M.H.A.C., *Second Biennial Report*, 1985–1987, para. 17.1).

Treatment: The *Code of Practice* covers treatment given to all categories of patients suffering from mental disorder (s.118(1)(b)).

Any aspect of the care and treatment: Note the extent of this power.

In hospitals, independent hospitals and care homes: But not in the community.

Subsection (5)

1–1003   Anyone who obstructs a person authorised by the Commission to carry out the review mentioned in subsection (4) commits an offence under section 129.

Subsection (6)

1–1004   *Secretary of State:* See subsection (2). With regard to the National Assembly for Wales, the Treasury approval requirement continues in effect so far as it relates to pensions (S.I. 1999 No. 672, art. 2, Sched. 1).

Subsection (7)

1–1005   *The Commission shall review:* The Commission's procedure in relation to its responsibilities under this provision is set out in paragraph 8.7 of Appendix 8 to its Sixth Biennial Report, 1993–1995:

"(A) *Introduction*

The powers of hospital managers to examine and withhold postal packets and their duties when they exercise those powers, are set out in section 134 of the Mental Health Act 1983 and the Mental Health (Hospital, Guardianship and Consent to Treatment) Regulations (S.I. 1983 No. 893). Where a packet or anything contained in it is withheld the duties include notifying within seven days, the patient and, if known, the person by whom the packet was sent, of a right of review of the decision by the Mental Health Act Commission.

By section 121(7) and (8) of the Act and the regulations, the Commission is given complete discretion in the way it should conduct this review (which must be made to it within six months of the receipt of the notice) and it may direct that the packet be not withheld.

(B) *Procedure for the exercise of the Commission's powers:—*
   (1) Relevant Special Hospital Panel (SHP) Executive Officer or visiting Commissioner receive "appeal" from patient and/or sender of package. This need not necessarily be in writing.
   (2) A minimum of two, and not more than three Commissioners nominated by the SHP convenor to review the decision.
   (3) Relevant Executive Officer notifies hospital of receipt of "appeal" and the arrangements made by Commissioners to hear it, and asks for their written explanation of the grounds for withholding the package or item within the terms of section 134(1) and (2) and the details of the procedure they have followed.
   (4) A visit should be arranged at which the following action should be taken.
      (a) If patient is appellant, Commissioners interview as on complaints visits.
      (b) If sender is appellant, Commissioners decide whether to invite him to be present or if written submission will suffice.
      (c) Commissioners should examine hospital's procedural documents to satisfy themselves that the requirements of the Act have been followed.
      (d) Commissioners to examine documents, article etc., withheld.

(e) Commissioners, at their discretion, to interview all staff who had any direct influence on the particular decision to withhold.

(f) Commissioners to interview the person appointed by the Managers, who has withheld the package or item, especially if considering overriding the decision.

(N.B.: If appropriate and parties agree, Commissioners could interview appellant and parties (e) and (f) together).

(5) Commissioners make decision and notify appellant(s) and managers in writing. If the Commissioners think it is desirable, and especially if the patient is mentally impaired, they may also tell the patient verbally.

(6) Commissioners consider whether case raises any issues which should be reported to SHP team meeting, relevant National Standing Committee meeting or [Management Board]."

An application: Regulation 18 of S.I. 1983 No. 893 (see subs. (9)) allows a wide discretion to the Commission to accept applications in any form which it sees fit. The Commission is empowered by this regulation to direct the production of such documents, information and evidence as it may reasonably require for the purpose of determining an application.

Subsection (9)
Regulations: See regulation 18 of the Mental Health (Hospital, Guardianship and **1–1006** Consent to Treatment) Regulations 1983.

Subsection (10)
Report: Responsibility for preparing the report has been given to the Management **1–1007** Board of the Commission (S.I. 1983 No. 894, reg. 7(2)(b)). The Commission's *Eighth Biennial Report* covering the period April 1997 to March 1999 was published in 1999.

Provision of pocket money for in-patients in hospital

122.—(1) The Secretary of State may pay to persons who are receiving **1–1008** treatment as in-patients (whether liable to be detained or not) in [...] hospitals wholly or mainly used for the treatment of persons suffering from mental disorder, such amounts as he thinks fit in respect of their occasional personal expenses where it appears to him that they would otherwise be without resources to meet those expenses.

(2) For the purposes of the National Health Service Act 1977, the making of payments under this section to persons for whom hospital services are provided under that Act shall be treated as included among those services.

AMENDMENT
The words omitted were repealed by the Health Act 1999, s.65, Sched. 5.

DEFINITIONS
    patient: s.145(1).   **1–1009**
    special hospital: s.145(1).
    hospital: s.145(1).
    mental disorder: ss.1, 145(1).

GENERAL NOTE
This section enables a patient in a psychiatric hospital to receive "pocket money" **1–1010** from the Secretary of State to cover his personal expenses, if he is without other resources. In practice, payments under this section are limited to patients who were admitted to hospital before November 17, 1975. Patients admitted after that date will be supported by the Department of Social Security if they come within the appropriate eligibility criteria.

Social Services authorities can provide money to cover the occasional personal expenses of children under 16 who are, or have been, suffering from mental disorder if they are being cared for in residential accommodation provided under the National Health Service Act 1977: see Schedule 8, paragraph 2 of that Act.

Subsection (1)

1–1011   *Secretary of State:* The functions of the Minister, so far as exercisable in relation to Wales, are exercised by the National Assembly for Wales (S.I. 1999 No. 672, art. 2, Sched. 1).

Transfers to and from special hospitals

1–1012   **123.**—(1) Without prejudice to any other provisions of this Act with respect to the transfer of patients, any patient who is for the time being liable to be detained [...] under this Act (other than under sections 35, 36 or 38 above) [in a hospital at which high security psychiatric services are provided] may, upon the directions of the Secretary of State, at any time be removed into any [other hospital at which those services are provided].

(2) Without prejudice to any such provision, the Secretary of State may give directions for the transfer of any patient who is for the time being liable to be so detained into a hospital [at which those services are not provided].

(3) Subsections (2) and (4) of section 19 above shall apply in relation to the transfer or removal of a patient under this section as they apply in relation to the transfer or removal of a patient from one hospital to another under that section.

AMENDMENTS

The amendments to subss. (1) and (2) were made by the Health Act 1999, Sched. 4, para. 67, Sched. 5.

DEFINITIONS

1–1013   patient: s.145(1).
special hospital: s.145(1).
hospital: s.145(1).

GENERAL NOTE

1–1014   This section enables the Secretary of State (or, in relation to Wales, the National Assembly for Wales) to direct the transfer of a patient from one high security psychiatric hospital to another (subs. (1)) and to direct the transfer of a patient from a high security psychiatric hospital to a hospital which is not a high security psychiatric hospital (subs. (2)). A patient who has been transferred under this section will be detained in the hospital to which he has been transferred as if the application for his compulsory admission had been made to that hospital (s.19(2)).

In *R. v. Secretary of State for the Home Department, ex p. Pickering*, May 25, 1990, the Court of Appeal held that a patient has no right to be consulted prior to a decision to transfer him under this section from one high security psychiatric hospital to another.

Subsection (1)

1–1015   *Other provisions:* See section 19.

Secretary of State: The functions of the Minister, so far as exercisable in relation to Wales, are exercised by the National Assembly for Wales (S.I. 1999 No. 672, art. 2, Sched. 1).

Removed: For general provisions relating to the conveyance of patients, see section 137.

Subsection (2)
    Give directions: Whether or not the hospital has agreed to accept the patient. **1–1016**
According to Larry Gostin and Phil Fennell, *Mental Health: Tribunal Procedure*
(1992), p. 218, this power is never used and transfers from high security psychiatric
hospitals to local hospitals take place under regulation 7 of the Mental Health
(Hospital, Guardianship and Consent to Treatment) Regulations 1983.

Default powers of Secretary of State
    124. [*Repealed by the National Health Service and Community Care Act* **1–1017**
1990, *s.*66(2), *Sched.* 10.]

Inquiries
    125.—(1) The Secretary of State may cause an inquiry to be held in any **1–1018**
case where he thinks it advisable to do so in connection with any matter
arising under this Act.
    (2) Subsections (2) or (5) of section 250 of the Local Government Act 1972
shall apply to any inquiry held under this Act, except that no local authority
shall be ordered to pay costs under subsection (4) of that section in the case
of any inquiry unless the authority is a party to the inquiry.

GENERAL NOTE
    This section provides the Secretary of State and the National Assembly for Wales **1–1019**
with a power to order a formal inquiry to be held into "any matter" which arises
under this Act. The Tribunals and Inquiries Act 1992 applies to an inquiry held under
this section to the extent provided for in the Tribunals and Inquiries (Discretionary
Inquiries) Order 1975 (S.I. 1975 No. 1379) art. 3, Sched., Pt. 1, para. 39.
    The following passage from the judgment of Kennedy J. in *R. v. Secretary of State
for Health, ex p. Prison Officers Association* [1992] C.O.D. 177 examines the nature
of inquiries, including inquiries established under this section:

> "It is important to bear in mind that this inquiry, whether with or without
> statutory powers, is like others that have gone before it—for example, Lord
> Scarman's Red Lion Square statutory inquiry and the non-statutory Strange-
> ways inquiry conducted by Woolf L.J.—just an inquiry. It is by nature
> inquisitorial, not adversarial. No one is on trial even if at times certain
> individuals feel tempted to suggest otherwise. So decisions such as which
> documents are seen, which witnesses are called and how the witnesses are
> handled in terms of how much evidence is led, what cross-examination is
> allowed and to what extent attention is paid to rules governing the admissibility
> of evidence are all matters for the Committee subject only to the overriding
> requirement that the proceedings shall be fair. Fairness may require some
> witnesses to be protected more than others, but what cannot be done is to say
> that the proceedings of any inquiry are fundamentally flawed just because, for
> example, formal discovery or cross-examination has not been permitted to go as
> far as it would normally go in a trial."

Subsection (1)
    Secretary of State: The functions of the Minister, so far as exercisable in relation to **1–1020**
Wales, are exercised by the National Assembly for Wales (S.I. 1999 No. 672, art. 2,
Sched. 1).
    Inquiry: The Secretary of State for Health established a Committee of Inquiry
under this section to investigate allegations of improper care and treatment at
Ashworth Hospital. The report of the Committee was published in two volumes in
1992, with the reference Cm. 2028. During the course of this inquiry the Special
Hospitals Services Authority applied to the High Court for a judicial review of the

Committee's order to the Authority to produce for inspection (and selection of the relevant documents) the personal file of a nurse against whom complaints had been made. The Authority submitted that the file was the subject of a bona fide claim for public interest immunity, made in respect of a class of documents, consisting of the files of nurses nursing at special hospitals. The application was dismissed by Schiemann J. who held that, in the context of the terms of reference of the inquiry, the public interest in disclosing any such document to the Committee and the public was manifestly greater than the public interest in concealing them. The judgment of Schiemann J., which is reproduced as Appendix 6J to the Committee's Report, established the principle that "subject to national or public security, the inquiring body is entitled to demand production to itself of all relevant material and to decide for itself whether the whole, or part only, of the material should be publicly disclosed" (*ibid.*, Ch. VI, p. 32).

Subsection (2)

1–1021   *Subsections (2) to (5) of section 250:* Under which the person appointed to hold the inquiry may by summons require any person to attend to give evidence or to produce any documents in his custody or under his control which relate to any matter in question at the inquiry; and may take evidence on oath (subs. (2)). Any person who refuses to attend, or to give evidence, or to produce a document or who interferes with the document commits an offence (subs. (3)). Subsections (4) and (5) are concerned with the costs of the inquiry.

PART IX

OFFENCES

GENERAL NOTE

1–1022   Section 128 of the Mental Health Act 1959 is not repealed by this Act. That section makes it an offence: (1) for a man on the staff of, or employed by, a hospital, independent hospital or care home to have extramarital sexual intercourse with a woman who is receiving treatment for mental disorder in that hospital or home either as an out-patient or an in-patient; and (2) for a man to have extramarital sexual intercourse with a woman who is subject to his guardianship or is otherwise in his custody or care. No offence is committed under section 128 if the man did not know, and had no reason to suspect, that the woman was a mentally disordered patient.

Forgery, false statements, etc.

1–1023   **126.**—(1) Any person who without lawful authority or excuse has in his custody or under his control any document to which this subsection applies, which is, and which he knows or believes to be, false within the meaning of Part I of the Forgery and Counterfeiting Act 1981, shall be guilty of an offence.

(2) Any person who without lawful authority or excuse makes or has in his custody or under his control, any document so closely resembling a document to which subsection (1) above applies as to be calculated to deceive shall be guilty of an offence.

(3) The documents to which subsection (1) above applies are any documents purporting to be—

(a) an application under Part II of this Act;

(b) a medical [or other] recommendation or report under this Act; and

(c) any other document required or authorised to be made for any of the purposes of this Act.

(4) Any person who—

420

(a) wilfully makes a false entry or statement in any application, recommendation, report, record or other document required or authorised to be made for any of the purposes of this Act; or

(b) with intent to deceive, makes use of any such entry or statement which
he knows to be false,

shall be guilty of an offence.

(5) Any person guilty of an offence under this section shall be liable—

(a) on summary conviction, to imprisonment for a term not exceeding six
months or to a fine not exceeding the statutory maximum, or to both;

(b) on conviction on indictment, to imprisonment for a term not
exceeding two years or to a fine of any amount, or to both.

AMENDMENT

In subs. (3)(b) the words in square brackets were inserted by the Mental Health
(Patients in the Community) Act 1995, s.2(1), Sched. 1, para. 17.

DEFINITIONS

statutory maximum: s.145(2).   1–1024
subject to after-care under supervision: ss.25A(2), 145(1A).

GENERAL NOTE

Under this section it is an offence either to forge or make false statements in 1–1025
applications, recommendations or other documents made under this Act.

Subsection (1)

Any person: Or corporation (Interpretation Act, s.5, Sched. 1).   1–1026
False: Is defined in section 9 of the Forgery and Counterfeiting Act 1981. An entry
or statement may be false on account of what it omits, even though the statement or
entry itself is literally true (*R. v. Lord Kylsant* [1932] 1 K.B. 442).
Offence: Proceedings can be instituted by a local social services authority (s.130).

Subsection (2)

To deceive: "To deceive is ... to induce a man to believe a thing to be true which is 1–1027
false, and which the person practising the deceit knows or believes to be false"; *per*
Buckley J. in *Re London and Globe Finance Corporation Ltd* [1903] 1 Ch. 728, 732. In
Welham v. D.P.P. [1961] A.C. 103 Lord Radcliffe extended the scope of Buckley J.'s
obiter remarks to include the inducing of a man to believe a thing to be false which is
true.

Ill-treatment of patients

127.—(1) It shall be an offence for any person who is an officer on the staff 1–1028
of or otherwise employed in, or who is one of the managers of, a hospital [,
independent hospital or care home]—

(a) to ill-treat or wilfully to neglect a patient for the time being receiving
treatment for mental disorder as an in-patient in that hospital or
home; or

(b) to ill-treat or wilfully to neglect, on the premises of which the hospital
or home forms part, a patient for the time being receiving such
treatment there as an out-patient.

(2) It shall be an offence for any individual to ill-treat or wilfully to neglect
a mentally disordered patient who is for the time being subject to his
guardianship under this Act or otherwise in his custody or care (whether by
virtue of any legal or moral obligation or otherwise).

[(2A) It shall be an offence for any individual to ill-treat or wilfully to neglect a mentally disordered patient who is for the time being subject to after-care under supervision.]

(3) Any person guilty of an offence under this section shall be liable—

(a) on summary conviction, to imprisonment for a term not exceeding six months or to a fine not exceeding the statutory maximum, or to both;

(b) on conviction on indictment, to imprisonment for a term not exceeding two years or to a fine of any amount, or to both.

(4) No proceedings shall be instituted for an offence under this section except by or with the consent of the Director of Public Prosecutions.

AMENDMENTS

In subs (1) the words in square brackets were substituted by the Care Standards Act 2000, s.116, Sched. 4, para. 9(8).

Subs. (2A) was inserted by the Mental Health (Patients in the Community) Act 1995, s.2(1)), Sched. 1, para. 18.

DEFINITIONS

1–1029　　the managers: s.145(1).
hospital: s.145(1).
patient: s.145(1).
mental disorder: ss.1, 145(1).
statutory maximum: s.145(2).
independent hospital: s.145(1).
care home: s.145(1).

GENERAL NOTE

1–1030　　This section creates three separate offences. Firstly, under subsection (1) it is an offence for an employee or a manager of a hospital, independent hospital or care home to ill-treat or wilfully to neglect an in-patient or out-patient of that hospital or home. Secondly, under subsection (2) it is an offence for a guardian or some other person who has the custody or care of a mentally disordered person who is living in the community to ill-treat or wilfully to neglect that person. Thirdly, under subsection (2A) it is an offence for any person to ill-treat or wilfully to neglect a patient who is subject to supervised discharge. It is an essential pre-requisite for each offence that the victim is a mentally disordered person within the meaning of section 1 of this Act at the time when the offence is committed.

In *R. v. Newington* (1990) 91 Cr.App.R. 247, the Court of Appeal said that "ill-treatment" could not be equated with "wilfully to neglect". Their Lordships therefore advised the Crown Prosecution Service that, when proceedings were brought under this section, charges of "ill-treatment" and of "wilfully to neglect" should be put in separate counts in the indictment.

Proceedings under this section can either be instituted by the Director of Public Prosecutions, or by a local social services authority with the Director's consent (s.130 and subs. (4)). Section 139 of this Act does not apply to proceedings brought under this section (s.139(3)).

In *R. v. Spencer* [1986] 2 All E.R. 928, the House of Lords held that a trial judge should warn the jury of the dangers of convicting on the uncorroborated evidence of witnesses each of whom had a criminal record and suffered from a mental disorder. This case, which was concerned with the alleged ill-treatment of Rampton Hospital patients contrary to section 126 of the Mental Health Act 1959, has limited applicability to cases involving mentally disordered people who have not committed any criminal offence. Lord Ackner described the Rampton patients as "men of bad character ... mentally unbalanced ... anti authoritarian, prone to lie or exaggerate ... [and who] could well have old scores which they were seeking to pay off" (at 937).

Subsection (1)
Officer on the staff of the hospital: See the note on section 17(3).   **1–1031**
Care home: Registration of such a home under the Care Standards Act 2000 is not the test of whether an establishment is a care home. The fact of being a care home triggers the obligation to register, not the reverse (*R. v. Davies and Poolton* [2000] Crim.L.R. 297, CA). This interpretation also applies to independent hospitals.

Ill-treat: A single act, such as slapping the patient's face on one occasion, could constitute ill-treatment under this section (*R. v. Holmes* [1979] Crim.L.R. 52, Bodmin Crown Court).

In *R. v. Newington*, above, the Court of Appeal held that for there to be a conviction of ill-treatment under this section (the case in question was brought under subs. (2)), the Crown would have to prove: (1) deliberate conduct by the accused which could properly be described as ill-treatment irrespective of whether it damaged or threatened to damage the victim's health; (2) a guilty mind involving either an appreciation by the accused that she was inexcusably ill-treating a patient, or that she was reckless as to whether she was inexcusably acting in that way; and (3) that the victim was a mentally disordered person within the meaning of section 1 of this Act. The Court disapproved of a direction given by the trial judge "that violence would inevitably amount to ill-treatment" on the ground that violence necessarily used for the reasonable control of a patient would not amount to ill-treatment. As the Court found that for the offence to have been committed there is no need for the prosecution to show that the treatment caused actual injury to the victim, it is clear that "ill-treatment" encompasses a wide range of conduct. M. J. Gunn has stated that the decision in *R. v. Newington* suggests that an offence of ill-treatment "might deal with matters such as inadequate feeding, heating, etc., or the use of harsh words and gratuitous bullying as well as what would be ordinarily understood to be ill-treatment" (*Journal of Forensic Psychiatry* (1990) 1(3), at p. 361; also see Gunn's commentary on this case at [1990] Crim.L.R. 595–597).

In *R. v. Davies and Poolton*, above, the Court of Appeal held that it was not a requirement of an offence under this section that the accused should be aware that the establishment where she worked was a mental nursing home (now an independent hospital or a care home) and that the victim of ill-treatment or wilful neglect was receiving treatment for mental disorder. The relevant *mens rea* is found in the element of ill-treatment or wilful neglect that is the gist of the offence.

Neglect: Is an objective state which is not defined in this Act. A failure to provide adequate medical aid to a patient would probably constitute neglect under this section.

Patient: There is no requirement under this subsection for the victim to have been detained under the provisions of this Act. The ill-treatment or wilful neglect of an *in-patient* need not have taken place on the hospital premises.

Subsection (2)
Mentally disordered patient: Is a person who is either suffering or appearing to be   **1–1032**
suffering from mental disorder (*R. v. Newington*, above). There is no need for the victim to be receiving treatment for his mental disorder, to have had a history of in-patient treatment in a hospital, or to have been a detained patient or a detained patient on leave of absence from a hospital. At the time of the offence the victim could, for example, be living in his own home, with relatives or friends, in accommodation registered under the Care Standards Act 2000, in local authority accommodation or in accommodation provided under an adult-placement scheme.

Otherwise in his custody or care: The custodians or carers could include social workers, residential care workers, teachers, relatives or friends. It is likely that the use of the term "moral obligation" extends the scope of this section to include a family member, friend or volunteer who is caring for the mentally disordered person. As to legal custody, see section 137.

Assisting patients to absent themselves without leave, etc.

1–1033   **128.**—(1) Where any person induces or knowingly assists another person who is liable to be detained in a hospital within the meaning of Part II of this Act or is subject to guardianship under this Act to absent himself without leave he shall be guilty of an offence.

(2) Where any person induces or knowingly assists another person who is in legal custody by virtue of section 137 below to escape from such custody he shall be guilty of an offence.

(3) Where any person knowingly harbours a patient who is absent without leave or is otherwise at large and liable to be retaken under this Act or gives him any assistance with intent to prevent, hinder or interfere with his being taken into custody or returned to the hospital or other place where he ought to be he shall be guilty of an offence.

(4) Any person guilty of an offence under this section shall be liable—

(a) on summary conviction, to imprisonment for a term not exceeding six months or to a fine not exceeding the statutory maximum, or to both;

(b) on conviction on indictment, to imprisonment for a term not exceeding two years or to a fine of any amount, or to both.

DEFINITIONS
1–1034   hospital: s.145(1).
absent without leave: ss.18(6), 145(1).
patient: s.145(1).
hospital: ss.34(2), 145(1).

GENERAL NOTE
1–1035   Under this section it is an offence to induce or to help a patient escape from custody or to absent himself from hospital without leave, or to harbour or prevent the recapture or return to hospital of such patients. Proceedings under this section can be instituted by local social services authorities (s.130).

Subsection (1)
1–1036   *Absent himself without leave:* Note that the patient does not commit an offence by absenting himself without leave.

Knowingly: The use of this term emphasises the requirement of *mens rea* (*R. v. Dunne, The Times*, March 16, 1998, CA).

Obstruction
1–1037   **129.**—(1) Any person who without reasonable cause—

(a) refuses to allow the inspection of any premises; or

(b) refuses to allow the visiting, interviewing or examination of any person by a person authorised in that behalf by or under this Act [or to give access to any person to a person so authorised]; or

(c) refuses to produce for the inspection of any person so authorised any document or record the production of which is duly required by him; or

(d) otherwise obstructs any such person in the exercise of his functions, shall be guilty of an offence.

(2) Without prejudice to the generality of subsection (1) above, any person who insists on being present when required to withdraw by a person authorised by or under this Act to interview or examine a person in private shall be guilty of an offence.

(3) Any person guilty of an offence under this section shall be liable on summary conviction to imprisonment for a term not exceeding three months or to a fine not exceeding level 4 on the standard scale or to both.

AMENDMENT

In subs. (1)(b) the words in square brackets were inserted by the Mental Health **1–1038** (Patients in the Community) Act 1995, s.2(1), Sched. 1, para. 19.

GENERAL NOTE

This section specifies when a person commits the offence of obstruction under this **1–1039** Act. The Committee of Inquiry into Complaints about Ashworth Hospital stated that they were "inclined to the view that the right of silence is abrogated by [this section] which makes it an offence for anyone, without reasonable excuse, to obstruct an authorised investigation" (Cm. 2028, Vol. 1, Ch. XIII, p. 126).

Subsection (1)

Any person: Or corporation (Interpretation Act 1978, s.5, Sched. 1). **1–1040**

Obstructs: Cases on the offence of obstructing a policeman in the execution of his duty suggest that an offence under this section: (1) need not involve physical violence (*Hinchcliffe v. Sheldon* [1955] 1 W.L.R. 1207); (2) is not committed on a mere refusal to answer questions (*Rice v. Connolly* [1966] 2 Q.B. 414) or on advising a person not to answer questions (*Green v. DPP* [1991] Crim.L.R. 782, DC); and (3) might be committed if a verbal warning of an impending inspection was given (*Green v. Moore* [1982] 2 W.L.R. 671). With regard to (2), see the General Note to this section. There is also authority to support the contention that an offence is committed if the defendant's conduct makes it more difficult for an authorised person to carry out his duties: see the dictum of Lord Goddard C.J. in *Hinchcliffe v. Sheldon*, above, at 1210 which was followed by the Divisional Court in *Lewis v. Cox* [1984] 3 W.L.R. 875. In *Swallow v. London County Council* [1916] 1 K.B. 224, a case on the Weights and Measures Act 1889, it was held that, in the absence of a legal duty to act, standing by and doing nothing did not amount to an obstruction.

Offence: Proceedings can be instituted by a local social services authority (s.130).

Subsection (2)

In private: Although an approved social worker is required to interview a patient **1–1041** "in a suitable manner" before making an application under Part II of this Act (s.13(2)), there is no express provision authorising him to interview the patient in private. A person who disrupts an approved social worker's interview with a patient would be guilty of an offence under subsection (1)(d) of this section. A doctor is given the power to interview a patient in private by section 24(1).

Prosecutions by local authorities

130. A local social services authority may institute proceedings for any **1–1042** offence under this Part of this Act, but without prejudice to any provision of this Part of this Act requiring the consent of the Director of Public Prosecutions for the institution of such proceedings.

DEFINITION

local social services authority: s.145(1). **1–1043**

GENERAL NOTE

This section empowers a local social services authority to institute proceedings for **1–1044** an offence alleged to have been committed under this Part.

Local authority staff who are charged with the duty of investigating offences under this Part must have regard to relevant provisions of the Codes of Practice issued under the Police and Criminal Evidence Act 1984 (*ibid.* s.67(9)). In particular, the following caution must be administered to a suspect before any questions about the offence are put to him: "You do not have to say anything. But it may harm your defence if you do not mention when questioned something which you later rely on in court. Anything you do say may be given in evidence" (*Code of Practice C*, paras. 10.1, 10.4).

Consent of the Director of Public Prosecutions: Is required by section 127.

PART X

MISCELLANEOUS AND SUPPLEMENTARY

Miscellaneous provisions

Informal admission of patients
1–1045   **131.**—(1) Nothing in this Act shall be construed as preventing a patient who requires treatment for mental disorder from being admitted to any hospital or [registered establishment] in pursuance of arrangements made in that behalf and without any application, order or direction rendering him liable to be detained under this Act, or from remaining in any hospital or [registered establishment] in pursuance of such arrangements after he has ceased to be so liable to be detained.

(2) In the case of a minor who has attained the age of 16 years and is capable of expressing his own wishes, any such arrangements as are mentioned in subsection (1) above may be made, carried out and determined [even though there are one or more persons who have parental responsibility for him (within the meaning of the Children Act 1989)].

AMENDMENTS
1–1046   In subs. (1) the words in square brackets were substituted by the Care Standards Act 2000, s.116, Sched. 4, para. 9(2).
        In subs. (2) the words in square brackets were substituted by the Children Act 1989, s.108(5), Sched. 13, para. 48(5).

DEFINITIONS
1–1047   patient: s.145(1).
        mental disorder: ss.1, 145(1).
        hospital: s.145(1).
        registered establishment: ss.34(1), 145(1).

GENERAL NOTE
1–1048   This section provides that a patient can either enter hospital for treatment for mental disorder on an informal basis, or remain in hospital on an informal basis once the authority for his original detention has come to an end. The *Code of Practice* considers informal admission at paragraphs 2.7 and 2.8. For a discussion of the informal status of psychiatric patients, see *Mental Health Law in Context: Doctor's Orders*, M. Cavadino, 1989, Ch. 7 and B. Andoh, "The Informal Patient in England and Wales" (2000) Med. Sci. Law, 2, 147–155. The circumstances of patients informally admitted to secure psychiatric units are considered by P. Sugarman and P. Collins in "Informal admission to secure units: a paradoxical situation", *The Journal of Forensic Psychiatry*, Vol. 3, No. 3, December 1992, pp. 477–485.
        In *R. v. Bournewood Community and Mental Health NHS Trust, ex p. L* [1998] 3 All E.R. 289, the House of Lords held that patients who are admitted to hospital under subsection (1) of this section without the formalities necessary for detention under this Act, fall into two categories: those who, having the capacity to consent to the admission, do consent ("voluntary patients") and those who, though lacking capacity to consent to the admission, do not object ("informal patients"); *per* Lord Steyn at 308: "section 131(1) permits the admission of compliant incapacitated patients where the requirements of the principle of necessity are satisfied." If a patient in the latter category is being detained in the hospital and subsequently indicates either verbally or through his actions that he is no longer content with being there, consideration should be given to making an application under Part II of this Act in respect of him (*Code of Practice*, para. 19.27). If he does not object to his

detention and such detention is in his best interests, justification for its use can be found in the common law doctrine of necessity. In *Bournewood* the House of Lords held for a patient to be "detained" there must *in fact* be a complete deprivation of, or restraint upon, the patient's liberty. Therefore, it could not be said that a mentally incapable patient who is being accommodated in an unlocked ward and who is not subject to restraint by staff, has been deprived of his liberty. The tort of false imprisonment would be committed in the absence of lawful authority (*i.e.* under this Act or under the common law doctrine of necessity) for the patient's detention. Also see the note on "The Human Rights Act 1998", below. Concern about relying on the doctrine of necessity to justify the detention of compliant but incapable patients was expressed by Lord Steyn, at 308, 309:

> "The common law principle of necessity is a useful concept, but it contains none of the safeguards of the 1983 Act. It places effective and unqualified control in the hands of the hospital psychiatrist and other health professionals. It is, of course, true that such professionals owe a duty of care to patients and that they will almost invariably act in what they consider to be in the best interest of the patient. But neither habeas corpus nor judicial review are sufficient safeguards against misjudgments and professional lapses in the case of complaint incapacitated patients."

Subject to section 5, informal patients have the right to leave hospital when they like. However, as Phil Fennell has pointed out, "for many—especially confused elderly or profoundly learning disabled people—this right remains purely theoretical since there is nowhere else for them to go and because they lack the capacity to express an informed desire to leave hospital" ("Informal Compulsion: The Psychiatric Treatment of Juveniles Under Common Law" (1992) J.S.W.F.L. 311–333, 314). The Mental Health Act Commission has expressed its concern about the "*de facto* detention" of this group of patients; see, for example, the Commission's First Biennial Report, 1983–1985, para. 8.10.

With the exception of the provisions of section 57, informal patients are not subject to the consent to treatment provisions contained in Pt IV of this Act and are therefore free to refuse treatment if they possess the required mental capacity: see the General Note to Part IV. If a patient who has been admitted informally fails to accept necessary treatment or refuses to co-operate with those who are caring for him, consideration should be given to either discharging him from the hospital or assessing him for possible detention under Part II.

There is no legally established mechanism for reviewing either the reasons for an informal patient's admission to hospital or the justification for his continued hospitalisation. Once an informal patient has been admitted to hospital no person or body is placed under any legal obligation to inform him of his legal status and the fact that he is free to leave hospital whenever he wishes. Neither is there any obligation to inform a detained patient that his period of detention has expired. Department of Health and Social Security Circular No. DS 89/75, dated March 7, 1975, addresses this issue: "From time to time the Department has been asked whether a patient and his nearest relative should be told what his position will be if he remains in hospital on an informal basis on the expiry of a period of detention authorised by the Mental Health Act. The experience of the Health Service Commissioner who has investigated a number of complaints from people who are or have been patients in psychiatric hospitals indicates that there is a need for general guidance on this point ... It is the Department's view that in these circumstances the patient and, providing he has no valid objection, his nearest relative, should be sent a letter explaining his position. This might be done by a letter written by the responsible medical officer and copies to the managers or by the hospital secretary on behalf of the managers copied to the responsible medical officer. In some cases it might be advisable to explain the position verbally to the patient as well. The letter could also contain advice about the hospital rules and the importance of being guided by the doctor in charge of the patient as regards further treatment but it should also make it clear that if the patient insists on leaving he will be free to do so unless exceptionally the hospital authorities find it necessary to take steps to authorise his detention under the Mental Health Act." At some date in the future the Mental Health Act Commission could have responsibility for keeping under review the care and treatment of informal patients (s.121(4)).

In *R. v. Kirklees Metropolitan Borough Council, ex p. C* [1992] 2 F.L.R. 117, Kennedy J., on an application for the judicial review of a decision by the local authority to consent to the admission of an adolescent girl to a psychiatric hospital, held that an admission to a psychiatric hospital can be lawful even though it does not take place within the framework of this Act, which did not cover all eventualities. His Lordship found that there is no reason to conclude that the right to arrange an informal admission is limited to the terms of this section. If that were the case it would produce the surprising result that no one, adult or child, who had not been diagnosed as being mentally disordered, could ever be admitted to a psychiatric hospital for assessment. This section did not apply to the applicant because there was no evidence that she required "treatment for mental disorder" (see subs. (1)). The local authority was entitled to consent on the applicant's behalf because a care order had been made in respect of her and at the material time she was not "Gillick competent"; see subsection (2). On affirming this decision at [1993] 2 F.L.R. 187, the Court of Appeal confirmed that although the informal admission of a patient for assessment is not covered by this section, there is nothing to prohibit such an admission taking place under common law. The effect of this decision is merely to fill a gap in the statutory scheme, a gap which was described by Lloyd L.J., at 190, as being "odd".

The Human Rights Act 1998

1–1049   Two challenges to the provisions of this section could be made under the European Convention on Human Rights:

1. It is likely that the common law detention of compliant mentally incapable adults patients (see the decision of the House of Lords in *Bournewood*, above) violates Article 5 of the European Convention on Human Rights in that:

> (a) the detention of persons of unsound mind must take place "in accordance with a procedure proscribed by law" (Art. 5(1)). The law in question must be "adequately accessible" and "formulated with sufficient precision to enable the citizen to regulate his conduct" (*Sunday Times v. United Kingdom* (1979) 2 E.H.R.R. 245, para. 49). As common law detention, which is not exercised in relation to any defined criteria, neither provides the patient with any procedural protection nor requires the psychiatrist to present objective evidence to any competent authority of the need for detention, it is difficult to argue that either this requirement or the guidance on what is required for detention to be lawful given by the European Court on Human Rights in *Winterwerp v. Netherlands* (1979) 2 E.H.R.R. 387, is satisfied (see the notes on Art. 5(1)(e)); and
>
> (b) as the common law does not provide for the review of the detention of such patients, there is almost certainly a violation of Article 5(4) of the Convention.

It should also be noted the European Court of Human Rights has held that for a patient to be deprived of his liberty for the purposes of Article 5, there is no need to show that the patient was subject to a direct physical restraint to prevent him from leaving the hospital: see the note on "detention" in Article 5(1)(e). This contrasts with the decision in *Bournewood* where the House of Lords held that a restraint on the freedom of movement of the patient was an essential element of detention; see generally, Philip Fennell, "Doctor Knows Best? Therapeutic Detention Under Common Law, the Mental Health Act, and the European Convention" (1999) 6 Med. L. Rev. 322–353.

2. Article 5 of the European Convention applies to children. Although the European Court held in *Nielsen v. Denmark* (1989) 11 E.H.R.R. 175, that no deprivation of liberty occurred when the mother of a 12 year old boy consented to his admission to a psychiatric hospital against his wishes, it has been doubted whether this case would be followed in future: see the note on "detention" under Article 5(1)(e). It is likely that the Court would hold that a parental consent to the admission of a mentally competent 16- or 17-year old child to a psychiatric hospital violates Article 5 if the child objects to the admission (see the notes on subs.(2)).

The compulsory admission of a child under this Act would violate Article 8 if the decision to make the application was made without an opportunity being made available to the child's parents to be involved in the decision-making process (see the General Note to Art.8).

Subsection (1)

Treatment: But not assessment (*R. v. Kirklees Metropolitan Borough Council, ex p.* **1–1050** *C*, above). The treatment and care of mentally incapable informal patients is authorised under the common law doctrine of necessity if such treatment and care is in the patient's best interests: see the General Note to Part IV.

Being admitted: The Mental Health Act Commission "is frequently asked to comment on whether or not older patients with dementia or other organic brain syndromes which impair their mental capacity to make reasoned judgments, should be detained for care and treatment under the provisions of the Act or can be admitted and cared for informally. There is, however, no hard and fast rule, the circumstances of every patient must be considered individually. The majority of older people with dementia who are mentally incapacitated are willing to accept the care and treatment offered to them. If admission is felt to be necessary, they can at present, be admitted as informal patients, if that is felt to be in their best interests under the authority of common law. The problem arises where the patient is actively refusing care and treatment and may persistently reject help from professional carers or actively seeks to leave the unit. In these cases, where the clinical team judges that the health or safety of the patient is at risk by allowing the patient freedom to remain outside the hospital or nursing home, then the team should seek an assessment for admission under the Act" (M.H.A.C., Fifth Biennial Report 1991–1993, para. 3.5(j)).

This opinion should now be read subject to the decision of the House of Lords in the Bournewood case, above. An application for admission could only be applied for in respect of a patient who "actively seeks to leave the unit". A mentally incompetent patient who is resistant to being treated, but who is compliant in respect of being in hospital, is not being detained and can be treated under common law powers: see the General Note to Part IV.

Without any application: Although informal admission should be the preferred mode of admission, there is nothing in this Act which expressly prevents an application being made in respect of a patient who is willing to enter hospital as an informal patient. While it is true that section 5 of this Act can be invoked to prevent an informal patient from leaving hospital, circumstances can arise which justify the use of compulsion on a "willing" patient. An example of a situation where compulsion might be thought to be justified is the patient who is known to be willing to enter hospital but unwilling to accept essential treatment. Also see paragraph 2.7 of the *Code of Practice*.

Subsection (2)

This provision states that a child who is between the ages of 16 and 18, and who is **1–1051** "capable of expressing his own wishes" can make his own decision on whether he is to be admitted to hospital as an informal patient. Such a person also has the power to take his own discharge. Persons who have parental responsibility for a child can agree to the informal admission of that child if he lacks the required capacity to consent on his own behalf. It is submitted that the test established in *Re C* (*Refusal of Medical Treatment*), noted under "capacity" in the General Note to Part IV, should be used to determine whether a child over the age of 16 has the required capacity. The medical treatment of children is considered in the General Note to Part IV.

The right of a child under the age of 16 to consent to an informal admission is governed by the common law. In *Gillick v. West Norfolk and Wisbech Area Health Authority* [1985] 3 All E.R. 402, the House of Lords held that a doctor had a discretion to give medical advice or treatment to a child under 16 without the parents' knowledge or consent provided that the child requested it and had achieved a sufficient understanding and intelligence to enable him or her to understand the nature and implications of the proposed treatment. Although the *Gillick* case was concerned with the issue of consent to treatment it is reasonable to assume that the courts would extend the principle established there to the related question of whether a child had capacity to agree to an informal admission to hospital. The *Gillick* case was considered in *Re W* (*A Minor*) (*Medical Treatment*) [1992] 4 All E.R. 627, CA, Lord Donaldson M.R. held, at 639, 640, that "no minor of whatever age has power by refusing consent to treatment to override a consent to treatment by someone who has parental responsibility for the minor and *a fortiori* a consent by the court. Nevertheless such a refusal is a very important consideration in making clinical judgments and for parents and the court in deciding whether themselves to give consent. Its importance increases with the age and maturity of the minor". This finding can be regarded as the authoritative statement of law on this issue. Although a court, in following *Re W*, is likely to hold that the parents of a *Gillick* competent non-consenting child can lawfully agree to her informal admission, the child's failure to agree to the admission would clearly influence the doctor's decision on whether to admit her informally.

An interested party, such as a local authority, which considers that the informal admission of a child might not be in the child's best interests could seek leave to apply to the court for a "specific issue" order under Part II of the Children Act 1989 or to invoke the inherent jurisdiction of the High Court (*ibid.* s.100(3)–(5)) to determine the issue. Also see the note on "The Human Rights Act 1998", above.

Under sections 85 and 86 of the Children Act 1989, where a child is to be accommodated by a Health Authority or NHS trust for a consecutive period of at least three months, or where a child is to be accommodated in a care home or independent hospital for a similar period, the accommodating authority or the person carrying on the hospital or home must notify the local authority for the area where the child is ordinarily resident. The local authority is then placed under a duty to determine whether the child's welfare is being adequately safeguarded and to consider whether it should exercise any of its functions under the 1989 Act in respect of the child.

Hospitals as "secure accommodation"

1–1052   Regulation 5 of the Children (Secure Accommodation) Regulations 1991 (S.I. 1991 No. 1505) provides that section 25 of the Children Act 1989, which sets restrictions on the use of secure accommodation for children, does not apply to a child who is detained under any provision of this Act, although it will apply if the child is granted leave of absence under section 17 (*Hereford and Worcester County Council v. S* [1993] 2 FLR 360). Section 25 will also apply if the child is either admitted informally under this section or is admitted under the common law powers identified in *R. v. Kirklees Metropolitan Borough Council, ex p. C*, above, and if the unit of the hospital where the child is being accommodated is "secure accommodation". Secure accommodation is defined as "accommodation which is provided for the purpose of restricting the liberty of children to whom section 25 [of the 1989 Act] applies" (reg. 2(1)). Paragraph 8.10 of the *Children Act 1989: Guidance and Regulations, Vol. 4, Residential Care*, HMSO, 1991, states that "it is important to recognise that any practice or measure which prevents a child from leaving a room or building of his own free will may be deemed by the court to constitute restriction of liberty." In *R. v. Northampton Juvenile Court, ex p. London Borough of Hammersmith and Fulham* [1985] F.L.R. 193 an adolescent "behaviour modification unit" of a private hospital where "the locking of the unit is part of the planned treatment regime which enables the medical staff to control, modify and eliminate aggressive and dangerous behaviour" was held to be "accommodation provided for the purpose of restricting liberty". Ewbank J. found that the purpose of the unit was to restrict the liberty of the children with a view to modifying their behaviour. A psychiatric unit which Douglas Brown J. held in *South Glamorgan County Council v. W and B* [1993] 1 F.L.R. 574, to be "just short" of a secure unit was described in the following terms: "Although Merrifield is not a secure unit, we would endeavour to prevent [the child] from leaving the premises unaccompanied and it will be important that we have clear permission from the court to do this, otherwise it would not be possible to admit [the child] to our unit without her consent."

These cases were referred to by Wall J. in *Re C* (*Detention: Medical Treatment*) 2 F.L.R. 180, where his Lordship held that a psychiatric unit for the treatment of eating disorders did not constitute secure accommodation. The primary purpose of the placement of a child in the unit "is to achieve treatment: the accommodation provides a structure for that treatment. The fact that such a structure includes a degree of restriction on the patient's liberty is ... an incident of the treatment programme, and the fact that steps can be taken to prevent [a child] leaving the premises does not, of itself, render the clinic secure accommodation" (at 192, 193). In doubting the finding of Cazalet J. in *A Metropolitan Borough Council v. DB* [1997] 1 F.L.R. 767, that a maternity ward to which entry and exit could only be effected by the use of a key out pass was secure accommodation, Wall J. said that the natural meaning of the words "provided for the purpose of restricting liberty" is "designed for, or having as its primary purpose" the restriction of liberty.

Subject to regulation 5, section 25 applies to children who are accommodated by health authorities, local authorities, National Health Service trusts or local education authorities and to children who are accommodated in independent hospitals or care homes (reg. 7). Regulation 10 specifies that a child may not be kept in secure accommodation without the authority of a court if he is kept in such accommodation for an aggregate period of 72 hours in any period of 28 consecutive days. The placing of children in secure accommodation is considered by the *Code of Practice* at paragraph 30.9.

The detention of informal child patients

In *Re C* (*Detention: Medical Treatment*), above, a 16-year-old child needed **1–1053** treatment for anorexia nervosa in a private psychiatric unit in circumstances where the unit would not accept patients who were detained under the 1983 Act and where there were sound reasons for not instituting care proceedings. Wall J. held that:

(1) the High Court has the power under the inherent jurisdiction to order the detention of a child in a specified institution for the purpose of medical treatment being administered to the child without her agreement (*Re W* (*A Minor*) (*Medical Treatment*), above);

(2) the court has power to authorise the use of reasonable force (if necessary) to detain the child in the institution and to ensure that any necessary treatment is received (*Norfolk and Norwich Healthcare* (*NHS*) *Trust v. W* [1996] 2 F.L.R. 613);

(3) as the clinic was not "secure accommodation" for the purposes of section 25 of the Children Act 1989 and the attendant regulations (see above), the inherent jurisdiction was not ousted. An application under section 25 for a secure accommodation order would have had to have been made if the clinic did constitute secure accommodation;

(4) although section 25 did not apply, the court should pay careful attention to the scheme laid down by Parliament under that section, and an order should not

431

be made under the inherent jurisdiction unless the section 25 criteria are, by analogy to the facts of the case, met. The rights given to a child who is the subject of a section 25 application should be made available, and equivalent safeguards to those provided for in section 25 should be built into the order; and

(5) although consideration should always be given to alternative avenues (for example, under section 31 of the Children Act or the Mental Health Act) a refusal to exercise the inherent jurisdiction on the basis that an alternative avenue was available could lead to the child falling between several statutory stools, and not receiving the treatment that he or she needs. A primary purpose of the inherent jurisdiction is to fill lacunae in the statutory schemes; if the court is satisfied that in the particular circumstances of the case no statutory scheme is available, it should not hesitate to use its powers under the inherent jurisdiction.

A minor: There is nothing in this Act which prevents a child from being compulsorily admitted to hospital under Part II.

Attained the age: At the commencement of his sixteenth birthday (Family Law Reform Act 1969, s.9(1)).

Duty of managers of hospitals to give information to detained patients

1–1054   **132.**—(1) The managers of a hospital or [registered establishment] in which a patient is detained under this Act shall take such steps as are practicable to ensure that the patient understands—

(a) under which of the provisions of this Act he is for the time being detained and the effect of that provision; and

(b) what rights of applying to a Mental Health Review Tribunal are available to him in respect of his detention under that provision;

and those steps shall be taken as soon as practicable after the commencement of the patient's detention under the provision in question.

(2) The managers of a hospital or [registered establishment] in which a patient is detained as aforesaid shall also take such steps as are practicable to ensure that the patient understands the effect, so far as relevant in his case, of sections 23, 25, 56 to 64, 66(1)(g), 118 and 120 above and section 134 below; and those steps shall be taken as soon as practicable after the commencement of the patient's detention in the hospital or [registered establishment].

(3) The steps to be taken under subsections (1) and (2) above shall include giving the requisite information both orally and in writing.

(4) The managers of a hospital or [registered establishment] in which a patient is detained as aforesaid shall, except where the patient otherwise requests, take such steps as are practicable to furnish the person (if any) appearing to them to be his nearest relative with a copy of any information given to him in writing under subsections (1) and (2) above; and those steps shall be taken when the information is given to the patient or within a reasonable time thereafter.

AMENDMENT

The words in square brackets in subss. (1), (2) and (4) were substituted by the Care Standards Act 2000, s.116, Sched. 4, para. 9(2).

DEFINITIONS

1–1055   the managers: s.145(1).
hospital: s.145(1).
registered establishment: ss.34(1), 145(1).
nearest relative: ss.26(3), 145(1).

This section, which is considered in chapter 14 of the *Code of Practice*, requires the **1–1056** managers of a hospital or registered establishment to inform a detained patient of his legal position and rights. Unless the patient requests otherwise, the information must also be given to the patient's nearest relative. A failure by the managers to take all practicable steps to ensure that the patient understands the relevant information may be referred to the Mental Health Act Commission for investigation (ss.120(1)(b)(i) (ii), 121(2)(b)).

In addition to the information provided for in this section "[t]he patient should also be told about any legal aid schemes which could help him obtain representation for a Mental Health Review Tribunal. Transferred patients should be told about any special Mental Health Review Tribunal rights" (*Memorandum*, para. 299). The patient should also be provided with information about welfare benefits.

Neither this section nor section 133 applies to patients who are subject to guardianship or to informal patients. For informal patients, see D.H.S.S. Circular No. DS 89/75 which is quoted in the General Note to section 131. For patients under guardianship, see paragraph 8 of D.H.S.S. Circular No. HC (83)17 which is referred to in the General Note to section 7.

Paragraph 301 of the *Memorandum* states: "When a patient is discharged from detention, or the authority for his detention expires, this fact should be made clear to him, whether he wishes to leave hospital or to stay on as an informal patient."

The Human Rights Act 1998

Although this section does not place an obligation on the managers to inform the **1–1057** patient of the facts that gave rise to his detention, the European Court of Human Rights has held that the provisions of Article 5(4) of the European Convention on Human Rights, which provides a detained person with a right to challenge the lawfulness of his detention speedily, would be breached if the person concerned is not "promptly and adequately informed of the facts and legal authority relied on to deprive him of his liberty" (*X v. United Kingdom* (1981) 1 B.M.L.R. 98, at 119; see also *Van der Leer v. Netherlands* (1990) 12 E.H.R.R. 567, at paras 27, 28. Also of relevance in this context is the requirement in Article 5(2) that anyone arrested or detained should be "informed promptly, in a language which he understands, of the reasons for his arrest . . ." The detention of a mentally disorded person is an "arrest" in Convention terms. Although the *Code of Practice* specifies that a detained patient should be informed of the reasons for his detention (at para. 14.5*b*), this section is silent on this point and therefore violates Article 5(2). In *Fox, Campbell and Hartley v. United Kingdom* (1991) 2 E.H.R.R. 287, the Court said that a detained person has a right to be provided with the reasons for his detention in "simple, non-technical language that he can understand" and that the reasons must contain "the essential legal and factual grounds for his [detention]." Although an approved social worker applicant might well have confirmed the facts that gave rise to the patient's detention during the interview required by section 13(2), it would be prudent for hospital staff to reinforce this information for such patients, and to provide such information to patients who were either admitted pursuant to a nearest relative application or were too unwell to absorb the information during the interview with the approved social worker; also see the note on Article 5(2) of the Convention.

Subsection (1)

Detained under this Act: There is no requirement to give information under this **1–1058** section to patients who are detained under this Act in places other than a hospital or registered establishment, *e.g.* a patient who is detained in a police station under section 136.

Such steps as are practicable: The steps must include giving the requisite information both orally and in writing (subs. (3)).

Ensure that the patient understands: If the patient initially fails to understand the information provided, the managers must persist with their efforts in an attempt to achieve the required level of understanding. In appropriate cases the managers should use an interpreter.

For the time being detained: This provision requires the patient to be provided with the relevant information when the section under which he is detained changes.

Rights of applying to a Mental Health Review Tribunal: If the patient (or his nearest relative) has missed an opportunity to apply to a tribunal because of a failure to provide him with the information set out in this provision, he (or his representative) should request that the Secretary of State refers the case to the tribunal under his discretionary powers contained in section 67 or 71.

As soon as practicable: Having regard to the patient's state of mind and his ability to understand the information. It is important not to equate "practicable" with "possible": see the note on "not reasonably practicable" in section 11(4).

Subsection (2)

1–1059   Sections 23, 25 and 66(1)(a) are concerned with the powers of the responsible medical officer, the hospital managers and the nearest relative to discharge the patient, sections 56 to 64 contain the consent to treatment provisions, section 118 provides for the publishing of the *Code of Practice*, section 120 is concerned with the Mental Health Act Commission's functions relating to the general protection of detained patients and section 134 deals with the withholding of detained patient's correspondence. Although this section does not require the managers to give reasons for any decision taken, the *Code of Practice*, at paragraph 14.1, states that patients should be given "as much information as possible about their care and treatment"; see further, the note on "The Human Rights Act 1998", above.

Subsection (3)

1–1060   *Orally and in writing:* These are not alternatives. Leaflets which can be used for giving the written information have been prepared by the Department of Health. The leaflets that have been prepared are listed in Appendix 4 to the Memorandum. They are available from The Stationery Office, Broadway, Chadderton, Oldham OL9 9QH.

Subsection (4)

1–1061   *Patient otherwise requests:* The patient should be informed of the provisions of this subsection at the same time as he is given the information required by subsections (1) and (2). A nearest relative will usually be informed about an admission under section 2 (s.11(3)) and consulted about an admission under section 3 (s.11(4)).

Appearing to them: The hospital managers must take reasonable steps to ascertain the identity of the patient's nearest relative.

Nearest relative: If the nearest relative is mentally incapable, an approved social worker should be asked to consider making an application to the court under section 29(3)(b) for an acting nearest relative to be appointed.

Copy of any information: Annex B to D.H.S.S. Circular No. HC(83)17 contains a series of draft covering letters which hospitals may wish to adapt and use to send to the nearest relative.

Duty of managers of hospitals to inform nearest relatives of discharge

1–1062   **133.**—(1) Where a patient liable to be detained under this Act in a hospital or [registered establishment] is to be discharged otherwise than by virtue of an order for discharge made by his nearest relative, the managers of the hospital or [registered establishment] shall, subject to subsection (2) below, take such steps as are practicable to inform the person (if any) appearing to them to be the nearest relative of the patient; and that information shall, if practicable, be given at least seven days before the date of discharge.

(2) Subsection (1) above shall not apply if the patient or his nearest

relative has requested that information about the patient's discharge should not be given under this section.

AMENDMENT
The words in square brackets in subs. (1) were substituted by the Care Standards Act 2000, s.116, Sched. 4, para. 9(2).

DEFINITIONS

1–1063
    patient: s.145(1).
    hospital: s.145(1).
    registered establishment: ss.34(1), 145(1).
    nearest relative: ss.26(3), 145(1).
    the managers: s.145(1).

GENERAL NOTE

1–1064
    This section places a duty on the managers of hospitals or registered establishments to inform the nearest relative of a detained patient that he is about to be discharged from detention. The duty does not arise if either the patient or his nearest relative has requested that this information should not be given.

Subsection (1)

1–1065
    Is to be discharged: This refers to a discharge from detention and not to a discharge from hospital.
    Order for discharge made by his nearest relative: Under section 23.
    Appearing to them: nearest relative: See the notes on section 132(4).
    Seven days: The duty under this section arises even though the patient is to be discharged immediately after the expiration of one of the short-term orders.

Correspondence of patients

1–1066
    134.—(1) A postal packet addressed to any person by a patient detained in a hospital under this Act and delivered by the patient for dispatch may be withheld from [the postal operator concerned].

    (a) If that person has requested that communications addressed to him by the patient should be withheld; or

    (b) subject to subsection (3) below, if the hospital is [one at which high security psychiatric services are provided] and the managers of the hospital consider that the postal packet is likely—

        (i) to cause distress to the person to whom it is addressed or to any other person (not being a person on the staff of the hospital); or

        (ii) to cause danger to any person;

and any request for the purposes of paragraph (a) above shall be made by a notice in writing given to the managers of the hospital, the registered medical practitioner in charge of the treatment of the patient or the Secretary of State.

    (2) Subject to subsection (3) below, a postal packet addressed to a patient detained [under this Act in a hospital at which high security psychiatric services are provided] may be withheld from the patient if, in the opinion of the managers of the hospital, it is necessary to do so in the interests of the safety of the patient or for the protection of other persons.

    (3) Subsections (1)(b) and (2) above do not apply to any postal packet addressed by a patient to, or sent to a patient by or on behalf of—

(a) any Minister of the Crown [or the Scottish Ministers] or Member of either House of Parliament [or a Member of the Scottish Parliament];
(b) the Master or any other officer of the Court of Protection or any of the Lord Chancellor's Visitors;
(c) the Parliamentary Commissioner for Administration, [the Welsh Administration Ombudsman] the Health Service Commissioner for England, the Health Service Commissioner for Wales or a Local Commissioner within the meaning of Part III of the Local Government Act 1974;
(d) a Mental Health Review Tribunal;
(e) a [Health Authority[, Special Health Authority or Primary Care Trust]], a local social services authority, a Community Health Council or a [local probation board established under section 4 of the Criminal Justice and Court Services Act 2000];
(f) the managers of the hospital in which the patient is detained;
(g) any legally qualified person instructed by the patient to act as his legal adviser; or
(h) the European Commission of Human Rights or the European Court of Human Rights.

(4) The managers of a hospital may inspect and open any postal packet for the purposes of determining—
(a) whether it is one to which subsection (1) or (2) applies, and
(b) in the case of a postal packet to which subsection (1) or (2) above applies, whether or not it should be withheld under that subsection;
and the power to withhold a postal packet under either of those subsections includes power to withhold anything contained in it.

(5) Where a postal packet or anything contained in it is withheld under subsection (1) or (2) above the managers of the hospital shall record that fact in writing.

(6) Where a postal packet or anything contained in it is withheld under subsection (1)(b) or (2) above the managers of the hospital shall within seven days give notice of that fact to the patient and, in the case of a packet withheld under subsection (2) above, to the person (if known) by whom the postal packet was sent; and any such notice shall be given in writing and shall contain a statement of the effect of section 121(7) and (8) above.

(7) The functions of the managers of a hospital under this section shall be discharged on their behalf by a person on the staff of the hospital appointed by them for that purpose and different persons may be appointed to discharge different functions.

(8) The Secretary of State may make regulations with respect to the exercise of the powers conferred by this section.

(9) In this section "hospital" has the same meaning as in Part II of this Act, [and "postal operator" and] "postal packet" [have] the same meaning as in [the Postal Services Act 2000].

AMENDMENTS

In subss. (1) and (2) the words in square brackets were substituted by the Health Act 1999, s.65, Sched. 4, para. 68. In subs. (3)(c) the words in square brackets were inserted by the Government of Wales Act 1998, s.125, Sched. 12, para. 22.

The words in square brackets in subs.(3)(a) were inserted by the Scotland Act 1998 (Consequential Modifications) (No.2) Order 1999 (S.I. 1999 No. 1820), art. 4, Sched. 2, para. 71.

In subs. (3)(e) the words in square brackets were substituted by the Health Authorities Act 1995, s.2(1), Sched. 1, para. 107(10), the Health Act 1999 (Supplementary, Consequential, etc., Provisions) Order 2000 (S.I. 2000 No. 90), Sched. 1, para. 16(7) and the Criminal Justice and Court Services Act 2000, s.74, Sched. 7, para. 74.

The reference to postal operator in subs. (1) and the amendments to subs. (9) were made by the Postal Services Act 2000, Sched. 8, para. 19, Sched. 9.

DEFINITIONS

    patient: s.145(1).   **1–1067**

    hospital: ss.34(2), 145(1).

    special managers: s.145(1).

    the managers: s.145(1).

    local social services authority: s.145(1).

    Health Authority: s.145(1).

    Special Health Authority: s.145(1).

GENERAL NOTE

This section provides authority for the inspection and withholding of a detained **1–1068** patient's outgoing and incoming mail. There is no power to withhold or inspect the mail of an informal patient. The *Code of Practice*, at paragraph 22.15, advises managers to have a written policy concerning the implementation of their powers under this section.

If either a detained or an informal patient is sent articles of potential danger, such as weapons, explosives or matches, through the mail, section 3(1) of the Criminal Law Act 1967 and the common law provide authority for hospital staff to take reasonable measures to prevent the patient from receiving or keeping the article in his possession (see, further, *Consultative Document*, para. 10.28 and the General Note to s.5). In *R. v. Franey, ex p. Warren*, January 1, 1998, Turner J., in refusing leave to bring judicial review proceedings, held that the decision of the Chief Executive of Broadmoor Hospital to remove, *inter alia*, personal computers from patients' rooms was a lawful decision which did not prevent patients from communicating with the authorities or the courts. Arrangements had been made for patients to have access to their computers in the hospital's day areas.

Further provisions relating to items brought to hospital premises for patients, patients' access to computer equipment and mobile phones, patients' post and patients' telephone calls for patients at Ashworth, Broadmoor and Rampton Hospitals can be found in the Safety and Security in Ashworth, Broadmoor and Rampton Hospitals Directions 2000. These Directions, which were made by the Secretary of State for Health under sections 16D, 17 and 126(4) of the National Health Service Act 1977 and section 4(5) of the Regulation of Investigatory Powers Act 2000, can be found at http://www.doh.gov.uk/hospitaldirections/.

The *Memorandum*, at paragraph 311, describes the procedure for reviewing decisions to withhold a patient's mail: "Section 121(7) gives the Mental Health Act Commission power to review any decision to withhold a postal packet under section 134(1)(b) or (2) provided an application to review such a decision is made within six months of the receipt of the written notice. The applicant should provide the Commission with a copy of the written notice. In the case of outgoing mail it is only the special hospital patient who may apply, but in the case of incoming mail, the special hospital patient or the sender may apply. When reviewing a decision to withhold a postal packet the Commission may inspect documents and evidence (including the withheld item) which it reasonably requires. The Commission has the power to release the withheld item to the addressee (s.121(8))". The procedure that has been adopted by the Commission in exercising its jurisdiction to review a decision to withhold mail is set out in the note to section 121(7).

The Malicious Communications Act 1988 makes provision for the prosecution of persons who send or deliver letters or other articles for the purpose of causing distress or anxiety.

For the procedure to be adopted when mail is opened and inspected, see regulation 17 of the Mental Health (Hospital, Guardianship and Consent to Treatment) Regulation 1983.

The Human Rights Act 1998

1–1069　It is likely that the power contained in this section does not contravene the European Convention on Human Rights, given the interpretation that the Court has given to Article 8(2) of the Convention in *Herczegfalvy v. Austria* (1993) 15 E.H.R.R. 432, at paragraphs 85 to 92: also see the note on Article 10(2) of the Convention.

Subsection (1)

1–1070　This subsection authorises a person appointed by the hospital managers (subss (4), (7)) to withhold a detained patient's outgoing mail from the Post Office if the addressee has requested that the communications addressed to him by the patient should be withheld. The outgoing mail of patients detained in a high security psychiatric hospital can also be withheld if it is felt that the communication is likely to cause distress or danger to any person. It is "intended that this power should be used to withhold, for example, threatening letters, letters to victims of crime, or dangerous objects" (*Memorandum*, para. 305). There is no provision equivalent to that which was contained in section 36 of the Mental Health Act 1959 which authorised the withholding of outgoing mail which would "be likely to prejudice the interests of the patient". A patient whose mail is withheld under subsection (1)(b) or (2) can appeal to the Mental Health Act Commission (s.121(7)).

Postal packet: Is defined in subsection (9).

Detained: Both in high security psychiatric hospitals and in other hospitals. This section does not apply to informal patients or to patients who are subject to guardianship.

Withheld: There is no authority for the hospital managers to censor correspondence, *i.e.* to strike out certain passages in a letter. However, there is power to withhold something contained in a postal packet (subs. (4)).

This section does not confer on a hospital a power to require the return of a patient's mail once it has reached its destination. In *Broadmoor Hospital Authority v. R.* [2000] All E.R. 727, the Court of Appeal refused the hospital's application for an injunction requiring the return of a draft manuscript of a book which had been sent by a patient to his agent. The hospital considered that the contents of the book, if published, would be prejudicial to the interests of the sender and would cause distress to the family of his victim. The court held that it could, if appropriate, grant an injunction to restrain an activity outside the hospital if it could be shown that it was having a sufficiently significant impact on the security of the hospital or the treatment of a patient; see further the General Note to this Act under the heading "Injunctions to support an authority's performance of its duties under this Act".

Paragraph (a): The review procedure set out in section 121(7)(8) does not apply to outgoing mail which is withheld under the provisions of this paragraph.

Requested: The Hospital Managers are not placed under a statutory obligation to inform the patient that such a request has been made.

Paragraph (b) managers of the hospital: Their functions shall be discharged by a member of the hospital staff (subs. (7)). Decisions made under this paragraph are routinely monitored by the Mental Health Act Commission (M.H.A.C., Fifth Biennial Report, 1991–1993, para. 8.1).

High security: Paragraph 22 of the Safety and Security in Ashworth, Broadmoor and Rampton Hospitals Directions 1999, which were made under section 17 of the National Health Service Act 1977 and annexed to Circular HSC 1999/150, states that a "hospital authority shall ensure that:

(a) all outgoing postal packets from patients, other than letters or cards, are packed and sealed by patients on their wards in the presence of a member of staff; and

(b) other outgoing postal packets from patients are opened and inspected from time to time by a member of staff, except where any postal packet is addressed to one of the persons or organisations referred to in [subsection (3) of this section]."

Subsection (2)

This subsection authorises the withholding of the incoming mail of a patient **1–1071** detained in a high security hospital if it is considered that such action is necessary in the interests of the safety of the patient or for the protection of other persons. Either the patient or the sender can appeal to the Mental Health Act Commission against a decision to withhold mail (s.121(7)). There is no power to withhold incoming mail on the ground that it would cause distress to the patient.

High security: Paragraph 20 of the 1999 Directions referred to in subsection (2), states that a "hospital authority shall ensure that, subject to the provisions of [this section] and regulation 17 of the 1983 regulations:

(a) all incoming postal packets addressed to a patient other than those opened or inspected centrally are, subject to sub-paragraph (b) below, opened and inspected by a member of staff in the presence of the patient and the contents recorded; and

(b) any postal packet which indicates on the outside that it is sent by or on behalf of one of the persons or organisations referred to in [subsection (3)] is opened in accordance with sub-paragraph (a) above."

There is no power to withhold the incoming mail of a patient who is detained in a hospital which is not a high security hospital.

The managers: See subsection (7).

Subsection (3)

This subsection excludes the provisions of subsections (1)(b) and (2) in respect of **1–1072** certain bodies and individuals. Any person listed in this subsection can, under subsection 1(a), request that communications addressed to him by the patient be withheld.

The Mental Health Act Commission "holds the view that patient telephone calls to the same organisations [listed in this subsection] should attract a similar degree of privacy and that whilst any supervision of phone calls should not generally include listening into the contents of the calls (in certain circumstances this may be necessary) such listening in should never take place when the patient's phone call is with one of the specific organisations referred to above" (M.H.A.C., Sixth Biennial Report, 1993–1995, para. 9.8). Any policy that restricts a patient's access to a telephone must be consistent with the patient's rights under Article 8 of the European Convention on Human Rights (*Valle v. Finland*, December 7, 2000).

Paragraph (c)

Parliamentary Commissioner: And the Scottish Parliamentary Commissioner for **1–1073** Administration (S.I. 1999 No. 1351, art.17).

Subsection (4)

The managers: See subsection (7). **1–1074**

Open. It will not usually be necessary to open the mail of patients who are not detained in high security hospitals, as the requirements of subsection (1)(a) can be met by looking at the addresses on patients' outgoing mail. However, it would be permissible for such mail to be opened if staff had a reasonable suspicion that a postal packet contained letters which the patient wanted the addressee to forward to people who had requested that mail be withheld. In high security psychiatric hospitals it will be necessary to open both outgoing and incoming mail if there is a reasonable suspicion that the provisions of either subsection (1) or (2) applies. If, as a result of the inspection, nothing is withheld from the patient, the procedure set out in regulation 17(1) of S.I. 1983 No. 893 should be followed.

Although the issue has not been tested in the courts, it is likely that the inspection of the contents of a postal packet can include viewing the contents of a computer disc.

Subsection (5)

1–1075   *Record:* See regulation 17(2) of the 1983 Regulations.

Withheld: The obligation to record does not apply to the opening of mail under subsection (4).

Subsection (6)

1–1076   *Notice:* See regulation 17(3) of the 1983 Regulations.

Subsection (7)

1–1077   *Shall be discharged:* The hospital managers must appoint a member of staff to discharge their functions under this section. It is "expected that the decision to withhold post would be made in consultation with the responsible medical officer" (*Memorandum*, para. 312).

Subsection (8)

1–1078   *Secretary of State:* The functions of the Minister, so far as exercisable in relation to Wales, are exercised by the National Assembly for Wales (S.I. 1999 No. 672, art. 2, Sched. 1).

Subsection (9)

1–1079   *Postal operator:* Means "a person who provides the service of conveying postal packets from one place to another by post or any of the incidental services of receiving, collecting, sorting and delivering such packets" (Postal Services Act 2000, s.125(1)).

Postal packet: Means "a letter, parcel, packet or other article transmitted by post" (*ibid.*).

Warrant to search for and remove patients

1–1080   **135.**—(1) If it appears to a justice of the peace, on information on oath laid by an approved social worker, that there is reasonable cause to suspect that a person believed to be suffering from mental disorder—

(a) has been, or is being, ill-treated, neglected or kept otherwise than under proper control, in any place within the jurisdiction of the justice, or

(b) being unable to care for himself, is living alone in any such place, the justice may issue a warrant authorising any constable [...] to enter, if need be by force, any premises specified in the warrant in which that person is believed to be, and, if thought fit, to remove him to a place of safety with a view to the making of an application in respect of him under Part II of this Act, or of other arrangements for his treatment or care.

(2) If it appears to a justice of the peace, on information on oath laid by any constable or other person who is authorised by or under this Act or under section 83 of the [Mental Health (Scotland) Act 1984] to take a patient to any place, or to take into custody or retake a patient who is liable under this Act or under the said section 83 to be so taken or retaken—

(a) that there is reasonable cause to believe that the patient is to be found on premises within the jurisdiction of the justice; and

   (b) that admission to the premises has been refused or that a refusal of such admission is apprehended,
the justice may issue a warrant authorising any constable [...] to enter the premises, if need be by force, and remove the patient.

   (3) A patient who is removed to a place of safety in the execution of a warrant issued under this section may be detained there for a period not exceeding 72 hours.

   (4) In the execution of a warrant issued under subsection (1) above, [a constable] shall be accompanied by an approved social worker and by a registered medical practitioner, and in the execution of a warrant issued under subsection (2) above [a constable] may be accompanied—

   (a) by a registered medical practitioner;

   (b) by any person authorised by or under this Act or under section 83 of the [Mental Health (Scotland) Act 1984] to take or retake the patient.

   (5) It shall not be necessary in any information or warrant under subsection (1) above to name the patient concerned.

   (6) In this section "place of safety" means residential accommodation provided by a local social services authority under Part III of the National Assistance Act 1948 [...], a hospital as defined by this Act, a police station, [an independent hospital or care home] for mentally disordered persons or any other suitable place the occupier of which is willing temporarily to receive the patient.

AMENDMENTS

   In subss (2) and (4) the words in square brackets which refer to the Mental Health (Scotland) Act were substituted by the Mental Health (Scotland) Act 1984, s.127(1), Sched. 3, para. 56. In subss (1) and (2) the words omitted were repealed by the Police and Criminal Evidence Act 1984, s.119, Sched. 7. In subs. (4) the words in square brackets were substituted by *ibid.*, s.119, Sched. 6, para. 26. In subs. (6) the words omitted were repealed by the National Health Service and Community Care Act 1990, s.66(2), Sched. 10 and the words in square brackets were substituted by the Care Standards Act 2000, s.116, Sched. 4, para. 9(9).

DEFINITIONS

   approved social worker: s.145(1).   **1–1081**
   mental disorder: ss.1, 145(1).
   patient: s.145(1).
   local social services authority: s.145(1).
   hospital: ss.34(2), 145(1).
   independent hospital: s.145(1)
   care home: s.145(1).

GENERAL NOTE

   This section provides for a magistrate to issue a warrant authorising a policeman to **1–1082** enter premises, using force if necessary, for the purpose of removing a mentally disordered person. A warrant under subsection (1) need not name the patient, but must specify the premises to which it relates. Note the distinction between warrants issued under subsections (1) and (2). Subsection (1) is used where there is concern about a person who is not liable to be detained under this Act. Subsection (2) is used where the person concerned is already liable to be detained. A warrant under this section would not be required if a co-owner or, possibly, a co-occupier of the premises gives permission for the mental health professionals to enter: see the note on "enter and inspect" in section 115. A patient who is detained under this section is not subject to the consent to treatment provisions contained in Part IV of this Act (s.56(1)(b)).

Section 15(1) of the Police and Criminal Evidence Act 1984 (PACE) states:

> "This section and section 16 ... have effect in relation to the issue to constables under any enactment, including an enactment contained in an Act passed after this Act, of warrants to enter and search premises, and an entry on or search of premises under a warrant is unlawful unless it complies with this section and section 16 ...."

Although it would appear from the heading of this section that a warrant issued to a constable under either subsection (1) or (2) comes within the scope of sections 15 and 16 of PACE, the wording of section 15(4), which states that the "constable shall answer on oath any question that the justice of the peace ... hearing the application asks him", suggests that the two sections only relate to warrants issued on the application of a constable. It is submitted that the better interpretation is that sections 15 and 16 apply to warrants issued under this section. This is the view of the Home Office (Personal Communication). The effect of this interpretation is that, in addition to the provisions of this section, the following requirements of PACE must be satisfied:

(i) the application for the warrant shall be made *ex parte* and the information laid before the magistrate must be in writing (s.15(3));

(ii) the warrant shall authorise an entry on one occasion only (s.15(5));

(iii) the warrant shall specify the name of the person who applies for it, the date on which it is issued and the fact that it was issued under this Act (s.15(6));

(iv) the warrant shall identify, so far as is practicable, the person to be sought (s.15(6));

(v) two copies shall be made of the warrant and the copies shall be clearly certified as copies (s.15(6)(7)). One copy is retained by the police and the other is handed to the occupier of the premises. It is suggested that a third copy be taken for retention by the person in charge of the place of safety to which the patient is removed;

(vi) entry and search under the warrant must be within one month from the date of its issue (s.16(3));

(vii) entry and search under the warrant must be at a reasonable hour unless it appears to the constable executing it that the purpose of a search may be frustrated on an entry at a reasonable hour (s.16(4));

(viii) if the occupier of the premises is present at the time when the constable seeks to execute the warrant, the constable shall (a) identify himself; (b) produce the warrant to him; and (c) supply him with a copy of it. If the occupier of the premises is not present but some other person who appears to the constable to be in charge of the premises is present, the above procedure will be followed in respect of that other person. If there is no person present who appears to the constable to be in charge of the premises, he shall leave a copy of the warrant in a prominent place on the premises (s.16(5)(6)(7));

(ix) a search under the warrant may only be a search to the extent required for the purpose for which the warrant was issued (s.16(8));

(x) the constable executing the warrant shall make an endorsement on it stating whether the person sought was found (s.16(9)); and

(xi) a warrant which has been executed, or which has not been executed within the time authorised for its execution, shall be returned to the clerk to the justices (for the petty sessions area for which the issuing justice of the peace acts) who shall retain it for a period of 12 months. During this period the occupier of the premises to which the warrant relates shall be allowed to inspect the warrant (s.16(10)(11)(12)).

Forms which are said to comply with this section and with sections 15 and 16 of the 1984 Act are available from Shaw and Sons Ltd, Shaway House, Crayford, Kent DA1 4BZ.

In *D'Souza v. Director of Public Prosecutions* [1992] 4 All E.R. 545, the House of Lords held that the power to obtain a warrant under subsection (2) of this section is not the exclusive method of gaining access to premises in order to retake a detained patient who has absconded from hospital and that an alternative is provided for in section 17(1)(d) of the Police and Criminal Evidence Act 1984. Section 17(1)(d) states that a policeman "may enter and search any premises for the purpose ... of recapturing a person who is unlawfully at large and whom he is pursuing". The leading speech in the House of Lords was given by Lord Lowry who said, at 556, that the

"verb in the clause 'whom he is pursuing' is in the *present continuous* tense and therefore, give or take a few seconds or minutes—this is a question of degree—the pursuit must be almost contemporaneous with the entry into the premises There must, I consider, be an act of pursuit, that is a chase, however short in time or distance. It is not enough for the police to form an intention to arrest, which they put into practice by resorting to the premises where they believe that the person whom they seek may be found".

His Lordship further held, at 553, 554, that if a person who is lawfully detained in hospital under section 6(2) of this Act goes absent without leave, he is by virtue of section 18(1) liable to be taken into custody and returned to the hospital, and is therefore "unlawfully at large" for the purposes of section 17(1)(d) of the 1984 Act. By virtue of section 117 of the 1984 Act a policeman "may use reasonable force, if necessary, in the exercise of the power [under section 17]". Also note that section 17(1)(e) of the 1984 Act provides the police with the power to enter and search any premises if such action is required to save "life or limb" or to prevent "serious damage to property". Section 17(1)(e) does not provide the police with authority to remove any person from the premises.

The Police and Criminal Evidence Act has not removed the common law power of the police to enter private premises without a warrant to prevent a breach of the peace occurring if they reasonably believe that an imminent breach of the peace is likely to occur on the premises (*McLeod v. Commissioner of Police of the Metropolis* [1994] 4 All E.R. 553, CA). The nature of a breach of the peace is considered in the General Note to section 5 under the heading "Further powers available to the staff of hospitals to detain and control patients".

The *Code of Practice*, at paragraph 2.20, states that "calling the police in order to see if they would exercise any relevant lawful power of entry" is an alternative to invoking this section.

Persons who have been removed to a police station as a place of safety under this section have the rights and protections afforded by the *Code of Practice* for the Detention, Treatment and Questioning of Persons by Police Officers which has been issued under section 66 of the 1984 Act: see the General Note to section 136.

The Human Rights Act 1998
Use of this section involves an interference with the mentally disordered person's **1–1083** home and private life that must be justified under Article 8(2) of the European

Convention on Human Rights. Entry to the person's home must be a proportionate measure in all the circumstances and the reasons adduced to justify the search must be relevant and sufficient (*McLeod v. United Kingdom* (1999) 27 E.H.R.R. 493). In *Camenzind v. Switzerland* (1999) 28 E.H.R.R. 458, para. 45, the European Court of Human Rights held that the state's governing legislation and practice must afford adequate and effective safeguards against abuse if the test of proportionality is to be satisfied. This suggests that the absence of notification to the mentally disordered person of an impending application under this section, which is required by section 15(3) of the Police and Criminal Evidence Act 1984, might breach Article 8. However, it is likely that a court would find that the adjudication of the application by a magistrate provides the "adequate and effective" safeguard required.

Subsection (1)

1–1084   This subsection enables an approved social worker to make an application to a magistrate for a warrant authorising a policeman to enter premises where a mentally disordered person is believed to be living for the purpose of removing that person to a place of safety so that his condition can be assessed. As a warrant issued under this subsection provides authority for the person to be detained in the place of safety for up to 72 hours there is no need for an application under Part II of this Act to be made once entry has been gained to the premises. The power to remove the person only applies if such action is thought to be necessary: see the note on "if thought fit", below.

The experience of the author differs from those respondents who agreed with the Law Commission's provisional view, expressed in Consultation Paper No. 130, that the power in this subsection is "of little help in practice," (The Law Commission, *Mental Incapacity*, 1995, para. 9.11).

Laid by: The approved social worker may lay the information before a magistrate at any time and at any location.

Approved social worker: Only an approved social worker can apply for a warrant to be issued under this subsection.

A person: This procedure can be invoked even though the name of the mentally disordered person is not known (subs. (5)).

Kept otherwise than under proper control: This phrase encompasses not only the situation where a person is being subjected to a degree of improper control, but also the situation where a person is suffering from the absence of control.

Unable to care for himself: This paragraph is aimed at a mentally disordered person who is unable to look after himself appropriately. As "care" is a broad term which encompasses matters that relate to a person's daily needs, it would seem that a warrant could be applied for where the main cause of concern is the apparent failure of the person to take essential prescribed medication.

Living alone: The suggestion by the Royal College of Psychiatrists that this section should also provide for a situation where two mentally disordered people were living together and were unable to care for themselves was not adopted (Cmnd. 7320, para. 2.21).

Authorising: The warrant does not require the constable to enter the premises. The arrival of the constable at the premises could have the effect of persuading the person concerned to admit the approved social worker and the doctor without the need for the warrant to be executed.

Constable: Any police officer can execute the warrant: see the note on "constable" in section 136(1). The constable must be accompanied by an approved social worker and a doctor (subs. (4)). The approved social worker need not necessarily be the person who applied for the warrant.

In which that person is believed to be: There should be some evidence to suggest that the person concerned is to be found at the specified premises.

If thought fit: This section does not specify whose decision this is. It is suggested that the policeman's role is to gain entry to the premises and to ensure the safety of the doctor and the approved social worker, whose joint role is to assess whether the patient should be removed to a place of safety.

Place of safety: Is defined in subsection (6). Local social services authorities have a duty to provide temporary protection for the property of persons admitted to hospital or to accommodation provided under Part III of the National Assistance Act 1948 (*ibid.* s.48).

Making an application in respect of him ... or ... other arrangements for his treatment or care: The authority to detain the patient ceases once it has been decided to take no action in respect of him.

Subsection (2)

This subsection provides for the issue of a warrant to a policeman to enter **1–1085** premises, using force if necessary, for the purposes of taking or retaking a patient who is *already* liable to be detained into custody. It also applies to a patient under guardianship who has absconded from a place where he is required to reside. Also note the power of the police under section 17(1)(d) of the Police and Criminal Evidence Act 1984 which is noted in the General Note to this section.

Any constable: Who *may* be accompanied by a doctor or any other person, such as an approved social worker, who is authorised to take or retake the patient (subs. (4)).

Authorised ... to take a patient to any place: The persons authorised to retake patients under section 18 of this Act are, in addition to a constable, any officer on the staff of the hospital, any approved social worker or any person authorised by the hospital managers, or, in the case of a patient subject to guardianship, any officer on the staff of a local social services authority, or any person authorised by the guardian or a local social services authority.

Remove the patient: To the place where he is required to reside under the terms of his detention or guardianship.

Subsection (3)

Removed: For general provisions relating to the conveyance of patients from one **1–1086** place to another, see section 137.

Place of safety: Is defined in subsection (6). "Only in exceptional circumstances should a police station be used as a place of safety. If a police station is used, the patient should remain there for no longer than a few hours while an approved social worker makes the necessary arrangements for his removal elsewhere, either informally or under Part II of the Act" (*Memorandum*, para. 315). If a hospital is used as the place of safety, a patient who is detained under this section cannot subsequently be transferred to another hospital under regulation 7 of the Mental Health (Hospital, Guardianship and Consent to Treatment) Regulations: see the note on section 19(1)(a), (2)(a).

72 hours: This is the maximum period of detention. It starts from the time when the person arrives at the place of safety. If the person escapes from the place of safety he cannot be retaken after the 72 hours have expired (s.138(3)).

Subsection (4)

Registered medical practitioner: This section does not provide the doctor with a **1–1087** power to override the objection of a mentally capable person to being mentally examined.

Subsection (5)

Name the patient: The name of the patient should be identified in the information **1–1088** or warrant if it is known.

Subsection (6)

1–1089   *Any other suitable place:* Which could be the home of a relative or friend of the patient.

Mentally disordered persons found in public places

1–1090   **136.**—(1) If a constable finds in a place to which the public have access a person who appears to him to be suffering from mental disorder and to be in immediate need of care or control, the constable may, if he thinks it necessary to do so in the interests of that person or for the protection of other persons, remove that person to a place of safety within the meaning of section 135 above.

(2) A person removed to a place of safety under this section may be detained there for a period not exceeding 72 hours for the purpose of enabling him to be examined by a registered medical practitioner and to be interviewed by an approved social worker and of making any necessary arrangements for his treatment or care.

DEFINITIONS

1–1091   mental disorder: ss.1, 145(1).
approved social worker: s.145(1).

GENERAL NOTE

1–1092   This section, which is considered in chapter 10 of the *Code of Practice*, empowers a policeman to remove a person from a public place to a place of safety if he considers that the person is suffering from mental disorder and is in immediate need of care or control. The power is available whether or not the person has, or is suspected of having, committed a criminal offence. The person can be detained in a place of safety for up to 72 hours so that he can be examined by a doctor and interviewed by an approved social worker in order that suitable arrangements can be made for his treatment or care. This section is usually invoked "where a person's abnormal behaviour is causing nuisance or offence" (Cmnd. 7320, para. 2.22). As the purpose of the section "is to allow for assessment within the shortest possible period, up to a maximum of 72 hours ... it should *not* therefore be treated, as in the case of some hospitals, as an admission section authorising 72 hours' detention" (Mental Health Act Commission, Second Biennial Report, 1985–87, para. 11.1(e)).

If the person concerned is on private premises, the police have common law and statutory powers to enter such premises to prevent a breach of the peace (see the note on the "The Human Rights Act 1998", below).

The *Code of Practice* recommends that local agencies work together to establish an agreed policy on the implementation of this section (para. 10). For a regionwide survey of arrangements made under this section see "Section 136 Agreements in a Regional Health Authority", M. Klÿnsma *et al.*, *Psychiatric Bulletin* (1994), 18, 36–38. The operation of this section has been the subject of a three stage investigation. The first stage is reported in *A Place of Safety*, A. Rogers and A. Faulkner, 1987, and the second and third stages are reported in *Out of Harm's Way*, P. Bean *et al.*, 1991. Philip Joseph reports that the use of this section by the police is "patchy and inconsistent and varies across the country" ("Mentally disordered offenders: diversion from the criminal justice system" (1990) *Journal of Forensic Psychiatry*, Vol. 1, No. 2, 133–138, at p. 135).

The power to arrest under this section was specifically preserved by section 26 and Schedule 2 to the Police and Criminal Evidence Act 1984 (PACE). This means that a person who has been removed to a place of safety under this section is given the following rights under PACE: to have another person of his choice informed of his removal (*ibid.*, s.56) and if held in a police station to consult a solicitor privately at any time (*ibid.*, s.58).

The *Code of Practice* for the Detention, Treatment and Questioning of Persons by Police Officers which has been issued under section 66 of PACE (HMSO 1995) applies to persons who have been removed to a police station as a place of safety under this section (*ibid.*, Code C para. 1.10). Code C, which is concerned with the "Detention, Treatment and Questioning of Persons by Police Officers", requires the police to secure the attendance of an "appropriate adult" if the person being detained appears to be mentally disordered. As the principle function of the appropriate adult is to protect the interests of a mentally disordered suspect during police questioning, it is difficult to see what role this person has to play under this section where the mentally disordered person is being detained for assessment by mental health professionals and not for questioning by the police. However, it could be argued that the early appearance of an appropriate adult could help to ensure that the detained person is aware of the effect of this section, is given information about what is to happen to him and has been informed of his rights under sections 56 and 58 of PACE. There can be no doubt that the attendance of an appropriate adult is necessary if a person who, having been detained under this section, is also going to be involved in a procedure under the criminal law. This happened in *Francis v. Director of Public Prosecutions, The Times*, May 2, 1996, where the Divisional Court held that detention under this section does not give rise to any legal bar to any subsequent use of the breath specimen procedure under section 7 of the Road Traffic Act 1988. The court said that the fact of detention under this Act, while giving rise to obligations on the police, was not determinative of the issue of whether the procedure could be used, and that the propriety or fairness of using the procedure in such circumstances fell to be decided on the facts. If a person who has been detained under this section does become involved in a procedure under the criminal law, the appropriate adult should not be the approved social worker who has been involved with that person's assessment.

Although paragraph 9.2 of the PACE Code C states that a person can be transferred from a police station to a place of safety, it is submitted that there is no power under this section to transfer the person from one place of safety to another because the reason for invoking the section is for the person to be "detained there," *i.e.* at the place of safety, to enable an assessment to take place (subs. (2)). The Mental Health Act Commission states that the "legality of the common practice of taking prospective patients to a police station en route to hospital needs clarification, but it may be unavoidable ... when the initial arrest may be for an offence and only later, while being transported to, or while at the station, may mental disorder be suspected" (Fifth Biennial Report 1991–1993, para. 10.7(c)). In these circumstances the constable cannot be said to have invoked this section as he will not have determined when the person was apprehended that the person was mentally disordered (see subs. (1)). In its Sixth Biennial Report 1993–1995 at paragraph 7.4, the Commission states that "it is illegal to move the subject from one place of safety to another once assessment has been instigated". The Commission does not provide any argument in favour of its implied contention that it is possible to move a patient from one place of safety to another before the assessment has started. In the absence of statutory language which supports such an approach (the transfer of patients detained under this section is not covered by s.19 or by the Mental Health (Hospital, Guardianship and Consent to Treatment) Regulations 1983), it should be assumed that no such power exists. This approach is endorsed by the *Code of Practice* at paragraph 10.5.

Paragraph 3.10 of the PACE Code C states that it "is imperative that a mentally disordered or mentally handicapped person who has been detained under section 136 of the Mental Health Act 1983 should be assessed as soon as possible. If that assessment is to take place at the police station, an approved social worker and a registered medical practitioner should be called to the police station as soon as possible in order to interview and examine the person. Once the person has been interviewed and examined and suitable arrangements have been made for his treatment or care, he can no longer be detained under section 136. In most cases the person should not be released until he has been seen by both the approved social worker and the registered medical practitioner." However, the person should be released before the attendance of the approved social worker if the assessing doctor concludes that that person is not mentally disordered: see the note on "registered medical practitioner in subsection (2). A person who has been arrested and detained in a police station other than under the provisions of this section can be subjected to a mental health assessment (Home Office Circular No. 66/90, paras 4(iii) and 7).

There is no statutory form that can be used to record an admission of a person to a hospital which is acting as a place of safety under this section. If such an admission takes place the hospital should not record it on Form 14 of the Schedule to the Mental Health (Hospital, Guardianship and Consent to Treatment) Regulations 1983 as no application has been made in respect of that person (*ibid.*, reg. 4(3)). The Metropolitan Police are advised in their standing orders to complete an administrative form if a patient is removed to a hospital as a place of safety under this section. The form is reproduced in Appendix C to *Out of Harm's Way*, above.

If a person is removed to a hospital or registered establishment under this section, the managers of the hospital or establishment are obliged to give him information under section 132. The *Code of Practice*, at paragraph 10.11, recommends that the written information required by section 132 be given to a patient who is removed to a police station under this provision.

The Human Rights Act 1998

1–1093   In *Winterwerp v. Netherlands* (1979) 2 E.H.R.R. 387, the European Court of Human Rights held that "except in emergency cases", an individual "should not be deprived of his liberty unless he has been reliably shown to be of 'unsound mind'" (para.39). The Court subsequently said that it cannot "be inferred from the *Winterwerp* judgment that [a medical report on the patient] must in all conceivable cases be obtained before rather than after the confinement of a person on the ground of unsoundness of mind" (*X v. United Kingdom* (1981) 4 E.H.R.R. 188, para.41). As the power under this section: (i) applies to a person who appears to be in *immediate* need of care or control; and (ii) lasts for a relatively brief period, it is highly likely that it would be treated as an emergency measure which complies with Article 5(1)(e) of the Convention The continued detention of a person under this section subsequent to a finding by the assessing doctor that the person was not mentally disordered would contravene the Convention as there would be no ground under Article 5(1)(e) to detain him.

The common law and statutory powers of the police to enter private premises to prevent a breach of the peace (which are preserved by section 17(6) of the Police and Criminal Evidence Act 1984) does not beach the Convention as such action can be said to be both "in accordance with law" and pursued for the legitimate aim of "the prevention of disorder or crime" for the purposes of Article 8(2). However, the action of the police must be a proportionate measure in all the circumstances (*McLeod v. United Kingdom* (1999) 27 E.H.R.R. 493). The nature of a breach of the peace is considered in the General Note to section 5 under the heading "Further powers to detain and control patients".

Subsection (1)

1–1094   *Constable:* Means the office of constable, and not the rank of constable (Police Act 1964, s.18, Sched. 2). Therefore, any police officer can exercise this power.

In *Clunis v. Camden and Islington Health Authority* [1998] 3 All E.R. 180, the Court of Appeal doubted whether the wording of this section places on the constable a duty to take care which gives rise to a claim for damages at the suit of the disordered person.

Place to which the public have access: This phrase is not defined. It probably includes: (1) places to which members of the public have open access, *e.g.* the public highway; (2) places to which members of the public have access if a payment is made, *e.g.* a cinema; and (3) places to which members of the public have access at certain times of day, *e.g.* a public house. It does not cover areas where members of the public have access by virtue of being visitors to private premises: see *R. v. Edwards* (1978) 67 Cr.App.R. 228, where the Court of Appeal held that the fact that the public can obtain access to a private house as visitors through the front garden does not make the garden a public place for the purposes of the Public Order Act 1936. In *Knox v. Anderton* (1983) 76 Cr.App.R. 156, a case under section 1(4) of the Prevention of Crime Act 1953, the Divisional Court held that a "public place" to which the public have access could include premises where there are no barriers or notices restricting access, such as the upper landing of a block of flats which could be entered by members of the public without hindrance. In the only reported case on this section, *Carter v. Metropolitan Police Commissioner* [1975] 1 W.L.R. 507, the Court of Appeal proceeded on the basis that a communal balcony in a block of flats was a "place to which the public have access." The Mental Health Act Commission reports that there "have been occasions when police, called to a disturbed individual in an Accident and Emergency Department, have declined to use section 136 on grounds that it is not a public place" (Fifth Biennial Report 1991–1993, para. 10.7(a)). As a hospital Accident and Emergency Department waiting area is a place at which members of the public can attend without hindrance for a particular purpose, such a place comes within the scope of this provision. A memorandum on the meaning of this phrase by Dr I. J. Keown is reproduced as Appendix D to *Out of Harm's Way*, above

In their examinations of the uses of this section in *Detained. Inspection of compulsory mental health admissions* (2001), the Social Services Inspectorate found a "significant minority" of cases where the police had used their power under this section unlawfully by removing "people from their own homes to a place of safety" (para. 6.8). If the person concerned is on private premises the police could consider using their common law and statutory powers to enter such premises to prevent a breach of the peace.

Necessary to do so: There is nothing to prevent the person from being escorted to hospital without this section being invoked if he is willing to be admitted as an informal patient and the hospital is prepared to accept him.

Appears to him: No medical evidence is needed. All that is required is that the constable has a reasonable belief that the person is mentally disordered within the meaning of section 1. It is for the constable to determine whether he is detaining a person under this section: he cannot make a determination which is conditional on a subsequent confirmation by a superior officer. Although some concern has been expressed about the ability of the police to recognise persons who are mentally disordered, research studies suggest that the police are able to diagnose psychiatric patients and are efficient sources of referrals: see P. Bean, *Compulsory Admissions to Mental Hospitals*, 1980, p. 73, A. Rogers and A. Faulkner, *A Place of Safety* (1987), p. 32, and T. A. Fahy, "The Police as a Referral Agency for Psychiatric Emergencies—A Review," (1989) 29 *Medicine, Science and the Law*, 315–22. P. Joseph suggests that a more cautious interpretation of such studies "would be that the police are missing many other cases of mental illness, hence the lack of false positives in their referrals" ("Mentally disordered offenders: diversion from the criminal justice system" above, at p. 135). A. E. Mokhtar and P. Hogbin report that patients removed under this section are very similar clinically to the most difficult to manage patients detained under section 2 or section 3 ("Police May Underuse Section 136" (1993) 33 *Medicine Science and the Law*, 188–196).

Care or Control: The police can intervene under this section if the person concerned appears to be in immediate need of care. The potential use of force by the police is not a pre-condition to use of this section.

May: The fact that the criteria set out in this subsection are satisfied does not oblige a police officer to detain a person under this section.

Protection of other persons: But not their property.

Remove: There is no power under this section to remove the person from one place of safety to another: see the General Note to this section. A person who is being conveyed to a place of safety is deemed to be in legal custody (s.137).

This section does not specify who, other than the constable, might have the power to convey the patient to the place of safety. The *Butler Committee*, at paragraph 9.2, had "no doubt" that the constable's power "extends to persons acting under his direction, such as the ambulance staff who are taking the disordered person to hospital."

Subsection (2)

1–1095   *Place of safety:* Is defined in section 135(6). The choice of place of safety is for the police, bearing in mind that a hospital is not legally obliged to act as a place of safety under this section. Paragraph 4(i) of Home Office Circular 66/90 recommends that the place of safety should, wherever possible, be a hospital rather than a police station. This is also the view of the Mental Health Act Commission (M.H.A.C., Sixth Biennial Report, 1993–1995, para. 7.4) and the joint Home Office and Department of Health review of health and social services for mentally disordered offenders (Final Summary Report, Cm. 2088, para. 5.2). The annual report of the Police Complaints Authority, 1998–1999, states that the Authority does not consider a police cell to be a suitable place of safety. The *Code of Practice*, at paragraph 10.5, states that as a "general rule" it is preferable the person to be detained in a hospital. Also see paragraph 315 of the *Memorandum* which is quoted in the note on s.135(3). Council Report CR61 of the Royal College of Psychiatrists, "Standards of Places of Safety under Section 136 of the Mental Health Act (1983)", contains recommendations relating to the physical facilities, staffing and policy in relation to the use of the place of safety.

If the person is taken to a hospital, the police officer is only legally obliged to remain there if his presence is required to respond to a breach of the peace. The Police Complaints Authority has said that where a hospital is used as a place of safety police management will need to ensure that, where necessary, police officers remain in attendance until skilled staff can assume responsibility for the care and custody of the person concerned.

May be detained: Not necessarily by the police. "The powers of detention given by section 136(2) are not conferred expressly on the police, but are given to any person who is a party to the detention of the disordered person once he has been brought to a place of safety" (*Butler Committee*, para. 9.2). As the purpose of this section is to provide the individual with a mental health assessment, assessment by both doctor and approved social worker should begin as soon as possible after his arrival at the place of safety. If an admission to a hospital acting as a place of safety takes place late at night it would seem reasonable to delay summoning the approved social worker until the following morning.

A person who is detained under this section is not subject to the consent to treatment provisions contained in Part IV of this Act (s.56(1)(b)).

72 hours: The power to detain the person under this section will lapse as soon as he has been examined and interviewed and it is considered that no further arrangements need be made for his treatment or care (*Code of Practice*, para. 10.8). As the 72 hour period starts from the time when the person arrives at the place of safety a record of his time of arrival there must be made immediately (*ibid.*, para. 10.7). This period should not be continued under section 5(2) or (4) (*ibid.*, para. 10.18(b)). If a person escapes from the place of safety he cannot be retaken after the 72 hours have expired (s.138(3)).

Registered medical practitioner: Who should wherever possible be approved under section 12 of this Act (*Code of Practice*, para. 10.12). The authority to detain under this section ends if the doctor's assessment leads him to conclude that the person who has been brought to the place of safety is not mentally disordered because appearing to be mentally disordered is a condition precedent to being detained under this provision: see the *Code of Practice* at paragraph 10.8a and the note on "The Human Rights Act 1998", above. The detention will not end on a finding by the doctor that the patient is not "sectionable" because the sectioning of the person is only one of the possible outcomes of the assessment.

Approved social worker: The role of the approved social worker "includes contacting the detained person's relatives, and ascertaining whether there is a history of psychiatric treatment. Should admission to hospital prove necessary this information may indicate which hospital would be most suitable; but he should always consider whether any course other than admission to hospital is appropriate. Knowing the range of resources which is available he is in a position to assess all the circumstances and is responsible for making sure whether treatment in hospital is the only solution" (*Butler Committee*, para. 9.1). The role of the approved social worker is also considered in the *Code of Practice* at paragraph 10.15.

In its Second Biennial Report, 1985–87, the Mental Health Act Commission reported that it had "found that doubt exists when the person brought to the hospital [under this section] has been examined by the doctor but no approved social worker is available to conduct the interview. The legal consequences of failure to provide an approved social worker interview are open to debate. Has the person to remain in detention even though the doctor does not consider that compulsory admission is necessary, until the approved social worker is available? Good practice would suggest that if the delay is going to be considerable (say more than four hours) then the requirements of the section shall be deemed to have been fulfilled so that detention may end. The case where the doctor decides that compulsory admission is appropriate is more controversial, since Parliament clearly intended that the approved social worker's opinion would be of great importance both in providing a safeguard for the rights of the individual and in deciding what arrangements are most appropriate to provide the care which the person needs" (para. 11.1(e)). It is submitted that the wording of subsection (2) clearly envisages the person being both examined by a doctor and interviewed by a social worker and that in both of the situations identified by the Commission the patient will remain subject to detention under this section until the interview by the approved social worker takes place or the 72 hour period expires. In the passage quoted the Commission appears to assume that the sole purpose of being removed to a place of safety is to assess the patient for possible compulsory admission. Such an outcome is, in fact, only one of a number of options that would be considered on an assessment. Although the authority to detain the patient would not end on a finding by the doctor that the person was suffering from mental disorder but did not satisfy the grounds for compulsory admission, it would end if the doctor found that the person was not suffering from a mental disorder: see the note on "registered medical practitioner", above.

Necessary arrangements: It is the responsibility of both the doctor and approved social worker to consider if any necessary arrangements for the person's treatment and care need to be made (*Code of Practice*, para. 10.17).

Provisions as to custody, conveyance and detention

137.—(1) Any person required or authorised by or by virtue of this Act to **1–1096** be conveyed to any place or to be kept in custody or detained in a place of safety or at any place to which he is taken under section 42(6) above shall, while being so conveyed, detained or kept, as the case may be, be deemed to be in legal custody.

(2) A constable or any other person required or authorised by or by virtue of this Act to take any person into custody, or to convey or detain any person

shall, for the purposes of taking him into custody or conveying or detaining him, have all the powers, authorities, protection and privileges which a constable has within the area for which he acts as constable.

(3) In this section "convey" includes any other expression denoting removal from one place to another.

GENERAL NOTE

1–1097 This section specifies the circumstances whereby a person is deemed to be in legal custody and provides that a person who is required or authorised to detain or convey a person who is in legal custody shall have the powers of a constable when so acting. A person who escapes from legal custody can be retaken under section 138.

Subsection (2)

1–1098 In *R. v. Broadmoor Special Hospital Authority and The Secetary of State for the Department of Health, ex p. SH and D*, February 5, 1998, Potts J. held that this subsection was concerned with the limited function of detention for the purpose of conveyance to hospital, not with detention once there. This finding was referred to, without comment, when this case reached the Court of Appeal: see [1998] C.O.D. 199.

Powers . . . which a constable has: Which include the power to arrest a person who is wilfully obstructing him in the execution of his duties and the power to require other persons to assist him in the execution of his duties.

Retaking of patients escaping from custody

1–1099 **138.**—(1) If any person who is in legal custody by virtue of section 137 above escapes, he may, subject to the provisions of this section, be retaken—

(a) in any case, by the person who had his custody immediately before the escape, or by any constable or approved social worker;

(b) if at the time of the escape he was liable to be detained in a hospital within the meaning of Part II of this Act, or subject to guardianship under this Act, by any other person who could take him into custody under section 18 above if he had absented himself without leave.

(2) A person to whom paragraph (b) of subsection (1) above applies shall not be retaken under this section after the expiration of the period within which he could be retaken under section 18 above if he had absented himself without leave on the day of the escape unless he is subject to a restriction order under Part III of this Act or an order or direction having the same effect as such an order; and subsection (4) of the said section 18 shall apply with the necessary modifications accordingly.

(3) A person who escapes while being taken to or detained in a place of safety under section 135 or 136 above shall not be retaken under this section after the expiration of the period of 72 hours beginning with the time when he escapes or the period during which he is liable to be so detained, whichever expires first.

(4) This section, so far as it relates to the escape of a person liable to be detained in a hospital within the meaning of Part II of this Act, shall apply in relation to a person who escapes—

(a) while being taken to or from such a hospital in pursuance of regulations under section 19 above, or of any order, direction or authorisation under Part III or VI of this Act (other than under section 35, 36, 38, 53, 83 or 85) or under section 123 above; or

(b) while being taken to or detained in a place of safety in pursuance of an order under Part III of this Act (other than under section 35, 36 or 38 above) pending his admission to such a hospital,

as if he were liable to be detained in that hospital and, if he had not previously been received in that hospital, as if he had been so received.

(5) In computing for the purposes of the power to give directions under section 37(4) above and for the purposes of sections 37(5) and 40(1) above the period of 28 days mentioned in those sections, no account shall be taken of any time during which the patient is at large and liable to be retaken by virtue of this section.

(6) Section 21 above shall, with any necessary modifications, apply in relation to a patient who is at large and liable to be retaken by virtue of this section as it applies in relation to a patient who is absent without leave and references in that section to section 18 above shall be construed accordingly.

DEFINITIONS

approved social worker: s.145(1).   **1–1100**
absent without leave: ss.18(6), 145(1).
restriction order: ss.41, 145(1).
patient: s.145(1).

GENERAL NOTE

This section provides for the retaking of persons who have escaped from legal **1–1101** custody. If a patient who has been made subject to an application under Part II of this Act escapes whilst on his way to hospital, he can only be retaken if he can be apprehended within the relevant period set out in either paragraph (a) or paragraph (b) of section 6(1). A person who assists another person who is in legal custody to escape commits an offence under section 128(2).

Subsection (1)

Retaken: This section does not provide authority for force to be used to enter **1–1102** premises where the patient is believed to be. An application to a magistrate under section 135 should be made if such action is deemed to be necessary.

Hospital within the meaning of Part II: See section 34(2).

Subsection (6)

The effect of this subsection is that if the patient is retaken within the last week of **1–1103** the period during which he can be retaken, the authority to detain him will end a week after the day he is retaken.

Protection for acts done in pursuance of this Act

139.—(1) No person shall be liable, whether on the ground of want of **1–1104** jurisdiction or on any other ground, to any civil or criminal proceedings to which he would have been liable apart from this section in respect of any act purporting to be done in pursuance of this Act or any regulations or rules made under this Act, or in, or in pursuance of anything done in, the discharge of functions conferred by any other enactment on the authority having jurisdiction under Part VII of this Act, unless the act was done in bad faith or without reasonable care.

(2) No civil proceedings shall be brought against any person in any court in respect of any such act without the leave of the High Court; and no criminal proceedings shall be brought against any person in any court in respect of any such act except by or with the consent of the Director of Public Prosecutions.

(3) This section does not apply to proceedings for an offence under this Act, being proceedings which, under any other provision of this Act, can be instituted only by or with the consent of the Director of Public Prosecutions.

(4) This section does not apply to proceedings against the Secretary of State or against a [Health Authority[, Special Health Authority or Primary Care Trust]] [or against a National Health Service trust established under the National Health Service and Community Care Act 1990].

(5) In relation to Northern Ireland the reference in this section to the Director of Public Prosecutions shall be construed as a reference to the Director of Public Prosecutions for Northern Ireland.

AMENDMENT

In subsection (4) the words in square brackets were added by the National Health Service and Community Care Act 1990, s.66(1), Sched. 9, para. 24(7) and the Health Authorities Act 1995, s.2(1), Sched. 1, para. 107(11). The reference to Primary Care Trusts was inserted by the Health Act 1999 (Supplementary, Consequential, etc., Provisions) Order 2000 (S.I. 2000 No. 90), Sched. 1, para. 16(8).

DEFINITIONS

1–1105   Health Authority: s.145(1).
Special Health Authority: s.145(1).

GENERAL NOTE

1–1106   This section provides that: (1) apart from proceedings against a Health Authority, a National Health Service trust, the Secretary of State or the National Assembly for Wales, and proceedings under section 127, no civil or criminal proceedings can be brought against any person in any court in respect of an act purporting to be done under this Act without the leave of the High Court or the Director of Public Prosecutions; and (2) for such proceedings to succeed the court must be satisfied that the person proceeded against acted in bad faith or without reasonable care. It does not affect the right of a patient to apply to the High Court for his discharge by means of a writ of *habeas corpus*: "If Parliament is to suspend *habeas corpus,* it must do so expressly or by clear implication"; *per* Lord Denning M.R. in *R. v. Governor of Pentonville Prison, ex p. Azam* [1974] A.C. 18, 31. *Azam* was referred to by Ackner L.J. in *R. v. Hallstrom and another, ex p. W* [1985] 3 All E.R. 775 where the Court of Appeal held that leave under this section is not required for applications for judicial review: see the note on "civil proceedings", below. During the course of this case all of the parties and the court accepted that this section would not bar an application for a writ of *habeas corpus*.

In *Winch v. Jones, Winch v. Hayward* [1985] 3 All E.R. 97, 102, CA, Sir John Donaldson M.R. said that this section "is intended to strike a balance between the legitimate interests of the applicant to be allowed, at his own risk as to costs, to seek the adjudication of the courts on any claim which is not frivolous, vexatious or an abuse of the process and the equally legitimate interests of the respondent to such an application not to be subjected to the undoubted exceptional risk of being harassed by baseless claims by those who have been treated under the Mental Health Acts."

Winch v. Jones was cited in *James v. Mayor and Burgesses of the London Borough of Havering,* (1992) 15 B.M.L.R. 1, CA, where Farquharson L.J. said that the effect of this section goes further than that identified by Sir John Donaldson M.R. in that "it is not only protection against frivolous claims; it is also a protection from error in the circumstances set out in [subsection (1)]." His Lordship described the point of this section as providing a protection for a social worker or a doctor "from the consequences of a wrong decision made in purported compliance with this Act" and said that "what one has to look at in deciding whether they are entitled to the protection of [this section] is what appeared to the social worker and the doctor at the time and how they reacted to it."

A successful application under subsection (2) of this section does not inhibit a judge on an application to strike out reaching a conclusion following fuller investigation that a statement of claim should be struck out as disclosing no reasonable cause of action (*X v. A, B and C and the Mental Health Act Commission* (1991) 9 B.M.L.R. 91).

This section is considered by D. Hewitt in "Something less than ready access to the courts: Section 139 and Local Authorities", (2000) 3 Journal of Mental Health Law 73–82. The impact of this section on the tort liability of approved social workers and their employers is examined by J. and A. Jaconelli in "Tort liability under the Mental Health Act 1983" (1998) 20(2) J.Soc.Wel. & Fam.L. 151–164.

The Human Rights Act 1989
The provisions of this section do not transgress a patient's right to a fair trial under **1–1107** the European Convention on Human Rights (see the note on Art. 6(1)).

Subsection (1)
"In my judgment this subsection does not create any cause of action and only **1–1108** relates to pre-existing possible liability. It creates a hurdle for a plaintiff to surmount" (*X v. A, B and C and the Mental Health Act Commission, ibid., per* Morland J. at 96).

Person: Or corporation (Interpretation Act 1978, s.5, Sched. 1).

Civil or criminal proceedings: The proceedings need not necessarily involve a patient.

Act purporting to be done in pursuance of this Act: Nearly all acts done "in pursuance of this Act" will relate to detained patients. During the passage of the 1982 Act the Government resisted an amendment to exclude the provisions of this section for informal patients on the ground that this would remove the protection given to someone who purports to do something under the Act when he *believes* that the patient is a detained patient. The Minister for Health gave the following illustration in support of this argument: "An ambulance man ... has a patient in his charge whom he believes is a detained patient because he is told so. Therefore, he is told that he should prevent the patient escaping. If the patient attempts to go off and he takes steps to stop him escaping, he might be liable to an action thereafter, but he would be protected if we retain [this section] with its present wording" (HC, Vol. 29, col. 173). This interpretation has not yet been tested in the High Court but there is Crown Court authority for the contention that this section does not cover acts done in respect of informal patients (*R. v. Runighian* [1977] Crim.L.R. 361). This section clearly applies to patients who are subject to the jurisdiction of the Court of Protection and to patients under guardianship and supervised discharge.

In *Pountney v. Griffiths* [1976] A.C. 314, the House of Lords quashed the conviction of a nurse who had been charged with assaulting a patient when ushering the patient to his ward after a visit from the patient's family, on the ground that leave to prosecute had not been obtained under subsection (2) of this section. Their Lordships approved the finding of Lord Widgery C.J. in the Court of Appeal that "when a male nurse is on duty and exercising his functions of controlling the patients in the hospital, acts done in pursuance of such control are acts within the scope of [section 139] and are thus protected by the section." Although this Act provides for the detention and treatment of patients, it nowhere explicitly refers to the control of patients. The House of Lords held that treatment necessarily involves the exercise of discipline and control, and that suitable arrangements for visits to patients by family and friends was an obvious part of the patient's treatment. *Pountney v. Griffiths* was cited by Auld L.J. in *R. v. Broadmoor Special Hospital and the Secretary of State for the Department of Health, ex p. S, H, and D* [1998] C.O.D. 199, where the Court of Appeal held that the power of detention carries with it a power of control and discipline, including, where necessary, a power to search patients with or without cause and despite individual medical objections (see further, ch. 25 of the *Code of Practice*). His Lordship said that both this Act and the 1959 Act "leave unspoken many of the necessary incidents of control flowing from a power of detention for treatment, including: the power to restrain patients, to keep them in seclusion ..., to deprive them of their personal possessions for their own safety and to regulate the frequency and manner of visits to them ..." The Report of the Committee of Inquiry into the Personality Disorder Unit, Ashworth Special Hospital (1999) made the following response to this judgment: "In the Special Hospitals there are fundamental requirements of security that must prevail and be seen to prevail. For far too long there has been uncertainty in this important area. We welcome the clarification provided by this judgment" (para. 2.12.28). Also see *R. v. Mental Health Act Commission, ex p. Smith* (1998) 43 B.M.L.R. 174, noted under section 120(1)(b)(ii) and the footnote to paragraph 25.3 of the Code of Practice.

In the unreported case of *Ashingdane v. Secretary of State for Social Services*, February 18, 1980, the Court of Appeal held that the immunity conferred by this section is confined to an act done by a person to whom authority to do an act of that type is expressly or impliedly conferred by this Act or by regulations made under it. Applying this test the Court held that the decision of a nurses' union not to allow patients who were subject to restriction orders to be transferred to a particular hospital was a policy decision which fell outside their express or implied authority and was not, therefore, covered by this section. *Per* Bridge L.J.: "[Subsection (1)] clearly propound[s] a subjective and not an objective test. If a person is acting honestly with the intention of performing, in the best way he knows how, the statutory functions or duties which are cast upon him, then it seems to me he is acting in purported pursuance of the statute."

Acted in bad faith or without reasonable care: In *Richardson v. London County Council* [1957] 1 W.L.R. 751 it was held: (1) that whether a person has acted in bad faith or without reasonable care is a question of fact with the burden of proof lying with the applicant; and (2) that this section offers protection even though the person proceeded against acted either without jurisdiction or misconstrued this Act, as long as the misconstruction was one which this Act was reasonably capable of bearing. Although a mistake about the law comes within the scope of this section, professional people who have functions placed upon them by this Act are under an obligation to acquire knowledge about the law they are operating. A person seeking a remedy for an alleged mistake of law would be advised to apply for a judicial review of the decision: see the note on "civil proceedings," below.

Subsection (2)

1–1109   *Civil proceedings:* This phrase does not include proceedings for judicial review. Acts purportedly done in pursuance of this Act can therefore be reviewed by the Divisional Court even if bad faith or lack of reasonable care are not alleged (*R. v. Hallstrom and another, ex p. W*, above). "This decision is to be applauded. By not imposing severe restrictions on applications for judicial review, it will permit the resolution of some complex problems of interpretation of the Act to the advantage of doctors and approved social workers, without having the traumatic effect on the professionals that a negligence or similar action has" (M. J. Gunn, "Judicial Review of Hospital Admissions and Treatment in the Community under the Mental Health Act 1983" [1986] J.S.W.L. 290, 292).

Leave: Proceedings instituted without leave being obtained are a nullity (*Pountney v. Griffiths* above). An appeal lies to the Court of Appeal against a judge's decision but either the leave of the judge or of the Court of Appeal is required before the appeal can be made (*Moore v. Commissioner of Metropolitan Police* [1968] 1 Q.B. 26). No appeal lies to the House of Lords from a refusal of the Court of Appeal of leave to appeal to the House (*Whitehouse v. Board of Control* [1960] 1 W.L.R. 1093, HL). The onus is on the applicant to satisfy the court or the D.P.P. that the proceedings should be commenced (*Carter v. Commissioner of Police for the Metropolis* [1975] 1 W.L.R. 507, CA).

The test to be applied by the court on an application for leave is "not whether the applicant has established a prima facie case or even whether there is a serious issue to be tried, although that comes close to it. The issue is whether, on the materials immediately available to the court, which, of course, can include material furnished by the proposed defendant, the applicant's complaint appears to be such that it deserves the fuller investigation which will be possible if the intended applicant is allowed to proceed" (*Winch v. Jones*, above, *per* Sir John Donaldson M.R., at 102). This test was applied by the Court of Appeal in *Simpson-Cleghorn v. Lancashire County Council*, July 5, 1999.

In *Furber v. Kratter, The Times*, July 21, 1988, Henry J. said that "it is really only if it is unfair to the defendants that there should be a trial at all that the court should refuse leave." In this case leave was granted to a patient who alleged that immediately after she had attacked a nurse she was placed in seclusion for 16 days during which there was a denial of nursing care to her and a denial of clothing, reading and writing materials. The patient alleged both negligence and false imprisonment against the nursing team. The judge rejected a submission made on behalf of the nurses that the detention of the patient, who was subject to a restriction order under section 41 of this Act, could not be made unlawful by a change in the conditions of her detention. Referring to *Middleweek v. Chief Constable of Merseyside* [1985] C.L.Y. 3386, the judge held that a lawful detention could become unlawful by a change in the conditions of the detention, although it is a matter of degree and could only happen in extreme cases.

Subsection (3)
Consent of the Director of Public Prosecutions: Is required for proceedings under **1–1110** section 127.

Subsection (4)
Does not apply: Note that the acts of a local social services authority performed in **1–1111** pursuance of this Act are protected by this section.
Secretary of State: This subsection shall have effect as if after these words there were inserted "the National Assembly for Wales" (S.I. 2000 No. 253, Sched. 3).

Notification of hospitals having arrangements for reception of urgent cases

140. It shall be the duty of every [Health Authority] to give notice to every **1–1112** local social services authority for an area wholly or partly comprised within the [Health Authority's area] specifying the hospital or hospitals administered by [or otherwise available] [to the Health Authority] in which arrangements are from time to time in force for the reception, in case of special urgency, of patients requiring treatment for mental disorder.

AMENDMENT
The amendment to this section was made by the National Health Service and Community Care Act 1990, s.66(1), Sched. 9, para. 24(8) and the Health Authorities Act 1995, s.2(1), Sched. 1, para. 107(12).

DEFINITIONS
Health Authority: s.145(1).   **1–1113**
local social services authority: s.145(1).
hospital: s.145(1).
patient: s.145(1).
mental disorder: ss.1, 145(1).

GENERAL NOTE
Paragraph 296 of the *Memorandum* states: "The attention of Health Authorities is **1–1114** drawn to the fact that the section 140 places a statutory duty on them to notify social services authorities, wholly or partly in their area, of hospitals which have arrangements for admitting emergencies. This duty will be met if the Health

Authority makes arrangements for social services authorities to be kept aware of psychiatric catchment areas for particular hospitals within the Region, with suitable notes explaining, for example, where the catchment area for elderly patients differs from that for younger patients." Also note the duty placed on Health Authorities by section 39, to provide the courts with information as to the availability of hospital places.

Reception: This section does not oblige the specified hospitals to admit patients.

Requiring treatment: Either as informal or detained patients.

Members of Parliament suffering from mental illness

1–1115   **141.**—(1) Where a member of the House of Commons is authorised to be detained on the ground (however formulated) that he is suffering from mental illness, it shall be the duty of the court, authority or person on whose order or application, and of any registered medical practitioner upon whose recommendation or certificate, the detention was authorised, and of the person in charge of the hospital or other place in which the member is authorised to be detained, to notify the Speaker of the House of Commons that the detention has been authorised.

(2) Where the Speaker receives a notification under subsection (1) above, or is notified by two members of the House of Commons that they are credibly informed that such an authorisation has been given, the Speaker shall cause the member to whom the notification relates to be visited and examined by two registered medical practitioners appointed in accordance with subsection (3) below.

(3) The registered medical practitioners to be appointed for the purposes of subsection (2) above shall be appointed by the President of the Royal College of Psychiatrists and shall be practitioners appearing to the President to have special experience in the diagnosis or treatment of mental disorders.

(4) The registered medical practitioners appointed in accordance with subsection (3) above shall report to the Speaker whether the member is suffering from mental illness and is authorised to be detained as such.

(5) If the report is to the effect that the member is suffering from mental illness and authorised to be detained as aforesaid, the Speaker shall at the expiration of six months from the date of the report, if the House is then sitting, and otherwise as soon as may be after the House next sits, again cause the member to be visited and examined by two such registered medical practitioners as aforesaid, and the registered medical practitioners shall report as aforesaid.

(6) If the second report is that the member is suffering from mental illness and authorised to be detained as mentioned in subsection (4) above, the Speaker shall forthwith lay both reports before the House of Commons, and thereupon the seat of the member shall become vacant.

(7) Any sums required for the payment of fees and expenses to registered medical practitioners acting in relation to a member of the House of Commons under this section shall be defrayed out of moneys provided by Parliament.

[(8) This section also has effect in relation to members of the Scottish Parliament but as it—
    (a) any references to the House of Commons or the Speaker were references to the Scottish Parliament or (as the case may be) the Presiding Officer, and
    (b) subsection (7) were omitted.]

[(9) This section also has effect in relation to members of the National Assembly for Wales but as if—
  (a) references to the House of Commons were to the Assembly and references to the Speaker were to the presiding officer, and
  (b) in subsection (7), for "defrayed out of moneys provided by Parliament" there were substituted "paid by the National Assembly for Wales".]

[(10) This section also has effect in relation to members of the Northern Ireland Assembly but as if—
  (a) references to the House of commons were to the Assembly and references to the Speaker were to the Presiding Officer; and
  (b) in subsection (7), for "provided by Parliament" there were substituted "appropriated by Act of the Assembly".]

AMENDMENTS
  Subsection (8) was added by the Scotland Act 1998, s.125, Sched. 8, para. 19, subsection (9) was inserted by the Government of Wales Act 1998, s.125, Sched. 12, para. 23 and subsection (10) was inserted by the Northern Ireland Act 1998, s.99, Sched.13, para.5.

DEFINITIONS
  hospital: s.145(1).   **1–1116**
  mental disorder: ss.1, 145(1).

GENERAL NOTE
  This section sets out the procedure for vacating the seat of a member of the House **1–1117**
of Commons, the Scottish Parliament (subs.(8)), the National Assembly for Wales
(subs.(9)) and the Northern Ireland Assembly (subs.(10)), who has been detained
under this Act on the ground that he is suffering from mental illness.
  "There is no similar provision in the Act for members of the House of Lords but
House of Lords Standing Order 77 requires a court or authority ordering the
imprisonment or restraint of a member of the House of Lords to give written notice
to the Clerk of the Parliaments. Where a member of the House of Lords is detained
under the Act, the managers of the hospital or mental nursing home where that
member is detained should inform the Clerk of the Parliaments, House of Lords,
SW1 in writing of the section of the Act under which that member is detained and the
date of his detention. The Clerk should also be informed when the member of the
House of Lords is discharged or given leave of absence, or if he absents himself
without leave. Where the member of the House of Lords is sent from a court or
transferred from prison, the court or prison will have informed the Clerk of the
Parliaments but when that member is discharged or given leave of absence, or if he
absents himself from the hospital or nursing home without leave, it will be for the
managers to inform the Clerk" (*Memorandum*, para. 319). Also see the General
Note to Part II.

Subsection (1)
  Authorised to be detained: This section does not stipulate that the detention need **1–1118**
be under *this* Act.
  Mental illness: This section does not apply to a member who is detained on the
ground that he is suffering from any other form of mental disorder.

Pay, pensions, etc., of mentally disordered persons
  142.—(1) Where a periodic payment falls to be made to any person by way **1–1119**
of pay or pension or otherwise in connection with the service or employment

459

of that or any other person, and the payment falls to be made directly out of moneys provided by Parliament or the Consolidated Fund [or the Scottish Consolidated Fund], or other moneys administered by or under the control or supervision of a government department, the authority by whom the sum in question is payable, if satisfied after considering medical evidence that the person to whom it is payable (referred to in this section as "the patient") is incapable by reason of mental disorder of managing and administering his property and affairs, may, instead of paying the sum to the patient, apply it in accordance with subsection (2) below.

(2) The authority may pay the sum or such part of it as they think fit to the institution or person having the care of the patient, to be applied for his benefit and may pay the remainder (if any) or such part of the remainder as they think fit—

(a) to or for the benefit of persons who appear to the authority to be members of the patient's family or other persons for whom the patient might be expected to provide if he were not mentally disordered, or

(b) in reimbursement, with or without interest, of money applied by any person either in payment of the patient's debts (whether legally enforceable or not) or for the maintenance or other benefit of the patient or such persons as are mentioned in paragraph (a) above.

(3) In this section "government department" does not include a Northern Ireland department.

AMENDMENT

The words in square brackets in subsection (1) were inserted by the Scotland Act 1998 (Consequential Modifications) (No.2) Order 1999 (S.I. 1999 No. 1820), art.4, Sched.2, para.71.

DEFINITION

1–1120   mental disorder: ss.1, 145(1).

GENERAL NOTE

1–1121   Under this section provision is made in the case of any pay, pension or similar payment payable by Parliament or the Government, for direct payment to the institution or person having the care of the patient. Any sums which remain can be paid to members of the patient's family, or to other persons for whom the patient might be expected to provide were he not mentally disordered, or to reimburse people who have paid his debts or helped to maintain him or his family. This section applies to any person who "is incapable by reason of mental disorder of managing and administering his property and affairs" and is not limited to either detained or hospital patients.

Subsection (1)

1–1121.1   *Government department:* Or the National Assembly for Wales (S.I. 2000 No. 253, Sched. 3).

Supplemental

General provisions as to regulations, orders and rules

1–1122   **143.**—(1) Any power of the Secretary of State or the Lord Chancellor to make regulations, orders or rules under this Act shall be exercisable by statutory instrument.

(2) Any Order in Council under this Act [or any order made under section

54A [or 65] above] and any statutory instrument containing regulations or rules made under this Act shall be subject to annulment in pursuance of a resolution of either House of Parliament.

(3) No order shall be made under section [45A(10)] 68(4) or 71(3) above unless a draft of it has been approved by a resolution of each House of Parliament.

AMENDMENTS

In subsection (2) the words in square brackets were inserted by the Criminal Justice Act 1991, s.27(3) and the Health Authorities Act 1995, s.2(1), Sched. 1, para. 107(13).

In subsection (3) the figure in square brackets was inserted by the Crime (Sentences) Act 1997, s.55, Sched. 4, para. 12(18).

GENERAL NOTE

Subsection (1)

Secretary of State: Or, in relation to Wales, the National Assembly for Wales (S.I. **1–1123** 1999 No. 672, art. 2, Sched. 1).

Power to amend local Acts

144. Her Majesty may by Order in Council repeal or amend any local **1–1124** enactment so far as appears to Her Majesty to be necessary in consequence of this Act.

Interpretation

145.—(1) In this Act, unless the context otherwise requires— **1–1125**

"absent without leave" has the meaning given to it by section 18 above and related expressions shall be construed accordingly;

"application for admission for assessment" has the meaning given in section 2 above;

"application for admission for treatment" has the meaning given in section 3 above;

"approved social worker" means an officer of a local social services authority appointed to act as an approved social worker for the purposes of this Act;

["care home" has the same meaning as in the Care Standards Act 2000;]

["Health Authority" means a Health Authority established under section 8 of the National Health Service Act 1977;]

["high security psychiatric services" has the same meaning as in the National Health Service Act 1977;]

"hospital" means—

(a) any health service hospital within the meaning of the National Health Service Act 1977; and

(b) any accommodation provided by a local authority and used as a hospital or on behalf of the Secretary of State under that Act; and "hospital within the meaning of Part II of this Act" has the meaning given in section 34 above;

["hospital direction" has the meaning given in section 45A(3)(a) above;]

"hospital order" and "guardianship order" have the meanings respectively given in section 37 above;

461

["independent hospital" has the same meaning as in the Care Standards Act 2000;]

"interim hospital order" has the meaning given in section 38 above;

["limitation direction" has the meaning given in section 45A(3)(b) above;]

"local social services authority" means a council which is a local authority for the purpose of the Local Authority Social Services Act 1970;

"the managers" means—

(a) in relation to a hospital vested in the Secretary of State for the purposes of his functions under the National Health Service Act 1977, and in relation to any accommodation provided by a local authority and used as a hospital by or on behalf of the Secretary of State under that Act, the [Health Authority or Special Health Authority] responsible for the administration of the hospital;

(b) [...];

[(bb) in relation to a hospital vested in [a Primary Care Trust or] a National Health Service trust, [...] the trust;]

[(c) in relation to a registered establishment, the person or persons registered in respect of the establishment;]

and in this definition "hospital" means a hospital within the meaning of Part II of this Act;

"medical treatment" includes nursing, and also includes care, habilitation and rehabilitation under medical supervision;

"mental disorder," "severe mental impairment," "mental impairment" and "psychopathic disorder" have the meanings given in section 1 above;

[...]

"nearest relative," in relation to a patient, has the meaning given in Part II of this Act;

"patient" (except in Part VII of this Act) means a person suffering or appearing to be suffering from mental disorder;

["Primary Care Trust" means a Primary Care Trust established under section 16A of the National Health Service Act 1971;]

["registered establishment" has the meaning given in section 34 above;]

["the responsible after-care bodies" has the meaning given in section 25D above;]

"restriction direction" has the meaning given to it by section 49 above;

"restriction order" has the meaning given to it by section 41 above;

["Special Health Authority" means a Special Health Authority established under section 11 of the National Health Service Act 1977;]

[...]

[...]

["supervision application" has the meaning given in section 25A above;]

"transfer direction" has the meaning given to it by section 47 above.

[(1A) References in this Act to a patient being subject to after-care under supervision (or to after-care under supervision) shall be construed in accordance with section 25A above.]

[(1AA) Where high security psychiatric services and other services are provided at a hospital, the part of the hospital at which high security psychiatric services are provided and the other part shall be treated as separate hospitals for the purposes of this Act.]

(2) [...]

(3) In relation to a person who is liable to be detained or subject to guardianship by virtue of an order or direction under Part III of this Act (other than under section 35, 36, or 38), any reference in this Act to any enactment contained in Part II of this Act or in section 66 or 67 above shall be construed as a reference to that enactment as it applies to that person by virtue of Part III of this Act.

AMENDMENTS

In subs. (1) the words in square brackets were substituted or inserted by the Registered Homes Act 1984, s.57(1), Sched. 1, para. 11, the National Health Service and Community Care Act 1990, s.66(1), Sched. 9, para. 24(9), the Health Authorities Act 1995, s.2(1), Sched. 1, para. 107(14), the Mental Health (Patients in the Community) Act 1995, s.2(1), Sched. 1, para. 20, the Health Act 1999, s.65, Sched. 4, para. 69, the Crime (Sentences) Act 1997, s.55, Sched. 4, para. 12(19), the Health Act 1999 (Supplementary, Consequential, etc., Provisions) Order 2000 (S.I. 2000 No. 90), Sched. 1, para. 16(9) and the Care Standards Act 2000, s.116, Sched. 4, para. 9(10). Subs. (1A) was inserted by *ibid.* The definition of "standard scale" and subs. (2) were repealed by the Statute Law (Repeals) Act 1993, s.1(1), Sched. 1, Part XIV, Group 2. The words omitted from para. (bb) of the definition of "the managers" were repealed by the Mental Health (Amendment) Act 1994, s.1. The definition of "special hospital" and para. (b) of the definition of "the managers" were repealed and subs. (1AA) was inserted by the Health Act 1999, s.65, Sched. 4, para. 69, Sched. 5. The definition of "mental nursing home" was repealed by the Care Standards Act 2000, s.117(2), Sched. 6.

GENERAL NOTE

Subsection (1)

Approved social worker: It is submitted that an "officer" of a local social services **1–1126** authority is a person who has a contract of employment with that authority. This submission is supported by paragraph 12 of D.H.S.S. Circular LAC(86)15, entitled "Mental Health Act 1983—Approved Social Workers", which refers to an "employing authority" having the right to withdraw approval from a social worker in certain circumstances.

Care Home: Under section 3 of the Care Standards Act 2000, an establishment is a care home if it provides accommodation, together with nursing or personal care for any of the following persons:

(a) persons who are or have been ill;
(b) persons who have or have had a mental disorder;
(c) persons who are disabled or infirm;
(d) persons who are or have been dependent on alcohol or drugs.

An establishment is not a care home if it is a hospital, an independent clinic or a children's home, or if it is of a description excepted by regulations.

High Security Psychiatric Services: These comprise "hospital accommodation and services for persons who are liable to be detained under the Mental Health Act 1983 and in [the opinion of the Secretary of State] require treatment under conditions of

463

high security on account of their dangerous, violent or criminal propensities" (National Health Service Act 1977, s.4(1)).

Hospital: This definition includes hospitals providing high security psychiatric services (see above) and hospitals which do not specialise in treating patients with mental disorder. The definition of "hospital within the meaning of Part II of this Act" includes a registered establishment (s.34(2)).

Prison "hospitals" are excluded from the definition as such facilities are not provided under the 1977 Act. The implications of this exclusion are considered by Professor J. Gunn: "The term 'hospital' as applied to prison facilities for the mentally disordered is also misleading as the Mental Health Act 1983 does not regard any facility within prison as a hospital. This prevents compulsory treatment within prison. The psychotic patient in prison is also deprived of the safeguards provided by the Mental Health Act Commission. In some prison hospitals, it is possible to see an acutely psychotic patient locked in a cell for the whole day. He may be clad only in a canvas shift with no possessions or furniture other than a mattress, possibly soaked in urine or soiled with faeces. Compulsory treatment can only be given in an emergency. Patients kept in such conditions in the health service would be the cause of public outcry and an enquiry. The situation is no more defensible when it occurs in prison" (*Mentally Disordered Prisoners*, J. Gunn *et al.*, Institute of Psychiatry, 1990, p. 65.) In *Knight v. Home Office* [1990] 3 All E.R. 237, Pill J. held that the standard of care provided for a mentally ill prisoner in a prison hospital was not required to be as high as the standard of care provided in a psychiatric hospital outside prison. His Lordship refused, at 243, to "speculate on what an appropriate standard might be".

Independent hospital: Under section 2(2) of the Care Standards Act 2000, an independent hospital is a hospital which is not a health service hospital.

Local social services authority: In England is a non-metropolitan county council, a metropolitan district council, a London borough council or the Common Council of the City of London. In Wales is a county council or a county borough council (Local Authority Social Services Act 1970, s.1). As far as the Isles of Scilly are concerned this expression shall, in relation to the Isles, mean the Council of the Isles constituted under the Isles of Scilly Order 1978: see the note on "Extent" in the General Note to this Act.

The managers: The functions of hospital managers are summarised in chapter 22 of the *Code of Practice*. Hospital managers are accountable for the lawfulness of each patient's detention under this Act (ss.6(2), 40(1)(b)). "The managers are primarily the people who 'detain' and therefore at common law are legally liable for any deprivation of liberty which is not justified by the Act" (Mental Health Act Commission, First Biennial Report, 1983–1985, para. 8.13).

Hospital vested in the Secretary of State: Or in the National Assembly for Wales for the purposes of its functions under the National Health Service Act 1997 (S.I. 2000 No. 253, Sched. 3).

The trust: Acting through its Board of Directors.

Medical treatment: The courts have interpreted this term very broadly. In *Reid v. Secretary of State for Scotland* [1999] 1 All E.R. 481, the House of Lords ruled that the definition of treatment contained in section 125 of the Mental Health (Scotland) Act 1984, which in all material respects is similar to the definition in this section, "is a wide one, which is sufficient to include all manner of treatment the purposes of which may extend from cure to containment". It "is also wide enough to include treatment which alleviates or prevents a deterioration of the symptoms of the mental disorder, not the disorder itself which gives rise to them" (*per* Lord Hope at 495, 497). Other cases have confirmed that the mere fact of being cared for or nursed in hospital under medical supervision is sufficient to constitute "medical treatment". See, for example, *R. v. South East Thames Mental Health Review Tribunal, ex p. Ryan*, June 30, 1987, DC, where Watkins L.J. adopted Denning L.J.'s definition (see *Minister of Health v.*

Royal Midland Counties Home for Incurables at Leamington Spa [1954] Ch. 530) of care as "the homely art of making people comfortable and providing for their well being" so far as their condition allows and *R. v. Mersey Mental Health Review Tribunal, ex p. Dillon, The Times*, April 13, 1987, DC, where the continued detention of the patient in hospital was upheld even though there was nothing other than nursing care that could be provided for him.

A decision to transfer a patient to another hospital could, in certain circumstances, be regarded as part of the patient's "medical treatment" (*R. (on the application of F.) v. Oxfordshire Mental Healthcare NHS Trust and Oxfordshire NHS Health Authority* [2001] EWHC Admin 535). *Per* Sullivan J.: "Treatment includes rehabilitation, and I can envisage cases where transfer to a particular institution because of the particular form of therapy available there would be a necessary step in the patient's rehabilitation" (para. 68).

"Habilitation" is defined in the *Shorter Oxford English Dictionary* as "the action of enabling or endowing with ability or fitness, capacitation, qualification". An illustration of the distinction between habilitation and rehabilitation was given by Mr Terry Davis M.P. at the Special Standing Committee: " 'Habilitation' would cover those cases in which someone, probably a child, was so severely mentally impaired that he had never learnt certain social skills such as being able to eat or communicate in some way. The remedying of that impairment cannot be called 'rehabilitation' because that person never had those skills, so one has to use the word 'habilitation' in its technical sense." (Sitting of June 22, 1982).

Nearest relative: Is defined in section 26.

Patient: In *R. v. Davies and Poolton* [2000] Crim.L.R. 297, the Court of Appeal considered a similar definition of patient found in section 22 of the Registered Homes Act 1984. The court said: "It is obvious that a person may be receiving treatment for mental disorder, without actually suffering from it, if he or she *appears* to be suffering from it. Much medical diagnosis and treatment is based on probability, not certainty or therefore, in some cases, actuality."

In *R. v. Merseyside Mental Health Review Tribunal, ex p. K* [1990] 1 All E.R. 694, CA, the appellant, a restricted patient, sought judicial review of the tribunal's decision on the ground that once it had found as a fact that he was not suffering from mental disorder he was no longer a "patient" as defined in this section and he was therefore entitled to an absolute discharge. The Court of Appeal affirmed the tribunal's decision to grant the patient a conditional discharge and held that a restricted patient remains a "patient" until he is discharged absolutely. *Per* Butler-Sloss L.J. at 699: "At the time the offender is detained under a hospital order he is a patient within the interpretation of section 145. By section 41(3)(a) a restricted patient continues to be liable to be detained until discharged under section 73 and, in my judgment, remains a patient until he is discharged absolutely, if at all, by the tribunal. Any other interpretation of the word 'patient' makes nonsense of the framework of the 1983 Act and the hoped-for progression to discharge of the treatable patient, treatable being a prerequisite of his original admission."

Subsection (3)

I gratefully adopt Phil Fennell's interpretation of this obscurely drafted provision: **1–1127** "For certain purposes, such as the renewal of detention, and entitlement to Mental Health Review Tribunals, parties liable to be detained under Part III are treated as if liable to be detained under section 3. What section 145(3) does is to ensure that this happens subject to the modifications specified in sections 40(4), 41(3) and (5), 55(4) and Sched. 1, Pt 1. ... The modifications relate to the powers to remand and to sentence to interim hospital orders. People who are on remand remain under the jurisdiction of the courts. They are liable to be detained, but they remain under the jurisdiction of the courts rather than the mental health system. The reason that they are expressly mentioned in section 145(3) is that they have no rights to seek discharge from a Mental Health Review Tribunal" ("Double Detention under the Mental Health Act 1984—A Case of Extra Parliamentary Legislation?" [1991] J.S.W.F.L. 200).

Application to Scotland

1–1128   **146.** Sections 42(6), 80, 88 (and so far as applied by that section sections 18, 22 and 138), 104(4), 110 (and so much of Part VII of this Act as is applied in relation to Scotland by that section), 116, 122, 128 (except so far as it relates to patients subject to guardianship), 137, 139(1), 141, 142, 143 (so far as applicable to any Order in Council extending to Scotland) and 144 above shall extend to Scotland together with any amendment or repeal by this Act or any provision of Schedule 5 to this Act relating to any enactment which so extends; but, except as aforesaid and except so far as it relates to the interpretation or commencement of the said provisions, this Act shall not extend to Scotland.

DEFINITION
1–1129   patient: s.145(1).

GENERAL NOTE
1–1130   This section provides for a limited application to this Act to Scotland. For an account of Scots law as it relates to mental health, see H. Patrick and A. Ward, *Mental Health (Scotland) Act 1984 & Adults with Incapacity Act 2000*, 2001.

Application to Northern Ireland

1–1131   **147.** Sections 81, 82, 86, 87, 88 (and so far as applied by that section sections 18, 22, and 138), 104(4), 110 (and so much of Part VII as is applied in relation to Northern Ireland by that section), section 128 (except so far as it relates to patients subject to guardianship), 137, 139, 141, 142, 143 (so far as applicable to any Order in Council extending to Northern Ireland) and 144 above shall extend to Northern Ireland together with any amendment or repeal by this Act of or any provision of Schedule 5 to this Act relating to any enactment which so extends; but except as aforesaid and except so far as it relates to the interpretation or commencement of the said provisions, this Act shall not extend to Northern Ireland.

DEFINITION
1–1132   patient: s.145(1).

GENERAL NOTE
1–1133   This section provides for a limited application of this Act to Northern Ireland.

Consequential and transitional provisions and repeals

1–1134   **148.**—(1) Schedule 4 (consequential amendments) and Schedule 5 (transitional and saving provisions) to this Act shall have effect but without prejudice to the operation of sections 15 to 17 of the Interpretation Act 1978 (which relate to the effect of repeals).

(2) Where any amendment in Schedule 4 to this Act affects an enactment amended by the Mental Health (Amendment) Act 1982 the amendment in Schedule 4 shall come into force immediately after the provision of the Act of 1982 amending that enactment.

(3) The enactments specified in Schedule 6 to this Act are hereby repealed to the extent mentioned in the third column of that Schedule.

Short title, commencement and application to Scilly Isles

1–1135   **149.**—(1) This Act may be cited as the Mental Health Act 1983.

(2) Subject to subsection (3) below and Schedule 5 to this Act, this Act shall come into force on September 30, 1983.

(3) Sections 35, 36, 38 and 40(3) above shall come into force on such day (not being earlier than the said September 30) as may be appointed by the Secretary of State and a different day may be appointed for each of those sections or for different purposes of any of those sections.

(4) Section 130(4) of the National Health Service Act 1977 (which provides for the extension of that Act to the Isles of Scilly) shall have effect as if the references to that Act included references to this Act.

GENERAL NOTE

Subsection (2)
Schedule 5: The provisions for approved social workers (ss.114 and 145(1)) came **1–1136** into force on October 28, 1984 (Sched. 5, para. 4).

Subsection (3)
Sections 35, 36, 38 and 40(3): Came into force on October 1, 1984 (S.I. 1984 No. **1–1137** 1537).

Subsection (4)
The Isles of Scilly (Mental Health) Order 1985 (S.I. 1985 No. 149) made under **1–1138** s.130(4) of the National Health Service Act 1977, extends this Act to the Isles of Scilly from March 12, 1985, with the modification that the expression "local social services authority" in this Act shall, in relation to the Isles, mean the Council of the Isles of Scilly.

SCHEDULES

Sections 40(4),   SCHEDULE 1
41(3) and (5),
and 55(4)

APPLICATION OF CERTAIN PROVISIONS TO PATIENTS SUBJECT
TO HOSPITAL AND GUARDIANSHIP ORDERS

PART I

PATIENTS NOT SUBJECT TO SPECIAL RESTRICTIONS

1. Sections 9, 10, 17, [21 to 21B], 24(3) and (4), [25C] to 28, 31, 32, 34, 67 and 76 shall apply in **1–1139** relation to the patient without modification.
2. Sections 16, 18, 19, 20, 22, 23, [25A, 25B] and 66 shall apply in relation to the patient with the modifications specified in paragraphs 3 to 9 below.
3. In section 16(1) for references to an application for admission or a guardianship application there shall be substituted references to the order or direction under Part III of this Act by virtue of which the patient is liable to be detained or subject to guardianship.
4. In section 18 subsection (5) shall be omitted.
5. In section 19(2) for the words from "as follows" to the end of the subsection there shall be substituted the words "as if the order or direction under Part III of this Act by virtue of which he was liable to be detained or subject to guardianship before being transferred were an order or

direction for his admission or removal to the hospital to which he is transferred, or placing him under the guardianship of the authority or person into whose guardianship he is transferred, as the case may be".

6. In section 20—

(a) in subsection (1) for the words from "day on which he was" to "as the case may be" there shall be substituted the words "date of the relevant order or direction under Part III of this Act;" and

(b) in subsection (9) for the words "the application for admission for treatment or, as the case may be, in the guardianship application, that application" there shall be substituted the words "the relevant order or direction under Part III of this Act, that order or direction".

7. In section 22 for references to an application for admission or a guardianship application there shall be substituted references to the order or direction under Part III of this Act by virtue of which the patient is liable to be detained or subject to guardianship.

8. In section 23(2)—

(a) in paragraph (a) the words "for assessment or" shall be omitted; and

(b) in paragraphs (a) and (b) the references to the nearest relative shall be omitted.

[8A. In sections 25A(1)(a) and 25B(5)(a) for the words "in pursuance of an application for admission for treatment" there shall be substituted the words "by virtue of an order or direction for his admission or removal to hospital under Part III of this Act".]

9. In section 66—

(a) in subsection (1), paragraphs (a), (b), (c), (g) and (h), the words in parenthesis in paragraph (i) and paragraph (ii) shall be omitted; and

(b) in subsection (2), paragraphs (a), (b), (c) and (g) [, and in paragraph (d), "(g)", shall be omitted.]

AMENDMENTS

The amendments to this Part were made by the Mental Health (Patients in the Community) Act 1995, s.2(1), Sched. 1, paras 6, 14, s.2(8).

PART II

PATIENTS SUBJECT TO SPECIAL RESTRICTIONS

1–1140   1. Sections 24(3) and (4), 32 and 76 shall apply in relation to the patient without modification.

2. Sections 17 to 19, 22, 23 and 34 shall apply in relation to the patient with the modifications specified in paragraphs 3 to 8 below.

3. In section 17—

(a) in subsection (1) after the word "may" there shall be inserted the words "with the consent of the Secretary of State";

(b) in subsection (4) after the words "the responsible medical officer" and after the words "that officer" there shall be inserted the words "or the Secretary of State"; and

(c) in subsection (5) after the word "recalled" there shall be inserted the words "by the responsible medical officer", and for the words from "he has ceased" to the end of the subsection there shall be substituted the words "the expiration of the period of [twelve] months beginning with the first day of his absence on leave".

4. In section 18 there shall be omitted—

(a) in subsection (1) the words "subject to the provisions of this section"; and

(b) subsections (3), (4) and (5).

5. In section 19—

(a) in subsection (1) after the word "may" in paragraph (a) there shall be inserted the words "with the consent of the Secretary of State", and the words from "or into" to the end of the subsection shall be omitted; [...]

(b) in subsection (2) for the words from "as follows" to the end of the subsection there shall be substituted the words "as if the order or direction under Part III of this Act by virtue of which he was liable to be detained before being transferred were an order or direction for his admission or removal to the hospital to which he is transferred" [and

(c) in subsection (3) after the words "may at any time" there shall be inserted the words ", with the consent of the Secretary of State",]

6. In section 22 subsection (1) and paragraph (a) of subsection (2) shall not apply.

7. In section 23—

(a) in subsection (1) references to guardianship shall be omitted and after the word "made" there shall be inserted the words "with the consent of the Secretary of State and"

(b) in subsection (2)—
  (i) in paragraph (a) the words "for assessment or" and "or by the nearest relative of the patient" shall be omitted; and
  (ii) paragraph (b) shall be omitted.

8. In section 34, in subsection (1) the definition of "the nominated medical attendant" and subsection (3) shall be omitted.

AMENDMENTS

The amendment to para. 3(c) was made by the Mental Health (Patients in the Community) Act 1995, s.3(3).

The word omitted in para. 5 was repealed by the Crime (Sentences) Act 1997, s.56(2), Sched. 6. Para 5(c) was inserted by *ibid.*, s.49(3).

DEFINITIONS

hospital order: ss.37, 145(1).   **1–1141**
patient: s.145(1).

Section 65(2)   SCHEDULE 2

MENTAL HEALTH REVIEW TRIBUNALS

1. Each of the Mental Health Review Tribunals shall consist of—   **1–1142**

(a) a number of persons (referred to in this Schedule as "the legal members") appointed by the Lord Chancellor and having such legal experience as the Lord Chancellor considers suitable;

(b) a number of persons (referred to in this Schedule as "the medical members") being registered medical practitioners appointed by the Lord Chancellor after consultation with the Secretary of State; and

(c) a number of persons appointed by the Lord Chancellor after consultation with the Secretary of State and having such experience in administration, such knowledge of social services or such other qualifications or experience as the Lord Chancellor considers suitable.

2. The members of Mental Health Review Tribunals shall hold and vacate office under the terms of the instrument under which they are appointed, but may resign office by notice in writing to the Lord Chancellor; and any such member who ceases to hold office shall be eligible for re-appointment.

3. One of the legal members of each Mental Health Review Tribunal shall be appointed by the Lord Chancellor as chairman of the Tribunals.

4. Subject to rules made by the Lord Chancellor under section 78(2)(c) above, the members who are to constitute a Mental Health Review Tribunal for the purposes of any proceedings or class or group of proceedings under this Act shall be appointed by the chairman of the tribunal or, if for any reason he is unable to act, by another member of the tribunal appointed for the purpose by the chairman; and of the members so appointed—

(a) one or more shall be appointed from the legal members;

(b) one or more shall be appointed from the medical members; and

(c) one or more shall be appointed from the members who are neither legal nor medical members.

5. A member of a Mental Health Review Tribunal for any area may be appointed under paragraph 4 above as one of the persons to constitute a Mental Health Review Tribunal for any other area for the purposes of any proceedings or class or group of proceedings; and for the purposes of this Act, a person so appointed shall, in relation to the proceedings for which he was appointed be deemed to be a member of that other tribunal.

6. Subject to any rules made by the Lord Chancellor under section 78(4)(a) above, where the chairman of the tribunal is included among the persons appointed under paragraph 4 above, he shall be president of the tribunal; and in any other case the president of the tribunal shall be such one of the members so appointed (being one of the legal members) as the chairman may nominate.

GENERAL NOTE

1–1143   An account of the roles of the legal member, the medical member and the lay member of the tribunal can be found in the Annual Report of the Mental Health Review Tribunals for England and Wales, 1997–98, pp. 86–89.

Paragraph 1

1–1144   *Legal member:* In the case of a restricted patient, the legal member must be chosen from a panel of legal members who have been approved by the Lord Chancellor to hear such cases (Mental Health Review Tribunal Rules 1983 (S.I. 1983 No. 942), r. 8(3)).

Medical members: Have a duty to examine the patient prior to the tribunal hearing and to form an opinion about the patient's mental condition (S.I. 1983 No. 942, r. 11). In practice the medical members are consultant psychiatrists.

The Lord Chancellor: Who, in the exercise of his functions under this provision in relation to Wales, is required to consult with the National Assembly for Wales with regard to appointments made under paragraphs (b) and (c) (S.I. 1999 No. 672, art. 5, Sched. 2).

Paragraph 4

1–1145   *Appointed by the chairman:* Members shall not be appointed in the circumstances set out in S.I. 1983 No. 942, r. 8(2).

Section 113   SCHEDULE 3

ENACTMENTS DISAPPLIED IN RESPECT OF PERSONS WITHIN
JURISDICTION UNDER PART VII

1–1146

Session and Chapter	Short title	Enactments
13 Geo. 3. c.81	The Inclosure Act 1733.	Sections 22 and 24.
7 Geo. 4. c.16.	The Chelsea and Kilmainham Hospital Act 1826.	Sections 44 to 48.
2 & 3 Will. 4. c.80.	The Ecclesiastical Corporation Act 1832.	Section 3.
1 & 2 Vict. c.106.	The Pluralities Act 1838.	Section 127.
4 & 5 Vict. c.38.	The Schools Sites Act 1841.	Section 5.
5 & 6 Vict. c.26.	The Ecclesiastical Houses of Residence Act 1842.	Section 12.
5 & 6 Vict. c.108.	The Ecclesiastical Leasing Act 1842.	Section 24.
8 & 9 Vict. c.16.	The Companies Clauses Consolidation Act 1845.	Section 79.
8 & 9 Vict. c.18.	The Lands Clauses Consolidation Act 1845.	Section 9.

8 & 9 Vict. c.118.	The Inclosure Act 1845.	Sections 20, 133, 134 and 137.
9 & 19 Vict. c.73.	The Tithe Act 1846.	Sections 5, 9 and 10.
17 & 18 Vict. c.112.	The Literary and Scientific Institutions Act 1854.	Section 5.
25 and 26 Vict. c.53.	The Land Registry Act 1862.	Section 116.
27 & 28 Vict. c.122.	The Improvement of Land Act 1866.	Section 24.
29 & 30 Vict. c.122.	The Metropolitan Commons Act 1866.	Section 28.
31 & 32 Vict. c.109.	The Compulsory Church Rate Abolition Act 1868.	Section 7.
36 & 37 Vict. c.50.	The Places of Worship Sites Act 1873.	Sections 1 and 3.
...	...	...
57 & 58 Vict. c.60.	The Merchant Shipping Act 1894.	In section 55, subsection (1).

AMENDMENT

The reference to the Colonial Stock Act 1877 was repealed by the Statute Law (Repeals) Act 1998, Sched. 1, Pt IV.

Section 148   SCHEDULE 4

CONSEQUENTIAL AMENDMENTS

[Not reproduced.]

Section 148   SCHEDULE 5

TRANSITIONAL AND SAVING PROVISIONS

1. Where any period of time specified in an enactment repealed by this Act is current at the **1–1147** commencement of this Act, this Act shall have effect as if the corresponding provision of this Act had been in force when that period began to run.

2. Nothing in this Act shall affect the interpretation of any provision of the Mental Health Act 1959 which is not repealed by this Act and accordingly sections 1 and 145(1) of this Act shall apply to any such provision as if it were contained in this Act.

3. Where, apart from this paragraph, anything done under or for the purposes of any enactment which is repealed by this Act would cease to have effect by virtue of that repeal it shall have effect as if it had been done under or for the purposes of the corresponding provisions of this Act.

4.—(1) Until the expiration of the period of two years beginning with the day on which the Mental Health (Amendment) Act 1982 was passed this Act shall have effect as if—

(a) section 114 were omitted;

(b) in section 145(1) the definition of an approved social worker were omitted and there were inserted in the appropriate place the following definition:—

" 'mental welfare officer' means an officer of a local services authority appointed to act as mental welfare officer for the purposes of the Mental Health Act 1959 or this Act";

(c) for paragraph 16(e) of Schedule 4 there were substituted—

"(e) in section 83(3)(a) for the words 'the Mental Health Act 1959' there were substituted the words 'the Mental Health Act 1983' ";

(d) for paragraph 47(e)(i) of Schedule 4 there were substituted—

"(i) in sub-paragraph (1)(d) for the words 'the Mental Health Act 1959' and 'Part IV or Part V' there were substituted respectively the words 'the Mental Health Act 1983' and 'Part II or III' "; and

(e) for any reference to an approved social worker there were substituted a reference to a mental welfare officer.

(2) Any appointment of a person as a mental welfare officer for the purposes of the Mental Health Act 1959 or this Act shall terminate at the expiration of the period mentioned in sub-paragraph (1) above but without prejudice to anything previously done by that person or to the continuation by an approved social worker of anything which is then in progress of being done by that person.

5. If no order has been made under section 11 of the National Health Service Act 1977 before September 30, 1983 establishing the Mental Health Commission the following shall be substituted for subsection (1) of section 121 of this Act—

"(1) The Secretary of State shall under section 11 of the National Health Service Act 1977 establish a special health authority to be known as the Mental Health Act Commission.".

1–1148 6. This Act shall apply in relation to any authority for the detention or guardianship of a person who was liable to be detained or subject to guardianship under the Mental Health Act 1959 immediately before September 30, 1983 as if the provisions of this Act which derive from provisions amended by section 1 or 2 of the Mental Health (Amendment) Act 1982 and the amendments in Schedule 3 to that Act which are consequential on those sections were included in this Act in the form the provisions from which they derive would take if those amendments were disregarded but this provision shall not apply to any renewal of that authority on or after that date.

7. This Act shall apply to any application made before September 30, 1983 as if the provisions of this Act which derive from provisions amended by sections 3 to 5 of the Mental Health (Amendment) Act 1982 and the amendments in Schedule 3 to that Act which are consequential on those sections were included in this Act in the form the provisions from which they derive would take if those amendents were disregarded.

8.—(1) Where on 30th September 1983 a person who has not attained the age of sixteen years is subject to guardianship by virtue of a guardianship application the authority for his guardianship shall terminate on that day.

(2) Section 8(1) of this Act has effect (instead of section 34(1) of the Mental Health Act 1959) in relation to a guardianship application made before the coming into force of this Act as well as in relation to one made later.

9.—(1) Section 20(1) of this Act shall have effect in relation to any application for admission for treatment and to any guardianship application made before October 1, 1983 with the substitution for the words "six months" of the words "one year".

(2) Section 20(2) of this Act shall have effect in relation to any authority renewed before October 1, 1983 with the substitution for the words "six months" of the words "one year" and for the words "one year" in both places they occur of the words "two years".

(3) Where an authority has been renewed on or before September 30, 1983 for a period of two years of which less than 16 months has expired on that date that period shall expire at the end of 18 months from the date on which it began.

10. Section 23(2)(a) of this Act shall have effect in relation to a patient liable to be detained in pursuance of an application under section 25 of the Mental Health Act 1959 made before September 30, 1983 as if the reference to the nearest relative of the patient were omitted.

11. Where at any time before September 30, 1983 an application to a Mental Health Review Tribunal has been made by a person who at that time was the patient's nearest relative and the application has not then been determined and by reason of the coming into force of section 26 of this Act that person ceased to be the patient's nearest relative on that date, that person shall nevertheless be treated for the purpose of the application as continuing to be his nearest relative.

12. A person—

(a) who was admitted to hospital in pursuance of an application for admission for treatment; or

(b) in respect of whom a guardianship application was accepted; or

(c) in respect of whom a hospital order was made,

before September 30, 1983 may make an application to a tribunal under section 66 of this Act in the cases mentioned in subsection (1)(b) and (c) of that section and under section 69(1)(b) of this Act within the period of six months beginning with day on which he attains the age of 16 years if that period is later than that which would otherwise apply to an application in his case.

13. Subsection (1) of section 68 of this Act does not apply to any patient admitted or **1–1149** transferred to hospital more than six months before September 30, 1983; and subsection (2) of that section applies only in relation to a renewal of authority for detention after that date.

14. Section 69(1)(b) of this Act shall have effect in relation to patients liable to be detained immediately before September 30, 1983 as if after the words "in respect of a patient" there were inserted the words "admitted to a hospital in pursuance of a hospital order or".

15. The provisions of this Act which derive from sections 24 to 27 of the Mental Health (Amendment) Act 1982 shall have effect in relation to a transfer direction given before September 30, 1983 as well as in relation to one given later, but where, apart from this paragraph, a transfer direction given before September 30, 1983 would by virtue of the words in section 50(3) of this Act which are derived from section 24(3) of the Mental Health (Amendment) Act 1982 have ceased to have effect before that date it shall cease to have effect on that date.

16. The words in section 42(1) of this Act which derive from the amendment of section 66(1) of the Mental Health Act 1959 by section 28(1) of the Mental Health (Amendment) Act 1982 and the provisions of this Act which derive from section 28(3) of and Schedule 1 to that Act have in relation to a restriction order or, as the case may be, a restriction direction made or given before September 30, 1983 as well as in relation to one made or given later, but—

(a) any reference to a tribunal under section 66(6) of the said Act of 1959 in respect of a patient shall be treated for the purposes of subsections (1) and (2) of section 77 of this Act in their application to sections 70 and 75(2) of this Act as an application made by him; and

(b) sections 71(5) and 75(1)(a) of this Act do not apply where the period in question has expired before September 30, 1983.

17. Section 91(2) of this Act shall not apply in relation to a patient removed from England and Wales before September 30, 1983.

18.—(1) Subsection (3) of section 58 of this Act shall not apply to any treatment given to a patient in the period of six months beginning with September 30, 1983 if—

(a) the detention of the patient began before the beginning of that period; and

(b) that subsection has not been complied with in respect of any treatment previously given to him in that period.

(2) The Secretary of State may by order reduce the length of the period mentioned in sub-paragraph (1) above.

19. In the case of a patient who is detained at the time when section 132 of this Act comes into **1–1150** force, the steps required by that section shall be taken as soon as practicable after that time.

20. The repeal by the Mental Health (Amendment) Act 1982 of section 77 of the Mental Health Act 1959 does not affect subsection (4) of that section in its application to a transfer direction given before September 30, 1983, but after the coming into force of this Act that subsection shall effect for that purpose as if for the references to subsection (6) of section 60, Part IV of that Act and the provisions of that Act there were substituted respectively references to section 37(8), Part III and the provisions of this Act.

21. Section 46(3) of this Act shall apply to any direction to which section 71(4) of the Mental Health Act 1959 applied immediately before the commencement of this Act.

22. Notwithstanding the repeal by this Act of section 53(5) of the Mental Health Act 1959, the discharge or variation under that section of an order made under section 52 of that Act shall not affect the validity of anything previously done in pursuance of the order.

23. For any reference in any enactment, instrument, deed or other document to a receiver under Part VIII of the Mental Health Act 1959 there shall be substituted a reference to a receiver under Part VII of this Act.

24. Nothing in this Act shall affect the operation of the proviso to section 107(5) of the Mental Health Act 1959 in relation to a charge created before the commencement of this Act under that section.

25. Nothing in this Act shall affect the operation of subsection (6) of section 112 of the Mental

Health Act 1959 in relation to a charge created before the commencement of this Act by virtue of subsection (5) of that section.

26. If the person who is the Master of the Court of Protection at the commencement of this Act has before that time duly taken the oaths required by section 115(1) of the Mental Health Act 1959 he shall not be obliged to take those oaths again by virtue of section 93(3) of this Act.

27. Nothing in this Act shall affect the operation of section 116 of the Mental Health Act 1959 in relation to orders made, directions or authorities given or other instruments issued before the commencement of this Act.

28. References to applications, recommendations, reports and other documents in section 126 of this Act shall include those to which sections 125 of the Mental Health Act 1959 applied immediately before the commencement of this Act and references in section 139 of this Act to the acts to which that section applies shall include those to which section 141 of the said Act of 1959 applied at that time.

29. The repeal by the Mental Health Act 1959 of the Mental Treatment Act 1930 shall not affect any amendment effected by section 20 of that Act in any enactment not repealed by the said Act of 1959.

30. The repeal by the Mental Health Act 1959 of the provisions of the Lunacy Act 1890 and of the Mental Deficiency Act 1913 relating to the superannuation of officers or employees shall not affect any arrangements for the payment of allowances or other benefits made in accordance with those provisions and in force on November 1, 1960.

31.—(1) Any patient who immediately before the commencement of this Act was liable to be detained in a hospital or subject to guardianship by virtue of paragraph 9 of Schedule 6 to the Mental Health Act 1959 shall unless previously discharged continue to be so liable for the remainder of the period of his treatment current on November 1, 1960.

(2) The patient may before the expiration of the period of treatment referred to in sub-paragraph (1) above apply to a Mental Health Review Tribunal.

1–1151   32. Any patient who immediately before the commencement of this Act was liable to be detained or subject to guardianship by virtue of an authority which had been renewed under paragraph 11 of Schedule 6 to the Mental Health Act 1959 shall unless previously discharged continue to be so liable during the period for which that authority was so renewed.

33.—(1) This paragraph applies to patients who at the commencement of this Act are liable to be detained or subject to guardianship by virtue of paragraph 31 or 32 above.

(2) Authority for the detention or guardianship of the patient may on the expiration of the relevant period, unless the patient has previously been discharged, be renewed for a further period of two years.

(3) Sections 20(3) to (10) and 66(1)(f) of this Act shall apply in relation to the renewal of authority for the detenton or guardianship of a patient under this paragraph as they apply in relation to the renewal of authority for the detention or guardianship of the patient under section 20(2).

(4) In this paragraph "the relevant period" means—

(a) in relation to a patient liable to be detained or subject to guardianship by virtue of the said paragraph 31, the period of his treatment referred to in that paragraph;

(b) in relation to a patient detained by virtue of the said paragraph 32, the period for which authority for the detention or guardianship of the patient has been renewed under paragraph 11 of Schedule 6 to the 1959 Act;

(c) in relation to a patient the authority for whose detention or guardianship has previously been renewed under this paragraph, the latest period for which it has been so renewed.

34.—(1) Any patient who is liable to be detained in a hospital or subject to guardianship by virtue of paragraph 31 above shall (subject to the exceptions and modifications specified in the following provisions of this paragraph) be treated as if he has been admitted to the hospital in pursuance of an application for admission for treatment under Part II of this Act or had been received into guardianship in pursuance of a guardianship application under the said Part II and had been so admitted or received as a patient suffering from the form or forms of mental disorder recorded under paragraph 7 of Schedule 6 to the Mental Health Act 1959 or, if a different form or forms have been specified in a report under section 38 of the Act as applied by that paragraph, the form or forms so specified.

(2) Section 20 of this Act shall not apply in relation to the patient, but the provisions of paragraph 33 above shall apply instead.

(3) Any patient to whom paragraph 9(3) of Schedule 6 to the Mental Health Act 1959 applied

at the commencement of this Act who fell within paragraph (b) of that paragraph shall cease to be liable to be detained on attaining the age of 25 years unless, during the period of two months ending on the date when he attains that age, the responsible medical officers records his opinion under the following provisions of this Schedule that the patient is unfit for discharge.

(4) If the patient was immediately before November 1, 1960 liable to be detained by virtue of section 6, 8(1) or 9 of the Mental Deficiency Act 1913, the power of discharging him under section 23 of this Act shall not be exercisable by his nearest relative, but his nearest relative may make one application in respect of him to a Mental Health Review Tribunal in any period of 12 months.

35.—(1) The responsible medical officer may record for the purposes of paragraph 34(3) above his opinion that a patient detained in a hospital is unfit for discharge if it appears to the responsible medical officer—

> (a) that if that patient were released from the hospital he would be likely to act in a manner dangerous to other persons or to himself, or would be likely to resort to criminal activities; or
> (b) that that patient is incapable of caring for himself and that there is no suitable hospital or other establishment into which he can be admitted and where he would be likely to remain voluntarily;

and where the responsible medical officer records his opinion as aforesaid he shall also record the grounds for his opinion.

(2) Where the responsible medical officer records his opinion under this paragraph in respect of a patient, the managers of the hospital or other persons in charge of the establishment where he is for the time being detained or liable to be detained shall cause the patient to be informed, and the patient may, at any time before the expiration of the period of 28 days beginning with the date on which he is so informed, apply to a Mental Health Review Tribunal.

(3) On any application under sub-paragraph (2) above the tribunal shall, if satisfied that none of the conditions set out in paragraphs (a) and (b) of sub-paragraph (1) above are fulfilled, direct that the patient be discharged, and subsection (1) of section 72 of this Act shall have effect in relation to the application as if paragraph (b) of that subsection were omitted.

36. Any person who immediately before the commencement of this Act was deemed to have **1–1152** been named as the guardian of any patient under paragraph 14 of Schedule 6 to the Mental Health Act 1959 shall be deemed for the purposes of this Act to have been named as the guardian of the patient in an application for his reception into guardianship under Part II of this Act accepted on that person's behalf by the relevant local authority.

37.—(1) This paragraph applies to patients who immediately before the commencement of this Act were transferred patients within the meaning of paragraph 15 of Schedule 6 to the Mental Health Act 1959.

(2) A transferred patient who immediately before the commencement of this Act was by virtue of sub-paragraph (?) of that paragraph treated for the purposes of that Act as if he were liable to be detained in a hospital in pursuance of a direction under section 71 of that Act shall be treated as if he were so liable in pursuance of a direction under section 46 of this Act.

(3) A transferred patient who immediately before the commencement of this Act was by virtue of sub-paragraph (3) of that paragraph treated for the purposes of the Act as if he were liable to be detained in a hospital by virtue of a transfer direction under section 72 of that Act and as if a direction restricting his discharge had been given under section 74 of that Act shall be treated as if he were liable by virtue of a transfer direction under section 47 of this Act and as if a restriction direction had been given under section 49 of this Act.

(4) Section 84 of this Act shall apply to a transferred patient who was treated by virtue of sub-paragraph (5) of that paragraph immediately before the commencement of this Act as if he had been removed to a hospital under section 89 of that Act as if he had been so removed under the said section 84.

(5) Any person to whom sub-paragraph (6) of that paragraph applied immediately before the commencement of this Act shall be treated for the purposes of this Act as if he were liable to be detained in a hospital in pursuance of a transfer direction given under section 48 of this Act and as if a restriction direction had been given under section 49 of this Act, and he shall be so treated notwithstanding that he is not suffering from a form of mental disorder mentioned in the said section 48.

38. Any patient who immediately before the commencement of this Act was treated by virtue of sub-paragraph (1) of paragraph 16 of Schedule 6 to the Mental Health Act 1959 as if he had been conditionally discharged under section 66 of that Act shall be treated as if he had been

conditionally discharged under section 42 of this Act and any such direction as is mentioned in paragraph (b) of that sub-paragraph shall be treated as if it had been given under the said section 42.

39. Upon a restriction direction in respect of a patient who immediately before the commencement of this Act was a transferred patient within the meaning of paragraph 15 of Schedule 6 to the Mental Health Act 1959 ceasing to have effect, the responsible medical officer shall record his opinion whether the patient is suffering from mental illness, severe mental impairment, psychopathic disorder or mental impairment, and references in this Act to the form or forms of mental disorder specified in the relevant application, order or direction shall be construed as including references to the form or forms of mental disorder recorded under this paragraph or under paragraph 17 of the said Schedule 6.

40. A person who immediately before the commencement of this Act was detained by virtue of paragraph 19 of Schedule 6 to the Mental Health Act 1959 may continue to be detained until the expiration of the period of his treatment current on November 1, 1960 or until he becomes liable to be detained or subject to guardianship under this Act, whichever occurs first, and may be so detained in any place in which he might have been detained under that paragraph.

41. Any opinion recorded by the responsible medical officer under the foregoing provisions of this Schedule shall be recorded in which form as may be prescribed by regulations made by the Secretary of State.

1–1153   42.—(1) In the foregoing provisions of this Schedule—

   (a) references to the period of treatment of a patient that was current on November 1, 1960 are to the period for which he would have been liable to be detained or subject to guardianship by virtue of any enactment repealed or excluded by the Mental Health Act 1959, or any enactment repealed or replaced by any such enactment as aforesaid, being a period which began but did not expire before that date; and

   (b) "the responsible medical officer" means—

      (i) in relation to a patient subject to guardianship, the medical officer authorised by the local social services authority to act (either generally or in any particular case or for any particular purpose) as the responsible medical officer;

      (ii) in relation to any other class of patient, the registered medical practitioner in charge of the treatment of the patient.

(2) Subsection (2) of section 34 of this Act shall apply for the purposes of the foregoing provisions of this Schedule as it applies for the purposes of Part II of this Act.

(3) The sentence or other period of detention of a person who was liable to be detained or subject to guardianship immediately before November 1, 1960 by virtue of an order under section 9 of the Mental Deficiency Act 1913 shall be treated for the purposes of the foregoing provisions of this Schedule as expiring at the end of the period for which that person would have been liable to be detained in a prison or other institution if the order had not been made.

(4) For the purposes of the foregoing provisions of this Schedule, an order sending a person to an institution or placing a person under guardianship made before March 9, 1956 on a petition presented under the Mental Deficiency Act 1913 shall be deemed to be valid if it was so deemed immediately before the commencement of this Act by virtue of section 148(2) of the Mental Health Act 1959.

43.—(1) Any order or appointment made, direction or authority given, or thing done which by virtue of paragraph 25 of Schedule 6 to the Mental Health Act 1959 had effect immediately before the commencement of this Act as if made, given or done under any provision of Part VIII of that Act shall have effect as if made, given or done under Part VII of this Act.

(2) Where at the commencement of this Act Part VIII of the Mental Health Act 1959 applied in any person's case by virtue of paragraph 25 of Schedule 6 to that Act as if immediately after the commencement of that Act it had been determined that he was a patient within the meaning of the said Part VIII, Part VII of this Act shall apply in his case as if immediately after the commencement of this Act it had been determined that he was a patient within the meaning of the said Part VII.

44. Where a person who immediately before November 1, 1960 was the committee of the estate of a person of unsound mind so found by inquisition was immediately before the

commencement of this Act deemed by virtue of paragraph 26 of Schedule 6 to the Mental Health Act 1959 to be a receiver appointed under section 105 of that Act for that person, he shall be deemed to be a receiver appointed under section 99 of this Act for that person and shall continue to have the same functions in relation to that person's property and affairs as were exercisable by him immediately before the commencement of that Act as committee of the estate and references in any document to the committee of the estate of that person shall be construed accordingly.

45. Section 101(1) of this Act shall apply in relation to any disposal of property (within the meaning of that section) of a person living on November 1, 1960, being a disposal effected under the Lunacy Act 1890 as it applies in relation to the disposal of property of a person effected under Part VII of this Act.

46. [...]

AMENDMENT

Para. 46 was repealed by the Health Authorities Act 1995, s.5(1), Sched. 3.

DEFINITIONS

local social services authority: s.145(1). **1–1154**
approved social worker: s.145(1).
application for admission for treatment: ss.3, 145(1).
patient: s.145(1).
nearest relative: ss.26(3), 145(1).
hospital order: ss.37, 145(1).
transfer direction: ss.47, 145(1).
restriction order: ss.41, 145(1).
restriction direction: ss.49, 145(1).
mental disorder: ss.2, 145(1).
hospital: s.145(1).
the managers: s.145(1).
severe mental impairment: ss.1, 145(1).
psychopathic disorder: ss.1, 145(1).
mental impairment: ss.1, 145(1).

GENERAL NOTE

This Schedule makes provision to cover the transition from the Mental Health Act **1–1155** 1959, as amended by the Mental Health (Amendment) Act 1982, to this Act. It therefore affects patients detained on or before the commencement date of this Act (September 30, 1983) and anything which was in the process of being done at that date. It is considered by Mike Gunn in *Mental Handicap,* Vol. 12, June 1984, p. 86 and in the *Memorandum,* paras. 299 to 322.

Paragraph 1

This paragraph states the general rule that any period of time specified in **1–1156** legislation which was in force on September 30, 1983 will be replaced by the corresponding provision in this Act, calculated from the time when the original order or application was made. This rule is subject to the important exceptions set out in paragraph 9.

Paragraph 2

The provisions of the Mental Health Act 1959 which were not repealed by this Act, **1–1157** *viz.* sections 8, 9 and 128, are to be interpreted by the use of the sections 1 and 145 of this Act.

Paragraph 6

This paragraph "ensures that the changes in the definitions of mental disorder will **1–1158** not affect the authority to detain somebody who was detained prior to September 30, 1983. This paragraph does not apply to the renewal of authority" (*Memorandum,* para. 303).

Paragraph 8

1–1159   Provides: (1) that guardianship ceases for patients who were under 16 on September 30, 1983; and (2) that the new powers of the guardian have immediate effect.

Paragraph 9

1–1160   "When an authority to detain a patient admitted for treatment or to subject a patient to guardianship is renewed before October 1, 1983 the duration of the authority applicable under the 1959 Act (of one or two years) will continue to apply. However, where the authority has been renewed for two years and less than 16 months has passed since the renewal by September 30, 1983, that period of detention will expire after 18 months rather than 2 years. If that detention is subsequently renewed the period of one year will apply" (*Memorandum*, para. 305).

Paragraph 31 to 42

1–1161   *Inter alia*, provide authority for the continued detention or guardianship of patents whose detention or guardianship commenced before the Mental Health Act 1959 came into force.

Section 134   SCHEDULE 6

1–1162   REPEALS

[*Not reproduced.*]

PART 2

DELEGATED LEGISLATION

MENTAL HEALTH (HOSPITAL, GUARDIANSHIP AND CONSENT TO TREATMENT) REGULATIONS 1983

(S.I. 1983 No. 893)

Dated June 23, 1983 and made by the Secretary of State for Social Services under the Mental Health Act 1983 (c. 20), ss.9, 19(1), (4), 32(1)(2), 57(1)(b), 58(1)(a), (64)(2), 134(8), Sched. 5, para. 41.

GENERAL NOTE

These Regulations are the principal regulations dealing with the exercise of **2–001** compulsory powers in respect of persons liable to be detained in hospital or subject to guardianship under the Mental Health Act 1983.

Part I contains general provisions affecting the interpretation of the Regulations and procedures required by the Act.

Part II contains provisions relating to the procedure for, and record of, hospital admissions, guardianship, re-classification and transfer of patients, and renewal of authority for detention or guardianship. Provision is also made for the classification, and record, of patients moved to England and Wales from Scotland, Northern Ireland, the Channel Islands or the Isle of Man. The forms for use in connection with these requirements are prescribed in Sched. 1.

Part III relates to the functions of guardians and nearest relatives of patients. Duties of guardians who are not local social services authorities, additional to those imposed by the Act, are prescribed, while the local social services authorities responsible for any patients subject to guardianship are required to visit such patients regularly. The nearest relatives of patients are empowered to authorise other persons to exercise their functions under the Act in respect of patients and provision is made in relation to the discharge of patients by nearest relatives. The forms for use in connection with discharge procedure are prescribed in Sched. 1.

Part IV concerns consent to treatment. It prescribes treatments (other than those specified in the Act) which are to require either consent and a second opinion or consent or a second opinion. The forms for use in connection with the consent procedure are prescribed in Schedule 1.

Part V contains provisions on the correspondence of patients. Procedures to be followed on opening postal packets and for making an application to the Mental Health Act Commission for review of a decision to withhold a postal packet or anything contained in it are set out.

Part IV contains transitional provisions and revocations. In particular provision is made so that the regulations apply to mental welfare officers during the transitional period before the introduction of approved social workers. The Mental Health (Hospital and Guardianship) Regulations 1960 are revoked.

Retention of records

The Secretary of State has made a direction under section 17 of the National **2–002** Health Service Act 1977 requiring Health Authorities to keep all records required to be made under these regulations for not less than five years commencing on the date on which the person to whom they relate ceases to be a hospital patient. This direction was extended to NHS trusts by a direction issued with Department of Health Circular No. HC(91)29: see the note on section 120(4) of the 1983 Act.

AMENDMENTS

2–003   The amendments to Form 13 in Schedule 1 were made by S.I. 1993 No. 2156, reg. 2(1) and S.I. 1998 No. 2624, reg. 2. The amendment to reg. 4(4) and the substitution of Forms 2–4, 7, 9–12, 14, 15, 21, 22, 24, 28–30 were made by S.I. 1996 No. 540. Reg. 10A and Forms 31A and 31B were inserted by S.I. 1997 No. 801.

ARRANGEMENT OF REGULATIONS

REG.

PART I

GENERAL

2–004 1. Citation and commencement
2. Interpretation
3. Documents

PART II

PROCEDURES AND RECORDS RELATING TO HOSPITAL ADMISSIONS
AND GUARDIANSHIP

4. Procedure for and record of hospital admissions
5. Procedure for and acceptance of guardianship applications
6. Procedure for and record of reclassification of patients
7. Transfer from hospital to hospital or guardianship
8. Transfer from guardianship to guardianship or hospital
9. Conveyance to hospital on transfer
10. Renewal of authority for detention or guardianship
11. Removal to England and Wales

PART III

FUNCTIONS OF GUARDIANS AND NEAREST RELATIVES

12. Duties of private guardians
13. Visits of patients subject to guardianship
14. Performance of functions of nearest relative
15. Discharge by nearest relative

PART IV

CONSENT TO TREATMENT

16. Consent to treatment

PART I

GENERAL

Citation and commencement
1. These regulations may be cited as the Mental Health (Hospital, **2–005**
Guardianship and Consent to Treatment) Regulations 1983 and shall come
into operation on September 30, 1983.

Interpretation
2.—(1) In these regulations, unless the context otherwise requires—   **2–006**

"the Act" means the Mental Health Act 1983;
"appropriate medical officer" has the same meaning as in section 16(5)
    of the Act;
"the Commission" means the Mental Health Act Commission;
"document" means any application, recommendation, record, report,
    order, notice or other document;
"private guardian", in relation to a patient, means a person, other than a
    local social services authority, who acts as guardian under the Act;
"served", in relation to a document, includes addressed, delivered,
    given, forwarded, furnished or sent.

(2) Except insofar as the context otherwise requires, any reference in
these regulations to—
  (a) a numbered section is to the section of the Act bearing that number;
  (b) a numbered regulation or Schedule is to the regulation in or Schedule
      to these regulations bearing that number and any references in a

regulation to a numbered paragraph is a reference to the paragraph of that regulation bearing that number;

(c) a numbered form is a reference to the form in Schedule 1 bearing that number.

Documents

2–007   **3.**—(1) Except in a case to which paragraph (2) or (3) applies, any document required or authorised to be served upon any authority, body or person by or under Part II of the Act (compulsory admission to hospital or guardianship) or these regulations may be served—

(a) by delivering it to the authority, body or person upon whom it is to be served, or upon any person authorised by that authority, body or person to receive it; or

(b) by sending it by prepaid post addressed to the authority or body at their registered or principal office or to the person upon whom it is to be served at this usual or last known residence.

(2) Any application for the admission of a patient to a hospital under Part II of the Act shall be served by delivering the application to an officer of managers of the hospital, to which it is proposed that the patient shall be admitted, authorised by them to receive it.

(3) Any order by the nearest relative of the patient under section 23 for the discharge of a patient who is liable to be detained under Part II of the Act, and the notice of such order given under section 25(1), shall be served either by delivery of the order or notice at that hospital to an officer of the managers authorised by them to receive it or by sending it by prepaid post to those managers at that hospital.

(4) Subject to sections 6(3) and 8(3) (proof of applications), any document required or authorised by or under Part II of the Act or these regulations and purporting to be signed by a person required or authorised by or under that Part II or these regulations to do so shall be received in evidence and be deemed to be such a document without further proof, unless the contrary is shown.

(5) Any document required to be addressed to the managers of a hospital in accordance with the Act or these regulations shall be deemed to be properly addressed to such managers if addressed to the administrator of that hospital.

(6) Where under these regulations a local social services authority or the managers of a hospital are required to make any record or report, that function may be performed by an officer authorised by that authority or those managers in that behalf.

DEFINITIONS

2–008   served: reg. 2(1).
document: reg. 2(1).

GENERAL NOTE

Regulation 3(1)

2–009   *Served:* It is submitted that this regulation does not apply to reports that have to be "furnished" to the hospital managers, such as reports made under the holding power contained in section 5(2): see the note on "time when the report is ... furnished" in that provision.

Person authorised: Although, unlike the position under regulation 4(2), the authorisation need not be in writing, good practice suggests that it should be.

Regulation 3(2)

Served: The application documents cannot be served by post.　　　　　　　　**2–010**

Delivering the application: A person who is authorised to receive documents on behalf of the managers should be available in hospitals out of office hours. Advice on the receipt and scrutiny of documents is contained in chapter 12 of the *Code of Practice.*

Officer ... authorised by them: See the note on "person authorised", above. An "officer" is an employee or a person who has been contracted to perform functions under these Regulations.

Regulation (3)

Served: In *Gary Kinsey v. North Mersey Community NHS Trust*, June 21, 1999, CA,　**2–011** the nearest relative of a patient who had been admitted to hospital under section 3 handed a letter to the ward receptionist requesting the patient's discharge. This took place on May 27. The nearest relative was told that the letter would be handed to the appropriate person, namely the Mental Health Act administrator. The letter was received by the administrator on June 3. On that day, as no barring report under section 25 had been issued, the nearest relative arrived on the ward, seeking the discharge of the patient. A barring report was then made. In rejecting an application for *habeas corpus* the court held that the purpose of this regulation was to ensure that an order for discharge came to the notice of the proper authorised person without delay. That being the case, the handing of the letter to the ward receptionist did not satisfy that requirement and was not good delivery. The notice was served when the letter was received by the administrator on June 3.

Regulation 3(4)

Without further proof: The officer scrutinising the document may therefore take　**2–012** certain statements at face value; for example he need not check that the doctor who states that he is a registered medical practitioner is so registered or that the social worker who states that he is an approved social worker has, in fact, been approved by his employing authority.

Part II

Procedures and Records Relating to Hospital Admissions and Guardianship

Procedure for and record of hospital admissions

4.—(1) For the purposes of admission to hospital under Part II of the　**2–013** Act—
    (a) any application for admission for assessment under section 2 shall be in the form set out—
        (i) where made by the nearest relative, in Form 1,
        (ii) where made by an approved social worker, in Form 2;

(b) any medical recommendation for the purposes of section 2 shall be in the form set out—
    (i) in the case of joint recommendations, in Form 3,
    (ii) in any other case, in Form 4;

(c) any emergency application under section 4 shall be in the form set out—
    (i) where made by the nearest relative, in Form 5,
    (ii) where made by an approved social worker, in Form 6;

(d) any medical recommendation for the purposes of section 4 shall be in the form set out in Form 7;

(e) any application for admission for treatment under section 3 shall be in the form set out—
    (i) where made by the nearest relative, in Form 8,
    (ii) where made by an approved social worker, in Form 9;

(f) any medical recommendation for the purposes of section 3 shall be in the form set out—
    (i) in the case of joint recommendations, in Form 10,
    (ii) in any other case, in Form 11;

(g) any report made under subsection (2) of section 5 (detention of patient already in hospital for 72 hours) by the registered medical practitioner in charge of the treatment of the patient shall be in the form set out in Form 12;

(h) any record made under subsection (4) of section 5 (power to detain an in-patient for a maximum of 6 hours) by a nurse of the class for the time being prescribed for the purposes of that subsection shall be in the form set out in Form 13.

(2) For the purposes of section 15 (rectification of applications and recommendations), the managers of the hospital to which a patient has been admitted in pursuance of an application for assessment or for treatment may authorise in writing any officer or class of officers on their behalf—

(a) to consent under subsection (1) of that section to the amendment of the application or any medical recommendation given for the purposes of the application;

(b) to consider the sufficiency of a medical recommendation and, if the recommendation is considered insufficient, to give written notice as required by subsection (2) of that section,

and the managers of a mental nursing home, if two or more in number, may authorise one of their number to exercise the functions mentioned in sub-paragraphs (a) and (b).

(3) Where a patient has been admitted to a hospital pursuant to an application under section 2, 3 or 4, or detained pursuant to a report under section 5(2), a record of admission shall be made by the managers of that hospital in the form set out in Form 14 and shall be attached to the application or, as the case may be, report.

(4) A record of the receipt of any recommendation for the purposes of section 4, and any joint recommendation or, as the case may be, the second medical recommendation shall be made by the managers of the hospital to which the patient is to be admitted in the form set out in [Form 14] and shall be attached to the recommendation.

(5) The time at which a patient ceased to be detained under subsection (4)

of section 5 or the arrival, if earlier, of the registered medical practitioner having power to furnish a report under subsection (2) of section 5 shall be recorded either by a nurse who made the record required by the said subsection (4) or by another nurse of the class prescribed under that sub-section, and authorised by the managers in that behalf, in the form set out in Form 16.

GENERAL NOTE

Regulation 4(1)
   Shall be in the form set out: See the General Note to Schedule 1.   **2–014**

Regulation 4(2)
   An officer: See the note on regulation 3(2). Advice on the receipt and scrutiny of **2–015** documents is contained in Chapter 12 of the *Code of Practice*.

Regulation 4(3)(4)
   Form 14 ... Form 15: If an application has been "duly completed" (s.6(1) of the **2–016** 1983 Act), a failure to comply with the requirement to complete these forms would not invalidate the admission because such an application is "sufficient authority" to detain the patient (s.6(2)). The relevant form should be completed on the omission being discovered.

Procedure for and acceptance of guardianship application
   5.—(1) For the purposes of section 7 (application for guardianship)—   **2–017**
   (a) an application for guardianship shall be in the form set out—
      (i) where made by the nearest relative, in Part 1 of Form 17,
      (ii) where made by an approved social worker, in Part I of Form 18;
   (b) where a person other than a local social services authority is named as guardian, the statement by that person that he is willing to act shall be in the form set out in Part II of Form 17 or, as the case may be, 18;
   (c) any medical recommendation shall be in the form set out—
      (i) in the case of a joint recommendation, in Form 19,
      (ii) in any other case, in Form 20.
   (2) A local social services authority may authorise in writing an officer or class of officers on behalf of the authority to consent under section 8(4) to any amendment of any guardianship application which the authority has accepted or any medical recommendation given for the purposes of that application.
   (3) Where such an application is accepted by the responsible local social services authority, the record of acceptance shall be in the form set out in Form 21 and shall be attached to the application.
   (4) The record of the receipt of any joint medical recommendation or, as the case may be, the second medical recommendation shall be made by the responsible social services authority in the form set out in Form 15 and shall be attached to the recommendation.

GENERAL NOTE

Regulation 5(2)
   Authorise ... an officer . See the note on regulation 4(2).   **2–018**

Procedure for and record of reclassification of patients

2–019   **6.** Any report for the purposes of section 16 (reclassification of patients detained in hospital or subject to guardianship) shall be—

    (a) in the case of a patient detained in hospital, in the form set out in Part I of Form 22;

    (b) in the case of a patient subject to guardianship, in the form set out in Part I of Form 23,

and the receipt of that report shall be recorded by the managers of the hospital, or as the case may be, the guardian in the form set out in Part II of Form 22 or 23 respectively.

Transfer from hospital to hospital or guardianship

2–020   **7.**—(1) This regulation shall apply in respect of any patient who is for the time being liable to be detained in a hospital under the Act, other than a patient transferred under section 19(3) (transfer between hospitals under the same managers) or section 123(1) and (2) (transfers between and from special hospitals) applies.

(2) A patient to whom this regulation applies may be transferred to another hospital where—

    (a) an authority for transfer in the form set out in Part I of Form 24 is given by the managers of the hospital in which the patient is liable to be detained; and

    (b) those managers are satisfied that arrangements have been made for the admission of the patient to the hospital to which he is being transferred within a period of 28 days beginning with the date of the authority for transfer,

and, on the transfer of that patient, the managers of the hospital to which he is transferred shall record his admission in the form set out in Part II of Form 24.

(3) A patient to whom this regulation applies may be transferred into the guardianship of a local social services authority, or of any person approved by a local social services authority, where—

    (a) an authority for transfer in the form set out in Part I of Form 25 is given by the managers of the hospital in which the patient is detained;

    (b) the transfer has been agreed by the local social services authority, which will be the responsible one if the proposed transfer takes effect, in the form set out in Part II of Form 25;

    (c) that local social services authority has specified the date on which the transfer shall take place; and

    (d) where the person named in the authority for transfer as a guardian is a person other than a local social services authority, the agreement of that person has been obtained and recorded in the form set out in Part III of Form 25.

(4) Where a patient to whom this regulation applies is detained in a mental nursing home—

    (a) he may be transferred from that home to another where both homes are under the management of the same managers, and paragraph (2) shall not apply;

(b) where he is maintained under a contract with a Regional Health Authority, District Health Authority or a special health authority, any authority for transfer required under paragraph (2)(a) or, as the case may be, (3)(a) may be given by an officer of that health authority, authorised by that health authority in that behalf, instead of by the managers.

(5) In this regulation the functions of the managers may be performed by an officer authorised by them in that behalf.

GENERAL NOTE

Regulation 7(1)
Liable to be detained: Including a patient who has been detained under section 2. **2–021**

Regulation 7(2)
Form 24: This form should not be signed until the arrangements for the transfer have **2–022** been finalised. "The managers and where relevant, Special Health Authorities, will probably wish to give a general authority to senior staff to authorise transfers" (*Memorandum*, para. 82). The authority to transfer is valid for 28 days (reg. 9).

Regulation 7(3)
   Transferred into ... Guardianship: Although the patient's nearest relative has no **2–023** statutory right to object to such a transfer, he can discharge the patient from guardianship (s.23(2)(b)).
   Date on which the transfer shall take place: Until that date the patient remains liable to be detained, but there is no reason why he should not be granted leave to take up residence in the place where he will be required to reside under guardianship before that date.

Transfer from guardianship to guardianship or hospital
   8.—(1) This regulation shall apply in respect of any patient who is for the **2–024** time being subject to guardianship under Part II of the Act.
   (2) A patient to whom this regulation applies may be transferred into the guardianship of another local social services authority or person where—
   (a) an authority for transfer is given by the guardian in the form set out in Part I of Form 26;
   (b) that transfer has been agreed by the local social services authority, which will be the responsible one if the proposed transfer takes effect, in the form set out in Part II of Form 26;
   (c) that local social services authority has specified the date on which the transfer shall take place; and
   (d) where the person named in the authority for transfer as proposed guardian is a person other than a local social services authority, the agreement of that person has been obtained and recorded in the form set out in Part III of Form 26.
   (3) An authority for transfer to hospital of a patient to whom this regulation applies may be given by the responsible local social services authority in the form set out in Form 27 where—

(a) an application for admission for treatment has been made by an approved social worker in the form set out in Form 9 and, for the purposes of that application, sections 11(4) (consultation with nearest relative) and 13 (duty of approved social worker) shall apply as if the proposed transfer were an application for admission for treatment;

(b) that application is founded on medical recommendations given by two registered medical practitioners in accordance with section 12 in the form set out—

(i) in the case of joint recommendations, in Form 28;

(ii) in any other case, in Form 29;

(c) that application has been accepted by the managers of the hospital to which it was addressed and the responsible local social services authority is satisfied that arrangements have been made for the admission of the patient to that hospital within the period of 14 days beginning with the date of the authority for transfer;

(d) the responsible local social services authority has taken such steps as are practicable to inform the person (if any) appearing to be the patient's nearest relative of the proposed transfer.

and, on the transfer of that patient, a record of admission shall be made by the managers of the hospital to which he is being transferred in the form set out in Form 14 and shall be attached to the application.

GENERAL NOTE

2–025   When a patient is transferred from guardianship to hospital he has a right to apply to a Mental Health Review Tribunal within six months of the day of the transfer (s.66(1)(e), (2)(e)). If he does not exercise this right the hospital managers must automatically refer his case to the tribunal (s.68(1)).

Regulation 8(2)(d)

2–026   *Person other than a local social services authority:* Who, after the transfer has been completed, must appoint a nominated medical attendant and send relevant details to the local services authority (reg. 12).

Regulation 8(3)

2–027   The provisions of section 15 concerning the rectification of applications and medical recommendations do not apply to documents given in support of a transfer. "The application and recommendations should be scrutinised carefully to make sure they comply with the requirements of the Act and regulations before the authority for transfer is signed" (*Memorandum*, para. 91).

Transfer to hospital: The patient must be admitted to the hospital within 14 days beginning with the date of the latter of the two medical examinations on which the medical recommendations are based (reg. 9).

Conveyance to hospital on transfer

2–028   **9.**—(1) Where the conditions of regulation 7(2) or 8(3) are satisfied, the authority for transfer given in accordance with those regulations shall be sufficient authority for the following persons to take the patient and convey him to the hospital to which he is being transferred within the periods specified—

(a) in a case to which regulation 7(2) applies, an officer of the managers of either hospital, or any person authorised by the managers of the hospital to which the patient is being transferred, within the period of 28 days beginning with the date of the authority for transfer;

(b) in a case to which regulation 8(3) applies, an officer of, or any person authorised by, the responsible local social services authority, within the period of 14 days beginning with the date on which the patient was last examined by a medical practitioner for the purposes of regulation 8(3)(b).

(2) Paragraph (1) shall apply to a patient who—

(a) is liable to be detained under the Act and is removed to another hospital in circumstances to which section 19(3) applies, as if the authority given by the managers for that transfer were an authority for transfer given in accordance with regulation 7(2);

(b) is liable to be detained in a special hospital and who, pursuant to a direction given by the Secretary of State under section 123(1) or (2), is removed to another special hospital or transferred to another hospital, as if that direction were an authority for transfer given in accordance with regulation 7(2).

(3) In a case to which regulation 7(4)(a) applies, an officer of or any other person authorised by the managers of the mental nursing home may take and convey the patient to the mental nursing home to which he is being transferred.

Renewal of authority for detention or guardianship

10.—(1) Any report for the purposes of section 20(3) (medical recommendation for renewal of authority to detain) shall be in the form set out in Part I of Form 30.   **2–029**

(2) Any report for the purposes of section 20(6) (medical recommendation for renewal of guardianship) shall be in the form set out in Part I of Form 31.

(3) Any renewal of authority for detention or guardianship under section 20(8) shall be recorded by the managers of the hospital in which the patient is liable to be detained or, as the case may be, the responsible local social services authority in the form set out in Part II of Form 30 or, as the case may be, 31.

[Detention or guardianship after absence without leave for more than 28 days

10A. Any report for the purposes of section 21B(2) (authority for detention or guardianship of patients who are taken into custody or return after more than 28 days):   **2–030**

(a) in relation to a patient who is liable to be detained, shall be in the form set out in Part I of Form 31A; and

(b) in relation to a patient who is subject to guardianship, shall be in the form set out in Part I of Form 31B.

and the receipt of that report shall be recorded by the managers of the hospital in which the patient is liable to be detained or, as the case may be, the responsible local social services authority in the form set out in Part II of Form 31A or, as the case may be, 31B.]

Removal to England and Wales

2–031   **11.**—(1) This regulation shall apply to any patient who is removed to England or Wales under Part VI of the Act or Part VI of the Mental Health (Scotland) Act 1960 (removal and return of patients within United Kingdom).

(2) The appropriate medical officer shall record, in the form set out on Form 32, his opinion as to the form or forms of mental disorder from which a patient to whom this regulation applies is suffering—

(a) where the patient is or becomes at the time of his removal subject to an order or direction restricting his discharge, or is treated as being so subject, as soon as is reasonably practicable after he ceases to be so subject; and

(b) in any other case, as soon as reasonably practicable after the patient's removal.

(3) Where a patient to whom this regulation applies is liable to be detained in a hospital, the managers of the hospital shall record in the form set out in Form 33 the date on which the patient is admitted to the hospital, and shall, as soon as reasonably practicable, inform the patient's nearest relative, if any, of the admission.

(4) Where a patient to whom this regulation applies is received into guardianship—

(a) the guardian shall record in the form set out in Form 33 the date on which the patient arrives at the place at which the patient is to reside on his reception into guardianship under the Act;

(b) the guardian shall, as soon as reasonably practicable, inform the patient's nearest relative, if any, that the patient has been received into guardianship under the Act; and

(c) a private guardian shall notify the responsible local social services authority of the date mentioned in sub-paragraph (a) and of the particulars mentioned in regulation 12(b) and (e).

GENERAL NOTE

Regulation 11(1)

2–032   *Part VI of the Mental Health (Scotland) Act* 1960. Now see Part VII of the Mental Health (Scotland) Act 1984.

Regulation 11(2)

2–033   *Appropriate Medical Officer:* See regulation 2(1) and section 16(5).

PART III

FUNCTIONS OF GUARDIANS AND NEAREST RELATIVES

Duties of private guardians

12. It shall be the duty of a private guardian—   **2–034**

(a) to appoint a registered medical practitioner to act as the nominated medical attendant of the patient;

(b) to notify the responsible local social services authority of the name and address of the nominated medical attendant;

(c) in exercising the powers and duties conferred or imposed upon him by the Act and these regulations, to comply with such directions as that authority may give;

(d) to furnish that authority with all such reports or other information with regard to the patient as the authority may from time to time require;

(e) to notify the authority—

    (i) on the reception of the patient into guardianship, of his address and the address of the patient,

    (ii) except in a case to which paragraph (f) applies, of any permanent change of either address, before or not later than 7 days after the change takes place;

(f) where on any permanent change of his address, the new address is in the area of a different local social services authority, to notify that authority—

    (i) of his address and that of the patient,

    (ii) of the particulars mentioned in paragraph (b),

    and to send a copy of the notification to the authority which was formerly responsible; and

(g) in the event of the death of the patient, or the termination of the guardianship by discharge, transfer or otherwise, to notify the responsible local social services authority as soon as reasonably practicable.

GENERAL NOTE

Nominated medical attendant: Who has the power to reclassify the patient (s.16) **2–035** and is responsible for examining the patient when authority for his guardianship is due to expire and for making a report renewing the guardianship, if appropriate (s.20). This doctor, who could be the patient's general practitioner, should only be appointed after consultation with the local social services authority (*Memorandum*, para. 43).

Visits to patients subject to guardianship

13. the responsible local social services authority shall arrange for every **2–036** patient received into guardianship under Part II of the Act to be visited at such intervals as the authority may decide, but in any case at intervals of not more than 3 months, and at least one such visit in any year shall be made by a practitioner approved by the Secretary of State for the purposes of section 12 (general provisions as to medical recommendations).

Performance of functions of nearest relative

2–037   **14.**—(1) Subject to the conditions of paragraph (2), the nearest relative of a patient may authorise in writing any person other than the patient or a person mentioned in section 26(5) (persons deemed not to be the nearest relative) to perform in respect of the patient the functions conferred upon the nearest relative by or under Part II of the Act or these regulations and may revoke such authority.

(2) The conditions mentioned in paragraph (1) are that, on making or revoking such authority, the nearest relative shall forthwith give the authority, or give notice in writing of the revocation of such authority, to—

    (a) the person authorised;

    (b) in the case of a patient liable to be detained in a hospital, the managers of that hospital;

    (c) in the case of a patient subject to guardianship, the responsible local social services authority and to the private guardian, if any.

(3) Any such authority shall take effect upon receipt of the authority by the person authorised, and any revocation of such authority shall take effect upon the receipt of the notice by the person authorised.

(4) A person for the time being authorised in accordance with the preceding paragraphs shall exercise the functions mentioned in paragraph (1) on behalf of the nearest relative.

DEFINITION

2–038   private guardian: reg. 2(1).

GENERAL NOTE

Regulation 14(1)

2–039   *May authorise:* "Such authorisation may be given at any time, whether a question of admission to hospital or guardianship has already arisen or not, and it may be revoked at any time. It lapses on the death of the person who made it" (*Memorandum*, para. 62). The nearest relative is not required to consult with the patient when exercising his discretion under this paragraph.

Any person: The person authorised need not be a relative of the patient. Although there is no requirement for the person concerned to have consented to the delegation, it must be assumed that such consent is a pre-condition to delegation.

Discharge by nearest relative

2–040   **15.**—(1) Any order made by the nearest relative of the patient under section 23 for the discharge of a patient who is liable to be detained under Part II of the Act shall be served upon the managers of the hospital where the patient is liable to be detained and may be in the form set out in Form 34.

(2) Any order made by the nearest relative of the patient under section 23 for the discharge of a patient subject to guardianship under the Act shall be served upon the responsible local social services authority and may be in the form set out in Form 35.

(3) Any report given by the responsible medical officer for the purposes of section 25 (restrictions on discharge by nearest relative) shall be in the form set out in Part I of Form 36 and the receipt of that report by the managers of the hospital in which the patient is liable to be detained shall be in the form set out in Part II of Form 36.

served: reg. 2(1).   **2–041**

GENERAL NOTE

Regulation 15(1)(2)
May be in the form: There is no requirement to use the statutory form.   **2–042**

PART IV

CONSENT TO TREATMENT

Consent to treatment
   16.—(1) For the purposes of section 57 (treatment requiring consent and a **2–043**
second opinion)—
   (a) the form of treatment to which the section shall apply, in addition to
        the treatment mentioned in subsection (1)(a) of that section (any
        surgical operation for destroying brain tissue or for destroying the
        functioning of brain tissue), shall be the surgical implantation of
        hormones for the purpose of reducing the male sexual drive;
   (b) the certificates required for the purposes of subsection (2)(a) and (b)
        of that section shall be in the form set out in Form 37.
   (2) For the purposes of section 58 (treatment requiring consent or a
second opinion)—
   (a) the form of treatment to which that section shall apply, in addition to
        the administration of medicine mentioned in subsection (1)(b) of that
        section, shall be electro-convulsive therapy; and
   (b) the certificates required for the purposes of subsection (3)(a) and (b)
        of that section shall be in the form set out in Forms 38 and 39
        respectively.

GENERAL NOTE

Regulation 16(1)(a)
Surgical implantation: The oral administration of sex hormones does not come **2–044**
within the scope of section 57.

PART V

CORRESPONDENCE OF PATIENTS

Inspection and opening of postal packets
   17.—(1) Where under section 134(4) (inspection and opening of postal **2–045**
packets addressed to or by patients in hospital) any postal packet is
inspected and opened, but neither the packet nor anything contained in it is
withheld under section 134(1) or (2), the person who so inspected and
opened it, being a person appointed under section 134(7) to perform the

functions of the managers of the hospital under that section "the person appointed"), shall record in writing—
(a) that the packet had been so inspected and opened;
(b) that nothing in the packet has been withheld; and
(c) his name and the name of the hospital,
and shall, before resealing the packet, place the record in that packet.
(2) Where under section 134(1) or (2) any postal packet or anything contained in it is withheld by the person appointed—
(a) he shall record in a register kept for the purpose—
(i) that the packet or anything contained in it has been withheld,
(ii) the date on which it was so withheld,
(iii) the grounds in which it was so withheld,
(iv) a description of the contents of the packet withheld or of any item withheld, and
(v) his name, and
(b) if anything contained in the packet is withheld, he shall record in writing—
(i) that the packet has been inspected and opened,
(ii) that an item or items contained in the packet have been withheld,
(iii) a description of any such item,
(iv) his name and the name of the hospital, and
(v) in any case to which section 134(1)(b) or (2) applies, the further particulars required for the purposes of 134(6),
and shall, before resealing the packet, place the record in that packet.
(3) In a case to which section 134(1)(b) or (2) applies—
(a) the notice required for the purposes of section 134(6) shall include—
(i) a statement of the grounds on which the packet in question or anything contained in it was withheld, and
(ii) the name of the person appointed who so decided to withhold that packet or anything contained in it and the name of the hospital; and
(b) where anything contained in a packet is withheld the record required by paragraph (2)(b) above shall, if the provisions of section 134(6) are otherwise satisfied, be sufficient notice to the person to whom the packet is addressed for the purposes of section 134(6).

Review of decisions to withhold postal packets

2–046   **18.**—(1) Every application for review by the Commission under section 121(7) (review of any decision to withhold a postal packet, or anything contained in it, under section 134)—
(a) shall be made in such manner as the Commission may accept as sufficient in the circumstances of any particular case or class of case and may be made otherwise than in writing; and
(b) shall be made, delivered or sent to an office of the Commission.
(2) Any person making such an application shall furnish to the Commission the notice of the withholding of the postal packet or anything contained in it, given under section 134(6), or a copy of that notice.
(3) For the purpose of determining any such application the Commission may direct the production of such documents, information and evidence as it may reasonably require.

DEFINITIONS
2–047   commission: reg. 2(1).
document: reg. 2(1).

PART VI

TRANSITIONAL PROVISIONS AND REVOCATIONS

Transitional provisions

19.—(1) Until the expiration of the period mentioned in paragraph 4(1) of **2–048** Schedule 5 to the Act (delay of introduction of approved social workers) for any reference in these regulations (and in any form in schedule 1 to these regulations) to an approved social worker there shall be substituted a reference to a mental welfare officer.

(2) Any opinion of the responsible medical officer recorded for the purposes of paragraph 39 of Schedule 5 to the Act shall be in the form set out in Form 32.

Revocations

20. The regulations and orders specified in column 1 of Schedule 2 are **2–049'** hereby revoked to the extent mentioned in column 3 of that Schedule.

Regulations 4–11, 15 and 16	SCHEDULE 1	**2–050**

GENERAL NOTE

The forms set out in this Schedule are available from the Stationery Office. Health authorities and local authorities can produce their own forms as long as the correct wording is used. The use of a form which failed to reproduce the exact wording set out in these regulations because it was either obsolete or defective would not necessarily invalidate the application or recommendation because minor departures from the statutory form would, in most circumstances, be regarded as being *de minimis*. This would not be the case if the statutory criteria set out in the defective form failed to reproduce the correct wording in some material respect.

A batch of forms were incorrectly printed with the NHS logo reproduced in the top right hand corner. This error was pointed out to the Department of Health by an approved social worker. In reply, the Department stated that no further forms would be printed with the NHS logo on them and that in the interim the logo should be struck out or covered with correction fluid before use.

It is submitted that a facsimile reproduction of a completed form can be acted upon as if it were an original document if: (1) the recipient confers with the signatory by telephone to confirm that the form was completed by the signatory; and (2) the original form is delivered to the recipient at the earliest opportunity. The Mental Health Act Commission has endorsed the use of faxed forms (M.H.A.C., Sixth Biennial Report, 1993–1995, para. 3.13).

**FORMS FOR USE IN CONNECTION WITH COMPULSORY
ADMISSION TO HOSPITAL, GUARDIANSHIP AND
CONSENT TO TREATMENT**

Regulation 4(1)(a)(i)   *Form 1*

2–051 **Mental Health Act 1983 section 2—application by nearest relative for admission for
assessment**

To the Managers of [name and address of hospital or mental nursing home]. I [your full name]
of [your address] hereby apply for the admission of [full name of patient] of [address of patient]
for assessment in accordance with Part II of the Mental Health Act 1983.

Complete (a) or (b)

(a) To the best of my knowledge and belief I am the patient's nearest relative within the
meaning of the Act
I am the patient's [state relationship].

*Delete the phrase
which does not
apply*

(b) I have been authorised to exercise the functions under the Act of the patient's nearest
relative by a county court/the patient's nearest relative.

A copy of the authority is attached to this application.
I last saw the patient on [date].
This application is founded on two medical recommendations in the prescribed form.
If neither of the medical practitioners knew the patient before making their recommendations,
please explain why you could not get a recommendation from a medical practitioner who did
know the patient:—

Signed ....

Date ....

Regulation 4(1)(a)(ii) **Form 2**

Mental Health Act 1983 section 2—application by an approved social worker for admission for assessment **2–052**

To the Managers of [name and address of hospital or mental nursing home].

I [your full name] of [your office address] hereby apply for the admission of [full name of patient] or [address of patient] for assessment in accordance with Part II of the Mental Health Act 1983.

I am an officer of [name of local social services authority] appointed to act as an approved social worker for the purposes of the Act.

Indicate clearly below if the nearest relative is known or not

The following section should be completed if nearest relative known

Indicate if (a) or (b) is applicable.

   (a) To the best of my knowledge and belief [name and address] is the patient's nearest relative within the meaning of the Act.

I have/have not yet* informed that person that this application is to be made and of his power to order the discharge of the patient.

Delete the phrase which does not apply OR

   (b) I understand that [name and address] has been authorised by a county court/the patient's nearest relative* to exercise the functions under the Act of the patient's nearest relative.

I have/have not yet* informed that person that this application is to be made and of his power to order the discharge of the patient.

   (a) I have been unable to ascertain who is the patient's nearest relative within the meaning of the Act.

OR

   (b) To the best of my knowledge and belief this patient has no nearest relative within the meaning of the Act.

The following section must be completed in all cases

I last saw the patient on [date].

I have interviewed the patient and I am satisfied that detention in a hospital is in all the circumstances of the case the most appropriate way of providing the care and medical treatment of which the patient stands in need.

This application is founded on two medical recommendations in the prescribed form.

If neither of the medical practitioners knew the patient before making their recommendations, please explain why you could not get a recommendation from a medical practitioner who did know the patient:—

      Signed ....

      Date ....

2–053 **Mental Health Act 1983 Section 2—joint medical recommendation for admission for assessment**

THIS FORM MUST ONLY BE COMPLETED IF BOTH DOCTORS ARE PRESENT

    We [full names and addresses of both medical practitioners], registered medical practitioners, recommend that [full name and address of patient] be admitted to a hospital for assessment in accordance with Part II of the Mental Health Act 1983.

I [name of first practitioner] last examined this patient on [date].

*I had previous acquaintance with the patient before I conducted that examination.

Delete if not applicable   *I have been approved by the Secretary of State under section 12 of the Act as having special experience in the diagnosis or treatment of mental disorder.

I [name of second practitioner] last examined this patient on [date].

*I had previous acquaintance with the patient before I conducted that examination.

Delete if not applicable   *I have been approved by the Secretary of State under section 12 of the Act as having special experience in the diagnosis or treatment of mental disorder.

    We are of the opinion

      (a) that this patient is suffering from mental disorder of a nature of degree which warrants the detention of the patient in hospital for assessment

AND

Delete the indents not applicable   (b) that this patient ought to be so detained
         (i) in the interests of the patient's own health
         (ii) in the interests of the patient's own safety
         (iii) with a view to the protection of other persons

AND

      (c) that informal admission is not appropriate in the circumstance of this case for the following reasons:—

(The full reason why informal admission is not appropriate *must* be given)

               Signed ....

               Date ....

               Signed ....

               Date ....]

Regulation 4(1)(b)(ii)   *[Form 4*

Mental Health Act 1983 Section 2—medical recommendation for admission for assessment   **2–054**

I [full name and address of medical practitioner], a registered medical practitioner, recommend that [full name and address of patient] be admitted to a hospital for assessment in accordance with Part II of the Mental Health Act 1983.

I last examined this patient on [date].

*I had previous acquaintance with the patient before I conducted that examination.

Delete if not applicable   *I have been approved by the Secretary of State under section 12 of the Act as having special experience in the diagnosis or treatment of mental disorder.

I am of the opinion

(a) that this patient is suffering from mental disorder of a nature or degree which warrants detention of the patient in a hospital for assessment

AND

Delete the indents not applicable   (b) that this patient ought to be so detained
     (i) in the interests of the patient's own health
     (ii) in the interests of the patient's own safety
     (iii) with a view to the protection of other persons

AND

(c) that informal admission is not appropriate in the circumstances of this case for the following reasons:—

(The full reason why informal admission is not appropriate *must* be given)

Signed ....

Date ....]

499

2–055 **Mental Health Act 1983 section 4—Emergency application by nearest relative for admission for assessment**

THIS FORM IS TO BE USED ONLY FOR AN EMERGENCY APPLICATION

To the Managers of [name and address of hospital or mental nursing home].

I [your full name] of [your address] hereby apply for the admission of [full name of patient] of [address of patient] for assessment in accordance with Part II of the Mental Health Act 1983.

Complete (a) or (b)

(a) To the best of my knowledge and belief I am the patient's nearest relative within the meaning of the Act.

I am the patient's [state relationship].

Delete the phrase which does not apply

(b) I have been authorised to exercise the functions under the Act of the patient's nearest relative by a county court/the patient's nearest relative.

I last saw the patient on [date] at [time].

In my opinion it is of urgent necessity for the patient to be admitted and detained under section 2 of the Act. Compliance with the provisions of Part II of the Act relating to applications under that section would involve undesirable delay.

This application is founded on one medical recommendation in the prescribed form.

If the medical practitioner did not know the patient before making his recommendation, please explain why you could not get a recommendation from a medical practitioner who did know the patient—

Signed ....

Date ....

Time ....

Regulation 4(1)(c)(ii)   Form 6

Mental Health Act 1983 section 4—Emergency application by an approved social worker for admission for assessment   2–056

THIS FORM IS TO BE USED ONLY FOR AN EMERGENCY APPLICATION

To the Managers of [name and address of hospital or mental nursing home].
I [your full name] of [your office address] hereby apply for the admission of [full name of patient] of [address of patient] for assessment in accordance with Part II of the Mental Health Act 1983.
I am an officer of [name of local social services authority] appointed to act as an approved social worker for the purposes of the Act.
I last saw the patient on [date] at [time].
I have interviewed the patient and I am satisfied that detention in a hospital is in all the circumstances of the case the most appropriate way of providing the care and medical treatment of which the patient stands in need.
In my opinion it is of urgent necessity for the patient to be admitted and detained under section 2 of the Act. Compliance with the provisions of Part II of the Act relating to applications under that section would involve undesirable delay.
This application is founded on one medical recommendation in the prescribed form.
If the medical practitioner did not know the patient before making his recommendation, please explain why you could not get a recommendation from a medical practitioner who did know the patient—

Signed ....

Date ....

Time ....

2–057 **Mental Health Act 1983 section 4—Medical recommendation for emergency admission for assessment**

THIS FORM IS TO BE USED ONLY FOR AN EMERGENCY APPLICATION

I [name and address of medical practitioner], a registered medical practitioner, recommend that [full name and address of patient] be admitted to a hospital for assessment in accordance with Part II of the Mental Health Act 1983.
I last examined this patient on [date] at [time].
*I had previous acquaintance with the patient before I conducted that examination.

Delete if not applicable *I have been approved by the Secretary of State under section 12 of the Act as having special experience in the diagnosis or treatment of mental disorder.
I am of the opinion—

(a) that this patient is suffering from mental disorder of a nature or degree which warrants the patient's detention in a hospital for assessment for at least a limited period.

AND

Delete the indents not applicable
(b) that this patient ought to be so detained
(i) in the interests of the patient's own health
(ii) in the interests of the patient's own safety
(iii) with a view to the protection of other persons

AND

(c) that informal admission is not appropriate in the circumstances of this case.

In my opinion it is of urgent necessity for the patient to be admitted and detained under section 2 of the Act. Compliance with the provisions of Part II of the Act relating to applications under that section would involve undesirable delay.
In my opinion an emergency exists, because I estimate that compliance with those provisions would cause about [   ] hours' delay, and I consider such a delay might result in harm as follows [state reasons] to
*(a) the patient
*(b) those now caring for him
*(c) other persons

I understand that the managers of the hospital to which the patient is admitted may ask me for further information relevant to this recommendation I was first made aware that his condition was causing anxiety, such that it might warrant immediate admission to hospital—
†(a) Today at [time]
Delete whichever do not apply †(b) Yesterday
†(c) On [date if within one week]
†(d) More than a week ago

Signed ....

Date ....

Time ....]

502

Mental Health Act 1983 section 3—Application by nearest relative for admission for treatment

2–058

To the Managers of [name and address of hospital or mental nursing home].
I [your full name] of [your address] hereby apply for the admission of [full name of patient] of [address of patient] for treatment in accordance with Part II of the Mental Health Act 1983.

Complete (a) or (b)

(a) To the best of my knowledge and belief I am the patient's nearest relative within the meaning of the Act.
I am the patient's [state relationship].

Delete the phrase which does not apply

(b) I have been authorised to exercise the functions under the Act of the patient's nearest relative by a county court/the patient's nearest relative.

A copy of the authority is attached to this application.
I last saw the patient on [date].
This application is founded on two medical recommendations in the prescribed form.
If neither of the medical practitioners knew the patient before making their recommendations, please explain why you could not get a recommendation from a medical practitioner who did know the patient—

Signed ....

Date ....

2–059 **Mental Health Act 1983 section 3—Application by approved social worker for admission for treatment**

To the Managers of [name and address of hospital or mental nursing home].

I [your full name] of [your office address] hereby apply for the admission of [full name of patient] of [address of patient] for treatment in accordance with Part II of the Mental Health Act 1983 as a person suffering from:

mental illness, mental impairment, severe mental impairment, psychopathic disorder [enter whichever of these is appropriate].

I am an officer of [name of local social services authority] appointed to act as an approved social worker for the purposes of the Act.

Indicate clearly below if the nearest relative had been consulted or not.

The following section should be completed where consultation has taken place.

Complete (a) or (b)

(a) have consulted [name and address] who to the best of my knowledge and belief is the patient's nearest relative within the meaning of the Act.

That person known as the nearest relative has not notified me or the local social services authority by who I am appointed that he/she objects to this application being made.

OR

*Delete the phase which does not apply

(b) I have consulted [name and address] who I understand has been authorised by a county court/the patient's nearest relative* to exercise the functions under the Act of the patient's nearest relative.

That person known as the nearest relative has not notified me or the local social services authority by whom I am appointed that he/she objects to this application being made.

The following section should be completed where no consultation has taken place

Indicate whether (a), (b) or (c) applies

(a) I have been unable to ascertain who is this patient's nearest relative within the meaning of the Act.

OR

(b) To the best of my knowledge and belief this patient has no nearest relative within the meaning the Act.

OR

(c) I understand that [name and address] is

Delete either (i) or (ii)

(i) this patient's nearest relative within the meaning of the Act
(ii) authorised to exercise the functions of this patient's nearest relative under the Act

AND in my opinion it is not reasonably practicable or would involve unreasonable delay to consult that person before making this application.

Mental Health Regulations 1983

The following section must be completed in all cases

I last saw the patient on [date].

I have interviewed the patient and I am satisfied that detention in a hospital is in all the circumstances of the case the most appropriate way of providing the care and medical treatment of which the patient stands in need.

This application is founded on two medical recommendations in the prescribed form.

If neither of the medical practitioners knew the patient before making their recommendations, please explain why you could not get a recommendation from a medical practitioner who did know the patient:—

Signed ....

Date ....]

2–060 **Mental Health Act 1983 section 3—Joint medical recommendation for admission for treatment**

THIS FORM MUST ONLY BE COMPLETED IF BOTH DOCTORS ARE PRESENT

We [full names and addresses of both practitioners], registered medical practitioners, recommend that [full name and address of patient] be admitted to a hospital for treatment in accordance with Part II of the Mental Health Act 1983.

I [name of first practitioner] last examined this patient on [date].

*I had previous acquaintance with the patient before I conducted that examination.

Delete if not applicable   *I have been approved by the Secretary of State under section 12 of the Act as having special experience in the diagnosis or treatment of mental disorder.

I [name of second practitioner] last examined this patient on [date].

*I had previous acquaintance with the patient before I conducted that examination.

*I have been approved by the Secretary of State under section 12 of the Act as having special experience in the diagnosis or treatment of mental disorder.

In our opinion this patient is suffering from—(*complete* (a) *or* (b))

  (a) mental illness/severe mental impairment** and his mental disorder is of a nature or degree which makes it appropriate for him to receive medical treatment in a hospital;

Delete the phrase which does not apply   (b) psychopathic disorder/mental impairment and his mental disorder is of a nature or degree which makes it appropriate for him to receive medical treatment in a hospital and such treatment is likely to alleviate or prevent a deterioration of his condition.

This opinion is founded on the following grounds—

[Give clinical description of the patient's medical condition]

We are of the opinion that it is necessary

Delete the indents not applicable   (i) in the interests of the patient's own health
  (ii) in the interests of the patient's own safety
  (iii) with a view to the protection of other persons

that this patient should receive treatment and it cannot be provided unless he is detained under section 3 of the Act, for the following reasons—

[Reasons should indicate whether other methods of care or treatment (e.g. out-patient treatment or local social services authority services) are available and if so why they are not appropriate, and why informal admission is not appropriate.]

Signed ....

Date ....

Signed ....

Date ....]

Regulation 4(1)(f)(ii)   [Form 11

Mental Health Act 1983 section 3—Medical recommendation for admission for treatment   **2–061**

I [full name and address of practitioner], a registered medical practitioner, recommend that [full name and address of patient] be admitted to a hospital for treatment in accordance with Part II of the Mental Health Act 1983.

I last examined this patient on [date].

*I had previous acquaintance with the patient before I conducted that examination.

*I have been approved by the Secretary of State under section 12 of the Act as having special experience in the diagnosis or treatment of mental disorder.

Delete if not applicable In my opinion this patient is suffering from—(*complete* (a) *or* (b))

(a) mental illness/severe mental impairment** and his mental disorder is of a nature or degree which makes it appropriate for him to receive medical treatment in a hospital;

The phrase which does not apply must be deleted

(b) psychopathic disorder/mental impairment** and his mental disorder is of a nature or degree which makes it appropriate for him to receive medical treatment in a hospital and such treatment is likely to alleviate or prevent a deterioration of his condition.

This opinion is founded on the following grounds—
[Give clinical description of the patient's mental condition]
I am of the opinion that it is necessary

delete the indents not applicable

(i) in the interests of the patient's own health

(ii) in the interests of the patient's own safety

(iii) with a view to the protection of other persons

that this patient should receive treatment and it cannot be provided unless he is detained under section 3 of the Act, for the following reasons—
[Reasons should indicate whether other methods of care or treatment (e.g. out-patient treatment or local social services authority services) are available and if so why they are not appropriate, and why informal admission is not appropriate.]

Signed ....

Date ....]

2–062 **Mental Health Act 1983 section 5(2)—Report on hospital in-patient**

To the Managers of [name of hospital or mental nursing home in which the patient is]

Delete the phrase which does not apply

I [full name] am the registered medical practitioner (responsible for the patient's treatment)/the nominee of the registered medical practitioner in charge of the treatment of [full name of patient], who is an in-patient in this hospital and not at present liable to be detained under the Mental Health Act 1983. I hereby report, for the purposes of section 5(2) of the Act, that it appears to me that an application ought to be made under Part II of the Act for this patient's admission to hospital for the following reasons—

[The full reasons why informal treatment is no longer appropriate *must* be given.]

Signed ....

Date ....

Time ....]

Regulation 4(1)(h)   *Form 13*

Record for the purposes of Mental Health Act 1983 section 5(4)   **2–063**

To the Managers of [name and address of hospital or mental nursing home]
[Full name of the patient]
It appears to me—

> (a) that this patient, who is receiving treatment for mental disorder as an in-patient of this hospital, is suffering from mental disorder to such a degree that it is necessary for the patient's health or safety or for the protection of others for that patient to be immediately restrained from leaving the hospital;

AND

> (b) that it is not practicable to secure the immediate attendance of a registered medical practitioner for the purpose of furnishing a report under section 5(2) of the Mental Health Act 1983.

I am [full name of nurse], a nurse registered—

> (a) in Part 3 (first level nurse trained in nursing persons suffering from mental illness);

delete the phrase [OR
which does not
apply

> (aa)in Part 4 (second level nurse trained in the nursing of persons suffering from mental illness (England and Wales));]

OR

> (b) in Part 5 (first level nurse trained in the nursing of persons suffering from [learning disabilities];

[OR

> (bb)in Part 6 (second level nurse trained in the nursing of persons suffering from learning disabilities (England and Wales));]

[OR

> (c) in Part 13 (nurses qualified following a course of preparation in mental health nursing);

OR

> (d) in Part 14 (nurses qualified following a course of preparation in [learning disabilities] nursing);]

of the professional register.

Signed ....

Date ....

Time ....

2–064 **Mental Health Act 1983 sections 2, 3, 4 and 5(2)—Record of receipt of medical recommendations(s) and formal admission to hospital**

(To be attached to the medical recommendation(s) and the application for admission or report)

[Name of hospital or mental nursing home.]
[Full name of patient]
The above named patient was—
admitted to this hospital on [date]
Statutory documentation relating to this patient's liability to be detained under the Mental Health Act 1983 was received by me on behalf of the managers and the patient was consequently formally detained under section [   ] on [date].
The patient was given information in accordance with section 132 of the Act on [date].

Delete the phrase which does not apply
The patient's nearest relative/the person authorised to exercise the functions of the nearest relative was informed of the patient's admission on [date].
The local social services authority of the area where the patient resided immediately before admission is [name of authority]. That authority was advised of the patient's admission on [date].

Signed ....
on behalf of the managers

Date ....

Time ....]

Mental Health Act 1983 section 7—Record of receipt of medical recommendations   **2–065**

(*To be attached to the medical recommendation or the joint medical recommendation or, as the case may be, the second medical recommendation*)

[Full name of patient]
This recommendation was received by me on behalf of the authority at [time] on [date] and the patient was received into guardianship on [date].

Signed ....

Date ....]

Regulation 4(5)   *Form 16*

2–066 Mental Health Act 1983 section 5(4)—Record of time at which power to detain under Mental Health Act 1983 section 5(4) elapsed

[Full name of patient]

Complete (a) or (b) whichever occurred first

      (a) Registered medical practitioner arrived at [time] on [date]
      (b) The patient ceased to be detained at [time] on [date].

Signed ....

Status ....

Regulation 5(1)(a)(i) and (b)   Form 17

Mental Health Act 1983 section 7—Guardianship application by nearest relative   **2–067**

PART I

(To be completed by the nearest relative)

To the [name of local social services authority]
I [your full name] of [your address] hereby apply for the reception of [full name of patient] of [address of patient] into the guardianship of [full name and address of proposed guardian] in accordance with Part II of the Mental Health Act 1983.

Complete (a) or (b)

    (a) To the best of my knowledge and belief, I am the patient's nearest relative within the meaning of the Act.
        I am the patient's [state relationship].

ete the phrase hich does not apply.

    (b) I have been authorised to exercise the functions under the Act of the patient's nearest relative by a county court/the patient's nearest relative.

A copy of the authority is attached to this application.

Complete (i) or (ii)

    (i) The patient's date of birth is [date]
OR
    (ii) I believe the patient is aged 16 years or over.
I last saw the patient on [date].
This application is founded on two medical recommendations in the prescribed form.
If neither of the medical practitioners knew the patient before making their recommendations, please explain why you could not get a recommendation from a medical practitioner who did know the patient—

Signed ....

Date ....

PART II*

mplete only if proposed ardian is not a local social ices authority.

(To be completed by the proposed guardian)

[Your full name and address]
I am willing to act as the guardian of [name of the patient] in accordance with Part II of the Mental Health Act 1983.

Signed ....

Date ....

Regulation 5(1)(a)(ii) and (b)   *Form 18*

2–068 **Mental Health Act 1983 section 7—Guardianship application by approved social worker**

PART I

(To be completed by the approved social worker)

To the [name of local social services authority]
I [your full name] of [your office address] hereby apply for the reception of [name of patient] of [address of patient] into the guardianship of [full name and address of proposed guardian] in accordance with Part II of the Mental Health Act 1983 as a person suffering from:
mental illness, mental impairment, severe mental impairment, psychopathic disorder [enter whichever of these is appropriate].
I am an officer of [name of local social services authority] appointed to act as an approved social worker for the purposes of the Act.

The following section should be deleted if no consultation has taken place

Complete (a) or (b)

  (a) I have consulted [name and address] who to the best of my knowledge and belief is the patient's nearest relative within the meaning of the Act;

OR

Delete the phrase which does not apply
  (b) I have consulted [name and address] who I understand has been authorised by a county court/the patient's nearest relative to exercise the functions under the Act of the patient's nearest relative.

That person has not notified me or the local social services authority by whom I am appointed that he/she objects to this application being made.

The following section should be deleted if consultation has taken place

Delete whichever do not apply
  (a) I have been unable to ascertain who is this patient's nearest relative within the meaning of the Act.

OR

  (b) To the best of my knowledge and belief this patient has no nearest relative within the meaning of the Act.

OR

  (c) [name and address] is
    (i) this patient's nearest relative within the meaning of the Act
Delete the phrase which does not apply
    (ii) authorised to exercise the functions of this patient's nearest relative under the Act

  AND in my opinion it is not reasonably practicable or would involve unreasonable delay to consult that person before making this application.

The following section must be completed in all cases
I last saw the patient on [date].

Complete (i) or (ii)

  (i) The patient's date of birth is [date].

OR

(ii) I believe the patient is aged 16 years or over.

This application is founded on two medical recommendations in the prescribed form.
If neither of the medical practitioners knew the patient before making their recommendations, please explain why you could not get a recommendation from a medical practitioner who did know the patient—

Signed ....

Date ....

omplete only if
proposed
ardian is not a
local social
vices authority

PART II*

(To be completed by the proposed guardian.)

I [Your full name and address] am willing to act as the guardian of [name of the patient] in accordance with Part II of the Mental Health Act 1983.

Signed ....

Date ....

2–069   **Mental Health Act 1983 section 7—Joint medical recommendation for reception into guardianship**

We [full names and addresses of both medical practitioners], registered medical practitioners, recommend that [name and address of patient] be received into guardianship in accordance with Part II of the Mental Health Act 1983.

I [name of first practitioner] last examined this patient on [date].

*I had previous acquaintance with the patient before I conducted that examination.

*I have been approved by the Secretary of State under section 12 of the Act as having special experience in the diagnosis or treatment of mental disorder.

I [name of second practitioner] last examined this patient on [date].

*(a) I had previous acquaintance with the patient before I conducted that examination.

*(b) I have been approved by the Secretary of State under section 12 of the Act as having special experience in the diagnosis or treatment of mental disorder.

In our opinion this patient is suffering from† of a nature or degree which warrants reception into guardianship under the Act. This opinion is founded on the following grounds—
[Give clinical description of the patient's mental condition.]
We are of the opinion that it is necessary

Delete if not applicable — (marginal note)

†Insert mental illness, severe mental impairment, psychopathic disorder or mental impairment — (marginal note)

Delete (i) or (ii) unless both apply — (marginal note)

(i)   in the interests of the welfare of the patient
(ii)   for the protection of other persons

that the patient should be so received for the following reasons:—
[Reasons should state why patient cannot appropriately be carried for without powers of guardianship.]

Signed ....

Date ....

Signed ....

Date ....

Mental Health Regulations 1983

Regulation 5(1)(c)(ii)   Form 20

Mental Health Act 1983 section 7—Medical recommendation for reception into guardianship   **2–070**

I [full name and address of practitioner], a registered medical practitioner, recommend that [name and address of patient] be received into guardianship in accordance with Part II of the Mental Health Act 1983.

I last examined this patient on [date].

*Delete if not applicable   *I had previous acquaintance with the patient before I conducted that examination.

*I have been approved by the Secretary of State under section 12 of the Act as having special experience in the diagnosis or treatment of mental disorder.

†Insert mental illness, severe mental impairment, psychopathic order or mental impairment   In my opinion this patient is suffering from† of a nature or degree which warrants the patient's reception into guardianship under the Act. This opinion is founded on the following grounds— I am of the opinion that it is necessary

delete (i) or (ii) unless both apply

    (i) in the interests of the welfare of the patient
    (ii) for the protection of other persons

that the patient should be so received for the following reasons—
[Reasons should state why patient cannot appropriately be cared for without powers of guardianship]

Signed ....

Date ....

2–071 **Mental Health Act 1983 section 7—Record of acceptance of guardianship application**

(*To be attached to the guardianship application*)

This application was accepted by/on behalf of the local social services authority on [date].

Signed ....

on behalf of the responsible social services authority

Date ....

The patient was informed of his/her right to apply to a Mental Health Review Tribunal on [date on which patient was informed].

Delete the phrase The patient's nearest relative/The person authorised to exercise the functions of the nearest
which does not relative was informed of the patient's reception into guardianship on [date].
apply

Signed ....

on behalf of the responsible social services authority

Date ....]

Mental Health Act 1983 section 16—Reclassification of patient detained for treatment   **2–072**

PART I

(To be completed by the responsible medical officer)

To the Managers of [name of hospital or mental nursing home in which the patient is detained].
[Full name of patient].
I have consulted [give name or names and status of at least one other person] who has/have been professionally concerned with the patient's medical treatment.
It appears to me that this patient who is recorded on the application for admission to this hospital is suffering from [original classification as amended by any previous reclassification] is now suffering from mental illness, severe mental impairment, psychopathic disorder, mental impairment*.

†In my opinion further medical treatment in hospital is likely to alleviate or prevent a deterioration of the patient's condition.

elete whichever
does not apply

†Delete unless
patient is
lassified above
suffering from
psychopathic
rder or mental
impairment

Signed ....
Responsible Medical Officer

Date ....

PART II

(To be completed on behalf of the managers)

This report was received by me on behalf of the managers on [date].
The patient was informed of the above report on [date].
    The patient's nearest relative/the person authorised to exercise the functions of the nearest relative was informed of the above report on [date].

elete the phrase
which does not
apply or both if
known nearest
relative

Signed ....

Date ....]

Regulation 6(b)   *Form 23*

2–073   Mental Health Act 1983 section 16—Reclassification of patient under guardianship

PART I

(*To be completed by the appropriate medical officer*)

To [name of guardian]
[Full name of patient]
I have consulted [give name or names and status of at least one other person]
who has/have been professionally concerned with the patient's medical treatment.
This is to inform you that the patient who is recorded on the application for guardianship as
suffering from [original classification as amended by any previous reclassification] is now
suffering from*

**Insert mental
illness, severe
mental
impairment,
psychopathic
disorder or mental
impairment.
†Delete whichever
does not apply.*

Signed ....
†Responsible Medical Officer
Nominated Medical Attendant

Date ....

PART II

(*To be completed by the guardian*)

This report was received by me on [date].
The patient was informed of this report on [date].
‡The patient's nearest relative

*‡Delete the phrase
which does not
apply or both if
no known nearest
relative, or if the
nearest relative is
also the guardian*

The person authorised to exercise the functions of guardian
was informed of the above report on [date].

Signed ....
Guardian (or where guardian is a local social security
authority, officer acting on behalf of the authority)

Date ....

Mental Health Act 1983 section 19 and Schedule I Part II—Authority for transfer from one   **2–074**
hospital to another under different managers

PART I

(To be completed on behalf of the managers of the hospital where the patient is detained)

Authority is hereby given for the transfer of [name of patient] from [name and address of hospital in which the patient is liable to be detained] to [name and address of hospital to which patient is to be transferred] in accordance with the Mental Health (Hospital, Guardianship and Consent to Treatment) Regulations 1983 within 28 days beginning with the date of this authority.

Signed ....
on behalf of managers of first named hospital

Date ....

PART II

RECORD OF ADMISSION

(This is not part of the authority for transfer but is to be completed at the hospital to which the patient is transferred)

This patient was transferred to [name of hospital] in pursuance of this authority for transfer on [date of admission to receiving hospital]. The nearest relative was informed on [date].

Signed ....
on behalf of managers of receiving hospital

Date ....]

2–075 Mental Health Act 1983 section 19—Authority for transfer from hospital to guardianship

PART I

(*To be completed on behalf of the managers of the hospital where the patient is detained*)

Authority is hereby given for the transfer of [name of patient] who is at present liable to be detained in [name and address of hospital] to the guardianship of [name and address of proposed guardian] in accordance with the Mental Health (Hospital, Guardianship and Consent to Treatment) Regulations 1983.

Signed ....
on behalf of the managers

Date ....

PART II

(*To be completed by the local social services authority which will be responsible if the transfer takes place*)

Delete the phrase which does not apply or both if nearest relative is not known This transfer was agreed by/on behalf of the [name of local social services authority] on [date of confirmation] and the transfer shall take place on [date].
The patient's nearest relative/The person authorised to exercise the functions of the patient's nearest relative was informed of the transfer on [date].

Signed ....
on behalf of the local
social services authority

Date ....

*Complete only if proposed guardian is not a local social services authority

PART III*
(*To be completed by the proposed guardian*)

I [your full name and address] am willing to act as the guardian of [name of the patient] in accordance with Part II of the Mental Health Act 1983.

Signed ....

Date ....

Regulation 8(2)   *Form 26*

2–076 **Mental Health Act 1983 section 19—Authority for transfer of a patient from the guardianship of one guardian to another**

PART I

(To be completed by the present guardian)

Authority is hereby given for the transfer of [name and address of patient] from the guardianship of [name and address of the present guardian] to the guardianship of [name and address of the proposed guardian] in accordance with the Mental Health (Hospital, Guardianship and Consent to Treatment) Regulations 1983.

Signed ....

Date ....

PART II

(To be completed by the local social services authority which will be the responsible authority if the transfer takes place)

Delete the phrase which does not apply or both if nearest relative is not known This authority for transfer was confirmed by/on behalf of [name of local social services authority] on [date] and the transfer shall take place on [date].
The patient's nearest relative/The person authorised to exercise the functions of the patient's nearest relative was informed of the transfer on [date].

Signed ....
on behalf of the local
social services authority

Date ....

Complete only if proposed guardian is not a local social services authority ## PART III

(To be completed by the proposed guardian)

I [your full name and address] am willing to act as the guardian of [name of the patient] in accordance with Part II of the Mental Health Act 1983.

Signed ....

Date ....

2–077 **Mental Health Act 1983 section 19—Authority for transfer from guardianship to hospital**

Authority is hereby given for the transfer of [full name and address of patient] who is at present under the guardianship of [name and address of guardian] to [name and address of hospital] in accordance with the Mental Health (Hospital, Guardianship and Consent to Treatment) Regulations 1983.

Signed ....

on behalf of the
local social services authority

Date ....

Regulation 8(3)(b)(i)   *[Form 28*

Mental Health Act 1983 section 19—Joint medical recommendation for transfer from   **2–078**
guardianship to hospital

We [full names and addresses of practitioners], registered medical practitioners, recommend
that [full name and address of patient] be transferred from guardianship to hospital in
accordance with the Mental Health (Hospital, Guardianship and Consent to Treatment)
Regulations 1983 and admitted to a hospital for treatment in accordance with Part II of the
Mental Health Act 1983.
I [name of first practitioner] last examined this patient on [date].

*Delete if not   *I had previous acquaintance with the patient before I conducted that examination.
applicable.   *I have been approved by the Secretary of State under section 12 of the Act as having special
experience in the diagnosis or treatment of mental disorder.
I [name of second practitioner] last examined the patient on [date].
*I had previous acquaintance with the patient before I conducted that examination.
*I have been approved by the Secretary of State under section 12 of the Act as having special
experience in the diagnosis or treatment of mental disorder.
In our opinion this patient is suffering from—(*complete* (*a*) *or* (*b*))

**Delete the   (a) mental illness/severe mental impairment **and his mental disorder is of a nature or
case which does   degree which makes it appropriate for him to receive the medical treatment in a hospital;
not apply.   (b) psychopathic disorder/mental impairment** and his mental disorder is of a nature or
         degree which makes it appropriate for him to receive medical treatment in a hospital and
         such treatment is likely to alleviate or prevent deterioration of his condition.
This opinion is founded on the following grounds—
[Give clinical description of the patient's mental condition]
We are of the opinion that it is necessary

delete the indents   (i) in the interests of the patient's own health
not applicable.   (ii) in the interests of the patient's own safety
        (iii) with a view to the protection of other persons
that this patient should receive treatment and it cannot be provided unless he is detained under
section 3 of the Act, for the following reasons—
[Reasons should indicate why transfer to hospital is recommended and, where other methods of
care or treatment (e.g. out-patient or local social services authority services) are available, why
they are not appropriate, and why informal admission is not appropriate.]

Signed ....

Date ....

Signed ....

Date ....]

2–079 **Mental Health Act 1983 section 19—Medical recommendation for transfer from guardianship to hospital**

I [full name and address of practitioner], a registered medical practitioner, recommend that [full name and address of patient] be transferred from guardianship to hospital in accordance with the Mental Health (Hospital, Guardianship and Consent to Treatment) Regulations 1983 and admitted to a hospital for treatment in accordance with Part II of the Mental Health Act 1983.

I last examined this patient on [date].

*Delete if not applicable.

*I had previous acquaintance with the patient before I conducted that examination.

*I have been approved by the Secretary of State under section 12 of the Act as having special experience in the diagnosis or treatment of mental disorder.

In my opinion this patient is suffering from—(*complete* (a) *or* (b))

**Delete the phrase which does not apply.

(a) mental illness/severe mental impairment** and his mental disorder is of a nature or degree which makes it appropriate for him to receive medical treatment in a hospital;
(b) psychopathic disorder/mental impairment** and his mental disorder is of a nature or degree which makes it appropriate for him to receive medical treatment in a hospital and such treatment is likely to alleviate or prevent a deterioration of his condition.

This opinion is founded on the following grounds—
[Give clinical description of the patient's mental condition]
I am of the opinion that it is necessary

Delete the indents not applicable.

(i) in the interests of the patient's own health
(ii) in the interests of the patient's own safety
(iii) with a view to the protection of other persons

that this patient should receive treatment and it cannot be provided unless he is detained under section 3 of the Act, for the following reasons—
[Reasons should indicate why transfer to hospital is recommended and, where other methods of care or treatment (*e.g.* out-patient treatment or local social services authority services) are available, why they are not appropriate, and why informal admission is not appropriate.]

Signed ....

Date ....]

Regulation 10(1)   *[Form 30*

Mental Health Act 1983 section 20—Renewal of authority for detention   **2–080**

PART I

(To be completed by the responsible medical officer)

To the Managers of [name of hospital or mental nursing home in which patient is liable to be detained].

I examined [name of patient] on [date of examination] who was admitted to hospital on [date of admittance to hospital under the Mental Health Act 1983].

In my opinion this patient is suffering from—*(complete (a) or (b) or both)*

Delete the phrase which does not apply.

(a) mental illness/severe mental impairment* and his mental disorder is of a nature or degree which makes it appropriate for him to receive medical treatment in a hospital and either

*(i) such treatment is likely to alleviate or prevent a deterioration of his condition,

OR

*(ii) the patient, if discharged, is unlikely to be able to care for himself, to obtain the care which he needs or to guard himself against serious exploitation,

(b) psychopathic disorder/mental impairment* and his mental disorder is of a nature or degree which makes it appropriate for him to receive medical treatment in a hospital and such treatment is likely to alleviate or prevent a deterioration of his condition.

I am of the opinion that it is necessary

Delete the indents not applicable

(i) in the interests of the patient's own health
(ii) in the interests of the patient's own safety
(iii) with a view to the protection of other persons

that this patient should receive treatment and it cannot be provided unless he continues to be detained under the Act, for the following reasons—

[Reasons should indicate whether other methods of care or treatment (*e.g.* out-patient treatment or local social services authority services) are available and if so why they are not appropriate, and why informal admission is not appropriate.]

Signed ....

Date ....

PART II

(To be completed by the managers)

This report has been considered by the managers/persons authorised to act on behalf of the managers, who have decided not to order that the patient be discharged. The patient was informed of the receipt of this report on [date].

Delete the phrase which does not apply or both if nearest relative not known.

The patient's nearest relative/the person authorised to exercise the functions of the patient's nearest relative was informed of this report on [date].

Signed ....
on behalf of the managers

Date ....]

527

2–081 **Mental Health Act 1983 section 20—Renewal of authority for guardianship**

PART I

(To be completed by the responsible medical officer or nominated medical attendant)

To [name of guardian]
[name of responsible local social services authority if it is not the guardian]
I examined [name of patient] on [date].

*Insert mental illness, severe mental impairment, psychopathic disorder or mental impairment

Delete (i) or (ii) unless both apply

I am of the opinion that this patient is suffering from* of a nature or degree which warrants his reception into guardianship.
It is necessary

    (i) in the interests of the welfare of the patient
    (ii) for the protection of other persons

that the patient should remain under guardianship under the Act beyond [the date on which authority for guardianship is due to expire if not renewed] for the following reasons—
[Reasons should indicate why other methods of care are not appropriate]

†Delete whichever does not apply.

Signed ....
†Responsible Medical Officer
Nominated Medical Officer

PART II

(To be completed on behalf of the responsible local social services authority)

This report has been considered by/on behalf of the local social services authority, who have decided not to order that the patient be discharged from guardianship.
The patient was informed of this report on [date].
The guardian was informed of this report on [date].

Signed ....
on behalf of the local
social services authority

Date ....

Regulation 10A(a) [Form 31A]

Mental Health Act 1983 section 21B—Authority for Detention after Absence Without **2–082**
Leave for More Than 28 Days

PART I

(*To be completed by the responsible medical officer*)

To the managers of [name of hospital or mental nursing home in which patient is liable to be detained].

I examined [name of patient] on [date of examination] who:

(a) was admitted to hospital on [date of admission to hospital under the Mental Health Act 1983];

(b) was absent without leave from hospital or the place where he ought to be beginning on [date absence without leave began];

(c) was/is* liable to be detained for a period ending on [date authority for detention would have expired, apart from any extension under section 21, or date on which it will expire]; and

Delete the phrase which does not apply (d) returned/was returned* to the hospital or place on [date].

In my opinion the patient is suffering from—(*complete either (a) or (b) or both*)

Delete the indents not applicable (a) mental illness/severe mental impairment* and the patient's mental disorder is of a nature or degree which makes it appropriate for him to receive medical treatment in a hospital and either:

(i) such treatment is likely to alleviate or prevent a deterioration of his condition or

(ii) the patient, if discharged, is unlikely to be able to care for himself, to obtain the care which he needs or to guard himself against serious exploitation,

Delete the phrase which does not apply (b) psychopathic disorder/mental impairment* and the patient's mental disorder is of a nature or degree which makes it appropriate for him to receive medical treatment in a hospital and such treatment is likely to alleviate or prevent the deterioration of his condition.

I am of the opinion that it is necessary:

Delete the indents not applicable (i) in the interests of the patient's own health

(ii) in the interests of the patient's own safety

(iii) with a view to the protection of other persons

that this patient should receive treatment and it cannot be provided unless the patient continues to be detained under the Act, for the following reasons:

[Reasons should indicate whether other methods of care or treatment (*e.g.* out-patient treatment or local social services authority services) are available and if so why they are not appropriate, and why informal admission is not appropriate].

†Complete if appropriate This report shall/shall not† have effect as a report duly furnished under section 20(3) for the renewal of the authority for the detention of the patient.

[The above declaration should be completed if the authority for the detention of the patient is due to expire within a period of two months beginning with the date the report is to be furnished to the managers].

Signed ....

Add name in block capitals..

....

Date ....

PART II

(To be completed by the managers)

Delete the phrase which does not apply or both if nearest relative not known This report was received by the managers/persons authorised to act on behalf of managers on [date]. The patient was informed of this report on [date]. The patient's nearest relative/the person authorised to exercise the functions of patient's nearest relative was informed of this report on [date].

Signed ....
on behalf of the managers

Date ....]

Regulation 10A(b)   [Form 31B

**Mental Health Act 1983 section 21B Authority for Guardianship After Absence Without   2–083
Leave for More Than 28 Days**

PART I

(To be completed by the responsible medical officer or nominated medical attendant)

To [name of guardian]

[name of responsible local social services authority if it is not the guardian]

*Delete the phrase
which does not
apply*

I examined [name of patient] on [date of examination] who:
(a) was received into guardianship on [date];
(b) was absent without leave from the place where he is required to reside beginning on [date absence without leave began];
(c) was/is† subject to guardianship for a period ending on [date authority for guardianship would have expired, apart from any extension under section 21, or date on which it will expire]; and
(d) returned/was returned† to that place on [date].

**Insert mental
illness, severe
mental
impairment,
psychopathic
disorder or mental
impairment*

I am of the opinion that this patient is suffering from* of a nature or degree which warrants the continuation of the guardianship.

*Delete (i) or (ii)
unless both apply*

It is necessary:
(i) in the interests of the welfare of the patient
(ii) for the protection of other persons
that the patient should remain under guardianship under the Act for the following reasons:
[Reasons should indicate why other methods of care are not appropriate]

*†Complete if
appropriate*

This report shall/shall not† have effect as a report duly furnished under section 20(6) for the renewal of the authority for the guardianship of the patient.
[The above declaration should be completed in the authority for the guardianship of the patient is due to expire within a period of two months beginning with the date the report is to be furnished to the responsible local social services authority].

*Delete whichever
does not apply*

Signed ....
†Responsible Medical Officer
Nominated Medical Officer

Date ....

PART II

(To be completed by the responsible local social services authority)

This report was received by/on behalf of the local social services authority on [date].
The patient was informed of this report on [date].
The guardian was informed of this report on [date].

Signed ....
on behalf of the responsible local social services authority

Date ....]

2–084 **Mental Health Act 1983 section 92(3) or schedule 5, paragraph 39—Classification of patient**

[Full name of patient]

*Delete the phrase which does not apply

For the purposes of section 92(3) of/paragraph 39 of Schedule 5 to * the Mental Health Act 1983 I am of the opinion that this patient is suffering from**

**Insert mental illness, severe mental impairment, psychopathic disorder or mental impairment

Signed ....

Responsible Medical Officer

Date ....

Regulation 11(3) and (4)   *Form 33*

Mental Health Act 1983 Part VI—Date of reception of a patient to England and Wales   **2–085**

*Delete as [Full name of patient] was *admitted to [name and address of hospital/*received into the
ppropriate guardianship of] [name and address of guardian] on [date].

> Signed ....
> on behalf of *managers/
> *guardian
>
> Date ....

2–086   **Mental Health Act 1983 section 23—Discharge by nearest relative of patient liable to be detained in hospital**

To the Managers of [name and address of hospital or mental nursing home where patient is detained]
[Your full name] of [your address]

Complete (a) or (b)

Delete the phrase which does not apply

    (a) I am to the best of my knowledge and belief the nearest relative within the meaning of the Act of [full name of patient].

    (b) I have been authorised to exercise the functions under the Act of the nearest relative of [full name of patient] by a county court/the patient's nearest relative.

I have given notice in writing to the managers of my intention to discharge the patient.
I hereby order the discharge of the above-mentioned patient.

Signed ....

Date ....

Time ....

Mental Health Act 1983 section 23—Discharge by nearest relative of patient subject to guardianship   **2–087**

To the [name of responsible local social services authority]
[Your full name] of [your address]

Complete (a) or (b)

Delete the phrase which does not apply

(a) I am to the best of my knowledge and belief the nearest relative within the meaning of the Act of [full name of patient].
(b) I have been authorised to exercise the functions under the Act of the nearest relative of [full name of patient] by a county court/the patient's nearest relative.

I hereby order the discharge from guardianship of the above-named patient.

Signed ....

Date ....

2–088 Mental Health Act 1983 Section 25—Report barring discharge by nearest relative

PART I

(*To be completed by the responsible medical officer*)

To the Managers of [name of hospital or mental nursing home in which patient is liable to be detained]
[Name of nearest relative] gave notice at [time] on [date] of his/her intention to discharge [name of patient]. I am of the opinion that the patient, if discharged, would be likely to act in a manner dangerous to other persons or to himself/herself.

Signed ....

Responsible Medical Officer

Date ....

PART II

(*To be completed on behalf of the managers*)

Delete the phrase which does not apply This report was received by me on behalf of the managers at [time] on [date]. The patient's nearest relative/The person exercising the functions of the patient's nearest relative was informed of this report on [date].

Signed ....

on behalf of the managers

Date ....

Mental Health Act 1983 section 57—Certificate of consent to treatment and second opinion   **2–089**

(*Both parts of this certificate must be completed*)

PART I

I [full name and address], a registered medical practitioner appointed for the purposes of Part IV of the Act, and we [full name, address and status], being two persons appointed for the purposes of section 57(2)(*a*) of the Act, certify that [full name and address of patient]

    (a) is capable of understanding the nature, purposes and likely effects of [give description of treatment or plan of treatment]

AND

    (b) has consented to that treatment.

Signed ....

Date ....

Signed ....

Date ....

Signed ....

Date ....

PART II

I [full name] a registered medical practitioner appointed for the purposes of Part IV of the Act have consulted [full name of nurse], nurse and [full name and status] who have been professionally concerned with the medical treatment of the patient named above and certify that, having regard to the likelihood of the treatment specified above alleviating or preventing a deterioration of the patient's condition, that treatment should be given.

Signed ....

Date ....

2–090 **Mental Health Act 1983 section 58(3)(a)—Certificate of consent to treatment**

Delete the phrase which does not apply   I [full name and address] the responsible medical officer/a registered medical practitioner appointed for the purposes of Part IV of the Act certify that [full name and address of patient]

> (a) is capable of understanding the nature, purpose and likely effects of [give description of treatment or plan of treatment]

AND

> (b) has consented to that treatment.

Signed ....

Date ....

Mental Health Act 1983 section 58(3)(b)—Certificate of second opinion   **2–091**

I [full name and address], a registered medical practitioner appointed for the purposes of Part IV of the Act, have consulted [full name of nurse], nurse and [full name and status] who have been professionally concerned with the medical treatment of [full name and address of patient].

I certify that the patient—

elete whichever
does not apply

    (a) is not capable of understanding the nature, purpose and likely effects of

OR

    (b) has not consented to

[give description of treatment or plan of treatment] but that, having regard to the likelihood of that treatment alleviating or preventing a deterioration of the patient's condition, it should be given.

Signed ....

Date ....

Regulation 20   SCHEDULE 2   **2–092**

REVOCATIONS

Regulations or Order 1	Reference 2	Extent of revocation 3
The Mental Health (Hospital and Guardianship) Regulations 1960	S.I. 1960/1241	The whole of the regulations
The Mental Health (Hospital and Guardianship) Amendment Regulations 1962	S.I. 1962/1593	The whole of the regulations
The National Health Service Reorganisation (Consequential Amendments) Order 1974	S.I. 1974/241	The whole of the Order
The Local Authorities (Social Services and Food and Drugs) Order 1974	S.I. 1974/273	Article 3(4)
The Mental Health (Hospital and Guardianship) Amendment Regulations 1975	S.I. 1975/1337	The whole of the regulations
The Health Services Act 1980 (Consequential Amendments) Order 1982	S.I. 1982/288	Paragraph 2 of Schedule 1

MENTAL HEALTH (AFTER-CARE UNDER SUPERVISION) REGULATIONS 1996

(S.I. 1996 No. 294)

2–093 *Dated February 14, 1996, and made by the Secretary of State for Health under the National Health Service Act 1977, (c. 49), s.16(1) and the Mental Health Act 1983 (c. 20), s.32(1), (2) and (3).*

GENERAL NOTE

These Regulations enable specified functions of Health Authorities and local social services authorities relating to supervised discharge to be performed by other persons or bodies on their behalf (reg. 2). They also prescribe forms for use in connection with supervised discharge (reg. 3 and Sched. 2).

Citation, commencement and interpretation

2–094 **1.**—(1) These Regulations may be cited as the Mental Health (After-care under Supervision) Regulations 1996 and shall come into force on 1st April 1996.

(2) In these Regulations unless the context otherwise requires—

"the 1977 Act" means the National Health Service Act 1977;
"the 1983 Act" means the Mental Health Act 1983.

(3) In these Regulations unless the context otherwise requires any reference—

(a) to a numbered regulation or a numbered Schedule is a reference to the regulation or Schedule bearing that number in these Regulations; and

(b) in a regulation to a numbered paragraph is a reference to the paragraph bearing that number in that regulation; and

(c) to a numbered form is a reference to the form bearing that number in Schedule 2.

Exercise of functions relating to After-care under Supervision

2–095 **2.**—(1) The "relevant provisions" for the purposes of this regulation are the provisions specified in column 1 of Schedule 1 to these Regulations, the subject matter of which is specified in column 2 of that Schedule.

(2) Subject to paragraph (5), where a Health Authority, which has or will have a duty under section 117 of the 1983 Act to provide after-care services to a patient, makes an arrangement under section 23 of the 1977 Act or section 4 of the National Health Service and Community Care Act 1990 for the provision, by another person or body, of services consisting of or including psychiatric and related services for that patient, it may authorise that other person or body to perform on its behalf its functions under the relevant provisions in respect of that patient.

(3) Subject to paragraph (5) a Health Authority may make arrangements for its functions under the relevant provisions to be exercised on its behalf by any of the persons or bodies specified in section 16(1)(a)(i) to (v) of the 1977 Act.

(4) Subject to paragraph (5), where a local social services authority has or will have a duty under section 117 of the 1983 Act to provide after-care services to a patient, and where the Health Authority which also has or will have a duty with respect to the patient has given an authorisation to, or made arrangements with, a person or body under paragraph (2) or (3), the local social services authority may authorise the same person or body to perform all of that local social services authority's functions under the relevant provisions in respect of the patient.

(5) Nothing in this regulation shall permit a Health Authority or local social services authority to authorise a person or body to exercise the functions under section 25E(1) and (3) of the 1983 Act so far as they relate to review and modification of after-care services provided (or to be provided) to a patient under section 117 of the 1983 Act.

GENERAL NOTE

Paragraph (3)
Specified in section 16(1)(a)(i) to (v) of the 1977 Act: The relevant persons and **2–096** bodies are set out in the General Note to s.25A of the 1983 Act under the heading "Delegation of functions".

Procedure for and acceptance of supervision applications and related matters
3. For the purposes of after-care under supervision under Part II of the **2–097** 1983 Act—
   (a) any supervision application under section 25A shall be in the form set out in Form 1S;
   (b) any written recommendation of a registered medical practitioner under section 25B(6)(a) shall be in the form set out in Form 2S;
   (c) any written recommendation of an approved social worker under section 25B(6)(b) shall be in the form set out in Form 3S;
   (d) any report furnished under section 25F(1) (reclassification of a patient subject to after-care under supervision) shall be in the form set out in Form 4S;
   (e) any report furnished under section 25G(3) (medical recommendation for renewal of after-care under supervision) shall be in the form set out in Form 5S;
   (f) any renewal of after-care under supervision under section 25G(7) shall be recorded in the form set out in Part II of Form 5S;
   (g) any direction under section 25H(1) (ending of after-care under supervision) shall be in the form set out in Form 6S.

2–098 Regulation 2(1)   **SCHEDULE 1**

PROVISIONS OF THE ACT CONFERRING FUNCTIONS ON
HEALTH AUTHORITIES AND LOCAL SOCIAL SERVICES AUTHORITIES

(1)	(2)
Provision of the Act **(a)**	*Subject matter*
Section 25A(6), (7) and (8)	Supervision applications—acceptance etc.
Section 25C(6)	Supervision applications—consent to amendment
Section 25D(1)	Imposition of requirements
Section 25E(1), (3), (4), (6), (8) and (11) **(b)**	Review and modification of requirements imposed
Section 25F(1) and (4)	Receipt of reclassification report
Section 25G(3) and (8)	Receipt of renewal report and notification
Section 25H(6)	Ending of after-care supervision and notification

   (a) Sections 25A to 25H are inserted in the Act by section 1(1) of the MH 1995 Act.
   (b) This is subject to the exception provided for in regulation 2(5).

SCHEDULE 2   *Regulations 1(3)(c) and 3*

Form 1S   *Regulation 3*

Supervision Application   *Mental Health Act 1983*
                                     Section 25B or Section 25f

PART I

2–099 [COMPLETE EITHER SECTION A OR SECTION B: SECTION A IF PATIENT IS LIABLE TO BE DETAINED AND
SECTION B IF PATIENT IS SUBJECT TO A COMMUNITY CARE ORDER UNDER THE MENTAL HEALTH
(SCOTLAND) ACT 1984]

Section A
[COMPLETE IN BLOCK CAPITALS]

(full name and   I, ...
professional address of
responsible medical   of ....
officer)
                          ....
                          ....
                          ....
                          ....

                          and the responsible medical officer of

(full name and address ....
of patient)
                          ....
                          ....
                          ....
                          ....

                          who is currently liable to be detained in pursuance of an application for
                          admission for treatment in

(name and address of   ....
hospital)
                          ....
                          ....
                          ....

<table>
<tr><td>*(delete whichever does not apply)*</td><td>(a) The patient's date of birth is ....
(b) The patient's exact date of birth is unknown but the patient is believed to have attained the age of 16.
I hereby apply for the above named patient to be subject to after-care under supervision in accordance with the terms of Part II of the Act.</td></tr>
</table>

MENTAL DISORDER

In my opinion the patient is suffering from—

(delete whichever does not apply)

    (i) mental illness
    (ii) severe mental impairment
    (iii) psychopathic disorder
    (iv) mental impairment

This opinion is founded on the following grounds:—

(give a clinical description of the patient's condition)

....
....
....
....
....
....
....
....

NEED FOR AFTER-CARE UNDER SUPERVISION

I am of the opinion that after-care under supervision is necessary for this patient because
(a) the patient is suffering from mental disorder, as specified above;
(b) if the patient did not receive section 117 after-care there would be a substantial risk of—

(delete whichever does not apply)

    (i) serious harm to the patient's health
    (ii) serious harm to the patient's safety
    (iii) serious harm to the safety of other persons
    (iv) serious exploitation of the patient

(state reasons)

because ....
....
....
....

and
(c) such supervision is likely to help secure that the patient receives section 117 after-care services because ....
....

CONSULTATION

The following people have been consulted about the making of this application and I have taken account of the views they expressed:—

(names, addresses and designations of those consulted)

....
....
....
....
....
....
....
....
....
....
....
....
....

(Any separate sheet on which this statement is continued shall be deemed to be part of the application.)

AFTER-CARE DETAILS

2–100

I attach details of the after-care services to be provided for this patient. I consider that the patient should be subject to the following requirements:—

(specify proposed requirements)

....
....
....
....
....
....
....
....

The following person will be the patient's community responsible medical officer and will be in charge of the medical treatment to be provided for the patient as part of the after-care services to be provided under section 117:—

(delete whichever does not apply)

(a) myself, or

(full name and professional address of proposed community responsible medical officer)

(b) ....
of ....
....
....
....
....
....

and a written statement from this person to that effect is attached at Part II.

The following person will be the patient's supervisor and will supervise the patient with a view to ensuring that the patient receives the after-care services provided under section 117:—

(delete whichever does not apply)

(a) myself, or

(full name, professional address and profession of proposed supervisor)

(b) ....
or ....
....
....
....

a ....

and a written statement from this person to that effect is attached.

This application is accompanied by two recommendations in the prescribed forms from an approved social worker and a registered medical practitioner.

Signed .... Date ....

Section B

[COMPLETE IN BLOCK CAPITALS]

(full name and professional address of applicant)

I, ...
of ....
....
....
....
....

am the proposed community responsible medical officer of

(full name)

....

who is currently subject to a community care order under the Mental Health (Scotland) Act 1984.

The patient's address in Scotland is

(current address of patient in Scotland)

....
....
....
....

The patient will be residing at

(proposed address of patient in England or Wales)

....
....
....

(a) The patient's date of birth is ....

(delete whichever does not apply)

(b) The patient's exact date of birth is unknown but the patient is believed to have attained the age of 16.

I hereby apply for the above named patient to be subject to after-care under supervision in accordance with the terms of Part II of the Act.

MENTAL DISORDER

I am satisfied that the patient is suffering from—

(delete whichever does not apply)

    (i) mental illness
    (ii) severe mental impairment
    (iii) psychopathic disorder
    (iv) mental impairment

This opinion is founded on the following grounds:—

(give a clinical description of the patient's condition)

....
....
....
....
....
....
....

NEED FOR AFTER-CARE UNDER SUPERVISION

I am of the opinion that after-care under supervision is necessary for this patient because

(a) the patient is suffering from mental disorder, as specified above; and

(b) if the patient did not receive section 117 after-care there would be a substantial risk of—

delete any which do not apply)

    (i) serious harm to the patient's health
    (ii) serious harm to the patient's safety
    (iii) serious harm to the safety of other persons
    (iv) serious exploitation of the patient

(state reasons)

because ....
....
....
....

and

(c) such supervision is likely to help secure that the patient receives section 117 after-care services because ....
....
....
....
....
....
....

CONSULTATION

The following people have been consulted about the making of this application and I have taken account of the views they expressed:—

2–101

545

(names, addresses and designations of those consulted)

....
....
....
....
....
....
....
....
....
....
....
....
....

(Any separate sheet on which this statement is continued shall be deemed to be part of the application.)

AFTER-CARE DETAILS

I attach details of the after-care services to be provided for this patient.

I consider that the patient should be subject to the following requirements:—

(specify proposed requirements)

....
....
....
....
....
....
....
....
....
....
....

The following person will be the patient's supervisor, and wil supervise the patient with a view to ensuring that the patient receives the after-care services provided under section 117:—

(delete whichever does not apply)
(full name, professional address and profession of proposed supervisor)

(a) myself, or

(b) ....

of ....
....
....
....
....
....

a ....

and a written statement from this person to that effect is attached at Part II.

This application is accompanied by two recommendations: one from the patient's special medical officer in Scotland or a registered medical practitioner and the other from the patient's after-care officer in Scotland or an approved social worker.

Signed .... Date ....

PART II

[COMPLETE IN BLOCK CAPITALS]

A. STATEMENT BY THE PROPOSED COMMUNITY RESPONSIBLE MEDICAL OFFICER

[THIS MUST BE COMPLETED IN ALL CASES INCLUDING WHERE THE APPLICANT IS TO BE THE PATIENTS COMMUNITY RESPONSIBLE MEDICAL OFFICER]

(full name and professional address of practitioner)

I, ...

of ....

....

....

....

am a registered medical practitioner approved for the purposes of section 12 of the Mental Health Act 1983 as having special experience in the diagnosis or treatment of mental disorder. I will be the community responsible medical officer of the patient specified in Part I of ths form and will be in charge of the medical treatment provided for him as part of the after-care services provided under section 117 of the Mental Health Act 1983.

Signed .... Date ....

B. STATEMENT BY THE PROPOSED SUPERVISOR

[THIS MUST BE COMPLETED IN ALL CASES INCLUDING WHERE THE APPLICANT IS TO BE THE PATIENTS SUPERVISOR]

(full name, professional address and profession of proposed supervisor)

I, ...

of ....

....

....

....

a ....

will be supervisor of the patient specified in Part I, and will supervise the patient with a view to ensuring that the patient receives the after-care services provided under section 117 of the Mental Health Act 1983.

Signed .... Date ....

PART III

('To be completed on behalf of the Health Authority)   **2–102**

This application was received by me on .... (date) accompanied by the required recommendations.

The local social services authority

.... (name) has been consulted about this application.

The patient was informed orally about the acceptance of this application and the effect in his case of becoming a person subject to after-care under supervision by .... (name) on .... and in writing on .... (dates)

(delete whichever does not apply)

(a) The patient's nearest relative

.... (name) of

....

....

....

....

was informed in writing on .... (date)

(b) The patient's nearest relative has not been informed because

(delete (i) or (ii))

(i) This was not practicable

(ii) the patient objected

(c) The patient has no known nearest relative

The following person(s) (not being professionally concerned with the after-care services to be provided) is believed to play a substantial part in the care of the patient:—

(name(s) and address (es))
....
....
....
....
....
....

and has been informed about the acceptance of this application.

(name of health authority) The bodies responsible for the patient's after-care under section 117 of the Act are

(name of local authority)
....
and
....

They were informed about the acceptance of this application on .... and .... (dates) respectively.

The patient's RMO .... (name)
was informed on .... (date)

The patient's community RMO .... (name)
was informed on .... (date)

The patient's supervisor .... (name)
was informed on .... (date)

The patient's GP .... (name)
was informed on .... (date)

Signed .... Date ....

Name .... Position ....

Regulation 3   Form 2S

**Medical recommendations for after-care
under supervision**

Mental Health Act 1983 **2–103**
Section 25B

[COMPLETE IN BLOCK CAPITALS]
RECOMMENDATION

(full name and   I, ...
professional address of of ....
practitioner)   ....
....
....
....
....

a registered medical practitioner, recommend that

(full name and address ....
of patient)   of ....
....
....
....

who is currently liable to be detained in

(name and address of   ....
hospital)   ....
....
....

be subject to after-care under supervision in accordance with Part II of
the Act.

MENTAL DISORDER

In my opinion the patient is suffering from—

(delete whichever does   (i)   mental illness
not apply)   (ii) severe mental impairment
(iii) psychopathic disorder
(iv) mental impairment

(Give a clinical   This opinion is founded on the following grounds:—
description of the   ....
patients conditions)   ....
....
....
....
....

NEED FOR AFTER-CARE UNDER SUPERVISION

I am of the opinion that (having regard in particular to the patient's
history) after-care under supervision is necessary for this patient
because

(a) the patient is suffering from mental disorder, as specified above;
and
(b) if the patient did not receive section 117 after-care there would be a
substantial risk of—

(delete whichever does   (i)   serious harm to the patient's health
not apply)   (ii) serious harm to the patient's safety
(iii) serious harm to the safety of other persons
(iv) serious exploitation of the patient

(state reasons)   because ....

....

....

....

....

....

and

(c) such supervision is likely to help secure that the patient receives
section 117 after-care services because ....

....

....

....

....

....

Signed ....   Date ....

Regulation 3   *Form 3S*

**Approved social worker's
recommendation for after-care
under supervision**

Mental Health Act 1983 **2–104**
Section 25B

[COMPLETE IN BLOCK CAPITALS]

*(full name and
professional address of
Approved Social
Worker)*

I, ...
of ....
....
....

am an officer of

*(name of local
authority)*

....

appointed to act as an Approved Social Worker under the Act.

I recommend that

*(full name and address
of patient)*

....
of ....
....
....
....

who is currently liable to be detained in

*(name and address of
hospital)*

....
....
....
....

be subject to after-care under supervision in accordance with Part Ii of
the Mental Health Act 1983.

I last interviewed the patient on .... (date)

I am of the opinion that (having regard in particular to the patient's
history) after-care under supervision is necessary for this patient
because

(a) if the patient were not to receive section 117 after-care there would
be a substantial risk of—

*(delete whichever does
not apply)*

    (i) serious harm to the patient's health
   (ii) serious harm to the patient's safety
  (iii) serious harm to the safety of other persons
  (iv) serious exploitation of the patient

(state reasons)

because ....
....
....
....
....

and

(b) such supervision is likely to help secure that the patient receives
section 117 after-care services because ....
....
....
....
....

Signed ....   Date ....

551

Regulation 3   Form 4S

2–105 **Reclassification of a patient
subject to after-care under
supervision**

PART I

[COMPLETE IN BLOCK CAPITALS]

*(full name and
professional address of
responsible community
medical officer)*

I, ...

of ....

....

....

....

....

am the community responsible medical officer of

*(full name and address
of patient)*

....

....

....

....

....

I last examined the patient on .... (date)

*(original classification
as amended by any
previous reclassifica-
tion)*

It appears to me that the patient who is recorded on the supervision
application as suffering from

....

is now suffering from—

*(delete whichever does
not apply)*

    (i) mental illness
   (ii) severe mental impairment
  (iii) psychopathic disorder
  (iv) mental impairment

This opinion is founded on the following grounds:—

*(give a clinical
description of the
patient's condition)*

....

....

....

....

....

....

....

....

....

(delete (a) or (b))

(a) I have consulted the following person(s) professionally concerned
with the patient's medical treatment:—

*(name(s), designation
(s) and professional
address(es) of person
(s) consulted, if any)*

....

....

....

....

....

....

....

....

(b) There is one other than myself professionally concerned with the
patient's medical treatment.

Signed .... Date ....

PART II

(To be completed on behalf of the responsible after-care bodies)

This reclassification report was received by me on .... (date)

The patient was informed orally about the reclassification on ...... (date)
by ....
.... (name) and in writing on .... (date)

(delete whichever does not apply)

(a) The patient's nearest relative
.... (name of
....
....
....
....

was informed in writing on .... (date)

(b) The patient's nearest relative has not been informed because

(delete (i) or (ii))
    (i) this was not practicable
    (ii) the patient objected

(c) The patient has no known nearest relative

Signed .... Date ....

Name .... Position ....

Regulation 3   *Form 5S*

2–106 **Renewal of after-care under supervision**

PART I

[COMPLETE IN BLOCK CAPITALS]

(full name and professional address of community responsible medical officer)

I, ...

of ....

....

....

....

....

am the community responsible medical officer of

(full name and address of patient)

....

....

....

....

....

I last examined the patient on .... (date)

[THIS MUST BE WITHIN TWO MONTHS OF THE DATE AFTER-CARE UNDER SUPERVISION IS DUE TO EXPIRE]

MENTAL DISORDER

In my opinion the patient is suffering from—

(delete whichever does not apply)

   (i) mental illness
   (ii) severe mental impairment
   (iii) psychopathic disorder
   (iv) mental impairment

This opinion is founded on the following grounds:—

(give a clinical description of the patient's condition)

....

....

....

....

....

....

....

....

NEED FOR AFTER-CARE UNDER SUPERVISION

In my opinion it is necessary that this patient should continue to be subject to after-care under supervision for the following reasons:—

(a) the patient is suffering from mental disorder, as specified above;

and

(b) if the patient did not receive section 117 after-care there would be a substantial risk of—

(delete whichever does not apply)

   (i) serious harm to the patient's health
   (ii) serious harm to the patient's safety
   (iii) serious harm to the safety of other persons
   (iv) serious exploitation of the patient

(state reasons)

because ....

....

....

....

554

....
....

and

(c) such supervision is likely to help secure that the patient receives section 117 after-care services because ....
....
....
....
....
....
....
....

CONSULTATION

The following people have been consulted and I have taken account of the views they expressed:—

(names, addresses and designations of those consulted)

....
....
....
....
....
....
....
....
....
....
....
....

(Any separate sheet on which this statement is continued shall be deemed to be part of this renewal report)

(full name, professional address and profession of supervisor)

The patient's supervisor is
....
of ....
....
....
....
....

a ....

Signed ....   Date ....

PART II

(To be completed on behalf of the responsible after-care bodies)

This renewal report was received by me on .... (date)

The patient was informed orally about the renewal of after-care under supervision and its effect in his case by .... (name) on .... and in writing on .... (dates)

(delete whichever does not apply)

(a) The patient's nearest relative
.... (name) of
....
....
....
....

(date)

was informed in writing on ....

(b) The patient's nearest relative has not been informed because

(delete (i) or (ii))

(i) this was not practicable

555

(ii) the patient objected

(c) The patient has no known nearest relative

The following person(s) (not being professionally concerned with the after-care services provided) is believed to play a substantial part in the care of the patient:—

(name(s) and address (es))

....

....

....

....

....

....

and has been informed about the renewal of after-care under supervision.

The bodies responsible for the patient's after-care under section 117 of the Act are

(name of health authority)

....

and

(name of local authority)

....

who have agreed to continue to provide such care.

(dates)

They were informed about the renewal of after-care under supervision on

.... and .... respectively.

The patient's supervisor .... (name)

was informed on .... (date)

Signed .... Date ....

Name .... Position ....

Regulation 3   Form 6S

Directing termination of after-care   **2–107**
under supervision

PART I

[COMPLETE IN BLOCK CAPITALS]

(full name and   I, ...
professional address of
community responsible   of ....
medical officer)   ....
                          ....
                          ....
                          ....
                          ....

                          am the community responsible medical officer of

(full name and address ....
of patient)   ....
                          ....
                          ....
                          ....

                          I hereby direct that this patient shall cease to be subject to after-care
                          under supervision because ....
(give reason)   ....
                          ....

                          The following people have been consulted about the giving of this
                          direction and I have taken account of the views they expressed:—

(names, addresses and   ....
designations of those   ....
consulted)   ....
                          ....
                          ....
                          ....
                          ....
                          ....
                          ....
                          ....
                          ....
                          ....
                          ....

                          (Any separate sheet on which this statement is continued shall be
                          deemed to be part of this direction.)

                          Signed ....   Date ....

PART II

(To be completed on behalf of the responsible after-care bodies)

                          This direction was received by me on .... (date)

                          The patient was informed orally about the ending of after-care under
                          supervision by .... (name)
                          on .... and in writing on .... (dates)

(delete whichever does (a) The patient's nearest relative
not apply)
                          .... (name) of
                          ....
                          ....

557

....
....
....

was informed in writing on .... (date)

(b) The patient's nearest relative has not been informed because

(delete (i) or (ii))

    (i) this was not practicable

    (ii) the patient objected

(c) The patient has no known nearest relative

The following person(s) (not being professionally concerned with the after-care services provided) is believed to play a substantial part in the care of the patient

(name(s) and address (es))

....
....
....
....
....
....

and has been informed about the ending of after-care under supervision.

The bodies responsible for the patient's after care under section 117 of the Act are

(name of health authority)

....

and

(name of local authority)

....

They were informed about the ending of after-care under supervision on .... and .... (dates) respectively.

The patient's supervisor .... (name)
was informed on .... (date)

The patient's GP .... (name)
was informed on .... (date)

Signed .... Date ....

Name .... Position ....

MENTAL HEALTH (PATIENTS IN THE COMMUNITY) (TRANSFERS FROM SCOTLAND) REGULATIONS 1996

(S.I. 1996 No. 295)

Dated February 14, 1996, and made by the Secretary of State for Health under **2–108**
the Mental Health Act 1983 (c. 20), s.25J(2).

GENERAL NOTE
These Regulations prescribe modifications to sections 25A to 25I and other provisions of the **2–109**
Mental Health Act 1983 to enable patients who are subject to community care orders made
under the Mental Health (Scotland) Act 1984, and who wish to move to England or Wales, to
become subject to supervised discharge.

Citation, commencement and interpretation
1. These Regulations may be cited as the Mental Health (Patients in the **2–110**
Community) (Transfers from Scotland) Regulations 1996 and shall come
into force on 1st April 1996.

Modifications of provisions of the Mental Health Act 1983
2. The provisions of the Mental Health Act 1983 set out in column 1 of the **2–111**
Schedule to these Regulations shall apply in relation to a patient in respect of
whom a supervision application is (or is to be) made subject to the
modifications prescribed in column 2 of the Schedule.

SCHEDULE   **Regulation 2**

MODIFICATIONS OF PROVISIONS OF THE MENTAL HEALTH ACT 1983 IN   **2–112**
RESPECT OF PATIENTS SUBJECT TO COMMUNITY CARE ORDERS IN
SCOTLAND WHO INTEND TO RESIDE IN ENGLAND OR WALES

(1) *Provision*	(2) *Modification*
Section 25A	As if for subsection (1) there were substituted the following subsection— "(1) Where a patient is subject to a community care order made under section 35(A)(3) of the Mental Health (Scotland) Act 1984 (in this and the next section referred to as a "community care order") an application may be made for him to be supervised upon his taking up residence in England or Wales, for the period allowed by the following provisions of this Act, with a view to securing that he receives the aftercare services provided for him under section 117 below".
	As if in subsection (2) for "left hospital" there were substituted "taken up residence in England or Wales".
	As if in subsection (4)(b) for "leaves hospital" there were substituted "takes up residence in England or Wales".
	As if in subsection (5) for "the responsible medical officer" there were substituted "the registered medical practitioner who is proposed to be the community responsible medical officer".
	As if in subsection (6) for "leaves hospital" there were substituted "takes up residence in England or Wales".
	As if subsection (9) were omitted.

(1) *Provision*	(2) *Modification*
Section 25B	As if in subsection (1) for "responsible medical officer" on both occasions the words appear there were substituted "practitioner".
	As if in sub-paragraph (ii) of subsection (2)(a) for "in hospital" there were substituted "whilst he was subject to a community care order" and as if at the end of that sub-paragraph there were inserted "and the patient's after-care officer (as defined in section 125(1) of the Mental health (Scotland) Act 1984".
	As if in subsection (2)(a)(iv) for "the responsible medical officer" there were substituted "the practitioner making the application" and as if for "leaves hospital" there were substituted "takes up residence in England or Wales".
	As if in subsection (2)(c) for "the responsible medical officer" there were substituted "the practitioner making the application".
	As if in subsection (3)(b) for "the responsible medical officer" there were substituted "the practitioner making the application".
	As if for paragraph (a) of subsection (5) there were substituted the following paragraph— "(a) that the patient is subject to a community care order";
	As if in subsection (5)(d) for "leaves hospital" there were substituted "takes up residence in England or Wales".
Section 25B	As if for paragraph (a) of subsection (6) there were substituted the following paragraph— "(a) where available to the practitioner making the application the written recommendation of the patient's special medical officer (as defined in section 125(1) of the Mental Health (Scotland) Act 1984 or, where this recommendation is not available to that practitioner, the written recommendation of any registered medical practitioner; and".
	As if for paragraph (b) of subsection (6) there were substituted the following paragraph— "(b) where available to the practitioner making the application the written recommendation of the patient's after-care officer (as defined in section 125(1) of the Mental Health (Scotland) Act 1984 or, where this recommendation is not available to that practioner, the written recommendation of an approved social worder.".
	As if in subsection (8) "social worker" there were substituted "person making the recommendation".
	As if in subsection (9)(a) and (b) for "leaves hospital" there were substituted "takes up residence in England or Wales".
	As if in subsection (10) for "responsible medical officer" there were substituted "practitioner making it".
	As if in subsection (11) for "leaves hospital" there were substituted "takes up residence in England or Wales".
Section 25C	As if subsection (3) were omitted.
	As if subsection (4) were omitted.
	As if subsection (5) were omitted.
Section 25D	As if in subsection (1) for "(or, if he has not yet left hospital, is to be so subject after he leaves hospital)" there were substituted "(or, if he has not yet taken up residence in England or Wales, is to be so subject when he does take up residence there)".

(1) Provision	(2) Modification
Section 25G	As if in subsection (1)(a) for "leaves hospital" there weere substituted "takes up residence in England or Wales". .
Section 72	As if in subsection (4A) for "(or, if he has not yet left hospital, is to be so subject after he leaves hospital)" there were substituted "(or, if he has not yet taken up residence in England or Wales, is to be so subject when he does take up residence there)".
Section 76	As if in subsection (1)(a) for "(or, if he has not yet left hospital, is to be subject to after-care under supervision after he leaves hospital)" there were substituted "(or, if he has not yet taken up residence in England or Wales, is to be subject to after-care under supervision when he takes up residence there)".

PART 3

PRACTICE AND PROCEDURE

MENTAL HEALTH REVIEW TRIBUNAL RULES 1983

(S.I. 1983 No. 942)

Dated June 28, 1983, and made by the Lord Chancellor under the Mental **3–001**
Health Act 1983, s.78.

GENERAL NOTE

These Rules provide for a code of procedure to be followed in proceedings before **3–002**
Mental Health Review Tribunals. They do not provide a tribunal with jurisdiction to
award costs against a party. The constitution and proceedings of tribunals are
considered in the General Note to section 65 of the 1983 Act.

Legal representation "in proceedings before a Mental Health Review Tribunal ...
where the client's case or application to the tribunal is, or is to be, the subject of the
proceedings" is available without reference to the client's financial resources
(Community Legal Services (Financial) Regulations 2000 (S.I. 2000 No. 516, reg. 3).
The Law Society has established a panel of solicitors with experience of tribunal
work to assist patients in finding a suitable legal representative. Inquiries about the
panel can be sent to: The Panel Administrator, Professional Standards and
Development Directorate, The Law Society, Ipsley Court, Berrington Close,
Redditch, Worcestershire B98 0TD. The Law Society has published "Representation
at Mental Health Review Tribunals: Guidelines for Legal Representatives" (1997).

The Council on Tribunals, which is established under the Tribunal and Inquiries
Act 1992, is required to keep under review the constitution and working of Mental
Health Review Tribunals (*ibid.*, s.1(a), Sched. 1). The Council's address is, 7th Floor,
22 Kingsway, London WC2B 6LE.

ARRANGEMENT OF RULES

PART I

INTRODUCTION

Title and commencement
1. These Rules may be cited as the Mental Health Review Tribunal Rules **3–004**
1983 and shall come into operation on September 30, 1983.

Interpretation
2.—(1) In these Rules, unless the context otherwise requires—   **3–005**

"the Act" means the Mental Health Act 1983;
"admission papers" means the application for admission under section
    2 of the Act and the written recommendations of the two registered
    medical practitioners on which it is founded;
"assessment application" means an application by a patient who is
    detained for assessment and entitled to apply under section
    66(1)(a) of the Act or who, being so entitled, has applied;
"the authority's statement" means the statement provided by the
    responsible authority pursuant to rule 6(1);
"chairman" means the legal member appointed by the Lord Chancellor
    as chairman of the Mental Health Review Tribunal under para-
    graph 3 of Schedule 2 to the Act or another member of the tribunal
    appointed to act on his behalf in accordance with paragraph 4 of
    that Schedule or section 78(6) of the Act as the case may be;
"decision with recommendations" means a decision with recommenda-
    tions in accordance with section 72(3)(a) [or (3A)(a)] of the Act;
"health authority" has the same meaning as in the National Health
    Service Act 1977;
["National Health Service trust" means a body established under
    section 5(1) of the National Health Service and Community Care
    Act 1990;]
"nearest relative" means a person who has for the time being the
    functions under the Act of the nearest relative of a patient who is
    not a restricted patient;
"party" means the applicant, the patient, the responsible authority, any
    other person to whom a notice under rule 7 or rule 31(c) is sent or
    who is added as a party by direction of the tribunal;
"president" means the president of the tribunal as defined in paragraph
    6 of Schedule 2 to the Act;
"private guardian" in relation to a patient means a person, other than a
    local social services authority, who acts as guardian under the Act;
"proceedings" includes any proceedings of a tribunal following an
    application or reference in relation to a patient;
"provisional decision" includes a deferred direction for conditional
    discharge in accordance with section 73(7) of the Act and a
    notification to the Secretary of State in accordance with section
    74(1) of the Act;
"reference" means a reference under section 67(1), 68(1) or (2), 71(1),
    (2) or (5) or 75(1) of the Act;

"registration authority" means the authority exercising the functions of the Secretary of State under the Nursing Homes Act 1975;
"responsible authority" means—

(a) in relation to a patient liable to be detained under the Act in a hospital or mental nursing home, the managers of the hospital or home as defined in section 145(1) of the Act; and

(b) in relation to a patient subject to guardianship, the responsible local social services authority as defined in section 34(3) of the Act; [and

(c) in relation to a patient subject to after-care under supervision, the Health Authority which has the duty under section 117 of the Act to provide after-care services for the patient;]

"the Secretary of State's statement" means a statement provided by the Secretary of State pursuant to rule 6(2) or (3);
"tribunal" in relation to an application or a reference means the Mental Health Review Tribunal constituted under section 65 of the Act which has jurisdiction in the area in which the patient, at the time the application or reference is made, is detained or is liable to be detained or is subject to guardianship [or is (or is to be) subject to after-care under supervision], or the tribunal to which the proceedings are transferred in accordance with rule 17(2), or in the case of a conditionally discharged patient, the tribunal for the area in which the patient resides.

AMENDMENTS
The amendments to this rule were made by S.I. 1996 No. 314, r. 2

GENERAL NOTE
3–006   *Nursing Homes Act 1975:* Now see Parts I and II of the Care Standards Act 2000.

PART II

PRELIMINARY MATTERS

Making an application
3–007   **3.**—(1) An application shall be made to the tribunal in writing, signed by the applicant or any person authorised by him to do so on his behalf.

(2) The application shall wherever possible include the following information—

(a) the name of the patient;

(b) the patient's address, which shall include—

(i) the address of the hospital or mental nursing home where the patient is detained; or

(ii) the name and address of the patient's private guardian; or

(iii) in the case of a conditionally discharged patient or a patient to whom leave of absence from hospital has been granted, the address of the hospital or mental nursing home where the patient was last detained or is liable to be detained; together with the patient's current address;

(c) where the application is made by the patient's nearest relative, the name and address of the applicant and his relationship to the patient;

(d) the section of the Act under which the patient is detained or is liable to be detained;

(e) the name and address of any representative authorised in accordance with rule 10 or, if none has yet been authorised, whether the applicant intends to authorise a representative or wishes to conduct his own case;

[(f) in the case of a patient subject (or to be subject) to after-care under supervision—

   (i) the names of the persons who are (or who are to be) the patient's supervisor and community responsible medical officer;

   (ii) the name and address of any place at which the patient is (or will be) receiving medical treatment;

   (iii) where the patient is subject to after-care under supervision his current address, or in the case of a patient who is to be subject to after-care under supervision upon leaving hospital, the address of the hospital where he is, or was last, detained or is liable to be detained.]

(3) If any of the information specified in paragraph (2) is not included in the application, it shall in so far as is practicable be provided by the responsible authority or, in the case of a restricted patient, the Secretary of State, at the request of the tribunal.

AMENDMENT
Paragraph 2(f) was inserted by S.I. 1996 No. 314, r. 3.

DEFINITIONS
   tribunal: r. 2.   **3–007.1**
   private guardian: r. 2.
   nearest relative: r. 2.
   the Act: r. 2.
   responsible authority: r. 2.

GENERAL NOTE

Paragraph (1)
   In writing: There is no prescribed form. Nevertheless, forms have been produced **3–007.2** for those who wish to use them, and copies are available from tribunal offices (D.H.S.S. Circular No. HC (83)17, para. 10).
   Person authorised by him: Such as a relative, social worker or nurse. The application could also be made by the patient's representative; see r. 10(4). This rule does not allow for an application to be made on the behalf of a patient whose mental incapacity is at a level which disables him from authorising a person to act for him.

Paragraph (2)
   Wherever possible: Failure to provide any of the information set out in this **3–007.3** paragraph does not invalidate the application.

Notice of application

3–007.4   **4.**—(1) On receipt of an application, the tribunal shall send notice of the application to—

(a) the responsible authority;

(b) the patient (where he is not the applicant); and

(c) if the patient is a restricted patient, the Secretary of State.

(2) Paragraph (1) shall apply whether or not the power to postpone consideration of the application under rule 9 is exercised.

GENERAL NOTE

Paragraph (1)

3–008   *Secretary of State:* Before starting to hear any application in respect of a restricted patient when the Home Secretary is not represented, a Mental Health Review Tribunal should ensure that he has been given notice of the application and of the hearing. A failure to provide the Home Secretary with the necessary notice and documentation has been held to invalidate the proceedings (*Secretary of State for the Home Department v. Oxford Regional Mental Health Review Tribunal* [1987] 3 All E.R. 8, HL).

Preliminary and incidental matters

3–009   **5.** As regards matters preliminary or incidental to an application, the chairman may, at any time up to the hearing of an application by the tribunal, exercise the powers of the tribunal under rules, 6, 7, 9, 10, 12, 13, 14(1), 15, 17, 19, 20, 26 and 28.

DEFINITIONS

3–010   chairman: r. 2.

tribunal: r. 2.

Statements by the responsible authority and the Secretary of State

3–011   **6.**—(1) The responsible authority shall send a statement to the tribunal and, in the case of a restricted patient, the Secretary of State, as soon as practicable and in any case within three weeks of its receipt of the notice of application; and such statement shall contain—

(a) the information specified in Part A of Schedule 1 to these Rules, in so far as it is within the knowledge of the responsible authority; and

(b) the report specified in paragraph 1 of Part B of that Schedule; and

(c) the other reports specified in Part B of that Schedule, in so far as it is reasonably practicable to provide them.

(2) Where the patient is a restricted patient, the Secretary of State shall send to the tribunal, as soon as practicable and in any case within 3 weeks of receipt by him of the authority's statement, a statement of such further information relevant to the application as may be available to him.

(3) Where the patient is a conditionally discharged patient, paragraphs (1) and (2) shall not apply and the Secretary of State shall send to the tribunal as soon as practicable, and in any case within 6 weeks of receipt by him of the notice of application, a statement which shall contain—

(a) the information specified in Part C of Schedule 1 to these Rules, in so far as it is within the knowledge of the Secretary of State; and

(b) the reports specified in Part D of that Schedule, in so far as it is reasonably practicable to provide them.

[(3A) Where the patient is (or is to be) subject to after-care under supervision paragraph (1) shall not apply and the responsible authority shall send a statement to the tribunal as soon as practicable, and in any case within 3 weeks of the responsible authority's receipt of the notice of application, and this statement shall contain—

  (a) the information specified in Part E of Schedule 1 to these Rules, in so far as it is within the knowledge of the responsible authority;
  (b) the reports specified in Part F of that Schedule;
  (c) the details of the after-care services being (or to be) provided under section 117 of the Act; and
  (d) details of any requirements imposed (or to be imposed) on the patient under section 25D of the Act;

and shall be accompanied by copies of the documents specified in paragraph 3 of Part E of that Schedule.]

  (4) Any part of the authority's statement or the Secretary of State's statement which, in the opinion of—

  (a) (in the case of the authority's statement) the responsible authority; or
  (b) (in the case of the Secretary of State's statement) the Secretary of State,

should be withheld from the applicant or (where he is not the applicant) the patient on the ground that its disclosure would adversely affect the health or welfare of the patient or others, shall be made in a separate document in which shall be set out the reasons for believing that its disclosure would have that effect.

  (5) On receipt of any statement provided in accordance with paragraph (1), (2) or (3), the tribunal shall send a copy to the applicant and (where he is not the applicant) the patient, excluding any part of any statement which is contained in a separate document in accordance with paragraph (4).

AMENDMENT
Paragraph 3A was inserted by S.I. 1996 No. 314, r. 4.

DEFINITIONS   **3–012**
  responsible authority: r. 2.
  tribunal: r. 2.
  the authority's statement: r. 2.
  the Secretary of State's statement: r. 2.

GENERAL NOTE
  This rule and Schedule 1 require the responsible authority to send information on **3–013** the patient to the tribunal within three weeks of being notified that an application has been made. If the patient is a restricted patient the information must also be sent to the Home Secretary who is obliged to send any further information that might be available to him to the tribunal within three weeks of receiving the authority's statement. A separate rule applies to conditionally discharged patients where the Home Secretary must send specified information to the tribunal within six weeks of being notified that an application has been made. For patients subject to supervised discharge, the responsible authority must send to the tribunal a statement containing the information specified in paragraph (3A) within three weeks of being notified that an application has been made. If these timescales are not met the tribunal should consider issuing a direction under rule 13. A failure to comply with the tribunal's direction might constitute a contempt of court: see *Pickering v. Liverpool Daily Post and Echo Newspapers plc* [1991] 1 All E.R. 622, HL, noted under r. 21(5).
  If the application is an assessment application the authority must provide such of

the information as can reasonably be provided in the time available (r. 32(1)). The hearing date of an assessment application must be within seven days of receipt of the application (r. 31(a)). The responsible authority can be required to provide further information to the tribunal (rr. 13 and 15) and the tribunal can subpoena a witness to appear before it or to produce any documents (r. 14).

The Human Rights Act 1998

3–014   In *R. (on the application of C.) v. Secretary of State for the Home Department* [2001] EWCA Civ 1110, the Court of Appeal held that:

(1) A uniform practice that tribunal hearings requested by patients who had been detained under section 3 of the Act would be fixed eight weeks after the date of application did not comply with Article 5(4) of the European Convention on Human Rights, which requires the lawfulness of the patient's detention to be decided speedily. Each application had to be heard as soon as reasonably practicable;

(2) However urgent the patient's demand for a hearing, such time could properly be allowed for preparation as was reasonably necessary to ensure that the tribunal was in a position adequately and fairly to adjudicate on the issues before it; and

(3) There was nothing inconsistent with Article 5(4) in having a target date of eight weeks maximum for the listing of hearings. In cases requiring eight weeks preparation that period would not conflict with the requirement that a decision on the application had to be reached speedily.

Per Lord Phillips M.R.: "It seems to me that a more informed stage at which to fix a [hearing] date would be after receipt of the statement required by Rule 6, when the scope of the remaining activities that would need to take place before the hearing would be clear" (para. 60).

Paragraph (1)

3–015   *The other reports specified in Part B:* Which refer to the patient's social circumstances. They could include "reports on the patient's home and family circumstances, attitude of his nearest relative, employment and occupation prospects, housing facilities if he were to be discharged, financial circumstances, community support and relevant medical facilities" (Larry Gostin and Phil Fennell, *Mental Health: Tribunal Procedure* (1992), p. 117). Responsibility for providing the report on social circumstances is, in practice, delegated to the social services authority which would be responsible for the patient's care if he were to be discharged. The preparation of social circumstance reports is considered by John Lloyd in *Social Work Today*, November 2, 1987, pp. 16, 17 and by Fenella Morris and Stuart Sinclair in the *Solicitors Journal* 1998, 142(28) Supp., 44–45.

Paragraph (2)

3–016   *Secretary of State:* The statement is prepared by the Mental Health Unit at the Home Office and "may include medical reports from previous tribunal applications, medical and other reports to the sentencing court and recent reports from psychologists or other health professionals; reports of the Aarvold Board are considered to be confidential to the Home Secretary but the statement will draw attention to the Board's conclusions or main concerns" (L. Gostin and P. Fennell, *supra*, p. 118). The tribunal will also receive from the Home Office a "statement outlining the offences which caused the patient to be admitted to hospital or prison and setting out its view on any proposal his doctor may have put to the Tribunal to transfer him to a different hospital or to discharge him" (Robert Baxter, "The mentally disordered offender in hospital: the role of the Home Office" in *The Mentally Disordered Offender* (Ed. K. Herbst and J. Gunn) (1991), p. 137).

Within three weeks: Or two weeks in cases where a reference has been made under s.75(1) (r. 29(c)).

Paragraph (4)

Should be withheld: The tribunal will consider whether the disclosure of the **3–017** documents would adversely affect the health or welfare of the patient (r. 12(2)). If it considers that disclosure would have this effect, it must record its decision not to disclose. This decision may be taken by the regional chairman before the tribunal sits (r. 5).

Reasons for believing: The reasons should be specific. It would not be sufficient merely to restate the wording of the ground set out in this paragraph.

Notice to other persons interested

7. On receipt of the authority's statement or, in the case of a [conditionally **3–018** discharged patient], the Secretary of State's statement, the tribunal shall give notice of the proceedings—

   (a) where the patient is liable to be detained in a mental nursing home, to the registration authority of that home;

   (b) where the patient is subject to the guardianship of a private guardian, to the guardian;

[(bb) where the patient is, or will upon leaving hospital be, subject to after-care under supervision, to the person who appears to be the patient's nearest relative, and the persons who are, or will be, the patient's supervisor and community responsible medical officer and in the case of a patient who has not yet left hospital, the person who has prepared the medical report referred to in paragraph 1 of Part F of Schedule 1 to these Rules;]

   (c) where the patient's financial affairs are under the control of the Court of Protection, to the Court of Protection;

   (d) where any person other than the applicant is named in the authority's statement as exercising the functions of the nearest relative, to that person:

   (e) where a health authority [or National Health Service trust] has a right to discharge the patient under the provisions of section 23(3) of the Act, to that authority [or trust];

   (f) to any other person who, in the opinion of the tribunal, should have an opportunity of being heard.

AMENDMENTS

The words "conditionally discharged patient" were substituted by S.I. 1998 No. 1189, r. 2(2). Paragraph (bb), and the words in square brackets in para. (e) were inserted by S.I. 1996 No. 314, r. 5.

DEFINITIONS

the authority's statement: r. 2.   **3–019**
the Secretary of State's statement: r. 2.
tribunal: r. 2.
registration authority: r. 2.
private guardian: r. 2.
nearest relative: r. 2.
health authority: r. 2.
National Health Service trust: r. 2.

GENERAL NOTE

Paragraph (f)

Any other person: This should include the person who would supervise the patient **3–020** in the community if he were to be the subject of a conditional discharge.

The tribunal should not use its power under this paragraph in a case where the patient has "indicated that he did not wish, for reasons of confidentiality or other good reason, for a particular person to be ... given notice" (R. (on the application of H.) v. Mental Health Review Tribunal, December 7, 2000, *per* Longmore J., at para. 39).

Appointment of the tribunal

3–021   **8.**—(1) Unless the application belongs to a class or group of proceedings for which members have already been appointed, the members of the tribunal who are to hear the application shall be appointed by the chairman.

(2) A person shall not be qualified to serve as a member of a tribunal for the purpose of any proceedings where—

(a) he is a member or officer of the responsible authority or of the registration authority concerned in the proceedings; or

(b) he is a member or officer of a health authority [or National Health Service trust] which has the right to discharge the patient under section 23(3) of the Act; or

(c) he has a personal connection with the patient or has recently treated the patient in a professional medical capacity.

(3) The persons qualified to serve as president of the tribunal for the consideration of an application or reference relating to a restricted patient shall be restricted to those legal members who have been approved for that purpose by the Lord Chancellor.

AMENDMENTS
    The words in square brackets in para. (2)(b) were substituted by S.I. 1996 No. 314, r. 6.

DEFINITIONS
3–022   tribunal: r. 2.
    chairman: r. 2.
    proceedings: r. 2.
    responsible authority: r. 2.
    registration authority: r. 2.
    health authority: r. 2.
    president: r. 2.
    reference: r. 2.
    National Health Service trust: r. 2.

GENERAL NOTE
3–023   Schedule 2 of the 1983 Act is concerned with the constitution of Mental Health Review Tribunals.

Paragraph (1)
3–024   *Class or group:* E.g. a reconvened tribunal following an adjournment and the further consideration of an application where a recommendation of a tribunal has not been implemented.
    Appointed: Where the tribunal has not been appointed, certain powers may be exercised by the chairman (r. 5).

Paragraph (2)
3–025   There is nothing to prevent the legal member of a tribunal from presiding over more than one hearing involving the same patient (*R. v. Oxford Regional Mental Health Review Tribunal, ex p. Mackman, The Times,* June 2, 1986). This ruling would

undoubtedly apply to other members of the tribunal. A member should refuse appointment to a tribunal if the appointment would raise legitimate questions about the member's ability to exercise an independent judgment.

Paragraph (3)
The purpose of this provision is to ensure that lawyers presiding over tribunals in **3–026** cases of patients who may pose a serious danger to the public have "substantial experience in the criminal courts"; *per* Lord Belstead, HL, Vol. 426, No. 28, col. 761.

Powers to postpone consideration of an application
9.—(1) Where an application or reference by or in respect of a patient has **3–027** been considered and determined by a tribunal for the same or any other area, the tribunal may, subject to the provisions of this rule, postpone the consideration of a further application by or in respect of that patient until such date as it may direct, not being later than—
  (a) the expiration of the period of six months from the date on which the previous application was determined; or
  (b) the expiration of the current period of detention, whichever shall be the earlier.
(2) The power of postponement shall not be exercised unless the tribunal is satisfied, after making appropriate inquiries of the applicant and (where he is not the applicant) the patient, that postponement would be in the interests of the patient.
(3) The power of postponement shall not apply to—
  (a) an application under section 66(1)(d) [or (gb)] of the Act;
  (b) an application under section 66(1)(f) of the Act in respect of a renewal of authority for detention of the patient for a period of six months [or an application under section 66(1)(gc) of the Act in respect of a report furnished under section 25G(3)(c) concerning renewal of after-care under supervision], unless the previous application or reference was made to the tribunal more than three months after the patient's admission to hospital [, reception into guardianship or becoming subject to after-care under supervision];
  (c) an application under section 66(1)(g) of the Act;
  (d) any application where the previous application or reference was determined before a break or change in the authority for the patient's detention or guardianship [or his being (or being about to be) subject to after-care under supervision] as defined in paragraph (7).
(4) Where the consideration of an application is postponed, the tribunal shall state in writing the reasons for postponement and the period for which the application is postponed and shall send a copy of the statement to all the parties and, in the case of a restricted patient, the Secretary of State.
(5) Where the consideration of an application is postponed, the tribunal shall send a further notice of the application in accordance with rule 4 not less than 7 days before the end of the period of postponement and consideration of the application shall proceed thereafter, unless before the end of the period of postponement the application has been withdrawn or is deemed to be withdrawn in accordance with the provisions of rule 19 or has been determined in accordance with the next following paragraph.
(6) Where a new application which is not postponed under this rule or a

reference is made in respect of a patient, the tribunal may direct that any postponed application in respect of the same patient shall be considered and determined at the same time as the new application or reference.

(7) For the purpose of paragraph (3)(d) a break or change in the authority for the detention or guardianship [or his being (or being about to be) subject to after-care under supervision] of a patient shall be deemed to have occurred only—

    (a) on his admission to hospital in pursuance of an application for treatment or in pursuance of a hospital order without an order restricting his discharge; or

    (b) on his reception into guardianship in pursuance of a guardianship application or a guardianship order; or

    (c) on the application to him of the provisions of Part II or Part III of the Act as if he had been so admitted or received following—

        (i) the making of a transfer direction, or

        (ii) the ceasing of effect of a transfer direction or an order or direction restricting his discharge; or

    (d) on his transfer from guardianship to hospital in pursuance of regulations made under section 19 of the Act [; or

    (e) on his ceasing to be subject to after-care under supervision on his reception into guardianship in accordance with section 25H(5)(b).]

AMENDMENTS
The amendments to this rule were made by S.I. 1996 No. 314, r. 7.

DEFINITIONS
3–028   reference: r. 2.
    tribunal: r. 2.

GENERAL NOTE
3–029   This rule enables the tribunal to postpone the consideration of a patient's application if an application or reference in respect of that patient has recently been determined.

Paragraph (7)
3–030   *Regulations made under section 19 of the Act:* See regulation 8 of the Mental Health (Hospital, Guardianship and Consent to Treatment) Regulations 1983.

PART III

GENERAL PROVISIONS

Representation, etc.
3–031   **10.**—(1) Any party may be represented by any person whom he has authorised for that purpose not being a person liable to be detained or subject to guardianship [or after-care under supervision] under the Act or a person receiving treatment for mental disorder at the same hospital or mental nursing home as the patient.

(2) Any representative authorised in accordance with paragraph (1) shall notify the tribunal of his authorisation and postal address.

(3) As regards the representation of any patient who does not desire to conduct his own case and does not authorise a representative in accordance

with paragraph (1) the tribunal may appoint some person to act for him as his authorised representative.

(4) Without prejudice to rule 12(3), the tribunal shall send to an authorised representative copies of all notices and documents which are by these Rules required or authorised to be sent to the person whom he represents and such representative may take all such steps and do all such things relating to the proceedings as the person whom he represents is by these Rules required or authorised to take or do.

(5) Any document required or authorised by these Rules to be sent or given to any person shall, if sent or given to the authorised representative of that person, he deemed to have been sent or given to that person.

(6) Unless the tribunal otherwise directs, a patient or any other party appearing before the tribunal may be accompanied by such other person or persons as he wishes, in addition to any representative he may have authorised.

AMENDMENT
The words in square brackets in para. (1) were inserted by S.I. 1996 No. 314, r. 8.

DEFINITIONS
    tribunal: r. 2.   **3–032**
    party: r. 2.

GENERAL NOTE
This rule enables a party to the proceedings to be represented before the tribunal **3–033** and gives the tribunal a discretion to appoint a representative for a patient who does not want to conduct his own case and does not authorise a representative to act for him.

"[B]efore starting to hear any application when the Secretary of State is not represented, [the Tribunal] should inquire, and note, whether he has been given notice of the application and when"; *per* Lawton L.J. in *R. v. Oxford Mental Health Tribunal* [1986] 3 All E.R. 239 at 247.

Paragraph (1)
    Represented: The patient should state in his application to the tribunal whether he **3–034** intends to be represented or to conduct his case himself (r. 3(2)(e)).

Paragraph (3)
    May appoint: The tribunal is not placed under a duty to appoint a representative **3–035** for the patient, nor is the patient bound to co-operate with the tribunals's appointee. If a mentally capable patient informs a solicitor who has been appointed under this rule that s/he does not wish to be represented, the solicitor should decline the appointment.

Paragraph (6)
    Such other person: Who could provide the patient with advice and support.   **3–036**

Medical examination
    11. At any time before the hearing of the application, the medical member **3–037** or, where the tribunal includes more than one, at least one of them shall examine the patient and take such other steps as he considers necessary to form an opinion of the patient's mental condition; and for this purpose the patient may be seen in private and all his medical records may be examined

by the medical member, who may take such notes and copies of them as he may require, for use in connection with the application [and in the case of a patient subject to after-care under supervision this rule shall also apply to such other records relating to any after-care services provided under section 117 of the Act].

AMENDMENT
The words in square brackets were inserted by S.I. 1996 No. 314, r. 9.

DEFINITION
3–038   tribunal: r. 2.

GENERAL NOTE
3–039   This rule requires the medical member of the tribunal to examine the patient in order to form an opinion of the patient's mental condition. Although the tribunal will doubtless be guided by the medical member on this issue, it is the tribunal as a whole which determines issues relating to the patient's mental condition in the light of their own experience and examination of the patient (*R. v. Trent Mental Health Review Tribunal, ex p. Ryan* [1992] C.O.D. 15, DC). The medical member may provide a written report or, more commonly, will discuss his opinion with the other two members during their deliberations.
The patient can commission a medical report on his condition that can be presented to the tribunal as evidence (see ss.67(2), 69(3) and 76).

The Human Rights Act 1998
3–040   Crane J., in *R. v. Mental Health Review Tribunal, North and East London Region, ex p. H*, September 15, 2000, considered submissions that the role of the medical member of the tribunal is anomalous. His Lordship noted that in *Johnson v. United Kingdom* [1997] 27 E.H.R.R. 296, the European Court of Human Rights had referred to the Mental Health Review Tribunal as "an expert review body which included a doctor who had interviewed the patient" (para.64). His Lordship said: "For my part, I do not accept that the role of the medical member is to be equated exactly to that of a witness. It is plain that there is an inquisitorial element in the procedure of the tribunal. It may be that that is more unusual in the eyes of English lawyers than it would be to lawyers in some other jurisdictions, to which the European Court of Human Rights has to have regard." Subsequent to this judgment, the Court, in *D.N. v. Switzerland*, March 29, 2001, held that the fact that a psychiatrist member of a "court" who, in his role as judge rapporteur, had previously prepared an expert opinion on the patient and had communicated his opinion on whether the patient's application should succeed to the "court", constituted a violation of Article 5(4) of the European Convention on Human Rights. The Court said that the psychiatrist's position in the proceedings gave rise to legitimate fears in the applicant that "he had a preconceived opinion as to her request for release from detention and that he was not, therefore, approaching her case with due impartiality" (para. 54). This case, which is considered in the note on "court" in Article 5(4), does not affect the validity of Crane J.'s judgment because the position of the judge rapporteur differs significantly from that of the medical member in that the former prepares a formal written report on the patient prior to the hearing which includes a recommendation, which is disclosed to the parties, on whether the patient's application should succeed. The medical member's role prior to a tribunal hearing is confined to forming an opinion of the patient's mental condition. This opinion is not disclosed to the parties prior to the hearing.
Medical member: The Council on Tribunals has expressed its concern that the medical member is "effectively a witness and a member of the tribunal deciding the validity of his own evidence, and that the applicant should have an opportunity of knowing what evidence he has given and commenting on it. Under the present

system a medical member examines an applicant before the hearing and then (generally in the course of the hearing) raises any material factors which in his view should be open for comment; he then advises the tribunal in private. While this is not ideal, it is probably the best that can be devised" (*The Annual Report of the Council on Tribunals* 1982–3 (1983) HMSO para. 3.22). The role of the medical member was considered in *R. v. Mental Health Review Tribunal, North and East London Region, ex p. H*, noted under "The Human Rights Act 1998", above.

Shall examine the patient: This rule is mandatory. The tribunal should consider using its power to adjourn under rule 16 on a refusal by the patient to be examined. If a patient who is subject to supervised discharge refuses to undergo a medical examination, his tribunal application is deemed to have been withdrawn (r. 19(2A)). The medical member will be protected by section 139 of the 1983 Act when acting under this rule.

An opinion of the patient's mental condition: The tribunal is entitled to rely on the evidence of its medical member even if the evidence of the patient's responsible medical officer and the patient's independent psychiatrist asserts that the patient is not suffering form a detainable mental disorder. However, any evidence or information which has only been made available to the medical member must be shown at least to the patient's representative so that he can have the opportunity to present countervailing arguments (*R. v. Mental Health Review Tribunal, ex p. Clatworthy* [1985] 3 All E.R. 699, DC). The Annual Report of the Mental Health Review Tribunals for England and Wales 1997–98, at pp. 83, 84, states that "natural justice requires that the medical opinion [of the medical member], if it differs significantly from other medical witnesses, should be made known in the course of the hearing because it would be contrary to a basic principle of natural justice if the tribunal members were to act on a basis known only to themselves." In *R. v. Mental Health Review Tribunal, North and East London Region, ex p. H*, above, Crane J. said that "what is required . . . as a matter of fairness and of natural justice at common law, is that if the medical member is taking into account or is drawing to the attention of other members, either evidence or his views as an expert, then the [patient] and his advisers should be alerted to such evidence and such views in sufficient detail, and sufficiently early in the proceedings, to enable them to deal with them."

Records: The tribunal may use its power under rule 14(1) to *subpoena* these records if there is a refusal to provide them.

Take such notes and copies of them as he may require: It is submitted: (1) that any notes that the medical member might make would not have to be disclosed to the applicant under rule 12(1), because such notes would not constitute a document *received* by the tribunal; and (2) that any copy of the patient's case notes made by the medical members would fall within the scope of rule 12(1) and would therefore have to be disclosed to the applicant.

Disclosure of documents

12.—(1) Subject to paragraph (2), the tribunal shall, as soon as practicable, **3–041** send a copy of every document it receives which is relevant to the application to the applicant, and (where he is not the applicant) the patient, the responsible authority and, in the case of a restricted patient, the Secretary of State and any of those persons may submit comments thereon in writing to the tribunal.

(2) As regards any documents which have been received by the tribunal but which have not been copied to the applicant or the patient, including documents withheld in accordance with rule 6, the tribunal shall consider whether disclosure of such documents would adversely affect the health or welfare of the patient or others and, if satisfied that it would, shall record in writing its decision not to disclose such documents.

(3) Where the tribunal is minded not to disclose any document to which

paragraph (1) applies to an applicant or a patient who has an authorised representative it shall nevertheless disclose it as soon as practicable to that representative if he is—

(a) a barrister or solicitor;

(b) a registered medical practitioner;

(c) in the opinion of the tribunal, a suitable person by virtue of his experience or professional qualification;

provided that no information disclosed in accordance with this paragraph shall be disclosed either directly or indirectly to the applicant or (where he is not the applicant) to the patient or to any other person without the authority of the tribunal or used otherwise than in connection with the application.

DEFINITIONS

3–042   tribunal: r. 2.

responsible authority: r. 2.

GENERAL NOTE

3–043   In *R. v. Parole Board, ex p. Bradley* [1990] 3 All E.R. 828, 841, DC, the court said that where applications are made to the Mental Health Review Tribunal "it is the practice, save in exceptional cases, that disclosure to the patient is made of medical reports so that he knows the reason for his continued detention. The evidence before the court from Dr Grounds, a forensic psychiatrist shows that this has worked well and had a beneficial effect."

The Access to Health Records Act 1990 provides patients with a right of access to their medical records. The patient's representative should obtain the written authority of the patient to apply for such access.

The Human Rights Act 1998

3–044   A decision by the tribunal not to copy a document to the patient under paragraph (2) would constitute an interference with the patient's right to respect for his private and family life under Article 8(1) of the European Convention on Human Rights. Article 8(2) proves a justification for such an interference on the ground of either protecting the patient's "health or morals" or the prevention of "disorder or crime". An interference of the general ground of protecting the "welfare of the patient" is not allowed for in Article 8(2). In *Winterwerp v. Netherlands* (app. no. 6301/73), the Commission said that the patient's lawyer had the right to examine the patient's file, but that it was not necessary for the patient to be informed of all the evidence or that he be allowed access to all of the information in his medical file. When reaching a decision under Article 8(2), the tribunal should balance the need to protect the patient or others from the consequences of disclosure against the requirement under Article 5(4) of the Convention for the patient to have an opportunity to be heard in the proceedings.

Paragraph (1)

3–045   *Every document it receives:* This would appear to cover the patient's case notes if they were examined by the tribunal either prior to, or during the course of the hearing. Peay reports that there is a divergence in practice on the application of this rule to such documents (*Tribunals on Trial*, 1989, p. 94).

To the applicant: Or his representative (r. 10(5)).

Secretary of state: See the General Note to rule 28.

May submit comments: This gives the patient or his representative an opportunity to comment on the incompleteness of any report received by the tribunal.

Paragraph (2)

3–046   *The tribunal shall consider:* This is a decision that may be taken by the chairman prior to the hearing (r. 5). L. Gostin and P. Fennell suggest that "all information should be disclosed to the applicant unless there are clear and specific reasons for not doing so" (*Mental Health: Tribunal Procedure* (1992), p. 122).

Adversely affecting the health or welfare of the patient: This should not be equated with adversely affecting the doctor–patient relationship.

Record in writing its decision: The tribunal is not required to give reasons for its decision.

Paragraph (3)

Solicitor: Or a recognised body (Solicitors' Incorporated Practices Order 1991 (S.I. **3–047** 1991 No. 2684), art. 4, Sched. 1).

Or to any other person: Such as an independent psychiatrist.

Directions

13. Subject to the provisions of these Rules, the tribunal may give such **3–048** directions as it thinks fit to ensure the speedy and just determination of the application.

GENERAL NOTE

Directions: This power enables tribunals to direct those who are late in producing **3–049** reports to do so forthwith. A failure to comply with such a direction could result in the tribunal using its power of subpoena under rule 14.

To ensure: A failure to comply with a tribunal's direction could constitute a contempt of Court (*Pickering v. Liverpool Daily Post and Echo Newspapers plc* [1991] 1 All E.R. 622, HL, noted under r. 21(5)).

Speedy: See the notes on Article 5(4) of the European Convention on Human Rights under the heading "speedily" and on rule 6, above, under the heading "The Human Rights Act 1998".

Evidence

14.—(1) For the purpose of obtaining information, the tribunal may take **3–050** evidence on oath and subpoena any witness to appear before it or to produce documents, and the president of the tribunal shall have the powers of an arbitrator under section 12(3) of the Arbitration Act 1950 and the powers of a party to a reference under an arbitration agreement under subsection (4) of that section, but no person shall be compelled to give any evidence or produce any document which he could not be compelled to give or produce on the trial of an action.

(2) The tribunal may receive in evidence any document or information notwithstanding that such document or information would be inadmissible in a court of law.

DEFINITIONS

    tribunal: r. 2.   **3–051**

    president: r. 2.

GENERAL NOTE

    Tribunal proceedings are not governed by the rules of evidence.   **3–052**

Paragraph (1)

Take evidence on oath: This is not normally done.   **3–053**

Subpoena any witness: According to L. Gostin and P. Fennell tribunals "have used subpoenas to compel attendance of a Director of Social Services where no social worker had attended to give a social circumstances report" (*Mental Health: Tribunal Procedure* (1992), p. 126). As it is the responsibility of the hospital managers, and not that of the social services authority, to prepare a social circumstances report in respect of patients who are liable to be detained, such action is legally questionable.

Paragraph (2)

3–054   *Inadmissible in a court of law:* This enables the tribunal to consider "hearsay evidence, opinions from non-professional witnesses and accounts of incidents from other patients. It will, of course, give appropriate weight to evidence according to its nature and source" (Gostin and Fennell, above, pp. 126, 127).

Further information

3–055   **15.**—(1) Before or during any hearing the tribunal may call for such further information or reports as it may think desirable, and may give directions as to the manner in which and the persons by whom such material is to be furnished.

(2) Rule 12 shall apply to any further information or reports obtained by the tribunal.

DEFINITION

3–056   tribunal: r. 2.

Adjournment

3–057   **16.**—(1) The tribunal may at any time adjourn a hearing for the purpose of obtaining further information or for such other purposes as it may think appropriate.

(2) Before adjourning any hearing, the tribunal may give such directions as it thinks fit for ensuring the prompt consideration of the application at an adjourned hearing.

(3) Where the applicant or the patient (where he is not the applicant) or the responsible authority requests that a hearing adjourned in accordance with this rule be resumed, the hearing shall be resumed provided that the tribunal is satisfied that resumption would be in the interests of the patient.

(4) Before the tribunal resumes any hearing which has been adjourned without a further hearing date being fixed it shall give to all parties and, in the case of a restricted patient, the Secretary of State, not less than 14 days' notice (or such shorter notice as all parties may consent to) of the date, time and place of the resumed hearing.

DEFINITIONS

3–058   tribunal: r. 2.
responsible authority: r. 2.

GENERAL NOTE

The Human Rights Act 1998

3–059   A request for an adjournment that is not made by the patient should be considered in the light of the patient's right to have a speedy determination of his application: see the notes to Art. 5(4) of the European Convention on Human Rights.

Paragraph (1)

3–060   *Adjourn:* In *R v. Mental Health Review Tribunal, ex p. Hall* (1999) 2 C.C.L.R. 383, 390 CA, Kennedy L.J. said: "The tribunal can adjourn ... to enable those involved to produce a care plan, and that adjournment can be finite. ... The tribunal can, if necessary call for reports (r.15) and even summon witnesses such as directors of Social Services or chairmen of Health Authorities (r.14) but in the end the tribunal can only gather information and impose conditions."

The power to adjourn under this provision can only be exercised in relation to a function which the Mental Health Act permits or requires the tribunal to do. This means that for a restricted patient the power of adjournment can only be exercised for the purpose of enabling the tribunal to decide whether there should be a discharge or not, whether conditions should be applied to such a discharge, or whether there should be a reclassification of the patient's mental disorder (see s.73 and *R v. South West Thames Mental Health Review Tribunal, ex p. Demetri* [1997] C.O.D. 44, CA, noted under s.72(5)). A tribunal cannot therefore adjourn for the *sole* purpose of assisting its determination of whether to exercise its non-statutory discretion to recommend the patient's transfer to another hospital. If the tribunal decides to adjourn, it must have and must give reasons which show that there was a proper purpose behind such adjournment (*R. (on the application of the Secretary of State for the Home Department) v. Mental Health Review Tribunal* [2001] A.C.D. 334).

It is unlawful to adjourn the proceedings so as to monitor the patient's progress in the hope that a projected course of treatment would eventually permit the tribunal to discharge the patient (*R. v. Nottinghamshire Mental Health Review Tribunal, ex p. Secretary of State for the Home Department; R. v. Trent Mental Health Review Tribunal, ex p. Secretary of State for the Home Department, The Times, October 12, 1988, CA*). In *R. v. Mental Health Review Tribunal, ex p. Cleveland* (1989) CO/819/88, Popplewell J. upheld the decision of a tribunal not to adjourn the proceedings to enable the applicant to submit further evidence on the ground that even if the evidence sought had been available it would not have effected the tribunal's decision.

Paragraph 6 of the Law Society publication "Representation at Mental Health Review Tribunals: Guidelines for Legal Representative" (1997) states that if it appears "that an adjournment is avoidable, an application should be made as early as possible, setting out the reasons. Where the delay is caused by late reports from the responsible medical officer, solicitors are advised to use the hospital complaints procedure, or to ask the Tribunal for directions."

Paragraph (4)
Parties: The nearest relative of a restricted patient will only become a party if he or **3–061** she has been given notice of the proceedings under rule 7(f) (*R. (on the application of H.) v. Mental Health Review Tribunal*, December 7, 2000).

Not less than 14 days' notice: Or for assessment applications, such notice as is reasonably practicable (r. 33(b)).

Transfer of proceedings
17.—(1) Where any proceedings in relation to a patient have not been **3–062** disposed of by the members of the tribunal appointed for the purpose, and the chairman is of the opinion that it is not practicable or not possible without undue delay for the consideration of those proceedings to be completed by those members, he shall make arrangements for them to be heard by other members of the tribunal.

(2) Where a patient in respect of whom proceedings are pending moves within the jurisdiction of another tribunal, the proceedings shall, if the chairman of the tribunal originally having jurisdiction over those proceedings so directs, be transferred to the tribunal within the jurisdiction of which the patient has moved and notice of the transfer of proceedings shall be given to the parties and, in the case of a restricted patient, the Secretary of State.

DEFINITIONS
3–063   tribunal: r. 2.
         chairman: r. 2.

Two or more pending applications
3–064   **18.**—(1) The tribunal may consider more than one application in respect
of a patient at the same time and may for this purpose adjourn the
proceedings relating to any application.
         (2) Where the tribunal considers more than one application in respect of
the patient at the same time, each applicant (if more than one) shall have the
same rights under these Rules as he would have if he were the only applicant.

DEFINITION
3–065   tribunal: r. 2.

GENERAL NOTE

Paragraph (1)
3–066   *More than one application:* This rule does not apply if an application and a
reference are both pending. In these circumstances the tribunal could proceed to
hear the reference and then use its power under rule 9 to postpone the hearing of the
application.

Withdrawal of application
3–067   **19.**—(1) An application may be withdrawn at any time at the request of
the applicant provided that the request is made in writing and the tribunal
agrees.
         (2) If a patient ceases to be liable to be detained or subject to guardianship
[or after-care under supervision] in England and Wales, any application
relating to that patient shall be deemed to be withdrawn.
         [(2A) Where a patient subject to after-care under supervision fails without
reasonable explanation to undergo a medical examination under rule 11, any
application relating to that patient may be deemed by the tribunal to be
withdrawn.]
         (3) Where an application is withdrawn or deemed to be withdrawn, the
tribunal shall so inform the parties and, in the case of a restricted patient, the
Secretary of State.

AMENDMENTS
         The amendments to this rule were made by S l. 1996 No. 314, r. 10.

DEFINITIONS
3–068   tribunal: r. 2.
         party: r. 2.

GENERAL NOTE

Paragraph (1)
3–069   *Withdraw:* If an application is withdrawn the applicant can make a further
application during the specified period (s.77(2)). Also note sections 68(5) and 71(6)
of the 1983 Act.
         In writing: There is no prescribed form.
         Tribunal agrees: The chairman may agree to the withdrawal on behalf of the
tribunal (r. 5).

PART IV

THE HEARING

Notice of hearing
20. The tribunal shall give at least 14 days' notice of the date, time and **3–070**
place fixed for the hearing (or such shorter notice as all parties may consent
to) to all the parties and, in the case of a restricted patient, the Secretary of
State.

DEFINITIONS
  tribunal: r. 2.   **3–071**
  party: r. 2.

GENERAL NOTE
  This rule does not apply where the Home Secretary has made a reference under **3–072**
section 75(1) (r.29(a)).
  Date: See the note on rule 6 under the heading "The Human Rights Act 1998".
  Secretary of State: See the note on rule 4. A failure to notify the Home Secretary
would invalidate the proceedings (*Secretary of State for the Home Department v.
Oxford Regional Mental Health Review Tribunal* [1987] 3 All E.R. 8, HL).

Privacy of proceedings
21.—(1) The tribunal shall sit in private unless the patient requests a **3–073**
hearing in public and the tribunal is satisfied that a hearing in public would
not be contrary to the interests of the patient.
  (2) Where the tribunal refuses a request for a public hearing or directs that
a hearing which has begun in public shall continue in private the tribunal
shall record its reasons in writing and shall inform the patient of those
reasons.
  (3) When the tribunal sits in private it may admit to the hearing such
persons on such terms and conditions as it considers appropriate.
  (4) The tribunal may exclude from any hearing or part of a hearing any
person or class of persons, other than a representative of the applicant or of
the patient to whom documents would be disclosed in accordance with rule
12(3), and in any case where the tribunal decides to exclude the applicant or
the patient or their representatives or a representative of the responsible
authority, it shall inform the person excluded of its reasons and record those
reasons in writing.
  (5) Except in so far as the tribunal may direct, information about
proceedings before the tribunal and the names of any persons concerned in
the proceedings shall not be made public.
  (6) Nothing in this rule shall prevent a member of the Council on
Tribunals from attending the proceedings of a tribunal in his capacity as such
provided that he takes no part in those proceedings or in the deliberations of
the tribunal.

DEFINITIONS

  tribunal: r. 2.   **3–074**
  responsible authority: r. 2.
  proceedings: r. 2.

GENERAL NOTE

Paragraph (1)

3–075   *Patient requests a hearing in public:* A nearest relative applicant has no power to make such a request. It seems that the request can be made at any time.

Paragraph (4)

3–076   *Any hearing:* Public or private.

Any person: Including the patient's nearest relative who has no automatic right to attend.

Paragraph (5)

3–077   *Shall not be made public:* In *Pickering v. Liverpool Daily Post and Echo Newspapers plc* [1991] 1 All E.R. 622, HL, the patient applied to the court under this paragraph for an injunction restraining the defendants from publishing in their newspapers any information about his application to a Mental Health Review Tribunal. The House of Lords held that:

(1) a tribunal is, by virtue of section 19 of the Contempt of Court Act 1981 and section 12 of the Administration of Justice Act 1960, a "court" whose proceedings are subject to the law of contempt;

(2) the functions of rule 21(5) is to ensure that the protection given by the law of contempt to the privacy of the proceedings generally applies to the subject matter of the hearing, except in so far as the tribunal may give a direction to the contrary;

(3) rule 21(5) does not give a cause of action for breach of statutory duty to a patient applying for his discharge to a tribunal in respect of the unauthorised publication of information about the proceedings on that application;

(4) the essential privacy which is protected by section 12 of the 1960 Act attaches to the substance of the matters which the "court" has closed its doors to consider; and

(5) the combined effect of rule 21(5) and section 12 of the 1960 Act is that:

(a) *the following information may be published*
   (i) the fact that the tribunal has been made by a named patient.
   (ii) the fact that an application or reference to a tribunal will sit, is sitting or has sat at a certain date, time or place.
   (iii) a direction made by a tribunal that the patient be discharged, either absolutely or conditionally.
(b) *the following information may not be published*
   (i) the recorded reasons for the tribunal's decision to the extent that they disclose the evidential and other material on which it is based.
   (ii) any conditions imposed by the tribunal.

Hearing procedure

3–078   **22.**—(1) The tribunal may conduct the hearing in such manner as it considers most suitable bearing in mind the health and interests of the patient and it shall, so far as appears to it appropriate, seek to avoid formality in its proceedings.

(2) At any time before the application is determined, the tribunal or any one or more of its members may interview the patient, and shall interview him if he so requests, and the interview may, and shall if the patient so requests, take place in the absence of any other person.

(3) At the beginning of the hearing the president shall explain the manner of proceeding which the tribunal proposes to adopt.

(4) Subject to rule 21(4), any party and, with the permission of the tribunal, any other person, may appear at the hearing and take such part in

the proceedings as the tribunal thinks proper; and the tribunal shall in particular hear and take evidence from the applicant, the patient (where he is not the applicant) and the responsible authority who may hear each other's evidence, put questions to each other, call witnesses and put questions to any witness or other person appearing before the Tribunal.

(5) After all the evidence has been given, the applicant and (where he is not the applicant) the patient shall be given a further opportunity to address the Tribunal.

DEFINITIONS   3–079
   tribunal: r. 2.
   president: r. 2.
   party: r. 2.
   proceedings: r. 2.
   responsible authority: r. 2.

GENERAL NOTE
   An account of tribunal procedure can be found in Appendix 4 to the Annual **3–080** Report of the Mental Health Review Tribunals for England and Wales, 1997–98.

Paragraph (1)
   Conduct the hearing: Most tribunal hearings take place in hospital committee **3–081** rooms.

Paragraph (2)
   May interview the patient: In practice the tribunal always interviews the patient **3–082** before reaching a decision, unless the patient positively objects.

Paragraph (3)
   Manner of proceedings: There is no requirement for the parties to be heard in any **3–083** particular order.

Paragraph (4)
   Responsible authority: There is no obligation placed on the patient's responsible **3–084** medical officer to give evidence about the patient's medical treatment. Another doctor who has been involved in the patient's treatment can be called to give such evidence as long as that doctor is thinking of the relevant issues independently and carefully and the evidence is up-to-date (*R. v. London North and East Mental Health Review Tribunal, ex p. Manns*, May 25, 1999).

Paragraph (5)
   The applicant: This paragraph allows the applicant or patient (or his representative **3–085** (r. 10(4)) to sum up his case and to add any final points.

PART V

DECISIONS, FURTHER CONSIDERATION AND MISCELLANEOUS PROVISIONS

Decisions
   23.—(1) Any decision of the majority of the members of a tribunal shall be **3–086** the decision of the Tribunal and, in the event of an equality of votes, the president of the Tribunal shall have a second or casting vote.

   (2) The decision by which the Tribunal determines an application shall be recorded in writing; the record shall be signed by the president and shall give

the reasons for the decision and, in particular, where the Tribunal relies upon any of the matters set out in section 72(1) [, (4) or (4A)] or section 73(1) or (2) of the Act, shall state its reasons for being satisfied as to those matters.

(3) Paragraphs (1) and (2) shall apply to provisional decisions and decisions with recommendations as they apply to decisions by which applications are determined.

AMENDMENT

In para. (2) the words in square brackets were substituted by S.I. 1996 No. 314, r. 11.

DEFINITIONS

3–087 tribunal: r. 2.
president: r. 2.

GENERAL NOTE

3–088 A Mental Health Review Tribunal has its statutory duty to perform and could not avoid that by accepting a submission that it is bound to follow another tribunal's decision, even though there had been no change of circumstances. It must come to its own decision, no doubt taking into account a previous decision. There could be no *res judicata* (the legal principle that a matter which has been settled by a court cannot be reopened or challenged as to the matter decided) (*R. v. South-West Thames Mental Health Review Tribunal, ex p. Demitri* [1997] C.O.D. 44, CA).

If a decision of a tribunal which appears to have been made without jurisdiction has not been quashed by proceedings which were properly commenced within time, the decision must be treated as being a valid decision (*Bath and North East Somerset Council v. A. J. C.*, December 8, 1999, Sullivan J.).

The Human Rights Act 1998

3–088.1 In *R. (on the application of H.) v. Mental Health Review Tribunal, North and East London Region* [2001] EWCA Civ 415, the Court of Appeal held that the provisions of section 72 and 73 of the Act, in so far as they place the burden on the patient to prove to a tribunal that the conditions for detention are met, are incompatible with Articles 5(1) and 5(4) of the European Convention on Human Rights. One of the practical implications of this decision is that where a tribunal refuses an application for discharge it should express its reasons as positive findings, *e.g.* "The patient's responsible medical officer has satisfied the tribunal that ...". The *H.* case is considered in the General Note to section 72 under this heading.

Paragraph (1)

3–089 *Decision:* Which must be given within seven days of the hearing (r. 24(1)).

Paragraph (2)

3–090 *Recorded in writing:* It is submitted that an oral announcement of the decision does not take effect until it and the accompanying reasons are recorded in writing.

Reasons for the decision: The importance of the requirement for a decision-maker to give reasons was emphasised by Sedley J. in *R. v. Solihull Metropolitan Borough Council Housing Benefits Review Board, ex p. Simpson* (1993) 26 H.L.R. 370 at 377:

> "A statutory duty imposed on a named decision maker to give reasons ... is not simply a bureaucratic chore or an opportunity for lawyers to find fault. It is, and is increasingly recognised as being, a fundamental aspect of good public administration (underpinned increasingly by law) because it focuses the decision maker's mind on exactly what it is that has to be decided, within what legal framework, and according to what relevant evidence and material. Experience shows that it will sometimes produce an opposite conclusion to that which was initially in the decision-makers mind before the rigour of formulating acceptable reasons was applied."

The tribunal is obliged to give full reasons for its decision which should be expressed as positive findings: see the note on "The Human Rights Act 1998", above. The reasons "must be read as a whole, in a common sense way, not as a legal treatise" (*R. (on the application of Epsom & St Helier N.H.S. Trust* v. *The Mental Health Review Tribunal,* [2001] EWHC Admin 101, *per* Sullivan J. at para. 49). They must be "adequate and intelligible ... and must grapple with the important issues raised" (*R. v. Mental Health Review Tribunal, ex p. Pickering* [1986] 1 All E.R. 99, *per* Forbes J. at 102). It is therefore not sufficient for the tribunal merely to reiterate the statutory grounds. In *Bone v. Mental Health Review Tribunal* [1985] 3 All E.R. 330, 333, Nolan J. said: "The tribunal, by failing to give reasons, have fallen into error. That is enough, strictly speaking, to dispose of the question put to me. It is right however that I should go further and amplify what I understand by the requirement that reasons should be given. I do so by quoting passages from two very well known authorities in which this matter has been considered. The first is a passage of Megaw J. in *Re Poyser and Mills' Arbitration* [1964] 2 Q.B. 467 at 478, where he said: 'Parliament provided that reasons shall be given, and in my view that must be read as meaning that proper, adequate reasons must be given. The reasons that are set out must be reasons which will not only be intelligible, but which deal with the substantial points that have been raised.' In *Alexander Machinery Ltd v. Crabtree (N.I.R.C.)* [1974] I.C.R. 120, Sir John Donaldson said: 'It is impossible for us to lay down any precise guidelines. The overriding test must always be: is the tribunal providing both parties with the materials which will enable them to know that the Tribunal has made no error of law in reaching its finding of fact?'"

Bone was referred to in the judgment of Mann J. in *R. v. Mental Health Review Tribunal, ex p. Clatworthy* [1985] 3 All E.R. 699 where his Lordship quashed the decision of a tribunal because the reasons given by it did not enable the applicant to know why the case advanced in detail on his behalf by his responsible medical officer and an independent psychiatrist had not been accepted. His Lordship stated, at 704, that "where a tribunal desires to proceed on the basis of some point which has not been put before it and which on the face of the matter is not in dispute, it is in my view in the highest degree desirable that the person whose case is being considered by the tribunal should be alerted to the possibility. ... Were it to be the case ... that this tribunal proceeded on some basis unknown to others but known to themselves, then I would have regarded that decision as flawed by reference to [the principle of natural justice which requires that a party should know the case against him.]"

Where a tribunal gives reasons for its decision "one must somehow be able to read from the reasons the issue to which the reasons are directed" (*R. v. Mental Health Review Tribunal, ex p. Pickering*, above, *per* Forbes J at 104) In this case Forbes J. said, at 101, that it is "essential" for the tribunal to distinguish between "the diagnostic question" of whether the patient is still suffering from a mental disorder and "the policy question" of whether it is safe to discharge him. In *R. v. Mental Health Review Tribunal, ex p. Booth* [1998] C.O.D. 203, Laws J. said: "It has to be remembered ... that the quality of reasons required of a Mental Health Review Tribunal has to be looked at in light of the fact that the decision is addressed to an informed audience. Those who receive it and who are concerned with it will be familiar with the essential documents in the case ... They will be familiar with what has been said at the tribunal by way of oral evidence and what the issues there were which had been argued. Given that necessary familiarity, if there was a case in which it could still be said that the parties simply were not told why the tribunal arrived at the decision it did, then no doubt there would be a sound basis for a legal challenge." Further guidance was given by Crane J. in *R. v. Mental Health Review Tribunal, North and East London Region, ex p. H*, September 15, 2000, where his Lordship said: "It is helpful, plainly, [for the tribunal] to address the issues in turn with the reasons for each conclusion and setting out, though not at great length, how any significant conflicts of evidence are to be resolved. [However], on the authorities, the tribunal is addressing an informed audience, in other words, people who know what the issues are." There is no need for the tribunal to state why alternatives to rejecting a patient's application for discharge were rejected when it gives reasons for its decision (*R. v. The Mental Health Review Tribunal for the South Thames Region, ex p. Smith* [1999] C.O.D. 148, Popplewell J.).

In *R. v. South West Thames Mental Health Review Tribunal, ex p. Demmetri* [1997] C.O.D. 445, Kay J. held that while he accepted the general proposition that a tribunal may find it difficult to give precise reasons why it prefers one expert's evidence to another, if the reasons are to be adequate they must demonstrate that the tribunal has considered the real issues and explain in so far as is possible why it has reached the conclusion that it has. His Lordship said that that there may be cases which had no exceptional features where it is sufficient to say "we have heard what both doctors say and whilst there is no inherent flaw in either we, nonetheless, are persuaded that one rather than the other is right".

Communication of decisions

3–091 **24.**—(1) The decision by which the tribunal determines an application may, at the discretion of the tribunal, be announced by the president immediately after the hearing of the case and, subject to paragraph (2), the written decision of the tribunal, including the reasons, shall be communicated in writing within 7 days of the hearing to all the parties and, in the case of a restricted patient, the Secretary of State.

(2) Where the tribunal considers that the full disclosure of the recorded reasons for its decision to the patient in accordance with paragraph (1) would adversely affect the health or welfare of the patient or others, the tribunal may instead communicate its decision to him in such manner as it thinks appropriate and may communicate its decision to the other parties subject to any conditions it may think appropriate as to the disclosure thereof to the patient; provided that, where the applicant or the patient was represented at the hearing by a person to whom documents would be disclosed in accordance with rule 12(3), the tribunal shall disclose the full recorded grounds of its decision to such a person, subject to any conditions it may think appropriate as to disclosure thereof to the patient.

(3) Paragraphs (1) and (2) shall apply to provisional decisions and decisions with recommendations as they apply to decisions by which applications are determined.

(4) Where the tribunal makes a decision with recommendations, the decision shall specify the period at the expiration of which the tribunal will consider the case further in the event of those recommendations not being complied with.

DEFINITIONS
3–092   tribunal: r. 2.
president: r. 2.
decision with recommendations: r. 2.

GENERAL NOTE
3–093   Guidance to tribunals on the announcement of decisions is contained in Appendix 8 to the Annual Report of the Mental Health Review Tribunals for England and Wales, 1997–98.

Paragraph (1)
    Within seven days of the hearing: Three days in the case of assessment applications **3–094**
(r. 33(d)).

Paragraph (4)
    Specify the period: If, at the end of this period, the recommendation has not been **3–095**
complied with the tribunal may reconvene the hearing under rule 25(2).

Further consideration
    25.—(1) Where the tribunal has made a provisional decision, any further **3–096**
decision in the proceedings may be made without a further hearing.
    (2) Where the tribunal has made a decision with recommendations and, at
the end of the period referred to in rule 24(4), it appears to the tribunal after
making appropriate inquiries of the responsible authority that any such
recommendation has not been complied with, the tribunal may reconvene
the proceedings after giving to all parties [...] not less than 14 days' notice
(or such shorter notice as all parties may consent to) of the date, time and
place fixed for the hearing.

AMENDMENT
    In para. (2) the words omitted were repealed by S.I. 1998 No. 1198, r. 2(3).

DEFINITIONS
    tribunal: r. 2.   **3–097**
    proceedings: r. 2.
    responsible authority: r. 2.
    party: r. 2.

GENERAL NOTE

Paragraph (2)
    Recommendation: The effect of this paragraph is limited to the circumstances **3–098**
where the 1983 Act empowers recommendation. It does not apply to the case of a
restricted patient (*R v Oxford Mental Health Review Tribunal, ex p. Smith*, January
25, 1995, CA).

Time
    26.—(1) Where the time prescribed by or under these Rules for doing any **3–099**
act expires on a Saturday, Sunday or public holiday, the act shall be in time if
done on the next working week.
    (2) The time appointed by these Rules for the doing of any act may, in the
particular circumstances of the case, be extended or, with the exception of
the periods of notice specified in rule 16(4), rule 20 and rule 25(2), abridged
by the tribunal on such terms (if any) as it may think fit.

DEFINITION
    tribunal: r. 2.   **3–100**

Service of notices, etc.
    27. Any document required or authorised by these Rules to be sent or **3–101**
given to any person may be sent by prepaid post or delivered—

(a) in the case of a document directed to the tribunal or the chairman, to the tribunal office;

(b) in any other case, to the last known address of the person to whom the document is directed.

DEFINITIONS

3–102   tribunal: r. 2.

chairman: r. 2.

Irregularities

3–103   **28.** Any irregularity resulting from failure to comply with these Rules before the tribunal has determined an application shall not of itself render the proceedings void, but the tribunal may, and shall, if it considers that any person may have been prejudiced, take such steps as it thinks fit before determining the application to cure the irregularity, whether by the amendment of any document, the giving of any notice, the taking of any step or otherwise.

DEFINITIONS

3–104   tribunal: r. 2.

proceedings: r. 2.

GENERAL NOTE

3–105   In *R. v. Oxford Mental Health Tribunal* [1986] 3 All E.R. 239, the Court of Appeal found that the failure to send relevant documents and notice of the hearing to the Secretary of State in contravention of rules 12(1) and 20 was an irregularity which could not be cured under this rule, as the Secretary of State had lost his right to make any representations. This decision was affirmed by the House of Lords at [1987] 3 All E.R. 8.

Determined an application: A decision to defer the conditional discharge of a patient determines an application (*R. v. Oxford Mental Health Tribunal*, above).

PART VI

REFERENCES AND APPLICATIONS BY PATIENTS DETAINED FOR ASSESSMENT

References

3–106   **29.** The tribunal shall consider a reference as if there had been an application by the patient and the provisions of these Rules shall apply with the following modifications—

(a) rules 3, 4, 9 and 19 shall not apply [and where a reference is made under section 75(1) of the Act rule 20 shall also not apply;]

(b) the tribunal shall, on receipt of the reference, send notice thereof to the patient and the responsible authority; provided that where the reference has been made by the responsible authority, instead of the notice of reference there shall be sent to the responsible authority a request for the authority's statement;

(c) rules 5, 6 and 7 shall apply as if rule 6(1) referred to the notice of reference, or the request for the authority's statement, as the case may be, instead of the notice of application [and where a reference is made under section 75(1) of the Act—

    (i) rule 6(2) shall apply as if the period of time specified therein was two weeks instead of three weeks; and

    (ii) on receipt of the authority's statement, the tribunal shall give notice of the date, time and place fixed for the hearing to any person whom the tribunal notifies of the proceedings under rule 7;]

[(cc) where a reference is made under section 75(1) of the Act, on receipt of the reference the tribunal shall—

    (i) fix a date for the hearing being not later than eight weeks, nor earlier than five weeks, from the date on which the reference was received;

    (ii) fix the time and place for the hearing; and

    (iii) give notice of the date, time and place of the hearing to the patient, the responsible authority and the Secretary of State;]

  (d) a reference made by the Secretary of State in circumstances in which he is not by the terms of the Act obliged to make a reference may be withdrawn by him at any time before it is considered by the tribunal and, where a reference is so withdrawn, the tribunal shall inform the patient and the other parties that the reference has been withdrawn.

AMENDMENTS

The amendments to this rule were made by S.I. 1998 No. 1189, r. 2(4).

DEFINITIONS

3–107

    tribunal: r. 2.

    reference: r. 2.

    responsible authority: r. 2.

    the authority's statement: r. 2.

GENERAL NOTE

The amendments to this rule, which set a time limit for a tribunal to hear the case of **3–108** a conditionally discharged patient who is recalled to hospital under s.75(1) of the 1983 Act, were made as a response to applications that had been made to the European Commission on Human Rights alleging a breach of article 5(4) of the European Convention on Human Rights which gives those detained a right to a speedy review by a court; see, for example, *Pauline Lines v. United Kingdom* (App. No. 24519/94).

Making an assessment application

    30.—(1) An assessment application shall be made to the tribunal in **3–109** writing signed by the patient or any person authorised by him to do so on his behalf.

    (2) An assessment application shall indicate that it is made by or on behalf of a patient detained for assessment and shall wherever possible include the following information—

  (a) the name of the patient;

  (b) the address of the hospital or mental nursing home where the patient is detained;

  (c) the name and address of the patient's nearest relative and his relationship to the patient;

(d) the name and address of any representative authorised by the patient in accordance with rule 10 or, if none has yet been authorised, whether the patient intends to authorise a representative or wishes to conduct his own case.

(3) If any of the information specified in paragraph (2) is not included in the assessment application, it shall in so far as is practicable be provided by the responsible authority at the request of the tribunal.

DEFINITIONS
3–110   assessment application: r. 2.
tribunal: r. 2.
nearest relative: r. 2.
responsible authority: r. 2.

GENERAL NOTE

Paragraph (2)
3–111   *Wherever possible:* A failure to provide any of the information set out in this paragraph will not invalidate the application.

Appointment of a tribunal and hearing date
3–112   **31.** On receipt of an assessment application the tribunal shall—
(a) fix a date for the hearing, being not later than seven days from the date on which the application was received, and the time and place for the hearing;
(b) give notice of the date, time and place fixed for the hearing to the patient;
(c) give notice of the application and of the date, time and place fixed for the hearing to the responsible authority, the nearest relative (whether practicable) and any other person who, in the opinion of the tribunal, should have an opportunity of being heard;
and the chairman shall appoint the members of the tribunal to deal with the case in accordance with rule 8.

DEFINITIONS
3–113   assessment application: r. 2.
tribunal: r. 2.
responsible authority: r. 2.
nearest relative: r. 2.
chairman: r. 2.

GENERAL NOTE
3–114   *Any other person:* Such as the approved social worker who made the application.

Provision of admission papers, etc.
3–115   **32.**—(1) On receipt of the notice of an assessment application, or a request from the tribunal, whichever may be the earlier, the responsible authority shall provide for the tribunal copies of the admission papers, together with such of the information specified in Part A of Schedule 1 to these Rules as is within the knowledge of the responsible authority and can reasonably be provided in the time available and such of the reports specified in Part B of that Schedule as can reasonably be provided in the time available.

(2) The responsible authority shall indicate if any part of the admission papers or other document supplied in accordance with paragraph (1) should, in their opinion, be withheld from the patient on the ground that its disclosure would adversely affect the health or welfare of the patient or others and shall state their reasons for believing that its disclosure would have that effect.

(3) The tribunal shall make available to the patient copies of the admission papers and any other documents supplied in accordance with paragraph (1), excluding any part indicated by the responsible authority in accordance with paragraph (2).

DEFINITIONS   **3–116**
    assessment application: r. 2.
    tribunal: r. 2.
    responsible authority: r. 2.
    admission papers: r. 2.

GENERAL NOTE
    This rule is concerned with the provision of admission papers and reports in **3–117** respect of a tribunal application made by a person who is detained under section 2 of the Act.

Paragraph (1)
    Responsible authority: See rule 2(1).   **3–118**
    Admission papers: There is no equivalent requirement to provide the tribunal with admission papers for patients who are detained under other provisions of the Act: see rule 6.
    Such of the information ... as ... can reasonably be provided: In its Annual Report for 1991 the Mental Health Review Tribunal for Wales states that with section 2 applications "there is often insufficient time for reports to be submitted to the Tribunal Office and almost invariably these are made available for tribunal members immediately before the hearing" (para. 6).
    Reports specified in Part B: See the note on rule 6.

General procedure, hearing procedure and decisions
    33. Rule 5, rule 8 and Parts III, IV and V of these Rules shall apply to **3–119** assessment applications as they apply to applications in so far as the circumstances of the case permit and subject to the following modifications—
    (a) rule 12 shall apply as if any reference to a document being withheld in accordance with rule 6 was a reference to part of the admission papers or other documents supplied in accordance with rule 32 being withheld;
    (b) rule 16 shall apply with the substitution for the reference to 14 days' notice, of a reference to such notice as is reasonably practicable;
    (c) rule 20 shall not apply;
    (d) rule 24 shall apply as if the period of time specified therein was 3 days instead of 7 days.

DEFINITIONS   **3–120**
    assessment applications: r. 2.
    admission papers: r. 2.

PART VII

TRANSITIONAL PROVISIONS AND REVOCATIONS

Transitional provisions

3–121   **34.** These Rules shall apply, so far as practicable, to any proceedings pending at the date on which they come into operation, and, where their operation is excluded by virtue of the foregoing provision, the rules in force immediately before that date shall continue to apply to such proceedings.

Revocations

3–122   **35.** Subject to rule 34, the rules specified in Schedule 2 to these Rules are hereby revoked.

Rules 6 and 32   **SCHEDULE 1**

3–123   **STATEMENTS BY THE RESPONSIBLE AUTHORITY AND
                                    THE SECRETARY OF STATE**

PART A

INFORMATION RELATING TO PATIENTS (OTHER THAN CONDITIONALLY DISCHARGED PATIENTS)
[AND PATIENTS SUBJECT (OR TO BE SUBJECT) TO AFTER-CARE UNDER SUPERVISION]

1. The full name of the patient.
2. The age of the patient.
3. The date of admission of the patient to the hospital or mental nursing home in which the patient is currently detained or liable to be detained, or of the reception of the patient into guardianship.
4. Where the patient is being treated in a mental nursing home under contractual arrangements with a health authority, the name of that authority.
5. Details of the original authority for the detention or guardianship of the patient, including the Act of Parliament and the section of that Act by reference to which detention was authorised and details of any subsequent renewal of or change in the authority for detention.
6. The form of mental disorder from which the patient is recorded as suffering in the authority for detention (including amendments, if any, under section 16 or 72(5) of the Act, but excluding cases within section 5 of the Criminal Procedure (Insanity) Act 1964).
7. The name of the responsible medical officer and the period which the patient has spent under the care of that officer.
8. Where another registered medical practitioner is or has recently been largely concerned in the treatment of the patient, the name of that practitioner and the period which the patient has spent under his care.
9. The dates of all previous tribunal hearings in relation to the patient, the decisions reached at such hearings and the reasons given. (In restricted patient cases this requirement does not relate to decisions before September 30, 1983).
10. Details of any proceedings in the Court of Protection and of any receivership order made in respect of the patient.
11. The name and address of the patient's nearest relative or of any other person who is exercising that function.
12. The name and address of any other person who takes a close interest in the patient.
13. Details of any leave of absence granted to the patient during the previous 2 years, including the duration of such leave and particulars of the arrangements made for the patient's residence while on leave.

594

PART B

REPORTS RELATING TO PATIENTS (OTHER THAN CONDITIONALLY DISCHARGED PATIENTS) [AND PATIENTS SUBJECT (OR TO BE SUBJECT) TO AFTER-CARE UNDER SUPERVISION]

1. An up-to-date medical report, prepared for the tribunal, including the relevant medical **3–124** history and a full report on the patient's mental condition.

2. An up-to-date social circumstances report prepared for the tribunal including reports on the following—
   (a) the patient's home and family circumstances, including the attitude of the patient's nearest relative or the person so acting;
   (b) the opportunities for employment or occupation and the housing facilities which would be available to the patient if discharged;
   (c) the availability of community support and relevant medical facilities;
   (d) the financial circumstances of the patient.

3. The views of the authority on the suitability of the patient for discharge.

4. Any other information or observations on the application which the authority wishes to make.

GENERAL NOTE

Paragraph 1
Prepared for the Tribunal: And not for some other purpose.   **3–125**

Paragraph 3
The authority: Means the responsible authority as defined in regulation 2.   **3–126**

Paragraph 11
The name and address of the nearest relative of a restricted patient should not **3–127** appear under this paragraph: see the definition of "nearest relative" in rule 2 and *R. (on the application of H.) v. Mental Health Review Tribunal,* December 7, 2000.

Paragraph 12
Other person: Although the nearest relative of a restricted patient could come **3–128** within this category, the responsible authority should not name a person under this paragraph "in a case where the patient indicated that he did not wish, for reasons of confidentiality or other good reason, for [either the nearest relative or any other particular person] to be named" (*R. (on the application of H.) v. Mental Health Review Tribunal,* above, *per* Longmore J. at para.39).

1. The full name of the patient.   **3–129**
2. The age of the patient.
3. The history of the patient's present liability to detention including details of offence(s), and the dates of the original order or direction and of the conditional discharge.
4. The form of mental disorder from which the patient is recorded as suffering in the authority for detention. (Not applicable to cases within section 5 of the Criminal Procedure (Insanity) Act 1964).
5. The name and address of any medical practitioner responsible for the care and supervision of the patient in the community and the period which the patient has spent under the care of that practitioner.
6. The name and address of any social worker or probation officer responsible for the care and supervision of the patient in the community and the period which the patient has spent under the care of that person.

REPORTS RELATING TO CONDITIONALLY DISCHARGED PATIENTS

3–130   1. Where there is a medical practitioner responsible for the care and supervision of the patient in the community, an up-to-date medical report prepared for the tribunal including the relevant medical history and a full report on the patient's mental condition.

2. Where there is a social worker or probation officer responsible for the patient's care and supervision in the community, an up-to-date report prepared for the tribunal on the patient's progress in the community since discharge from hospital.

3. A report on the patient's home circumstances.

4. The views of the Secretary of State on the suitability of the patient for absolute discharge.

5. Any other observations on the application which the Secretary of State wishes to make.

DEFINITIONS
3–131   health authority: r. 2.
nearest relative: r. 2.
tribunal: r. 2.

[PART E

INFORMATION AND DOCUMENTS RELATING TO PATIENTS SUBJECT (OR TO BE SUBJECT) TO AFTER-CARE UNDER SUPERVISION

3–132   1. The full name, address and age of his patient.

2. The date of the acceptance of the supervision application in respect of the patient.

3. A copy of the original supervision application, details of the after-care services provided (or to be provided) under section 117 of the Act, details of any requirements imposed (or to be imposed) under section 25D(1) of the Act, a copy of any report furnished under section 25G(3)(b) of the Act in relation to renewal of the supervision application and a copy of any record of modification of the after-care services provided.

4. Any reclassification of the form of mental disorder from which the patient is recorded as suffering in the supervision application reported in accordance with section 25F(1) of the Act.

5. The name and address of the person who is (or is to be) the community responsible medical officer and the period (if any) during which he has been in charge of the patient's medical treatment.

6. The name and address of the person who is (or is to be) the patient's supervisor.

7. Where a registered medical practitioner other than the community responsible medical officer is or has recently been largely concerned in the treatment of the patient, details of the name and address of that practitioner and the period which the patient has spent under his care.

8. The name and address of any place where the patient (if he has been discharged) is receiving medical treatment.

9. The name and address of the hospital where the patient was detained or liable to be detained when the supervision application was made.

10. The dates of any previous tribunal hearings in relation to the patient since he became subject to after-care under supervision, the decisions reached at such hearings and the reasons given.

11. Details of any proceedings in the Court of Protection and of any receivership order made in respect of the patient.

12. The name and address of the patient's nearest relative or of any other person who is exercising that function.

13. The name and address of any other person who takes a close interest in the patient.

PART F

REPORTS RELATING TO PATIENTS SUBJECT (OR TO BE SUBJECT) TO AFTER-CARE UNDER SUPERVISION

3–133   1. An up-to-date medical report, prepared for the tribunal by the patient's community responsible medical officer or, if he has not yet left hospital, his responsible medical officer (or, where there is none, his last responsible medical officer), including the relevant medical history and a full report on the patient's mental condition.

2. Where the patient is subject to after-care under supervision an up-to-date report prepared for the tribunal by the patient's supervisor including reports on the following—

(a) the patient's home and family circumstances, including the attitude of the patient's nearest relative or the person so acting and the attitude of any person who plays a substantial part in the care of the patient but is not professionally concerned with any of the after-care services provided to the patient;

(b) his progress in the community whilst subject to after-care under supervision including an assessment of the effectiveness of that supervision.

3. Where the patient has not yet left hospital an up-to-date social circumstances report prepared for the tribunal by a person professionally concerned with the nature of the patient's social circumstances including reports on the following—

(a) the patient's home and family circumstances, including the attitude of the patient's nearest relative or the person so acting;

(b) the opportunities for employment or occupation and the housing facilities which would be available to the patient upon his discharge from hospital;

(c) the availability of community support and relevant medical facilities;

(d) the financial circumstances of the patient.]

AMENDMENTS

The amendments to this Schedule were made by S.I. 1996 No. 314, r.12.

SCHEDULE 2

Rule 35   REVOCATIONS   3–134

Titles	References	Extent of Revocation
The Mental Health Review Tribunal Rules 1960	S.I. 1960/1139	The whole Rules.
The Mental Health Review Tribunals (Welsh Forms) Rules 1971	S.I. 1971/1772	The whole Rules.
The Mental Health Review Tribunal (Amendment) Rules 1976	S.I. 1976/447	The whole Rules.

CIVIL PROCEDURE RULES 1998

(S.I. 1998 No. 3132)

SCHEDULE 2

CCR ORDER 49

Miscellaneous Statutes

.   .   .   .   .   .

Mental Health Act 1983

3–135 12.—(1) In these rules—

a section referred to by number means the section so numbered in the Mental Health Act
1983 and "Part II" means Part II of that Act;

"place of residence" means, in relation to a patient who is receiving treatment as an
in-patient in a hospital or other institution, that hospital or institution;

"hospital authority" means the managers of a hospital as defined in section 145(1).

(2) An application to a county court under Part II shall be made by a claim form filed in the
court for the district in which the patient's place of residence is situated or, in the case of an
application made under section 30 for the discharge or variation of an order made under section
29, in that court or in the court which made the order.

(3) Where an application is made under section 29 for an order that the functions of the
nearest relative of the patient shall be exercisable by some other person—

(a) the nearest relative shall be made a respondent to the application unless the application is
made on the ground set out in subsection (3)(a) of the said section or the court otherwise
orders, and

(b) the court may order that any other person, not being the patient, shall be made a
respondent.

(4) On the hearing of the application the court may accept as evidence of the facts stated
therein any report made by a medical practitioner and any report made in the course of his
official duties by—

(a) a probation officer, or

(b) an officer of a local authority or of a voluntary organisation exercising statutory functions
on behalf of a local authority, or

(c) an officer of a hospital authority;

provided that the respondent shall be told the substance of any part of the report bearing on his
fitness or conduct which the judge considers to be material for the fair determination of the
application.

(5) Unless otherwise ordered, an application under Part II shall be heard and determined by
the court sitting in private.

(6) For the purpose of determining the application the judge may interview the patient either
in the presence of or separately from the parties and either at the court or elsewhere, or may
direct the district judge to interview the patient and report to the judge in writing.

General Note

3–136   This rule is concerned with applications to the county court under sections 29 and
30 of the Mental Health Act 1983. The court, on hearing an application under section
29, has the power to make an interim order; see the General Note to section 29.

Proceedings under this rule are listed in Section B of the Practice Direction "How
to Make Claims in the Schedule Rules and Other Claims". Paragraph B8 of the
Practice Direction requires the use of Part 8 claim form. Paragraph B12 provides that
the defendant (*i.e.* the nearest relative) is not required to serve an acknowledgement

of service. Under Paragraph B13 the court may, on the hearing date, either deal with the case or give case management directions.

The Human Rights Act 1998

In *Perrin v. Jay* (2001) 4 C.C.L.R. 3 a county court judge refused permission to a   **3–137**
patient to be represented at a displacement application on the ground that he had no power to disapply rule 12(3)(b) on the basis that it was incompatible with the patient's rights under Articles 6 and 8 of the European Convention on Human Rights. The patient appealed on the basis that section 6 of the 1998 Act does not provide the judge with a defence if his reliance on the rule is incompatible with the patient's Convention rights. Permission to appeal has been granted and the appeal referred to the Court of Appeal.

Paragraph (4)

To comply with the requirement of the proviso, it is sufficient if a report is handed   **3–138**
to the respondent's legal adviser in circumstances where the legal adviser can give advice and take instructions *(B(A) v. B(L) (Mental Health: Patient)* [1980] 1 W.L.R. 116).

Paragraph (5)

The publication of information relating to proceedings before any court sitting in   **3–139**
private shall be a contempt of a court where the proceedings are brought under Part VIII of the Mental Health Act 1983, or under any provision of that Act authorising an application or reference to be made to a Mental Health Review Tribunal or to a county court (Administration of Justice Act 1960, s.12(1)(b)).

Paragraph (6)

The Judge: A district judge may not make an order under this rule (Practice   **3–140**
Direction "Allocation of Cases to Levels of Judiciary", para. 11.1).

PART 4

GOVERNMENT GUIDANCE

CODE OF PRACTICE MENTAL HEALTH ACT 1983

PUBLISHED MARCH 1999, PURSUANT TO SECTION 118 OF THE ACT

DEPARTMENT OF HEALTH AND WELSH OFFICE   **4–001**

CONTENTS

601

INTRODUCTION

4–002 1. This revised Code of Practice has been prepared in accordance with section 118 of the Mental Health Act 1983 by the Secretary of State for Health and the Secretary of State for Wales, after consulting such bodies as appeared to them to be concerned, and laid before Parliament. The Code will come into force on 1 April 1999. The Act does not impose a legal duty to comply with the Code but as it is a statutory document, failure to follow it could be referred to in evidence in legal proceedings.

2. The Code provides guidance to registered medical practitioners, managers and staff of hospitals and mental nursing homes and approved social workers (ASWs) (who have defined responsibilities under the provisions of the Act), on how they should proceed when undertaking duties under the Act. It should also be considered by others working in health and social services (including the independent and voluntary sectors), and by the police.

3. The Code makes a number of references to the Memorandum on Parts I to VI, VIII and X of the Act (revised 1998) which gives a detailed description of some of the Act's provisions. Authorities, Trusts and other service providers are responsible for seeking their own legal advice on any matters of doubt.

4. The Secretaries of State are required to keep the operation of the Code under review. The Mental Health Act Commission will be monitoring experience of using the Code and will take this into account in drawing up proposals for any necessary further modification in due course. The Commission also publishes from time to time Practice and Guidance Notes containing advice on particular points which have been drawn to its attention. A list of the current Practice, Guidance and other Notes is given at Annex A.

5. Finally a note on presentation. It is hoped that the Code will be helpful not only to those for whom the Act requires it to be written but also to patients, their families, friends and others who support them. It has been

drafted as far as possible with this aim in mind. Throughout the Code the Mental Health Act 1983 is referred to as "the Act". Where there is reference to sections of other Acts, the relevant Act is clearly indicated.

6. In accordance with the requirements of the Welsh Language Act, this publication is available in the Welsh Language. Details can be obtained from

Robert Booth or Dominic Worsey
PCH4
Welsh Office, Health and Social Work Service
Cathays Park
Cardiff CF1 3NQ
Telephone: Robert Booth 01222 823998
             Dominic Worsey 01222 823480

1. GUIDING PRINCIPLES

1.1 The detailed guidance in the Code needs to be read in the light of the **4–003** following broad principles, that people to whom the Act applies (including those being assessed for possible admission) should:

- receive recognition of their basic human rights under the European Convention on Human Rights (ECHR);
- be given respect for their qualities, abilities and diverse backgrounds as individuals and be assured that account will be taken of their age, gender, sexual orientation, social, ethnic, cultural and religious background, but that general assumptions will not be made on the basis of any one of these characteristics;
- have their needs taken fully into account, though it is recognised that, within available resources, it may not always be practicable to meet them in full;
- be given any necessary treatment or care in the least controlled and segregated facilities compatible with ensuring their own health or safety or the safety of other people;
- be treated and cared for in such a way as to promote to the greatest practicable degree their self determination and personal responsibility, consistent with their own needs and wishes;
- be discharged from detention or other powers provided by the Act as soon as it is clear that their application is no longer justified.

Care Programme Approach and Care Management

1.2 The delivery of all mental health services is framed within the Care **4–004** Programme Approach (CPA) set out in Circular HC(90)23/LASSL(90)11, and in the Welsh Office Mental Illness Strategy (WHC(95)40). The CPA provides the framework for all patients, both in hospital and in the community and Health Authorities, Trusts and Social Services Authorities are responsible for ensuring that the Act is always be applied within this context.

The key elements of the CPA are:
- systematic arrangements for assessing people's health and social care needs
- the formulation of a care plan which addresses those needs;

— the appointment of a key worker to keep in close touch with the patient and monitor care;

— regular reviews and if need be, agreed changes to the care plan.

Similarly Social Services Authorities also have a responsibility to undertake assessments of individuals' social care needs and design care plans in accordance with care management procedures. These two systems should as far as possible be integrated.

Communicating with patients

4–005   1.3 As a general principle, it is the responsibility of staff to ensure that effective communication takes place between themselves and patients. All those involved in the assessment, treatment and care of patients should ensure that everything possible is done to overcome any barriers to communication that may exist.

1.4 Local and Health Authorities and Trusts should ensure that ASWs, doctors, nurses and others receive sufficient guidance in the use of interpreters and should make arrangements for there to be an easily accessible pool of trained interpreters. Authorities and Trusts should consider co-operating in making this provision.

1.5 Barriers to communication may be caused by any one of a number of reasons, *e.g.* the patient's first language is not English or he or she may have difficulty understanding technical terms and jargon; he or she may have a hearing or visual impairment or have difficulty reading. There may also be barriers to communication associated with the person's mental disorder, for example, the patient may lack mental capacity.

1.6 Staff need to be aware of how communication difficulties affect each patient individually so that they can address the needs of patients in ways that best suit them. This will require patience and sensitivity. Specialist help should always be made available to staff as required, either from within the hospital itself, or from the local social services authority or a voluntary organisation. The patient's relatives or friends should not normally be used as an intermediary or interpreter. When the need arises, staff should make every attempt to identify interpreters who match the patient in gender, religion, dialect, and as closely as possible in age.

1.7 It will at times be necessary to convey the same information on a number of different occasions and frequently check that the patient has fully understood it. Information given to a patient who is unwell may need to be repeated when they have improved.

Confidentiality

4–006   1.8 Managers and staff in all Trusts, Authorities, Mental Nursing Homes, Social Services Departments and other organisations which provide services for patients should be familiar with the Department of Health (DH) Guidance on confidentiality (*The Protection and Use of Patient Information, Department of Health 1996*, HSG(96)18). Ordinarily, information about a patient should not be disclosed without the patient's consent. Occasionally it may be necessary to pass on particular information to professionals or others in the public interest, for instance where personal health or safety is at risk. Any such disclosure should be in accordance with the principles set out in the

Guidance (*see also Building Bridges (para 1.5), Department of Health, February 1996, and guidance the power to disclose information under section 115 of the Crime and Disorder Act, Home Office, 1998*).

Victims

1.9 Where a patient detained under Part III of the Act is both competent **4–007** and willing to agree to the disclosure of specified information about his or her care, this should be encouraged to enable victims and victims' families to be informed about progress. It can be important to a patient's rehabilitation that victims understand what has been achieved in terms of modifying offending behaviour. Disclosure of such information also serves to reduce the danger of harmful confrontations after a discharge of which victims were unaware. Without prejudice to a patient's right to confidentiality, care teams should be ready to discuss with him or her the benefits of enabling some information to be given by professionals to victims, within the spirit of the *Victim's Charter (Home Office, 1996)*. The patient's agreement to do so must be freely given and he or she will need to understand the implications of agreeing to information being given to the victim(s). Care must be taken not to exert any pressure on the patients or this may bring into question the validity of the consent.

Information

1.10 The Hospital Managers have a statutory duty to give information to **4–008** detained patients, and to their nearest relatives, unless the patient objects. A definition of the nearest relative under the Act is given at section 26. The Department of Health publishes leaflets about the information which should be given to detained patients.

1.11 All patients, including those subject to guardianship, should be given full information, both verbally and in writing, to help them understand why they are in hospital, or subject to guardianship, and the care and treatment they will be given. Informal patients who are capable of expressing consent should be told that they may leave at any time. Where mentally incapacitated patients have been admitted informally their position should be explained to them as far as possible and their close relative, carer or advocate should be kept informed about the arrangements for their care.

1.12 Information should be clearly displayed on ward notice boards and in reception areas. All patients should be given admission booklets, information about the Mental Health Act Commission and complaints leaflets for the Hospital, Trust and local Social Services Department. More details on the giving of information is in Chapter 14.

1.13 Authorities and Trusts should keep records of the ethnicity of all patients admitted under the Act. The NHS Executive's Information Management Group guidance *Collecting ethnic group data for admitted patient care—implementation guidance and training material (Department of Health 1994)* should be followed. The Department of Health's standard ethnicity codes should be used, namely:

0 White
1 Black Caribbean

2 Black African
3 Black other
4 Indian
5 Pakistani
6 Bangladesh
7 Chinese
8 Any other
9 Not given

and should establish a system to monitor admissions by race and sex.

2. ASSESSMENT

General

4–009   2.1 This chapter is about the roles and responsibilities of ASWs and doctors when making assessments of the needs of a person with mental health problems, where the assessment may lead to an application for admission to hospital under the Act.

2.2 An individual should only be compulsorily admitted if the statutory criteria are met and other relevant factors have been considered as set out in para 2.6 below. A decision *not* to apply for admission under the Act should be supported, where necessary, by an alternative framework of care and/or treatment. The decision should also be clearly recorded in the patient's medical notes.

2.3 Doctors and ASWs undertaking assessments need to apply professional judgment, and reach decisions independently of each other but in a framework of co-operation and mutual support. Good working relationships require knowledge and understanding by the members of each profession of the other's distinct role and responsibilities. Unless there are good reasons for undertaking separate assessments, assessments should be carried out jointly by the ASW and doctor(s). It is essential that at least one of the doctors undertaking the medical assessment discusses the patient with the applicant (ASW or nearest relative) and desirable for both of them to do this.

2.4 Everyone involved in assessment should be alert to the need to provide support for colleagues, especially where there is a risk of the patient causing physical harm. Staff should be aware of circumstances where the police should be called to provide assistance, and how to use that assistance to minimise the risk of violence.

The objective of assessment under the Act

4–010   2.5 All those assessing for possible admission under the Act should ensure that:
   a.   they take all relevant factors into account;
   b.   they consider appropriate alternatives to compulsory admission;
   c.   they comply with the legal requirements of the Act.

The factors to be taken into account at assessment

2.6 A patient may be compulsorily admitted under the Act where this is **4–011** necessary:
— in the interests of his or her own health, *or*
— in the interests of his or her own safety, *or*
— for the protection of other people.
Only one of the above grounds needs to be satisfied (*in addition to those relating to the patient's mental disorder*). However, a patient may only be admitted for treatment under section 3 if the treatment cannot be provided unless he or she is detained under the section. In judging whether compulsory admission is appropriate, those concerned should consider not only the statutory criteria but should also take account of:
— the guiding principles in Chapter 1
— the patient's wishes and view of his or her own needs;
— the patient's social and family circumstances;
— the nature of the illness/behaviour disorder and its course;
— what may be known about the patient by his or her nearest relative, any other relatives or friends and professionals involved, assessing in particular how reliable this information is;
— other forms of care or treatment including, where relevant, consideration of whether the patient would be willing to accept medical treatment in hospital informally or as an out-patient and of whether guardianship would be appropriate (see Chapter 13);

— the needs of the patient's family or others with whom he or she lives;
— the need for others to be protected from the patient;
— the burden on those close to the patient of a decision not to admit under the Act.
Ordinarily only then should the applicant (in consultation with other professionals) judge whether the criteria stipulated in any of the admission sections are satisfied, and take the decision accordingly. In certain circumstances the urgency of the situation may curtail detailed consideration of all these factors.

Informal admission

2.7 Where admission to hospital is considered necessary and the patient is **4–012** willing to be admitted informally this should in general be arranged. Compulsory admission powers should only be exercised in the last resort. Informal admission is usually appropriate when a mentally capable patient consents to admission, but not if detention is necessary because of the danger the patient presents to him or herself or others. Compulsory admission should be considered where a mentally capable patient's current medical state, together with reliable evidence of past experience, indicates a strong likelihood that he or she will have a change of mind about informal admission prior to actually being admitted to hospital, with a resulting risk to their health or safety or to the safety of other people.

GENERAL NOTE
Last resort: The Act states that compulsory powers to be used where the ASW **4–013** considers this to be the "most appropriate" way to proceed (s.13(2)).

2.8 If at the time of admission, the patient is mentally incapable of consent, but does not object to entering hospital and receiving care or treatment, admission should be informal[1] (see paras 15.9–15.10 for assessment of capacity and 15.18–15.22 for the treatment of mentally incapacitated patients). The decision to admit a mentally incapacitated patient informally should be made by the doctor in charge of the patient's treatment in accordance with what is in the patient's best interests and is justifiable on the basis of the common law doctrine of necessity (see para 15.21). If a patient lacks capacity at the time of an assessment or review, it is particularly important that both clinical and social care requirements are considered, and that account is taken of the patient's ascertainable wishes and feelings and the views of their immediate relatives and carers on what would be in the patient's best interests.

Protection of others

4–014   2.9 In considering the protection of others (see sections 2(2)(b) and 3(2)(c) of the Act) it is essential to assess both the nature and likelihood of risk and the level of risk others are entitled to be protected from, taking into account:
— reliability of evidence including any relevant details of the patient's clinical history and past behaviour including contact with other agencies;
— the degree of risk and its nature. A risk of physical harm, or serious persistent psychological harm, to others is an indicator of the need for compulsory admission;
— the willingness and ability to cope with the risk, by those with whom the patient lives, and whether there are alternative options available for managing the risk.

The health of the patient

4–015   2.10 A patient may be admitted under sections 2 or 3 solely in the interests of his or her own health or safety even if there is no risk to other people. Those assessing the patient must consider:
— any evidence suggesting that the patient's mental health will deteriorate if he or she does not receive treatment;
— the reliability of such evidence which may include the known history of the individual's mental disorder;
— the views of the patient and of any relatives or close friends, especially those living with the patient, about the likely course of the illness and the possibility of it improving;
— the impact that any future deterioration or lack of improvement would have on relatives or close friends, especially those living with the patient, including an assessment of their ability and willingness to cope;
— whether there are other methods of coping with the expected deterioration or lack of improvement.

---

[1] *R. v. Bournewood Community and Mental Health NHS Trust, ex parte L.* [1998] 3 All E.R. 289.

Interests of his or her own health: Although this paragraph focuses on the patient's **4–016**
mental health, the patient's physical health is also covered by this phrase.

Individual professional responsibility—the Approved Social Worker

2.11 It is important to emphasise that an ASW assessing a patient for **4–017**
possible admission under the Act has overall responsibility for co-ordinating
the process of assessment and, where he or she decides to make an
application, for implementing that decision. The ASW must, at the start of
the assessment, identify him or herself to the person, members of the family
or friends present and the other professionals involved in the assessment.
They should explain in clear terms the ASW's own role and the purpose of
the visit, and ensure that the other professionals have explained their roles.
ASWs should carry with them at all times documents identifying them as
ASWs.

GENERAL NOTE
"There is not a requirement under [this paragraph] that the approved social **4–018**
worker must make it clear for the purposes of which section he or she is
operating. What is required is that the role of the social worker and the purpose
of the visit must be explained by someone, not necessarily by the social worker
himself, given the plural word 'they' as to who should explain in paragraph 2.11"
(*Re G.M. (Patient: Consultation)* [2000] M.H.L.R. 41 *per* Burton J. at para. 71).

2.12 The ASW must interview the patient in a "suitable manner", taking
account of the guiding principles in Chapter 1:
   a.   It is not desirable for a patient to be interviewed through a closed door
        or window except where there is serious risk to other people. Where
        there is no immediate risk of physical danger to the patient or to
        others, powers in the Act to secure access (section 135) should be
        used.
   b.   Where the patient is subject to the effects of sedative medication, or
        the short-term effects of drugs or alcohol, the ASW should consult
        with the doctor(s) and, unless it is not possible because of the patient's
        disturbed behaviour and the urgency of the case, either wait until, or
        arrange to return when, the effects have abated before interviewing
        the patient. If it is not realistic, or the risk indicates that it would not be
        appropriate to wait, the assessment will have to be based on whatever
        information the ASW can obtain from all reliable sources. This
        should be made clear in the ASW's report.
2.13 The patient should ordinarily be given the opportunity of speaking to
the ASW alone but if the ASW has reason to fear physical harm, he or she
should insist that another professional be present. If the patient wants or
needs another person (for example a friend, relative or an advocate) to be
present during the assessment and any subsequent action that may be taken,
then ordinarily the ASW should assist in securing that person's attendance
unless the urgency of the case or some other reason makes it inappropriate
to do so. Deaf or hearing impaired patients may feel more confident with a
friend or advocate who is also deaf or hearing impaired.
2.14 The ASW must attempt to identify the patient's nearest relative as
defined in section 26 of the Act (*see paras 62–63 of the Memorandum*). It is
important to remember that the nearest relative for the purposes of the Act

may not be the same person as the patient's "next of kin", and also that the identity of the nearest relative is liable to change with the passage of time. The ASW must then ensure that the statutory obligations with respect to the nearest relative set out in section 11 of the Act are fulfilled. In addition, the ASW should where possible:

   a. ascertain the nearest relative's views about both the patient's needs and the relative's own needs in relation to the patient;

   b. inform the nearest relative of the reasons for considering an application for admission under the Act and the effects of making such an application.

Applications under section 2

4–019   2.15 It is a statutory requirement to take such steps as are practicable to inform the nearest relative about an application for admission under section 2 and of their power of discharge (section 11(3)). If the ASW has been unable to inform the nearest relative before the patient's admission, he or she should notify the hospital as soon as this has been done.

Applications under section 3

4–020   2.16 Consultation by the ASW with the nearest relative about possible application for admission under section 3 or reception into guardianship is a statutory requirement unless it is not reasonably practicable or would involve unreasonable delay (section 11(4)). Circumstances in which the nearest relative need not be informed or consulted include those where the ASW cannot obtain sufficient information to establish the identity or location of the nearest relative or where to do so would require an excessive amount of investigation. Practicability refers to the availability of the nearest relative and not to the appropriateness of informing or consulting the person concerned. If the ASW has been unable to consult the nearest relative before making an application for admission for treatment (section 3) he or she should persist in seeking to contact the nearest relative so as to inform the latter of his or her powers to discharge the patient under section 23. The ASW should inform the hospital as soon as this has been done.

GENERAL NOTE

4–021   *Practicability refers to … availability:* It is submitted that this statement does not represent the correct legal position: see the note on section 11(4).

Delegation of nearest relative's functions

4–022   2.17 If the nearest relative would find it difficult to undertake the functions defined in the Act, or is reluctant for any reason to do this, regulation 14[2] allows him or her to delegate those functions to another person. ASWs should consider proposing this in appropriate cases.

   2.18 If the nearest relative objects to an application being made for admission for treatment or reception into guardianship it cannot proceed at that time. If, because of the urgency of the case, and the risks of not taking forward the application immediately, it is thought necessary to proceed with

---

[2] Mental Health (Hospital, Guardianship and Consent to Treatment) Regulation 1983.

the application, the ASW will then need to consider applying to the county court for the nearest relative's "displacement" (section 29), and Local Authorities must provide proper assistance, especially legal assistance, in such cases. It is desirable for social services authorities to provide clear practical guidance on the procedures, and this should be discussed with the relevant county courts.

2.19 In so far as the urgency of the case allows, an ASW who is the applicant for the admission of a patient to hospital should consult with other relevant relatives and should take their views into account.

2.20 The ASW should consult wherever possible with others who have been involved with the patient's care in the statutory, voluntary or independent services. Deaf patients may be known to one of the specialist hospital units for mental health and deafness.

2.21 Having decided whether or not to make an application for admission the ASW should tell (with reasons):
— the patient;
— the patient's nearest relative (whenever practicable);
— the doctor(s) involved in the assessment;
— the key worker, if the patient is on CPA;
— the patient's GP, if he or she was not involved in the assessment.
When an application for admission is to be made the ASW should plan how the patient is to be conveyed to hospital and take steps to make the necessary arrangements (see Chapter 11).

GENERAL NOTE
The patient's nearest relative: The patient's permission should be obtained if **4–023** confidential information is contained in the "reasons": see para. 1.8.

Individual professional responsibility—the doctor

2.22 The doctor should: **4–024**
a. decide whether the patient is suffering from mental disorder within the meaning of the Act (section 1) and assess its seriousness and the need for further assessment and/or medical treatment in hospital;
b. consider the factors set out in para 2.6, and discuss them with the applicant and the other doctor involved;
c. specifically address the legal criteria for admission under the Act and, if satisfied that they are met, provide a recommendation setting out those aspects of the patient's symptoms and behaviour on which that conclusion is based;
d. ensure that, where there is to be an application for admission, a hospital bed will be available.

Medical examination

2.23 A proper medical examination requires: **4–025**
— direct personal examination of the patient's mental state;
— consideration of all available relevant medical information including that in the possession of others, professional or non-professional;
— that the guiding principles in Chapter 1 are taken into account.

2.24 If direct access to the patient is not immediately possible, and it is not desirable to postpone the examination in order to negotiate access, consideration should be given to calling the police in order to exercise their lawful power of entry set out in the Act (section 135).

2.25 It may not always be practicable for the patient to be examined by both doctors at the same time; but they should always discuss the patient with each other.

2.26 It is desirable for both doctors to discuss the patient with the applicant. It is essential for at least one of them to do so (see para 2.3).

Joint medical recommendations

4–026   2.27 Joint medical recommendations forms (3 and 10) should only be used where the patient has been jointly examined by two doctors. It is desirable that they are completed and signed by both doctors at the same time.

2.28 In all other circumstances separate recommendation forms should be used (forms 4 and 11).

The second medical recommendation

4–027   2.29 Unless there are exceptional circumstances, the second medical recommendation should be provided by a doctor with previous acquaintance with the patient (that is, one who knows the patient personally in his or her professional capacity). This should be the case even when the "approved" doctor (who is, for example, a hospital-based consultant) already knows the patient. Where this is not possible (for example the patient is not registered with a GP) it is desirable for the second medical recommendation to be provided by an "approved" doctor (see paras 2.41 and 2.42).

GENERAL NOTE

4–028   *Exceptional circumstances:* The Act establishes a less stringent practicability criterion in section 12(2).

2.30 Where a Trust manages two or more hospitals which are in different places and have different names one of the two doctors making the medical recommendations may be on the staff of one hospital and the second doctor may be on the staff of one of the other hospitals.

A decision not to apply for admission

4–029   2.31 Most compulsory admissions require prompt action to be taken. It should be remembered that the ASW has up to 14 days from having personally seen the patient to complete an application for admission under section 2 or 3. The duly completed application and the medical recommendations provide the ASW with the authority to convey the patient to hospital and, in the case of an application for admission under section 2 or 3, such authority lasts for 14 days from the date when the patient was last examined by a doctor with a view to making a recommendation for his or her admission. Where a decision not to apply for a patient's compulsory admission is taken, the ASW must decide how to implement those actions (if any) which his or her assessment indicates are necessary to meet the needs of the patient including, for example, referral to other social workers or services within the social services department. It is particularly important that any keyworker concerned with the patient's care be fully involved in the taking of such decisions. The professionals must ensure that the, the patient and (with the patient's consent except where section 13(4) applies) the patient's nearest relative and any other closely connected relatives have a clear understanding of any alternative arrangements. Such arrangements and any plans for re-viewing them must be recorded in writing and copies made available to all those who need them (subject to the patient's right to confidentiality).

2.32 The ASW must discuss with the patient's nearest relative the reasons for not making an application and should advise the nearest relative of his or her right to do this. If the nearest relative wishes to pursue this the ASW should suggest that he or she consult with the doctors. Where the ASW has carried out an assessment at the request of the nearest relative (section 13(4)) the reasons for not applying for the patient's admission must be given to the nearest relative in writing. Such a letter should contain sufficient details to enable the nearest relative to understand the decision whilst at the same time preserving the patient's right to confidentiality.

GENERAL NOTE

Must discuss with the patient's nearest relative the reasons: The use of the **4–030** mandatory term "must" in this context is unfortunate. Giving reasons to a nearest relative for not making an application is only a legal requirement in the circumstances set out in section 13(4). As the imparting of information to a nearest relative about the patient's situation is a breach of the patient's right to respect for his private life under Article 8(1) of the European Convention on Human Rights, a justification for taking such action must be found in Article 8(2).

Particular practice issues—disagreements

2.33 Sometimes there will be differences of opinion between assessing **4–031** professionals. There is nothing wrong with disagreements: handled properly these offer an opportunity to safeguard the interests of the patient by widening the discussion on the best way of meeting his or her needs. Doctors and ASWs should be ready to consult colleagues (especially keyworkers and other community care staff involved with the patient's care) while retaining for themselves the final responsibility. Where disagreements do occur, professionals should ensure that they discuss these with each other.

2.34 Where there is an unresolved dispute about an application for admission, it is essential that the professionals do not abandon the patient and the family. Rather, they should explore and agree an alternative plan, if necessary on a temporary basis, and ensure that the family is kept informed. Such a plan and the arrangements for reviewing it should be recorded in writing and copies made available to all those who need it (subject to the patient's right to confidentiality).

The choice of applicant for admission

2.35 The ASW is usually the right applicant, bearing in mind professional **4–032** training, knowledge of the legislation and of local resources, together with the potential adverse effect that an application by the nearest relative might have on the latter's relationship with the patient. The doctor should therefore advise the nearest relative that it is preferable for an ASW to make an assessment of the need for a patient to be admitted under the Act, and for the ASW to make the application. When reasonably practicable the doctor should, however, advise the nearest relative of the rights set out in section 13(4) (see para 2.38) and of his or her right to make an application.

GENERAL NOTE

4–033 *The doctor should ... advise the nearest relative:* This is not a legal requirement. As the doctor's prime responsibility is to his patient, he should involve the nearest relative only if such involvement serves to protect the patient's best interests and does not involve a breach of the doctor's duty of confidentiality to his patient.

2.36 The doctor should never advise the nearest relative to make an application in order to avoid involving an ASW in an assessment.

Agency responsibilities—the Local Authority

4–034 2.37 A nearest relative should not be put in the position of having to make an application for admission under the Act because it is not possible for an ASW to attend for assessment. Subject to resources, local authorities should provide a 24 hour ASW service to ensure that this does not happen.

GENERAL NOTE

4–035 *Subject to resources:* It is submitted that local authorities are legally required to provide a 24–hour ASW service: see the note on "sufficient number" in section 114(1) of the 1983 Act.

Section 13(4)

4–036 2.38 Local Authorities are required, if requested by a nearest relative, to an ASW to make an assessment and:
    (a) should have explicit policies on how to respond to repeated requests for assessment where the condition of a patient has not changed significantly;
    (b) should give guidance to ASWs as to whether nearest relative requests can be accepted by way of GPs or other professions. (Such requests should certainly be accepted provided the GP or other professional has been so authorised by the nearest relative.)

GENERAL NOTE

4–037 *To direct an ASW to make an assessment:* A request by a nearest relative under section 13(4) does not oblige an ASW to make an assessment. The obligation is to "take the patient's case into consideration" under section 13(1): see the notes on section 13(4).
Repeated requests for assessment: See above.

Emergencies out of hours, etc.

4–038 2.39 Arrangements should be made to ensure that information about applications is passed to professional colleagues who are next on duty. For example, where an application for admission is not immediately necessary but might be in the future, the necessary arrangements could be made for an ASW to attend the next day.

Agency responsibilities—the Health Authority

Doctors approved under section 12

2.40 The Secretary of State has delegated to Health Authorities the task of **4–039** approving medical practitioners under section 12(2).

2.41 Health Authorities should:
a. take active steps to encourage sufficient doctors, including GPs and those working in the Health Care Service for Prisoners, to apply for approval;
b. seek to ensure a 24 hour on-call rota of approved doctors sufficient to cover the area;
c. maintain a regularly updated list of approved doctors which indicates how each approved doctor can be contacted and the hours that he or she is available;
d. ensure that the up-to-date list of approved doctors and details of the 24 hour on-call rota are circulated to all concerned parties including GPs, mental health centres and social services.

2.42 Authorities and Trusts should consider including in the job description for new consultant psychiatrists with a responsibility for providing a catchment area service obligations to become approved under section 12 of the Act, to keep such approval up-to-date and to participate in the 24 hour on-call approved doctors' rota.

Health Authorities/Trusts Local Authorities

2.43 Good practice requires that Health Authorities, Trusts and local **4–040** Social Services Authorities should co-operate in ensuring that regular meetings take place between professionals involved in mental health assessments in order to promote understanding, and to provide a forum for clarification of their respective roles and responsibilities. Professionals should also keep in mind the interface with the criminal justice agencies, including the probation service and the police.

3. PART III OF THE ACT—PATIENTS CONCERNED WITH CRIMINAL PROCEEDINGS (ASSESSMENT PRIOR TO POSSIBLE ADMISSION)

General

3.1 People subject to criminal proceedings have the same right to **4–041** psychiatric assessment and treatment as other citizens. Any person who is in police or prison custody, who is in need of medical treatment for mental disorder which can only be satisfactorily given in a hospital (or mental nursing home) as defined by the Act, should be admitted to such a hospital. If criminal proceedings are discontinued it may be appropriate for the police to alert the relevant local social services department to allow them to consider whether an application under Part II of the Act would be appropriate.

3.2 All professionals involved in the operation of Part III of the Act should remember:

    a.   that mentally disordered people in police or prison custody may be very vulnerable. The risk of suicide or other self destructive behaviour should be of special concern;

    b.   that a prison health care centre is not a hospital within the meaning of the Act. Comprehensive treatment facilities are rarely available, and the provisions of Part IV of the Act do not apply.

Individual professional responsibilities

4–042   3.3 All professionals concerned with the operation of Part III of the Act should be familiar with:

— the relevant provisions of the Act *[see paras 141–211 of the Memorandum]*;

— Home Office and Department of Health guidance relating to mentally Department disordered offenders including Home Office Circular 12/95;

— their own professional responsibilities and those of other disciplines and authorities and agencies;

— available facilities and services.

Agency responsibilities

4–043   3.4 Health Authorities should:

    a.   be able to provide in response to a request from a court under section 39 of the Act, or other proper requests, up-to-date and full information on the range of facilities that would be available for a potential patient from their area, including secure facilities *[see para. 173 of the Memorandum]*;

    b.   appoint a named person to respond to requests for information.

3.5 Section 39A which was introduced under sections 27 of the Criminal Justice Act 1991 requires a local social services authority to inform the court if requested, if it or any other person is willing to receive the offender into guardianship and how the guardian's powers would be exercised.

3.6 Local Authorities should appoint a named person to respond to requests from the courts about mental health services provided in the community including guardianship.

Assessment by a doctor

4–044   3.7 A doctor who is asked to provide an opinion in relation to a possible admission under Part Ill of the Act should:

    a.   identify him or herself to the person being assessed, explain who has requested the report and the limits of confidentiality in relation to the report, including that the data and the opinion could be relevant not only to medical disposal by the Court but also to the imposition of a punitive sentence, or to its length (see para 3.12);

    b.   request relevant pre-sentence reports, the Inmate Medical Record, if there is one, previous psychiatric reports as well as relevant documentation regarding the alleged offence. If any of this information is not available, the doctor's report should say so clearly.

The report should, where possible, be prepared by a doctor who has previously treated the patient. The doctor, or one of them if two doctors are preparing reports, should have access to a bed or take responsibility for referring the case to another doctor who does (see para 3.18).

3.8 The doctor should where possible identify and access other independent sources of information about the person's previous history (including convictions), including information from GP records, previous psychiatric treatment and patterns of behaviour.

3.9 Assessment for admission of the patient is the responsibility of the doctor but other members of the clinical team who would be involved with the person's care and treatment should also be consulted. A nursing assessment should usually be undertaken if admission to hospital is likely to be recommended. The doctor should also contact the person who is preparing a pre-sentence report, especially if psychiatric treatment is recommended as a condition of a probation order.

3.10 In cases where the doctor cannot state with confidence at the time of sentencing whether admission to hospital will be beneficial, he or she should consider recommending an interim hospital order under section 38 of the Act. This order provides for the person to be admitted to hospital for up to 12 weeks (which may be extended for further periods of up to 28 days to a maximum total period of 12 months) so that recommendations as to treatability and the appropriateness of continuing treatment in hospital can be fully informed.

Reports to the court

3.11 The weight of the clinical opinion is particularly important in helping **4–045** courts to determine the sentence to be passed. In the case of patients subject to criminal proceedings the doctor's report should set out clearly:

a. the data on which the report is based;
b. how this relates to the opinion given;
c. where relevant, how the opinion may relate to any medical condition defence, or other trial issue;
d. factors relating to the presence of mental disorder that may affect the risk that the patient poses to him or herself, or to others, including risk of re-offending; and
e. if admission to hospital is recommended, what, if any, special treatment or security is required and how this would be addressed.

The report should not comment on guilt or innocence.

3.12 When sentencing mentally disordered offenders the court is bound by the requirement in section 4 of the Criminal Justice Act 1991 to consider any information before it which relates to the patient's mental condition. Except where the offence is one for which the law requires a life sentence the court must, before passing sentence, consider the effect of a custodial sentence on the offender's mental disorder and on the treatment which may be available for it.

3.13 A medical report will be of crucial importance in determining whether or nor a sentence of life imprisonment should be imposed where this is not mandatory.

3.14 In a report submitted to the court it may be appropriate to include recommendations on the disposal of the case including any need for a further report in the event of conviction. In making recommendations for disposal

the doctor should consider the longer term, as well as immediate, consequences. Factors to be taken into account include:
    a.   whether the court may wish to make a hospital order subject to special restrictions *[see paras 162–164 of the Memorandum]*;
    b.   whether, for restricted patients, the order should designate admission to a named unit within the hospital.

3.15 The power of the courts to order admission to a named unit was introduced by the Crime (Sentences) Act 1997 to enable the court or the Home Secretary to specify a level of security in which the patient needs to be detained. A named hospital unit can be any part of a hospital which is treated as a separate unit. It will be for the court to define what is meant in each case where it makes use of the power. Admission to a named unit will mean the Home Secretary's consent will be required for any leave or transfer from the named unit, whether the transfer is to another part of the same hospital or to another hospital.

3.16 The need to consider the longer term implications of a recommended disposal is particularly important following the introduction of powers under section 45A of the Act (introduced under the Crime (Sentences) Act 1997). This provides a new option, if the offender is diagnosed as suffering from psychopathic disorder within the meaning of section 1 of the Act (with or without an additional category of mental disorder), for the court to attach a hospital direction and limitation direction to a prison sentence. Where either a hospital order under section 37 or a prison sentence with a hospital direction under section 45A is available to the court the choice rests with the court. The making of a hospital direction and a limitation direction will mean that from the start of his or her sentence the offender will be managed in hospital as if he or she was a transferred prisoner (under section 47 and 49). Thereafter the responsible medical officer (rmo) will have the option of seeking the patient's transfer to prison at any time before his or her release date if no further treatment is likely to be beneficial.

3.17 It is a matter for the discretion of the court whether to make a hospital order subject to restrictions. A hospital direction must always be accompanied by a limitation direction which applies restrictions. It is also for the courts to decide whether to name a hospital unit.

Availability of places

4–046   3.18 If the doctor has concluded that the person needs treatment in hospital but is not able to identify a suitable facility where the person could be admitted immediately, he or she should consider seeking advice from the NHS forensic mental health service or learning disability services for the person's home area. Once advice has been sought, written details of the type of provision required should be sent to the responsible Health Authority, together with relevant supporting information which the authority will need in order to discharge their responsibilities.

Requests for ASW assessment

4–047   3.19 When an ASW is requested to undertake an assessment in prison or court with a view to making an application for admission under section 2 or section 3 or guardianship, he or she must be given as much notice as possible, and time and facilities to interview the prisoner. The ASW should be given access to the pre-sentence report and any other relevant records and reports.

Transfer of prisoners to hospital

13.20 The need for in-patient treatment for a prisoner should be identified **4–048** and acted upon quickly and contact made immediately between the prison doctor and the hospital doctor. The Home Office Mental Health Unit should be informed as soon as the statutory requirements for transfer are in place so that consideration can be given to issuing a direction under the Home Secretary's powers. Supporting reports should take account of the guidance on reports to the courts in paras 3.11 and 3.14 above.

3.21 The transfer of a prisoner to hospital under the Act should take place as soon as possible after the need has been identified. A transfer close to the expected date of release may be seen by the prisoner as being primarily intended to extend detention and result in an unco-operative attitude towards treatment.

4. PRIVATE PRACTICE AND THE PROVISION OF MEDICAL RECOMMENDATIONS

4.1 The Act restricts the provision of medical recommendations by certain **4–049** categories of doctor in private practice. Thus:
a.　where an individual is to be admitted to a mental nursing home or as a private patient to a hospital, neither medical recommendation can be provided by a doctor on the staff of the hospital or mental nursing home (section 12(3));
b.　no medical recommendation can be provided by a doctor who receives, or has an interest in the receipt of, any payment made on account of the maintenance of the patient (section 12(5)(d)).

4.2 It is the personal responsibility of any doctor providing a medical recommendation to ensure that he or she is complying with these legal requirements; if in doubt legal advice must be sought.

4.3 It is undesirable for a doctor to provide a recommendation where he or she will receive payment from the patient (or a relative or friend or an insurance company) for medical services to be provided after he or she has been admitted as a private patient to a hospital or mental nursing home.

4.4 If there could be any suspicion (however unjustified) that a doctor providing a medical recommendation is doing so for pecuniary advantage, then arrangements should be made for another doctor to make the recommendation.

4.5 Where the patient is currently receiving treatment from a doctor that doctor should be consulted by the doctor(s) providing the medical recommendation.

5. SECTION 2 OR SECTION 3?

The choice

5.1 Which admission section should be used? Professional judgment must **4–050** be applied to the criteria in each section and only when this has been done can a decision be reached as to which, if either, section applies. Detention under section 3 can last for any period of time, and need nor last its full course.

5.2 Section 2 pointers:

a. the diagnosis and prognosis of a patient's condition is unclear;

b. a need to carry out an in-patient assessment in order to formulate a treatment plan;

c. a judgment is needed as to whether the patient will accept treatment on a voluntary basis following admission;

d. a judgment has to be made as to whether a particular treatment proposal, which can only be administered to the patient under Part IV of the Act, is likely to be effective;

e. the condition of a patient who has already been assessed, and who has been previously admitted compulsorily under the Act, is judged to have changed since the previous admission and further assessment is needed;

f. the patient has not previously been admitted to hospital either compulsorily or informally and has not been in regular contact with the specialist psychiatric services.

5.3 Section 3 pointers:

a. the patient is considered to need compulsory admission for the treatment of a mental disorder which is already known to his clinical team, and has been assessed in the recent past by that team. In these circumstances it may be right to use section 3 even where the patient has nor previously been admitted as an in-patient;

b. the patient is detained under section 2 and assessment indicates a need for treatment under the Act for a period beyond the 28 day detention under section 2. In such circumstances an application for detention under section 3 should be made at the earliest opportunity and should not be delayed until the end of section 2 detention. The change in detention status from section 2 to section 3 will not deprive the patient of a Mental Health Review Tribunal hearing if the change takes place after a valid application has been made to the Tribunal but before that application has been heard. The patient's rights to apply for a Tribunal under section 66(1)(b) in the first period of detention after his change of status are unaffected.

5.4 Decisions should not be influenced by the possibility that:

a. a proposed treatment to be administered under the Act will last less than 28 days;

b. a patient detained under section 2 will get quicker access to a Mental Health Review Tribunal than one detained under section 3;

c. after-care under supervision will only be available if the patient has been admitted under section 3 (see Chapter 27). The use of section 3 must be justified by the patient's need to be admitted for treatment under the terms of that section, not considerations about what is to happen after his or her eventual discharge;

d. a patient's nearest relative objects to admission under section 3.

5.5 If the nearest relative unreasonably objects to admission under section 3 an application should be made to the county court under section 29 of the Act for the functions of the nearest relative to be transferred to the local Social Services Authority or another person. A further section 2 application cannot be made if the patient is already in hospital following admission under section 2.[3] The section 29 application should be made as soon as it is clear that the patient will need to be detained under section 3 and that the nearest relative unreasonably objects to this.

GENERAL NOTE

The choice of admission section is considered in the General Note to section 2 **4–051** under the heading "Section 2 or section 3".

Paragraph 5.3a

Has been assessed in the recent past by that team: This requirement is often ignored **4–052** by those who advocate admission under section 3 for the "well known" patient; see, for example, the Mental Health Act Commission's *Seventh Biennial Report* 1995–1997, para. 3.1.1. Those assessing the patient for section 3 admission are often confined to the applicant and the recommending doctors.

Paragraph 5.5

A further section 2 application cannot be made: The effect of the *Wilson* decision is **4–053** to prevent an *initial* application under section 2 from being made if the motive for the application is to avoid the consequences of a nearest relative's objection to a section 3 application: see the General Note to section 2. This interpretation is adopted by the *Memorandum* at paragraph 19.

6. ADMISSION FOR ASSESSMENT IN AN EMERGENCY (SECTION 4)

(Para. 24 of the Memorandum)

General

6.1 Application for admission for assessment under section 4 should be **4–054** made only when:
  a. the criteria for admission for assessment are met (see para 5.2); and
  b. the matter is of urgent necessity and there is not enough time to get a second medical recommendation.

6.2 Section 4 should be used only in a genuine emergency, never for administrative convenience. "Second doctors" should be available to assist with assessments prior to admission.

Admission

6.3 An emergency arises where those involved cannot cope with the **4–055** mental state or behaviour of the patient. To be satisfied that an emergency has arisen, there must be evidence of:
  — an immediate and significant risk of mental or physical harm to the patient or to others; and/or
  — the danger of serious harm to property; and/or
  — the need for physical restraint of the patient.

GENERAL NOTE

There must be evidence of: Section 4 can be invoked if the criteria in section 4(1)(2) **4–056** are satisfied. The factors mentioned here do not have to be present if the patient's

---

[3] *R. v. Wilson, ex parte W.* [1996] C.O.D. 42.

urgent need for hospitalisation outweighs the desirability of an attendance by the second doctor.

6.4 Patients should not be admitted under section 4 rather than section 2 because it is more convenient for the second doctor to examine the patient in, rather than outside, hospital. Those assessing an individual's need must be able to secure the attendance within a reasonable time of a second doctor and in particular an approved doctor.

6.5 If the ASW is considering an application for admission and no second doctor is available, he or she should discuss the case with the doctor providing the recommendation and seek to resolve the problem. If this is not possible he or she should have access to an officer in the local Social Services Authority who is sufficiently senior to take up the matter with the Health Authority or Trust. The ASW's Local Authority should make it clear that the ASW in these circumstances is under an obligation to report the matter in this way.

6.6 Hospital Managers should monitor the use of section 4 and seek to ensure that second doctors are available to visit a patient within a reasonable time after being so requested.

6.7 If a patient is admitted under section 4 an appropriate second doctor should examine him or her as soon as possible after admission, to decide whether the patient should be detained under section 2.

7. PART III OF THE ACT—PATIENTS ADMITTED FROM PRISON OR REMAND CENTRE

Admission

4–057 7.1 The following documents should be sent from the prison or remand centre to the hospital at the time of transfer:
— an up-to-date medical report including details of medication
— a report from Prison Health Care staff covering the patient's day-to-day care and management including risk factors
— any relevant pre-sentence reports prepared by the probation service.
It is important that all information is made available to the patient's rmo and other professional staff concerned.

Restricted patients

4–058 7.2 When a person is transferred from prison to hospital under sections 47 or 48 as a restricted patient, it is the responsibility of the Hospital Managers and the rmo to ensure that the patient has received, and as far as possible, understood the letter from the Home Office explaining the roles of Hospital Managers and rmos in relation to restricted patients. Patients should also be given patient leaflets 18 and 20 which explain prison/hospital transfers under these sections.

Patients on remand/subject to an interim hospital order

4–059 7.3 For patients detained under sections 35, 36, 37 and 38 it is the court's responsibility to organise appropriate transport from the court to the receiving hospital.

8. DOCTOR'S HOLDING POWER (SECTION 5(2))

(Paras 25–27 of the Memorandum)

8.1 Good practice depends upon: **4–060**
(a) the professionals involved in implementing the holding power (and in particular the doctor invoking it correctly understanding the power and its purpose;
(b) the Health Authority, Trust and local Social Services Authority making necessary arrangements and agreeing performance standards to ensure that when the power is used, the patient is assessed as quickly as possible for possible admission under the Act by an ASW and doctors; and
(c) the Hospital Managers monitoring the use of the power.

Nature of the power

8.2 The power, which authorises the detention of the patient for up to 72 **4–061** hours, can be used only where the doctor in charge of the treatment of an informal in-patient, or that doctor's nominated deputy, concludes that an application for admission under one of the relevant sections of the Act is appropriate. For this purpose, informal in-patients include those being treated for physical disorders who need treatment for a mental disorder. The period of detention commences at the moment the doctor's report (form 12) is delivered to the Hospital Managers, or someone authorised to receive such a report on their behalf.

8.3 Detention under section 5(2) will end immediately where:
(a) an assessment for admission under section 2 or 3 is made and a decision is taken not to make an application for detention under section 2 or 3;
(b) the doctor decides that no assessment for possible detention under section 2 or 3 needs to be carried out.

The patient should be informed that he or she is no longer detained under the doctor's holding power. The decision, the reasons for it, and its time should be recorded preferably on a form prepared for the purpose. The power cannot be renewed, but circumstances may arise where, subsequent to its use and the patient's reversion to informal status, its use can be considered again.

8.4 For the purposes of section 5(2), informal patients are usually voluntary patients, that is, those who have the capacity to consent and who consent to enter hospital for in-patient treatment. Patients who lack the capacity to consent but do not object to admission for treatment may also be informal patients (see para 2.8). The section cannot be used for an out-patient attending a hospital's accident and emergency department. Admission procedures should not be implemented with the sole intention of then using the power in section 5(2).

8.5 Where a report under section 5(2) is provided in relation to a patient under the care of a consultant other than a psychiatrist, the doctor invoking the power should make immediate contact with a psychiatrist.

8.6 Where a patient is receiving treatment for a physical disorder and a mental disorder for the purposes of section 5(2) the consultant psychiatrist is the doctor in charge of treatment.

Information

4–062   8.7 Where a patient is detained under section 5(2), the Hospital Managers must ensure that the requirements of section 132 to give information are fulfilled (see Chapter 14).

Treatment

4–063   8.8 Part IV of the Act does nor apply to a patient detained under section 5(2). A patient detained under Section 5(2) who has the capacity to consent can only be treated if he or she consents to the treatment. A patient who lacks capacity to consent may be treated under the common law doctrine of necessity in their own best interests (see Chapter 15).

The doctor's role

4–064   8.9 Section 5(2) should only be used if at the time it is nor possible or safe to use section 2, 3 or 4. Section 5(2) is not an admission section under the Act.
8.10 The patient's doctor, or nominated deputy, should only use the power immediately after having personally examined the patient. The doctor should not complete a section 5(2) form and leave it on the ward with instruction for others to submit it to the Hospital Managers if, in their view, the patient is about to leave.

GENERAL NOTE
4–065   The practice described in this paragraph should not be followed because it would result in the unlawful detention of the patient.

Hospital Manager's responsibilities

4–066   8.11 The patient may only be detained when the doctor's section 5(2) report has been delivered to the Hospital Managers, or somebody author-ised to receive it on their behalf. It is therefore important that there is no delay in delivering the report to the Hospital Managers and that sufficient staff are authorised to enable reports to be received at any time. The doctor or nominated deputy must always be aware of who the authorised person is.

GENERAL NOTE
4–067   *Delivered:* See the note on "time when the report is … furnished" in section 5(2).

Assessment for admission while a patient is "held" under section 5(2)

4–068   8.12 All the normal procedures apply, including the use of either section or section 3 if compulsory admission is thought necessary.

Nominated deputies—section 5(3)

4–069   8.13 The registered medical practitioner in charge of an in-patient's treatment may nominate a deputy to exercise section 5(2) powers during his or her absence from the hospital. That deputy will then act on his or her own responsibility and should be suitably experienced.

8.14 Some safeguards:

a. Where the nominated deputy is a junior doctor, the nominating doctor must be satisfied that the deputy has received sufficient guidance and training to carry out the function satisfactorily.

b. Wherever possible the nominated deputy must contact the nominating doctor or another consultant, where the nominated deputy is not a consultant, before using section 5(2). The nominated deputy should have easy access to the nominating doctor or the consultant psychiatrist on call.

c. Only registered medical practitioners who are consultant psychiatrists should nominate deputies.

d. The nominated deputy should report the use of section 5(2) to the nominator as soon as possible.

e. All relevant staff should know who is the nominated deputy for a particular patient.

GENERAL NOTE

Only ... consultant psychiatrists should nominate deputies: As section 5(3) clearly **4–070** gives non-psychiatrists a power to nominate deputies, it is difficult to identify the rationale for this guidance. Relevant staff from non-psychiatric hospitals should receive training on common law and statutory powers that are available for use in emergency situations involving patients.

8.15 It is unlawful for one nominated deputy to nominate another.

8.16 It is usual practice outside normal working hours for the nominated deputy to be the junior doctor on call for the admission wards. Where this occurs the nominating doctor is responsible for ensuring that all the doctors liable to be on duty are competent to act as the nominated deputy and that they are adequately trained, and that an individual doctor has been nominated for every duty period.

Transfer to other hospitals

8.17 It is not possible for patients detained under section 5(2) to be **4–071** transferred to another hospital under section 19 (because they are not detained by virtue of an application made under Part II of the Act). Guidance on the implications of this, and on the circumstances in which such patients may be lawfully transferred, is given in the Mental Health Act Commission's Practice Note 3 (March 1994).

9. NURSE'S HOLDING POWER (SECTION 5(4))

(Paras 28–29 of the Memorandum)

The power

9.1 A psychiatric emergency requires the urgent attendance of a doctor. In **4–072** practice, a doctor may not be immediately available. This chapter sets out the circumstances in which a nurse of the "prescribed class"[4] may lawfully

---

[4] [See the note on section 5(7) of the 1983 Act.]

prevent an informal in-patient, receiving medical treatment for mental disorder, from leaving the hospital. The holding power may only be applied for up to 6 hours or until a doctor with the power to use section 5(2) in respect of the patient arrives, whichever is the earlier, and can only be used when the patient is still on the hospital premises. The holding power cannot be renewed. It is the personal decision of the nurse who cannot be instructed to exercise this power by anyone else. Part IV of the Act does not apply to patients detained under section 5(4).

Assessment before implementation

4–073   9.2 Before using the power the nurse should assess:
    a. the likely arrival time of the doctor as against the likely intention of the patient to leave. Most patients who express a wish to leave hospital can be persuaded to wait until a doctor arrives to discuss it further. Where this is not possible the nurse must try to predict the impact of any delay upon the patient;
    b. the consequences of a patient leaving hospital immediately—the harm that might occur to the patient or others—taking into account:
       — the patient's expressed intentions including the likelihood of the patient committing self-harm or suicide;
       — any evidence of disordered thinking;
       — the patient's current behaviour and in particular any changes in usual behaviour:
       — the likelihood of the patient behaving in a violent manner;
       — any recently received messages from relatives or friends;
       — any recent disturbances on the ward;
       — any relevant involvement of other patients;
    c. the patient's known unpredictability and any other relevant information from other members of the multi-disciplinary team.

Acute emergencies

4–074   9.3 Normally assessment should precede action but in extreme circumstances it may be necessary to invoke the power without carrying out the proper assessment. The suddenness of the patient's determination to leave and the urgency with which the patient attempts to do so should alert the nurse to potentially serious consequences if the patient is successful in leaving.

Reports

4–075   9.4 The nurse entitled to use the power does so by completing form 13. This must be delivered to the Hospital Managers, or to an officer appointed by them, as soon as possible after completion. It is essential that:
    a. the reasons for invoking the power are entered in the patient's nursing and medical notes;
    b. a local incident report form is sent to the Hospital Managers;
    c. details of any patients who remain subject to the power at the time of a shift change are given to staff coming on duty.
9.5 At the time the power lapses the nurse of the prescribed class who is responsible for the patient at that time must complete form 16.

Use of restraint

9.6 A nurse invoking section 5(4) is entitled to use the minimum force **4–076** necessary to prevent the patient from leaving hospital. The general principles that should be applied when the use of restraint has to be considered are set out in paras 19.6–19.8.

Management responsibilities

9.7 The use of section 5(4) is an emergency measure and the doctor with **4–077** the power to use section 5(2) in respect of the patient should treat it as such and arrive as soon as possible. The doctor should not wait six hours before attending simply because this is the maximum time allowed. If the doctor has not arrived within four hours, the duty consultant should be contacted and should attend. Where no doctor has attended within six hours an oral report (suitably recorded) should be made immediately to the responsible senior manager, and a written report should be submitted to that manager and the Hospital Managers on the next working day. The responsible senior manager should nominate a suitable person to supervise the patient's leaving.

GENERAL NOTE

If the doctor has not arrived within four hours: As this provision will only be used in **4–078** a psychiatric emergency (para. 9.1), the non-arrival of a doctor within this period would constitute prima facie evidence of negligent behaviour.

9.8 The holding power lapses upon the arrival of the doctor. The six hour holding period counts as part of the 72 hour holding period if the doctor decides to report under section 5(2).

9.9 A suitably qualified, experienced and competent nurse should be on all wards where there is a possibility of section 5(4) being invoked, particularly acute admission wards, and wards where there are acutely disturbed patients, or patients requiring intensive nursing care.

9.10 While it is desirable that a nurse who invokes the power should be qualified in the speciality relevant to the patient's mental disorder the legislation does not require this. Where a nurse may have to apply the power to patients from outside his or her specialist field it is good practice for employers to arrange suitable post-basic education and training, especially in the use of section 5(4). Close working between nurses in different specialities is also important.

10. THE POLICE POWER TO REMOVE TO A PLACE OF SAFETY (SECTION 136)

(Para. 317 of the Memorandum)

Good practice

10.1 This depends on: **4–079**
a. the local Social Services Authority, Health Authority, Trust and the Chief Constable establishing a clear policy for use of the power;

b.   all professionals involved in its implementation understanding the power and its purpose, and the person's other rights and following the local policy concerning implementation.

The local policy

4–080   10.2 The purpose of removing a person to a place of safety (as defined in section 135(6)) under section 136(2) is to enable him or her to be examined by a doctor and interviewed by an ASW and for any necessary arrangements for his care and treatment to be made. The local policy should ensure that these assessments are conducted effectively and quickly.

10.3 The policy should define the responsibilities of:

a.   police officers to remain in attendance where the patient's health or safety or the protection of others so require, when the patient is taken to a place of safety other than a police station;

b.   police officers, doctors and ASWs for the satisfactory returning to the community of a person assessed under section 136 who is not admitted to hospital or immediately placed in accommodation.

10.4 The policy should include provisions for the use of the section to be monitored so that:

a.   a check can be made of how and in what circumstances it is being used, including its use in relation to ethnic minorities;

b.   the parties to the policy can consider any changes in the mental health services that might result in the reduction of its use.

The place of safety

4–081   10.5 The identification of preferred places of safety is a matter for local agreement. However, as a general rule it is preferable for a person thought to be suffering from mental disorder to be detained in a hospital rather than a police station. Regard should be had to any impact different types of place of safety may have on the person held and hence on the outcome of an assessment. Once the person has been removed to a particular place of safety they cannot be transferred to a different place of safety.

Good practice points

4–082   10.6 Where an individual is removed to a place of safety by the police under section 136 it is recommended that:

a.   where he or she is to be taken to a hospital as a place of safety immediate contact is made by the police with both the hospital and the local social services department;

b.   where the police station is to be used as a place of safety immediate contact is made with the local social services authority and the appropriate doctor.

The local policy for the implementation of section 136 should ensure that police officers know whom to contact.

Record keeping

4–083   10.7 A record of the person's time of arrival must be made immediately he or she reaches the place of safety. As soon as detention under section 136 ends the individual must be so advised by those who are detaining him or her. The managers of the place of safety should devise and use a form for recording the end of the person's detention under this section (similar to the form used for section 5(4)).

10.8 Section 136 is not an emergency admission section. It enables an individual who falls within its criteria to be detained for the purposes of an assessment by a doctor and ASW, and for any necessary arrangements for his or her treatment and care to be made. When these have been completed within the 72 hour detention period, the authority to detain the patient ceases.

    a.   Ordinarily, neither a hospital nor the police should discharge an individual detained under section 136 before the end of the 72 hour period without assessments having been made by a doctor and ASW within that period. Where the doctor, having examined the individual, concludes that he or she is not mentally disordered within the meaning of the Act then the individual can no longer be detained under the section and should be immediately discharged from detention.

    b.   Where a hospital is used as a place of safety it may be better for the patient not to be formally admitted although he or she may have to be cared for on a ward. Where such a policy is adopted it is essential to remember that the patient must be examined by a doctor in the same way as if formally admitted.

    c.   Where a police station is used as a place of safety speedy assessment is desirable to ensure that the person spends no longer than necessary in police custody but is either returned to the community or admitted to hospital.

Information about rights

10.9 Where an individual has been removed to a place of safety by the **4-084** police under section 136.

    a.   the person removed is entitled to have another person, of his or her choice, informed of the removal and his or her whereabouts (section 56 of the Police and Criminal Evidence Act 1984);

    b.   when the person removed is in police detention (that is, a police station is being used as a place of safety) he or she has a right of access to legal advice (section 58 of the Police and Criminal Evidence Act 1984);

    c.   where detention is in a place of safety other than a police station access to legal advice should be facilitated whenever it is requested.

It is important to recognise that although the Act uses the term "remove", it is deemed to be an "arrest" for the purposes of the Police and Criminal Evidence Act 1984.

10.10 Where the hospital is used as a place of safety the Hospital Managers must ensure that the provisions of section 132 (giving of information) are complied with.

10.11 Where the police station is a place of safety, although section 132 does not apply, the local policy should require that the same information is given in writing on the person's arrival at the place of safety. There may be scope for co-operation between hospitals and the police in preparing suitable leaflets or letters.

Assessment

4–085 10.12 The local implementation policy should ensure that the doctor examining the patient should wherever possible be approved under section 12 of the Act. Where the examination has to be conducted by a doctor who is not approved, the reasons for this should be recorded.

10.13 Assessment by both doctor and social worker should begin as soon as possible after the arrival of the individual at the place of safety. Any implementation policy should set target times for the commencement of the assessment and the Health Authority, Trust and local Social Services Authority should review local practice against these targets.

10.14 The person must be seen by *both* the doctor and the ASW, unless the circumstances set out in para 10.8(a) apply. The local policy should include the necessary arrangements to enable the person to be jointly assessed.

  a. If the doctor sees the person first and concludes that admission to hospital is unnecessary, or the person agrees to informal admission, the individual must still be seen by an ASW, who must consult with the doctor about any other arrangements that might need to be made for his or her treatment and care.

  b. It is desirable for a consultant psychiatrist in learning disabilities and an ASW with experience of working with people with learning disabilities to be available to make a joint assessment if it appears that the detained person has a learning disability.

10.15 The role of the ASW includes:

— interviewing the person;
— contacting any relevant relatives/friends;
— ascertaining whether there is a psychiatric history;
— considering any possible alternatives to admission to hospital;
— making arrangements for compulsory admission to hospital;
— making any other necessary arrangements.

Treatment

4–086 10.16 Part IV of the Act does not apply to persons detained under section 136. In the absence of consent, the person can only be treated in accordance with the provisions of the common law (see Chapter 15).

Necessary arrangements

4–087 10.17 Once the assessment has been concluded it is the responsibility of the doctors and ASW to consider if any necessary arrangements for the person s treatment and care have to be made.

10.18 Where compulsory admission is indicated:

  a. where the hospital is the place of safety the person should be admitted either under section 2 or section 3, as appropriate. When the approved doctor providing one recommendation is on the staff of the hospital, the second recommendation should be provided by a doctor with previous knowledge of the person, for example his or her GP. When a person detained under section 136 is not registered with a GP, the second opinion should be provided by a second approved doctor;

b. persons detained under section 136 in hospital pending completion of their assessment should not have their detention extended by use of section 5(2) or section 5(4);

c. where the police station is the place of safety then compulsory admission should be under section 2 or 3 as appropriate. Section 4 may be used if there is an urgent need to move the person to hospital.

GENERAL NOTE

Paragraph (b)
Should not have their detention extended: Because the courts would be most likely **4–088** to declare such a practice to be unlawful: see *R. v. Wilson, ex p. Williamson* [1996] C.O.D. 42, noted in the General Note to section 2.

Section 135

10.19 Powers of entry under section 135(1) or (2) may be used when it is **4–089** necessary to gain access to a mentally disordered person who is not in a public place and, if necessary, remove him or her to a place of safety. Local authorities should issue guidance to ASWs on how to use the power.

11. CONVEYANCE OF PATIENTS

(Para. 31 of the Memorandum)

Powers

11.1 A properly completed application for admission under the Act, **4–090** together with the required medical recommendations, gives the applicant (ASW or nearest relative) the authority to convey the patient to hospital. In the case of patients subject to after-care under supervision, the supervisor has the power to take and convey the patient to a place where he or she is required to attend for medical treatment, occupation, education or training (see Chapter 28).

General

11.2 Authorities, including the ambulance service and the police, who are **4–091** involved in conveying patients should agree joint policies and procedures to include:

a. a clear statement of the roles and obligations of each authority and its staff;

b. the form of any authorisation to be given by the ASW, or supervisor, to others to convey the patient;

c. guidance on powers in relation to conveying patients.

11.3 The ASW, or supervisor, has a professional obligation to ensure that the most humane and least threatening method of conveying the patient is used, consistent with ensuring that no harm comes to the patient or to others. The ASW or supervisor should take into account:

— the patient's preferences;
— the views of relatives or friends involved with the patient;
— the views of other professionals involved in the application or who know the patient;
— his or her judgment of the patient's state of mind, and the likelihood of the patient behaving in a violent or dangerous manner;
— the impact that any particular mode of conveying the patient will have on the patient's relationship with the community to which he or she will return.

11.4 When conveying a patient to hospital the ASW has the power of a police constable. The task of conveying the patient may be delegated eg. to ambulance staff or the police. The ASW or supervisor retains ultimate responsibly to ensure that the patient is conveyed in a lawful and humane manner and should give guidance to those asked to assist.

11.5 If the patient is conveyed by ambulance, the ASW or supervisor may accompany the patient. Where requested by the applicant, the ambulance authority should make the necessary arrangements. The patient may be accompanied by another person, provided the ASW or supervisor is satisfied that this will not increase the risk of harm to the patient or others.

11.6 The patient should not be conveyed by car unless the ASW or supervisor is satisfied that this would not present danger to the patient or others. There should *always* be an escort for the patient other than the driver.

11.7 If the patient is likely to be violent or dangerous the police should be asked to help. Where possible an ambulance should be used. Otherwise a police vehicle suitable for conveying such a patient should be used. While the police may have to exercise their duty to protect persons or property while the patient is being conveyed they should, where possible, comply with any directions or guidance given by the ASW or supervisor.

Conveying into hospital

4–092   11.8 If an ASW is the applicant, he or she has a professional responsibility for ensuring that all the necessary arrangements are made for the patient to be conveyed to hospital.

11.9 If the nearest relative is the applicant, the assistance of an ASW should be made available if requested. If this is not possible, other professionals involved in the admission should give advice and assistance.

11.10 The ASW should telephone the receiving hospital to ensure that the patient is expected and give the likely time of arrival. If possible the ASW should ask the name of the person who will be formally receiving the admission documents.

11.11 The ASW must ensure that the admission documents arrive at the receiving hospital at the same time as the patient. If the ASW is not travelling in the same vehicle as the patient, the documents should be given to the person authorised to convey the patient with instructions for them to be presented to the officer authorised to receive them.

11.12 If the ASW is not travelling with the patient, he or she should arrive at the hospital at the same time or as soon as possible afterwards. He or she should ensure that the admission documents have been delivered, that the admission of the patient is under way and that any relevant information is passed to the hospital staff. The ASW should remain in the hospital with the patient until satisfied that the patient has been detained in a proper manner.

GENERAL NOTE

He or she should arrive at the hospital: Following this advice would not be **4–093** practicable if the receiving hospital was located a considerable distance from the ASW's home area. In these circumstances relevant information could be communicated to the hospital staff by telephone or by fax. Section 6(1) of the Act enables the ASW to delegate responsibility for conveying the patient to hospital to another.

11.13 The ASW should leave an outline report at the hospital when the patient is admitted, giving reasons for the admission and any practical matters about the patient's circumstances which the hospital should know and, where possible, the name and telephone number of a social worker who can give further information. Social services departments should consider the use of a form on which ASWs can make this outline report. A full report should also be prepared for the formal social services department record.

11.14 A patient who has been sedated before being conveyed to hospital should whenever possible be accompanied by a nurse, a doctor or a suitably trained ambulance person experienced in the management of such patients.

11.15 If the ASW or authorised person is refused access to the premises where the patient is, and forcible entry will be needed to remove the patient, an application should be made for a warrant under section 135(2).

12. RECEIPT AND SCRUTINY OF DOCUMENTS

(Paras 44–54 of the Memorandum)

12.1 The Hospital Managers should formally delegate their duties to **4–094** receive and scrutinise admission documents to a limited number of officers, with a knowledge of the relevant parts of the Act, who can provide 24 hour cover. A general manager should take overall responsibility on behalf of the Hospital Managers for the proper receipt and scrutiny of documents.

12.2 There is a difference between "receiving" documents and "scrutinising" them. Documents should be scrutinised at the same time as they are received, if possible, otherwise as soon after as possible.

Receipt of documents

12.3   **4–095**
   a. If the Hospital Managers' obligation to receive documents is delegated to nursing staff such delegation should be to the nurse in charge of the ward. If the nurse is below the grade of first level nurse, he or she should seek the advice of a first level nurse when "receiving" documents.
   b. The hospital should have a checklist for the guidance of those delegated to receive documents, to detect errors which cannot be corrected at a later stage in the procedure (see section 15).

c. When the patient is being admitted on the application of an ASW the person "receiving" the admission documents should check their accuracy with the ASW.

d. The "receiving" officer should have access to a manager for advice, especially at night.

"Scrutinising documents"

4–096 12.4

a. Where the person delegated to receive the documents is not authorised by the Hospital Managers to rectify a defective admission document, the documents must be scrutinised by a person who is authorised immediately on the patient's admission or during the next working day if admitted at night, during weekends or on public holidays when such a person is not available.

b. The Hospital Managers must arrange for the medical recommendations to be medically scrutinised, to ensure that they show sufficient legal grounds for detention. The clinical description of the patient's mental condition should include a description of his or her symptoms and behaviour, not merely a diagnostic classification. This scrutiny should be carried out at the same time as the administrative scrutiny.

Hospital Managers

4–097 12.5

a. The Hospital Managers are responsible for ensuring that patients are detained lawfully. They should therefore monitor the receipt and scrutiny of admission documents on a regular basis.

b. Those delegated to scrutinise documents must be clear about what kind of errors on application forms and medical recommendations can and cannot be corrected *[see paras 46–49 of the Memorandum]*. If no original pink forms are available photocopies of an original form can be used. Current statutory versions of the forms must be used.

c. Details of defective admission documents, whether rectifiable or not, and of any subsequent action, must be given to the Hospital Managers on a regular basis.

d. Hospital Managers should ensure that those delegated to receive and scrutinise admission documents understand the requirements of the Act, and if necessary receive appropriate training.

GENERAL NOTE

Paragraph 12.5(b)

4–098 *Current statutory versions of the forms must be used:* Any document, including a handwritten one, which reproduces the wording of the relevant form set out in Schedule 1 to the Mental Health (Hospital, Guardianship and Consent to Treatment) Regulations would be legally valid.

13. GUARDIANSHIP (SECTION 7)

(Paras 38–42 of the Memorandum)

Purpose of guardianship

13.1 The purpose of guardianship is to enable patients to receive care in **4–099** the community where it cannot be provided without the use of compulsory powers. It provides an authoritative framework for working with a patient, with a minimum of constraint, to achieve as independent a life as possible within the community. Where it is used it must be part of the patient's overall care and treatment plan.

13.2 After-care under supervision provides an alternative statutory framework for the after-care of patients who have been detained in hospital for treatment and meet the criteria set out in section 25A of the Act. Detailed guidance on after-care under supervision is given in Chapter 28.

Assessment for guardianship

13.3 ASWs and doctors should consider guardianship as a possible **4–100** alternative to admission to, or continuing care in, hospital.

13.4 An application for guardianship should be accompanied by a comprehensive care plan established on the basis of multi-disciplinary discussions. It is important that any procedures instituted by social services departments are no more than the minimum necessary to ensure the proper use of guardianship and that guardianship can be used in a positive and flexible manner.

Components of effective guardianship

13.5 A comprehensive care plan is required (under the Care Programme **4–101** Approach (CPA) in England) which identifies the services needed by the patient and who will provide them. The care plan should include care arrangements, suitable accommodation, treatment and personal support. For those subject to guardianship the care plan should also indicate which of the powers under the Act are necessary to achieve the plan. If no powers are required guardianship should not be used.

13.6 Key elements of the plan should include:
a. depending on the patient's level of "capacity", his or her recognition of the "authority" of, and willingness to work with, the guardian;
b. support from the Local Authority for the guardian;
c. suitable accommodation to help meet the patient's needs;
d. access to day care, education and training facilities;
e. effective co-operation and communication between all persons concerned in implementing the care plan.

The guardian should be willing to "advocate" on behalf of the patient in relation to those agencies whose services are needed to carry out the care plan

Duties of Social Services Departments

4–102   13.7 Each Local Authority should establish a policy setting out the arrangements for:
  a. receiving, considering and scrutinising applications for guardianship. Such arrangements should ensure that applications are properly but speedily dealt with;
  b. monitoring the progress of the guardianship including steps to be taken to fulfil the authority's statutory obligations in relation to private guardians and to arrange visits to the patient;
  c. ensuring the suitability of any proposed private guardian, and that he or she is able to understand and carry out the statutory duties, including the appointment of a nominated medical attendant;
  d. ensuring that patients under guardianship receive, both orally and in writing, relevant aspects of the information that Hospital Managers are required to give to detained patients under section 132 (patient leaflets 10 and 11);
  e. ensuring that the patient is aware of his or her right to apply to a Mental Health Review Tribunal and that a named officer of the local authority will give any necessary assistance to the patient in making such an application;
  f. maintaining detailed records relating to the person under guardianship;
  g. ensuring the review of the guardianship towards the end of each period of guardianship;
  h. discharging the patient from guardianship as soon as it is no longer required.

The powers of the guardian

4–103   13.8 Section 8 of the Act sets out the three powers of the guardian as follows:
  a. to require the patient to live at a place specified by the guardian. This does not provide the legal authority to detain a patient physically or remove the patient against his or her wishes. A patient who is absent without leave from the specified place may be returned within the statutory time limit *[see paras 72–74 of the Memorandum]* by those authorised to do so under the Act;
  b. to require the patient to attend at specified places for medical treatment, occupation, education or training. If the patient refuses to attend, the guardian is not authorised to use force to secure such attendance, nor does the Act enable medical treatment to be administered in the absence of the patient's consent;
  c. to require access to the patient to be given at the place where he or she is living to persons detailed in the Act. A refusal without reasonable cause to permit an authorised person to have access to the patient is an offence under section 129 but no force may be used to secure entry.
If the patient consistently resists the exercise of the guardian's powers it can be concluded that guardianship is not the most appropriate form of care for that person and the guardianship order should be discharged.

GENERAL NOTE
The three powers of the guardian: The guardian also has an implied duty to act for the welfare of the patient (*R. v. Kent County Council, ex p. Marston,* noted under s. 8(1)(a)).

This does not provide the legal authority to detain a patient physically: For a **4–104** consideration of the legal position of a patient who is being detained in a community setting, see the note on section 8(1) under the heading "reside".

13.9 Points to remember:

a. Guardianship does not restrict the patient's access to hospital services on an informal basis. A patient who requires treatment but does not need to be detained may be admitted informally.

b. Guardianship can also remain in force if the patient is admitted to hospital under section 2 or 4 but not under section 3.

c. It is possible in certain circumstances for a patient liable to be detained in hospital by virtue of an application under Part II of the Act to be transferred into guardianship and for a person subject to guardianship under Part II of the Act to be transferred into the guardianship of another local social services authority or person approved by such authority or to be transferred to hospital. (See section 19 and regulations 7–9 of the Mental Health Hospital. Guardianship and as Consent to Treatment) Regulations 1983).

13.10 Particular practice issues:

a. Guardianship must not be used to require a patient to reside in hospital except where it is necessary for a very short time in order to provide shelter whilst accommodation in the community is being arranged.

b. Where an adult is assessed as requiring residential care, but owing to mental incapacity is unable to make a decision as to whether he she wishes to be placed in residential care, those who are responsible for his or her care should consider the applicability and appropriateness of guardianship for providing the framework within which decisions about his or her current and future care can be planned.

Guardianship under section 37

13.11 Guardianship may be used as an alternative to hospital orders by **4–105** courts where the prescribed criteria, which are similar to those of a hospital order, are met. The court should be satisfied that the Local Authority or named person is willing to act as guardian. The Local Authority should be satisfied with the arrangements. In considering the appropriateness of guardianship they should be guided by the same principles as apply under Part II of the Act. The powers and duties conferred on the local authority or private guardian and the provisions as to duration, renewal and discharge are the same as in guardianship applications except that the power to discharge is not available to the nearest relative.

14. INFORMATION FOR DETAINED PATIENTS, THOSE SUBJECT TO GUARDIANSHIP AND NEAREST RELATIVES

(Paras 297–302 of the Memorandum)

4–106　14.1 Under section 132 the Hospital Managers must ensure that all detained patients are given and understand:

    a.   specific information as soon as is practicable after their admission *[see section 132 and para. 297 of the Memorandum]*;

    b.   particular information in so far as it is relevant to the patient *[see section 132(2) and para 298 of the Memorandum]*.

14.2 The managers are also required to ensure that the above information is given in writing to the patient's nearest relative—unless the patient wishes otherwise. Health Authorities and Trusts are reminded that sample letters to nearest relatives were circulated at Annex B of Circular HC(83)17.

14.3 Under Section 133 the Hospital Managers should, if the patient does not object, give the nearest relative of a detained patient at least seven days notice of his or her discharge from detention in a hospital or mental nursing home (unless the nearest relative requests not to be kept informed). It is good practice, if the patient agrees, for the nearest relative to be provided with details of any care the patient will be receiving once discharged from detention in hospital.

The Hospital Managers' information policy

4–107　14.4 In order to fulfil their statutory duties Hospital Managers should implement a system which is consistent with the principles set out in Chapter 1 and ensures that:

    a.   the correct information is given to the patient;

    b.   the information is given in a suitable manner and at a suitable time and in accordance with the requirements of the law;

    c.   the member of staff who is to give the information has received sufficient training and guidance and is identified in relation to each detained patient;

    d.   a record is kept of the information given, including how, when, where and by whom it was given;

    e.   a regular check is made that information has been properly given to each detained patient, and understood by them.

Specific information

14.5

a. Information on consent to treatment

4–108　The patient must be informed;

    — of the nature, purpose and likely effects of the treatment which is planned;

    — of their rights to withdraw their consent to treatment at any time and of the need for consent to be given to any further treatment;

— how and when treatment can be given without their consent, including by the second opinion process and when treatment has begun if stopping it would cause serious suffering to the patient.

b. In formation on detention, renewal and discharge

The patient should be informed: **4–109**
— of the provisions of the Act under which they are detained, and the reasons for their detention;
— that they will not automatically be discharged when the current period of detention ends;
— that their detention will not automatically be renewed when the current period of detention ends;
— of their right to have their views about their continued detention or discharge considered before any decision is made.

c. Information on applications to Mental Health Review Tribunals

Patients and nearest relatives must be informed: **4–110**
— of their rights to apply to Mental Health Review Tribunals;
— about the role of the Tribunal;
— how to apply to a Tribunal;
— how to contact a suitably qualified solicitor;
— that free Legal Aid—Advice By Way Of Representation (ABWOR) may he available;
— how to contact any other organisation which may be able to help them make an application to a Tribunal.

d. Information on the Mental Health Act Commission **4–111**

Patients must be informed:
— about the role of the Mental Health Act Commission;
— when the Commission is to visit a hospital or unit;
— of their right to meet the Commissioners;
— of their right to complain to the Commission.

15. MEDICAL TREATMENT

(Paras 212–230 of the Memorandum)

Introduction

15.1 This chapter gives guidance on medical treatment, capacity (see paras **4–112** 15.9–15.12), consent to treatment (see paras 15.13–15.17) and the treatment of those without capacity (see paras 15.18–15.24).

Duty of rmo

15.2 Everyone involved in the medical treatment of mental disorder **4–113** should be familiar with the provisions of Part IV of the Act, related statutory instruments, relevant circulars and advice notes. But it is for the rmo to ensure that there is compliance with the Act's provisions relating to medical treatment.

Duty of the Hospital Managers

4–114   15.3 The managers should monitor compliance with the provisions of Part IV of the Act. (For a more detailed discussion of Part IV of the Act see Chapter 16.)

Medical treatment

4–115   15.4 For the purposes of the Act, medical treatment includes nursing and care, habilitation and rehabilitation under medical supervision, *i.e.* the broad range of activities aimed at alleviating, or preventing a deterioration of, the patient's mental disorder. It includes physical treatment such as ECT and the administration of drugs, and psychotherapy.

Treatment plans

4–116   15.5 Treatment plans are essential for both informal and detained patients. Consultants should co-ordinate the formulation of a treatment plan in consultation with their professional colleagues. The plan should form part of a coherent care plan under the CPA, for patients in England, and be recorded in the patient's clinical notes.

15.6 A treatment plan should include a description of the immediate and long term goals for the patient with a clear indication of the treatments proposed and the methods of treatment. The patient's progress and possible changes to the care programme should be reviewed at regular intervals.

15.7 Wherever possible the whole care programme should be discussed with the patient, with a view to enabling him or her to contribute to it and express agreement or disagreement. The care programme should he discussed with the patient's relatives or carers, with the consent of the patient if he or she is capable of giving consent, and, if the patient is not capable, on the basis of whatever discussions are necessary in the best interests of the patient.

Capacity and consent to treatment: introduction

4–117   15.8 Under the common law, valid consent (see para 15.13) is required from all patients before medical treatment can be given, except where common law or statute provides authority to give treatment without consent. The common law may authorise treatment where the patient is incapable of consenting or, rarely, where the patient may be capable of consent. Treatment may be authorised by statute for example under Part IV of the Act (see Chapter 16).

Capacity to make treatment decisions

4–118   15.9 The assessment of a patient's capacity to make a decision about his or her own medical treatment is a matter for clinical judgment, guided by current professional practice and subject to legal requirements. It is the personal responsibility of any doctor proposing to treat a patient to determine whether the patient has capacity to give a valid consent.

Capacity: the basic principles

15.10 An individual is presumed to have the capacity to make a treatment **4–119** decision unless he or she:
— is unable to take in and retain the information material to the decision especially as to the likely consequences of having or not having the treatment; or
— is unable to believe the information; or
— is unable to weigh the information in the balance as part of a process of arriving at the decisions.[5,6]
It must be remembered that:
— any assessment as to an individual's capacity has to be made in relation to a particular treatment or admission proposal;
— capacity in an individual with a mental disorder can be variable over time and should be assessed at the time the admission or treatment is proposed;
— all assessments of an individual's capacity should be fully recorded in the patient's medical notes.
15.11 Where an individual lacks capacity at a particular time it may be possible to establish that there was an advance refusal of treatment in the past. To be valid an advance refusal must be clearly verifiable and must relate to the type of treatment now proposed. If there is any reason to doubt the reliability of an advance refusal of treatment, then an application to the court for a declaration could be made.[7] The individual must have had the capacity to make an advance refusal when it was made. An advance refusal of medical treatment for mental disorder does not prevent the authorisation of such treatment by Part IV of the Act in the circumstances where those provisions apply.
15.12 Mental disorder does not necessarily make a patient incapable of giving or refusing consent. Capacity to consent is variable in people with mental disorder and should be assessed in relation to the particular patient, at the particular time, as regards the particular treatment proposed. Nor everyone is equally capable of understanding the same explanation of a treatment plan. The explanation should be appropriate to the level of his or her assessed ability.

Consent: the basic principles

15.13 "Consent" is the voluntary and continuing permission of the patient **4–120** to receive a particular treatment, based on an adequate knowledge of the purpose, nature, likely effects and risks of that treatment including the likelihood of its success and any alternatives to it. Permission given under any unfair or undue pressure is not "consent".

[5] *Re C. (Refusal of Treatment)* [1994] 1 F.L.R. 31.
[6] *Re M.B.* [1997] 2 F.C.R. 541.
[7] See Guideline 3 in *R. v. Collins, ex parte S. (No. 2)* [1998].

1t from patients with capacity to consent

ǀ It is the duty of everyone proposing to give treatment to use reasonable care and skill, not only in giving information prior to seeking a patient's consent but also in meeting the continuing obligation to provide the patient with adequate information about the proposed treatment and alternatives to it.

15.15 The information which must be given should be related to the particular patient, the particular treatment and the relevant medical knowledge and practice. In every case sufficient information must he given to ensure that the patient understands in broad terms the nature, likely effects and risks of that treatment including the likelihood of its success and any alternatives to it. Additional information is a matter of professional judgment for the doctor proposing the treatment.

15.16 The patient should be invited to ask questions and the doctor should answer fully, frankly and truthfully. There may be a compelling reason, in the patient's interests, for not disclosing certain information. A doctor who chooses not to disclose must be prepared to justify the decision. If a doctor chooses not to answer a patient's question, he or she should make this clear to the patient so that the patient knows where he or she stands.

15.17 The patient should be told that his or her consent to treatment can be withdrawn at any time and that fresh consent is required before further treatment can be given or reinstated. The patient should receive an explanation of the likely consequences of not receiving the treatment. (See para. 16.11 on withdrawing consent in relation to treatment administered under Part IV of the Act.)

Treatment of those without capacity to consent

4–122   15.18 The administration of medical treatment to people incapable of taking their own treatment decisions is a matter of much concern to professionals and others involved in their care. It is the personal responsibility of professionals to ensure that they understand the relevant law.

15.19 Principles governing a child's capacity to consent to treatment are set out in Chapter 31.

15.20 An adult patient may be mentally incapable of consenting to treatment or refusing treatment (see paras 15.9–15.12). The mental incapacity may be due to temporary factors such as delirium, shock, pain or drugs, or mental incapacity may be more long-lasting as with patients who have severe learning disabilities or some patients who suffer from a degenerative condition such as Alzheimer's disease.

15.21 There are particular considerations that doctors must take into account in discharging their duty of care for those who lack capacity to consent. Treatment for their condition may be prescribed for them in their best interests under the common law doctrine of necessity.[8] According to the decision in the case of in *Re F.*, if treatment is given to a patient who is not capable of giving consent "in the patient's best interests", the treatment must be:

[8] See the decisions in the House of Lords in *Re F.* [1990] 2 A.C. 1 and *R. v. Bournewood Community and Mental Health NHS Trust, ex parte L.* [1998] 3 All E.R. 289.

— necessary to save life or prevent a deterioration or ensure an improvement in the patient's physical or mental health; and

— in accordance with a practice accepted at the time by a reasonable body of medical opinion skilled in the particular form of treatment in question".[9]

GENERAL NOTE

The scope of the best interests test has been extended by *Re Y. (Mental Incapacity;* **4–123** *Bone Marrow Transplant)* [1996] 2 F.L.R. 787, which is noted in the General Note to Part IV of the 1983 Act under the heading "The treatment of incapable patients".

15.22 There are exceptional circumstances in which the proposed treatment should not be carried out on mentally incapacitated patients without first seeking the approval of the High Court by way of a declaration. Sterilisation, according to the House of Lords in *Re F.*, is one such circumstance.

15.23 The procedures to be used when applying for a declaration that a proposed operation for sterilisation is lawful were set our initially by Lord Brandon of Oakbrook in *Re F.* and developed by the Official Solicitor.[10] In outline, the procedure is as follows:

a. applications for a declaration that a proposed operation for sterilisation of a patient can lawfully be carried our despite the inability of such patient to consent thereto should be by way of Originating Summons issuing out of the Family Division of the High Court;

b. the applicant should normally be the person(s) responsible for the care of the patient or intending to carry our the proposed operation or other treatment, if it is declared to be lawful;

c. the patient must always be a party and should normally be a respondent. In cases in which the patient is a respondent the patient's guardian *ad litem* should normally be the Official Solicitor. In any cases in which the Official Solicitor is not either the "next friend" or the guardian *ad litem* of the patient or an applicant he shall be respondent;

d. with a view to protecting the patient's privacy, but subject always to the judge's discretion, the hearing will be in chambers, but the decision and the reasons for that decision will be given in court.

15.24 *The Handbook of Contraceptive Practice (Department of Health 1990)* considers the effect of *Re F.* on operations for sterilisation, as well as other matters relating to the sexuality of people with learning disabilities.

Treatment of those who may have capacity to consent where consent is not given

15.25 A patient capable of giving consent can only be given medical **4–124** treatment for mental disorder against his or her wishes in accordance with the provisions of Part IV of the Act. In an emergency, where it is not possible immediately to apply the provisions of the Mental Health Act, a patient suffering from a mental disorder which is leading to behaviour that is an immediate serious danger to him- or herself or to other people may be given

---

[9] The test that was originally laid down in *Bolam v. Friern Hospital Management Committee* [1957] 1 W.L.R. 582.

[10] *Practice Note (Official Solicitor: Sterilisation)* [1996] 2 F.L.R. 111.

such treatment as represents the minimum necessary response to avert that danger. The administration of such treatment is nor an alternative to giving treatment under the Mental Health Act and its administration should not delay the proper application of the Act to the patient at the earliest opportunity (see Chapter 16).

GENERAL NOTE

4–125 For an expression of doubt as to the correctness of the advice contained in this paragraph, see the General Note to Part IV of the 1983 Act under the heading "The treatment of capable patients".

16. MEDICAL TREATMENT AND SECOND OPINIONS

(Paras 212–230 of the Memorandum)

4–126　16.1 The common law (see Chapter 15) applies to patients detained under the Act but additional provisions affecting medical treatment of detained patients are to be found in Part IV of the Act. Part IV of the Act provides specific statutory authority for forms of medical treatment for mental disorder to be given to most patients liable to be detained, without their consent in certain circumstances. It also provides specific safeguards. Patients "liable to be detained"are those who are detained or have been granted leave of absence (section 17). Part IV also provides specific safeguards to all patients (whether detained or not) in relation to treatments that give rise to special concern.

16.2 The provisions of Part IV can be summarized as follows:
   a.　Section 57—Treatments requiring the patient's consent and a second opinion—psychosurgery and the surgical implantation of hormones for the reduction of male sexual drive. These provisions apply to all patients whether or not they are liable to be detained.
   b.　Section 58—Treatments requiring the patient's consent or a second opinion—the administration of medicine beyond three months and treatment by ECT at any time. These provisions apply to all patients liable to be detained except those detained under section 4, sections 5(2) or 5(4), sections 35, 135, 136 and 37(4); also patients conditionally discharged under section 42(2) and sections 73 and 74. Patients subject to those sections can be treated under common law.
   c.　Section 62—Urgent Treatment—in certain circumstances the safeguards in sections 57 and 58 do not apply where urgent treatment is required (see para 16.40–16.41). Section 62 is only applicable to those patients and types of treatments set out in (a) and (b) above.
   d.　Section 63—Treatments that do not require the patient's consent—all medical treatments for mental disorder given by or under the direction of the patient's rmo and which are nor referred to in sections 57 or 58. This provision applies to the same patients as section 58.

16.3 Everyone involved in the operation of Part IV of the Act should be familiar with:
   a.　the provisions of Part IV of the Act;
   b.　*paras 212–230 of the Memorandum*;
   c.　DHSS circular Dear Doctor Letter (DDL) (84)4.

In addition, rmos should obtain copies of "Advice to Second Opinion Appointed Doctor" published by the Mental Health Act Commission.

16.4 A detained patient is not necessarily incapable of giving consent. '. patient's consent should be sought for all proposed treatments which m lawfully be given under the Act. It is the personal responsibility of tl patient's current rmo to ensure that valid consent has been sought. The interview at which such consent was sought should be properly recorded in the medical notes.

16.5 Part IV of the Act applies to medical treatment for mental disorder. Medical treatment may be interpreted as including care and treatment to alleviate the symptoms of mental disorder.[11] Part IV does not apply to the treatment of physical disorders unless it can reasonably be said that the if physical disorder is a symptom or underlying cause of the mental disorder. If in doubt the rmo should seek legal advice. (See also the Mental Health Act Commission's Guidance Note 3 on Anorexia Nervosa.)

GENERAL NOTE

Medical treatment for mental disorder: A patient can be treated under Part IV if **4–127** such treatment is regarded as being ancillary to the core treatment that the patient is receiving for his mental disorder: see the notes on section 63 of the 1983 Act.

Section 57—Treatments requiring consent and a second opinion

16.6 A decision to give treatment under section 57 requires careful **4–128** consideration because of the ethical issues and possible long-term effects. Procedures for implementing this section must be agreed between the Mental Health Act Commission and the hospitals concerned.

16.7 Before the rmo or doctor in charge of treatment refers the case to the Mental Health Act Commission:

a. the referring doctor should personally satisfy him or herself that the patient is capable of giving valid consent and has consented;

b. the patient and, if the patient agrees, his or her close relatives and caters should be told that the patient's willingness to undergo treatment does not necessarily mean that the treatment will be given. The patient should be made fully aware of the provisions of section 57;

c. for psychosurgery, the consultant considering the patient's case should have fully assessed the patient as suitable for psychosurgery;

d. for psychosurgery, the case should be referred to the Commission before the patient is transferred to the neuro-surgical centre for the operation. The Commission organises the attendance of two appointed persons and a doctor. The appointed persons and the doctor will usually visit and interview the patient at the referring hospital at an early stage in the procedure;

e. for surgical implantation of hormones for the purpose of reducing male sexual drive, the relationship of the sexual disorder to mental disorder, the nature of treatment, the likely effects and benefits of treatment and knowledge about possible long-term effects require considerable care and caution should be observed.

16.8 Section 57 refers to the surgical implantation of hormones only for the reduction of male sexual drive where it is administered as a medical treatment for mental disorder. If there is any doubt as to whether it is a

[11] *R. v. Croydon HA* [1995] 2 W.L.R. 294.

mental disorder which is being treated, independent legal and medical advice must be sought. The advice of the Mental Health Act Commission should also be obtained about arrangements for implementing section 57 where necessary.

Section 58—Treatments requiring consent or a second opinion: ECT

4–129 16.9 When ECT is proposed valid consent should always be sought by the patient's rmo:
- a. if the patient consents the rmo or the Second Opinion Appointed Doctor (SOAD) should complete form 38 and include on the form the proposed maximum number of applications of ECT. In addition a record of the discussion with the patient with reference to his or her capacity to consent should be made by the rmo in the medic notes. Such information should be included in the patient's treatment plan;
- b. if:
   - — the patient withdraws consent which has been given, or
   - — there is a break in the continuity of the patient's detention, or
   - — there is a change in the rmo,
   the form 38 lapses and consent should be given again on a fresh form 38 or a second opinion obtained. Arrangements should be made for ensuring that invalid consent forms are clearly marked as lapsed;
- c. if the patient's valid consent is not forthcoming, or is withdrawn, or if his or her wishes appear to fluctuate and the rmo plans to proceed with the treatment, the rmo must comply with the requirements of section 58, which should be initiated as soon as possible (see paras 16.20–16.34).

GENERAL NOTE

Paragraph b
4–130 *A change in the rmo:* A properly completed form 38 provides legal authority for the patient to be treated under section 58. Section 58 neither states nor implies that this authority will lapse on a change in the patient's rmo; also see the note on paragraph 16.35.

16.10 Patients treated with ECT should be given a leaflet which helps them to understand and remember, both during and after the course of ECT, the advice given about its nature, purpose and likely effects.

Section 58—Treatments requiring consent or a second opinion: medication

a. The first three months

4–131 16.11 The three month period gives time for the doctor to develop a treatment programme suitable for the patient's needs. Even though the Act allows treatment to be given without consent during the first three months the rmo should ensure that the patient's valid consent is sought before any medication is administered. The patient's consent or refusal should be recorded in the case notes. If such consent is not forthcoming or is withdrawn during this period, the rmo must consider whether to proceed in the absence of consent, to give alternative treatment or no further treatment.

16.12 The three month period starts on the occasion when medication for mental disorder was first administered by any means during a period of continuing detention. This does not include detention under sections 5(2) or 5(4) (holding power), section 35 (remand to hospital), section 37(4) (court order for detention in a place of safety), section 135 (warrant for removal to a place of safety), and section 136 (removal to a place of safety). The medication does not necessarily have to be administered continuously throughout the three months. The definition of this period is not affected by renewal of the patient's detention, withdrawal of consent, leave of absence or change in or discontinuance of the treatment. A fresh period will only begin if there is a break in the patient's liability for detention. Detention should never be allowed to expire as a means of enabling a fresh three month period to start.

b. Medication after three months

16.13 A system should be in place for reminding both rmos and patients at least four weeks before the expiry of the three months. Before the three month period ends the patient's current rmo should personally seek his or her consent to any continuing medication, and such consent should be sought for any subsequent administration of medication. A record of the discussion with the patient with reference to his or her capacity to consent should be made by the rmo in the medical notes.

16.14 If the patient consents, the rmo must certify accordingly (form 38). On the certificate the rmo should indicate all drugs proposed, including medication given "as required", either by name or, ensuring that the number of drugs authorised in each class is indicated, by the classes described in the British National Formulary (BNF). The maximum dosage and route of administration should be clearly indicated for each drug or category of drugs proposed.

16.15 Specific advice relating to the inclusion of clozapine in a treatment programme is given in the Mental Health Act Commission's Practice Note 1 (June 1993).

16.16 The original form 38 should be kept with the original detention papers, and copies kept in the case notes and with the patient's medicine chart, so as to ensure that the patient is given only medication to which he or she has consented. It is important that all such additional copies are cancelled if the patient's consent is withdrawn (see para 16.19 below). If the patient's consent is not forthcoming the rmo must comply with the safeguard requirements of section 58. For urgent treatment section 62 may apply (see paras 16.40–16.41).

16.17 The rmo should satisfy him- or herself that consent remains valid. It is advisable to seek a second opinion under the section 58 procedures if there is doubt about whether the patient is consenting or not, or if his or her wishes appear to fluctuate.

c. Nurses and the administration of medication

16.18 Advice on the position of nurses in relation to the administration of medication is given in the Mental Health Act Commission's Practice Note 2 (March 1994)

Withdrawal of consent

4–132   16.19 A patient being treated in accordance with section 58 may withdraw consent at an time. Fresh consent or the implementing of section 58 procedures is then required before further treatment can be carried out or reinstated. Where the patient withdraws consent he or she should receive a clear explanation, which should be recorded in the patient's records:
— of the likely consequences of not receiving the treatment;
— that a second medical opinion under Part IV of the Act may or will be sought, if applicable, in order to authorise treatment in the continuing absence of the patient's consent;
— of the doctor's power to begin or continue urgent treatment under section 62 until a second medical opinion has been obtained, if applicable.
All consent forms which have become invalid because the patient has withdrawn consent must be clearly marked as cancelled.

Procedure for second opinions

a. The Role of the Second Opinion Appointed Doctor (SOAD) [see paras 216–221 of the Memorandum]

4–133   16.20 The role of the SOAD is to provide an additional safeguard to protect the patient's rights. When interviewing a patient the SOAD must determine whether he or she is capable of giving valid consent. If the patient does not give or is not capable of giving consent, the SOAD has to determine whether the treatment proposed by the rmo is likely to alleviate or prevent a deterioration of the patient's condition and should be given.
16.21 The SOAD acts as an individual and must reach his or her own judgment as to whether the proposed treatment is reasonable in the light of the general consensus of appropriate treatment for such a condition. In reaching this judgment the SOAD should consider not only the therapeutic efficacy of the proposed treatment but also, where a capable patient is withholding consent, the reasons for such withholding, which should be given their due weight.
16.22 The SOAD should seek professional opinion about the nature of the patient's disorder and problems, the appropriateness of various forms of treatment including that proposed, and the patient's likely response to different types of treatment. The SOAD should take into account any previous experience of comparable treatment of a similar episode of disorder. The SOAD should give due weight to the opinion, knowledge. experience and skill of those consulted.

b. Responsibilities of the Hospital Managers

16.23 In anticipation of, and preparation for, a consultation under Part IV, the Hospital Managers and their staff should ensure that:
a.   the statutory documents are in order and available to the SOAD;
b.   a system exists for reminding the rmo prior to the expiry of the limit set by section 58 and section 61 and for checking the doctor's response;

c. a system exists for letting the patient know towards the expiry of the "3 month period" that his or her consent, or a second opinion, is required;

d. appropriate personnel, including a person other than a doctor or nurse professionally concerned with the patient's care are available (see para 16.31(b)).

c. Arranging and preparing for the visit of the SOAD

16.24 If a SOAD visit is required, the patient's rmo has the personal responsibility of ensuring that the request is made. He or she should ensure that the arrangements are made with the Mental Health Act Commission. Ordinarily, the Commission aims to arrange for a visit from a SOAD to take place within two working days of the request where ECT is proposed, and, in the case of medication, five working days.

16.25 The treatment proposal for the patient, together with notes of any relevant multidisciplinary discussion, must be given to the SOAD before or at the time of the visit. The Hospital Managers, in consultation with the rmo, are responsible for ensuring that the patient is available to meet the SOAD and that the following people are available in person at the time the SOAD visits:

— the patient's rmo:
— the statutory "consultees" (see para 16.31);
— any other relevant persons;

and that the following documents are available:

— the patient's original detention documents wherever possible or copies of such documents. The original document should be available for viewing by the SOAD if he or she requests;
— all the patient's case notes including records of past responses to similar treatment.

It is desirable that a single professional record is kept for each patient which contains all records relating to that patient. Adequate facilities must be made available for the visit.

d. The visit of the SOAD

16.26 During a visit the SOAD should:

a. in the case of a treatment under section 58, satisfy him- or herself that the patient's detention papers are in order;

b. interview the patient in private if possible. Others may attend if the patient and the SOAD agree, or if it is thought that the doctor would be at significant risk of physical harm from the patient;

c. discuss the case with the patient's rmo face to face, or on the telephone in exceptional circumstances;

d. consult with two other persons professionally concerned with the patient's care as statutorily required (*i.e.* the "statutory consultees"). The SOAD should be prepared, where appropriate, to consult a wider range of persons professionally concerned with the patient's care than those required by the Act and, with the patient's consent, the patient's nearest relative, family, carers or advocates.

4–134   *The SOAD should . . . satisfy him- or herself that the patient's detention papers are in order:* Although the SOAD should satisfy himself that the patient is a detained patient by ensuring that either signed application and medical recommendation forms or a relevant court order exist in respect of the patient, it is not appropriate for the SOAD to subject these forms to detailed scrutiny. If the SOAD detects an apparent error on the face of the forms this will not affect the patient's detained status as the application will remain in place until it is either discharged under section 23, or by a tribunal, or set aside by a court. The SOAD should draw any apparent errors to the attention of the hospital managers ; also see Circular No. DDL (84)4, para. 23.

16.27 The SOAD may not be able to reach a decision at the time of the first visit. In these circumstances the patient should be told of the delay. Once a decision has been reached, it is the rmo's responsibility to inform the patient of the SOAD's decision. Only when the SOAD has signed form 39 may treatment be given without the patient's consent, except as provided in section 62. The SOAD may direct that a review report on the treatment be sent to the Mental Health Act Commission at a date earlier than the next date for review under section 61.

16.28 Every attempt should be made by the rmo and the SOAD to reach agreement. If the SOAD is unable to agree with the rmo, the rmo should be informed by the SOAD personally as soon as possible. It is good practice for the SOAD to give reasons for his or her dissent. Neither doctor should allow a disagreement in any way to prejudice the interests of the patient. If agreement cannot be reached, the position should be recorded in the patient's case notes by the rmo who will continue to have responsibility for the patient's management.

16.29 The opinion given by the SOAD is the latter's personal responsibility. It cannot be appealed against to the Mental Health Act Commission.

16.30 If the patient's situation subsequently changes the rmo may contact the Mental Health Act Commission and request a further second opinion. In these circumstances it is the policy of the Commission to ask the same SOAD to return.

e. Role of the "statutory consultees"

16.31 The SOAD must consult:
a.   a nurse, who must be qualified (nursing assistants, auxiliaries and aides are excluded) and has been professionally concerned with the patient's care;
b.   another person similarly concerned, who has direct knowledge of the patient in their professional capacity, and who is neither a nurse nor a doctor; for example, a social worker, occupational therapist, psychologist, psychotherapist, or pharmacist.

16.32 Any person whom the SOAD proposes to consult must consider whether he or she is sufficiently concerned professionally with the patient's care to fulfil the function. If not, or if the person feels that someone else is better placed to fulfil the function, he or she should make this known to the patient's rmo and the SOAD in good time.

16.33 Both consultees may expect a private discussion (only in exceptional cases on the telephone) with the SOAD and to be listened to with consideration.

16.34 Amongst the issues that the "consultees" should consider commenting upon are:
— the proposed treatment and the patient's ability to consent to it;
— other treatment options;
— the way in which the decision to treat was arrived at;
— the facts of the case, progress, attitude of relatives, etc.;
— the implications of imposing treatment upon a non-consenting patient and the reasons for the patient's refusal of treatment;
— any other matter relating to the patient's care on which the "consultee" wishes to comment.
" Consultees" should ensure that they make a record of their consultation with the SOAD which is placed in the patient's records.

Review of treatment

a. General

16.35 All treatments, whether or not section 61 applies to them, should be **4–135** regularly reviewed and the patient's treatment plan should include derails of when this will take place. Where a patient is receiving treatment under section 58(3)(a), *i.e.* the patient has consented and form 38 has been completed, the form should always have been completed by either the patient's rmo or the SOAD. Although the Act does not direct review of the validity of form 38, it is good practice for them to be reviewed at regular intervals. When such a review is carried out and it is found that the conditions are satisfied a new form 38 should be completed, if appropriate. A new form should also be completed:
— if there is a change in the treatment plan from that recorded;
— if consent is re-established after being withdrawn;
— when there is a break in the patient's detention;
— when there is a permanent change of rmo;
— when the patient's detention is renewed (or annually, whichever is earlier);
— if there is a change in the hospital where the patient is detained.
If the patient no longer consents and it is considered that the treatment should still be given, a second opinion must be sought.

GENERAL NOTE
The implication contained in this paragraph that Form 38 lapses on a change of the **4–136** patient's responsible medical officer, on the renewal of the patient's detention or on the patient being granted leave of absence to be treated in another hospital, is incorrect. The validity of Form 38 will only lapse in the circumstances identified in the note on section 58(3)(a) under the heading "certified". A statutory form should only be completed as a response to a statutory requirement: it should not be completed in order to comply with notions of "good practice".

b. Section 61

16.36 When a patient has been treated under section 57 or section 58, when a SOAD has authorised treatment in the absence of the patient's consent, a review by the Mental Health Act Commission on behalf of the Secretary of State has to take place:

    a.   in the circumstances set out in section 61 (all professionals involved should be familiar with the procedures for completing form MHAC1);

    b.   where the SOAD has time limited his or her certificate or made it conditional on the making of a review report on the treatment at a date earlier than the first statutory review (See MHAC1).

Once the treatment has been reviewed and form MHAC1 completed, a copy of that form should be given to the patient.

16.37 When submitting a report under section 61, the rmo should advise the Mental Health Act Commission if a patient for whom a certificate of second opinion has previously been issued has since given consent and the consent is still valid. After receipt of a review report, the Mental Health Act Commission will, when necessary, send a SOAD to reassess the patient and decide whether the treatment should continue.

Section 63 treatments not requiring the patient's consent

4–137   16.38 Apart from the forms of treatment specified in sections 57 and 58, treatment for the patient's mental disorder which is given by or under the direction of the rmo does not require the patient's consent—although consent should always be sought. As well as medication in the first three months (see paras 16.11–16.12) section 63 covers a wide range of therapeutic activities involving a variety of professional staff and includes in particular psychological and social therapies. Medical treatment is defined in section 145 (see para 16.5 for a reference to relevant case law).

16.39 In practice, it is unlikely that these psychological and social therapies could be undertaken without the patient's acceptance and active co-operation. Acceptance in relation to such procedures requires a clear expression of agreement between the patient and the therapist before the treatment has begun. The agreement should be expressed positively in terms of willingness to co-operate rather than as an indication of passive submission (see also paras 18.1–18.10).

Urgent treatment

4–138   16.40 Any decision to treat a patient urgently under section 62 is a responsibility of the patient's rmo or, in the rmo's absence, of the doctor for the time being in charge of his or her treatment. The rmo, or other doctor, should bear in mind the following considerations:

    a.   Treatment can only be given where it is immediately necessary to achieve one of the objects set out in section 62 and it is not possible to comply with the safeguards of Part IV of the Act. It is insufficient for the proposed treatment to be simply "necessary" or "beneficial."

    b.   The section specifically limits the use of "irreversible" or "hazardous" treatments. The patient's rmo, or other doctor, is responsible for judging whether treatment falls into either of these categories, and whether therefore the Act allows it to be given, having regard to generally accepted medical opinion.

    c.   Urgent treatment given under section 62 can only continue for as long as it is immediately necessary to achieve the statutory objective(s).

d.   Before deciding to give treatment under section 62 the patien
or the doctor for the time being in charge of his or her trea
should wherever possible discuss the proposed urgent treatment
others involved with the patient's care.

It is essential that rmos, or the doctor for the time being in charge of t
patient's treatment, have a clear understanding of the circumstances whe
section 62 applies (see para 16.2.c).

16.41 The Hospital Managers should monitor the use of section 62 in their
hospitals. They should ensure that a form is devised to be completed by the
patient's rmo or the doctor for the time being in charge of the patient's
treatment, every time urgent treatment is given under section 62, giving
details of:

—   the proposed treatment;
—   why it is of urgent necessity to give the treatment;
—   the length of time for which the treatment was given.

Responsibility for operating Part IV

16.42 Promoting the welfare of the patient by the implementation of Part   **4–139**
IV and its safeguards requires careful planning and management. The
patient's rmo is personally responsible for ensuring that Part IV procedures
are followed in relation to that patient. Such responsibility is a continuing
one and will apply even if a doctor other than the rmo acts under section 62.

16.43 Overall responsibility for ensuring that the provisions of the Act are
complied with rests with the Hospital Managers who should ensure that
proper arrangements are made to enable rmos to discharge their responsibilities, but all professional staff involved with the implementation of Part IV
should be familiar with its provisions and the procedures for its implementation in the hospital.

16.44 Patients have a statutory right to be informed about the provisions
of Part IV of the Act as it relates to them. They should be reminded by letter
in addition to receiving the statutory leaflet when either their consent to
treatment is needed or a second opinion is due.

17. PART III OF THE ACT—PATIENTS CONCERNED WITH CRIMINAL PROCEEDINGS

Treatment and care in hospital

17.1 A patient who is remanded to hospital for a report (section 35) or for   **4–140**
treatment (section 36) is entitled to obtain, at his or her own expense, or
through Legal Aid, an independent report on his or her mental condition
from a registered medical practitioner of the patient's choosing for the
purpose of applying to court for the termination of the remand. The Hospital
Managers should help in the exercise of this right by enabling the patient to
contact a suitably qualified and experienced solicitor, or other adviser.

17.2 The consent to treatment provisions of the Act do not apply to
patients remanded under section 35, so in the absence of the patient's
consent, treatment can only be administered in an emergency under the
provisions of the common law (see Chapter 15).

17.3 Where a patient remanded under section 35 is thought to be in need
of medical treatment for mental disorder under Part IV of the Act, the

patient should be referred back to court as soon as possible with an appropriate recommendation, and with an assessment of whether he or she is in a fit state to attend court. If there is a delay in securing a court date, consideration should be given to whether the patient meets the criteria for detention under section 3 of the Act.

17.4 A report prepared in pursuit of a section 35 remand order should contain:

— a statement as to whether a patient is suffering from a specified form of mental disorder as required by the section, identifying its relevance to the alleged offence. The report should not comment on guilt or innocence. It may be appropriate to suggest that a further report be submitted to the court between conviction and sentence;

— relevant social factors;

— any recommendations on care and treatment, including where and when it should take place and who should be responsible.

18. PSYCHOLOGICAL TREATMENTS

4–141   18.1 Psychological treatments carried out competently can be beneficial to patients. If carried out incompetently they can be harmful. Some treatments interfere with patients' basic human rights and it is important that no one deprives a patient of food, shelter, water, warmth, a comfortable environment, confidentiality or reasonable privacy (both physical and in relation to their personal feelings and thoughts). The possibility of misapplication of techniques and serious errors in therapy can be reduced by ensuring that people offering such treatments (on an individual or group basis) are appropriately qualified and supervised, and that they demonstrate a commitment to evidence-based practice. Recruitment and selection procedures should ensure appropriate qualification, using appropriate external assessors. A medical or nursing qualification does nor, in itself, confer competence to practise psychotherapeutic treatment. Membership of, or affiliation to, an appropriate professional body may help to promote the maintenance of a high standard of professional practice.

18.2 The Hospital Managers must ensure that psychological treatment programmes are set out clearly so that they can be understood by staff, patients and relatives. Guidelines should include procedures for noting and monitoring their use. A person with sufficient skills in implementing programmes should be available to monitor procedures as well as the progress of patients.

18.3 Any programme of psychological treatment should form part of a patient's previously agreed care programme. At no time should it be used as a spontaneous reaction to a particular type of behaviour.

18.4 A decision to use any psychological treatment programme for an individual patient should be preceded by a full discussion with the professional staff concerned with the patient.

18.5 Such a programme should be regularly reviewed in the case of each patient, and abandoned if it has proved ineffective or otherwise modified if necessary.

18.6 Patients and, with the patients' consent, their relatives, should be fully informed of the planned use of any such methods as part of a patient's treatment and the patient's consent should always be sought.

18.7 Psychological treatments may proceed in the absence of a patient's consent only where this is justified legally (see Chapters 15 and 16). If consent is not or cannot be given, and the patient is detained, or mentally incapacitated, a locally agreed procedure should be adopted in which the rmo should seek the advice of a suitably qualified person who is not a member of the clinical team responsible for the patient. This could be a psychologist, doctor, social worker or nurse who has received special training that equips them to supervise psychological procedures.

18.8 The rmo can authorise other members of staff to use such programmes. It remains the rmo's responsibility to ensure that those who are so authorised have adequate skills and abilities to carry out the procedures to the required standard. The Hospital Managers must ensure that such members of staff have received relevant training and have regular professional supervision.

Time out

18.9 Time out is a behaviour modification technique which denies a **4–142** patient, for a period of no more than 15 minutes, opportunities to participate in an activity or to obtain positive reinforcers immediately following an incident of unacceptable behaviour. The patient is then returned to his or her original environment. Time out should never include the use of a locked room and should be clearly distinguished from seclusion which is for use in an emergency only and should never form part of a behavioural programme. Time out should:
— form part of a programme which enables the patient to achieve positive goals as well as reducing unwanted behaviour;
— enable a patient, following a change of behaviour, to be subject to fewer restrictions;
— ordinarily not take place in a room which is used for seclusion on other occasions;
— be used only as part of a planned approach to managing a difficult or disturbed patient.

18.10 Hospitals should have clear written policies about the use of time out. These should include a clear definition of this form of therapy and procedures for noting and monitoring its use on individual patients.

19. PATIENTS PRESENTING PARTICULAR MANAGEMENT PROBLEMS

19.1 Patients, or people who may become patients, may behave in such a **4–143** way as to disturb others around them, or their behaviour may present a risk to themselves or others around them or those charged with their care. These problems may occur anywhere, and the issues addressed here relate to general health care settings as well as to psychiatric facilities. It is important to distinguish:
— the needs of patients who pose an immediate threat to themselves or those around them and where techniques for the immediate management and control of a difficult situation must be used; and

655

— the need for some patients to remain in a secure environment as a result of a perceived risk to the general public or as a result of pending or past decisions of the courts, but who pose no immediate threat to those around them.

Behaviour contributing to problems in management

4–144   19.2 Patients' behaviour should be seen in its context. Professionals should not categorise behaviour as disturbed without taking account of the circumstances under which it occurs or assume that a previous history of disturbance means the patient will behave that way again. However they should also recognise that though they may experience the disturbed behaviour as intermittent, fellow residents or carers will experience it through 24 hours.

19.3 Behaviour which can give rise to managerial problems can include:

— refusal to participate in treatment programmes;
— prolonged verbal abuse and threatening behaviour;
— destructive behaviour;
— self-injurious behaviour;
— physical attacks on others;
— going missing.

Possible causes

4–145   19.4 In exploring preventive methods staff should be aware of some possible, often very evident causes of problem behaviours:

— boredom and lack of environmental stimulation;
— too much stimulation, noise and general disruption;
— overcrowding;
— antagonism, aggression or provocation on the part of others;
— influence of alcohol or substance abuse;
— an unsuitable mix of patients;
— the rewarding of undesirable behaviour by attention.

General preventive measures

4–146   19.5 In addition to individual care plans much can be done to prevent behaviour problems by examining the ward or other environment and pinpointing problem areas. Among such general measures are:

— keeping patients fully informed of what is happening and why;
— giving each patient a defined personal space and a secure locker for the safe keeping of possessions;
— ensuring access to open space;
— organising the ward (in hospital) to provide quiet rooms, recreation rooms, single sex areas and visitors' rooms;
— providing all necessary help for patients with any type of disability or impairment;
— ensuring access to a telephone;
— providing structured activities by professional staff;
— seeking patients' co-operation, and encouraging their participation in the general running of the ward;

— identifying those patients most at risk and ensuring appropriate levels of observation;
— encouraging energetic activities for younger patients;
— providing training for staff in the management of disturbed behaviour, including de-escalation techniques, diversional therapies and other non-physical intervention skills;
— monitoring the skill mix of staff;
— monitoring the mix of patients;
— developing a therapeutic relationship between each patient and a key worker/nurse;
— consistent application and monitoring of any individual programme;
— ensuring that patients' complaints are dealt with quickly and fairly.

Restraint

19.6 Restraint may take many forms. It may be both verbal and physical **4–147** and may vary in degree from an instruction to seclusion. The purposes of restraint are:
— to take immediate control of a dangerous situation;
— to contain or limit the patient's freedom for no longer than is necessary; and
— to end or reduce significantly the danger to the patient or others.
The most common reasons for restraint are:
— physical assault;
— dangerous threatening or destructive behaviour;
— non-compliance with treatment;
— self-harm or risk of physical injury by accident;
— extreme and prolonged over-activity likely to lead to physical exhaustion.
19.7 The basic considerations which should underlie any methods aimed at reducing and eliminating unacceptable behaviour should take account of:
— the need for individual care planning;
— the physical condition of the patient;
— the physical environment of the ward or unit;
— the need to maintain adequate staffing levels.
Where the risk of problem behaviour is identified in a group of patients, but its onset cannot be predicted, an agreed strategy for dealing with such behaviour should be developed. This should include continuing risk assessment and management.
19.8 If the patient is not detained but restraint in any form has been deemed necessary, whether as an emergency or as part of the patient's treatment plan, consideration should be given to whether formal detention under the Act is appropriate, especially if restraint has occurred on a repeated basis.

GENERAL NOTE
Consideration should be given to whether formal detention under the Act is **4–148** *appropriate:* It would only be lawful for the use of restraint to lead to the detention of a patient under the Act if the restraint was used:
(1) to prevent a mentally capable patient from leaving hospital;
(2) to ensure that a mentally capable patient received treatment for his mental disorder; or

(3) to prevent a mentally incapable patient from leaving hospital.

The use of restraint on a mentally incapable patient to ensure that necessary treatment is given or as a response to a behavioural disturbance is authorised under common law, even if the restraint "has occurred on a repeated basis". The use of the Act in these circumstances would be unlawful as the "detention of the patient" would not be "warranted" for the purposes of section 2(2)(a) and criterion in section 3(2)(c) that the patient's treatment "cannot be provided unless he is detained under [section 3]" could not be satisfied.

Training

4–149 19.9 Staff in NHS hospitals and private mental nursing homes who are ordinarily likely to find themselves in situations where training in the management of actual or potential aggression might be necessary should attend an appropriate course taught by a qualified trainer. The trainer should have completed an appropriate course of preparation designed for health care settings and preferably validated by one of the health care bodies (English National Board or Royal College of Nursing Institute).

Methods of restraining behaviour

4–150 19.10 Physical restraint should be used as little as possible. Restraint which involves tying (whether by means of tape or by using a part of the patient's garments) to some part of a building or to its fixtures or fittings should never be used. Staff must make a balanced judgment between the need to promote an individual's autonomy by allowing him or her to move around at will and the duty to protect that person from likely harm. Where physical restraint is used staff should:

— record the decision and the reasons for it;
— state explicitly in a care plan under what circumstances restraint may be used;
— record what form the restraint may take and how its application will be reviewed; and
— document and review every episode of restraint.

19.11 Restraining aggressive behaviour by physical means should be done only as a last resort and never as a matter of course. It should be used in an emergency when there seems to be a real possibility that significant harm would occur if no intervention is made. Any initial attempt to restrain aggressive behaviour should, as far as the situation will allow, be non-physical:

a. assistance should be sought by call system or orally;
b. one member of the team should assume control of the incident;
c. the patient should be approached where possible and agreement sought to stop the behaviour, or to comply with a request. Approaches to deaf and hearing impaired patients should be made within their visual field (not from behind) and gestures used to engage them in calm communication;
d. where possible an explanation should be given of the consequences of refusing the request from staff to desist;
e. other patients or people not involved in the use of restraint should be asked to leave the area quietly.

19.12 A large number of staff acting in an uncoordinated way in attempting to restrain a patient can be counter-productive whereas fewer, but well briefed staff are likely to be more effective. If non-physical methods have failed or immediate action is needed, the person in control of the incident may decide to use physical restraint and should organise a small number of staff members to assist in managing the incident. Any restraint used should:

— be reasonable in the circumstances;
— apply the minimum force necessary to prevent harm to the patient or others:
— be used for only as long as is absolutely necessary;
— be sensitive to gender and race issues.

In doing so staff should:

a. make a visual check for weapons;
b. aim at restraining arms and legs from behind if possible, and seek to immobilise swiftly and safely;
c. continuously explain the reason for sustaining the action;
d. enlist support from the patient for voluntary control as soon as possible. If the patient is deaf or hearing impaired he or she must be able to see the staff member in control of the incident so that the attempt to communicate can be sustained;
e. not use neck holds;
f. avoid excess weight being placed on any area, but particularly on stomach and neck;
h. not slap, kick or punch.

Post-incident analysis and support should be developed for both staff and patients.

GENERAL NOTE
See the General note to section 5 of the 1983 Act for a consideration of the **4–151** common law powers available to staff.

Restraint and complaints

19.13 The Hospital Managers should appoint a senior officer who should: **4–152**
— be informed of any patient who is being subjected to any form of restraint that lasts for more than two hours;
— see the patient as soon as possible;
— visit and talk to the patient about the incident and ascertain if he or she has any concerns or complaints and if so assist in putting them forward.

The senior officer may delegate this task to a member of staff who has a good relationship with the patient.

Policy on restraint

19.14 All providers should have clear, written policies on the use of **4–153** restraint of which all staff should be aware. The policy should include provision for review of each incident of restraint, and its application should be audited and reported to the Hospital Managers.

Medication

4–154   19.15 Medication to reduce excitement and activity may be useful to facilitate other therapeutic interventions. Other than in exceptional circumstances, the control of behaviour by medication should only be used after careful consideration, and as part of a treatment plan (see Chapters 15 and 16). Medication which is given for therapeutic reasons may become a method of restraint if used routinely for prolonged periods. Before medication is given, the doctor in charge should consider whether it would be lawful and therapeutic in the longer term. Medication should never be used to manage patients in the absence of adequate staffing.

Seclusion

4–155   19.16 Seclusion is the supervised confinement of a patient in a room, which may be locked to protect others from significant harm. Its sole aim is to contain severely disturbed behaviour which is likely to cause harm to others.
   Seclusion should be used:
   — as a last resort;
   — for the shortest possible time.
   Seclusion should not be used:
   — as a punishment or threat;
   — as part of a treatment programme;
   — because of shortage of staff;
   — where there is any risk of suicide or self-harm.
   Seclusion of an informal patient should be taken as an indicator of the need to consider formal detention.
   19.17 Hospitals should have clear written guidelines on the use of seclusion which:

   — ensure the safety and well being of the patient;
   — ensure the patient receives the care and support rendered necessary by his or her seclusion both during and after it has taken place;
   — distinguish between seclusion and "time-out" (see paras 18.9–18.10);
   — specify a suitable environment taking account of patient's dignity and physical well being;
   — set out the roles and responsibilities of staff;
   — set requirements for recording, monitoring, reviewing the use of seclusion and any follow-up action.

Procedure for seclusion

4–156   19.18 The decision to use seclusion can be made in the first instance by a doctor or the nurse in charge. Where the decision is taken by someone other than a doctor, the rmo or duty doctor should be notified at once and should attend immediately unless the seclusion is only for a very brief period (no more than five minutes).
   19.19 A nurse should be readily available within sight and sound of the seclusion room at all times throughout the period of the patient's seclusion, and present at all times with a patient who has been sedated.
   19.20 The aim of observation is to monitor the condition and behaviour of

the patient and to identify the time at which seclusion can be terminated. The level should be decided on an individual basis and the patient should be observed continuously. A documented report must be made at least every 15 minutes.

19.21 The need to continue seclusion should be reviewed
— every 2 hours by 2 nurses (1 of whom was not involved in the decision to seclude), and
— every 4 hours by a doctor.

A multidisciplinary review should be completed by a consultant or other senior doctor, nurses and other professionals, who were not involved in the incident which led to the seclusion if the seclusion continues for more than:
— 8 hours consecutively; or
— 12 hours intermittently over a period of 48 hours.

If the need for seclusion is disputed by any member of the multidisciplinary team, the matter should be referred to a senior manager.

GENERAL NOTE

1 of whom was not involved in the decision to seclude: In *R. v. Ashworth Special* **4–157**
Hospital Trust, ex p. Munjaz, September 28, 2000, this requirement did not feature in the hospital's seclusion procedure on the ground that, in the context of Ashworth Hospital, it might not be practicable for every review of seclusion to be carried out by two nurses, one of whom had no involvement with the original decision. Jackson J., in holding that there was no justification for the total abandonment by the hospital of this requirement, said that the Seclusion Procedure ought to contain a provision along the following lines: "Where practicable, one of the nursing staff who carries out a review of seclusion should not have been involved in the original decision to seclude."

Every 4 hours by a doctor: In the *Ashworth* case, above, the hospital's seclusion procedure required that after three days a patient's seclusion need only be reviewed by a doctor once a day. Jackson J. held that:

(i) the Code of Practice is directed at all instances of seclusion, including those that last for more than three days;
(ii) the review of seclusion by doctors has an important function in that it provides a second opinion from an objective and independent source;
(iii) the hospital's policy represented too great a departure from the Code;
(iv) a review by a doctor twice a day subsequent to the patient being secluded for three days would be appropriate; and
(v) the statement in the "Report of the Committee of Inquiry into Complaints about Ashworth Hospital" (Cm. 2028-I) that "the ending of seclusion ... should never in any sense be liked to the patient expressing remorse or sorrow for any assault or damage that had occurred" (p.203) goes too far. If a patient is genuinely remorseful for earlier acts of violence, that is a factor favouring the end of seclusion that should not be ignored.

Conditions of seclusion

19.22 The room used for seclusion should: **4–158**

— provide privacy from other patients;
— enable staff to observe the patient at all times;
— be safe and secure;
— not contain anything which could cause harm to the patient or others;
— be adequately furnished, heated, lit and ventilated;

— be quiet but not soundproofed and with some means of calling for attention; the means of operation should be explained to the patient. Staff may decide what a patient may take into the seclusion room, but the patient should always be clothed.

Record keeping

4–159   19.23 Detailed and contemporaneous records should be kept in the patient's case notes of any use of seclusion, the reasons for its use and subsequent activity, cross-referenced to a special seclusion book or forms which should contain a step-by-step account of the seclusion procedure in every instance. The principal entry should be made by the nurse in charge of the ward and the record should be countersigned by a doctor and a senior nurse. The Hospital Managers should monitor and regularly review the use of seclusion.

Locking ward doors on open ward

4–160   19.24 The management, security and safety of patients should be ensured by means of adequate staffing. Service providers are responsible for ensuring that staffing is adequate to prevent the need for the practice of locking patients in wards, individual rooms or any other area.

19.25 The nurse in charge of any shift is responsible for the care and protection of patients and staff and the maintenance of a safe environment. This responsibility includes the care of patients who have been detained in hospital because they are considered a danger to other people. The nurse in charge of a shift has discretion for all or part of that shift to lock the door of the ward, to protect patients or others, because of the behaviour of a patient or patients. The nurse in charge should:

    a.   inform all staff of why this action is being taken, how long it will last and a notice to that effect should be displayed at the entrance to the ward;

    b.   inform the patient or patients whose behaviour has led to the ward door being locked of the reasons for taking such action;

    c.   inform all other patients that they may leave on request at any time and ensure that someone is available to unlock the door;

    d.   inform his or her line manager of the action taken;

    e.   inform the rmo or nominated deputy;

    f.   keep a record of this action and reasons, and make use of an incident reporting procedure.

19.26 When handing over to the relieving shift the nurse in charge should discuss in detail the reasons for the action taken. Where the relieving nurse considers it necessary to keep the door locked, (a) to (f) above apply. Where any ward is locked for three consecutive shifts (excluding night duty) the senior manager responsible for that ward should be informed.

19.27 The safety of informal patients who would be at risk of harm if they wandered out of a ward or mental nursing home at will, should be ensured by adequate staffing and good supervision. Combination locks and double handed doors should be used only in units where there is a regular and significant risk of patients wandering off accidentally and being at risk of harm. There should be clear policies on the use of locks and other devices and a mechanism for reviewing decisions. Every patient should have an individual care plan which states explicitly why and when he or she will be prevented from leaving the ward. Patients who are not deliberately trying to leave the ward, but who may wander out accidentally, may legitimately be deterred from leaving the ward by those devices. In the case of a patient who persistently and/or purposely attempts to leave a ward or mental nursing home, whether or not they understand the risk involved, consideration must be given to assessing whether they would more appropriately be formally detained under the Act in a hospital or a mental nursing home registered to take detained patients, than remain as informal patients (see Chapter 2).

General Note

A patient who persistently and/or purposely attempts to leave a ward: A patient's **4–161** purposeful attempt to leave a ward need not be persistent for it to justify a Mental Health Act assessment. Consideration should be given to assessing the compliance of those patients who lack the physical ability to make persistent and/or purposeful attempt to leave a ward.

Locked wards and secure areas

19.28 There are some detained patients in general psychiatric hospitals **4–162** and mental nursing homes who may be liable to cause danger to themselves or others. For these patients professional judgment, or the requirement of a Court as an alternative to imprisonment, may point to the need for varying degrees of security. In such cases, where the need for physical security is a prerequisite, the patient's rmo, in consultation with the multi-disciplinary team, should ensure that:

a. he or she has carefully weighed the patient's individual circumstances and the degree of danger involved;
b. he or she has assessed the relative clinical considerations of placing the patient in a physically secure environment, in addition to or as opposed to providing care by way of intensive staffing;
c. treatment in secure conditions lasts for the minimum necessary period;
d. arrangements are made to enable his or her speedy return to an open ward when physical security is no longer required.

19.29 Service providers should ensure that:

a. a ward/area is specifically designated for this purpose with adequate staffing levels;
b. written guidelines are provided, setting out:
— the categories of patient for whom it is appropriate to use physically secure conditions;
— those for whom it is nor appropriate;
— a clear policy for practice, procedure and safeguards for treatment in secure conditions.

Observation, care and management of patients at risk of self injury

19.30 Patients must be protected from harming themselves when the drive **4–163** to self injury is a result of mental disorder for which they are receiving care and treatment. On admission, all patients should be assessed for immediate

and potential risks of going missing, suicide, self harm and self neglect, taking into account their social and clinical history. Individual care plans should include:
— a clear statement of the degree of risk of self harm;
— the measures required to manage the risk safely;
— the level of observation needed to ensure the patient's safety.
Staff must balance the potentially distressing effect on the patient of close observation, particularly when one-to-one observation is proposed for many hours, against the risk of self injury. Levels of observation and risk should be regularly reviewed and a record made of agreed decisions.

19.31 Staff should observe changes in the patient's:
— general behaviour;
— movement;
— posture;
— speech;
— expression of ideas;
— appearance;
— orientation;
— mood and attitude;
— interaction with others;
— reaction to medication.

Deprivation of daytime clothing

4–164 19.32 Patients should never be deprived of appropriate daytime clothing during the day, with the intention of restricting their freedom of movement. They should not be deprived of other aids necessary for their daily living.

Staff

4–165 19.33 Staff must try to gain the confidence of patients so that they can learn to recognise potential danger signs. Staff should understand when to intervene to prevent harm from occurring. Continuity of staffing is an important factor both in the development of professional skills and consistency in managing patients.

Management responsibilities

4–166 19.34 Staff who take part in incidents involving control and restraint may experience a degree of stress. Hospital Managers should ensure that they are given the opportunity to discuss these issues with them (the managers) and with colleagues. Hospital Managers should formulate and make available to staff a clear written operational policy on all forms of restraint, including post-incident analysis and support for patients and staff.

20. LEAVE OF ABSENCE (SECTION 17)

4–167 20.1 A patient who is currently liable to be detained in a hospital or a specified hospital unit, can only leave that hospital, or hospital unit, lawfully—even for a very short period—by being given leave of absence in accordance with the provisions of section 17 or by way of transfer to another hospital under section 19. Leave of absence can be an important part of a patient's treatment plan. Only the patient's rmo, with the approval of the Home Secretary in the case of restricted patients, can grant a detained patient leave of absence. Rmos are not entitled to grant leave of absence to patients detained under sections 35, 36 or 38. Except where the patient is detained in a specified hospital unit, no formal procedures are needed to allow a patient to go to different parts of the hospital or hospital grounds as part of the care programme.

GENERAL NOTE

For the position where a patient is moved to a facility in the hospital which is administered by a different NHS Trust, see the note on "from the hospital" in section 17(1). **4–168**

20.2 Leave of absence can be granted by the rmo for specific occasions or for longer indefinite or specific periods of time. The period of leave may be extended in the patient's absence. The granting of leave should not be used as an alternative to discharging the patient.

20.3 **The power to grant leave (section 17)**

a. Unrestricted patients

The rmo cannot delegate the decision to grant leave of absence to any other doctor or professional. The rmo is responsible for undertaking any appropriate consultation, and may make leave subject to conditions which he or she considers necessary in the interests of the patient or for the protection of other people. Only the rmo can grant leave of absence to a patient formally detained under the Act. In the absence of the rmo (for example, if he or she is on annual leave or otherwise unavailable) permission can only be granted by the doctor who is for the time being in charge of the patient's treatment. Where practicable this should be another consultant psychiatrist, a locum consultant or specialist registrar approved under section 12(2) of the Act. The granting of leave cannot be vetoed by the Hospital Managers. **4–169**

b. Restricted patients

Any proposal to grant leave has to be approved by the Home Secretary who should be given as much notice as possible, together with full details of the proposed leave. **4–170**

GENERAL NOTE

Paragraph (b)

Has to be approved by the Home Secretary: See the guidance on leave of absence which was published by the Home Office in June 1996. **4–171**

Short-term leave

20.4 The rmo, with the authority of the Home Secretary if the patient is subject to restrictions, may decide to authorise short-term local leave, which may be managed by other staff. For example, the patient may be given leave **4–172** for a shopping trip of two hours every week, with the decision on the particular two hours left to the discretion of the responsible nursing staff. It is crucial that such decisions fall within the terms of the grant of periodic leave by the rmo, and that he or she reviews decisions and their implementation from time to time and explicitly records the outcome in writing (see para. 20.6).

Longer periods of leave

4–173 20.5 Leave of absence should be properly planned, if possible well in advance. Leave may be used to assess an unrestricted patient's suitability for discharge from detention. The patient should be fully involved in the decision to grant leave and should be able to demonstrate to the professional carers that he or she is likely to cope outside the hospital. Subject to the patient's consent there should be detailed consultation with any appropriate relatives or friends (especially where the patient is to reside with them) and with community services. Leave should not be granted if the patient does not consent to relatives or friends who are to be involved in his or her care being consulted.

Recording and information

4–174 20.6 The granting of leave and the conditions attached to it should be recorded in the patient's notes and copies given to the patient, any appropriate relatives or friends and any professionals in the community who need to know. Hospitals should adopt a local record form on which the rmo can authorise leave and specify the conditions attached to it.

Care and treatment while on leave

4–175 20.7 The rmo's responsibilities for the patient's care remain the same while he or she is on leave although they are exercised in a different way. The duty to provide after-care under section 117 includes patients who are on leave of absence.

20.8 A patient granted leave under section 17 remains "liable to be detained" and the provisions of Part IV of the Act continue to apply. If it becomes necessary to administer treatment in the absence of the patient's consent under Part IV, consideration should be given to recalling the patient to hospital. The refusal of treatment would not on its own be sufficient grounds for recall (see para 20.11). Such a recall direction should be in writing.

Patients in custody or in other hospitals

4–176 20.9 The rmo may direct that the patient remains in custody while on leave of absence, either in the patient's own interests or for the protection of other people. The patient may be kept in the custody of any officer on the staff of the hospital or of any person authorised in writing by the Hospital Managers. Such an arrangement is often useful, for example, to enable patients to participate in escorted trips, or to have compassionate home leave.

20.10 The rmo may also require the patient, as a condition of leave, to reside at another hospital and he or she may then be kept in the custody of an officer of that hospital. The patient's detention can be renewed during a period of leave. However, consideration should be given as to whether it would be more appropriate to move the patient from one hospital to another under the provisions of section 19 rather than being given section 17 leave.

Recall to hospital

20.11 The rmo may revoke a patient's leave at any time if he or she **4–177** considers this to be necessary in the interests of the patient's health or safety or for the protection of other people. The rmo must consider very seriously the reasons for recalling a patient and the effects this may have on him or her. For example a refusal to take medication would not on its own be a reason for revocation; the rmo would have to be satisfied that this was necessary in the patient's interests or for the safety of others. The rmo must arrange for a notice in writing revoking the leave to be served on the patient or on the person for the time being in charge of the patient. The reasons for recall should be fully explained to the patient and a record of such explanation placed in the patient's case notes. A restricted patient's leave may be revoked either by the rmo or the Home Secretary.

20.12 It is essential that any appropriate relatives and friends, especially where the patient is residing with them whilst on leave, and other professionals in the community who need to know should have easy access to the patient's rmo if they feel consideration should be given to the return of the patient to hospital before his or her leave is due to end.

Duration of leave/renewal of authority to detain

20.13 A period of leave cannot last longer than the duration of the **4–178** authority to detain which was current when leave was granted. If the authority to detain an unrestricted patient might express whilst the patient is on leave the rmo may examine the patient and consider writing a report renewing the detention when the patient is still on leave, if the rmo thinks that further formal in-patient treatment is necessary and statutory criteria are met.[12]

21. ABSENCE WITHOUT LEAVE (SECTION 18)

(Paras 70–71 of the Memorandum)

21.1 Section 18 provides powers for the return of patients who are absent **4–179** from hospital without leave, fail to return to hospital at the end of an authorised leave of absence or when recalled, or are absent without permission from an address where they have been required to live either by the conditions of their leave of absence, or by their guardian. The hospital must know the address of a person on leave of absence.

21.2 A patient who is liable to be detained in hospital may be taken into custody and returned to hospital or the place where he or she is required to live by an ASW, any officer on the staff of the hospital, any police officer, or any person authorised in writing by the Hospital Managers.

[12] *R. v. Managers of Warley Hospital, ex p. Barker* [1998] C.O.D. 309.

21.3 A patient who has been required to reside in another hospital as a condition of leave of absence can also be taken into custody by any officer on the staff of that hospital or by any person authorised by the managers of that hospital. Otherwise responsibility for the safe return of the patient rests with the detaining hospital. If the absconding patient is initially taken to another hospital that hospital may, if authorised by the managers of the detaining hospital in writing, detain the patient while arrangements are made for his or return. Such authority can be provided by fax.

21.4 A person absent without leave while under guardianship may be taken into custody by any officer on the staff of the local social services authority, or by any person authorised in writing by the guardian or the local social services authority.

Local policies

4–180 21.5 It is the responsibility of the Hospital Managers, and of the local Social Services Authority where guardianship is concerned, to ensure that there is a clear written policy in relation to action to be taken when a detained patient or a person subject to guardianship goes absent without leave. All staff should be familiar with this policy.

21.6 The policy should include guidance as to:

a. the immediate action to be taken by any member of staff who becomes aware that a patient has gone absent without leave, including the requirement that they immediately inform the nurse in charge of the patient's ward who should in turn ensure that the patient's rmo is immediately informed;

b. the circumstances when a search of the hospital and its grounds should be initiated;

c. the circumstances when other local agencies with an interest, including the social services authority, should be notified, in the case of a patient detained in hospital;

d. the circumstances when the police should be informed, in the case of a patient detained in hospital. This should be the subject of agreed local arrangements with the police. The police should be asked to assist in returning a patient to hospital only if necessary, but they should always be informed immediately of the absence without leave of a patient who is considered to be vulnerable, dangerous or who is subject to restrictions under Part III of the Act. There may be other cases where, although the help of the police is not needed, a patient's history makes it desirable to inform them that he or she is absent without leave in the area. Whenever the police are asked for help in returning a patient they must be informed of the time limit for taking him or her into custody;

e. how and when the patient's nearest relative should be informed. In almost all cases the patient's nearest relative should be informed immediately the patient goes absent without leave and any exceptions to this requirement should be clearly set out in the policy;

f the action that should be taken in the case of someone received into guardianship who is absent without leave from the place where he or she is required to reside. This should include immediate notification of the specified guardian and the social services authority.

22. DUTIES OF THE HOSPITAL MANAGERS

22.1 The Hospital Managers have a central role in operating the **4–181** provisions of the Act. In England and Wales, in general, NHS Hospitals are owned by NHS trusts. For these hospitals the Trusts themselves are defined as the "managers" for the purposes of the Act. But the three special hospitals are owned by the Secretary of State and Hospital Managers' functions are exercised on behalf of the Secretary of State by the Special Health Authorities which have been set up to manage those hospitals as Special Hospital Authorities. In the case of a mental nursing home the person or persons in whose name the home is registered are managers for the purposes of the Act.

22.2 It is the Hospital Managers who have the power to detain patients who have been admitted under the Act. They have the key responsibility for seeing that the requirements of the Act are followed. In particular they must ensure that patients are detained only as the Act allows, that their treatment and care accord fully with its provisions, and that they are fully informed of, and are supported in exercising, their statutory rights.

22.3 The main responsibilities which the Act confers on the Hospital Managers are set out in paras 22.7–22.16 More detailed guidance is given in the relevant chapters of the Code. The exercise of the Hospital Managers' powers to discharge patients is dealt with in Chapter 23.

Exercise of the Hospital Managers' functions

22.4 The Trust or Hospital Authority should appoint a committee or **4–182** sub-committee to undertake the Hospital Managers' functions. The legislation allows such a committee to be made up of Directors of the Trust or Hospital Authority, or outside people, or a mixture of the two. Most of the Hospital Managers' responsibilities may be delegated to officers of the Trust or Hospital Authority but the power to discharge patients may only be exercised by three or more committee members who are nor also employees of the Trust (see Chapter 23). The Hospital Managers retain responsibility for the performance of all delegated duties and must ensure that those acting on their behalf are competent to undertake them.

22.5 The Trust or Hospital Authority retains the ultimate responsibility for the performance of the Hospital Managers' duties, and in view of this the committee should, where possible, include members of the Trust or Hospital Authority Board. The committee should report formally to the Board with an account of its activities not less than once a year. Trusts and Hospital Authorities must ensure that all those appointed to exercise the Hospital Managers' functions are properly informed about the working of the Act and receive suitable training in their role. Such appointments should be made for a fixed period and reappointments should be preceded by a review.

22.6 For detained patients placed in a mental nursing home under a contract with a Trust, the Trust committee which is appointed to undertake

Hospital Managers' functions should also monitor the way those functions are performed by the managers of the mental nursing home.

Specific duties

Admission

4–183 22.7 It is the Hospital Managers' duty to ensure that the grounds for admitting the patient are valid and that all relevant admission documents are in order. Any officer to whom the responsibility is delegated must be competent to make such a judgment, and to identify any error in the documents which may require rectification. Guidance on the receipt, scrutiny and rectification of documents is given in chapter 12 and *paras 44–54 of the Memorandum.*

22.8 Where a patient is admitted under the Act following an application by his or her nearest relative, the Hospital Managers should request the relevant local social services department to provide them with the social circumstances report required by section 14.

Transfer between hospitals

4–184 22.9 Section 19 of the Act, and the regulations[13] made under it allow the Hospital Managers to transfer a detained patient from one hospital to another. Officers to whom this responsibility is delegated must ensure that the transfer is being made for valid reasons and that the needs and interests of the patient have been fully considered. For restricted patients, the Hospital Managers' power is subject to the prior agreement of the Home Secretary.

GENERAL NOTE

4–185 The hospital managers can also use section 19 to transfer a detained patient into the guardianship of a local social services authority, or of any person approved by the authority.

Discharge

4–186 22.10 Section 23 provides for the rmo to discharge a detained patient by giving an order in writing. The Hospital Managers should ensure that a suitable form is available upon which this order can be given and that it is received and acknowledged by someone authorised to receive and scrutinise documents on their behalf.

22.11 The exercise of the Hospital Managers' own powers to discharge patients is dealt with in Chapter 23.

Information for health and local authorities

4–187 22.12 Where a Tribunal hearing has been arranged, the Hospital Managers should inform Health and Local Authorities so that they are able to consider the need for a section 117 care planning meeting before the

[13] Regulations 7 and 9 of the Mental Health (Hospital, Guardianship and Consent to Treatment) Regulations 1983 (S.I. 1983 No. 893) amended by the Mental Health (Hospital, Guardianship and Consent to Treatment) (Amendment) Regulations 1996 (S.I. 1996/540).

Tribunal takes place and, if necessary, provide a report to the Tribunal (see para 27.7).

Information for patients and relatives

22.13 Sections 132 and 133 require the Hospital Managers to give certain **4–188** information to detained patients and their relatives. Guidance on the exercise of this duty is given in Chapter 14.

Correspondence of patients

22.14 Section 134 allows the Hospital Managers to withhold outgoing mail **4–189** from detained patients if the addressee has requested this in writing to the Hospital Managers, the patient's rmo or the Secretary of State. The fact that mail has been withheld must be recorded in writing and the patient must be informed.

22.15 The Hospital Managers of the special hospitals have wider powers under section 134 to withhold both incoming and outgoing mail from patients in certain circumstances. This is subject to review by the Mental Health Act Commission. The Hospital Managers of the special hospitals should have a written policy for the exercise of these powers which should be discussed with the Commission.

Access to Mental Health Review Tribunals

22.16 If a patient, or the patient's nearest relative, does not exercise his or **4 190** her right to apply to a Mental Health Review Tribunal, section 68 requires the Hospital Managers to refer a patient's case to the Tribunal:
  a. when six months have elapsed since the patient was admitted under section 3 or transferred from guardianship under section 19 if the patient has not applied for a Tribunal during the first six months (this does not apply to patients admitted under a hospital order or transferred from prison to hospital); and
  b. at the time when the patient's detention is renewed if he or she has not then had a Tribunal review for three years or more; this applies also to unrestricted patients admitted under a hospital order or prison transfer direction.
The reference should be made within one week of the patient's detention being renewed.

22.17 The Hospital Managers should ensure that a patient who wishes to apply to a Tribunal is given all necessary help with his or her application.

22.18 The Hospital Managers should ensure that when a Tribunal hearing has been arranged officers of the Trust provide reports (including any reports about after-care) to the Tribunal within the time limits set in the Tribunal rules.

23. THE HOSPITAL MANAGERS' POWER OF DISCHARGE (SECTION 23)

23.1 Section 23 gives the Hospital Managers (see para 22.1) the power to **4–191** discharge an unrestricted patient from detention. Discharge of a restricted patient requires the consent of the Home Secretary. The power may be exercised on behalf of the Hospital Managers by three or more members of a committee or sub-committee formed for that purpose. In the case of a Trust or Hospital Authority the committee or sub-committee must not include any employee or officer of the Trust or Hospital Authority concerned.

GENERAL NOTE

4–192   *Discharge of a restricted patient:* Although hospital managers have the power to order the discharge of a restricted patient under section 23, this power is exercisable only with the consent of the Home Secretary (s.41(3)(c)(iii)). A restricted patient is therefore entitled to request the hospital managers to consider whether they should conduct a review of his detention. A blanket refusal by the managers to consider such cases would be unlawful. A review need not necessarily be conducted by way of a hearing (see the note on para. 23.9).

Principles

4–193   23.2 The legislation does not define either the criteria or the procedure for reviewing a patient's detention. However the exercise of this power is subject to the general law and to public law duties which arise from it. The Hospital Managers' conduct of reviews must satisfy the fundamental legal requirements of fairness, reasonableness and lawfulness:
   a.   they must adopt and apply a procedure which is fair and reasonable:
   b.   they must not make irrational decisions, that is, decisions which no body of Hospital Managers, properly directing themselves as to the law and on the available information, could have made: and
   c.   they must not act unlawfully, that is, contrary to the provisions of the Act, any other legislation and any applicable regulations.

GENERAL NOTE

4–194   *The hospital managers' conduct of reviews:* As the managers are performing a quasi-judicial function when exercising their discretion under section 23, they must abide by the rules of natural justice. These rules require decision makers to act fairly, in good faith and without bias and to afford each party the opportunity to adequately state his case. Reasons must be given to justify the decision reached.

Review panels

4–195   23.3 The Trust or Hospital Authority retains the final responsibility for the proper performance of the Hospital Manager duties in considering whether or not patients should be discharged. To reflect this the review panel should, if possible, include a non-executive member of the Board. The panel must have at least three members. The Board must ensure that all those appointed to this role are properly informed and experienced and receive suitable training (see also para 22.5).

GENERAL NOTE

4–196   *At least three members:* A majority decision would suffice.
         23.4 The person or persons registered in respect of a mental nursing home see para 22.1) retain final responsibility for the performance of the Hospital

Managers' duties in considering whether or not patients should be discharged. They may delegate their discharge function to a committee or sub-committee. It is desirable that detention is reviewed by people who are neither on the staff of the home nor have a financial interest.

23.5 Mental nursing home managers, and Trusts and Health Authorities should, where possible, co-operate over exercising their respective functions in relation to the discharge of patients detained in mental nursing homes.

When to review

23.6 The Hospital Managers should ensure that all patients are aware that **4–197** they may seek discharge by the Hospital Managers and of the distinction between this and their right to a Mental Health Review Tribunal hearing.

23.7 The Hospital Managers may undertake a review at any time at their discretion, but they must review a patient's detention when the rmo submits a report under section 20(3) renewing detention. Such reports should normally be submitted not less than two weeks before the current period of detention expires, to enable the review to take place as close as possible to the expiry date.

GENERAL NOTE
There are four points to note on this paragraph: (1) a request from the patient is **4–198** not a pre-condition to a review taking place; (2) the only legislative requirement placed on managers were a report under section 20(3) is submitted is to "consider" the report (see Part II of Form 30); (3) as the rmo must submit a section 20(3) report to the managers within two months of the expiry date of the patient's detention, the two-week deadline would appear to be unnecessarily tight; and (4) it is lawful for the managers' review to take place after the expiration of the current period of detention (*R. v. Managers of Warlingham Park Hospital, ex p. B* (1992) 22 B.M.L.R. 1).

23.8 The Hospital Managers must consider holding a review:
a.   when they receive a request from a patient;
b.   when the rmo makes a report under section 25(1) opposing a nearest relative's application for the patient's discharge.

GENERAL NOTE
A review need not necessarily be conducted by way of a hearing (see the note on **4–199** para. 23.9).

23.9 The Hospital Managers should consider carefully whether it is appropriate to hold a review in the case of patients detained for treatment, if there has been a review in the last 28 days and there is no evidence that the patient's condition has changed or a Mental Health Review Tribunal hearing is due in the next 28 days.

GENERAL NOTE
It is difficult to see how the managers could "consider carefully" the appropriate- **4–200** ness of having a review without actually undertaking the review. A distinction should be made between having a review of the papers concerning the patient, which would include a report by the patient's rmo, and having a hearing. A review of the papers (with, perhaps, one member of the panel interviewing the patient) could lead the managers to conclude that there had been no significant change in the patient's circumstances since the previous review. A hearing could be held if such a change was identified. If a patient makes a request for a review in circumstances where a Mental Health Review Tribunal hearing in respect of that patient is imminent, it is suggested that the review be adjourned until after the hearing and that the managers then

conduct a paper review. A managers' hearing should only be held if a significant change in the patient's circumstances had occurred subsequent to the tribunal hearing.

23.10 In the cases covered by para 23.8(a) and (b) above the patient, or nearest relative, will be actively seeking his or her discharge. In the case where the rmo submits a report renewing detention, the Hospital Managers are under a statutory obligation to consider the renewal even if the patient does not object to it. The procedures adopted need to differentiate "uncontested" renewals from reviews where detention is contested by the patient (see paras 23.13–23.19).

Criteria

4–201   23.11 The Act does not define specific criteria to be applied by the Hospital Managers when considering the discharge of a patient who is detained or liable to be detained. The essential yardstick in considering a review application is whether the grounds for admission or continued detention under the Act are satisfied. To ensure that this is done in a systematic and consistent way the review panel should consider the following questions, in the order stated:
—   Is the patient still suffering from mental disorder?
—   If so, is the disorder of a nature or degree which makes treatment in a hospital appropriate?
—   Is detention in hospital still necessary in the interests of the patient's health or safety, or for the protection of other people?
If the panel is satisfied from the evidence presented to them that the answer to any of these questions is "no", the patient should be discharged.

GENERAL NOTE
4–202   The managers should also consider questions relating to the "treatability test" and to whether a patient who has been granted section 17 leave needs to be subject to the responsible medical officer's recall power, if such questions are relevant to the patient's circumstances: see the note on "the managers" in section 23(2).

Immediate discharge from detention or a decision not to order the patient's discharge are not the only options open to managers when undertaking a review: adjourning the hearing, making recommendations relating to supervised discharge or guardianship, and ordering either the conditional or deferred discharge of the patient are other options that could be considered: see the note on "the managers" in section 23(2).

23.12 In cases where the rmo has made a report under section 25(1), the managers should not only consider the three questions above but also the following question:
—   Would the patient, if discharged, be likely to act in a manner dangerous to other persons or to him- or herself?[14]
This question focuses on the probability of dangerous acts, such as causing serious physical injury, not merely the patient's general need for safety and others' general need for protection: it provides a more stringent test for continuing detention. If, on consideration of the report under section 25(1) and other evidence, the managers disagree with the rmo and decide the answer to this question is "no" they should usually discharge the patient.

[14] *R. v. Riverside Mental Health NHS Trust, ex parte Huzzey* (1998).

Likely to act in a manner dangerous: Dangerous behaviour is probably not **4–203** confined to behaviour that is likely to cause physical injury: see the note on "dangerous" in section 25(1).

They should usually discharge the patient: In the *Huzzey* case, below, Latham J. said that on making such a finding the managers "would be likely, in almost all circumstances" to order the discharge of the patient.

Conduct of reviews—where detention is contested

23.13 The review should be conducted so as to ensure that the case for **4–204** discharging, or continuing to detain, the patient is properly considered against the above criteria and in the light of all relevant evidence. This means that the review panel needs to have before it sufficient information about the patient's past history of care and treatment, and details of any future plans. The main source of this will be the patient's CPA documentation or care plan. It is essential that the panel is fully informed about any history of violence or self-harm, and any risk assessment which has been conducted.

23.14 In advance of the hearing the review panel should obtain written reports from the patient's rmo and others who are directly involved in the patient's care such as the key worker, named nurse, social worker and clinical psychologist. The patient should receive copies of the reports unless the Hospital Managers are of the opinion that the information disclosed would be likely to cause serious harm to the physical or mental health of the patient or any other individual. The patient's nearest or most concerned relatives, and any informal carer should be informed of the review, if the patient consents. Relatives and carers may be invited to put their views to the panel in person. If the patient objects to this a suitable member of the professional care team should be asked to include the relatives' and/or carer's views in his or her report.

Cause serious harm: It would be more appropriate for the managers to use the **4–205** same test that Mental Health Review Tribunals are required to consider in these circumstances, *i.e.* would disclosure of the report "adversely affect the health or welfare of the patient or others" (MHRT Rules, r. 12(2)).

23.15 The report submitted by the rmo should cover the history of the patient's care and treatment and details of his or her CPA or care plan, including all risk assessments. Where there is a rmo report under section 20 renewing detention (form 30) the panel should also have a copy of it before them. This should be supplemented by a record of the consultation undertaken by the rmo in accordance with section 20(5). The written reports should be considered by the panel alongside the documentation compiled under the CPA.

23.16 The procedure for the conduct of the hearing is for the Hospital Managers to decide, but generally it needs to balance informality against the rigour demanded by the importance of the task. Key points are:
— The patient should be given a full opportunity, and any necessary help, to explain why he or she wishes to be discharged.
— The patient should be allowed to be accompanied by a friend or representative of his or her own choosing to help in putting his or her point of view to the panel.

— The rmo and other professionals should be asked to give their views on:
  — whether the patient's continued detention is justified; and
  — the factors on which those views are based.
— The patient and the other parties to the review should, if the patient wishes it, be able to hear each other's statements to the panel and to put questions to each other. However the patient should always be offered the opportunity of speaking to the panel alone.

GENERAL NOTE

Conduct of the hearing: See the General Note to paragraph 23.2.

4–206   *Opportunity of speaking to the panel alone:* As the managers are obliged to abide by the rules of natural justice, the patient cannot be given an undertaking that this discussion will remain confidential. If the patient reveals previously unknown information which is pertinent to his detained status, fairness would dictate that the information be shared with his responsible medical officer.

23.17 While the panel must give full weight to the views of all the professionals concerned in the patient's care its members will not, as a rule, be qualified to form clinical assessments of their own. If there is a divergence of views about whether the patient meets the clinical grounds for continued detention, especially in relation to matters such as risk assessment, the panel should consider an adjournment to seek further medical or other professional advice.

GENERAL NOTE

4–207   *Clinical grounds for continued detention:* No such grounds exist, although the questions that the managers are recommended to address in paragraph 23.11 clearly have a clinical dimension to them. If, having considered those questions, the managers are of the opinion that they require further information to enable them to arrive at a decision they should adjourn to enable that information to be presented to them. The mere fact that they do not accept a "clinical" opinion would not, of itself, justify an adjournment.

23.18 In applying the criteria in para 23.11 and 23.12, and deciding in the light of them whether or not to discharge the patient, the panel needs to consider very carefully the implications for the patient's subsequent care. The presence or absence of adequate community care arrangements may be critical in deciding whether continued detention is necessary in the interests of the patient's health or safety or for the protection of others. It the panel conclude that the patient ought to be discharged but arrangements for after-care need to be made, they may adjourn the panel, for a brief period, to enable a full CPA/care planning meeting to take place.

Decision

4–208   23.19 The Hospital Managers' decision following the review, and the reasons for it, should be recorded. The decision should be communicated immediately, both orally and in writing, to the patient, to the nearest relative with the patient's consent, and to the professionals concerned. At least one of the members of the panel should see the patient to explain in person the reasons for the decision. Copies of the papers relating to the review, and the formal record of the decision, should be placed in the patient's records.

Reasons: It is not sufficient for the managers merely to reiterate the statutory **4–209** grounds: the reasons must deal with the substantial points that have been raised at the review; also see the notes on rule 23(2) of the Mental Health Review Tribunal Rules 1983.

Uncontested renewals

23.20 If a patient's detention is renewed under section 20, and the patient **4–210** has indicated that he or she does not object to this, the review panel should meet to consider the papers and should interview the patient and his or her key worker. If the panel then agree that the patient should not be discharged the review can be concluded and the outcome recorded in the patient's records.

24. COMPLAINTS

24.1 Guidance on the arrangements introduced in April 1996 for dealing **4–211** with complaints about NHS treatment and services is contained in the document *Complaints: Listening … Acting … Improving. Guidance on implementation of the NHS Complaints Procedure (EL(96) 19)*, and parallel guidance issued in Wales in March 1996. All providers of NHS services have been directed under the Hospital Complaints and Procedures Act 1985 to have complaints handling arrangements in place.

24.2 Trusts and Authorities are responsible for ensuring that staff are adequately trained in the requirements and procedures of the new system, and in dealing with complaints. Staff have the responsibly of bringing to the attention of all patients, both orally and in writing, the procedures for making a complaint through the NHS complaints system, and, in relation to detained patients, their rights to complain to the Mental Health Act Commission. If a patient is unable to formulate a complaint, he or she should be given reasonable assistance to do so by staff. It is the personal responsibility of all members of staff involved in a patient's care to give such assistance where necessary.

Recording

24.3 The guidance on the NHS complaints system states that as a matter of **4–212** good practice complaints records should be kept separate from health records. Patients' health records should contain only information which is strictly relevant to their care and treatment.

25. PERSONAL SEARCHES

25.1 Managers of hospitals and mental nursing homes admitting patients **4–213** under the Act should ensure that there is an operational policy on the searching of patients and their belongings. The policy should be based on legal advice.

25.2 The purpose of the policy is to meet two objectives which may, at least in part, be in conflict: firstly the creation and maintenance of a therapeutic environment in which treatment may take place; and secondly, the maintenance of the security of the establishment and the safety of patients, staff and the public.

25.3 The policy may extend to routine and random searching without cause, but only in exceptional circumstances, for example, where the dangerous or violent criminal propensities of patients create a self evident and pressing need for additional security.[15]

GENERAL NOTE

4–214   In the *Broadmoor* case (see footnote) the Court of Appeal held that the express power of detention must carry with it a power of control and discipline, including, where necessary, a power of search with or without cause and despite individual medical objection. The specific regime of random and/or routine searches proposed by a hospital falls to be judged by *Wednesbury* principles. This means that the specific regime adopted by a hospital must be proportionate to the level of risk posed by the patient population to the maintenance of a safe and therapeutic environment. A search policy must also take account of a patient's right of respect for his private life under Article 8 of the European Convention on Human Rights. The court endorsed the provision of the *Broadmoor* search policy which requires the responsible medical officer "to consider whether a proposed search would harm the patient's mental health and, if that is his view, to refer it to the Medical Director for decision, who should take into account that view and the interests of security and safety of the individual and the hospital."

The searching of patients at Ashworth, Broadmoor and Rampton Hospitals is governed by the Safety and Security in Ashworth, Broadmoor and Rampton Directions 2000. These Directions, which are made by the Secretary of State for Health under the sections 16D, 17 and 126(4) of the National Health Service Act 1977 and section 4(5) of the Regulation of Investigatory Powers Act 2000, are also concerned with the searching of members of staff, contractors, visitors and visiting children and other issues relating to the security of those hospitals. The Directions can be found at http://www.doh.gov.uk/hospitaldirections/.

25.4 In all cases, the consent of the patient should be sought before a search is attempted. If consent is duly given, the search should be carried out with due regard for the dignity of the individual and the need to ensure maximum privacy.

25.5 If consent is refused, the rmo for the patient should first be contacted so that any clinical objection to a search by force may be raised. If no such objection is raised, the search should proceed as set out in para. 25.8.

25.6 If a clinical objection is raised by the rmo, but the person empowered to search wishes nonetheless to proceed, the matter should be referred to the medical director of the hospital for decision.

25.7 Any delay in respect of paragraphs 25.5 and 25.6 should be kept to a minimum. While the matter is being resolved, a patient should be kept under observation and isolated from other patients. The patient should be told what is happening and why, in terms appropriate to his or her understanding.

25.8 If a search is to proceed without consent, it should be carried out with due regard for the dignity of the individual and the need to ensure maximum privacy. The minimum force necessary should be used. A search of a patient's person should be carried out by a member of the same sex unless necessity dictates otherwise.

25.9 If items belonging to a patient are removed, the patient should be given a receipt for the items and informed where they are being kept.

[15] *R. v. Broadmoor Special Hospital Authority, ex p. S.* [1998] C.O.D. 199.

26. VISITING PATIENTS DETAINED IN HOSPITAL OR REGISTERED MENTAL NURSING HOMES

The right to be visited

26.1 All detained patients are entitled to maintain contact with and be **4–215** visited by anyone they wish to see, subject only to some carefully limited exceptions. Maintaining contact with friends and relatives is recognised as an important element in a patient's treatment and rehabilitation. The decision to prohibit a visit by a person whom the patient has requested to visit or agreed to see should be regarded as a serious interference with the rights of the patient and to be taken only in exceptional circumstances. This should only occur after other means to deal with the problem have been exhausted. Any decision to exclude a visitor should be fully documented and available for independent scrutiny by the Mental Health Act Commission.

GENERAL NOTE

All detained patients are entitled to . . . be visited: Hospital authorities have the right **4–216** to control who is allowed to be at the hospital and under what circumstances. Under common law visitors to a hospital are licensees and the person who has responsibility for a hospital ward can, on behalf of the hospital and at her absolute discretion, withdraw the license and request the visitor to leave. If the visitor does not leave the ward on such a request being made, he becomes a trespasser and reasonable force can be used to remove him.

The Report of the Committee of Inquiry into the Personality Disorder Unit, Ashworth Special Hospital (1999) said that it "should be clearly understood that the Special Hospitals have the right to refuse entry to the Hospital to a visitor who refuses to be searched" (para. 2.12.31).

Grounds for excluding a visitor

26 2. There are two principal grounds which may justify the exclusion of a visitor:

a. Restriction on clinical grounds

It will sometimes be the case that a patient's relationship with a relative, **4–217** friend or supporter is anti-therapeutic (in the short or long term) to an extent that discernible arrest of progress or even deterioration in the patient's mental state is evident and can reasonably be anticipated if contact were not to be restricted. Very occasionally, concern may centre primarily on the potential safety of a particular visitor to a disturbed patient. The grounds for any decision by the rmo, taken after full discussion with the patient's multi-disciplinary care team, should be clearly documented and explained to the patient and the person concerned, orally and in writing.

b. Restriction on security grounds

The behaviour of a particular visitor may be, or have been in the past, disruptive to a degree that exclusion from the hospital or mental nursing home is necessary as a last resort. Examples of such behaviour include: incitement to abscond, smuggling of illicit drugs/alcohol into the hospital, mental nursing home or unit, transfer of potential weapons, or unacceptable aggression or unauthorised media access. A decision to exclude a visitor on the grounds of his or her behaviour should be fully documented and explained to the patient orally and in writing. Where possible and appropriate the reason for the decision should be communicated to the person concerned.

GENERAL NOTE
4–218   The exclusion of a visitor to a detained patient will not contravene the European Convention on Human Rights if one of the grounds in Article 8(2) of the Convention is satisfied.

Visiting of patients by children

4–219   26.3 Hospitals should have written policies on the arrangements about the visiting of patients by children, which should be drawn up in consultation with local social services authorities. A visit by a child should only take place following a decision that such a visit would be in the child's best interests. Decisions to allow such visits should be regularly reviewed.

GENERAL NOTE
4–220   Further guidance to NHS trusts, Health Authorities and Social Services Authorities on the implementation of this guidance is set out in Department of Health Circular HSC 1999/222.

Directions, issued under section 17 of the National Health Service Act 1977, governing visits by children to the special hospitals, were made on July 23, 1999 to Ashworth, Broadmoor and Rampton Hospital Authorities as Circular HSC 1999/160. They came into force on September 1, 1999 and were amended on August 10, 2000 (see Part A of Circular HSC 2000/027). These Directions were found to be lawful and not in breach of Article 8 of the European Convention on Human Rights in *R. (on the application of L) v. Secretary of State for Health* [2001] 1 F.L.R. 406. *Per* Scott Baker J.: "If there are special circumstances in which the patient has good reason for being visited by a child who is not within the permitted category relationship the remedy is to apply to the court for an order under the Children Act 1989." Guidance to local social services authorities on the steps to be undertaken by an authority in receipt of a request by a special hospital on whether it is in the best interests of a child to visit a named patient is contained in Department of Health Circulars LAC (99) 23 and LAC (2000) 18.

Child: i.e., a person under the age of 18. The potential child visitor could be married to the patient.

Facilitation of visiting

4–221   26.4 The hospital or mental nursing home should be sufficiently flexible to enable regular visits to the patient, if he or she wishes. Ordinarily, inadequate staff numbers should not be allowed to deter regular visiting. The facilities provided for visitors should be comfortable and welcoming, and for children, child-friendly. Consideration should be given to meeting the needs of visitors who have travelled long distances.

GENERAL NOTE
4–222   *Ordinary, inadequate staff numbers should not be allowed to deter regular visiting:* Unsupervised visits should not be allowed if this would compromise the security of high security hospitals: see paragraph 2.12.33 of the Ashworth Report, above.

Other forms of communication

26.5 Every effort must be made to assist the patient, where appropriate, to **4–223** make contact with relatives, friends and supporters. In particular patients should have readily accessible and appropriate day time telephone facilities and no restrictions should be placed upon dispatch and receipt their mail over and above those referred to in section 134 of the Act.

GENERAL NOTE
Telephone facilities: The Ashworth Report, above, recommended "that it is **4–224** essential to control and monitor the use of ward-based telephones carefully in order to prevent abuse, control fraud and prevent the introduction into the Hospital of prohibited substances and articles" (para. 2.12.37). In *R. (on the application of N.) v. Ashworth Special Hospital Authority and the Secretary of State for Health* [2001] EWHC Admin 339, a patient challenged a provision in the Safety and Security in Ashworth, Broadmoor and Rampton Hospital Directions 2000, which confers a discretionary power on each hospital authority to record and subsequently listen to, a random 10 per cent of the outgoing and incoming telephone calls of patients at the hospitals (Direction 29(3)). Newman J. held that the provision of random monitoring, whilst constituting an interference with patients' rights under Article 8 of the European Convention on Human Rights, is directed to a legitimate aim, namely the discharge of the Secretary of State's duty under section 4 of the National Health Service Act 1977, and that the direction was a proportionate response to the permitted purpose of reducing the security risks at the three hospitals. The application for judicial review was dismissed.

Hospital Managers

26.6 Hospital Managers should regularly monitor the exclusion from the **4–225** hospital or mental nursing home of visitors to detained patients.

27. AFTER-CARE

27. 1 While the Act defines after-care requirements only in very broad **4–226** terms, it is clear that a central purpose of all treatment and care is to equip patients to cope with life outside hospital and function there successfully without danger to themselves or other people. The planning of this needs to start when the patient is admitted to hospital.

27.2 These objectives apply to all patients receiving treatment and care from the specialist psychiatric services, whether or not they are admitted to hospital and whether or not they are detained under the Act. They are embodied in the Care Programme Approach (CPA) set out in Circular HC(90)23/LASSL(90)11, and in the Welsh Office Mental Illness Strategy (WHC(95)40). The key elements of the CPA are:
— systematic arrangements for assessing people's health and social care needs;
— the formulation of a care plan which addresses those needs;
— the appointment of a key worker to keep in close touch with the patient and monitor care;
— regular review and if need be, agreed changes to the care plan.

27.3 Section 117 of the Act requires Health Authorities and local Social Services Authorities, in conjunction with voluntary agencies, to provide after-care for certain categories of detained patients. This includes patients given leave of absence under section 17. The after-care of detained patients should be included in the general arrangements for implementing the CPA, but because of the specific statutory obligation it is important that all patients who are subject to section 117 are identified and records kept of them. There is a section 117 after-care entitlement when the patient stays in hospital informally after ceasing to be detained under the Act, and also when a patient is released from prison, if they have spent part of their sentence detained in hospital. There are special considerations to be taken into account in the case of patients who are subject to restrictions under Part III of the Act (see Chapter 29).

27.4 NHS Managers and Directors of Social Services should ensure that all staff are aware of the CPA and related provisions. Further guidance on the discharge of mentally disordered people and their continuing care in the community is given in HSG(94)27/LASSL(94)4 and WHC(95)7 and WHC (96)26. The relationship between the CPA, section 117 after-care and local authority arrangements for care management is more fully explained in *Building Bridges—Guide to arrangements for inter-agency working for the care and protection of severely mentally ill people (Department of Health 1995)*.

27.5 Before the decision is taken to discharge or grant leave to a patient, it is the responsibility of the rmo to ensure, in consultation with the other professionals concerned, that the patient's needs for health and social care are fully assessed and the care plan addresses them. If the patient is being given leave for only a short period a less comprehensive review may suffice but the arrangements for the patient's care should still be properly recorded.

27.6 The rmo is also responsible for ensuring that:
— a proper assessment is made of risks to the patient or other people;
— in the case of offender patients, the circumstances of any victim and their families are taken into account;
— consideration is given to whether the patient meets the criteria for after-care under supervision, or under guardianship (see Chapters 13 and 28); and
— consideration is given to whether the patient should be placed on the supervision register established in accordance with HSG(94)5.

Mental Health Review Tribunals and managers' hearings

4–227 27.7 The courts have ruled[16] that in order to fulfil their obligations under section 117 Health Authorities and Local Authority Social Services Authorities must take reasonable steps to identify appropriate after-care facilities for a patient before his or her actual discharge from hospital. In view of this, some discussion of after-care needs, including social services and other relevant professionals and agencies, should take place before a patient has a Mental Health Review Tribunal or managers' hearing, so that suitable after-care arrangements can be implemented in the event of his or her being discharged (see para 22.12).

[16] *R. v. Ealing District Health Authority ex parte Fox* [1993] 3 All E.R. 170.

Who should be involved

27.8 Those who should be involved in consideration of the patient's **4–228** after-care needs include:
— the patient, if he or she wishes and/or a nominated representative;
— the patient's rmo;
— a nurse involved in caring for the patient in hospital;
— a social worker/care manager specialising in mental health work;
— the GP and primary care team;
— a community psychiatric/mental health nurse;
— a representative of relevant voluntary organisations;
— in the case of a restricted patient, the probation service;
— subject to the patient's consent, any informal carer who will be involved in looking after him or her outside hospital;
— subject to the patient's consent, his or her nearest relative[17];
— a representative of housing authorities, if accommodation is an issue.

27.9 It is important that those who are involved are able to take decisions regarding their own and as far as possible their agency's involvement. If approval for plans needs to be obtained from more senior levels (for example, for funding) it is important that this causes no delay to the implementation of the care plan.

Considerations for after-care

27.10 Those concerned must consider the following issues: **4–229**
a.   the patient's own wishes and needs, and those of any dependents;
b.   the views of any relevant relative, friend or supporter of the patient;
c.   the need for agreement with authorities and agencies in the area where the patient is to live;
d.   in the case of offender patients, the circumstances of any victim and their families should be taken into account when deciding where the patient should live;
e.   the possible involvement of other agencies, *e.g.* probation, voluntary organisations;
f.   the establishing of a care plan, based on proper assessment and clearly identified needs, including:
     — day time activities or employment
     — appropriate accommodation
     — out-patient treatment
     — counselling, and personal support
     — assistance in welfare rights and managing finances
     — a contingency plan should the patient relapse.
g.   the appointment of a key worker (see para 27.2) from either of the statutory agencies to monitor the care plan's implementation, liaise and co-ordinate where necessary and report to the senior officer in their agency any problems that arise which cannot be resolved through discussion;
h.   the identification of any unmet need.

---

[17] There are special considerations governing consultation with the nearest relative of a patient subject to after-care under supervision: see Chapter 28.

27.11 The professionals concerned should establish an agreed outline of the patient's needs, taking into account his or her social and cultural background, and agree a time-scale for the implementation of the various aspects of the plan. All key people with specific responsibilities with regard to the patient should be properly identified. Once plans are agreed it is essential that any changes are discussed with others involved with the patient before being implemented. The plan should be recorded in writing.

27.12 The care plan should be regularly reviewed, It will be the responsibility of the key worker to arrange reviews of the plan until it is agreed that it is no longer necessary. The senior officer in the key worker's agency responsible for after-care arrangements should ensure that all aspects of the procedure are followed.

28. AFTER-CARE UNDER SUPERVISION

(Paras 113–140 of the Memorandum)

4–230   28.1 After-care under supervision was introduced in April 1996 by the Mental Health (Patients in the Community) Act 1995. In the introductory guidance, HSG(96)11/LAC(96)8, it is referred to as "supervised discharge".

Purpose

4–231   28.2 After-care under supervision is an arrangement by which a patient who has been detained in hospital for treatment under the provisions of the Act may be subject to formal supervision after he or she is discharged. Its purpose is to help ensure that the patient receives the after-care services to be provided under section 117 of the Act. It is available for patients suffering from any of the four forms of mental disorder in the Act but is primarily intended for those with severe mental illness.

Criteria for use of supervision

4–232   28.3 The Act may be used to ensure after-care is provided for patients who:
— have been detained for treatment;
— need suitable after-care in respect of their mental disorder to prevent substantial risk of serious harm to themselves or other people, or of serious exploitation.

28.4 Before the patient is discharged, he or she must have a community rmo, who will be responsible for treatment after discharge. The patient must also have an identified supervisor who is a suitably qualified and experienced member of the multi-disciplinary community team. For patients living in England, the supervisor will also fulfil the role of key worker under CPA.

28.5 If a patient needs to receive after-care within a formal structure but he or she does not meet all the criteria for after-care under supervision guardianship under section 7 of the MHA 1983 (see Chapter 13) may be used.

Implementation

28.6 Before the supervision application is made the responsible Health **4–233** Authority, or the service provider acting for the authority, should meet the responsible Local Authority and seek to agree the arrangements for providing the after-care, including the requirements to be imposed on the patient under the Act. The procedure for this needs to be agreed as part of local liaison arrangements, which should identify the officer who is to act for the local Social Services Authority. The after-care arrangements will have to be drawn up as part of the normal discharge planning process, following the principles of the CPA in England and the Welsh Office Mental Illness Strategy (WHC(95)40) in Wales and in accordance with the formal consultation requirements in the Act.

28.7 The rmo who makes the supervision application is responsible for consulting both the current and the proposed future care team about the arrangements for after-care and the requirements to be imposed. The rmo should ensure that agreement about a care plan is reached between all involved. Details of the after-care to be provided must be attached to the supervision application and the rmo must list the requirements to be imposed and name the supervisor and rmo.

Admission to hospital

28.8 After-care under supervision will end completely if the patient is **4–234** admitted to hospital under section 3 or 37 of the Act. If the patient is admitted to hospital under section 2, or informally, the after-care will merely be suspended: the patient temporarily ceases to receive after-care and have requirements imposed. The period of after-care under supervision will continue to run whilst the patient is in hospital and if it does not expire it will continue after discharge for the remainder of the period, if any. In the case of an informal patient, if the period of after-care under supervision would expire before the expected date of discharge, the need for renewal should be considered in the normal way and any necessary action taken. In the case of a patient admitted under section 2, if the period expires before discharge it will be deemed to be extended for 28 days after discharge for the purpose of renewal. The same will apply if the period of after-care under supervision has up to 28 days to run after the discharge of a patient detained under section 2.

Further guidance

28.9 Further guidance on after-care under supervision can be found in **4–235** *Guidance on Supervised Discharge (After-care under Supervision) and Related Provisions* which was published under HSG(96)11/LAC(96)8 and WHC(96)11 and which remains extant.

29. PART III OF THE ACT—PATIENTS CONCERNED WITH CRIMINAL PROCEEDINGS

Discharge and supervision

4–236   29.1 Those involved in the supervision of a conditionally discharged restricted patient should have copies of and be familiar with *Supervision and After-Care of Conditionally Discharged Restricted Patients* (HO/DHSS notes of guidance 1987 and the guidance for social supervisors in this series updated in 1997) and *Recall of Mentally Disordered Patients subject to restrictions on discharge* (HSG(93)20/LAC(93)9).

Recall

4–237   29.2 If a conditionally discharged restricted patient requires hospital admission, it will nor always be necessary for the Home Secretary to recall the patient to hospital. For example,

a. The patient may be willing to accept treatment informally. In these circumstances, however, care should be taken to ensure that the patient's consent is freely given, if he or she is capable of giving consent. If the patient is incapable of giving consent, it is advisable to consider whether treatment may be given under the common law doctrine of necessity or whether the Home Secretary should recall the patient.

b. In some cases it may be appropriate to consider admitting the patient under Part II of the Act as an alternative.[18]

c. It may not always be necessary to recall the patient to the same hospital from which he or she was conditionally discharged. In some cases recall to hospital with a lesser, or greater degree of security will be appropriate.

29.3 When a recall is being considered this should be discussed between the doctor, the social supervisor and the Mental Health Unit of the Home Office.

29.4 When a patient is recalled, the person taking him or her into custody should explain that the patient is being recalled to hospital by the Home Secretary and will be given a fuller explanation later. As soon as possible after admission to hospital, and in any event within 72 hours of admission, the rmo or deputy, and an ASW or a representative of the hospital management, should explain to the patient the reason for the recall and ensure, in so far as the patient's mental state allows, that he or she understands. The patient should also be informed that his or her case will be referred to a Mental Health Review Tribunal within one month.

29.5 The patient's rmo should ensure that:

— the patient is given assistance to inform his or her legal adviser (if any);

— subject to the patient's consent, his or her nearest relative and/or other relative or friend is told.

---

[18] *R. v. North West London Mental Health Trust, ex parte Stewart* (1998).

Return to court

29.6 All professionals concerned with ensuring the return to court of a **4–238** patient on remand or under an interim hospital order should be familiar with the contents of paras 31–33 of Home Office circular number 71/1984 on the implementation of sections 35, 36, 38 and 40(3) of the Mental Health Act. When a patient has been admitted on remand or subject to an interim hospital order, it is the responsibility of the hospital to return the patient to court as required. The court should give adequate of time to confirm the arrangements for escorting the patient to and from notice of the hearing. The hospital should liaise with the courts in plenty hospital. The hospital will be responsible for providing a suitable escort for the patient when travelling from the hospital to the court and should plan for the provision of necessary staff to do this. The assistance of the police may be requested if necessary. Once on the court premises, the patient will come under the supervision of the police or prison officers there.

GENERAL NOTE
Home Office Circular No. 71/1984: The relevant paragraphs are reproduced in the **4–239** note on section 35(9).

30. PEOPLE WITH LEARNING DISABILITIES

General

30.1 The guidance given elsewhere in the Code applies to patients with **4–240** learning disabilities. This chapter gives guidance on a number of particular issues of importance to this group of patients.

30.2 Very few people with learning disabilities are detained under the Act. Where people with learning disabilities fall within the legal definition of mental disorder they may be considered for admission under section 2 and detention under sections 5, 135 and 136. Other admission sections can only be considered if the person falls within the legal definition of mental impairment or severe mental impairment. But admission of a person with learning disability for treatment under the Act may also be considered if he or she also suffers from another form of mental disorder (for example mental illness).

Communication

30.3 The assessment of a person with learning disabilities requires special **4–241** consideration to enable communication with the person being assessed. Where possible the ASW should have had experience of working with people with learning disabilities or be able to call upon someone who has. It is important that someone who knows the patient and can communicate with him or her is present at the assessment. The ASW should seek assistance from the community team for learning disabilities.

Assessment

4–242 30.4 No patient should be classified under the Act as mentally impaired or severely mentally impaired without an assessment by a consultant psychiatrist in learning disabilities and a formal psychological assessment. This assessment should be part of a complete appraisal by medical, nursing, social work and psychology professionals with experience in learning disabilities, in consultation with a relative, friend or supporter of the patient. Contact with the specialist hospital units for deafness and mental health may help to forestall deaf people being wrongly assessed as learning disabled. These procedures should also be followed, except in emergencies, where it is proposed that a patient is to be admitted under section 2 on the grounds of mental disorder.

Mental impairment/severe mental impairment (legally defined in section 1)

4–243 30.5 The identification of an individual who falls within these legal categories is a matter for clinical judgement, guided by current professional practice and subject to the relevant legal requirements. Those assessing the patient must be satisfied that he or she displays a number of characteristics; these are difficult to define in practice. The following is general guidance in relation to the key factors or components of these legal categories.

Incomplete or arrested development of mind. This implies that the features that determine the learning disability were present at some stage which permanently prevented the usual maturation of intellectual and social development. It excludes persons whose learning disability derives from accident, injury or illness occurring after that point usually accepted as complete development.

Severe or significant impairment of intelligence. The judgment as to the presence of this particular characteristic must be made on the basis of reliable and careful assessment.

Severe or significant impairment of social functioning. The evidence of the degree and nature of social competence should be based on reliable and recent observations, preferably from a number of sources such as social workers, nurses and psychologists. Such evidence should include the results of one or more social functioning assessment tests.

Abnormally aggressive behaviour. Any assessment of this category should be based on observations of behaviour which lead to a conclusion that the actions are outside the usual range of aggressive behaviour, and which cause actual damage and/or real distress occurring recently or persistently or with excessive severity.

Irresponsible conduct. The assessment of this characteristic should be based on an observation of behaviour which shows a lack of responsibility, a disregard of the consequences of action taken, and where the results cause actual damage or real distress, either recently or persistently or with excessive severity.

30.6 A person who has severe learning disabilities and lacks the capacity to make personal health care decisions may be admitted to hospital on an informal basis if he or she does not object to being an in-patient. In that case the patient's admission and care must in his or her best interests and in accordance with the common law doctrine of necessity (see paras 2.8 and 15.21).

31. CHILDREN AND YOUNG PEOPLE UNDER THE AGE OF 18

Introduction

31.1 The Code of Practice applies to all patients including children and **4–244** young people under the age of 18 (referred to in this Chapter as children). This Chapter gives guidance on a number of issues of particular importance affecting children. There is no minimum age limit for admission to hospital under the Act (but only a person who has attained the age of 16 can be subject to guardianship or after-care under supervision).

GENERAL NOTE
  Also see the notes on section 131(2) of the 1983 Act.   **4–245**

The legal framework and legal advice

31.2 The legal framework governing the admission to hospital and **4–246** treatment of children is complex. It is the responsibility of all professionals, local social services authorities and education authorities and Trusts to ensure that necessary information (including the Code of Practice, the Act, the Children Act and in particular volumes 1, 4, 6 and 7 of the Children Act Guidance) is available to all those responsible for the care of children.
31.3 Where it is considered necessary to require a child's residence in a particular place and/or to require them to undergo medical treatment the choice between the Act and the Children Act is not always easy. When considering which provisions to use it is particularly important to identify the primary purpose of the proposed intervention. For example, a seriously mentally ill child may require treatment under the Act, whereas the needs of a behaviourally disturbed child may be more appropriately met within secure accommodation under the Children Act. Professional staff who address these questions should:
  a. be aware of the relevant statutory provisions and have easy access to competent legal advice;
  b. keep in mind the importance of ensuring that the child's care and treatment is managed with clarity, consistency and within a recognisable framework; and
  c. attempt to select the option that reflects the predominant needs of the child at that time whether that be to provide specific mental health care and treatment or to achieve a measure of safety and protection. Either way the least restrictive option consistent with the care and treatment objectives for the child should be sought.

GENERAL NOTE
  It is suggested that the following factors should influence a decision about statutory **4–247** intervention:

  (i) use of the Mental Health Act is likely to be appropriate where the predominant issue in a case is the discrete need for a child to receive treatment for a mental disorder;

689

(ii) intervention under the Children Act is likely to be appropriate if the child's mental disorder is only one factor in a dysfunctional family situation which requires a range of interventions aimed at both the child and the family; and

(iii) the right of the child's nearest relative, usually a parent, to order the discharge of the child from detention under the Mental Health Act can make it inappropriate to use that Act if the child comes from a dysfunctional family.

Guiding principles

4–248   31.4 The guidance set out in Chapter 1 applies equally to children although in the case of children there will be special considerations. In particular:

a.   children should be kept as fully informed as possible about their care and treatment, and their views and wishes ascertained and taken into account, having regard to their age and understanding. It is important to remember; including in the case of older children, that the impact of the child's wishes on the parents or other person with parental responsibility should always be considered;

b   any intervention in the life of a child considered necessary by reason of their mental disorder, should be the least restrictive possible and result in the least possible segregation from family, friends, community and school; and

c.   all children in hospital should receive appropriate education (see joint DH/DFEE guidance—The Education of Sick Children, DFEE 4 Circular number 12/94, DH circulars LAC(94)10 and HSG(94)24, May 1994).

31.5 Whenever the care and treatment of a child under the age of 16 is being considered, the following questions (amongst many others) need to be asked. it may also be appropriate to ask the following questions in the case of the older child:

a.   Who has parental responsibility for the child? It is essential that those responsible for the care and treatment of the child always request copies of any court orders for reference on the hospital ward. These orders may include care orders, residence orders, contact orders, evidence of appointment as the child's guardian, parental responsibility agreements or orders under section 4 of the Children Act and any order under wardship;

b.   If the child is living with either of the parents who are separated, whether there is a residence order and if so in whose favour. It may be necessary to consider whether it is appropriate to contact both parents;

c.   What is the capacity of the child to make his or her own decisions in terms of emotional maturity, intellectual capacity and mental state? (see Chapter 15 and paragraph 31.11);

d.   Where a parent or other person with parental responsibility refuses consent to treatment, how sound are the reasons and on what grounds are they made?; and

e.   Could the needs of the child be met in a social services or educational placement? To what extent have these authorities carefully considered all possible alternative suitable placements?

Informal admission to hospital

Children under 16

31.6 The parents or other person with parental responsibility may arrange **4–249** for the admission of children under the age of 16 to hospital as informal patients. Where a doctor concludes that such a child has the capacity to make such a decision for him or herself (*i.e.* he or she is of sufficient intelligence and understanding to make that decision that is to say "Gillick competent", see paragraph 31.11) and the child objects to such admission then the consent of the person with parental responsibility may be sufficient authority to enable the child to be admitted against their wishes. Where a "Gillick competent" child wishes to discharge him or herself as an informal patient from hospital, the contrary wishes of any person who has parental responsibility will ordinarily prevail. In either circumstance consideration should be given to whether the use of the Act, if applicable, would be appropriate (see also paragraph 31.13).

31.7 Where a "Gillick competent" child is willing to be admitted but the parents or other person with parental responsibility object, their views should be seriously considered and given due weight but their objections to such admission will not prevail.

16 or 17 year olds

31.8 Section 131(2) of the Act provides that any 16 and 17 year old "capable of expressing his own wishes" can admit him or herself as an informal patient to hospital, irrespective of the wishes of his or her parent or guardian. Where a 16 or 17 year old is unwilling to remain in hospital as an informal patient, consideration may need to be given to whether he or she should be detained under the Act.

31.9 Where a 16 or 17 year old is incapable of expressing his own wishes, the consent of the parents should be obtained or consideration given to the use of the Act.

Consent to medical treatment (see Chapters 15 and 16)

31.10 It is normal practice in relation to the treatment of a child to obtain **4–250** the consent of the parent (or other person with parental responsibility) as an exercise of their parental responsibility. There are circumstances, however, in which the child will decide for him or herself.

GENERAL NOTE
Notes on "The medical treatment of children" can be found in the General Note to **4–251** Part IV of the 1983 Act.

Children under the age of 16

31.11 A "Gillick competent" child can give a valid consent to medical treatment. A child may be regarded as "Gillick competent" if the doctor concludes that he or she has the capacity to make the decision to have the proposed treatment and is of sufficient understanding and intelligence to be capable of making up his/her own mind.[19]

31.12 The refusal of a "Gillick competent" child to be medically treated can be overridden by the courts or by their parents.[20]

31.13 The assistance of the court may be sought, in particular in the following circumstances:

— in the case of a child who is not 16 or "Gillick competent" where treatment decisions need to be made and the person with parental responsibility cannot be identified or is incapacitated, for example in dealing with a child who is accommodated by a local authority;

— where a person with parental responsibility may not be acting in the best interests of the child in making treatment decisions on behalf of the child.

A child's refusal to be treated is a very important consideration in making clinical judgements and for parents and the court in deciding whether themselves to give consent. Its importance increases with age and maturity of the child.

31.14 In cases involving emergency protection orders, child assessment orders, interim care orders and full supervision orders, the Children Act specifically provides that a child may refuse assessment, examination or treatment. (See respectively Children Act section 44(8), section 43(8), section 38(6) and section 35 and Schedule 3 Part I paragraph 4(4)). However, the inherent jurisdiction of the High Court can be used to override a child's refusal, where it considers it should do so.[21]

16 and 17 year olds

31.15 Section 8(1) of the Family Law Reform Act 1969 provides that a child of 16 years or over may consent "to any surgical, medical or dental treatment which, in the absence of consent, would constitute a trespass to his person, [and the consent] shall be as effective as it would be if he were of full age; and where a minor has by virtue of this section given an effective consent to any treatment, it shall not be necessary to obtain any consent for it from his parent or guardian."

31.16 Where a 16 or 17 year old is regarded as incapable of consenting to treatment the consent of the parents or other person with parental responsibility should be obtained. The refusal of a competent 16 or 17 year old to be medically treated can be overridden by their parents or other person who has parental responsibility for that 16 or 17 year old or by the court. Consideration should be given to whether the use of the Act, if applicable, would be appropriate.

---

[19] *Gillick v. West Norfolk and Wisbech Area Health Authority and Another* [1986] A.C. 112. Capacity is dealt with in Chapter 15, paragraph 15.9 *et seq.* although it is important in assessing whether a child is to be regarded as "Gillick competent" to have regard to the decision of the Court of Appeal in *Re R.* [1992] 1 F.L.R. 190. In that case the Court of Appeal stated that "'Gillick—competence' is a developmental concept and will not be lost or acquired on a day to day or week to week basis. In the case of mental disability, that disability must also be taken into account, particularly where it is fluctuating in its effect."

[20] *Re W.* [1992] 4 All E.R. 627.

[21] *South Glamorgan C.C. v. W. & B.* [1993] 1 F.L.R. 57.

Emergency treatment

31.17 In an emergency situation a doctor may undertake treatment if **4–252** delay would be dangerous (see para 15.25). It is good practice in that situation to attempt to obtain the consent of the parents or other person with parental responsibility.

Children looked after by the local authority

31.18 Where children are looked after by the local authority (see section **4–253** 20 of the Children Act), treatment decisions should usually be discussed with the parent or other person with parental responsibility. If a child is voluntarily accommodated by the local authority, the consent of the parent or other person with parental responsibility to the proposed treatment should be obtained. If the child is subject to a care order, the parents share parental responsibility with the local authority and it will be a matter for agreement/negotiation between them as to who should be consulted although it should be remembered that local authorities can, in the exercise of their powers under section 33(3)(b) of the Children Act limit the extent to which parents may exercise their parental responsibility.

Parents/guardians consent

31.19 The fact that a child has been informally admitted by parents or **4–254** other person with parental responsibility should not lead professionals to assume that they have consented to all components of a treatment programme regarded as "necessary". Consent should be sought for each aspect of the child's care and treatment as it arises. "Blanket" consent forms should not be used.

Information

31.20 The advice concerning the giving of information (see Chapter 14) **4–255** applies with equal force to children. In particular where such patients are detained under the Act, it is important that assistance is given to enable their legal representation at any Mental Health Review Tribunal.

31.21 Children's rights to confidentiality should be strictly observed. It is **4–256** important that all professionals have a clear understanding of their obligations of confidentiality to children and that any limits to such an obligation are made clear to a child who has the capacity to understand them (see paragraphs 4.10 and 4.11 of the DH Guidance on confidentiality *The Protection and Use of Patient Information, Department of Health, March 1996*, HSG(96)18).

Placement

31.22 It is usually preferable for children admitted to hospital to be **4–257** accommodated with others of their own age group in children's wards or adolescent units, separate from adults. If, exceptionally, this is not practicable, discrete accommodation in an adult ward, with facilities, security and staffing appropriate to the needs of the child might provide the most satisfactory solution.

Complaints

4–258   31.23 See Chapter 24.

Welfare of certain hospital patients

4–259   31.24 Local authorities should ensure that they arrange for visits to be made to:
— children looked after by them whether or not under a care order who are in hospital, and
— those accommodated or intended to be accommodated for 3 months or more by Health Authorities, Trusts, local education authorities or in residential care, nursing or mental nursing homes (see Review of Children's Cases Regulations 1991 S.I. 1991/895 as amended and sections 85 and 86 of the Children Act). This is in addition to their duty in respect to children in their care in hospitals or nursing homes in England and Wales as required by section 116 of the Act. Local authorities should take such other steps in relation to the patient while in hospital or nursing home as would be expected to be taken by his or her parent. Local authorities are under a duty to:
— promote contact between children who are in need and their families if they live away from home and to help them get back together (paragraphs 10 and 15 of Schedule 2 to the Children Act); and
— to arrange for persons (independent visitors) to visit and befriend children looked after by the authority wherever they are if they have nor been regularly visited by their parents (paragraph 17 of Schedule 2 to the Act).

ANNEX A

MENTAL HEALTH ACT COMMISSION PRACTICE AND GUIDANCE NOTES

4–260   [Current versions of all of the Commission's Practice and Guidance Notes can be found at the Commission's website: www.mhac.trent.nhs.uk/].

ANNEX B

SUMMARY OF REFERENCED CASES

4–261 **Case name and Law Report Reference (where available)**	**Subject**	**Paragraph**
B. v. Croydon Health Authority [1995] 2 W.L.R. 294	Medical treatment of symptoms of mental disorder (naso-gastric feeding)	16.5

R. v. Managers of Warley Hospital, ex parte Barket [1998] C.O.D. 309	Renewal of detention while patient on leave of absence	20.10 20.13
Gillick v. West Norfolk and Wisbech Area Health Authority [1986] A.C. 112	When child under 16 has capacity to consent to treatment without consent of parent	31.11
R. v. Bournewood Community and Mental Health NHS Trust, ex parte L. [1998] All E.R. 319	Informal admission and treatment of mentally incapacitated patients	2.8 8.4 15.21 30.6
R. v. Broadmoor Special Hospital Authority, ex parte S. [1998] C.O.D. 199	Power to search patients detained under the Act	25.3
R. v. Collins, ex parte S. (No. 2) [1998]	Refusal to consent to invasive treatment (Guidelines)	15.11
R. v. Ealing District Health Authority, ex parte Fox [1993] 3 All E.R. 170	Duty to provide section 117 aftercare services	22.12 27.7
R. v. North West London Mental Health Trust, ex parte Stewart (1998)	Part II admission of conditionally discharged patient	29.2(b)
R. v. Riverside Mental Health NHS Trust, ex parte Huzzey (1998)	Discharge by managers after nearest relative's discharge barred	23.12
R. v. Wilson, ex parte W. [1996] C.O.D. 42	No successive section 2 applications	5.5
Re C. [1994] 1 F.L.R. 31	Capacity to decide on leg amputation	15.10
Re F. [1990] 2 A.C. 1	Treatment of mentally incapacitated patient: doctrine of necessity	15.21
Re M.B. [1997] 2 F.C.R. 541	Test of capacity to consent to invasive treatment	15.10
Re R. [1992] 1 F.L.R. 190	Fluctuating mental disorder and Gillick competency	31.10
Re W. [1992] 4 All E.R. 627	Refusal of treatment by Gillick competent child	31.12

MENTAL HEALTH (PATIENTS IN THE COMMUNITY) ACT 1995—GUIDANCE ON SUPERVISED DISCHARGE (AFTER-CARE UNDER SUPERVISION) AND RELATED PROVISIONS

SUPPLEMENT TO THE *Code of Practice* published August 1993 pursuant to section 118 of the Mental Health Act 1983

DEPARTMENT OF HEALTH—WELSH OFFICE

GENERAL NOTE

4–262 This guidance remains extant: see paragraph 28.9 of the *Code of Practice*. References to the current edition of the Code have been inserted in the text.

CONTENTS
Introduction

Supervised Discharge

SUPERVISED DISCHARGE (AFTER-CARE UNDER SUPERVISION) AND RELATED PROVISIONS

Introduction

1. This supplement to the Mental Health Act *Code of Practice*,[22] gives **4–263** guidance on the new provision for after-care supervision, referred to throughout as supervised discharge. This becomes effective from April 1, 1996 on the implementation of the Mental Health (Patients in the Community) Act 1995 which amends the Mental Health Act 1983 (referred to in this guidance as "the Act).

2. The 1995 Act contains two other main provisions (apart from amendments to the equivalent Scottish legislation). The first is to remove the previous six-month time limit on the period for which a detained patient may be given leave of absence under section 17 of the Act. The effect of this is explained in paragraph 71 below. The second is to extend the period during which a patient who is absent without leave from detention or guardianship may be returned. This is explained in the Appendix to this guidance.

SUPERVISED DISCHARGE

The purpose of supervised discharge

3. Supervised discharge is an arrangement by which a patient who has **4–264** been detained in hospital for treatment under the provisions of the 1983 Act may be subject to formal supervision after he or she is discharged. Its purpose is to help ensure that the patient receives the after-care services to be provided under section 117 of the Act. It is available for patients suffering from any of the four forms of mental disorder in the Act but is primarily intended for those with severe mental illness (see paragraph 14). The provisions incorporate the key principles of the Care Programme Approach, as defined in circular HC(90)23/LASSL(90)11, and those set out in the Welsh Office Mental Illness Strategy (WHC(95)40, Draft Guidance on the Care of People in the Community with a Mental Illness). They also reflect the Department of Health's Guidance on the Discharge of Mentally Disordered People and their Continuing Care in the Community (HSG(94)27/LASSL(94)4).

4. The above initiatives are directed to ensuring that there are effective **4–265** after-care services for all discharged patients based on close co-operation between all the agencies concerned at local level. In particular, before a patient is discharged from hospital, a risk assessment should be carried out, a care plan established based on a systematic assessment of need and a key

---

[22] The guidance contains a number of references to existing paragraphs of the Code. This means that the general principles underlying those paragraphs apply to the operation of supervised discharge, even though their wording was drawn up before it was introduced.

worker identified to monitor the patient's progress and the delivery of care in the community. The services provided should then be kept under regular review in the list of the patient's needs. The relationship between section 117 after-care, the Care Programme Approach, and local authority arrangements for care management is explained in "Building Bridges—A Guide to arrangements for inter-agency working for the care and protection of severely mentally ill people" (DH 1995).

4–266 5. These principles apply to all patients receiving care from the specialist psychiatric services in the community, whether or not it follows a spell in hospital. Supervised discharge is intended for patients whose care needs to be specially supervised in the community because of risk to themselves or others. This applies particularly to "revolving door" patients who have shown a pattern of relapse after discharge from hospital. Relapses often follow the breakdown of arrangements for care in the community, for example when a patient stops taking medication. The legal framework which supervised discharge provides should help to prevent such failures provided that the care arrangements which it underpins have been fully agreed between the agencies concerned. Its purpose is to complement and reinforce existing arrangements under the Care Programme Approach, and supervised discharge procedures should be integrated with those operating under the CPA.

4–267 6. Patients who are placed under supervised discharge will have been assessed as presenting a substantial risk of serious harm to themselves or other people, or of being seriously exploited, if they do not receive suitable after-care. They should normally be included in the supervision registers established in England in accordance with HSG(94)5 (and the corresponding local lists in Wales) to identify patients in the care of the psychiatric services who are at significant risk. However, not all patients who are on supervision registers will be suitable for supervised discharge. For example, the registers will also include patients who have not been detained—and indeed may not have been in hospital at all—and cannot therefore be subject to supervised discharge under the Act.

7. The duty to provide after-care services under section 117 extends to all patients who have been detained for treatment under the relevant sections of the Act (see paragraph 15). Patients should not be placed under supervised discharge simply with a view to ensuring that these services are provided for them, but only if they meet the criteria set out in paragraphs 13 and 15 below.

Supervised discharge and guardianship

4–268 8. Guardianship under section 7 of the Act remains available as an option when considering the arrangements to be made for a patient's care in the community. Where a patient is detained in hospital and meets the criteria, supervised discharge has advantages in the specific legal provision it offers for making and reviewing after-care arrangements and the roles assigned to the community responsible medical officer and supervisor. Where a patient needs a degree of formal structure in his or her after-care arrangements but does not fully meet the criteria for supervised discharge responsible medical officers and their professional colleagues may well want to consider proposing guardianship. This may be particularly suitable for patients with learning disability, providing they meet the Mental Health Act definition of "mental impairment" or "severe mental impairment".

Statutory responsibilities

9. The Act places a number of responsibilities for the supervised discharge **4–269** procedure—particularly relating to the initial application—on the Health Authority which is to be responsible for the health element of the after-care services to be provided under section 117 of the Act. Some other responsibilities relating to the operation of supervised discharge are placed jointly on that Health Authority and the corresponding local authority responsible for the social services element of the section 117 after-care (who the Act defines together as the "responsible after-care bodies"). It is recommended that health and local authorities develop local protocols on the implementation and working of supervised discharge. Some suggested issues for inclusion are set out at Annex C.

10. The Mental Health (After Care under Supervision) Regulations 1996 allow the Health Authority's responsibilities under the 1995 Act, and the *joint* responsibilities of the Health Authority and local authority in their capacity as the "responsible after-care bodies", to be delegated to a body with whom the Health Authority has contracted to provide section 117 services. Such a body is referred to throughout this guidance as the provider unit. This would in most cases be an NHS Trust, but could be an independent or voluntary sector provider. Otherwise (for example where a small provider unit does not have the administrative back-up to fulfil all the documentary requirements) the powers may be delegated to an officer of the Health Authority itself, or to an officer of another Health Authority if there are joint purchasing agreements in place and it has been agreed that such functions should be undertaken by only one of the parties. The functions may also be delegated to a committee of the Health Authority.

11. These provisions make it possible for a single body to fulfil the **4–270** procedural requirements of supervised discharge on behalf of the health and local authorities. The functions which may be delegated are listed in Annex D. It is for each authority to decide whether its functions should be delegated to the health service provider, and if they are, to satisfy itself that there are suitable arrangements for fulfilling its statutory obligations. The actual provision of section 117 after-care services cannot be delegated under the regulations—though in the case of the Health Authority this will normally be secured through NHS contracts, and in practice the services will be delivered jointly by health and social services staff working as members of the patient's care team.

12. The new Act does not assign any functions to the hospital managers, though it would be open to a Trust to assign a monitoring role to a committee similar to that formed to exercise the managers' functions under the Act.

Applying for supervised discharge (s.25A)

13. An application for supervised discharge (a supervision application) **4–271** may be made only by the patient's responsible medical officer (RMO) at a time when the patient is liable to be detained under the Act. The RMO's role

is a key point of difference with the procedure for applications for admission to hospital under the Act, which are usually made by an approved social worker (ASW). In supervised discharge cases the ASW makes a recommendation in support of the application (see paragraph 30 below). The RMO should consider making an application if he or she is satisfied:

— that the patient is suffering from one of the four categories of mental disorder defined in section 1(2) of the Act; *and*
— that there would be a substantial risk of serious harm to the health or safety of the patient or the safety of other people, or of the patient being seriously exploited, if the patient did not receive after-care services under section 117 of the Act; *and*
— that supervision is likely to help ensure that the patient receives those services.

All three of these conditions must be met.

While the duty to make the application rests solely with the RMO, this does not preclude others with professional knowledge of the patient's condition and needs proposing supervised discharge to the RMO for his or her consideration.

14. Supervised discharge is primarily intended for severely mentally ill people but may be suitable for some patients suffering from other forms of mental disorder. In the case of those suffering from mental impairment or severe mental impairment the question of potential exploitation may be particularly relevant, though the RMO should then always consider whether guardianship might offer a better option for the patient's after-care.

4–272   15. The RMO must also be satisfied:

— that the patient is 16 years of age or over;
— that he or she is currently liable to be detained under section 3, 37, 47 or 48 of the Act (this includes patients who have been granted leave of absence under section 17); *and*
— that he or she is an unrestricted patient, that is not subject to restrictions under section 41 or 49 (conditional discharge under section 42 of the Act is available for restricted patients). An application may however be made if the patient was formerly subject to restrictions which have been lifted or have expired.

Patients who have been admitted under section 2 of the Act may be considered for supervised discharge only if they have subsequently been detained under section 3. The difference should *not* influence the choice between admission under these two sections, the criteria for which are set out in Chapter 5 of the Code.

16. A patient must be liable to be detained in hospital at the time when the application is made. Supervised discharge takes effect when the patient leaves hospital or, in the case of patients on section 17 leave, at the point when he or she is discharged from liability to detention. If for any reason a patient remains in hospital on an informal basis after ceasing to be liable to be detained, the supervision application may still take effect when he or she eventually leaves provided this is within six months of the application being accepted. However it is preferable to avoid long delays as a patient's circumstances may change. Where a patient's liability to be detained would end before the after-care arrangements can be implemented the RMO should consider whether the criteria in section 20 of the Act are met and if so

whether the detention should be renewed. Otherwise there will be nothing to prevent the patient from leaving hospital without the aftercare arrangements having been completed (and there is no provision for such a patient to be treated as absent without leave).

17. A supervision application may be made on behalf of a patient who is subject to a Community Care Order under the Mental Health (Scotland) Act 1984—the equivalent provision to supervised discharge in Scotland—and who wishes to live in England or Wales. This is governed by a separate procedure which is explained (with the corresponding arrangements for patients wishing to move from England to Scotland) in paragraphs 55 and 56 below.

After-care arrangements

18. The arrangements for after-care under supervision will need to be **4–273** drawn up as part of the normal discharge planning process, following the principles of the Care Programme Approach in England and WHC(95)40 in Wales and in accordance with the formal consultation requirements in the Act (see below). Chapter 27 of the Code is also relevant. The professional team providing care in the community will need to consider and plan the services to be provided, including as may be appropriate daytime activities, accommodation, treatment, personal and practical support, 24-hour emergency cover and assistance in welfare rights and financial advice. They will also need to consider how often the patient is likely to need particular services. Support for informal carers should not be overlooked as the care plan may be to some degree dependent on their role.

19. The Act defines requirements which may be imposed when a patient is subject to supervised discharge. These are:
— that the patient should live in a particular place;
— that the patient should attend a particular place at set times for medical treatment, occupation, education or training;
— that the supervisor, or a person authorised by the supervisor, should be allowed access to the patient at his or her place of residence (see paragraph 51 below).
The reasons for imposing requirements should be explained to the patient, and details of them should be included in the care plan. A requirement to attend for medical treatment does not carry with it any power to impose medication or other treatment against the patient's wishes.

Consultation (s.25B)

20. The RMO is responsible for ensuring that both the current and **4–274** proposed future care team (if different) are consulted about the arrangements to be made for the patient's care after discharge from hospital, and about any requirements to be imposed (see paragraph 19 above) and that agreement about the care plan is reached between all involved.

21. The Act specifies certain people who must be consulted about the making of the supervision application. These are:
— the patient;
— one or more members of the team caring for the patient in hospital;
— one or more members of the team who will be caring for the patient in the community (if different from the hospital care team). It will be

important to involve and secure the agreement of the social services representative to the care plan;

— the person, if anyone, who will be acting as an informal carer; that is someone who the RMO believes will play a substantial part in the care of the patient in the community but will not be professionally concerned in the provision of after-care services (for example spouse, relative, or friend).

— the patient's nearest relative, as defined in section 26 of the Act, unless there is no practicable way in which he or she can be contacted. Except where the nearest relative is also to be an informal carer this is subject to the provision for a patient to object explained in paragraph 27 below.

4–275 22. The Act stipulates that the local social services authority which has the duty to provide after-care under section 117 must be consulted by the health authority about the application after it has been made. But since the application must be accompanied by a statement of the after-care services which will be provided it follows that the local authority's agreement to the care plan and the supervision arrangements will in fact need to be secured before the application is made. The procedure for this needs to be agreed as part of local liaison arrangements. The care team in the community is likely to include local authority staff and the most straightforward arrangement may be for consultation with the authority to be channelled through them. It is important that any other agencies who will be involved in providing after-care services to the patient but who may not part of the care team—for, example voluntary agencies or a housing department—are also consulted (subject to the necessary safeguards for confidentiality of patient ihformation).

23. The RMO is responsible for ensuring that all those whom the Act specifies are consulted. While he or she is not obliged to undertake all the consultation personally this responsibility should be delegated only with the RMO's express agreement. Those who are consulted must be given a genuine opportunity to comment on the proposed arrangements and account must be taken in making the application of any views they have expressed. The arrangements clearly will not work without a substantial measure of agreement on the part of those responsible for them and this also needs to be taken into account.

4–276 24. While the Act does not require the patient's agreement to supervised discharge it is unlikely to be effective unless the patient, and any informal carer, has understood and accepted its terms. The RMO must ensure that the patient has a genuine opportunity to take part in discussions about the proposals for after-care. The patient should always be given a copy of the care plan in its final form, preferably at least three days before discharge.

25. The patient, any informal carer and the nearest relative (subject to paragraph 27 below) should have the opportunity to speak to the RMO, or any person the RMO has agreed should undertake the consultation, alone if they wish. The patient may wish a friend, relative or advocate to be present during the discussion and such a wish should be respected unless there are exceptional reasons for excluding a particular person.

26. Patients, informal carers and nearest relatives must be consulted in a

suitable and sensitive manner. Where those involved cannot understand each other's language sufficiently, recourse to a trained interpreter who understands the terminology and conduct of a psychiatric interview is to be preferred. Where anyone involved has a hearing or speaking difficulty, help should be enlisted from someone with relevant communication skills (if practicable a professional or trained interpreter). The RMO and the other professionals involved must take into account the possibility of misunderstandings resulting from assumptions person's gender, social background, ethnic origin, sexual orientation or religion or from other medical/health conditions including deafness. Further guidance on suitable interviewing is given in [chapter 2] of the Code.

Nearest relatives

27. The Act requires a patient's nearest relative to be consulted (unless it **4–277** is impracticable to do so) about the initial application for supervised discharge and subsequently about its review, renewal or ending. A patient may however object to consultation with the nearest relative, unless he or she will also be acting as the patient's informal carer. The RMO may then consult the nearest relative only if the patient is known to have a propensity to violent or dangerous behaviour towards others and the RMO thinks such consultation appropriate. The patient's objection should not lightly be set aside and it is for the RMO to judge whether the patient has a propensity to violent or dangerous behaviour (which must be directed to other people) and if so whether consultation with the nearest relative is advisable in all the circumstances. Matters which the RMO is likely to want to consider include what is known about the patient's history, the seriousness of any past violence, against whom it has been directed, how the patient has responded to treatment and how much consultation with the nearest relative is likely to help in the assessment of the patient's present condition and needs. RMOs may also want to refer to the general discussion of risk assessment in the Department of Health's "Guidance on the Discharge of Mentally Disordered People and their Continuing Care in the Community" published in May 1994 (HSG(94)27 and LASSL(94)4). The RMO should record the reasons for his or her decision.

Submitting the supervision application (s.25B)

28. The application for supervised discharge should be made on Form 1S. **4–278** The application must include the names of the supervisor and community responsible medical officer (these roles are explained in paragraphs 43 and 44 below) as well as those of the nearest relative (if any) and of any informal carer who has been consulted about the application.

29. The supervision application will normally be submitted to the provider unit which is responsible for the health component of the after-care services (see paragraph 10 above). The provider unit needs to identify an individual officer who will be responsible for handling the documentation. This would be a suitable role for a Mental Health Act Administrator where there is one appointed.

Supporting documentation (ss.25B & 25C)

4–279   30. The application must be supported by the written recommendation of an approved social worker (using Form 3S) and another doctor (using Form 2S). The Act requires that the latter should if possible be a doctor who will be professionally concerned with the patient's medical treatment in the community. This should normally be the community responsible medical officer (see paragraph 44 below) unless the patient's RMO in hospital will also be acting in that role. In the latter case it is preferable for the recommendation to be given by the patient's general practitioner. If the RMO is unable to identify another doctor who will be involved in the patient's treatment after he or she leaves hospital the recommendation may be made by any other doctor, including a member of the hospital staff (but not one who works under the direction of the RMO). The ASW making the recommendation may also be the patient's proposed supervisor.

GENERAL NOTE
The statement that a medical recommendation cannot be given by a doctor who works under the direction of the responsible medical officer is an assertion of good practice and not of law: see section 25B(6)(a).

31. For the purpose of deciding whether to make a recommendation, the doctor the approved social worker should each visit and interview the patient and the should also examine the patient following the guidance in [chapter 2] of the Code. Wherever possible the ASW and the doctor should visit the patient within a week of each other and it is good practice for them to see the patient together. To ensure that their recommendations are based on a fully informed judgement they should examine any records relating to the patient's detention or treatment in hospital, and the after-care services to be provided.

4–280   32. A written recommendation in support of the supervision application may not be made by:
—   the RMO or a close relative of the RMO;
—   anyone who would have a financial interest as specified in chapter 4 of the Code;
—   a close relative of the patient or of the other professional supporting the recommendation.
"Close relative" for these purposes is defined as husband, wife, father, father-in-law, mother, mother-in-law, son, son-in-law, daughter, daughter-in-law, brother, brother-in-law, sister or sister-in-law.
33. A supervision application must also be accompanied by
—   signed statements from the community RMO and the supervisor that they are willing to act in those capacities (these are included in the application form 1S);
—   a statement of the after-care services to be provided (as in the care plan).
—   details of any requirements to be imposed on the patient (see paragraph 19).

Accepting the supervision application (ss.25A & 25C)

4–281   34. Supervised discharge can only come into effect after the application is accepted. By this time the after-care arrangements should have been agreed

704

between all those involved and there should be no question of the application being rejected unless it appears not to have been properly made—for example, if it does not have the required signatures, or if there are inconsistencies either in the application itself or in any of the accompanying information. The scrutiny of the application may be undertaken by suitably experienced members of staff of the provider unit or Health Authority, provided that account is taken of the principles set out in Chapter 12 of the Code. A defective application or supporting recommendation may be amended within 14 days of being accepted.

35. Before accepting the application, the Health Authority (or provider unit) must consult the local authority named in the application to confirm that those elements of the after-care services for which it will be responsible have been agreed. This should be a check that the arrangements, on which the local authority should already have been consulted, will be in place in time for the patient's discharge. The officer who is to act for the local authority should be identified as part of local liaison arrangements.

36. Supervised discharge cannot take effect until the patient is discharged from hospital. But, for the purpose of determining when supervision would expire (unless renewed), it will be deemed to have effect from the date the application was accepted.

Informing the patient (s.25B)

37. The Act sets out specific requirements governing information to be **4–282** given to patients and other people. But in any case the patient should as a general principle be given as much information as he or she needs to exercise rights and understand requirements.

38. The RMO must inform the patient (both orally and in writing) and anyone else who has been consulted that an application is being made; what after-care services it is proposed will be provided; any requirements to be imposed on the patient; and the names of the community RMO and supervisor. An outline of a possible model letter is attached at Annex A to this guidance and RMOs may wish to adapt this to the circumstances of individual cases.

39. The Health Authority (or provider unit) must inform the patient (orally and in writing) that the supervision application has been accepted and the implications of this for the patient (a further model letter is at Annex B). In particular the patient's right to apply to a Mental Health Review Tribunal must be explained. A patient's information leaflet will be available for this purpose, and the general guidance in paragraph [14.5c] of the Code on informing patients of their Tribunal rights also applies. The local authority and anyone else who has been consulted must be told when the application is accepted. Copies of the patient's information leaflet should also be sent to the patient's nearest relative (where he or she has been consulted) and any informal carer.

The operation of supervised discharge

40. The following paragraphs explain how the new powers will work once **4–283** an application has been accepted and the patient discharged from hospital (or liability to detention).

Professional responsibilities (Sched. 1)

4–284   41. The Act gives specific responsibilities to designated individual members of the care team, namely the supervisor and the community responsible medical officer. The principle of allocating responsibilities to individuals is not new since the Act already defines the responsibilities of approved social workers, responsible medical officers when a patient is detained in hospital and guardians. Staff undertaking duties defined in the Act remain professionally and managerially accountable for them in the normal way. The possibility of personal legal liability would only arise if there were a culpable professional failure which fell outside the protection afforded by section 139 of the Act.

42. Suitable training should be provided for members of the care team who are to fulfil specified roles in relation to supervised discharge.

4–285   43. The **supervisor** is responsible for monitoring the supervised discharge arrangements and for liaising with other members of the community team and coordinating their work where necessary. He or she must be a suitably qualified and experienced member of the patient's care team in the community who has agreed to take on this role. In England, the supervisor would normally also fulfil the role of key worker under the CPA. The supervisor should ensure that the team reviews the patient's after-care plan well before the date when it falls to be reviewed, and whenever any shortfall in the arrangements is identified (see paragraphs 46 and 47 below). The supervisor has powers to require entry to the patient's place of residence and to convey the patient to a place where he or she is required to live or attend (see paragraphs 48–50). The supervisor performs a key role in supervised discharge and it is important that this is supported by a proper framework of training, accountability and clear reporting lines within his or her employing organisation. Close working links between the supervisor and the community responsible medical officer are essential.

4–286   44. The **community responsible medical officer** (CRMO) is responsible for the patient's psychiatric treatment in the community. He or she must be a registered medical practitioner approved by the Secretary of State for the purposes of section 12 of the Act as having special experience in the diagnosis or treatment of mental disorder. The right person to undertake this will usually be a consultant psychiatrist. Often he or she may also have been the patient's RMO in hospital, but if not there must be a handover of responsibility when the patient leaves hospital (or, if already on leave of absence, ceases to be liable to be detained). The CRMO has powers (set out in paragraphs 57–66 below) to renew and terminate supervised discharge, and to reclassify the patient's mental disorder, in each case after taking into account views expressed during consultation with a range of people as set out below.

4–287   45. A patient's **general practitioner** does not as such have a statutory role defined in the Act in the operation of supervised discharge (though a GP who is approved under section 12 may be appointed as the CRMO). Nevertheless good practice requires that the CRMO and the supervisor ensure that the OP is involved in decisions which affect the patient's medical treatment in the community. As with anyone leaving hospital steps should be taken to ensure that the patient is registered with a GP, not least because severely mentally ill people often have substantial physical health needs. The OP should receive a copy of the care plan before the patient's discharge and know who are the patient's supervisor and CRMO and which member of the care team can be contacted in an emergency. The OP should be kept up to date with any developments. A patient's OP may make the medical recommendation which is required to support a supervision application (see paragraph 30 above).

Review and modification of Supervised Discharge (s.25E)

46. The supervisor needs to maintain sufficiently close contact with the **4–288** patient to be satisfied that he or she is receiving the agreed after-care services and is complying with any requirements. If for any reason either is not happening the supervisor must convene a meeting of the after-care team to review the case and consider whether any changes to the care plan are needed, or whether supervised discharge is still appropriate. The supervisor and the care team should also be alive to signs of deterioration and other warning signals which may require the services to be reviewed. They should make themselves accessible to people with whom the patient is living and be ready to listen to concerns they may express. Good practice requires close contact between the members of the team, especially between the supervisor and the CRMO who has the power to terminate supervised discharge (see paragraphs 65 and 66 below). The review and monitoring arrangements should be integrated with those established under the Care Programme Approach.

47. If the care team consider that any part of the care plan, or any **4–289** requirement placed upon the patient, needs to be changed they must (on behalf of the health authority and local authority who are responsible for section 117 after-care) consult the following people about the modifications

— the patient;
— any informal carer;
— the patient's nearest relative, where practicable and unless the patient objects, subject to what is said in paragraph 27 above.

and take their views into account. If changes are made the patient and any person consulted should be informed. The patient must be told both orally and in writing, and should be given a copy of the revised care plan and requirements. The patient's nearest relative (if consulted) must be told in writing about the modifications. Those concerned must be informed in the same way if there is a change of CRMO or supervisor for any reason— including the case where the patient has moved from one area to another (see paragraph 54 below).

Power to convey a patient (s.25D)

48. The Act gives the supervisor the power to take and convey a patient to **4–290** a place where he or she is required to reside or to attend for medical treatment, occupation, education or training. It follows that the power is available only where the supervised discharge arrangement includes such requirements.

49. The circumstances in which this power should be used need to be **4–291** carefully considered and those concerned may find it helpful to draw up a local inter-agency protocol defining the circumstances in which it may (or may not) be used and the records which should be kept. The supervisor may decide to use the power if a patient has got into a situation which is putting

him or her, or other people, at risk and needs to be taken home urgently. The supervisor may also wish to consider using the power if the patient is not attending for medical treatment and it is thought that this might be overcome by taking him or her to the place where treatment is to be given. The patient cannot then be required to accept medical treatment and the power should only be used in these circumstances if the supervisor is satisfied (where necessary in the light of consultation with other members of the care team) that it is likely to lead to the patient co-operating with the services being provided. The supervisor should record the reasons for using the power. The supervisor should also consider (again, consulting other members of the team as necessary) whether the problem might be overcome by some adjustment to the package of services, or conversely whether it may point to a need to reassess the patient for possible readmission to hospital under the Act.

4–292   50. If the power is used, the supervisor may authorise any responsible adult to convey the patient. Given the potential difficulties it will normally be advisable to obtain the support of the ambulance service and the supervisor may also seek the help of the police. The patient should always be accompanied by the supervisor or another duly authorised adult, preferably a member of the health or social services staff who is known to the patient. Any person authorised must carry some form of documentary evidence to that effect. The care team may wish to maintain a list of people who can be called upon in an emergency to fulfil this role. Unreasonable force must never be used when conveying a patient, and neither should the power (or the threat of using it) be used to coerce a patient into accepting medication or treatment. Where a patient has been conveyed medical and other staff need to be satisfied that his or her consent to any subsequent treatment is genuine and not forced. A patient who has been conveyed to a clinic and then insists on leaving cannot be kept there or given treatment against his or her will (except in the circumstances allowed by common law where it may be permissible to administer treatment in order to deal with the immediate emergency).

Access to the patient (s.25D)

4–293   51. The terms of supervised discharge may include a requirement to allow access to the patient, at his or her place of residence, by the supervisor, a registered medical practitioner, an approved social worker or a person authorised by the supervisor. Any person who seeks access to the patient must carry some form of documentary evidence of his or her entitlement. If a patient refused to allow access it would lead to a review of the case (see paragraph 46 above). It would be an offence under section 129 of the 1983 Act for any other person to prevent access to the patient (see paragraph [13.8c] of the Code). If the supervisor considered that forced entry to the premises was justified because the patient was at risk, this could only be authorised by a warrant from a magistrate, which would need to be executed by the police.

Readmission to hospital (s.25E)

4–294   52. If at any time the team believe that the patient's condition warrants his or her readmission to hospital under the Act they should either contact an approved social worker for this purpose or, if the patient agrees, seek an informal admission. If the patient is readmitted under section 3 of the 1983 Act supervised discharge will be terminated. If the patient is readmitted under section 2 or is admitted informally supervised discharge is suspended (see paragraphs 68–70 below).

53. If the team concludes that supervised discharge is no longer appropriate and the patient does not need to be readmitted to hospital the CRMO has the power to terminate the arrangements. This is explained more fully in paragraphs 65–67 below.

Patients moving within England and Wales (s.25E)

54. If the patient wishes to move to an area in England or Wales covered **4–295** by a different health and local social services authority, the supervisor will need to take the lead, before the patient moves, in contacting the professionals who will be responsible for section 117 after-care services in the new home area. There will need to be direct contact between the present CRMO and his or her counterpart in the new area. It will be for the health and local authorities in the new area to decide whether to continue the supervised discharge arrangements. If so the arrangements set out in paragraph 47 above for consulting and informing the patient and others about modifications to the care plan will apply.

Patients moving to or from Scotland (s.25J)

55. A supervision application may be made for a patient who is subject to a **4–296** community care order (the Scottish equivalent of supervised discharge) under the Mental Health (Scotland) Act 1984 and who wishes to move to England or Wales. In these cases the application will normally be made by the prospective CRMO in England and Wales. The details are set out in the Mental Health (Patients in the Community) (Transfers from Scotland) Regulations 1996. The applicant will be responsible for consulting members of the care team in Scotland, the person (if anyone) who will be acting as the patient's informal carer and the nearest relative (subject to paragraph 27 above) as well as members of the care team in England and Wales. It will be essential before making the application to ensure that both the health authority and the local authority agree to provide section 117 after-care for the patient. In practice the initiative is likely to be taken by the care team in Scotland and the application should if possible be supported by recommendations from the patient's special medical officer (the equivalent in Scotland of the CRMO) and the patient's after-care officer in Scotland. If (exceptionally) a recommendation cannot be obtained from either the special medical officer or the after-care officer it may be given by, respectively, another registered medical practitioner or an approved social worker. Once the application is accepted and the patient has moved the arrangements are as for anyone else subject to supervised discharge.

56. There are similar arrangements for patients subject to supervised discharge wishing to move from England or Wales to Scotland. In that event the special medical officer in Scotland will be required to consult the English

or Welsh care team, any informal carer and the patient's nearest relative about the proposed community care order.

Reclassification of a patient (s.25F)

4–297 57. The CRMO may submit a reclassification report, using Form 4S, to the Health Authority (or the provider unit), stating that the patient is suffering from a mental disorder other than that shown on the supervision application, provided that he or she has ensured that at least one other person concerned with the patient's medical treatment (unless there is none) has been consulted. Medical treatment is defined in paragraph 15.4 of the Code. The supervision application will then be treated as if the revised classification had been specified in the first place. The patient must be informed both orally and in writing and his or her nearest relative must be informed in writing (if practicable and unless the patient objects). The patient has the right to apply to a Mental Health Review Tribunal against the reclassification, as does his or her nearest relative within 28 days of the reclassification report being furnished.

Renewal of supervised discharge (s.25G)

4–298 58. Supervised discharge will apply initially for a maximum period of six months, and can thereafter be renewed for a further six months and then for periods of a year at a time. The CRMO must examine the patient in the two months preceding the expiry date. The CRMO must also ensure that the following are consulted and their views taken into account:
— the patient;
— the supervisor;
— one or more persons professionally concerned with the patient's medical treatment in the community;
— at least one member of the patient's care team (preferably a representative of the local social services);
— any informal carer;
— the patient's nearest relative (if practicable and unless the patient objects, subject to what is said in paragraph 27 above).
Consultation with the care team will normally take place as part of the regular review process (see paragraphs 46 and 47 above) and should be integrated with existing CPA procedures.

4–299 59. If supervised discharge is to be renewed, the CRMO must submit a renewal report (using Form 5S) to the Health Authority (or provider unit) stating:
— that the patient is still suffering from one of the four categories of mental disorder defined in section 1(2) of the Act; *and*
— that there is still a substantial risk of serious harm to the health or safety of the patient or to the safety of other people, or of the patient being seriously exploited, unless the aftercare is supervised; *and*
— that supervision will help to ensure that the patient continues to receive the section 117 services.
The Act requires the renewal report to be submitted to the responsible health and local authorities. However if both the health and local authorities have delegated their functions to the provider unit or another body (see

paragraph 10 above) the CRMO will need to submit the report only to that body.

60. The body receiving the report must ensure that the following people are informed:
— the patient, orally and in writing. The implications of renewal for the patient must be made clear. In particular, the right to apply to a Mental Health Review Tribunal must be explained (see paragraph [14.5c] of the Code);
— any informal carer;
— the nearest relative, in writing (if practicable and unless the patient objects, subject to what is said in paragraph 27 above)

that supervised discharge has been renewed.

Appeals against supervised discharge (Sched. 1)

61. A patient, and his or her nearest relative, have the right to appeal to a **4–300** Mental Health Review Tribunal against the imposition or renewal of supervised discharge during each period of supervision. Legal representation for the patient is free of charge under the legal aid scheme. The patient and the nearest relative also have the right to apply to a tribunal when the patient's mental disorder has been reclassified. As with guardianship there is no provision for appeal to the managers of the service.

62. The tribunal must terminate supervised discharge if it is satisfied that the patient does not meet the criteria defined in the Act, and has discretion to terminate it in other cases. To help it make its decision, the tribunal will be given full access to records including the detailed care plan.

63. Where a tribunal does not terminate supervision it has the power to reclassify the patient's mental disorder if this is appropriate (see paragraph 57 above).

64. A tribunal considering an application for a patient's discharge from hospital may also recommend that consideration should be given to making him or her subject to supervised discharge.

Ending of supervised discharge (s.25H)

65. The CRMO may at any time direct that the patient should cease to be **4–301** subject to supervised discharge. Before doing so, he or she must ensure that the people who would have had to be consulted if a renewal application were being made (see paragraph 58) are consulted and must take their views into account. The CRMO should make the direction on Form 6S to the Health Authority (or provider unit). The Health Authority (or provider unit) must inform the local authority that supervised discharge has been terminated and should note on the form that this has been done. A possible option may be to transfer the patient from supervised discharge to guardianship if, say, compliance with medication has been achieved but the delivery of social care still requires a degree of legal backing in the patient's interests.

66. When a patient ceases to be subject to supervised discharge the same people must be informed as if supervision were being renewed (see paragraph 60 above).

67. The duty upon the health authority and the local social services authority to provide after-care services under section 117 does not end

simply because the supervision arrangements have been terminated. That duty continues until the two authorities are satisfied that after-care services are no longer needed.

Readmission to hospital etc

4–302   68. Supervised discharge will automatically be ended if a patient is readmitted to hospital for treatment (under section 3 of the Act) or is received into guardianship. It also ends when a patient has been detained in prison or remanded in custody for more than six months, beginning on the date of the relevant court order.

69. When a patient is imprisoned or remanded in custody for six months or less or is detained in hospital under section 2 of the Act, the arrangements for supervised discharge will be suspended. On the patient's release or discharge, supervised discharge will be re-activated and continue for the remainder of the original period. If supervised discharge would have lapsed whilst the patient was detained in custody or in hospital, it will be deemed to have been extended for 28 days after his or her release or discharge. Any renewal (and associated examination) must be made during this period.

70. An emergency admission under section 4 of the Act, or admission to a hospital as a "place of safety" under section 136, will not end supervised discharge unless the patient is then detained under section 3 for treatment. If a patient subject to supervised discharge is admitted to hospital on an informal basis, the arrangements for supervision are put into suspense and reactivated when the patient leaves hospital.

Annex A

MODEL LETTER FROM RESPONSIBLE MEDICAL OFFICER

4–303   Dear **[name of patient]**

APPLICATION FOR SUPERVISED DISCHARGE

I told you on **[date of meeting/conversation]** that I had decided to make an application for supervised discharge when you are discharged from hospital/ your leave of absence ends.

I have made an application today to **[name of health authority/provider unit]**. They will be writing to you as soon as possible to let you know when the application has been accepted.

The arrangements for your supervised discharge have been discussed fully with all those concerned with your care. The following after-care services should be provided for you under section 117 of the Mental Health Act 1983:— **[Section 117 services to be provided]**
(For use as appropriate)
*When the application has been accepted you will be required to
[list of requirements]   1)
                                            2)
                                            3)
Your supervisor will be **[name of supervisor]**. He/she will try to make sure

that the arrangements for your care in the community are working. If you have any problems about these, please contact him/her at **[address/tel. no.]** on **[when available]**.

I/**[name of CRMO]** will be your community responsible medical officer in charge of the medical treatment for your mental disorder. I/he/she can be contacted at **[address/tel. no.]** on **[when available]**. If you have any other health needs, speak to your GP.

If you are put on supervised discharge and you are unhappy with any of the services provided or anything you are asked to do, you should speak to your supervisor about your worries. You must however keep to the arrangements which have been made unless it is decided that they should be changed. If you do not do this, a review of the supervised discharge arrangements will take place. This may include considering whether you should be assessed again for possible admission to hospital under the Mental Health Act 1983.

You will have the right to appeal against the decision to put you on supervised discharge to a Mental Health Review Tribunal. The details of how to appeal will be explained to you when you are told that the supervision application has been accepted.

A copy of this letter is being sent, for information, to **[names of any informal carer(s) and nearest relative (if consulted about application)]**.

Yours sincerely

[Name]

Responsible Medical Officer

Annex B

MODEL LETTER OF ACCEPTANCE FROM HEALTH AUTHORITY/PROVIDER UNIT

This should be dated the same day as acceptance of the supervision **4–304** application.

Dear **[name of patient]**

APPLICATION FOR SUPERVISED DISCHARGE

I am writing to let you know that **[name of RMO]**'s application for you to be put on supervised discharge has been accepted by/on behalf of the **[name of health authority]**.

The arrangements set out in **[name of RMO]**'s letter of **[date]** to you have been agreed.

You have the right to apply to a Mental Health Review Tribunal (MHRT) against this decision to put you on supervised discharge. If you wish to appeal, you should **[gives details of local arrangements]**. A legal representative can be provided free of charge under the legal aid scheme.

Your community responsible medical officer (CRMO) can decide to end supervised discharge at any time but will not do so before consulting everyone concerned, including you. If supervised discharge is still in place six months from the date of this letter, your CRMO will decide whether it should be renewed. If, after consulting all concerned, he or she decides that supervised discharge should continue, you will be able to appeal to a MHRT against the decision.

I enclose a copy of a leaflet which explains more about supervised discharge.

A copy of this letter is being sent, for information, to [**names of RMO and any informal carer and/or nearest relative consulted**].

Yours sincerely

On behalf of

[**name of HA**]

Annex C

JOINT PROTOCOLS ON SUPERVISED DISCHARGE: ISSUES FOR LOCAL INTER-AGENCY AGREEMENT

4–305 Shared understanding needed on—
* Risk assessment procedure
* Consultation procedures between the Health Authority/provider unit and the local authority, especially important when supervised discharge is being first considered and when the documentation is being completed and the supervision application accepted
* Reviewing and monitoring
* Role of supervisor and experience required.
* Power to convey: when to use, when not to use, records and who is authorised to use, involvement of local ambulance service and police.
* Appeals and complaints

Making the procedure work—
* How to provide advocacy and interpretation
* What joint procedures to use if patient does not attend for treatment
* How best to integrate CPA and care management assessments and policies with supervised discharge.
* IT systems to integrate CPA with supervision registers
* Performance standards
* Involvement of users and carers

Implementation planning—
* Training for supervisors and other professionals
* after-care arrangements discussed with probation, housing, police and GPs

Annex D

FUNCTIONS OF THE HEALTH AUTHORITY OR OF THE RESPONSIBLE AFTERCARE BODIES WHICH MAY BE DELEGATED TO A PROVIDER UNIT

Provision of the Act[23]	**Subject matter**	**4–306**
Section 25A(6), (7) and (8)	Supervision applications: receipt; consultation with local authority; acceptance; and notification	
Section 25C(6)	Supervision applications and recommendations—amendments where incorrect or defective	
Section 25(D)1	Imposition of requirements	
Section 25E(1), (3), (4), (6), (8) and (11)[24]	Review and modification of requirements imposed	
Section 25F(1) and (4)	Receipt of reclassification report	
Section 25G(3) and (8)	Receipt of renewal report and notification	
Section 25H(6)	Ending of after-care under supervision and notification	

[23] Sections 25A to 25H are inserted in the 1983 Act by section 1(t) of the 1995 Act.
[24] Review and modification of the after-care services cannot be delegated.

PART 5

MENTAL HEALTH ACT COMMISSION PUBLICATION

FORM MHAC 1

General Note

This form has been published by the Mental Health Act Commission to assist **5–001** responsible medical officers with their duties under section 61 of the 1983 Act.

Mental Health Act 1983 Review of Treatment

(Section 61)

This form must be completed by the Responsible Medical Officer and **5–002** forwarded to the Mental Health Act Commission when a patient is being treated under section 58(3)(b) on the occasions referred to at note 5 within this form. Although the notes refer to patients being treated under section 57(2) (psychosurgery and the surgical implantation of hormones for the suppression of male sexual drive), this form only applies to the treatments (ECT and Medication) referred to in section 58.

5–003 **I examined**
(*Name of patient*)
of

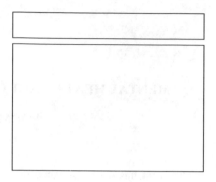

(*Name of hospital or mental nursing home in which the patient is liable to be determined*)

on
(*Date of examination*)

who was detained on
(*Date first detained in this period of detention*)

and is currently under section

on whom a certificate (Form 39) was last given

by a registered medical practitioner appointed under Section 58 of the Act for the purpose of the Secretary of State

To expire on (give date if applicable)

Please indicate whether Form 39 is for ECT or Medication.
*(Delete as applicable)

Medication*   ECT*

Describe the treatment given.
Please state:
a) present medication by drug name, route and dosage, or
b) number of ECT given

Form MHAC 1

Progress made:

```
┌─────────────────────────────────────────────────────────────────────┐
│                                                                     │
│                                                                     │
│                                                                     │
│                                                                     │
│                                                                     │
│                                                                     │
│                                                                     │
└─────────────────────────────────────────────────────────────────────┘
```

*a) It is intended to continue the treatment as authorised.

*b) The patient is now consenting to the treatment and I have completed a Form 38, a copy of which is enclosed with this report. *Completion of Form 38 is taken to cancel Form 39. Should the patient subsequently refuse or become unable to consent, the Mental Health Act Commission should be contacted for a further second opinion.*

Signed: _____ Date: _____

      (Responsible Medical Officer

* = Please circle as appropriate

MENTAL HEALTH ACT 1983—REVIEW OF TREATMENT, SECTION 61

NOTES TO AID THE COMPLETION OF FORM MHAC 1

5–004 1 Section 57 of the Mental Health Act 1983 is concerned with certain form of medical treatment for mental disorder which require the consent of the patient and a second opinion.

2 Section 58 relates to treatment requiring consent or a second opinion.

3 Section 61 provides for reports to be given in relation to treatments given under Section 57 or 58.

4 This note is issued by the Mental Health Act Commission acting for the Secretary of State and notifies:

a) Health Authorities;

b) National Health Service Trusts; and

c) Mental Nursing Homes, registered to take detained patients

of the arrangements for reports to be given by responsible medical officers (RMO) under Section 61 of Mental Health Act 1983.

5 Section 61 provides that where a patient is given treatment in accordance with Section 57(2) or Section 58(3)(b)—i.e. where a treatment plan has been authorised by a doctor appointed by the Mental Health Act Commission, a report on the treatment and the patient's condition shall be given by the responsible medical officer to the Mental Health Act Commission, acting for the Secretary of State:—

a) on the next and subsequent occasions that the authority for the patient's detention is renewed under Section 20(3);

b) at any other time if so required by the Commission; and

c) in the case of patients subject to a restriction order, at the end of the first six months. If treatment began during this period, and subsequently on each occasions that the RMO is statutorily required to report to the Secretary of State.

6 Unless the treatment was initially authorised on Form 39, a report is not required when the treatment has been given after the responsible medical officer has certified on Form 38 that the patient is capable of understanding the nature, purpose and likely effects of the treatment, and has consented to it.

7 When a report has been given to the Commission, as required by Section 61, permission to continue treatment as authorised may be assumed to be given unless the Commission gives notice of the withdrawal of Form 39. If such notice is given a further certificate will be required before treatment may be continued, except for urgent treatment given under the provisions of Section 62.

8 Please issue a copy of this document to the patient on completion (*Code of Practice*: [16.36]).

9 Completed forms and requests for further supplies of MHAC 1's should be sent to:

Mental Health Act Commission
Maid Marian House
56 Hounds Gate
Nottingham
NG1 6BG
Tel: 0115 943 7100   Fax 0115 943 7101

PART 6

HUMAN RIGHTS ACT 1998

(1998 c. 42)

An Act to give further effect to rights and freedoms guaranteed under the European Convention on Human Rights; to make provision with respect to holders of certain judicial offices who become judges of the European Court of Human Rights; and for connected purposes.   **6–001**

[9th November 1998]

*   *   *   *

GENERAL NOTE

Introduction

The Second World War and its associated horrors caused an upsurge in **6–002** international concern for human rights. The European Convention for the Protection of Human Rights and Fundamental Freedoms, commonly known as the European Convention on Human Rights, emerged out of that concern. It was concluded under the auspices of the Council of Europe in 1950, was ratified by the United Kingdom in 1951 and entered into force in 1953. Opposition to the right of individual petition was strong, and the United Kingdom did not accept this right until 1996.

The Commission and the Court

One of the most distinctive features of the Convention has been the role played by **6–003** two organs, the European Commission of Human Rights ("the Commission") and the European Court of Human Rights ("the Court"), in building up a substantial body of case law in the course of deciding petitions brought by individuals. Until recently, such petitions have been required to pass through two hurdles. Initially, the case has been examined by the Commission to determine whether it is "admissible". More than 90% of cases brought before the Commission have been found to be inadmissible. In 1998 the role of the Commission was abolished and there are now only two European institutions, the Court and the Committee of Ministers of the Council of Europe, that administer the Convention.

Interpreting the Convention

The Court has said: **6–004**

> "Inherent in the Convention is a search for a fair balance between the demands of the general interest of the community and the requirements of the protection of the individual's fundamental rights" (*Soering v. U.K.* (1989) 11 E.H.R.R. 439).

721

The Court has developed a standard approach when considering cases:

1. Has there been an interference with a Convention right, bearing in mind the need to construe the Convention broadly in order to give it practical effectiveness?
2. If there has been an interference with a non-absolute Article, is it justified?
3. To be justified the interference must be: (a) lawful; (b) intended to pursue a legitimate aim (*i.e.* one of the aims listed in Articles 8(2), 9(2), 10(2) or 11(2)); (c) necessary in a democratic society; and (d) not be discriminatory.

With regard to 3, the Court has said that:

(a) Lawfulness involves more than merely formal authorisation. It requires that "the law must indicate the scope of any such discretion conferred on the competent authorities and the manner of its exercise with sufficient clarity, having regard to the legitimate aim of the measure in question, to give the individual adequate protection against arbitrary interference" (*Malone v. U.K.* (1985) 7 E.H.R.R. 14, para. 68). The law in question, which can be either statute or common law, must be "adequately accessible" and be "formulated with sufficient precision to enable the citizen to regulate his conduct" (*Sunday Times v. United Kingdom* (1979) 2 E.H.R.R. 245, para. 49).

(b) To be "necessary in a democratic society" the limitation or restriction must fulfil a pressing social need and be "proportionate to the legitimate aim pursued" (*Handyside v. U.K.* (1976) 1 E.H.R.R. 737, para. 49). This means that even if a particular policy or action that interferes with a Convention right pursues a legitimate aim this will not justify the interference if the means used to achieve the purpose are excessive. Proportionality must be assessed by the standards of a "democratic society", characterised by "pluralism, tolerance and broadmindedness" (*ibid.*).

(c) The second principle that the Court has developed under 3(c) is the "margin of appreciation". This principle, which means the range of discretion open to national authorities without violating Convention provisions, is a refection of the fact that national authorities, including national courts, "are in principle in a better position than the international judge to give an opinion on the exact content of" restrictions on Convention rights (*ibid.*, para. 48). In *R. (on the application of N) v. Ashworth Special Hospital Authority and the Secretary of State for Health* [2001] EWHC Admin 339, para. 21, Newman J. said: "In my judgment the obligation not to interfere with human rights save to a degree necessary to achieve a permitted purpose does not place a straightjacket upon public authorities, the design of which is dictated by the exercise of objectively reasonable prescience and considerations of a range of certainties. A risk assessment involves regard being paid to the possibility of an event occurring in circumstances which are not foreseeable and which cannot be predicted with any degree of precision. The assessment will involve a significant element of subjectivity. The jurisprudential definition or recognition of this subjectivity is the doctrine of the margin of appreciation."

The Court, in a number of cases, has said that the Convention is a "living instrument" which must be interpreted in the light of present day conditions (see, for example, *Tyrer v. U.K.* (1978) 2 E.H.R.R. 1). This approach was emphasised in *Selmouni v. France* (2000) 29 E.H.R.R. 403, para. 101, where the Court said that "the increasingly high standard being required in the area of protection of human rights and fundamental liberties correspondingly and inevitably requires greater firmness in assessing breaches of the fundamental values of democratic societies." The interpretation of Convention rights will need to be subject to constant re-appraisal in order for them to adapt to present day conditions.

The Human Rights Act 1998

This Act is one of the most significant pieces of constitutional legislation enacted in **6–005** the United Kingdom. It incorporates provisions from the European Convention on Human Rights into U.K. law. The relevant provisions of the Convention are reproduced in Schedule 1 to the Act, which is set out below. The Act is ultimately subject to the sovereignty of Parliament, in that:

1. It does not provide the courts with a power to strike down primary legislation that is inconsistent with the Convention.
2. It leaves Parliament free, if it chooses to do so, to enact and maintain legislation that is incompatible with the Convention.
3. The Act is not entrenched against repeal.

Within these constraints, the Act attempts to achieve the Government's aim to "bring rights home" (*Rights Brought Home: the Human Rights Bill,* Cm. 3782 (1997)) by operating through three mechanisms:

1. Courts and tribunals are required to construe all legislation (past and future) "so far as it is possible to do so ... in a way which is compatible with Convention rights" (s.3). When doing so the court or tribunal must take account of the case law of the Court and the Commission. This requirement means that domestic courts must search for a construction that would prevent the making of a "declaration of incompatibility" (see below and *Re K. (A Child) (Secure Accommodation Order: Right to Liberty)* [2001] 2 All E.R. 719, *per* Butler-Sloss P. at 732).
2. All public authorities, including all courts and tribunals, are required to act in accordance with the Convention, within the scope permitted by primary legislation (s.6) and to have regard to European jurisprudence (s.2). "An act" includes a failure to act (s.6(6)). Public authorities include central and local government, the police, NHS Trusts, Health Authorities, hospital managers and any person "certain of whose functions are functions of a public nature" (s.6). Approved social workers, responsible medical officers, doctors, and nurses are therefore public authorities for the purposes of the Convention when they perform functions under the Mental Health Act.
3. The higher courts are able to make a "declaration of incompatibility" in respect of a provision of primary legislation, which the court considers to be incompatible with a Convention right (s.4). Such a declaration does not affect the validity, continued operation or enforcement of the provision in respect of which it is made (s.4(6)(a)) but it may lead to the correction of the legislation by Parliament making a "remedial order" which has the effect of bypassing the full legislative process (s.10). In *R. v. D.P.P., ex p. Kebeline* [1998] 3 W.L.R. 972, at 981, Lord Steyn said: "It is crystal clear that the carefully and subtlety drafted Human Rights Act preserves the principle of Parliamentary Sovereignty. In a case of incompatibility ... the courts may not disapply the legislation. The court may merely issue a declaration of incompatibility which then gives rise to a power to take remedial action." Where it is not possible to interpret subordinate legislation so as to be compatible with the Convention, the courts have power to disapply it unless the primary legislation prevents removal of the incompatibility (s.4(4)(b)).

Proceedings

Under section 7 of the Act, a person who claims that a public authority has acted **6–006** (or proposes to act) in a way which is incompatible with a Convention right may (a) bring civil proceedings for damages against the authority under the Act or (b) rely on the Convention right concerned in any criminal or civil proceedings, but only if he is (or would be) a victim of the act. It is anticipated that the great majority of cases will fall within route (b). A public authority cannot be a "victim" for the purposes of the Convention (*Ayuntamiento de M.* v. *Spain* (1991) D&R 209).

Approach of the courts to the Act

6–007 The courts should give "a broad and purposive approach, not a rigid approach, to the language of the Convention, an approach which will make the Convention a valuable protection of the fundamental rights of the individual members of the public as well as society as a whole" (*R. v. Lambert; R v. Ali: R. v. Jordan* [2001] 1 All E.R. 1014, per Lord Woolf CJ at para. 13). The Convention "is to be construed as an autonomous text, without regard to any special rules of English law ..." (*Re A (Children) (Conjoined Twins: Surgical Separation)* [2000] 4 All E.R. 961, *per* Robert Walker L.J. at 1068.

In *R v. Mental Health Review Tribunal for North East Thames Region, ex p. Secretary of* State *for the Home Department, The Times,* February 20, 2001, Collins J. said at para.77:

"The United Kingdom has of course been a signatory to the European Convention since its outset in 1951. Since 1966 it has granted the right of individual access, and there have been a considerable number of cases against the United Kingdom before the court. We now have incorporated the Convention into our law by the Human Rights Act of 1998. But, as it seems to me, the view that that makes a sea change is an erroneous one. We have had, over the years since 1951, to comply with the terms of the Convention. Sometimes, as decisions of the court have made plain, we have not succeeded in doing so. But for the most part, the practices and procedures carried out in this country do comply with the terms of the Convention, and it is wrong to approach the matter with a view that there may be a breach. Rather, as it seems to me, the approach should be that the court will not accept a breach unless persuaded and satisfied that there is one."

SCHEDULE 1

THE ARTICLES

PART I

THE CONVENTION

RIGHTS AND FREEDOMS

ARTICLE 2

RIGHT TO LIFE

6–008 1. Everyone's right to life shall be protected by law. No one shall be deprived of his life intentionally save in the execution of a sentence of a court following his conviction of a crime for which this penalty is provided by law.

2. Deprivation of life shall not be regarded as inflicted in contravention of this Article when it results from the use of force which is no more than absolutely necessary:

(a) in defence of any person from unlawful violence;

(b) in order to effect a lawful arrest or to prevent the escape of a person lawfully detained;

(c) in action lawfully taken for the purpose of quelling a riot or insurrection.

GENERAL NOTE

6–009 The European Court of Human Rights has stated that this Article "ranks as one of the most fundamental provisions in the Convention and, together with Article 3 of the Convention, enshrines one of the basic values of the democratic societies making up the Council of Europe" (*Cakici v. Turkey* [2001] E.H.R.R. 5, para. 86). The object and purpose of the Convention requires that this Article be interpreted and applied so as to make its safeguards practical and effective (*McCann and others v. United Kingdom* (1996) 21 E.H.R.R. 97, paras 146–147).

In *Kelly and others v. United Kingdom*, May 4, 2001, the Court said:

"The text of Article 2, read as a whole, demonstrates that it covers not only intentional killing but also the situations where it is permitted to 'use force' which may result, as an unintended outcome, in the deprivation of life. The deliberate or intended use of lethal force is only one factor however to be taken into account in assessing its necessity. Any use of force must be no more than 'absolutely necessary' for the achievement of one or more of the purposes set out in sub-paragraphs (a) to (c). This term indicates that a stricter and more compelling test of necessity must be employed from that normally applicable when determining whether State action is 'necessary in a democratic society' under paragraphs 2 of Articles 8 to 11 of the Convention. Consequently, the force used must be strictly proportionate to the achievement of the permitted aims" (para. 93).

In *Osman v. United Kingdom* (2000) 29 E.H.R.R. 245, the Court said that it was common ground that the state's obligation under this Article:

"extends beyond its primary duty to secure the right to life by putting in place effective criminal law provisions to deter the commission of offences against the person backed up by law-enforcement machinery for the prevention, suppression and sanctioning of such provisions. It is thus accepted by those appearing before the Court that Article 2 of the Convention may also imply in certain well-defined circumstances a positive obligation on the authorities to take preventive operational measures to protect an individual whose life is at risk from the criminal acts of another individual" (para. 115).

The Court said that for this positive obligation to be breached it must be established to the Court's satisfaction "that the authorities knew or ought to have known at the time of the existence of a real and immediate risk to the life of an identified individual or individuals from criminal acts of a third party and that they failed to take measures within the scope of their powers which, judged reasonably, might have been expected to take to avoid that risk" (para. 116). The Court also said that this obligation "must be interpreted in a way which does not impose an impossible or disproportionate burden on the authorities" (*ibid.*). In *Barrett v. United Kingdom* (1997) 23 E.H.R.R. CD 185, the Commission found that no breach of this Article had occurred in the case of a Naval Airman whose death on a naval base had been caused by excessive alcohol consumption. However, the Commission said: "Where a State provides facilities for drinking in circumstances where there is an obvious and substantial risk of excessive consumption the absence of any measures designed to discourage drinking to excess and, in the event, to secure adequate care and treatment, is likely to raise issues under Article 2."

The *Osman* case places professionals who are performing functions under the Mental Health Act under a positive obligation to take appropriate preventative measures in respect of patients who they know (or ought to have known) to be so dangerous as to be a threat to the lives of others. A positive obligation to save the life of a detained patient who is on hunger strike could also arise (see *Application N. 10565/83 v. Germany,* noted in Art. 3 under "degrading"). Under common law principles, by analogy with the position of a prisoner, there is a duty to take reasonable care to prevent the suicide of a detained patient, irrespective of the patient's mental capacity, and of a mentally incapable informal patient. This duty arises "from the complete control which the police or prison authorities have over the prisoner, combined with the special danger of people in prison taking their own lives" (*Reeves v. Commissioner of Police for the Metropolis* [1999] 3 All E.R. 897, HL, *per*

725

Lord Hoffmann at 903). The duty will arise where there is a "real and immediate risk of suicide" (*Keenan v. United Kingdom,* April 3, 2001, para. 92).

In *Scialacqua v. Italy* (1998) 26 E.H.R.R. CD 164, the Commission said:

> "[E]ven assuming that [this Article] can be interpreted as imposing on States the obligation to cover the costs of certain medical treatments or medicines that are essential in order to save lives, the Commission considers that this provision cannot be interpreted as requiring States to provide financial cover for medicines which are not listed as officially recognised medicines."

The procedural element contained in this Article "imposes the minimum requirement that where a State or its agents potentially bear responsibility for loss of life the events in question should be subject to an effective investigation or scrutiny which enables the facts to become known to the public, and in particular to the relatives of any victim" (*Taylor, Campton and Gibson families v. United Kingdom*, app. no. 23412/94). The Court has said that the investigation must be independent, effective, be reasonably prompt, have a sufficient element of public scrutiny and the next of kin must be involved to the appropriate extent (*Jordan v. United Kingdom*, May 4, 2001, paras. 106 to 109). Where the "events at issue lie wholly, or in large part, within the exclusive knowledge of the authorities as, for example, in the case of persons within their control in custody, strong presumptions of fact will arise in respect of injuries and death which occur. Indeed the burden of proof may be regarded as resting on the authorities to provide a satisfactory and convincing explanation" (*Kelly and others v. United Kingdom*, above, para. 92). Hospitals are required to have regulations for the protection of patient's lives, and an effective system for establishing the cause of a death which occurs in hospital and any liability on the part of the medical practitioners concerned (*Erikson v. Italy* (1999) 29 E.H.R.R. CD 152).

Everyone's life shall be protected by law: The Commission has said that the "concept that 'everyone's life shall be protected by law enjoins the State not only to refrain from taking life intentionally but, further, to take appropriate steps to safeguard life" (*Association X v. United Kingdom* (1978) 14 DR 31).

The extent to which this Article can be invoked to protect the life of an unborn child is uncertain: see the note on "The Human Rights Act 1998" under section 3 of the Mental Health Act.

ARTICLE 3

PROHIBITION OF TORTURE

6–010   No one shall be subjected to torture or to inhuman or degrading treatment or punishment.

GENERAL NOTE

6–011   This article prohibits conduct which has a serious physical or psychological impact on the person concerned. One of its main purposes is to protect "a person's dignity and physical integrity" (*Tyrer v. United Kingdom* (1978) 2 E.H.R.R. 1, para. 33). In *Tekin v. Turkey*, [2001] E.H.R.R. 4, the Court said that:

> "... in respect of a person deprived of his liberty, recourse to physical force which has not been made strictly necessary by his own conduct diminishes human dignity and is in principle an infringement of the right set forth in Article 3" (para. 53).

In *A. v. United Kingdom* (1999) 27 E.H.R.R. 611, the European Court of Human Rights held that this Article requires "States to take measures designed to ensure that individuals within their jurisdiction are not subjected to torture or inhuman or degrading treatment or punishment, including such ill-treatment administered by private individuals" (para. 22). These measures "should provide effective protection, in particular, of children and other vulnerable persons and include reasonable steps to prevent ill-treatment of which the authorities had or ought to have had knowledge" (*Z and others v. United Kingdom*, May 10, 2001, para. 73). The scope of this Article therefore extends to both public authorities and to individuals.

In *Assenov v. Bulgaria* (1998) 28 E.H.R.R. 652, the Court held that this Article, like Article 2, imposes an obligation to investigate. The investigation "should be capable of leading to the identification and punishment of those responsible" (para. 102).

According to the Court, the ill-treatment that the person is subjected to:

"must attain a minimum level of severity if it is to fall within the scope of Article 3. The assessment of this minimum is, in the nature of things, relative; it depends on all the circumstances of the case, such as the duration of the treatment, its physical or mental effects and in some cases, the sex, age and state of health of the victim, etc." (*Ireland v. United Kingdom* (1978) 2 E.H.R.R. 25, para. 162).

In *Selmouni v. France* (2000) 29 E.H.R.R. 403, the Court said that it:

"has previously examined cases in which it concluded that there had been treatment which could only be described as torture. However, having regard to the fact that the Convention is a 'living instrument which must be interpreted in the light of present-day conditions', the Court considers that certain acts which were classified in the past as 'inhuman and degrading treatment' as opposed to 'torture' could be classified differently in future. It takes the view that the increasingly high standard being required in the area of the protection of human rights and fundamental liberties correspondingly and inevitably requires greater firmness in assessing breaches of the fundamental values in a democratic society" (para. 101).

This significant statement means that the concept of inhuman or degrading treatment will inevitably expand to encompass conduct that was previously outside the scope of this Article.

The nature of the acts or omissions covered by this Article were considered by the Court in *V. v. United Kingdom* (2000) 30 E.H.R.R. 121:

"Treatment has been held by the Court to be 'inhuman' because, *inter alia,* it was premeditated, was applied for hours at a stretch and caused either actual bodily injury or intense physical or mental suffering, and also 'degrading' because it was such as to arouse in its victims feelings of fear, anguish and inferiority capable of humiliating and debasing them. In order for a punishment or treatment associated with it to be 'inhuman' or 'degrading', the suffering or humiliation involved must in any event go beyond that inevitable element of suffering or humiliation connected with a given form of legitimate treatment or punishment. The question whether the purpose of the treatment was to humiliate or debase the victim is a further factor to be taken into account but the absence of any such purpose cannot conclusively rule out a finding of a violation of Article 3" (para.71).

Authorities are under an obligation to protect the health of persons deprived of liberty (*Hurtado v. Switzerland*, Comm. Report, July 8, 1993), and the lack of appropriate medical treatment for such a person may amount to treatment contrary to this Article (*Ilhan v. Turkey,* Judgment, June 27, 2000, para.87).

The assessment of whether a particular treatment or punishment is incompatible with the standards of this Article has, in the case of mentally ill persons, to take into consideration their vulnerability and their inability, in some cases, to complain coherently or at all about how they are being affected by any particular treatment (*Keenan v. United Kingdom*, Judgment, April 3, 2001, para. 110). In this case the Court said that the "treatment of a mentally ill person may be incompatible with the standards imposed by Article 3 in the protection of fundamental human dignity, even though that person may not be able, or capable of, pointing to any specific ill-effects" (para. 112).

The Court has been reluctant to categorise either psychiatric treatment or institutional conditions as "inhuman or degrading treatment". In *Herczegfalvy v. Austria* (1993) 15 E.H.R.R. 432, the patient had been handcuffed to a security bed with a belt placed around his ankles. The Court, in holding that medical treatment could, in principle reach a level of severity sufficient to amount to "inhuman or degrading treatment" contrary to this Article, said:

> "The Court considers that the position of inferiority and powerlessness which is typical of patients confined in psychiatric hospitals calls for increased vigilance in reviewing whether the Convention has been complied with. While it is for the medical authorities to decide, on the basis of recognised rules of medical science, on the therapeutic methods to be used, if necessary by force, to preserve the physical and mental health of patients who are entirely incapable of deciding for themselves and for whom they are therefore responsible, such patients nevertheless remain under the protection of Article 3, the requirements of which permit no derogation ... [H]owever, the evidence before the Court is not sufficient to disprove the Government's argument that, according to the psychiatric principles generally accepted as the time, medical necessity justified the treatment in issue" (paras 82, 83).

This interpretation involves the application of principles very similar to those in *Bolam v. Friern Barnet Hospital* [1957] 1 W.L.R. 582, which means that treatment which would be considered by a responsible body of psychiatrists as being therapeutically necessary could not be regarded as inhuman or degrading. However, in *Herczegfalvy*, the Court said that it "must nevertheless satisfy itself that the medical necessity has been convincingly shown to exist" (para. 82).

In *NHS Trust A v. M; NHS Trust B v. H* [2001] 1 All E.R. 801, Butler-Sloss P. held that this Article "requires the victim to be aware of the inhuman and degrading treatment which he or she is experiencing or at least be in a state of physical or mental suffering" (para.49). This is a surprising finding which has the effect of removing the protection afforded by this Article from a group of extremely vulnerable citizens, *i.e.* insensate patients.

In *R. v. North West Lancashire Health Authority, ex p. A, D and G* (1999) 2 C.C.L.R. 419, a case brought by transsexuals who had been refused funding for gender reassignment, Auld L.J. said, at 437, that this Article "was not designed for circumstances of this sort of case where the challenge is to a Health Authority's allocation of finite funds between competing demands."

An admissibility decision of the Commission in *Grare v. France* (1992) 15 E.H.R.R. CD 100, suggests that psychiatric treatment in the form of medication with unpleasant side-effects could involve a breach of this Article if the side-effects were sufficiently serious: see O. Thorold "The Implications of the European Convention on Human Rights for United Kingdom Mental Health Legislation" [1996] E.H.R.L.R. 619–636, at 620. If the medication is therapeutically justified, an application on this ground would have no prospect of success unless it could be shown that there was alternative medication available which was equally efficacious and had significantly less serious side effects. In *Grare* the Commision found that although the treatment in question constituted an interference with applicant's right to private life under Article 8(1), it was justified by the need to preserve public order and the protection of the applicant's health under Article 8(2).

Although the courts will doubtless be reluctant to interfere in matters of pure clinical judgment, the Commission, in *Tanko v. Finland*, app. no. 23634/94, said that it "does not exclude that a lack of proper care in a case where someone is suffering from a serious illness could in certain circumstances amount to treatment contrary to Article 3."

The detention of persons of unsound mind in an unsatisfactory or non-therapeutic environment could amount to a violation of this Article if the ill-treatment of the patient attains a minimum level of severity (*Aerts v. Belgium* (2000) 29 E.H.R.R. 50). A patient who is kept in conditions of high security, which his clinical condition did not warrant, could consider basing an application on this decision. In *Aerts* the Court held that, where the sole basis of detention is unsoundness of mind, an anti-therapeutic environment may contravene Article 5(1), even if it is not severe enough to amount to inhuman and degrading treatment under this Article: see the note on Art. 5(1)(e).

Removal from association, such as the seclusion of a mentally disordered patient, does not normally amount to inhuman or degrading treatment, but it will depend upon the conditions, duration, purpose and the effects on the person concerned (*Koskinen v. Finland* (1994) 18 E.H.R.R. CD 146 and *A v. United Kingdom*, app. no. 6840/74). In *Dhoest v. Belgium* 12 E.H.R.R. 97, the Commission said that it had stated that "complete sensory deprivation, coupled with total social isolation, can destroy the personality and constitutes a form of treatment which cannot be justified by the requirements of security or for any other reason. It has moreover drawn a distinction between this and removal from association with other prisoners for security, disciplinary or protective reasons, and would not normally consider that this form of segregation from the prison community amounts to inhuman or degrading treatment. The same reasoning applies *mutatis mutandis* to persons who have been committed to a mental hospital in the framework of criminal proceedings" (para. 117).

In *Vilvarajah v United Kingdom* (1992) 14 E.H.R.R. 248, the Court said that:

"expulsion by a Contracting State of an asylum seeker may give rise to an issue under Article 3, and hence engage the responsibility of that State under the Convention, where substantial grounds have been shown for believing that the person concerned faced a real risk of being subjected to torture or to inhuman or degrading treatment or punishment in the contrary to which he was returned" (para. 103).

The Court will assess the risk of inhuman or degrading treatment at the time of its **6–012** own consideration of the case (*D v. United Kingdom* (1997) 24 E.H.R.R. 423, para. 50). In *D*. the Court said that "aliens ... who are subject to expulsion cannot in principle claim any entitlement to remain on the territory of a contracting state in order to continue to benefit from medical, social or other forms of assistance provided by the expelling state during their stay" (para. 54). Also note *R. v. Secretary of State for the Home Department, ex p. K.*, February 16, 2000, CA, where Sir Christopher Staughton said that it would not be inhuman or degrading treatment to send the applicant, who was suffering from AIDS, back to Uganda on the ground that he may or may not be able to afford all the treatment that he requires.

Similar considerations would apply to the exercise by the Home Secretary of his power to deport an "alien patient" under section 86 of the Mental Health Act: see *R. v. Secretary of State for the Home Department, ex p. X.*, *The Times*, January 9, 2001, where the Court of Appeal rejected a submission that to move someone with a medical problem from conditions where it was being contained in circumstances where that removal would lead to an increased risk of self harm and the deterioration in mental health and might not be in the patient's best interests, amounted to a breach of this Article. In *Bensaid v. United Kingdom*, February 6, 2001, the Court held that the fact that the applicant's circumstances with regard to the treatment of his mental illness in Algeria would be less favourable than those enjoyed by him in the United Kingdom was not decisive from the point of view of this Article. The Court said that the case did not disclose "the exceptional circumstances" of the *D*. case, above, where the applicant was in the final stages of a terminal illness, AIDS, and had no prospect of medical care or family support on expulsion to St. Kitts" (para. 40). In *Bensaid* the Court found that medical treatment for his mental disorder would be available to the applicant in Algeria. A less restrictive approach was adopted by Rafferty J. in *R. (on the application of Njai) v. Secretary of State for the Home Department,* December 1, 2001, where her ladyship referred to the following passage from the decision of the Commission in *SCC v. Sweden* (2000) 29 E.H.R.R. CD 245 at 249:

> "According to established case-law aliens who are subject to expulsion cannot in principle claim any entitlement to remain in the territory of a Contracting State in order to continue to benefit from medical, social or other forms of assistance provided by the Contracting State. However, in exceptional circumstances an implementation of a decision to remove an alien may, owing to compelling humanitarian considerations, result in a violation of Article 3."

Her Ladyship, in what she described as a "difficult decision", found that such "compelling humanitarian considerations" existed where the deportation of a mentally ill man to Gambia would subject him to a "risk of physical and mental suffering" because of an anticipated difficulty in obtaining supplies of the drug risperidone.

The guarantees of this Article apply in deportation cases irrespective of the reprehensible nature of the conduct of the person in question (*Chahal v. United Kingdom* (1996) 23 E.H.R.R. 413).

Aspects of mental health practice that could be challenged under this Article include:

(a) the placing of female patients with a history of sexual abuse by men in mixed sex wards;

(b) the automatic handcuffing of patients when the police are involved in the transporting of patients to hospital;

(c) the unjustified use of CS spray; and

(d) the imposition of control and restraint techniques on a patient where neither the patient's history nor a current assessment justify their use.

If the treatment is not of sufficient severity to bring it within this Article, it might be possible to bring an application under Article 8 if the patient was mentally competent to refuse the intervention. The Court's caselaw does not exclude the possibility that treatment which does not reach the severity of treatment under this Article may nonetheless breach Article 8 in its private life aspect where there are sufficiently adverse effects on physical and moral integrity (*Costello-Roberts v. United Kingdom* (1995) 19 E.H.R.R. 122).

Degrading: Treatment may be considered degrading "if it is such as to arouse in its victims feelings of fear, anguish and inferiority capable of humiliating and debasing them and possibly breaking their physical and moral resistance. Moreover, it is sufficient if the victim is humiliated in his or her own eyes (*Smith and Grady v. United Kingdom* (2000) 29 E.H.R.R. 493, para. 120). The fact that the object of the treatment was not to humiliate or debase the person concerned cannot conclusively rule out a finding of violation of this Article (*Price v. United Kingdom*, July 10, 2001, para. 24). In this case the Court held that "to detain a severely disabled person in conditions where she is dangerously cold, risks developing sores because her bed is too hard or unreachable, and is unable to go to the toilet or keep clean without the greatest of difficulty, constitutes degrading treatment contrary to [this Article]" (para. 30).

In *App. No. 10565/83 v. Germany* 7 E.H.R.R. 152, the Commission said that "the forced feeding of a person does involve degrading elements which in certain circumstances may be regarded as prohibited by Article 3... Under the Convention the High Contracting parties are, however, also obliged to secure to everyone the right to life as set out in Article 2. Such an obligation should in certain circumstances call for positive action on the part of the Contracting Parties, in particular an active measure to save lives when the authorities have taken the person in question into their custody. When, as in the present case, a detained person maintains a hunger strike this may inevitably lead to a conflict between an individual's right to physical integrity and the High Contracting Party's obligation under Article 2 . . .– a conflict which is not solved by the Convention itself." In *R. v. Ashworth Hospital Authority, ex p. Brady,* March 10, 2000, Kay J., having considered submissions on the point, decided not to make a finding on whether the State has either the power or the duty to prevent the suicide of a mentally capable patient.

ARTICLE 4

PROHIBITION OF SLAVERY AND FORCED LABOUR

6–013

1. No one shall be held in slavery or servitude.
2. No one shall be required to perform forced or compulsory labour.
3. For the purpose of this Article the term "forced or compulsory labour" shall not include:
(a) any work required to be done in the ordinary course of detention imposed according to the provisions of Article 5 of this Convention or during conditional release from such detention;
(b) any service of a military character or, in case of conscientious objectors in countries where they are recognised, service exacted instead of compulsory military service;
(c) any service exacted in case of an emergency or calamity threatening the life or well-being of the community;
(d) any work or service which forms part of normal civic obligations.

ARTICLE 5

RIGHT TO LIBERTY AND SECURITY

6–014

1. Everyone has the right to liberty and security of person. No one shall be deprived of his liberty save in the following cases and in accordance with a procedure prescribed by law:
(a) the lawful detention of a person after conviction by a competent court;
(b) the lawful arrest or detention of a person for non-compliance with the lawful order of a court or in order to secure the fulfilment of any obligation prescribed by law;
(c) the lawful arrest or detention of a person effected for the purpose of bringing him before the competent legal authority on reasonable suspicion of having committed an offence or when it is reasonably considered necessary to prevent his committing an offence or fleeing after having done so;
(d) the detention of a minor by lawful order for the purpose of educational supervision or his lawful detention for the purpose of bringing him before the competent legal authority;
(e) the lawful detention of persons for the prevention of the spreading of infectious diseases, of persons of unsound mind, alcoholics or drug addicts or vagrants;
(f) the lawful arrest or detention of a person to prevent his effecting an unauthorised entry into the country or of a person against whom action is being taken with a view to deportation or extradition.

2. Everyone who is arrested shall be informed promplty, in a language which he understands, of the reasons for his arrest and of any charge against him.

3. Everyone arrested or detained in accordance with the provisions of paragraph 1(c) of this Article shall be brought promptly before a judge or other officer authorised by law to exercise judicial power and shall be entitled to trial within a reasonable time or to release pending trial. Release may be conditioned by guarantees to appear for trial.

4. Everyone who is deprived of his liberty by arrest or detention shall be entitled to take proceedings by which the lawfulness of his detention shall be decided speedily by a court and his release ordered if the detention is not lawful.

5. Everyone who has been the victim of arrest or detention in contravention of the provisions of this Article shall have an enforceable right to compensation.

GENERAL NOTE

The purpose of this Article was described by the European Court of Human **6–015** Rights in *Shiesser v. Switzerland* [1979] 2 E.H.R.R. 417, at 425:

"The Court views Article 5 as designed to ensure that no one should be arbitrarily dispossessed of his liberty. This overall purpose entails, in the area covered by paragraph 4, the necessity of following a procedure which has a 'judicial character' and gives 'guarantees appropriate to the kind of deprivation of liberty in question' without which it would be impossible to speak of a 'court'."

This Article embraces the detention and release of the mentally disordered, but not a right to treatment (*Winterwerp v. Netherlands* below at para. 51).
The Court has said that:

"... the list of exceptions to the right to liberty secured by Article 5(1) is an exhaustive one and only a narrow interpretation of those exceptions is consistent with the aim and purpose of that provision, namely to ensure that no one is arbitrarily deprived of his or her liberty" (*Quinn v. France* (1996) 21 E.H.R.R. 529, para. 42).

Although the list in paragraph 1 is exhaustive, "the applicability of any one ground does not necessarily preclude that of another; a detention may, depending on the circumstances, be justified under more than one sub-paragraph (*Eriksen v. Norway* (2000) 29 E.H.R.R. 328, para. 76).

Paragraph 1

6–016   *Everyone:* Including children (*Nielsen v. Denmark* (1989) 11 E.H.R.R. 175, at para. 58).
Procedure prescribed by law: The law in question is domestic law. "However, the domestic law must itself be in conformity with the Convention, including the general principles expressed or implied therein. The notion underlying [this term] is one of fair and proper procedure, namely that any measure depriving a person of his liberty should issue from and be executed by an appropriate authority and should not be arbitrary" (*Winterwerp v. Netherlands* (1979) 2 E.H.R.R. 387, para. 45). This requirements does not mean that the common law cannot grow or shape itself to changing social conditions and perceptions (*SW and CR v. U.K.* (1996) 21 E.H.R.R. 363). It means that "any such change must be principled and predictable"; *per* Sedley L.J. in *Re F (Adult: Court's Jurisdiction)*, [2000] F.L.R. 512, 531, CA.

Paragraph 1(a)

6–017   *Conviction:* A mentally disordered offender who is convicted of a criminal offence and ordered to be detained in a psychiatric hospital will be detained under both Article 5(1)(a) and 5(1)(e) (*X v. United Kingdom* (1981) 4 E.H.R.R. 188, para. 39).

Paragraph 1(e)

6–018   In *Anderson v. The Scottish Ministers*, Court of Session, Inner House, *The Times*, June 21, 2000, the Lord President summarised the principles to be derived from the authorities on this paragraph:

"The admission and detention of a person of unsound mind must be in conformity with a procedure laid down in domestic law. The domestic law relating to the detention of such persons must conform to three criteria: a true mental disorder must be established before a competent authority on the basis of objective medical expertise; the mental disorder must be of a kind or degree warranting compulsory confinement; and the valditity of the patient's continued detention depends upon the persistence of such a disorder. Moreover, Article 5(1)(e) does not require that the detention of persons of unsound mind be for the purpose of treatment, but it should be in a hospital, clinic or other appropriate institution authorised for the purpose. Detention under Article

5(1)(e) is justified where it is necessary to serve a legitimate social purpose, which may be the protection of the public."

In this case the court, having considered the reasoning of the European Court of Human Rights in *Litwa v. Poland*, April 4, 2000, concluded that:

   (i) detention under this paragraph can be justified on the ground of social policy, including the protection of the public, as long as the detention is necessary in the circumstances, and other measures are insufficient to achieve that end; and

  (ii) it is lawful to continue to detain a mentally disordered person who is admitted to hospital on the satisfaction of a treatment condition and who now no longer satisfies that condition although he does satisfy another Convention condition, such as the protection of the public.

Lawful: Lawfulness implies the absence of any arbitrariness (*Bozano v. France* (1987) 9 E.H.R.R. 297, para. 59). It also implies that "the deprivation of liberty is in keeping with the purpose of the restrictions permissible under Article 5(1)" (*Bouamar v. Belgium* (1989) 11 E.H.R.R. 1, para. 50). In *Litwa v. Poland*, above, the Court said that the "detention of an individual is such a serious measure that it is only justified where other, less severe measures have been considered and found to be insufficient to safeguard the individual or public interest which might require that the person concerned be detained. That means that it does not suffice that the deprivation of liberty is executed in conformity with national law but it must also be necessary in the circumstances" (para. 78).

Detention: This Article is concerned with deprivation of liberty and not with mere restrictions on liberty of movement which are governed by Article 2 of Protocol No. 4 (*Ashingdane v. United Kingdom* (1985) 7 E.H.R.R. 528, para. 41). Article 2 of Protocol No. 4 has not been ratified by the United Kingdom. In *Ashingdane* the Court said that the applicant's liberty had been "circumscribed both in fact and in law". The applicant, who was subject to a restriction order, was "detained" even though he had been cared for in an open ward after his transfer from Broadmoor to a local hospital. Also note *L v. Sweden*, 45 D. & R. 181, where the Commission said that "a person detained in a psychiatric hospital would clearly be regarded as 'deprived of his liberty' even if he was occasionally allowed to leave the hospital premises." In *Guzzardi v. Italy* (1981) 3 E.H.R.R. 333, the Court observed that "the difference between deprivation of and restriction upon liberty is nonetheless merely one of degree or intensity, and not one of nature or substance" (para. 93). The Court must have regard to the patient's actual situation in the hospital, taking into account such factors as the type, duration, effects and manner of implementation of the restrictions placed upon the patient (*Ashingdane*, at para. 41).

The Convention does not guarantee "for a person who has been ordered to undergo compulsory psychiatric treatment, the right to choose the place of his detention" (*Valle v. Finland*, March 16, 2000).

This Article does not cover individuals who have consented to the constraint on their liberty, for example, patients who have consented to be informal psychiatric patients. Consent must be clearly established in such cases (*De Wilde, Ooms and Versp v. Belgium* (1971) 1 E.H.R.R. 373).

In *Nielsen v. Denmark*, above, the Court found that no deprivation of liberty had occurred when the mother of a 12-year-old boy consented to his admission to a psychiatric hospital against his wishes and that of his father. Among the factors that were cited in support of this decision, the Court emphasised, at paragraph 72:

  (1) the fact that the mother was the sole holder of parental resonsibility in respect of the child. The Court said that the "care and upbringing of children

normally and necessarily require that the parents or an only parent decide where the child must reside and also impose, or authorise others to impose, various restrictions on the child's liberty." However, it accepted that "the rights of the holder of parental authority cannot be unlimited and that it is incumbent on the State to provide safeguards against abuse";

(ii) that the "restrictions to which the [child] was subject were no more than the normal requirements for the care of a child of 12 years of age receiving treatment in hospital"; and

(iii) its view that the child "was still of an age at which it would be normal for a decision to be made by the parent against the wishes of the child.

The Court concluded by stating that it "must be possible for a child like the applicant to be admitted to hospital at the request of the holder of parental rights, a case which is clearly not covered by paragraph 1 of Article 5." This statement was made because the child, not having been diagnosed as being mentally ill, was not detained as a person of unsound mind so as to bring the case with this sub-paragraph.

It has been said that although Nielsen is a recent decision, "there must be doubt how far, if at all, [it] will be followed in future. In considering any similar issue today, account should be taken of the Convention of the Rights of the Child 1989" (S. Grosz, J. Beatson, P. Duffy, *Human Rights: The 1998 Act and the European Convention*, (2000), p. 199).

6–019 *Persons of unsound mind:* In *Winterwerp v. Netherlands*, above, the Court held that in order for a detention on the ground of unsoundness of mind to be lawful the Government has to be able to show by reliable medical evidence before a competent national authority that:

(i) except in emergency cases, a true mental disorder has been established by objective medical expertise;

(ii) the detention must be effected in accordance with a procedure prescribed by law;

(iii) the mental disorder is of a kind or degree warranting compulsory confinement; and

(iv) the validity of continued confinement depends upon the persistence of such a disorder.

Taking these requirements in turn:

(i) The Court held that the term "persons of unsound mind" is "not one that can be given a definitive interpretation ... it is a term whose meaning is constantly evolving as research in psychiatry progresses, an increasing flexibility in treatment is developing and society's attitude to mental illness changes, in particular so that a greater understanding of the problems of mental patients is becoming wide-spread. In any event, Article 5(1)(e) obviously cannot be taken as permitting the detention of a person simply because his view or behaviour deviate from the norms prevailing in a particular society" (para. 37). In *X v. Federal Republic of Germany*, 6 D. & R. 182, the Commission found that the term "unsound mind" did not just mean mental illness, but must be understood in a wider sense to include abnormal personality disorder.

Neither the Court nor the Commission has set out the nature of the Convention obligations that apply in a situation where a person of unsound mind is detained in an emergency. In *X v. United Kingdom*, above, the Court said that it is sufficient for emergency procedures not to be arbitrary and not to exclude observance in individual cases of the principles stated in the *Winterwerp* judgment (para. 31). The medical evidence referred to in the *Winterwerp* judgment need not be obtained on the emergency recall to hospital of a restricted patient by the Home Secretary under section 42(3) of the 1983 Act (*X v. United Kingdom*, above). In *Winterwerp*, the Court concluded that a period of emergency detention which lasted for six weeks before a medical opinion was obtained from a general practitioner did not violate this Article. In *Kay v. United Kingdom*, 40 B.M.L.R. 20, the Commission found that there had been a violation of this requirement where the Home Secretary, in a non-emergency situation, had used his powers under section 42(3) to recall a conditionally discharged patient who was nearing the end of a prison sentence without obtaining up-to-date medical evidence about his mental health.

(ii) This places an obligation on the Government to "conform to the substantive and procedural rules" of national law so as to "protect individuals from arbitrariness" (*Herczegfalvy v. Austria* (1993) 15 E.H.R.R. 432, para. 63): also see paragraph 45 of the *Winterwerp* judgment noted under "procedure prescribed by law", above.

(iii) This requirement is satisfied by the 1983 Act: see sections 2(2)(a) and 3(2)(a) and the interpretation given to "nature or degree" by Popplewell J. in *R. v. The Mental Health Review Tribunal for the South Thames Region, ex p. Smith*, noted under section 3(2)(a). Also see the decision of the Court of Appeal in *R (on the application of H.) v. Mental Health Review Tribunal, North and East London Region*, with is noted in the General Note to section 72. It is frequently the case that tribunals and hospital managers find that a patient is not suffering from a mental disorder of a nature or degree warranting detention if appropriate after-care services could be provided for him. The question whether the failure to discharge a patient in these circumstances would constitute a violation of this Article was considered by the Court of Appeal in *R. v. Camden and Islington Health Authority, ex p. K.*, which is noted in section 117 of the 1983 Act under the heading "The Human Rights Act 1998".

(iv) This requirement links to the review procedure provided for under paragraph 4 of this Article. In *Johnson v. United Kingdom* (1997) 27 E.H.R.R. 296, the Court rejected the submission of the applicant, a restricted patient, that once there had been a finding by an expert authority, in this case the Mental Health Review Tribunal, that the mental disorder had ceased, he should as a consequence have been immediately and unconditionally released. The Court said:

> "Such a rigid approach to the interpretation of that condition would place an unacceptable degree of constraint on the responsible authority's exercise of judgment to determine in particular cases and on the basis of all the relevant circumstances whether the interests of the patient and the community into which he is to be released would in fact be best served by this course of action. It must also be observed that in the field of mental illness the assessment as to whether the disappearance of the symptoms of the illness is confirmation of complete recovery is not an exact science" (para. 61).

A responsible authority is therefore entitled to exercise a "measure of discretion in deciding whether in the light of all the relevant circumstances and interests at stake it would in fact be appropriate to order the immediate and absolute discharge of a person who is no longer suffering from the mental disorder that led to his confinement" (para. 63). Also note *Luberti v. Italy*, February 23, 1984, Series A No. 75, where the Court said that the responsible authority was entitled to "proceed with caution" in effecting the release of a mentally disordered offender who had been convicted of homicide (para. 29).

In the *Johnson* case the tribunal deferred the conditional discharge of the patient until arrangements had been made for him to be cared for in suitable hostel accommodation. Attempts to find the accommodation proved unsuccessful. The Court held that this paragraph had been violated because the "lack adequate safeguards including provision of judicial review to ensure that the applicant's release from detention was not unreasonably delayed" (para. 63). The Court commented that in between reviews by the tribunal "the applicant could not petition the tribunal to have the terms of the hostel residence condition reconsidered; nor was the tribunal empowered to monitor periodically outside the annual reviews the progress made in the search for a hostel and to amend the deferred conditional discharge order in the light of the difficulties encountered by the authorities" (para. 66). Compliance with this ruling will require tribunals to be given powers to ensure that discharge arrangements will not be unduly delayed.

In the *Winterwerp* case, above, the Court held that "a mental patient's right to treatment appropriate to his condition cannot as such be derived from Article 5(1)(e)" (para. 51). In *Ashingdane v. United Kingdom*, above, the Court said that this Article "is not in principle concerned with suitable treatment or conditions" (para. 44). However, if the absence of appropriate treatment has a severe effect on the patient it might be possible to argue that this constitutes a violation of Article 3. In *Aerts v. Belgium* (2000) 25 E.H.R.R. 50, the applicant, who was an offender patient, was placed in provisional detention in the psychiatric wing of a prison for seven months before a place became available in a psychiatric institution. The Court heard evidence that the wing was not regarded as an appropriate insitution for persons of unsound mind, as there was no regular medical attention and it was not a therapeutic environment. The Mental Health Board found that the situation was harmful to Mr Aerts who was not receiving treatment for his disorder. The Court held that, in principle, the detention of a person of unsound mind will only be lawful for the purposes of this paragraph "if effected in a hospital, clinic or other appropriate institution authorised for that purpose" (para. 44). In this context "for that purpose" must mean purpose of caring for the mentally disordered. The detention of the applicant violated this paragraph because the "proper relationship between the aim of the detention and the conditions in which it took place was . . . deficient" (para. 49). This implies that there must be some therapeutic involvement with the patient. The Court further found that the conditions in which the applicant was detained were not sufficiently severe to lead to a finding of inhuman or degrading treatment under Article 3. It follows that where detention is justified under this paragraph, complaints about the conditions in the patient's place of detention are better brought under this Article rather than Article 3. It is likely that the Court would need evidence that standards relating to the provision of services and/or the quality of conditions in the place of detention had fallen very low for it to be satisfied that this Article had been violated.

Alcoholics: Persons who are not medically diagnosed as "alcoholics", but whose conduct and behaviour under the influence of alcohol pose a threat to public order or themselves, can be taken into custody for the protection of the public or their own interests, such as their health or personal safety (*Litwa v. Poland*, April 4, 2000, para. 61).

Paragraph 2

6–020   In the psychiatric context, the purpose of this paragraph is to adequately inform the patient of the reason for his detention so that he may judge its lawfulness and take steps to challenge it if he thinks fit, thus availing himself of the right guaranteed by Article 5(4).

In *Van der Leer v. Netherlands* (1990) 12 E.H.R.R. 567, the Court held that the term "arrest" extends beyond the realm of criminal law measures and embraces deprivation of liberty on the ground of unsoundness of mind (para. 27). A patient who is detained under the 1983 Act must therefore be informed promptly, in language that he understands, of the reasons for his detention. Merely providing the patient with a copy of the application for his detention would not satisfy this requirement. The information provided must be sufficient to enable the patient to know why he is being detained. The mere recital of the legal basis for the detention is insufficient (*Fox, Campbell and Hartley v. United Kingdom* (1991) 13 E.H.R.R. 157). It is likely that the Court would hold that information could be withheld if it might cause psychological harm to the patient. In this situation, the patient's legal representative should be provided with the relevant details.

Paragraph 4

This paragraph and paragraph 1 are "separate provisions and observance of the **6–021** former does not necessarily entail observance of the latter" (*Douiyed v. Netherlands* (2000) 30 E.H.R.R. 790, para. 57).

In *De Wilde, Ooms and Versp v. Belgium*, above, the Court said that the purpose of this paragraph "is to assure to persons who are arrested or detained the right to a judicial supervision of the lawfulness of the measure to which they are thereby subject" (para. 76). It does not require the reviewing body to have any other control of the detention process, such as decisions regarding leave of absence (*Roux v. United Kingdom* (1986) 48 D&R 263, at 268).

The principles which emerge from the Court's case law on this paragraph as they apply to the detention of person of unsound mind were summarised in *Megyeri v. Germany* (1993) 15 E.H.R.R. 584, at para. 22. They include the following:

(i) A person of unsound mind who is compulsorily confined in a psychiatric institution for an indefinite or lengthy period is in principle entitled, at any rate where there is no automatic periodic review of a judicial character, to take proceedings "at reasonable intervals" before a court to put in issue the "lawfulness"—within the meaning of the Convention—of his detention (see *X v. United Kingdom*, above, at para. 52).

(ii) Article 5(4) requires that the procedures followed have a judicial character and give to the individual concerned guarantees appropriate to the kind of deprivation of liberty in question; in order to determine whether a proceeding provides adequate guarantees, regard must be had to the particular nature of the circumstances in which such proceedings takes place (see *Wassink v. Netherlands*, Sept. 27, 1990, Series A, No. 185–A, p. 13, para. 30).

(iii) The judicial proceedings referred to in Article 5(4) need not always be attended by the same guarantees as those required under Article 6(1) for civil or criminal litigation. None the less, it is essential that the person concerned should have access to a court and the opportunity to be heard either in person or, where necessary, some form of representation. Special procedural safeguards may prove called for in order to protect the interests of persons who, on account of their mental disabilities, are not fully capable of acting for themselves (see *Winterwerp v. Netherlands*, above, at para. 60).

(iv) Article 5(4) does not require that persons committed to care under the head of "unsound mind" should themselves take the initiative in obtaining legal representation before having recourse to a court (*ibid.*, para. 60).

The Court went on to say that it "follows from the foregoing that where a person is **6–022** confined in a psychiatric institution on the ground of the commission of acts which constituted criminal offences but for which he could not be held responsible on account of mental illness, he should—unless there are special circumstances— receive legal assistance in subsequent proceedings relating to the continuation, suspension or termination of his detention. The importance of what is at stake for him—personal liberty—taken together with the very nature of his affliction— diminished mental capacity—compel this conclusion" (para. 23).

Although the Court has been prepared to borrow some of the general concepts of fairness in judicial proceedings from Article 6, this does not mean that the process required for conformity with this Article must also be in conformity with Article 6. That would conflate the Convention's control over two sets of proceedings, which have different objects (*R. (on the application of the Director of Public Prosecutions v. Havering Magistrates Court; R. (on the application of McKeown v. Wirral Borough Magistrates Court, The Times,* February 7, 2001, *per* Latham L.J., at para. 36).

In *Anderson v. The Scottish Ministers*, above, the Court held that when a patient invoked his right to have the legality of his detention reviewed, the fact that the ground to be reviewed was, as a result of a new law (the Mental Health (Public Safety and Appeals) (Scotland) Act 1999), different from the original ground for his detention, did not contravene this paragraph. In this case the court proceeded on the basis that the principle of equality of arms, which has been expounded by the Court in relation to hearings governed by Article 6, applies to hearings required by this paragraph. This principle "means that a person must be afforded a reasonable opportunity of presenting his case to the court under conditions do not place him at a substantial disadvantage *vis-à-vis* his opponent" (S. Grosz *et al., op. cit.* p. 246).

The Commission has said that a patient does not have a right to obtain an independent psychiatric opinion in a situation where the psychiatric evidence before the court was "sufficient in scope and nature to provide a reasonable basis for the courts' ... decisions" (*M v. Federal Republic of Germany* (1984) 38 D. & R. 104, 113, para. 5).

In the *Winterwerp* case, above, the Commission said that the patient's lawyer had the right to examine the patient's file, but that it was not necessary for the patient to be informed of all the evidence or that he be allowed access to all of the information in his medical file. The Commission also said that it was not necessary for the proceedings to take place in public (app. no. 6301/73, paras 98, 101). The Court did not comment on these guidelines.

Lawfulness of his detention: Detention lasts from the time when the detention is authorised to the time when it is officially lifted, even if the patient is not physically detained during the whole of this period, *i.e.* it covers periods of leave of absence and absence without leave (*Van der Leer v. Netherlands*, above, para. 35).

In *X v. United Kingdom*, above, the Court specified the nature and scope of the judicial review that must be made available to the detained patient:

> "The right guaranteed by Article 5(4) to test the lawfulness of detention does not incorporate a right for the court to substitute its discretion for that of the decision-making authority; but the scope of the judicial review must be sufficient to enable enquiry to be made whether, in the case of detention of a mental patient, the reasons which initially justified the detention continue thereafter to subsist" (para. 58).

Fennell states that this finding "means that judicial review and habeas corpus are not adquate remedies since they go to lawfulness in a less substantive sense that that required by the Convention. They do not enable the domestic court to examine whether the substantive reasons for detention continue to subsist" (P. Fennell, "Doctor Knows Best? Therapeutic Detention Under Common Law, the Mental Health Act, and the European Convention", (1998) 6 Med.L.Rev. 322–353, at 349).

Speedily: "In the Court's view, this concept cannot be defined in the abstract; the matter must ... be determined in the light of the circumstances of each case" (*Sanchez-Reisse v. Switzerland* (1987) 9 E.H.R.R. 71, para. 55). The Commission has said that the authorities must make a patient's right to a speedy review "practical and effective" (*Luberti v. Italy*, (1982) app. no. 9019/80, para. 69). Where there has been a delay in undertaking a review, the Court must determine whether the delay can be attributed to the authorities (*Luberti v. Italy* (1982) E.C.H.R. Ser. A, No. 75, para. 34).

In *R. (on the application of C.) v. Secretary of State for the Home Department* [2001]

EWCA Civ 1110, the Court of Appeal said that decisions of the Court such as *E. v. Norway* (1994) 17 E.H.R.R. 30, where a delay of eight weeks between application and hearing was held to violate this paragraph, were not attempts to decide as of principle whether a particular practice or policy of setting a specified time for a hearing was in breach of this paragraph. What the Court had made clear was that each case was to be decided upon its own particular circumstances. The Court of Appeal held that this approach was not compatible with a policy of automatically listing cases for hearing eight weeks after the application had been made: see the note on rule 6 of the Mental Health Review Tribunal Rules 1983 under the heading "The Human Rights Act 1998".

In an *Cottenham v. United Kingdom,* app. 36509/97, the Court, in an admissibility decision, found that the tribunal could not be criticised for a delay of ten months which had been caused by the patient's solicitor's request for an adjournment to obtain an independent psychiatric report. The Court said that it "does not rule out that, given the particular problems of detained patients, where it appears that the legal representatives of such a person are acting negligently or in some way causing unjustified delay in the presentation of an application to a MHRT, the tribunal would be under a duty to make enquiries and to ensure that the application is proceeded with expeditiously."

Less urgency is required when the patient makes a further application in pursuance of his right to a periodic review of his detention. A delay of over four months in these circumstances has been held by the Court to be incompatible with this paragraph (*Koendjbiharie v. Netherlands* (1990) 13 E.H.R.R. 820). In *X v. United Kingdom* (1981) app. no. 6998/75, para. 138, the Commission said that a delay of six months between the decision of the Home Secretary to recall a conditionally discharged patient to hospital and the subsequent tribunal hearing violated this Article.

Court: This term has a much wider meaning under the Convention than in English law. A body can be a court if it is independent of the executive and of the parties to the case and has a judicial character (*De Wilde, Ooms and Versp,* above, para. 76). A Mental Health Review Tribunal qualifies as a court for the purposes of the Convention (*X. v. United Kingdom* (1981) 4 E.H.R.R. 188).

Paragraph 5

This paragraph requires an enforceable claim for compensation before a national **6–023** court if a breach of any of the other paragraphs in this Article has occurred. The Court has held that "... there can be no question of 'compensation' where there is no pecuniary or non-pecuniary damage to compensate" (*Wassink v. Netherlands,* above, para. 38).

The court must also be impartial. In *D.N. v. Switzerland,* March 29, 2001, the Court said that "impartiality must be determined by a subjective test, that is on the basis of the personal conviction of a particular judge in a given case, and also by an objective test, that is ascertaining whether the judge offered guarantees sufficient to exclude any legitimate doubt in this respect" (para. 44). The Court also said that "any judge in respect of whom there is legitimate reason to fear a lack of impartiality must withdraw. In deciding whether in a given case there is a legitimate reason to fear that a particular judge lacks impartiality, the standpoint of the parties concerned is important but not decisive. What is decisive is whether this fear can be held to be objectively justified" (para. 46). In applying these criteria to the role of the judge rapporteur in Swiss law, the Court found a violation of this paragraph: see the note on rule 11 of the Mental Health Review Tribunal Rules 1983.

ARTICLE 6

RIGHT TO A FAIR TRIAL

1. In the determination of his civil rights and obligations or of any criminal charge against him, **6–024** everyone is entitled to a fair and public hearing within a reasonable time by an independent and

impartial tribunal established by law. Judgment shall be pronounced publicly but the press and public may be excluded from all or part of the trial in the interest of morals, public order or national security in a democratic society, where the interests of juveniles or the protection of the private life of the parties so require, or to the extent strictly necessary in the opinion of the court in special circumstances where publicity would prejudice the interests of justice.

2. Everyone charged with a criminal offence shall be presumed innocent until proved guilty according to law.

3. Everyone charged with a criminal offence has the following minimum rights:

    (a) to be informed promptly, in a language which he understands and in detail, of the nature and cause of the accusation against him;

    (b) to have adequate time and facilities for the preparation of his defence;

    (c) to defend himself in person or through legal assistance of his own choosing or, if he has not sufficient means to pay for legal assistance, to be given it free when the interests of justice so require;

    (d) to examine or have examined witnesses against him and to obtain the attendance and examination of witnesses on his behalf under the same conditions as witnesses against him;

    (e) to have the free assistance of an interpreter if he cannot understand or speak the language used in court.

GENERAL NOTE

6–025   Although this Article, which provides for the right to a fair hearing in civil or criminal proceedings, is the Convention's single most frequently invoked provision, its direct relevance to the detention of mentally disordered patients is limited (*A.R. v. United Kingdom*, below). However, the lawfulness of the detention of such patients can be challenged under Article 5(4) and the European Court of Human Rights, in its interpretation of that paragraph, has been prepared to borrow some of the concepts of fairness in judicial proceedings from this Article.

Wachenfeld states that "[g]uardianship proceedings must comply with the standards of Article 6(1) because it involves the determination of a civil right. See for example, Commission Admissibility Decision *X, Y and Z v. Switzerland*, app. no. 6916/76, 6 D&R 107, 112, 12 March 1976" (Margaret G. Wachenfeld, "The Human Rights of the Mentally Ill in Europe" (1991) 60 *Nordic Journal of International Law*, 109–292, at 224).

Paragraph 1

6–026   The Court's case law on this paragraph was examined in *Z and others v. United Kingdom*, May 10, 2001. The Court said that:

    (i) This paragraph "extends only to *contestations* (disputes) over (civil) 'rights and obligations' which can be said, at least on arguable grounds, to be recognised under domestic law; it does not itself guarantee any particular content for (civil) rights and obligations' in the substantive law of the Contracting States. It will however apply to disputes of a 'genuine and serious nature' concerning the actual existence of the right as well as to the scope or manner in which it is exercised" (para. 87);

    (ii) This paragraph "may be relied on by anyone who considers that an interference with the exercise of one of his (civil) rights is unlawful and complains that he has not had the possibility of submitting that claim to a tribunal meeting the requirements of [this paragraph]. Where there is a serious and genuine dispute as to the lawfulness of such an interference, going either to the very existence or the scope of the asserted civil right, [this paragraph] entitles the individual 'to have this question of domestic law determined by a tribunal' " (para. 92); and

    (iii) "The right [to have the question determined by a tribunal] is not however absolute. It may be subject to legitimate restrictions, for example, statutory limitation periods, security for costs orders, regulations concerning minors and persons of unsound mind. Where the individual's access is limited either by operation of law or in fact, the Court will examine whether the limitation imposed impaired the essence of the right and in particular whether it pursued a legitimate aim and there was a reasonable relationship of proportionality between the means employed and the aim sought to be achieved. If the restriction is compatible with these principles, no violation of Article 6 will arise (para. 93).

The Court found that there "is no reason to consider the striking out procedure which rules on the existence of sustainable causes of action as *per se* offending the principle of access to court" (para. 97).

In *A.R. v. United Kingdom* (1996) E.H.R.L.R. 324, the Commission said:

"According to the Commission's case-law . . . , proceedings regarding a person's detention in a psychiatric hospital do not concern the determinations of that person's 'civil rights and obligations' within the meaning of Article 6(1) ... unless it is found that the detention had indirect effects on the detained person's right to administer his property or to carry out legal transactions (see *e.g. Neumeister v. Austria* (1979–80) 1 E.H.R.R. 91, para. 23, *Winterwerp v. Netherlands* (1979) 2 E.H.R.R. 387, para. 73 and *Wassink v. Netherlands*, September 27, 1990, series A, No. 185–A, para. 64)".

This Article is applicable where the purpose of the proceedings is to determine whether or not legal capacity can be restored to the applicant (*Matter v. Slovakia* (2001) 31 E.H.R.R. 32, para. 51).

In *Winterwerp v. Netherlands* (1979) 2 E.H.R.R. 387, the Court, in holding that the capacity to deal personally with one's property involves the exercise of private rights and hence affects "civil rights and obligations", said: "Whatever the justification for depriving a person of unsound mind of the capacity to administer his property, the guarantees laid down in Article 6(1) must nevertheless be respected" (para. 75).

Although detention under the Mental Health Act 1983 does not lead either to the direct or indirect deprivation of the patient's right to administer property, it is likely that the absence of an opportunity for the patient to be heard on an application being made to invoke the jurisdiction of the Court of Protection constitutes a breach of paragraph 1 of this Article: see the Court of Protection Rules 1984 (S.I. 1994 No. 3046) and the General Note to Part VII of the Mental Health Act.

In *Ashingdane v. United Kingdom* (1984) 7 E.H.R.R. 528, the Court found that the restrictions on bringing legal proceedings placed on patients by section 141 of the Mental Health Act 1959 (now see section 139 of the 1983 Act) did not transgress the patient's "right to a court" under this paragraph. The Court said: "Certainly, the right of access to the courts is not absolute but may be subject to limitations; these are permitted by implication since the right of access 'by its very nature calls for regulation by the State, regulation which may vary in time and in place according to the needs and resources of the community and of individuals' (*Golder v. United Kingdom* (1975) 1 E.H.R.R. 524, para. 38). In laying down such regulation, the Contracting States enjoy a certain margin of appreciation. Whilst the final decision as to observance of the Convention's requirements rests with the Court, it is no part of the Court's function to substitute for the assessment of the national authorities any other assessment of what might be the best policy in this field" (para. 57).

In the determination: This phrase "refers not only to the particular process of the making of the decision but extends more widely to the whole process which leads up to the final resolution" (*R. (on the application of Alconbury Developments Ltd) v. Secretary of State for the Environment, Transport and the Regions)* [2001] 2 All E.R. 929, HL, *per* Lord Clyde at para. 152).

Fair ... hearing: Among the rights that the Court and the Commission have identified as comprising the right to a fair hearing are: the right to adversarial proceedings, the right to have a hearing within a reasonable time, the right to equality of arms, the right to know the grounds on which a decision is based and access to information necessary to bring the case effectively; see further S. Grosz *et al*, *Human Rights; The 1998 Act and the European Convention* (2000), pp. 244 *et seq.* The fairness of proceedings should be assessed with regard to the proceedings as a whole (*Pélisser and Sassi v. France* (2000) 30 E.H.R.R. 715, at para. 46).

In the *Winterwerp* judgment, above, the Court held that the fact that the emergency confinement of the patient directed by the burgomaster did not afford the patient the opportunity of being heard, either in person or through a representative, did not satisfy the requirement of a "fair hearing" (at para. 74).

Public hearing: A private hearing is possible. "[W]hile the need to protect professional confidentiality and the private lives of patients may justify holding proceedings in camera, such an occurrence must be strictly required by the circumstances" (*Diennet v. France* (1996) 21 E.H.R.R. 554, para. 34).

Reasonable time: "The reasonableness of the length of proceedings is to be assessed in the light of the particular circumstances of the case, regard being had to the criteria laid down in the court's case-law, in particular the complexity of the case, the applicant's conduct and the conduct of the competent authorities" (*Pélissier and Sassi v. France*, above, at para. 67).

Tribunal: There must be a right of access to a court with "full" jurisdiction. In *Le Compte, Van Leuven and De Meyere v. Belgium* (1982) 4 E.H.R.R. 1, para. 51, the Court defined the concept of access to a court of full jurisdiction in the following terms:

> "... Article 6(1) draws no distinction between questions of fact and questions of law. Both categories of question are equally crucial for the outcome of proceedings relating to 'civil rights and obligations'. Hence, the 'right to a court' and the right to a judicial determination of the dispute cover questions of fact just as much as questions of law."

In order to establish whether a tribunal is "independent" for the purposes of this paragraph, regard must be had, *inter alia,* to the manner of appointment of its members and their term of office, the existence of safeguards against outside pressures and the question whether it presents an appearance of independence (*Incal v. Turkey* (2000) 29 E.H.R.R. 449, para. 65).

ARTICLE 7

NO PUNISHMENT WITHOUT LAW

6–027   1. No one shall be held guilty of any criminal offence on account of any act or omission which did not constitute a criminal offence under national or international law at the time when it was committed. Nor shall a heavier penalty be imposed than the one that was applicable at the time the criminal offence was committed.

2. This Article shall not prejudice the trial and punishment of any person for any act or omission which, at the time when it was committed, was criminal according to the general principles of law recognised by civilised nations.

ARTICLE 8

RIGHT TO RESPECT FOR PRIVATE AND FAMILY LIFE

6–028   1. Everyone has the right to respect for his private and family life, his home and his correspondence.

2. There shall be no interference by a public authority with the exercise of this right except such as is in accordance with the law and is necessary in a democratic society in the interests of national security, public safety or the economic well-being of the country, for the prevention of disorder or crime, for the protection of health or morals, or for the protection of the rights and freedoms of others.

GENERAL NOTE

6–029   In *Glaser v. United Kingdom* [2000] 1 F.L.R. 153, the European Court of Human Rights said (at 167–168 (para.63)):

> "The essential object of Article 8 is to protect the individual against arbitrary

interference by public authorities. There may however be positive obligations inherent in an effective "respect" for family life. These obligations may involve the adoption of measures designed to secure respect for family life even in the sphere of relations between individuals, including both the provision of a regulatory framework of adjudicatory and enforcement machinery protecting individuals' rights and the implementation, where appropriate, of specific steps (see among other authorities, *X and Y v. Netherlands* (1986) 8 E.H.R.R. 235, and, mutatis mutandis, *Osman v. United Kingdom* (2000) 29 E.H.R.R. 245). In both the negative and positive contexts, regard must be had to the fair balance which has to be struck between the competing interests of the individual and the community, including other concerned third parties, and of the state's margin of appreciation (see, among other authorities, *Keegan v. Ireland* ((1994) 18 E.H.R.R. 342)."

The Court has applied the concept of positive obligation in a number of areas including requiring a state to enable the guardians of a mentally defective girl to lodge a complaint with a view to instituting criminal proceedings against a man who had sexually abused her (*X and Y v. Netherlands*, above); to establish a fair system whereby the question of access to the personal files of a child in public care will be determined (*Gaskin v. United Kingdom* (1990) 12 E.H.R.R. 36); and to take all reasonable steps to facilitate reunion between a child in public care and his parents (*Hokkanen v. Finland* (1995) 19 E.H.R.R. 139); see further, S. Grosz, J. Beatson and P. Duffy, *Human Rights: The 1998 Act and the European Convention* (2000), p. 266. This Article imposes no positive obligations to provide medical treatment (*R. v. North West Lancashire Health Authority, ex p. A, D and G* (1999) 2 C.C.L.R. 419).

The combined effect of the *Glaser* and *Netherlands* cases, above, and of the provisions of section 12(3) of the Human Rights Act 1998 requires a court to have regard to the Convention in private law cases: see *Venables v. News Group Newspapers Ltd* [2001] 1 All E.R. 908, *per* Butler-Sloss P. at 917 and *Douglas v. Hello! Ltd* [2001] I.P. & T. 391, *per* Sedley L.J. at 425.

The Commission has recognised that public authorities might have to take particular steps to protect the mentally disordered in order to fulfil their obligations under this Article: "... the impossibility for the above category of persons [the mentally disabled] to form or express their will calls for protective measures on behalf of the authorities which go beyond what is required with regard to persons who are in full possession of their physical and mental capacities" (*X and Y v. Netherlands* (1983) E.C.H.R., Ser. B, No. 74, para. 81).

In *Ciliz v. Netherlands* [2000] 2 F.L.R. 469, 482, the Court said that whilst this Article contains no explicit procedural requirements, the decision-making process leading to measures of interference must be fair and such as to afford due respect to the interests safeguarded by the Article:

"[W]hat ... has to be determined is whether, having regard to the particular circumstances of the case and notably the serious nature of the decisons to be taken, the parents have been involved in the decision-making process, seen as a whole, to a degree sufficient to provide them with the requisite protection of their interests. If they have not, there will have been a failure to respect their family life and the interference resulting from the decision will not be capable of being regarded as 'necessary' within the meaning of Article 8 (see *W. v. United Kingdom* (1987) 10 E.H.R.R. 29, paras 62, 64; and *McMichael v. United Kingdom* (1995) 20 E.H.R.R. 205, para. 86)".

It is therefore the case that a violation of this Article will occur if an application is

743

made to detain a child under the Mental Health Act in circumstances where the parents of the child have not been offered the opportunity of being involved in the decision making process.

Paragraph 1

6–030   In *Passannante v. Italy* (1998) 26 E.H.R.R. CD 153, a case where the applicant had waited five months to see a hospital specialist, the Commission stated that "where the State has an obligation to provide medical care, an excessive delay of the public health service in providing a medical service to which the patient is entitled and the fact that such delay has, or is likely to have, a serious impact on the patient's health could raise an issue under Article 8(1) of the Convention." Also see *Scialacqua v. Italy* (1998) 26 E.H.R.R. CD 164, noted under Article 2.

Respect: This Article provides that everyone has the right to "respect" for certain aspects of his life, not that they have the right to a private and family life. In *Sheffield and Horsham v. United Kingdom* (1998) 27 E.H.R.R. 163, the Court said:

> "The Court reiterates that the notion of 'respect' is not clear cut, especially as far as the positive obligations inherent in that concept are concerned: having regard to the diversity of the practices followed and the situation obtaining in the Contracting States, the notion's requirements will vary considerably from case to case. In determining whether or not a positive obligation exists, regard must be had to the fair balance that has to be stuck between the general interests of the community and the interests of the individual, the search for which balance is inherent in the whole of the Convention" (para. 52).

Private . . . life: "Private life is a broad term not susceptible to exhaustive definition . . . Mental health must be regarded as a crucial part of private life associated with the aspect of moral integrity" (*Bensaid v. United Kingdom*, February 6, 2001, at para. 47). In *Botta v. Italy* (1998) 26 E.H.R.R. 241, the Court said that "private life . . . includes a person's physical and psychological integrity; the guarantee afforded Article 8 is primarily intended to ensure the development, without outside interference, of the personality of each individual in his relations with other human beings" (para. 32). In this case the Court's case law on the concept of private live was described being "based on a pragmatic, common-sense approach rather than a formalistic or purely legal one" (para. 27). In *Niemietz v. Germany* (1992) 16 E.H.R.R. 97, para. 29, the Court said that respect for private life must "comprise to a certain degree, the right to establish and develop relationships with human beings". Private life covers a person's sexual relations (*X and Y v. Netherlands* (1986) 8 E.H.R.R. 235, para. 22, but possibly not a person's sexuality (*R. v. North West Lancashire Health Authority, ex p. A, D and G* above, *per* Buxton L.J. at 442). In *Amann v. Switzerland* (2000) 30 E.H.R.R. 843, the Court said that there appears "to be no reason why . . . the notion of 'private life' should be taken to exclude activities of a professional or business nature" (para. 65).

A person has a right under this Article to have access to files concerning his own life. Any restriction on this right in domestic law must meet the requirements of paragraph 2. If a public authority is not able to secure the consent of a person who has contributed to the file to have that material disclosed, there must be an independent authority that can decide whether the material should be disclosed (*Gaskin v. United Kingdom*, above). The Court has said that "the protection of personal data, not least medical data, is of fundamental importance to a person's enjoyment of his or her right to respect for private and family life . . . Respecting the confidentiality of health data . . . is crucial not only to respect the sense of privacy of a patient but also to preserve his or her confidence in the medical profession and in health services in general. [Disclosure must be justified by] an overriding requirement in the public interest" (*Z v. Finland* (1998) 25 E.H.R.R. 371, paras 95, 96); also see *K & T v. Finland*, noted under "rights and freedoms of others", below.

The appointment of a guardian for a mentally disordered patient is an interference with that person's private life because the guardian is given power to make personal decisions on behalf of that person (*X v. Federal Republic of Germany* (1980) 20 D.&R. 193). Although the Convention does not place any restrictions on the guardian's powers, the exercise of such powers must fall within one of the limitations set out in paragraph 2. Guardianship proceedings are governed by Article 6(1) because they involve the determination of a person's civil right (see the note on Art. 6).

The searching of a mentally disordered detained patient would violate this Article in the absence of a justification under paragraph 2. It has been stated that the Court "has exercised particular judicial vigilance where the authorities are empowered under national law to order and effect searches without a judicial warrant. Very strict limits on such powers are called for in such cases in order to protect individuals from arbitrary interference by the authorities with "the rights guaranteed under [this Article (*Camenzind v. Switzerland* (1999) 28 E.H.R.R. 458)]" (S. Grosz *et al.*, above, at p. 285).

The use of surveillance techniques, such as CCTV, in hospitals and care homes will involve Article 8 rights. In *Khan v. United Kingdom*, (2000) *The Times*, 23 May, a case involving the use of a covert listening device by the police, the Court said: "The Court recalls, with the Commission in the case of *Govell* (paras.61,62), that the phrase 'in accordance with the law' not only requires compliance with domestic law but also relates to the quality of that law, requiring it to be compatible with the rule of law (see *Halford v. United Kingdom*). In the context of covert surveillance by public authorities, in this instance the police, domestic law must provide protection against arbitrary interference with an individual's right under Article 8. Moreover, the law must be sufficiently clear in its terms to give individuals an adequate indication as to the circumstances in which and the conditions on which public authorities are entitled to resort to such covert measures (*Malone v. United Kingdom*)" (para. 26). Surveillance operations conducted by local authorities and NHS trusts must comply with the provisions of Part II of the Regulation of Investigatory Powers Act 2000 which was passed partly as a result of the decisions in *Khan* and *Halford*.

In *Marzari v. Italy* (1999) 28 E.H.R.R. CD 175, the Commission said, at 179, 180, that, "although Article 8 does not guarantee the right to have one's housing problem solved by the authorities, a refusal of the authorities to provide assistance in this respect to an individual suffering from a serious disease might in certain circumstances raise an issue under Article 8 . . . because of the impact of such a refusal on the private life of the individual."

Family . . . life: This Article "makes no distinction between the 'legitimate' and the **6–031** illegitimate' family" (*Marckz v. Belgium* (1979) 2 E.H.R.R. 330, at para. 31). The concept of family life embraces, even where there is no co-habitation, the tie between a parent and his or her child (*Boughanemi v. France* (1996) 22 E.H.R.R. 228). The range of family relationships that have been held to amount to "family life" under this Article are identified by S. Grosz, *et al.*, *op. cit.* at pp. 270, 271. In *R. (on the application of L.) v. Secretary of State for Health* [2001] 1 F.L.R. 406, Scott Baker J. considered the jurisprudence on this Article. He said: "Family life it seems to me, is an elastic concept that depends very much on the facts of the individual case. In some cases the existence of family life will be immediately obvious; in others the reverse will be true. But the onus of establishing family life in each case is in my judgment on the applicant."

The purpose of this Article "is to assure within proper limits the entitlement of individuals to the benefit of what is benign and positive in family life. It is not to allow other individuals, however closely related and well intentioned, to create or perpetuate situations which jeopardise their welfare"; *per* Sedley L.J. in *Re F (Adult: Court's Jurisdiction)* [2000] 2 F.L.R. 512, 532, CA. *Re F.* is considered in the General Note to section 8 of the Mental Health Act under the heading "The protection of mentally disordered adults".

Phil Fennell argues that the decision in the *Bournewood* case (see the General Note to s.131 of the 1983 Act) to deprive the patient of access to his carers with whom he had lived for over three years and they to him, might be a violation of this Article: see Philip Fennell, "Doctor Knows Best? Therapeutic Detention Under Common Law, the Mental Health Act, and the European Convention" (1999) 6 Med. L. Rev. 322–353. Fennell's argument is strengthened by the decision in *K and T v. Finland* [2000] 2 F.L.R. 79, where the Court held that this Article had been violated in a case where children had been taken into pulbic care because of the risks caused by the mother's mental health and disturbed behaviour. The making of the care orders led to restrictions being placed on the mother's access to the children. Although the mother, who had been diagnosed with schizophrenia, had been subject to compulsory hospitalisation, the Court found that the reasons adduced to justify the care orders and the methods used in implementing those decisons were excessive.

In *R. v. Secretary of State for the Home Department, ex p. Mahmood* [2001] A.C.D. 38, at paragraph H17, the Master of the Rolls identified the approach that the courts should adopt when considering the potential conflict between the respect for family life and enforcement of immigration controls.

Home: This does not have to be the sole or main place of residence (*Mentes v. Turkey* (1998) 26 E.H.R.R. 595). In *North and East Devon Health Authority, ex p. Coughlan* (1999) 2 C.C.L.R. 285, the Court of Appeal held that the enforced move of a patient by an NHS Trust from accommodation that had been promised as her home for life, a move that would be both emotionally devastating and seriously anti-therapeutic, was a breach of this Article that was not justified by paragraph 2. Couglan was applied by Jackson J. in *R. v. Merton, Sutton and Wandsworth Health Authority, ex p. Perry and others*, July 31, 2000, where the Health Authority's decision to close a hospital for the learning disabled was quashed, partly on the ground that the Authority had failed to take into acocunt the fact that the families of patient's had been given promises that the hospital would provide a home for life for their relatives. If the residents of a local authority residential care home had been promised that the home would be their "home for life", it could be argued that the closure of that home was justified under paragraph 2 on the ground that the "economic well-being" of the council would be prejudiced if continuing to operate the home would be grossly uneconomic. A document, such as a residents' handbook, which appears to raise an expectation that residents had a "home for life" should not be construed as if it were a legal text being read by a lawyer. The test is what would the ordinary resident think the document was attempting to convey (*R. (on the application of Bodimeade and others) v. London Borough of Camden* [2001] EWHC Admin 271, *per* Turner J. at para. 26).

This Article could be used to challenge a decision following an assessment under section 47 of the National Health Service and Community Care Act 1990 to meet the community care needs of an individual by the provision of residential accommodation, if it would have been possible to meet those needs by the less cost effective means of providing services in the patient's home. The removal of the individual from his home would have to be justified by one of the criteria in paragraph 2. This Article could also be invoked in a situation where a patient had to remain in hospital for social reasons after the completion of treatment because of a failure to fund a care package that would enable the patient to return home.

Correspondence: A law which allows for state interference with correspondence must not leave the authorities too much latitude. It must "indicate with reasonable clarity the scope and manner of the exercise of the relevant discretion conferred on the public authorities" (*Domenichini v. Italy*, ECHR, November 15, 1996, para. 33). In *Klass v. Germany* ((1978) 2 E.H.R.R. 214) the Court held that this Article protects telephone conversations as well as written corespondence. A similar finding would almost certainly be made on other forms of communication, such as e-mail.

Paragraph 2

The concept of necessity requires that the interference permitted by this paragraph **6–032** should correspond to a pressing social need, and must be proportionate to the aim pursued (*Silver v. United Kingdom* (1983) 5 E.H.R.R. 347). The "graver the impact of the decision in question upon the individual affected by it, the more substantial the justification that will be required" (*R. v. Secretary of State for the Home Department, ex p. Mahmood*, above, *per* Laws L.J., at para. 19).

In *Re W. & B. (Children): Re W. (Children)*, above, para. 54, Hale L.J. said that an interference under this paragraph can only be justified if three conditions are fulfilled:

(i) it must be "in accordance with the law". This means more than it must have a basis in domestic law; the domestic law must be adequately accessible and formulated so that it is reasonably foreseeable; and there must be adequate and effective safeguards in that law to prevent arbitrary interference; see *Sunday Times v. United Kingdom* (1979) 2 E.H.R.R. 245; *Silver v. United Kingdom* (1983) 5 E.H.R.R. 347; *Malone v. United Kingdom* (1985) 7 E.H.R.R. 14; and *Halford v. United Kingdom* (1997) 24 E.H.R.R. 523. Subject to that, however, the need for flexibility and discretion are also recognised;

(ii) It must be in pursuit of one of the legitimate aims provided for in this Article; and

(iii) It must be "necessary in a democratic society": that is to say, the reasons for the interference must be "relevant and sufficient". It must correspond to a "pressing social need" and be "proportionate" to the legitimate aim pursued; see *Olsen v. Sweden (No. 1)* (1998) 11 E.H.R.R. 259. The more serious the intervention, the more compelling must be the justification; see *Johanssen v. Norway* (1996) 23 E.H.R.R. 33.

The principles which govern the court's approach in determining whether an interference with an Article 8 right can be justified under this paragraph were identified by Newman J. in *R. (on the application of N.) v. Ashworth Special Hospital Authority and the Secretary of State for Health* [2001] EWHC Admin 339, at para. 9. "They are:

(i) When considering whether an interference with a Convention right is proportionate the burden lies on the State to justify its actions.

(ii) the interference must go no further than is strictly necessary to achieve its permitted purpose.

(iii) The more substantial the interference the more that is required to justify it.

(iv) The court should anxiously scrutinise a decision of the executive which interferes with human rights and should consider applying an objective test 'whether the decision maker could reasonably have concluded that the interference was necessary to achieve one or more of the legitimate aims recognised by the Convention'.

(v) The mode of such objective review is more intrusive, or it could be said, more demanding than the conventional *Wednesbury* test.

(vi) The court should give due deference or allow a margin of appreciation to the decision maker."

In this case, Newman J. held that Direction 29(3) of the Safety and Security in Ashworth, Broadmoor and Rampton Hospitals Directions 2000, which confers a discretionary power on each hospital authority to record and subsequently to listen to a random 10 per cent of the outgoing and incoming telephones calls of patients at the hospitals, did not violate this Article.

This paragraph permits hospital managers to ban a particular visitor, including a close relative, that a detained patient wishes to see, as long as one of the specified grounds is satisfied.

The common law and statutory powers of the police enter private to prevent a breach of the peace, which are preserved by section 17(6) of the Police and Criminal Evidence Act 1984, do not contravene this paragraph as they are "in accordance with law" and are pursued with the legitimate aim of the "prevention of disorder or crime" for the purposes of this paragraph. The use of this power by the police must be a proportionate measure in all the circumstances (*McLeod v. United Kingdom* (1999) 27 E.H.R.R. 493).

In *X & Y v. Switzerland* (1978) 2 D.R. 105, the Commission said that an interference with family life which is justified under this paragraph cannot at the same time consistute a violation of Article 12.

In accordance with the law: The "law", which can be judge made law as well as legislation, should be foreseeable in its effects (*Malone v. United Kingdom* (1985) 7 E.H.R.R. 14, para. 66). The fact that it confers discretion on a professional, such as a doctor, is not in itself inconsistent with the requirement of foreseeability, subject to the proviso that "the scope of the discretion and the manner of its exercise are indicated with sufficient clarity, having regard to the legitimate aim of the measure in question, to give the individual adequate protection against arbitrary interference" (*Gillow v. United Kingdom* (1989) 11 E.H.R.R. 335, para. 51).

In *Lambert v. France* (2000) 30 E.H.R.R. 346, the Court said that this expression "requires firstly, that the impugned measure should have some basis in domestic law; it also refers to the quality of the law in question, requiring that it should be accessible to the person concerned, who must moreover be able to foresee its consequences for him, and compatible with the rule of law" (para. 23).

Necessary in a democratic society: In *Z and others v. United Kingdom*, May 10, 2001, the Court said: "In determining whether the impugned measures were 'necessary in a democratic society', the Court will consider whether, in the light of the case as a whole, the reasons adduced to justify them were relevant and sufficient for the purposes of [this paragraph]" (para. 70). The Court also said that whilst this Article "contains no explicit procedural requirements, the decision-making process involved in measures of interference must be fair and such as to afford due respect to the interests safeguarded by Article 8" (para. 72).

Protection of health: In *L v. Sweden*, 45 D. & R. 181, the Commission held that a decision provisionally to release a patient who had been detained in a psychiatric hospital constituted an interference with his right to respect for family life under this Article. However, the Commission went onto declare the application manifestly ill-founded as the decision was justified in the interests of the patient's health. The reason for not discharging the patient absolutely was that there were reasons to believe that she would stop taking her medication if this happened, and that this would lead to a deterioration in her health. This decision sanctions both the granting of leave to, and the conditional discharge of, a detained patient on conditon that the patient continues to accept medication, as long as the terms of this paragraph are satisfied.

Rights and freedom of others: In *TV v. Finland*, app. no. 21780/93, the Commission held that the disclosure that a prisoner was HIV positive to prison staff directly involved in his custody and who themselves were subject to obligations of confidentiality was justified as being necessary "for the protection of the rights and freedoms of others." Similar considerations would apply to a patient who had been assessed as being a danger to other patients or to staff.

ARTICLE 9

FREEDOM OF THOUGHT, CONSCIENCE AND RELIGION

6–033   1. Everyone has the right to freedom of thought, conscience and religion; this right includes freedom to change his religion or belief and freedom, either alone or in community with others and in public or private, to manifest his religion or belief, in worship, teaching, practice and observance.

2. Freedom to manifest one's religion or beliefs shall be subject only to such limitations as are prescribed by law and are necessary in a democratic society in the interests of public safety, for the protection of public order, health or morals, or for the protection of the rights and freedoms of others.

ARTICLE 10

FREEDOM OF EXPRESSION

1. Everyone has the right to freedom of expression. This right shall include freedom to hold **6–034** opinions and to receive and impart information and ideas without interference by public authority and regardless of frontiers. This Article shall not prevent States from requiring the licensing of broadcasting, television or cinema enterprises.

2. The exercise of these freedoms, since it carries with it duties and responsibilities, may be subject to such formalities, conditions, restrictions or penalties as are prescribed by law and are necessary in a democratic society, in the interests of national security, territorial integrity or public safety, for the prevention of disorder or crime, for the protection of health or morals, for the protection of the reputation or rights of others, for preventing the disclosure of information received in confidence, or for maintaining the authority and impartiality of the judiciary.

GENERAL NOTE
The courts "have frequently stated that in the field of freedom of speech there is no **6–035** difference in principle between English law and [this Article]—see, for instance, *A-G v. Guardian Newspapers Ltd (No.2)* [1990] 1 A.C. 109, 283–4 *per* Lord Goff; *Derbyshire County Council v. Times Newspapers* [1993] A.C. 534 at 551 *per* Lord Keith; *R. v. Home Secretary, ex p. Simms* [1999] 3 W.L.R. 328 at 336 *per* Lord Steyn"; *per* Lord Philips MR in *Ashworth Security Hospital v. M.G.M. Ltd* [2001] 1 All E.R. 991, CA, at para. 71.

Paragraph 1 of this Article guarantees the right to freedom of expression. An interference with this right entails a violation of the Article if it does not fall within one of the exceptions provided for in paragraph 2. In *Handyside v. United Kingdom* (1976) 1 E.H.R.R. 737, the Court said:

> "Subject to Article 10(2), [this Article] is applicable not only to 'information' or 'ideas' that are favourably received or regarded as inoffensive or as a matter of indifference, but also to those that offend, shock or disturb the State or any sector of the population. Such are the demands of that pluralism, tolerance and broadmindedness without which there is no democratic society. This means, amongst other things, that every 'formality', 'condition', 'restriction' or 'penalty' imposed in this sphere must be proportionate to the legitimate aim pursued" (at para. 49).

In *Goodwin v. United Kingdom* (1996) 22 E.H.R.R. 123, 137, the Commission expressed the view that only in "exceptional circumstances where vital public or individual interests are at stake" can an order requiring journalists to disclose their sources be justified. The Court of Appeal found that such circumstances did exist in *Ashworth Security Hospital v. M.G.N. Ltd.*, noted above.

This Article with often overlap with an Article 8(2) claim, especially with regard to a claim concerning access to information.

Paragraph 2

6–036

In *Kelly v. B.B.C.* [2001] 1 All E.R. 323, Munby J. said at 335:

> "Well known jurisprudence of the European Court on Human Rights estab-lishes: (i) that the exceptions in paragraph 2 must be narrowly interpreted; (ii)

that if a restraint is to be justified under paragraph 2 it must be 'necessary in a democratic society'—that is to say, the necessity for any such restriction must be 'convincingly established' by reference to the existence of a 'pressing social need', and the restriction must be 'proportionate to the legitimate aim pursued'; and (iii) that the restriction must be 'prescribed by law'—that is, the law must be 'adequately accessible to the citizen and must be 'formulated with sufficient precision to enable a citizen to regulate his conduct: see *Rantzen v. Mirror Group Newspapers* (1986) Ltd. [1993] 4 All E.R. 975 at 990, citing *Sunday Times v. United Kingdom* (No. 1) (1979) 2 E.H.R.R. 245 and *Sunday Times v. United Kingdom* (No. 2) (1991) 14 E.H.R.R. 229."

The provisions of section 134 of the Mental Health Act 1983, under which a patient's correspondence can be withheld, are likely to be held to be in accordance with this paragraph in that the restrictions in the section "are necessary in a democratic society, in the interests of ... public safety, ... for the protection of health or morals, [or] for the protection of the reputation or rights of others ..."

ARTICLE 11

FREEDOM OF ASSEMBLY AND ASSOCIATION

6–037   1. Everyone has the right to freedom of peaceful assembly and to freedom of association with others, including the right to form and to join trade unions for the protection of his interests.
2. No restrictions shall be placed on the exercise of these rights other than such as are prescribed by law and are necessary in a democratic society in the interests of national security or public safety, for the prevention of disorder or crime, for the protection of health or morals or for the protection of the rights and freedoms of others. This Article shall not prevent the impositon of lawful restrictions on the exercise of these rights by members of the armed forces, of the police or of the administration of the State.

ARTICLE 12

RIGHT TO MARRY

6–038   Men and women of marriageable age have the right to marry and to found a family, according to the national laws governing the exercise of this right.

GENERAL NOTE
6–039   While this Article is confined to legally formalised heterosexual relationships, Article 8 is far broader in its scope. An interference with family life which is justified under Article 8(2) cannot at the same time constitute a violation of this Article (*X & Y v. Switzerland* (1978) 13 D.R. 105).
The Marriage Act 1983 places no restrictions on mentally disordered patients, whether detained or not, from marrying as long as they have sufficient mental capacity to contract a marriage (see the General Note to the Mental Health Act 1983 under the heading "Marriage"). Any substantial interference with this right would violate this Article. However, the Commission in *Hamer v. United Kingdom* ((1981) 4 E.H.R.R. 139) left open whether it might, exceptionally, be possible to prohibit a patient's marriage on the grounds of special dangerousness, and the consequential risk posed to the partner: see O. Thorold, "The Implications of the European Convention on Human Rights for United Kingdom Mental Health Legislation", [1996] E.H.R.L.R. 619–636, at 634.
The Commission has considered the right to sexual relations in a number of cases. In *X v. United Kingdom* (1975) 2 D.R. 105, a long-term prisoner complained of being deprived both of his conjugal rights and of the exercise of his paternal rights. In giving its opinion, the Commission said:

"With a view to his family rights the applicant has also complained that he has been prevented from 'founding further family'. It is true that Article 12 of the Convention secures to everyone of marriageable age the right to found a family ... Although the right to found a family is an absolute right in the sense that no restrictions similar to those in paragraph 2 of Article 8 of the Convention are expressly provided for, it does not mean that a person must at all times be given the actual possibility to procreate his descendants. It would seem that the situation of a lawfully convicted person detained in prison in which the applicant finds himself falls under the his own responsibility, and that his right to found a family has not otherwise been infringed."

A similar finding was made by the Commission in *X & Y v. Switzerland*, above, where, in an application founded on Article 8, it was held that that Article does not require conjugal visits, even if the husband and wife are detained in the same prison. The rationale of this finding was based on the need to prevent "disorder or crime".

Different considerations would apply to the position of mentally disordered detained patients, as they are not "responsible" for their hospitalisation. Thorold argues that conjugal visits "can help to preserve a patient's marital relationship and thereby improve longer-term mental health prognosis. Any limitation on sexual relationships between patients, or a patient and a spouse, would have to be strictly justified. A prohibition which was expressed in general terms would be in grave danger of breaching Article 12. It may therefore be necessary for a policy to be formulated which permits sexual relations subject to well-defined exceptions, of which danger to another person would clearly be one" (*op. cit.*, at 635). In *Secretary of State for the Home Department, ex p. Mellor* [2001] EWCA Civ 472, the Court of Appeal concluded that the qualifications on the right to respect for family life that are recognised by Article 8(2) apply equally to rights under this Article (*per* Lord Phillips M.R. at para. 39). This means that justification for the exceptions referred to by Thorold must be found in Article 8(2).

Right to marry: Even if there is no prospect of cohabitation (*Hamer v. United Kingdom*, above).

ARTICLE 14

PROHIBITION OF DISCRIMINATION

The enjoyment of the rights and freedoms set forth in this Convention shall be secured **6–040** without discrimination on any ground such as sex, race, colour, language, religion, political or other opinion, national or social origin, association with a national minority, property, birth or other status.

GENERAL NOTE

This Article does not provide a free-standing prohibition on discrimination. It **6–041** prohibits discrimination only in relation to enjoyment of rights and freedoms guaranteed by the Convention. In *Botta v. Italy* (1998) 26 E.H.R.R. 241, the Court said:

"Article 14 complements the other substantive provisions of the Convention and its protocols. It has no independent existence, since it has effect solely in relation to 'the enjoyment of the rights and freedoms' safeguarded by those provisions. Although the application of Article 14 does not presuppose a breach of one or more of those provisions—and to this extent it is autonomous—there can be no room for its application unless the facts of the case fall within the ambit of one or more of the latter" (para. 39).

Not every difference of treatment in the exercise of Convention rights and freedoms is forbidden by this Article:

"Article 14 does not prohibit distinctions in treatment which are founded on an objective assessment of essentially different factual circumstances and which, being based on the public interest, strike a fair balance between the protection of the interests of the Community and respect for the rights and freedoms safeguarded by the Convention" (*Belgium Linguistic Case (No. 2)* (1968) 1 E.H.R.R. 252, para. 7).

S. Grosz *et al.* state that when examining a complaint under this Article the Court will ask itself the following questions:

(a) Do the facts of the case fall within the ambit of one or more of the other substantive provisions of the Convention?
(b) Was there a difference in treatment?
(c) Were the objects of such differential treatment placed in analogous situations?
(d) Did the difference of treatment have an objective and reasonable justification, i.e. does it pursue a legitimate aim and does the differential treatment bear a reasonable relationship of proportionality to the aim sought to be achieved? (*Human Rights: The 1998 Act and the European Convention* (2000), pp. 326, 7).

Any ground such as: The list that follows is illustrative, not exhaustive.
Other status: Which could include the mentally disordered.

ARTICLE 16

RESTRICTIONS ON POLITICAL ACTIVITY OF ALIENS

6–042   Nothing in Articles 10, 11 and 14 shall be regarded as preventing the High Contracting Parties from imposing restrictions on the political activity of aliens.

ARTICLE 17

PROHIBITION OF ABUSE OF RIGHTS

6–043   Nothing in this Convention may be interpreted as implying for any State, group or person any right to engage in any activity or perform any act aimed at the destruction of any of the rights and freedoms set forth herein or at their limitation to a greater extent than is provided for in the Convention.

ARTICLE 18

LIMITATION ON USE OF RESTRICTIONS ON RIGHTS

6–044   The restrictions permitted under this Convention to the said rights and freedoms shall not be applied for any purpose other than those for which they have been prescribed.

PART II

THE FIRST PROTOCOL

ARTICLE 1

PROTECTION OF PROPERTY

6–045   Every natural or legal person is entitled to the peaceful enjoyment of his possessions. No one shall be deprived of his possessions except in the public interest and subject to the conditions provided for by law and by the general principles of international law.

The preceding provisions shall not, however, in any way impair the right of a State to enforce such laws as it deems necessary to control the use of property in accordance with the general interest or to secure the payment of taxes or other contributions or penalties.

ARTICLE 2

RIGHT TO EDUCATION

No person shall be denied the right to education. In the exercise of any functions which it **6–046** assumes in relation to education and to teaching, the State shall respect the right of parents to ensure such education and teaching in conformity with their own religious and philosophical convictions.

ARTICLE 3

RIGHT TO FREE ELECTIONS

The High Contracting Parties undertake to hold free elections at reasonable intervals by **6–047** secret ballot, under conditions which will ensure the free expression of the opinion of the people in the choice of the legislature.

PART III

THE SIXTH PROTOCOL

ARTICLE 1

ABOLITION OF THE DEATH PENALTY

The death penalty shall be abolished. No one shall be condemned to such penalty or **6–048** executed.

ARTICLE 2

DEATH PENALTY IN TIME OF WAR

A state may make provision in its law for the death penalty in respect of acts committed in **6–049** time of war or of imminent threat of war; such penalty shall be applied only in the instances laid down in the law and in accordance with its provisions. The State shall communicate to the Secretary General of the Council of Europe the relevant provisions of that law.

INDEX

755